W9-BNY-114

EDGAR RICE BURROUGHS

EDGAR RICE BURROUGHS

The Man Who Created Tarzan

Irwin Porges

Hulbert Burroughs, pictorial editor

Introduction by Ray Bradbury

Brigham Young University Press
Provo, Utah 84602

Library of Congress Catalog Card Number: 75-15980
International Standard Book Number: 0-8425-0079-0
Brigham Young University Press, Provo, Utah 84602
© 1975 by Brigham Young University Press (text only)
© 1975 by Edgar Rice Burroughs, Inc. (illustrations only)
All rights reserved. First edition, third printing 1976
Printed in the United States of America
76   7M   16040

All illustrations have been printed by permission of
Edgar Rice Burroughs, Inc., Tarzana, California 91356.

Library of Congress Cataloging in Publication Data
Porges, Irwin.
Edgar Rice Burroughs: the man who created Tarzan

Includes bibliographical references and index.
1. Burroughs, Edgar Rice, 1875–1950. I. Edgar
Rice Burroughs, inc.
PS3503.U687Z84   813′.5′2 [B]   75-15980
ISBN 0-8425-0079-0

To my wife Cele,
not only for the years of research, but for
her spirit and enthusiasm that transformed
this formidable task into an adventure.

CONTENTS

Editor's note: Almost all source material in the book is of a primary nature (i.e., correspondence, poems, drawings, scrapbooks, ERB's *Autobiography,* published novels and stories, and unpublished manuscripts) and is on file at Edgar Rice Burroughs, Inc., at Tarzana, California. Because of this, and because the notes provide thorough information for other sources as well, a separate bibliography has not been included with the back matter. Quoted material has been left in its original form, complete with any misspellings and errors in punctuation and grammar. Only occasionally has a change been made and then only for the sake of clarifying meaning. Burroughs, a prolific writer of notes and letters, often dashed these off in haste, using his own type of shorthand. The term *sic* is used only rarely to call attention to otherwise confusing errors. Titles published in book form appear in italics; titles published in magazines, and also unpublished titles, are placed inside quotation marks. Most of the photographs have been taken by ERB, his son Hulbert, and his daughter Joan.

FOREWORD

The publication of Irwin Porges' biography of Edgar Rice Burroughs is a timely milestone and the ultimate addition to the literature of Burroughsiana. It not only marks the centennial of ERB's birth, but more importantly it is the first and only true and definitive account of the life and work of this remarkably successful author.

Mr. Porges is the first and only researcher who was afforded complete and uncensored access to all of the Burroughs family's personal files as well as those of Edgar Rice Burroughs, Inc. My editorial work on the manuscript involved corrections, addition of interesting material unknown to Porges, and the preparation and production of illustrative matter. No attempt whatever was made to produce a sympathetic book.

Cele Porges, Irwin's talented wife, devoted nearly three years researching the voluminous archives at our company offices and warehouse in Tarzana. The result is a fascinating and well-written story of a man and his career.

Contributing significantly to this volume is the wealth of photographic and illustrative material. Seldom has the subject of a major biography possessed the combined talents of writer, photographer, and artist. Sometime in the 1890s ERB became interested in photography and from then on recorded the people and places in his life. A major portion of the photographs in this book are from his own photo albums and negative files. His pen-and-ink sketches and cartoons are both humorous and documentary. The sheer quantity of good pictorial material available and our realization that only a very limited number could be included because of space limitations presented a rather frustrating challenge. From thousands of photographs and drawings I selected about six hundred for enlargement to 8 × 10 size. I shall never forget the four days I spent with charming Kerril Sue Rollins, chief project editor of the biography at Brigham Young University Press in Provo, Utah, selecting and placing each picture on the appropriate page of text and the hard and painful decisions we made in reducing the number from 600 to about 270. Had it not been for the firm hand and character of Kerril Sue, the book might well have contained an extra fifty pounds of photos! We swore that some day we would publish an ERB photobiography.

I think my Dad would have been pleased with this book. Irwin Porges has organized and presented a great wealth of material in a way that gives the reader a real insight into ERB the man. I knew him, of course, first as a father. As such he was an extremely loving and kindly man — perhaps overly generous and protective. He set a strong example of love of country, honor, and integrity, as well as loyalty to family and friends. Porges has captured the true essence of ERB with all his strengths and weaknesses. This book will be a prime, standard source for all future Burroughs researchers.

I thank and congratulate Irwin and Cele Porges for their prodigious effort in researching and writing this book. The good people at Brigham Young University Press will always have a special place in my heart. Without the sincere dedication of Gail Bell, Kerril Sue Rollins, Jean Paulson, Mac Magleby, and the other great people of BYU Press, I doubt that this massive volume could have been published.

We are all greatly indebted to Ray Bradbury

for his splendid introductory essay. If ERB were alive today, he would be especially pleased for the many times Ray has so generously acknowledged his indebtedness to ERB as the inspiration for his own highly successful writing career. I never cease to wonder at the number and diversity of the minds that have been and are still being influenced by the imagination of Edgar Rice Burroughs. Most important, ERB is gradually receiving the critical acclaim he was denied in his lifetime. No longer is *Tarzan of the Apes* considered mere entertainment — for Tarzan *is* the "Naked Ape," the tribal ancestor of Marshall McLuhan. And ERB's wild imaginings among the stars are no longer beneath the notice of serious men; they have become subjects for scholars and an inspiration to a new generation of writers of imaginative fiction.

Burroughs is remembered as a modest man who never took himself or his work too seriously. His friends recall his ready sense of humor, his great love of the outdoors, and his unbounded pride in his country. One scholar suggests that the very last line of the last Tarzan novel may be taken as ERB's own unintentional valedictory to a very meaningful life: "Thank God for everything."

Hulbert Burroughs
Tarzana, September 1, 1975

PREFACE

The idea of writing a biography of Edgar Rice Burroughs, which I had only tentatively considered, received a strong stimulus in 1962 as a result of my puzzlement and curiosity.

In my early years I had read the Burroughs stories — a number of the *Tarzan* books and the science-fiction adventures on Mars, Venus, and other worlds. I admired Burroughs for the unlimited bounds of his imagination, for his ingenuity in creating scientific environments for his fantastic civilizations, and for reasons almost impossible to explain that his characters, although unreal and narrowly slanted versions of virtue and vice, somehow lived on vividly and permanently in the reader's mind.

I became convinced that the publicized "ERB," the one known to the readers and the public, was a patchwork of bits and pieces of biography in newspapers and magazines, much of this exaggerated and contradictory. Superficial details — mere lists of data or summary highlights of a person's life — can only produce a superficial man. But an added factor was at work. As a consequence of his wildly imaginative writings and the furor they caused, Burroughs, the individual, was somehow lost — forgotten. *Tarzan of the Apes* alone was potent enough to overwhelm the author. The *author* Burroughs emerged, but not the *man*. Through the years, when he supposedly wrote about himself, he was really supplying the familiar information about his writings or repeating a thin biographical sketch. The *man* Burroughs did not exist — a flesh-and-blood man who had faced conflicts and suffered frustrations and agonies — was unknown.

Why should this have happened? An ironical thought occurred: perhaps there was an assumption that one so strongly identified with worlds of fantasy, a writer who avoided real-life situations, was himself without real-life identification — a disembodied creature. But the puzzling question of why no definitive biography had been written prompted me to get in touch with Edgar Rice Burroughs, Inc., located nearby in the small community that owed its name to ERB — Tarzana, California.

The company is owned and controlled by the author's two sons, Hulbert Burroughs and John Coleman Burroughs. An only daughter, Joan Burroughs Pierce, died in December 1972. My meeting with Hulbert took place in December 1962. The building that housed the Burroughs' offices was unlike anything I had pictured. It was a Spanish-styled bungalow, typical of those popular in Los Angeles from the 1900s on, with one story, walls of yellow-tinged stucco, and a long ivy-festooned veranda across the front. It was the original building, erected by Burroughs in 1927, its exterior unchanged. Set back from busy Ventura Boulevard and secluded behind a weathered redwood fence and huge mulberry trees, the building could easily escape the notice of passers-by who, if they noticed it, might assume it to be a private residence.

Hulbert Burroughs chatted with me, at times seated behind the desk that had belonged to his father, a desk of glowing walnut decorated ornately with Moorish figures — heads of women, rams, circular flowerlike carvings, exotic lamps — and on occasion arising to show me valuable books, illustrations, and Burroughs mementoes. In the adjoining room was a large table, even more elaborate in design than the matching Moorish desk. In facial characteristics

Hulbert resembles both his mother and his father; physically, with his broad shoulders, and large hands, he takes after his father. Our discussion was pleasant and the brief tour of the offices highly interesting, but as far as the biography was concerned, I was given no encouragement. Hulbert informed me that he and his brother Jack had plans to write their father's story.

Five years later, the project forgotten, I had turned to other writing when, in October 1967, I received a letter from Robert M. Hodes, the new vice-president and general manager of the Burroughs firm. It contained a proposal that I undertake the biography. After a period of consideration, I agreed to do so. My wife, Cele, an experienced, efficient researcher, began the task of collecting information, much of it contained in documents in the warehouse that adjoined the offices. The warehouse had been built by Burroughs who intended to rent it as a store, but when it remained vacant, he used it at first as a garage. The willing cooperation of the family — Joan, Jack, and Hulbert — was evident from our earliest interviews and tapings. But I had no concept of the complexity of the project I had undertaken.

It was during the early stages of my preparing to write the biography of Edgar Rice Burroughs, and before a single sentence had been composed, that I arrived at a dismaying realization: I had shouldered the task unsuspectingly and with a degree of naivete that already appeared incredible — and would appear increasingly so, I was certain, in the light of developments. For awhile I became convinced that confronting me was a unique situation, unparalleled in the annals of biographies. However, the passage of time (three years of poring through documents on my wife's part, plus the joint searching, sorting, assembling, corresponding, and interviewing by the two of us, and then, of course, the writing and revising) has given me a more temperate and realistic perspective. Undoubtedly my blithe confidence and misapprehension of the difficulties that

awaited me have been matched in the experiences of other biographers. But the completion of the biography, accompanied by calm appraisal, has made plain that in one aspect — the huge mass of materials, mainly first sources — the reconstruction of Burroughs' life has posed problems beyond those encountered by the average biographer.

My first view of the warehouse piled to the ceiling with cases of documents and records came as a shock. Before me was a biographer's dream — or nightmare. In the warehouse were seventy-eight large storage file boxes, each the size of a legal file drawer, containing papers that dated to 1911. The labels themselves were an indication of the formidable task that lay ahead: Tarzana Ranch and E.R.B. Personal, 1918-1937, boxes 1-6; Real Estate, 1924-49, boxes 9-12; Motion Pictures, Miscl., and Burroughs-Tarzan Enterprises, Inc., 1918-47, boxes 14-16. Other cases, at random, included Book Publishing — for example, A. C. McClurg & Co., 1914-41 — five boxes marked Fans, with letters from every state and from foreign countries; Tarzan Radio Serials, Tarzan Merchandise Franchises, Tarzan Daily Strips, Tarzan Sunday Pages.

Inside some of the sliding file boxes were rows of folders filled with letters, lists, and mimeographed material; many of these had not been examined for years or had not been opened since Burroughs' death in 1950. Valuable original documents had been saved, including correspondence covering Burroughs' first stories — the exchange of letters with Munsey editor Thomas Metcalf concerning "Under the Moons of Mars," *The Outlaw of Torn,* and *Tarzan of the Apes.* Among these was Metcalf's famous eight-word letter: "For the love of Mike! Don't get discouraged!" sent after Burroughs, deeply disappointed and ready to leave the writing field, had remarked, "I can make money easier some other way."

All of these papers would have to be read, and many of them contained material that had to be copied. The amount of general correspondence, letters, and replies by Burroughs was appalling. It had been noted that ERB up to the last years of his life, and except for periods of illness, answered almost everybody who wrote to him. Voluminous is an understated term to describe his letter-writing. With unbelievable patience and care he furnished detailed information to those who sought it, responded to acquaintances, replied to his fans, and even good-humoredly answered cranks who didn't deserve the time and energy he expended.

In response to a writer who accused him, because of a scene in one of his stories, of encouraging distressed persons to end their lives, Burroughs wrote, "I thought only of the dramatic value of the situation, and had no intention of glorifying suicide. I feel that very few readers will interpret it as you have. I hope not."

Carbon copies of most of the letters were saved. A survey not only of the warehouse but of other storage rooms and cabinets leads to the

Tarzana storeroom of Edgar Rice Burroughs, Inc., housing files researched by the author, Irwin Porges, and his wife.

indisputable conclusion that Edgar Rice Burroughs was the king of savers. He had inherited a tendency from ancestors who formed a long line of savers of the most meticulous type. The papers in the warehouse were only part of the collection. In other storage places are documents of greater importance to a biographer, those relating personally to Burroughs, revealing his background and illuminating his character and problems, and the family records that in some cases travel back to the ancestral origins in seventeenth-century England.

A favorite means of preservation was the scrapbook. Mary Evaline, Burroughs' mother, kept one, and on the other side Emma Burroughs' parents, the Hulberts, saved several large books of clippings and other references. In addition, Mary Evaline, at her sons' urgings, had written the recollections of her Civil War experiences, and these, together with genealogical information, were printed in a small volume. The family books were augmented by the numerous albums of photos from both the Burroughs family and the Hulberts, photos marked on the backs with vital details.

The custom of keeping records in book form was adopted by Burroughs. His series of desk diaries with brief notations about his stories and comments about daily happenings cover the period of 1921-49. Further records and mementoes are contained in his school scrapbook and other books relating to the past. In the office files are various workbooks in which he methodically prepared story outlines, casts of characters, plot suggestions, definitions for his invented languages, and geographical explanations. His early financial accounts include a precise card index of story sales, dates, and the amounts paid.

But besides all these letters, documents, and records, not to exclude certain personal belongings also saved because, as Burroughs' fame increased, they had a value in themselves, there were of course his writings, both fiction and nonfiction, published and unpublished. A definitive biography is of course written to offer the reader some integration of the man and his works. Awaiting me were some seventy published novels to read — about twenty of these to re-read, since I had read them in my youth — plus many unpublished works. In addition, original manuscripts of published stories, in some cases handwritten, had to be checked for Burroughs' notations and revisions that could be of importance. Applying especially to ERB's writings was a further reading task: his unchanging popularity with science-fiction and Burroughs fan organizations had resulted in the publication of numerous analyses of his works. It was necessary for me to familiarize myself with the ideas expressed in these.

Possibly the most intimate aspects of a man's character emerge through contacts with the people who knew him personally — relatives, friends, business associates. Burroughs throughout his life had a facility for forming friendships, many of these being in the publishing, theatrical, and motion picture fields. Much valuable information has been provided by relatives and friends through correspondence, interviews, and tapings. A list of names is contained under the acknowledgements section.

In summary, I might say that while Burroughs, as with all individuals, revealed himself through his actions, through what he said and what others said about him, as a writer he operated in an additional dimension to expose himself. Even a man who escapes into fantasies of other worlds uncovers himself with every page he creates. Through his writings — and this idea he would have been happy to accept — we obtain a most significant understanding of Edgar Rice Burroughs.

ACKNOWLEDGMENTS

The following people have given me valuable information and assistance in the preparation of this book.

An acknowledgment beyond any words that I could devise must go to my wife Cele for her labors of more than three years among the mounds of paper in the Burroughs storerooms at Tarzana. To the enormous task she brought not only a remarkable ability in research and organization, but also an enthusiasm and a spirit of adventure that swept me through the periods of discouragement. Without her, the biography would have been impossible.

I thank the following members of Edgar Rice Burroughs' family and other relatives: Hulbert Burroughs; John Coleman Burroughs; Joan Burroughs Pierce; James Pierce; Marion Burroughs; Danton Burroughs; Mrs. Carlton D. McKenzie, Harry Burroughs' daughter, for numerous letters and a taped interview; George T. Burroughs, III, for letters and a taped interview; Joyce Burroughs Goetz, George's daughter; Marie Burroughs, Studley Burroughs' widow; June Burroughs, Studley's daughter, for a taped interview; Katherine Burroughs Konkle, Frank Burroughs' daughter, for numerous letters; Dorothy Westendarp Aitchison, niece of Edgar Rice Burroughs, for letters.

I also thank Florence Gilbert, Burroughs' second wife, for a taped interview; Florence's daughter, Caryl Lee (Cindy Cullen), for a taped interview; Lee Chase, Florence's son, for an interview; Ed Gilbert, Florence's brother, for interviews.

I am grateful to the following Burroughs fans who have given me important varied information: Dale R. Broadhurst, for valuable information about Burroughs' Idaho days; Stan Vinson; Vernell Coriell; Henry Hardy Heins; and Sam Moskowitz. I express appreciation to Ray Bradbury for his most appropriate introductory essay.

Mildred Jensen, Burroughs' secretary, has provided interviews and tapings. Ralph Bellamy and Rochelle Hudson have given taped interviews; Sol Lesser, a taped interview; and Hal Thompson, correspondence. General Thomas H. Green, retired, has supplied a letter and a tape; General Kendall Fielder, retired, numerous letters; Phil Bird, an interview; Herbert Weston, Jr., letters; Sterling and Floye Adams, a letter. Mrs. Zeamore Ader has given me information on Burroughs' Chicago background. The Chicago Historical Society, Miss Margaret Scriven, librarian, has provided information on Burroughs' early years in Chicago. The Phillips Academy, Andover, Massachusetts, has also given me valuable information, with special assistance from Charles W. Smith, alumni secretary, and Mrs. Waters Kellogg, associate archivist. I extend my appreciation to all of these people.

Irwin Porges
November 1, 1974

INTRODUCTION

Tarzan, John Carter, Mr. Burroughs,
and the Long Mad Summer of 1930

In the summer of 1930 if you had got off a train and walked up through the green avenues of Waukegan, Illinois, you might have met a mob of boys and girls running the other way. You might have seen them rushing to drown themselves in the lake or hide themselves in the ravine or pop into theatres to sit out the endless matinees. Anything, anything at all to escape . . .

What?

Myself.

Why were they running away from me? Why was I causing them endless flights, endless hidings-away? Was I, then, that unpopular at the age of ten?

Well, yes, and no.

You see my problem was Edgar Rice Burroughs and Tarzan and John Carter, Warlord of Mars.

Problem, you ask. That doesn't sound like much of a problem.

Oh, but it was. You see, I couldn't stop reading those books. I couldn't stop memorizing them line by line and page by page. Worst of all, when I saw my friends, I couldn't stop my mouth. The words just babbled out. Tarzan this and Jane that, John Carter here and Dejah Thoris there. And when it wasn't those incredible people it was Tanar of Pellucidar or I was making noises like a tyrannosaurus rex and behaving like a Martian thoat, which, everyone knows, has eight legs.

Do you begin to understand why Waukegan, Illinois, in the summer of 1930 was so long, so excruciating, so unbearable for everyone?

Everyone, that is, save me.

My greatest gift has always been falling in love.

My greatest curse, for those with ears, has been the expression of love.

I went to bed quoting Lord Greystoke.

I slept whimpering like Cheetah, growling like Numa, trumpeting like Tantor.

I woke, called for my head, which crawled on spider legs from a pillow nearby, to sit itself back on my neck and name itself *Chessman* of Mars.

At breakfast I climbed trees for my father, stabbed a mad gorilla for my brother, and entertained my mother with pithy sayings right smack-dab out of Jane Porter's mouth.

My father got to work earlier each day.

My mother took aspirin for precipitant migraine.

My brother hit me.

But, ten minutes later I hit the door, the lawn, the street, babbling and yodeling ape cries, ERB in my hand and in my blood.

How came it so?

What was it that Mr. Burroughs did to several dozen million scores of boys all across the world in the last sixty years?

Was he a great thinker?

He would have laughed at that.

Was he a superb stylist?

He would have snorted at that, also.

What if Edgar Rice Burroughs had never been born, and Tarzan with him? Or what if he had simply written Westerns and stayed out of Nairobi and Timbuctoo? How would our world have been affected? Would someone else have become Edgar Rice Burroughs? But Kipling had his chance, and didn't change the world, at least not in the same way.

The Jungle Books are known and read and loved around the world, but they didn't make most boys run amok pull their bones like taffy and grow them to romantic flights and farflung jobs around the world. On occasion, yes, but more often than not, no. Kipling was a better writer than Burroughs, but not a better romantic.

A better writer, too, and also a romantic, was Jules Verne. But he was a Robinson Crusoe humanist/moralist. He celebrated head/hands/heart, the triple H's shaping and changing a world with ideas. All good stuff, all chockful of concepts. Shall we trot about the world in eighty days? We shall. Shall we rocket to the Moon? Indeed. Can we survive on a Mysterious Island, a mob of bright Crusoes? We can. Do we clear the seas of armadas and harvest the deeps with sane/mad Nemo? We do.

It is all adventurous and romantic. But it is not very wild. It is not impulsive.

Burroughs stands above all these by reason of his unreason, because of his natural impulses, because of the color of the blood running in Tarzan's veins, because of the blood on the teeth of the gorilla, the lion, and the black panther. Because of the sheer romantic impossibility of Burroughs' Mars and its fairytale people with green skins and the absolutely unscientific way John Carter traveled there. Being utterly impossible, he was the perfect fast-moving chum for any ten-year-old boy.

For how can one resist walking out of a summer night to stand in the middle of one's lawn to look up at the red fire of Mars quivering in the sky and whisper: *Take me home.*

A lot of boys, and not a few girls, if they will admit it, have indeed gone "home" because of such nights, such whispers, such promises of far places, such planets, and the creator of the inhabitants of those planets.

In conversations over drinks around our country the past ten years I have been astonished to discover how often a leading biochemist or archaeologist or space technician or astronaut when asked: what happened to you when you were ten years old? replied:

"Tarzan."

"John Carter."

"Mr. Burroughs, of course."

One eminent anthropologist admitted to me, "When I was eleven I read *The Land That Time Forgot.* Bones, I thought. Dry bones. I will go magic me some bones and resurrect a Time. From then on I galloped through life. I became what Mr. Burroughs *told* me to become."

So there you have it. Or almost have it, anyway. The explanation that we, as intellectuals, dread to think about. But that we, as creatures of blood and instinct and adventure, welcome with a cry. An idea, after all, is no good if it doesn't *move.* Toynbee, for goodness sake, teaches us that. The Universe challenges us. We must bleed before the challenge. We must waste ourselves in Time and Space in order to survive, hating the challenge, hating the response, yet in the welter and confusion, somehow loving it all. We are that creature of paradox that would love to sit by the fire and only speak. But the world, other animals more immediately practical than ourselves, and all of outer space says otherwise. We must die in order to live. The settlers did it before us. We will imitate them on the Moon, on Mars, and bury ourselves in graveyards among the stars so that the stars themselves become fecund.

All this Burroughs says most directly, simply, and in terms of animal blood and racial memory every time that Tarzan leaps into a tree or Carter soars through space.

We may know and admire and respect and be moved by Mr. Verne, but he was too polite, wasn't he? You always felt that in the midst of Moon-stalking, his gents might just sit down to tea, or that Nemo, no matter how deep he sank in the Sargasso, still had time for his organ and his Bach. Very nice, very lovely. But the blood does not move so much with this, as does the mind.

In sum, we may have liked Verne and Wells and Kipling, but we loved, we adored, we went quite mad with Mr. Burroughs. We grew up into our intellectuality, of course, but our blood always remembered. Some part of our soul always stayed in the ravine running through the center of Waukegan, Illinois, up in a tree, swinging on a vine, combating shadow-apes.

I still have two letters tucked away in my First Edition *Tarzan of the Apes*. They were written by Mr. Burroughs to me when I was seventeen and still fairly breathless and in fevers over him. I had asked him to come down and speechify the Science Fiction League which met every Thursday night in Clifton's Cafeteria in Los Angeles. It was a great chance for him to meet a lot of mad young people who dearly loved him. Mr. Burroughs, for some strange reason, cared not to join the mob. I wrote again. This time Mr. Burroughs wrote back and assured me that the last thing in the world he would dream of doing was make a public lecture. Thanks a lot but no thanks, he said.

What the hey, I thought, if *he* won't talk about Tarzan, *I will*.

I gabbed and blabbed and gibbered about Tarzan for well over an hour. I had Clifton's Cafeteria emptied in ten minutes, everyone home in twenty, everyone with aspirins for migraine in their mouth five minutes short of an hour.

The summer of 1930 madness had struck again. When I stopped babbling, my arms ached from swinging on all those vines, my head rang from giving all those yells.

I guess that about sums it up.

A number of people changed my life forever in various ways.

Lon Chaney put me up on the side of Notre Dame and swung me from a chandelier over the opera crowd in Paris.

Edgar Allan Poe mortared me into a brick vault with some Amontillado.

Kong chased me up one side and down the other of the Empire State.

But Mr. Burroughs convinced me that I could talk with the animals, even if they didn't answer back, and that late nights when I was asleep my soul slipped from my body, slung itself out the window, and frolicked across town never touching the lawns, always hanging from trees where, even later in those nights, I taught myself alphabets and soon learned French and English and danced with the apes when the moon rose.

But then again, his greatest gift was teaching me to look at Mars and ask to be taken home.

I went home to Mars often when I was eleven and twelve and every year since, and the astronauts with me, as far as the Moon to start, but Mars by the end of the century for sure, Mars by 1999. We have commuted because of Mr. Burroughs. Because of him we have printed the Moon. Because of him and men like him, one day in the next five centuries, we will commute forever, we will go away . . .

And never come back.

And so live forever.

Ray Bradbury
Los Angeles, California
May 8, 1975

1 THE CREATIVE DECISION

On a July day in 1911 Edgar Rice Burroughs sat in a small office at the intersection of Market and Monroe streets in Chicago. He had borrowed desk space from a friend in order to launch his latest enterprise, an agency for the sale of pencil sharpeners. The salesmen who responded to his ads were sent out on a commission basis. "They did not sell any pencil sharpeners," he noted, "but in the leisure moments, while I was waiting for them to come back to tell me that they had not sold any . . ."[1]

What else was there to do? He began to write, the pen seeming oddly small in his heavy fingers. He bore little resemblance to the image of a writer, but there was even less in his appearance to suggest the typical businessman. Since he would seldom draw upon real-life experiences, where would he find the story plots that he needed? His search for excitement, for high adventure in his early years had ended in disappointment. Whatever he found fell far short of his expectations. His youthful spirit of

adventure, still unrealized, was temporarily thrust aside. At night, in a happy release from the monotonous daytime routines, it returned to spur his imagination to life. He often lay awake devising fantastic situations and creating his own characters, superhumans who performed incredibly heroic feats in strange worlds and on distant planets.

Now his instincts turned him to the freedom of imagination. His pen swept across the only paper available — orange, blue, and yellow sheets were mixed with white. The blue and yellow ones were old letterheads. He used the backs, shaping words hastily so that they emerged with distinctive flattened or unfinished letters. The u's, r's, m's and n's rose in vague curves above the line, the i's were barely visible, and the crossbars of the t's were dabbed in late beyond the line, out of place, like an afterthought.

Formed in his daydreams and imaginings, the ingredients for many stories — strange encounters, daring rescues, hairbreadth escapes, glorious battles — awaited his summons. As he wrote, the real world of the commonplace became the unreal one; it vanished, and in its place he conjured up a strange fierce civilization set in the midst of a dying planet. The new world closed around him, all sounds of the old were gone, and he was a man lost in a perilous land where science battled against savagery, beauty against ugliness.

The Edgar Rice Burroughs of summer 1911 who entered hesitantly into the field of writing was almost a dual personality. To relatives and close friends he was a delightful man, a humorous practical joker and composer of fairy tales and clever drawings for favorite nieces and nephews. Yet in the business world where he struggled desperately for success he was matter-of-fact, never disclosing the creative imagination of a writer. For example, in a letter discussing his first story he used the stilted jargon of commerce: "It is purely a business proposition with me and I wish to deliver the goods in accordance with your specifications." Though this seems ludicrous, it must be remembered that Burroughs bore not only a suppressed talent but an accumulation of buried hopes, regrets, and frustrations. Approaching thirty-six, he probably viewed his present unhappy circumstances and the past years of random ventures and short-lived occupations with bewilderment and confusion. He had reached a dead end, unable to discover goals or direction.

The reasons for his unplanned, helter-skelter life were unclear to him. All he knew was that he had held on to nothing, that nothing had become permanent. Even the experience he had gained, astonishing in its variety, was of doubtful value. He had floundered about in the business field, vacillating between being an employee and an entrepreneur.

Burroughs lived under the spell of the dominant creed of the times: that success for an individual of the middle-class fringe, especially one without a skill or profession, could be found only in business. A man could begin in a small way with a routine office position, waiting hopefully for promotion, or, if impatient and inclined to gamble, he could invest some tiny capital in business and operate on dreams and a shoestring. There was always the possibility of a get-rich-quick scheme that would work.

Caught in the problems of day-to-day living, Burroughs obtained employment which demanded all his attention and exhausted him; there wasn't time to pause for self-analysis and to identify the creativity that had been struggling for expression since early childhood.

What turned him to writing was not a sudden perception but rather desperation. He wouldn't understand until some time later that a career solely in the business world was not for him. But now, with all the year's efforts adding up to zero, Burroughs was ready to concede that he was a failure. The distinction, subtle but important — the difference between being a failure and being simply a misplaced man — was beyond him. His mind, to elaborate upon the old saw of the pegs, was designed for stretching a round universe of elastic boundaries, for pushing the boundaries out; there was no way he could exist or fit into the universe of square partitions, of offices, of adding machines, sales, profits, and losses.

The turning point came at a time of bitter realization. He had been involved in still another impossible project, hardly knowing why, and with little faith left. Failure was inevitable. "My business venture," he wrote, "went the way of all other enterprises and I was left without money, without a job and with a wife and two babies."[2]

Ironically, with thirty-five years gone and all else tried, he was ready to put his ideas on paper. But strangely, the experiences he had undergone, the colorful characters he had known — soldiers, cowboys, Indians, and miners — these, the stuff of realism and the reminders of an unstable past, he instinctively avoided. These experiences had physically shaped him into what he was — a solid, muscular man, sturdily framed, with broad shoulders and strong arms. His large hands, a family inheritance, with their thick, powerful fingers drew immediate attention. A masseur in a Turkish bath examined Burroughs' hands and remarked, "We get all kinds of people in here, but this is the first time I ever massaged a blacksmith."[3] Athletics, a vigorous outdoor life, cowpunching and horseback riding — at military school he had vaulted easily into the saddle from a standing position — had combined to develop a physique that altered little through the years.

Now, in writing, the strange characters and settings of a favorite fantasy, one to which his mind had often retreated, sprang to life easily with the rapid movement of his pen. Within any man's fantasy there is always a superhero, and of course the role is reserved for him alone. Edgar Rice Burroughs *was* his main character, playing the scene his imagination approved. At the story's opening he, the protagonist, was in a period of enforced return, the wild adventures temporarily over. He was a brooding, suffering man, dragged back without his consent, fated to walk the earth in agony, to tell of events that seemed crowded into the past: "I am a very old man; how old I do not know. Possibly I am a hundred, possibly more; but I cannot tell because I have never been like other men. I remember no childhood . . ."

That was the key, the prayer of all escapists — *not to be like other men.* Burroughs knew little about the techniques of writing but he understood that those who read his story would have their own dreams and fantasies, their own yearnings to get away from painful reality.

As he wrote he compiled a brief glossary of names and of special words used in the story, to him a fascinating task. A man is true master of a civilization when he can dictate its language, concocting such words as *Barsoom* — Mars; *Iss* — River of Death; *Woola* — a Barsoomian calot or dog; *Dejah Thoris* — a Princess of Helium; and *Helium* — the empire of the grandfather of Dejah Thoris.

The list was short, nothing approaching a complete vocabulary, but the words gave a genuine touch to the characters and scenes set on a planet millions of miles distant. The paradox of attempting to weld fantasy with reality and science with the wildest of fiction did not deter him. It was here that Burroughs first demonstrated one of the secrets of his success as a writer — he was able to make the most impossible tale seem as though it were really happening. It had been plausible in his imagination; he was willing to suspend disbelief and he presumed that the reader would respond the same way.

The protagonist, John Carter, was a romantic hero in the most glorious tradition. He was a chivalrous soldier of fortune, an adventurer, a man whose "only means of livelihood" had been fighting. In the foreword, a kind of prologue that is vital to the story, Burroughs describes Carter as:

. . . a splendid specimen of manhood, standing a good two inches over six feet, broad of shoulder and narrow of hip, with the carriage of the trained fighting man. His features were regular and clear cut, his hair black and closely cropped, while his eyes were of a steel gray, reflecting a strong and loyal character, filled with fire and initiative. His manners were perfect, and his courtliness was that of a typical southern gentleman of the highest type.

Burroughs created a character whose background and physical accomplishments were a super version of his own. "His horsemanship, especially after hounds," he wrote, "was a marvel and delight even in that country of magnificent horsemen." Carter had been cautioned about his "wild recklessness," but would respond with a laugh and say "that the tumble that killed him would be from the back of a horse yet unfoaled."

While prospecting in Arizona, Captain Carter strays into the dangerous territory of the Apaches, a situation duplicated by Burroughs in his activities with the Seventh Cavalry. But Arizona was selected as the briefest of settings; once Carter had faced the hostile Indians, all realism was discarded. Mysteriously transported through space, he finds himself among a race of huge green Martians whose young are hatched in glass incubators from eggs two-and-one-half feet in diameter.

It was a beginning, a tentative release of the bonds that had confined Ed's imagination. He wrote freely, all restraints overcome, and by August of 1911 a substantial section of the Mars story was finished. He had worked "very surreptitiously," commenting, "I was very much ashamed of my new vocation and until the story was nearly half completed I told no one about it, and then only my wife. It seemed a foolish thing for a full grown man to be doing — much on a par with dressing myself in a boy scout suit and running away from home to fight Indians."[4] Another, practical circumstance impelled him to secrecy. He still believed his future awaited him in the business world. What would his associates and prospective employers think of a man who abandoned his sober surroundings and projected himself into unbelievable scenes on another planet? Ed feared that both his reputation and his career would be irreparably damaged.

Moreover, he was a novice to publishing; he knew nothing about magazine editors or the procedures for sending a story to them. When he had written twelve chapters, about 180 pages, he sat back to contemplate his work, convinced he had produced enough to demonstrate that he could write. He was pleased to realize that he still had a great deal of material left. The matter of a title became a problem. Uncertain, he settled for "My First Adventure on Mars," a title both weak and colorless. Shortly afterward he lined it out and inserted "The Green Martians"; this too he found unsatisfactory. He was beginning to appreciate the difficulty that all writers face in selecting titles.

Burroughs considered and in the right corner of the manuscript jotted down "Dejah Thoris Martian Princess," following it with question marks. Beneath the title he wrote an odd nom de plume — *By Normal Bean*. This choice was a measure of his own insecurity and of his modestly humorous appraisal of his writing ability. He wished to stress his ordinariness — that he had a very common head. But his adoption of a pen name was also dictated by his fear of identification with so fantastic a work. The solution was a refuge in anonymity.

Impressed by the popular *All-Story* magazine, he submitted his story to the magazine's editor and offered a brief summary of the plot:

The story is supposedly from the manuscript of a Virginian soldier of fortune who spends ten years on Mars, among the ferocious green men of that planet as well as with the highly developed and scientific race of dominant Mar-

Part of ERB's foreword to "Under the Moons of Mars" in original form; published in book A Princess of Mars, 1917.

STORIES TOLD AND RETOLD

A PRINCESS
OF MARS

Edgar Rice Burroughs

OXFORD UNIVERSITY PRESS

Cover of A Princess of Mars, *Oxford University Press, 1962; book selected for series* Stories Told and Retold.

tians, who closely resemble the inhabitants of Earth, except as to color. It is a member of this latter race which gives the story its name and at the same time infuses the element of love into the narrative.

Burroughs explained that the manuscript, the first part of *Dejah Thoris, Martian Princess,* totaled about 43,000 words and that he could offer "about two more parts of the same length." He couldn't resist including a personal endorsement that had the tone of a sales-pitch: "The story contains sufficient action, love, mystery and 'horror' to render it entertaining to a large majority of readers."

On August 24, 1911, the answering letter came from the Frank A. Munsey Company in New York, carrying the signature of the managing editor of *All-Story* Magazine, Thomas Newell Metcalf. An analyst par excellence and a man of succinct habits in writing, he mixed the good news with the bad. "There are many things about the story which I like," he said, "but on the other hand, there are points about which I am not so keen. Undoubtedly the story shows a great deal of imagination and ingenuity; but I am unable to judge . . . the total effect, on account of its unfinished condition.

Then he came to grips with the story's weaknesses: it was "too slow in getting under way." Obviously, at least for magazine purposes, he didn't care for the long, wordy foreword that described Captain Carter's background, his return after sixteen years, and his strange death. Metcalf also commented that Burroughs treated "too casually and vaguely Carter's leaving the earth and arriving upon Mars." He complained about the author's "long-windedness" and his tendency to tell many things that were unessential to the story.

Metcalf, with a dry humor, refers to the supposed "taciturnity of the Martians" which Burroughs had emphasized. ". . . yet you have one of the ladies tell a story of a couple of thousand words and often the Tharks talk to a great extent. Somehow, it seems to me you are hardly consistent." The lady was a young green-Martian woman assigned to Carter with combined duties of guide, housekeeper, and tutor.

Metcalf, after some hesitation, eliminated the chapter titled "Sola Tells Me Her Story," but Burroughs restored it later in the book form.

Setting a 70,000-word limit, Metcalf went on to end the letter encouragingly: "If it would be possible for you to compress into that length a story as ingenious as is the greater part of what I have read, I should be . . . glad to consider it."

Burroughs was not at all perturbed by the editor's criticisms and suggestions for revision. In his letter of August 26 he displayed an eagerness to rewrite the story. He reverted curiously to the cold, practical philosophy of the businessman in explaining his reasons for writing: "I wrote this story because I needed the money it might bring, and not from motives of sentiment. . . ." (Sentiment was taboo — this from an author who wrote exaggeratedly romantic stories with beautiful heroines and noble, dashing heroes.) His added comment was a giveaway: ". . . although I became very much interested in it while writing." Ashamed to admit any sentiment about the characters who occupied his dreams, he hoped to avoid exposure through this deception and the often-repeated statement, obviously false, that money was his only motive for writing.

When Burroughs showed some confusion about the problem of the garrulous Tharks and the long account given by Sola, Metcalf, struggling to balance a natural asperity against a fear of being overblunt, fell into a style that was amusing in its own longwindedness, ". . . may I say that it will be perfectly easy to correct the inconsistency of which we have talked merely by neglecting to say that the Tharks are a taciturn people? At the same time, I believe that you can eliminate a good deal of their conversation."

In the letter of August 26, Burroughs had also outlined important sections of the last half of the story for Metcalf, including a vague and unsatisfactory ending scene for his hero, John Carter:

. . . later attempts to explore the mysterious Valley Dor at mouth of River Iss. Is caught in

mighty air currents above the valley and borne high aloft into cold and darkness. Loses consciousness and awakens in his Arizona cave.

Metcalf, two days later, had his own suggestion for the ending, inquiring, "why would it not be possible to have the Martian city attacked by some kind of a plague, or something of that sort?" The Martian princess would then die, and afterward John Carter would contract the illness and find himself dying; he would awaken in the cave in Arizona.

This suggestion for the last scene proved an inspiration to Burroughs. On September 28 he commented, ". . . worked out the ending along the line you suggested, which is much more satisfactory than that I originally had in mind." But what he had devised far exceeded this modest statement. He had invented an unresolved ending, with the reader (protestingly, as it later developed) clutched and squirming in unbearable suspense. From this first Mars story on, his specialty was to be the unfinished ending and the inescapable sequel.

With the completed revisions the full manuscript was mailed. Perhaps the most thrilling letter of an author's career is the one announcing the first sale. On November 4 Metcalf wrote:

The Martian Princess' story is in perfectly good form now and I should like very much to buy it for publication in The All-Story Magazine. I therefore offer you for all serial rights, $400.00.

His acceptance included a request for permission to change the title and to do some cutting, especially at the beginning. In later years Burroughs commented: "The check was the first big event of my life. No amount of money today could possibly give me the thrill that that first $400 check gave me."

Burroughs' elation was tempered by a businessman's cold analysis of the payment versus the time consumed. On November 6, he evaluated a future writing profession with considerable skepticism:

This story business is all new to me, but I like the work provided I can make it pay. However, I know that it would not be worth my while to devote all my time to it at this rate, as I started this story in July, which makes the remuneration equivalent to about $100.00 per month.

Metcalf had informed Burroughs that the title would be "In the Moons of Mars," but when the February 1912 *All-Story* appeared with the first installment, the "In" had been changed to "Under." More surprising was the discovery of an alteration in the author's name: it was printed as "Norman" Bean. The assumption was that an enterprising proofreader, dubious that such a name as "Normal" could be correct, had made the change.

Annoyed, Burroughs indicated in his letter of February 2 that as a result of the printer's blunder he was discarding his nom de plume. In sending a new manuscript he commented acidly:

You will also note that I have used my own name as author. I have done this because what little value was attached to my "trade" name was rendered nil by the inspired compositor who misspelled it in the February '11 Story — or was it the artist? ['11 is an obvious error.]

He finished by taking a humorous, more indulgent attitude:

I liked his illustration so well, however, that I easily forgave him; though I cannot forgive the printer who let "animal" get by for "mammal" twice.

The publication of "Under the Moons of Mars" was a beginning. Burroughs, while encouraged, accepted this first sale with caution and would not allow his expectations to soar. A full-fledged writing career was not as yet within his grasp. Nothing had changed, and the necessity to support his family sent him out again on a search for employment. But the most significant thing had been accomplished: he had attained an insight, a vision of his suppressed creativity. A fuller confidence and understanding were not far away. He was on the verge of finding himself.

2 CHILDHOOD AND A FIRST ADVENTURE

Ed Burroughs grew up in a busy environment. The three-story brick house on Chicago's West Side, Washington Boulevard between Lincoln and Robey Streets, solid and substantial, was in itself a symbol of middle-class prosperity. With its many rooms (and the customary basement) the house was well-designed for a large family. Ed, as the youngest child, became a fascinated spectator of the numerous activities of his father and three brothers. He was a sensitive child, observant, and eagerly attentive. An impression of lightness — pale skin and golden-brown hair — conveyed also the image of delicate health that concerned his parents.

Admiring his older brothers, he wished to emulate them, but he was not at all like brothers George, Harry, and Frank. His quick sense of humor was evident in these earliest years, along with his search for creative expression. Curious and imaginative, he liked to shape words and thoughts on paper, turning first, at the age of five, to rhyme:

I'm Dr. Burroaghs come to town,
To see my patint Maria Brown

An account of his education refers jokingly to "an advanced course in a private kindergarten," where the major activity seemed to be "weaving mats from strips of colored paper."[1] But most memorable were the years spent at the old Brown School on the West Side of Chicago, only a few blocks from the Burroughs home, the same school that George, Harry, and Frank had attended.

Secure within a close-knit circle of family and friends, Ed found this period a happy one. Four blocks to the east was Union Park, a quiet, grassy oasis set in the midst of busy city streets. One of the park's functions was to serve as a grazing area for the neighborhood cows brought there each day by the herdsmen. Major George was among those who kept a cow to supply fresh milk. In their rambles around the neighborhood, Ed and his friends visited the park for

9

another reason: they enjoyed tossing peanuts to Old Bob, the grizzly bear.

The Brown School friends who grew up with Ed were William (Billy) Carpenter Camp; Alson Clark, the painter; Ben Marshall, a successful Chicago architect; and Mancel T. Clark, a wealthy paint manufacturer. Florenz Ziegfeld, the celebrated theatrical producer, was also a pupil at the Brown School. Here, Ed was assigned to what he jokingly listed as his first army experience. Within a list titled My Wonderful Military Career, he noted that he had been "Right Guard, Brown School Cadets," and added in parentheses, "Wooden gun."[2]

Near the Burroughs home on Washington Boulevard resided Alvin Hulbert, his wife Emma Theresa, and their children. For George's four sons the normal neighborly relationships were made more attractive because of the four lively Hulbert sisters — Leila, the oldest, Julia, Jessie, and Emma — who occupied the three-story family residence at 194 Park Avenue. Walking to and from the Brown School, young Ed and Emma often met and formed an early habit of being together.

From the age of six Ed showed an interest and delight in letter writing, enjoying opportunities to correspond with members of his family when they were away from home. On February 19, 1882, his father, while staying in Washington, D. C., received a letter from Ed, written in heavy capitals, reading, "HOW ARE YOU. I MISS YOU VERY MUCH. WE ARE ALL WELL."[3]

In 1885 George Jr. and Henry (Harry) were sent to Yale University by their father, and they enrolled in the Sheffield Scientific School. George, the older of the two, had his education delayed because of illness, and as a result, the brothers entered Yale together.[4] Ed, in this first long separation from his brothers, missed them keenly. He corresponded regularly, eager to hear of their activities and to tell about his. These letters reveal much about the beginnings of his creativity, not only in his writing and poetry, but also in his drawings and cartoons,

Major George Tyler Burroughs, father of ERB, 1861.

10

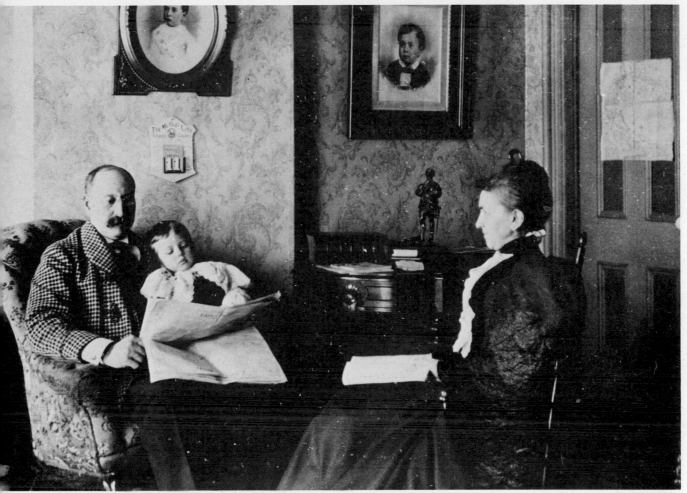

Mr. and Mrs. George Tyler Burroughs and grandson Studley in home at 646 Washington Boulevard, Chicago, 1896.

Mary Evaline Burroughs, ERB's mother.

which, often humorous, served as illustrations for his comments, news items, or poems. The letters present an intimate picture of the warm, sympathetic relationships between all of the brothers.

On February 13, 1887, Ed sent his brother George a valentine, and George responded on February 22 to thank him: ". . . it was the only one we received. Did you get many?"

Ed had evidently told of a burglary in the neighborhood, for George wrote:

You must have had quite an exciting time with Dr. Adolphus' burgular. I should think neither the doctor nor Mr. Simington would feel very safe with vacant houses next to them which afford burglars so easy an entrance.

11

Alvin Hulbert family home at corner of Robie and Park Avenue, Chicago; the boy in the surrey is Alvin Hulbert, Jr.

George reveals Ed's interest in reading:

I am glad you are reading "Tales of Ancient Greece" and am not surprised that you enjoy it. I know I did when I read it.

Now if you will take one of our "Barnes General Histories" that I asked Mother to send to us, and read up the history of Greece, which you will find some what closely related to its Mythology, that is the early history, your reading will be more interesting as well as instructive.

In continuing, George tells of an incident that might have been serious:

About half the University & half the freshman crew had a nice mud bath down at the boathouse Sat. A platform broke, dropping us about six feet into the slimiest mud I ever saw. I landed square on top of another fellows & so, fortu- *nately, came off somewhat better than I otherwise would, but I was a sight.*

George explains about privileges at Yale:

There is still one saloon which we cannot enter and unless our nine, that is the freshman nine defeat the Harvard freshmen in the Spring we are not allowed to sit on the "fence." I think you will find an account of this custom in that book I gave the folks Christmas.

In a joint letter to Harry and George, dated March 27, 1887, Ed, age eleven and one-half, draws a picture, presumably of himself, holding a telephone receiver to his ear while he addresses his brothers. He tells of watching experiments of "crystalizing" under the "micrescope" which were "fine." Ed compliments Harry, telling proudly that the man who performed the experiments said that "the fly wing you mount-

Alvin Hulbert family; seated, left to right: Emma Theresa Hulbert and Alvin Hulbert; standing, left to right: Alvin Hulbert, Jr., Leila, Emma Centennia, Julia, and Jessie.

ed was mounted as well if not better than any he had. I saw it too." At the close of his letter to Harry he says, "I will be glad when the time comes for you boys to come home."

In the section intended for George, Ed begins:

As I wrote to Harry first I have pretty near emptied my fertile brain but will try to think of some thing more, For instance How are you getting along in your studies? I am getting along first rate backwards. As I lose every letter I get I cant answer them atall. A boy and I have gone into the yeast business x x x x x And broken up. "A Boy" has offered me some pigeons (two) and I expect to get them some time before I die. .

At the top of the second page Ed has drawn a picture of the American flag floating from the top of a pole that extends vertically along the left margin of the sheet almost to the bottom. A man in a cowboy suit and hat has climbed more than half way up the pole. We see that he has dropped his gun and that it is falling through the air. On the ground at the foot of the pole an odd-appearing little animal is waiting. All of this is designed to illustrate the poem which Edgar "made up . . . this morning. . . ."[5]

The lure of cartooning that drove him, even at this early age, to drawing his small illustrations and comical figures in the margins of his letters and poems was also evident in his school textbooks. Within the covers and in the margins of the pages he drew his cartoons; their presence creates the suspicion that his attention could stray from his school work to an activity he found more stimulating.

A more significant part of his creativity was demonstrated in the delight he took in making up stories. Because of his low resistance to colds and infections, he was often confined to bed. At these times he became impatient with the old fables that his mother told him, prefer-

13

ring to create his own imaginative tales and tell them to her.[6]

Ed's poetry writing as an outlet for his imagination was just one part of his youthful development. Major George, always the practical businessman, took the opportunity to provide his son with an experience in the field of commerce. A note dated February 21, 1887, and signed by George Burroughs was evidently used in a business transaction involving Ed. George, using formal terminology, devised a legal form for his twelve-year old son:

On or before March 1st 1888 for value received I promise to pay Edgar R. Burroughs Twenty Seven & 50/100 ($27 50/100) with interest at the rate of six percent per annum.

Whether George purchased something belonging to Ed, or whether he borrowed some of his son's money has not been ascertained. The transaction may have been part of a business game, and not viewed as a real obligation, for George appears to have forgotten about it until years later. But he did discover it and pay it off — with interest. Written across the note is the statement "Paid March 31st 1898 $46.12."

Possibly because of the death of Ed's two infant brothers, his parents became cautious about his health, and when the city was swept by an epidemic of diptheria, they decided to take him out of the public schools. He was midway through the sixth grade, but his parents, unwilling to take chances, began a search for a private school. The only one available on the West Side was Mrs. K. S. Cooley's School for Girls.

To a twelve-year-old boy the prospect was appalling. Ed reacted to the situation with an attitude of extreme distaste. It was little consolation to him that the parents of a half-dozen of his closest friends were following the Burroughs' example. Billy Camp, Ben Marshall, Mancel Clark, and others were placed in Miss Cooley's school. Ed spent only a brief period there, later commenting, "I know that we all got out of Miss Cooley's Maplehurst School for Girls as

An 1885 sketch by ERB, at age ten, of an Indian mounted on an

An 1885 pencil sketch by ERB at age ten.

14

quickly as unfeeling parents would permit."

A report card issued by Miss Cooley, dated "April 9th to May 11th 1888," reveals that Ed was a better-than-average student. He received high marks of 98 in geography and 95 in reading. His lowest mark, 80, was in composition.

The Burroughs family had always stressed good health habits and exercise, and this was evidenced in the letters written by brother George while he was at Yale in 1887 and 1888.[7] Concerned about reports of illness, he wrote to his father on December 4, 1887:

I am sorry that Mother & Eddie are not well. I am afraid that neither of them get enough outdoor exercise to keep their systems in order.

Plain food, regular habits good hours & plenty of exercise keep me in such perfect health that I want to prescribe the same for every one who is not feeling well.

George was both firm and frank in emphasizing his objections to a program of excessive studying at the expense of physical fitness. He clearly had no patience with the student who turned himself into a grind, and in a letter of January 9, 1887, commented:

. . . When I came down here I had hopes that I might distinguish myself in my studies (in some one), but I find that impossible and when I look at those of my classmates who do the best, I feel thankful that I am not like them, for with a few exceptions the "digs" are a poor, sickly looking lot. I hope however that I will know as much as any of them at the end for I will learn from them in recitations & when I get hold of a thing once I remember it. I tell you this for I want you to understand that even if I don't make a mark I am working and not wasting my time.

On April 8, 1888, again from Yale to his father, George, concerned about Eddie's health, wrote:

. . . I am glad Eddie has a bicycle, & hope he will have some inducement to keep him riding it.

I dont think any of us ever realized how much good our bicycles did Harry & I how much time we spent on them out of doors when

THE HOTEL WORLD

Issued Every Saturday. THE HOTEL AND TRAVELERS' JOURNAL. Issued Every Saturday.

25th Yr.-Vol. L. CHICAGO, ILL., SATURDAY, FEB. 10, 1900. NO. 6.

Masthead of cover of Hotel World *magazine, February 10, 1900.*

we would otherwise have been in the house.

Frank & Eddie are neither of them as strong & well as they ought to be and I think it is because they do not take exercise enough in the open air. Not that it would do either of them any good to force them to do something distasteful to them. . . .

As Eddie spent more time outdoors, his health improved. Bicycle riding became a source of enjoyment, and on Chicago's Warren Avenue, where a first stretch of experimental asphalt pavement had been laid, running west from Ogden Avenue to Western, he rode his bike for many hours.[8]

Although it cannot be documented, it is assumed that during this period the Hulbert and Burroughs families were probably in neighborly association, and Ed found his attachment to Emma growing stronger. A youthful romance was developing, and he soon preferred to devote most of his attentions to her.

Emma's father, Alvin Hulbert, had acquired a position of esteem in Chicago business circles; he was respected as a civic leader, and his reputation in the community was comparable to that held by George Burroughs. Alvin had shown an early interest in the hotel business and had worked as a clerk in the old Sherman House in Chicago. He and W. S. Eden later became owners of the Tremont and Great Northern Hotels. Alvin's ventures were highly successful, and in October 1871, after the Sherman House was burned to the ground, he made arrangements for the erection of a new hotel with 250 rooms. As its genial landlord, known for his "urbanity and pleasant manners," he received the enthusiastic approval of the hotel guests.[9] He was also associated with the Lindell Hotels in St. Louis.

Alvin's entry into politics in the primary of March 26, 1880, resulted in his defeating his opponent R. P. Williams and being elected Alderman of the Twelfth Ward. He ran on the regular Republican ticket, and in a letter to the *New York Times* (date unknown) protested about the *Times*' error in referring to him as an independent Democrat. He maintained that he had always been a stalwart Republican.[10]

While Emma continued to attend the Brown School, Ed, happy to escape from Miss Cooley's Maplehurst School for Girls, in the fall of 1888 entered the Harvard School on 21st Street and Indiana Avenue. His brother Frank (called Coleman) had been a student at Harvard for a year. Ed remarked, "I was never a student — I just went to school there."[11]

He had vivid recollections of the period:

Benny Marshall, the Chicago architect, was one of my classmates. We used to sneak down to the lake and sit on the breakwater and smoke cubeb cigarettes, thinking that we were regular devils.

While I was attending Harvard School, we lived on the west side on Washington Boulevard, about four blocks west of Union Park; and I often rode my pony to school, keeping it in a livery stable near Twenty-Second Street. It would be difficult to imagine riding a pony from the west side to Twenty-First and Indiana today.[12]

He explained that the West Side was "where everybody made his money in those days and then moved to the South Side to show off." In good weather Ed either drove or rode to school. He remembered other details clearly:

In inclement weather, I took the Madison Street horsecars to Wabash, a cable-car to 18th Street, and another horse-car to school. Sometimes, returning from school, I used to run down Madison Street from State Street to Lincoln Street, a matter of some three miles, to see how many horsecars I could beat in that direction. It tires me all out even to think of it now. I must have been long on energy, if a trifle short on brains.[13]

Of the school staff young Burroughs never forgot Principal John C. Grant, of whom he was "scared to death," and Professor John J. Schobinger, also listed as principal, who was determined that the students should learn Greek and Latin grammar before turning to a study of English. A *Harvard School* report card, issued on September 7, 1891, covers the period of September 1890 to February 1891, and lists average marks on a scale of 100: Arithmetic, 62; English, 67; Algebra, 79; Latin, 83.

Evidently because of the concentration on Latin, Ed was far stronger in this subject than he was in English.[14] The disparity between the marks on arithmetic and algebra is difficult to explain. In a letter of September 3, 1891, addressed to "Whom this may concern," and signed by both Schobinger and Grant, there is a statement that "he [Ed] leaves the school of his own accord, in good standing." Ed had left the

school months earlier, and this certificate of moral character was obviously issued at the request of his father, who needed it for Ed's next school — Phillips Academy. A later combination of report card and character reference, written on the seventh, explains that Ed is "of good moral character and he left our school on account of ill-health." This new version of the reasons for Ed's departure from Harvard may have been demanded by George Burroughs, who was undoubtedly sensitive about his son's weak achievement at the school. Burroughs may have removed his son because of a fear of an epidemic of la grippe which had spread throughout Chicago. Another possibility is that Harvard itself may have been temporarily closed, for a later reference about this school period mentions that ". . . epidemics had closed two schools that I had attended."[15]

That Ed's departure was abrupt is indicated in the exchange of letters (three in all) between Schobinger and Burroughs. On September 7 the Professor wrote:

Your letter being dated Sept 6th and Edgar not having called, I suppose he is gone by this time. I therefore send you the required certificate by mail, as requested. . .[16]

At any rate, when Ed left Harvard School in midsemester, some time after February 1891, he must have done so with relief. The typical school studies, the lessons in Greek and Latin, he found dreary tasks. Highly imaginative, he could discover in these subjects nothing to motivate him. But the new plans for the coming months created a feeling of joy and excitement. His destination, for a fifteen-year-old boy, was like something out of his dreams. Awaiting him was the high road to adventure.

Upon their graduation from Yale in 1889, George and Harry returned to Chicago where they went to work in their father's American Battery Company. Harry, at his desk job in an atmosphere filled with battery fumes, quickly developed a cough which worsened as the days went by; his lungs appeared to show the first

Front of American Battery Company business card.

signs of consumption. The doctor insisted that a change of climate was imperative. Through a friend, Major George arranged at once to purchase land for a cattle ranch in southern Idaho. Lew Sweetser, a Yale classmate, whose father also supplied some of the money, joined in the Burroughs' venture. The vigorous outdoor life of a cowpuncher built up Harry's damaged lungs and restored him to good health.

Located in Cassia County, Idaho, on a section of the extensive ranges owned by "Cattle King" Jim Pierce, the Burroughs-Sweetser spread occupied land along the lower Raft River, in the southeastern part of the state. The ranch was about thirty miles from American Falls, the railway station and shipping point for the cattle. To honor their alma mater the brothers called their ranch the *Bar Y*, and after persuading the federal government to establish a post office near the ranch, paid further tribute to their college by naming the post office *Yale*.

It was to the state of Idaho, newly admitted to the Union on July 3, 1890, that Ed was sent by his father. To a big city boy the sudden removal to a rough, primitive country was a thrilling adventure. From the strict discipline of school and the close supervision of his father he now found himself in the free-and-easy atmosphere of ranch life and under the indulgent care of brothers George and Harry. His friends were rugged and sometimes wild cowboys and miners who because of their vigor and individuality appeared like characters out of a western

American Battery Company office, 172-174 South Clinton Street,

adventure novel. In contrast, Ed was probably looked upon as a true tenderfoot. His only practical experience, pony riding on city streets, was of only rudimentary value on the *Bar Y* Ranch.

The story of his Idaho cowboy days is colorfully narrated in his *Autobiography*:

I did chores, grubbed sage brush and drove a team of bronchos to a sulky plow. I recall that once, after I unhooked them, they ran away and evidently, not being endowed with any too much intelligence, I hung onto the lines after tripping over a sage brush and was dragged around the country three times on my face. . . .[17]

He aroused the amazement of the cowboys and won "instant distinction" when he tried to pay for a drink with pennies:

No one in Idaho had ever before seen a penny. Two drinks were "two-bits"; one drink was "two-bits"; a cigar was "two-bits"; things were "two-bits," "four-bits," "six-bits." There were no pennies and there was no paper money. Everything was silver or gold; at least I understand there was gold there, though I never saw any of it.

The greenest of ranch hands, young Burroughs began to gain his experience in the most painful ways.[18] His brothers George and Harry were hard put to find some tasks he could do. ". . . as I had proven more or less of a flop as a chore boy," Ed noted, "they appointed me mail carrier." He rode daily to the railroad at American Falls, either on horseback or, if there was

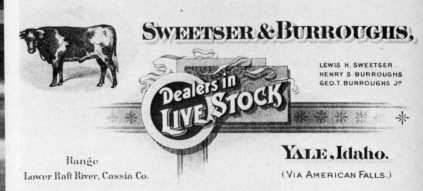

Business card of Sweetser and Burroughs Bar Y Ranch ($\overline{Y}$).

Chicago, about 1901.

19

ERB at age sixteen in Idaho.

freight to bring back, with a team and wagon. When he went on horseback, he made the round trip of sixty miles in one day.

His most exasperating experiences were with horses:

The team that I drove consisted of two outlawed bronchos; one was locoed and the other was too mean to ride. One day the wagon went through a bridge and I had to go about five miles to a ranch house to borrow the necessary tools to get it out. Being a tenderfoot, a horse to me was a horse and not knowing anything about the past lives or reputations of either of the team I naturally climbed aboard the bad one and rode him bareback five miles to the ranch. Here I loaded up with shovels, picks and crowbars and climbed back onto the broncho, riding the five miles back to the stalled wagon with assorted hardware bumping him on all his corners, which goes to show that Providence really does look after a certain class of people.

In another incident which demonstrated that naivete and good luck seemed to go together, he was asked to go to the pasture and bring some horses back to the corrals. They belonged to a newly arrived cow outfit. Everybody assumed that Ed would take one of the ranch horses for the trip to the pasture, but instead he chose a strange horse that was standing saddled and bridled. He was unaware of its bad reputation and that it was being ridden by Hi Rice, a famous bronco-buster. Neglecting also to look at the cinch, he climbed hastily aboard and rode away.

As they approached a steep bank of the Raft River, the horse clambered up and the saddle suddenly slipped off over his tail. Ed went head-over-heels, landing on the ground behind the animal. "He should have killed me," Ed said, "but instead he stopped with the cinch around his hind feet and turned an inquiring glance back at me." Later, when he had replaced the saddle, rounded up the horses, and returned to the corrals, a "goggle-eyed group of cowpunchers" was waiting for him, "including a couple of terrified brothers." They all stared as he rode in, "safe and alive, on the worst horse in Cassia County."[19]

These incidents, humorously exaggerated, do not give credit to Ed's knack in handling horses, evident even at this early age. His love of horses and riding — "when I got my leg over a horse I owned the world" — was matched by a sensitive and understanding attitude toward almost all animals.[20]

"At this time," he commented, "I learned. . . to take care of my horses, especially their backs, and I became proud of the fact that I never gave a horse a sore back, nor have I in my life." During a fall roundup he was given two horses with sore backs and both of them were healed while he was riding them.

Ed had noticed one horse, a beautiful black gelding, "fat as butter, with a long mane and a tail that almost dragged the ground." The condition of the tail indicated that the horse hadn't been ridden for some time since it was the custom to thin out the tail hairs so that the tail would not get full of burs and sagebrush.[21] The significance of this and other revealing facts about the horse, Whisky Jack, escaped Ed:

He had killed one man and maimed several others, but he was the only horse that was in good condition and it seemed a shame to ride our poor worn out crow baits while he was running in sleek and glossy idleness.

Eager to ride Whisky Jack, Ed pleaded with Jim Pierce until he was given permission. The men had to throw and hogtie the animal before they could saddle and bridle him. Then they put a blind on the horse while Ed mounted. When they removed the blind, Whisky Jack took two jumps, slipped, and fell, with Ed beneath him.

He didn't break anything in me, but I certainly hurt. However, I had to hide it for fear the boss wouldn't let me try it again. He was surprised when he found that I wanted to; he even grew enthusiastic. It had now become a sporting proposition with him and he offered to give me the horse if I could ride him.

21

Ed mounted the horse again, doubtful himself that he would last very long. But Whisky Jack adopted a more tractable attitude: "I stayed on him all that day because I was afraid if I got off I could never get on again. . . ." He rode the horse as long as he remained in Idaho, never bridling him but using a hackamore and a shoelace for a head-stall. Kindness changed Whisky Jack remarkably; with Ed he was always docile, but he would still refuse to allow any other man to handle him.

Whisky Jack's reaction was violent, although not unexpected, the first time Ed used him to carry the mail:

The Government furnished leather mail bags that went over the horse's rump behind the saddle and hung down on either side. They were equipped with metal staples and padlocks that rattled. I had to blindfold Jack to get them on him at all, then I mounted and jerked off the blind. He took a few steps, felt the bags against his sides, heard the rattle of the padlocks and started to leave the country. The road wound through foothills and he ran for ten miles before he became resigned to the fact that he couldn't leave the mail bags behind.

On another occasion Whisky Jack, startled by something, began to buck wildly when Ed mounted him for the return trip from American Falls to Yale:

There was a little gulley on the way out of town and some Chinamen lived in a dugout there. . . . Whisky Jack elected to buck up onto the roof of this dugout. That roof must have been constructed of railroad ties. If it had been of any lighter construction, we should have gone through. I had a fleeting glimpse of a dozen wild eyed Chinamen scurrying from the interior, and then Jack bucked off down the road relieving me of considerable embarrassment.

Ed recalled those early Idaho days with some nostalgia:

. . . I slept on the floor of a log cabin and in the winter time the snow drifted in under the door.

When I got up at four o'clock in the morning to do the chores, I had only two garments to put on, my hat and my boots. The hat went on easy enough, but the boots were always frozen. I wonder why we recall such hardships as among the happiest experiences of our lives.

Cassia County of the 1890s, a section of raw, frontier America, naturally bred rough, violent men. The images of the tough men Ed knew remained vivid in his memory. One, an old man named Blanco, "stammered terribly and cursed like a pirate." Because of his utter fearlessness and uncontrollable temper, nobody dared oppose him in any way. Ed's first experience with him was in a saloon in Albion. Noting the stick pin Ed was wearing, a miniature replica of a cartridge, Blanco walked calmly up to him, removed it from his tie, and stuck it in his own shirt. Ed had heard of Blanco and decided, with discretion, not to offer any protest. "I thought it better to show my deference for age," he said, "and let it go at that."[22]

Texas Pete, a young cowpuncher who arrived at the Burroughs' ranch dead broke, was another one whom Ed remembered. Pete, given a job grubbing sagebrush at seventy-five cents an acre, was charged, according to custom, the usual amount for his board. After working for several weeks, he decided to leave. His earnings were totaled, his board bill deducted, and he was paid the difference. Pete got the full amount — "six-bits" — which Ed then won from him in a crap game.

Ed found Pete to be very likable, "but like most Texans always ready to fight":

I saw him fighting with another puncher one day during a roundup. They went into a clinch on the ground and each one was spurring the other in the back with long roweled Mexican spurs. The foreman used to take their guns away from them in camp; so they had to use spurs.[23]

About Pete, Ed commented, "He had the reputation of being a bad man, but there was nothing bad about him."[24] The events had a tragic outcome. Pete, wanted for some minor law violation, attempted to evade arrest by rowing across the Snake River. He was shot by the sheriff.[25]

Although he was only sixteen, Ed's imagination and powers of observation were stimulated by the colorful characters who surrounded him. Their actions, attitudes, and mannerisms were recorded in his memory. Of the sheriff, Gum Brown, he recalled:

Whenever anyone had to be arrested or a posse was formed, Gum would go around the saloon and point to the cowboys saying, "I deputize yo'; I deputize yo'", and nobody would pay any attention to him. It was a standing joke in Albion.[26]

Other memorable characters were Hank Monk, a cook on the ranch, and Sam Lands, a garrulous cowpuncher who specialized in tall stories. About Monk, Ed remarked, "I could always tell when we were going to have baking powder biscuits: Monk would have flour in his ears and nose. . . .The less one saw of Hank cooking, the better his appetite."[27]

And Lands had an unforgettable story about a bad horse he had ridden:

. . . the horse threw him but his foot caught in the stirrup; and, he said, the horse "drug" him for three days and three nights and that all he had to drink was when he "drug" him through a river, and that all he had to eat was when he "drug" him through a strawberry patch.[28]

To Ed everything that occurred on the ranch was exciting and adventurous. One of his most enjoyable chores was "chasing bulls out of the alfalfa":

There were quite a number of imported Hereford bulls on the range, and there never was a fence built that would hold them. They put their necks under the lower wire and either lifted the post out of the ground or pulled the staples all out. Then we would have maybe three or four of them in our alfalfa. It was my job to take a shotgun loaded with very fine shot, go down on horseback and chase them out. Upon these occasions I played Buffalo Bill, pretending that the bulls were buffalo. I would ride along beside them and pepper them in the seat.[29]

On one occasion Ed had a real scare. The enraged bull whirled about suddenly to charge him. With the animal very close, Ed fired, hitting him right between the eyes. The bull turned a "complete somersault." Ed rode back to the ranch in a panic, convinced he had killed a three- or four-thousand-dollar bull. Later he was relieved to discover that the animal displayed no symptoms of pain or injury.[30]

Those were the days of bitter rivalry between the cattle and sheep ranches that led to violence and shootings. Unaware at first when the spring roundup began, Ed soon discovered that the man riding with him was a "very likable murderer." As they were resting on a hillside, his friend described how he had killed a man named Paxton and Ed took it in stride:

It was perfectly all right because each of the two men had been hired to kill the other and though Paxton got the drop on him across the dinner table, my friend came out alive and Paxton didn't.[31]

This brief Idaho period in 1891 had given Ed freedom and a touch of the kind of carefree, adventurous life he would seek again. A restlessness and a need to express his masculinity remained with him, governing some of his future actions. But now a summons from his father brought him, regretfully, back to Chicago and a resumption of his education.[32] In contrast to the exciting days he had spent with cowboys and badmen, and the exhilarating physical challenge he had encountered, a program of classroom studies could only appear dull and boring. Major George had already made preparations for Ed's enrollment in school, but he found his son uninterested in a return to books and exams — and even rebellious. The days ahead were to be ones of tension at home, unhappiness for Ed, and disappointment and irritation for his father.

3
SCHOOLING, REBELLION, AND DISCIPLINE

Ed's scrapbook, a bulky collection of papers, cards, and clippings, all reminders of his school days, displays at the beginning a page of the printed entrance examination to Phillips Academy, Andover, Massachusetts, dated September 1891. The page contains problems in mathematics, covering "Algebra to Simple Equations" and "Simple Equations to Quadratics." Written in ink at the bottom is the notation "Passed, Mark 20."

While the Phillips catalog advised that "No age is prescribed for admission," it offered more specific information in its statement that "boys fourteen years of age usually possess sufficient maturity for the responsibilities of school-life here."[1] Ed, just sixteen, and probably overage for a new student, was required to fill out the school's entrance form containing eighteen questions. At the top he listed himself as a candidate for the "Junior Middle E class" (English), adding the projected date of graduation — class of 1894.

He answered the questions in a clear, firm handwriting. Under question six, *Father's business or Profession,* he wrote, "Vice Pres. Anglo American Battery Co." The reason for his own version of the company name is not clear. Under *Father's Titles* he wrote "Major in late war." His mother's birthplace was listed only as "State of Indiana." After *Church Denomination* Ed drew a long line, indicating "none." He of course gave his last school as "Harvard School, Chicago," and the "Chief Instructor" as "Prof. J. J. Schobinger." Other answers revealed that he took room and board with Mrs. C. A. Morrill, presumably in Andover, and that his brother Frank Coleman Burroughs had attended the school in 1890 and 1891. To be exact, Frank was in the English Department for two years, 1890-92, as a Junior Middler and Senior Middler.[2]

Phillips Academy, already 113 years old, had first opened for instruction on April 30, 1778. It had been founded by Samuel Phillips, his brother John, and Samuel Phillips, Jr., in that year, although not incorporated until October 4, 1780. As part of the Academy's remarkable history, a most distinguished visitor and speaker, George Washington, on November 5, 1789, addressed the students assembled on the Old Training Field.[3] The fourth principal was John Adams, and during his term the second schoolhouse was burned in 1818, and a new brick Academy was built. This was the "classic hall" described in Oliver Wendell Holmes' centennial poem, "The School-Boy."[4]

The principal at the time of Ed's enrollment was Dr. Cecil F. P. Bancroft, in charge from 1873 until his death in 1901. He is described as "a man of foresight and clear vision, patience and shrewd discrimination."[5] During his administration, attendance increased from 262 to more than 400 pupils. When Ed attended, 1891-92, the exact number was 440, with 184 in the English Department and 256 in the Classical department. The pupils came from thirty-eight states and from Hawaii, Japan, Canada, and even Turkey. The tuition for the fall term was $30, winter term, $25, and spring term, $20.

As a Junior Middler in the English department Ed would be required to follow the course of study emphasizing mathematics and the "Natural Sciences, with History, Latin, Modern Languages, and Literature." The catalog states that "The Course of Study is designed to furnish a broad and thorough preparation for the Sheffield Scientific School of Yale University, the Massachusetts Institute of Technology, and other scientific schools and colleges"[6]

All Junior Middle Year students were required to study Latin, but in the Middle Year, French or German was substituted, with Latin becoming elective. The course of study for the Junior Middlers in the Latin department included both Latin (notably Caesar's Gallic Wars) and Greek, plus mathematics and English, in the first term. The second term maintained a Latin sequence with selections from *Ovid* and part of the *Aeneid* of Virgil. Additional Greek, mathematics, and English were required.

The serious scholastic atmosphere of Phil-

lips Academy must have been disconcerting to young Ed Burroughs. But as always he was quick to make friends and was eagerly accepted by the other students. The popularity he quickly achieved with his classmates may be explained, at least partially, by the colorful anecdotes he probably told them about his Idaho days. Since for some unexplained reason he arrived with a guitar in his luggage, he was urged to join the Mandolin Club and given a further invitation to the Glee Club.

In regard to the Mandolin Club, he recalled that "I agreed with alacrity, although I cannot conceive that I could have done so without misgivings, inasmuch as I had never played a guitar, am totally devoid of any sense of music and did not know one note from another."[7] He further comments, "They must have been embarrassed when they discovered that I could not play guitar. Anyhow my engagement with the glee club was brief."[8]

While there appeared to be no doubt about his musical limitations, he soon began to express his natural creativity in the familiar directions. Ed turned to the *Mirror,* a publication sponsored by the Philomathean Society, the literary organization of the school. The *Mirror,* printed once a term, was designed as an outlet for Philomathean members, providing "an opportunity for writing stories, poems and grinds, and for making cuts."[9] Grinds seemed to be quotes by well-known authors, usually witty or humorous, submitted by students who either signed their names or used fictitious names. The grind might apply aptly to the student himself, in a joking way, or to other students.[10]

Ed submitted material for the *Mirror* of Fall 1891 and Winter 1892. There are no grinds printed with his name beneath, but some may have appeared under a pseudonym, for in the issue of 1891 the editorial review contains an acknowledgment stating, "We are also indebted for grinds and cuts to E. R. Birroughs." A number of cuts or cartoons, mainly humorous in nature, are Ed's work (they are initialed E.R.B. in his copy of the 1891 *Mirror*). The first illustration, on the table of contents page, consists of eight human figures spaced about the perimeter of the box that encloses the magazine's contents. These figures perch there or are engaged in various climbing actions. A typical humorous example is a drawing of an odd little machine titled The Mirror Grinding Machine, described beneath as a "Head Reducer." Sketches of a boy are shown, the head at first large and then reduced in size. A caption reads, "Before and After Using."

Another page in the *Mirror* of fall 1891 displays cuts of horses, Ed's favorite subject for drawing. The horses, although small, are skillfully and realistically done.

In the *Mirror* of Winter 1892, the editorial comment refers to a poetry contest and explains, "1st prize for Poem to S. A. Dickerson and in connection with this we are obliged to state that the judges, on account of the lack of competition in poems, deemed it best to award no second prize. . . ." But whether considered worthy of a prize or not, the poem printed in this issue (author unnamed) bears the stamp of Ed's particular humor and style. Titled "Possum et Coona," it stresses a clever distortion of Latin.[11]

The poem tells the story of two boys who go hunting with their dog. When they proudly bring a possum home, displaying him to their parents, comparisons of their glory are made with David, Samson, Caesar, and others. But when they wake in the morning they find that the possum was not really dead, he was playing possum — "the possum est ressurectum." He has fled and they are quite crestfallen. The poem ends: "Pueri think non plus of Caesar, Coad urcum, Shalmeneser;/Take your laurels, cum the honor, Since ista possum is a goner."

The *Mirror* of 1892, in its list of contributors, expresses indebtedness to E. R. Burroughs for cuts only. None of these has been identified. Ed is listed as a member of the Athletic Association and as president of his class. This award of the highest honor by his fellow classmates, presumably stemming from Ed's personal popularity, was also announced on January 20, 1892, in *The Phillipian*, the school newspaper. The brief note contains a misspelling of the new president's name:

Elections. A class meeting of P.S. '94 was held Wednesday noon and the following officers were elected: President, Burrows; vice-president, Clark; secretary and treasurer, Finch.[12]

Commenting on both his selection as class president and the class colors of P.S. '94 — pale blue and orange — Ed wrote, "when one considers their choice of a presiding officer the selection of blue seems nothing short of an inspiration, but the fruit should have been lemon."[13]

In the passing days he devoted much of his time to extracurricular activities.[14] A side interest in sports, but neither as a participant nor spectator, is revealed in a letter pasted in his scrapbook. Dated November 23, 1891, the letter, concerned with the placing of a bet, was addressed to him at Andover and came from the office of Stoddard & Kendall in Boston. The firm, according to the items printed on its letterhead, handled a large variety of sports equipment. On the list are fishing tackle, skates, baseball supplies, lawn tennis, and gymnasium goods. The miscellaneous merchandise includes cutlery and hair clippers. The letter to Ed advises:

Dear Sir

I enclose you a check for stake on the Amherst Williams game as it resulted in a tie.

Respty yours
J. L. Crafts[15]

Unfortunately, from the moment of his arrival at Phillips, Ed showed little inclination to concentrate on his studies. His reaction to the formal curriculum at the Academy, with its familiar emphasis upon Latin and Greek, was hardly enthusiastic. He had been equally unimpressed by the same subject requirements at Harvard School.[16] His lack of effort and achievement came to the attention of Principal Bancroft. "Banty," as the students called him, believed that a semester's trial was enough; he reached the limit of his patience. Once the holidays were over, and shortly after school reconvened for the new term on January 15, 1892,

Banty made his decision known. George Burroughs received a firm request for the withdrawal of his son. Ed's stay at Phillips terminated as abruptly as it began. It appears that his election as president and his dismissal from the school occurred close enough in date to almost coincide. Obviously, at the class graduation in 1894 President Burroughs would not officiate.[17]

Though his annoyance and disappointment were great, George Burroughs still exhibited unusual control and managed to accept his son's return with an attitude of tolerance and understanding.[18] But he had no intention of abandoning Ed's schooling. Perhaps a more disciplined environment was the answer. Retired Major Burroughs turned to a popular solution, often adopted by parents of problem sons: Ed would be sent to a military school.

The chosen institution was Michigan Military Academy, situated at Orchard Lake, twenty-six miles northwest of Detroit. It had been in existence for fifteen years. Ed later wrote with wry amusement that the academy had a "sub rosa reputation as a polite reform school."[19]

Whether the academy's requirements were really stricter than those of similar schools is doubtful. Certainly, as expected in a military school, the cadets' activities were severely regimented. Emphasis was upon army routine, drilling, and above all discipline and obedience. Physical development was an important goal, and to achieve it the cadets led a hard, rough-and-tumble life.

At the time Ed enrolled, Colonel J. Sumner Rogers was the superintendent and Adelbert Cronkhite, the commandant.[20] Cronkhite's tenure was brief, as was that of Captain Charles King who succeeded him; and in the Michigan Military Academy catalog of 1893 Lieutenant Frederick S. Strong, 4th U.S. Artillery, is listed as commandant. The catalog's register of cadets for 1892-93 displays the name *Edgar Rice Burroughs*, with the course identified as *Sc.* (scientific). Preparatory studies required in the scientific course include English grammar, civil government, arithmetic, and English composition. The curriculum for the first year, divided under first and second terms, contains rhetoric and composition as requirements in both terms. It appears, as far as the catalog is concerned, that the academy did stress the study of grammar and composition.[21]

Among the cadets who entered the academy at the same time as Ed were two who became close and long-lasting friends, Robert D. Lay and Herbert (Bert) T. Weston. Lay's course was listed in the catalog as *Ac.*(academy).[22]

The beginning of Ed's life in a military environment brought no change in his rebellious nature. He was obviously not ready to settle down, and not ready to adapt himself to the academy's strict discipline and regulation. His first semester at the school (second term, 1892) found him in numerous difficulties. A natural nonconformist, he seemed unable to follow school rules or to suppress impulsive actions that usually led him into trouble.

One of Ed's early experiences at the academy during his plebe year had to do with the popular pastime of hazing, carried on by the "old boys" or upper classmen. In Ed's *Autobiography,* where the practice is described as the "refined and unrefined torture of hazing," various details are offered. For what occurred in one particular case, Ed can hardly be blamed. The commandant at the start of the term, Adelbert Cronkhite, who was far from being one of Ed's favorites, appeared to have a pet aversion to plebes:

I think that he looked upon us with absolute contempt and loathing. At noon one day, during the winter, he made a speech in the mess-hall. It was to the effect that the plebes were too fresh and that it was up to the old boys to put them in their place. This, coming from the high authority of the commandant of cadets, brought immediate effects, one of which was that immediately after the meal the entire plebe class scattered in all directions, taking to the woods, not only figuratively, but literally. Several of us, I recall, just beat it — whither, we did not know.

"Any place would have been better than the Michigan Military Academy on that bleak Sat-

Michigan Military Academy cavalry platoon; ERB second from left.

urday afternoon," Ed remarked. Although he was "as usual" under arrest for "various and diverse infractions of discipline," under these emergency circumstances the arrest became unimportant as did the regulations against going off-limits and, more serious, going off off-limits.

After the panicky escape, Ed and his friends walked twelve miles through the snow to a nearby town. There, although he was wearing rubber boots, he attended a village dance that evening. At a late hour, after the dancing was over, the boys reluctantly decided that they must return to the barracks. This posed a problem:

We also discovered simultaneously that we did not want to walk back and that we had no money. I managed, however, to pawn my watch for three dollars with which we rented a horse and rig, thus coming back to school and sneaking into our quarters while the old boys were asleep.

"I do not recall how much additional punishment I got for this escapade," Ed wrote, "but it could not have meant anything to me as I already was undergoing a life sentence."

Approximately two months after his arrival at the Academy, the Easter vacation began, and all the cadets were excused to return home. From Chicago, where Ed was spending the vacation with his family, his father wrote to Colonel Rogers on March 23, 1892, requesting an extension of Ed's leave. Two days later Rogers replied, ". . . Of course we shall extend cadet Burroughs' permit, as you request, although it is to his disadvantage to be absent from work at this time. School is moving along very pleasantly under our new commandant."[23]

The new commandant, replacing Adelbert Cronkhite, was Captain Charles King, a well-known author of novels centered about army life in the West. Although he remained at the academy for only a brief period, his firm atti-

29

tude tempered with justice and consideration and his numerous accomplishments created in Ed an intense admiration which was close to worship.

Ed continued to find the discipline and restrictions of a military life impossible to cope with; as described in his *Autobiography,* the penalties seemed endless:

The first year was the hardest. I accumulated so many hours of unwalked punishment that if I had remained there the rest of my life I could never have walked it all, as we had only forty-five minutes a day for recreation, except Saturdays and Sundays and as I recall it we were not compelled to walk punishment on Sunday.

Desperate, and "burdened by a harrowing contemplation of the future," he fled from the academy:

I sneaked out of barracks at dusk and walked four and a half miles to Pontiac. I crept fearfully through the woods, for all the time I heard the cavalry pursuing me, my budding imagination being strong even then.

In Pontiac I hung around the railroad yards waiting for the Chicago train. Every man I saw was a detective searching for me and when the train pulled in and the inspectors passed along it with their flares, I knew they were looking for me, but I hid out between two freight cars until the train started. Those were the good old days before anyone had thought of solid vestibule trains, so I had no difficulty in flipping it and eluding the regiment of detectives that loitered about.[24]

Reaching home on April 15, 1892, Ed told his version of conditions at the academy and the harsh treatment he believed he had suffered. His father, indignant, wrote a letter to Colonel Rogers the same day. But the arrival of a telegram the next day, with its terse, abrupt wording, made Ed's behavior appear serious. The telegram from Commandant Charles King read: "Your son deserted Thursday letter will follow."

"Your son deserted" telegram from General Charles King.

General Charles King.

That George Burroughs, a retired army major, accustomed to military discipline, should protest about the treatment accorded Ed indicates that matters can be different when one's own son is involved. Commandant King's reply to Burroughs' letter, written on April 18, in the absence of Superintendent Rogers, revealed also that King, while refusing to budge an inch, was a master of tact and diplomacy:

That you should think, after hearing your son's side of the story, that the commandant is too severe is most natural, and being a father himself, the Commandant has every sympathy with your distress. Now, however, let us look at the soldier side of the question.

He then proceeded to explain in detail the offenses that Ed had committed; George Burroughs must have found the list painfully incredible. "Since his return from vacation, a week or more behind time," King wrote, "Cadet Burroughs has received an extraordinary number of reports for not one of which has he tendered to the authorities the faintest explanation or excuse. They include some of the most serious known to our records both in the Academic and military departments, as you may see from the specimens enclosed herewith."

Of the "specimens" submitted for Burroughs' verification, King commented that the academy had always had a "standard of punishments" for these — the penalties Cadet Burroughs received were nothing new. King offered a mild reproof and reminder to Burroughs:

The severity of which you complain may possibly exist in these long established rules, but as an old soldier yourself, you should understand that the Commandant is simply carrying out the orders in the case, and although he might with propriety say that he feels no obligation to defend his course, on the other hand he prefers to invite the better judgement of a Companion of the Loyal Legion upon the facts in the case.

King remarked with some restraint that "it is to be regretted that Cadet Burroughs for his own sake was not willing to explain." By this time George Burroughs must have realized that

his son, to put it euphemistically, had been quite "unwilling" to explain.

Other facts emerged, revealing a debatable question of Ed's supposed "illness":

As to the accusation of harshness in not permitting the young man to remain in bed and have his meals sent to his room, I will say that when one doctor pronounces a Cadet able to be up and about, it is considered ill advised on the part of the Commandant to interpose. In Cadet Burroughs' case, as stated by himself, both doctors pronounced him able to get up and to go to meals.

King, continuing to write in his objective third person, stated, "It was the severe Commandant who ventured to oppose his judgement and permit the boy to go to bed again."

As to the confusion arising over Ed's claims that he didn't consider himself "in confinement" even though Professor Loveland had given him the order, following which he had *reported* for confinement, King offered a comment that was a masterpiece of understatement. Ed's explanation "is necessarily looked upon with much surprise, if not with grave doubt as to his sincerity."

King gave further details of Ed's behavior. On the morning of Wednesday, April 13, Ed, while in confinement by orders of Professor Loveland, climbed through the window of the barracks to make his escape. He was accompanied by another cadet "who has since deserted under still more serious accusations." When questioned by the cadet officer, Ed admitted that he was leaving for the depot. Taken before the commandant and "invited to explain his extraordinary breach of orders and discipline," he replied that "he had nothing to say." In the letter King pointed out, "As an old soldier you must know that the Commandant had then no recourse but to administer the punishment required 'by the custom of war' in like cases, as he found it at this Academy."

Ed's attempt to escape, on this morning, had evidently not been very determined. But on the next day, April 14, he made a successful escape and returned to his home in Chicago where, shortly afterward, King's "desertion" telegram was received.

King offered some consoling words to George Burroughs in the letter:

Cadet Burroughs' offenses have been most serious, but not irretrievably so. He has been reckless; not vicious. He has found friends here including the Commandant, who best knew the boy in the Cavalry squad and on drill, and it is not impossible for him to return and wipe out his past.

Ed's father, displaying a most unexpected reaction for a veteran army officer, made demands that King considered unreasonable. They were firmly rejected:

. . . while I am unprepared to say what will be the action of the faculty, this I can say that under no circumstances will your demand that he be given a "clean sheet" and allowed to start in all free again without any punishment whatsoever, be acceded to. If granted to him, it would have to be granted, perhaps, to many another.

King went on to insist firmly that Ed would not be relieved from duty merely because he complained of being sick, but only "when having been examined by the doctor, he is *pronounced* sick." King added to this, with some acidity, that "if cadets were relieved from duty and excused whensoever they complained of feeling ill, at least half the battalion would be off duty every day."

In closing, he referred to George Burroughs' complaint that no boy could undergo the academy discipline without having his spirit crushed. "Permit me to say," King wrote, "that as the result of over thirty years observation of cadets here and elsewhere, I find that more than nine-tenths of the corps take kindly to the discipline and are as spirited and soldierly a lot of young fellows as one could ask to see."

Of the incident and his flight from Michigan Military Academy, Ed noted, "I should have thought that my father would have been about fed up with me by this time." He recalled how he had been received "with open arms and with

no reproaches when he was fired from Andover" and added, "but I think that to him, a soldier, this was by far the greater disgrace, yet he put it directly up to me to decide for myself whether I should return or not."[25]

Ed was not long in making a decision. "I think it was the word 'deserted' in the telegram that got me, and the next day I was back at Orchard Lake walking punishment."

By the fall of 1892 Ed had begun to channel some of his excess energies into sports. Football offered the kind of physical challenge that was always important to him; he traveled with the team as they played games away from home.

In a letter of October 19, 1892, in which he explains to his parents, "I owe you all letters I guess so I will write to all of you at once," he discusses the games and school news:

They are not going to send us to Chicago this week, we are going to Pontiac though to march in their procession.

The shin protectors came, and I am much obliged to you for them. Do not be afraid of my getting hurt in foot-ball. I dont play hard enough, besides its worth while when I can go around to the different towns and play and wear a big M on my sweater and a little MMA on my jacket.

Ed, amused by his parents' concern and their concept of football as a rough and hazardous game, encloses some "illustrations," presumably his typical cartoons, "for the manner in which Foot-Ball is *not* played, though you folks evidently imagined it was." Of the possibility of promotion he notes that "appointments" could be announced within the next two days; "I have been expecting them every day so have not written you hoping to be able to tell you what the fellows whom you know got."

About his own prospects Ed wrote, "I won't get anything, because I haven't been here a year yet." But he added, with some pride, "I am treated by all the fellows that I like and by *all* the fellows who were old-boys last year as if I had been here three or four years. I don't care anyway, so I guess that is the reason."

As a boy away from home for a lengthy period, he was evidently lonely, for he inquired about his brother Harry and Harry's wife Ella (Nellie) Oldham, who had been married less than a year, remarking wistfully that he wished he could see them:

When are some of you coming out? Can't Harry leave his business one Saturday and bring Nell up here: they could leave 8-15 P.M. Friday; spend Sat. here and be back 7 AM Sund. or leave Sat and be back Mon. I will expect Frank most any day.[26]

By the end of the year Ed appeared to be making some adjustments to the academy routine and to be doing better in his studies. His father, continuing an over-solicitous attitude, wrote regularly to Superintendent Rogers about various matters. On December 14, 1892, Rogers reported that "Cadet Burroughs has made excellent progress in his studies during the last three months and is satisfactory in discipline. We hope for still better results after Christmas." Possibly apprehensive, Rogers tempered his praise with a cautionary reminder: "You will aid us materially by him report [sic] promptly January 17th, so that he may have all his lessons on the next day."

Rogers included a laudatory statement about the academy's high reputation and the honor it had recently received:

After fifteen years of earnest effort we feel that we can with becoming modesty claim that we have succeeded in establishing a model school for the complete training of boys. In a list of forty "Leading Secondary Schools in the United States" selected by President Eliot of Harvard University, as President of a special committee of the National Educational Association, this Academy is honored in being one of the number chosen; and the only military school in this important list.

In the letter he also told of plans to increase the academy's attendance during the holiday vacation with a view to creating a battalion of 180 cadets. This battalion would be taken to the World's Fair Columbian Exposition in Chicago in June of the following year. The cadets would camp "in close proximity to if not within, the Exposition Grounds," remaining there for about three weeks. The instructors would accompany the cadets, and the objective was to make a careful and systematic study of the exposition and of exhibits that illustrate and enforce work done at the academy. Rogers explained, "By this plan we are convinced that we shall be able in three weeks to obtain a better knowledge of the people and industries of the World than would probably be acquired in several years' travel."

The change in dates of the Christmas holidays, beginning on December 22 with an extension to January 17, was caused by a decision to omit the Easter vacation. "We think that more satisfactory work can be accomplished by following this plan," Rogers said. The cadets were scheduled to leave about June 10 for the World's Fair, with a possibility that the commencement exercises might be held in Chicago.

On the same date as Rogers' letter, and again on December 16, George Burroughs had written about a problem Ed seemed to be having with his eyes. The exchange of letters appeared to indicate that Ed's father was somewhat annoyed at the fact that Rogers allowed an oculist to treat his son. Burroughs had suggested that Ed be sent to the oculist, and what he had in mind was not clear. Rogers wrote on December 17 with an evidence of impatience:

. . . would say that in accordance with your suggestion in your first dispatch I sent Cadet Burroughs to Detroit to an oculist of high standing to ascertain if his eyes were in a condition to allow him to study. Had no idea that he was to give him any treatment; and thought very likely that he could fit him with a pair of glasses so that he could go on with his work until the vacation began. I do not think that I exceeded my authority in any way.

The nature of the oculist's diagnosis is unknown, but the result was an early vacation dismissal for the patient. Rogers ended his letter with a curt comment, "He returned last night with the report of Dr. Frothingham, and upon his recommendation I have this day sent him home. He will explain the matter fully to you."

Whether Ed had a tendency to exaggerate his illnesses, or even to malinger, is difficult to tell. The record of his early years and the details contained in his brothers' letters from Yale reveal that he had been a delicate child, not as sturdy as his brothers, and more susceptible to common illnesses. That his health had caused both concern and worry to his parents is quite evident.

On January 26, 1893, in a letter to his mother he writes that he has been ill for some time. His complaints about the school are quite bitter; the tone of the entire letter is one of gloom and resentment. However, in this case, there is little doubt that his illness is severe:

Excuse me for not writing sooner but I have been sick and didn't feel very much like writing. I am still in bed. I have had a very sore throat and membraneous formation in my throat, headache, pains all over my body and have been sick to my stomach for the last three days. I am terrible sick at my stomach today but my head and throat are better.

He explained that the doctor had seen him yesterday, and although he had asked them not to send him again, the doctor made a second visit that day. ". . . I guess it was about as well," Edgar wrote, "for if he hadn't called they would have made me get up at noon, as it was he told me to stay in bed and keep quiet." After the vivid description of his illness, he attempts to reassure his parents; "Dont worry as I am not very sick; just thought I would write and let you know that I was still alive," and he adds, "Excuse writing as I am lying down and am rather weak. . . ." His P.S. offers more details and complaints:

To let you see what attention is paid to a fellow on the sick report: There's a jar out in the hall that was brought up yesterday morning and that I have used ever since and thrown up all my meals into it and it has never been emptied;

and it never would be if I stayed here ten years with it.

I have lain on this hard bed for so long that my right side is really raw, the bottom of my stomach is raw from having the top sag down and up against it and my throat is raw from the extra work of having each meal go through two ways.

Ed, as with most young people of his age, was not a regular correspondent. He apologizes about his failure to write, and on April 25 offers as an excuse that he had hurt his finger with a sword. He remarks, "I looked over some of my letters the other day and I find that I never acknowledged the letter in which you sent that check I thought I had done so and I am very much ashamed of myself consequently."

He tells of receiving perfume and candy from his mother, adding, "it was fine and went to the right place." The obvious reference is to a girl friend, unidentified, but probably Emma Hulbert.

He inquires, "How is the kid?" a query about his nephew Studley, born only a month before on December 26, 1892, and continues jokingly:

From all of your letters I will expect to find him riding a bicycle and reading Caesar on my return in the summer. Don't rush him too much, he may get brain fever. Just tell him to follow after his uncle: — if he wants to be a blooming idiot.

From his early years, as part of a remarkable sense of humor, Ed exhibited a delight in playing practical jokes. It almost seemed that in devising little schemes at other people's expense he was satisfying some need of his imagination. It was done without malice and no harm was ever intended.[27] But the tendency to lapse into pranks and escapades, to yield to temptations impulsively, was part of his character. He would retain this tendency in lesser degree through his lifetime, and during his school years it would lead him into trouble.

In his letter of April 25, 1893, to his father he reports, with a customary glee, that "Lt.

Reeder, who was cadet Capt. and adjutant last year, is going to sleep over in Graves room to-night and Graves, Cox and I were just in there folding up the under sheet in his bed and tying knots in his night shirt. I hope he don't find out who did it."

After telling of this prank he turns to his favorite subject — horses. He had always dreamed of owning one, and now approached the matter obliquely, posing a question to his father with more than a hint of guile:

Would you like to make some money or help me make some? I have an elegant chance to buy Captain, the horse I told you of that I think so much of, for about $150.00 or $125.00 — He is a fine Kentucky horse perfectly sound, very showy and well gaited for a saddle horse; he is broken to harness as well; he is a very fine and fast singlefooter; his action is something superb.

There was of course a special reason why the colonel wanted to sell the horse: ". . . he is too fiery and too good a horse for a lot of boys to ride. I am the only cadet that rides him." The story sounds familiar — a scene from Ed's past in Idaho. And one can read between the lines.

The fiery and hard-to-handle ones, the outlaws — these were the horses whose beautiful wildness Ed admired, that offered the challenge he couldn't resist. He used a torrent of words to try to persuade his father:

If I had $200 and could buy a horse to keep I would buy him in preferance to most any horse I ever rode; in Chicago this year that horse would sell for a good $250.00, I am very sure. If I bought him now for $125.00 or even $150.00 I could have him to ride and get a lot of good out of him until school closes and then or before, ride him down to Detroit and sell him so as to make from $25 to $75.00 off of him anyway.

Carried away by his appeal to his father's practical business instincts, he began to expand the money-making possibilities:

The money I have paid the Col. for cavalry the rest of this term would pay for his board here and I could drop cavalry — for having a horse of my own I would not need to take it as I could do anything I wanted in the way of riding.

"I wish you could see the horse," he said,

A drawing from the Michigan Military Academy Adjutant *depicting an exhibition drill.*

"I know you would think it a bargain." Another idea occurred: "You might loan me $150.00 for 3 months at 6%." The letter ended on a humorous note: "Enclosed please find rough sketch of my room mate and myself figuring out the interest on $150.00 for 3 months at 6%."

It appears that Ed's father, powerless to resist his son's blandishments, or to withstand his barrage of dollars and percentages, may have purchased the horse. Ed rode Captain later in exhibitions at the Detroit Riding Club.

As a member of the cavalry troop at Michigan Military Academy Ed had the opportunity to develop a remarkable skill in riding. In recollection, he wrote, "We did a great deal of trick riding in those days — bareback, Cossack, Graeco-Roman and all the rest of it. It was known as 'monkey drill,' and if a man did not lose his nerve and quit, he had to become a good horseman."[28]

News of the astonishing ability of the academy cavalry had reached the ears of the Detroit Riding Club, and a selected group of riders was chosen to appear for an exhibition. A souvenir program of the Columbian Saddle Horse Show describes the events of Tuesday, April 4, through Thursday, April 6, 1893. The Orchard Lake Cadets' exhibition drill, with saddle and full equipment on the first night, was listed as "Event No. 5" on the program. The Drill Master was Hugh Thomason, and of the fourteen cadets in the platoon, Cadet Private E. R. Burroughs is listed as number seven; his friend Robert Lay was number twelve and the color bearer.[29]

On Wednesday April 5 the cadets presented an exhibition drill "with blankets, without equipments." On the final evening, April 6, a newspaper reported the results: "The Orchard Lake cadets took part in a competitive drill, which was an exciting affair. Their vaulting and dismounting and mounting drew applause, and the judges had a hard time picking the winners."[30]

The decision was made: "They finally had T. T. Harker, Ed R. Burroughs and F. R. Graves step out, and after an exhibition by each of them gave the prizes in the order named. . . ."[31] Ed's second prize was a gentleman's riding crop, while his horse, Captain, received a red ribbon. In the newspaper accounts of the exhibition, (April 4-7, 1893) the cadets' riding drew a eulogy:

. . . These young men ride in the natural and easy position of a cavalry man, and their mounting and dismounting on bareback is wonderful. . . .

The dashing cavalry from Orchard Lake gave one of the most attractive exhibits of the evening, commanded by Hugh Thomason, first sergeant troop F, U.S. cavalry. Hard riding and difficult evolutions, sweep of flashing sabres through the air and a volley of shots as a wind up, wrought the audience up to a pitch of applause that was deafening. . . .

The drill wound up in the manner of the wild west show. Drawing their revolvers the cadets dashed madly around the ring, firing in all directions, and then rallied in the center, after which they left the ring.

In a news story of April 5, the astonishment of the viewers, and their realization of the differences in style between the sedate, stiff English riders who normally appeared at the horse shows, and the vigorous, natural riding of the cadets is revealed. The writer made it plain that he preferred the American cavalry horsemanship:

These horrid cavalry horses did not have the fashionable English trot or gallop, nor did the rider sit in the English way, but they were plain Americans. The cadets ride like the vaqueros dash through the chapparel, ride like the fleet South American gauchos, the most skillful and daring riders in the world. But the cadets are not fashionable riders.

The cadets are what might be called strong riders. Their stirrups are long, their seats are firm, they never forsake the motion of the horse. There is an abandon, a smoothness, a naturalness, a spirit to their horsemanship, that breathes forth the wild wind, the long road, the cheerfulness of outdoors. . . .

It is not military horsemanship. It is American horsemanship, it is Mexican horsemanship, it is South American horsemanship. It is riding of men who live in the saddle.

A less enthusiastic description of the English rider is added:

The fashionable rider is not part of his horse, he is perched on his horse; he is bobbing, he is making an art of riding, his horse is giving an exhibition of what a saddler should be, and is showing how a rider should retain his seat. . . .

The cadets' type of horsemanship, as reported in a story of April 6, included bareback riding feats that "recalled the exhibitions by Buffalo Bill's cowboys." This riding skill and love of horses developed by Ed in his academy years would always remain with him.

The summer of 1893 saw the start of Ed's lifelong fascination with the automobile when he became involved in the exhibition staged by his father's American Battery Company at the World's Columbian Exposition in Chicago. He was given the enviable assignment of driving an electric automobile around the fairgrounds. George Burroughs had installed the auto at the World's Fair to demonstrate the company's storage batteries. One writer, in calling the vehicle an "electrical horseless carriage," goes on to report that Ed drove "a nine-seater horseless surrey about the fairgrounds, starting runaways every hundred feet or so."[32] In another account the writer claims that Ed drove the first automobile in Chicago, and describes how "at night, circling about the Fair grounds, it threw off sparks and flashes of blue flame."[33]

In the passing months Ed became immersed in a variety of school activities. Starting from his plebe year, his interest in football had increased until, after successive semesters, he had made the team. As cadet sergeant major he was evidently responsible for preparing the football

ERB passbook to World's Columbian Exposition, Chicago, 1893, where he drove an electric auto powered by batteries.

Michigan Military Academy football team prior to 1895; ERB first on left in front row.

lineups. On November 18, 1893, in the game between Michigan Military Academy and Ypsilanti, the lineup lists "Left-H.B. — Burroughs." His friend Bob Lay was scheduled to play fullback, and Bert Weston was right tackle. The name *Ed Burroughs*, together with his rank, is stamped officially at the bottom of the lineup.[34] The score was MMA, 36, Ypsilanti, 22.

The Adjutant, the academy's monthly magazine, reports Ed playing mainly quarterback and on one occasion right end. An article about the games in *The Adjutant* tells of the contest between the school and *Ypsilanti Normal*, with the final score "Academy 24; Normals, 10." Ed is given credit for making one touchdown.[35]

In *The Adjutant*, Senior Number, June 1895, Ed is placed on the Champion Prep School Team of the West, 1894. Statistics show

him as "Captain, age 19, weight 169, height 5 feet, 10½ in., position Quarter Back." In the December 1895 issue, a listing is again made of a championship team of the year; Ed is shown as "Captain-Quarterback, Height 5-10, Weight 165, Age 20 years, 4 mos."[36]

About his football playing Ed wrote:

I made the football team, which I captained the last two years. We had an unusually good prep school team, cleaning up everything in our class and a number of teams that were out of our class. About the only teams that could beat us were such teams as Notre Dame and the University of Michigan, and at that we once held to a tie score the University of Michigan team that had held Harvard 4 to 0.[37]

". . . In those days," Ed noted, "it was a national football upset of the first magnitude, and

ERB in football uniform, Michigan Military Academy, 1895.

our showing against this great Michigan team was equally as remarkable. I know that one of the results was that I was offered flattering inducements to come to Michigan after I graduated from Orchard Lake." Because his brothers George and Harry were graduates of Yale, he had made that college his first choice; as a result, he rejected the Michigan offer.[38]

But his interests were not limited to sports. He would always find a fascination in drawing, even if his sketches and humorous figures were done only occasionally in letters or in moments of relaxation.[39] In addition, as at *Phillips Academy*, he could not resist the lure of the school magazine. In *The Adjutant* for October, November, and December 1895, Ed, now a second lieutenant, headed the list of ten editors. It is assumed that he was editor-in-chief or managing editor. *The Adjutant* for January, February and March of 1896 again displays the name "Lieutenant E. R. Burroughs" above a group of ten other editors. He had returned to the academy after graduation.[40]

The launching of a newspaper, *The Military Mirror*, may have been one of Ed's projects. Volume 1, number 1, is dated January 30, 1894, and on the editorial page the paper is described as "a journal devoted to the Interests of Cadets and ex-Cadets of the Michigan Military Academy." Printed beneath are the names Lt. Burt Barry, Lt. Chas. H. Campbell, Lt. Ed. R. Burroughs, editors. Of interest is the fact that the paper was called *The Mirror,* reminiscent of the Phillips Academy publication to which he had contributed.

By the end of 1893 a continuing improvement in his studies was evident. On December 20 a faculty member, C. Leslie Lewis, wrote a letter of commendation to Ed's father:

At the close of the first session of our school year, I take pleasure in speaking of the good record which your son has made here this year.

In spite of the fact that we of the faculty are marking closer than ever before, yet Cadet Burroughs has carried heavy work, and maintained a high standing.

Lewis reported Ed's marks: "Physics 87; French 86; Rhetoric 92; Military Science 90; Junior Rhetoricals 92; giving him an average of 89.4%. His deportment marks show that he has 16 merits to his credit. We look upon him as one of our best boys."

Ed's marks were in the 60s and 70s at Harvard School, but only three years later show remarkable improvement. He had not, however, become totally angelic. He couldn't resist the temptation to indulge in wild pranks. The wildest of all escapades, one which Ed described amusedly as "the means for breaking the monotony of the long Michigan winters in barracks," was a contrived incident involving Ed and First Lieutenant Charles H. Campbell.[41] "We had quarreled," Ed wrote, "and were not on speaking terms. It occurred to one of us that we might make capital out of our well known dislike for one another. . . ."[42] There is little question about the identity of the "one of us" to whom the idea occurred. On an evening when Ed was officer of the day there was a "prear-

ranged altercation in front of the battalion after it had formed for mess."[43]

The affair, on December 11, 1893, is detailed in Ed's *Autobiography:*

. . . Just before assembly sounded for supper, at a time when the entire corps of cadets was in front of barracks, Campbell made some insulting remark to me and I struck him across the face with my glove, whereupon we immediately mixed, but were presently separated by our friends, one of whom, First Lieutenant Barry, took me into his room until assembly had sounded.

The plan had been for some of the cadets to break up the fight, ". . . but unfortunately for us," Ed wrote, "'they were more interested in watching the scrap than in stopping it. Someone finally interfered, much to our relief. . . .'"[44]

Later that evening Campbell's second, Captain Risser, delivered the expected challenge:

Sir: For having grossly insulted me in the presence of witnesses and without provocation, I claim it as a right, if you are possessed of any honor, to meet at the earliest possible opportunity and give me the satisfaction my insult demands.

Yours Very Respect.
Charles H. Campbell

In reply, Ed sent his second, Lieutenant Barry, to arrange the details. Someone decided that the weapons should be Springfield rifles at fifty paces. There is some confusion as to who made the choice, but in one account Ed notes, "I . . . being the challenged party, selected the weapons. . . ."[45] They ran into difficulties with Risser, who, Ed observed, was a "solid, substantial sort of chap of a serious turn of mind . . . endowed with a little intelligence, with the result that he positively refused to have anything to do with the matter, and threatened to report the whole thing to the commandant immediately if we did not drop it."[46] Reluctantly, they were forced to let Risser in on the joke; he was then willing to play his part. Captain Buel, selected as referee, was also aware that the whole incident was a hoax.

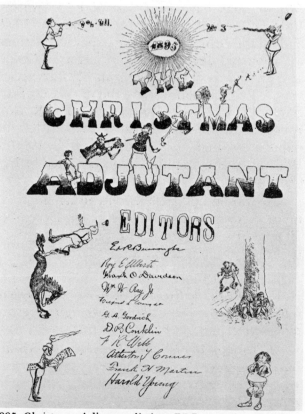

1895 Christmas Adjutant *listing ERB as editor in chief; pen and ink drawings were probably ERB's work.*

The duel was to take place at Cass Lake on the ice, about a mile from the academy, at 4:20 Tuesday afternoon. Among the cadets the news of the duel spread rapidly and the entire school was in a fever of excitement. ". . . Why the authorities heard no inkling of it," Ed wrote, "I have never been able to guess, except that the entire corps of cadets was so anxious to see blood shed that none of them wanted to let the powers that be have an opportunity to prevent the meeting."[47]

Wild rumors spread throughout the school. Ed was approached in haste by a friend who informed him that Campbell's group was planning to murder him during the night. The cadet wished to sleep in Ed's room to protect him, and was only dissuaded when Ed explained that he was a light sleeper and would keep a loaded revolver within reach. The "old boys" at the school, determined to keep the entertainment to themselves, had informed the plebes that they were not permitted to watch the event. "But when I approached the field of honor on that bleak Michigan winter morning," Ed wrote, "the bare trees all around the shore of the lake were decorated with plebes who had sneaked off limits ahead of us and gained points of vantage at the ringside."[48]

At 4:00 p.m. Ed had jumped out of the back window of his barracks, and accompanied by his second, started for the "field of honor." Ahead of them, several cadets were carrying the guns. As Ed turned to look at the school, he observed, with satisfaction, that there was a string of cadets "a mile long" following him. The important details of the duel were taken care of: the cartridges were blanks and Ed carried a "bloodied" handkerchief in his blouse.

Shortly afterward some of Campbell's group could be seen hurrying toward the chosen spot. Ed's friends began to shake hands with him and bid him goodbye; overcome at the prospect of his death, several burst into tears. But when the group arrived, headed by Captain Risser, Campbell's second, it was evident that Ed's opponent was not among them. Risser reported that

someone had blabbed to the commandant, that Campbell had been placed under arrest and locked up. The commandant, Lieutenant Frederick F. Strong of the 4th Artillery, a West Pointer, sent a very peremptory order to Ed: he was to report to the office immediately. "It was a long, cold walk back to school," Ed wrote. "I would much sooner have faced Campbell with Springfields at twenty paces than to have faced the Commandant, and when I entered his office and saw his face I realized that my judgment was still perfectly good."[49] Ed never forgot Strong's reaction:

. . . He was terrible upset by what had occurred and by the extremely narrow margin by which a bloody tragedy had been averted, for Springfield rifles at fifty paces in the hands of boys who knew how to use them would have meant sudden death for at least one of the principals.

I could see that he was laboring under a great nervous strain and it was with difficulty that he controlled his natural feelings, which I imagine would have prompted him to turn me over his knee and spank me, but as was his custom, he asked me for my story and listened to it, though somewhat impatiently when I told him that the whole thing had been a joke.[50]

Strong asked Ed if discharging Springfield rifles at one another at fifty paces was his idea of a joke. The incident had been so well planned that Ed had difficulty in convincing Strong that it was a hoax. Fortunately, he was able to show Strong the blank cartridges and the white handkerchief stained with red ink. ". . . He was so relieved," Ed wrote, "that we all got off with a simple reprimand and a warning to put a curb in the future on our peculiar senses of humor. But the worst was yet to come. When the cadets learned the truth they wanted to mob us and for a while we were far from being the most popular members of the corps."[51]

On December 15, 1893, soon after the "duel," he wrote a letter to his mother. Both she and his father had evidently written to mention their concern about him and the absence of any news from him. He expressed his regret and said he was in good health, except for "that tired feeling." Then, with pride, he proceeded to give the details of the hoax, telling the story gleefully.

"Campbell, Barry and I started the joke and made all the arrangements before hand, practiced our parts, faked some cartridges etc.," he wrote. Toward the end of the letter he admitted that when the hoax was revealed, "the fellows wanted to kill us both." But he added that "The Lieut. [Commandant Strong] thought it was the best joke he had ever heard of and laughed as much as any one."

At Orchard Lake he had what he described as his "first, last and only stage experience." The cadets formed a company to present a play titled "The End of His Tether." After a school performance the company went on the road during the Easter vacation. The only impression that remained with him, outside of the fact that the play was a "terrible flop," was a most vivid one about the incredible whiskers he wore:

They were a full set fastened to a wire, the ends of which curved over my ears, thus, supposedly, holding the hirsute appendage properly in place, a fact which they accomplished in theory only, since, when I started to speak my lines, my breath blew the whiskers outward until they were suspended at an angle of forty-five degrees and I was talking beneath them.[52]

Of the towns where the cadet actors appeared, Flint, Michigan, was especially memorable. ". . . we played to an audience consisting of the owner of the theater and a couple of members of his family. There was not a paid admission and the only reason the owner was there was because he had to be in order to turn out the lights and lock the doors when we had departed."[53]

When financial matters reached a crisis, the familiar telegram, a duplicate of numerous others sent home by unsuccessful thespians, was dispatched to George Burroughs: "Wire five show busted Hotel Vincent Saginaw."[54]

The year 1894 brought no change in Ed's penchant for ignoring the rules and getting into trouble. An extract of "Special Order No. 49," issued on April 12, contained serious charges:

For gross neglect of duty as Officer of the Day on the 11th Inst. Cadet 2nd Lieut. Burroughs is hereby reduced to the ranks and confined to "Reduced Limits" until June 10, 1894.
By order of Col. Rogers
R. S. Spilman 2nd Lieut. M.M.A. Adjutant

Ed's father was undoubtedly notified of this; but he received a further shock when Rogers' letter of April 17 referred to "Special Orders No. 52." It was Rogers' "unpleasant duty" to forward an extract of these orders to Burroughs. The Colonel stated, "Your son has doubtless written you the particulars of his offense. If not, I will write you fully, explaining to you his breach of disipline."

In a reply to Rogers, dated April 20, George Burroughs exhibited mixed emotions of anguish and helplessness. He refers to the "Special Orders" enclosed in Rogers' letter:

I need not tell you that its contents brought to me humiliation and pain. What more can I say? My Son knows what I expect of him, his sense of duty to his school and his parents should guide all his actions, and make him obedient to every rule. I do not know what, if anything, I can do in the premeses? If he will not obey, he must take the consequences, and his parents must suffer with him.

But he could not conceal a fear about the extent of his son's punishment:

He has not written home about the matter, and I will thank you to explain fully to me in what his "neglect of duty" consisted, and also what you mean in "Orders" when you say "Confined to reduced limits". I hope it does not mean confinement in his room for such a long time when we are likely to have hot weather. His offense must have been great, if a reduction to the ranks would not be regarded sufficient punishment.

Ed's offense, as described by Rogers on April 23, was almost beyond the bounds of any that the colonel had ever encountered at the academy. While on duty as officer-of-the-day, Ed had "not only permitted but encouraged one of the cadets to assault one of the cadet officers whom he relieved but a few moments before for official acts done in the performance of his duty and in accordance with the commands of the Commandant; i.e., he reported this man for smoking."

Rogers stressed that he found it very humiliating to even admit that "such a disgraceful breach of discipline could take place in this Academy." He ended with a softer note, adding that "while it is a severe lesson for your son, I am pleased to say that he seems to consider the punishment merited and is faithfully attending to his duties."

The colonel's belief that Ed, considering himself at fault, had turned contrite, was clearly contradicted in the indignant letter George Burroughs received from his son. On April 20 Ed wrote to explain that he had hesitated to tell his side of the story because he didn't wish to upset them. After reflection he had decided that they would feel much worse if they heard the story from "some other source and without knowing the details."

The account, as Ed gave it, involved one of his friends, Second Lieutenant Ed Rohrbaugh.[55] On April 10 Lieutenant F. B. Ward, officer-of-the-day, was making his customary inspection tour when he saw Rohrbaugh leaning out of a window. "I was also in the room," Ed wrote, "but he says he didn't see me. We had gone in there to call to a cadet in the area." According to Ed, Ward didn't like Rohrbaugh, was quick to assume he was smoking, a violation of rules, and reported him.

The next day, Ed explained, when he was O.D., he saw Rohrbaugh follow Ward up to his room, and, alerted to possible trouble between the two, hurried upstairs after them. It seems plain that Rohrbaugh and Ward were quarreling, and that Rohrbaugh, angry at being reported, made some threats. Ward said he would tell the colonel if "anyone did anything to him."

Rohrbaugh then lost his temper and struck Ward in the chest.

Ed, as officer-of-the-day and peacemaker, stepped in to prevent any more blows, and the two men "appeared to cool off." Carrying out his duty, Ed claimed, he reported Rohrbaugh for striking Ward. But unfortunately he couldn't refrain from taking his friend's side and in telling Ward off, including some threats of his own, that Ward "would have to settle with me for some things he had said. . . ." The reference was obviously to some four-letter words which Ed said he couldn't write.

In the meetings with the faculty and administration after the incident, Ed explained to his father that he talked to them "the way I would to you if I were in trouble." He told them not only what he "honestly thought" but also that he despised Ward. "I didn't use any tact," he confessed. "I didn't think I had to, I believed that justice would be given by them, the same way that you would see justice done. It turned out however that I was running down a favorite of the Colonel and Lt. Strong. . . ." Ed said that later Colonel Rogers called him a liar and Rohrbaugh a bully and coward.

In continuing his story, Ed told how all the other cadets gave their support to him. When the order reducing him to the ranks was read in the mess hall, there was a commotion, and "the whole battalion . . . began to hiss and cry 'Lynch him', and 'Kill him,' meaning Ward." Later, when Ward was Officer-of-the-Guard, "the men cut pillows up and threw them at him and spit on him and stepped on him and cryed, 'Drag him out' and 'Lynch him.' It was because the Col. and Comm't liked that . . . man better than they did me that I was reduced."[56] The faculty appeared to be on Ed's side:

Rohrbaugh and I came very nearly being fired, the Col. and Lieut Strong wanted to but most of the younger profs didn't so they compromised. A man said to one of the profs the day I went down that he didn't see why I was reduced and the Prof said: "I'll be darned if I do either."

Ed devoted a section of his letter to urging his parents not to get discouraged, while at the same time making no attempt to conceal his own gloomy attitude:

Please don't *feel sorry for me. I have enough sand in me to take my punishment, however unjust without grumbling (too much) but if I could only feel that you and mother hadn't lost confidence in me again on acct of this; it wouldn't be so hard. I have not shown that I felt injured by my reductions. I have done what I thought you would want me to do, braced up and done what I thought would put me on the road to work up all over again. I have been on guard twice and rec'd orderly to the commanding Officer for being the neatest man and having the cleanest gun in the guard.*

Toward the end of the letter he found it difficult to control his emotions:

I think I have rec'd no demerits since my reductions, I have studied just as hard if not harder. And I tell you Father its not for myself I am doing it, either, as far as I am concerned I don't give two whoops in hades whether school keeps or not. I am both home-sick and discouraged, because it looks as though a fellow never could get up again, when he had all headquarters to buck against . . .

He signed himself "Your affect. son," using his full name, Ed R. Burroughs, and placing his new, reduced rank beneath in a kind of bitter defiance: "Cadet Private Co. A."[57]

Obviously, his reduction to ranks affected him very deeply; his hurt and resentment were strong because he believed that the punishment was unjustified and that prejudice was involved. Unable to find a release for his anger and frustration, he turned to one of his favorite pastimes — cartooning. On a piece of cardboard he drew a tombstone in a pyramidal shape. In the center he printed his own version of his sentence, giving it the appearance of an epitaph:

April 12, 1894 — Cadet 2nd Lieut. Ed. R. Burroughs, Company "A", is hereby reduced to the ranks and confined to reduced limits until the 10th of June 1894, for "Alleged" gross neglect of

duty while Officer of the Day. By Col J. S. Rogers and Lt. F. S. Strong without the sanction of the Faculty of M.M.A. . . .

That Ed had sufficient determination to recover from his reduction in rank and start the uphill climb again is demonstrated by the events of the succeeding year. He was advanced to first sergeant, and by his senior year in 1895 was appointed second ranking captain and assigned to the "D" company.[58]

At the academy the fact that he was regularly promoted and given positions of responsibility seemed to indicate he was overly severe in his judgments of Superintendent Rogers and Commandant Smith. His accusations that they were prejudiced against him and in favor of others may have been more emotional than rational. The opinions (and his actions) were part of a period of youthful rebellion. When he examined his academy career in the calmness of retrospect, his estimate was quite different.

In his *Autobiography* he comments:

During my second and third years at Orchard Lake I held various offices, including that of corporal, 1st-sergeant, sergeant-major and 2nd-lieutenant. I was reduced to the ranks a couple of times, for what I do not recall, but realising now what a young ass I must have been it is not so surprising that I was reduced to the ranks as that I was ever reappointed to office again.

From the distance of time he now views the actions of Rogers and others in charge as unbiased:

There was practically no such thing as "pull" at Orchard Lake and little or no favoritism was shown in the appointment of non-commissioned officers and commissioned officers, and as I look back upon it now I cannot understand why it was that I was so often promoted. I was not particularly neat in my personal appearance, except at ceremonies; I was not particularly amenable to discipline, and in the matter of observing regulations I was a rotten soldier, for I broke them all; but I loved everything mili-

ERB on horse "Belle," Michigan Military Academy, April 1895.

tary. The little United States Infantry Drill Regulations was my bible and I took great pride in the military correctness and precision of my every act and word when on duty.

The lure of military life, the fascination it had for him — these can be understood through a consideration of his age, his nature, and his total personality. He was young and restless, in need of excitement and challenge. But beyond what his age required, he was naturally vigorous and active, bored by too long application to books, in need of a continuous physical outlet. He was fiercely competitive, and in a military life, where in riding and drilling, physical skill was demanded, and promotion depended upon this skill, he found the stimulation that was vital to him.

Strangely, his home environment during that period did not appear to be as important an influence as the factors listed. His father, although an army major, had made no attempt to drive his son toward a military career. His main concern had been to see that Ed received a good education. In his letters Major George Burroughs had been revealed more as an indulgent father rather than as an army disciplinarian. If anything, he appeared to have a mistrust of harsh army regulations and punishments. After all, it was significant that following the Civil War, although an officer, he made no further attempt to find a career for himself in the army, but chose to abandon a military life at the age of thirty-three for a turn at business.

Once promoted to captain, Ed showed a disposition to take quite a different attitude when violations of school rules were committed by the cadets under his command. In an amusing incident, a private was reported by Captain Burroughs for "direct disobedience to orders at supper." The cadet, King Taylor, on March 16, 1895, submitted his own explanation of matters to Commandant Strong:

I would respectfully state that I was laughing when Captain Burroughs told me to wipe it off, and I tried to as quick as I could. But it is not an easy thing to wipe it off when you are laughing hard, and I think I wiped it off so soon after

that it would not be called "Dirrect Disobedience to orders" for he didint give me time to wipe it off.

Taylor's protest was sent to Ed with a note attached: "Respectfully referred to Cadet Captain Burroughs for statement of facts in this case." It was signed by the commandant. There is no record of Ed's response.

With his graduation from Michigan Military Academy scheduled for June 1895, Ed realized that plans must be made for his future. The prospect of a military career, especially as a commissioned officer, appealed strongly to him. But the first step to achieve this was a difficult one: somehow he must secure an appointment to the Military Academy at West Point. The support of an influential person, preferably someone in an important government position was needed, and brother George set the political wheels in motion.

George and Harry Burroughs together with their friend Lew Sweetser were still operating as Sweetser & Burroughs, Dealers in Livestock, at their ranch in Yale, Idaho. Their colorful letterhead included an engraving of a steer and a miniature replica of their brand — a large Y with a bar above it. Shipping was still via American Falls. As a respected Idaho businessman, George was able to obtain the help of Congressman Edgar Wilson, a member of the United States House of Representatives. The appointment came through quickly. On May 6, 1895, George sent a telegram to Ed: "You have principal appointment. Prepare for examination on June 13."

George wrote on the same day to give a full explanation:

. . . I enclose letter from Hon. Edgar Wilson to me when you have read same please return. Allow me to extend to you my most sincere congratulations. I consider you very much to be envied and you yourself cannot be any more pleased than I am at the result. Your friends have done all for you now that is in their power to do; your future rests with yourself.

Continuing, George cautioned his younger brother:

I will write you at length in a day or so the steps that have been taken in your behalf and to whom besides yourself you are indebted. Mr. Ramsey, State Auditor, to whom Mr. Wilson refers is a Cassia Co. man and a friend of ours. I feel sure you will pass, Ed, but remember the exam is a rigid one, don't spare yourself in the short time left you to prepare.

George suggested that Ed write a note of appreciation to Congressman Wilson, of whom he noted, "He is a young man and I think a graduate of the University of Mich. If you ever have any opportunity to make his acquaintance do so. I think he has a very bright future before him and he may rise to almost any position."

George's belief was that Wilson would look upon Ed as "a sort of protege," would watch his career with interest, and "will like any man feel gratified if you show that you feel the obligation you are under to him."

Soon after, Ed received the official document from the War Department, dated May 10, 1895. It was addressed to him at what was assumed to be his legal residence, Yale, Cassia County, Idaho, and in an opening notification stated:

You are hereby informed that the President has conditionally selected you for appointment as a Cadet of the United States Military Academy at West Point, New York.

Should you desire the appointment, you will report in person to the Superintendent of the Academy on the 13th day of June, 1895, for examination. . . .[59]

The *Boise Statesman* reported the story at the same time, one of its headlines reading "Edgar R. Burroughs Appointed by Congressman Wilson." The lead paragraph also referred to Albert Brunzell of Reynolds, Owyhee County, who had been named as alternate.

It was interesting to note that Albert Brunzell, the alternate, had been appointed once before, but had failed the examination. The situation was further explained:

Congressman Wilson hopes that one or both of these young men will be successful in the examination so that Idaho may have a creditable representative in the great military school, one who will go through and graduate with honors to himself and to the state.[60]

The statement is puzzling. Whether Wilson was aware of the fact that Ed, born and raised in Illinois, had visited Idaho only briefly, is not clear. But another aspect must be considered. Idaho, a newly-formed frontier state, had only a small number of inhabitants who were born in the state, or who had lived there for any long period. The population consisted mainly of newcomers who had drifted in from other states. Thus a choice of candidates for West Point would be limited.

A further point is that the educational opportunities were limited in this pioneer state. Those hoping for admission to West Point would naturally be forced to choose schools in other states for preparation and training. This would explain the official attitude adopted toward Ed, who, although not in Idaho at the time of his appointment, was noted to be "receiving training and instruction" at Michigan Military Academy.

Unfortunately, as far as candidate Edgar R. Burroughs was concerned, the hopes of Congressman Wilson and the dreams of the state of Idaho were not to be realized. The dismal outcome was reported succinctly in Ed's *Autobiography:* "During the end of my senior year I received an appointment to West Point, where I went for examination with a hundred and eighteen other candidates, only fourteen of whom passed, I being among the one hundred and four." The *Boise Statesman* had mentioned the limited number who had been successful previously: ". . . of 181 examined in March, only 57 passed, while of those examined at New Orleans not one went through successfully." But since on June 13 only fourteen passed, Ed's group made an even poorer achievement than the one that preceded it.

With the news of his failure, both Ed's discouragement and the disappointment at home must have been profound. One can also imagine the humiliation of brother George who had worked so hard to obtain Congressman Wilson's assistance. Ed's father, who had been remarkably tolerant of his son's earlier escapades at the academy, was reaching the limits of his patience. A survey of all the later happenings from 1894 on made it plain that Ed was still not ready to take a serious view of life. He was nearing twenty and groping toward maturity, as yet unsteady and without a goal or objectives.

Nothing awaited; there were no new plans to be formed. He followed the obvious, accepting the only offer: he would return to the academy. On July 4, 1895, Colonel J. Sumner Rogers wrote a letter to "E. P. Burrows," 646 Washington Boulevard, Chicago, explaining:

You will be appointed to the place at the same compensation Spellman [Spilman] & Bisco receive i.e. $35 per month, for the nine school months with room and board. I have not time to write you fully at this time, but I hope that you will take up the work at once with your natural enthusiasm and help us fill every room with desirable cadets — Gentlemen — With kind regards to your father. . . .

Although Ed's behavior had shown improvement in his senior year, it must be admitted that Rogers, like George Burroughs, Sr., displayed great patience and an unusually forgiving nature. Not only did he welcome Ed back, but he was willing to place him in a position of authority. This action proved Rogers to be a man of some discernment. In Ed Burroughs, beyond his erratic and rebellious conduct, were the high spirits, the "natural enthusiasm" Rogers had mentioned, of a young man who took pride in physical achievement, loved military drill and horsemanship, and was willing to work hard at tasks that interested and challenged him.

Ed's position for the fall term of 1895-96 was to be that of assistant commandant, an office which included the duties of cavalry and gatling gun instructor, tactical officer — and professor of geology.

chool was out, and the arrival of the summer vacation found Ed at home in Chicago. Too restless to accept the weeks of inactivity, he began a search for employment. His friend and roommate from Orchard Lake, Bob Lay, came forward with an offer. They would both work for the Knickerbocker Ice Company, 134 Van Buren Street, whose owner was Bob's uncle. They were appointed collectors, and Ed's area was in Grand Crossing, a suburb of Chicago.

The job turned out to be anything but mundane. In his *Autobiography,* the experiences he describes most vividly are those involving encounters with unfriendly dogs:

I never was much of a runner, although once I did win a pearl-handled penholder for coming in second in a mile race at Pontiac, after smoking several cigarettes and eating a bag of popcorn, but there was one occasion in Grand Crossing that summer when I broke all existing records for sustained flight without refueling. A dog and I discovered each other simultaneously in a dark hallway upon the third floor of a ramshackle flat building. You know the kind, with the back porches sticking out behind and the stairs zig-zagging from the upper porch to the ground. The dog was young and agile and I only had about fifteen feet start on him, but I beat him down those zig-zag stairs and over the back fence, my banking at the turns being perfect.

On another occasion, in his round of collections, he arrived at a Victorian mansion "set far back from the street in grounds surrounded by a high fence." As he entered he could hear angry barking coming from the stables in the rear of the house. He hesitated, pondering "the advisability of attempting to collect the bill by mail," but he then heard the clank of a chain and felt reassured, believing that the dog was tied up. He walked to the front porch, some distance from the entrance, his fears calmed by the steady clanking of the chain. But as he pressed the doorbell, he became aware of an ominous change in the sound from the rear of the house:

The barking and growling became louder and seemed to be approaching and the clanking of the chain had become a rattle — it was dragging along the ground. I was almost paralyzed, for the dog sounded like a large dog, and when he came careening around the corner of the house I saw that he was a large dog; in fact, he was a Great Dane.[61]

He could think of nothing to do except "gluing" his finger to the bell button as the dog galloped toward him. The memory of what his brother George had once said — that if you stand perfectly still a vicious dog will not bite you — returned to him. "I stood so still," he wrote, "that he must have thought that I was a new statue for the front lawn." The dog sniffed at him for some time and then sprawled at full length across the front of the porch, entirely blocking his escape.

He could hear the continuous ring of the bell and began to fear that there was no one at home:

. . . but presently, to my great relief, a maid opened the door. I told her about the ice bill, but she said that there was no one home to pay it, and then I asked, "Does this dog bite?" To which she replied, "Yes," and slammed the door in my face. Imagine my embarrassment.

Somehow he gathered sufficient courage to step over the dog and start away from the house, managing "to stroll slowly and nonchalantly down to the gate, which was now at least two miles from the front porch." The dog merely stared after him.

His most ludicrous adventure as a bill collector came when he "parked" his horse, tying it to a tree in front of a house. He had several stops to make at homes nearby. He had failed to notice that the horse was stationed near some young trees and also that the horse was hungry. "When I returned," he said, "I found that he

had eaten the trees and that an irate householder was waiting for me." The householder happened to be Lieutenant Bondfield of the Chicago Police Department. Bondfield told him off in emphatic language and then sent for one of his sergeants who lived nearby. Ed was placed under arrest. He described what followed:

I was taken to the Police Station and put in a cell in the basement. It was a Saturday afternoon and the Lieutenant evidently planned to keep me there until Monday, for no effort was made to reach either my employers or my father, but I succeeded in making such a damned nuisance of myself that they finally got in touch with the Knickerbocker Ice Company and I was released on bail. Monday, when I appeared in court, my father and the judge discovered that they had won the Civil War together and Lieutenant Bondfield learned that I was going back to Michigan Military Academy as Assistant Commandant, where one of his sons was a cadet, so we all kissed and made up.[62]

When the summer was over, and Ed reported to Orchard Lake for his new position, he could undertake his military tasks with a degree of confidence. But at first consideration his assignment as "Professor of Geology" appeared ludicrous. In his *Autobiography* he describes his return to the academy, the events that followed, and his reactions to the assignment. "The fact that I had never studied geology seemed to make no difference whatever," he commented. "They needed a professor of geology and I was it. . . . The men knew that I knew nothing about geology and naturally they made the most of it, but they did not get away with much because I studied geology harder than they did and always kept about one jump ahead of them."

The commandant was now Captain Fred A. Smith of the regular army. As assistant commandant under him, Ed was responsible for discipline and for detecting any violations of school rules. "Colonel Rogers could scarcely have selected a better man," he noted, "as I had broken every regulation myself while I was a cadet and knew just how it was done."

He would enter the plebes' rooms and go directly to what they presumed was a safe hiding place for their cigarettes or chewing tobacco. They began to view him with awe, not realizing that he had used the same places to hide his own forbidden objects. He describes an inspection of the room of Cadet Martin of Marshalltown, Iowa. Ed went to his desk, pulled out a drawer, and reaching behind it, found a box containing candy:

Now I had not known that there was anything back of that drawer, but Martin was a plebe and the plebes always hid their tobacco, at first at least, in some such obvious hiding place. When I opened the box and found that it was candy I knew that there was something wrong, since candy was not taboo. Therefore I became suspicious and cutting into one of the pieces found that it was chewing tobacco coated with chocolate.

He was well acquainted with all the popular hiding places for the contraband, usually cigarettes or chewing tobacco. The sash weight wells on either side of the windows were often used; at the bottom of the sash was a little panel which could be unscrewed. Other favorite spots were the inside of mattresses or pillows and holes in the floors beneath the rugs. Books were suspect; at times the centers were cut out and the contraband inserted. But the number of hiding places was limited, because the cadets were quartered in small, bare rooms, two to a room. Most of the men learned to carry their tobacco in their socks, "but only when there was little danger of inspection as it was easy to run one's hand down the inside of a man's trouser leg below the knee and feel the package of cigarettes or plug of tobacco beneath."

Ironically, Ed, who had taken delight in breaking many of the rules when he was a cadet, now turned into a strict disciplinarian. Any popularity he may have had began to vanish. In one instance somebody threw electric light bulbs and ink bottles at him when he walked past the barracks at night. Discovering that only one or two men were involved, he gave a stern warning. When it was repeated, he gave the corps an ultimatum: they must produce the guilty man in twenty-four hours. If they didn't, and any more missiles were thrown, the entire corps would be punished. The threat brought no change in the situation:

I did not expect that they would turn in the offender and I should have been ashamed of them if they had, but I thought that at least they would prevent him from throwing any more ink bottles at me. However, the following night I was again attacked whereupon I routed out a bugler, had a long roll sounded and marched the whole corps around the country for about two hours.

This drastic action merely increased his problems. The cadets, exhausted because of a lack of sleep, all failed their recitations the next morning. They blamed Ed, and as a result he was severely criticized by the faculty. A short while later, when he ordered another long roll and a midnight march, he aroused the anger of everybody, and this procedure was strictly forbidden.[63]

The position of assistant commandant with its authority and prestige had at first appeared very enticing to Ed, but as the weeks passed he discovered it had serious disadvantages. Separated from the cadets, viewed by them as a member of the staff, he was now unable to form the friendships that had been so important during his first four years. He realized that he now had a "lonesome job." He lived alone above the quartermaster's office on one side of the quadrangle, while almost all of the other staff and faculty members lived some distance away in cottages. But as far as they were concerned, even if they had lived closer, Ed, at his age, could have little in common with them; what he missed above all was the opportunity to join with the young cadets and be accepted by them.

The weight of his duties as cavalry and gatling gun instructor, tactical officer and professor of geology — plus his responsibilities in supervising the cadets — did not prevent him from being active in sports. On the letterhead of the Michigan Military Academy Athletic Association he is listed as one of the three directors in charge of football. Captain F. A. Smith, the commandant, is the secretary of the organization while Cadet A. T. Conner has replaced Ed as the "Foot-Ball and Base-Ball Captain." But *Lieut. E. R. Burroughs* is now given the title of "Foot-Ball and Baseball Manager."

In these capacities he was given full authority to arrange the game schedules. His contacts with coaches from other schools and universities, evidenced in the original telegrams preserved in his scrapbook, demonstrate that he conducted negotiations and set up times and dates for the games. A telegram from Hyde Park, dated November 13, 1895, is addressed to E. R. Burroughs and reads: "Can Have Them for Morning Game. We Play in Afternoon. Collect 25c. A. A. Stagg."

Another from Notre Dame, Indiana, on November 20, reads: "Will Guarantee $100.00 or One-Half Gate. Reply. (Signed) P. B. McManus."

Other telegrams are indicative of the negotiations. From Faribault, Minnesota, November 19, Newhall writes, "Must stand by my first telegram. This is final." A telegram from Milwaukee, Wisconsin, dated November 19, advised, "Will play if guarantee expenses $90.00 and game is played in afternoon. Answer. Have written." It is signed "Smythe."

He still found time for his duties with the school magazine. The *Adjutants* of November and December 1895 list Lieutenant E. R. Burroughs at the head of ten other editors, and in the issues running from January through March of 1896 his name appears in the same position.

His lonesomeness as assistant commandant was partially alleviated by the friendship of another man who for a few months was given the same title. Emelio Figerallo, Count de-Gropello, was a captain of cavalry on leave from the Italian army. He and Ed spent time together when they were off duty. To the cadets, Emelio, with his emotional behavior, his typical Italian gestures and expressions, and his blun-

dering attempts at the English language, was a constant source of amusement. It was a period in which Ed, also, had insufficient maturity to understand Emelio. He had noted with some distaste that Emelio's manners at the table were far from what he expected of a European nobleman. But in retrospect, in his *Autobiography,* he describes Emelio with a regret for his old narrowness of vision and with the mature perception of age. Without doubt Emelio was a "great big overgrown boy; a lovable chap who could never understand us or our ways and who, when gauged by the narrow provincialism of a small American private school in those days, could not be understood by us." Emelio, simple and natural, "horrified the members of the faculty by his casual references to natural phenomena, which in those days were not mentioned in the presence of ladies." In summarizing, Ed wrote:

Now, after the passing of years and a broader experience of people, I realize that he was, perhaps, the only human being among us. I know that he had a heart of gold. . . . His family owned a whole town and he had a gorgeous watch that had been presented to him personally by the King of Italy. When he left us he went to South America and I have often wondered what became of him.

By the spring of 1896 Ed's impatience with his confining duties, the routine of school schedules, of supervisory tasks, reached a climax. His restlessness, part of his nature but also of his age, was caused by his urgent need for action and adventure — the challenge of something different. He had spent five years at the academy, was weary of it, and found no interest even in his position of assistant commandant and in chances for future promotions. At twenty Ed was too young and too doubtful about himself to accept permanency or the prospect of being tied down. In contrast to the restrictive atmosphere of a school, he had a dream of a freer, more exciting life. His decision and his departure from the academy came suddenly and, as in the past, impulsively.

4
THE SEVENTH CAVALRY AND BEYOND

Toward the end of 1894, six months before graduation from Michigan Military Academy, Ed had already made his own decision about the future. His studies had improved and he had done better in a variety of subjects, but the army — and especially the cavalry — remained his prime interest. A motivating influence was his love of horses and riding, as well as his love for the outdoors. Added to this was another factor: he had passed four years of military life and had risen in ranks to be a cadet officer. His dream now was to be a commissioned officer in the regular army; and with the experience and training he had acquired at the academy, the appointment might be possible. But if it could not be obtained, he was prepared to serve an apprenticeship as an enlisted man and was planning for the commission that was bound to come.

During the same period Major George Burroughs yielded to pressure from his son and gave him a letter of consent. Required because Ed was underage, the letter of December 1, 1894, gave a complete authorization:

To any Recruiting Officer
    U.S. Army

This is to certify that the bearer, my son Edgar R. Burroughs who is underage; has the consent of his parents to enlist in the Cavalry Service of the U.S. Army.

        Very Respectfully
        Geo. T. Burroughs[1]

As events turned out, the letter was not used. By May of 1895 Ed's plans had changed; awaiting him was the possibility of an appointment to the United States Military Academy. His failure to pass the examination led to his return to Michigan Academy that fall. But with the tediousness of academy duties he once more sought refuge in his dreams of a career in the cavalry.

When Ed had accepted the position of instructor and assistant commandant, Colonel

Rogers had assumed he would stay for the school year. Now, sometime in April or the first part of May 1896, he quit his position abruptly. From Orchard Lake he went to the army recruiting station at Detroit. Enlisting was not as simple as he thought. In telling the complete story of his army experience in his *Autobiography*, Ed noted that they wouldn't accept his word that he was twenty-one, adding "which incidentally I was not." He would be twenty-one on September 1. He gave the details:

The fact that I wore good clothes made them suspicious as they had recently had some trouble because of having enlisted a son of Deering, the reaper man, while he was still under age. There was some delay while permission was obtained from my father and then there was a still further delay when I asked to be sent to the worst post in the United States, for they had to get special permission from Washington to send me outside of that department in which Detroit is located.[2]

Ed waited with impatience at the recruiting station, where he recalled having his first experience with wharf rats. "They used to play around at night in the room where we slept and there were some among them that were fully as large as a housecat. We occupied our time throwing shoes at them until we fell asleep."

When permission finally came through from Washington, Ed was assigned to the Seventh Cavalry at Fort Grant, Arizona Territory. He was assured by the recruiting sergeant that it was "absolutely the worst assignment in the United States Army."

In a small brown memorandum book which he had carried with him at Michigan Military Academy, Ed kept a record of his height and weight and jotted down names and addresses. On December 27, 1895, he shows his weight, dressed, as 175 and one-fourth pounds. Some five months later, on May 13, 1896, the date of his enlistment, he notes that his weight stripped is 153 and his height five feet nine inches. Records of ERB's height show some variation. In 1894, as captain of the MMA football team, his height is listed as five feet ten and one-half

inches. Hulbert Burroughs said that his father's height was closer to five feet nine inches. A further entry indicates that his arrival at the Fort was one day early: "Sworn in 9 am. Assigned to Troop B 7th U.S. Cav. May 24th 1896. Arrived Fort Grant May 23rd."[3]

The journey to the fort began with a railroad trip to Wilcox, Arizona. The government paid for coach transportation only, and Ed used his own money to take Pullman accommodations to Kansas City, the first stopover. Viewing the ride as a lark, Ed spent most of his money in Kansas City and as a result was forced to complete the remainder of the long trip in a day coach. He also faced a more urgent problem — what to do about food. "I was very hungry," he said, "so hungry in fact that at one of the stops I swiped the lunch of a Mexican who had gotten off to stretch his legs."

When the train arrived at Wilcox, he discovered he would have to pass the night there; the stage for Fort Grant did not leave until the next morning. His funds were now reduced to a single dollar, and the question was, how to spend it. Although he was "terrible hungry" and "equally sleepy," he settled for a bath, which he wanted most of all. Later, in a hotel, he was allowed to sleep in a sample room used by traveling salesmen. It contained a cot but no lights, and he had barely lain down when he discovered that the cot was swarming with bedbugs. Sleep was impossible, and he dressed, planning to go outside; but as he picked up his suitcase, it burst open, spilling all the contents on the floor. He spent a half hour crawling about on his hands and knees in the dark, searching for his belongings. Then he went out to sit on the edge of the porch for the remainder of the night, his feet dangling into the street.

Fort Grant in 1896 was a dreary collection of dusty barracks and tents set in the midst of parched Arizona country. The bleakness of the natural environment was more than matched by the drudging monotony of the life and work at the fort and the bad relationships between the officers and enlisted men. The duties, a prisonlike form of hard labor, consisted of road work, ditchdigging, and what Ed described as "boulevard building". The commanding officer, enormously fat, and lazy, set an uninspiring example of leadership for the other officers. Ed commented scathingly about the colonel that he "conducted regimental maneuvers from an army ambulance. It required nothing short of a derrick to hoist him onto a horse. He was then and is now my idea of the ultimate zero in cavalry officers."

Similarly lethargic, and reluctant to exert themselves by calling the men out for drill or maneuvers, the officers under the colonel's command were quite willing to accept his philosophy. To the commander, who was known as a "pick-and-shovel man," this philosophy was simple and pragmatic. Ed gave his own version of it: the way to keep soldiers occupied was to have them "building boulevards in Arizona where no one needed a boulevard." Ed further explained that "Fort Grant was superimposed upon a chaos of enormous boulders, some of them as large as a house. . . ." The soldiers' first appalling task was to remove these before the road work began; obviously, as Ed phrased it, the daily labor was "anything but a sinecure."

Ed soon made the acquaintance of two other men from whom he would take orders. About the top sergeant of B Troop, an Irishman named Lynch, Ed wrote, "He would have been nice to me if I had bought beer for him and if I had it to do over again, I would keep him soused indefinitely, for by that route would come favors and promotion." But about the other man, Lieutenant Tompkins, Ed wrote:

Tommy Tompkins was our troop commander. I think he was a first lieutenant then. He had risen from the ranks. Tommy had a set of mustachios that were the pride of the regiment. He could curl the ends back over his ears and the yellow cavalry stripes on his breeches were so wide that little of the blue could be seen. Tommy was a great character and at drill he was a joy. He called us long-eared jackasses and a great many other things, but this is the only one that is printable; yet none of the men ever took

offense. There were many other officers in the post who were cordially hated, but Tommy was universally loved.

After being quartered with the rest of the B Troop in Sibley tents, Ed received his initiation in army routine. But it was soon evident that he knew the typical rookie drill by heart; the only new skill to be learned was the use of the saber, and this he mastered quickly. Within a brief period the sergeant was convinced that Ed didn't belong in the beginning dismounted squad, and he was sent to the drill master for instruction in cavalry riding. Ed reported the results with amusement: "I had been in his squad only a few days when he came to Lynch and complained. 'Why in hell did you send me that bird?' he inquired. 'He can ride better than I can.' "[4]

The area surrounding Fort Grant, arid, and baked by the sun to a desertlike dryness, was hardly appealing to a newcomer. Ed was first informed that it hadn't rained for seventeen years; however, soon after his arrival, nature staged a violent reversal of policy. A series of torrential electrical storms began. The drinking water became contaminated and Ed contracted dysentery. Although he resisted for a while, he was finally forced to go to the hospital. The experience was one that remained vivid in his mind, especially as it concerned the hospital steward, a man named Costello, "the one man whom I have ever sworn to kill," and the drunken doctors assigned to the post. Ed described his days in the hospital:

I was so weak that I could scarcely stand and they would not give me anything to eat, which I suppose was the proper treatment; that is they would not give me anything but castor oil, which it seemed to me in my ignorance that I did not need. I was absolutely ravenous for food and one day one of the men on the opposite side of the ward had a crust of toast that he did not want and he told me that I might have it. He was too weak to bring it to me, so I managed somehow to totter over and get it.

55

Unfortunately, Costello, in hiding, was watching to see if any such attempt would be made, and he appeared in time to take the food away and punish Ed for violating the rules. In a rage, Ed "spent the next few weeks concocting diabolical schemes for killing Costello, after subjecting him to various sorts of torture." He also broadcast the threat that as soon as he was discharged from the hospital and had regained his health, he intended to kill the steward. "I do not know whether he believed it or not," Ed wrote, "but before I was able to carry out my threat he deserted and I have never seen him since."

In later recollections of the incident, Ed could view it with more tolerance: "Time is a mellower; if I should meet him now the chances are that we would have a bottle of home brew together and that I should find him a most delightful fellow."

What Ed termed "the most disagreeable part of his service" centered about his contacts with the doctors. The two medical officers, a major-doctor and a captain-doctor, were a sorry pair:

The principal difference between them being that at times the captain-doctor was not quite so drunk as the major-doctor. However, drunk or sober, their word was law. When they made the rounds of the hospital they referred to us as "this" and "it." To them we were less than human beings and if they decided that one of us was dead, we were dead.

Costello, the steward, who was given to telling anecdotes about the hospital and the doctors, relished repeating a story that fitted his peculiar idea of how to entertain and cure patients:

A colored trooper was very ill. One of the doctors pronounced him dead. "Have it taken out," he said to Costello, according to whom it was their custom to carry the dead from the main ward and drop them through a trap door into the cellar until the time for burial arrived. . . . It seems that as they were about to drop the

. . . trooper into the cellar he gained consciousness and objected, insisting that he was not dead. "The doctor said you were dead," replied Costello, and pushed him through the trap door.

Ed, soon after his arrival at the Fort, was examined by the major-doctor. To his consternation the doctor recommended an immediate discharge because of heart disease. Ed hardly knew what to think. "I did not wish to have heart disease," he commented, "neither did I wish to be discharged from the army." All he could do was wait to see what procedure would be followed. After awhile, when an order came from Washington to have him re-examined, the assignment was given to the captain-doctor. The diagnosis was the same; but Ed believed that the reason was obvious — the captain didn't dare to differ with his superior.

After another waiting period a further communication from Washington ordered Ed to be held for observation. This advice he evaluated pessimistically, "it evidently being cheaper to bury me then to pay transportation back to Detroit." Naturally quite disturbed, he went to the captain-doctor to find out what his chances were. "He was quite reassuring," Ed wrote. "He told me that I might live six months, but on the other hand I might drop dead at any moment."

Ed's recollection of the doctors and their drunkenness led him to describe an amusing incident:

The major-doctor had an orderly who had a highly developed sense of humor. According to military usage, he followed so many paces behind the major-doctor whenever the latter went abroad. I have seen them crossing the parade ground with the major-doctor laying a most erratic course and always, no matter where or how he staggered, his orderly would stagger similarly the required number of paces to his rear.

Ed faced the difficulty of adjusting to an existence at the fort where the soldiers' morale and the level of discipline were extremely low. He became convinced that the recruiting sergeant's opinion had been accurate — one could hardly imagine a worse post than Fort Grant.

He was quickly aware of the atmosphere of thinly repressed violence, of enmity between the enlisted men and officers. Ed saw an officer dragged from his mount and beaten up by a soldier; he heard other men in the post canteen who swore that they would kill any officer they found after dark. Few officers walked the grounds at night, and it was seldom that either the officer of the day or the officer of the guard ventured out for evening inspection. The unfortunate situation, Ed believed, was the result of the attitude and behavior of Colonel Sumner, "which was reflected by his subordinates."

Some officers received a measure of respect, and there were others, like Tommy Tompkins, for whom the men showed a comradely affection. As Ed made friends with the men, he realized they were neither incorrigible nor vicious; they had the basic qualities of good soldiers and would have responded to a fair and reasonable discipline. But their natural response to a callous, repressive treatment could only be one of hostility and hatred.

The fort and its surrounding area teemed with excitement and apprehension. In the wide stretches of Arizona country the actions of the Indians, restless and resentful, could not be predicted. The Apaches had been confined at a nearby post, but everybody expected them to break loose and go on a rampage. A dangerous outlaw, The Apache Kid, was roaming the country side with his band of cutthroats, while there were reports of towns being raided by another bandit called Black Jack. To Ed these depredations became a source of hope rather than fear; he wrote, "We were always expecting boots and saddles and praying for it, for war would have been better than camp life at Fort Grant under Colonel 'Bull' Sumner."

The opportunity came. Ed, having lied himself out of the hospital and still being weak from dysentery, heard that his troop was scheduled to leave on an urgent mission. A man and his daughter had been murdered on the Solomonsville Trail; their wagon had been burned, and the assumption was that the Apache Kid

and his band of Indians were the guilty ones. Ed's B Troop, allotted three days rations, was given the task of capturing the Apache Kid. Although in no condition to undertake an active campaign, Ed, by further lying and pleading, managed to rejoin his troop.

The soldiers began a nightmarish journey which took them across the Arizona mountains. Tommy Tompkins was in command, and a young officer acted as a guide to show them a shortcut to Solomonsville. The "shortcut" was revealed as a direct climb across the jagged peaks:

I knew that there was an army wagon with us part of the time, because I remember distinctly assisting it along mountain trails where there was only room for the wheels on one side of the wagon. We would pass ropes from the opposite side over the top of the wagon and the entire troop dismounted and clinging to the mountainside above the wagon would manage to keep the whole business from pitching into the abyss below, while the mules stumbled and slithered along ahead like a bunch of mountain goats.

Ed vaguely recalled that somewhere along the route the wagon was lost. He became a rider weaving blindly in and out of the column, unable to think of anything but his severe abdominal pains. These were aggravated by the fourteen pounds of ammunition and weapons fastened to his waist. As his suffering grew more acute, Ed found it impossible to wait for permission to fall out. He noted that he fell out, "just far enough to clear the horses behind me and then I would tumble off, usually headfirst onto the ground while the troop went on. At first the sergeants used to bawl me out for not getting permission, but after a while they got used to it and paid no attention to me, since I always managed to catch up later."

Their arrival after dark at Solomonsville, a Mormon settlement, launched them on the first of a series of misadventures and blundering escapades. The inhabitants were responsible for the troops being there since they had sent an urgent request for army protection, but their actions in no way resembled those of a welcoming committee. They greeted the exhausted, thirsty soldiers by padlocking the wells, and then proceeded to set their dogs on the men. The enraged B Troopers broke the padlocks and drove the dogs away.

The hunt for the Apache Kid began in the rain. Ed described the soldiers' discomfort:

We each had two blankets that the men, recently from Fort Sheridan, had nicknamed the Chicago Heralds because they were so thin. One of these blankets we used as a saddle blanket during the day, and the other was in a roll at our cantel, but as it had no protection it was always wet both from rain and horse sweat. At night we laid them on the wet ground with our saddles at one corner and starting at the opposite side we rolled ourselves up in blankets until our heads reached our saddles. This is great for dysentery.

A running guard was kept, and in alphabetical order each enlisted man was required to take one hour of guard duty. The sentry was armed only with a revolver, and because the belt and holster were too heavy and uncomfortable, those on guard followed a custom of jamming the revolver into one of their leggings. The problem was to know when the hour was up and the next man was to be awakened. Fortunately, Ed had brought his watch, the only one in the troop, an open-faced silver watch he had received for a present on his sixteenth birthday. It became indispensable.[5]

The men displayed a naivete about Indians that Ed later viewed as incredible. Two soldiers patrolled the Indian trails all day, exposing themselves easily to attack by the Indians. "It was just as well for us that there were no renegades about," Ed commented, "for these patrols would have been nothing more than animated targets that no self-respecting renegade could have ignored." To him it appeared that the soldiers were being set up as bait; a dead trooper would have proved that there were hostile Indians in the area.

Ed exhibited his own share of blissful ignorance. With a man named Kunze he discovered

a hillside cave that was evidently the habitat of a silver-tipped bear. The two men decided to enter the cave and kill the bear, but as Ed noted, "Kunze, having all the brains in the party, remained at the bottom of the hill and held the horses, while I climbed up the steep trail to the cave, armed only with a revolver. A rubber band and a couple of spitwads would have been equally as useful."

Ed was deeply disappointed to find that the bear was not at home. About their actions he wrote in summation, "I mention this incident merely as a suggestion that there must be some power that watches over idiots."

The general ignorance of the men was also revealed in an experience with a gila monster which had been captured and then escaped from its box. The troop, terror-stricken, combed the camp until midnight in a search for the reptile. They believed that its bite meant instantaneous death and that the monster could kill merely by exhaling its venomous breath on any living thing.

Confusion and carelessness were part of normal procedure. Ed, on sentry duty, was given strict orders not to allow anyone to approach the camp, and to follow regulations by challenging twice and then firing. On this dark, rainy night Ed caught the movement of a shadowy figure, apparently dodging from tree to tree. When the figure drew nearer, Ed hurled a challenge, but the man kept moving without any reply. Ed continued to challenge him, and by the time he cried, "Halt or I fire", they were only a few feet apart. In the blackness he couldn't tell whether the man was a soldier or an Indian. He recalled what happened:

I had him covered and my finger was on the trigger of my revolver and then I saw him reach for his hip pocket. That was an occasion where a hunch was worth more than brains for I certainly was warranted in shooting him, and I should have shot him, but I didn't. I waited to see what he was going to pull out of his hip pocket. It was fortunate for one of us that it was a flask instead of a gun. When he asked me to have a drink I recognized his voice and discov-

ered that he was one of our sergeants drunk as a lord.

With their three-days rations gone, the troop was reduced to a diet of potatoes, which they bought in the area, and to a main dish of the only game available — jackrabbits. Ed described the rabbits vividly: "The muscles of those we killed were filled with large white grubworms as big as one's thumb. Sometimes the cook found them and dug them out, though I am under the impression that he missed many." Ravenously hungry, Ed ate the jackrabbit stew.

The men were given an occasional pass to go to the nearby town of Duncan, and Ed got involved in a poker game there, losing all his money to Mexican vaqueros. He conceived the idea of borrowing money from his commanding officer, Tommy Tompkins, hardly dreaming that the attempt would be successful. But Tommy's response raised him forever in Ed's esteem. "He listened to me patiently," said Ed, "told me he only had a dollar and a half and then gave me half of it."

Apparently the hunt for the Apache Kid had long since been forgotten. Since the men never went anywhere and merely lazed around the camp on the Gila River, the possibilities of catching him became quite remote. After a while they were ordered to return to the post. The journey was exhausting and dangerous. A heavy rainstorm turned the arid Arizona flatland into a torrential river; in places it was more than a mile wide, and the soldiers had to march fifty miles out of their way to get around it.

Upon arriving at the post Ed was still weak from his illness and unable to resume his active duties. He refused to go to the hospital, and Tommy Tompkins, again showing an unusual kindness, gave him a special "coffee-cooling" job, an assignment that removed him from drill, guard duty, and boulevard building. But the job was not exactly a sinecure. "I was placed in charge of headquarters stables," Ed noted, "where all I had to do was to take care of fourteen horses. I cleaned them and their stables, hauled manure, hay, and grain, and doctored those that were sick."

For men who led dreary, monotonous lives all year, the Thanksgiving and Christmas holidays were events to look forward to. In these brief periods at least, there was a relaxation of the army discipline; a festive atmosphere prevailed, and the soldiers for a time could escape from the tensions and boredom. Special holiday dinners were prepared, although they could not have been as deluxe as the Thanksgiving dinner displayed on Troop C's menu of November 26, 1896. The menu, found among Ed's souvenirs, included such choice items as Blue Point Oysters, roast venison, and roast pork, probably the result of some soldier's wry sense of humor. The Christmas menu for Troop C listed beef, turkey, and mutton. But about the B Troop and their dinner, Ed noted in disgust:

Our Christmas table groaned beneath a load of bottled beer and I hope to God that for once in his life Lynch got all the beer he wanted. For the rest, B Troop had only an ordinary dinner, but it sloshed in the same beer that one could buy any day at the post canteen.[6]

During this period Ed was part of a trio that organized "The May Have Seen Better Days Club." The men, all from different troops, had one thing in common: they really had seen better days and came from prosperous families. Ed could recall very few names, but wrote:

There was one chap whose father was a wealthy merchant from Boston; another was a Canadian; and the third was a chap by the name of Napier who had been an officer in the English army. We met in my quarters at the headquarters stables once a month, immediately after payday when we were flush. We usually managed to rake up a pretty good feed and plenty of wine, and then through the balance of the month we were broke, for thirteen dollars does not go far, especially when one has a lot of canteen checks to redeem on payday.[7]

By this time it had become apparent to Ed that life as an enlisted man was anything but romantic or adventurous. Still, it wasn't really soldiering that he now viewed with disgust, but the dreary duties of ditchdigging and boulevard building, " 'Bull' Sumner's idea of preparing men to serve their country in time of war." Ed was happiest when he was his own boss at the stables, even though he worked very hard. One of his duties was to haul hay and grain on a two-wheeled army cart pulled by a horse. He would pile the loose hay as high as possible so as to save the work of extra trips, and then climb atop the hay for the return to the stables. His carelessness led to all sorts of mishaps:

Once I slipped off the top bringing most of the load with me, fell astride one of the thills, turned completely over and stood on my head between the horse's hind feet and the cart. Again I had reached my corral and was bouncing down a little incline with the horse at a trot when the top of the load slipped off and took me with it. I bounced off the horse's rump and fell under the wheel, which passed over the small of my back. I thought that I was killed and for several seconds I was afraid to try to move for fear that I should discover definitely that my back was broken.

Although his back was extremely sore for weeks afterward, nothing could have made him disclose his pain to anybody. His fear was that he might lose his "coffee-cooling" job or be sent back to the hospital.

Among Ed's recollections were those of the 24th Infantry, a Negro regiment that was quartered at Fort Grant. He remembers them as "wonderful soldiers and as hard as nails," recalling their belief that "a member of the 24th was a rookie until he was serving his third enlistment." That they were respected by the army is evidenced by the fact that their noncommissioned officers were ranked unusually high, and one of their sergeants had the highest rank in the service.

On several occasions Ed remembered working under a black sergeant in such menial tasks as day labor or cleanup details, and he commented, ". . . without exception they were excellent men who took no advantage of their authority over us and on the whole were better to

work under than our own white sergeants."

He made only one friend among the Indian scouts — possibly because he bought whisky for him — a man called Corporal Josh, who may have been a chief at one time. Josh had not surrendered with Geronimo, but had remained a renegade, joining the Apache Kid's band. After a while he decided to give himself up and tried to think of some plan to win favor and forgiveness. There was a reward for the Kid, but Josh didn't dare attempt to bring him in. Ed offered the gruesome details of what followed:

. . . he did the next best thing and killed one of the Kid's relatives, cut off his victim's head, put it in a gunny sack, tied it to the horn of his saddle and rode up from the Sierra Madres in Mexico to Fort Grant, where he dumped the head out on the floor of the headquarters and asked for forgiveness and probably for a reward, so they let him enlist in the Apache scouts and made him a corporal.

Restricted to the monotony of army life, Ed's need for a creative outlet brought him back once more to a field in which he had shown unmistakable talent — that of sketching and water coloring. A keen observer of people and animals, aware always of the unusual and picturesque, he found stimulating subjects for his art in Fort Grant and its environs. He took delight in drawing the soldiers in colorful uniforms, in differing poses, and performing various duties.[8]

Always fascinated by horses, he developed an ability to draw them in precise detail, capturing subtle lines and impressions so that each animal emerged with individuality. No matter what soldier was mounted upon the horse, its beauty and grace were never obscured.

Some of his sketches were highlighted with water colors applied with skill and realism. At the bottom of one page of sketches in various colors he wrote humorously, "Please notice the Impressionist coloring."

Other sketches, typical of his interest, were titled *An Apache Scout, On Herd Guard* (a mounted soldier) and *An Old Soldier.* The Christmas Eve entertainment program pro-

Sketches ERB made during his service with 7th U.S. Cavalry, Fort Grant, Arizona Territory.

61

"No savvy trot."

Citizen Packer.

Sketches ERB made during his service with 7th U.S. Cavalry, Fort Grant, Arizona Territory.

vided him with an opportunity to make a group of drawings and cartoons. These included *Wing Dancer,* and one of a soldier carrying a child's hobby horse and toy wagon, with the caption, "How you can tell the 'Married Man'." Ed's sense of humor couldn't be repressed, and one of his cartoons is described as "A Drawing of Sitting Bull presenting Geo. Washington to Victoria of England. The Prince of Wales may be seen in the background." The Prince is shown as a curious but shy child, peering from behind Victoria's skirts.[9]

Ed's disillusionment with the life of an enlisted man at Fort Grant was inevitable. He had arrived on May 23 eager and excited at the prospect of an adventurous career in the cavalry, convinced that this period of training would lead to promotion and the attainment of the commission he had so desired. But two months of drudging labor and monotonous camp life, as well as illness, deflated his romantic ideas and made him realize that a career in the cavalry, especially at Fort Grant, was unthinkable. Whatever were the prospects of advancement, and these appeared remote, Ed couldn't conceive of any circumstances that would persuade him to stay in his present situation.

Toward the end of July 1896 or the first part of August he began writing complaining and even imploring letters to his father. His hopes were centered upon a procedure that had often been followed in cases similar to his: the army permitted a soldier to buy his way out of the service. He discussed this in correspondence with his father and was sustained by a confidence that his father would use money and influence to bring about his discharge. George Burroughs had never wanted Ed to enlist in the army and had undoubtedly yielded against his better judgment. But now, as with his son's impulsive actions and escapades of the past, he would be compelled to come to his rescue.

On August 25 Ed wrote to his father, acknowledging receipt of a letter of August 20, and then went on to reveal his misery and plead for help:

I learned something today which "makes my heart grow sad." A fellow wrote me that he had just heard that some law had been passed lately taking away a soldier's privilege of buying himself out. I don't know whether or not it is so and I can not find out here with-out asking an officer and if Tommy learned that I expected to buy out in the spring he might not like it.

In the event that the rumor was true, and a soldier could not buy his way out, Ed had an alternative suggestion:

I hope it is not true as I was beginning to look forward already to the time when I should be home again. If it is so would you be willing to have me try to borrow the transportation (about $50 including meals) and put in an application for transfer to the 1st Cavalry 2 troops of which are to be stationed at Sheridan (Fort Sheridan, Illinois) if not already there. I should make application for one of those troops. An applicant has to be able to show that he has the cash *for transportation.*

He also has to have the approval of his troop Commander, Post Commander and Secy of War and the Troop Commander of the troop he is going to has to express his willingness to accept him. I think the only stumbling block would be Col. E. V. Sumner, Post Commander. They say he objects to transfers without good cause.

Ed's youthful bravado and daring that drove him to request the worst assignment in the United States Army had been considerably dissipated by this time. A transfer to Fort Sheridan, near his home in Chicago, was pleasant to contemplate. But he offers to resign himself to his present situation if no change is possible: "If you think best I will make no attempt to transfer. I made my bed and I will lie in it. . . ." He is unable to conceal an acute homesickness:

. . . I think that if I ever get home again that I shall never leave, unless you drive me away and then I will go and sit on the curb stone in front of Rease's house and look at HOME.

I am glad you are to vote for Bryan electors. Hope you are still well at home. Love to all from your affectionate son Ed.

His loneliness may have also provoked wistful thoughts of Emma. From Coldwater, Michigan, where she was spending a vacation, with relatives, she mailed her picture. A notation on the back read, "1896 Sent to E. R. Burroughs — and received on his 21st Birthday at Duncan Arizona. Camp of the 7th U.S. Cavalry."

As Ed discovered, in matters involving decisions of any type, the army cannot be hurried. By the end of the year he was still waiting. On December 2, 1896, he wrote to Colonel J. Sumner Rogers at the Michigan Military Academy. One can only conjecture as to his reasons. He may have hoped to obtain Rogers' help either in getting a discharge or a transfer to the 1st Cavalry. Possibly, he was contemplating a return to the academy. The letter's main purpose may have been to offer an apology to Rogers. Ed, upon reflection, and with a little more maturity gained through his sequence of shattering experiences, might view his behavior at the academy, and his precipitate departure when the colonel was depending upon him, with guilt and a new understanding of his faults.

Rogers' reply on December 26 showed that the colonel had remarkable powers of patience and forgiveness:

I have read your favor of the 2nd inst with both interest and pleasure. While I still think that you acted imprudently and unkindly to me, I do not permit a single escapade in which your worst qualities were brought into requisition to blind me to the fact that you possess many admirable traits, and your letter still further causes me to forget your mistake.[10]

Ed had evidently stated that he planned to remain in the army, for Rogers referred to this point:

I assure you that I hold no malace against you, and wish you success in your profession of soldier. Your letter confirms my faith in your good heart, which is much to a soldier as well as civilian.

In stressing his friendly feelings, Rogers

wrote that Ed would always receive a cordial welcome at the Academy, adding:

It is my desire to remember you just as I remember other ex-cadets who have made a good record at the Academy, — with kindness and sincere good wishes for their prosperity, and I am glad to know that your feelings toward your school are warm and kind.

Concerning the Academy's financial condition, Rogers commented that "Considering the very hard times, we are holding our own in a most encouraging way."

George Burroughs, faced once more with the task of extricating his son from an unpleasant situation, began contacting people of influence. In March 1897 he wrote to a friend, W. D. Preston of the Griffin Wheel Company, requesting him to write to R. A. Alger, secretary of war. Preston, in his letter of March 11, explains the circumstances of Ed's enlistment with his father's consent, and refers to his ambition "to adopt a military profession." Then Preston bases his appeal upon Ed's supposed health problem:

It was his intention, as he is a young man of good ability and education to endeavor to pass the examinations and ultimately to get a commission, but it seems that after he was sent to Arizona he did not pass the proper Medical Inspection and the Medical Inspectors recommended that he be discharged. He has however not been discharged and is still held at Fort Grant.

Ed's main goal, according to Preston, was now unattainable:

This report of the Medical Examiners would undoubtedly prevent his getting a Commission even though he passed the proper examination, and as that was his idea on entering the Service, both he and his parents are now very anxious that he should get a regular discharge, as he has two very fine openings in Commercial lines.[11]

Preston adopted a sentimental tone in mentioning that "His Mother is in poor health and is very much worked up over the matter. . . ."

He stated that "from a thorough knowledge of all the circumstances it would appear to me that it would be . . . proper for you to grant the discharge. . . ." George Burroughs' influence with people in high places is revealed in Preston's reference to "Senator Mason of this city," with a comment that the Senator "will undoubtedly present the matter to you in proper form. . . ."

Another of George Burroughs' friends, E. G. Kieth, wrote much along the same lines on March 11 to Secretary Alger, mentioning a "medical examination which was unsatisfactory"; he presented the case from a rather peculiar viewpoint, shifting the blame to Ed's shoulders: ". . . his father is now quite anxious for his discharge, feeling that the young man was inconsiderate in enlisting without a Medical examination."

These intercessions achieved the desired results, and on March 19, 1897, Ed received a telegram from his father which read: "Discharge has been ordered. Will mail draft today."

In his *Autobiography* Ed explains concisely that "owing to the fact that I had twice been recommended for discharge because of heart disease, once by the major-doctor and once by the captain, it seemed wholly unlikely that I should pass a physical examination for a commission, and my father therefore obtained my discharge from the army through Secretary of War Alger."[12]

The discharge, dated March 23, 1897, refers to special orders of March 15 and reports in error that Ed was twenty-one and eight-twelfths years of age at the time of enlistment. He was actually twenty and eight-twelfths years old. His height is listed as five feet eight and one-half inches, his complexion fair with "Brown #3" eyes and dark brown hair, and his occupation as "Student." Tommy Tompkins, his commanding officer, rated his character as "excellent." Information about his military record is contained on the reverse side of the discharge.[13]

His service with the Seventh Cavalry ended, Ed, aware of past failures and disappointments, chose to review his entire sequence of military experiences with a satirical attitude. Beginning with his childhood, he prepared a list of the successive ranks he had held and headed the list "My Wonderful Military Career." On it he listed eleven steps:

1. *Right Guard Brown School Cadets (wooden gun)*
2. *High Private Harvard School Cadets (no gun)*
3. *Plebe — Orchard Lake*
4. *Corporal — Orchard Lake*
5. *Sergeant Major — Orchard Lake*
6. *2nd Lieut — Orchard Lake*
7. *Private — Orchard Lake*
8. *1st Sergeant — Orchard Lake*
9. *Captain — Orchard Lake*
10. *2nd Lieut M.M.A. Tactical Officer, Assistant Commandant, Adjutant of the Academy — Orchard Lake*
11. *Private — 7th U.S. Cavalry*

At the bottom he noted, "Between 4 and 5 there should also be a Private and Corporal."

Ed, who had spoken of his homesickness in the letter to his father, may have planned to return to Chicago immediately, but at Fort Grant he learned of his brothers' latest venture in the cattle business and received an invitation from them that was too enticing to turn down. The outfit of Sweetser & Burroughs, while continuing to raise cattle at the Idaho ranch, had discovered that success was becoming more and more elusive. Now, Lew Sweetser had gone to Mexico and purchased an entire brand of cattle, and Harry, at Nogales, Arizona, was awaiting the arrival of the animals. They were to be shipped to Kansas City.

Always eager to be with his brothers, Ed agreed to join Harry at Nogales and help in the loading of the cattle. The experience turned out to be one that he had not anticipated. In his *Autobiography* he gives the details of his second brief period in the cattle business. Accustomed to handling the big Idaho Herefords, Ed was amused by the appearance of the scrubby Mexican animals; they looked "about the size of jackrabbits." He viewed them with con-

tempt, and even went into the loading pens on foot to drive them up the runways to the cars. But he quickly changed his opinion:

They may have been small in stature, but they were large in initiative and they did not wish to go up the runways into the cars. They went part way and then all of a sudden they turned around and came toward me. I was not afraid of them, and on the other hand they appeared to be even less afraid of me. Those in the front rank knocked me down and the others galloped over me, after which I let somebody else load them.

As the train journeyed toward Kansas City, Ed's problems increased. Starting with seven cars of Mexican cattle, he later picked up other cars, including some at La Junta with Texas longhorns. Ed's only helper was an old man whom he described as "a poor consumptive trying to work his way East." The cattle were in poor shape, underfed and underwatered, and at a number of stops they had to drag seven or eight dead animals out of each car. The stops included one at Albuquerque, where, he remembered, he was given a hotel room that apparently belonged to somebody else. ". . . in a drawer were two beautiful six-guns. It was a good thing for the owner that I was honest."[14]

Ed thought he had experienced all possible difficulties, but soon a new one arose. The cattle, weak from starvation, would suddenly fall down. In order to save their lives, somebody would have to crawl into the cars and "tail them up." Since the old man was unable to do it, Ed had no choice but to volunteer for the task. Climbing down through the trap in the roof of each cattle car, he lowered himself among the close-packed, wild Texas steers. He described his task:

After I had got past their horns and down between them it was not so bad for about the worst they could do was step on me. The old fellow helped me at first, but finally he got kicked so badly that I had to do it alone and with the animals swaying and crowding it was a strenuous job to get an animal back on its feet after it had fallen down. Of course it is physically impossible for a man to lift a steer, but if you get hold of the tail and heave up the natural inclination of the beast is to help itself and about all you do is to balance it while it gets its feet under itself, though at that there is considerable heavy lifting.

Ed found that he had to perform this difficult job every time the train stopped; afterward, with the train in motion, his dangerous return route was along the tops of the swaying cars. "As a rule," he wrote, "the wind was blowing so hard across the Kansas prairies that I should have been blown off the top of the train before I reached the caboose, so I used to sit down and cling to a brake handle until the next stop."

With the cattle shipment completed, he was free to return home and to readjust to a family life and activities that must have appeared sedate in comparison to his days in Arizona. In the summer of 1897 he resumed friendships and took part in a varied social life.[15] Separation from Emma Hulbert had, if anything, increased his interest in her. In the small brown memo book that he carried with him at Fort Grant, he had printed the names Jessie D. Hulbert and Emma C. Hulbert, with the address 194 Park Avenue. But there was no question that he now preferred Emma. They dated regularly, went to parties at friends' homes and to the theater. Emma, a year younger than Ed, had been born on January 1, 1876, in Chicago, and her birth year accounted for her unusual middle name of *Centennia* adopted in honor of the 100th anniversary of the Declaration of Independence.

Temporarily, Ed accepted the most readily available occupation — helping his father in the American Battery Company. However, for the first time he considered turning to a creative field for a profession. The lure of drawing and cartooning, especially as a means of using his imagination to present characters in a humorous or satirical way, had always been strong. He had even been intrigued by the possibility of becoming a political cartoonist. Now, with a new surge of interest, he enrolled in classes at the Art Institute on Michigan Boulevard.[16]

Unfortunately, his studies were brief. His lack of perseverance may again be attributed to the personality problems that he still could not conquer. At twenty-two Ed was painfully indecisive, uncertain of goals or directions, and as yet without any understanding of himself or his nature. He was unable to subdue an impatience and a fierce restlessness that drove him into impulsive courses of action. He was motivated by sudden enthusiasms, as in his study of art, but was as quickly discouraged when he perceived that the period of development would be long and difficult. At present only the physical appealed to him: he was still dominated by a desire to obtain a commission and to make the army his career. In the physical and the active lay his confidence — in these he had proved himself, but in other areas he felt insecure.

The reasons for his failure to continue his study of art were not only personal. Certainly George Burroughs, impatient with Ed's past mistakes and his tendency to vacillate, could offer little encouragement to his son in this choice of a possible profession. Above all, to George, a hard-headed businessman, the very idea of art as a way of making a living was rejected as unthinkable. Ed's father, while attempting to be tolerant, would view his son's latest project as completely impractical, or as a whim which would soon be forgotten.

In his opinion that Ed would find no serious motivation George Burroughs was correct, for his son was not willing to follow a thorough study of drawing and painting, with exposure to all forms and subjects. According to one report, when Ed was placed in a life class which stressed the ability to understand human anatomy and draw the body realistically, he lost interest at once. Presumably, he made it plain that he cared only to draw horses.[17]

Other influences, powerful in their attraction, were destroying his creative impulse. He wanted to be with his brothers George and Harry, and, as always, he could not resist the lure of the rugged outdoor life of Idaho. But the army still exerted the stronger fascination,

How would you like to be a Russian?

One of ERB's political cartoons.

and while the 7th Cavalry experience had been an unhappy one, Ed did not believe that this worst post in the army was in any way typical of other units.

On February 22, 1898, Ed wrote to his former commandant from the academy, Captain Fred A. Smith, then stationed at Fort Niobrara, Nebraska, to inquire about enlistment. Smith's reply of the twenty-fifth was friendly, but not encouraging about any possibility of enlistment: "I am sorry that I cant hold forth any hope or promise to you just now as I have no place or even expectation at the present writing. . . ."

Ed's plaintive letter to his father at the time he was hoping for an army discharge had con-

tained a promise that if he ever got home again he would never leave unless driven away. But with the passing months he was again confronted with the problem of his future — of choosing some type of career. He could not consider remaining permanently at the American Battery Company; to work there performing routine tasks under the close supervision of his father would hardly be a happy situation. Without any other choice, he decided in April of 1898 to rejoin his brothers at Pocatello, Idaho.

The first stage in the train trip to Pocatello included a stopover at Denver. Here he ran into an old 7th Cavalry friend, a former member of "The May Have Seen Better Days Club." A celebration seemed in order, and as Ed con-

Slightly Handicapped
But still a safe bet.

One of *ERB*'s political cartoons.

fessed in his *Autobiography,* the succeeding events became quite hazy. For some reason he and his friend hired a band and paraded along the downtown streets of Denver with the band marching ahead. "This left our exchequer rather depleted, but a kindly disposed gambler came to our rescue the next morning and especially opened his place of business for us at about ten o'clock, so that we could recoup our fallen fortune. But that something must have gone wrong is indicated by a telegram which I find in my scrapbook. It was addressed to my brother, Harry, in Pocatello: "Lost roll. Wire twenty-five."

At Pocatello, where George and Harry greeted him, their pleasure at his arrival was evident, but it soon became equally clear that they had no permanent employment for him. In fact, the cattle shipping operations had been far from successful, and the brothers were facing financial difficulties. A letter of May 26, 1898, written by Harry from Yale, Idaho, to his father, reveals that he had been unable to make payments on the money that Major George had lent him at an earlier period:

I enclose check for $80 to cover interest on the $1000 note for one year. Had the check made out before I thought of the exchange but will include it in the check I will send for the purchases Mother is making for us. I should have sent this on the 1st when it was due, but did not have the amt. in bank at the time.

After explaining that he would probably go to Denver with the cattle in the following week, Harry wrote, "Ed and I have been driving cattle and will put in the next few days helping Walter and John Sparks gather what we are going to ship. Ed is at the camp up in the hills now, and I start for there tonight."

Even on the small ranch in Idaho, so remote from the center of the nation, Ed had become aware of the turbulent events that were arousing the nation, driving Americans to a fever pitch of patriotism. The sinking of the battleship *Maine* in Havana Harbor on February 15, 1898, had provided a climax to the already tense situation between America and Spain. Congress, in a joint resolution of April 19, authorized President McKinley to use force to drive Spain out of Cuba. Four days later, after being empowered to call on the states for volunteers, McKinley requested 125,000 men.

These stirring actions and the hope that the crisis might create a need for soldiers were a stimulus to Ed's military ambitions. Most exciting to him was the news that Theodore Roosevelt had assembled his Rough Riders to join in the battle. He wrote directly to Roosevelt, volunteering for the Rough Riders; the response was prompt, terse, and disappointing:

> First Regt. U.S. Vol. Cavalry
> In Camp near
> San Antonio, Texas,
> May 19th, 1898.

Edgar Rice Burroughs,
Pocatello, Idaho.

Dear sir,

I wish I could take you in, but I am afraid that the chances of our being over-enlisted forbid my bringing a man from such a distance.

> Yours very truly,
> T. Roosevelt
> Lt. Col.

The typed note bore Roosevelt's sprawling signature.

Earlier, in his search for army employment, Ed, on April 26, had sought the help of Colonel Rogers. Rogers' reply of May 3 was cordial: "I know you will be a credit to yourself in such service as you wish to enter. I am just about arranging now to go to Washington and I assure you that I shall gladly say what I can in your behalf. . . ." But a critical report of Ed's attitude toward enlistment contained the accusation that he had refused to join a local group: "A Pocatello barber organized a company of militia that went to the Philippines and served with distinction. But Burroughs was too proud of his military background to go with these raw recruits."[18]

As in the past, Ed's desire to adopt the army as a career was frustrated at every turn. In addition, the employment situation appeared bleak; no openings were available. Adrift without any plans, he was persuaded to launch his first venture as a businessman. Sometime in June 1898, at the urging of his brother Harry, who supplied the money, Ed became the proprietor of a stationery store in Pocatello, Idaho. He bought out the owner, Victor Roeder, a long-time resident of the town. The store, on West Center Street, had a large newsstand and a cigar counter and specialized in the sale of photographic materials and in the development and printing of Kodak pictures.

In his *Autobiography* Burroughs notes that "the girl who attended to that did her work so well that we used to receive films from all over the United States for development and printing." The store, of course, handled books, magazines, and newspapers, and Ed even established a newspaper route. At times, when he couldn't find a carrier, he delivered the papers himself, making his rounds on a black horse he had purchased and named Crow.

He devoted both his imagination and unlimited energies to trying to make the store a success. His printed photo bill announces "Finishing for Amateurs a specialty," states that cameras are rented, and refers to "Two Hundred Snap Shot Views of Pocatello and Vicinity from which we print to Order." Beneath the list of charges is a statement, "No deduction

Interior of ERB's Pocatello, Idaho, store; dictionary stand in center is still in use in offices of ERB, Inc.

can be made for Developing Failures as they require the Same Labor as Successful Exposures."

That Ed was ingenious and enterprising is revealed in the publicity given to the store in the *Pocatello Tribune* (now the *Idaho State Journal*). In the issue of June 25, 1898, a notice under "Local Brevities" announces the change of ownership:

Mr. V. C. Roeder has sold his book and stationery store to Mr. E. R. Burroughs who is now in charge. Mr. Roeder has not yet decided upon what he will do, but if he does not go to war with the volunteer engineers now being recruited by Mr. F. E. J. Mills at Salt Lake, will probably locate somewhere in California. Mr. Roeder's departure from Pocatello is a matter of genuine regret to all. He is one of the old timers of Pocatello and will be missed by everybody.

Mr. Roeder's successor, Mr. Burroughs, is a recent arrival in Pocatello, but a young man of fine abilities and we have no doubt "Roeder's", as it has always been known, will continue as popular as ever under his management.[19]

The "Local Brevities" from July through most of October 1898 contained various bits of publicity for the store: "July 2 (?): United States flags from six for five cents to forty cents each; Cuban flags for ten cents at Burroughs, successor to Roeder." The war against Spain and the nationwide sympathy for the oppressed Cubans had made Cuban flags very popular.

July 2: Flags for the Fourth at Burroughs, successor to Roeder.

July 6: E. R. Burroughs, successor to V. C. Roeder, has an assortment of latest vocal and instrumental music.

New novels and magazines every day at Burroughs'. Capt. Chas. King's latest, "A Wounded Name", just received.

July 9: Come to Burroughs' and get a photo of your Fourth of July float.

You can get a cigar at Burroughs' that you don't have to go out in the back yard to smoke.[20]

Other publicity notices include offers to deliver any paper or magazine, American or foreign, to the home, and announcements of the Junius Brutus Havana cigars sold at the store. A news story on page one for October 12 and 15 is headed "The Autograph Quilt." It reports that "a feature of the Congregational church Fair will be a new advertising medium — an autograph quilt," and lists "enterprising Pocatello firms who have already secured space. . . ." Among them appears the name *E. R. Burroughs.*[21]

In spite of the enthusiasm and determination that Ed displayed in launching the business, the stationery store was not destined to be a success. The complete reasons for the failure are difficult to assess. Possibly, his capital was insufficient. A small business, re-established under new ownership, might require time for acceptance and patronage by the community. This would result in a waiting period and a need for a capital reserve. But a personal element was also involved: the new proprietor would have to possess both patience and persistence, plus, of course, a continuing interest in the business. The first two qualities were the ones that Ed had failed to display in the past. After an enthusiastic start he had a habit of losing interest and becoming discouraged. Slowly developing long-range projects that required sustained determination were not for him.

In later years, reminiscing about the store, Ed commented:

I had a book shop in Pocatello, Idaho, when cheap editions cost me fourteen cents and Munsey's Magazine sold for ten cents and cost me nine and weighed over a pound and the postage was a cent a pound and I am still trying to figure where my profits occured, especially in those recurring periods that it was non-returnable.[22]

Toward the end of 1898 or first part of 1899 the former owner of the stationery store re-

turned and was quite willing to buy the store back. In his *Autobiography* Ed remarked, "My store was not a howling financial success and I certainly was glad when Victor Roeder, the man from whom I purchased it, returned to Pocatello and wanted it back."

To this, he added, "God never intended me for a retail merchant!"

In his unoccupied moments, Ed again turned to creative writing for stimulation. His scrapbook contains newspaper clippings, evidently from the *Pocatello Tribune*, date unknown, of two poems. One, titled "The Black Man's Burden," is a parody of Kipling's famous poem, "The White Man's Burden." While the parody contains no author's name, a brief explanatory note heading the poem supplies reasonable evidence that Ed was the author: "The following clever lines, in imitation of a recent very celebrated poem, are the composition of one of the well-known young men of Pocatello — Ed."

The parody, mocking Kipling's poem, offers a satirical and bitter comment upon the plight of the black man and his mistreatment by the whites. The first line of each stanza, as in Kipling, reads "Take up the white man's burden," but the remaining lines contain a searing description of this "burden" which the Negro has been forced to accept. The poem includes such statements as:

The white man's culture brings you
The white man's God, and rum.

Take up the white man's burden;
Take it because you must;
Burden of making money;
Burden of greed and lust;

Other lines speak of the "poor simple folk" who must "abandon nature's freedom" and then accept the white man's "Liberty" which makes them free only in name, while the white goddess in her heart still "brands" them as slaves.

It is significant that both in tone and content the poem parallels the philosophy so repeatedly expressed by Ed in later years — his bitter indictment of civilization and its destructive, degrading effects upon the simple natives and the animals. (As further supporting evidence of authorship, the very fact that Ed saved these two poems throughout the years must be given some weight.)[23]

Having disposed of the stationery store, Ed, now without any prospect of employment, followed his customary procedure of joining his brothers George and Harry. On Crow, his black horse, he began his journey to the Mule Shoe Ranch on the Snake River, where he planned to help later with the spring roundup.

"There had been a terribly hard winter in Canada and Northern Idaho," he noted in his *Autobiography*, "with the result that timber wolves were driven way down into our back yards, which seemed to be the only places left where they might pick up a bite to eat."

I had never been to the Mule Shoe Ranch before; and the first thing that I did was to get myself lost, turning up the Snake after I reached it instead of down.

By the time I was thoroughly convinced that I was going in the wrong direction, night had overtaken me. There was no trail; and so I followed a barbed wire fence, which ran along a side hill. My horse showed signs of unusual nervousness; but he had nothing on me, for I have always been scared of a barbed wire fence and especially so on a trailless side hill after dark.

However, it was not the side hill that seemed to be worrying Crow. It was something above us on the top of the hill, or rather the low ridge below which we were riding. Presently I discovered the cause of his perturbation. A number of animals were paralleling our course along the summit of the ridge. Occasionally I could see them outlined against the sky. I hoped that they were coyotes, but I had never seen so many coyotes together in one pack. I think I counted seven or eight of them. It was about this time that I recalled the fact that the wolves had been driven down by the hard winter. I did not know that they were wolves; I do not know now, but I have never heard of coyotes running in packs

or following horsemen; and for the next hour I wished that I were somewhere else, but at that I think I was more afraid of the barbed wire fence than I was of my companions.

I was unarmed, unfamiliar with the country, and it was quite dark; so that it was with a sense of considerable relief that I saw the lights of a ranch house twinkling in the distance; but when I got to the gate and dismounted I found that I had jumped from the frying pan into the fire, for no sooner had I opened the gate than I was set upon by a pack of dogs that seemed much more enthusiastically vicious than whatever had been following me for the past hour.[24]

Once at work on the ranch, Ed demonstrated his love of horses and his ability to handle them. He had a confirmed philosophy about cowboys and their horses which he expounded in his *Autobiography*:

The majority of our cow horses have fool tricks of some nature due exclusively to the fact that they are usually broken by fools. As a horseman, the American cowpuncher is very much overrated. He may be a good rider, but there is lots more to horsemanship than riding.

In civilized countries where they know how to train a horse they have no word analogous to breaking. Their horses are not broken; they are trained. Cow horses were broken, which results in either a disspirited plug or an unruly animal with bad traits.

Ed, as an example, described what had happened to Whisky Jack. The horse had been broken by a Mexican who, according to reports, "beat him over the head and neck with a club until the horse's neck was so swollen that he could not turn his head in any direction and to the day of his death he carried the scars of spur marks almost from his ears to the root of his tail. No wonder that he killed men." Ed maintained that various "tortures" were applied to horses, and that during his years in Idaho "the proper feeding, grooming and care of a horse were practically unknown."

Always indignant about any manifestation of cruelty toward an animal, Ed tells the story in his *Autobiography* of a minister who was his neighbor on the Raft River, and "who had his own ideas about applying the teachings of Christ." The man was especially annoyed because the horse that pulled his buckboard had a tendency to balk. Ed reported the details of what occurred on a day when the minister lost his patience:

Pushing, pulling and beating had accomplished nothing, so he built a fire underneath her. With the stubborn asininity that is one of the symptoms of balkiness, she lay down in the fire, whereupon the sky pilot shoveled coals on top of her.

For the spring roundup the foreman insisted that the men camp near a little mountain stream just below a crossing where the cattle were herded back and forth. As a result, the drinking water turned to "a thick mixture of cow manure and mud." Ed developed a severe case of mountain fever and rode down to the railroad with a temperature in the 100's. "... I was, fortunately, out of my head most of the time," he wrote. "How I stuck in the saddle I do not know."

It was during this Idaho period that Ed suffered an odd and distressing experience that he never forgot. As a bystander in a saloon at the time a quarrel erupted, he got in the way of a policeman's billy club. He received a severe blow on the head and wound up in the hospital where stitches were taken in his scalp. Long afterward, he complained of dizziness and reported having strange hallucinations. In later years, responding to a general questionnaire from the Boston Society for Psychic Research, he offered his recollections of the happening and of an unusual incident that followed:

In 1899 I received a heavy blow on the head which, while it opened up the scalp, did not fracture the skull, nor did it render me unconscious, but for six weeks or two months thereafter I was the victim of hallucinations, always after I had retired at night when I would see figures standing beside my bed, usually shrouded. I invariably sat up and reached for them, *but my hands went through them. I knew they were hallucinations caused by my injury and did not connect them in any way with the supernatural, in which I do not believe.*[25]

Ed then described an occurrence that took place, "for which," he maintained, "I have never been able to find any explanation other than that I was guided by my sub-conscious mind in performing this act."

It was my habit at this time to carry my keys, three or four in number, on a red silk cord about an eighth of an inch in diameter. The ends of the cord were tied in a hard knot and then cut off so closely to the knot that the ends were not visible. I had carried my keys in this way for some time with the result that the silk, which was originally of a very bright color, was much darkened by use, though that portion inside of the knot must have been as fresh and bright as when first tied.

At night I hung my clothes on hooks in a large bathroom which I used for a dressing room. The two doors leading from my bedroom and bath were locked from the inside, yet one morning, when I had occasion to use my keys, I found that one of them had been removed from the cord, though the knot was still tied in precisely the same way that it had been; the ends were not protruding, nor was there any of the clean, bright colored portion visible.

This key could have been removed only by untying the knot and then re-tying it precisely as it had been, which would have been practically impossible for anyone to accomplish without evidence of the knot having been tampered with being apparent.[26]

Ed added a theory he had developed as a result of this odd incident: "While the above appears to have not much bearing upon the subject of your investigation, it has suggested to me, when considered in the light of the fact that it is the only occurrence of its kind in a lifetime of over fifty years, that much other, perhaps all, so-called supernatural phenomena are the result of injured or diseased brains. Prior to my injury I had no hallucinations; subsequent to my recovery I have had none."[27]   Being a creator of fantasies of other worlds filled with unrealistic incidents that might be considered wilder than any hallucinations was one thing. But as a man of science in a real world, he firmly rejected the improbable or unprovable.

Before the spring roundup was over, Ed, again in his desperate search for employment, continued his efforts to obtain a commission in the army. He had heard the news that on March 3, 1899, the War Department obtained official authorization to organize a volunteer army of 25,000. On March 25, he wrote to the War Department to inquire. But the reply that he received four days later offered nothing definite. The acting secretary of war, after acknowledging Ed's application for a commission, wrote, "As it has been decided not to organize at this time the 25,000 volunteers, authorized by the act of March 3, 1899, your letter has been placed on file for consideration should the future turn of events make this possible."

Also on March 25, Ed took the opportunity to seek the help of Congressman Edgar Wilson of Idaho who had sponsored his appointment to West Point. Wilson responded, ". . . I am advised that Idaho has received her full quota of appointments in the Army, so there would not be an opportunity for you to secure a place. However, if you could bring to bear any influence from Michigan, or the east anywhere, I would be glad to second the application and give the best endorsement possible." Wilson further suggested that Ed write to friends in Chicago and Michigan who might have influence with the secretary of war.

July of 1899 found Ed in New York. Whether he was there because of some business transactions in connection with the American Battery Company, or whether he was in search of employment or trying to contact someone who might help him get a commission is impossible to ascertain. A letter of July 16 was sent to Colonel Rogers, and Rogers' reply of the twenty-second is addressed to Ed at "No. II East 17th Street" in New York. Rogers, writing from the Pay Department of the Army in Washington, where he had evidently been assigned because of the Spanish-American War, refers to not having a vacation "since entering the service" and states that "the work has been very arduous during the war." About to take a short leave, he anticipates "a good rest at Orchard Lake."

Rogers indicates that he would be quite willing to help Ed, but points out that "an army officer's influence amounts to little where Senators and Congressmen, and in fact, Cabinet Officers, are so numerous." He urges Ed to get one of these to intercede for him if he wishes to get a commission in the regular service. "I am sure your father could get some influential politician in Chicago to look after your case," Rogers writes.

But all of Ed's attempts to get a commission were in vain.[28] Resigned to the inevitable, he returned to Chicago to accept a job again in his father's American Battery Company. In his *Autobiography* he comments, "I started at the bench and learned the business from the ground up." Some time afterward he became the treasurer of the company.[29]

An 1899 item, possibly of minor import, could, however, lead to some interesting speculations. The item, a book preserved throughout the years in Burroughs' personal library, is *Descent of Man,* by Charles Darwin (2nd Edition, Century Series, American Publishers Corporation, N.Y., 1874). On the flyleaf appears a notation "E. R. Burroughs Jan '99," and beneath it a pencil drawing by Ed of a large monkey or ape in a typical position, somewhat crouching, knuckles resting on the ground. On the right of the drawing he had written "Grandpa." Young Ed, only 23, and given to mischievous pranks, was poking fun at Abner Tyler Burroughs, his grandfather. The drawing and his early exposure to Darwin's theories can naturally raise questions about *when* the Tarzan-of-the-apes idea was born. Was there a mere glimmering, an intriguing notion of an ape-man at this time, and did the idea lie dormant for many years until some creative necessity summoned it?

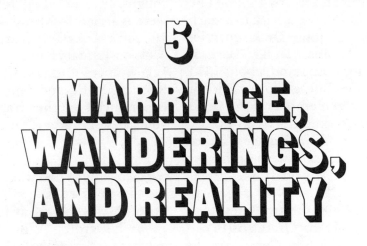

5
MARRIAGE, WANDERINGS, AND REALITY

Through the years, Ed's unchanging devotion to Emma had proved to be an element of constancy in his erratic life. It was not surprising, therefore, that their attachment to each other should reach its natural romantic peak. Since Ed had presumably given up his wandering ways and was ready to settle down to the sober role of a businessman, marriage was obviously on the horizon. He had shown some adjustment to his position in the American Battery Company and to the social activities of his circle of friends.[1]

From the earliest days when they both attended the Brown School, he had considered Emma to be his girl. According to one account, "When Ed was fourteen . . . he began proposing to a little girl named Emma Hulbert. . . . For ten years 'Ed' Burroughs haunted her, when he wasn't out West, or in the army, or at school, and for ten years he kept proposing and she continued to say 'no.' "[2]

The growing-up period for Emma, the youngest of four sisters, was one of calm and security. Alvin Hulbert, her father, highly successful in his hotel enterprises, had ample income to provide not only the material comforts for his family, but to afford some of the luxuries typical of wealthy families. These even included a trip to Europe for his daughter Leila. An unidentified clipping reports the event: "Miss Leila Hulbert, eldest daughter of Mr. Alvin Hulbert, of the Tremont and Great Northern Hotels, left on Tuesday via the Michigan Central Railway for New York, where she will spend a few days prior to sailing on Saturday for a three months' tour of Europe."

Emma spent her early years in the normal patterns of schooling, home duties, and social affairs, but displayed a special interest in music, taking private voice lessons. Her formal education ended with her graduation from the Brown School in 1892; however, she continued her work in music. The family suffered a serious tragedy and an interruption of all activities with the death of the only son, Alvin, Jr., at the age of fourteen.[3]

The Hulberts, as with both sides of the Burroughs family, could establish a British ancestry. The family line, traced by Emma Theresa (Mrs. Alvin) Hulbert, went back to as early as 1413 when a certain John Drake married Christiana Billett. Thomas Drake, born in Colyton, Devon County, England, about 1635, then carried the Drake lineage to America in 1653-54.[4] Distinguished members of the Drake family fought in the Continental Army at Lexington and at Bunker Hill. Emma Theresa Drake and her husband Alvin were both born in Rochester, New York, she on July 24, 1850, and he on January 29, 1829. With their marriage on October 12, 1868, the two lines, Hulbert and Drake, were joined. On the birth certificate of their daughter, Emma Centennia, the twenty-two year difference stands out: Alvin was forty-six at the time, Emma Theresa, twenty-four.[5]

Although their daughter Emma had grown quite serious about Ed, the Hulberts could hardly view him with any enthusiasm as a prospective son-in-law. In fact, his visits to the Hulbert home provoked vigorous opposition. Ed could recall the circumstances at a later period:

... as you probably know, parental interference often results in defeating its own purpose. Mrs. Hulbert forbade me the house before Emma and I were married. Perhaps, had she adopted an opposite policy and insisted on my coming to dinner every day, Emma would have gotten so fed up on seeing me around that she would have dropped something in my coffee some evening. ...[6]

The Hulberts, leading stable, sedate lives, with the emphasis upon regularity in one's tasks, whether at home or in the business world, had observed Ed's past antics with disapproval. A young man who appeared unable to settle down, unable to choose some type of career or occupation, was not one they could consider suitable for their daughter. But the lovers' determination made it plain that resistance was futile. Alvin and Emma Theresa Hulbert had to capit-

ulate, and on Wednesday, January 31, 1900, Ed and Emma were married in Chicago.[7]

That made three brothers who were married in the same month and year. George T. Burroughs, Jr., and Edna McCoy of Bellvue, Idaho, were married in Minidoka, Idaho, on January 10; and Frank (Coleman) married Grace Stuart Moss on January 24 in Chicago. Harry had wed Ella Frances Oldham in 1891. Soon after the wedding of Ed and Emma the Hulbert family experienced another tragedy. On February 4, 1900, Alvin Hulbert, Sr., died at the age of 71.

Working at his father's battery company and starting married life with Emma seemed to pose no problems for Ed at first. In his *Autobiography* he wrote, "When I was married I was getting fifteen dollars a week and immediately thereafter received a raise to twenty. Owing to the fact that we could eat as often as we pleased

Emma and ERB about 1900.

at Mrs. Burroughs' mother's home or at my mother's, we got along very nicely."

During the years 1901-2 Ed made a serious attempt to adjust to his work and to assume the responsibilities of a married man. He and Emma, as with all newlyweds, were experiencing the ordinary problems of running a household. Ed's salary of twenty dollars was barely sufficient to meet daily expenses, and little was left to pay for extras. He had taken out an insurance policy with the New York Life Insurance Company, but in October 1902 was forced to borrow on the policy in order to meet his premium.[8] In the same year he was ill for some time with typhoid fever.[9]

By 1903 he was finding the situation at the American Battery Company increasingly difficult. Working under the supervision of his father, as in the past, created tension and conflict. Also, Ed could generate little interest in the business. His impatience was sharpened

with envy at the thought that his brothers were in Idaho, living the kind of active, unrestricted life that had always appealed to him.

George and Harry, discouraged after years of struggle and small profit, had given up their cattle ranch. They conceived of a new enterprise, one that offered rich opportunities. From their Bar Y Ranch property, as it bordered on the Snake River, the brothers and their partner Lewis Sweetser had observed the many itinerant miners who traveled along the river banks panning for gold. To the three Yale engineers, graduates of the Sheffield Scientific School, this method appeared slow and antiquated. They discussed the possibility of removing the gold by suction with a large dredge. As a result, in about 1897, the Yale Dredging Company was formed, and soon after, a dredge was constructed. At a later period, at the end of 1898 or the

Ella Oldham Burroughs and ERB's brother Henry Studley Burroughs in 1891 shortly after their marriage.

El Nido *(the nest), houseboat built by partners in gold-dredging adventure.*

Sweetser-Burroughs tug, Snake River, Idaho.

first part of 1899, the partners had another inspiration: in order to be close to their operations, and to have a mobile home that could accompany the dredge to new sites, they began to build a houseboat. They and their families had been living in Pocatello. The Yale Dredging Company was now expanded to the Sweetser-Burroughs Mining Company, which at first listed only three officers: George T. Burroughs, Jr., as president and treasurer; Walter S. Sparks, vice-president; and Lewis H. Sweetser, secretary. Sweetser, the brothers' close friend and Yale classmate, had been with them since graduation. The company's location was at Minidoka, Idaho. Frank and Harry Burroughs had joined in the project, and later, Harry assumed the position of treasurer.

The houseboat, christened El Nido (the nest), was an example of remarkable planning and construction. Providing accommodations for all the members of the company and their families, it contained eighteen rooms and included a spacious living room thirty feet long and fifteen feet wide. The double-decked houseboat, with dimensions of sixty by thirty feet, had porches six feet wide, railings on the upper porches, and two twelve-foot planks to allow for walking along the sides.

On the houseboat were George and Edna Burroughs; Harry Burroughs and his wife Nellie and their children Studley and Evelyn; Walter and Frieda Sparks; Lewis Sweetser, then unmarried; and of course Frank Burroughs who had arrived alone, but had returned to Chicago to marry his fiancée Grace Moss. In February 1900, after their honeymoon, the couple came back to live on the houseboat.

The dredge, a platformlike contrivance with a towering funnel, contained a suction hose to draw up the gravel, sand, and gold. At the front of the dredge were tables covered with burlap; as the sand washed over the tables, the gold particles were left behind, caught in the burlap. The houseboat and dredge, naturally, were inseparable. The dredge worked up- or downstream, floating through whatever open channels it could find, leaving large mounds of gravel and sand in its wake. Each move re-

Sweetser-Burroughs Mining Company dredge, Snake River.

quired a new campsite; the dredge had to work within reasonable distance of some level shoreland where the houseboat, a tug, and some barges could be tied up.

The various tasks were apportioned, and Frank (Coleman) and Grace were given the job of traveling along the shore to find suitable campsites. George, whose specialty was organization and planning, took charge of the daily work schedules. The dredge ran on three eight-hour shifts, 6 a.m. to 2 p.m., 2 p.m. to 10 p.m., and 10 p.m. to 6 a.m., and since the men were dependent upon rowboat transportation up and back, George made certain that the changing shifts were ready on time. The company employed a crew of four to six men who were assigned living quarters on a smaller houseboat.[10]

While the operation of the dredge was generally smooth and uneventful, there was at least one occasion when an emergency arose. The main danger area, always to be watched, was in the dredge's caulking; if this were washed away, the dredge could quickly sink to the bottom. In her recollections of these gold-mining days, Grace Moss Burroughs tells of a frightening occurrence:

A signal had been set up so that in case of an emergency the men on the dredge could blow a whistle. Early one morning, shortly after midnight, this terrifying whistle resounded as though from a cannon, routing all of us from our beds. . . . The men all made for the rowboats which were fastened to the houseboat at all times, and made for the dredge some several hundred feet away. The wives waited tensely for some sound which would indicate the nature of the problem and what was being done about it. Soon we realized that the calking must have loosened, permitting the dredge to take in water; for, almost immediately, the pumps began to operate. After hours of strenuous labor, the caulking was replaced and the dredge floated again. But it had been a tense ordeal. We wives sent coffee in relays all night long, for the men could not leave their posts and risk the terrible loss which loomed as a very real and disastrous possibility.[11]

The wives, Edna, Nell, Freda, and Grace shared the housekeeping chores among them.[12] The only two children, Studley and Mary Evelyn, about eight and five years old at the time, were delighted with the adventurous outdoor living and never forgot their experiences.

Although during this period Ed's lifelong creative compulsion became more and more manifest, it would be another ten years before he would finally discover the talent that had been struggling beneath the surface for so many years. In 1900-1901 his interest in poetry, drawing, and cartooning took a more concrete form. About this time he composed his first complete, unified works. Dedicated to his niece Evelyn, with some poems written for her, the three booklets contained original verses and accompanying cartoons.

The booklet that appears to represent his earliest work is of a family nature, featuring humorous references to Ed's brothers, offering advice to little Evelyn on future marriage choices, and commenting about the family ancestral line. Idaho gold-dredging activities are also mentioned. The first page with its poem about the distinguished genealogy of Evelyn's (Marie's) family indicates clearly that the original emphasis upon ancestry resulted from Ella Oldham Burroughs' interest and research into this subject. The page contains a large drawing of George Washington holding a baby on his knee, and the poem follows:

You're descended from the **Burghs** *of
    Normandy
From the Naegles and the Burkes
And in your veins there lurks
The blue blood of the Washingtons, Marie
You never can complain
Of Your Old ancestors fame
For your Great Grandmother sat on George's
    Knee.*[13]

Ed is not hesitant about ridiculing himself and in one poem mentions his drawing ability and concludes that it is best demonstrated when he hastens to draw his pay. A cartoon portrays him running frantically to do so. In the same family booklet he has devised a page of "Uncle Ed's Finger Plays" for his niece Evelyn. Drawings of the fingers and hands show how to create impressions of certain objects, animals, and places that are listed in the poem. These include a well, a corral, a long-horned steer, a bucking bronco, a milking stool, and a mule.[14]

A second booklet of poems, handwritten, artistically lettered and dated 1900, is titled "Snake River Cottontail Tales." The booklet, marked "Author's Autographed Edition E. R. Burroughs Limited To One Copy of Which This is No. 1," contains children's poems with watercolor drawings, all composed expressly for Evelyn Burroughs. In its twelve pages with alternating poems and cartoons, the booklet features rabbits as the main characters and observers of animal antics; at times a baby rabbit is being informed about events by its mother. In these creations Ed also reveals that he is a keen and careful observer of nature. He shows his proclivity for puns and

Cover (upper left), autograph page (upper right), and first two pages (bottom) of ERB's Snake River Cotton-Tail Tales.

double puns. One cartoon depicts a bull fiercely rushing toward a man who is leaping head-
long over the fence to escape the animal. A rabbit onlooker comments:

"A Bull Rush in the meadow,
As the Blue-Jay on the wing,
Informs me," said the rabbit,
"That we'll see an early spring."

In the play on words the "bullrush" is also a
plant, the cattail, and of course the "early
spring" is matched by the man's "spring" over
the fence.

Another cartoon shows a cow sliding down a
steep incline on its rump, while two rabbits
watch through a fence. A poem describes the
action:

"When I see the little cow-slip,"
Said the Rabbit to his chum,
"I can read the story plainly
That another Fall has come."

Ed cannot resist the puns on "cow-slip" and the
animal's "fall."

A baby rabbit, peering in confusion at a hen,
remarks to its mother:

"That great big ugly egg-plant, ma,
Just bit me on the leg."
"That is a hen you foolish child."
"Well I saw her lay an egg."[15]

The third booklet of fourteen pages, displaying alternate recipes and cartoons, is titled
Grandma Burroughs' Cook Book, and the dedication reads, "For Miftrefs Evelyn Christmas
1901." The recipes, real ones, are deliberately
prepared in small quantities for a child's use —
gills, drops, and pinches. They include ingredients and instructions for the making of
cookies, fried chicken and gravy, angel's food
cake, three kinds of candy and ice cream, and
sponge cake.

Ed again reveals himself as a close observer,
even in the kitchen. The meticulous nature of
the recipes is demonstrated by the one for strawberry ice cream; after the details are presented,
an admonition follows: "mixing the sugar with

Emma Burroughs on stage coach at watering stop for horses betw

Emma Burroughs in baggage car between Blackfoot and
Mackay, Idaho, May 1903.

84

Challis and Robinson's Bar, Stanley Basin country, Idaho, May 1903.

ERB on train platform en route to Stanley Basin, Idaho, on Union Pacific, 1903.

the berries prevents cream from curdling." Instructions for the preparation of other dishes are offered with equal care and accuracy.[16]

Ed, convinced that he could not remain with the American Battery Company, waited for some encouragement from his brothers to rejoin them in Idaho. The invitation finally came, and in the spring of 1903 he and Emma said goodbye to Chicago and started their journey west. It appears that the trip may have been financed through a loan from his brother Coleman through a series of notes totaling $300.[17]

Since they planned to establish a permanent home in Idaho, Ed and Emma brought all of their possessions, their furniture, and even their collie dog, Rajah. They soon discovered that transporting Rajah posed problems. Whether a dog was allowed on the train at all depended upon the consent of the express messenger in whose car the passengers rode. ". . . as there were seven divisions on the Union Pacific between Chicago and Pocatello," Ed noted in his *Autobiography*, "it was necessary to beseech the aid of seven express messengers en route."

Because he had fortunately brought with him "the ingredients for numerous cocktails," he was able to smooth the way and eliminate any difficulties: "We spent practically all of our time in the express cars, going back to our Pullman only at night, and we were usually surrounded by the entire train crew with the exception of the engineer and fireman."

From Pocatello, Ed and Emma proceeded to Mackay and then on from there to the Stanley Basin, where the Burroughs brothers' dredge was located. Riding on what Ed described as "an old-time Concord stage coach drawn by four horses," they perched on top during the day and slept inside at night. Ed remembered the vivid beauty of the wild country:

Stanley Basin is in the heart of the Sawtooth Mountains, the most beautiful spot in the United States. There granite peaks rise far above the timber line and the summits of the higher mountains are covered with perpetual snow, while nestled in the valleys is a series of beautiful lakes and numerous mountain streams.

The country itself he recalled was "almost untouched even as late as 1903 and abounded in game of many varieties, including deer, mountain sheep and grizzly bear." Ed and Emma set up housekeeping in a tent at first and then began planning a more permanent home. Lumber was no problem; they selected a site, and with the aid of the men who worked at the mine, felled some of the adjacent trees. Ed gave details of the building of the cabin: "My plan was to set posts in the ground to the height of the eaves, nail slabs on the inside and outside and fill the interstices with dirt. It was an excellent idea or would have been if the dirt had not leaked out through the sides between the slabs."

While working on the new house, Ed employed an Italian to construct a "one-holer" for him, he disclosed in his *Autobiography*. The results were not at all what he had anticipated:

The Italian could not understand English and I could not understand Italian, so I marked out a rectangle on the ground and handed him a long handled shovel, then I went away and left him. I think I must have forgotten him until late in the afternoon for when I got back he had dug himself out of sight and I found him at the bottom of a deep shaft from which I had to drag him into the light of day at the end of his shovel. Nothing short of a parachute could have imparted a feeling of safety in the subsequent use of this famous one holer, which was, to be technically accurate, of the Kansas single rail type.

The Sweetser-Burroughs Mining Company was doing very well. A newspaper story describes the placer mining in the vicinity of Minidoka and notes that "The owners do not make boasts of what they are doing, but their success is attested by the fact that they have kept the plant in operation night and day all this season."[18] The company was also reported as having moved the machinery that year, drifting downstream during the winter and starting

dredging in a new place in the summer.

In this hectic period with the dredge working around the clock and the company employing four to six additional men, the feverish activities seemed to duplicate those of the Gold Rush of '49. For the three brothers and their wives and the two children, Studley and Mary Evelyn, life on the houseboat was a far cry from the quiet days in Chicago. About the only possible resemblance was that the brothers, as in Chicago, kept a cow to provide milk for the children.[19]

When the gold production in the Minidoka area began to dwindle, the company sought richer fields. Ed recalled the various enterprises, noting that his brothers had operated gold dredges on the Snake River in Idaho "over a stretch of about sixty miles, until they had worked out the gravel in this district." Following this, George moved a dredge up to Stanley Creek in the Sawtooth Mountains of Idaho, while Harry took over the management of a dredge on the Snake River in Oregon near Parma, Idaho.[20]

His employment at the Stanley Basin evidently had little appeal for Ed. After a short stay he and Emma decided to join Harry at Parma. The move may have been made as a result of some differences with George or even an outright quarrel. One account indicates that Ed showed little inclination to do his share of mining and preferred to spend his time in romantic walks with Emma along the river bank. George, annoyed, is supposed to have told him to stop the walks and get down to work. Ed's departure soon followed.[21]

Traveling usually created hazards and temptations for Ed; the short trip to Parma was no exception. He described the journey in his *Autobiography*:

We loaded our belongings onto a freight wagon and started for Hadley, where we arrived in due time with a collie dog and forty dollars. Forty dollars did not seem much to get anywhere with, so I decided to enter a stud game at a local saloon and run my capital up to several hundred dollars during the night.

ERB and Emma waiting for train in Parma, Idaho, 1904.

Main Street of Parma, Idaho, 1904.

One member of the poker game whom he never forgot was a "one-eyed tinhorn, who would put the side of his head with the good eye flat on the table, raise the corner of his hole card and while he was pretending to look at it endeavor to see mine if I raised it off the table." Based upon Ed's previous gambling escapades, the outcome of this one was easily anticipated. He noted the aftermath briefly: "When I returned to the room that we had rented we still had a collie dog; otherwise we were flat broke."

As usual, brother Harry came to the rescue, providing him with funds to reach Parma. There Ed showed some temporary adjustment to his gold-mining chores. But in his spare time he turned again to creative expression. He still maintained an interest in his drawing and water coloring. A letter of October 9, 1903, to his

father reveals that Ed was taking correspondence lessons in drawing. His main purpose in writing was to send a birthday greeting: on October 13 his father would be seventy. The letter contains one of Ed's typical illustrations at the top, that of a man bent to drink from an outdoor pump, a cowboy hat held in his hand. After writing, "Here's wishing you many happy returns of the day," he continues with, "Have completed three of my drawing lessons. Two have returned and the criticisms are very favorable."

He refers to a previous letter from his father: "Am glad you are going to close Saturday afternoon. Am also very glad to hear of your good sales for this year. Am always interested in hearing about the business. . . ."

From at least one source there is evidence that Ed had not relinquished his dream of being a cartoonist. In a biography sent to Charles

Lederer of the Chicago Press Club, he remarks, "It was while I was at Parma, Idaho, that you had hopes of making a cartoonist of me. . . ."[22] But more important evidence reveals that during this period or shortly thereafter he made his first creative venture into the field of fiction, improvising a delightfully fanciful story titled "Minidoka 937th Earl of One Mile Series M. An Historical Fairy Tale."[23] The recent discovery of this unnoticed manuscript clearly established that it antedates the story assumed to be Burroughs' first — "Under the Moons of Mars."

Handwritten on odd sheets of paper including the backs of letterheads of the Yale Dredging Company, Minidoka, Idaho, photo bills from the stationery store at Pocatello, and letterheads of the American Genealogical Society, 1102 Woman's Temple, Chicago, the story is composed of eighty-two pages. The Burroughs handwriting, unmistakable, sweeps across the pages in a hasty scrawl, as though his pen were dashing to keep pace with the ideas that tumbled forth. Yet, despite the apparent haste, there are not many corrections. The first part of the story is somewhat scratchy, with lined-out phrases and with sentences and words inserted or changed; but the author's imagination soon breaks free, and the incidents, as improbable as any ever created, soon flow along with only brief and minor corrections.

"Minidoka" is a captivating, highly imaginative fairy story that presages the Edgar Rice Burroughs talent that was to flower ten years later. Idaho was naturally the setting for the fairy tale, and Ed created two imaginary kingdoms separated by the Raft River and "forever at war." The tone of the writing is of course humorous and satirical, and in the opening Ed pokes fun at the Irish.

The year 1903 passed with Ed aiding his brother Harry in the gold dredging on the Snake River in Oregon near Parma, Idaho. In the spring of 1904 Ed conceived of a new idea — he would enter politics and run for the office of town trustee. Competition in Parma was between the incumbent Citizens' Ticket and an opposing group seeking office. In the election of April 5, 1904, 104 of the 108 registered voters cast their ballots. The *Parma Herald* of April 9 broadcast the result, the headline reading "Old Board of Trustees Re-Elected With One Exception. Large Vote Cast." The lead paragraph reported, "Parma's first election since becoming a municipality passed off in a very dignified manner."

The "one exception" was E. R. Burroughs; and his winning margin, in defeating Pat Hanratty, was *one vote*, 49 to 48. Ed had run as an independent, not being selected for either ticket, but had still managed to secure enough votes to edge his way in. In his *Autobiography* Ed humorously disclosed the secret of his success:

. . . There was to be an aldermanic election. I do not know how I came to be nominated unless I nominated myself. I was running against a popular party named Hanratty, who was already an alderman. My campaigning methods were simple. I button-holed every voter that I met, told him that I was running for office and that I did not want to be embarassed by not getting a single vote and asking him as a personal favor to cast his vote for me, with the result that enough of them tried to save me from embarrassment to cause my election.

Ed's Certificate of Election reads:

Know all men by these presents:
This is to certify that E. R. Burroughs was duly elected as a Trustee of the Village of Parma, Canyon County Idaho, at the General Election held within said Village on the 5th day of April 1904, for the term of one year, or until his successor is duly elected, appointed and qualified.
Attest.
R. K. (?) Sammons
Clerk of the Village
Parma, Canyon County, Idaho, April 11th 1904[24]

But fate, appearing to have other plans for Ed, yanked him abruptly from his first and only political office. The gold-dredging enterprise, which had first operated profitably, ran into disaster. According to one story, an eastern syndicate persuaded the brothers to take over property on the Salmon River and dredge there. The gold deposits were ample, and success seemed assured, but because the period allowed for the payment of their various obligations was impossibly short, they were unable to meet their creditors' demands and went bankrupt.[25] Another account stresses that the brothers' troubles began when they bought a new claim on the Snake River. After taking their dredge apart, they faced the difficult and dangerous feat of hauling the heavy equipment over the rapids — accomplished by their throwing lines across. The move took weeks. And when the exhausted men arrived, they found they had been swindled. The claim was salted.[26]

Ed in his *Autobiography* records briefly, "The company for which my brother was working failed and Mrs. Burroughs and I found ourselves again in possession of nothing but a collie dog." Again through the efforts of his brother Harry he was to find a new type of employment. The sight of the luxurious private cars reserved for railroad executives (especially presidents and vice-presidents) caused Ed to drift temporarily into a world of illusion. "I decided to devote my life and talents to railroading," he wrote in his *Autobiography*, recalling his willingness to start at the bottom and "work up to a private car." He added, "As a matter of fact the only interest that I had in railroading, I think, was the ultimate private car. . . ."

To oblige his friend Harry Burroughs, Howard V. Platt, a division superintendent of the Oregon Short Line Railroad Company at Salt Lake City, offered Ed a job. Ed had been willing to start in as a fireman, but there were no vacancies. He was persuaded to accept the only opening available — that of railroad policeman. When notified that Ed was broke, the accommodating Platt even sent passes for the trip from Parma to Salt Lake.

In April of 1904 Ed and Emma said their farewells to Idaho, the adventurous days of a near-frontier life forever behind them, and departed for Salt Lake City. Upon arrival they took rooms at 111 North First West.[27] The pro-

ERB hanging out laundry, probably in Salt Lake City.

90

Emma in rooms at 111 North Fifth West Street, Salt Lake City, Utah, 1904.

cedure for appointment as a special railroad policeman included the approval of the chief of police and Salt Lake City Council. A letter of May 12 from the recorder's office to Ed contains the official statement: "At a meeting of the City Council held May 9th, 1904, your appointment by the Chief of Police as special policeman to serve without pay from the City, was presented and the appointment confirmed on unanimous roll call vote." He would of course be paid by the Oregon Railroad Company. His classification was "depot policeman," and he was outfitted with a blue uniform with gleaming brass buttons and carried a club.[28]

For Bob Davis's column in the *New York Sun*, July 20, 1940, Ed recalls the days:

... now an experienced man, I married, settled down in Salt Lake City with a job on the police force as a special officer. My beat was in the railroad yards where after nightfall I rambled and fanned bums off the freight cars and the blind baggage of the Butte Express. Kept good hours and always came home with fifty pounds of high-grade ice, which I swiped while the watchman slept. I was always a good provider.

In his *Autobiography* Ed provides details of his and Emma's experiences in Salt Lake City, noting that he was kept busy "rushing bums out of the railroad yards and off the passenger trains." He adds, "It was not very exciting for the bums and yeggs were seldom as hard boiled as they are painted and only upon one or two occasions did I even have to flash my gun."[29] He considered drunks to be the worst. "If you have never tried to eject a drunk from a day coach," he wrote, "you have no idea how many arms and legs a man can have."

Notified that a murderer was hiding in the railroad yard, and "being more conscientious than intelligent," he hunted through numerous dark coaches and box cars without finding the man.

On their own for the first time, without any help from their families or from Ed's brothers, the young couple struggled to solve their house-hold problems. Because his small salary was barely sufficient to meet necessary expenses, Ed had to perform all sorts of unaccustomed tasks:

Neither one of us knew much about anything that was practical, but we had to do everything for ourselves including the family wash. Not wishing to see Mrs. Burroughs do work of this sort I volunteered to do it myself. I took all of our soiled clothes and put them in the bath tub, turned the water on them and let them soak over night. I did not know until next morning that I should have separated the white clothes from the colored ones and thereafter it would have made no difference since they were all colored. I got along fairly well, however, until I came to iron the sheets. I tried to iron them flat on a little ironing board without folding them. The sheets were so large that they trailed on the floor and got tangled up in my feet. They had not been very clean — the sheets I mean — when I got through washing them. When I got through ironing them no one could have recognized them as sheets.[30]

During those months in Salt Lake City Ed half-soled his own shoes — and even bottled his own beer. Meanwhile, he could hardly feel any enthusiasm about his duties as a railroad policeman, and the prospect of a fireman's job seemed too remote to contemplate. In a letter home, undated, he wrote:

... Made an arrest last night and after waiting half an hour for the wagon turned the man loose. I can imagine the Chicago patrol taking a half hour to answer a call.

The fellow was drunk, dressed up and disorderly, refused to leave the yd. and resisted me.

Can't say I am stuck on the job of policeman. . . .

Once again his illusions had vanished, and with them went his vision of the glamorous private car, dissipated by the cold light of reality. Seeing no future in railroading, on October 14, 1904, Ed resigned. An official acceptance letter from the Oregon Short Line Railroad Company, dated October 17, states, "Conduct, services and capabilities satisfactory."

Two of ERB's sketches of the "cop" and the "cook," made during his employment as a policeman in Salt Lake City.

On October 16 he wrote home, addressing his letter to "Dear Little Mother," explaining that the exact time of departure for Chicago was uncertain, but that he and Emma would, upon arrival, go directly to the Hulbert's home on 194 Park Avenue, and not to the Burroughs' place at 493 Jackson Boulevard until a later evening. "I quit work yesterday," he wrote, "as they had my successor down here from Ogden." He speaks of his cold being so bad that he "welcomed the opportunity of staying indoors nights," and explains that "Emma also has a bad cold and as we have no heating stove we are longing for Tuesday to come so that we can go somewhere and get warm."

Ed illustrates his letter with a small cartoon in a lower corner; the caption beneath it reads, "The Passing of the Cook and the Cop" and he symbolizes his and Emma's duties in Salt Lake by outlining the dotted forms of a policeman and cook, and then drawing Emma and himself in heavy lines as they emerge in their new forms —Ed jaunty, with derby and cane, and Emma all dressed up and wearing a flowered hat. Clearly, Ed had little regret at the passing of their Salt Lake period. But, his policeman's job had lasted only five months.

In their plans to return home, the couple encountered their most serious obstacle: they had no money for the railroad fare. At this time they conceived a brilliant idea. All they possessed of value was the household furniture, dragged with them "all over Idaho and Utah." This they would auction off, hoping to obtain enough money for the journey to Chicago.

About the results Ed wrote in his *Autobiography:*

That auction was a howling success. I never imagined people would buy such utterly useless things and pay real money for them. The only decent things that we had brought little or nothing, but the junk brought about ten times what it was worth, and so we got home again, traveling first class.

The pattern was depressingly repetitive — he was again unemployed. When his search for a job proved futile, he appealed to his close friend and former Michigan Military Academy classmate, Bob Lay. The only opening Bob could find was that of a timekeeper at a site where a seventeen story brick and concrete warehouse was being constructed. Ed was willing to take anything, and although he had no experience in this field and was made dizzy by heights, he soon found himself crawling about on narrow steel girders high in the air. One day he saw a workman tumble from the heights, pulling a wheelbarrow of concrete after him. Ed was shaken by this and grew even more apprehensive, but he forced himself to walk across the girders. He described the closest he came to catastrophe:

> *Once I was tight-roping across a steel girder on the ninth or tenth story with nothing on either side of me. About twelve feet ahead of me planks were laid across two other girders, making an oasis in the desert of mid-air. Somehow I lost my balance after I started across that girder. At an angle of about forty-five degrees I ran a few steps and jumped for the oasis. That I am here today is sufficient evidence that I hit it, but thereafter I swallowed my pride, straddled the girders and hitched myself across.*[31]

The job, obviously, was one that Ed could not endure, and the hunt continued. Work that promised interest and stimulation, a position with permanency and a future, seemed non-existent. Ed grabbed at the only work available; he became a door-to-door book salesman, peddling Stoddard's collected lectures. As part of his training he memorized a sales talk he was prepared to deliver at the moment a housewife opened the door. In a letter of February 12, 1921, to Herbert Hungerford, editor of the *American News Trade Journal*, Ed supplied the details:

> *... I was equipped with a long thing that telescoped like an accordian and Mrs. Burroughs made me a little black bag with a shoulder strap, that I put on over my vest. I carried the thing in the little black bag hidden under my coat tails. It might have looked as though I was ashamed of it; but I was not supposed to be and I was. And I wandered around a large city shoving my foot inside front doors before weary house-wives could slam the doors in my face and if I succeeded in getting in and planting myself on their best plush furniture I commenced to recite, parrot-like, a long and hideous lie, interpersed occasionally with facts. The initial and most colossal falsehood of that shameful aggregation still haunts my memories. It was: "Mr. Stoddard has asked me to call on you, Mrs. Brown." Even now I blush as I type it.*

The "thing" must have been a folding series of book covers and illustrations, in facsimile, which Ed displayed to the housewives. He recalled that he had actually sold several sets of Stoddard's Lectures, but commented, "I think my victims were moved more by compassion for me than for any desire for the lectures."[32] During these months he also tried selling electric light bulbs to janitors and candy to drugstores. Unsuccessful in this, he found an advertisement in the *Chicago Tribune* for an "expert accountant." Without having the faintest idea of the duties of an accountant, he applied for the job at E. S. Winslow Company and was accepted.

In his *Autobiography* Ed notes that the breaks or luck are as important as one's ability and explains that "my employer knew even less about the duties of an expert accountant than I did." Winslow was so impressed by Ed's procedures in opening an entire new set of books that he gave him a permanent job as his office manager. "I was with him for a couple of years," Ed wrote, "and I think that in all that time he never really found me out, for when I left him it was of my own accord."

Ed's jobs and business ventures cannot always be identified. For example, a postcard saved in Emma's album is dated January 18, 1906, and addressed to Ed at Room 409, Western Union Building, Jackson and La Salle Streets, Chicago. Whether this was his office or his place of employment has not been determined. But his search for success through a bewildering variety of occupations brought him into two strange mysterious enterprises. He had saved the stationery of what appeared to be defunct businesses. One yellow letterhead reads American Genealogical Society with the address beneath as 1102 Woman's Temple, Chicago, and to the left the phone number, Main 949. A blue letterhead reads "Moss & Burroughs, Forwarding Agents," with the same address and phone number. On this stationery, in addition, appear two printed names: E. R. Burroughs at top right and Earl C. Moss at top left.[33]

The precarious living, the changes from job to job, and the inability to find a type of employment that could challenge him and sustain his permanent interest, brought him back once more to an ambition that had never died. His hope of obtaining some kind of military position, either as an instructor or as a commissioned officer, where his skill in horsemanship could be utilized, became dominant again. In March 1906 he wrote a series of letters to acquaintances to inquire about possible openings for instructor in horsemanship and cavalry tactics or to request letters of recommendation for such a position. The first person he wrote to, naturally, was the man whom he still idolized in his memory — Charles King, Brigadier General U.S.A. (West Point, 1866). King was then superintendent of St. John's Military Academy in Delafield, Wisconsin.

On March 3 King replied to a letter from Ed that had evidently contained a request for his advice. A logical assumption is that Ed was uncertain that he still possessed the skill and knowledge needed to qualify as a cavalry instructor in a military academy. King, in his response, offered Ed reassurance:

You rode well in 1892 and with all your later experience ought now to be an expert teacher of the soldier school of horsemanship — which is far more exacting than the Park or English system. For civil life, however, one needs to be at home in the latter, as I dare say you have discovered and have made it, too, a study.

Ed wrote again, hard on the heels of his first letter, but whether he hinted about the possibility of a position at St. John's Academy is difficult to tell. King, three days later, does not refer to any request, but states, "Your letter went right to my heart. Twelve of the boys wrote me in '98 asking for staff positions but I had none to give. Every now and then I meet some of the old battalion and it does me good." King enclosed some photos of himself.

Although King had been commandant at Michigan Military Academy for only a short period, and his dealings with Ed had been brief, his forthrightness, attitude of simple humanity, and emphasis upon principle and justice had left an indelible impression in Ed's mind. In recollections of the academy, Ed wrote glowingly of King:

. . . The Commandant was Capt. Charles King, author of the best army stories that ever were written; a man who has been an inspiration to me all my life because of his outstanding qualities as a soldier, a cavalryman and a friend. But the inspiration he gave me had nothing to do with writing. He made me want to be a good soldier.[34]

King, whose blunt telegram of April 16, 1892, to Ed's father read, "Your son deserted yesterday," a telegram that Ed preserved and reread in the passing years, was the same man who became a well-known author of novels about army life in the West. Ed communicated with him periodically and sought his advice about writing and publishing.[35]

That Ed, a boy of sixteen separated from his home and family, lonesome, and possibly seeking a father figure in the stern but kindly King, may have created an unreal image of the general, in certain aspects is entirely possible. The picture of King may have been exaggerated or romanticized, especially because of his soldierly qualities and colorful horsemanship. An exchange of letters with a former Orchard Lake classmate offers some evidence in this direction. C. C. Matteson, who had read a biography of Ed in the *Los Angeles Times*, wrote to him about King, commenting, "Why stress the short term as commandant of Captain King, as I remember it he was there for only three months, during which time he was mostly drunk. . . ."

Ed replied on November 6, 1929:

. . . The article in the Times *was a condensation of an autobiography that my publishers hounded out of me. They picked the parts that they thought would prove interesting. In the original you may be sure that I did not neglect General Strong, for whom I had and still have the highest admiration. I gave Adelbert Cronkhite hell and possibly it was just as well that they left that out.*

As for General King — I conceived a boyish enthusiasm for him because he was a strict disciplinarian and at the same time just, and because he stood so high in the estimation of the regular army as a tactician. I fully understood his weakness — a weakness for which he paid very dearly and which he regretted more than any man, but it did not lessen my admiration for him. He is a fine character and very much loved by everyone with whom I have come in contact who has known him at all well. . . .

Another former commandant of Michigan Military Academy to whom Ed wrote in 1906 was Frederick F. Strong, a major in the artillery corps, stationed in Washington. Ed requested a letter of reference and Strong was happy to oblige, commenting on March 5, "Of course I must rely upon my knowledge of you some years ago, but am confident you have not changed very much." In his reference, headed "To Whom it May Concern," Strong described Ed as "one of the best horsemen ever at the academy and a good soldier in all respects," adding that "unless he has greatly changed I am glad to recommend him for the position of Cavalry Instructor and Tactical Officer."

Ed, motivated by the hope of finding a position of interest that would provide a degree of security, turned March into a month of busy correspondence. He received letters of recommendation from various friends and business acquaintances: one on March 12 from George C. Ball of the firm of T. A. McIntyre and Company, stockbrokers, and separate letters on March 14 from the partners in a Chicago insurance company, C. E. Rollins, Jr., and Arch O. Burdick.[36] An old friend, Lew Sweetser, wrote from Yale, Idaho, on March 15 to contribute his recommendation.

The two letters Ed also wrote in March addressed to Fred A. Smith, another former commandant from the academy, were sent to Governor's Island and, since Smith had been assigned elsewhere, did not reach him until mid-July. Smith, now a colonel in the 8th United States Infantry, responded from the headquarters at Camp Jassman, Guimaras, Philippine Islands, on July 17, 1906. His letter of reference described Ed as "energetic and fully qualified to instruct in all the branches, Infantry, Cavalry or Artillery but particularly excellent in Cavalry." His accompanying note read:

I would not have you think for a moment that I did not esteem your friendship and often think of the pleasant hours we spent together in the Commandant's office. I take pleasure in forwarding with this a letter such as I think you desire but for God's sake if you have a good position do not forfeit it for the military business.

The scare in China seems to have blown over but I was reading today that the Chinese are employing Japanese Officers as Instructors and why not you.

Smith explained that he was in charge of operations in the island of Samar, where his task would be "to subjugate the 'Pulajanes' a disaffected crowd who rob their friends and foes." Smith's suggestion about seeking a position with the Chinese Army had already been anticipated by Ed. On March 12 he wrote to Major George W. Gibbs, addressing him "% Chinese Imperial Reform Assn.," at 345 South Clark Street in Chicago. Ed stated, "Am seeking a commission in the Chinese Army and beg to ask if you can give me information relative to the proper parties to whom I should go."

Gibbs's lengthy hand-written reply of March 19 was on the letterhead of the 1st Batallion, 2nd Regiment Infantry, 1st Brigade Imperial

Army and was sent to Ed at 194 Park Place. Gibbs supplied a detailed explanation of the circumstances:

. . . I have no information that the Chinese Gov't is looking for military men for their army. From items published in the press, it would appear that they were seeking such men, but from the best authority of the Chinese themselves they tell me it is false. From the numerous letters I have on file I believe I could furnish several hundred such parties if they were needed. I presume these letters were sent me because I am mentioned as an instructor at the American Chinese Empire Reform Academy, an institution incorporated under the State Laws of Ill.

He described the academy as a school "maintained by the Chinese Empire Reform Ass'n, another incorporated organization, for the purpose of instructing the Chinese in the English Language, Western Civilization, International Law and Military Science and Tactics." He then wrote with some fervor about China's new role among the nations of the world:

China has no idea of attacking any other nation, but she is going to create an army on modern ideas, for the purpose of defending herself, for example she don't propose to have any more outside countries use the chinese territory for a place to settle disputes of war to the distress and loss of her own people. She is also going to demand the respect of other countries in the treatment of Chinese subjects that they may receive at least the treatment and courtesy that other nations receive.

Major Gibbs (a "late 1st Lieutenant, Utah Artillery, U.S. Volunteers") promised that if military men "with first class records" were needed in the future he would notify Ed. He commented that "the newspapers seem to be writing up a lot of fairy stories in an endeavor to get next to the inside." But he did reveal that a commission for the Chinese Army had "a specification for a contract for 1 million rifles and 3 thousand guns for light artillery." Gibbs invited Ed to visit the drill hall and school at 345 South Clark Street, third floor, and closed with the statement, "I write you at length for the trouble you took to reach me."

On March 17, two days before receiving Gibbs's reply, Ed wrote to the Imperial Chinese Legation in Washington. Their response of the 20th was blunt: ". . . there are no openings in the Chinese army for American officers or those of any other nationality, so far as this Legation is informed. The report that the Chinese Government is engaging such officers has no foundation whatever."

Thus, from the Spanish-American War period of 1898 through March of 1906 all of Ed's efforts to return to military life either as a soldier, officer, or instructor had proved fruitless. His attempts to find a permanent career in the army or at a military academy were at an end. But his interest in military life and his intense patriotism would drive him to seek other associations with the army in the future. It is significant to note that in all of Burroughs' attempts to obtain a commission in the army or as an instructor at an academy, he relied on letters of recommendation. Invariably he sought the help of someone who might have influence with the authorities in obtaining for him officer's rank. Except for the relatively brief stint with the 7th Cavalry, Burroughs made no attempt to enlist in the Army with the idea of working his way up the ladder for a commission. He wanted to start as an officer.

For Ed and Emma the early period of their marriage, the years of struggle and discouragement, were also the years of constant moving, often from one shabby flat to another. When their marriage was launched in 1900 they took a room in the large, three-story Hulbert home at 194 Park Avenue. The collection of photos in the old family album, with precise notations on their backs, chronicles the frequent changes of address. They are shown at 88 Park Avenue in 1901; 35 South Robey Street from April 1902 to May 1903; and upon their return from Idaho and Salt Lake City in 1904, they stayed with Emma's family again at 194 Park Avenue. By 1908 they had moved across the street, taking a

ERB's drawing of Sears, Roebuck stenographic department.

flat at 197 Park Avenue in a building owned by the Hulberts. The addresses of cards sent through the mail indicate that in July 1909 they still lived at 197 Park Avenue, but by October had moved to 2008 Park Avenue. 1910 found them at 821 South Scoville Avenue in Oak Park, a suburb of Chicago.[37]

The search for employment continued. Impressed by the reports of unusual opportunities in the mail order business, Ed, in 1907, applied for a job at Sears, Roebuck and Company. He was given a position in the correspondence department. His promotion came quickly; an interoffice bulletin, addressed to managers and assistant managers, dated April 17 and issued by L. E. Asher, reads, "Mr. E. R. Burroughs has been appointed Manager of the Stenographic Department (159)." Ed, in describing the Sears, Roebuck period in his *Autobiography,* said, "After a few months, I was made manager of a clerical department, in which all the correspondence was handled and typed."

That Ed's efficient methods and business ingenuity focused attention upon him is illustrated in a letter of November 30, 1907, sent by R. C. Blanchard to the general office manager, P. V. Bunn. It opens with enthusiastic praise:

I found the Stenographic Department to be in very satisfactory condition. The department is well managed by Mr. Burroughs, who is handling the department in a business like and rather professional manner. He seems to be conversant with every detail of the department; knows all that goes on, and is in every respect all that could be expected of a Manager.

After further complimentary remarks, Blanchard says, "In all the department shows a remarkable improvement over its condition a year ago, and I think that Mr. Burroughs and his division heads should be given due credit for what they have done."

Ed, the man who "knows all that goes on," was quick to demonstrate that even the most minor of inefficiencies and unwarranted expenditures could not escape his scrutiny. A discovery of his, which Mr. Blanchard considered of great value, was that from January of that year the graphophone and shorthand letters had gradually increased in length from about twelve lines to an average of sixteen lines per letter. As a result of Ed's perception, Blanchard analyzed the letters and reported that in some

ERB's drawing of activity in stenographic department at Sears, 1907.

cases "eight or ten lines could be cut out of a letter and it would be equally if not more forcible." At the rate of 4,000 letters a day, and a cost of thirty cents per hundred lines, if four lines were removed, the savings would be $48 per day, $288 a week, or $14,976 a year.[38]

About the situation Ed wrote, "It was a large department in which we turned out a tremendous volume of business and as I was able to cut costs materially, I was acclaimed as a howling success. I had my problems there, including the young lady who couldn't do as much work in the winter time as she could in the summer time because the days were shorter."

On December 7, 1907, Ed issued a comparison report of the four weeks ended November 23 against the corresponding four weeks of 1906 to explain how he had cut costs. L. E. Asher described the results as "indeed very satisfactory," forwarded the paper to Mr. Bunn who in turn sent the report to Julius Rosenwald, the head of Sears, Roebuck, with the comment "interesting and gratifying." He wrote across the paper, "Very Fine. J.R." The figures were impressive: Ed had turned out 36 percent more lines while reducing the payroll 21 percent. His cost per 100 lines was 35.2 cents as compared

with the 1906 cost of 61.5 cents, an improvement of 42.7 percent.

Ed's recollections of Mr. Rosenwald were pleasant. He noted in a letter of March 3, 1937, to M. R. Werner of New York that "my contacts with Mr. Rosenwald were not of any great importance, either to Sears, Roebuck & Co. or to the world at large, but they did give me a slight insight into Mr. Rosenwald's character." As manager of a stenographic department which employed approximately 150 stenographers and typists, all of whom worked in one room, Ed could expect regular visits and inspections by company executives, who often brought business acquaintances and friends. The department was a kind of showroom. Ed remembered that although he was "a very minor cog in the machinery of the mail-order business," Mr. Rosenwald was always very careful to ask his permission courteously before bringing anyone to his department and never forgot to thank Ed when he left the room.

In a letter of September 13, 1926, to John M. Stahl of Sears, Roebuck radio station WLS in Chicago, while noting that he still kept up an acquaintance with O. C. Doering, a general superintendent for Sears, Roebuck,[39] Ed recalled Julius Rosenwald's visits again and remarked, "Only a thorough gentleman would remember always to accord an inferior such a courtesy."

Even the cold efficiency of the mail order business could not stifle Ed's creative impulses. He was happy to find an opportunity to write some of his humorous verse. On January 16, 1908, a letter sent to Rosenwald encloses a copy of a screed "which has been going around through the country press, entitled 'Ninety and Nine,' and which has just appeared in the Emporia Kansas Gazette." The letter refers to "Mr. Burroughs of 159" who has added a verse of his own "from the Seroco standpoint" (Seroco was a brand of Sears pants). The author of the letter, an unidentified company official, explains that the plan is to get both verses started around among the country papers. A memo to Ed at the bottom of the typed note reads: "I took a few liberties with your verses but not many."

The original screed poked fun at Sears, Roebuck and the type of customers who dealt with them:

There were ninety and nine who blew their wads, in Emporia stores each day, when they purchased their clocks or their lightning rods, their soap or their bales of hay; but one would send to the roebuck sears and he was the object of gibes and jeers. . . .

It pictured the ninety and nine as "rich and fat" and living on "oysters and pumpkin pie"; but the one "who bought of roebuck sears, had never the price of a pair of beers." While the ninety and nine at death could look forward to a ride in "the smoothest hearse in town," the sorry creature "who deals with the roebuck sears, will be hauled away by a pair of steers."

Ed responded with his own screed, composed in the same verse form, and offered a defense of Sears, Roebuck by explaining what would happen in the hereafter. The ninety and nine found quite a different situation when they approached the "golden gates" where St. Peter commented that "oysters and pie weren't served

in Heaven with beer." He identified the one "intelligent ghost, with elegant coat and vest" and recognized the Seroco pants of Sears. The others are sent to a place "where fires are furnished free," because they "hadn't the brains to know Sears, Roebuck quali-tee."[40]

In December 1907, Ed addressed letters to a book dealer and to public libraries in Chicago requesting information about certain types of publications. Attempts to explain the reasons for these inquiries have led to a number of speculations. A response from A. C. McClurg & Company, 215 South Wabash Avenue, dated December 12, was sent to Ed at 194 Park Avenue. After referring to his letter "of recent date," it listed books and prices:

Holt. Care and Feeding of
*   Children*   net 75 cts.
Finger Prints, Classification and uses,
*   by Henry.*   net 80 cts.
Finger Print Directories by Galton.   net $2.00
Decipherment of Blurred
*   Fingerprints.*   net 1.00

McClurg's noted that the "first mentioned title" was in stock, but that the others "would have to be imported from England, which would require at least two months time."

A logical explanation for Ed's interest in books on the raising of children may be found in his anticipation of the birth of his first child, only a month away. But his unusual inquiry about books on fingerprints, plus two additional requests for information sent out at the same time, does not yield so easily to explanation. On December 10 he wrote to both the John Crerar Library in Chicago and the Chicago Public Library, and in response these libraries offered lists of books on the same subject, including those by Francis Galton and E. R. Henry, and others by Roscher and Windt, German language publications. These replies from McClurg's and the libraries have been preserved in one of Ed's notebooks along with an article "The Telltale Fingers" by Harry H. Seckler (source unknown) that describes the fingerprint system of identification used by departments of the federal government. It presents case histories and stresses the superiority of this system to the Bertillion method.

As indicated, there have been various conjectures as to what lay behind Ed's curious interest in fingerprints during this 1907 period. The explanations either deal separately with his inquiries for children's books and fingerprinting books, or attempt, ingeniously, to unite the two. The reasoning and evidence will be familiar to readers of *Tarzan of the Apes*.[41]

By 1908, Ed's record at Sears, Roebuck and his business efficiency and imagination had marked him in the eyes of the company executives as a man to be watched. A successful, stable career with steady advancement awaited him. Then, in a typically impulsive gesture, he abandoned his prospects and his future at Sears, Roebuck.

The previous failures to find anything permanent had left him undaunted. He decided to go into business for himself.

He left Sears, Roebuck during August of 1908, and on August 14 received a letter of commendation from P. V. Bunn, the general office manager. Bunn, who was away on a vacation and had missed saying goodbye to Ed, wrote to him at 197 Park Avenue:

Your record with the house has been a fine one, and the work you have done in straightening out the Stenographic Department and bringing it down to a proper level as to cost output has been much appreciated, and if ever at any time you wish to return to us, I am sure the House will be glad to give your request for reinstatement its best consideration.

Contrary to his own statements in various brief autobiographical articles that he failed in every job he attempted, Ed did not fail at Sears. He obviously performed well there and had excellent chances for a successful future.

Ed's action appears even more bewildering in view of the anticipated event that occurred early that year: on January 12, 1908, at the Park Avenue Hospital, Emma had given birth to a daughter. The arrival of Joan Burroughs meant, of course, a new responsibility for Ed to shoulder. It seemed hardly a time to throw over security and an established future.

At a later period, in his *Autobiography*, Ed could joke about the birth of Joan: ". . . the collie dog, that had shared our vicissitudes with us for so many years, was compelled to take a back seat along with me. . . ." The arrival of a daughter was also the occasion for some humorous writing, in this case an article that joked about the care of babies, the selection of a nurse and doctor, and the duties of the mother, father, and grandmother. In the 1908 article, titled "What Every Young Couple Should Know," Ed, evidently enjoying himself, went on at length creating some 3,000 words of comical exaggeration about a home with a baby. This tone is set at once in the opening.[42]

Although Burroughs made no attempt to submit "What Every Young Couple Should Know" to any publication at that time, the article had a later revival, far in the future. On May 5, 1937, in a letter to Gertrude Lane, Editor of *Woman's Home Companion*, he wrote:

I am sending you, herewith, copy of a manuscript that I wrote about twenty-nine years ago, shortly after the birth of my first child. This was before I started writing and was merely for the amusement of my family and friends. I recently found it among some old papers; and as it seems to be quite as up-to-date today as it was twenty-nine years ago, I thought it might have some interest for your readers. . . .

The manuscript referred to was undoubtedly "What Every Young Couple Should Know"; there is no record of acceptance by any magazine.

In 1908, while capable of joking about the advent of a daughter, Ed must have faced reality, understanding that as a married man with a child it was time to view his obligations more seriously. But what he did not understand was the uncontrollable part of his nature — the part that would not allow him to settle for a routine life, the part that drove him on blindly in a quest, undefinable, for something different, something that matched his imagination.

THE ALL-STORY

VOL. XXII   FEBRUARY, 1912.   No. 2

Under the Moons of Mars

by Norman Bean

RELATIVE to Captain Carter's strange story a few words, concerning this remarkable personality, are not out of place.

At the time of his demise, John Carter was a man of uncertain age and vast experience, honorable and abounding with true fellowship. He stood a good two inches over six feet, was broad of shoulder and narrow of hip, with the carriage of the trained fighting man. His features were regular and clear-cut, his eyes steel gray, reflecting a strong and loyal character. He was a Southerner of the highest type. He had enlisted at the outbreak of the War, fought through the four years and had been honorably discharged. Then for more than a decade he was gone from the sight of his fellows. When he returned he had changed, there was a kind of wistful longing and hopeless misery in his eyes, and he would sit for hours at night, staring up into the starlit heavens.

His death occurred upon a winter's night. He was discovered by the watchman of his little place on the Hudson, full length in the snow, his arms outstretched above his head toward the edge of the bluff. Death had come to him upon the spot where curious villagers had so often, on other nights, seen him standing rigid—his arms raised in supplication to the skies.

—*Editor's Note.*

CHAPTER I.

IN THE MOUNTAINS.

I AM a very old man; how old, I do not know. Possibly I am a hundred, possibly more; but I cannot tell, because I have never aged as other men, nor do I remember any childhood. So far as I can recollect, I have always been a man, a man of about thirty. I appear to-day as I did forty years and more ago, and yet I feel that I cannot go on living forever; that some day I shall die the real death from which there is no return.

I do not know why I should fear death, I who have died twice and am still alive; yet I have the same horror of it as you who have never died, and it is because of this terror of death, I believe, that I am so convinced of my mortality.

6
FRANTIC YEARS AND A TASTE OF SUCCESS

In preparing to write his *Autobiography*, Ed made a rough outline, jotting down in words or phrases the events still sharp in his memory. Whatever a man recalls from the past — and especially from a past of fifty years crowded with experiences — must be of importance to him. In the eight pages that he headed "Thoughts on Auto Biog," the section relating to the seven or eight years that followed his return from Salt Lake City is quite detailed. "The next few months encompassed a series of horrible jobs," Burroughs wrote. The list of positions or projects abandoned, the impression of deep discouragement, are reminders of the years when Ed's fortunes deteriorated steadily to their lowest point:

I get a job as Time Keeper on a construction job
   dizzy heights
I sell Stoddards lectures
   candy
   lt bulbs
I am a Flop

Get job as expert accountant
make good
Office Manager for E. S. Winslow
Go to Sears
Joan born
Go into business with Dentzer
Fail
Get job with Stace
Hulbert born about this time
Stace-Burroughs Co
Flop
Head aches for years — no vacation — lunches
Sell pencil sharpeners
Am just about ready to give up
Start writing A Princess of Mars
in corset jobbers office at Market & Monroe
Champlain Yardley Co
1/2 story accepted
My first check
Write Outlaw of Torn   rejected
Great poverty
pawning watch

Get job with System
E. W. Shaw
Jack born
Give up my job & decide to depend solely on writing
Everyone thinks I am crazy including myself

Impatient with any moderate and gradual climb up the ladder of success, Ed preferred to exchange a career at Sears, Roebuck for a more stimulating scheme with get-rich-quick possibilities. The enterprise, a partnership, was started with a man named Dentzer. A small brown business card, saved in one of Ed's scrapbooks, reads, "Burroughs & Dentzer, Advertising Contractors/610 — 134 E. Van Buren Street, Chicago."

One writer has described the business as an advertising agency based upon a correspondence course in salesmanship that prepared the students for active selling.[1] Ed, not at all deterred by his meager knowledge of salesmanship, had supposedly written the course. The situation and its outcome are vividly pictured in a magazine article:

Burroughs and his partner thought there were millions in it. They regarded themselves as aluminum kings about to corner the pot-and-pan trade with the help of peddlers who would pay tuition fees for the privilege of peddling. But the students all quit when they got to the field-work stage. Some failed to send back either the money or the pots and pans.[2]

This type of project, involving a few weeks of study by correspondence followed by door-to-door selling of pots and pans, appears to duplicate, in many respects, an enterprise that occurred at a later period during Ed's partnership with Dr. Stace.

Ed left Sears, Roebuck in August 1908, and the card he sent to Emma from South Bend, Indiana, shortly afterward indicates that he was preparing for some new enterprise or engaged in making contacts or purchases for his partnership with Dentzer. Dated September 15, 1908, the card was addressed to Emma at 197 Park Avenue. It reads: "This isn't a half bad little town. Haven't accomplished much yet. Not even my lunch — 12:15 p.m." On the same date he sent little Joan a card containing one word: "Google."

Whatever the business was, Ed, in his *Autobiography*, could summarize its collapse with wry amusement: "Having a good job and every prospect for advancement I decided to go into business for myself, with harrowing results. I had no capital when I started and less when I got through."

The circumstances were familiar; the struggle continued. From the run-down flat at 197 Park Avenue where he, Emma and baby Joan lived, Ed resumed the quest for employment. Meanwhile, the fortunes of Ed's own family had undergone some change. With the failure of their gold dredging projects in Idaho, brothers George, Harry, and Coleman returned to Chicago. Major George Tyler Burroughs, at an advanced age, still headed his company, but the income had declined steadily. During this difficult period his deep love for Ed and the unfailing kindness of his nature were demonstrated in the letter he sent to his son on December 25, 1908. Written on the letterhead of the American Battery Company at 172 South Clinton Street, it is addressed to "My Dear Son Edgar" and contains a most unusual Christmas present:

Kindly accept from me the within paid notes. I have had them for quite a long time, and I think it only right, at this time to give them to you, that your mind may be relieved of just this burden. They would never have troubled you, had I retained them, it is just as well for you to have them. Coleman has been paid in full. It is better for you not to mention this transaction to either Geo. or Coleman as the latter did not wish to let me have them and only did so after repeated importunities. He did not wish to hurt your feelings. There is no reason why they should be. Coleman could not afford to carry these notes and you could not take them up at that time, therefore I did the only proper thing, I think. I took them myself. I hope you will soon be in shape to pay any other indebtedness

104

you have, and now wishing you & Emma a Merry Christmas & a happy New Year.

Thus, Major George, without saying anything, had paid off the notes for the $300 Ed had borrowed from Coleman in May 1903. Through the years he had kept this deed a secret from Ed. The signature of the major was as touching as his action; in closing, he wrote, "I am, and always affctly. Your friend and Father."

From the rented home on 646 Washington Boulevard that George and Mary Evaline had occupied for so many years they had finally moved to 493 Jackson Boulevard (later renumbered 1418). A brief biography of the major was printed on the occasion of his birthday, Wednesday, October 13, 1909: "George T. Burroughs Sr. of 1418 West Jackson boulevard, president of the American Battery company and a native of Massachusetts, is 76 today. He carried a gun throughout the civil war and came to Chicago in 1868."[3]

For Ed the year 1909 brought an added responsibility. The family, now at 2008 Park Avenue, was increased to a total of four, with the birth of a son on August 12. He was named Hulbert, after Emma's side of the family.[4] Meanwhile, Ed had accepted a position as office manager for the Physicians Co-Operative Association at 1006 South Michigan Boulevard in Chicago. The firm, under the ownership of Dr. Stace, sold a nostrum called Alcola, publicized as a cure for alcoholism.

Stace, whom Ed found very likable, had grown ashamed of the patent medicine business and was casting about for a more reputable type of livelihood. His qualms may have been reinforced by the dubious attitude of the United States Government: "Alcola cured alcoholism all right, but the Federal Pure Food and Drug people took the position that there were worse things than alcoholism, and forbade the sale of Alcola."[5] Soon a new organization was formed, the Stace-Burroughs Company, with Ed listed as secretary-treasurer and with the office at the same address on Michigan Boulevard.

Although his failure in his own business, a recent occurrence, must have been fresh in his mind, he was unable to resist the temptations of this new get-rich-quick scheme. Stace had conceived of a partnership project and Ed blithely and eagerly acceded.

The ingenious nature of the enterprise seemed to indicate that it was an inspired product of Ed's imagination. The partner's first task, quickly completed, was to devise a course on "scientific salesmanship." It was writing, Ed confessed, "which I should have been eminently fitted to do since I knew about everything that a salesman should not do."[6] The twenty-one booklet course was sold to prospective salesmen at a reasonable price, actually less than similar courses being sold elsewhere, but in about the third or fourth lesson the catch appeared. Salesmen needed practice, which could only be obtained, of course, through selling the company's products; from these sales Stace-Burroughs would naturally make a generous profit. The trainees could choose from a wide variety of items, ranging from aluminum pots to pianos, these to be sold in door-to-door fashion. Ed did not overlook the firm and explicit reminders that the money should be remitted to the home office in Chicago.

Shortly after he started to work for Dr. Stace, Ed received a summons from Sears, Roebuck; he was offered the position of assistant manager of one of the merchandising departments. "If I had accepted it," he wrote in his *Autobiography,* "I would probably have been fixed for life with a good living salary, yet if I had, the chances are that I should never have written a story, which proves that occasionally it is better to do the wrong thing than the right thing."

The partnership scheme with Stace, which closely resembled Ed's project with Dentzer, was doomed. Its collapse, caused again by the lack of enthusiasm on the part of the student-trainees, was inevitable. Ed's comment in his *Autobiography* about the depressing outcome was brief: "The Stace-Burroughs Company sank without a trace and I was again out of a job." In these recollections of the period Ed states that he had reached the lowest depths of discouragement, a condition bordering on desperation:

I had worked steadily for six years without a vacation and for fully half of my working hours of that time I had suffered tortures from headaches. Economize as we could, the expenses of our little family were far beyond my income.

"Three cents worth of ginger snaps constituted my daily lunches for months," he wrote. "At this time I approached as near financial nadir as one may reach. I had no job and no money. I had to pawn Mrs. Burroughs' jewelry and my watch to buy food." It was a period that remained painfully sharp in his memory, one that shaped his often-quoted philosophy about poverty:

I loathed poverty and I should have liked to have gotten my hands on the party who said that poverty is an honorable estate. It is an indication of inefficiency, and nothing more. There is nothing honorable and nothing fine about it.

To be poor is quite bad enough, but to be poor and without hope — well, the only way to understand it is to be it.[7]

His equating of poverty with "inefficiency" is based upon the success-in-business goal that had ruled his life. In this competitive world the individual rises above poverty through efficiency.

A more intense condemnation of poverty is contained in a brief poem he had written, presumably several years earlier. In its extreme bitterness the poem becomes even more representative of his feelings during this period of his most acute struggles. The poem, marked "Written about 1908," succeeds, despite its heavy, stilted language, in depicting poverty with hatred and disgust:

POVERTY!
Accurst and cursing.
Thou Drab of Sin and Vice and Misery;
Thou spur to Fortune.
From thy shrunk womb a Lincoln springs.
Engulfest thou a thousand who might have
　　Lincolns been.

Seducer, thou, of Health and Happiness and
　　Love;
Murdress of countless children, wan and
　　pinched.
Honor in thee? Forefend us God!
Who lies with thee reeks of thy filth,
The butt of Ridicule the jest of Fate,
Loathing and loathed to a dishonored grave.

rom an analysis of Burroughs' early career in a wide variety of jobs and business enterprises, two basic facts emerge. Although frequently on the verge of bankruptcy he was not afraid to abandon a comparatively well-paying job such as that at Sears for the exciting prospects of a new enterprise offering quicker riches. Furthermore, because of his restless and highly imaginative nature he seemed to know he could never be content in a routine and uninspiring job. Had he been imbued with the same fears that stifle so many of us, he would have pursued the safe and secure course and remained at Sears. And so, despite his frequent and periodic totterings on the brink of disaster and the consequent feelings of hopelessness and frustration, he never gave up in his continuing search for success. It was this same indomitable will to succeed that he was soon to write into his fictional hero, John Carter of Mars. When Carter faced such insurmountable odds that death seemed certain, his defiant exclamation was "I still live!"

A list typed by Ed and dated September 1909 illustrates his struggles to make ends meet on the small salary he earned with the Stace organization:

Salary per week		$30.00
Grocery & Market	10.00	
Gas	1.75	
Girl	5.00	
Laundry	.75	
Milk	1.85	
Telephone	.70	
Jno. M. Smythe & Co.	5.00	
Car fare (ERB)	.60	
Interest	.47	

One of ERB's Christmas cards.

Total	*26.12*
Balance	*3.88*

This balance of $3.88 is mostly required for clothing, medicine and incidentals for a family of four.

Next month when I have to commence buying coal I shall have a weekly deficit of $1.12.[8]

The end of the year brought no change in his financial problems. He had no money to purchase the few Christmas cards he wished to send to his family and friends, and in these circumstances decided to use his own imagination and skill. Ed drew the cards in ink and created his own verses. Even those somber times could not repress his sense of humor. His Christmas card to F.C.B. (Frank Coleman Burroughs) read:

Please accept this little token
It would be more were I not broken.

In the drawings of two men on the card, one man is presenting the other with a paper containing the words, "Lease to 25th floor of any 24 floor bldg." This was Ed's comical idea of the only "little token" he could afford. On another card he printed "Merry Christmas to Mother" and in one corner drew a picture of a woman in joyous pose, while in the opposite corner, next to a "Merry Christmas to Father," Ed outlined a child's speckled rocking horse. His verse reads:

To giving you the things we'd like
We cannot come a mile
But its purpose will be well fulfilled
If this card brings a smile.

It is signed "Emma & Ed."

A card addressed to his nephew Studley Oldham Burroughs at 1418 Jackson Boulevard is dated December 25, 1909, and Ed's verse is headed in large capitals "St.O.B." Again, he jokes about his financial state:

Please accept from Edgar Rice
The best he's got to give — advice.

Uncertainty as to the movements of a certain stock has decided Santa Claus to remain where he is for an indefinite period. We are therefore sending you only our best wishes for A Merry Christmas and A Happy New Year

One of ERB's Christmas cards.

In the illustration the "advice" being handed out is simple: "Start a Bank Account."[9]

The immediate day-to-day pressure of providing for his growing family left him little time or energy to implement his other creative thoughts and ideas. In his *Autobiography* he recorded:

Evidently there was not a job to be had in Chicago. I got writer's cramp answering blind ads and wore out my shoes chasing after the others. Then, somehow, I got hold of a few dollars and took an agency for the sale of a lead pencil sharpener and borrowed office space from a friend of mine, Bert Ball, who was a corset jobber with an establishment at the corner of Market and Monroe Streets in Chicago.

I would not try to sell the lead pencil sharpeners myself, but I advertised for agents and sent them out. They did not sell any sharpeners, but in the leisure moments, while I was waiting for them to come back to tell me that they had not sold any, I started writing "A Princess of Mars," my first story.

The incredible plot concerning a certain princess on a far-off planet had probably passed through a long period of gestation. In July 1911 he started writing. The words flowed swiftly, the details clear and vivid in his mind.

As the story progressed, the pencil sharpener business ground to a halt and then expired. Ed

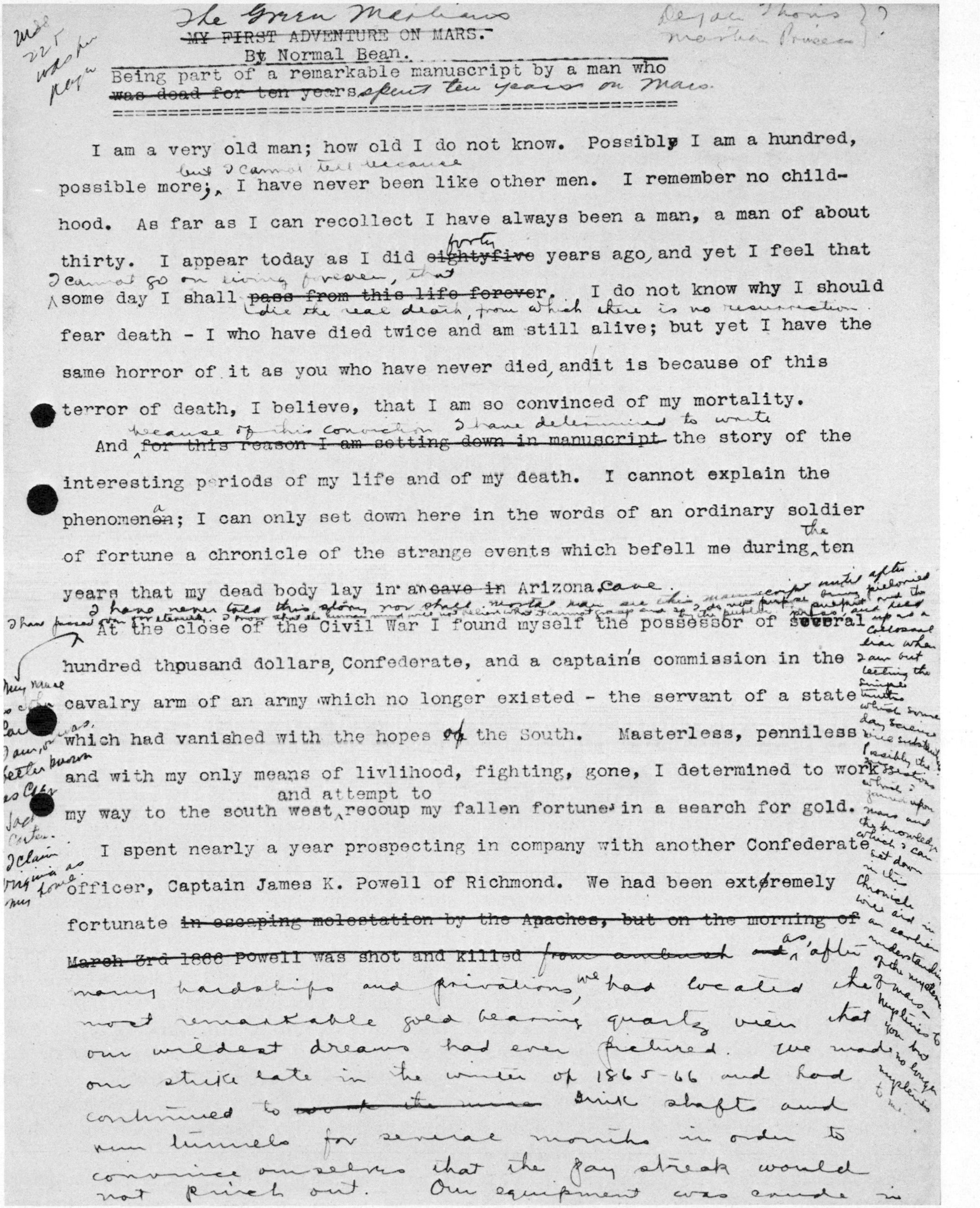

The Green Martians

~~MY FIRST ADVENTURE ON MARS.~~

By Normal Bean.

Being part of a remarkable manuscript by a man who ~~was dead for ten years~~ spent ten years on Mars.

I am a very old man; how old I do not know. Possibly I am a hundred, possible more; but I cannot tell because I have never been like other men. I remember no childhood. As far as I can recollect I have always been a man, a man of about thirty. I appear today as I did ~~eightyfive~~ forty years ago, and yet I feel that I cannot go on living forever, that some day I shall ~~pass from this life forever~~ die the real death, from which there is no resurrection. I do not know why I should fear death - I who have died twice and am still alive; but yet I have the same horror of it as you who have never died, and it is because of this terror of death, I believe, that I am so convinced of my mortality.

And ~~for this reason I am setting down in manuscript~~ because of this conviction I have determined to write the story of the interesting periods of my life and of my death. I cannot explain the phenomena; I can only set down here in the words of an ordinary soldier of fortune a chronicle of the strange events which befell me during the ten years that my dead body lay in an ~~cave in~~ Arizona cave.

At the close of the Civil War I found myself the possessor of several hundred thousand dollars, Confederate, and a captain's commission in the cavalry arm of an army which no longer existed - the servant of a state which had vanished with the hopes of the South. Masterless, penniless and with my only means of livlihood, fighting, gone, I determined to work my way to the south west and attempt to recoup my fallen fortunes in a search for gold.

I spent nearly a year prospecting in company with another Confederate officer, Captain James K. Powell of Richmond. We had been extremely fortunate ~~in escaping molestation by the Apaches, but on the morning of March 3rd 1866 Powell was shot and killed~~ as, after many hardships and privations, we had located the most remarkable gold bearing quartz vein that our wildest dreams had ever pictured. We made our strike late in the winter of 1865-66 and had continued to sink shafts and run tunnels for several months in order to convince ourselves that the pay streak would not pinch out. Our equipment was crude in

First page of manuscript of "Under the Moons of Mars;" original manuscript was written longhand.

The Green Martians
~~MY FIRST ADVENTURE ON MARS.~~
By Normal Bean.
Being part of a remarkable manuscript by a man who
~~was dead for ten years.~~ spent ten years on Mars.
===

I am a very old man; how old I do not know. Possibly I am a hundred,
possible more; but I cannot tell because I have never been like other men. I remember no child-

hood. As far as I can recollect I have always been a man, a man of about

thirty. I appear today as I did ~~eightyfive~~ forty years ago, and yet I feel that
I cannot go on living forever, that some day I shall ~~pass from this life forever.~~ die the real death, from which there is no resurrection.   I do not know why I should

fear death - I who have died twice and am still alive; but yet I have the

same horror of it as you who have never died, and it is because of this

The American Genealogical Society

1102 WOMAN'S TEMPLE

Telephone Main 949

Chicago,

Part of first page of first "Under the Moons of Mars" manuscript and business stationery on which ERB wrote the story.

went to work for his brother Coleman, who now owned the Champlain-Yardley Company, a firm that in Ed's words "might be grandiloquently described as manufacturing stationers — we made scratch pads." In the company's office at 222 West Kinzie Street he continued his writing and completed the first half of the story. On August 14, 1911, he mailed the manuscript, together with an explanatory letter, to *Argosy Magazine*, New York, preferring to use his business address rather than that of his home on 2008 Park Avenue.

Of his first story and its submission Ed recalled that at the age of thirty-five (he was within a few weeks of thirty-six) he knew nothing about writing technique, and remarked:

I had never met an editor, or an author or a publisher. I had no idea how to submit a story or what I could expect to get in payment. Had I known anything about it at all I would not *have thought of submitting half a novel. I do not know that any writer has ever done it successfully before or since.*[10]

With the sale of "Under the Moons of Mars" Ed arrived at a decision: he would make writing his career. He started at once on a second story, a romantic serial, its setting suggested by Metcalf. But in spite of his first, promising success, his financial situation was unchanged. Coleman's business would not support two families, and Ed once more began a search for work. The year 1912 found him working for *System*, the magazine of business, as manager of the System Service Bureau. The offices were at Wabash and Madison Avenues in Chicago, but the magazine also maintained offices in New York and London.[11]

System had achieved great respect and popularity in the world of commerce. Termed

"The Magazine of Efficiency" by its publisher, it was sometimes described as "the businessman's bible." A writer explains the reasons for its astonishing success: "It was a pioneer in introducing charts and graphs. Many businessmen worshipped charts and graphs as religious symbols. It was their belief that, if they stared long enough at these mystic curves and angles, red ink would turn into black."[12]

Ed, as manager of the Service Bureau, was assigned the task of giving business advice to the subscribers. He viewed this as somewhat unbelievable, noting in his *Autobiography:*

I knew little or nothing about business, had failed in every enterprise I had ever attempted and could not have given valuable advice to a peanut vendor; yet I was supposed to solve all the problems of our subscribers, among which were some very big concerns.

The inquiries were numerous, for upon payment of fifty dollars a year, a businessman could write to *System's* Bureau as often as he liked and demand detailed advice on his business dilemmas.

Ed especially remembered a milling company in Minneapolis or St. Paul that sent him intricate problems to be solved. "Had God asked me to tell Him how to run heaven," he wrote, "I would have known just as much about it as I did about the milling business."[13] But he was not the only member of the staff who had this type of responsibility. He could recall with amusement that a young man of about nineteen was hired to give advice to bankers. His sole banking experience "consisted in his having beaten his way around the world."[14]

In one version, Ed is depicted as a counselor who used great care to avoid any statements of a specific nature — statements that might be clearly interpreted:

Burroughs sat at his desk from morning until night, writing counsel to merchant princes and captains. He used words that rumbled with portentous business wisdom, but were too vague to enable any industrial baron to act on them. Burroughs had a conscience, and it was always

his fear that, if his advice ever became understandable, it would land his clients in the bankruptcy courts. With his letters he would enclose some of the awe-inspiring hieroglyphics now known as "barometries."[15]

The writer insists that Ed's advice never brought a complaint, and that "he may have been as good as anybody else in this field"; concerning the science of "barometries" it is humorously noted that "nothing is definitely known on the subject today except that the more the charts and graphs flourish, the faster the business decays."[16]

About the magazine *System*, its service bureau, and its owner, A. W. Shaw, Ed, in his *Autobiography,* offered some severely critical comments:

Ethically it was about two steps below the patent medicine business. One of the many differences between Stace and Shaw was that Stace was ashamed of what he did, notwithstanding the fact that he was constantly showered with unsolicited testimonials evidencing the fact that his treatment cured drunkenness.

Of Shaw himself, Ed wrote, "I never so thoroughly disliked any employer. He was an overbearing, egotistical ass with the business morality of a peep show proprietor."

Possibly during the period of varied business enterprises, Ed turned once more to his nom de plume of Normal Bean in writing a brief anecdote. Titled "Selling Satisfaction — an Anecdote," it presents, in its three pages, pointed advice on the businessman's obligations to his customers. The article, undated, was evidently not submitted to any commercial publications, although Ed, at the time he wrote it, may have contemplated offering it for sale to a magazine or sending it to a business "house organ." The emphasis upon "Selling Satisfaction" brings up the familiar Sears, Roebuck guarantee and could indicate that the article was written during his employment there or some time afterward.

He chose the anecdotal form with the entire article constructed in dialogue: "We had been discussing the failure of a competitor; the general manager and I. . . ." The competitor had been Lounsbury, head of a one-man concern. The company had failed in spite of the fact that "their goods were right, their prices right and they had an excellent organization, both sales and executive." The General Manager knew the reason for Lounsbury's failure; the policy he had followed "would wreck any house in this day of satisfaction-guaranteed-merchandising, where competition is as keen as in our line."

As Normal Bean, Ed recounts, in conversation, how he had run a general store in Montana, competing with Lounsbury. At the start, Lounsbury with his old established store had the bulk of the trade, but soon Ed acquired most of his customers. One important account, how-

Title page of ERB's "The Violet Veil."

A page from "The Violet Veil;" ERB gave the book to Johnny and Danton Burroughs in 1944.

112

ever, that of a wealthy miner and cattleman, Ed was unable to get. As the anecdote develops, a customer returns to Ed's store to complain about a pick handle that had broken. The customer does not expect any adjustment since the purchase was three months old, but Ed at once offers him a choice of selecting a new handle or getting his money back. The wealthy miner, who has witnessed the scene, is so impressed by Ed's business methods that he orders one hundred dollars worth of goods; he explains that he is quitting Lounsbury who has refused to do anything about a broken harness. Lounsbury's policy was that a purchased item belongs to the customer, and if it is defective, the storekeeper, who has not made it, cannot be responsible. "I reckon," the miner said, "that his logic is O.K., but I like your way of doing *business*."

Ed explained that this incident had given him a permanent understanding: ". . . from that day to this I have studied to perfect a policy which I had unconsciously adopted without realizing its immense value as a business builder." This was the "satisfaction-guaranteed-policy," in which the businessman is saying to any customer, "I am as much responsible for the *value* of the goods I sell you, after you buy them as I was before."

During the years of poverty, of irregular employment, and of an equally irregular income, Ed, before he turned to writing fiction, had, as in the past, found time for whimsical and humorous expression through poetry. He had shown that he loved to create children's poems; these allowed his imagination a further outlet — the poems lent themselves naturally to his colorful illustrations and cartoons. The narrative style of poetry, similar to the verses he had inserted in "Minidoka 937th Earl of One Mile Series M.," appeared to be his favorite, and he evidently enjoyed devising wildly improbable fairy-tale plots with nonsensical ideas and phrases reminiscent of Edward Lear and Lewis Carroll. As in "Minidoka," he sensed that children's interest lay mainly in animals — that to them, the concept of animals personified, talking and acting like humans (ridiculous ones), was joy-provoking.

A sixteen-page booklet titled "The Violet Veil" is a remarkable example of Ed's talent in creating a unified work of art. Here he integrates a lengthy children's poem with watercolor drawings of animals. Ed, in a note following the title page, has written in his typical self-deprecating style, "This thing was committed prior to 1913." Within an inked rectangle drawn on the third page he presents an amusing description of the work:

THE VIOLET VEIL

A Treely Truly Story
by
E. R. Burroughs
Profusely Illustrated in 18 colors
By the Author

Emma, Ed, Rajah & Co. Publishers
194 Park Avenue Chicago

Since the address listed is at 194 Park Avenue, this might indicate that the booklet was completed some time between 1904 and 1907; Emma's maroon leather postcard album is inscribed "194 Park Avenue From 1904 to 1907."[17]

The *Rajah* listed as one of the publishers is the collie dog Ed and Emma took with them on their trips to Idaho and Salt Lake City.

Page two contains a dedication to Ed's two grandsons, obviously written many years later, "To Johnnie and Danton Burroughs with love from their grandfather Edgar Rice Burroughs, Tarzana 25 Nov. 1944." John Ralston and Danton are the children of Ed's youngest son, John Coleman Burroughs.

In "The Violet Veil" Ed returns to his favorite theme of kindness to animals, and the moral may possibly be interpreted as a warning against altering nature's perfect creations and changing their accustomed environments. Man's cruelties, often based upon whims, and his irrationally destructive acts toward the animals are being censured. The poem, in its simple objective, offers this moral lesson for children, stressing kindness to animals and revealing that nature's creatures are not to be tampered with by man.

7
THE OUTLAW OF TORN

The sale of "Under the Moons of Mars" to *All-Story* Magazine was the stimulus that Ed needed to revive suppressed dreams of success. The sequence of misfortunes through the years had sobered him somewhat, given him a cautious viewpoint on life and its occurrences; but past failures in themselves had little effect in altering the basic impulsiveness of his nature — they could only temper it. A powerful influence was his conditioning in the business world, an emphasis upon dollars-and-cents practicality that had been started in the earliest years of his childhood and reinforced during his later employment experiences. This acquired habit, or quality, now seemed to act in an advisory or appraising manner to balance Ed's more imaginative tendencies.

In his letter of November 6, 1911, to Thomas Metcalf, the E. R. Burroughs of Sears, Roebuck, of hours of labor as against output, takes charge. The influence extends to his use of stiff business phrases: "While the remunera-tion is not exactly in proportion to the time and effort expended, I realize that for a first story it is considerably above the average, were one to include the rejected manuscripts."

In the same letter of November 6, succumbing once more to the pragmatic side of his nature, Ed advanced a skeptical view of writing as an occupation. "Does the price at which I have sold you this first manuscript establish the rate for future stories?" he inquired. His comment was made in a grumbling tone:

This story business is all new to me, but I like the work provided I can make it pay. However, I know that it would not be worth my while to devote all my time to it at this rate, as I started this story in July, which makes the remuneration equivalent to about $100.00 per month.[1]

Upon receipt of the $400 check Ed noted that the form of endorsement did not guarantee him the stipulated book rights, and on November 17 he reminded Metcalf of this agreement. The editor replied to assure him that the omission of book rights was a technical error, and that *these* did belong to him.

Before filing the carbon of the November 6 letter, Ed wrote across the top, "Check $400 recd Nov 17 — 1911 ERB." He was initiating a system of meticulous care in noting pertinent data and keeping records of transactions, a method that he would maintain throughout the years.

Metcalf had asked for references, presumably to offer some assurance that the story was original, and Ed pointed out that since it was his first story, he could not give any publishers as references. "I do not know any," he wrote, adding, "The story is absolutely original and I believe the best proof to you must be the fact that I wrote the ending along lines of your own suggestion."[2] Ed did offer three personal references: Robert D Lay, his friend and classmate from Michigan Military Academy, now with the National Life Insurance Company; Arch O. Burdick and Charles E. Rollins of a Chicago insurance firm; and two Sears, Roebuck officials, O. C. Doering, general superintendent, and Maurice D. Lynch, director of correspondence.[3]

In his acceptance letter of November 4 Metcalf laid down some conditions:

. . . I should like to stipulate that I might change the title and that I shall very likely do some cutting especially at the very beginning of the story, and also very likely entirely eliminate Solar's story, as the latter does not seem to me to be necessary to the rest of the story.

It was Metcalf, in the same letter, who persuaded Ed to create his next story in a different setting, a world almost as remote as that of the red and green Martians. Somewhat unhappily, Ed found himself returning to the thirteenth century to write a pseudo-historical romance about a gallant outlaw. To Ed, an anxious beginner, a suggestion from so distinguished an editor as Metcalf was both a challenge and a command. Metcalf wrote:

I was thinking last night, considering with how much vividness you described the various fights, whether you might not be able to do a serial of

the regular romantic type, something like, say "Ivanhoe", or at least of the period when everybody wore armor and dashed about rescuing fair ladies. If you have in mind any serials, or anything of that sort, and if you think it worth your while, I should be very glad indeed to hear from you in regard to them.

Ed's response was to offer the first demonstration of his amazing ability to write at a feverish pace. Approximately three weeks after receiving Metcalf's suggestion, he had completed the story. In his letter of November 29, sent from the Champlin-Yardley Company at 222 West Kinzie Street, Ed reported the dispatch, by United States Express, of "The Outlaw of Torn"; again, only the serial rights were for sale. He explained that the story was set in medieval England, and described it by repeating Metcalf's phrase, "when everybody wore armor and dashed about on horseback rescuing fair ladies."

Ed could not refrain from presenting the same type of sales pitch he had used with his Martian story. About his hero, the fictitious second son of Henry III, he wrote glowingly, "The story of his adventurous life, and his love for a daughter of the historic Simon de Montfort, Earl of Leicester, gives ample opportunity for thrilling situations, and hair raising encounters." His obvious awareness of the limited nature of his research as well as his apprehension about any story that might require strong realism gave him a feeling of insecurity. As a result, he preferred to joke about the matter, pointing out that "while the story hinges, in a way, upon certain historic facts in connection with The Barons' War of that period, I have not infused enough history, scenery or weather in it to in any way detract from the interest of the narrative." He signed the letter, in parentheses, "Normal Bean."[4]

The plot, quite ingenious, and with no actual basis in fact, concerns the incredible revenge of Sir Jules de Vac, French fencing master in the household of Henry III, for the insult he has suffered from the English King. But if Ed had assumed that a quick first sale would put him on the easy road to success, he was doomed to disappointment. To a critical reader, "The Outlaw of Torn" was nothing more than a ragged patchwork of assorted characters and incidents, hastily conceived and ineffectively bundled together. Even as a picaresque romance with the customary string of loosely related adventures it was a failure. The semblance of a medieval atmosphere, which Ed attempted to create through brief descriptions and bits of historical reference, was completely unconvincing. Metcalf, on December 19, 1911, offered a summary of the novel's defects:

I am very doubtful about the story. The plot is excellent, but I think you worked it out all together too hurriedly. You really didn't get the effect of the picturesqueness of Torne. Opportunities for color and pageantry you have entirely missed. The worth of some of the figures of which you might make a great deal, you do not seem to realize. As, for instance, the old fencer whom you use for about three chapters and then ignore entirely until the very end of the story. In him you have a kind of malevolent spirit who might pervade the whole book.

The criticism simply revealed that Ed, a novice writer, lacked the experience and understanding to attempt a work of this nature. Metcalf termed this letter as "cursory," promising to send a more detailed one. Ed showed no discouragement in his reply of December 21; in fact, his attitude was aggressive, and he devoted much of the letter to defending his concept of what the novel required. His belief had been that *All-Story* would want something with a good plot and "as rapid action as possible, so as to not entail too much matter." He conceded that since this story was completed so soon after his first one, a reader might receive an impression that it was hurriedly written; this was clearly not the case, he insisted. "I work all day and late into the night studying my references and writing alternately. An experienced writer would doubtless cover much more ground in the same time." A period of some twenty-five

days to complete a novel did not seem exceptionally brief to Burroughs.

In his reply to Metcalf he exhibited a supreme confidence that was close to cockiness. The flaws in "The Outlaw of Torn," ones that Metcalf rated as quite serious, were of minor consequence — "errors" subject to speedy correction. He was inclined to pooh-pooh them: "I can see no reason why I cannot make the story satisfactory to you, for the errors you cite are purely of omission, and they can easily be remedied."

Ed's confidence was shaken somewhat when Metcalf, keeping his promise, devoted his two-page letter of December 21 to a devastating analysis of the novel. His opening statement set the tone: "I think you have neglected great opportunities." He believed that Ed's first chapter should have been "full of color and excitement." After a brief summary of the plot, Metcalf referred to the ending: "I am not sure that there is any particular value in the happy ending. It seemes to be more legitimate to have both De Vac and the outlaw die in the end, leaving the lady dissolved in tears, possibly on her way to become a nun."

To Metcalf, who obviously disagreed with Ed, the story's weaknesses were the result of excessive haste in writing: "It would almost seem that you were in such a hurry to get the story done that you muddled and underplayed many of the situations. . . ." About the development of so colorful a chracter as de Vac, Metcalf maintained that Ed had "fallen down very badly," noting that de Vac had been dropped entirely for almost ninety pages. In this connection Metcalf offered good advice to a beginning author:

I think this is a shortcoming in your work. When you are not using any one or any number of your charactors you sort of lay them away in a drawer, so to speak, and seem apparently to forget all about them. I think it is necessary in a good story for the author always to keep in the reader's mind the fact that no matter which of the characters is in the limelight, the others are all drawing breath somewhere else out of sight or across the ocean, or wherever they may be.

A series of specific suggestions followed; and further in the letter Metcalf stressed that Ed ought to take time "to give the impression of the gorgeous barbarity of the times." He urged Ed to read Maurice Hewlett's *Forest Lovers* and Howard Pyle's *Men of Iron,* among other romantic novels, to acquire a stronger background. He presumed that Ed was acquainted with *Ivanhoe.*[5] ". . . I would not find it worth my while to be so explicit if I did not believe in your ability," Metcalf remarked, and stressing Ed's meager writing experience, added: ". . . you cannot, having been so short a time in the writing game, turn out wholly available stuff by working at a great rush, because I do not believe that you are as yet thoroughly sure of yourself."

Metcalf's appraisal of the manuscript evidently convinced Ed of the necessity for careful, studied revision, for he now worked slowly, not returning "The Outlaw of Torn" until February 2, 1912. A letter written from 2008 Park Avenue on this date was the one in which he notified Metcalf that he planned to use his real name from then on, since the compositor who had altered his pseudonym of "Normal Bean" had destroyed its future value. He was taking no chances and explained that he had devised two separate endings for the story, "one happy and the other tending toward the opposite, but leaving the matter somewhat in the reader's hands." His own preference was made plain:

For business reasons I lean to the "happy" one, because as all classes read fiction purely for relaxation and enjoyment, I imagine they do not care particularly for stories which leave a bad taste. However, I leave it to your greater experience.

Ed received no response from Metcalf during the month of February. The editor was suffering his own mental agonies as he tried to decide the fate of the novel. He later confessed, "I have been rather distraught as to exactly what my decision in regard to the story might be." Whether impatient of the delay, or already convinced that Metcalf would not accept the story, Ed sent an inquiry elsewhere, making his first contact with a book publisher. In his letter of February 29, which offered *two* stories for sale, he included a description of "Under the Moons of Mars." On March 4 a response came from Houghton Mifflin Company in Boston; it was not encouraging, and the letter, in its tone and wording, gave the impression that this staid firm viewed a novel of adventure on Mars as something so fantastic as to be detached from any world of either belief or consideration:

We thank you for your letter of the 29th ult in regard to two manuscripts that you wish to dispose of. It is not at all probable, we think, that we can make use of the story of a Virginia soldier of fortune miraculously transported to Mars, but the historical novel of the time of Henry III might be available for us. We ought to say, however, that it is almost certain that we could not use it this year, as our fiction engagements are already quite as numerous as we think desirable for next fall.

On the same date Ed received Metcalf's decision: the editor rejected "The Outlaw of Torn." "With the exception of one or two places," he wrote, "I do not feel that your rewritten version is very much of an improvement over the first copy of 'The Outlaw' which you sent me. The incidents, as a rule, seem rather wooden, and the color which you now introduce seems rather perfunctory, and you have not successfully concealed your artistry."

Metcalf, at whose instigation Ed had attempted this historical romance, now confessed, as though first aware of the idea, that "it must be a rather difficult thing to write a medieval story, unless one is pretty well steeped and interested in the period." But he then went on to make the kind of offer that Ed had never anticipated. Because he believed "so thoroughly" in the plot, Metcalf proposed to buy it and turn it over to a man in New York who had an extensive background in medieval history. The editor offered $100 for the plot and promised that when the story appeared, Ed would be listed as one of the authors.

Although Ed's financial situation, as in the past, was far from satisfactory, and the $100 offer must have been tempting, he had no intention of surrendering his plot to Metcalf. His refusal, somewhat curt and impatient, was based upon a businessman's evaluation of the amount of work and of the total hours expended. His letter of March 6 firmly closed the door on any suggestion of this sort: "I am very sorry that you do not find "The Outlaw of Torn" available in its present form; but I thank you for your alternative offer, which, however, in view of the time I have put on the story, I cannot see my way to accept."

Even at this early period, and as a novice writer striving for acceptance, Ed exhibited the two qualities of self-confidence and unyielding independence that characterized him throughout his career. These qualities, developed mainly through his conditioning and business environment, provided a simple but explicit guide for his actions: a writer's work, plainly no different from any commodity that was placed on the market, deserved a fair price, and its value, in at least one respect, was determined by the number of hours required to complete the work.

Concerning Metcalf's suggestion for a new story, Ed explained that he had been considering a Martian sequel; however, business had picked up lately and he was finding less time for writing. Metcalf may have persuaded himself with deep feelings of relief that "The Outlaw of Torn" was now consigned to whatever place an author reserved for his rejected manuscripts. But in the correspondence of succeeding months, this belief was revealed as an illusion. The first hint came in Ed's letter of March 14:

I really think your readers would have liked that story. I am not prone to be prejudiced in favor of my own stuff, in fact it all sounds like rot to me, but I tried the Mss on some young people; extremely superior, hypercritical young people, and some of them sat up all night reading it.

Warming up, Ed became doggedly argumentative. His study of the medieval period had convinced him "that nobody *knows* any-

thing about the manners, customs or speech of 13th century England. . . . So who may say that one story fairly represents the times and that another does not?"

If I had written into The Outlaw of Torn my real conception of the knights of the time of Henry III you would have taken the Mss with a pair of tongs and dropped it in the furnace. I made my hero everything that I thought the men of the time were not.

Metcalf, it appears, could not be goaded into a response, but on April 3, 1912, he wrote to Ed requesting material; and explained that *All-Story* was changing its policy and was again in the market for full-length novels of from 60,000 to about 80,000 words.

Ed's eager reply, fired back two days later, was what Metcalf should have expected. ". . . I have 'The Outlaw of Torn' on hand — What will you give me for the serial rights?" His scrawled postscript read: "By the way — do you suppose The Cavalier could use The Outlaw Mss? Provided of course that Allstory don't want it, or do you decide on the stories for both publications?"

In mentioning the story, Ed's use of the phrase "on hand" may have been subject to interpretation. On March 18, more than two weeks earlier, despite only the faintest encouragement, he had sent it to Houghton Mifflin Company, and he had not yet received any response from them. Whether he planned to forward another copy of the novel to Metcalf, or whether he believed there was little danger of the editor wanting it, is a moot point. But as Ed had probably anticipated, Metcalf's rejection was firm and prompt, and on April 9 he also made it plain that the manuscript had no chance for acceptance by *The Cavalier,* a weekly Munsey publication. Disappointment piled on top of disappointment. On May 7 Houghton Mifflin sent a letter of rejection which stressed the weakness of the story, but gave no details:

A careful consideration of the story left us with so much doubt of practical success that we do not think it expedient to make you an offer for the manuscript. The amount of fiction of all kinds that is constantly issuing from the press nowadays is very great and the natural competition is correspondingly large. We have doubted whether your historical romance will win out in the contest, and hence the decision we have stated above.

Much of the optimism raised by a first sale had vanished when the months of writing brought no further success. Ed continued his struggle to make a living, working as manager of the System Service Bureau for *System* magazine. He revealed his discontent in a letter of May 30 to Metcalf: "I wish that there was enough in fiction writing for me so that I could devote all my time to it for I like it. My specialties; advertising and business methods and selling command a bully salary, but they give me a highly localized pain."

The subject of "The Outlaw of Torn" remained quiescent for several months, but despite this fact, Metcalf must have understood that he was dealing with a man who would never give up. On October 30, while discussing other matters, Ed noted, "Am working on The Outlaw of Torn and think that I am whipping a good story out of it. Do you really think it worth while submitting it to you or would you suggest that I fire it to some other magazine?" He jokingly referred to Metcalf's frank discussion of editors in *All-Story's* column, "The Table Talks," in what amounted to an admission that editors "are but human after all" and given to mistakes.

"It is my job, you know, to read manuscripts as many times as authors see fit to chuck them my way," Metcalf replied, "and I am perfectly willing to do this so long as I have the enthusiasm I have had and always shall have for your work."

However, in sending the story to him on November 19, Ed indicated in his cover letter he had little hope for its acceptance, saying, "Please don't return it to me. When you are through with it let me know and I will send you a shipping paster and the coin to forward it elsewhere." He offered a positive prediction: "I know that you will not like it any better than

Dust jacket for A. C. McClurg and Company's first edition of The Outlaw of Torn, *1927, J. Allen St. John, illustrator.*

you did before," and as though baffled, added, "It's funny too, for everyone who has read it except yourself has thought it by far the most interesting story I have written."

The rejection was inevitable, even though Metcalf waited until December 18 to inform Ed; then, undoubtedly torn with guilt and regret, Metcalf said in his letter, "I should like to have sent you some kind of a check around Christmas time. . . ." Ed refused to voice any unhappiness, sending Metcalf instead what resembled an announcement of determination, or a proclamation of defiance: "I am going to do it over again when I have time — I shall stick to The Outlaw of Torn until it is published — I come of a very long lived family."[6]

Ed's struggle with the novel the year before

from November 1911 through January 1912 had resulted in three versions: an original longhand story of 215 pages; a typed manuscript, quite similar but with small corrections; and the expanded, detailed form, dated February 2, 1912, which he had submitted to Metcalf. In the first longhand version, Ed, with methodical care, began his system of recording the dates of manuscripts. The starting date on page one is noted as "Nov. 7, 1911 1:25 p.m.," and at the end Ed has written "Finished Nov. 23, 1911."[7]

In both the original longhand and typed forms the opening section thrusts the reader abruptly into the action (*in medias res*), focusing at once upon the wily, villainous De Vac and the incident leading to his terrible revenge. This opening differs from later ones:

De Vac had grown old in the service of the Kings of England, but he hated all things English, and all Englishmen. The dead King he had loved, but with the dead king's bones De Vac's loyalty to the house he served had been buried in Westminister.[8]

The revised manuscript of 1912, a collection of handwritten and typed pages, and even of odd pieces pasted in as corrections, offers evidence of what must have been exhausting writing. Some of the changes were probably based upon additional research — Ed's hasty hunt for information about the medieval period in order to give his work an authentic atmosphere. A box typed in an outline on the title page contains Ed's pen name and a statement of the theme.[9]

Ed's first two openings were discarded, and in the final published version of "The Outlaw of Torn" a more leisurely introductive section appeared. Leading into the quarrel between King Henry III and Simon de Montfort, this section substitutes an informal approach for the taut, compressed style of the other openings. It is the one familiar to Burroughs readers:

Here is a story that has lain dormant for seven hundred years. At first it was suppressed by one of the Plantagenet kings of England. Later it was forgotten. I happened to dig it up by accident. The accident being the relationship of my wife's cousin to a certain Father Superior in a very ancient monastery in Europe.[10]

Because it had the advantage of bringing the author directly into the story, this type of personalized introduction was popular with writers of the day. Having previously used it in "Under the Moons of Mars" (where it had become quite lengthy) Ed, perplexed over the various choices of openings, may have returned to it as a kind of refuge and as the easiest way to solve the problem.

At the close of 1912 "The Outlaw of Torn" remained unsold. Discouraged but not defeated, Ed had vowed to Metcalf, "I am going to do it over again when I have time." His most noticeable revision was in the introductory paragraphs; these took the final, personalized form. It was not until eight months later, after some dickering with A. L. Sessions, Editor of the *New Story* magazine, that Ed's obstinancy paid off. Sessions, in a letter of August 18, 1913, agreed to take "The Outlaw of Torn" for $500 for the first serial rights, and to pay two cents a word more if the story, according to reader response, proved to be successful.[11]

From a businessman's standpoint, as he balanced the long hours of revision and research against the net return, Ed undoubtedly considered "The Outlaw of Torn" to be a poor investment. Still, he had gained the satisfaction of another sale and had demonstrated the power of sheer stubbornness. Above all, through his unhappy experience with medieval times, castles and knighthood, he had learned that the historical romance, with its emphasis upon realistic atmosphere, was not the best outlet for his talents.

Ed's problems with "The Outlaw of Torn" during 1912 turned out to be of minor importance, however, for late in 1911 he had become engrossed in an astonishing plot, the wildest that his imagination had so far projected. As he wrote, the story, fully shaped in his mind, flowed across the pages with ease and certainty.

Tarzan of the Apes

8
TARZAN
OF THE APES

"I have been working at odd moments on another of the 'improbable' variety of tale...."[1] In this modest, somewhat apologetic report to Thomas Newell Metcalf, Ed made his first reference to a *most* "improbable" tale, one launched in pathos and depicting the tragedy of a young English nobleman, initially named John Clayton, Lord Bloomstoke, but by page six of the manuscript retitled Lord Greystoke, a name that sounded more aristocratic. The tale — its ingredients consisting of a crew of mutineers, an unfortunate Lord and Lady Greystoke set ashore on an African coast, and the events that happened after their death — was called "Tarzan of the Apes." Derived from a language Burroughs had invented for his fictional tribe of anthropoid apes, the name *Tar-Zan* meant "white-skin." It was a product of his fascination with odd syllables and strange sounding names which he repeated aloud in varying combinations until, with the approval of both his ears and intuition, he made a final choice.

Ed's tone, in his statement to Metcalf, reflected sensations new to him, those of hesitancy and doubt, a reversal of the confidence he had felt after his sale of "Under the Moons of Mars." His elation and his dreams of a successful career had been shaken by Metcalf's blunt rejection of the revised "Outlaw of Torn." Now, Ed was a man driven back to reality — back to the dreary but practical haven of business. His attitude displayed unemotional acceptance of the situation. To Metcalf he mentioned that business "has picked up" and that "the time and necessity for writing stories are much less than of a few months ago."

In this same letter of March 6, 1912, he proceeds to tell Metcalf about his latest tale, maintaining a precise, formal English so that no hint of his own feelings would emerge:

The story I am on now is of the scion of a noble English house — of the present time — who was born in tropical Africa where his parents

Part of first page of "Tarzan of the Apes" manuscript and pen ERB used to write it and "Under the Moons of Mars."

died when he was about a year old. The infant was found and adopted by a huge she-ape, and was brought up among a band of fierce anthropoids.

The mental development of this ape-man in spite of every handicap, of how he learned to read English without knowledge of the spoken language, of the way in which his inherent reasoning faculties lifted him high above his savage jungle friends and enemies, of his meeting with a white girl, how he came at last to civilization and to his own makes most fascinating writing and I think will prove interesting reading, as I seem especially adapted to the building of the "damphool" species of narrative.

Ed's phrase "the 'damphool' species of narrative" is an early example of his humorous self-deprecation and an expression of his life-long feelings of inferiority. Although he has still used a "sales pitch," he finishes by stating, "If it sounds good to you let me know and I will send on a copy when it is completed."

He had commented about "working at odd moments" on the story without offering any hint of when he started it, but on the original, a thick longhand manuscript of 504 pages, Ed had noted, "Commenced Dec. 1 1911 8:00 p.m."[2] Thus, approximately one week after he had completed the first version of "The Outlaw of Torn," he had turned to the creation of "Tarzan

Page 71 of "Tarzan of the Apes" manuscript where ERB created the name Tarzan; *on the eighth line the first name he used appears to have been* Zantar; *next he tried* Tublat-Zan — *Tublat was Kala's mate and Tarzan's foster father — referring to the white child as white Tublat; finally he created* Tarzan; *in the language of the great apes of the tribe of* Kerchak, Zan *means skin and* Tar *means white; in line 10 ERB changed the name* Bloomstoke *to* Greystoke.

of the Apes." Story ideas, of course, may be spontaneous, the result of sudden inspiration; story plots, however, as in the case of "Tarzan," so neatly and logically worked out, appear to require more time for pondering, testing and rejecting, and seasoning. That the plot of "Tarzan" may have been retained somewhere deep in Ed's imagination and summoned up in his fantasies to be reshaped and even relived at various times is entirely conceivable. The "Tarzan" embryo may have gestated for long years in Ed's mind before he scratched the first story lines on paper.[3]

Metcalf, in his letter of March 11, 1912, displayed an immediate enthusiasm for Ed's theme: "I think your idea for a new serial is a crackerjack and I shall be very anxious to have a look at it." The editor must have condemned himself many times for having urged Ed to write a historical romance. Highly sensitive, he could imagine, with all the accompanying guilt feelings, Ed's intense struggles that led only to failure; in addition, he could not easily forget his own agonies in making a final decision to reject the story. From this unhappy experience he emerged with a perception and conviction: Ed's talents were best expressed through his own wildly imaginative creations. Metcalf's letter included an appreciation and an implied apology:

Chicago

III

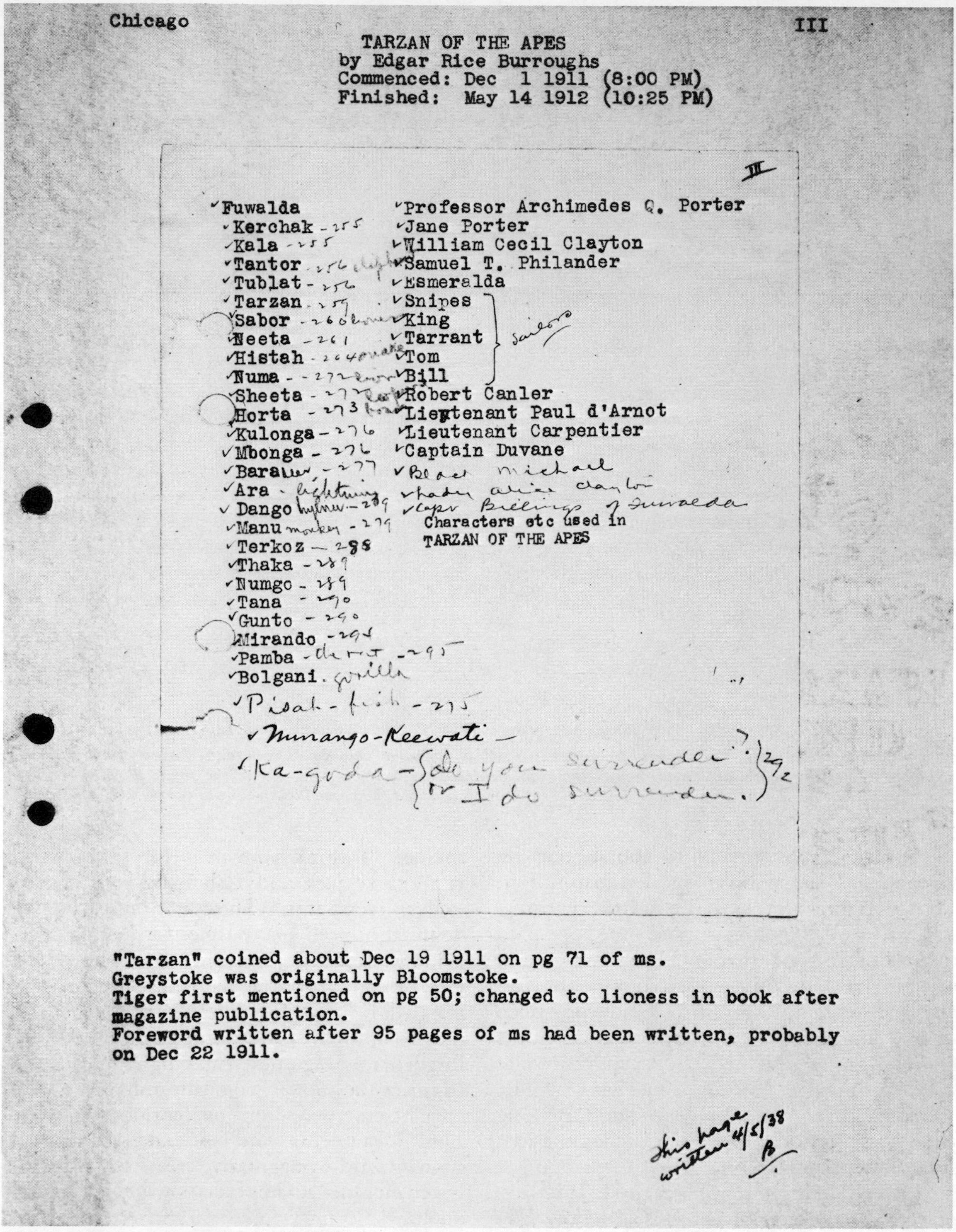

TARZAN OF THE APES
by Edgar Rice Burroughs
Commenced: Dec 1 1911 (8:00 PM)
Finished: May 14 1912 (10:25 PM)

III

Fuwalda
Kerchak - 255
Kala - 255
Tantor - 256 elephant
Tublat - 256
Tarzan - 259
Sabor - 260 lioness
Neeta - 261
Histah - 264 snake
Numa - 272 lion
Sheeta - 272 leopard
Horta - 273 boar
Kulonga - 276
Mbonga - 276
Bara deer - 277
Ara - lightning
Dango hyena - 279
Manu monkey - 279
Terkoz - 288
Thaka - 289
Numgo - 289
Tana - 290
Gunto - 290
Mirando - 294
Pamba - the rat - 295
Bolgani. gorilla
Pisah - fish - 295
Munango-Keewati -
Ka-goda - {do you surrender? / or I do surrender.} 292

Professor Archimedes Q. Porter
Jane Porter
William Cecil Clayton
Samuel T. Philander
Esmeralda
Snipes
King
Tarrant
Tom
Bill } sailors
Robert Canler
Lieutenant Paul d'Arnot
Lieutenant Carpentier
Captain Duvane
Black Michael
Snader alias Clayton
Capt Billings of Fuwalda

Characters etc used in
TARZAN OF THE APES

"Tarzan" coined about Dec 19 1911 on pg 71 of ms.
Greystoke was originally Bloomstoke.
Tiger first mentioned on pg 50; changed to lioness in book after magazine publication.
Foreword written after 95 pages of ms had been written, probably on Dec 22 1911.

this page written 4/5/38
B.

ERB's notebook page, prepared April 5, 1938, for "Tarzan of the Apes"; center portion, pasted on, is from earlier notebook.

You certainly have the most remarkable imagination of anybody whom I have run up against for some time, and I have come to the conclusion that I had very likely better not butt in on any of your schemes, but let you go ahead as you and your imagination see fit.

Ed had no intention of allowing anyone to come between him and his imagination. Still employed by *System* magazine, he was writing furiously in his spare time, racing to complete "Tarzan of the Apes."[4] In the correspondence that followed, Ed's letters resembled progress reports, while Metcalf's displayed an uncontrollable eagerness to read the story:

Glad you like scheme of new serial.
                              [Ed, March 14, 1912]

Will try to finish up "Tarzan of the Apes" in the next few weeks.   [Ed, April 5]

I cannot tell you how keen I am to see your story "Tarzan of the Apes", when you get it done.   [Metcalf, April 9]

How are you getting along with that serial? I am very anxious to see it.   [Metcalf, May 27]

In about a week now I should be able to send on the serial you ask about in yours of the 27th.

Have had but little time to work on the story as I am managing the System Service Bureau for The System Company, publishers of the System magazine. Am also writing a course in salesmanship for them and a new "How" book.
                              [Ed, May 30]

By United States Express I am sending you manuscript of Tarzan of the Apes.

May I have an early decision?
                              [Ed, June 11]

Although spurred on by Metcalf's inquiries to write "evenings and holidays,"[5] Ed was not working with any strong feeling of elation or optimism. With the rejection of "The Outlaw of Torn" he had become dubious about his writing ability. As a result, he now had little faith that "Tarzan" would be accepted. "... When I finished it I knew that it was not as good a story

Last page of "Tarzan of the Apes" manuscript, with date and time referring to completion.

as 'The Outlaw of Torn'," he commented, "and that, therefore, it would not sell. . . ."[6] The actual completion date, marked at the top of the original manuscript, read: "May 14, 1912 (10:25 p.m.)."

The sequence of correspondence, like one of Ed's stories, rose naturally to its climax — Metcalf's acceptance of "Tarzan of the Apes" and his payment — truly an unexpected climax, one that Ed had not dared hope for. (Unfortunately, this most important letter, listing the amount of the check, with a probable statement about the story, has vanished.)

On June 26, 1912, Metcalf wrote, "I suppose by this time you have got a small souvenir from us to remind you of our attitude toward 'Tarzan of the Apes'." Evidently, normal procedures were followed in a separate mailing of the check by the Munsey business office, also under the date of June 26. The payment for "Tarzan of the Apes" — established through other sources and records — was $700.[7] Ed's acknowledgement two days later read, "Your check and letter came together on this morning's mail and I thank you for both. The endorsement on the reverse of check covered all rights, though I assume that it was as before but an error, as I only sold you the serial rights."

The question of Ed's nom de plume of *Norman Bean* was brought up by Metcalf, who explained that the readers had been demanding more stories by the author of "Under the Moons of Mars." In apologizing for the change from *Normal* to *Norman,* Metcalf inquired, "Do you think it would be advisable to run this story ["Tarzan of the Apes"] under the name *Norman Bean,* or shall I ignore any requests for some of that gentleman's work and run it under *Normal Bean,* or your own name?"[8]

Ed's response of June 28 revealed that the printer's alteration of his name was still a touchy subject:

In the matter of the pen name, why not run this story as by Norman Bean (Edgar Rice Burroughs) and then, should I write another one *run that as by Edgar Rice Burroughs (Norman Bean), thereafter dropping the pen name entirely?*

This may not accord with your policy, but I think you will agree that you owe me a concession in the matter of names, for you sure did smear up the original.

It seems to me that it would be unwise to attempt to revive Normal Bean now.

At the end of the letter he asked, "By the way, when will Tarzan of the Apes happen?"

The *All-Story* of October 1912 featured "Tarzan of the Apes" as a "book," marked "complete in this issue." Metcalf accepted Ed's second suggestion, listing the author as *Edgar Rice Burroughs (Norman Bean),* the last time that Ed's pen name would appear on a printed story.

Various theories have been advanced that Ed found his inspiration both for his stories of other planets and for the Tarzan idea in fictional works by well-known authors. He often insisted that in his adult years fiction held little interest for him, but had conceded that "as a boy and as a young man I read practically nothing else."[9] The question of where he *might* have obtained his themes, especially for his earliest works, deserves examination.

In referring to an author whose novel features elements common to many stories of strange civilizations, Ed again stressed his reading habits: "I did read a part of Sir Arthur Conan Doyle's Lost World several years ago but never finished it for as a matter of fact I read practically no fiction although I remember that I was much impressed with the possibilities suggested by the story."[10] Ed's "Under the Moons of Mars" (1911) predated "The Lost World" (1912) by one year; this very fact precluded any possibility of Ed's using Doyle's novel as a source. Moreover, any comparison of the two works reveals them as completely dissimilar.

The first claim that one of Ed's stories resembled a work of another author did appear, however, in connection with *A Princess of Mars.* Ed expressed his concern in a letter to Joseph

Bray, A. C. McClurg & Company editor, on May 31, 1918:

Will you tell me, please, when H. G. Wells wrote his Martian stuff or rather when it appeared? One critic calls attention to the fact that this story of Wells' and another story which I never heard of, suggested my Princess of Mars. As a matter of fact, I never read Wells' story and as mine was written in 1911, it is possible that it anticipated Wells'. Just for curiosity I should like to know.

In this case Ed's concept of the dates is inaccurate. Presumably, the reference is to Wells' main Martian novel, *The War of the Worlds*, published in 1898, far ahead of *A Princess of Mars*. Eleven of Wells' science-fiction or fantasy novels appeared before 1911, and Wells continued to produce a steady flow of similar works through 1937. But any theory that *The War of the Worlds* even "suggested" *The Princess of Mars* is without logical evidence. Wells' novel, written in his coldly precise style in an attempt to create scientific realism, bears no resemblance to Ed's freely imaginative work with its fantastic characters and setting.

In Wells' plot, centered about an invasion of our planet *from Mars,* the Martians become grotesque monsters; he makes no effort to develop them as individuals or to characterize them. Ed creates a bizarre civilization *on Mars;* in doing so, he was concerned with neither reality nor with scientific plausibility, although he did supply sufficient and ingenious details to give some semblance of reality. Students of Burroughs attribute much of his success as a storyteller to his knack of making the impossible seem as if it could really happen. His characters, surprisingly, were projected with vividness despite the fact that they were not individualized; actually, they were stereotypes. Yet, in a way not easily explained, they became unforgettable. Beyond all this, Ed's concept of a story, in contrast to Wells', was exaggeratedly romantic; he utilized all the popular ingredients — a beautiful lady, a dashing hero, a warped, sadistic villain, and, of course, a love that surmounted all obstacles.

In his most spectacular work, *Tarzan of the Apes,* Burroughs had to face a far heavier barrage of speculations, theories, and accusations concerning the possible sources for his famous theme. *Tarzan* may have been written, according to one explanation, with the aid only of "a 50c Sears dictionary and Stanley's *In Darkest Africa. . .,*"[11] but Ed on several occasions explained that the ancient tale of the founding of Rome had provided his first stimulus:

As a child I was always fascinated by the legend of Romulus and Remus, who were supposed to have been suckled and raised by a she-wolf. This interest, I presume, led to conjecture as to just what sort of an individual would develop if the child of a highly civilized, intelligent and cultured couple were to be raised by a wild beast without any intercourse whatsoever with members of the human race. It was because that I had played with this idea on my mind at various times, I presume, that I naturally embodied it in the story after I started writing.[12]

I started my thoughts on the legend of Romulus and Remus who had been suckled by a wolf and founded Rome, but in the jungle I had my little Lord Greystoke suckled by an ape.[13]

While the story of Romulus and Remus may have been an important source for the Tarzan idea, Ed was apparently drawing a more direct inspiration from a work by a master storyteller — Rudyard Kipling. The link is found in the *Jungle Books,* fiction that Ed recalled reading in his early years:

As a boy I loved the story of Romulus and Remus, who founded Rome, and I loved too, the boy Mowgli in Kipling's "Jungle Books". I suppose Tarzan was the result of those early loves.[14]

. . . I presume that I got the idea for Tarzan from the fable of Romulus and Remus who were suckled by a she-wolf, and who later founded

Rome; and also from the works of Rudyard Kipling, which I greatly enjoyed as a young man....[15]

On February 13, 1931, in a letter to the editor of *The Bristol Times*, Bristol, England, Ed replied to a statement accusing him of stealing his themes from the British writers Kipling, Wells, and Haggard. Ed tempered his reaction to the accusation by adding the phrase "unintentionally perhaps." After noting that "for some reason English reviewers have always been particularly unkind to me," Ed proceeded to a frank discussion of the authors: "To Mr. Kipling as to Mr. Haggard I owe a debt of gratitude for having stimulated my youthful imagination and this I gladly acknowledge, but Mr. Wells I have never read and consequently his stories of Mars could not have influenced me in any way."

In denying that he took Kipling's original idea and exploited it to his own profit, Ed wrote:

The Mowgli theme is several years older than Mr. Kipling. It is older than books. Doubtless it is older than the first attempts of man to evolve a written language. It is found in the myths and legends of many peoples, the most notable, possibly, being the legend of Romulus and Remus, which stimulated my imagination long before Mowgli's creation.

Ed again acknowledged that Kipling may have influenced him, adding, "but I am also indebted to many other masters as, doubtless, Mr. Kipling would acknowledge his debt to the vast literature that preceded him...." He reiterated firmly, "... to Mr. Wells, whom I have never read, I owe nothing."[16]

In a lengthy correspondence Ed tried to explain the origins of the Tarzan idea to Professor Rudolph Altrocchi of the University of California at Berkeley. Altrocchi, in the Department of Italian, first wrote to Ed on March 29, 1937, stressing that he was *not at all* a fan-writer" but one interested in "folkloristic and narrative motifs." Curious about "the mysterious processes of literary creation," he had previously communicated with such famous authors as Mary Roberts Rinehart, George Santayana, Richard Le Gallienne, and Edgar Lee Masters.

Ed made it plain that he could only speculate, or search his memory "for some clue to the suggestions that gave me the idea," as he had often done for the numerous people who made inquiries during "the past twenty years":

... As close as I can come to it I believe that it may have originated in my interest in Mythology and the story of Romulus and Remus. I also recall having read many years ago the story of the sailor who was shipwrecked on the Coast of Africa and who was adopted by and consorted with great apes to such an extent that when he was rescued a she-ape followed him into the surf and threw a baby after him.

Then, of course, I read Kipling; so that it probably was a combination of all of these that suggested the Tarzan idea to me. The fundamental idea is, of couse, much older than Mowgli, or even the story of the sailor; and probably antedates even Romulus and Remus; so that after all there is nothing either new or remarkable about it.

I am sorry that I cannot tell a more interesting story concerning the origin of Tarzan....[17]

The story of the shipwrecked sailor, one that Altrocchi was unfamiliar with, aroused his excitement. Eager to discover where Ed had found it, he wrote again, apologetic, offering a pun that deprecated his own accomplishments, ". . . the distinction should be made . . . between one who *is* Burroughs and one who just burrows in literary motifs."[18]

Ed replied, "The story of the shipwrecked sailor was not the basis of any book, as I recall it, but merely an anecdote that was supposed to be authentic; but where it originated or where I saw it, I cannot now recall. Anyway, it is probably not true. . . ."[19]

The determined Altrocchi embarked upon a six months' search for the anecdote, without success, and in a further inquiry posed a series of questions in the hope that they might stimulate Ed's memory. "I shall not have peace, — at least literary peace," Altrocchi wrote, "until I have located this confoundedly elusive tale."[20] Ed again had no recollection, but in his response he offered an amused reaction to Altrocchi's feverish search: "I may say, however, that you have me started now, and that life will seem quite worthless unless I can recall further details. Possibly I shall be able to do so, and if I am successful I shall communicate with you immediately."[21]

Any belief Ed might have entertained that the matter was ended proved to be illusory. Two years later, on June 13, 1939, the dedicated Altrocchi revealed that his mission — the hunt for the shipwrecked sailor story — was continuing. The professor, assuming that Ed must have read the story in some 1912 publication, had done exhaustive research within this period but had found nothing. However, he did unearth two old sources involving relationships between humans and apes. These, he noted, "are in such inaccessible books that I do not see how they could have been read by you. In fact both were then inaccessible to anybody, or almost so." The two works he identified as Guazzo's *Compendium Maleficarum*, written in Latin in the seventeenth century and "only recently translated," and an unnamed adventure novel published in 1635. He summarized the themes:

In the first a woman who had committed a crime is relegated to an uninhabited island where she is seduced by an ape and has two babies from him before she is rescued; in the second, with a similar situation, the ape-husband follows her into the surf and throws the baby after her, when she is rescued.

Altrocchi hoped that these folk-tales might revive some dormant memory of the magazine where Ed supposedly had read about the sailor. "Otherwise," he announced resignedly, "I'll have to continue my search." Ed again had no recollection, but, anxious to help, he speculated, ". . . I may have found it in some book in the Chicago Public Library at the time I was searching for material for a Tarzan book. . . ."[22] This brought an eager reply from Altrocchi who was suddenly struck with a new idea: could Ed have done research in other languages, and if so, what languages?[23]

Ed quickly understood that his reference to the Chicago library had created a mistaken impression: ". . . I am afraid that I have misled you if I have suggested that I ever made any research for a source for Tarzan. My research was for data concerning the fauna and flora of Africa and the customs of native tribes." He emphasized the important point: "I had already found Tarzan in my own imagination."[24]

Altrocchi's literary investigations and his correspondence finally culminated with a letter to Ed, on November 13, 1939, containing an announcement of his plan to read a paper at the annual meeting of the Philological Association of the Pacific Coast, the subject being, "Ancestors of Tarzan." The paper, an abbreviated version of the original fifty-four typewritten sheets, was to be read at the University of Southern California on November 24. Ed, of course, was invited.

The invitation had to be declined. Ed wrote to explain that he was leaving for New York on the twenty-first. He hoped that if the paper were printed Altrocchi might send him a copy. The more than two years Altrocchi had spent in tracing the sources of the Tarzan theme had produced little that was directly related to the Burroughs novel. Altrocchi, however, as in the two seventeenth-century references to humans and apes, demonstrated that the theme had roots deep in the past, and in his total research assembled information of high interest to folklorists, historians, and the general reader.[25] Unhappily, the source that the incredibly persistent professor had hoped to discover — the tale of the shipwrecked sailor — was never found. His letter to Ed containing an invitation to the reading expressed the hope "to have, at last, the pleasure of meeting you personally." During the two years of correspondence Altrocchi, the scholar, engrossed in his musty documents, displayed no interest in making the acquaintance of the living man — the author whose creation, *Tarzan,* had driven him into an obsessive search. Altrocchi, as in his finished work, an essay titled "The Ancestors of Tarzan," remained in the remote past, never attempting to bridge his abstract paper world with the world of human reality. The two men never met.

The claim that Ed, in *Tarzan of the Apes*, had taken his theme from Kipling's *Jungle Books,* works that he freely admitted reading as a child, was one that occasionally drew Ed's ire. But while responding in annoyance to the *Bristol Times* writer who had hinted at plagiarism, Ed also acknowledged his indebtedness to the man, saying, "He has reawakened my interest in my set of Kipling, which I have not opened for many years, and which I may still enjoy above the works of later writers, despite the disparaging remarks that I understand Mr. Kipling has made relative to my deathless contributions to the classics."[26]

Kipling's references to *Tarzan* and its author, appearing in the autobiographical *Something of Myself,* offers actual praise of Ed's creation; but through the use of the word "imitators," and the avoidance of mentioning the name "Burroughs," as though one could not bother to recall the writer of a work so superficial as *Tarzan,* Kipling achieves an air of condescension and lofty tolerance:

. . . If it be in your power, bear serenely with imitators. My Jungle Book *begot Zoos of them. But the genius of all genii was the one who wrote a series called* Tarzan of the Apes. *I read it, but regret I never saw it on the films, where it rages most successfully. He had jazzed the motif of the* Jungle Books, *and, I imagine had thoroughly enjoyed himself. . . .*[27]

Kipling made this final comment about Ed: "He was reported to have said that he wanted to find out how bad a book he could write and 'get away with,' which is a legitimate ambition."

While not addressing himself directly to Kipling, Ed noted that one could offer a different interpretation of plagiarism if the ancient legend of Romulus and Remus were accepted as the first and original source for all the variations that followed:

That Mr. Kipling selected a she-wolf to mother a man-child might more reasonably subject him to charges of plagiarism than the fact that I chose a she-ape should condemn me on a similar count.

It is all very silly, and perhaps noticing such charges is sillier yet, but no man enjoys being branded a thief.[28]

Ed had shown himself quite willing to answer questions about the possible sources of *Tarzan* and to conjecture as to how the idea came to him. But one point should be emphasized: he was responding to those who had already formulated theories concerning *Tarzan's* origin. In other words, these theories *were not his.* Until the critics began to analyze his works, he made no attempt to search his mind or probe his memory in the hope of recalling some source from the dim past. Once the discussions began, he agreed readily that elements of the Romulus and Remus tale and of Kipling's *Jungle Books* could have provided him with his original inspiration. This theory was logical and possible. However, an awareness of the various qualifying phrases Ed used in his answers — "I presume," "I suppose," "as close as I can come to it," and others — makes it plain he was only conjecturing. He could not identify *any source* with certainty.

Ed knew only that the Tarzan idea came from somewhere deep in his imagination. He was willing to concede that the imagination is stimulated by what one reads, but he understood that beyond this, the creative process worked in mysterious ways that often defied analysis. ERB's son Hulbert, in an interview at Tarzana, commented: "I am frequently amused and sometimes irritated by those who constantly seek to prove that there are no new ideas, that ERB *had* to have direct sources for the Tarzan and Mars themes, that he stole his ideas from other writers. I am probably biased, but it seems to me that Ed Burroughs' remarkable imagination, demonstrated in many stories over the years, was certainly capable of developing a *new* idea and that perhaps Tarzan and John Carter *were* original with him. Nobody accuses Edison of stealing a light bulb."

The answer Ed preferred to give in later years to the inevitable question, "How did you happen to write Tarzan?" exhibited his familiar uncertainty, but offered a simple, commonsense explanation:

I've been asked that hundreds of times and ought to have a good answer thought up by now, but haven't. I suppose it was just because my daily life was full of business, system, and I wanted to get as far from that as possible. My mind, in relaxation, preferred to roam in scenes and situations I'd never known. I find I can write better about places I've never seen than those I have seen.[29]

Aside from his efforts to explain the origins of the Tarzan idea, Ed was at times drawn into a discussion of the theories or philosophies he was trying to develop in his story, or those that others believed were inherent in his story. In relation to this, the question was also asked, "what does Tarzan, as a human in an animal environment, represent or symbolize?"

The philosophic themes that were generally associated with *Tarzan of the Apes* may be listed as follows: the conflict of heredity and environment; the lone man pitted against the forces of nature; the search for individual freedom; escapism — flight from the boring routines of daily life; a destructive civilization, with man, its representative, displaying all its vices, as opposed to the simple virtues of nature's creatures.

Regarding the basic scientific controversy of heredity vs. environment, Ed stated, "I liked to speculate as to the relative values of heredity, environment, and training in the mental, moral, and physical development of such a child, and so in Tarzan I was playing with this idea."[30] At present, environment is viewed as the decisive force in shaping or conditioning the individual. Possibly without being aware of it, Ed, in *Tarzan of the Apes,* created a unique situation in

which heredity, within a civilized setting the lesser influence, now emerged as the greater. Clearly, heredity's victory in the conflict was inevitable. Tarzan, even the infant Tarzan, could not repress his human attributes, his intelligence. These led to his curiosity about his surroundings and about his parents, his observation of differences between the apes and him, his discovery of weapons, his motivation to learn to read, and eventually his rejection of the jungle life and a return to civilization. The outcome might be interpreted in another way: Tarzan and his circumstances represent abnormality; within this strange situation nature's irresistible pressure for a righting, a balance, forces heredity to assume its proper place.

An early analysis of the Tarzan theme describes it as "the Robinson Crusoe idea over again" and explains:

The lone man or boy fighting for his existence single-handed against nature always attracts readers when it is well done. This interest comes doubtless from something within us which goes back to the time when our ancestors were doing this kind of thing themselves.[31]

The lone man is of course ourselves, the evertriumphant hero of our daydreams. This Ed understood instinctively, assuming that as he lived vicariously in the role of John Carter or Tarzan, so did others live in their own illusory roles.

Associated with the concept of man versus nature is his search for individual freedom, stemming from society's restrictions and man's rebellion against the "social contract." Although we yield to civilization's controls, we yearn to break out of our confines: "Tarzan always represents individual freedom . . . which is always present with us. There is not a man or woman who occasionally does not like to get away into a more or less primitive wilderness where he is 'monarch of all he surveys.' "[32]

Viewed with differing emphasis is the concept of escapism; Ed related this to the monotony of existence:

Perhaps the fact that I lived in Chicago and yet hated cities and crowds of people made me write my first Tarzan story.... Tarzan was, in a sense, my escape from unpleasant reality. Perhaps that is the reason for his success with modern readers. Maybe he takes them, too, away from humdrum reality.[33]

The escapism, according to another writer, was Ed's personal release from a dreary environment: "He was nearing forty; his life was still monotonous and insecure. It was perhaps natural that he should imagine a young demigod of superhuman strength and agility, living a life of freedom in the jungle...."[34]

Man's numerous vices, his greed, hypocrisy, and deceit, as well as his irrational and cruel behavior, opposed to the instinctive order and justice of nature — this theme has become familiar to most readers of the Tarzan stories. In *Tarzan of the Apes* elements of the theme are stressed in connection with Tarzan's human inheritance:

He (Tarzan) killed for food most often, but being a man he sometimes killed for pleasure, a thing which no other animal does; for it has remained for man alone among all creatures to kill senselessly and wantonly for the mere pleasure of inflicting suffering and death.

The natives' sadistic treatment of a prisoner is both a shock and a revelation to Tarzan:

As he was dragged, still resisting, into the village street, the women and children set upon him with sticks and stones, and Tarzan of the Apes, young and savage beast of the jungle, wondered at the cruel brutality of his own kind.
Sheeta, the leopard, alone of all the jungle folk, tortured his prey. The ethics of all the others meted a quick and merciful death to their victims.
He saw that these people were more wicked than his own apes, and as savage and cruel as Sabor, herself. Tarzan began to hold his own kind in but low esteem.

Man, whose actions the animals are all too familiar with, creates fear wherever he goes:

"No longer was there safety for bird or beast. Man had come." The fierce beasts who prowl the jungle may cause the weaker ones to flee, but they return again when the danger is over. Man's arrival is a signal for a different response: "When he comes many of the larger animals instinctively leave the district entirely, seldom if ever to return; and thus it has always been with the great anthropoids. They flee man as man flees a pestilence."

In his article "The Tarzan Theme," Burroughs, in retrospect, discussed the background of *Tarzan of the Apes* and offered a thorough analysis of his motivations and of the most popularly suggested themes. Concerning his favorite theme — destructive man with all his vices in contrast to the simple creatures who merely carry out the dictates of nature — Ed wrote, "It pleased me. . . to draw comparisons between the manners of men and the manners of beasts and seldom to the advantage of men. Perhaps I hoped to shame men into being more like beasts in those respects in which beasts excel men, and these are not few."[35] In continuing, he discussed man's harmful actions:

I wanted my readers to realize that man alone of all the creatures that inhabit the earth or the waters below or the air above takes life wantonly; he is the only creature that derives pleasure from inflicting pain on other creatures, even his own kind. Jealousy, greed, hate, spitefulness are more fully developed in man than in the lower orders. These are axiomatic truths that require no demonstration.

To further develop this idea, Ed maintained that the lion is actually "merciful when he makes his kill"; this, of course, is not intentional, but the result of "the psychology of terror" which contributes to "the swift mercy of his destruction." Ed noted that men who have been mauled by lions "felt neither fear nor pain during the experience," and to support this statement, he recalled Livingston's near fatal encounter with a lion in which his body was terribly scratched and torn and his shoulder crushed. Explorer Livingston, who may have been the first to record an incident of this sort, wrote:

Growling horribly close to my ear, the lion shook me as a terrier does a rat. The shock produced a stupor similar to that which seems to be felt by a mouse after the first shake of the cat. It caused a sort of dreaminess, in which there was no sense of pain nor feeling of terror.[36]

Ed commented, "Compare this, then, with the methods of the present day gangster who cruelly tortures his victim before he kills him. The lion sought only to kill, not to inflict pain. Recall the methods of the Inquisition. . . ."

To reinforce his theory, Ed included a quote from an English officer who had been clawed and bitten by a lion:

Regarding my sensations during the time the attack upon me by the lion was in progress, I had no feeling of pain whatever, although there was a distinct feeling of being bitten; that is, I was perfectly conscious, independently of seeing the performance, that the lion was gnawing at me, but there was no pain. To show that the feeling, or rather want of it, was in no wise due to excessive terror I may mention that, whilst my thighs were being gnawed, I took two cartridges out of the breast pocket of my shirt and threw them to the Kaffir who was hovering a few yards away, telling him to load my rifle.[37]

The assumption that Ed has drawn from these illustrations is that Nature, having established the necessity for killing among her lower creatures for food only, has mercifully eliminated the pain through her creation of a "psychology of terror," which numbs the sensations of the wounded animals and allows them to die with a minimum of suffering.

In his analysis of "The Tarzan Theme" Ed explained that while writing *Tarzan of the Apes* he had been interested "in playing with the idea of a contest between heredity and environment," and, as a result, had thrown an infant child "into an environment as diametrically op-

posite that to which he had been born as I might well conceive." However, Ed was careful to emphasize that he was *not dealing with reality*; furthermore, he had no illusions that under real-life circumstances the young Tarzan's development would have followed the same path:

As I got into the story I realized that the logical result of this experiment must have been a creature that would have failed to inspire the sympathy of the ordinary reader, and that for fictional purposes I must give heredity some breaks that my judgement assured me the facts would not have warranted.[38]

Thus, Tarzan was endowed not only with the "best characteristics of the human family," but also with the best qualities of the wild beasts.

Ed, in another statement on the subject, revealed the same dubious attitude about the actual outcome of a situation involving a human being raised by apes:

. . . I do not believe that any human infant or child, unprotected by adults of its own species, could survive a fortnight in such an African environment as I describe in the Tarzan stories, and if he did, he would develop into a cunning, cowardly beast, as he would have to spend most of his waking hours fleeing for his life. He would be under-developed from lack of proper and sufficient nourishment, from exposure to the inclemencies of the weather, and from lack of sufficient restful sleep.[39]

Tarzan, Ed pointed out, "was merely an interesting experiment in the mental laboratory which we call imagination."[40]

On occasion Ed could not resist presenting a humorous picture of how Tarzan might have turned out. When questioned about his "conception of a modern person of high birth who had been brought up by apes," Ed replied:

When I first conceived the story, that is what he started out to be; but the more I thought about it, the more convinced I became that the resultant adult would be a most disagreeable person to have about the house. He would probably have B.O., Pink Toothbrush, Halitosis, and Athlete's Foot, plus a most abominable disposition; so I decided not to be honest, but to draw a character people could admire.[41]

etcalf, highly enthusiastic about "Tarzan of the Apes," had given it advance publicity in the *All-Story Magazine*, and at the same time, had extended an apology to Ed for the unfortunate change in his pen name. In the "Table-Talk" column of September 1912 a bold heading reported, "Blind Blunders of an Editor," and beneath it was written Metcalf's "confession," which he introduced with the parenthetical statement, "If it surprises you to learn that editors can make mistakes, we might say that once we, too, believed they were infallible, but that was a long, long time ago." He supplied the details:

When the manuscript of "Under the Moons of Mars" came to us, the name signed was Normal (with an "l") Bean. When we came to run the story — from enthusiasm or some other worthy sentiment — we beefed it and called the author Norman (with an "n") Bean.

The editor noted that in spite of the mistake, "Mr. Bean was very decent to us," adding, "then we found out that his real name wasn't Bean, anyway." Metcalf continued:

Really he is Edgar Rice Burroughs, and he does some important stunt or other in Chicago, using the name Bean [an obviously confused statement]. *Considering the general mess we made of his* nom-de-plume, *it has been decided by all hands to return to his real name....*

The forthcoming appearance of "Tarzan of the Apes" in the next issue of *All-Story* was heralded in glowing phrases:

If you will stop and realize how many thousands of stories an editor has to read, day in, day out, you will be impressed when we tell you that we read this yarn at one sitting and had the time of our young lives. It is the most exciting story we

have seen in a blue moon, and about as original as they make 'em.

Through a series of catastrophes an English baby boy is kidnaped by a tribe of huge anthropoid apes. He grows up among them. The fact that he is a reasoning animal makes a difference in his development, and then the forces of civilization obtrude. Zowie! but things happen!

The October *All-Story* featured "Tarzan of the Apes, A Romance of the Jungle," with the cover illustration by Clinton Pettee showing Tarzan in deadly battle with a lion. He is astride the animal's back, his legs clamped vise-like, and has one powerful arm around the lion's throat. Its head jerked back, the lion is rearing; Tarzan has a long knife upraised, ready to plunge it downward. The story brought a flood of approving letters from excited readers. Among them was, however, at least one who struck a sour note. He was a reader who demanded accuracy and authenticity, and he may have been the first to note the existence of an animal character who was out of context. In the "Table-Talk" of December 1912, "G.T.M." of Springfield, Massachusetts, launched a spirited controversy:

In "Tarzan of the Apes" the author stumbled into what has often proved an effective trap for the unwary. One of his principal quadruped characters is Sabor, the tiger, who is thoughtlessly placed on the continent of Africa, where he does not belong.

The tiger is not and never has been included in the fauna of the African continent. Neither history, science, nor the personal experience of the explorer or hunter records the tiger as being indigenous to Africa.

The newspaper cartoonists blundered into the same pitfall at the time of Colonel Roosevelt's hunting trip, and the surprising thing is that no one seemed to care enough about the matter to correct them.

Ed was mortified over his blunder, realizing he should have done his research more carefully. Other letters followed, with a number of readers hastening to defend Ed's creation of

Cover of All-Story Magazine, October 1912; first publication of "Tarzan."

Sabor the tiger. Several produced convincing data:

It seems to me that it is about time that some one came to the rescue of our friend Mr. Burroughs and his much belabored African tiger, "Sabor."

. . . I quote from the introduction to Mr. Jekyll's very interesting book, "Jamaican Song and Story."

"All over South Africa leopards are called 'tigers' by Dutch, English and Germans. 'Tiger' is used in the same sense in German Kamerun and probably elsewhere in West Africa.[42]

The writer directed scathing comment at those who had complained: "Mr. Burroughs undoubtedly knows all this, but probably like some others of us, he is too busy wearing out the point of his fountain-pen to start a primary school class 'for critics only.' " At the end of the letter the writer proposed a solution, tongue-in-cheek, to the entire problem: ". . . why doesn't Mr. Burroughs gather together all his 'tiger' critics in that little hut on the edge of the African jungle, get old 'Sabor' headed in the right direction, and — let go of his tail?"

A second letter in "Table-Talk" contained other facts to support Ed's use of the word "tiger." The writer, from Cape Town, South Africa, stated:

From the Cape to the Zambezi you can scarcely pick up a newspaper but the chances are that a record is there of a "tiger" hunt, or of a "tiger" having destroyed sheep, et cetera.

Colonials all call it a "tiger" over here; scientifically it may be known as a leopard or a panther, but to South Africans — Dutch or English speaking — it is a tiger.[43]

These letters mention the South African custom in using the word "tiger" rather generally and loosely to apply to a number of members of the cat family. But Ed unfortunately described Sabor as a tiger in his magazine story, referring to the animal's "beautiful skin of black and yellow." He made careful corrections and deletions before the book was published. Sabor received both a new gender and identity; the

male tiger became a female — now Sabor the lioness. Her skin was merely described as beautiful, with the colors "black and yellow" omitted.

In one other important respect Sabor, as a representative of the tigers, received a character change and an exoneration. The magazine story had stated, "Sabor, the tiger, alone of all the jungle folk, tortured his prey." In the book version this calumny against the race of tigers was rectified. The bloodthirsty villain became Sheeta the leopard. Ed made certain that the tiger never again appeared in his African stories.

The publication of "Tarzan of the Apes" brought an admiring letter from Ed's old friend Bert Weston, who on September 28, 1912, wrote:

I was in the western part of the state about 2 wks ago, and thinking that I was going to have 3 hrs of day train with nothing to do, bought an All Story, *having got the habit from the Moons of Mars. It was a very pleasant shock to find that that naked young hero of a Lion-Killer on the cover was a child of your fertile brain. That is a great tale. Better I think than the Moons. . . . I hope that you combed them down good and strong for the sous for that tale, and that you are very prosperous and that your literary prosperity has only commenced. . . .*

In a previous letter of March 16, Weston had commented about "Under the Moons of Mars," making it clear that his assumptions about Ed's writing had changed after he read the story:

. . . Speaking further of babies, that is a very ingenious idea to have the Martians lay eggs and hatch them. . . . I am fain to confess that the style of your tale (Moons of Mars) was very surprising to me. I had an idea someway that your stories would be like your drawings. This one isn't. You are mighty versatile, and this is mightily to your credit. . . .

Among the many letters of praise for "Tarzan of the Apes" were those including comments on Ed's "unfinished" ending — his scheme of deserting the reader in the midst of unresolved suspense. The readers who had expressed dismay over the same type of ending in "Under the

Moons of Mars" now believed they were confronted with an author who was going to make it a habit. Remarks ranged from humorous jibes and entreaties for a sequel to indignant or even disgusted statements about a writer who would dare construct disappointing endings of this nature.[44]

In "Under the Moons of Mars" Ed's ending device, somewhat different, had been a real cliff-hanger: John Carter sinks unconscious before the opening door of the atmosphere plant and awakens in the cave on the planet Earth; both he and the reader are left in anxiety and doubt concerning Mars' survival. Here, Ed's suspenseful ending, worked out with some hesitation, was a daring device — in every sense an inspiration.[45] (Actually, it was in the best tradition of the old-time storyteller who kept his circle of eager listeners on tenterhooks awaiting the next episode.)

After the success of his Mars story Ed was quite willing to undertake a sequel. In response to Metcalf's suggestion that he write another John Carter romance, he replied, "I have had in mind a sequel to the Martian story. . . ."[46] This, he made plain, would be his next task upon the completion of "Tarzan." From his statements it would appear likely that in "Under the Moons of Mars" Ed was planning a sequel at the time he created his ending.

However, with "Tarzan of the Apes," he exhibited an uncertainty. While dangling the possibility of a sequel before the tantalized reader, Ed was really dubious, not at all convinced that it would be either desirable or successful. Metcalf had first brought the matter up, mentioning the approving letters being received at *All-Story*. He added a qualifying remark, gleefully predicting Ed's response, ". . . everyone has cursed out the end, which, of course will do your soul good," and continued, "Most everybody now is talking about a sequel."[47] Admitting he had no definite suggestion, Metcalf wrote, ". . . but the jungle is still there and I suppose that Tarzan having become generally disgusted with human nature could go back and try to lord it once more over the apes. Keep your hyperbolic imagination at work on this and see if you can do anything."[48]

Ed, in his answer to Metcalf, displayed the attitude of a man seeking to be persuaded: "About a sequel to Tarzan. Candidly I don't think it would be a go, although I have a really bully foundation in mind for one. These sequel things usually fall flat. I'll be glad to think it over, however, and later if you decide that it will be wise to try it I'll tackle it. . . ."[49] Some of this hesitancy was to b expected with a beginning writer. But the frustrating failure of "The Outlaw of Torn" was still affecting him. Despite a second sale, Burroughs was wary; he would not be lured by glittering visions of the future. Nevertheless, stubborn reserves of confidence that neither doubt nor caution could destroy remained within him. The very fact that he could be considering a sequel was in itself an indication of his faith in his ability.

He sought encouragement. On October 2 he wrote, "About a score of readers have threatened my life unless I promised a sequel to Tarzan — shall I?" Metcalf's response was tactfully affirmative:

I have been thinking over the necessity of a sequel to "Tarzan" and it certainly looks as though we ought to have one, don't you think so? Of course, as you say, sequels are never quite as good as the originals, but with such a howling mob demanding further adventures of your young hero, it looks to me as though it would be a very good move to bring him again to the notice of the great public.[50]

Metcalf, meanwhile, found it good business practice to keep his readers in a state of anticipation through regular comments about a possible sequel. These appeared in consecutive issues of *All-Story* in the "Table-Talk" section:

. . . Lots of folks don't seem to like the finish and are sitting round and barking for a sequel.

It would seem that no editorial comment were necessary. But we are tempted to say — oh, why should we? [A note about Ed's letter and his query about a sequel follows.]

[December 1912]

139

August 20, 1913.

Dear Sir:

        We are returning under separate
cover The All-Story magazine (Oct.1912)
containing your story, "Tarzan of the Apes."
        We have given the work careful con-
sideration and while interesting we find
it does not fit in with our plans for the
present year.
        Thanking you for submitting the story
to us, we are

                    Yours very truly,
                        Rand McNally & Co.
                            H.

Mr. Edgar Rice Burroughs,
    2008 Park Avenue,
    Chicago.

Letter of rejection typical of those ERB received from book publishers regarding "Tarzan of the Apes."

We have a good deal of correspondence with Mr. Burroughs in re a follow-up story for Tarzan.

We believe we can persuade Mr. Burroughs to frame up a few more stunts for Tarzan.
                            [*January 1913*]

Letters still come in about "Tarzan." Also about the proposed sequel. We have done our best with Mr. Burroughs, and now we can only lie down and wait. He is a good-humored man, however, and we should not be surprised if at some odd moment he would flash something on us.
                            [*February 1913*]

The pleas and demands of the readers, and Metcalf's urgings, had little effect upon Ed's plans. His imagination and pen were working at high speed on the project he had given priority — a sequel to "Under the Moons of Mars." (On October 2, 1912, he completed the story, "The Gods of Mars," and sent it to Metcalf.)

But it was evident that in the midst of all this furious writing, the next step, a most important one, had already occurred to him. "Am glad your readers liked Tarzan," he had remarked to Metcalf. "One of them wrote me a very nice letter. In this connection I am wondering if you destroy letters of this kind when you are through with them. If so might I have them instead?"[51] Considered practically and from a businessman's viewpoint, the letters were forms of references or testimonials. He explained, "I have an idea that I could show them to publishers to whom I might wish to submit my Mss for the Book part of it. . . ." Then he joked with Metcalf about the printed confession that "editors can make mistakes." Ed wrote, "Let me thank you for the very acceptable bull con you handed me via the Table Talks — you are a real artist."[52]

His mind made up, on October 5, 1912, he chose A. C. McClurg & Company, Chicago publishers, for his first inquiry. The letter in his precise business style was written from 2008 Park Avenue:

Herewith magazine copy of a story, Tarzan of the Apes, which I submit for your consideration.

I have received several letters from readers in different parts of the country indicating that the story made a hit with them at least, and the Editor of All Story writes me that the magazine has had a great quantity of laudatory letters relative to this story.

These facts suggested that if published in book form the story might be successful.

The acknowledgement of the receipt of his letter and the magazine copy came three days later, bearing a signature that would become quite familiar to Ed Burroughs in the future — that of editor Joseph Bray. On October 31 a full response followed; the letter offered no concrete evaluation of the story, contenting itself with praise — and polite rejection:

You have written a very exciting yarn in "Tarzan of the Apes" and we think it deserved all the success you say it had as a Magazine story.

Although there are many points in its favor and it is quite possible that it might sell fairly well in book form, yet we are unable to convince ourselves altogether of its availability.

We hope to have the priviledge of seeing more of your work....

The perfunctory wording of the letter, its tone of kindly encouragement to a writer assumed to be a novice, and its choice of so vague a term as "availability" as an excuse for rejection, make clear that Bray was decidedly unimpressed by both the story and Ed's sales points.

Undiscouraged, Ed expanded his letter to include more details of the popularity of "Tarzan of the Apes" with *All-Story* readers. He explained that the approving comments came not only from the United States, but from Panama, Canada, and England, thus demonstrating that "the story appealed to sufficiently widely distributed and varied classes of readers to warrant the belief that it would make a successful book." He offered to send the readers' letters to the book publisher.

On November 3, 1912, he sent this form, with a copy of the magazine, to The Bobbs-Merrill Company of Indianapolis, Indiana, and Reilly & Britton of 1006-8 South Michigan Avenue in Chicago. Bobbs-Merrill's rejection, received about two weeks later, resembled the ones sent automatically to thousands of aspiring authors:

We are sorry to have to send you an adverse decision in regard to the manuscript, Tarzan of the Apes, but after careful consideration on the part of our editorial readers, we can not feel that it makes a place for itself on our list.

We are grateful for the privilege of seeing this story and only regret that we have not more favorable news to send you....[53]

The firm of Reilly & Britton, early in 1913, was still struggling to arrive at a decision. The same letter, sent to Dodd, Mead and Company in New York, brought a note of rejection.[54]

At this stage Ed wrote again to the man he idolized, his old commandant of Michigan Military Academy. On January 15, 1913, in a letter to Charles King at Milwaukee, Wisconsin, he asked the general for advice; Ed, optimistic, chose to believe that Reilly & Britton's delay was a good sign, an indication that a book contract might be in the offing. To the general he explained, "I am threatened with a book, and as it is my first I want to ask what royalty I should expect, or if I sold the book rights, about what would be a fair cash price?"

He mentioned his sales of "three short novels" to the Munsey Company, adding, "This of course has been in addition to my regular work." In connection with Reilly & Britton he noted that he had seen Reilly that day, and "he seems very keen for the story. From what he said I think they will make me a proposition shortly, and of course I should like to know what I am talking about when they do — *if* they do." He sent Charles King a copy of *Tarzan of the Apes*.[55]

Ed's hopes were not to be realized — his persistent search for a publisher would not yet be successful. The debut of "Tarzan" in book form was still more than a year away.

New terms, names, characters, places etc mentioned in 2nd John Carter Mss

Old Ben or Uncle Ben - the writer's body servant (colored)

Holy Therns - a martian religious cult.

Otz Mountains - surrounding the Valley Dor and the Lost Sea of Korus.

plant men of Barsoom - a strange race inhabiting the Valley Dor.

Golden Cliffs - walls of Otz mountains facing the Valley Dor.

Issus - Goddess of Death, whose abode is upon the banks of the Lost Sea

    of Korus.

banth - Barsoomian lion -see Chap III pg 36 orig mss
silian - slimy reptiles inhabiting the sea of Korus
Sator Throg - a Holy Thern of the Tenth Cycle 55
Tenth Cycle - a sphere or plane of eminence among the holy therns 55
Thuvia - a red Martian girl - prisoner of the holy therns 55
Father of Therns - 55
Matai Shang, Father of Therns - 55
thewian - chief of the Lesser Therns 57
Black Pirates of Barsoom 63
pimalia - a gorgeous flowering plant 65
Dator- Chief or Prince among the First Born 70
First Born - black race - the Black Pirates
Phaidor - daughter of Matai Shang
hekkador - title of Father of Therns
Thuria - the nearer moon
skeel - a Martian hard wood 86
sorapus (same) 86
Xodar - Dator among the First Born
Shador - island in Omean
Omean - the buried sea
Thurid - another black Dator 107
Thabis - Issus' chief 123
Zithad - another Dator 134
Torith - officer of the guards at submarine pool
Yersted - commander of sub-marine
Tan Gama - Warhoon warrior
Kab Kadja - Jeddak of the Warhoons of the South 159
Hor Vastus - padwar in navy of Helium 174
Xavarian - a Helium war ship
Zat Arrras - Jed of Zodanga
Temple of Reward - 182
Avenue of Ancestors 183
Gate of Jeddaks 183
tal - second)
zat - minute) see table
zode - hour)
Aisle of Hope
Throne of Righteousness
Pedestal of Truth 186
Ptarth - Thuvia's country
Hastor - a city of Helium 198
Parthak - the Zodangan who brought food to Carter in the pits of Zat Arrras 206
dwar - captain
utan - a company of 100 men (military)
Gur Tus - dwar of 10th Utan 231
Djor Kantos - son of Kantos Kan 231

1st zode 6 am (accurate
2 —— 8:24 am
3 —— 10:48
4 —— 1:12 Pm
5 —— 3:36
6 —— 6:00
7 —— 8:24
8 — 10:48
9 — 1:12 am
10 — 3:36 am

TABLE of TIME (MARTIAN)
200 tals = 1 xat - 2 mines 57.24 s
50 xats - 1 zode
67 PADANS = 1 TEEAN (month)   10 zodes - 1 PADAN (DAY)
10 TEEANS = 1 ORD (YEAR)   1 revolution of
Mars upon its axis
10 zodes - 88,620 Earth seconds
1,477 " minutes
24 hrs 37 min Earth time
1 zode = 2 hrs 27 min 42 sec or 2.46

1 xat = 2 min 57.3 sec

686 days = 1 Martian Year (Earth
670 " = 1
669 " in
Century and in
divisible by 4
each century) there is also
necessary an additional correction

9

THE PROLIFIC PERIOD

In the fall of 1912, encouraged by Metcalf's acceptance of three of his stories, Ed embarked with determination upon a writing schedule that would demonstrate his ability to produce a variety of works in an unbelievably short period. Metcalf, by now convinced of Ed's talent, had suggested the sequel which became "The Gods of Mars" — a story idea which appears to have stimulated Ed's imagination. On March 4, 1912, Metcalf's letter contained this idea:

. . . I was wondering if you could not write another romance about John Carter, introducing the Valley Dorr, the River Iss and the Sea of Korus, or those other semi-religious semi-mystical regions which you mentioned, but I believe never used in "Under the Moons of Mars." You could pretend that the adventures you would be writing about in this romance occurred between the time of Carter's marriage to the Martian Princess and the catastrophe you relate in the serial now running in The All-Story.

Metcalf's view of the logical theme for the new work, proceeding naturally from Ed's references in "Under the Moons of Mars," was one that may have already occurred to Ed — the false religion of the Martians. Metcalf explained:

Carter might get into some terrific rows, apropos of religion, with some of the Martian priests. You might cook up some kind of a story showing that all this section of Mars where Carter finally lands is governed by a hierarchy of dissolute religionists, and Carter might go to work and smash the superstition into a thousand pieces and readjust the running of the country.

Metcalf was obviously intrigued by Ed's geographical inventions: "The mystical appeal of all these rivers, valleys and seas, which you mentioned only casually in 'Under the Moons of Mars' I believe would be very strong. . . ."

During this period Ed had been involved with his first revision of "The Outlaw of Torn";

143

his efforts to persuade Metcalf to accept the story would continue until the end of 1912. But that was only a small portion of his writing. In response to Metcalf's request for a "Mars" sequel, he had informed the editor that the Tarzan story was in progress — "another of the 'improbable' variety of tale." Ed wrote, ". . . if I ever finish it I shall see what I can do in the way of a John Carter sequel." "Tarzan of the Apes," of course, was completed by the end of June.

The astonishing writing pace continued. On September 20 he reported, "Speaking of sequels. I have the second John Carter tale nearly completed. I can't tell you anything about it because I am no judge. I think it will prove as readable as the first."[1]

Perhaps still meditating over Metcalf's original suggestion for an ending that led to the death of the Martian Princess, Ed added, "I doubt if I can kill Dejah Thoris though." He revealed his basic sentimentality, in contradiction to the stoical attitude and dollars-and-cents practicality he liked to assume, by stating, "You know I told you that I was purely mercenary insofar as my work is concerned, but when it comes to the characters I find that I develop a real affection for them — funny, isn't it?"

With its theme established, the new Martian work could have only one title — "The Gods of Mars." In its finished form, sent to Metcalf on October 2, Ed proved again the power of his imaginative vision to project far beyond Metcalf's basic idea. To him the entire Martian religion became a sham, a hoax created for the gratification of sadistic gods — a hoax accepted with blind devotion by all the races of Mars. Around this concept Ed devised a remarkable structure, a stratum of Martian life that included the plant men, the great white apes, the Holy Therns, and the black men. Again, he developed his geographical inventions, the River Iss, Valley Dorr, Lost Sea of Korus, mountains and valley of Otz, and Sea of Omean. The elements of conflict and suspense, which Ed instinctively understood as vital to any story, are at once apparent, not only in John Carter's opposition to the Martian religion, but in the hostility between the various races.

In "The Gods of Mars" the Burroughs device of a foreword in which he establishes the personal relationship to "Uncle Jack" (John Carter) is again used, with the story opening after a lapse of twelve years. Carter returns to earth, and at a meeting with his nephew informs him that he now has learned the secret of journeying through space between the two planets. In presenting the written story of his adventures, he says, "Give them what you wish of it, what you think will not harm them, but do not feel aggrieved if they laugh at you."

Carter implies that this will be his last visit to the earth, stating, "I doubt that I shall ever again leave the dying world that is my life." Ed, as his nephew, comments, "I have never seen Captain John Carter, of Virginia, since." But in later works, Ed, as the author, found the original situation too tempting to resist, and in *The Chessmen of Mars* (1922) and *The Swords of Mars* (1934) uncle and nephew meet once more on earth. Ed revives the foreword (or prelude) that he has not used in intervening Mars novels.

In creating a super-race, the First Born of Barsoom (Mars), Ed chose the black men. This may have been his way of satirizing the earthly white man's treatment of the Negro as he had done in his parody of Kipling's poem.[2] In "The Gods of Mars" Xodar, a black man, explains proudly to John Carter:

The First Born of Barsoom are the race of black men of which I am a Dator, or, as the lesser Barsoomians would say, Prince. My race is the oldest on the planet. We trace our lineage, unbroken, directly to the Tree of Life which flourished in the centre of the Valley Dorr twenty-three million years ago.

Ed's evolutionary scheme for the development of the First Born and the lesser races of Mars is both ingenious and amusing. The buds on The Tree of Life were like large nuts, about a foot in diameter, and divided into four sections. "In one section grew the plant man, in another a sixteen-legged worm, in the third the progenitor of the white ape and in the fourth

144

the primaeval black man of Barsoom." When the buds burst, the plant man remained attached to his stem, but the other three sections fell to the ground. The "imprisoned occupants," unsuccessful in their attempts to escape, had to content themselves, through countless ages, with merely hopping about in their shells. It was the black man, however, whose initiative and adventurous spirit led to the freeing of the "imprisoned occupants":

Countless billions died before the first black man broke through his prison walls into the light of day. Prompted by curiosity, he broke open other shells and the peopling of Barsoom commenced.

Ed has Xodar explain that the black man is the only *pure* man on Mars:

The pure strain of the blood of this first black man has remained untainted by admixture with other creatures in the race of which I am a member; but from the sixteen-legged worm, the first ape, and renegade black man has sprung every other form of animal life on Barsoom.

In a later section of "The Gods of Mars" the black men are described as a type of aristocracy: "We are a non-productive race, priding ourselves upon our non-productiveness. It is criminal for a First Born to labour or invent. That is the work of the lower orders, who live merely that the First Born may enjoy long lives of luxury and idleness."

Ed had not as yet finished with his structuring of the races. The First Born, who live in an inner world beneath the surface of Mars, maintain a system of slavery. "The places of the outer world and the temples of the therns have been robbed of their princesses and goddesses that the blacks might have their slaves." Ed goes into detail:

The First Born are all "noble." There is no peasantry among them. Even the lowest soldier is a god, and has his slaves to wait upon him.
The First Born do no work. The men fight — that is a sacred privilege and duty; to fight and die for Issus. The women do nothing, ab-
solutely nothing. Slaves wash them, slaves dress them, slaves feed them. . . .

Other than the races of the First Born and therns, Ed, in "The Gods of Mars," created the plant men who learned to detach themselves from The Tree of Life before it died. They are bisexual like true plants and move about guided purely by instinct: ". . . The brain of a plant man is but a trifle larger than the end of your smallest finger." Curiously, the plant men's diet consists of both vegetation and the blood of animals: ". . . Their brain is just large enough to direct their movements in the direction of food, and to translate the food sensations which are carried to it from their eyes and ears. They have no sense of self-preservation and so are entirely without fear in the face of danger. That is why they are such terrible antagonists in combat."

Ed's invention of the Martian gods included the supreme deity, Issus. When John Carter is commanded to turn and gaze upon the "holy vision" of Issus' "radiant face," the sight is not at all what he had anticipated:

On this bench, or throne, squatted a female black. She was evidently very old. Not a hair remained upon her wrinkled skull. With the exception of two yellow fangs she was entirely toothless. On either side of her thin, hawklike nose her eyes burned from the depths of horribly sunken sockets. The skin of her face was seamed and creased with a million deepcut furrows. Her body was as wrinkled as her face, and as repulsive.
Emaciated arms and legs attached to a torso which seemed to be mostly distorted abdomen completed the "holy vision of her radiant beauty."

The name Issus obviously calls to mind the Egyptian diety Isis, also worshipped by the Greeks and Romans. (Ed's acquaintance with mythology has been previously mentioned. His "Lost Sea of Korus" may have resulted from some recollection of the son of Isis, by coincidence named Horus.)

Xodar, the First Born, convinced at last that he has been deceived, gives an evaluation of the false religion that may approximate Ed's philosophy:

The whole fabric of our religion is based upon superstitious belief in lies that have been foisted upon us for ages by those directly above us, to whose personal profit and aggrandizement it was to have us continue to believe as they wished us to believe.

Beyond the exciting plot and the invention of a complex civilization, Ed displayed an ability for vivid description; that he was able to construct colorful passages in a story written so quickly is quite remarkable. A number of these depict the bizarre Martian environment:

There is no twilight on Mars. When the great orb of day disappears beneath the horizon the effect is precisely as that of the extinguishing of a single lamp within a chamber. From brilliant light you are plunged without warning into utter darkness. Then the moons come; the mysterious, magic moons of Mars, hurtling like monster meteors low across the face of the planet.

His imaginative use of military tactics, based possibly upon his readings while at military school, and his descriptions of the massive forces engaged in battle at the climax of the story give "The Gods of Mars" a convincing reality. John Carter offers precise instructions for the deployment of the huge fleet of battleships of the air:

Form the balance of the battleships into a great V with the apex pointing directly south-southeast. Order the transports, surrounded by their convoys, to follow closely in the wake of the battleships until the point of the V has entered the enemies' line, then the V must open outward at the apex, the battleships of each leg engage the enemy fiercely and drive him back to form a lane through his line into which the transports with their convoys must race at top speed that they may gain a position above the temples and gardens of the therns.

The appeals and complaints of readers concerning the Burroughs proclivity for "suspended" endings could not persuade him to change this practice. The cliff-hanger fitted his particular sense of humor, and of course it was a commercial device planned for a sequel that was certain to follow. In "The Gods of Mars" he left his readers in suspense once more, creating an ending that in a few pages turned a glorious victory into a temporary defeat.

On October 9, 1912, he inquired about the story and admitted that he had forgotten to title the chapters, a task that he dreaded.[3] Metcalf, in accepting "The Gods of Mars" two days later, made it plain that he also viewed the job "with considerable sinking of heart," and on October 15 Ed obliged by sending a list of titles for twenty-two chapters, commenting, "Never again. I'd rather write a whole story."

At this early period in his writing career Burroughs had his first disappointing and annoying experience with an editor in the matter of the promised payment. He viewed his writing, in one sense, as no different from any job that required an investment in time and work; he was insistent upon fair payment, even as a beginner. Upon receiving Metcalf's check for "The Gods of Mars," he sent a blunt complaint:

You promised me at least 1c a word and the Lord knows that is little enough, by comparison with what other magazines pay. As I remember it there were 245 pages of Mss. It averaged from what I counted 12 words to the line and 30 lines to the page. Allowing ample deduction for chapter heads and ends I figured that 86,000 words was giving you good measure, but if you will send me a check for another $100.00 I shall be satisfied.[4]

He thanked Metcalf for sending him a number of readers' letters that had been published in "Table-Talk" and added, "Don't forget the balance of the letters when you are through with them. My father and mother fairly gloat over them. I think they may help with some publisher; am going to try it anyway."

Metcalf's reply contained an apology for

having "forgotten" his word "in regard to that one cent a word stuff." He asked Ed's permission to "make up the deficit" on the next manuscript, promising to pay one cent a word for it and add $100 to that amount.

The *All-Story* for December 1912 followed its usual custom of publicizing the next issue. A box beneath the table of contents announced new works by William Patterson White and Edgar Rice Burroughs, explaining that "the latter has written a sequel to 'Under the Moons of Mars' and has called it 'The Gods of Mars.' " In "Table-Talk," Metcalf, using his informal chatty style and florid vocabulary, described Ed as "Battling" Burroughs and wrote enthusiastically of the forthcoming Martian serial: "The author's imagination again riots over the periphery of our terrestrial neighbor. Once more we play with thoats and snarks and so forth, and six-legged gents, and the scientific paraphernalia that can exist nowhere except on Mars, where, as we learn from our savants, 'they do those things better.' " Beginning in the January 1913 issue of *All-Story*, "The Gods of Mars" ran as a five-part serial and was completed in the May 1913 issue.[5]

During 1912, with all of Ed's intensive writing done in his spare time — he was still working for Shaw's *System* organization — he could not resist an experiment with another type of fiction, the short story. So far, his imagination had found its best outlet in the longer works; his interest in creating full settings, complex scientific details, and a large gallery of characters seemed to exclude him from more condensed writing. Early in the year he wrote a story of some 3,500 words titled "The Avenger," and followed this in the fall with "For the Fool's Mother," of about the same length and written in only two days. Ed, probably having become aware of the short story market, chose to avoid his fantasy themes and attempt to construct "down-to-earth" plots.

However, in "The Avenger" he devises a plot which at its climax becomes grim and repellent, and the actions of the main character have not been developed so as to make them logical or convincing.

In February 1912, probably for the first time, "The Avenger" was submitted to The Associated Sunday Magazines, a group that handled a feature section for various newspapers. An editor's letter of February 20 commented, " 'The Avenger' is both interesting and strong, but too gruesome to make a commendable feature of our Sunday Magazine. . . ." Sent out later in the year, the story was again rejected.[6]

Ed's second attempt at short story writing, a Western drama titled "For the Fool's Mother," was completed on October 5, 1912.[7] In a letter to Donald Kennicott of the Story-Press Corporation, Ed, on October 6, appeared undecided about the title, referring to his submission as "For the Mother of a Fool, or, For a Fool's Mother." He stated, "I have in mind a series of short stories, each complete in itself, with The Prospector as the principal character. I hope that you find this one in good form. . . ."

"For the Fool's Mother" is the first of Ed's stories to make actual reference to persons he had known, in this case to acquaintances of his Idaho cattle ranch days.[8]

Once more Ed returns to a feature he had reserved for several of his heroic characters. The Prospector is described as "straight, grey-eyed," and having "keen grey eyes"; of course the picture is familiar, recalling John Carter's "keen grey eyes," "undimmed" by time, and the steely *gray* eyes of Tarzan, Lord *Grey*stoke.[9]

In this period of feverish writing Burroughs was stretching his imagination to devise a plot for his sequel to *Tarzan of the Apes*. Again, a germ of the idea came from Metcalf, who on October 11, 1912, wrote:

I have been wondering whether it would not be possible to have him (Tarzan) after receiving his congé from the girl, make a stagger at being highly civilized in some effete metropolis, like London, Paris or New York, where he very quickly finds the alleged diversions of civilization to be only as ashes in his mouth.

After this, Metcalf suggested, Tarzan then returns to the jungle and tries unsuccessfully to find happiness there. As a result of frustration, he becomes erratic, even "develops extreme cruelty and runs the gamut of doing all kinds of almost insane things with the various animals and also with the blacks." Metcalf conceived of the idea of introducing a young woman who had been "marooned in the wilderness" and like Tarzan, had grown up to be a savage.

Apologetically, Metcalf remarked, "I don't offer this line of guff as anything more than a suggestion. It may be that you may find in it something which your superior ability might whip into shape. . . ."

On October 30 Ed submitted a rough outline of his sequel. Metcalf's idea about "some effete metropolis" had evidently taken root, for Ed referred to his sequel as "Monsieur Tarzan," a name he had already used in *Tarzan of the Apes,* and indicated that some of the action would take place in Paris. He had shown an interest in France and the French language in *Tarzan.* Lord Greystoke's diary, the only book Tarzan had been unable to read, was written in French. Lieutenant D'Arnot, of course, is given an important role, and, as a result, Tarzan's first spoken language is French; under D'Arnot's tutelage he takes on the polish of a French gentleman, and at a later period the full name on his personal card is *M. Jean C. Tarzan.*[10]

Concerning Ed's outline of the sequel, Metcalf was critical of the shipwreck or mutiny incidents. In "Tarzan" Ed had twice devised mutinies to get his characters to an African shore. Now he proposed in his latest work to have two more similar incidents, one centered about Tarzan and Hazel Strong, and the other about Jane and Clayton. Metcalf referred tactfully to this device as being "overdone."[11]

Another of Ed's ideas received a firm rejection. "I am afraid that I must definitely taboo your suggestion concerning the cannibalism of the people in the boat where Jane and Clayton are," Metcalf wrote. "Really, now, that is going a little bit too far."[12] Worried that Ed was not giving the right emphasis to the "jungle" aspects

of his sequel, Metcalf sent a follow-up letter with detailed instructions. He noted that the most popular incidents were those involving Tarzan's jungle adventures and commented, ". . . you ought to have no more actual civilization in the new story than you had in the old," adding farther on, ". . . the best thing to do would be to exactly reverse the main thread of the first story and instead of having the animal become civilized, have your plot deal very largely with the unhappy and necessarily unsatisfactory attempts of Tarzan to renounce his lately won civilization."[13]

Ed was quick to agree with Metcalf's analysis and on December 5 offered an outline of the sequel that was far more precise and detailed than his previous one. His intention was to develop one of his favorite ideas — an encounter with a "strange race" who inhabit the heart of Africa, living in the ruins of a former great city.[14]

At the close of the letter he wrote, "I have two other bully stories mulling around in my head. One of them has possibilities far beyond any I have yet written — I don't mean literary possibilities, but damphool possibilities. It will be based on an experiment in biology the result of which will be a real man and a real woman — not monsters. I have it practically all planned out in my head."[15]

Metcalf had continued to send him the readers' letters that poured in, most of them containing comments about "Tarzan." Concerning these, the editor remarked, "They come in so often and ask for more of your work that I am tempted to believe we had better call the magazine the 'All-Burroughs Magazine.' "[16]

The letters, especially those with protests about Ed's unfinished ending to "Tarzan," amused him and also stimulated the mischievous side of his nature. He viewed them with glee as a challenge for further teasing or tantalizing of the impatient readers. On December 20 he wrote:

There is so much reference to the "punk ending" that I am inclined to think that that is the very feature of the story that really clinched their interest. For two cents I'd give them another surprise in the sequel. I have a bully little Arab girl, daughter of a sheik, who is the only logical mate for a savage like Tarzan. I am just "thinking," however, and probably shall not do it, though it would be quite artistic.

He reported to Metcalf that the sequel was "progressing finely" and would soon be finished: "The result is that I am working about 25 hours a day, approximately."[17]

Through December 1912 and the first part of January Ed had worked hard on the long sequel. With its completion on January 8 he remained uncertain about the title. In his correspondence with Metcalf he had called the manuscript "Monsieur Tarzan"; now he titled it "The Ape-Man."[18] To the editor a day later he wrote, "The Ape-Man goes forward to you by express tomorrow. As you will see I have changed the name from what I at first purposed calling it — I never did like the other." He was not at all reticent about reminding Metcalf of the rates he had promised to pay and of the money that was still owed him from "The Gods of Mars."

He spoke of another "bully" letter he had received, one that praised "Tarzan" highly, and he commented, "Mrs. B. says I never will write another such story — cheerful, isn't it, for one who has only just started?"

In the remainder of the letter Ed turned to a problem which, even at this early period, loomed large in his mind and would contribute to the feeling of inadequacy that plagued him throughout his writing career. Oversensitive about what he conceived to be his deficiencies in English grammar, he was inclined to view this supposed weakness as a serious handicap to his writing. To Metcalf he wrote, "That reminds me of something that I have wanted to ask you about a number of times — I refer to my English. I imagine it is pretty rotten, and I wish that you would tell me frankly if you agree with me."

Ed then gave a resumé of what had hap-

pened in his school days; this was a topic that he would discuss again, often jokingly, in the future. The very fact that it kept recurring, even with a humorous emphasis, is an indication that it troubled him.

I never studied English grammar but a month in my life — while I was cramming for West Point. I was taken out of public school before I got that far, and sent to a private school here — the old Harvard School on Indiana avenue; you may recall it — where they had a theory that a boy should learn Greek and Latin grammar before he took up English grammar. Then before I got to English grammar I was sent to Andover, where I was supposed to have had English before I came, and started in on Greek and Latin again.

As a result, Ed noted, he had studied Latin for eight years and had never learned English. He described this process as "my notion of a bum way to educate a boy" and then inquired, "I have been thinking of getting hold of an English tutor. What do you think about it?"[19]

Metcalf, who could see no reason for Ed's concern, responded that there was nothing wrong with Ed's grammar; he didn't think it was worthwhile for Ed to find a tutor, stating, ". . . you did become a little too involved every once in a while when you tried to use archaic terms in 'The Outlaw of Torn,' but otherwise —no." He suggested that if Ed were to get a good rhetoric "like Sherman Adam Hill's," this might prove valuable; but he didn't believe that "anything more serious" was necessary.[20]

Ed found Metcalf's answer reassuring. He had expected that the editor's opinion "would not be colored by any fear of offending." . . noting that a person naturally assumes his English to be good, Ed remarked, ". . . my trouble is that I don't *know*." In the same letter he sought Metcalf's advice about possible dealings with a book publisher; it appeared that a firm was about to offer him a contract for "Tarzan of the Apes." The firm was Reilly & Britton in Chicago, and Ed had just stopped into their offices to deliver some readers' letters.[21] Metcalf, on January 17, gave him information about royalties and publishers' contracts, but said nothing about the "Tarzan" sequel. Ed, who had previously described himself as a "bum waiter," could contain himself no longer. "Have you finished The Ape-Man?" he queried. "How do you like it? I am rapidly choking to death with curiosity."[22]

The bad news — what might have been described as a prelude to a rejection — came a few days later. On January 22 Metcalf wrote, ". . . I have read a great deal of 'The Ape-man' and I am very sorry to say that I am pretty doubtful so far. What I feel more than anything else is a kind of lack of balance. . . ." Ed was stunned. He had felt more certain of acceptance of "The Ape-Man" than anything else he had previously submitted. The editor's disapproval, equivalent to outright rejection, was sufficient to thrust him into the deepest gloom and depression. In his letter of January 24 his emotions vary from frustration and pessimism about the future to bitterness and self-condemnation:

Sorry you don't like the Ape-Man. I put a lot of work on it. Mapped it out carefully so that I was quite sure that it would be smooth and consistent. You approved of the plans, and I did not deviate from them except in such minor details as seemed necessary. I don't understand what you mean by "lack of balance".

There is so much uncertainty about the writing game — the constant feeling, for me at least, that I don't know how my stuff is going to hit you that I am entirely discouraged. I certainly can not afford to put months of work into a story thinking it the best work that I had ever done only to find that it doesn't connect. I can make money easier some other way.

In continuing, he referred to a letter from John S. Phillips of *The American Magazine* expressing interest in his work. Ed commented gloomily, "I presume that if I worked a couple of months on something for him he would come back with the 'not convincing' or 'lack of balance' dose." He concluded by blaming himself and rejecting the entire writing game:

That's the trouble, I can't tell that what I am writing is what the other fellow wants. I prob-ably lack balance myself — a well balanced mind would not turn out my kind of stuff. As long as I can't market it as it comes out it is altogether too much of a gamble, so I think I'll chuck it.

As though the matter were all settled and his writing days were ended, Burroughs wrote in ironic humor, "Let me thank you once again for your many courtesies during the period of my incursion into litrachoor."[23]

The letter of John S. Phillips, Editor of *American Magazine*, dated January 21, had been quite complimentary; Ed was offered an opportunity in a publication of prestige whose payment rates were much higher than *All-Story*: "I have been interested for a long time in your stories. If you ever write any short stories or a short novelette of anywhere from 12 to 30,000 words. . . . You have a wonderful imagination. I would like to get some of it into the American magazine."

Ed of course hastened to reply to him. Meanwhile, Metcalf had sent a final rejection of "The Ape-Man," stating that after careful consideration he was "very much afraid" that he could not use it. "This makes me feel very bad," he wrote, "because of course I was very keen indeed, both for your sake, for mine and for the sake of all those insistent readers who wanted a sequel to 'Tarzan'. . . ." On the same day, January 27, alarmed by Ed's complete pessimism and his intention to abandon his writing career, he dispatched another letter, brief and urgent, typed in capitals: "For the love of Mike! Don't get discouraged!"

Ed may have plunged into depths of discouragement for a short period, but it was not his nature to brood over misfortune or failure. Although he possessed all of the basic uncertainties of a beginning writer, he still managed to preserve elements of confidence in his ability and judgement. To him the only response to discouragement was to find some sort of positive action. As far as he was concerned, Metcalf had been given a chance, had refused it, and now the time had come to try a new market. On January 24 he wrote to Street & Smith, describing the enthusiastic reception *Tarzan of the Apes* had received, and offering them the sequel. He added frankly, "Another consideration which prompts me to write you is that I understand that your rates are higher than those paid by the *All-Story*."

Street & Smith showed an immediate interest. Their letter of February 8, sent shortly after they received "The Ape-Man," was one that justified Ed's faith in his sequel. The price they proposed to pay, an indication of the story's value, was far in excess of any amount he had dreamed of. From A. L. Sessions, Editor of Street & Smith's *New Story Magazine,* came an offer of $1000 for first serial rights. Ed accepted two days later.

"The Return of Tarzan" opens with a skillful use of the *in medias res* device: unintroduced characters, the Count and Countess de Coude, are conversing aboard an ocean liner that is three days out from New York and en route to Paris. ERB launches immediately into the development of Paris as the "effete metropolis" that Metcalf had suggested. The story contains the first of the foreign villains to appear in Burroughs' works; in this case they are the Russians, Nikolas Rokoff and Alexis Paulvitch, villains, without any redeeming features.

The indictment of the civilized society is resumed, with Tarzan, the simple jungle creature, baffled by the peculiarities of human behavior. Later, Tarzan encounters the Arab tribal chief, Sheik Kadour ben Saden, and in the Sheik and his "stern and dignified warriors" he discovers people he deeply admires.

In a criticism of society, Ed took the occasion to express his philosophy about hunting and to reveal his intense feelings about the indiscriminate killing of animals: "The ape-man could see no sport in slaughtering the most harmless and defenseless of God's creatures for the mere pleasure of killing." Tarzan pretended to hunt, but allowed the gazelles to escape: ". . . to come out of a town filled with food to shoot down a soft-eyed, pretty gazelle — ah, that was crueller than the deliberate and cold-blooded murder of a fellow man."

In the tentative outline of "The Return of Tarzan" Metcalf had disapproved of the incident involving cannibalism. Nevertheless, Ed created a lengthy section (later titled "The Lottery of Death") in which Jane and Clayton, adrift in a lifeboat with the villainous Rokoff and sailors from the *Lady Alice,* await the prospect of cannibalism in helpless horror as each day brings it nearer. The cannibalism is fortunately averted, and the two are saved with the arrival of rain and the discovery of land.

The plot of "The Return of Tarzan" posed a special problem, previously discussed by Metcalf, in what might be described as "civilization-to-jungle logistics." The perplexing question was how to get both Tarzan and Jane back to the coast of Africa and do it without reverting to the old ship's mutiny device. A temporary sojourn in Paris was necessary, but Tarzan must be returned to his primitive surroundings. The public demanded it; the ape-man without his jungle became nonfunctional and, more importantly, unsalable. It was at once obvious that the most fertile imagination could not create anything original: Tarzan and Jane must board ships in order to arrive in Africa. The best Ed could do was to have the *Lady Alice,* carrying Jane and Clayton, wrecked in a collision with a derelict. And Tarzan, en route from Algiers to Capetown by steamer, is tumbled overboard by the villains Rokoff and Paulvitch.

Retitled "The Return of Tarzan," the story was typical, fast-moving Burroughs. According to some critics it was marred by several instances of Burroughs' use of improbable coincidences. While these coincidental devices, exhibited also in Ed's later works, are weak links in his plots and are subject to criticism, they should be viewed with a consideration of his writing practices and the philosophy he chose to adopt. Possibly, a slower writing pace might have led to longer reflection and resulted in plotting that was more ingenious and convincing. But this is idle speculation; it was not Ed's nature to write slowly. In the matter of his philosophy, or attitude toward writing, his earliest published story, "Under the Moons of Mars," provides a good basis for deductions. The opening events — John Carter's mystic, unscientific, and unexplained journey or transmigration through space — are an indication of Ed's belief that the reader of his works would be entirely capable of accepting certain events *without explanation*, especially within the context or framework that Ed constructed. The reader received sufficient reward and stimulation from the amazingly imaginative plots and settings to compensate for any lapses into repetition, contrived devices, and coincidences.

On one occasion Ed preferred to view these illogical story elements humorously, commenting to his brother Harry about the supposedly scientific environment of Mars:

I had already read Dr. Abbot's pathetic theory relative to the inhabitability of Mars. If you will kindly compare his sources of information with mine you will readily see that there is no argument whatsoever.

He guesses *that Mars is nearly one hundred degrees colder than earth; he* guesses *that there is practically no water vapor in the atmosphere; he* guesses *therefore that Mars cannot support either vegetable or animal life. On the other hand, I have not had to guess, having had presented to me in manuscript form the unquestioned evidence of an actual observer of Martian conditions.*

If this statement does not entirely clear away your doubts, permit me to very respectfully refer you to His Royal Highness, John Carter, Prince of Helium and War Lord of Mars.[24]

For "The Return of Tarzan" Ed prepared his customary work sheet; in this case he did not include a glossary but merely listed characters not appearing in "Tarzan of the Apes" and matched the chapters and their headings with the manuscript page numbers. An unusual addition, attached to the work sheet, is Ed's "Sketch Map of Eastern Algeria for use with The Ape-Man." His source was apparently a relief map of Algeria, and Ed reproduced the northeast corner of the country with its cities,

villages, and mountains. This marked the first of many maps Burroughs drew in his working notebook to assist him in his desire for accuracy, believability, and consistency in his stories. His maps of both hemispheres of Barsoom (Mars) demonstrate the care and detail involved. For some stories he sketched the bizarre animals he had created; in others he invented the languages, alphabets, and numbers. He dotted in the course of the railway from Constantine to Biskra. Towns mentioned in the story, including Bouira, Aumale, Bou Saada, and Djelfa are shown on his map, and Ed even entered the names of the hotels at which Tarzan stopped — the Hotel Grossat in Aumale and the Hotel du Petit Sahara in Bou Saada, both of these hotels marked as being in "garrison towns." With his usual meticulousness Ed noted the completion date as "Jan. 8 1913 — 9 P.M."

Metcalf, in rejecting "The Ape-Man," had commented about its "lack of balance"; his use of this vague phrase had baffled Ed, since in writing the story he had twice submitted outlines, making changes to incorporate the editor's ideas, and had finally in a letter of December 10, 1912, received Metcalf's unqualified approval of the plot.[25] However, the "lack of balance" may have been a justifiable evaluation by Metcalf if, as appears probable, he was referring to the abrupt introduction of a new setting and series of episodes late in the story. The Waziri's description of a "ruined city of gold" spurs Tarzan into a journey to Opar, but the adventures that follow, the encounters with the crooked-legged, hairy Oparians and the meeting with the Priestess La, do not relate to the theme already established. They give the appearance of a subplot, in this case one that departs too widely from the preceding actions and characters and tends to create an effect of disunity. This brief new section, inserted toward the end of the story, might better have been saved for the opening of another novel.[26]

Circumstances at home were altered during the month of February 1913 as a result of two important occurrences — one happy and the other tragic. On February 28 the Burroughs's third child, a boy, was born. There could be no doubt about the choice of a name. *John* was the name Ed most admired; he had made that clear in his creation of John Carter of Mars and in his famous John Clayton, Lord Greystoke. He had often expressed regret at not having been named John instead of Edgar. Even in later years, on January 10, 1939, he mentioned this to his brother Harry: "... I don't blame you for dropping the Henry. I should like to drop Edgar; but it is too late now. I always wanted to be named John, which is one reason why I named one of my boys John. ..." Also chosen from an ancestral line, Coleman became the child's middle name.

The $1,000 windfall for the sale of "The Return of Tarzan" to *New Story Magazine* was opportune; certainly, now, more than ever, Ed, convinced that he must soon leave Shaw's *System*, could use money.

Earlier in the month, on February 15, George Tyler Burroughs, age seventy-nine, had

George Tyler Burroughs, Sr., October 13, 1903.

died. About his death, Evelyn Burroughs, Harry's daughter, commented:

I will always believe that he died of a broken heart. He was nearly eighty — had seen one fortune go after many years of prosperity, but pulled himself out of that failure and was doing well with the American Battery Company. There, at the last he found that one of the distillery company partners had been over a number of years bilking him out of what should have been his, if he hadn't been so trusting. He went to bed, refused to eat, and just died. His doctor told us later he had put "heart failure" on the death certificate because there wasn't a thing organically wrong with him, and he didn't want to falsify the record.

Ed's fond recollections of his father, and the appreciation and understanding of a parent that time and maturity often bring to a son, were evidenced in a practice that Ed later followed. An October 13 entry in his diary was made regularly; it might read, "Father's birthday today," or, as noted in a 1940 entry, "My father was born in Warren, Mass. 107 years ago today."

Major Burroughs, once doubtful that his son Ed would amount to anything, had lived to witness the launching of his writing career. The sale of "Under the Moons of Mars," followed by the spectacular success of "Tarzan of the Apes," made apparent by the furor it caused and the flood of readers' letters — Ed's statement that "My father and mother fairly gloat over them" indicated that George had read the letters avidly — surely swept away much of the Major's pessimism and gave him hope for his son's future.

Ed's jubilance over the sale of "The Return of Tarzan" was countered by an unexpected reaction from Metcalf, one that appeared to have no reasonable basis. The editor's letter was indignant and accusing:

I must say that I was nonplussed upon first hearing that Street and Smith had bought the Tar-

zan sequel. It struck me as fairly incredible, but then your letter came and settled the matter. I realise, of course, that you were quite justified in disposing of the manuscript, wherever you may have chosen, but somehow your course of action doesn't strike me as having been more than friendly.[27]

Metcalf displayed petulance and an inclination to take the matter personally: "I wonder if you weren't a little disgruntled at what you considered my unkind criticism and determined to show me. Well, you did." The sale of the "Tarzan" sequel, as far as he was concerned, did not indicate it was a well-constructed story: "I am also pretty certain that I did your literary reputation more good by rejecting the story than Street and Smith will have done by publishing it. I don't mean to be nasty, I really believe this."

At the close of the letter Metcalf returned again to his concept of fair dealings and friendship:

I suppose it was my appreciation of your real ability that made me what you doubtless consider commercially stupid. But it is too bad you couldn't see your way to working the story over and giving us — and me incidentally — not alone a square deal, but even more than a square deal. That's what friendly relationships amount to, anyway.

If Metcalf was "nonplussed" and "struck fairly incredible" over the sale, Ed was, in turn, astounded and bewildered over the editor's response. In his letter of March 1 he displayed far more tact than Metcalf had, and in fact, attempted to be conciliatory:

. . . It is so difficult to put things on paper and make them sound just as we would really say them face to face that I am trying to pound it in my thick skull that you actually had no intention of really making that letter carry the impression to me that the first reading did.

If you had said that I was a dummy, and a boob, and a plain damn fool, and didn't know when I was well off, or what was best for me, I might have been mad; but I shouldn't have been hurt.

Ed then proceeded with cold logic, point by point, to demonstrate to Metcalf that there was no reasonable basis for his attitude. To begin with, it was only because of his friendship for the editor that he submitted "The Ape-Man" to *All-Story* — otherwise it would have been sent to a different magazine. "I know that you have paid me a very low rate for my stories," Ed stated, and it would have been "only good business" for him to have tried another magazine, but he had not done so because he believed that in all fairness, Metcalf should have "first crack" at the story.

Ed was no doubt thinking of the exhausting hours of work he had spent on *The Outlaw of Torn*, to no avail, when he demanded:

Isn't it rather unjust to accuse me of unfriendliness because I sold to another magazine a story that you had refused, and criticized as ruthlessly as you did The Ape-Man? As a matter of fact wouldn't you think a man crazy who spent a month or more in rewriting a story for you without the slightest guarantee that you would like the second version any better than the first, when he could sell the original mss for more then he could get from you for the rewritten story?

As a further point Ed stressed the fact that Street & Smith was satisfied to buy the first serial rights only and that inquiries had already been made about syndication of the story. "I should hate to lose your friendship," Ed wrote, "and I don't think I shall. You were a bit sore when you wrote that letter, and you hadn't done very much thinking about the matter *from my side*." Ed noted an obvious fact, one Metcalf must have recognized, concerning the line of separation between friendship and business: "You don't take my stories because of friendship — you take them because you think they are good buys. I am not writing stories because of friendship — I am writing because I have a wife and three children."

Metcalf's letter conveyed an impression that

the editor believed Ed was gloating over his sale. Ed denied this, pointing out that although he had received an offer from Street & Smith for "The Ape-Man" on February 10, he had not told Metcalf about it until twelve days later. This was hardly the action of a "gloating" man.[28]

In Ed's dealings with Metcalf and the Munsey Company his future problems would be similar to the ones he had already encountered, mainly relating to amounts or rates of payment. He had determined to search for other markets. Responding on January 23 to the interest shown by John S. Phillips, editor of the *American Magazine,* Ed sought more definite information. Concerning possible submissions to the magazine, he explained that he had written only long novelettes of from seventy to a hundred thousand words. He felt he knew pretty well now what his readers liked: ". . . it is as easy for me to write one of these long stories as it would be to write half as many words in a number of short stories." Phillips had inquired about stories of less than thirty-thousand words.

Ed admitted that he wished to "enlarge" his market and "graduate into the better grade magazines," but he was not clear as to the type of story Phillips wanted. "For example — was it one of the Martian Stories or the ape-man story which struck your fancy?" he inquired. He described his latest work, even more apologetic than usual about its fantastic theme:

I happen to be working now on a very improbable type of yarn along the line of the Martian stuff. It is so wildly ridiculous that I am quite sure you would not care for it — yet I have worked it out so in accordance with known scientific facts that it sounds reasonable.

If there was a chance that it might appeal to *American* readers, Ed noted, he might be able to condense it to the desired length.

In his reply Phillips stated, "I don't know that I liked your ape-man story any more than your Martian stories. I have simply been taken with the imagination you show. I would like to see anything you do."[29] A few days later Ed sent a section of "The Inner World" that he had just completed and included an explanation:

The drawings which accompany it I made before I commenced the story — while I was thinking it out. I had in mind that they would prove helpful to the artist who did the illustrating, and I am including them with what I send you that the creatures in the text may seem more real.

I can complete the story inside of 30,000 words, or less. I should prefer to do it in less, if possible.[30]

From the start of the correspondence it is doubtful that Phillips was giving serious consideration to Ed's writings. Nothing of this type had ever appeared in the conservative *American,* and its readers would have reacted with shock or bewilderment if they had discovered "The Inner World" in their magazine. Phillips took only a few days to return the story, stating, in his letter of February 4, "I am hurrying back to you your story. It's got all the wonderful imagination in it that you show in your others. . . . It is just a little unbridled for us for a serial. . . . Won't you let me see the next thing you do?" Ed had not allowed himself to be over-expectant. "It was no surprise to me that you found it unavailable," he wrote, "though of course I hoped that you *might* decide in its favor."[31]

Ed's blunt answer to Metcalf had a salutory effect, for in a letter of March 7 the editor displayed a cautious and diplomatic attitude. "Let us allow this matter to drop and start all over again," he said. His proposal now was that he was willing to accept a payment plan which Ed might suggest, a plan that would guarantee Metcalf a first refusal on Ed's novels and would provide for a reasonable amount of revision. Ed replied promptly, referring to other demands for his work — those from Street & Smith, and the *American Magazine,* and also requests for syndication. "Under these circumstances," he wrote, "I should think that 5c a word for the first refusal on my novels, with the right to one reasonable revision, would be fair. This to give you the serial rights and leave the other rights in my hands. The arrangement to be in force for one year from the date of your acceptance."[32]

Metcalf's return offer was two cents a word for first serial rights only. Ed, surprisingly, compromised at once, writing, "I accept your proposition under date of March 14th for my 1913 crop." He reported another matter of interest to him: "Mr. Reilly, of Reilly & Britton, has asked me to compete in their ten thousand dollar prize novel contest. Of course there isn't one chance in ten million that I could win out in it, but I should like to have your permission to enter a mss. . . ."[33]

While Metcalf had no objection to his entering the novel contest, Ed very quickly lost his enthusiasm. At a later date he commented to Metcalf, "Quit in the middle of my $10,000.00 prize story. Realized the futility of attempting to compete in a field so far removed from my own as is Mr. Reilly's ideal. Have been writing one of my own kind of stories since, and expect to send it on for your amiable consideration soon."[34]

Ed's awareness of money-making opportunities in another area — that of newspaper syndication — was sharpened by events that occurred early in 1913. In the sale of his stories he had at first relinquished all serial rights to the Munsey Company. This included "Tarzan of the Apes," "A Princess of Mars," and "The Gods of Mars." At a later date, through an unexplained oversight, he sold all serial rights to "The Inner World."

The Munsey Company had arranged with the New York *Evening World* for the serialization of "Tarzan of the Apes," and with the appearance of successive installments, beginning on January 6, 1913, the popularity of Tarzan created an eager market in other newspapers.[35] To Ed the possibilities for syndication of his future works became quickly apparent. An opportunity first came in a letter of inquiry, dated February 25, from Albert Payson Terhune, editor of the *Evening World:*

We have been running your "Tarzan of the Apes" as a serial. It has been extremely popular with our readers; and we would like to make arrangements for newspaper serial publication of its sequel, after its appearance in a magazine.

If you have in mind any story of similar vein to "Tarzan" — with the scene laid in the jungle or possessing some equally unusual interest — please send such story or scenario of it for our consideration. . . .[36]

In the resulting correspondence Terhune agreed to purchase the New York City newspaper serial rights for "The Ape-Man." On March 15 he wrote, "For these, Mr. Tennant, the managing editor, commissions me to offer you $300. This is just six times the sum we paid the Munsey Company for 'Tarzan of the Apes'. . . ." Ed's acceptance of course was prompt. The vision of a nationwide syndicated outlet for his stories led to his insistence upon one type of sales contract: magazine editors could purchase *first serial rights only.*[37] Through inexperience he had surrendered the lucrative rights to "Tarzan of the Apes." There had been no demand for the syndication of his "Mars" stories, but he intended to take the necessary precautions with future works.

With syndication on his mind, it occurred to him that perhaps the serial rights to *Tarzan* had not been sold to a Chicago newspaper. His attempts to obtain these rights from the Munsey Company were unsuccessful, but not at all deterred he proceeded with his plan to syndicate "The Ape-Man" and other works, using the list of "Tarzan" newspapers he had obtained from Metcalf.[38] Terhune and the *Evening World* were his most important contacts. In May he wrote to Terhune to request his check for "The Ape-Man," commenting, "I see that The New Story is running it as The Return of Tarzan, which I think is very good. . . ."[39] The story ran as a seven-part serial from June through December 1913. But in the same month he also contacted the *Cleveland Press,* explaining:

"The Return of Tarzan" will be ready for news-
paper publication about the first of August....
I am getting about six times as much for The
Return of Tarzan as was paid for Tarzan of the
Apes; but those who have read the mss think it a
better story, and there is unquestionably a very
considerable demand for it....[40]

Other sales to the *Evening World* would
follow. Unfortunately, in the case of "The Inner World," which Ed sent to Metcalf on February 6, he wrote, ". . . the magazine rights
which I wish to sell." The payment of $420
covered all rights. About a week earlier Metcalf
had rejected "The Ape-Man," and this rejection
had thrust Ed into a state of insecurity and depression. This may have weakened his confidence in "The Inner World" and made him
hesitant about insisting upon first serial rights
only.[41]

Continuing reader comments about his story
endings were a source of amusement and stimulation to Ed, but in his letter of February 22,
1913, to Metcalf he made an astute observation
clearly based upon his analysis of these endings.
That he believed they had a significant value
was revealed in his statement that ". . . the unsatisfactory ending left much to the readers
imagination — it forced him to create a story
after his own liking — it made him think more
about the story than as though the ending had
been satisfactory and commonplace, and so it
made the story its own press agent."

In the same letter he reported to the editor
that for his next story he was "having a little fun
with higher education," and then followed with
a brief summary of the plot:

A young man from Bosting is cast ashore some-
where. He is all intellect. Falls in with a bunch
of cliff dwellers — aboriginal men and women.
Accident throws him with a young female. She
is strong, husky and intellectual as a she ape.
He is a physical weakling filled with the knowl-
edge of an encyclopaedia. Yet circumstances,
environment and the laws of sex find her the

brains and him the brawn of the combination.
I am having a lot of fun with it.

It is worth noting that the plot does not follow
the expected and unoriginal path but rather
takes a surprising and ingenious direction.

Now able to joke about Metcalf's rejection
of "The Ape-Man" — he had sold it for a good
price in spite of the editor's diagnosis that it
"lacked balance" — Ed offered to submit this
latest work if Metcalf would "promise not to say
that 'it is not convincing,' or 'lacks balance.' "
Ed wrote, "Just fire it back quick if you don't
like it."[42]

On March 22, the story titled "The Cave
Girl," was sent to Metcalf. It was a novelette,
about the same length as "The Inner World,"
and in his letter Ed stipulated, "If you take it
please see that the endorsement on check covers
no more than 1st serial rights." A few months
later, after publication, he forwarded "The
Cave Girl" to Terhune, who commented, "I
have read it with considerable interest. In
parts it is *almost* as good as 'Tarzan of the
Apes'. . . ."[43]

For some time Ed had been struggling to arrive at a decision about his future. He had been
dubious about the writing field as a full-time
occupation and as a source of regular income,
but the successive sales led him to change his
mind. On a number of occasions he had asked
his brother Harry to read his stories and had also
sought Harry's advice. His brother had been
enthusiastic about the stories, but in the consideration of whether Ed should quit his job
and concentrate on writing, Harry advised
against this step; to him it seemed too much of a
gamble. But there never had been any question
of Ed's willingness to gamble.[44]

In his *Autobiography* Ed noted that with
the birth of his third child, John Coleman, he
had decided to give up his job with Shaw's *Sys-*
tem and devote himself to writing. "Everyone,
including myself, thought I was an idiot," he
wrote, "but I had written five stories and sold
four, which I felt was a good average, and I

knew that I could write a great many more stories."

Further correspondence with Terhune of the *Evening World* brought Ed an understanding of the difficulties he would encounter in an effort to syndicate his stories nationally. Business matters involving one newspaper only, *The World*, made a steady exchange of letters necessary. All of this consumed Ed's writing time. In addition, the inquiries that came from all parts of the country included requests for quotations of charges. Here, Ed was at a loss; he had no idea what an acceptable charge should be. The greatest newspaper demands were for the serialization of "The Return of Tarzan." In this connection he sought Terhune's advice, writing:

I have been asked to quote on the newspaper serial rights for Cleveland, Cincinnati, Toledo, Akron, Columbus, Des Moines, Oklahoma City, Denver, Memphis, and Los Angeles; and I have no idea what to ask. I presume that the price would be governed largely by either the population of the city in question or the circulation of the newspaper. Can't you help me out — I shall certainly appreciate it.[45]

Ed, overambitious, had maneuvered himself into an impossible position. To even imagine the difficulties he now faced, one should remember that he had no office, was operating out of a crowded apartment on 2008 Park Avenue shared by his wife and three small children, and that, at the same time, he was attempting to maintain his incredible output of stories. Both "The Inner World" and "The Cave Girl" had been completed in the period between January 9, and March 22, 1913. Recognizing that the situation was beyond him, he decided to find an agency to handle the newspaper syndication. On May 26 he informed Terhune of this decision:

I have turned the handling of the newspaper syndicating over to the International Press Bureau, after a talk with Mr. W. G. Chapman, *their president. This for The Return of Tarzan exclusive of New York City. At first he wouldn't consider it when he learned that I had personally handled the sale of the New York City newspaper rights.*

Terhune had indicated an interest in "The Cave Girl," recently purchased by Metcalf, and in the same letter Ed wrote, "The Cave Girl mss will go forward to you as soon as I get it back from my mother who has been reading it." He also requested information about Ralph Danenhower of the Associated Publishers Syndicate Service, who had offered to handle "The Return of Tarzan."[46]

For some time Ed had been keeping a close count of the number of words in each story, in some cases actually listing the page numbers and totaling the words on the page. This was undoubtedly caused by the rate of payment problem he had already experienced with Metcalf. Payment, of course, was by the word, and Ed's care in counting obviously indicated his suspicion of an "under-count." In his letter of April 4 to Metcalf he acknowledged receipt of $600 for "The Cave Girl" and then demanded, "Howinel do you figure the number of words? By the most conservative estimate I cannot make it as little as 30,000. What's to be done about it? . . ."

Metcalf replied that he had totaled the word count by the same method he had used for "The Inner World," allowing an average of 320 words to a page, thus making for 89 pages, "not very much over 30,000 words."[47] Concerning the entire matter of counting, Ed, a month later commented to Metcalf that it had not been fair for him to assign the task of computing words entirely to the editor and then complain when the tallies did not agree. He indicated his future plan to list the exact number of words at the time the story was submitted.[48] Ed's meticulous work sheets, containing lists and descriptions of characters, tables, maps, and glossaries of terms, often included page-by-page word counts.

The agreement with William G. Chapman of the International Press Bureau in Chicago was finalized in Chapman's letter of June 3, 1913. Ed retained his responsibility for operations in New York and for the syndication of "The Return of Tarzan" in all other areas; Chapman's organization was to pay Ed a royalty each month of sixty percent of the gross sales. The next work for syndication, handled by Chapman later that year, was "The Cave Girl."[49]

In the midst of Ed's heavy writing schedule he still found time to aid Metcalf in a scheme the editor had devised for his "Table Talk" column. Metcalf had often referred to the cheerful and carefree manner in which his *All-Story* authors promised him the stories he requested, as though the writing of these stories was a simple and easy task. In reality, of course, the editor wrote, the writer was "sweating blood over a typewriter and hoping to goodness that he was going to be able to get this story to me." Metcalf proposed that his writers send in humorous letters refuting his cheerful account and "explaining how really sad is an author's life and how cruel an editor."[50] Ed, on February 26, sent in his humorous letter; headed "From the Man Who Knows Mars," it appeared in "Table-Talk" of May 1913. He joked about the "natural inference . . . that writers associate, on terms of equality, with editors," exaggerating the relationship to make it seem just the opposite — that writers occupy a lofty position which editors find unapproachable. In the "Table-Talk" letter Ed complains about the treatment of his man James who delivers the manuscripts to the editor and is kept waiting for the check "as long as ten minutes." Ed adds, "I do not wish to appear harsh, but I must insist that this must not occur again — James' time is very valuable."[51]

The cover designs of the October 1912 *All-Story* containing "Tarzan of the Apes" and of the June 1913 *New Story* with "The Return of Tarzan" had drawn Ed's interest and admiration. On June 1 he wrote to Metcalf to inquire whether he could purchase the original of the All-Story cover from the artist, Clinton Pettee: "I am to get the one illustrating the sequel and I

thought I should like to have them both. If you will find out the price that is wanted, and let me know, I'll be thankful."

At the same time he addressed a letter to A. L. Sessions, Editor of *New Story*, concerning the purchase of N. C. Wyeth's illustration. Metcalf, in his response of June 10, wrote in bold ink across the top of the page, "This is absolutely unofficial," and went on to explain that after consulting the Art Editor, he had learned that it was "the custom of the house" to sell these originals for fifty percent of the cost. In this case the asking price would be fifty dollars:

I believe, however, and of course this is strictly entre nous, that we would entertain an offer of $25.00, so if you feel at all interested you might write me a letter, very ingenuously pretending that I have not written to you, as I am now doing, and suggest that you would like to buy the cover in question if you could have it for $25.00.

My methods may seem peculiar, but I have adopted them only after considerable cogitation and discussion.

Ed's hope of purchasing the *New Story* original was not, however, to be realized. Wyeth's price, stated by Sessions on June 4, was $100, more than Ed could afford. He responded to Sessions, "I want to thank you for the trouble you have taken relative to the cover design by Mr. Wyeth. I am afraid, however, that Mr. Wyeth wants it worse than I do, so I shall be generous and let him keep it."[52] His inability to buy the Wyeth design appeared to discourage Ed, for on June 14 he wrote to Metcalf explaining that he had wanted the two cover illustrations as "companion pictures," and since he could not pay Wyeth's price, he had decided "to let the matter drop entirely."

Ed would have needed mystic powers as fantastic as any of those possessed by his creatures of other worlds to even dream that the matter of the Wyeth illustration, seemingly buried and forgotten, would rise from the past. Some fifty-two years later an astonishing postscript was to be written to the Wyeth affair.[53]

Ed's success in selling his stories had stimu-

"The Return of Tarzan" cover of New Story Magazine, *August 1913; illustrated by N. C. Wyeth, father of A. Wyeth.*

lated the ambitions of Ella (Nellie) Burroughs, Harry's wife. Her creative interest had been known to the family for some time, and she had shown both imagination and ability in her poems and stories. Her fictional themes were not of any world of fantasy comparable to Ed's, but dealt rather with human relationships, simple characterizations, and realistic settings. In her long story, "The Bride," appearing in 1913 in the popular magazine *The Metropolitan*, she creates a situation in which a delicate, protected Southern girl finds herself, as a young wife, abruptly transferred to a ranch in a rough frontier area. Here, Ella may have been recalling her own Southern background and her unanticipated experiences after she had married

Harry and moved with him to Idaho where she faced a difficult adjustment to life in a primitive country.

As a writer Ella displays a skill in description and in the development of atmosphere, but beyond this she reveals an unusual sensitivity in painting the intense feelings, the inner struggle, of the bewildered young bride. For the bride's artist son, Ella's model was obviously her son Studley and in this creation she was expressing all her hopes for his future. Studley was then displaying an interest in drawing and painting and would later illustrate some of the Burroughs books.

In the summer of 1913, possibly at her request, Ed sent a group of her stories to Thomas Metcalf. While there is no record of his evaluation, it is possible that Ella's stories did not contain sufficient elements of action and of excitement or adventure to meet *All-Story*'s requirements.[54]

Ed's relationship with Metcalf had developed through the constant correspondence into a warm association, almost as though the two were personal friends. Much of this feeling had resulted from a mutual informality of their natures which was expressed in the free-and-easy style used by both in their letters. A first meeting took place when Ed spent two days in New York — July 30 and 31 of 1913. Burroughs' purpose in making the trip, in addition to meeting Metcalf, was to confer with the editor about future stories.[55]

Continuing his intensive writing schedule, Ed had completed an unusual story which had been stored in a corner of his mind for some time; months before, in writing to Metcalf, he had spoken of it as based upon a biological experiment.[56] On May 20, in mailing it to the editor, he titled the story "Number Thirteen." His work sheet listed the starting and completion dates as March 31 and May 10, 1913.[57] Almost immediately he set to work on a sequel to "The Gods of Mars" which both Metcalf and the *All-Story* readers had been demanding. He titled it "The Prince of Helium" and in sending it to Metcalf on July 6, described it as "the last of the John Carter Martian stories."

I hope the ending will suit everybody — especially you.

. . . Am not sure that you will find the title commercially fit. I had difficulty in finding one to suit me. First I called it The Yellow Men of Barsoom; but that didn't describe the story. I also thought of The Fighting Prince of Mars, and The War Lord of Barsoom. How would something like Across Savage Mars do?

Well, if you like the story, and I hope you will, you can dope out your own title — my think tank is exhausted.[58]

Metcalf himself was responsible for Ed's undertaking an additional writing chore. The editor felt that "The Inner World" deserved expansion; he commented to Ed that "the reptilian part . . . could stand a lot of alteration and the whole story could be made very much more interesting. . ." He wondered whether Ed "might not add 10,000 or 15,000 more words to the middle of that story and deal with these peculiar over-sensitized lizards so that the great reading public might satisfactorily shudder. . . ." Ed quickly agreed to make the changes.[59]

During the spring and summer of 1913 Ed's efforts to find a book publisher for "Tarzan of the Apes" continued, but without success. Reilly & Britton of Chicago had held the story since November 1912, and Ed had remained hopeful because of Reilly's encouraging attitude. But this lengthy period of consideration brought no result. Ed's brief comment, written beneath the Reilly & Britton letter acknowledging receipt of the story, supplies the details: "March 4 1913 — By phone Mr. Reilly explained that the syndication of Tarzan of the Apes by the N.Y. World had killed it for their purposes." The lack of vision displayed by this firm and others who had viewed "Tarzan" as a poor risk is difficult to understand. It is also difficult to understand how the syndication of "Tarzan" which created a nationwide demand for the story could have destroyed its value. On May 23 Ed left a copy of the story at Rand McNally & Company in Chicago. His memorandum read, "Submitted Tarzan of the Apes to Mr. Clow. . . . Was to

have decision in about ten days." Worried about whether the company was aware of the growing demand for "Tarzan," Ed four days later sent a follow-up letter with a lengthy sales talk. Addressed to H. B. Clow, the letter first described the intense interest in the "Tarzan" sequel:

The newspaper syndicating of the sequel ("The Return of Tarzan") has been placed with the International Press Bureau, 1st National Bank bldg., and two other syndicating companies have also asked me for these rights although the story will not be available for them before November 15th. Over three months ago the New York Evening World solicited the New York City rights, and I sold them these for $300.00 (their own figure), which I understand is a rather good figure.

Neither *The World* nor the syndicating companies had read "The Return of Tarzan," Ed pointed out, and the fact that they were eager to take it sight unseen was ample evidence of "Tarzan's" popularity. In closing Ed wrote, "If you would care to see the letters of comment from readers, and the correspondence relative to the newspaper rights to the sequel I shall be glad to bring them down at any time you suggest."

Clow responded briefly on June 3, "I have read your story 'Tarzan of the Apes.' Will be pleased to talk with you on the subject at your leisure." Once again a publisher had no confidence in "Tarzan's" success as a novel. On August 20, 1913, Rand McNally & Company returned the story, offering nothing more than a conventional statement of rejection: "We have given the work careful consideration and while interesting we find it does not fit in with our plans for the present year."

In another area, that of sales of stories to Albert Payson Terhune and the *New York World*, Ed was having some success. Terhune explained that both he and the general manager, J. H. Tennant, liked "The Cave Girl," adding, ". . . we like all your stuff that we've read. Mr. Tennant wants to keep on using your stories and to see any new ones you may turn out." The *World's* offer for "The Cave Girl" was $200, and Terhune wrote, "Unofficially, let me say that $200 is the largest sum we have paid for any serial, except 'The Return of Tarzan,' for a long time."[60] Ed, in accepting, commented, ". . . I feel that I owe you a great deal for the bully treatment you accorded me when I was entirely new to the game."[61]

During July and August he began two new stories, "The Girl from Harris's" and "The Mucker." In what appeared to be a change of pace and setting, he temporarily left the world of fantasy to deal with earth-bound characters in familiar situations. Probably for material needed in "The Girl from Harris's" he contacted John McWeeny, the general superintendent of the Chicago Police Department, who in turn gave him a letter of introduction to Lieutenant W. R. Darrow of the 2nd District: "This will introduce Mr. Edgar Rice Burroughs who desires certain information concerning methods of handling prisoners. You will kindly favor him with all the information and assistance he requires."[62]

In the first half of 1913, from January to July, Ed had completed four long novelettes or serials, "The Inner World," "The Cave Girl," "Number Thirteen," (A Man without a Soul"), and "The Warlord of Mars." These four totaled more than 186,000 words.

With "The Inner World," retitled "At the Earth's Core" when it appeared in *All-Story*, he returned to his favorite "frame" structure, devising a brief prologue in which Ed, as the writer or story-teller, encounters the main character, David Innes, in the Sahara Desert. Innes has passed ten years in the fantastic inner world of Pellucidar, deep beneath the earth's crust, with an old inventor named Perry who had constructed the "iron mole" that transported them there. Innes's strange adventures occur in a land in which humans are helpless creatures who duplicate the condition of animals on earth; in this inner world great reptiles, the Mahars, who communicate with each other by

means of a "sixth-sense fourth-dimension language," rule sadistically over their human chattels. Here Ed, who had previously invented the settings for his dying planet of Mars and had created his own weird animals, for the first time devises a prehistoric setting — that of the Stone Age — and offers paleontological classifications for the monsters that Innes meets.[63]

At the story's end he created a "mystery" which in its reference to a count and countess who had vanished, and the finding of their locket on a deserted island, used familiar elements from "Tarzan of the Apes." By this time convinced that the ire of a small group of readers was hardly significant when compared to the large number who eagerly awaited his next story, Ed contrived the most indefinite of suspended endings, naturally with the inevitable sequel in mind.[64]

"Number Thirteen," published as "A Man Without a Soul," appears to have been thoroughly plotted by Ed before the end of 1912. In this early year of his writing he was already exhibiting the remarkable flexibility of an imagination able to shape several complicated stories at the same time. In his letter of December 5 to Metcalf he spoke of "bully stories mulling around in my head" and used his favorite phrase "damphool possibilities" in referring to "Number Thirteen."

Ed's unsuccessful venture into the short story field, as evidenced in "For the Fool's Mother" and "The Avenger," had provided convincing proof that his creative ideas were not designed for compression. On the contrary, they needed expansion — expansion of details, settings, incidents, and characters. As his writing progressed from story to story, his gallery of characters became larger and larger. In "Number Thirteen" the main characters, Professor Maxon, his daughter Virginia, Dr. Van Horn, and the Chinese Sing, are supplemented by a large variety of lesser ones and a cast of "extras" that would gladden the heart of a Hollywood producer. Included among minor characters are a Malay first mate, a Malay rajah, and a head warrior of a Dyak tribe. The participants in a succession of bloody battles are groups of Dyak warriors or pirates and an astonishing aggregation of thirteen "soulless" monsters. Ed had created a temporarily mad scientist who made Frankenstein's performance appear tame.

The professor, in his attempt to create life in his laboratory, has unfortunately overstressed physical perfection; his twelve experiments have resulted in twelve deformed monsters of superhuman strength. "You have overdone it," his assistant von Horn tells him, "with the result that the court of mystery is peopled by a dozen brutes of awful muscularity, and scarcely enough brain among the dozen to equip three properly." Bulan, who emerges as the hero of the story, is supposedly the product of Professor Maxon's thirteenth experiment. He is "a handsome giant, physically perfect," but he is soon revealed as the possessor of a high intelligence and of such virtues as courtesy, bravery, and unselfishness. In the story Ed naturally reserved a surprise for the end, and what was a greater surprise to his readers — a completely finished ending, with no possibility of the prolonged waiting for a sequel.[65]

Ed's major work during this period, completed within one month, from June 7 to July 8, 1913, was "The Warlord of Mars," at first titled "The Prince of Helium." The narrative is resumed after the suspenseful ending of "The Gods of Mars," with Dejah Thoris "entombed" in the Temple of the Sun and John Carter awaiting in agony the moment when the revolving shaft will permit the cell door to be opened so that he can learn whether his wife is alive or dead. The familiar characters of Ed's preceding Martian stories appear again, but of course there are additions, including Salensus Oll, Jeddak of Okar, and Kulan Tith, Jeddak of Kaol. Ed's imagination was especially given to the devising of new civilizations, races, and geographical settings that were unique. As though determined to achieve a variety of skin colors, he now added to his red, green, black, and white Martians, a race of yellow men, "fierce, black-bearded fellows with skins the color of a ripe lemon," who inhabit the forbidding arctic

region of Mars near the North Pole. A spectacular Burroughs invention is "The Carrion Caves," the only route "through the ice-barrier of the north to a fertile valley at the pole." He describes the yellow men's fight for survival against the other races and how, fleeing, they discovered the caves:

At the opening to the subterranean passage that led to their haven of refuge a mighty battle was fought in which yellow men were victorious, and within the caves that gave ingress to their new home they piled the bodies of the dead, both yellow and green, that the stench might warn away their enemies from further pursuit.

And ever since that long-gone day have the dead of this fabled land been carried to the Carrion Caves, that in death and decay they might serve their country and warn away invading enemies. Here, too, is brought, so the fable runs, all the waste stuff of the nation — everything that is subject to rot, and that can add to the foul stench that assails our nostrils.

Ed is also adept at creating new hideous animals. In "The Warlord of Mars" John Carter encounters the huge sith and the terrifying apt. The sith, a "bald-faced hornet . . . grown to the size of a prize Hereford bull" has a poisoned sting and "myriad facet eyes" that cover most of its grotesque head. The apt is presented in graphic detail:

It is a huge, white-furred creature with six limbs, four of which, short and heavy, carry it swiftly over the snow and ice; while the other two, growing forward from its shoulders on either side of its powerful neck, terminate in white, hairless hands, with which it seizes its prey.

The creature has two great horns that protrude from its lower jawbone, and its most astonishing feature is the eyes that extend "in two vast, oval patches from the center of the top of the cranium down either side of the head to below the roots of the horns, so that these weapons really grow out from the lower part of the eyes, which are composed of several thousand ocelli each."

Apparently feeling it necessary to provide a scientific explanation for the apt's bizarre features, Ed wrote:

This eye structure seemed remarkable in a beast whose haunts were upon a glaring field of ice and snow, and though I found upon minute examination of several that we killed that each ocellus is furnished with its own lid, and that the animal can at will close as many of the facets of his huge eyes as he chooses, yet I was positive that nature had thus equipped him because much of his life was to be spent in dark, subterranean recesses.

"The Warlord of Mars," ending happily with John Carter and his beloved Dejah Thoris united, was accepted by Metcalf for *All-Story*.[66] As Ed had previously stated, this novel was "the last of the John Carter Martian stories" — at least, for the time being.

The Martian trilogy of *A Princess of Mars, The Gods of Mars,* and *The Warlord of Mars* is considered by many people, including science-fiction authorities and Burroughs afficionados, as a classic in the field of fiction. In a truly remarkable feat of creativity Burroughs not only told a gripping tale, but invented on the planet Mars entire multiracial civilizations complete with nations, religions, gods, and science.

Before the summer was over, Ed succeeded in making a sale which may have provided him with a greater satisfaction than any of the other ones. At the close of 1912 "The Outlaw of Torn" remained unsold. Discouraged but not defeated, Burroughs had vowed to Metcalf, "I am going to do it over again when I have time."

An observation about writing, contained in the Burroughs *Autobiography,* was one that other authors have noted: "The stories that are easiest to write usually sell easy." From this it may be assumed that the converse is often true. "The Outlaw of Torn," which Ed described as "the story I had worked the hardest on," appeared unsalable. On February 24 A. L. Sessions, editor of *New Story,* wrote, "I hope, now that we have established communication with

you, you are going to give us a chance to read many more of your stories." Ed hastened to reply, referring to "The Outlaw of Torn" and explaining that it had been previously submitted.[67]

When Sessions stated, "I have no recollection of seeing the story," and showed an interest in reading it, Ed sent it to him. A month later the manuscript was returned with a brief statement of rejection.[68] Ed made no further overtures to Sessions, but by the summer of 1913, the growing furor over *Tarzan,* created mainly through its widespread syndication, was a factor in prompting the editor to seek another story, no matter what type, as long as it bore the Burroughs name. On July 19 he wrote, "If you have not disposed of the serial rights of your story "The Outlaw of Torn," I would like to consider it again for the New Story Magazine."

Ed rushed the story to him; however, on July 30, the best offer Sessions would make was $350 for first serial rights. He had some apprehensions regarding Ed's response to an offer so low and was careful to explain his reasons:

Anticipating what will probably be your feeling, that this is a rather modest sum for a story of this length, I ought to say that the reason is because we have not hitherto used anything approaching historical romance, or, indeed, any sort of material that is not what is popularly known as "up-to-date" in plot, characters, and action. So "The Outlaw of Torn" will be more or less of an experiment with us. If you are willing to accept this sum, I will see that you receive a check promptly.

As a result of Sessions' purchase of "The Return of Tarzan" Ed had promised him first refusal on the next "Tarzan" story. There appears little doubt that this opportunity to acquire a valuable Tarzan serial was dominating Sessions' thoughts and actions. The editor, eager to prod Ed into starting this new serial, offered a plot suggestion:

Another matter that I wish to bring to your attention is the question of another story of Tarzan. It has occurred to us that Tarzan's adven-

tures might be continued still further, and if the idea appeals to you, would like to suggest that he could be taken back to Africa once more as the authorized agent of the Smithsonian Institution, heading an expedition to investigate the talking apes and possibly to bring back specimens. Doubtless you have heard of Prof. Garner's reports that monkeys have a language of their own, and possibly have read accounts of his alleged researches. . . .

Sessions believed that this idea, taken as a theme, might lead to an exciting adventure story. Despite his difficulties in marketing "The Outlaw of Torn," and the fact that this was the first offer *anybody* had made, Ed had no intention of accepting the $350. With a dogged determination, he persisted in valuing the story according to the long hours of work he had devoted to it. On July 31, while in New York to visit Metcalf, he had a conference with Sessions. Later, across the top of Sessions' letter containing the offer, Ed noted:

Saw Sessions in N.Y. 7/31 asked $1000 for Outlaw of Torn & $3000 contract for sequel to Ret of Tarzan Feb 1914 delivery.

For a while it appeared that the negotiations would reach an impasse and Ed would again be left with the manuscript on his hands. But the dickering continued, with Sessions raising his offer to $500. Ed, on August 15, accepted, with the proposal previously referred to,[69] in which Ed had stipulated, "After the story has appeared in your magazine, if you find from the comments of your readers that it has proven successful you are to pay me a further sum of 2c per word, less the $500.00 previously paid."[70] On August 18 Sessions sent a prompt agreement to these conditions.

From a businessman's standpoint, as he balanced the long hours of revision and research against the net return, Ed undoubtedly considered "The Outlaw of Torn" as a poor investment. Still, he had gained the satisfaction of another sale and had demonstrated his power of determination. Above all, through this un-

happy experience with medieval times, castles, and knighthood, he had learned that the historical romance, with its emphasis upon realistic atmosphere, was not the best outlet for his talents. He would, however, later return to ancient history as the setting for a fantastic novel.

Thus, the summer's end in 1913 found Ed with a future unquestionably committed to the field of writing, the thoughts of returning to the business world thrust firmly aside. His successes had given him the confidence of a man who knows his worth. With this confidence he even dared to estimate the beginning dates of new stories and the approximate dates of completion. In a letter of August 21 he wrote to A. L. Sessions, "As to the next Tarzan story. . . . I intend starting it the first of the year, and shall have a considerable part of it ready by the first of February. . . ."[71]

In negotiations with Burroughs, editors and publishers soon realized they were encountering a type of writer they had not previously known. Shrewd and demanding, aware he was marketing a product everybody wanted, Ed sought the highest bidder. The editors who were accustomed to viewing authors' stories as so much merchandise, purchasable in a buyer's market in which they set the prices, now received a rude awakening. By their rules the acquisition of stories was a straightforward business transaction. If these were to be the rules, Ed proposed a logical extension — selling stories was also a business transaction. And the author of "Tarzan" intended to make an important change in the rules: within the limits of his powers, *he* would set the prices for his stories. The editors for the first time were confronted by a man whose shrewd business instincts and perception more than matched their own. They had no choice but to bargain with him.

Ed, in his future dealings, established himself as an unusual combination, a kind of dual personality. Seldom had a writer joined a soaring imagination with a cold dollars-and-cents practicality. He became the businessman-writer par excellence.

June 10 1914

My dear wife:

Do you recall how we waited in fear and trembling the coming of the post man for weary days after we sent the Tarzan Mss to Metcalf?

And will you ever forget THE morning that he finally came.

Not even this, our first book, can quite equal that unparalleled moment.

That we may never have cause for another such is the wish of your devoted husband

Ed R Burroughs

10
A
CALIFORNIA
SOJOURN

Ed's impulsive nature, restrained awhile by family responsibilities and by the discipline of his self-imposed writing goals, once more drove him to seek change and a touch of adventure. His first concession to success, a decidedly daring one for the times, was to buy an automobile — a used Velie. He recalled the matter with amusement in his *Autobiography:* "My stories were now selling as fast as I could write them and I could write them pretty rapidly, so I bought a second-hand automobile and became a plutocrat."

This festive mood demanded a greater and more impulsive gesture. Although family duties required that he control his restless or whimsical nature, he was still, as always, prepared to gamble in a surprising and unpredictable way. On September 6, 1913, Metcalf, who might have believed he had seen the end of Ed's unexpected actions, discovered he was wrong. The letter offered an abrupt announcement:

"Am leaving for California tonight. My address until further notice will be General Delivery, San Diego. When we're located I'll send you permanent address."

Ed's own comment about the sudden move was humorous: ". . . I had decided that I was too rich to spend my winters in Chicago so I packed my family, all my furniture, my second-hand automobile and bought transportation for Los Angeles."[1] Emma, who from the moment of her marriage to Ed had known little stability, and had been transported to the wilds of Idaho, may have by this time been conditioned to his whimsical decisions. Though she loved and trusted Ed, she must have been concerned by the difficulties of making a cross-country trip with three small children — Joan, age five, Hulbert, four, and John, an infant of not quite six months — and by the plan that included a repetition of past events — the shipping of all household belongings, the relocation, and the

House ERB and Emma rented in Coronado, California, at 550 A Avenue, September 25, 1913; auto is old Velie Ed took on the train with him; Emma and the three children are on porch.

setting up of housekeeping in strange surroundings.

Of this California expedition, Ed wrote in his *Autobiography:*

From Los Angeles we drove to San Diego and spent the winter in Coronado and San Diego. We were a long way from home. My income depended solely upon the sale of magazine rights. I had not had a book published at that time and, therefore, no book royalties were coming in. Had I failed to sell a single story during these months it would have been over the hills to the poorhouse for us, but I did not fail. That I had to work is evidenced by a graph that I keep on my desk showing my word output from year to year since 1911. In 1913 it reached its peak with something like four hundred and thirteen thousand words for the year. By glancing at this graph I can always tell when the sheriff has been camping on my coat-tails.

Metcalf wrote to inquire, "Are you going to stay definitely in California or are you going to be there for the winter? I hope you have a very fine time anyway, and I hope that literature flourishes like a streak out there. . . ."[2] Ed responded, "I think it is going to be great here. We came on the children's account. We have three, and the Chicago winters have always meant a round of sickness and worry. We have taken a house at Coronado — I do not know the street number, nor does anyone else; but if you will address me as follows I shall get your letters all right: A avenue, bet. 7th & 8th, Coronado, California."[3]

On business matters Ed noted, "The two short stories ["The Avenger" and "For the Fool's Mother"] came the other day. I did not cry myself to sleep over them. I told you they were rotten, but you asked to see them anyway." These had been rejected with the briefest of comments by Metcalf. Ed, neither surprised

Emma and the children on visit to Tijuana, Mexico, in the old Velie, 1914.

nor disappointed, considered the editor's opinion as a confirmation of his own belief — that he was not destined to be a short story writer.[4]

He hastened to maintain his other business correspondence. William G. Chapman of the International Press Bureau, who had already received a notification of the change of address, wrote to discuss the syndication of "The Cave Girl." As Ed had discovered earlier, the process of serializing stories in newspapers was a complicated one that seldom ran smoothly. Chapman was willing to handle "The Cave Girl" on the same basis as "The Return of Tarzan," his guarantee to be forty percent of the gross amount, but Sessions, editor of *New Story*, had not as yet sent the needed proofs of "The Return of Tarzan," and Chapman was inquiring if Ed was prepared to bear half the costs of printing the story so that it could be distributed.[5]

The syndication problems and the request for money were sufficient to revive Ed's worries about finances. Far from home and completely on his own, he had risked supporting his family and household solely through his writings; his concern was understandable. On October 3 he wrote to Chapman, "I find that one can use money to advantage in this neck of the woods," and later, in an inquiry about the syndication, he asked, ". . . is there any money coming in? I am starving to death among strangers."[6]

On October 7 Chapman finally had some good news to present: Sessions had sent fifty copies of each issue of *New Story* containing "The Return of Tarzan," and Chapman was now negotiating with the American Press Association and the Scripps MacRae newspapers.[7] Chapman's letter of December 20 offered a more substantial encouragement — a check for $150, Ed's sixty percent of the money paid by Scripps MacRae for "The Return of Tarzan."

Metcalf of course wrote to discuss matters of importance or of interest to Ed. On October 2 he commented, "I think 'The Man Without a Soul' ought to go pretty well." Presumably the November *All-Story* in which it would appear, complete in one issue, was out or about to come out. Metcalf reported also that "The Warlord of Mars" would begin in installments the following month, and then added one of his promotional suggestions which usually resulted in extra work for Ed: "It has just occurred to me that we could get some entertainment by publishing a line cut of the geography of Mars. Could you fake up something, seeing that you have traveled so thoroughly over that globe, which we could run?"[8]

Ed wrote, ". . . shall also see what I can do with a map of Mars — you will recall that I showed you my working map when I was in New York; but it was too meager for your purposes."[9] Again, with the payment foremost in his mind he remarked, "It is such a deuce of a way out here, and takes so long to get word back and forth that I am hoping you will favor me (again) with one of your early decisions."[10] (By this time Ed's California address had been established as 550 A. Avenue, Coronado.)

Ed's map of Mars (Barsoom), evidently drawn in response to the request, presents the planet in spherical views from two sides — first the exposed half of the eastern hemisphere progressing to one half of the western hemisphere, and then the other side of the globe with the hemispheres in reverse. He has drawn the lines of latitude and longitude and has entered important surface features and cities, including The Atolian Hills, Toonolian Marshes, Greater and Lesser Helium, Zodanga, Ptarth, and even the location of "The Hordes of Torquas."

The map contains a table of Martian measurements and a scale based upon "haads." In devising, as usual, his special terminology, he lists a "sofad" as equal to 11.69 plus earth inches, an "ad" as 9.75 minus earth feet, and a "haad" as 1949.05 earth feet. He notes that there are about 2.709 haads to an English mile and estimates the "speed of fast fliers" to be about 450 haads or 166.1 earth miles per hour.[11]

For the *All-Story* "Table-Talk" of October 1913, Metcalf, on his own initiative, arranged a glossary of Martian terms. In the column he commented, "Mr. Burroughs had all the terms at hand and we simply put them in alphabetical order and are printing them hereinafter, so that all who read the Martian stories may know exactly what is what." His glossary was divided into categories of "Proper Names" and "Common Names."[12]

The confusion over the use of Ed's pen name, "Norman Bean," for "Under the Moons of Mars" led to an amusing complaint from an *All-Story* reader. In the October "Table-Talk", writing from Hawaii, the reader commented about "The Gods of Mars":

The sequel, I notice, is written by "Burroughs" and the original tale by "Norman Bean." How is this?

Burroughs is undoubtedly one of your best writers, and the sequel is well written, but I do not think he has continued the story in the way the original author would have done, which makes it, to my idea, far less interesting. Another thing — he leaves the tale in an unfinished condition.

The reader explained, "My wife says had she known the abrupt finish to the story she would rather not have read it." Again, he urged Metcalf, "in the interest of all your readers," to induce "Norman Bean" to write "the continuation of this otherwise splendid story and finish it in a way satisfactory to all," later repeating the statement to "Try and get the finish to 'Under the Gods of Mars'" and to afterward "induce the same author — or one equally good" to write stories of life on other planets.

Ed's amusement over this suggestion must have been heightened by the blundering note from a reader in the Philippines whose letter of "heartfelt sympathy to the friends and relatives of Mr. E. R. Burroughs" appeared in the December 1913 *All-Story*. "His death must have been very sudden," the reader stated. "I liked his stories very much. It is too bad he could not have finished 'The Gods of Mars.'"

In this busy California period Ed continued

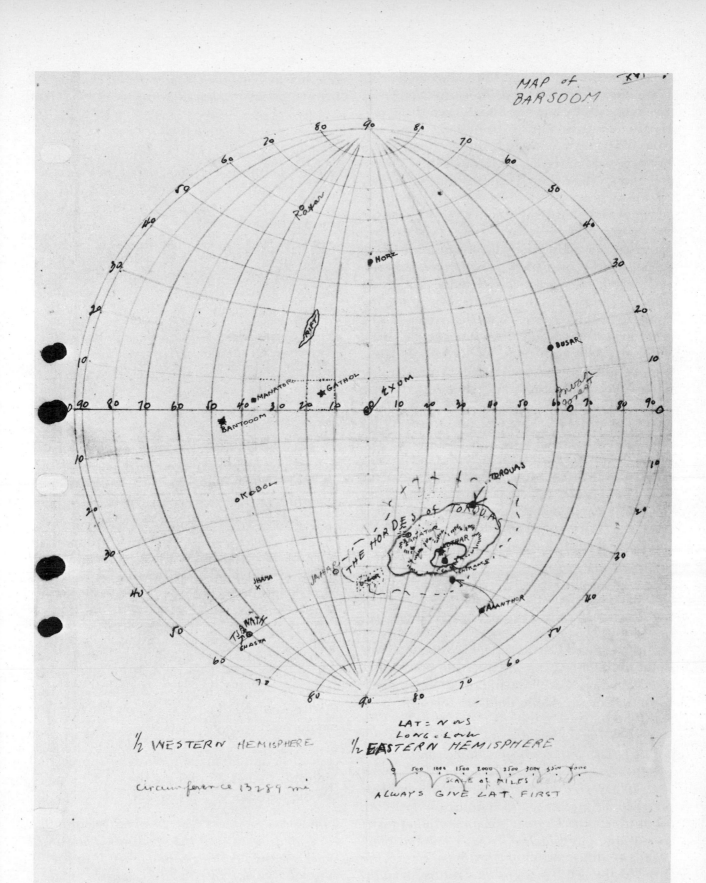

ERB's map of Barsoom (Mars), which he drew to help him maintain accuracy and realism in his geographical locations.

to have many irons in the fire. Arrangements for serialization of his stories in the *New York Evening World,* a project he was handling personally, occupied part of his time. About "The Man Without a Soul," scheduled to appear in the newspaper after publication in the October *All-Story,* Ed wrote to Terhune somewhat over-optimistically, "I sort of have an idea that this story is going to take almost as well as Tarzan of the Apes . . ."[13]

He was working speedily on the addition to "The Inner World" that he had promised Metcalf, and in sending the completed section to the editor he wrote, "At the time Mr. Innes recounted his adventures to me he presented me with several rough pencil drawings he had made before he left Pellucidar. Believing that you may be interested in seeing these I am sending them along with the mss."[14] He noted that the addition totaled forty-nine pages or about 16,170 words.[15]

Only two weeks earlier he had finished "The Mucker," a long story he had begun in Chicago on August 16, according to his workbook, and sent it to Metcalf. Now, with only a brief period allowed for the editor's evaluation, he sent a reminder: "Let me know about *The Mucker.* I am just as childishly impatient as when I sent my first story to you."[16]

In the midst of all this feverish writing he was making plans for new sequels and commented to Metcalf, "If your readers do not tire of Mars I should like to write another story of Helium around Carthoris — Carter's son, you know."[17] Concerning the question of a sequel to "The Cave Girl," he inquired, "Has there been any considerable demand for one?" and went on in detail to discuss the story:

I noticed in a letter from a reader a comment on the "rottenness" of the ending. Do [you] imagine this referred to the fact that the principals were not brought back to civilization, or to the suggestion of the rather unconventional (as it were) relations which may have marked their companionship after they went back into the forest together? To my mind a return, to civilization and the snobs I pictured his friends and

relatives as being would have meant the shattering of a pretty romance.[18]

"I hated to do it — " he commented, "and then, there is always the sequel!"

Letters referring to "The Mucker" may have crossed, because Metcalf's, dated a day earlier than the inquiry from Ed, contained the editor's verdict: it was an outright rejection. He used the expression Ed had objected to previously — "I might say that I don't think the story balances." Metcalf presented a long analysis of "The Mucker's" defects, concentrating first on the section describing Billy Byrne's activities aboard the *Halfmoon:*

Ninety-nine pages, pretty nearly half the story, were spent on the ship in circumstances that are not highly original. . . . it seems to me that you have resorted altogether too much to very lengthy conversations. The effect is one of repetition and slowness.[19]

In the last half of the story, Metcalf noted, Ed erred in taking an exactly opposite approach:

. . . When you get them ashore on the island, and introduce the decadent Japanese race and situations, which at least in color are more or less unusual, you hurry through it with great speed. The whole latter part of the story is so condensed and so hastily worked up that your effects are not always gained. . . .[20]

Metcalf added some penetrating and accurate remarks about Ed's failure to achieve a convincing characterization of Billy Byrne, the "Mucker," and commented, "I have a feeling that you started to write this story without having doped it out very carefully. . . ."[21]

Ed's response had a tone of gloom and dejection, although he made it plain he appreciated Metcalf's patience in taking the time "to point out the weak spots." Ed wrote:

I think that maybe I have been falling into that thing of dragging out the openings of late and I shall certainly try to guard against it in the future. I did not intend to hasten the ending, but toward the close I recalled one of your let-

*ters in which you stated that you were not par-
ticularly keen for stories of over seventy thousand words.*[22]

Metcalf's criticism of overlong introduc-
tions or opening sections recalls, of course, his
analysis of Ed's first story, "Under the Moons
of Mars," with its original four-page foreword,
which was finally reduced to several paragraphs
of summary and placed on the title page.

While in "The Mucker" Ed departed from
the fantasy or other world settings he often used,
he nevertheless returned to a favorite theme,
similar to the one he had developed in "The
Cave Girl." It was based upon the regeneration
of a weak or dissolute character following his removal from a physically and/or morally destructive environment to a rugged and somewhat primitive environment of nature. Here,
while he is being forced to battle for survival,
two strong influences operate to transform him
into a healthy, moralistic individual: one is the
result of a rigorous outdoor life and the other
develops from his encounter with a particularly
wholesome specimen of womanhood whose approval and love he desperately wants.

In "The Mucker" Ed used another story element upon which he would depend even more
heavily in the future — that of a strange lost or
misplaced race. On the island the passengers
from the wrecked ship are being watched by "a
little brown man with beady, black eyes set in
narrow fleshy slits." The man, who wore
"strange medieval armor" and carried "two
wicked-looking swords," was described as "Oda
Yorimoto, descendant of a powerful daimio of
the Ashikaga Dynasty of shoguns who had fled
Japan with his faithful samurai nearly three
hundred and fifty years before upon the overthrow of the Ashikaga Dynasty."

Ed's concept of a lost race, as with the Oparians in "The Return of Tarzan," led him to
create a people who were decadent and sadistically warped:

*Upon this unfrequented and distant Japan-
ese isle the exiles had retained all of their medi-*

*eval military savagery, to which had been added
the aboriginal ferocity of the head-hunting natives they had found there and with whom they
had intermarried. The little colony, far from
making any advances in arts or letters had, on
the contrary, relapsed into primeval ignorance
as deep as that of the natives with whom they
had cast their lot — only in their arms and armor, their military training and discipline did
they show any of the influence of their civilized
progenitors.*

The inhabitants of the island, the samurai,
"cruel, crafty, resourceful wild men trapped in
the habiliments of a dead past," represented
Ed's favorite version of the "lost race" theme;
later variations involved a race (or races) reverting to primitive life or savagery and surviving on the ruins and remnants of an ancient civilization which, in some cases, was far more advanced than theirs. The anachronism — the
idea of a group of people living in isolation and
clinging to odd customs and fearful rites of a remote period — was evidently intriguing to Ed.

In the development of "The Mucker" with
its rather loose-knit structure, Ed for the first
time used a variety of "earthbound" settings.
Billy Byrne flees from Chicago to San Francisco,
is shanghaied, and then shipwrecked on a
Malaysian island, and at the story's end turns up
in New York, where he meets Barbara Harding,
the girl he loves, and gallantly renounces her
and tells of his plans to return to Chicago and
his "own kind."

Although Ed may have expressed his gratitude for Metcalf's criticism of "The Mucker,"
he had no intention of getting involved in extensive revisions until he had tried the story
elsewhere. However, his submission of "The
Mucker" to Sessions at *New Story* brought a
firm rejection.[23] Resigned to the inevitable, he
then began revisions, shortening the story to
about 58,000 words.[24] Past experiences with
rejections by Metcalf made him dubious about
"The Mucker's" chances at *All-Story*, and on
December 22 he chose instead to submit it to
Adventure. His letter to Arthur S. Hoffman,

173

the editor, revealed his doubts that the story would be accepted: ". . . If "The Mucker" doesn't meet your requirements I'll be glad if you will let me know wherein it falls short, so that I may have another try later. . . ." Within weeks "The Mucker" was once more brought to Metcalf's attention:

Have rewritten The Mucker cutting out those parts you did not like, lopping off several closing chapters, changing the ending, and shortening the whole thing by some ten or eleven thousand words. It is out now with a magazine for which it is totally unfitted so I am expecting it back daily. Would you care to see it?[25]

At the same time Ed announced a change of address; he was now at 4036 3rd Street in San Diego:

. . . I have again been in the throes of moving. Coronado was too low and damp and we are now situated in a rose bowered (!) bungalow on the hills of S. D. By standing on tip toe we can peek over the mountains to the east and see almost to Schenectady.[26]

As expected, "The Mucker" was returned by *Adventure*, but Ed, continuing the intensive California writing schedule begun in early fall, had little inclination to brood over this failure. On October 26, he had turned again to royal adventure in "The Mad King of Lutha," completing it within a month. Continuing his rapid writing pace, Ed launched at once into "Nu of the Neocene," a shorter 25,000-word story that he finished in only twenty days.[27]

In "The Mad King of Lutha" Ed assembles familiar elements found in pseudo-historical romances of the day — a young king deprived of his rightful position, a villainous regent, a beautiful princess, and a courageous young American, Barney Custer of Beatrice, Nebraska, who is merely a tourist in the kingdom of Lutha, his mother's native land. Barney, because of a lost election bet is not permitted to shave for a year; his full red beard gives him a superficial resemblance to the escaped "mad" king, and as a re-

sult he becomes embroiled in danger and intrigue. Ed, in imitation of the settings adopted by other historical novelists, chooses to give his kingdom of Lutha an Austrian or German flavor, creating such characters as Peter of Blentz, Prince Ludwig von der Tann, Lieutenant Otto Butzow, and others. The heroine, Princess Emma von der Tann, is of course named after Ed's wife. The selection of Beatrice, Nebraska, as Barney's home town, and the emphasis this small town receives, is explained by Ed's close friendship with Herbert (Bert) T. Weston who had been his classmate at Michigan Military Academy. Weston, with his wife, Margaret, and their children, lived in Beatrice, Nebraska, and from there maintained a lifelong correspondence with Ed.[28]

Instead of establishing a historical period of the past, as he had done in "The Outlaw of Torn," Ed preferred to modernize "The Mad King" and in the story makes his first use of the automobile. Barney Custer drives into Lutha in a gray roadster and soon afterward maneuvers the car daringly to rescue Emma, the heroine, from a runaway horse. The presence of the automobile at once removes the story from the customary Victorian setting and places it in the twentieth century.

"The Mad King of Lutha," a melange of unoriginal devices and incidents, is hardly an example of Burroughs' imaginative best. Its plot, based upon the chance circumstances that force a visitor to a tiny kingdom to impersonate its king, closely resembles that of *The Prisoner of Zenda*, by Anthony Hope, published in 1894.

In accepting "The Mad King" Metcalf commented that it was "a pretty fair yarn,"[29] and on December 8 Ed replied to thank him for the early check that came in "mighty fine for Christmas."[30] The main subject of concern to Ed was the coming expiration of his agreement with the Munsey Company; in this, for the past year, he had granted them first refusal on all stories. Ed explained his views diplomatically:

I am anxious to try for other magazines for purely business reasons. Personally I should rather write for you than any of them, for no one could have accorded me more courteous treatment than I have received at the hands of The Munsey Company. I feel, however, that though I may never receive as decent treatment from others I should be making some effort to discover what other magazines want, and, if I can, enlarge the market for my stories.[31]

On December 17 Metcalf replied with an offer for first refusal on all of Ed's 1914 output: the Munsey Company would agree to pay two and one-half cents a word. Metcalf pointed out that Ed's market would not be limited, since "whatever we feel we cannot use you will be able to send immediately to other magazines, and you will thus learn what their needs are. . . ."

Ed, evidently weighing Metcalf's proposal, was in no hurry to commit himself, responding only after a second query from the editor,[32] and then making a terse counter-proposal: "As to the 2½c proposition, 3½c would be infinitely

more interesting."[33] This offer included certain reservations, specifically in the matter of the third Tarzan story which Ed had promised to submit to Sessions for *New Story Magazine.* Ed wrote:

I do not see that it would be right to do otherwise, though I am not bound to accept his offer for it, nor is there any reason why you should not see it and make me an offer for it if you choose; but if we reach a mutually satisfactory arrangement for 1914 this story will, of course, have to be excepted.[34]

Ed then inquired, "How would an arrangement covering each alternate story that I write strike you?"[35]

During the exchange of letters Metcalf revealed the new plans to transform *All-Story* into a weekly and noted, "This means that I can use all manner of stuff, novels 30,000 to 40,000

ERB and lifelong friend, Bert Weston, about 1901.

words long, serials and short stories. This is the chance of a life time for a brilliant young author."[36]

He also included critical comments about one of Ed's favorite practices: ". . . I would like to suggest that you do *not* use the present tense in writing at any time. There is no particular advantage to it. It has gone out of fashion nowadays and it is pretty awkward to the average reader."[37] In replying, Ed expressed a willingness to accept the suggestion: "Thanks for the present tense criticism. Will try to dodge it in future. I'll appreciate it if you'll tip me off to any other little oddities of style that my stuff would be better off without. . . ."[38]

The negotiations over a new agreement with Munsey revealed that Ed's worries and uncertainties over his writing future, although temporarily thrust aside during this successful period, could easily return. On January 19, 1914, he wrote:

Am still up in the air about the $.025 stunt, — or was it three and a half? I feel that it would result in selling all my best stuff at two and a half cents and not being able to sell what you didn't like at any price, even though it was not entirely rotten, and so I wouldn't have any chance to break into a wider field, and then when I have shot my wad as far as the All-Story readers are concerned I shall be just where I was when I first started to write, as far as other magazines are concerned. . . .

His strongest fear, the one that plagued many writers, was the fear of running out of ideas, of being *written out*. To Metcalf he explained:

. . . I cannot forget what you once told me about the majority of writers playing out after a couple of years. I imagine they play out with readers who have followed them for that long, as in two years a fellow pretty nearly exhausts his stock of situations, phrases and the like.[39]

"I feel that most of mine are already worn to a frazzle," Ed remarked gloomily. "If I knew

that you were going to take it all it might make a difference; but of course neither of us can know that."[40]

His comment about writers whose ideas were exhausted, and especially his mention of "a couple of years" as a time limit, when considered in the light and length of his future career, of course seem incongruous. But to Ed's personal insecurity at the time were added his doubts about writing as a permanent profession with an assured income. These combined factors account for the fears that were further sharpened by Metcalf's statement.

Ed thus revealed a painful awareness of the limited nature of the themes, incidents, and devices he had been repeating. It undoubtedly appeared inconceivable to him that he could build a successful writing career on this slim stock-in-trade — continuing variations of "Tarzan," discoveries of lost races and primitive societies, sequels to "Mars" and other-world stories, and occasional "historical" romances. In later years Ed referred with caustic amusement, and some satisfaction, to the dire predictions of critics that his popularity could not last.

His final remark to Metcalf indicated his concern about the future: "Wish that I might talk to you about it — writing is most unsatisfactory."[41]

On January 29 Metcalf's reply urged Ed to accept an agreement for 1914 based upon the offer of two and one-half cents a word; the editor emphasized that with *All-Story* now a weekly, "we very likely could use 50,000 words of yours a month which, at the rate of 2½ cents a word would mean practically an income from us alone of something considerably over $10,000 a year. That's a pretty good proposition, it seems to me."

Metcalf noted that based upon past occurrences Ed would have no difficulty in marketing any stories that were rejected by the Munsey Company. Accordingly, a year's contract would in no way harm his chances for sales. "I pay you, as it is, the highest rate I pay anybody, which, of course is a matter between you and me alone. . . ," Metcalf wrote.[42]

Surprisingly, as in the past year, Ed capitulated without further argument; perhaps Metcalf's logic had proved convincing. "I'll accept your 2½c per word offer for my 1914 output — first serial rights only — with the exception of the Tarzan story I am now finishing," he replied.[43] This was the story on which he had promised first refusal to Sessions at *New Story Magazine*. However, he restated his plan to send copies of the new *Tarzan* story to both magazines at the same time with the understanding that the best offer would be accepted. The agreement with Metcalf presented an opportunity which Ed was prompt to seize. With his usual persistence he hastened to advise the editor that he was sending a copy of the "revised Mucker," explaining once more that the revisions accorded with Metcalf's suggestions. Ed had eliminated "useless conversations, shortening it considerably more than ten thousand words."[44]

Undoubtedly influenced by the readers' clamor for more stories bearing the Burroughs name, as well as by the improved structure of "The Mucker," Metcalf now agreed to purchase it. On March 3, 1914, Ed received the largest amount he had so far been paid for any of his works — $1,450.00.[45]

Two months earlier Metcalf had taken "Nu of the Neocene," a story involving a double passage in time, first to the future and then to the past. Nu, a stone age man, after being buried in a cave for one hundred thousand years, awakens in modern times; later, accompanied by an American girl of the twentieth century, he is transported back to the prehistoric period. The story, titled "The Eternal Lover" when it appeared in *All-Story*, depends upon familiar names for its sequence of adventures. The heroine Victoria, from Beatrice, Nebraska, is the sister of Barney Custer, leading character of "The Mad King." Since the setting is in Africa on the vast estate of Lord and Lady Greystoke, where Victoria and Barney are guests at a hunt, brief parts are provided for Tarzan and Jane. This is the first reference to the estate and to the fact that the Greystokes are making their permanent home in equatorial Africa.[46]

From the restrictive and imitative plot and characters of "The Mad King" Ed must have returned to the fantasy world with a feeling of relief. His favorite subjects — the primitive life, the savage and his mate, fierce combat in the jungle, and of course the creation of Nu of the Neocene, mighty-muscled hunter of Oo, the saber-toothed tiger, as another version of Tarzan — allowed him to be freely imaginative and to devise situations amid familiar backgrounds.

In "The Eternal Lover," possibly as a result of hasty writing, Ed runs into occasional problems of appropriate language and style. At the beginning, in what appears to be an unnecessary explanation and a peculiar viewpoint intrusion by the author, he refers to Barney Custer as having come to the Greystoke estate "to hunt big game — and forget," and then adds:

But all that has nothing to do with this story; nor has John Clayton, Lord Greystoke, who was, once upon a time, Tarzan of the Apes, except that my having chanced to be a guest of his at the same time as the Custers makes it possible for me to give you a story that otherwise might never have been told.

Strangely, this author's viewpoint has no further development; no mention is again made of Burroughs as a guest or observer at the Greystoke estate, he offers no personal comment and he does not play a part in any of the scenes that follow.

An awkward writing practice, probably the one that provoked Metcalf's disapproving remarks about the use of the present tense, is demonstrated in Ed's shifts in verbs from the past to the present. In doing this he may have felt he was making the action more vivid and dramatic. After such uses of the past tense as "the hunter loosened the stone knife. . ." or he "drove his heavy spear deep. . . ," Ed then in other paragraphs changes to the present and writes, "Oo is creeping upon him now. The grinning jaws drip saliva. . ." or ". . . the beast succeeds. The paw closes upon the spear. . . ."

During this intensive writing period, with a

succession of stories being completed and dispatched to Metcalf, the editor may have felt like a man buried beneath a deluge of words. He gave understandable indications of being both stunned and confused. Concerning Ed's gallery of characters, especially in stories that had been purchased but not yet published, he seemed, on one occasion, to have lost track of both identifications and relationships. In sending a check for "Nu of the Neocene" he evidently displayed uncertainty about Barney Custer, who is assigned a limited role in the story.[47] Ed explained in detail:

Barney Custer appears first in The Mad King of Lutha. His mother was Victoria Rubinroth. I created a sister for him — Victoria Custer — to use as leading lady in Nu of the Neocene. I also used Barney in the latter story, as well as Lieutenant Butzow from The Mad King, and Tarzan and some of his characters. As I needed several minor characters I thought I might as well call upon old friends to give the tale additional human interest to those of your readers who happen to be familiar with these various characters. Those who have never heard of them before will find the story no less interesting because of them.[48]

He commented that he planned to use Barney again in another Lutha story; stressing his intention to include Butzow also "as the principal of a future yarn," he remarked, "I liked him exceedingly."[49]

On January 7, 1914, he turned his creative energy to the writing of the story awaited by his readers and both Metcalf and Sessions — the third Tarzan story. He had mentioned to Metcalf on February 3 that it was near completion, and a week later he wrote to announce it was en route and to reveal the title he had selected: "The Beasts of Tarzan." He was careful to again emphasize the conditions:

. . . This is the one I am forced to withhold from our 1914 arrangement owing to my promise to submit it to another publisher, as previously explained.

I can however entertain other offers for the first serial rights to it, and if you like the story I hope you get it.[50]

Months earlier, in writing to Sessions, he had discussed plans for the new Tarzan story, obviously attempting to gauge the extent of Sessions' interest and even predicting that the story would be started by the first of the year, with "a considerable part of it ready by the first of February. . . ."[51] That he should make a prediction of such astonishing accuracy — "The Beasts of Tarzan" was completed within the period of January 7 to February 9 — is an indication of the remarkable efficiency and discipline Ed Burroughs maintained in his work. Although Sessions, during the summer of 1913, had displayed an eagerness to obtain a Tarzan story and had been not at all perturbed by Ed's advance price tag of $3,000, his later correspondence appeared to show a lessening of interest, or so Ed interpreted the matter. Ed had written, "As to the next Tarzan story. I took it from your last letter that you desired to do nothing about cinching this for New Story, and so did not mention it further."[52] Ed chose to become idealistic about his objectives:

Whether you make a contract with me or not I am going to try to make this as nearly as good as Tarzan of the Apes and The Return of Tarzan as a sequel can be, with the hope of improving on both stories if it's in me. I realize that the Tarzan stuff is what put me on the map, and that if I fall down on the next Tarzan story it would have been better for me never to have written it at all.[53]

With the forwarding of "The Beasts of Tarzan" to Metcalf and Sessions at the same time, Ed inaugurated the kind of brazen bidding that no author had ever before attempted with an editor. It was a record "first" in the annals of story marketing. His opening maneuver, a week later, consisted of a follow-up letter to Metcalf in which, after explaining that he had written "The Beasts of Tarzan" entirely with the editor's "needs and desires in mind," he continued with an amusingly exaggerated sales pitch about

"Tarzan's" popularity: "The other two Tarzan stories have been read by some eighty nine million English speaking peoples, each of whom sat up all night to finish them. The entire civilized world is lying awake waiting for this sequel. I think, under these circumstances, that it might increase Munsey's circulation. Don't you?"[54] (The reference is to *Munsey's Magazine*, the top publication of the Munsey Company. It rated far above *All-Story* in prestige and paid higher rates; as a result, Ed had for some time hoped to place a story in the magazine.)

More seriously, Ed proceeded to the financial details:

I hope this tale will net me about twice what my best previous effort has brought. I refused a bona fide offer of $1500.00 for a contract for it before it was written, and have been told since that my request for $3000.00 would be no bar to its purchase.

With the popularity of its predecessors, which not even my blushing modesty prevents me from realizing, I think the story worth all of the latter sum, if not considerably more....[55]

The competitive bidding between Metcalf and Sessions was conducted mainly through a series of telegrams between San Diego and New York. Metcalf initiated the contest with an offering price, one he must have realized would not be accepted: "Feb. 17, 1914. Two thousand for Tarzan. If yes wire. Check immediately."

Ed promptly wired Sessions that he awaited his offer. But a complication had arisen; the manuscript sent to *New Story* had not arrived and was apparently lost in transit. The dickering was temporarily delayed while Wells Fargo was asked to trace the manuscript. On February 18 Ed wrote to Metcalf, "Did not think it worth while wiring you until I had something definite to say. I thank you for the offer, though, and hope you get the story — at a higher figure."

Too impatient to wait, and apprehensive that the bargaining might come to a halt, Ed sent a telegram to Metcalf: "Feb. 24, 1914: Sessions Tarzan manuscript lost. Kindly loan him yours on request." In his determination to keep the contest going, Ed appeared unconcerned about his astonishing request that one bidder share his copy of the manuscript with his competitor. Whatever Metcalf's initial reaction may have been, he nevertheless acceded to this unheard-of request. Negotiations reached a climax on February 28 in a rapid-fire sequence of telegrams:

A. L. Sessions
79 Seventh Ave
New York City

Will consider three thousand or more. Wire best to-day.   *E R Burroughs*
    Collect

Thomas Newell Metcalf
175 Fifth Ave
New York City

If can increase Tarzan offer materially wire best to-day.   *E R Burroughs*
    Paid

Edgar R Burroughs
4036 Third St San Diego Cal

Very sorry cannot offer more than two thousand   *A L Sessions*

E R Burroughs
4036 Third St San Diego

Do not want to be party to dickering name price will accept or reject immediately have a heart   *Metcalf*

Thomas Newell Metcalf
New York City

You can have for twenty five hundred. Wire.   *E R Burroughs*

    Paid

Ed's eagerness to complete the sale the same day, now that only one prospective buyer remained, was not matched by any haste on Metcalf's part. $2,500 was probably the largest amount of money that *All-Story* had ever considered paying for a manuscript, and the editor obviously intended to weigh his decision with care.

Several days passed, and on March 3, nervous over the silence from Metcalf's office, Ed wrote:

. . . I don't know whether you have decided to take the story or not. Since last August I had fixed the price in my mind at $3000.00 That is what I asked them [Sessions]. The concession to you was to demonstrate that I have a heart.

If you don't take it I shall wait until I get my $3000 — someone will give it. I really think you should have been glad to in consideration of the small sum the first Tarzan story cost you. Anyhow, I hope to beat the band that you get it even if I lose $500. . . .

On the same day the letter was mailed, a telegram came from Metcalf. The purchase of "The Beasts of Tarzan" for $2,500 was confirmed in two words: "All right."[56]

About the use of the same manuscript, Ed, on March 3, commented, "Probably I shattered all the age old ethics of the publishing business by suggesting that you loan Sessions yours. Howsomeever I saw no other way, and when there is but one and that requires shattering there is nothing to do but shatter."

The plot of "The Beasts of Tarzan" is centered once more around the schemes of the two **Russians, Rukoff and Paulvitch,** the villains of "The Return of Tarzan." Their plan for revenge leads to the kidnapping of the Greystoke's infant son Jack and the luring of both Tarzan and Jane aboard the steamer Kincaid, where they are made prisoners. Tarzan is set ashore on a jungle island and there, through a note written by Rokoff, learns the details of "the hideous plot of revenge":

You were born an ape. You lived naked in the jungles — to your own we have returned you;

but your son shall rise a step above his sire. It is the immutable law of evolution.

The father was a beast, but the son shall be a man — he shall take the next ascending step in the scale of progress. He shall be no naked beast of the jungle, but shall wear a loin-cloth and copper anklets, and, perchance, a ring in his nose, for he is to be reared by men — a tribe of savage cannibals.

Tarzan is also informed of the terrible fate reserved for his wife.

The jungle setting, with Tarzan returning to his savage life, and the favorite technique of maintaining suspense through alternating scenes, unresolved, in which Tarzan or Jane face new terrors, are of course familiar Burroughs fare. But Ed gives an original twist to his story with the introduction of an amazing crew composed of Sheeta the panther, a native named Mugambi, and a dozen huge apes led by the superintelligent Akut; all are trained by Tarzan to work as a unit and to respond to his summons for help. In endowing his beasts with almost-human attributes, Ed far exceeds the animal development he had devised in "Tarzan of the Apes," and equips the savage pack with an intelligence, discipline, and esprit de corps that strain the bounds of all belief. Among other accomplishments the "Beasts of Tarzan" — the panther, apes, and Mugambi, the native — become the most awe-inspiring crew to ever occupy a dugout or canoe; these seasoned mariners make hasty forays across the waters when Tarzan or Jane need rescuing.

In the exchange of letters with Metcalf, Ed brought up a new topic in regard to the ability of his young nephew Studley Burroughs. The son of Harry and Ella, Studley had from an early age shown unusual skill in drawing and illustrating and had chosen to make art his field of study. Ed wrote to inquire about possible opportunities:

By the way, if my nephew cared to submit a cover design with one of my future stories would it receive consideration? He's a mighty clever

SATURDAY — MAY 16 — TEN CENTS

ALL-STORY CAVALIER WEEKLY

13

The Beasts of Tarzan

by Edgar Rice Burroughs

ANOTHER ROMANCE OF THE "APE-MAN"

"The Beasts of Tarzan" cover of All-Story Cavalier Weekly, *May 16, 1914.*

young chap, and I don't know of anyone I'd rather see him get a start with than you. He's doing fairly well now, but nothing very steady, and his work is improving wonderfully. . . .[57]

About his latest writing, Ed remarked, "Am finishing up a story that Mrs. Burroughs says you will like. She has called the turn on all of them so far. So I have hopes. . . ."[58] He also disclosed his plans to leave California on March 28, returning to Chicago and his old address at 2005 Park Avenue. The new story, identified in his next letter, was called "The Lad and the Lion." Ed was somewhat dissatisfied with the title: "If you take it you may wish to change the title, and as several suggested themselves to me I'll pass them along to you for what they are worth: The Lord of the Lions. The Lion-Man. The Brother of the Lion. The Lion's Brother. Aziz-El-Adrea. The Prince and the Lion.[59]

To Ed's inquiry about the possible acceptance of art work by his nephew Studley, Metcalf replied that a cover design might be submitted. Ed wrote, "When I get home I'm going to get my nephew to try for one."[60] In the same letter he explained, "It will be some time now before I shall be able to send you another story as from now until the middle of May we shall be all muddled up with moving, house hunting and settling, though I may find a way to knock out another in the mean time."[61]

In commenting humorously about Metcalf's purchase of "The Beasts of Tarzan" after the frenzied round of bargaining, Ed noted, "Was glad to have your 'All right' telegram, and to know once more the w.k. solar system could continue on its accustomed trail, breathing regularly."[62] Ed included a reference to the $10,000 prize short story contest sponsored by Reilly & Britton. He had contemplated submitting a work in the contest but had changed his mind during the summer of 1913 and had "abandoned" the story after the completion of some sixty-seven pages. To Metcalf he remarked, "It is about half done — provided I cut it down to a short novelette, so I think that I shall finish it up now and let you have a look at it."[63] The story was revealed to be "The Girl from Harris's," and Ed required only thirteen more days

to finish it, sending the manuscript to Metcalf on March 20.[64]

Continuous correspondence with Metcalf covered matters of writing and publication. Concerning "The Eternal Lover," about to appear in the March 7, 1914, *All-Story* (the first issue as a weekly), Ed, upon re-reading the story, noted that it wasn't "half bad." When it was first completed, he had been disgusted with it and had begun a revision, but changing his mind had decided, "Oh Hell, let's wait 'til Metcalf makes me." He showed his dependence upon Emma and the importance he placed upon her opinions: "Mrs. Burroughs hadn't been able to read it ["The Eternal Lover"] before I sent it away, or I should have known that it was all right, for she has read it now and likes it immensely."[65]

Some months earlier he had indicated an interest in doing another Mars story, one centered about Carthoris, John Carter's son. Now Metcalf urged him to write the sequel and offered suggestions. On March 13 Ed wrote, ". . . I don't know about bringing Carthoris down to earth. But I might take Tarzan up to Mars, although with two such remarkable personalities in the same story I might find difficulty in doing credit to either. . . ." In continuing, he noted, "My plan for a Carthoris story centered principally about a little love affair between that young hybrid and Thuvia of Ptarth." A subject of further discussion was "The Mucker," and both Ed and Metcalf agreed that a better ending was needed. Ed commented, "The present close is beautifully artistic, but it's rotten at that. . . ." Of the editor, who had agreed to pay for revisions, Ed inquired, "How many more thousand words will you stand for? And, how soon do you want them?"[66]

Once more, an apparent misunderstanding on the part of Metcalf, relating to serial rights, this time hardly believable, caused strained relationships. In a postscript to his letter of March 13, Ed complained, "They made the old mistake on the Beasts of Tarzan check that they used to at first — the endorsement covered all rights, whereas I only offered you the first serial rights. Please have the proper formal letter of release sent me."

Metcalf, in his response, freely admitted that the fault lay with him; because of the large amount ($2,500) Munsey had paid for "The Beasts of Tarzan," the editor had assumed that all serial rights were included. He described the situation at the time of the purchase:

... We were discussing whether or not we could afford to buy this story. I was talking with Mr. Munsey about it, and he said: "If we pay him this sum, which will be considerably more than four cents a word, we will, of course, get all serial rights." And I said, "Why, yes, certainly." I explained very carefully to the clerical end of our manuscript department that when the cards were made out for our filing system it should be distinctly noted that we owned all serial rights on this latest Tarzan story.[67]

In a personal appeal to Ed, Metcalf wrote, "... I find myself very uncomfortably placed, because I am having a cover made for the yarn, which I suppose by this time is practically finished, and the story is entirely scheduled, and all that sort of thing. So you can see I am pretty much up a tree."[68]

As the disagreement over serial rights grew more intense, with Ed's impatience and annoyance growing, certain shifts and changes were taking place at the Munsey Company. In the previous month Metcalf had written to hint about these: "... it may be that I shall be given control of some other magazine in the house. I cannot speak in any way definitely. . . . Please don't say anything about this matter. . . . I am sure I may rely on your discretion."[69]

Ed viewed this possible change as a chance to improve his own fortunes. He wrote, "About the thing you suggested in your last. There is nothing I'd like better than following you where ever your rising star of fortune leads. I know that if the change should put me in line for a publication which payed more than *All-Story* that you would look after my interests."[70]

With the shift of positions Metcalf now became the editor of *Argosy Magazine* and Robert

H. Davis was given the editorship of the amalgamated *All-Story-Cavalier* weekly. Not directly informed of the changes, Ed heard about them from William G. Chapman, his agent for newspaper syndications. A concern about his future writing agreement with Munsey and uncertainty over other matters drove Ed into a state of agitation. His hasty inquiry to Metcalf echoed all his worries: he wanted to know if the "successor" on *All-Story* still cared to have "The Mucker" changed, and if so, in how many words; and what about the words in the Carthoris story? Or did the new editor *want* the story?[71] From these lesser problems Ed progressed to a more serious subject, one that aroused his familiar fears of wasting his writing efforts:

I was just thinking that possibly this change might put some one in who isn't keen for my brand of litrachoor, and if such is the case won't you use your good offices to obtain a release from my arrangement with Munsey. Otherwise I might write my head off on stuff that wouldn't do for any other magazine only to have it turned down. Take sequels, for instance. I knew pretty well what you wanted, but I don't know what the other fellow wants, so I don't want to write any sequels until I hear something definite.[72]

Notwithstanding the confidence Ed had expressed in Metcalf, and his willingness to follow the editor wherever his "rising star of fortune leads," he had no intention of relinquishing the serial rights to "The Beasts of Tarzan." That newspaper serialization of his stories would prove highly profitable had already been demonstrated, especially in the *New York Evening World*; through Chapman's International Press Bureau Ed was currently distributing "The Return of Tarzan," and he planned to follow the same procedure with "The Beasts. . . ." His letter to Metcalf contained a cold rejection of the editor's plea:

... I cannot see how there can be any chance for a misunderstanding. Months ago I distinctly stated that I only wished to offer the first serial rights to my stories. There was nothing said to the contrary about this story. I should have

been mad to have sold you all the rights for $2500.00. The newspaper rights to the Return of Tarzan have already brought in $950.00 and are still selling.[73]

A comparison of the returns from his own newspaper sales with those of the Munsey Company was highly revealing. It was clear that Ed, with his acute business and bargaining instincts, could give a lesson in salesmanship to the magazine's syndication department. His comment was bluntly critical:

Another thing, and the most important to me; if the newspaper rights are sold by your syndicating department at anything like their usual rates it will tend to ruin the market for my future stories as I will have been getting much more all along the line than your syndicating department sells mss for; — as much as six times what they sold Tarzan of the Apes for in one instance.[74]

His letter contained a threat to take an action that could lead to a complete break with the Munsey Company: "If Mr. Munsey insists upon holding me to the technicality of the check endorsement the only thing that I can see to do is to buy the story back from you. I hope that this will not be necessary for I wish you to have it. . . ."[75] He stressed his hopes for a satisfactory agreement, noting that one of his greatest pleasures in writing for the Munsey Company would disappear if he felt he might be "similarly misunderstood at any moment in the future," and that his interests "were not unquestionably safer" in their hands than in those of other publishers.[76]

With the changes in the editorial staff and the resulting confusion the matter remained unsettled. Ed's protests were unanswered, but with a bulldog tenacity he continued his one-sided campaign to acquire a clear ownership of his serial rights to "The Beasts of Tarzan." His succession of letters in the following months, written to both Metcalf and Davis, contained repeated references to the subject. To Metcalf he forwarded a personal appeal:

. . . The present policy of ignoring me does not set very well.

I asked several questions that should have been answered, which, you advise me, you relayed to the Proper authority; but I've heard nothing.

And about the Beast of Tarzan rights: I can understand that you made an honest mistake in perfectly good faith; but I can less well afford to suffer by it than The Frank A Munsey Company.

They got a story that their readers wanted for what they paid, while I will get nothing at all for a loss of several thousand dollars.

It would mean very little to The Munsey Company either way, but a great deal to me, and I shall never let my rights to this story go without contesting it to the utmost.[77]

"So keenly do I feel the injustice of it," he wrote, "that I am seriously considering writing nothing more until my arrangement with The Munsey Company is up the 31st of December."[78] In a second letter of the same date to Metcalf he stated, "I have heard nothing further about the several rights to The Beasts of Tarzan, and as a matter of form I should be very glad if the formal release such as was sent me in previous instances should be sent to me, releasing all but first serial rights. . . ."[79]

By this time the Munsey Company could entertain no illusions that Ed would forget the matter. In fact, it appeared plain that he would never allow *them* to forget it. To Robert Davis, the new editor of *All-Story-Cavalier*, he wrote, ". . . Just at present I am particularly concerned with the matter of the several rights to The Beasts of Tarzan, relative to which I have written Mr. Metcalf in the letters which you mention. . . . I state specifically that I can entertain offers for the first serial rights, nor anywhere in any letter have I even remotely suggested that I sought to dispose of any other rights."[80]

The battle may have been protracted, but the Munsey Company, at an early stage, might have perceived that in dealing with a man of Burroughs' dogged determination their chances were nil. The inevitable surrender came in a

184

letter from Davis: "This shall be your authority to exercise for your own account all rights in your story entitled "The Beasts of Tarzan," which ran serially in The All-Story Cavalier Weekly from May 16 to June 13, 1914, save the first serial rights."[81]

Ed continued to expend his unlimited energies in other directions. Syndication was very much on his mind, and an inquiry from the *Tacoma Tribune* prompted him, on February 26, to write to Chapman, who agreed to contact the newspaper concerning the two available Tarzan stories. Chapman revealed that the Munsey Company had granted him "the privilege" of making sales of "Tarzan of the Apes"; because of the small payments received by the syndication department, the company had evidently lost interest in marketing the story. Chapman's report that he had offered to release both "Tarzan of the Apes" and "The Return of Tarzan" to the *Tribune* for a mere $75 was hardly cause for elation. But the *Tribune* was one of the lesser outlets; newspapers of this type all over the country were included in Ed's ambitious plan to find some type of mass market for serialization of his stories.[82]

Ed was still plagued by a regret that he had relinquished the serial rights of "Tarzan of the Apes." His past attempt to repurchase these rights had been unsuccessful, and now, in an inquiry to Chapman, he again discussed the possibility of obtaining them. Chapman's reply was discouraging; about the story he wrote, "Nothing can be done. . . . They won't let go of it."[83]

Ed continued to conduct his own negotiations with Terhune at the *Evening World.* His telegram of March 11, 1914, to the editor read: "You may have New York City newspaper rights Eternal Lover for one cent per word. Immediate payment." Terhune, on the same date, wired a protest:

One cent a word for "Eternal Lover" would be three times as much pro rata as we paid for "Return of Tarzan" and nearly ten times prorata price of "Tarzan of Apes." We want the story but not at so prohibitive a price. Won't you re-

consider terms and telegraph. We consent to immediate payment as you propose.

In a letter of March 13 Ed presented a lengthy exposition of his sales philosophy. His statements were again based upon a businesslike analysis of the market value of his wares:

If the prices I asked for the New York City newspaper rights to The Eternal Lover seems high it must be remembered that my stories are worth more now than at first.

I am not viewing the matter from an egotistical standpoint. I have always tried, and I think succeeded in eliminating ego from my business consideration of my work — otherwise I might be prompted to give my yarns away.

He offered a logical comparison of past and present values:

. . . My last story brought six times what Tarzan of the Apes brought, and over ten times that which I received for the story that preceded it —my first. I only asked you three times as much as you paid for the first story you bought of me, which I think you will admit was very generous of me.

Ed brought up a further point, which he felt was "the most potent":

. . . Two large publishing houses shied at Tarzan solely on account of the fact that it had run in the newspapers. Some day someone will put my stories into books; but in the mean time I am losing just that much by allowing them to be syndicated, so I do not feel that I can afford the luxury without ample remuneration.

His final comment to Terhune was that "$300.00 is not an exorbitant price for such a story as The Eternal Lover if your readers like it. Of course, by the yard, it may seem a high price, but who would purchase works of art by the yard!"[84]

In answering on March 20, Terhune again stressed that the terms were prohibitive, adding, "I'm sorry, on my own account; and chiefly because of the thousands of Evening World readers who love Tarzan and are so eager to read every word about him." He offered $200 for

"The Eternal Lover" and pointed out that this was a record fiction price for his "twenty years of service" at the *World*. The magnetism of the Burroughs' name *on any story* and its power to lure readers was already demonstrated, even at this early period. As a result of this popular demand Ed had altered, or to a certain extent reversed, the normal author-editor relationship with the editor dictating the terms. That Ed was the dominant party, negotiating from a position of strength, was revealed in Terhune's personal plea, most unusual in that it came from the editor of one of the country's greatest newspapers. In continuing his letter Terhune implored, "Won't you reconsider on that basis? We should be your debtors and so should our readers. Telegraph in such event; and a check for $200 will be sent you by the next mail."

Concerning the rejection of "Tarzan" by book publishers, Terhune wrote, "If you will refer any future publishers to us, we shall be only too glad to testify to the tremendous interest the story has aroused among our readers. . . ."[85] Before the combined appeal of the editor's plea and his praise of "Tarzan," Ed's resistance collapsed. On March 25 he wired, "Two hundred dollars. . . Eternal Lover acceptable. Remit to Chicago address."

The two stories that signaled the end of the prolific California writing period were entirely dissimilar in their plots, settings, and styles. "The Girl from Harris's" (when finally published, the name Harris was changed to Farris), begun in Chicago a year earlier, depicted big city corruption, creating at times the effect of an exposé. It established some elements of realism, while, in contrast, the second work, "The Lad and the Lion," returned to fantasy and to a transparent repetition of situations and devices that had given "Tarzan" its popularity.

In "The Girl from Harris's" Ed adopts the role of a social reformer, commenting bluntly and witheringly about the alliance, in Chicago, between certain vice interests, scheming politicians, and powerful real estate groups and property owners. In addition, through his portrait of a hypocritical clergyman he offers a caustic view of religious do-gooders and of society's narrowly puritanical standards. Ed's characters are created with a sentimentality that weakens the story's realistic effect. The heroine, first introduced as "Maggie Lynch," is revealed to be a prostitute, an employee of Abe Harris, described as "the most notorious dive keeper in the city." Later events show that the supposed connection with a man's death has enabled Harris to blackmail her and keep her in his establishment against her will.

Maggie, aided by Ogden Secord, a handsome young businessman, and inspired by his faith in her, attempts to start a new life and takes a position as a typist, now using her real name — June Lathrop. Another character, the Reverend Theodore Pursen, exemplifies, as a minister, the worst qualities of false piety.

Ed, in developing the plot, devises an ironic twist or reversal of the roles of the two main characters. Ogden Secord receives a blow on the head during a robbery in his office and as a result, his memory and his power to think clearly are impaired. With the loss of his prosperous business he deteriorates, in the end becoming an alcoholic. The changing situations allow June Lathrop, now leading a respectable life, an opportunity to assist the man who had given her needed encouragement.

In the last few chapters the setting is abruptly shifted, and both Ogden and June are transported from Chicago to Idaho. June turns up as a waitress, hundreds of miles from Chicago, in the town of Goliath, the very same town where Ogden, a down-and-out drunk, has wandered. Once more Ed returns to his theme of a man's regeneration through a combination of a healthful outdoor life and a woman's faith and love. Ogden works as a miner, washing gold as Ed and his brothers had done. Actual towns are referred to: Ketchum on the Salmon River near Sun Valley, and Shoshone, farther south.[86]

As he had done in "The Mucker," Ed attempted to give his dialogue a realistic flavor through the use of the argot of the lower or criminal classes. The heroine, in her first role as Maggie, slips into the coarse slang of the times.[87] From the extremes of the vernacular Ed moves, in other sections, to the use of dialogue which is stilted, unnatural, and which gives a melodramatic effect: "You can't help being kind and sweet, for your soul is pure and true — I can read it in your eyes; but even that can't blind you to the bald and brutal fact of what I am — a drunken bum."

"The Lad and the Lion" presents an opening deliberately made vague, with brief, mysterious hints of the Lad's noble birth. The fourteen-year-old boy aboard the ship is summoned by "Old Jagst," a faithful attendant, when a shipwreck is imminent. Jagst says, "Quick, Your Highness," and later there is a reference to "royal blood"; but the Lad receives no name and the kingdom is not identified. The boy reveals his courage by refusing to enter a lifeboat, insisting that the place be given to a woman. As the ship goes down, he is struck on the head by a piece of timber, finds himself in the water and then climbs into a drifting lifeboat. The blow on his head has destroyed his memory.

Later, the story develops bizarre elements. The Lad is taken aboard a derelict ship whose only occupant is an odd creature, a half-mad epileptic, an old man who is also a deaf-mute. On the same ship is a young lion in a cage. The old man, who has derived a sadistic pleasure from teasing and torturing the animal, now begins to mistreat the boy, and in the passing months subjects him to threats and beatings. The Lad is required to learn the sign language of the deaf-mute. He shows kindness and sympathy toward the lion, and the two develop a strong bond of affection.

Four years of this life continue, until the lion kills the old man. The ship then drifts ashore on the coast of northern Africa, and the pair enter the desert together. A romance emerges between the Lad and Nakhla, the exotic daughter of Sheik Ali-Es-Hadji, complicated by the customary evil schemes of a villain, Ben Saada. From Nakhla the Lad finally receives a name, Aziz, meaning "beloved" in Arabic. With the introduction of Marie, the daughter of Colonel Joseph Vivier, commander of the French garrison, Ed devises the typical conflict of a love triangle.

The familiar device of a loss of memory is accompanied by its equally familiar solution: clubbed on the head in a battle with the Arabs, Aziz regains his memory. In the very last section of the story, the past returns to him. He recalls the ship and the "gray old man" who had cried, "Quick, Your Highness!" Beyond the ship he also sees, as in a vision, "a stately pile of ancient masonry," and a scene returns to him of a little boy being saluted by soldiers. He realizes that he is a royal prince and that a throne awaits him.

In its final love scene between the Lad and Nakhla, the story remains somewhat cryptic and inconclusive. The Sheik, when informed by Aziz that he would wed Nakhla and the two would then dwell in the family douar, had only accepted because he appeared to have no choice. As a foreigner, Aziz had been viewed with contempt by the Arabs, and had been called a "dog" and a "pig" by them. Now, with a realization of his royal birth, the Lad's feelings of inferiority are replaced by a sudden pride: "No longer was he a dog, or a pig. Now he knew precisely what he was and what awaited his coming upon another continent. . . ." He gazed into the eyes of Nakhla, "and then with all the ease and grace of centuries of breeding behind him, he dropped to one knee before her, lifting her slim brown hand to his lips. 'My Queen,' he said. 'My Queen — forever!' "

Whether the Lad intended to marry Nakhla and live in the Arab douar with her, or whether he planned to return with her to his unnamed kingdom is uncertain. The story is without a definite resolution. The typical Burroughs stratagem must be suspected: the possibility of a sequel was being held in abeyance.[88]

Ed was to achieve one more success, valued by him above all, before his return to Chicago. In February 1914 events began moving rapidly toward his long-desired goal — the acceptance of "Tarzan of the Apes" for book publication. The serial installments of the story, especially in the New York *Evening World*, had spread its fame and popularity. In the passing months the public's response had grown until it could be better described as a fascination with the very idea of Tarzan and his jungle environment. But Ed was not depending solely upon newspapers and public interest to promote the book possibilities. According to one report, for a period of several months he had made daily trips to A. C. McClurg & Company's store on South Wabash Avenue in Chicago to talk to Herbert Gould, McClurg editor and an old friend, and to others at the publishing company. Ed was a single-minded man, and the sole topic of discussion was the appearances of Tarzan stories in magazines and newspapers and how they were causing "Tarzan's" popularity to soar. Ed's dogged campaign was almost sufficient in itself to overcome the resistance.[89]

The Tarzan fame prompted John G. Kidd of Stewart & Kidd Company, Cincinnati, Ohio, on February 20, to express an interest in acquiring "Tarzan of the Apes" for publication. In his response Ed displayed a confident attitude. He knew there was a public demand for "Tarzan" in book form and that this demand would increase when "The Beasts of Tarzan" appeared in *All-Story*. The struggles and uncertainties of 1912 were long gone. He could afford to wait now until he received an attractive offer.[90] Nevertheless, he was curious about Stewart & Kidd and he sought information from Herbert Gould. His main concern was whether the firm had enough experience and capital to handle the book successfully. ". . . Have they a reputation for square dealing?" he also inquired.[91] Gould, on March 13, rated Stewart & Kidd as "first class," explaining that they had been in the book business and were "ambitious" to turn to publishing. "I have my doubts," he confessed. ". . . They certainly do not have the facilities for handling a novel as it should be handled." Undoubtedly to Ed's surprise and elation, Gould made a counter offer: "If you have not gone too far, it might be possible for you to again submit to us the manu-

script of your story 'Tarzan of the Apes.' I will be glad to have our publishing department reconsider their decision of last Fall about publishing it."[92]

Acceptance of "Tarzan of the Apes" by A. C. McClurg & Company was now a certainty. However, as negotiations continued, Ed preferred to let his agent William Chapman handle them. The sale of "Tarzan of the Apes" to a book publisher was the climax of two years of struggles and a sign of personal and creative triumph. But if Ed considered it so, his actions at this moment of success defy all explanation. With Europe in a turmoil and events moving rapidly toward declarations of war by the various powers, he arrived at a rather surprising decision: he wanted to be a war correspondent. Toward the end of April 1914 he sent his request to Albert Payson Terhune at the *Evening World*. Terhune was clearly incredulous:

Rare first edition of Tarzan of the Apes *(hardback).*

I've turned over your war correspondent application to Mr. Tennant, the Managing Editor. Though why a man who can write such fiction as you write should want to do press work, is beyond my understanding. In any case, I wish you all the luck there is.[93]

On April 25, with the "Tarzan" sale assured, Ed dispatched instructions to Chapman. The matter was one quite obviously dear to his heart:

I wish to have appear on the fly leaf of Tarzan of the Apes:

*To
Emma Hulbert Burroughs*

Or,

*Emma Hulbert Burroughs
Her Book*

The latter is rather irregular, but it fits the case — Mrs. Burroughs has always had a partiality for Tarzan, calling it her story from the first.

Will you please see to this for me.

Thanks.

Chapman, on May 1, notified Ed that the final agreement with McClurg had been reached.[94] A day later in a letter to Terhune Ed indicated that his desire to be a war correspondent was a mere impulse, subsiding as quickly as it had arisen. He wrote, ". . . I guess that war correspondent job will have to lie over until Teddy comes in again in 1916. . . ."[95]

Seldom did Burroughs display in his business correspondence the warm sensitivity and emotions that were so much a part of his private nature. His feelings about Emma and "Tarzan of the Apes" — Her Book — were touchingly revealed in the autograph he penned to Emma in a first edition copy of the book, published on June 17, 1914, at this milestone in his career:

June 10, 1914

My dear wife:

Do you recall how we waited in fear and trembling the coming of the postman for many days after we sent the Tarzan Mss to Metcalf?

And will you ever forget the morning that he finally came?

Not even this, our first book, can quite equal that unparalleled moment.

That we may never have cause for another such is the wish of your devoted husband

Ed R Burroughs

Delighted by the Fred J. Arting illustration of Tarzan in moonlit silhouette on the title page of the book, Ed pasted a miniature sticker of the drawing onto the letter of July 20 that he wrote to Bob Davis. Beneath the tiny rectangle showing Tarzan poised on a tree branch, Ed typed, "Ain't this a cute little sticker?"

The end of the California period and the return to Chicago brought this comment from Ed in the final lines of his *Autobiography:*

Before we left San Diego for the East I must have been feeling flush again for I ordered a new automobile for delivery in Chicago when we arrived.

Once again we auctioned our belongings, including the old second-hand Velie.

His earnings, collected during the summer of 1913 before he left California, totaled more than $4,600 from sales of stories and from the *Evening World* syndication. In California, from October through mid-March 1914, five completed stories and syndication payments from Chapman had brought him approximately $6,000.[96] He had written approximately 413,000 words. He was hardly in danger of going "over the hills to the poorhouse" and was well ahead of the sheriff.

11
THE
WRITER
AT HOME

With his return to Chicago at the end of March 1914, Ed, his financial situation now secure, planned to purchase his own home in a neighborhood suitable for the raising of his three children, Joan, six, Hulbert, five, and Jack, barely one year old. Ed had stayed temporarily at the Hulbert home at 2005 Park Avenue, renumbered from its original 194. He directed his mail to be forwarded there, but intended to remain there for only a brief period. He decided to buy a home in the upper middle-class suburb of Oak Park, at 414 Augusta Street, near Ridgeland, and on May 11 he moved his family into the large five-bedroom home which was advertised as having "the best hot-water heating plant in Oak Park."[1]

In the productive schedule of writing that he continued to maintain, Ed certainly demonstrated himself to be the least temperamental of writers. He had approached his story creations in the past with a businesslike, matter-of-fact attitude, and success had not changed him. Noises or distractions had little effect upon the flow of his ideas; he required neither complete silence nor isolation. While at work in his study, he permitted the children to enter and leave at will, and even had no objection to stopping in the middle of a passage to answer questions or play with them. As Ed typed a story, it was not unusual for Jack, then three or four, to climb up and perch himself on his father's knee.[2] A writer of the period reported:

Three beautiful children, Joan, Hulbert and Jack, the oldest six, clamber over Mr. Burroughs' anatomy, and desk and typewriter while he is turning out the tales you all clamor for. "Were I literary," he says, "and afflicted with temperament I should have a devil of a time writing stories. . . .[3]

In these early Oak Park days Ed's office was in his home. He had already adopted a schedule

191

that would become a habit with him, one that he would adhere to for the remainder of his writing career. Finding the morning hours most productive, he was at his typewriter at seven or seven-thirty, worked until noon, and after a pause for lunch, perhaps continued for an hour or so longer. In later years he wrote only in the morning. He followed this schedule five or six days a week, and on occasion worked in the evenings, especially when he corrected the pages he had written during the day. The corrections, though brief, sometimes involved typing errors or the substitution of one word for another, but Ed seldom rewrote or did lengthy revisions unless these were requested by a publisher.[4]

He was unaffected by the kind of temperament often evidenced in writers who went through agonizing struggles in a search for ideas and who claimed that they had to wait for the inspiration to arrive. His later philosophy revealed an impatience with these writers; he did not understand their inspirational requirements — he simply sat down to write and the ideas came.

At this time he typed all his stories himself, and having no training in the touch system, he used a two-finger method, pecking away rapidly and with an accuracy that was quite remarkable. His daily output averaged from ten to twelve pages, double-spaced. His approach did not include rough drafts, a practice followed by many authors who then revise or polish their material. Instead, he reflected upon each sentence, carefully working out the structure in his mind. He might sit silent for a long while, meditating, head down, in intense concentration, before turning to type the complete sentence. With this method he seldom found it necessary to make changes.

Ed maintained that often, as he wrote, and the fantastic characters and actions sprang from his imagination, he had no idea of what was coming next. This was clearly a humorous exaggeration; the plot and its general direction were already established in his mind. However,

he would never depend upon a strict, detailed outline, claiming that this would restrict him, tie him down in a way that would hamper his imaginative flights. The closest thing to an outline might be a summary of several sentences in which the theme or essence of a forthcoming chapter was briefly stated. Ed admitted, with amusement, that because of his spur-of-the-moment writing or improvising, he would sometimes get his character into a seemingly impossible situation and not know how to extricate him. Nevertheless he always did.

While in his writing he was freely imaginative, preferring to devise incidents as he went along, in his record keeping, as previously explained, he was thoroughly businesslike and methodical. (His card index of sales and payments has already been referred to.) With his first published story, "Under the Moons of Mars," he began his worksheets, using Roman numerals. On these sheets he noted beginning and completion dates, chapter headings, and page numbers, often with word counts, and listed his characters — later, because of his sequels, consisting only of new characters not involved in the previous stories.[5]

At this stage Emma was the first to read his stories, and she became his most valued critic. In seeking the opinions of his brothers, however, he naturally turned to Harry, who had been closest to him and had helped him through many difficult situations in the past. Earlier, when his first Martian story was in progress (then titled "Dejah Thoris, Martian Princess"), he had brought sections to Harry and his wife Ella (always addressed as Nell or Nellie) for their reading and reactions. They had of course been enthusiastic about the story and, at a later reading, about "Tarzan of the Apes." Their children, Evelyn and Studley, through family discussions and their own reading, became familiar with Ed's creations.[6] When, with these successes, Ed had considered quitting his job, he sought Harry's advice. Cautious, and without very much confidence in writing as a career, Harry advised Ed to stay where he was, remind-

A PRINCESS OF MARS
(Under the Moons of Mars)

-Iss - River of Death.
-Tars Tarkas - a chieftan; 2nd to Lorquas Ptomel.
-sak - jump.
- Sola - young green-Martian woman.
-Lorquas Ptomel - Jed among the Tharks.
-Woola - a Barsoomian calot.
-Sarkoja - a green-Martian woman.
-Thark - city and name of a green Martian horde.
-Tal Hajus - Jeddak of Thark.
-Dejah Thoris - Princess of Helium.
-Mors Kajak - a jed of Helium, her father.
-Helium - the empire of the grandfather of Dejah Thoris.
-Barsoom - Mars.
-Jeddak - Emperer.
-Jed - King.
-Dor - Valley of Heaven.
-Korus - lost sea of Dor.
-Korad - a dead city of ancient Mars.
-thoat - green martian "horse".
-Tardos Mors - grandfather of Dejah Thoris.
-Zad - Tharkian warrior.
-o mad - man with one name.
-Dotar Sojat - Captain Carter's Martian name, from the surnames of the
              two warrior-chieftans he first killed.
-sorak - a little pet animal among the red martian women; about the
         size of a cat.
-Warhoon - another community of green men; enemies of Thark.
-zitidars - mastadonian draught animals.
-calot - dog.

     A Community:(figures are approximate only)
                    500 warriors
                     20 chieftans
                    250 women
                    250 youths
                    500 children (immediately after a hatching)
                    250 chariots
                   1000 thoats
                    300 zitidars
                    500 calots
   July 14 1912 - commenced sequel to "Under the Moons of Mars" GODS OF MARS   IV
Bar Comas - Jeddak of Warhoon.
Dak Kova - Jed among the Warhoon (later Jeddak)
kaor - greeting
Kantos Kan - padwar of Helium navy.
padwar - lieutenant.
Zodanga - Martian city of red men, at war with Helium.
Ptor - family name of three brothers - Zodangans.
darseen - chameleon.
Sab Than - prince of Zodanga.
Than Kosis - Jeddak of Zodanga.
Notan - royal psychologist of Zodanga.
Gozava - Tar Tarkas' dead wife.
                    (Above Martian names and words used in Under the Moons of Mars)

ERB's notebook page for "A Princess of Mars"; ERB recorded information included in each of his stories which, when he started writing sequels, helped him keep characters and other facts in order.

ing him of his responsibilities to his wife and children. He urged Ed to view the writing merely as a part-time occupation.

Ed's family and friends had often commented about the names he devised for the strange characters in his stories. His ability to create exotic civilizations and races and surround them with an other-world atmosphere that appeared scientifically plausible and realistically convincing was matched, and necessarily so, by his adeptness in inventing names that fitted naturally into his bizarre settings. He formed his names, at times, by combining odd syllables, selecting and sounding them while he listened for the odd, foreign effect he was seeking. On occasion he chose or modified words from foreign languages, especially Latin. His ear, the final judge, told him when the sound was right. Above all, the name must fit the character. *Tars Tarkas* seemed natural for a brave Martian chief, and *Tal Hajus* for a cruel, villainous ruler (the sound was hard and cacophonic enough), while *Dejah Thoris* was perfect for a beautiful Martian princess. The name *Tarzan* itself appeared uniquely chosen — as though no other name could have possibly been accepted.

In devising names for his animal characters Ed was equally skillful. Somehow *Tantor* seems appropriate for a towering, majestic, and kindly elephant, *Sheeta* menacing enough for a leopard, and *Akut* just right for a protective ape companion. While many names were formed through the combining of syllables, Ed freely admitted he may have used actual names that somehow remained in his memory. In a letter of July 2, 1923, to his brother Harry who had inquired about his methods, Ed wrote:

. . . I try to originate all the peculiar names for people, places and animals in my stories. Sometimes I must unconsciously use a word or name that I have read and forgotten, as for instance Numa the lion. There was a Roman emperor, Numa, of whom I had forgotten until I was recently rereading Plutarch's Lives. The name must have been retained in my sub-conscious brain, later popping out as original. . . .

The other-world effect was also evident in the geographical names he invented. Such words as *Barsoom* for Mars, the *Otz Mountains, Ptarth, Phutra, Zodanga,* and others, through their strange, alien sounds, helped achieve a natural atmosphere for Ed's fantastic civilizations.

On a number of occasions Ed had expressed his preferences among his own writings, revealing that he liked his Martian stories better than the Tarzan stories; he had also been quite explicit about his choice of reading, his favorite authors — and his aversions. He liked Kipling's poetry but found his stories boring. He detested Dickens; according to one biographer this feeling may have resulted from Major Burroughs' habit of reading aloud to his young son:

When, for example, his father read Dombey and Son, Edgar hated Dombey and had the impression that Dombey and Dickens were one and the same person. When he learned the difference, it was too late for him to overcome his ingrained prejudice against Dickens. . . .[7]

At some period during his early years Ed had developed a dislike for Shakespeare which he could never overcome. On the other hand, his school studies and readings in Latin, including Caesar's *Commentaries* and the works of Gibbons, had given him a permanent interest in the Romans. This led to an intense admiration for Thomas Babington Macauley's *Lays of Ancient Rome;* in the vigorous style of these ballads, their regular meter, stirring narration, and martial tone Ed found pleasure and excitement.[8]

His early readings in fiction had made certain authors his favorites. These included Jack London, George Barr McCutcheon with his *Graustark* novels, Anthony Hope with his *Prisoner of Zenda*, and Zane Grey with his stories of the West. Much of his later nonfiction reading was done for research, but he had found the adventurous works of Richard Haliburton highly enjoyable.[9]

Hulbert, Emma, Jack, and Joan Burroughs, about 1915.

In the home life of the Burroughs family Ed naturally turned his vivid imagination loose to create the most fantastic of stories for his three children. Storytelling, which he first practiced as a child, reversing the normal procedure by telling his mother the stories he made up, had always been his special delight. For his children he invented such characters as Grandpa Kazink, an old man with a flowing white beard who embarked in his own flying machine for the wildest of escapades. Accompanying him, and sharing in the hair-breadth escapes was a little girl named Saphronia.[10] In later years Ed invented Arabella the Coyote who was involved in animal adventures that might include pursuits by lions or tigers.[11] Ed's procedure in telling his stories to the children at bedtime was a duplicate of the to-be-continued, cliff-hanging style he adopted in his published stories.

Grandpa Kazink, as well as the others, went on and on with continuing new sequences:

When the children were very small, it was Burroughs' job to tell them bedtime stories and, after a hard day's writing, pacing in the corridor outside their rooms, he broadcast improvisations wholesale. Characteristically, he had several serials going at the same time. In one of them "Grandpa Kazink and his Flying Machine," Grandpa, something of an interplanetary superman on a child's level, was constantly rescuing his girl friend Saphronia from other-world savages. After Burroughs had worked the kids up to an unbearable pitch, with Grandpa hanging on to the edge of Mars while six-legged Moaks hacked away at his tiring fingers, he would call, "That's all, children. Now go to sleep." . . .[12]

The Burroughs' Augusta Street home in Oak Park was typical of any home where three children were being raised. Included in its activity and excitement were the noises of children at play, the barking of dogs, and the sounds of music — singing and piano playing. Ed had always liked children, enjoyed playing with them and devising games for them, and Emma had her heart and interest centered in her home and family. As a result, the relationships of parents and children were warm and close. In their childhood Ed and Emma had developed a lasting fondness for dogs, and they soon acquired two airdale terriers. The male, naturally named Tarzan, became a permanent pet who would also, in the future, become a traveler, journeying with them to California.[13]

While Ed often made joking references to his voice, his inability to carry a tune, and freely admitted that his musical tastes were limited — he liked only marches, martial music, and hymns, claiming they were the only kind of music he understood — he nevertheless regretted his lack of musical background. As a result, he was pleased to have music become an important activity in his home. Emma, who had studied voice in the hope of becoming an operatic singer, entertained the family and friends. They encouraged all the children to take piano or singing lessons.

The Burroughs family early became aware of the strange and often frightening nature of their father's dreams. Throughout his adult years Ed was subject to nightmares. These occurred regularly and involved the kind of situation, familiar to many dreamers, where some fearful creature or unidentified peril was approaching the room, and the individual, aware of his danger, tried desperately to move but found himself paralyzed. Ed would twist about, moan and cry out loudly and awaken the family. Sometimes Emma soothed him until he became calm. Statements or suppositions that these nightmares contained fantasy scenes of other worlds or dangerous encounters with creatures of the type created by Ed in his stories, and that he would draw upon these nocturnal adventures for his plots, are unfounded. His nightmares

The Burroughs children in front of home at 414 Augusta Street, Oak

196

should not be confused with his daydreams during which he might devise characters and situations for his stories.[14]

At the time when he first turned to writing, Ed developed an illness that became troublesome. The sharp pain in his left shoulder was diagnosed as "neuritis." His most acute suffering occurred at night. The Burroughs children sometimes awakened in the middle of the night to see their father pacing the floor, unable to sleep because of the pain.[15] After a number of years the "neuritis" apparently vanished, or so Ed believed; on June 22, 1918, in a letter to his friend Bert Weston concerning the illness of Weston's wife, he discussed the matter:

I was mighty sorry to learn from your letter received today that Margaret is afflicted with neuritis. It is a mighty painful disease as I know from seven years experience with it. I am pretty well shut of it now and it may interest Margaret to know that my improvement immediately followed the taking of a medicine which I obtained while in Coldwater [Michigan] the 1st of March.

I do not take much stock in patent medicines but after a fellow has had neuritis for seven years he would take almost anything to be rid of it. — I even tried Christian Science once. This dope which I obtained is put up by a druggist in Coldwater from a prescription given to one of the Coldwater plutes by a traveling salesman — but where the traveling salesman got the prescription, deponent sayeth not. Anyhow, it costs one and a half bucks per bottle and is absolutely guaranteed to be harmless.[16]

Noting that Dr. Earle had scoffed at the idea of the medicine having any effect, Ed wrote, ". . . it was a remarkable coincidence that immediately after commencing to take it the pain left me for the first time in years and I have been steadily improving since."[17]

Whatever relief Ed may have obtained, real or imaginary, it was evident that the medicine did not provide a permanent cure. A year later he revealed that the pain had not disappeared:

197

For a considerable part of the past seven or eight years I have suffered the tortures of the damned with neuritis; but I have studiously avoided the use of drugs, preferring the pain to the possibility of acquiring a habit that always had seemed peculiarly revolting to me. . . .[18]

Again, in a letter to his brother Harry three years later concerning Nellie's (Ella's) illness, Ed also discussed his troublesome neuritis:

. . . Was very sorry to learn that Nellie had been suffering so from neuritis. Mine has come back again, after leaving me for two to three years, though it is not as bad as it used to be. I learned yesterday of a theory that acids aggravate it; therefore let us leave acids alone.[19]

Whether by modern diagnostic methods the illness would be called "neuritis" is doubtful. To his nephew Studley, who many years afterward complained about arthritis, Ed responded, ". . . . It hurts like hell. I know. But I am over mine. I also had bursitis. . . ."[20] The entire problem may have simply resulted from inaccurate diagnosis and treatment.

Despite his periodic suffering from neuritis, Ed continued to indulge in a recreation that was one of his greatest sources of pleasure. He had always loved automobiles and driving. The 1914 biographical sketch written for William G. Chapman (author unknown) comments about this:

Next to Mr. Burroughs' devotion to his family comes his love of motoring. Rain or shine, summer or winter, you may see him every afternoon with his family upon the Chicago boulevards or far out on some delightful country road beyond the city's limits. . . .

The author writes jokingly about Ed's ability in sports:

His tennis is about the funniest thing I ever saw, and his golf is absolutely pathetic, yet he loves them both, and baseball too, though he couldn't hit a flock of balloons with the side of a barn door, and if he did probably he would be as likely to run for third base as first.

Even at this early period, the fact that Ed was not a good social mixer was evident:

. . . Whatever Edgar Rice Burroughs may be he is unquestionably the world's poorest conversationalist, nor does that fact cause him the slightest concern. Unlike most people who cannot talk he is an equally poor listener. He believes that the average man or woman has little or nothing worth saying and that they spend so much of their waking lives in saying it that they have no time to think — they exercise their vocal organs while their brains atrophy.

Much of this attitude toward people at social affairs, and his impatience with the type of light chatter that went on in groups, remained with him in later years. He commented, on a number of occasions, that most people bored him, and at times, in crowds, he made little attempt to conceal this boredom. (According to his son, Hulbert, this reaction to large social gatherings was largely due to a natural shyness. Among close friends he was at ease.)

With the passing of the years, circumstances had of course changed for the remaining members of the Burroughs family. After the death of her husband, Major George Tyler Burroughs, in 1913, Mary Evaline continued an active life. She especially enjoyed traveling and visiting her sons, and at a later period adopted a custom of spending three months of the year with each son and his family.

The failure of their gold-dredging enterprise in the Stanley Basin of Idaho forced George and Harry Burroughs to seek new occupations.[21] After returning to Chicago, where he was unable to find satisfactory employment, George again succumbed to the lure of Idaho and in 1904 went to the small town of Burley, not far from his old location at Minidoka. George tried various occupations, finally establishing himself in the Burley Hardware Company, in later years adding a garage and car agency to the business.[22]

At the time the two brothers were attempting to wind up the affairs of the Sweetser-

Burroughs Mining Company and to salvage whatever they could, Harry had an unfortunate accident. He was chopping some kindling for the stove and was struck in the eye by a piece of wood. His eye was severely injured and his vision impaired. With regular medical treatment he appeared to be recovering, but there were complications; a bad inflammation of the optic nerve developed and soon spread to the other eye.[23] For a year he was virtually blind. Medical treatment continued, with Harry traveling back and forth from Parma, Idaho, where the family lived, to Boise to see the specialist, Dr. Buffem.[24] His condition remained unchanged, and as a result he decided to return to Chicago to seek new medical help. After a year of treatment, he began to improve, and regained partial vision.[25]

Harry found employment of various types, including a position as office manager for the Physicians Co-Operative Association, the same organization for which Ed had worked. Harry entered the new field of the automatic telephone, taking a job with the Automatic Electric Company. He became a telephone installer, and at the time his two children Evelyn and Studley were in high school, he was struggling to make an adequate living. Ella had even taken an office job — an almost unheard-of thing for a gentlewoman of the times.[26]

Frank Coleman Burroughs, closest in age to Ed, had remained in Minidoka, Idaho, after the others left, later returning to Chicago. Evelyn, Harry's daughter, recalled his activities:

He had seen the need for a general store where the people living there and on ranches for miles around could order staples and yard goods etc. from Eastern cities. So he built a house near the railroad and after his marriage brought his bride there to try the experiment of running a general store. It was quite successful, but difficult, and eventually fire destroyed most of the store and its contents — after the fire Uncle Coleman and Auntie Grace went back to Chicago.[27]

Katherine Burroughs Konkle, in recollections of her father Frank, noted:

After growing up in Chicago and attending school in Massachusetts, (Andover) he fell in love with the West and loved the small town life. However, after being twice burned out — both business and home — in a town where water was at a premium and there was no fire department, he brought his little family back to Chicago.[28]

Upon his return to Chicago sometime between 1906 and 1908, Frank and his wife Grace finally settled in the suburb of Wilmette. At this time he was working for the Champlin-Yardley Company, dealers in stationery. Ed had worked there also and had used the office and the mailing address in his early writing period. Frank later took a position with the Pullman Company.[29]

The association between Harry and George and their Yale classmate Lewis Hobart Sweetser had been close and continuous. With the collapse of the gold-dredging project, Sweetser remained in Idaho. In 1901 he had started a new venture, sheep ranching, but met with only limited success; he ceased operating it three years later.[30]

Sweetser next decided to try his fortunes in politics. He achieved a steady success, serving two terms in the Idaho legislature, following which he was twice elected lieutenant governor, in 1908 and again in 1910. As Republican candidate for governor in 1912 his chances for election seemed excellent, but unfortunate personal circumstances forced him to withdraw from the race.[31] He continued in a variety of business activities in Idaho.

Through the years 1913-15 Ed devoted spare moments to what might be described as his only creative hobby — the writing of light verse. Here, in sharp contrast to the practical money-making attitude he had adopted for his story writing, he chose to write, often humorously, for plain enjoyment. A number of these poems were submitted to two columns in the *Chicago Tribune*, first to "In the Wake of the News" by Hugh E. Keogh (HEK) and then to "A Line-

Burroughs family on a Sunday drive, Illinois, 1914; auto is ERB's Hudson.

O'-Type Or Two" by Bert Leston Taylor. Many of these appeared in print, mainly from 1914 to 1915, but several had been published earlier, possibly as early as 1909. In these newspaper contributions Ed maintained the only use of the pen name he had devised years before — Normal Bean.[32]

In these poems Ed had on occasion shown a strong interest in the Chicago Cubs baseball team, revealing himself to be a staunch fan. One of the earliest poems, saved in his collection, dated September 16, 1911, appeared in "In the Wake of the News" and was titled "O, Yes; It's Getting Thick"; its humorous subject is about the differing effects of the Cubs' losses and victories:

My dear, he said at breakfast time,
The Cubs have lost some more;
But as a loser I'm sublime,
'A Good Game Loser,' that is I'm;
List' not, you'll hear no roar.

Say, what in _____ is this _____ stuff?
It tastes to me like slops;
As coffee it's a rotten bluff.
This steak is raw and awful tough;
Those market guys are wops.

Then at the office: "Say, how much
Do you folks think I'll stand?
That straight front blonde'll get in Dutch
If she ain't here on time. Lord, such
A bunch should all be canned.

"Say, boy, you ain't no brickybrack,
You're paid to do some work.
Hike out o' here, and don't come back.
Who wrote these credits here in black?
Where's that _____ billing clerk?

"My sweet," he said, at eats that night,
"Although it's naught to me,
I note the Cubs played outosight
Today. They'll nail that pennant right.
This is delicious tea."

On the "In the Wake of the News" world series staff, jokingly appointed by Hugh E. Keogh, Normal Bean occupied a prominent spot. The group of "correspondents" was announced in the column:

To cover the world's series, The Wake of the News has come to an understanding with the fetchingest staff ever turned loose on a sporting event. We have gathered and enshrined under this roundtop the greatest collection of literary pinch hitters unpinched and the finest bunch of mot makers that ever fed sweetmeats to a gaping populace....[33]

Ed's letter, addressed to HEK from Austin, Illinois, and printed in the column, announced his readiness for the assignment: "Arrived at Fifty-second avenue at 7:10 a.m. Expect to reach Chicago, via Oak Park limited, by Saturday to cover assignment. Normal Bean."[34]

In his poem "Must Fight or Run Out" Ed offers a philosophical defense of prizefighting and sportsmanship. He is critical of the high-

brows' view that Rome declined because the gladiators took to fighting each other, or that the fighting bulls caused Spain's downfall. He reminds these highbrows that "The fact that Caesar loved a scrap/ Was what put Rome upon the map;" and ends by stating:

To those who say the fighter's worst
I might remark: "He's also first
Because some ancient guy could fight
You owe the fact you're here tonight."[35]

In answering the charges of brutality leveled at the prizefighting game — charges that Ed seemed unusually concerned about — he took the side of the supposed "lowbrow" who attended the fights, as opposed to the highbrow who went to auto races. Ed's opinion is expressed in a poem printed in "In the Wake of the News" and titled "Look on This Picture, Then on That." An introductory description of the poem is offered by HEK:

A study in contrasts shuffled up and presented by Dr. Normal Bean of Oak Park, an adept with the physical and metaphysical speculum, a man of broad and deep perspective and withal some pinch hitter at making verses. Cut the cards.[36]

The lowbrows, who "reek of stables and of bars" are pictured watching "two husky guys" pound each other until one is knocked out.

In Canto II he depicts the highbrows "attired like clowns on circus day" attending the auto races with their wives and children. He creates a scene of havoc and death:

A punctured tire — a deadly curve —
A mangled heap of blood and nerve —
A broken gear —a lost control —
A dead man mussing up the goal

After the tragedy which includes "a dying son — a sweetheart dead," Ed develops his contrast in a short stanza titled "The Wind Up":

The highbrowed gent, it seems to me,
Who takes his wife and kids to see
The mangled entrails, tortured bones,
And hear the shrieks and moans and groans,

Can learn a lesson from the dope
Of lowbrow's game, of "white man's hope"
He may not have a massive dome,
But — wife and kids he left at home.

Ed's defense of the lowbrow and the supposed lower-class sport of prizefighting, and his derision for the highbrow are revelatory of his identification with the common man. This had been evidenced in his almost defiant choice of Normal Bean as his pen name. With his insistence on being considered ordinary and his championing of ordinary tastes and attitudes, he was announcing belligerently that he belonged with the masses. But this self-relegation to the ranks of the ordinary was also an indication of something else — the feelings of inferiority he had long possessed. This inferiority was to be intensified with the poor reception his stories would receive in literary circles and from highbrow critics, along with his own understanding of his limitations and of the fact that he was not a "literary" writer. In the future he would continue to class himself with the common man and as the writer for the average or ordinary person — with repeated emphasis upon his philosophy that entertainment, not literary style, was the purpose of writing.

From San Diego Ed sent two poems to Bert Leston Taylor's "A Line-O'-Type Or Two." These poems represented a Chicagoan's critical appraisal of Southern California and the treatment the tourist received. The first one, later titled "Nay, It Hath Not Gone" by Taylor and reduced to four stanzas, was mailed by Ed on January 24, 1914, in its original six-stanza form:

I've missed The Wailing Place of Late,
And glean it hath been swiped.
  I'm full of rails and eke of wails —
  With sorrow I am piped.

Oh, who hath copped The Wailing Place?
I ask you, dear old pal.
  No Place they keep where one may weep
  In sunny southern Cal.

And if The Wailing Place hath gone
Forever and for keeps

What shall we do (whom all do do)
For where to spill our weeps?

The butcher man he robs me blind;
Robs me, the grocer deft;
  The brigand cruel who sells me fuel
  He taketh what is left.

The garage man (accent the gar),
Unmindful of my groans,
  He wrecks my car with loud Har! Har!
  And later picks my bones.

And now The Wailing Place is gone
Where shall we find us rest?
  Unless you say: "Come hither, pray,
  "And weep upon my vest."

                              Normal Bean[37]

Other poems by Ed appeared in "A Line-O'-Type Or Two" from 1914 and 1915. His poetry scrapbook contains poems of various types: these include printed poems with his pen name, Normal Bean, but updated; printed poems with both column or source and name missing; and typed poems which may or may not have been printed in a newspaper. Pasted on a page in his scrapbook are five printed poems, four of these from "A Line-O'-Type Or Two," but without an author's name. They appear to be in Ed's humorous, satirical style. Two of the four contain the earliest printed dates of any poems so far discovered — August 21, 1909, and October 23, 1909.[38]

Possibly in the period of 1908-09, Ed had also written a song-poem, not intended for submission to the newspaper. Titled "Joan's Pick-Me-Up Song," it was composed for his daughter born January 12, 1908. The three-stanza poem imaginatively represents the crooning song of an infant who wishes to be picked up:

  I am not crying 'cause anything's wrong;
I am just singing my Pick-me-up song.
  Pick me up, mamma, and then if you do
I'll show you how nicely I gurgle and coo.
  I have been sleeping so all the day long
That now I will sing you my Pick-me-up song.

After a changing second stanza, the third becomes a repetition of the first. Ed's penchant for writing on the backs of old letterheads from defunct businesses is again demonstrated in this typed poem. The letterhead, with *Burroughs* printed at the top and beneath it a listing of eight different titles, carries an address of 82 Sherman Street in Chicago.

Ed's past, as with the past of many famous individuals, had a way of returning. Letters from old acquaintances and friends often stirred his memories and caused him to reminisce. A letter from Edward H. Doughtery, Sales Manager for Foster & McDonnell, Chicago publishers, referred to the early days when Ed was sending his poems to the *Chicago Tribune*:

A copy of the "War Chief" by Edgar Rice Burroughs, was just laid on my desk, with a letter asking for a review of this book as soon after September 15th., as possible. It struck me as a coincidence and will appreciate your advising Mr. Burroughs of my receipt of same.

It was my privilege to be his office boy some fifteen years ago, when his chief effort was in "making" The Line, and my main duty as office boy, was carrying these efforts to the office of B. L. T. . . . .[39]

Ed, in his response, chose to joke about the lethal effects of both his poetry and prose:

. . . How many changes have occurred since the days when you carried my immortal lines to B. L. T.!

H. E. K., who conducted "In the Wake of the News" on the sporting page of the Tribune, died after publishing several of my gems. It took me longer to kill B. L. T., and I was nearly ten years disposing of Frank A. Munsey, and then there was Ogden McClurg, who succumbed after publishing more than twenty of my novels. The man who made my first motion picture died shortly after it was released, and so I cut my bloody swath across the literary fields of the twentieth century, but fortunately for me a few of my readers still survive. . . .[40]

The California sojourn being over, Ed resumed his intensive writing schedule; in mid-April 1914 he began what he had described as "a Carthoris story" (later titled "Thuvia, Maid of Mars").[41] Robert H. Davis, who had replaced Metcalf as the editor of the amalgamated *All-Story Cavalier*, wrote to Ed on May 29 to state that he would soon offer suggestions about future writing plans. These came in a letter of June 12:

I have read "The Mucker" and "The Girl from Harris's". . . familiarized myself with Tarzan. . . .

. . . my opinion that you and I ought to have a conference and that at an early date. . . five things I want to talk with you about.

1. . . . rehabilitation of Tarzan. 2. . . . plan to lengthen "The Girl from Harris's". . . . 3. "The Mucker" should be concluded. . . . 4. . . . sequel to perhaps "The Mad King" or "At the Earth's Core." 5. . . . the pleasure of seeing you.

If you are on for this suggestion, we will supply you with transportation both ways, and a one day's conference will be sufficient. . . .

In his reply Ed displayed a cooperative attitude, discussing Davis' points in order. Concerning the "rehabilitation" of Tarzan he was somewhat dubious: ". . . I may as well tell you frankly that I have never written anything in accordance with another's suggestions that has proved satisfactory to the other, although I am perfectly aware that the other fellow's ideas are probably much better than mine — the thing is that I can't ever seem to grasp what is wanted."[42] Ed was willing to accept the remaining suggestions: he could "easily" lengthen "The Girl from Harris's"; at the start he had intended to make it a full-length novel. In the story a problem had arisen about the elder Secor; Davis believed he should be eliminated. Ed commented, ". . . we can talk of that when I see you; but it seems to me that whatever plot the tale has hinges on the old gent."[43]

In the matter of a conclusion for "The Mucker" Ed explained he had previously written a different ending and was now forwarding it to Davis. He groaned at the mention of "sequels," commenting, "I am sick of writing sequels; but I appear to be doomed. The Mad King sequel seems less appalling than that to The Eternal Lover. However, I can write sequels for both if they are wanted."[44] He expressed pleasure at Davis' invitation to a conference, volunteering to travel to New York within the following two weeks, but preferably in the early part of the next week. He actually arrived in New York on June 23.[45] He had hastened to mail the ending of "The Mucker" to Davis, and about it noted, ". . . I tried to make him do a big thing simply. I hope the readers will get it. . . ."[46]

Writing at a furious pace, he had only a few days before he notified Davis of the mailing of the story he still titled "Carthoris." His letter mentioned "another Martian story, the first serial rights to which I wish to sell for use in the *All-Story Cavalier Weekly*."[47] He proceeded methodically to another task. Davis' remarks about "The Girl from Harris's" had included a disapproval of the role of John Secor, the wealthy old man who dupes the heroine, June Lathrop, into a false marriage. After Secor's death June and the old man's son Ogden fall in love and at the story's end are planning to get married. Davis had commented, "It's hell for a man to wind up as the husband of his father's mistress."[48]

Aware of this odd situation, Ed nevertheless had no intention of eliminating John Secor from the story; this would have required extensive revision. He searched for the easiest way out of the dilemma, and on July 11 wrote to Davis "about The Girl from Farris's." (Note the title had now been changed.) "If I make the old man his uncle or foster father will he cease to offend you? I think I could do it better that way than another. Please let me know by return mail as I am all set." From Davis came a prompt agreement. He preferred the foster father and remarked, "Anything to eliminate the blood relationship. . . ."[49]

Ed's labor-saving approach resulted in brief revisions centered about two pages, plus minor changes throughout the story. In sending the new version to Davis on July 21, Ed explained, ". . . have substituted 'Abe' Farris for 'Al' Harris wherever the latter appeared. However, it might be well to warn proof readers, or whoever do such stunts, to look out for any instance where I may have neglected to make the change. It is a tiresome job — I wouldn't have done it for anybody but you. . . ."[50]

To solve the problem, Ed had contrived the simplest and most abrupt device. The nonplussed reader, arriving at the story's end, encounters a sudden, amazing revelation that John Secor is not Ogden's father. The explanation is given by Ogden to June: "I was the foster son of John Secor's brother. When he died I went to live with the John Secors, and after the death of their only son I entered Mr. Secor's office, taking the place of the son he had lost, later inheriting his business."[51]

"The Girl from Farris's," with Ed's creation of Maggie Lynch (June Lathrop) as a prostitute and an occupant of a house of ill-repute owned by Abe Farris, "the most notorious dive keeper in the city," constituted a surprising departure from his usual fantasy and adventure stories. Whatever prompted him to make this abrupt turn from "Tarzan" and "Mars and the Inner World" to the subject of vice in Chicago — a subject that in 1914 would have to be handled with discretion — is difficult to tell. That Ed himself felt uncomfortable with the theme, or even doubtful that he had been wise in developing it, is indicated in his letter of September 19, 1914, to Davis:

In this connection, though it is none of my business, I am wondering if it might not be a good plan to run The Girl from Farris's in something other than The All-Story Cavalier whose readers appear to have a considerable antipathy for smut. I should hate to offend them as they have been very kind to me.

"Smut" is a strong word, and Ed's use of it to characterize his own writing reveals his sen-

Thuvia, Maid of Mars *frontispiece by St. John, 1920.*

sitivity to the supposedly sordid theme he had chosen. But the word is also revealing of limitations of Ed's moral attitude and conditioning. Bob Davis, an experienced editor who would have certainly rejected any material that might have been offensive to his readers, had offered no criticism of the theme. Obviously, he had found nothing wrong with it and the manner in which it was developed. His only objection had been to the relationship of the two Secors.

In the short period of contact with Davis, including the personal conference in New York, Ed's relationship with the editor had reached a pleasant, informal level. The correspondence of both men carried a friendly and jesting tone, similar to the one maintained by Metcalf and Ed. On June 29, 1914, Davis wrote to thank Ed for "one handsome copy of 'Tarzan of the Apes' " and referred to the autographed note: "Those flippant lines in 'Tarzan' in which you take a wallop at my parlor English are delightful. You and I alone understand what it means."[52] Davis acknowledged the additions to "The Mucker" and remarked:

I have performed the laparotomy and Wednesday will send you a check for the additional 5,400 words. You've got old Euclid tied in a clove hitch when it comes to mathematics. But I forgive you because the brand of words you spill seems to please a large number of readers, and those are the people we are after. . . .

Prompted by the request of Joseph Bray, McClurg editor, for publicity in connection with the publication of Tarzan in book form, Ed had written several times to suggest that a notice be inserted in All-Story Cavalier. On July 2 Davis forwarded a page proof from the forthcoming July 18 issue of the magazine; the "Heart to Heart Talks" contained an announcement about the Tarzan novel.[53] Davis continued to be cooperative, and a month later sent a copy of All-Story Cavalier in which Ed's letter discussing sequels was featured.[54]

In the months that followed, the flow of correspondence was steady, while the writing, because of requests for revisions, became more intensive and exhausting. But even though he had grown tired of the interminable sequels, he was still able to joke about them to Davis and to reveal, at the same time, the formidable writing tasks he had set for himself:

In reply to your recent query relative to The Cave Girl, The Mad King, The Eternal Lover, and At the Earth's Core, let me assure you that but half of each of these stories has yet been told.

You see I couldn't know that any of them would interest the All-Story Cavalier readers sufficiently to warrant prolonging them, and in the case of the Pellucidar narrative the fate of David Innes was not cleared up until quite recently, so that I couldn't have gone on with that one, anyway.

In the near future I rather expect I'll have all the data complete on each of these, when I shall be very glad to submit all the evidence to my bully friends of the All-Story Cavalier.[55]

With the changes in the Munsey staff and the assignment of Bob Davis as editor, the status of Metcalf had become uncertain.[56] On June 28 Ed received a card from Metcalf, mailed from the Harvard Club at 27 West 44th Street, New York, explaining the situation:

The Munsey Co. and I have split. It has been brewing — if splits may be said to "brew" — for some time. I have nothing definite in mind as yet, but when I do — if it is a business in which we may deal together I shall, of course let you know.

I am sure that your relations with Davis will be wholly satisfactory so don't worry about that end of it. If there is anything I may undertake for you, don't hesitate to write me. You may always address me here.

Ed responded, ". . . Cannot tell you how badly I felt to hear that you are no longer with Munsey. I hope that when you connect up again it will be in a way that will permit us to work together as in the past. . . ."[57]

Thousands of words produced, stories dispatched, revisions demanded, word counts disputed — this was the pattern of the last half of 1914. On August 17 "The Cave Man," a sequel to "The Cave Girl," was mailed to Davis. In the bickering that ensued, Ed first conceded that he had overestimated the word total, but nevertheless accused the Munsey Company of under-counting:

I made a bull in my word count of The Cave Man. Before I started it I figured the number of pages that should be necessary to give 40,000 words, and then I gave you what I thought a couple of thousand words for good measure. When the check came, for which by the way I thank you, I was surprised to see that it was for less than $1000. So I got busy and counted the words — suffering a second surprise when I discovered that there were less than 40,000, though at that whoever counted them at the other end short-changed me still further.[58]

With the forwarding of his next story, "Sweetheart Primeval," Ed explained that he had used the same method for his word count, and as a result of this inaccuracy the total was below the 50,000 words requested by Davis. "I am very sorry," Ed wrote, "but if you take the story, please plead with the Appollonius Pergasus who computes the remuneration to be generous upon my side this time."[59] He was hardly exaggerating when he added, "I am working like a wall-eyed part-horse, and hope to complete all your commissions this year."[60]

He had enclosed a check for $6.00 for two subscriptions to *The All-Story Cavalier*, one of these intended for his mother.[61] Davis evidently had decided by this time that the only safe and effective way of dealing with Ed was to kid him and to respond with the same type of humorous insults that Ed hurled at him. Upon

INCOME from stories		
Under the Moons of Mars	1911	400.00
The Outlaw of Torn	1913	500.00
Tarzan of the Apes	1912	700.00
The Gods of Mars	1912	750.00
The Return of Tarzan	Feb 1913	1000.00
The Inner World	Feb "	420.00
The Cave Girl	Apr	600.00
A Man Without a Soul		1165.00
War Lord of Mars		1141.00
The Return of Tarzan (N Y World)		300.00
The Cave Girl (N Y World)		200.00
The Ret of Tzn(Am Prss Assn)$200-60%		120.00
Inner World (addition to)		320.00
OVER		7616.00

First of ERB's many file cards on which he entered income from story sales and book royalties.

receipt of Ed's check, Davis addressed him as "My dear Colonel Burroughs" and commented, "A letter from you containing real money is such a startling proposition that I dare not tarry acknowledgement. . . ."[62]

Concerning the word counts, Davis somewhat despairingly suggested that Ed should list the exact number of words in his manuscript. "God knows," Davis said, "everybody in this shop tries to count your manuscripts so that there will be no argument. Life is too short to rush every issue to the Supreme Court. . . ."[63] About "Sweetheart Primeval" Davis asked, "What, in your opinion, is the exact number of words. . . ? Disregard everything else and deal only with this particular manuscript. Let us strike a basis for reckoning that will be permanent."[64]

At the close of the letter Davis again became humorously insulting:

Sorry you weren't with me this summer. I could have made it very pleasant for you at times and disagreeable at others. I think the only way to get good results out of you is to hand you the four seasons — spring, summer, autumn and winter. Continuous perfect weather is a bad thing for Burroughs. Somebody must step up and bite you or hit you with a stone axe or push you into a bottomless pit or clamp an abyss on you before you really begin to get human.[65]

Although appreciative of Davis' goodnatured sarcasm, Ed could not be sidetracked and clung doggedly to the issue of the word count in "Sweetheart Primeval." He replied with his own brand of humor:

You have been so good to me always that it tears my heartstrings to haggle over this business, but every time a heartstring starts to tear, up comes a word at 2½c per and bleats in its ear. The result is that I am immediately "torn by conflicting emotions". . . .[66]

As Davis had requested, Ed enclosed his exact count of "Sweetheart Primeval," at the same time pointing out that this could not be used as a permanent standard since the length of lines varied in different stories. Unable to repress his business instincts — an almost obsessive fear of being underpaid — he explained, "The Cave Man ran 11.44 words per line, while this one shows 11.9."[67] He added:

If it will be of service to you I am perfectly willing to submit a similar word count for each story — it would require but a couple of minutes each day to keep it up as I write.

I don't want to ask anything out of the ordinary, though, so if you would rather do it your way, why go ahead — though I must reserve my inalienable right to howl. . . .[68]

A week later, on September 29, Davis conceded that Ed's method was "pretty nearly exact," and urged him to continue his word counts. Davis remarked humorously, "I want to remove any possibility of your howling at my conclusions, because, believe me, Burroughs, you are one hell of a howler and the uttermost confines of the world are not sufficiently remote to escape the tremendous reverberations of your throaty protests." In noting that he planned to eliminate about 2,000 words or more, Davis wrote, "I am going to tie a can to some of those deep-sea reptiles and chase a little slime off the page."

Concerning these prehistoric monsters, Ed replied, "Of course the pterodactyles, plesiosaurs, ichthyosaurs, and the like are perfectly all right in a pre-glacial dream, but if you don't like them, why can them. Sir Conan got away with them, though, in a tale of the 20th Century — hold on now, I know I aint."[69] Reflecting over the shortened manuscript, Ed commented, "I suppose I really ought to howl, so that you won't find it too easy to fall into the habit of slicing great hunks of hard earned mazuma out of my mss. My artistic temperament writhes in contemplation of those fifty-odd bucks going into your waste basket; but possibly, were you to rush along the check for the balance, it might survive the shock. . . ."[70]

Ed, like a runner leaping over obstacles at

a breakneck speed, continued his writing schedule of one sequel after another. "Barney Custer of Beatrice," the sequel to "The Mad King," was sent to Davis on November 2. Ed would not permit himself a breather, writing, "I shall immediately start in on the sequel to At the Earth's Core, and after that will come, in order, The Son of Tarzan. . . ."[71] Contemplating 1914, past and future, he added, ". . . subsequent to which I think I shall lie me doon an' dee, for I sure have put in one hell of a year at hard labor — and all for you. I wouldn't have done it for anyone else on earth."[72]

The "hard labor" was compounded by further demands for revisions; Davis was far more difficult to please than Metcalf. The tone of his letters remained lightly ironic, but his criticisms were blunt and scathing. Upon receipt of "Barney Custer of Beatrice" he wrote, "In all your previous work you have established a reputation for speed and plot and movement. That is why you are getting large money these days. Also, you are A-1 for originality."[73] Then he proceeded to aim devastating blows at Ed's fictional cliches:

I will forgive you for having the King and Barney look alike, although it is the oldest device in modern fiction. But it isn't fair for Barney to make his escape by stealing two automobiles in Chapter V and Chapter VI hard-running. There is no art to that, Burroughs, and no ingenuity. A man can go on writing sequels for the balance of his lifetime if he is permitted to resort to these time-worn stunts.[74]

Davis' criticism continued with reference to page 27 of the manuscript in which the way the hero escaped the firing squad was "nothing short of preposterous." Davis commented, "Falling forward on one's face goes on skating rinks and in the presence of district leaders, but it is beneath you to pull it in fiction."[75] The reactions of the magazine's readers were his main concern: ". . . I do not want the sequel to be so much worse than the first part that the reader is dissatisfied. "The Mad King" made considerable of an impression and a large number of readers are waiting for this sequel,

which I have announced."[76] Davis exclaimed, "But great international God, Burroughs, don't hand them a hack story."[77]

Speaking frankly, Davis stressed the point that he would accept the story "even in its present form," but urged Ed to consider the criticisms and see if he couldn't "do better by the reader and the publication." He noted Ed's complaint about "one hell of a year at hard labor." As a new editor, Davis had made suggestions for sequels which, to a man as ambitious and hard-driving as Ed, were equivalent to orders. Ed's furious writing pace was the result of his own compulsiveness, his need to demonstrate that he could do the seemingly impossible; it was not caused by unreasonable demands on the part of Davis. Actually, the editor advised caution and a slow-down:

If you are already exhausted, after writing " 'Barney' Custer," what kind of a sequel will you turn out to "At the Earth's Core"? And where, oh where, will "The Son of Tarzan" wind up for the grand finish? I don't ask you to break your neck or wear yourself out with this thing. I would much prefer you to take your time and do something you are proud of. Any man who starts out as tired as you say you are ought to be seated somewhere along the line of march and take a little rest.[78]

Davis' joking tone at the end — "You may consider, under all circumstances, old Tarzan, that I am yours to a cinder. . . ." — may have helped to soften the severe criticisms. On November 13, 1914, in a night letter to Davis, Ed stated, "Feelings not lacerated. Will at once make changes you suggest; but as you accept the story for the love of Mike send a check. Five Hundred bucks advance will help a lot. Spare coin tied up in real estate and need money for current bills."

The money, dispatched at once by telegram, arrived the next day. Ed wrote again to explain that he had devised changes for "Barney Custer." He planned to complete them and return the manuscript quickly. "Have taken a two weeks rest," he said, "and shall start on sequel to At the Earth's Core today or Wednesday —

Tuesdays I play golf with increasingly pitiful results."[79] It was clear that Davis' admonitions would have little effect in diverting him from his hectic schedule. On November 16 the "Barney Custer" manuscript was sent to Davis, the changes indicated in Ed's letter:

Instead of having Barney dodge the bullet, I let it go as a bum shot which merely creased his head, which of course is quite reasonable.

And I changed the stealing of the second auto, which so grated upon your artistic temperament, so that he didn't have to steal one after all.

By this time Davis must have realized that any Burroughs revisions would cost the Munsey Company money. Ed appeared constitutionally unable to revise by eliminating or condensing. Ed wrote, "These changes have added 900 words to the mss."[80] Concerning Davis' worried remarks about overwork, Ed responded:

Who said I was tired? Can't a fellow lie down and die if he wants to without being tired? Nay, I am not, and furthermore I have seldom worked more enthusiastically upon a story than upon this last one. I enjoyed it and really thought that it was better than most of them — so you can see what a shock your letter was. I wish that you would be more careful what you eat before you pass on my stuff.[81]

Flabbergasted at Ed's ingenious method of revision, Davis, on November 24, after noting that a check for the $825.00 balance due on " 'Barney' Custer of Beatrice" was en route, remarked, "I swear to God, old man, I can't see how you got in 900 extra words without increasing the number of pages. I am figuring the whole thing out now at 53,000 flat, which I trust will pacify your tempestuous soul. . . ."

During the latter part of 1914 Ed continued his newspaper syndications, maintaining his personal contact with Terhune at the New York *Evening World.* Answering Terhune's request, Ed, on November 14, sent him "The Beasts of Tarzan"; and to open price negotiations, point-

ed out that although the story was shorter than "The Return of Tarzan," the payment for it had been two and one-half times as much. Ed explained that he would not ask for any such increase from Terhune. He wrote, "I will be perfectly satisfied with the same price for the New York City newspaper rights as you paid for The Return of Tarzan; namely, $300.00." Ed attempted to dicker, but Terhune remained firm at $200, a price that Ed finally accepted.[82] In the same period there was regular correspondence with Chapman about national syndications, and the dealings with his agent revealed that at this time he turned to a new and unexpected type of writing.

The outbreak of World War I in Europe in 1914 had revived his interest in military matters and his patriotic concern about the state of the U. S. Army. In a letter of September 24 to Chapman, he asked the agent to examine the "enclosed" and let him know whether it might be syndicated in the papers that had printed *Tarzan* stories. He remarked:

It struck me that owing to the interest in martial stuff it might take on, my idea being primarily that it would be good general publicity stuff for the Tarzan stories. It could be run as, by Edgar Rice Burroughs, author of Tarzan of the Apes.

If you could get real money for it — fine! If not the publicity would be our reward.

Chapman responded on the 25th, referring to the "Army MS" Ed had sent and indicating that it would be forwarded to the Journal. The *Journal* was presumably the *Army-Navy Journal,* because four years later another Burroughs article titled "A National Reserve Army," was published in that service magazine on August 31, 1918. Chapman wrote, ". . . I hardly think that papers would be inclined to pay money for it; I believe it will have to be considered publicity stuff."

The "Army MS" was an article of approximately 2,200 words, titled "What Is the Matter with the United States Army?" It was Ed's first professional article, and in writing it he drew upon his own military background and made specific proposals for the creation of an army with a "new purpose." His unrewarding experiences at Fort Grant, where he had not found the "real soldiering" he had sought, remained vivid in his memory, and drove him to view the army's methods with contempt and disgust. He recalled his commander at Fort Grant as a "pick and shovel man" and bitterly described his assignments under this commander. Ed noted that he had become "one of the loveliest little ditch diggers in the army," had proceeded from there to a "coffee-cooling" job, and then to being a stableboy, his task consisting of "chamber work for fourteen horses." He described the situation graphically (and with some guilt): "My comrades poked fun at me — and were envious. Mine was a sinecure. I was a gentleman of leisure. They — poor devils — had to work. They had to *soldier* while I loafed. I carried and fed and watered fourteen horses. I hauled hay and oats for them. I made their beds at night and unmade them in the morning, and as I rode luxuriously across the parade ground on top of a load of manure I saw my fellows sweatingly engaged in plucking house-size boulders out of the virgin soil of Arizona."

In introducing his plan, he offered some statistics about the army of his times:

We are spending nearly $100,000,000.00 each and every year to maintain our standing army — an army that half a dozen of the new Krupp guns would wipe out of existence in about forty-seven minutes.

We spend one hundred million dollars, then, to train eighty-five thousand recruits, and six hundred million to board and lodge them for the remaining six years of their enlistment. To my mind we are throwing away the six hundred millions.[83]

"How much better it would be," he said, "were we to turn eighty-five thousand trained men into private life every year and spend their board and lodging money in training eighty-five thousand more!" His familiar businessman's efficiency was now at work. He conceded that a yearly eighty-five thousand enlistment under present conditions would be impossible,

and proposed to change these conditions, the first target being the seven years enlistment law — four years active service and three in the reserve. His indignation stirred him to rhetorical extremes:

Seven years! What grey-beard conceived such an eternity of time for a young man? Or was it suggested by a jealous foreign power that wished to see our little army dwindle to nothingness? Were you ever young? Then you will recall that seven years was a mighty long time. Would you enlist in any man's army in times of peace for seven long, weary years? Neither would I.

As a first step, service in the regular army would be set at one year, but not the kind of service he had suffered — "that wouldn't make a soldier in seven years or seventy." After emphasizing that the young men, in whom "the spirit of Romance and Adventure breathes strong," do not want to dig ditches all day long, Ed turned to specific suggestions for the army with a "new purpose." Ditch digging should be done by hired laborers; soldiers and officers should devote an eight-hour day to military theory and practice. Under this program a recruit would not need a year for training — three months would be sufficient. A further result would be an increase in the soldier's pride; he would acquire an "esprit de corps which is so essential in a military organization, and which you seldom see among ditch diggers."

Under Ed's plan, the year in the army would be part of a total three-year requirement, the remainder, at the soldier's option, to be served either in the regular army or in any state militia. This would provide the National Guard with a steady reserve of trained men.[84]

There is no record of any publication of the article "What is the Matter with the United States Army? or of further communications with Chapman on the matter.

An early statement of Ed's philosophy concerning "Tarzan of the Apes" was contained in a letter addressed to M. N. Bunker, publisher of *The Naturopath*, Salina, Kansas. Bunker's inquiry about the *Tarzan* novel had been forwarded to Ed by Joseph E. Bray, McClurg Editor. On August 24, 1914, Bray wrote:

... I take it you will have a peach of a time explaining just why you wrote Tarzan, *because as I understand it, you did it because you hoped to make money out of it. Writers, however, are not supposed to compose their masterpieces for this sordid reason.*

Mr. Bunker (whose name, by the way, has a rather suspicious sound) evidently wants to get an argument for Physical Culture out of Tarzan. ...

In noting that he had answered Bunker's letter, Ed, on August 26, wrote to Bray:

Had I more time I could give him quite a spiel on the physical culture possibilities of Tarzan; but I am in the midst of another story and way behind my schedule. However, I imagine Mr. B. to be much better qualified to get the physical culture germs out of the book than I. ...

To Bunker, on the same date, Ed explained,

Of course the primary motive of a story like Tarzan of the Apes is to entertain, yet in writing this and other stories I have been considerably influenced by the hope that they might carry a beneficial suggestion of the value of physical perfection and morality.[85]

Because Tarzan led a clean, active, outdoor life he was able to accomplish mental as well as physical feats that are so beyond the average man that he cannot believe in their possibility, and if that idea takes root in the mind of but a single young man, to the end that he endeavors through similar means to rise above his environment, then Tarzan of the Apes will not have lived in vain.

Ed's statement of his primary writing motive as entertainment was of course the one he later preferred to stress. Perhaps the idealistic purposes he offers in the letter had influenced him in the creation of "Tarzan of the Apes"; perhaps they were ideas he had produced on the moment's inspiration purely for Bunker's benefit.

Similar ideas — themes, motifs — may always be discovered through analysis after a work is completed. Nevertheless, the philosophy of physical perfection that is so vital to the idea of a Tarzan relates closely to the Burroughs family's early goals of fitness, exercise and sports, and vigorous outdoor living. The transference to the "Tarzan" story came as part of a natural expression of belief.

Bunker had also inquired about the origin of the "Tarzan" plot. Ed responded:

In answer to your second question, the story is not founded on fact, though in greater part the life of the apes is more or less true to nature. The earthen drums of the anthropoids have been found and described by reputable travellers and explorers, and the natives of certain central African tribes insist that there is a race of apes of immense size and of much greater intelligence than the gorilla.

Upon publication of his review of *Tarzan of the Apes,* Bunker sent Ed the page from *The Naturopath* containing the review. At the bottom of the page Ed typed the notation "Ackd Nov. 14, 1914". The review appeared in the Physical Culture section, and Bunker glowingly summarized the book as "Natural Healing gotten up in a splendid fiction form." Important points are copied from Ed's letter: the primary function of books such as Tarzan of course was to entertain. But stories of this type carry a "beneficial suggestion of the value of physical perfection and morality." The novel, Bunker explained, provides a moral lesson "because Tarzan led a clean, active outdoor life. ..."

In another review of *Tarzan of the Apes* appearing a month later, the writer offered some precise criticism and made an amusing analysis of the Burroughs style. The review in the Chicago Press Club's *The Scoop* of December 12, 1914, referred to Ed's writing as "uneven" and commented on his "occasional habit of writing excessively long sentences." A particularly elongated sentence that became a paragraph was quoted. Introducing the "fierce, mad, intoxicating revel of the Dum-Dum," and comparing this ritual of the apes to our modern functions, the sentence begins, "From this primitive function has arisen, unquestionably, all the forms and ceremonials of modern church and state, for through all the countless ages, back beyond the last, uttermost ramparts of a dawning humanity. . . ."

The writer chose to compare the Burroughs style to that of Thomas Macauley, noting pungently, "In his preface to the *History of England* (fifty thousand words) Macauley wrote one perfectly limpid sentence of over two hundred words. Burroughs runs Macauley a prosperous second with a paragraph of a hundred and eleven words." The Burroughs paragraph, consisting of one sentence, utilizes commas, but remarkably does not contain a single semicolon. That the reviewer should have mentioned Macauley is oddly coincidental, since Ed, from his earliest studies in Latin, had become acquainted with Macauley's writings and had developed a deep admiration for them. In later years he could, on occasion, recall *The Lays of Ancient Rome*, with its stirring poem "Horatius."[86]

The 1914 Chicago writing period — the nine months that followed Ed's return from California — brought the completion of four stories and the near-completion of another. "Pellucidar," a sequel to "At the Earth's Core," was begun on November 23 but not finished until January 11, 1915.[87]

"Thuvia, Maid of Mars," the fourth of the Martian series, was completed on June 20, 1914, after two months of writing. It contains familiar plot elements; its action is launched with the abduction of the beautiful princess of Ptarth and a scheme to implicate Carthoris, John Carter's son, in Thuvia's disappearance. Although there is little freshness in the plot, Ed, as usual, produces some original devices. Anticipating an invention of modern times, the automatic pilot, Ed has Carthoris contrive an instrument for blindflying, described as "a clever improvement of the ordinary Martian air compass, which when set for a certain destination will remain constantly fixed thereon, making it only necessary to keep a vessel's prow always in the direc-

tion of the compass needle to reach any given point upon Barsoom by the shortest route." This was supplemented by an auxiliary steering device that upon arrival at the destination "brought the craft to a standstill and lowered it, also automatically, to the ground."

To avoid the possibility of collision with another craft, Ed has Carthoris invent an "obstruction evader," a type of "radium generator diffusing radio-activity in all directions to a distance of a hundred yards or so from the flier." Carthoris, in the story, explains the "evader's" workings in detail:

Should this enveloping force be interrupted in any direction a delicate instrument immediately apprehends the irregularity, at the same time imparting an impulse to a magnetic device which in turn actuates the steering mechanism, diverting the bow of the flyer away from the obstacle until the craft's radio-activity sphere is no longer in contact with the obstruction, then she falls once more into her normal course.

If an aircraft should approach from the rear, both the speed control and the steering gear are actuated, and as a result Carthoris' flyer either shoots ahead or moves evasively up or down. Other contingencies have been anticipated:

In aggravated cases, that is when the obstructions are many, or of such a nature as to deflect the bow more than forty-five degrees in any direction, or when the craft has reached its destination and dropped to within a hundred yards of the ground, the mechanism brings her to a full stop, at the same time sounding a loud alarm which will instantly awaken the pilot. . . .

In "Thuvia, Maid of Mars," Ed's most imaginative feat, startlingly original, is the creation of the Phantom Bowmen of Lothar. Seeking a safe haven from the green hordes, the last of the race of Lotharians had retreated to an impregnable fortress. Only men had arrived — some twenty thousand of them, the women and children having died en route. Faced with extinction of their race, the Lotharians, after realizing the Great Truth — that mind is all — developed superhuman mental powers. Through these they overcame death, which, after all, was "merely a state of mind."

The next step was to create their "mind-people," described as "the materialization of imaginings." These are the Phantom Bowmen who are summoned from nothingness to battle the enemy. To Carthoris, Jav, the Lotharian, explains:

We send out our deathless archers — deathless because they are lifeless, existing only in the imaginations of our enemies. It is really our giant minds that defend us, sending out legions of imaginary warriors to materialize before the mind's eye of the foe.

They see them — they see their bows drawn back — they see their slender arrows speed with unerring precision toward their hearts. And they die — killed by the power of suggestion.

In order that the enemy, the Torquasians, not suspect that they are fighting imaginary creatures, the Lotharians arrange for some of the bowmen to "die" on the battlefield. They are "pictured" as being killed, "to lend reality to the scene." If the Torquasians once learned the truth, "no longer would they fall prey to the suggestion of the deadly arrows, for greater would be the suggestion of the truth, and the more powerful suggestion would prevail — it is law."

Since there is neither food nor water in Lothar, those who call themselves "realists" create these substances through their imaginations. By "materializing food-thoughts" and then eating, they cause digestion and assimilation. The argument advanced by the "etherealists" among the Lotharians is that substance is nonexistent. However, the others believe that "mind has the power to maintain substance even though it may not be able to create substance." Thus Jav, a realist, explains, "We chew, we swallow, we digest. All our organs function precisely as if we had partaken of material food. And what is the result? What must be the result? The chemical changes take place through both direct and indirect suggestion, and we live and thrive."[88]

Next in order on Ed's list of sequels was "The Cave Man"; completed in less than a month, on August 17, 1914, it continued the exploits of Waldo Emerson Smith-Jones in his transformation from a skinny weakling to a powerfully muscled fighting man renamed Thandar, "the brave one." The plot weaves about his love for Nadara, the half-savage cave girl, and his plans to return to civilization with her. Waldo cannot bring himself to take Nadara as his mate according to the primitive customs of the cave people: "She — his wonderful Nadara — must become his through the most solemn and dignified ceremony that civilized man had devised." Waldo's thoughts, expressed in this stuffy language, reveal his prudish attitude, and place him in contrast to Nadara, child of nature, who can find no need for a ceremony and wishes simply to mate with the man she loves.

Nadara's father, himself baffled by Waldo's strange behavior, describes how he took his wife many years before by dragging her to his cave and beating her. No argument, however, can budge Waldo from his noble determination to give Nadara a civilized wedding, and through numerous hair-breadth escapes he clings unwaveringly to this goal, until, at the end, the two are transported back to Boston on the Smith-Joneses' yacht, the *Priscilla*. Waldo's blue-blood snobbery is satirized by Ed, and before the story is finished both Waldo and his mother appear to have overcome this snobbery. Ed seems also, on first impression, to be satirizing Waldo's and society's conventional morality, but the emphasis upon marriage as the only possible solution, and the ending with the triumph of legality and respectability, indicate an acceptance of society's standards. That Ed might have been opportunistic, catering to what he believed his moralistic readers would expect, must of course be considered. However, in "The Cave Man" this seems doubtful. This story, as with many stories, offers some revelations about the author: Ed's moral convictions — at least of circa 1914 — are clearly evident.

Curiously, while approving the convention of marriage, Ed, in this early work, vigorously rejected the funeral ceremony. His attitude emerges from the description of the death of Nadara's foster-father, following which the body was deposited at the top of a cliff. "There was no ceremony. In it, though, Waldo Emerson saw what might have been the first human funeral cortege — simple, sensible and utilitarian — from which the human race has retrograded to the ostentatious, ridiculous, pestilent burials of present day civilization." Through this indignant and almost violent criticism, Ed's philosophy of death and modern funerals is revealed. It would remain unchanged throughout his life.

Once more, in his plot devices, Ed falls into repetition, this time returning to a "Tarzan of the Apes" incident. A man and woman float ashore on the island of the cave people. The man is dead, but the woman lives long enough to give birth to a little girl, who of course turns out to be Nadara. Apparently reluctant to give his blessing to a union between the aristocratic Waldo Emerson and a savage cave girl, Ed, at the end of the story, makes the marriage more palatable by producing one of his predictable "surprises": the cave girl's mother is identified as Eugenie Marie Celeste de la Valois, Countess of Crecy, and so, happily, when the wedding takes place, the minister is able to enter another aristocratic name on the certificate — Nadara de la Valois.[89]

"Sweetheart Primeval," a sequel to "The Eternal Lover," was also completed in less than a month, on September 14, 1914.[90] To continue the adventures of the time travelers, Victoria Custer and her "troglodyte" lover Nu, Ed again reverts to his needed device — the earthquake. In the cave when the earthquake occurs, Victoria awakens as the primitive Nat-ul, making her journey "Back to the Stone Age." The entire story takes place in the prehistoric past and includes encounters with other savage races — the Boat Builders and the Lake Dwellers. At the end, after another earthquake tremor, Victoria is transported to modern times, finding herself in the familiar surroundings of Lord Grey-

stoke's bungalow on his African estate. With her are brother Barney, William Curtiss, the suitor she can never accept because of her love for Nu, and Lieutenant Butzow, who had left Lutha to accompany Barney to Beatrice, Nebraska.

Davis' revisions of "Sweetheart Primeval," to which Ed had grudgingly acceded, had undoubtedly eliminated certain prehistoric monsters — plesiosaurs, ichthyosaurs, and others — but some, including a pterodactyl and several unidentified mammoth reptiles, remained in the story.[91] For orientation Ed drew a brief map. The points of the compass are shown at the top, and to the east he has marked "The Restless Sea." A river winds away to the north, and just south and west of it, the habitation of the cave-dwellers, "The Barren Cliffs," is entered on the map. Far south Ed shows "The Cliffs of Nu" and "The Cave of Oo." At the extreme southern end of the map the area of "The Boat Builders" is marked, and near it Ed has drawn the "Mysterious Country (Islands)."[92]

In the sequel to "The Mad King," titled " 'Barney' Custer of Beatrice," the story opens in staid Nebraska surroundings, with sister Victoria present at the start, but only in a minor role. As a tribute to his friend Bert Weston, Ed had selected the town of Beatrice to be the setting for the original story, and now in continuing he even makes reference to Bert and his wife Margaret. Victoria, at the beginning of the story, wants to go motoring with Lieutenant Butzow and regrets her promise to Margaret to play bridge.[93]

Barney, in whose veins the royal blood of Rubinroth flows (his mother, the Princess Victoria, having fled from the kingdom of Lutha to marry Barney's father), is "stagnating" in Beatrice; he still dreams of Emma von der Tann, the woman he loves, and recalls the exciting days in Lutha, when, because of his close resemblance to Leopold, he had been mistaken for the king. Mysterious bombings in Beatrice are revealed to be the work of Captain Ernest Maenck, and in pursuit of the captain, Barney travels to Austria and then to Lutha.

The adventures that follow are similar to those created in "The Mad King," and Ed depends upon coincidence for a number of his plot devices. On two separate occasions Barney finds himself situated so that he can overhear important conversations coming from adjoining rooms. Lined up against a wall with a group of others fated for execution by a firing squad, Barney once more finds chance on his side. He is the only one to emerge alive, his skull merely creased when the volley of bullets is fired.

However, in " 'Barney' Custer of Beatrice," Ed displays ingenuity; for the first time he uses a real earth-type airplane. Lutha's sole plane is assigned a lookout post high above the battlefield and hovers there while its occupant scans the horizon for signs of the approaching allies, the Serbians. Barney's eyes "were fixed upon the soaring aeroplane"; he could wait only fifteen minutes for the vital signal. Then it came:

. . . there fluttered from the tiny monoplane a paper parachute. It dropped for several hundred feet before it spread to the air pressure and floated more gently toward the earth and a moment later there burst from its basket a puff of white smoke. Two more parachutes followed the first and two more puffs of smoke. Then the machine darted rapidly off toward the northeast.

Ed uses another imaginative device so that Barney can gain entrance to a garage. Unable to smash a window because the sounds would be heard, Barney recalls how a thief had cut a "neat little hole" in the window of a jeweler's shop on State Street in Chicago. The thief used a diamond. Barney borrows Princess Emma's diamond ring, scratches a "rough deep circle" close to the lock, and then taps the glass out.

Ed makes even greater use of the rather typical coincidence he had adopted for "The Mad King of Lutha" — the similarity in appearance of Barney and the cowardly King Leopold. The two men change roles, and their identities are confused several times. But Ed, with no sequel in mind, avoided his familiar

"open" ending and provided a firm and happy finish for Barney and Emma.[94]

" 'Barney' Custer of Beatrice" was written between September 26 and November 1, 1914. His next story, "Pellucidar," revealed elements of Burroughs' philosophies. His longheld belief in the rejuvenating effects of vigorous outdoor living are demonstrated in Abner Perry's physical condition:

. . . instead of appearing ten years older than he really was, as he had when he left the outer world, he now appeared about ten years younger. The wild, free life of Pellucidar had worked wonders for him.

Ed's dubious view of religion is illustrated through Perry's fears and what follows:

Perry was almost overcome by the hopelessness of our situation. He flopped down on his knees and began to pray.

It was the first time I had heard him at his old habit since my return to Pellucidar, and I had thought that he had given up his little idiosyncrasy; but he hadn't. Far from it.

Beyond this lies the characterization of Innes and, for that matter, of all of ERB's heroes who face dangers and seemingly hopeless situations undauntedly and with a refusal to yield to discouragement. With these men the solution always is found in action, not in "flopping down" to pray. This rejection of passivity — a resignation to fate or quietism — was part of Burroughs' practical view of life, that when a difficult situation arises, a man must do something to solve it on his own.

His antiwar philosophy is revealed in this comment by David Innes:

What we have given them (the Pellucidarians) so far has been the worst. We have given war and the munitions of war. In a single day we have made their wars infinitely more terrible and bloody than in all their past ages they have been able to make them with their crude, primitive weapons.

Through David Innes, Burroughs revealed

his own love of animals. To him a man's life was not complete without a dog. Concerning the primitive tribes of the inner world, Innes, as ERB's spokesman, stated:

...I had never guessed what it was that was lacking to life in Pellucidar, but now I knew that it was the total absence of domestic animals.

Man had not yet reached the point where he might take time from slaughter and escaping slaughter to make friends with any of the brute creations. . . .

On impulse David Innes is driven to saving the life of a fierce wolf-dog, a hyaenodon, injured when it plunged after him from the top of a sheer cliff into the sea. Watching the animal as it seemed on the verge of drowning, Innes was seized by pity: "The look of dumb misery in his eyes struck a chord in my breast, for I love dogs. I forgot he was a vicious, primordial wolf-thing — a man-eater, a scourge and a terror. I saw only the sad eyes that looked like the eyes of Raja, my dead collie of the outer world."

In gratitude, the wolf-dog later saved Innes' life, and with a bond of affection and trust established, the animal was given the name *Raja*. "Somehow all sense of loneliness vanished," Innes said. "I had a dog!"

As in his other stories of fantasy worlds, "Pellucidar" rises toward Ed's favorite climax — a furious battle scene on a grand scale. Abner Perry has succeeded in building the navy of the empire of Pellucidar. Against this fleet and an army supplied with guns and gunpowder, the forces of Hooja and the evil Mahars are helpless.

Innes' goal of moving Pellucidar into the twentieth century leads to the establishment of a political and economic system that modern scientists would have scrutinized in disbelief. The monarchy with David I as emperor depends for its support on various chieftains and naval officers who have been given the titles of king and duke. It is like a medieval empire. Ed's choice of a super-ruler is revealing of the philosophy he accepted — that somehow a be-

nevolent dictator was needed to direct the lives and affairs of the lower groups and to transform a primitive country into an ideal nation.

The economic system of Pellucidar is reduced to its simplest level through an elimination of money. Commerce, restricted by unusual regulations, becomes a matter of bartering:

A man may exchange that which he produces for something which he desires that another has produced; but he cannot dispose of the thing he thus acquires. In other words, a commodity ceases to have pecuniary value the instant that it passes out of the hands of its producer. All excess reverts to government; and, as this represents the production of the people as a government, government may dispose of it to other peoples in exchange for that which they produce. Thus we are establishing a trade between kingdoms, the profits from which go to the betterment of the people — to building factories for the manufacture of agricultural implements, and machinery for the various trades we are gradually teaching the people.

Thus the Empire of Pellucidar became a combination of opposites, truly strange bedfellows: rampant special-privileged royalty and nobility were assigned the task of developing a system of economic socialism.

"Pellucidar" offers examples of Ed's ingenuity in his creation of the "Brute-Men," skilled rope-throwers who dispatch their foes by lassoing them and hauling them to the top of the cliff.

The light and sometimes jesting tone, the loose style, and the rambling plot structure do not allow for sufficient development of excitement, suspense and conflict. These vital elements, normally Ed's stock-in-trade, are weak and unsustained in "Pellucidar."[95]

Among the items outlined for his *Autobiography* Ed had noted, "In 1914 I write 400,000 words, everything sells." Ed's 1914 production, exclusive of revisions or additions, consisted of eight stories, the shortest, "The Lad and the Lion," containing 40,000 words, and the longest, "Pellucidar," totaling more than 60,000 words.[96]

12 FILM FRUSTRATION

Early in 1914, through an initial step taken by Albert Payson Terhune of the *New York Evening World*, Ed began a new search for success — this time in the motion picture field. On March 20 Terhune had written, "By the way, I gave Stern & Co. [playbrokers and moving picture managers], your address today; and advised them to try at once to secure from you the dramatic rights on Tarzan."

From Edna Williams of Joseph W. Stern & Company of New York came an inquiry about *Tarzan of the Apes* and any other works with dramatic possibilities.[1] In his reply Ed explained that he had so far made no attempt to do anything with the motion picture rights of Tarzan, adding, "Am open to suggestions and an offer. If this story should succeed as a picture play I have others which might then be open for consideration."[2]

This contact brought no tangible result, but Ed's interest had now been aroused, and several months later, through the efforts of Bob Davis, Munsey editor, Ed communicated with Cora C. Wilkening of the Authors Photo-Play Agency of New York. He had sent her a copy of *Tarzan of the Apes*, and in his letter of June 24 presented his usual sales talk about *Tarzan* and *The Return of Tarzan* having appeared in newspapers from coast to coast, and asked, "Won't you please write me at your convenience confirming the conditions under which you undertake to place Tarzan with a moving picture producing company. . . ."

Mrs. Wilkening, apparently eager to handle Ed's work, wrote, "I think I know the company who will be delighted to put on your "Tarzan." I will submit all offers to you first for your approval."[3]

On July 10, upon returning from "a little vacation in the country," Ed responded, mentioning his file of letters from magazine readers "from nearly every English speaking corner of the globe and from every state in the Union." He voiced his main concern humorously:

By the way, still in the role of the modest violet by the mossy stone: I wish, in case you make a deal with a producer, that you would stipulate that my full name as author appears at the beginning of each reel — if that is what you call them. . . .

The passing weeks brought no word from Mrs. Wilkening. Impatient, Ed, on August 20, queried, "What's the matter?" The reply was glowingly optimistic: "I am now negotiating with two concerns who are considering the book on a royal basis with cash advance. . . . It will make a splendid feature — something absolutely original, and I am confident of being able to secure an excellent offer. . . ."

Ed was pleased to hear that things were going well, but noted that he was puzzled over the word "royal." He assumed it was intended to be "royalty" and commented, ". . . it sounds so much like a king's ransom that I get quite excited whenever I think of it. Anyhow, let's hope that the results will be 'royal'."[4] On August 31 he asked Joseph Bray at McClurg to forward three copies of *Tarzan* to Mrs. Wilkening and on the same date cautioned her, "In closing with anyone for the moving picture rights to Tarzan I hope you will be guided even more by the ability of the purchaser to produce properly and by his reputation for square dealing than by the size of the royalty or advance offered."

Ed's next contact with an agent was truly a comedy of errors. On November 9, 1914, a letter from the Frank Henry Rice Agency of New York referred to the subject of motion picture rights. Howard A. Archer, with whom Ed had previously communicated, explained that upon his return to New York he had found an inquiry concerning "The Cave Man" (seemingly a confusion in title for "The Cave Girl"). Archer wrote, "Please let me know if you will accept five percent on gross royalties with an advance of not less than five hundred dollars. It may be possible to obtain one thousand dollars advance against ten percent." An agency contract was forwarded for Ed's signature.

Ed was quite willing to allow the Rice Agen-cy to handle "The Cave Girl"; with the signed agreement he noted, "I think The Cave Girl as good as any for photo-play purposes, and really a better story than its sequel."[5] Once more he requested that his full name be displayed as the author at the beginning of each reel; he also insisted that in any contract with a producer, a clause should be added stating this requirement.[6]

However, whatever hopes Ed may have had were quickly shattered. On November 18 Frank Henry Rice wrote, ". . . I have found that the play for which I have an inquiry is entitled 'The Cave Man' which is an adaption of 'Lady Mechante' by Gelett Burgess, and not 'The Cave Girl' which is written by yourself." Rice, however, promised to seek offers for any other Burroughs stories suitable for motion pictures, and on November 21 Ed sent him a copy of "A Man Without a Soul."

Earlier, Ed had again written to Mrs. Wilkening to inform her that three agencies were interested in Tarzan. "I have been holding them off hoping to hear something favorable from you," he said. "I wish that you would let me know just what is wrong. If the producers don't want the story I should like to know it, so that I can get it out of my system and forget it. If they do want it, please tell me why they don't take it."[7] He emphasized that his interest in motion picture possibilities was "greater than formerly." Mrs. Wilkening responded that *Tarzan* was being considered by several companies. "I will do my utmost to close the matter during the coming week. . . ." she wrote.[8] But Ed's patience was running out. On November 28 he sent a succinct order to Mrs. Wilkening: "Please yank Tarzan off the movie market. I thank you for your efforts in his behalf." However, several days later, through Mrs. Wilkening's efforts, a new and hopeful prospect appeared.

William N. Selig of the Selig Polyscope Company was searching for material suitable for motion picture production. That Selig was an important contact was evidenced by the fact that Mrs. Wilkening hastened to journey from New York to meet him in Chicago for a conference.[9] On December 3 Ed wrote to Selig at the Chicago studios: "At Mrs. Wilkening's suggestion I am asking McClurg to send you a copy of Tarzan of the Apes. And herewith I am handing you a copy of The Lad and the Lion in mss. . . ."

He explained that although the Munsey Company had purchased the story, it had not yet appeared in magazine form, and under the circumstances no production could be begun without Munsey's agreement.[10] Ed added, "Mrs. Wilkening also suggested that you might wish to talk with me relative to these stories, and to this end I asked her to arrange with you to take lunch with me at your convenience — say Monday or Tuesday of next week, or later if you prefer."[11]

From William G. Chapman of the International Press Bureau, who was still acting as Ed's syndication agent, came an inquiry about Tarzan of the Apes. Chapman, on December 22, sought permission to submit the story to the Universal Film Manufacturing Company. Ed replied in a letter, sent a day later, and explained the situation, "One of the largest and best equipped producers in the country is now considering Tarzan of the Apes, favorably. However, they have no option on it. If you care to go ahead with the Universal people I have no objection."

Stressing his terms — "a good sized cash advance and a generous royalty," Ed stated, "Whoever makes me the best offer first can have it. It might be well to quote me liberally in writing to your prospect."

Chapman's request to act as a Burroughs agent in this new field made Ed aware that some explicit agreement was needed. In his response of December 23 he restated the terms, "I do not recall that we ever had any understanding about your commission in event of your placing Tarzan as a movie. 10% is customary. All the agents that have written me have mentioned this same commission. If this is satisfactory to you it is to me."

To Chapman Ed presented an attitude of indifference about the difficulties of finding a producer for Tarzan. It was of course an attitude assumed by him to conceal his disappointment. "To be perfectly candid," he remarked, "I am no longer 'het up' about placing Tarzan. I do not believe that any of the first class producers will be crazy about tackling it, or that they will want to pay enough for it to interest me. In other words, so far as Tarzan of the Movies is concerned, I am as independent as a hog on ice."

He commented to Chapman that Selig's company was his choice to make the movie — they have "the best zoo equipment of any of them." He explained the past situation: "Several weeks ago I yanked Tarzan off the movie market, but a New York agency wanted to submit it to one more prospect and they are the people who are now considering it." His annoyance was indicated in a final statement: "I shall close with some one by the first of January or I shall again grab it off and keep it off," to which he added, "I am getting bored by it."

Universal displayed no serious interest in Tarzan, but as a result of the contact that Chapman had made, Ed would later begin a submission of other works to them.

Meanwhile, with the end of 1914 came the first inquiry about a foreign language translation of Tarzan of the Apes. In December Joseph Bray forwarded a letter from Dr. Ralph Julian Sachers of New York requesting German rights to the famous story. Ed was inclined to view the whole matter with skepticism. The European situation, with World War I in full swing, made a request for terms on German translation rights appear particularly inappropriate. On December 22 Ed wrote to Bray, "It seems to me that if there is anything in this at all that the time is most inopportune for anything of the sort."

Aware of the strong animosities of the opposing sides, England and France vs. Germany, Ed commented, "In the first place it is doubtful if Germany would prove a profitable field at this time even for a novel of the first magnitude;

and in the second the popular interest in a novel featuring an English lordling and a French Officer in heroic roles would be notable for its absence."

However, he stressed that if Dr. Sachers could obtain a "bonafide cash offer for the rights from a reputable German Publisher" who would also handle the translation, the matter might be considered more seriously.[12]

With the negotiations for the "The Lad and the Lion" continuing, Mrs. Wilkening had telegraphed Ed to inquire about a price that would be acceptable to him. Ed could offer nothing definite: "I have less idea of the value of The Lad & the Lion than you. I do not know how many reels it will make, and if I did I shouldn't be much better off. I am sure that Mr. Selig is very keen for it, from what he has said to me, on the several occasions we have spoken of it."[13] Upon Selig's return to Chicago, Ed planned to discuss the price with him, but he urged Mrs. Wilkening, in the meantime, to suggest what she thought a fair price might be.

In this short period of his first contacts with the motion picture field and the use of scenarios, Ed had already acquired a skeptical attitude, made evident in his remark to Mrs. Wilkening: "As I told you once before, for the labor involved and the plots wasted I don't think much of the prices paid for scenarios that I have heard of at least; but of course I can tell more about it when I know what they will give me for The Lad & the Lion."[14] In the same letter he noted that he "liked Mr. Selig immensely and should be glad to write for him regularly."[15]

Toward the end of January 1915, Ed reached an agreement with Selig for the sale of the movie rights to "The Lad and the Lion" and a story in synopsis form titled "Ben, King of Beasts." Ed's pessimism about the payments received for film material was clearly justified. The price was $100 a reel, with "The Lad and the Lion" figured at five reels and "Ben, King of Beasts" at three, for a total of $800. Mrs. Wilkening's commission was fifty dollars.[16]

Plagued by the problem of inadequate payment for film stories, and worried about the forthcoming royalties from McClurg for *Tarzan*, Ed turned to The Authors' League of America for advice. Located in New York, the League displayed an impressive roster of officers with Winston Churchill as president and Theodore Roosevelt, vice-president. (Its British agent, Curtis Brown, in London, later became Burroughs' agent.) Ed applied for membership in January 1915 and was accepted a month later. In correspondence with Eric Schuler, secretary of the League, Ed at once brought up the matters that were troubling him. His first concern was with the McClurg royalties; he noted that the League's publication in its March *Bulletin* of an article titled "No Business-Man" had "raised a ghost that has been haunting me for a long time."[17]

Ed described his background in the business world, mentioning his practical education in "the school of experience" and explaining:

I even took an expert accountant job once, and "brought home the bacon"; but I am free to admit that I have quailed before the idea of demanding from McClurg an examination of their books, though I have fully realized that it was the proper thing to do.[18]

In seeking information about a point headed "Number 2," Ed wrote:

I recently sold the motion picture rights of two stories to The Selig Polyscope Company, and I wish to know if I received a fair and reasonable price for them.

It is my first experience in this line, of which I know less than nothing.[19]

He provided the details:

One story I submitted in mss form just as it had been accepted by a New York magazine that has not yet published it. Mr. Selig liked this story very much. He is the only member of his company who has read it, and until it came to making me an offer for it I dealt with no one else. He also read the other and accepted it — it was simply a synopsis.[20]

Ed, after listing the amounts received, noted that he was to be paid, in addition, $100 per reel for each extra reel that might be made in production. His appeal to the League for information brought little of consequence. It was clear that in this new field of motion picture writing, the League had nothing specific or practical to offer. Obviously, any stimulating or innovative ideas on the marketing of manuscripts would come from Burroughs, not from the League.

On the subject of second serial rights and the necessity for authors not to relinquish them, Ed could become eloquent. He had never forgiven himself for his early ignorance about these rights. The article "No Business-Man" in *The Bulletin* was concerned with syndication, and this was sufficient to arouse Ed's interest and cause him to express his own ideas on the matter. In sending a "communication" to *The Bulletin* on March 9, 1915, he commented: "If you feel that the subject merits the space necessary to give it publicity I only ask that you do not publish it over my name — the initial Z will do unless another uses Z, in which case the alphabet is at your disposal."[21]

The ideas contained in Ed's brief article "Syndication" were part of a philosophy he had discussed on previous occasions. He was anxious to awaken writers "to the possibilities for profit which they are throwing away — and worse than throwing away — when they permit the second serial rights to their manuscripts to pass out of their hands without receiving for them, in real money, what they are worth."

Jabbing in humorous disparagement his attitude, as a new writer, in feeling "fully qualified to spill advice promiscuously among my betters," he nevertheless pointed out, "I am making more real money out of the second serial rights to my stories than some famous authors whose work is of infinitely greater value than mine." Ed explained:

I sold three stories to magazines before I discovered that second serial rights had a value. [Actually the total is four if his first story, "Under the Moons of Mars," *is included.] From then I have retained these rights and the fourth story has already brought in $729.00 in cash and is still selling. I have received as high as $300.00 for the newspaper rights to a story for a single city. I have repeatedly sold to publishers who maintain a syndicating bureau of their own without the slightest demur on their part as to the retention of my second serial rights by me. I have sold for use in a single city to a newspaper that maintains a syndicating service covering many cities.*[22]

Ed's most important suggestion was that the League should form a syndicating bureau which would be allowed a "reasonable commission" for its services. This, he maintained, could not only make the bureau self-supporting, but could also "reimburse the League for the loss of literary agents advertising in *The Bulletin*." If a bureau were created, Ed indicated he would submit a list of the newspapers that had purchased his stories, together with the prices they had paid. Other writers might then do the same, and the collected information would establish a price basis suitable for all syndication dealings between authors and newspapers.[23]

The appearance of the article in *The Bulletin* of April 1915 brought a response and inquiry from author Walter Prichard Eaton. The signature of "Z" had proved to be no secret, since secretary Schuler had identified Burroughs to Eaton. Seeking further details, Eaton wrote:

. . . Your letter interested me strangely, seeing's how I never get a red cent out of any second rights of a single story of mine. It's only lately that I've had intelligence enough to hang on to the 2nd rights, anyhow. And now that I've got 'em, what am I goin' to do with 'em? Your letter gives me a glimmering hope that maybe you are a sort of Moses, to lead us sheep-like authors into the promised land. Why don't you organize a little 2nd rights bureau, and handle stuff for some of the rest of us, and let us pay you a commish or something? Have you got a

scheme? If so, for Heavens sake, let's hear it![24]

Ed, in his response of May 20, noted, "Yes, I had a lovely scheme, but Schuler blue penciled it. It was to have the League establish a syndicating bureau." He then restated the paragraph that Schuler had deleted from the article before it was printed. This contained the reference about a League bureau supported by commissions from newspaper sales. Schuler's reason for removing this paragraph was obvious: he was fearful of antagonizing the literary agents who might then withdraw their ads from *The Bulletin*. Ed's contention that the commissions would "more than reimburse" the League for loss of revenue from agents' ads was apparently unconvincing to Schuler. In the long letter to Walter Prichard Eaton, Ed presented other ideas:

There is, however, an alternative; but, to be perfectly candid, I don't know that it would work. It is for a few of us to organize a bureau, pay regular commissions to it for placing our work and depend upon the profits for the reduction of our personal commissions.

By this means we could do a regular agency business including book, magazine, newspaper and photo-play rights for the general writing public, and have a medium of our own for marketing such of our own rights as we did not care to handle ourselves.[25]

Concerning Eaton's suggestion that Ed organize and direct the bureau, he replied, ". . . it is out of the question — I am too dinged lazy; but I could easily find a manager who could devote all his time to it." Ed commented about the problem of raising capital, but believed that it should not be too difficult to get a contribution from each author. The man he had in mind for manager of the projected bureau was his brother Harry.

I was talking with my brother about it last evening, seeing if I could interest him in it. He has considerable mail order experience, which is just what a man would need to handle this work successfully, and the idea rather appealed to him. I think he might be willing to manage a bureau, though I am not sure.[26]

Ed demonstrated that in the business world his ideas possessed the same imagination and originality that he displayed in his stories. He envisioned the future — a plan only in the dream stage: "Way in the backs of our heads we could harbor the hope that some day the bureau could develop into that ideal (for the writer) organization — an authors' publishing house, by means of which we could not only get our royalties, but also a share of the profits from our books," and added, "I *know* that there are great possibilities in such a hope. I have even dreamed of a magazine, but as 999.9 of all magazines fail there is a legitimate doubt as to the feasibility of the latter."

In this letter of May 20 to Eaton, Ed recalled his position as department manager for the A. W. Shaw Company, publishers of *System, The Magazine of Business*, and commented, ". . . accept it from me, there is money in a sanely conducted magazine and publishing business combined."

Ed's visions of the future were not merely the vague and stimulating illusions that drift beyond the grasp of individuals; they were based upon practical business instincts. They resulted from his characteristic impatience with those who could not appreciate the value of his stories, or those who were handicapped by overcaution and limited imagination. He had exhibited both this business confidence and impatience in the past. When book publishers were reluctant to gamble on "Tarzan of the Apes," he seriously considered publishing the story himself. And when *All-Story's* syndication bureau appeared satisfied to settle for meager payments, Ed, contemptuous, proceeded to prove that newspaper sales could be highly profitable.

The differences between Burroughs, the man of action, and writers such as Eaton, were clearly emphasized in Eaton's response of May 23, in which he deplored Ed's refusal to direct the proposed bureau. Eaton, lost in business matters, spoke of his "abysmal ignorance" of the whole subject and confessed helplessly that he had not the faintest idea as to what to do with his second serial rights. Representative of the average writer, Eaton, richly imaginative, lived in his world of creativity, concentrated as did the others on producing his characters and situations, and was willing to leave business dealings to editors and agents. Through custom and convention the artist, whether a painter, musician, or writer, had always been pictured as a creative but wholly impractical individual. Burroughs, the paradox, now shattered this old-fashioned concept. He demonstrated that an author not only could, but should combine a business acuity and determination with his writing imagination.

That his visions *were* practical would be proved in the future. With Burroughs an idea was appraised, gripped firmly — and then made inevitable. When the time was right, he would accomplish two objectives: establish his own publishing company and arrange for the production of his own motion pictures.

915 brought a succession of dealings or contacts with agents and individuals about varied writing projects. All of these proved time-consuming and fruitless. On January 29 Ed wrote to Frank Henry Rice, "If you haven't done anything by this time with A Man Without a Soul, kindly let it drop, as I have decided to withdraw it. I enclose 4c for return of copy." Ed's faith in agents was rapidly vanishing, and Rice's response offered nothing to strengthen it: "Your magazine story, 'A Man Without a Soul' has been submitted to a producer for reading. . . ."[27] It was a typical agent's report — one that had brought no result in the past. Searching for new outlets, Ed on January 29 queried the Universal Film Corporation in New York, mentioning that his stories in magazine form possessed "photoplay possibilities." He noted, "One that I have in mind has a panther in it, but there are others in which no wild animals figure, so, if you care to see one, please let me know which class you prefer. . . ." On February 4 a

reply from Anthony P. Kelly, editor of the scenario department, indicated that Universal was interested. Kelly, who signed his letter "Yours for Universal Peace", wrote, "Only please, Mr. Burroughs, enclose a brief concise synopsis with each one of the stories submitted. . . ."

The hope of establishing a syndication bureau to handle all types of story and photoplay rights was soon abandoned. Whether insufficient interest was displayed by other authors, or whether the entire matter was impractical is difficult to ascertain. However, Ed still placed reliance upon The Author's League and turned to it for assistance. A letter from Alec Lorimore, president of the National Movement Motion Picture Bureau of New York, contained a proposal that Ed should novelize "a serial photo drama," evidently for submission in a contest. Ed doubted that he could afford "the expenditure of time," but added:

If Bob Davis, after reading the scenario, were to say that he believed I could write a novelization that would be acceptable to him, I should not hesitate to attempt it provided of course that my net remuneration was satisfactory.

As to the title of authorship, in case I wrote the novelization, I have very decided convictions on that subject, and should expect credit for the novelization only.[28]

Ed had been in communication with Eric Schuler of The Author's League, this time seeking information about copyrights. Schuler had sent details, but Ed, as in the past, was ready with one of his own imaginative schemes. He wrote, "There should be some way that an author could copyright his work before sending it to a publisher. Has any plan ever been suggested or considered? It seems to me that one might copyright the first and last pages of a mss., sending duplicate copies of each with fee in accordance with the regular procedure, or, perhaps, copyright a synopsis of the story, which would cover the plot and title. I wonder if it would be legal."[29] In the same letter he included an inquiry about the reputation of Lorimore and his company and remarked, "If I am becoming a pest you must thank yourself, for I recall that we are urged to make use of The League. Anyway, I thank you from the bottom of my heart for your patience and kindness, and when I can reciprocate shall be delighted to do so." Concerning Lorimore, Schuler could discover nothing: ". . . I found it difficult to get any information . . . and when I did finally . . . the information . . . was certainly not such as to warrant my recommending it to you."[30]

Although Selig had purchased "The Lad and The Lion" and "Ben, King of Beasts" for motion picture production he apparently showed no real interest in *Tarzan of the Apes*. Ed had discussed the story with him in a conference in December 1914. Perhaps Selig believed that the difficulties of producing such a jungle epic would be insurmountable. However, an inquiry from H. Morris Friedman of Ottumwa, Iowa, led to a reply from Ed revealing that Selig still had *Tarzan* under tentative consideration. Friedman, whose letter of March 11, 1915, was forwarded by McClurg, sought the photoplay rights to *Tarzan*. Ed replied, ". . . I rather doubt if I should care to close with a producer at this time, as one company already has a man in Africa trying to get bona fide ape-life pictures for an elaborate production of Tarzan. . . ."[31]

This unusual action of Selig was mentioned in Ed's letter of January 13, 1915, addressed to Terhune at the *Evening World:*

Mr. Selig, who is considering Tarzan of the Apes, is sending a man to Africa next week. A part of his equipment is a copy of the Tarzan book, and included in his instructions are orders to take moving pictures of ape life in the jungle. When that is released Tarzan should boom.[32]

To Ed the whole idea of a cameraman attempting to locate the African apes in the jungle, and to creep up on them and take moving pictures, appeared hilarious. He could readily imagine the difficulties the man was going to encounter. His humorous report of this near impossible feat, addressed to Mrs. Wilkening at

the Authors Photo-Play Agency, led her, on February 8, to comment appreciatively:

I am very much amused in regard to your remarks concerning the success of the man who thinks he is going to take pictures of the apes in the African jungles. You have given this subject considerable study and I imagine you know the lively time the poor man will have.

A steady flow of communications with Selig about "The Lad and the Lion" and other matters followed. On March 12 Selig noted, "We expect to shortly start work on the scenario . . . find we are in need of another copy of the book. . . ." A day later, in sending his only copy, Ed requested its return, explaining that "as the magazine often makes changes which I do not care for, I like to have a copy of the original against the possibility of book publication."

On behalf of his sister-in-law Ella, who displayed writing ability, Ed wrote to Selig to ask that she be given a tryout as an actress. "It is not the emotional notoriety-longing of a young girl," he said, "but the desire of a mature woman to utilize her talents and training for purposes of bread winning. . . . It is with a full realization of the fact that you must be bored to death with similar requests from people who have a right to ask favors of you, which I have not, that I ask this of you."[33] Selig's reply, sent from Los Angeles, was courteous: ". . . upon my return will be pleased to give your sister-in-law a fair trial. Will keep you posted as to the exact time of my return to Chicago."[34]

Eager to write material for the motion pictures or to adapt his own stories for film use, Ed found himself baffled and frustrated by the scenario form. He called a story outline a "synopsis," while Selig, in his letters, preferred the term "scenario." This type of explicit characterization plus a plot or action summary was contrary to the full and detailed novel style that had become second nature to him. In this new writing area he once again had all the sensations of a beginner, his old doubts and insecurities returning. He viewed the synopses he completed with disapproval or evaluated them as outright failures; it was plain to him that he did not, as yet, understand this special writing form.

He had written to John F. Pribyl of the Selig Polyscope Company to request a copy of a scenario to be used as a model. Pribyl had forwarded a copy of "In the Tentacles of the North" by James Oliver Curwood, and in a letter of January 9, 1915, had given valuable advice on motion picture writing:

The script will give you a general idea of the construction of a scenario. The importance of your story will determine the number of reels, whether one, two, three, four, or even five. The chief purpose in writing a scenario is to get as much action in each reel as possible and each reel is to contain a strong punch, all leading up to a final climax. If a two reel story can not have a big incident in each reel it is better to crowd all of the incidents in one reel.

Pribyl brought up the matter of expense. "If a photoplay is in one reel," he wrote, "it will not justify an expensive production, but if the production runs into three or more reels there is a possibility of economy in one or more reels to offset an expensive construction in the balance of the story, thus the general average of cost will be the same as if we were making single reel productions."

Pribyl expressed the belief that in discussions with Selig Ed had acquired "a general idea as to what is feasible for a camera." He stressed the point that a writer must look at all situations through the camera, commenting that, "anything that can not be photographed should not be written. Unfortunately, the camera has not the advantages of printers' type in this respect." Pribyl's succinct summary of instructions for film writing would be as relevant today as in 1915. On January 11 Ed thanked him for "loan of scenario," stating, "I'll get it back to you in good order in a few days. I want to keep it at hand while I experiment on one of my own."

Despite Pribyl's advice and the use of a scenario, Ed continued to have difficulties. To Selig, in seeking an offer for photoplay rights, he wrote, ". . . I am sending a rather bum synopsis of The Mad King . . . ," and by way of apology added, "The scenario would, I think have to be written from the magazine copy, as I have omitted many details and situations from the synopsis which are necessary to the interest and continuity of the story. I am not exactly hep to the writing of a synopsis. . . ."[35] And to Pribyl a few days later, he wrote, "Am sending you herewith synopsis of a comedy. Even though it may not be adapted to your uses it may help me to discover just what you can use, so do me the kindness to look it over."[36] Ed's pencil notation on the letter identified the comedy as "His Majesty: The Janitor"; it was Ed's first venture into a comedy synopsis designed for the movies.

His uncertainty about film writing was illustrated in his letter to Anthony P. Kelly of the Universal Film Manufacturing Company of New York. Kelly had earlier suggested that he submit one of his stories in synopsis form, and on August 28 Ed replied, "The trouble is that I haven't an idea as to how to go about it — whether merely the bare argument of the story is all that is necessary, or a summary showing all the principal situations and carrying the plot throughout. . . ."

However baffled he may have felt over motion picture writing, Ed, determined to enter this new field, displayed the same dogged persistence that had marked his past efforts in story selling. Unaffected by rejections, he dispatched queries and a stream of stories and synopses to various film companies. The summer and fall of 1915 was an especially hectic period. On August 19, Pribyl acknowledged "His Majesty: The Janitor," remarking, "Yes, it's funny, but don't know if the balloon stuff can be made. Have passed the script along to Colonel Selig. He knows things I don't know — and that's a hell-uva lot! You'll hear about this later. . . ." In the synopsis Jerry, the janitor, fleeing from a policeman, escapes in a balloon. Later, he falls out of the balloon and crashes through the ceiling of the royal palace.

Selig quickly rejected the comedy and other material Ed had sent him, and on August 27 wrote, ". . . returning your two scenarios, a western story and a comedy. The western story contains a theme which has been done over and over again and is not new. The comedy is not just suitable for our purpose, but we believe should be good for others. The other one I am still reading and expect to give you an answer within a day or two." The western story was evidently "For the Fool's Mother," written in 1912, or possibly a synopsis expansion of it, "The Prospector," completed later.[37] The "other one" referred to by Selig was Ed's synopsis of "The Mad King."

These rejections caused Ed to remark gloomily to Selig, "As a photoplay writer I'm a fine little chauffeur. Am enclosing another, which is even rottener than those you returned. It's mighty good of you to read them, and I appreciate it."[38] The enclosed material, Ed's second comedy synopsis, was titled "The Lion Hunter." On August 31, J. A. Berst, Vice-President of the Selig Company referred to Ed's synopsis of "The Mad King" and explained that the two books would make a five-reel picture. Evidently the "synopsis" was not suitable for motion picture production; Berst inquired how much Ed wanted for his story and also if he intended to write the "scenario." Concerning the comedy "The Lion Hunter," Berst advised that it would make a one-reel picture. ". . . We offer you $60.00 for same, as that is what it is worth to us," he wrote. An assignment of rights was enclosed for Ed's signature.

Having had only limited contacts with writer Burroughs, the Selig Company could not know, as both Metcalf and Davis had learned, that they were dealing with a man who was adamantly stubborn about what constituted a fair price for his stories. Of course, the company's piddling offer had confirmed the dubious view he already had of the motion picture business, but that did not prevent him from trying elsewhere. He at once sent "The Lion Hunter" and "The Mad King" to the Universal Film Manufacturing Company in Universal City, California.[39] To Kelly, Universal's scenario editor, he had, on August 28, sent "His Majesty: The Janitor." With no reply received, he tried to dicker with Selig, requesting a higher offer for "The Lion Hunter" and $100 a reel for "The Mad King."[40] Berst, in his reply, was unresponsive to both proposals:

. . . $100 a reel for "The Mad King" is too high, as we have to write the scenario and this is going to cost us also quite some money.

It is well-known by me that many of your novels have been published by newspapers and magazines, but it is not much of an asset for picture work as the public does not care so much who wrote the scenario. They are looking for a good story properly acted.

"The Mad King" is worth to us at a maximum $80 per reel. Of course, if it was in scenario form, ready to produce, we would be willing to pay more. . . .[41]

It appeared that Ed's customary references to the popularity of his printed works had made no impression upon Berst. In his letter of September 21 Ed apologized for a delay in answering the Selig offer; he had been ill. The illness was undoubtedly a recurrence of the neuritis that had troubled him for a number of years. The periodic flare-ups seemed to result from overwork and anxiety or tension, and more specifically, to be caused also by the many hours of storywriting or typing, in which the arm, shoulder, and neck may be held in a rigid position.

A further attempt by Ed to persuade Universal to purchase "The Lion Hunter" and "The Mad King" was unsuccessful.[42] The prospects of turning these into motion pictures were hardly encouraging. However, as demonstrated in the past, Ed had a constitutional resistance to wasting any of the material he had labored on. Possibly a comment of Berst — that a scenario form would be worth more money — may have motivated him. More than a month later he again sent "The Mad King" to Selig, this time as a scenario. But the work had been in vain. On November 30, Selig replied, "I have read your scenario 'The Mad King' and regret to state that we will not be able to use it for the reason that we already own three or four plays of that kind. . . ."

Among minor business matters that occupied Ed's time was a connection with a newspaper clipping bureau, that of Henry Romeike, Inc., of New York; Ed had subscribed to the service in June 1914, paying five dollars for one hundred clippings. When later billed for renewal, he wrote to Romeike with some asperity:

I have kept an accurate record of all clippings received from you, and including the last batch which came subsequent to your letter I have received but ninety five all told. These include a number of worthless cuttings such as publisher's notices like the attached.

Of course if you think it right to include these, go to it; but I really should have the full one hundred clippings that I have paid for.

Another thing. Under the contract, I believe, I was to receive clippings for a year. My advance payment was for the first one hundred. The balance up to the expiration of the contract were to be charged to me at 5c each, and the contract still has about three months to run.

The entire matter is trivial. If you say so, I'll send you another five; but I wish you would tell me: Why is an agreement?"[43]

Tarzan's popularity continued to bring inquiries from agents, among them Edna Williams, now with the International Theatrical Play Bureau of New York; she had written Ed several times about film possibilities and on April 16 explained that "a very large manufacturer" was seeking a scenario which would use some trained animals. It occurred to her that *Tarzan* would allow him to plan outside scenes for these animals; she was thinking of a serial which might combine *Tarzan* and *The Return of Tarzan*. Ed, unimpressed by agents' projects, replied that *Tarzan* was being considered by a producer. ". . . And so I should not care to submit it to another," he said, adding, "To be perfectly candid, I am not much excited about the movie end of my writing — there is not enough in it."[44]

Miss Williams was stubbornly persistent, and her letters finally wore Ed down. On May 25 he wearily responded:

If you wish to submit Tarzan of the Apes and The Return of Tarzan to some one producer other than The Selig Polyscope Company I do not know that I have any particular objections, other than a natural desire to obviate useless effort on your part, for, in the first place, it is impossible to produce these stories properly, and, in the second place, I would want more for my rights than anyone would pay me.

He authorized her only "to receive and transmit" offers. His statement that the *Tarzan* stories could not be produced "properly" was both surprising and unexpected. Selig's hesitancy led to an obvious interpretation — a huge jungle film of this type posed too many production difficulties and was, in fact, unfeasible. Such doubts would of course have contributed to Ed's negative attitude. Selig selected "The Lad and the Lion" as a motion picture vehicle because the story had fewer complications of plot and setting.

Ed's dubious view of *Tarzan of the Apes* as a suitable story for movie production did not change in the months that followed. However, evidenced in a letter of September 2, 1915, to Kelly at the Universal Film Company in Los Angeles, he had modified his doubts about the second *Tarzan* story. In planning to meet Kelly, he wrote, "Among other things, I want to talk over the movie possibilities of *The Return of Tarzan*, which could be much more easily produced than *Tarzan of the Apes*, which I have always considered unproducable."

Once more the question of translating *Tarzan* into German arose, this time in a proposal by Dr. Arthur Meyer of Paterson, New Jersey.[45] Ed was unenthusiastic, indicating on November 8 that he was not sure what advantages would "accrue" to him through this translation, and was equally uncertain that Meyer could translate the work "in a style that would insure it a place among the best fiction in the German language. . . ." Again, with the war in mind, he wrote, "The hero is an Englishman, his best friend is a Frenchman, and the author is an American — do you think Germans would wax very enthusiastic over such a combination, especially at such a time as this?"

In a letter describing his qualifications, Meyer noted that since a German copyright for *Tarzan* had not been obtained, anybody would be free to translate the book. He stressed, however, his desire to work with the author. He proposed that Ed pay him $150 for translating *Tarzan* and for securing a German publisher.[46] Now worried about the German copyright situation, Ed wrote to Schuler of the Author's League, inquiring whether the best procedure might be to contact a reputable German publisher directly.[47] Without sufficient information about existing copyrights on *Tarzan of the Apes,* Schuler could give no definite advice.[48]

The Selig Polyscope Company was having its difficulties with "The Lad and the Lion." Plans had been made to schedule the motion picture release to coincide with the publication of the story in *All-Story* magazine. On March 28 Ed remarked to Bob Davis, "Selig tells me you and he are going to pull off The Lad & the Lion simultaneously. He is all het up about the story and is figuring on making a big feature production of it with the great Kathlyn in the lead. It should be of a lot of benefit to both the play and the magazine to have them come together, and incidentally to that modest violet, the author."[49] On April 26 Davis wrote:

I had a talk with Mr. Selig a few weeks ago about "The Lad and the Lion". I shall schedule it so that it will terminate in the issue of October 30, simultaneous with its appearance on the screen throughout the United States. I am going to make some noise about this thing and give it lots of publicity. . . .

Because of delays at the studio, Davis's schedule could not be followed. Months later the production of "The Lad and the Lion" was still in a state of uncertainty and Ed, in contact with Berst, learned that "the scenario . . . was not satisfactory to him. . . ." To Davis Ed explained, ". . . he (Berst) expected to get busy on it himself very soon; but he did not mention any other difficulty, and spoke as though the obstacles might be easily overcome. I gathered from what he said that production would be completed early this winter, though he stated nothing definite as to time. . . ."[50] On December 1 Ed confessed to Davis, "I can't learn anything from Selig, and as the only other man there I was well acquainted with has left them, my sources of info in that quarter are nil. . . ."

1915 drew to a close with all of Ed's strenuous efforts to find a motion picture producer for *Tarzan* proving futile. Except for "The Lad and the Lion" and "Ben, King of Beasts," described as a "wild animal scenario," dealings with Selig had brought no result. In acknowledging the return of the scenario for "The Mad King," Ed wrote, "You also have another of mine, The Lion Hunter, which Mr. Berst made me an unsatisfactory offer on. Will you kindly return that, as well. . . ."[51]

"His Majesty, the Janitor," Ed's first experiment with the comedy-synopsis form, is constructed around a series of wildly slapstick incidents that rival those contained in a Mack Sennett comedy. In fact, many of Jerry the Janitor's brash and insolent actions appear Chaplinesque. For his concept of Jerry as a character, Ed adopted and exaggerated a prototype — that of the old-time apartment building janitor who ruled his domain and his tenants with the supreme authority of a king.[52]

In a second comedy-synopsis, "The Lion Hunter," Ed devises a situation of mistaken identity involving Algernon D. Simpson, an inept ribbon counter clerk who has just been fired, and the great French explorer and lion hunter, Alphonse de Sachet. At a boarding house where he is about to apply for a job as a porter, Algernon, because of the initials A.D.S. on his suitcase, is assumed to be de Sachet. Influenced by the adoring glances of a pretty girl, Algernon decides to continue his impersonation of the famous lion hunter.

The series of escapades that develops is

clearly slapstick, giving "The Lion Hunter" the appearance of a Chaplin or Laurel and Hardy comedy. When de Sachet finally arrives at the boarding house, Algernon, who has even arranged for a circus photographer to fake a picture of him with one foot on a lion's carcass, is exposed as a fraud and scorned by the pretty girl. His chance to redeem himself comes with the entry of an unexpected visitor to the boarding house — a lion that has escaped from the circus. De Sachet, the intrepid hunter, flees in panic and hides under a sofa, while Algernon emerges as a hero, routing the lion with a broom. The predictable romantic ending occurs.[53]

"Ben, King of Beasts," purchased by Selig for $300, is a fourteen-page synopsis with highly complicated plot elements. The characters travel from the original setting in Virginia to the wilds of Africa and back. The theme — one of Ed's favorites — centers about the close bonds between Dick Gordon, the hero, and Ben, a huge African lion.[54]

Burroughs' frustrated struggles with the movie synopsis form — a type of writing he felt he could never master — led him, about 1914-15, to scrawl in despair on the front of an unfinished work, "Synopsis of a bum photoplay." The plot of the handwritten, fourteen-page synopsis centers about the hazards faced by Hiram Huston, inventor of a highly explosive powder and a wireless detonator, and his daughter Deodora, the only one who knows where her father's notes and data are concealed. Other characters include Carter Colfax, Deodora's fiancé, whose father owns a large powder plant; Borsted, Covalla, and Klein, secret agents of a foreign government, Covalla having special powers as a hypnotist; Horta, an alluring female spy working with the trio; and Smith, Huston's secretary, a young man of weak character.

Huston, in an effort to interest the government in his invention, journeys to Washington. When Congress refuses to appropriate funds to purchase the invention, Huston visits Theodore Roosevelt at Oyster Bay; at Roosevelt's request Huston promises not to dispose of his invention to any foreign power.

The four agents, determined to steal the invention, concentrate first on Smith, Huston's secretary, and through the wiles of the lovely Horta, persuade him to join them and to spy on his employer. The plot develops complicated twists, with Burroughs reverting to one of his favorite and most convenient devices — that of switched identities. Colfax is drugged, and Borsted, who closely resembles him, takes his place; the conspirators also capture Huston. They set off an explosion at the experimental field, arrange for bits of Huston's clothing to be found, and convince Colfax, who has been hypnotized by Covalla, that he is responsible for the inventor's death.

The succession of incidents includes the police hunt for Huston's "murderer," the hypnotizing of Deodora, Colfax's awakening realization that he is not guilty, based upon such clues as the bloodless shreds of clothes and a duplicate walking stick, and, quite unbelievably, a reverse switch with Colfax now assuming the identity of the villainous Borsted.

Ed's persistent attempts during 1915 to break into the motion picture field had been severely disappointing. The minor sales of "The Lad and the Lion" and "Ben, King of Beasts" to Selig were hardly impressive when balanced against the producer's rejection of *Tarzan of the Apes*. The delay in production of "The Lad and the Lion" was exasperating, and as far as "Ben, King of Beasts" was concerned, Selig was making no plans at all to turn the story into a motion picture.

Various queries to Selig concerning "The Lad and the Lion" produced no definite information. Selig was evidently having production difficulties. In an exchange of letters between Ed and Bob Davis of the Munsey Company, both revealed their frustration:

Have you learned anything definite about the production of The Lad & the Lion? I imagine not. I am told that it will be useless to wait on Selig....

[*Ed to Davis, April 27, 1916*]

Motion picture set of The Lad and the Lion; *Joan Burroughs at age eight took photo with her Kodak Brownie camera.*

I think I will notify Selig that I am going to put "The Lad and the Lion" to press without any further delay from them. At least it will have the effect of flashing an answer. Then I will let you know what they say.
[*Davis to Ed, May 4, 1916*]

"The Lad and the Lion" I am withholding until I hear from the Selig people. If they don't come across soon, I shall print it regardless of them.
[*Davis to Ed, October 25, 1916*]

I think you are a nut to wait . . . for The Lad and the Lion Production. . . .
[*Ed to Davis, November 21, 1916*]

I think I will let Selig go over the dam on the "Lad and the Lion."
[*Davis to Ed, November 27, 1916*]

I note that you are going to let Selig slide. . . .
[*Ed to Davis, December 3, 1916*]

I was out at Selig's Zoo the other day and learned that they expect to start on The Lad and the Lion soon; but. . . .
[*Ed to Davis, February 10, 1917*]

Davis, who had purchased "The Lad and the Lion" on April 2, 1914, first serial rights only, had withheld publication, acceding to Ed's request that the appearance in *All-Story* be timed so as to coincide with the movie release. To Davis's astonishment, without prior consultation, Selig, on April 21, 1917, informed the editor of a planned prerelease of the film, to "take place in New York, Chicago and one or two more of the larger cities," and of a general release scheduled for June. Davis, irked, hastened to reply: ". . . These dates make it impossible for us to present this story in the proper manner in the *All-Story Weekly* and we do not feel justified in permitting a pre-release to come out before we can give the story publication."[55]

Davis reminded Selig of Munsey's purchase of the story in 1914, commenting, ". . . in 1915

Los Angeles set of Selig Polyscope Company during filming of ERB's story The Lad and the Lion, *1916.*

when we were about ready to put this story to press, Mr. Burroughs asked us to hold it back until the Selig Polyscope Co. could present it on the screen. We have been carrying it now as you will see, for nearly three years, during which time you have been unable to make your production. Our rights come first. . . ."[56]

Nevertheless, in a conciliatory approach, Davis noted that the "issue" was "purely reciprocal" and assumed that Selig would not wish "to depreciate the value of a property . . . held exclusively by us." He offered a compromise proposal: Selig was to hold the prerelease until June 13 so as to allow *All-Story* sufficient time to publish "The Lad and the Lion"; in this way the cooperative plan could still be followed.[57]

On May 14, 1917, in a note to Ed marked "Confidential," the editor described the outcome of the situation:

Yes, Mr. Selig has settled the matter, and the "Lad and the Lion" will appear in the films May 14th.

Davis added, "So far as you are concerned, Edgar, not a cloud hovers in the sky between us and you can crack my safe or my ice-box for all it contains. I am going to see that 'The Lad and the Lion' by Edgar Rice Burroughs gets a good square deal in all our publications. I know you will like the cover. Will send you one as soon as it is ready." Davis signed his letter, "Yours to a cinder."[58] In his reply Ed expressed appreciation to Davis, saying, "You are the best scout I ever did business with and if the time comes when I feel that I must pick pockets for a living you may feel perfectly secure."

Davis, despite his anger at Selig, allowed the movie reasonable publicity when the story, the first of three parts, appeared in the *All-Story Weekly* of June 30, 1917. The magazine featured a colorful cover illustration of the Lad and his lion companion. A motion picture announcement was printed at the bottom edge of

"The Lad and the Lion" cover of All-Story Weekly, *June 30, 1917.*

the cover. It stated briefly, "On the Screen Selig Polyscope Company."

In the movie, Selig's departure from the original story was evident from the beginning. He had removed Burroughs' hints that the Lad was of royal birth and had made him William Bankington, son of a millionaire, played by Will Machin. Others in the cast were Vivian Reed as the Arab girl Nakhla; Charles Le Moyne as Dan Saada; Al W. Filson as Sheik Ali-Es-Hadji; and Lafayette McKee as James Bankington.[59]

Selig also removed from the story the half-crazed old epileptic who mistreats both the boy and the lion, the years aboard the drifting ship, and the odd scenes with the old man, a deaf-mute, instructing the boy in sign language; he replaced the old man with a brutal stowaway, Broot. Thus, the opening incidents are drastically revised:

James Bankington, a millionaire, consents to his only son, William, making a trip to Africa. The boy takes passage with Captain Tagst. . . . They pass a sailing vessel carrying a caged lion to America. In the hold is a stowaway named Broot, and the pipe he smokes starts a fire. Knowing there is a consignment of powder the captain and crew abandon the ship. The stowaway extinguishes the blaze and discovers the lion.

Captain Tagst's ship is wrecked and William is left alone on a raft. The stowaway rescues the lad. Fright and exposure have robbed him of his memory. Time passes and the lad has made friends with the lion, for both are kicked and cuffed by Broot, the stowaway. Later the lion escapes and Broot springs overboard.[60]

The major action takes place in a North African Arab village where the Lad falls in love with Nakhla. A band of brigands, whose chief falls in love with Nakhla, is introduced; a love triangle develops; the Lad has his memory restored by a blow on the head in a fight with the brigand chief; and the lion springs upon the chief and kills him. Aware of his identity, the Lad still proclaims his love for the simple Arab girl. Ed's original story complications are followed in the major action.

During the 1915 period, when ERB's interest in screen writing had been stimulated, he devised two other synopses. The first of these, an eleven-page manuscript, "The Prospector," develops the plot of "For a Fool's Mother" (1912), but expands the story with additional action. "For a Fool's Mother" has no romantic interest, so Ed introduces two suitors for the seventeen-year-old Mary Turner. He also indicates familiarity with the scenario form, with emphasis on the visual, and such cues as: "Show Kid Turner, ragged, coughing, and weak, tramping along railway through desert country."

The plot includes many popular ingredients of the Western story — the escape from the sheriff, the recapture, a mob storming the jail and preparing to lynch the Prospector, and the nick-of-time testimony by a wastrel which saves the Prospector's life.

The synopsis ends with a happy future promised the lovers and Cole, the rival for the girl's hand, making a heroic sacrifice. Shaking the Prospector's hand, he says: "I'm going back east tomorrow but I'd like to leave a good superintendent in charge of the camp. Will you take my job — my secretary goes with it."[61]

A brief handwritten synopsis, completed on August 31, 1915, and titled "The Zealots," may be described as the original medical or doctors story. There is no record of its ever having been submitted to a motion picture producer. The love interest between an "M.D. Allopath," and his hometown sweetheart become minor as the story emphasizes conflicts based upon the opposing theories and practices of two doctors, and, in addition, the beliefs of Christian Science. Ed's paradoxical theme with its opposing elements of condemnation and approval for different healing practices is best explained at the end with a statement by one doctor that "there is good in all men and in all schools." The title unifies the theme well and offers symbolic interpretation: all three major characters, as exponents of certain healing methods, are zealots. In the end, zealotry is defeated, and balance and moderation triumph.[62]

13 AUTO-GYPSYING

Before the arrival of summer 1916, Ed, plagued by severe neuritis pains in his shoulder, and exhausted by months of intensive writing, was devising plans for a long vacation. His fascination with automobiles and driving would allow him to consider only one type of vacation as desirable: he and the family must embark upon an extended motoring and camping trip. The destination was the Maine woods, specifically Moosehead Lake, and afterward they would visit Portland, where his father and mother had lived for two years, and where his brothers George and Harry had been born. An automobile trip of this type, in some respects daringly "pioneer" for 1916, required careful preparation; first of all, information was needed, and Ed sent an inquiry to *Camp and Trail* magazine concerning campsites in the eastern states. His letter was forwarded to another author, Raymond S. Spears of Little Falls, New York, who on May 21 sent details of eastern

routes and campsites. Sears, explaining that there would be no difficulty in finding these sites, wrote, ". . . I met dozens of camping parties last summer, running a motorcycle from this city (Little Falls) to South Dakota. . . ."[1]

Commenting about the Adirondack region, which contained the only "wild country," Spears noted humorously, "I suppose, from Tarzan, that you want primitive conditions, and the Adirondacks will give you a kind of 'wilderness.' " To Spears, the purpose of traveling was mainly to find materials and sources for writing —the rich regional and native color, picturesque characters and settings, and elements preserved in Americana. About other areas, again through a writer's eyes, he remarked, ". . . Thoreau, for example, at Cambridge, camped just out of town — and around there are still to be had camping grounds. . . . On Chesapeake Bay, west side, you will find countless places of interest — Potomac River is the sailing land of the Maryland Oyster Pirates to this day, and they used to shanghai preachers, lawyers and poets — if they could catch them — to work oyster boats." Spears spoke of Warm Springs, Virginia, where Ed would find "moonshiner country." Spears' fascination with the people of the isolated "closed-off" regions and their unique cultures was evident:

Somewhere in that territory is a colony of Irish immigrants, with a brogue as broad as Cork, who never heard of Ireland, except by ancient tradition and fairy lore. Most of the Hill Billies are of English descent, however — primitive — and you can hardly go amiss, so far as material is concerned. The stories would come to your camp, in blue poke sunbonnets, figures unrestrained by stays and blue-eyed amazement. Don't fail to attend Mountain Preachin'.

He also advised that in the foothills of Kentucky Ed could find the "feud and night rider country," adding that if he were to camp on the Ohio Bottoms "almost anywhere, but especially at a loquacious ferryman's site," he could discover "endless material and river lore."[2]

Ed's letter to *Camp and Trail* had given Spears the impression that Ed planned to collect material and to write while on his camping trip. But the acquisition of material from real-life sources had never been one of Ed's prime objectives. Here the differences between the two writers were obvious. Spears was an author who delighted in the discovery of colorful characters, people with odd customs or traditions, and all the richness of folklore. On the other hand, Ed drew his characters and events of fantasy worlds from his imagination. A summary of his writing approach was made in the *Detroit Journal* at the time of his vacation trip: ". . . he has found that he can't write about anything he is thoroughly familiar with. . . ." And to this jesting statement with its basis of truth, Ed himself added, "The less I know about a thing the better I can write about it."[3]

Several weeks earlier Ed had ordered some camping equipment, listing items on a familiar form, headed (naturally) Sears, Roebuck and Company, Chicago. The list included folding camp beds and chairs, a kerosene oil-gas stove, fifty yards of canvas, and four pieces of mosquito netting.[4]

Spears urged Ed to stop off at Westfield where Jay Brown, Spears' cousin, had a farm. "Speaking of Gypsying," Spears wrote, "have you read The Romany Rye, the Bible in Spain and The Zincali by George Borrow? . . . While they may not help much in camping lore, yet they give zest to the meeting of Gypsies whom you are certain to meet or pass along the way."[5] He added, "I've never had any trouble on the road — no one is more cordial to a note-book man than feud fighters, bad men (particularly a Sears-Roebuck bad man) and river pirates."[6] Spears' previous invitation to Ed to visit the Spears' home at Little Falls was followed later with a hasty dispatch — "I thought I ought to let you know that measles have become epidemic in this city. . . ."[7]

The itinerary for the trip listed distances between cities, route numbers, and projected campsites. Familiar places were included: Coldwater, Michigan, the site of the Hulbert Sunnyside Farm; Orchard Lake, where Michigan Military Academy was located; Portland, Maine; and of course Warren, Massachusetts, noted "Father's birthplace." Moosehead Lake was marked "Terminal Camp Turn Back," and after one more northern stop at Bangor, the plan was to head south to Portland and then proceed to New Hampshire, to other eastern states en route to New York City, and finally to Washington, D.C.[8]

Ed was naturally prepared to keep a detailed account of the trip. Headed "Auto Gypsying," it opened, "June 14, 1916. Left Oak Park, Illinois, 5:30 P.M. Wednesday. Odom. 7664." This meticulous approach, so typical of his nature, had been illustrated also in his painstaking records of story sales and payments. The remainder of the trip diary is thick with minute details. The camping tour members were humorously introduced:

DIARY OF AN AUTOMOBILE CAMPING TOUR
Undertaken in 1916
by
Edgar Rice Burroughs
Emma Hulbert Burroughs
Joan Burroughs
Hulbert Burroughs
Jack Burroughs
&
TARZAN

Title page of ERB's diary of 1916 trip.

The party leaving 414 Augusta street, Oak Park, upon this fateful day consisted of Emma Hulbert Burroughs, Joan Burroughs (8½), Hulbert Burroughs (6½), 'Jack' Burroughs (3¼), Theresa Witzmann, maid, Louis J. Ziebs, chauffeur; Edgar Rice Burroughs, Emma Hulbert's husband; Dickie, canary bird; and the Jinx.

The Jinx, who made himself evident at the very start when Ed slammed the front door and then discovered he had locked all his keys inside, was to be very prominent during the journey and at times would dominate it. Also included, and described as "the most important member of the party" was Tarzan, the airedale terrier pup.

The "rolling stock" was listed as a Packard Twin Six 1-35 motor carriage, "vulgarly" known as a touring car; an Overland delivery car named *Happy Thought*, and a trailer, fittingly titled *Calamity Jane*. The machinations of The Jinx were undoubtedly aided at the start by the Burroughs' plans to carry an immense amount of supplies and baggage. Ed explained:

Had planned to leave in the morning but it took longer to load than we had anticipated. Louis could not help me much as he had two flat tires to attend to on the Overland. After we had crammed the Overland full and still had a mountain of equipment left on the garage floor we discovered that the rear fenders were resting on the tires — she seemed tiring rather early in the game. It was then that the use of a trailer occurred to me as an easy escape from our dilemma, and I bought one that is made by an Oak

1.

June 14, 1916 - Left Oak Park, Illinois, 5:30 P.M. Wednesday. Odom
7664. Had planned to leave in the morning but it took longer to load
than we had anticipated. Louis could not help much as he had two flat
tires to attend to - on the Overland. After we had filled the Overland
and still had a mountain of equipment left on the garage floor, we discovered that the rear fenders were resting on the tires - she seemed tiring
rather early in the game. It was then that the use of a trailer occurred
to me as an easy escape from our dilemma, and I bought one which is made
by an Oak Park concern. It was designed to trail a Ford and carry pianos.
Unfortunately we had not thought to bring a piano. The afternoon was
consumed in having the couplings altered so that the trailer could be attached to the Overland. It seemed a little thing at the time that it became necessary to invert the coupling clasps; but that was before we had
to do it on a hot, dusty country road with a heavy load on the trailer.
Just as we were ready to leave I discovered that I had forgotten something
and went back into the house, laying the garage key and front door key on
the billiard table. Then I came out and locked the front door after me -
just a playful antic of the Jinx which had already attached itself to us.
Mr. Whitaker, my neighbor, promised to send for a locksmith to rescue the
keys.

The party leaving 414 Augusta street consisted of Emma Hulbert Burroughs
Joan Burroughs (8-1/2), Hulbert Burroughs (6-1/2), "Jack" Burroughs (3-1/4),
Theresa Witzmann (maid), Louis J. Ziebs (chauffeur), Edgar Rice Burroughs
(Emma Hulbert's husband), Dickie (canary bird), and the Jinx. The rolling

First page of diary of 1916 trip.

Entire Burroughs expedition on road through Indiana, 1916.

Park concern. It was assigned to trail a Ford and carry pianos. Unfortunately about the only thing we had neglected to include in our equipment was a piano.

At the first stop, in Chicago, the travelers picked up Emma's mother and a little later dropped the canary bird Dickie at brother Harry's house. The peculiar Burroughs caravan, unparalled for the times, at once attracted attention and throughout the trip continued to draw amazed and disbelieving onlookers. But the chronicle of the tour was one of misfortunes, of heavy rains and muddy, almost impassable roads, of constant car trouble and regular breakdowns. Each day brought new and exasperating obstacles:

June 14:   Happy Thought, the trailer... illuminating gas gone... no headlights, tail lamp broken... I ran behind it shining my headlights on it... quite an interesting pastime....

June 15:   Near Gary... pole of the trailer stuck its nose into the road... a sheaf of tent poles did the same, breaking three of them and ramming a hole in the bottom of the steamer trunk.... decided to go in camp... commenced to rain... Louis and I had never put up the tent together... I had had a canvas floor sewed to it ... The poor egg who had done the work had started to sew with a twelve foot end of the floor against a twenty foot side wall, and gone merrily around until he met his starting point. The result was appalling... occurred to me that we might rip out the floor... we got the tent up... it was a frightful job driving those enormous two foot wooden stakes into the ground in the dark... We have named this Camp Despair....

241

"Camp Disaster" near Rolling Prairie, Indiana, June 18, 1916.

June 17: ...*got our usual early start about 11 a.m. . . . . a questionable road. . . . Happy Thought and Calamity Jane stopped in the heaviest part of it — to rest, presumably... backed up and hitched the Packard to them... road gang called something. . . trying to tell me that Calamity Jane had broken off — diplomatic relations I was about to say but there was about as much diplomacy in a mule as there was in Calamity Jane. . . .Hired a scraper team to tow Calamity Jane to camp. This is* Camp Disaster. . . .*It rained hard during the evening. . . .*[9]

June 19: *Reached South Bend, Indiana. . . . We towed Happy Thought and Calamity Jane up nearly every hill and at one railroad crossing we pushed them across by hand, much to the amusement of a carload of tourists. I think Happy was on her last legs. At South Bend I bought a new ¾ ton Republic Truck that had*

just been brought down from the factory at Alma, Michigan, for an ice man. I beat the ice man to it, probably the first time an ice man ever got the worse of it. . . . Left the old transport at South Bend to be sold on commission and started off once more about 6 p.m. We are perfect gluttons for this evening start stuff. . . . located a camp site with my spot light. In driving in through tall grass Louis hit a hidden stump and bent the steering rod of the nice, new truck into a U. . . .

June 20: ... *Had steering rod straightened at Mishawaka. . . . Reached Coldwater 3 p.m. Just inside city limits truck motor commenced to pound and Louis stopped her. . . . found we had burned out a connecting rod bearing. Made about 90 miles today. Much better than Happy Thought and Calamity Jane could make in five days.*

June 26:   ...Louis and I started for Alma, Michigan, about 1 p.m. in the truck, as we found while replacing one bearing that others were in bad shape...damage due to running without oil in crank case...oil gauge had shown Full....started out again about 1:30 a.m. Driving a new road on a cloudy night without headlights...the barn lantern was all that saved us. Reached Alma about 9:30 a.m.... take two days to repair the truck...started back for camp by R.R....about 140 miles from Alma to Morrisons Lake by auto; but it took us twelve hours to make it by train, taking four different lines of road....Michigan is a great state but it is through no fault of the railroads — they are doing and have done, always, their best to keep people out of Michigan. As far back as I can recall, Michigan has had the poorest train service of any state in the Union....[10]

At Morrison's Lake, near Coldwater, the travelers set up Camp Branch,[11] so named because it was the lakeside vacation cottage of Roy and Julia Branch, Emma's sister. From there they went on to Detroit. About the city that he had not seen in some time, Ed commented:

Detroit is a night-mare of a place to drive a car —narrow, winding streets, packed solid on both sides with cars where ever the law permits them to park...Detroit has grown like a weed since I last visited it...To me it has lost much of its charm and beauty in the last twenty five years, and I regretted the days when they used to stop the street cars to watch a dog fight, as I have seen done in the past....[12]

As demonstrated by his past actions, the unexpected was on occasion to be expected from Ed Burroughs. In a sudden decision, all of the detailed plans and itinerary for the tour of eastern states, all of the information furnished by Spears, and the destination of Moosehead Lake, Maine, were discarded. On July 15 Ed recorded the decision in his diary: "Emma and I have decided to give up the eastern trip and head for

Los Angeles instead. The prevalence of infantile paralysis in the east has frightened us...." This decision would shape and change the entire course of his life. "We are pretty nearly ready to start," Ed claimed, but they remained at Camp Branch until July 27, spending a total of thirty-seven days there before launching the caravan on the road. The first destination was Oak Park and home, and on the twenty-eighth they were at 414 Augusta Street, back where they had started.[13]

Departure was scheduled for August 7, and on that day Ed wrote:

Have all the furniture in storage after nine days at home, and to-day we set out for Los Angeles at 10:15 a.m. Odometer 10145.0....Got a new chauffeur while in Chicago. Ray [Hebert] is his name. Lewis was afraid to attempt the trip west owing to the return of an old trouble for which he was once operated on. Truck almost stalled on steep grade out of Starved Rock Park. Weighed the truck at Sandwich — 5965 lbs. gross, or about 2700 for the load. Some camp equipment. Those who doubt this statement should unload it after a long day's drive and load it again in the morning after a rotten night.... camp at school house about seven miles east of Ottawa, Illinois. The flies were awful. We call this Camp Fly.

On August 8 Ed noted, "Joan is ailing — another of her bilious attacks, I think," but on the next day, after a dosage of calomel and a cathartic she was much better, and Ed recorded proudly, "Joan and Hulbert drove the Packard all day to-day. They steered and used the foot accelerator....All that I did was to sit ready to save us from sudden death....Joan is eight and a half and Hulbert will be seven Saturday."[14]

Although the Burroughs travelers had reversed their destination to the western side of the continent, the weather remained the same — unalterably bad. The account was repetitive: "Storm brewing. Put side curtains on Packard....commenced to pour about 1:30... came down in torrents for a long time...." On August 11, at Camp Point, Illinois, Ed recorded what had become a type of normal catastrophe:

Ed Burroughs at Morrison Lake, Michigan, June 1916.

. . . commenced to rain. . . roads became suddenly frightful. . . . We skidded from the verge of one ditch to the brink of the opposite for a mile . . . futile to go on, so we turned around, which was quite some stunt in itself, and started back for Camp Point. In half a mile the truck went into a ditch. I couldn't get traction to pull it out, though I tried. Ray and I were in mud to our hips. Finally I left him and drove on for help. Just inside town I went into the ditch myself, worse than the truck had gone in.[15]

In the midst of the struggles and hardships Ed forgot about the neuritis in his shoulder and the fact that he was traveling for his health. After pushing the truck uphill, he commented, "Last winter Elsie or Theresa had to help me on with my overcoat. Now I run about the country with loaded motor trucks on my shoulder. There is nothing like the simple life for invalids."

On August 12 the Republic truck was towed into Hannibal, Missouri, while the vacationers took rooms at the Mark Twain Hotel. The rain continued as did repair work on the truck, and the Burroughs family took the opportunity to visit Twain's boyhood home in Hannibal. The fifteenth found them still in town, with work being done on the Packard — Tarzan had "knocked out" the glass from three rear windows. A group of Hannibal's bankers and businessmen welcomed the Burroughs and volunteered to take them on a tour of Mark Twain's famous cave. Ed described the experience:

Joan, Hulbert and I went, the others not caring to. Mr. Mainland fastened candles on the ends of sticks and after he had smashed the padlock which secures the door of the cave we filed in. . . . The corridors are quite narrow and winding and seem to be myriad, running in all di-

ERB's yacht, Morrison Lake, "Camp Branch"; left to right: Judson Branch, Joan Burroughs, Theresa Witzmann, Hulbert Burroughs, Emma Burroughs, Jack Burroughs, and Julia Branch.

245

ERB in front of Mark Twain's boyhood home, Hannibal, Missouri, August 15, 1916.

rections through the hill. They say that some even wind down beneath the river, and that the cave never has been fully explored. I am quite sure that I should not care to explore it in company with a little girl of eight and a little boy of seven, each armed with a lighted candle at the end of a long stick, and each gazing in every possible direction except at the business end of their candle. . . . This is the cave in which Tom Sawyer hid, or was lost; or was it Huckelberry Finn?

About the atmosphere Ed wrote, "It was cold and damp, silent and inky dark. To be left there without a light must be a trying experience. Three minutes after we entered I could not have found my way out alone, even with a battery of arc lights. How the characters in some of my stories get along so well in 'Stygian blackness' is beyond me, yet they do it. . . ."[16]

The hectic journey through Missouri and Kansas continued with the familiar succession of bad weather, breakdowns and repairs.[17] On

August 28 at Emporia, Kansas, Ed visited an author whose poems he had admired very much, noting, "Called on Walt Mason this afternoon, and found him a real human being, whom no one could help but like. . . . Lying hospitably he said that he had read all the Tarzan stories and liked them. . . ."[18] Two days later, at Newton, Kansas, the travelers encountered some unanticipated danger:

Ray [Hebert] placed his cot some distance from the tent under thick trees. . . . Something woke him and he saw two grim beasts sneaking about him in the darkness. . . . Together we searched for the intruders. . . . All night someone not far distant was firing a rifle. . . sat up until 2:45 waiting for the wild beasts to return. . . . We were told the next day that our prowling visitors were coyotes; but I doubt it. Coyotes howl. These beasts did not. . . . We named yesterday's camp Camp Coyote.

At the dinner table in Larned, Kansas, the Burroughs family was surprised to discover that the distinguished William Jennings Bryan was seated near them; he had come to open a chautauqua series. Ed, disapproving of Bryan's pacifist philosophy, commented disparagingly about him: "He is not as large a man, physically, as I had thought. His face belies his peace-at-any-price character. I have no admiration for him; but I imagine he would fight as well as the next man if necessity arose. It is sad to see one of his ability striving to paint a whole nation yellow and making them like it. . . ."[19] The arrival of September 1, his birthday, found Ed twelve miles west of Dodge City, and caused him to reminisce: "Am 41 today. Twenty years ago this Sept. 1st I rode south from Fort Grant, Arizona, with 'B' Troop of the 7th Cavalry after the Apache Kid and his band, and I was about as uncomfortable as I have been on this trip. . . ."[20] As the caravan entered Colorado the hardships and difficulties increased; the succeeding days were filled with troubles and problems:

September 6: . . . Started to search for a camp site in the mountains above Manitou. . . Drove the Packard up Ute Pass in search of a camp site. Could find nothing. Went as far as Cascade. . . turned back toward Colorado Springs. . . . Tried to reach Bear Creek. . . . Pushed truck by hand up 20% grade and discovered another, a down grade, even steeper. . . turned back again. . . . Joan has been sick. We are all discouraged and 1403 miles from Los Angeles. Since we left Oak Park August 7th we have driven 1365 miles by the Blue Book, so have come less than half way. . . .

September 7: Joan sick all day. After supper she stiffened out as though dying. . . drove into town. . . got Dr. Tucker to come out. . . doctor said it was merely reflex action following a bilious attack. . . .[21]

Joan's illness and the problems with the other children brought Ed and Emma to a decision: they would abandon camping out. Ed wrote, "NEVER AGAIN! At least not with three little children. It is impossible to keep the flies away from them, the food is improperly cooked, the meals are irregular, cold and unpalatable. . . . if one of them should be taken sick in a camp a long way from a big town I do not know what we could do. And I don't intend to find out. . . ."

The hazards also included poisonous snakes. Ed described his encounters with these:

Ray found a snake near camp today and I went out with my automatic to slay it. It was a copperhead, three feet long. A few days ago, in Kansas, I shot one, hitting it in the neck the first shot; but this last one was not so accommodating. Emptied the magazine and did not hit him at all. . . . This is our third copperhead in a week. . . glad we are quitting the camping business, as the children wouldn't have a chance in the world against one of them. . . .

With the camping definitely finished, Ed, on September 9, remarked, "Have shipped the bulk of equipment by freight to lighten load. Shall drive through to Los Angeles over the Santa Fe Trail as rapidly as possible, Ray following

Breaking camp for last time.

with truck more slowly. . . ." The unexpected hardships of the camping tour had made writing impossible. As a result, concerning his decision to hasten to Los Angeles, he noted, "It is just as well as I am close to being behind in my contract with The Blue Book Magazine, and find that I cannot, or at least do not write on the road. In fact I have to be at the threshold of the poor house with the sheriff levying on my coat-tails before I can really buckle down to work properly. . . ."

About the two Kansas farmers who had inspected the caravan with all its paraphernalia, with one remarking, "This, by hen, is a mighty inexpensive way to travel," Ed wrote, "Sure it is. I could only have taken my family around the world three or four times, with side trips to Mars and Orion, for what it has cost — and the end is not yet." The entire Los Angeles trip had of course resulted from an impulsive decision, and Ed's tendency to yield to these impulses was clearly demonstrated in his actions in Colorado, involving one particular excursion of September 10:

It was a cloudy, threatening day, so, with my w.k. acumen I selected it to drive up to the top of Pikes Peak. . . . We all went — Ray, Theresa, Tarzan. It is a long pull — about ten miles from Colorado Springs to the foot of the Pikes Peak Road, and all up grade, then eighteen miles to the summit. . . . It rained, hailed, snowed and fogged — principally fogged. It was a cold, dispiriting, uncomfortable, frightful trip — a regular pleasure exertion. The children wore socks, while I disported myself in a summer suit, B.V.D.'s and no overcoat. . . . At the top there was nothing but fog and out-houses. When the fog blew around a bit we had fleeting glimpses of the out-houses. It was a wonderful view from the top of Pikes Peak.

On September 12 Ed noted that he had shipped two trunks and seven suitcases to Los Angeles, and on that day, according to plan,

248

Rare photo of ERB and his camera.

Ray Hebert started off early with the truck. Ed followed later with the Packard, and about passing Hebert on the road commented, "We each experienced a strange sensation as we saw the truck ahead and again as we left it for the last time. It is odd that we can grow fond of inanimate objects, yet we do. I remember when we sold our first car the day before we left San Diego, the old Velie. When the poor egg who bought it wobbled down the street in it a lump rose in our throats. It was like parting with an old friend — an old friend who was about to experience four blowouts. . . ."

With the rains of Kansas and Colorado behind him, Ed was happy to drive through Arizona and New Mexico, covering distances of from 140 to 200 miles daily on roads that were at least temporarily dry.[22] However, there was little improvement in the quality of the roads. Of the one from Holbrook to Winslow, Arizona, described by Ed as "a sad, uncanny, practical joke," he reported having heard that in the rainy season as many as fourteen cars had piled up on this one stretch of road. He thought one story deserved repeating:

A young woman with her elderly aunt were touring alone. They left Winslow and running into this mud hole were unable to get out, so they camped in the ruts. The young lady slept in the car, her aunt in a cot attached to the running board and covered by one of those tents which attach to the top of a car. Probably they did not light their tail lamp; for after dark, while they were both asleep, another car came along and hit the old lady's cot. She must have been a nimble old lady and a light sleeper, for while the cot was demolished she herself escaped by leaping. After that some nine or ten more cars came along and stuck all around them, trying to pass them, I imagine, so that by the next noon there was quite a company. They stayed there two or three days, getting out at last only by placing boards in front of the cars, one at a time, and placing them in front again.[23]

On September 20, en route through Arizona, the Burroughs family saw the wreck of the Santa Fe California Limited. It had been derailed at a sharp curve and in the accident four or five people were killed. "At Yucca," Ed wrote, "we struck the Mojave Desert and from there to Topock the road was hideous. There was no road — merely wheel tracks where other damn fools had come or gone. . . . Was so tired that I dozed at the wheel several times. . . ." The difficult late-night driving continued the next day with the travelers reaching Barstow at eleven p.m. and Ed again dozing at the wheel and during one period, even falling asleep and dreaming. About the area and the matter of desert driving, Ed, in making a prediction, offered an amusing account of his mistaken beliefs:

Some day a paved boulevard will connect Kingman and San Bernardino, and when that day comes the desert will cease to exist in so far as it is of any concern to motorists. So much had been told us of the dangers of the desert crossing that we were prepared to discover the landscape dotted with the bleached bones of motorists who

"At the Summit of Cajon Pass our troubles ended" (ERB's caption), September 22, 1916.

had died of thirst there, and to see poor wretches crawling on hands and knees, raving for water, while every few yards some thirst-crazed Forder turned his Henry upside down to drain between his parched and swollen lips the seven drops of water remaining in the radiator. As a matter of fact the desert is monotonously devoid of danger, if one can keep awake — I mean the one who is driving.[24]

Saturday September 23 saw the Burroughs caravan leaving San Bernardino for the last brief lap of the trip. Ed reported, "We arrived in Los Angeles a little after noon, terminating three months and nine days of touring and camping with a total of 6008 miles recorded by the odometer. All are here and all are well. The odometer also shows that I have driven the Packard 3527 miles between Oak Park and Los Angeles."

About the supposed motive for the cross-country journey, he wrote, "The trip, which was undertaken in the hope that it would rid me of neuritis, has not been entirely successful in this; but my general health is much better. Last winter I had to have assistance in putting on an overcoat; now I can lift a trunk to my shoulder and perform other Herculean stunts — that is I could if I were not so lazy."

On this final day, in meditating over the hardships of these past months, Ed conceded that neither he nor Emma would care to undertake such a trip again, nor would they, on the other hand, wish to "part with the memory of the summer's experiences." If the 1916 tour were ever again to be attempted, he might suggest only one change in equipment: the bathtub and the typewriter could be eliminated, "as neither seem to have been in great demand." He would also suggest the addition of another driver for the Packard and a "general roustabout or camp boy" for the truck. He closed his diary of the trip with a sentimental observation:

However, if I had the choice of three children from all the children in the world, and one or more wives from all the wives in the world, for another similar trip, I could not find any better than those with which God has blessed me.

Now I lay me down to sleep.[25]

Hulbert Burroughs, who was only seven years old at the time, has some vivid memories of the trip:

To me as a child, and with none of the responsibilities, the 1916 trip from Chicago to California was an exciting adventure. Memories that come to mind are the occasions when we drove at night and the car's headlights illuminated the glowing eyes of mysterious wild animals fleetingly visible on the road ahead. Through parts of Colorado, New Mexico, and Arizona there were still thousands of prairie dogs and jackrabbits. I recall how my Dad would let our dog, Tarzan, out of the car for exercise, and how the big Airedale took out after the jackrabbits. There were so many that he was never on the trail of the same one for more than a few seconds at a time. I can still recall hearing his frustrated hunting yelps as he sought vainly to catch one.

It is difficult today in this era of the great transcontinental freeway system, to envision the primitive condition of most of the roads along what was then rather grandiloquently called the Lincoln Highway. They can best be compared to the tortuous Mexican Baja California road, scene of the famous Baja 1000 road race, prior to the recent completion of the newly paved "Trans-peninsular Highway."

I recall with vivid clarity a particularly horrible section of road through the Glorietta Mountains of New Mexico west of Santa Fe. It was called La Bajada Grade — where the route west descended out of the mountains down the cliffs in a series of steep and tight hairpin curves. By tight, I mean the radius of the arc of each curve was such that the big Packard Twin-Six could not negotiate them in one pass. My Dad had to extend the front wheels as far as possible to the brink of the abyss, then set the large emergency hand brake while he laboriously turned the steering wheel preparatory to backing up the few feet necessary to finally round the curve. My poor mother was so terrified of these steep grades that she would insist on leaving the car with us three children while Ed wrestled the car to safety. I don't know what she planned to do if Ed and the car had hurtled into the void.

The only pavement we encountered was in some of the more affluent cities and towns. Such pavement usually consisted of red bricks and in some cases four-by-four wooden blocks. One of the most interesting stretches of roadway was across the vast California desert sand dunes west of Yuma, Arizona. Because of the soft, shifting sands, a one-lane wooden plank road was constructed with occasional wider turnout sections for passing oncoming cars. Remnants of that old plank road can still be seen in a few places near the present high-speed freeway on Interstate 8.

Travel with three young children necessitated frequent stops. To minimize such delays to his westward progress, Ed partially solved the problem by inserting a funnel in the wooden floorboard of the tonneau.

During the camping tour Ed had maintained some correspondence with Bob Davis at the Munsey Company, sending him several Kodak photos which Davis, on August 28, described as "the Burroughs family ravaging the Michigan frontier," and adding, "the picture taken near Rolling Prairie, where Calamity Jane laid down and spit out such life as happened to be in her, interests me greatly because it shows Burroughs sitting down while the balance of his family stands up. . . ."

After a brief stay at the Hollenbeck Hotel, Ed had moved to a rented house at 355 South Hoover Street in Los Angeles, and from there he wrote to Davis, offering to send the editor the lengthy diary of the trip. Davis indicated willingness to read the diary and remarked, "What a devil of a time you must have had on that tour. You ought now to wear epaulets and a medal on

End of trip; house at 355 South Hoover Street, Los Angeles, September 1916.

your left breast with the following inscription: 'Bill Burroughs, the peace maker of the Piute Indians.' Any guy that can slip across a continent with a lot of his own female relatives in the same tent is not an enemy to society. . . ."[26]

Davis's comment that he had lived in Los Angeles himself, on Pico Street (now Boulevard), off Figueroa, brought a reply from Ed on November 21 in which he claimed he had driven around those streets but could find "no monument commemorating the historic fact. . . ."

To Ray Long, editor of *Blue Book Magazine*, who had contracted for a series of *Tarzan*

short stories, Ed confided his fondness for Los Angeles and his approval of the Hoover Street home he had rented:

You ask when we expect to return. Have rented this house until June 4 and shall probably stay the limit. To my surprise I like it here very much. I do not know when I have been more contented. We have a very pretty little place with many flowers and trees, and a good lawn. . . . The children are playing out in front now with no wraps, and wearing sox. . . .[27]

He suggested that the editor and his wife might live in Los Angeles, pointing out that Long could edit just as well there "as in a snowstorm." Ed also wrote, "There are oodles of writers here, too, so that you would be close to a supply. Am trying to get Walt Mason out here. If I could establish a colony of human beings it would be a nice place to live permanently."[28]

In letters of November 21 to both Long and Davis he spoke of the diary of his trip, informing Long that he had completed the manuscript — a total of 37,000 words, and reminding Davis of his promise to read it:

I am going to send it to you; but you don't have to read it. I just finished typing it from notes made on everything from Old Hampshire Bond to toilet paper at ten cents the roll. I thought that it was going to be interesting; but it is not. Please send it back to me when you have kept it long enough to make believe you have read it.

His hesitancy and his apologies about the diary reveal that, as in the past, he had little confidence in any writings that departed from his fictional style. This was more strongly demonstrated by his decision, a week later, not to send the diary at all; he explained to Davis:

. . . when Mrs. Burroughs had read it she opined that it was so dinged uninteresting that it would be a crime to inflict it on anyone outside the family. No one else on earth could cross a continent, spending three months and nine days in touring and camping, run off six thousand and eight miles on the odometer and fail to encounter a single thing that would interest anyone outside his own kitchenette. This is my unique record.[29]

It was not until two years later that Ed gathered sufficient courage to send the diary to Bob Davis.[30] In his humorous analysis of the thirty-six page "Diary of an Automobile Camping Tour," Davis noted that "it ought to be divided into three installments, as follows: Rain, Mud, Curtain," and remarked, "It is perfectly plain to me now, Edgar, that you could move Ringling Brothers circus across the continent and not lose a single elephant."[31]

ERB and children, Jack, Joan, and Hulbert, en route to San Diego from Los Angeles, 1916.

Concerning Tarzan, the Airedale pup, Davis said, ". . . he is as near to the saber-tooth tiger as any animal you ever came upon." About Ed's difficulties Davis wrote, "It is perfectly absurd that the man who wrote Tarzan and the Martian stories, and who has turned pain and bloodshed and a diet of grasshoppers into a small fortune, would be perfectly helpless in a jungle covering more than a single acre."

Davis' banter was directed at various happenings on the trip:

You carefully neglected throughout the entire story to tell us what became of the canary bird. Was he eaten by The Jinx?

As a ditcher you appear to be the world's champion. If you were touring Italy through the Appian Way you would probably back yourself into the Tiber three times a day. . . .

Of course you pensioned the chauffeur,

having ruined him for life. The next time I see a shattered old veteran holding out his hand asking for alms, I will ask him if he isn't the guy who made the transcontinental drive with Edgar Rice Burroughs in 1916.

Sorry your neuritis didn't entirely depart away from you. You speak of assistance to put on your overcoat. The last time you were in New York City it kept me busy seeing that you didn't put on some other fellow's overcoat when you left the restaurant.[32]

The cross-country trip caused Ed to digress briefly for an unanticipated type of writing, a promotional article done at the request of the Republic Motor Truck Company of Alma, Michigan. In his diary, early in the trip, on July 1, Ed had commented enthusiastically about the helpfulness of the "Republic Truck people" and of the assistance given by T. F. Bates of the service department in attempting to repair the Packard Twin-Six. In a letter of July 21 from Bates, sent to Ed at Coldwater, Michigan, after his return from the aborted eastern tour, the service manager was pleased to note that "the truck came through in good shape" and that it was being equipped with a "Prairie Schooner" top. In his diary Ed referred to *Kodak* No. 12 which "shows *Camp Branch* from rear with Packard, and Republic fitted with prairie schooner top made by W. H. Schmedlen of Coldwater." Later, Ed jokingly titled the outfit the Burroughs Yacht. Bates wrote, "I think you will enjoy the trip West much more than if you had decided to go East," adding a hope that Ed might find some way to "boost" the Republic truck, and thanking him for a copy of *The Beasts of Tarzan.*[33]

On December 9, W. A. Somerville, Republic advertising manager, wrote Ed in Los Angeles to offer a writing proposition:

We would like to get out, in De Luxe form, a little book, detailing your experiences with your Republic truck, on your recent transcontinental journey. We would like to have you give us this information in the form of a story; say about

1000 to 1500 words in length. We would also like you to furnish us your photograph, so that we may use it as a frontispiece in this little book.

Somerville explained that in return for this courtesy, the company would publicize Burroughs in these booklets as the author of four Tarzan novels, and stressed that since the small book would have a circulation of about a quarter of a million, it would be as valuable to him as to the Republic Company.

In his reply Ed made clear that he was quite willing to accept the assignment: "It will be a pleasure to me to partially reciprocate the kindness shown me by yourself and my other friends at Alma, and if a little story of the truck on the hike is what you want I'll do the best I can."[34]

The completed article of approximately 1900 words was titled "An Auto-Biography," and Ed wrote it in a whimsical vein, creating the truck as a first-person character recounting the story of the adventurous journey. Ed's personality comes through, as does his penchant for ridiculing his own actions and viewing himself as the most illogical and blundering of travelers. The Republic truck establishes its own character from the start:

Without undue vanity and with no intention of boasting I think I am warranted in saying that I have probably crowded more real living into the first four months of my life than the majority of my brothers and cousins experience in all the years which intervene between the factory and their ultimate burial ground — the junk pile.

How little did I imagine in my brief childhood as I purred through the quiet streets of Alma or rolled along the shady country roads beyond, what lay in store for me! Ah, but those were clean and happy days! The testing and the tuning were my playtimes, and always then were they careful of me. They never took me out without plenty of oil in my crank case and water in my radiator, and one would have thought me a petted child of luxury designed to transport nothing less ethereal than a Parisian gowned debutante to her first ball so careful were they of my paint and varnish. . . .[35]

AN AUTO-BIOGRAPHY

By Edgar Rice Burroughs

author of

Tarzan of the Apes
The Return of Tarzan
The Beasts of Tarzan
The Son of Tarzan

COMPLIMENTS OF THE
REPUBLIC MOTOR TRUCK COMPANY
(INCORPORATED)
ALMA, MICH.

Title page of ERB's "Auto-Biography," story of 1916 trip as told by Republic truck.

The truck, "born" in the early days of June, told of a score or more of brothers and cousins who were "delivered daily from the womb of our mother, The Factory"[36] and who were allowed very little time at home before being "hustled out into the world." The truck had dreamed of "nothing less than Chicago" where many other Republic trucks had gone; it had hoped to be purchased by a large packing company, and, in this case, would be envied by "less fortunate fellows." But fate had determined otherwise: "It was in the midst of one of these day dreams that I was sold to an ice-man in South Bend. I wept bitterly."

Arriving on June 18, the truck waited unhappily for its new owner: "I was still sobbing when The Agent brought a man to look at me. At first I thought it was the ice-man and made up my mind that I would run over him the first time he cranked me; but when I saw his garb I commenced to doubt, for I had seen the ice-man at Alma and he, I recalled distinctly, did not wear corduroy riding breeches, tan leather puttees or a deer skin coat. . . ."

The Man and a uniformed chauffeur both peeked under the bonnet and "looked wise," and after the purchase the truck was backed up to "a disreputable looking outfit consisting of a delivery car and a trailer, both heavily laden." The truck, its "side lamps opened pretty wide" stared disbelievingly at the objects as they were transferred: "There was an enormous refrigerator, a cook stove, a fireless cooker, a hat box, galvanized iron tanks, a phonograph, folding cots, stools, tables, a bath tub, two trunks, countless suit cases and bags, seven rolls of bedding, toys, a flag, tent poles and stakes, a great tent. . . ."

The truck could not comprehend why anyone would want to transport "all this junk clear to the Atlantic Ocean" until it learned that The Boss was "one of these writer fellows, for whose mental functionings there is no accounting." Overloaded with a ton and a half of equipment, the truck joined in the wild journey that followed, "up and down the sides of mountains, through sand, through mud, through rivers. . . ." Despite its suffering, the truck had periods of contentment when The Boss bragged about its performance. It was especially pleased at night when they went into camp: ". . . they used to hoist Old Glory at the end of a staff that fitted into a socket at the front end of the top. I liked that, and I can tell you that I was mighty proud, and happy, too."[37]

After the travels through nine states and the arrival in California, the truck's odyssey was at an end; it now had a new assignment, but could not forget its glorious past: "It is all over now and I am hauling boxes for a new Boss in Los Angeles; but to the day I am junked I shall carry the pride and the memory of my Fame ever uppermost in my mind, and strive to be what I always have been and what my brothers and my cousins are — the best motor trucks for the money that ever were built — a *Republic*."[38]

At the beginning of 1915, Davis, while pleased with the steady flow of stories from the Burroughs pen, waited impatiently for the *Tarzan* sequel Ed had promised. On January 20, after noting that "Sweetheart Primeval" had been given the cover illustration on *All-Story Cavalier*, Davis wrote, "I am very good to you, Edgar. Now, young feller, sit down and write 'Tarzan's Son', or God have mercy on your soul."[39] Ed sent a progress report:

Yes, I am working on The Son of Tarzan, *and I have been working on him for several months. I have written but little, but I've thought a lot. I am going to give you a good Tarzan story. Almost all of it will be in the jungle. But it will, if I can make it so, be entirely different from the other Tarzan stories. I shall base it on the fundamental suggestion that you made while I was in New York — that is of the boy and the ape running away together from London to Africa. The difficult part is to keep from a tiresome repetition of stunts that I have pulled in the three other Tarzan Tales, but I believe that I can fairly well succeed.*[40]

Ed's fear of repetition brought some joking repartee from Davis: "Come now, Burroughs, for God's sake don't cramp your correspondence like this, because when it comes to pulling duplicate dope and getting away with it, you hold the Charles K. Fox diamond belt."[41]

The completion of "The Son of Tarzan" obviously posed more problems than Ed had anticipated; the manuscript was not mailed until May 12. During the intensive writing, a period of four months, Ed was ill. He informed Davis, "It has taken me two months longer to write it than I expected, and so it has cost me already three times what it should have — due to the fact that I have had to devote a lot of time trying to get well — treatments here and a couple of weeks away...."[42] Davis' acceptance came quickly, although minor changes were later suggested.[43]

Earlier, on May 1, the first installment of "Pellucidar" had appeared in *All-Story Cavalier;* and printed with it, in four of the five issues, was Ed's map of the strange inner world. Ed joked about the map: "It should prove quite instructive. If The National Geographic Magazine wishes to reproduce it I have no objection...."[44]

The hasty acceptance of "The Son of Tarzan" was contrasted with an equally hasty rejection of "Ben, King of Beasts." Ed, on June 10, described the manuscript as "the novelization of a wild animal scenario I recently sold to the Selig people," adding, "I understand that they do not expect to release it until after The Lad & the Lion...." Davis, who had reached a stage where he had misgivings about turning down *any* Burroughs story, and had always regretted Metcalf's failure to buy "The Return of Tarzan," had been careful to use group evaluation on "Ben, King of Beasts." On June 17 he wrote:

I have no doubt it will make a corking movie, but it does not seem to have the proportions of Burrough's regular novels. Four of us tried our durndest to get interested in it, but it did not hook any of us.... Kneel down and pray for me. I know I'm crazy. But there are four other nuts here who feel the same about this as I do.[45]

Later in the summer Ed experienced his second rejection in a row, this time with a story that differed startlingly from his familiar otherworlds creations. "Beyond Thirty," set in the year 2137 on our earth, but with a Europe and Asia that had reverted to a primitive, savage existence, is one of only two Burroughs stories of the future.[46] About it, Davis commented:

'Beyond Thirty' reminds me of a magnificent piece of scenery with no play. You have drawn an extraordinary picture and set the stage for a stupendous thing. Then the curtain falls.

You must not, however, regard this criticism as a protest against your style, for it is full of the "Burroughs" quality, and I have not any doubt that some people will like to read this story. However, I am trying to escape war, rumors of war and themes kindred to war. That is the particular reason why I pass "Beyond Thirty" back to you....[47]

In this 1915 period Ed was in contact with A. L. Sessions, editor of Street & Smith's *New Story,* and had queried him about "Ben, King of Beasts." When Sessions expressed an interest, Ed, on June 10, sent the manuscript to him, but the result was only a noncommittal rejection. Attempts in August to sell "Beyond Thirty" to the higher-paying markets were similarly unsuccessful. Rejections came from the *Saturday Evening Post, Colliers* and *American Magazine,* whose editor remarked, "I'm mighty sorry but this story of Europe's reversion to savagery two hundred years hence doesn't get me...."[48]

Having exhausted the prestige markets, Ed now turned to Sessions. The editor had been previously involved in the Burroughs dickering and was cautious, laying down conditions in advance: "... 'Beyond Thirty'... will be glad to retain it if we can agree upon a price. The circumstances being what they are in the magazine business at the present, I do not feel justified in offering you more than $400.00...."[49] Ed's procedure could have been predicted; he would never succumb to a first offer. He reminded Sessions that the editor had purchased "The Outlaw of Torn" for only $500, one of the low-

SATURDAY   MAY 1   TEN CENTS

ALL-STORY
CAVALIER
WEEKLY

Sequel to
"At the
Earth's Core"

Pellucidar
by Edgar
Rice Burroughs

"Pellucidar" cover of All-Story Cavalier Weekly, *May 1, 1915.*

est prices ever paid for a Burroughs story. This was the compromise amount for "Beyond Thirty," a "dinged low" figure, which Sessions could not afford to turn down.[50]

Ed, as usual, was keeping all of his varied irons in the fire. Payments for newspaper syndications came in steadily, both through his own negotiations with Terhune at *The New York World*, and through the dealings of Chapman, his syndication agent. On January 11, 1915, Terhune inquired about any unpublished Tarzan stories, while at the same time commenting enthusiastically about the readers' response to "The Eternal Lover," previously sold to *The World*. Ed suggested that Terhune might consider "Sweetheart Primeval," then appearing in *All-Story Cavalier*.[51] Terhune, who was also well acquainted with Ed's bargaining tactics, on March 15 queried him about "The Mucker" and "Sweetheart Primeval," adding a somewhat stern note of warning:

May I suggest, unofficially, that war times are not flush times and that the most rigid economy governs every newspaper today? If you can see your way to letting us have this story at a low rate, we shall be gratified; and you will find that no other New York paper is prepared, just now, to offer more.

I hope for our readers' sakes and for ours that you will quote Mr. Tennant a price he can accept.

After some protestations, Ed explained that he would not do any haggling; he was evidently impressed by Terhune's severe attitude. He offered a concession if Terhune would accept both stories — five hundred dollars for the two. He added, "I didn't intend to come down any when I started this letter; but now you see I've gone and done it after all — I suppose it was that sob stuff about the war; though why the devil Mr. Tennant should hold me responsible for the great European conflict is beyond me."[52] Terhune sent a prompt acceptance.

In response to one of Chapman's misguided marketing attempts, Ed wrote a letter whose tone was both panicky and humorous. "For the love of Mike," he exclaimed, "have I been letting you sell newspaper rights to *At the Earth's Core*? I don't own the serial rights to this story — I sold them all to Munsey. . . ." At the end he stated, "I am enclosing a list of my stories, showing ownership of serial rights, and you had better paste it in your hat, or we'll both be breaking rock at Leavenworth."[53]

Ed had also maintained a steady flow of communications with Joseph Bray at McClurg, as preparations were being made for book publications. *The Return of Tarzan*, contracted for on December 5, 1914, appeared on March 10, 1915, with a dust jacket illustration by the distinguished American artist Newell C. Wyeth, the same picture that had been drawn for the *New Story Magazine* cover. Next to be accepted by McClurg was "The Beasts of Tarzan," contracted for on October 1, 1915; it would not appear in print until March 4, 1916.[54]

Ed's shrewd business instincts, as always, drove him to search for new marketing opportunities. In the past he had dealt with newspapers on second serial rights only, after the first rights to his stories had been sold to magazines. Now he conceived the idea of selling the first rights directly to the newspapers, in other words, allowing them the privilege of printing a *new* Burroughs story. He tentatively experimented with the plan, making up a form which he sent to various newspapers and syndicates, and in this case concentrating upon one story, "Ben, King of Beasts," based upon the scenario still retained by the Selig Polyscope Company. The responses were not encouraging. A number of rejections followed, but on October 18, 1915, the *New York Evening World* purchased all newspaper rights to the story, now retitled "The Man-Eater" by Ed — the price, $350. The sale of the 37,000-word "novelization" established a first and only instance of a Burroughs story going directly to a newspaper.[55]

This first experience did not, however, cause Ed to abandon his plan. In a letter of October

The Return of Tarzan *book cover, 1915; N. C. Wyeth, illustrator (same illustration used on magazine cover, June 1913).*

8 in which he had accepted Terhune's offer for "The Man-Eater" and "The Man Without a Soul,"[56] Ed brought up the subject of direct newspaper sales, urging the editor to read an article in the September *Bulletin* of The Author's League. The article, titled "A Crying Need," contained an interview with George D. Smith, Editor of the *Newark Star*, which Ed summarized:

. . . he states that newspapers would prefer to purchase first serial rights to stories, and pay a much higher price for them than for the "stale" fiction which they now pay $35 to $50 for. He says that an original novel by a well known writer would bring $100 and up in five hundred newspapers throughout the country, and that sooner or later someone is going to form a syndicate for this purpose.

Ed appeared quite excited over the prospect of receiving money in this amount from more than five hundred newspapers. To Terhune he presented a comparison of the total payments from a magazine plus syndications vs. newspaper sales only, and explained that he would be willing to experiment with an original *Tarzan* story, certain to have the highest nationwide appeal, for direct sale to the newspapers.[57] On first sight the scheme offered great possibilities. Ed's past was filled with schemes eagerly conceived and quickly abandoned, and this one followed the same pattern. The main reasons may have been physical. Even his astonishing energy had its limitations — perhaps his illnesses and neuritis resulted from states of exhaustion. And of course there were the limitations of time.

During the years Burroughs received a number of queries about the correct pronunciation of "Tarzan." The first, on October 19, 1915, came from Davis: ". . . Many readers have made the inquiry. I'll leave it entirely to you. He is your offspring, not mine. This is a case where a man's monkey shines shine brilliantly. . . ."

Ed's reply was in the same humorous vein: "It should be pronounced in low, barking gutturals, after the manner peculiar to huge, hairy anthropoids. I have heard a termangani pronounce it with the o silent, as in mice. Personally, I never pronounce it — I merely think it; but since you have forced the issue upon me, I should say that Tär-zan is about right."

To a fan who later raised the question, Ed wrote, ". . . My conception of the word Tarzan was originally that neither syllable should be accented, but, as a matter of fact, I find that in using the word I always accent the first and rather slur the second, in accordance with the American lazy method of speech. However, pronounce it the way it sounds best to you and you will have it as correct as anyone."[58]

An inquiry from Charles E. Funk of *The Literary Digest* brought a response that Tarzan was pronounced with the accent on the first syllable, "the first *a* as in *arm,* the second *a* as in *ask.*" Ed noted that this was supposed to be the correct pronunciation, but added, "I and my family have always slurred the second syllable, pronouncing it as though it were spelled *zn.*"[59]

The question finally came up in a letter from G. & C. Merriam Company, received by Ralph Rothmund, Burroughs' secretary, and forwarded by him to Ed who was then in Hawaii. Rothmund commented, ". . . will you please give me a copy of your reply for permanent filing here at the office. After being around here for more than thirteen years, I too, would like to know how to pronounce the damn name!"[60] To the Merriam Company Ed responded:

The pronunciation of Tarzan (tär' zăn) given in the 1934 edition of Webster's is the correct official pronunciation.

The word derives from the simian tar, *meaning white, and* zan, *meaning skin. It is, therefore, wholly descriptive; and both syllables should be pronounced.*

The fact that I, personally, slur the last syllable merely reflects my sloppy diction.

With this weighty matter now permanently

settled, I trust that the planets will return to their orbits.[61]

Perhaps influenced by a differing pronunciation he heard in later years, Ed, on occasion, accented the last syllable and pronounced it fully, not slurring it. This is revealed on a dictaphone cylinder in which the *zan* is drawn out, with the "a" pronounced as in *man*.[62]

Once more, although on a more limited scale, Ed attempted to set up a competitive bidding situation between *All-Story* and *New Story* magazines for his latest *Tarzan* story. Completed on October 19, 1915, it was titled "Tarzan and the Jewels of Opar." Editor Sessions at *New Story* had always been eager for a Tarzan story to increase the circulation of his magazine; after his purchase of "The Return of Tarzan" in 1913, he had been promised a "refusal" on the next one, but in the bidding that followed he had lost the story "The Beasts of Tarzan" to Metcalf. Later, without very much enthusiasm, Sessions had accepted "The Outlaw of Torn," but as a result of Ed's price demands, the atmosphere between the two men had become quite strained.

Later, in negotiating with Sessions for the purchase of "Beyond Thirty," Ed mentioned his new *Tarzan* story, again indicating that the editor would be given a chance to make an offer for it. This was probably Ed's way of dangling a reward if Sessions would buy the lesser work, "Beyond Thirty." On October 20, 1915, to signal the start of a hoped-for competition, "Tarzan and the Jewels of Opar" was mailed to both Sessions and Davis. Ed commented to Davis, ". . . I imagine you won't want another Tarzan story so soon; and I shouldn't have written one so soon had I known that I was going to be able to dispose of *The Man Eater* and *Beyond Thirty*; but for a time it looked as though these two were doomed never to sell."[63]

Sessions pondered over the story for more than a month before explaining his reactions. The value of the story, he contended, had become somewhat speculative because another Burroughs work, "The Son of Tarzan," was

about to appear in *All-Story*. Sessions referred to an announcement that advertised Jack Clayton, Tarzan's son, as the hero, and remarked:

The purpose of the announcement is, of course, to transfer the interest of the reader from father to son, the assumption being, I suppose, that the reading public has become more or less indifferent to Tarzan, or if not actually indifferent, it is at least in a mood to welcome a change. . . . If this turns out to be the case you will doubtless agree that "Tarzan & the Jewels of Opar" will hardly have the same value for our magazine as the other.[64]

Based upon this reasoning, Sessions was prepared to offer only $1,000 for the story.[65] Indignant, Ed wired that he would not accept less than $2,500. He annoyedly refuted the editor's argument about the reduced value of the story, stressing that "the conclusion of The Son of Tarzan leaves Tarzan of the Apes still the dominant figure in the cast." He noted, "I was unable to arouse in myself any such enthusiasm for the son as I had conceived for the father, and I think the same will be true of the readers. The public is not tiring of Tarzan."[66] He urged Sessions to consult Terhune and Bray about the public demand for *Tarzan*. Anger spurred him to an insulting accusation: "I am not asking an exorbitant figure for this story, and I feel that you have tried to take advantage of me by offering what you did for it."[67]

Meanwhile, Davis, having read "Tarzan and the Jewels of Opar," was fairly critical of it, expressing the opinion that it was weaker than the previous *Tarzan* stories. "It contains nothing new," he wrote on November 20. "You have introduced the old wallop-on-the-bean idea for the purpose of side-tracking Tarzan's intelligence. A good deal of stuff where the ferocious guy breakfasts on caterpillars, grasshoppers, etc., will have to be cut." Although he felt that the story was not worth what he had paid for the last one, nevertheless he believed that all of Burroughs' work belonged in the Munsey magazines.[68] Ed, now worried, departed for New

York on the 22nd to see Davis. After a two-day get-together, Ed wrote a memo: "He will take story at satisfactory price to be decided on later." Shortly afterward, Ed telegraphed to specify that the payment must be $2,500.

Upon receiving Ed's accusation, Sessions, irate, ended all dealings and returned the story. He stated icily, "I have had a long and somewhat varied editorial experience, but this is the first time that an author has ever interpreted my offer to buy his story as an attempt to take advantage of him."[69] Although the sale was apparently completed with Davis, Ed did not notify Sessions, and made it appear that the proper offer would be accepted. On December 9 Davis bought the story at Ed's price.[70]

In the midst of all the bargaining and correspondence, Ed still found time to finish his latest, a 40,000-word royal romance titled "H. R. H. The Rider." Rejected by *Redbook*, it was sent to Davis, who ushered in the new year of 1916 by purchasing it, on January 2, for $800.[71]

An incident involving the actions of an imposter, the first of its type, was experienced by Ed in the passing year. A letter addressed to *All-Story* from Ithaca, New York, inquired whether or not Edgar Rice Burroughs was in the city, and explained that a man was "masquerading" under that name and "claiming the 'Tarzan' stories as his." The writer said, "This person is indebted for room rent and it is in the interest of his landlady that I am writing this."[72] The events that followed were amusing. The imposter, evidently alerted to the fact that inquiries were being made, moved hastily to a new location in Ithaca, but still maintained his false identity. A week later the same type of letter about a "certain Edgar Rice Burroughs" was received from a concerned occupant of the second house. In this case the imposter, described as an "author," was using the name of Frank Davis, but claimed he was really Burroughs. However, in his second try he apparently had as little success convincing people as on the first occasion.[73]

On November 8 Ed notified *All-Story* that he had twice written to the chief of police at Ithaca, and remarked, "I realize that in a college town hoaxes are often pulled off, and this may be a hoax. If so, I am hectic to discover upon whom rests the joke." On the seventeenth Ed noted "the termination of The Imposter of Ithaca case." His attitude, in writing to Bob Davis, was without resentment and exhibited a kindly tolerance and a tendency to poke fun at himself:

In my first letter to the Chief I told him that I did not care to prosecute the man. As a matter of fact anyone who is simple enough to try to get anything on my name has my sincerest sympathy.

If you vindicate me in The Heart-to-Heart Talks you won't, of course, publish the poor gink's name? — that's a dear.

During 1915 Ed's creative energies had been partially directed to the writing of motion picture synopses, a diversion that resulted only in frustration and disillusionment. His output of stories had been smaller than the previous year. Upon completion of "Pellucidar" on January 11, he turned to "The Son of Tarzan," a work in which elements of the plot were carefully planned and woven together. Jack, Lord Greystoke's son, has been kept ignorant of his father's jungle background. However, through the arrival in London of Akut, Tarzan's former ape companion who has been placed on exhibition by Paulvitch, a vengeful enemy of Tarzan, and events that follow, he learns of his father's upbringing. Akut and Jack become close friends, and in his defense the ape is forced to kill two men — Paulvitch and a thief named Condon. Certain that he will be charged with murder, Jack, accompanied by the ape, flees to Africa. There, as he duplicates the jungle feats of his father, he is named Korak — meaning "Killer" —by Akut.

Aware, as always, of romantic necessities, Ed introduces ten-year-old Meriem, supposedly an Arab girl who is cruelly mistreated by Sheik Amor ben Khatour. In reality she is Jeanne Jacot, the abducted daughter of Captain Armand Jacot of the French Foreign Legion. Inevitably, the story's plot calls for her to join Korak in his free jungle life and to become almost as adept as he in swinging through the trees.

Other characters include two new villains, this time Swedes named Jenssen and Malbihn, and the "Hon." Morison Baynes, freshly transplanted from England to the Greystoke's African estate. Baynes becomes a familiar Burroughs type, the handsome, effete young man, not inherently bad, whose weakness leads him to take part in villainies involving the lovely heroine — in this case Meriem, who is being temporarily sheltered by Tarzan and Jane. Before the story's end Baynes repents of his evil deeds and cowardice, redeems himself in heroic actions, and dies of his wounds. When little Meriem's true identity is finally revealed, Ed cannot resist inserting one of his favorite devices: Armand Jacot, a man of modesty, is disclosed to have the title of Prince de Cadrenet, and this of course makes his daughter Jeanne, the former "Arab waif," a princess in her own right.

Ed, producing some new ideas and incidents, limits the attributes that Korak has inherited from his famous father. The son, after killing Sheeta the panther, has a "strange desire," raises his face toward heaven, and opens his mouth "to voice a strange, weird cry." But the victory cry of the bull ape does not come from his lips. Unlike his father Tarzan, Korak, despite a powerful emotion, will remain silent after all future kills.

In "The Son of Tarzan" animal behavior, as in other stories, is both interesting and amusing. Hordes of baboons, for the first time, are enlisted for an organized rescue effort. Placing faith in the theory about the elephant's indelible memory, Ed has Tantor recognize Malbihn as the evil ivory poacher who many years before had killed the elephant's mate. Tantor takes his just revenge, stamping out the life of the villain.[74]

"The Man-Eater," a Burroughs-expanded development of the synopsis "Ben, King of Beasts," utilizes a prologue for exposition of a tragic drama that occurred in the African jungle nineteen years before the main story opens. The coming of Jefferson Scott, Jr., and his friend Robert Gordon to the Methodist mission; the marriage of Scott to Ruth Morton, the missionary's daughter; and the deaths of the older Mortons and Scott at the hands of the savage Wakandas are all detailed. With the passing of years, the story then shifts to the Virginia home of Jefferson Scott, Sr., his death, and the matter of the will and the inheritance of the property. The heroine Virginia Scott, hero Richard Gordon, and dissolute villain Scott Taylor remain the same, and the story closely follows and fills in the plot outlined in the synopsis.

Devoid of originality, "The Man-Eater" becomes a mixture of overused devices. The action of course must be set in the African jungle; there are the usual natives, and the situation involving the Man-Eater, the familiar "huge, black-maned lion," is a repetition of the idea presented in "The Lad and the Lion." This time the beast acquires a gratitude and affection for Richard Gordon, the man who rescued him from a lion pit. The unabashed use of coincidence in having the lion turn up at the Virginia home after a conveniently planned railroad wreck nearby produces a rather unconvincing effect.

The scenes involving Negroes in "The Man-Eater" are of course not the first created by Burroughs; his other works contain unflattering characterizations of blacks as individuals and demeaning views of them in groups or tribes — the natives. The obvious criticisms can be made; it is no longer possible to accept the false picture of the Negro as servile, treacherous, fiendishly sadistic, cowardly, and without loyalty or honor. But viewing him understandingly in modern times and depicting him according to assumptions, distorted and prejudiced, of earlier periods are two different matters. Burroughs, forced to devise African jungle settings continuously, accepted the popular concept of the black native, considering him as a

ALL-STORY WEEKLY

The
Son of
Tarzan

*A Sequel to all the Tarzan Tales
by* Edgar Rice Burroughs

"*The Son of Tarzan*" cover of All-Story Weekly, *December 4, 1915.*

customary stage prop to accompany a jungle drama. There was neither malice nor prejudice in his attitude; in fact, he often created noble blacks — witness the faithful and courageous Waziri, Tarzan's retainers — and his worst villains were depraved whites who were shown as inhuman in their mistreatment and torture of innocent natives.

Burroughs' action in adopting the Negro as primitive or savage in order to utilize him for jungle setting or atmosphere was, as part of the times, a mere writing device. In real life, during his army career at Fort Grant, he had praised the colored regiment as "wonderful soldiers and as hard as nails," noted that they were held in high esteem, and recalled that in doing menial tasks under a black sergeant, he had found the man to be fair and considerate. Burroughs had also shown sympathy and compassion for the Negro. In his Pocatello days he had saved Kipling's poem "The White Man's Burden," pierced through its hypocrisy, and written his own version of "The Black Man's Burden," exposing how the white man's culture had ruined the helpless Negro. It should be stressed that in his earliest writing years, with the creation of "The Gods of Mars," he established the black men as the "First Born," the aristocracy and rulers of the planet Mars.[75]

In "Beyond Thirty," begun while he was vacationing at the Hulbert family farm in Coldwater, Michigan, and completed at Oak Park, Ed devised a plot of unusual originality. For some two hundred years after a devastating "Great War," the Western Hemisphere had lived in complete isolation from the belligerent, ever-warring Eastern Hemisphere. All relationships between the two halves of the world had been permanently severed. As a result of a Pan-American Federation, the Western Hemisphere was linked "from pole to pole under a single flag." Young Jefferson Turck, the protagonist and commander of the *Coldwater,* an aero-submarine, notes that since the world division, "peace had reigned from the western shores of the Azores to the western shores of the Hawaiian Islands, nor has any man of either hemisphere dared cross 30W. or 175W. From 30 to 175 is ours — from 30 to 175 is peace, prosperity and happiness."

As a child he had been brought up to regard "beyond thirty" as the "great unknown." The Eastern Hemisphere did not even exist on the maps or in the histories of Pan-America. All mention of it was forbidden. To travel "beyond thirty" or cross 175W. was high treason, with death as a possible punishment.

In the early section, well launched, the story appears to have interesting possibilities. But presumably as a result of hasty writing, Ed did not give sufficient care to the development and structure of the story and to the many ingenious situations that could have been devised. The provocative plot of "Beyond Thirty" deserved a full, imaginative development; it was unfortunate that Ed did not devote the time and thought that might have made this one of his best stories.[76]

Another of Ed's 1915 works, "Tarzan and the Jewels of Opar," opens with Tarzan's enforced return to the treasure vaults of the ruined city in search of ingots — the cause being the failure of a British company in which all his money was invested. The villain of "Opar" is Belgian Lieutenant Albert Werper, who after murdering his commanding officer, joins the outlaw band of Achmet Zek, Congo slave trader and ivory poacher. The ingredients of the story are familiar. Tarzan is deep in the rocky vaults of the Oparians when an earthquake occurs. Struck on the head by a jagged fragment that tumbles from the roof, he becomes unconscious; he awakes to a loss of all memory of his identity as Tarzan and as Lord Greystoke. The repetition of this old device brought a disapproving comment from Davis. Both the treasure ingots and a bag of jewels motivate the evil deeds of Werper, Zek, and others. Inevitably, Jane, Lady Greystoke, is kidnapped, escapes and faces peril in various forms. In Werper, Ed creates a man who reveals some remnants of honor in his behavior toward Jane, but does not, as in previous stories, become the villain or weakling who redeems himself and makes the supreme sacrifice. Werper's misdeeds continue to the end and contribute to his death.

Interestingly, in "Tarzan and the Jewels of Opar," Ed establishes the specific origin of High Priestess La and the Oparians, originally described in "The Return of Tarzan" as a lost race of whites who were the survivors of a kingdom that had sunk into the sea. The kingdom was the legendary Atlantis, first mentioned by Plato; Ed explains, "When Atlantis, with all her mighty cities and her cultivated fields and her great commerce and culture and riches sank into the sea long ages since, she took with her all but a handful of her colonists working the vast gold mines of Central Africa." The race of "gnarled men of Opar" was bred from these and their "degraded slaves and a later intermixture of the blood of the anthropoids," but in La, the old Atlantean strain of females had been passed down in its purest form.[77]

"H.R.H. the Rider," completed December 5, 1915, resumes the fascination with miniature kingdoms and lovely princesses that Ed had displayed in "The Mad King." In the story Ed also repeats a plot element he had used in "The Mad King" — the introduction of an American, this time a certain Hemmington Main, into the royal complications that follow. The plans for an arranged marriage, one deemed necessary to assure friendly relationships between two royal houses, require that Princess Mary of Margoth and Prince Boris of Karlov, who have never seen each other, accept the union obediently. However, both of them rebel, and as the plot develops, Ed reverts again to a favorite device — the exchange of identities. In this case not two, but four individuals are involved in the exchanges. Prince Boris and a notorious bandit, "The Rider," trade roles, while Princess Mary is mistaken for Gwendolyn Bass, the daughter of an American millionaire. Gwendolyn's desire to wed Hemmington Main, the man she loves, is frustrated by her socially conscious mother who has "higher ambitions" for the future of her daughter. The typical incidents occur, many of them involving conflict, dangerous encoun-

ters and shootings, but in the expected happy ending the loving couples are properly and finally joined.[78]

Although Davis purchased "H.R.H. the Rider," he was frank in discussing its weaknesses, noting the situations in the story that "strain the probabilities" but admitting, "I do not suppose anybody is justified in analyzing this type of yarn too closely."[79] With 1915 drawing to a close, Davis was more concerned about marketing plans for next year's crop of Tarzan stories. During Ed's sales efforts for "Tarzan and the Jewels of Opar," Davis had stressed, "I am not going to make this a bidding contest by any means, and regardless of what conclusion we may arrive at, I am to be acquitted of juggling rates with you. . . ."[80] On December 11 Davis demanded, "Would you mind giving us some idea as to future rates for this particular simian hero? We do not seem to be in unity at all on tariff. I cannot help but feel that Tarzan belongs to us; and that we should not be obliged to bid against other magazines. . . ."

Concerning Ed's temporary concentration on a new character, Korak, son of Tarzan, and the confusion caused by his return to Tarzan in ". . . the Jewels of Opar," Davis doubted that "we ought to ball the family up by pulling the son and then harking back to the father," and joked, "I suppose old grandpop will come along some day and pop at me like a jack-in-a-box. If he does, Edgar, I'll bean him as sure as you are born."[81]

Ed, in response, exhibited uncertainty as to what proposition to offer Munsey for the year 1916. He stated bluntly that he could not refuse to sell stories elsewhere if the payment were higher. "From all I hear," he wrote, "I am the only boob in the country who gets less than 5c a word, and were it not for my excessive modesty I should remark right here that there's lots of 5c stuff that isn't pulling as well as our old friend Tarzan."[82] The two men finally agreed to follow the past procedure. A copy of every Burroughs story would be submitted to Davis. Ed promised not to ask him to bid against a competitor, but would reserve the right to accept or reject the Munsey price.[83]

14 WRITER-PATRIOT

His first attempt to enter the motion picture field, based mainly on the hope of finding a producer for *Tarzan of the Apes,* had left Ed in a state of deep frustration. The distrust he acquired for producers, because of this experience, would undergo very little change in the future. On one occasion he wrote to Chapman, "You have several of my scripts (?) which are of no earthly use to anyone, so, if you will please return them to me, I will see if I can't sell them for a few hundred thousand dollars,"[1] and Chapman requested permission to continue marketing them. Ed's answer was bitter: "No, I'd rather you'd send the photo-play stuff back to me. I shall never again peddle any of that stuff around. The majority of producers are petty crooks and when I deal with any of them I wish to personally select my own crook."[2]

The disappointments of this early motion picture period brought a response that was typical of Ed's character. As in the past when his goals were blocked, the unsatisfying circumstances aroused his impatience and drove him to action. He usually turned to schemes of his own. On March 4, 1916, he informed Davis:

There are tangible indications that a company will shortly be formed to film Tarzan. The men back of it number several who have backed other features that have made their millions. I won't let it go ahead unless I am assured of success, and that it will be a ripping big thing.

In carrying out his plan to reserve stock for his friends, he offered Davis an opportunity to join the venture, but urged, "Keep this under your hat until it is ripe. . . ."

When Davis expressed an interest, Ed promised to supply more details later, and explained, about *Tarzan,* "There are four outfits after it now, so I am waiting for the best proposition. My hope is to form a company of my own and produce not only my own stuff, but a lot of the other that is now unavailable because of the suspicions which many writers harbor concerning the present-day producers."[3] He could see no reason why a producing company should not operate in as organized and legitimate a fashion as a publisher, so that authors would receive a "perfectly square deal devoid of even a suspicion of sharp practice."[4]

On April 12, Davis, after some consideration, revealed a change of attitude toward the proposition; because of his connection with the Munsey Company, he believed it inadvisable to become involved in the project, either as a stockholder or director.[5] And a week later, in an abrupt decision caused by his agonies with neuritis, Ed announced, ". . . I have about decided to abandon my venture for the time at least. . . ." Instead, he was making plans for the summer 1916 "gypsying" tour.[6] At the same time, however, he contacted David H. Watkins, a friend who was acting as a negotiator between him and the National Film Corporation of America, to indicate he was now "willing to entertain an offer for the photo-play rights to Tarzan of the Apes — cash and a royalty."[7]

Only two days before his departure from Oak Park on the camping tour, and in the midst of the feverish preparations for the trip, he still found time to complete arrangements with William Parsons, president of the National Film Corporation, for the production of *Tarzan of the Apes*. The agreement for the project stipulated that Ed was to be given $5,000 in cash, $50,000 in capital stock, and five percent of the gross receipts.[8]

With the creation of a new board of directors, Parsons, on July 7, notified Ed that his old boyhood friend, Robert Lay, secretary of the National Life Insurance Company in Chicago, had been elected vice-president, and Henry Carr, another Chicagoan, assistant treasurer. Parsons later moved his office to the Steger Building in Chicago.[9] The plans called for Ed to assume the presidency of the company, and upon Lay's advice — "I rather think it is to your interest to do so," he accepted the position.[10] Little action was expected in the summer months, but Parsons predicted that in the fall,

with Watkins in charge of the campaign (he was described as "the father of 'Tarzan of the Apes' motion picture" by Parsons), the company would raise the required capital without difficulty. However, money problems arose at once. Unable to pay Ed the promised $5,000, Parsons stalled by paying $1,000 for extensions until December 1916.[11] Discouraged, he wrote to Ed, then in Los Angeles, "I had about made up my mind that I cannot count on Watkins. . . ." On the verge of dropping the project, he decided to go ahead with it, because "at the last moment things looked so bright."[12]

Ed's suggestion, upon accepting the presidency, was that an assistant be selected to serve as his representative in dealings with Parsons; the man he had in mind was his brother Frank. Past unhappy experiences with producers had firmly conditioned the attitude of pessimism and suspicion which Ed continued to display. The beginning difficulties made him expect the worst; in a letter of October 7 to Parsons he remained dubious, waiting to be convinced. A most important provision had not been carried out. Ed mentioned that "the transfer of the $50,000.00 worth of stock to me as called for in our agreement," adding, "This, I think, you have overlooked."[13] He had struggled so far to express his disappointment tactfully and with some attempt to be patient; however, on October 18, his restraint vanishing, he wrote bluntly to Parsons to reveal his displeasure: ". . . Am as anxious as you that the company succeeds; but am in no position to know just what the prospects of success are. Up to date I cannot say that I have been much encouraged." He reminded Parsons that both he and Watkins had been "extremely sanguine and enthusiastic," and that Watkins had claimed he could easily raise money for the Tarzan picture "in Chicago, in Wyoming, in Tampa, in Jacksonville." Both of them, Ed conceded, were salesmen of "high ability"; yet, in four months they had raised "something like two thousand dollars on a proposition which should have at least fifty thousand in the bank before a wheel turns."

Parsons himself had stated a dissatisfaction with Ed's failure to cooperate, especially in the matter of seeking subscriptions from his friends. Ed, by this time, had made it clear that he had not sufficient faith in the company to ask his friends for money, noting he still had not received his capital stock and other monies due him. He resented Parson's implication that he had not lived up to his part of the agreement and commented, "As a matter of fact I did not agree to ask my friends to subscribe. Once, many years ago, I did a thing like that, with disastrous results, and since, I have not ever done it — nor shall I."[14] Ed stressed, in addition, that he did not want the presidency of National Film Corporation — he had taken it only because his friend Robert Lay had advised him to do so.

One of Parson's first acts had been to print new stationery for the film corporation. The Arting silhouette of Tarzan poised on a tree limb, drawn for the book's dust jacket, was reduced to a rectangle three inches high by one and three-fourths inches wide and placed in the center of the sheet. In bold type, divided above and below the illustration, was the phrase, "The Wonder Story of the Age."[15]

Ed's rejection of the presidency, and other problems in finding officers for the corporation, led to changes. He now accepted the position of director general; the stationery, reprinted, showed Parsons as president, Robert D. Lay as vice-president, and Sherman L. Smith as secretary and treasurer.[16] Plans to include Frank (Coleman) Burroughs in the corporation had not materialized. Eager to placate Ed, Parsons again offered him the presidency, volunteering to step down to the office of vice-president and general manager and then go out into the field as a salesman.[17]

Frustrated by the difficulty of communicating caused by the distance between Chicago and Los Angeles, and also by Ed's aloof attitude of noninvolvement, Parsons appealed to him to grant the power of attorney to brother Frank so the two could work together in making plans and decisions. Parsons wrote plaintively, "I am willing to do more than my share but I would like some help and you were to give me that and you ran away to Gods Country and left me to do it all alone. . . ."[18]

Ed continued to view both Parsons and the project with little confidence. Once more he refused the presidency — "I do not believe it sound business practice for a company to have any but *active* officers."[19] He noted coldly that he could see no reason why his brother Frank should be given the power of attorney. Concerning Parson's appeal for help, he replied that he would be happy to assist in the production of the film, as he had promised, but not in the promotion, of which he wrote, "I know nothing and care less."[20]

Corporation matters and Burroughs-Parsons relationships deteriorated steadily. Robert Lay, the vice-president, while conceding that Parsons would be able to raise the needed money, expressed doubt that he had sufficient financial background to administer the corporation's funds. Possibly infected by Burroughs' suspicions, Lay resigned his position.[21] Even the dispatching of 10,000 shares of corporation stock to Los Angeles, in fulfillment of the contract, could not dissipate Ed's pessimism about the venture. Desperate in his search for a president, Parsons urged Ed to suggest somebody. While doubtful that he knew anybody who had "the time, money and ability," Ed mentioned his old friend Watterson Rothacker, head of a film company, and also enclosed a letter of introduction to Carl Meyer of the law firm of Mayer, Meyer, Austrian & Platt in Chicago.[22]

On January 9, 1917, Ed informed Parsons, "This is my first day at work since coming out of the hospital where I was laid up for a short time by a minor operation."[23] Ed discussed his meetings with William E. Wing, the man chosen by Parsons to write the scenario of *Tarzan,* noting that he liked him "immensely," but that the two did not agree on one point:

He has the dyed-in-the-wool movie conviction that every story has to be altered before it can be filmed; while I am still firmly convinced that to change Tarzan, even though the change made a better story of it, would be to ruin it for the million or so people who have read the story. I have also called his attention to the fact that you have secured the rights to but one story and the moment you change the ending of that story you take something from the second book which you have not purchased and at the same time ruin the moving picture possibilities of the second story.

About these contemplated changes in *Tarzan*, Ed's idea was to get "an expression of opinion from a large number of readers throughout the country." This would also serve as publicity for the motion picture. "Possibly a circular letter to the several hundred names I have would do it," he wrote.[24] He had always taken pride in his fan letters, had answered them zealously, and had used them to promote his sales to newspapers. The letters, in a bound volume, were sent to Parsons, and accompanying them was his own sample draft of a circular letter for the group of readers. Cautious, as always, he instructed Parsons to send him a copy before the form was printed — "inasmuch as it is going out over my signature I wish to know precisely what is going to be said — my bloomin' signature being one of my assets."[25] On March 12, 1917, Parsons noted that Ed's files had contained only a hundred letters, enclosed a copy of the form letter to be circulated, and inquired, "When do you expect to be back in Chicago?"

The letter, addressed to a Chicago reader, pointed out that the screen has "certain limitations which the novel has not" and mentioned "a few slight changes and contractions" that "are absolutely imperative." Questions were then posed for the reader to consider:

Shall we adhere to the rather unpopular ending of the first Tarzan story in which Tarzan renounces his birthright and the woman he loves, or shall we take something from the second story and have a happy ending? And shall we confine the entire production to the jungle, which is the natural setting for Tarzan's life and romance? Or, shall we follow the story verbatim?

The forthcoming film was termed "*The animal classic of motion photography*"; the animals, actions, and jungle settings were vividly described:

. . . the largest and finest specimens of apes to be found . . . not two or three lions, but a herd of twenty or thirty . . . lions will be actually roped and killed by Tarzan . . . two or three thousand cannibals will take part in the battle and village scenes under Mbonga, the chief. . . hyenas, wild boar, leopards, antelope, and all the other numerous fauna of Central Africa will appear. . . .

In closing, the circular stressed that "the advice of every friend of Tarzan" was being sought, and urged the reader to respond.[26]

In the summer of 1917 Parsons' National Film Corporation acquired a studio in Los Angeles at Santa Monica Boulevard and Gower Street for the production of "The Wonder Story of the Age." The distances were the same, although reversed — Ed returned to Oak Park on April 3 of that year, and the communication gap remained unchanged.[27] His desire to purchase a larger and more elaborate home had prompted Ed to correspond with W. H. Gardner; a sale was quickly arranged, with Ed taking the two-story residence at 700 Linden Avenue in Oak Park.[28]

Ed apparently had no objection to Parsons' subscription forms and newspaper advertisements offering the film corporation's stock at five dollars a share. Notices in the *Oak Leaves* of May 5 and 12 were obviously inserted because Ed had become Oak Park's most celebrated citizen, and the paper may even have been chosen at his suggestion.[29]

Because of Ed's almost violent dislike of Wing's scenario, and his suspicion that he was not receiving an accurate financial accounting, the relationships between him and Parsons neared the breaking point. Upon his return to Chicago Ed had not tried to see Parsons, even though he knew the producer was at his office there. In July Ed took his family to Coldwater,

Michigan, for a summer vacation, and on the twenty-eighth of the month wrote a bitter and threatening letter to Parsons. With this, much of Parsons' restraint came to end; in two letters, as he struggled to control himself, he broke forth into angry comments about Burroughs' behavior:

Aug. 2: I am really quite upset over your letter and I don't feel that I am in a frame of mind to answer it. We never agreed to submit anything to you, but for your edification will say, that Mr. Wing's scenario was not used. We have had one written that is rather a composite of five different men. I am quite certain that it is your "ignorance of what is being done" that has caused you to write a letter of that kind. Considering the foolish price that was paid for this story I certainly don't like that part where you say "you will take means to prevent the coupling of your name or that of Tarzan with any film produced in accordance with Mr. Wing's story."

If I get in a better frame of mind regarding this letter I'll write you.

Aug. 3: After a night's thought . . . I am still as peeved as ever . . . have been working night and day on this proposition . . . many of the things you promised to do you have been unable to do. . . .

. . . you, yourself, stated that you had no desire to have anything to do with the production because of your complete ignorance of that phase of the business. . . . I still cannot understand how you dare to threaten me and it still rankles. . . . I suggest that you read it (your letter) and then ask yourself how you would like to get one from a person who has been getting all the best of it.

. . . this morning finds me provoked beyond measure at your daring to offer a threat such as was contained in your note, and I certainly feel that unless an explanation or apology is forthcoming that it will be useless for us to correspond.[30]

At National Film's Los Angeles studio, as reported in *The Moving Picture World* of August 11, unusual preparations were being made for the production of *Tarzan of the Apes.*

The work of E. M. Jahraus, chief property man, was described. He and a corps of assistants were engaged in making costumes to simulate the apes; presumably, the costumes were for those "ape" companions of Tarzan who had roles to play, while the real apes were to be used as jungle setting. The costumes consisted of a hairy covering for the body, and a head and face cleverly devised to be lifelike: "By the use of a peculiar spongy material and ingenious arrangement of wires, opening the mouth pulls back the lips from the teeth of the mask, and wrinkles the skin of the cheeks." The brown goatskins used for these outfits were prepared at a special studio tannery.

The *New York Times* of February 3, 1918, in addition to reporting that "sixty tailored ape suits were made from specifications supplied by Darwinian students," presented colorful details of the production:

Trips were made to Manaos, Brazil; Iquitos, Peru; New Iberia, La.; Great Bear Lake, Cal. and Banff, Canada. . . . In all 12,000 miles were traveled by train and over 6,000 miles by steamer. . . . Three hundred native huts were built in the Brazilian jungles. Two thousand native Negroes de Costa (Amazon River Negroes intermarried with Peruvian Indians), twenty principals, a working crew, directors and supervisors were transported from New York to Manaos on the steamer Madeirense and then a nine-car train chartered for the trip to New Iberia and thence to the studios at Los Angeles.

The *Times* account included other information:

Eleven hundred natives were used in the production. . . . Forty high priced aerial acrobats were engaged and paid for an entire season's work, although required but one month. Four lions, six tigers, several elephants, eighteen living apes (all that exist in this country) . . . were purchased and transported to the various locations. Wooden huts, similar to those at our army cantonments, fully screened against insect invasion, were built in the jungle at a small place called Itejuca, sixty miles inland from the Amazon River. . . .

Among the unusual happenings, as part of the plot, the three hundred native huts were built, burned to the ground, re-built and burned again. During the three-month period in this location near the equator, the company experienced fourteen serious accidents, one death and a delay of two weeks caused by "an outbreak of ulcers from which almost all the white players suffered great agony."[31]

Parsons, in his determined efforts to raise capital, had gone as far afield as Wyoming, and there secured the support of J. M. Rumsey, president of The Stock Growers National Bank in Rawlins. The roster of officers of the film corporation, with Parsons still president, now included Robert Middlewood of the Rawlins bank as vice-president, Fred L. Porter of Los Angeles as treasurer and secretary, and Rumsey himself as director.[32]

Ed's dissatisfaction was aggravated by a magazine report which caused him to demand of a friend in Culver City, "Can you tell me what the Parsons person is doing with, or to, Tarzan? Jimmie Quirk says he is producing it in a back-yard. . . ."[33] In a letter that was a combination of inquiry, complaint and accusation, Ed wrote to Rumsey concerning Parsons' activities; Rumsey responded in defense of Parsons and chided Burroughs:

We here in Wyoming invested because the chief feature was your production and that you were connected with it. We had every faith in Mr. Parsons and we believe that if you handle him right that you will have no trouble in having him do whatever you desire. . . .[34]

Rumsey scolded Ed as though he were a misbehaving child: "Now, I urge that you handle Parsons diplomatically and I believe everything will come out all right."[35]

These fatherly attempts at mediation did little to alter Ed's impatience and his distrust of Parsons. He could muster no faith in the corporation, and on December 12, 1917, seized the opportunity to sell his ten thousand shares of capital stock, valued at $50,000, to David H. Watkins for a mere $5,000.[36] He remained bitter about the motion picture industry, and in a letter to E.V. Durling of the Los Angeles *Morning Telegraph,* who had sought suggestions about forming a film company, commented, "As far as my own work is concerned there is very little of it adapted to the screen. In fact, of late, I have made it a point to write things which could not be produced, and which, therefore, could not be stolen. . . ."[37]

On January 16, 1918, with *Tarzan of the Apes* scheduled to open at the Broadway Theatre in New York on the 27th, Harry L. Reichenbach, publicity manager for the National Film Corporation, advised Ed that a box was being held for him. The Burroughs reply was frosty and succinct: "Thank you for your invitation to the opening of the Tarzan picture, which I shall have to decline."[38] Throughout the years of waiting, Ed had experienced rebuffs and rejections in his numerous attempts to have *Tarzan* produced, and the repeated statements about the difficulties of adapting the jungle story to the screen had almost convinced him that a *Tarzan* film was impossible. Yet, it was produced, and was advertised in *The New York Times* of the twenty-seventh as "from the original story by Edgar Rice Burroughs," while its author, as a result of petty quarrels and irritation over a scenario he could not approve, refused to attend its premiere.

Tarzan of the Apes, directed by Scott Sidney, was an eight-reel film that followed the Burroughs story in most respects but discarded or changed certain incidents in the plot. In the book, Tarzan's transition to a spoken human language had been in French, with Lieutenant D'Arnot as his tutor; the film, for very practical reasons, eliminated both D'Arnot and the French instruction sequences. These scenes involving the two men would not have been of sufficient importance to justify the introduction of a French character and a foreign language, and they might have proved confusing to American viewers. Instead, Tarzan learns English directly from a sailor named Binns. The original ending, with Tarzan's "noble act of self-renunciation," now became less definite. To satisfy the movie-goers' demand for a resolution with happier possibilities, a closing scene showed Tarzan and Jane embracing, indicated plans for them to return to England together, and implied that somehow their love would finally triumph.

Tarzan, the boy, was played by Gordon Griffith, a well-known child star, while for the role of the adult Tarzan, Elmo Lincoln, whose real name was Otto Elmo Linkenhelt, was chosen. Lincoln replaced a New York actor originally assigned the part. The powerful, twenty-eight-year-old Lincoln had been given his screen name by D. W. Griffith, and the famous director had used him in a number of movies, including *Birth of a Nation, The Kaiser,* and *Intolerance.* The role of the heroine, Jane Porter, was taken by Enid Markey.[39]

With the passing months of 1918, Ed's anger at Parsons, and his belief that the National Film Corporation was not paying him the royalties to which he was entitled, led him to consult his friend Carl Meyer, a Chicago attorney. The argument had now become technical, the question being whether National, under the Burroughs contract, was allowed to sell the distribution rights of *Tarzan;* this action, because of payments to the distributing company, resulted in smaller royalties.[40] Meanwhile, Ed, feeling that he needed a Los Angeles attorney, had engaged the services of Harry C. Levey. The issue of distribution rights was soon eclipsed by a larger one. In May 1918, a small item in Kitty Kelly's *Chicago Examiner* column alerted Ed to a situation which at first seemed incredible: Parsons was making *another* Tarzan film.[41] On May 29 Levey reported a rumor he had heard: ". . . from what I can gather there is another copy or film of your story that someone back in Wyoming has. Parsons had a hand in it. . . . you had better have things looked after to determine whether you are getting your proper share. They look like a bad bunch. . . ."[42]

Parsons' explanation was simple and ingenious. He was *not* producing an unauthorized film; he had bought the complete *Tarzan*

of the Apes novel and was now adapting the last half of the book as a movie sequel. Ed's shocked protest to attorney Carl Meyer brought a discouraging response: "If . . . the new film is really the second half of your book . . . there may be some difficulty in stopping its production. . . ."[43] In a letter to Levey of June 17, Meyer explained that the First National Exhibitors Circuit of New York was now distributing *Tarzan of the Apes:*

This company advanced the National Film Corporation of America the sum of $125,000. when they took over the distribution of the picture. The information which Mr. Burroughs has received is to the effect that the picture is making big money, and that the pictures which have been the biggest money makers for the last six months are the Charlie Chaplin Film, Gerard's Four Years in Germany, and Tarzan of the Apes. . . .

With Parsons apparently unperturbed by threats of legal action, Ed, unable to receive any accurate information on the corporation's earnings, sought the services of his friend Watterson Rothacker, head of an industrial film company, to act as his representative and to confer with Parsons. Changes in National Film had brought in Harry M. Rubey as president, with Parsons shifted to treasurer. In a conciliatory tone Parsons emphasized that the new picture would not affect "The Return of Tarzan," should Ed decide to sell it for film production. For the second Tarzan movie Parsons had selected the title "The Romance of Tarzan"; he believed that this title would lure a large audience to the box office. Urging Ed to arrange with him for the filming of "The Return of Tarzan," Parsons boasted, "No company in existence can do more justice to the 'Return of Tarzan' than we, because we have learned something from each picture."[44] About their personal conflicts, he wrote:

I have come to the conclusion, Mr. Burroughs, that our trouble has been that we have done business through other people. I think most of the stories told me as coming from you have been lies, and undoubtedly, same has taken place in stories told you. In the future, if I have anything to say, or you have anything to say, let's say it to each other.[45]

Ed now adopted a conciliatory attitude, maintained that he liked the title "The Romance of Tarzan," and through the mediation of Rothacker, agreed to accept an advance of $2,500 on the new film.[46] He even advised he was "looking forward with pleasure to seeing this film" and hoped that if it were shown privately in Chicago, he would be notified.[47] After refusing to attend the premiere of *Tarzan of the Apes,* he had seen a later performance, and even made the admission that he "thoroughly enjoyed it."[48]

Released in September 1918, *The Romance of Tarzan,* directed by Wilfred Lucas, again starred Elmo Lincoln and Enid Markey. In the film, which was hastily improvised and had little relationship to the book, Tarzan is wrongly suspected by Jane of having an affair with another woman, played by Cleo Madison. The scenario, written by Bess Meredyth, established the Porter home in San Francisco, and Tarzan, deserting his jungle environment, follows Jane there. In the big city scenes he not only discards his loincloth, but dons a tuxedo. Viewers who had found Lincoln highly stimulating as the bare-chested ape-man were critical of his transformation to a gentleman in dress suit. They had become accustomed to thinking of Elmo and Tarzan as the primitive, half-clad savage. It became obvious that in *The Romance of Tarzan* too many scenes had been cast in a civilized setting; Tarzan out of his jungle surroundings for lengthy periods was like a fish out of water.

During the course of the years the tremendous popularity of the *Tarzan* stories, especially among the young readers, led to the formation of a number of Tarzan clubs. The first of these appeared in the fall of 1916. On November 21 Ed wrote to Bob Davis, "There is a very enthusiastic boy down in Virginia at Staunton who is forming a Tribe of Tarzan. He says Tarzan has made a man of him. If he writes you be good to him and encourage him. His name is Herman Newman." Ed was honored with membership card number one, dated 1916, and signed by Acting Chief Newman and Secretary Gilbert Wheat. Davis replied jokingly, "More strength to Herman Newman, Emperor of the Tribe of Tarzan . . ." and added a hope that all the members would subscribe to *All-Story* for twenty years in advance.[49] Ed, not amused, rated the project as worthwhile, noting that the boys were "in real earnest" and that their interest was undoubtedly shared by other young readers. He offered two reasons why *All-Story* should become the official organ of The Tribe of Tarzan: the obvious one was for circulation-building purposes, but more important was the opportunity to "accomplish something for the good of the boys. . . ."[50] Davis remained reluctant about sponsoring the group, but agreed to run an announcement which Ed had written:

The boys of Staunton, Virginia, have organized the first Tribe of Tarzan. They would like to hear from boys in other cities and towns who are interested in forming tribes in their own jungles. The men of Staunton are helping the boys of Staunton. The latter have a Tribe Room where they hold their meetings; they have grass ropes, bows and arrows, hunting knives, and the author of Tarzan of the Apes is having medallions struck for them symbolic of Tarzan's diamond studded golden locket. Boys who are interested are invited to write to Herman Newman, Acting Chief of The First Tribe of Tarzan, 113 N. Jefferson street, Staunton, Va.[51]

The announcement appeared in the Heart to Heart Talks of *All-Story* on January 20, 1917. About it, Ed remarked:

I rather imagine that Herman Newman, Esq. will be swamped by mail. I hope so. He has kept me busy for months; but when I think of Frank Baum I realize that I should not complain. He gets about a hundred and fifty letters a week from kids and answers them all longhand. . . . all Los Angeles loves him. . . .[52]

276

PITTSBURGH JUNGLE

TRIBE of TARZAN

This is to Certify That_____

OF_____

IS A MEMBER IN GOOD STANDING IN

THE _____ TRIBE

_____ SCRIBE   _____ CHIEF

TARZAN CODE

A Tarzan Tribesman will always be truthful, honest, manly and courageous.

He will obey the laws of health and cleanliness.

He will smile in defeat and will be modest in victory.

He will do unto others as he would have others do unto him.

One of the cards, front and back, issued to members of the Tribe of Tarzan, founded in honor of ERB by Herman Newman of Staunton, Virginia.

At a later date, Ed wrote to urge the *Chicago Herald* to promote the Tribe of Tarzan through a special department in the newspaper, but the *Herald's* response was negative.[53] Through Ed's contacts with Joseph Bray, McClurg undertook to give the Tribe some publicity, and in their *Bulletin* of August-September 1918, in the section "Literary Items of Interest," a column was devoted to the organization, its founder, Herman Newman, now heading another Tribe in Covington, Virginia.

McClurg's *Bulletin* provided details of the rules that had been established for members of the Tribe of Tarzan. The purposes of the organization were idealistic — health, courage, and chivalry — and members were required to take an oath to be honest and truthful; to "think clean thoughts"; and to protect the weak.[54] The bronze medal that members still wore about their necks "symbolized the studded locket that Tarzan wore." With the United States at war, it was noted that the Tribe at Covington had sold $28,000 worth of Liberty Bonds and was now "working in the Thrift Stamp Campaign and for the Red Cross."[55]

The problems and irritations of film controversies in 1916 did not stifle the flow of Burroughs' story imagination. In two cases he mulled over ideas for unusual works, based upon subjects that departed from his customary patterns. On January 3, in writing to Davis, he appeared intrigued by an odd theme:

Another thing I have had in mind is The Autobiography of Cain, a monkey-man story of our revered ancestors who chewed upon one end of a ripe caterpillar while the green juice ran out at the other upon their hairy chests. Of course you could emasculate the mss later. I would reveal to a waiting and eager world the long hidden secret that Cain has been a much maligned party, and was, really, rather a decent sort.

Davis found the idea amusing but offered a cautious warning that it might be "a pretty hot proposition," which could result in his being entangled "with the Presbyterian Synod, the Methodist Conference and the Episcopalian Bishop...."[56] Ed explained that his idea was to create the story of Cain's childhood and develop the family life outside the garden of Eden. He would not overlook the opportunity to "drag in" a few prehistoric animals, and in succeeding episodes would "tell of the quarrel between Cain and Abel and give the real facts which led up to the killing, then follow Cain on his wanderings which led to the Land of Nod, his finding and fighting for a mate there."[57]

Ed noted frankly, "I want to be irreverent; but I know that you wouldn't stand for it, so I'll just hover around the verge without offending anyone." He joked, "There are a number of things in that part of Genesis which need explaining, and as Cain and I know all about them we'll clear matters up a bit. . . ."[58] He was blunt about the religious aspects: "Because I am not religious don't think that I couldn't write a religious story. It's just a matter of imagination, and I can easily imagine myself a religious bigot; and anyway I wouldn't make it too damn religious."[59] Possibly because Davis was not overly enthusiastic about the theme, and because of motion picture and other involvements, Ed allowed the idea of a Cain autobiography to fade away; he made no efforts to revive it.[60]

A second topic of an even more unusual nature, in a serious nonfiction area that Ed had never before contemplated, occurred to him late in 1916. In December he queried Bruce Barton of *Every Week* and the *Associated* of New York, expressing an interest in writing a biography of Jack London. With his entire success lying in his freely improvised fiction, that he should consider a severely structured form, such as a biography, is surprising. However, he had always admired London and his works. London had died that year. On December 19 Barton replied:

I happen to know that Mr. Sterling has already begun work on the life of Jack London, which is being offered in New York at this time. I don't see how we could use the life of Mr. London. Whether one of the other magazines would have a place for it I cannot tell, but I should think there was a sufficiently good chance to justify you in writing to some of the editors.

ERB also wrote to Davis, the indication being that in this case Ed was thinking of an article about London rather than a full biography. Davis answered, "Just between you and me, I don't give a whoop about Jack London's 'rough neck days on San Francisco Bay.' " But he offered advice and encouragement: "The people who will be interested are those who have been printing his stuff, notably Hearst's, Cosmopol-

itan and the Saturday Evening Post. I don't think you will have any trouble selling your dope."[61] Whether Ed made any further inquiries is not known. The plan to write about Jack London became another of his discarded projects.

Once more there was a return to the never-ending Burroughs catalog of "unfinished business" — the list of stories that had been left dangling for the inevitable sequels. "The Mucker," mentioned to Davis, brought the editor's response: "Yes, the poor wretch seems to demand rehabilitation of some sort," and a strong hint about any future plans for "The Mucker": ". . . conclude his career so that the scalawags who like your sort of fiction will regard the curtain as down for all time on that classic personality."[62] From the start, Davis had been lukewarm about "The Mucker."

On March 16, 1916, Ed sent the sequel, titled "Out There Somewhere" to Davis, along with a customary word count. The adventures of Billy Byrne, falsely accused of the murder of old man Schneider and still sought by the Chicago police, are continued, with Billy captured, sentenced to life imprisonment, and then escaping. He travels west and south, and for the first time there is a Burroughs setting in Mexico; Billy, happy in the midst of excitement and danger, is pleased to accept a captaincy under General Pesita, a Mexican bandit. His love for Barbara Harding and her faith in him had led to his reform, and the thought of her still served to control his actions. But curiously, in the sequel, Burroughs introduces a new inspirational force to affect Billy — almost incredibly it is the force of poetry. To Billy, poetry now becomes a revelation; its impact is powerful, and about the poets he says, "I always had an idea they was sissy fellows, but a guy can't be a sissy and think the thoughts they musta thought to write stuff that sends the blood chasin' through a feller like he'd had a drink on an empty stomach."

The particular poem which provides the greatest inspiration is Henry Herbert Knibbs' "Out There Somewhere," a favorite of Ed's and one that became both the title of his story and

Formerly "New Story Magazine"

| Vol. XI | FEBRUARY, 1916 | No. 4 |

Beyond Thirty.

By Edgar Rice Burroughs.

CHAPTER I.

SINCE earliest childhood I have been strangely fascinated by the mystery surrounding the history of the last days of twentieth-century Europe. My interest is keenest, perhaps, not so much in relation to known facts as to speculation upon the unknowable of the two centuries that have rolled by since human intercourse between the Western and Eastern Hemispheres ceased—the mystery of Europe's state following the termination of the Great War—provided, of course, that the war had been terminated.

From out the meagerness of our censored histories we learned that for fifteen years after the cessation of diplomatic relations between the United States of North America and the belligerent nations of the Old World, news of more or less doubtful authenticity filtered, from time to time, into the Western Hemisphere from the Eastern.

Then came the fruition of that historic propaganda which is best described by its own slogan: "The East for the East—the West for the West,"

and all further intercourse was stopped by statute.

Even prior to this, transoceanic commerce had practically ceased, owing to the perils and hazards of the mine-strewn waters of both the Atlantic and Pacific Oceans. Just when submarine activities ended we do not know; but the last vessel of this type sighted by a Pan-American merchantman was the huge Q 138, which discharged twenty-nine torpedoes at a Brazilian tank steamer off the Bermudas in the fall of 1922. A heavy sea and the excellent seamanship of the master of the Brazilian permitted the Pan-American to escape and report this last of a long series of outrages upon our commerce. God alone knows how many hundreds of our ancient ships fell prey to the roving steel sharks of blood-frenzied Europe. Countless were the vessels and men that passed over our eastern and western horizons never to return; but whether they met their fates before the belching tubes of submarines or among the aimlessly drifting mine fields, no man lived to tell.

"Beyond Thirty," All Around Magazine, *February 1916.*

an interwoven romantic theme. Concerning the poem, Ed later explained to a fan, "I saw it first in a magazine many years ago and was so greatly taken by it that I could not resist the temptation of using it in my book."[63] In the story, lines from the poem are chanted often by the character Bridge, a hobo who is paradoxically a man of sensitivity and refinement. This unusual man-of-the-road arouses in Billy a new appreciation of a culture he had once derided. The most compelling lines are about the woman who is waiting, in a sense, for every lonely, wandering man: "And you, my sweet Penelope, out there somewhere you wait for me,/With buds of roses in your hair and kisses on your mouth." Bridge, the personable vagabond, also displays a fondness for Kipling and Robert Service, and in "Out There Somewhere" quotes passages from Service's poems.[64]

The publication of "Out There Somewhere," carrying the magazine title of "The Return of the Mucker," brought a letter from Knibbs, a Los Angeles resident, who had not known that Burroughs was staying temporarily in the same city. On October 18, 1916, Ed replied sentimentally:

I, too, dreamed of a Penelope. On night herd beneath the brilliant stars along the Snake, I dreamed of her, and amidst the dark, nocturnal shadows of the cottonwoods beside the Gila, while the troop slept and I stood guard, I dreamed of her. For ten long years I dreamed, and then my dream came true.

Penelope and I are here, and we'd like mighty well to have you come and see us.

We are old and bald-headed now, and have eight or eleven children and very few teeth; but the spirit of romance still burns brightly in our withered hearts. . . .[65]

When the book later appeared in 1921 as *The Mucker,* it combined both stories, and Knibbs' poem drew numerous reader queries that led to responses by Burroughs.[66]

Since 1916 was the year of the "Auto Gypsying" tour and the extended California vacation, Burroughs' remaining literary output consisted of the first eight of twelve stories in "The

New Stories of Tarzan," a series of short stories purchased by Ray Long, editor of *The Blue Book Magazine.* Davis had been uninterested in these brief *Tarzan* tales, and had even inquired, "Who was so foolish as to take . . . the series?" To this Ed answered, "It was Ray Long, but for the luvomike, don't tell him he was foolish."[67]

Previous attempts to write short fiction with the characters and settings drawn from ordinary life had resulted in stories that were mawkish and trite. Examples of these are "For the Fool's Mother" and "The Avenger." But when Burroughs dealt with the purely imaginative and with material that interested and stimulated him, his writing, as demonstrated in "The New Stories," could emerge with a sensitivity and philosophical subtlety not present in his longer works. These stories, flashbacks to Tarzan's early years and his growth to manhood in a jungle environment, portray his learning-through-experience and, beyond that, his gropings toward the unknown and his struggles to penetrate the primitive world of superstition that enclosed him.

One facet of his human intellect, man's most persistent and prodding impulse — curiosity — lifted him high above his animal associates. It allowed Tarzan no rest, drove him to search and inquire. So began his search for an understanding of nature, of the baffling behavior of the sun and moon, and above all, for an explanation of the word *God* he had found in his dictionary, a word identifying a Being whose awesomeness, mystery, and power he both reasoned and sensed.

Among the twelve short tales that compose "The New Stories," one, "The God of Tarzan," develops young Tarzan's attempt to discover some definite meaning behind the vague concept of God. His ape friends' superstitious belief that Goro, the Moon, is the all-powerful force causes Tarzan to hurl a challenge at the moon, but this brings no result and drives him to hunt elsewhere. In the native village he sees a grotesque figure with the head of a buffalo, a long tail, and the legs of a man. Tarzan does not know of the witch doctor's disguise and is ready to believe that this strange creature, half-man, half-animal, is the god he seeks. Once again, however, he is disappointed; he finds that the buffalo hide conceals a black man who cringes in terror before him. In a rage he kills the man. But later, as he is about to kill Mbonga, the native chief, he sees that he is clutching a helpless old man who "seemed to wither and shrink to a bag of puny bones beneath his eyes." Tarzan, for the first time, is seized by the sensation of pity; he leaves Mbonga unharmed.

Through this episode Burroughs creates a beginning of Tarzan's vision of God: some "strange power" had "stayed his hand. . . . It was as though someone greater than he had commanded him to spare the life of the old man." Was this the mysterious force behind everything, he wonders, the God associated with the word "create," the God who made all things different, the ape unlike the deer, the panther unlike the rhinoceros, and Tarzan himself unlike the others? The rescue of Teeka, the female ape, and her baby from the grip of Histah, the snake, an instinctive act done at the risk of his own life, brings the final revelation to Tarzan. Teeka herself, despite her fears, had leaped "into the embrace of death" to save her baby. Why did she do it, and what made him do such things? The answer comes, "Somebody more powerful than he must force him to act at times." He recalls the word he had read: "all-powerful."

These involuntary acts were commanded by God because they were right and good. This was proved by what had occurred. And from these he reasons further:

The flowers and trees were good and beautiful. God had made them. He made the other creatures, too, that each might have food upon which to live. He had made Sheeta, the panther, with his beautiful coat; and Numa, the lion, with his noble head and his shaggy mane. He had made Bara, the deer, lovely and graceful.

To Tarzan, unaware of the limitations of human reasoning, it appears for a time that he has solved the mystery of God. But Burroughs confronts him abruptly with the gap in his neat pattern of logic. An inconsistency becomes suddenly apparent. Stunned, Tarzan hurls the question: "Who made Histah, the snake?" In a powerful climax Burroughs thrusts Tarzan back into humanity's constant puzzlement about God and His actions. Tarzan cannot be granted escape; like any other human, he cannot be given assurance. He must remain, still questioning, in his world of uncertainty. And in Tarzan's dilemma, Burroughs poses the familiar, age-old philosopher's problem: Why did God, the Creator of all things good and beautiful, also create Evil?

The development, in a short story, of certain interpretations of God's role, raises the question of Burroughs' personal attitude toward religion. In one of his earliest fantasy works, "The Gods of Mars," while exposing the Martian "Heaven," the priesthood, and the entire concept of the established church as a cruel and sadistic hoax, he was giving more than a hint about his own religious convictions. To begin with, here and in other works he made plain his distrust and rejection of organized religion. But the indirect presentation of his religious views, the inferences drawn from the statements or thoughts of his fictional characters, does not constitute the only evidence. Burroughs, as always, was not hesitant about stating his opinions bluntly and directly. A letter to Hulbert, written later, contained a severe condemnation of the church:

I was pained to discover how sadly you misinterpreted my attitude toward religion. I have no quarrel with religion, but I do not like the historic attitude of any of the established churches. Their enthusiasms and sincerity never ring true to me and I think that there has been no great change in them all down the ages, insofar as the fundamentals are concerned. There is just as much intolerance and hypocrisy as there ever was, and if any church were able to obtain political power today I believe that you would see all the tyranny and injustice and oppression which has marked the political ascendancy of the church in all times.[68]

This criticism of the established church, he stressed, "does not mean that I am not religious. I am a very religious man, but I do not subscribe to any of the narrow, childish superstitions of any creed."[69] In his letter he spoke of "the disgusting lust for publicity, which animates many divines." But Burroughs, as a man of science and a staunch believer in Darwin's theories, reserved his greatest contempt for the church in its attitude toward scientific progress and "toward the promulgation of the truth in art and literature. . . ." Between the established religions and their narrow beliefs, and the rationality of science, there was an irreconcilable conflict:

A man can be highly religious, he can believe in a God and in an omnipotent creator and still square his belief with advanced scientific discoveries, but he cannot have absolute faith in the teachings and belief of any church, of which I have knowledge, and also believe in the accepted scientific theories of the origin of the earth, of animal and vegetable life upon it, or the age of the human race; all of which matters are considered as basic truth according to the teachings of the several churches as interpreted from their inspired scriptures.[70]

Burroughs, in expressing his views on God, could at times become jokingly irreverent. In a letter of October 28, 1920, to Father Dom Cyprian, a priest with whom he had previously corresponded, Burroughs' comments about the Lord's actions had a humorous tinge:

I was very sorry to know that rheumatism has been bothering you. It seems to me that the Lord should look after you better than he does as you certainly must have earned more of his gratitude than a poor pagan such as I; yet, notwithstanding my ungodliness my neuritis has almost left me. Inscrutable indeed are the ways of Providence.

Father Cyprian's quoting of a remark by Dr. Barton brought a pointed reply: "I do not understand your reference to Dr. Barton and his belief that I am a godless man. You have aroused my curiosity and now you must relieve it. My daughter is in a Catholic convent and I am smiled upon by the Reverend Mother and a number of the Sisters which would never be true were I so godless as your remark suggests."

In his stories Ed's depiction of nature as the all-wise creator of living things, the Great Perfectionist who demonstrated her perfection in her scheme of things — the animals, plants, and their environments — indicated that his religious philosophy tended toward pantheism. His further statement to Father Cyprian supports this view: "Really, I think I have a more satisfactory God than Dr. Barton for I am not afraid of my God and I enjoy His company every day in the sunshine and flowers and the beautiful hills and I do not have to crawl into a dark closet to pray to him."[71] Ed's skepticism about the church did not affect his attitude of good-humored tolerance and helpfulness; beneath his letter to Father Cyprian is his scrawled note: "$1.00 bill enclosed with this letter."

Through the years his comments about God continued to be in a jesting tone. To his brother Harry Ed revealed his happiness about his Tarzana ranch and wrote, "It took God millions of years to get Tarzana and me together but I can see now that He was evidently working to that end since it occurred to Him to create Earth, and I have to give Him credit for pulling off at least one very successful job."[72]

His reply to the Reverend L. Eugene Wettling of Religious Films, Inc., New York, June 14, 1928, made clear his disapproval of the church:

Permit me to assure you of my appreciation of the honor conferred upon me by election to your Honorary Advisory Board.

My religious convictions are such, however, as to make such a connection incongruous, and as it might cause embarrassment to all concerned I sincerely hope that you will withdraw my name. . . .

His remarks, while of a joking nature, implied, on occasion, some acceptance of God's role as Creator. To a fan who had commented about the absence of snakes from his stories, Ed conceded that he had "fought more or less shy of them" because he felt they were "anathema" to his readers and editors, but added, "However, I may be able to invent something better than a snake, to try and put an extra thrill into my stories, as I have already created almost as many strange creatures as God; though He remains one up on me with the creation of Man."[73]

Burroughs, attempting to be open-minded on matters of religion, was particularly careful to avoid influencing his children or dictating to them. He advised his son Hulbert, then at school, in this manner: "You will be wise if you attend church occasionally, at least, if not regularly. It is a very necessary part of the education of all cultured men and women. Your own good judgment will tell you what to accept and what to reject."[74]

However, individual rights in a religious choice were quite different from any plan to introduce compulsory religion on a mass basis. In response to the query of Henry Goddard Leach, editor of *The Forum*, "Shall We Force Religion into the Schools?," Ed was vehemently on the negative side: "Compulsory religious training in any form in schools supported by taxpayers seems to me to be contrary to the highest ideals of American democracy."[75] He noted that even in endowed colleges religious subjects should be electives, and about the Bible, could see no practical way of using it in the public schools. He conceded that the "historical and literary phases" might be of value for study, but insisted that if the Bible were used, equal time should then be devoted to the Talmud, the Koran, and other works. Since, in his opinion, the material was not needed, and the school hours were insufficient for all these religious works, it was best that these subjects should be excluded from the public school curricula.[76]

In discussions with his sons Hulbert and Jack, Burroughs stated his religious attitude clearly: he did not believe in the Bible, Christ, the Immaculate Conception, or God. He called

himself an atheist. To his sons, Burroughs, who did not attend church, had often expressed his dislike for any form of organized or sectarian religion. At times, especially because of his efforts to be tolerant about other people's religious views, he gave the impression of being an agnostic. On occasion when he termed himself a "religious" man, he was referring to his objectives of following the moral or ethical precepts taught by Christ or found in the philosophies of the Greeks and the Romans. Concerning the typical religious attitudes displayed by characters in his stories, both of his sons have maintained that these should not be interpreted as representing Burroughs' beliefs — they are merely inserted as necessary elements in the story, or to create the particular effect he was seeking.[77]

For a period of exactly one year, from March 17, 1916, to March 18, 1917, Burroughs worked on his series of "The New Stories of Tarzan," dispatching them individually to *The Blue Book Magazine* and receiving a prompt $350 for each. They appeared in *Blue Book* one each month in issues dated September 1916 through August 1917. On March 29, 1919, they were published in book form by A. C. McClurg & Co. under the title *Jungle Tales of Tarzan*. In *Blue Book* the first story bore only the series title, but as Chapter One of the book it was titled "Tarzan's First Love." The remaining eleven had subtitles in the magazine, which later became chapter titles two to twelve in the book.

The series had been launched in Oak Park, one story even completed on the camping tour and the remainder finished in Los Angeles.[78] The stories, containing some of Burroughs' best writing, were highly praised by Ray Long; however, there were exceptions, one being number six, "The Witch-Doctor Seeks Vengeance." Here, the opening scene establishes a satirical comparison between the "civilized" Lord Greystoke, William Cecil Clayton, who had assumed the title and lands of Tarzan, and the real Lord Greystoke, the young savage of the jungle. Burroughs had used this same comparison in *Tar-*

Burroughs home at 700 Linden Avenue, Oak Park, Illinois, 1917.

zan of the Apes. His satire, again stressing one of his strongest aversions, the hunting and killing of animals, described how the British Lord Greystoke had shot "many more birds than he could eat in a year," while Tarzan in the African jungle killed only what he needed for food. Burroughs had also repeated another device — Tibo, the native child, seized by Tarzan in the previous story, is now stolen again by the witch doctor. About story number six Long noted:

I don't care for those references to the Lord Greystoke in England. Unless you object very heartily, we will take those references out. I also felt it was a mistake to return to that child. He was all right for one story, but he was not a good character for two....[79]

Ed offered no serious objection: "The references to Lord Greystoke in England were made for artistic contrast. Something similar in the first Tarzan novel has been commented upon very favorably. I thought they were real cute; but if you prefer, however, you may cut them

out. I am seldom so hectic about the children of my brain but that I can see them murdered without a sigh — if they are going to be paid for...."[80]

Early in 1917, still in Los Angeles, Ed had taken time from his writing chores to join the Uplifters, a purely social group, described by him to Davis as "a select bunch of millionaires, clerks, and other celebrities, all members of the Los Angeles Athletic Club, who meet weekly for luncheon and occasionally evenings for dinner and have a heck of a good time. Frank Baum, the fairy tale man, introduced me to them."[81] But these pleasant occasions were more than offset by personal health problems and illnesses in the family. On January 22, in correspondence with Joseph Bray about plans for a British edition of *Tarzan of the Apes,* Ed reported his troubles with his tendency, as usual, to exaggerate financial difficulties:

I may need some money before pay day. I have recently come out of the hospital after a minor operation performed by a surgeon who has no superior in his specialty. I have not yet had his bill. God alone knows what it will be. My oldest boy has been under the care of another high priced specialist for a month. My littlest boy has diptheria. He has it mildly and is about well; but the bills will presently materialize.[82]

However, the world situation was drawing his attention away from these personal problems. The United States' policy of neutrality in the European War could not conceal the country's strong anti-German sentiment. Undoubtedly, to Ed, an entrance into the war on the Allies' side appeared inevitable. Driven, as in the past, by an intense patriotism, he had already begun preparations for some type of military service. Because of his army experience, he naturally thought of the cavalry and in the fall of 1916 enrolled in the Los Angeles Riding Academy for a brush-up course in horsemanship. Here, in contrast to the free, rough-and-tumble riding he had learned at Michigan Military Academy, he was drilled in the formal English style of riding.[83]

The war situation had both aroused his patriotism and created apprehensions about continued story sales. Of Davis he inquired, "What will a war with Germany do to poor boobs who write fiction?" and he then followed with the familiar request: "If you have a pull get me a commission, . . ." mentioning his army career but admitting "that was in the days of cross-bows and catapults."[84] Meanwhile, deciding that the most practical approach would be to seek a commission in the reserves, he reverted to past habits and wrote to his old mentor, General Charles King, who advised him to apply for a captaincy in the cavalry — Officers Reserve Corps — and to get various letters of recommendation. "I will add a corker," said King, "and War or no War we'll have you on the List. . . ."[85] A reply from another former Michigan Military Academy commandant, Frederick Strong, now a major general in the army's Hawaiian headquarters, noted Ed's inability to enter active service because of his age and suggested that he join the Quartermaster Officers' Reserve Corps.[86]

In the past, when seeking military appointments, Ed had gone all out to acquire letters of recommendation from his friends and associates, but on this occasion he far exceeded all previous records, amassing a total of thirteen letters or statements. Included in these were recommendations from Brigadier General Fred Smith; W. H. Butts, his former teacher, now at the University of Michigan; Isaac K. Friedman of Wilmette, Illinois; Joseph Bray of McClurg; Robert D. Lay of the National Life Insurance Company; and Jacob Vogt of the Los Angeles Riding School. Ed also forwarded a copy of his March 15, 1897, army discharge, signed by Colonel Simmons with a character reference by Lieutenant Tompkins.[87] Under these circumstances it was not at all surprising that his commission was granted. The United States declaration of war against Germany came on April 6, 1917, and after his return to Oak Park, where he purchased a home at 700 Linden Avenue, Ed received the official notification from the state of Illinois; his appointment as captain in the reserves was issued as of July 19, 1917, Company A, Second Infantry.

Until the appointment came through, Ed had continued to seek a war correspondent's job. Davis confessed that he had no idea how to get him an assignment covering the war front, explained that there were "a thousand applications to every job," and added that "on our three newspapers we receive at least fifty appeals per diem. . . ."[88] He offered some typical raillery about Ed's qualifications:

You would make all previous war correspondents look like a lot of lame ducks tied in a coop. You know more about blood and trouble and pain and anguish than any other five scribes in the business. I don't know that it would improve your style any to go to the front, but it is a certainty you would improve the war.

. . . Between pronging a Hun and getting his opinion as to how well you executed the job, you could easily subtract enough material to write three serials and then three sequels to those serials.[89]

Despite all these inquiries, Ed, in the sum-

ERB as a captain in Illinois Reserve Militia, Oak Park, Illinois, 1918.

mer of 1917, managed to complete another story, "Bridge and the Oskaloosa Kid," and to indulge in his usual vacation at Coldwater, Michigan.[90] In the fall he turned to the first of his patriotic writings, undertaken at the request of John N. Willys of the War Camp Community Fund, who in a circular of October 9 requested that authors contribute articles to help the war effort. The specific need was for articles "advocating the opening of American homes to boys in the uniform of the army or navy." Ed had agreed promptly to write articles and to offer one each week to newspapers that had printed his stories. About the opening of homes to soldiers, on October 16 he suggested to John Willys that "after proper investigation and under proper authority" a flag be issued to each private home or public facility willing to accept soldiers; this flag would serve as a kind of beacon to the man "walking the streets of a strange city" and call his attention to a place where he might find a "ready welcome."

Ed sent three articles of four hundred words each to Jerle Davis of the Western Newspaper Union in Chicago and asked that he print fifty proofs to distribute to other newspapers, to which Davis agreed.[91] The three articles, titled "To the Mother," "To the Home Girl," and "To the Woman on the Town" (asking prostitutes to stay away from soldiers) were all on the same theme — aiding the lonely soldier adrift on the streets of the big city.[92]

Toward the end of April or the first part of May 1918, Ed took an office in a small brick building at 1020 North Boulevard, Oak Park; although the office was to function as a study and permanent business address, Ed, at times, was quite willing to use it for one of his favorite projects — the recruiting of men for the reserve militia. Summer activities were mainly of a military nature. From August 12 to 25 Ed joined his Oak Park company in training at Camp Steever, Geneva Lake, Illinois, under Commandant F. L. Beals. After his return in September came the announcement of his promotion to major and to the command of the First Battalion, Second Infantry of the Illinois Reserves. But he was convinced that a further

contribution was necessary: his writing skill must be dedicated to the war effort. As a result, in 1918 a stream of patriotic articles poured from the Burroughs pen. These included the following:

Do Boys Make Good Soldiers?
Patriotism by Proxy and Who's Who in Oak Park, both published in *Oak Leaves*.
Home Guarding for the Liberty Loan, a speech delivered at Flag Day exercises, Oak Park, June 14, 1918.
A National Reserve Army Proposed.
Go to Pershing.
Peace and the Militia.[93]

Despite his past censure of the army for its bungling and inefficiency, and curiously, despite the fact that in his own youthful army career he had been unable to adjust to the discipline, had been a rebel, and had implored his father to get him out of the cavalry as quickly as

Front cover of The Oak Parker *magazine with photo of ERB as a major, September 28, 1918.*

possible, the arrival of a national emergency aroused his pride in the military and stimulated an intensely chauvinistic attitude. In common with many other Americans he blindly accepted the vicious anti-German propaganda. An illustration of this is found in "Home Guarding for the Liberty Loan," with its bloodthirsty references to the "Hun" and "Boche":

Each and every one of us pines to go over the top and spear a Hun. . . . Next to sticking a bayonet through a Hun's gizzard, you can inflict the greatest pain upon him by jabbing him in the pocket-book. . . . watching the home Boche wriggle when you get his purse pinned down.

In this and other articles Ed revealed how he had been influenced by the wave of public suspicion directed at German-Americans. He admitted that his methods for selling Liberty Bonds may not have been ethical: "We went out in selected groups decked out in all the panoply of war and armed with a bunch of yellow cards each of which bore the name of some suspected German sympathizer, included in which were those who had subscribed for no liberty bonds or to the Red Cross or to the Y.M.C.A. fund." He endorsed this as a way to "spear a Hun right here at home."

These bitter attacks on those who did not conform to his rigid standards of patriotism were also illustrated in articles about the reserve militia. In "Patriotism by Proxy" Ed used a combined approach of lecturing, scolding, and hurling invective at men who had not joined the reserve: "Are you in the service of your country? If you are not and might be, you are either a traitor or a slacker. . . ." He referred to various kinds of patriotism. "Patriotism of the head" prompted a man to buy Liberty Bonds; this was laudable, but only a beginning. The highest form of patriotism was in service. Those able-bodied men who have contented themselves with lesser contributions to the war effort and have not enlisted in either the armed forces or the reserves, are "patriots by proxy."[94]

Concerning "Who's Who in Oak Park," Ed explained that the title, like the big guns at the war front, was camouflaged. In the article he commented scathingly about the men who had not joined the reserves. "The real title should be 'Who Ain't in Oak Park' for it deals with alibi artists and other lizards, as well as some well-meaning people who rear up on their hind legs and paw the air if anyone suggests that they are not rabid patriots."

Some of the opposition to the militia was displayed by labor union members who, because of the past actions of the national guard, were convinced that one of its main functions was strike-breaking. The contemptuous description of a union member, in the article, revealed unfortunately that Ed had insufficient background in labor history:

I recall one narrow chested, pimple-faced, chinless, anthropoid creature who met me at the door in his bare feet. I wouldn't have had him in my company if he'd been the only male thing in the world; but we put the question to him in the hope that there might be a human being around the place whom we did want. It seemed there was not; but he explained that the reason he couldn't join was that the militia was organized to shoot workingmen! I regret that my vocabulary is too limited to allow me to comment adequately upon this statement. . . .

About the man who had signed an application and then changed his mind because he had heard that the militia was used for strikebreaking, Ed noted, ". . . this man must have been deliberately misinformed by some disloyal acquaintance. . . ."

Ed was equally intemperate in his comments about churchgoers who chose to attend Sunday morning services rather than drill, and about ministers who have been opposed to these drills. Members of the militia, he maintained, were "performing a religious duty" and in defending the churches and homes against "the forces of disloyalty, disorder and lawlessness" were being far more positive than those persons who went to church and "prayed to God to do it for us." He supported the practical reasoning of "The Lord helps him who helps himself": "We are showing Him that we believe that these institutions for which He stands are worth fighting for.

. . ." His attacks on the clergy were violent:

To those who have preached against our drills let me say that I consider you a menace to the cause and welfare of the state; I believe you to be as disloyal at heart as any other pro-German and I am very far from being alone in that belief. . . . Let me tell you that Oak Park's loyal clergy should start a thorough house cleaning. Beside the men who preach against enlistment in the reserve militia there is at least one who has preached against enlistment in the federal forces, and he has a German name that smells to heaven.[95]

In his article "Do Boys Make Good Soldiers?" Ed's answer was in the affirmative; as evidence he cited his training at Camp Steever, where young instructors, all under twenty-one, showed remarkable ability, poise and efficiency in handling men, many of whom were far older than they.[96] His Flag Day speech of June 14 was highly emotional in tone: it had been a fad among "so-called intellectuals," he remarked, "to scoff at the puerile sentimentality of flag worship," and he used to believe that something was wrong with him, "some taint of mental weakness," when tears came to his eyes as the colors passed by. Now he knew that "the trouble was with the scoffers"; we should be glad that we can "choke up" when soldiers march past.

His article "A National Reserve Army Proposal," published in the Army and Navy Journal, August 31, 1918, contained an explanation of the weaknesses of a volunteer reserve militia and a demand for the formation of a compulsory national reserve army. ". . . Every man should be compelled to serve in some capacity. . . ." and the enforced training of these men, in addition to furnishing recruits for the regular army, would provide the states with "protection against internal disorders."

"Go to Pershing," written as the war neared its end, again extolled the virtues of military training and predicted that civilian training camps would be continued in peace time. Indications were, the article pointed out, that the new Camp Pershing, to be situated in Kentucky, would be the greatest of its kind. Ed's support of these camps was not primarily for military reasons; he believed other factors were more important. For the older man especially, after years of sedentary life, the program of exercise, drills, and vigorous outdoor activities would restore some physical fitness and bring back "the fire of youth." Other values of military training were the creation of friendships and the development of efficiency, tact, and resourcefulness — qualities, Ed stressed, that would be particularly useful to the businessman and employer. In "Peace and the Militia," published November 16, 1918, after the armistice was declared, Ed repeated his familiar demand for a continuation of the Illinois Reserve Militia, needed in peacetime to suppress certain elements at home that he conceived to be dangerous or disloyal:

. . . it is very possible that we shall see loosed upon the community a raft of street-corner orators of the I.W.W. and Bolshevik types.

The events of the last few days have clearly demonstrated that German propagandists are still among us.

We have thrashed the trouble makers of Europe and it is within the range of possibilities that we may have to deal with similar cattle here.[97]

The harsh attitude he displayed toward those who did not meet his exacting standards of patriotism and service to the country were no more severe than his assessment of his own contributions. His desire, above all, had been to enter active service at the war front; this could not be realized because of his age — almost forty-two when war was declared. The reserves were a compromise that did not at all satisfy him. He had been forced also to yield to Emma's opposition; to his friend Bert Weston, on September 17, 1918, he complained that militia work was "the only military activity which Emma will permit me to indulge in. . . ."

This combination of superpatriotism and disappointment in his own war performance led to feelings of guilt which drove him to resigning from the Military Order of the Loyal Legion of the United States, an organization which he had esteemed because his father had belonged to it. On January 15, 1919, in a letter to Lieutenant Colonel George V. Lauman, he explained the reasons for his resignation:

I applied for membership in the order out of respect for the memory of my father who had answered the call in his day in defense of the flag. When my opportunity came with the present war unfortunate circumstances prevented me from going and I now feel that to wear the insignia of the legion or claim membership is equivalent to assuming as my own the honors that were worn by another man. I did not have this feeling prior to the recent war as I felt that I had not had my chance and therefore I was warranted in showing a just pride in my father's service.

Though undeserved, he accepted the blame for a war record that he considered inadequate:

I feel very keenly the unfortunate circumstances which prevented me from entering active service and I cannot ever again wear the button of the legion without a sense of humiliation, for even though it was through no fault of my own that I did not serve, the fact, however, remains that I did not. . . .

Ed stated that if Colonel Lauman believed he should continue to be a member, he would pay dues but would not wear the legion button.

During 1917-18 Ed maintained his association with William G. Chapman, who continued to be his syndicating agent. On February 10, 1917, Ed reported with obvious satisfaction to Chapman, ". . . they sold only 30,000 copies of Tarzan of the Apes during the six months ending Dec. 31; which seems pretty good for the third year of something what aint literatoor. If it had been the chances are it would have been dead long since." Chapman, representing the Burroughs stories for all newspapers except those in New York City, forwarded inquiries from Henry M. Eaton, managing editor of the Philadelphia *Evening Ledger* concerning "Tar-

zan and the Jewels of Opar" and "The Jungle Tales of Tarzan." The numerous requests from readers who wished to get in touch with Burroughs personally were forwarded by Eaton to Chapman's press bureau in Chicago.

In the summer of 1918, while authorizing Chapman to accept newspaper offers for the Tarzan stories he had been handling, Ed insisted that he now planned to take over all syndication himself. On May 14, he wrote to Chapman that this was caused "by the necessity for increasing my income to take care of a part of the additional expenses I am bearing on account of my connection with the reserve militia." He maintained that the syndication could not produce enough money for two persons. Two days later Ed notified Davis that he was arranging to handle his own syndicating and requested that Chapman's agreement with the Munsey fiction syndicate be transferred to him. To Joseph Bray at McClurg, on May 27, he sent information of the change and commented in frank disapproval of Chapman as an agent:

Confidentially, I have been very much disappointed in Chapman's handling of all my work. He seems to lack pep and force and he certainly has not only brought me practically no new accounts, but has lost one or two of the profitable ones which I turned over to him.

In further correspondence with Davis, Ed suggested a plan for mutual cooperation in marketing the stories, but, on May 25, commented pessimistically about those works whose rights belonged to Munsey — "Tarzan of the Apes," "Under the Moons of Mars," "The Gods of Mars," and "At the Earth's Core" — stating, ". . . as a matter of fact I do not think that what are left of the syndicate rights of those stories which you own are worth a tinker's dam." Davis did not agree, noting on May 29 that these stories were "salable for an indefinite period" and explaining that the Munsey business department "intends to make another drive" to sell the stories. Discussions on the matter continued into the fall, with little result. A. T. Locke of the Munsey Bureau on October 31, 1918, rejected Ed's plan to issue a combined circular to be distributed to newspapers and to contain a brief description of all the Burroughs stories. Locke's opinion was that *Tarzan of the Apes* had been syndicated "just about the limit" and was "practically a dead issue anyway because it has been picturized." He believed it would be best for Ed to adopt an individual plan "featuring Edgar Rice Burroughs only." Thus, with 1918 drawing to a close, Ed, already overburdened with other activities, had added the personal handling of his newspaper sales.

To answer the public demand for more books by Burroughs, McClurg, beginning in the fall of 1914, had arranged for the publication of the second *Tarzan* novel — *The Return of Tarzan*. With its appearance on March 10, 1915, others were scheduled to follow. They included *The Beasts of Tarzan*, March 4, 1916; *The Son of Tarzan*, March 10, 1917; *A Princess of Mars*, October 10, 1917; *Tarzan and the Jewels of Opar*, April 20, 1918; and *The Gods of Mars*, September 28, 1918.

Tarzan of the Apes had been dedicated by Ed to his wife, and continuing this practice, he dedicated succeeding novels to members of his family: *The Return of Tarzan* to Mrs. George Tyler Burroughs, his mother; *The Beasts of Tarzan* to daughter Joan; *The Son of Tarzan* to his oldest son Hulbert; and *A Princess of Mars* to his son Jack. Because Bray had overlooked Ed's instructions concerning the dedication of *The Son of Tarzan*, none appeared in the first edition. On December 3, 1916, Ed had written, "Please see that this book is dedicated to Hulbert Burroughs and win my undying regards." Ed expressed disappointment over the omission, noting on March 12, 1917, "I wanted a book dedicated to each of my children. . . ." In later printings the dedication was added.

During the publication of the various novels, interesting matters were developed in the correspondence. In connection with *The Gods of Mars*, Bray, recalling Burroughs' remark that the *All-Story* version was somewhat abbreviated, requested the original manuscript. Ed's notation of April 24, 1918, read, "Del'd mss of 'Gods of Mars' to Bray . . . in person."

The assignment of illustrating the first two of the *Mars* series, *A Princess of Mars* and *The Gods of Mars*, was given to Frank E. Schoonover by Joseph Bray. Schoonover, whose dust jacket and illustrations appeared in both the McClurg and British Methuen editions of *A Princess of Mars,* made a careful analysis of the Burroughs stories and extracted details of the costumes, ornaments, and weapons of the varied Martian races. The meticulous nature of his preparation for the drawings in *A Princess of Mars* is revealed in his letter of July 27, 1917, to Bray; Schoonover enclosed a copy of the notes he had made for his own use — notes based upon the galley proofs and containing a list of information drawn from Burroughs' statements and descriptions. To Bray, Schoonover wrote:

You will find recorded all that the author has to say regarding costume. . . . you will observe in galley 11 that mention is made of ornaments strapped upon the head. If the Tharks had decorations upon their ugly top pieces, how much easier it would be for the people of Helium to wear them. So I imagine that Dejah Thoris had just about what I have painted, plus the diamonds as mentioned in galley 50. Also there is ample authority for the scabbard — see galley 42 — "drawing long sword" — and gal. 71 — "sheathing my bloody blade."

Schoonover's determination to faithfully portray the Burroughs costumes and to make the illustrations as authentic as possible is demonstrated in further comments to Bray, with reference to the guiding notes he had made:

These few notes were written after two or three days study and after making dozens of sketches. There has been worked out a sort of sliding scale of design for body decorations for the hordes of Barsoom. Their costumes can be made brutal and rough or refined to suit the Martian tribe under depictment. This, it seems to me, is absolutely necessary if there is to be a series of Martian books. . . . I am thoroughly at heart in the matter and I believe I have gotten some real originality in the make of the "metal". For example, in the picture that you have in hand now, there are some true Tharkian touches. The pistol butt is absolutely correct:

Frontispiece and cover illustration of A Princess of Mars, *1917; Frank Schoonover, illustrator.*

it is true Thark. The belts are also common to the same tribe and can only be found upon the green men that roam the dead sea bottoms. You can depend upon it — that is correct. The white metal is a mark of a true Tharkian: silver is common to the Zodangans while the people of Helium love the finely wrought ornaments of gold.

Schoonover, convinced that *A Princess of Mars* had been written "with an idea of a sequel or even a third volume," insisted that "it would be well to establish a foundation of costume that can be elaborated and refined or brought to the level of the dead sea bottom according to the custom of the tribe pictured." In adhering to this plan, he had invented a collection of belts and guns that could be altered "to suit the locality to be portrayed."

The "artist's visualization," Schoonover stressed, must be based upon "solid reasoning"; in creating his costumes he had made notes of all Burrough's descriptions of "body adornment." Schoonover's fascination with the story was evident: ". . . my imagination has been aroused to such an extent that I hardly see how Mr. Burroughs can drop the Martian curtain without telling us a little more." Schoonover posed questions that needed answers:

What, for example, is at the mouth (?) of the river Iss. Men or beasts or nothing.
What happens under ground.
What goes on at the source of the water supply.
What eventually happens to Carter, Dejah Thoris and the egg.
Is the egg saved. (It is)
And so on.

With the publication of the second of the *Tarzan* series, *The Return of Tarzan*, McClurg employed J. Allen St. John as the illustrator; St. John's association with the Burroughs books would continue for many years, and his colorful and exciting drawings would bring him fame. For *The Return of Tarzan* McClurg created a dust jacket using the picture drawn by N. C. Wyeth for the August 1913 cover of *New Story Magazine;* St. John's contribution consisted only of twenty-six small sketches placed as chapter headings. However, in the remaining novels of the 1917-18 period, *The Beasts of Tarzan, The Son of Tarzan,* and *Tarzan and the Jewels of Opar,* the dust jackets and all illustrations were done by St. John.

Ed, in his 1917 output, completed varied stories designed for magazine publication. Among these, "Bridge and the Oskaloosa Kid" received an incredulous reception and firm rejection from Davis. Ed had returned to his hobo favorite, the brave and gallant Bridge (who continued to quote poetry by Henry Herbert Knibbs), and involved the vagabond with a strange and diverse aggregation of characters. There were Abigail Prim, daughter of Jonas Prim, Oakdale's wealthiest citizen; no less than six hoboes, all either criminals or murderers; Giova, a gypsy girl, and Beppo, her trained bear; the Cases, a farm couple, and their son Willie, an amateur detective; and a long list of others.

Burroughs' scenes, devised for the slender Oskaloosa Kid, who had apparently burglarized the Prim home, and the suave Bridge, take place in a "haunted" house, the terrifying apparition being "The Thing," a creature that drags a clanking chain along with it. The Thing turns out, unbelievably, to be Beppo the bear. A surprise ending is the disclosure that the Oskaloosa Kid, who has traveled about with Bridge and with the gang of hoboes, is really the charming Abigail Prim, disguised in men's clothes. This was too much for Davis; his protest combined indignation with disgust:

None of us can swallow the fact that the "Oskaloosa Kid" is a pullet. Lord! Edgar, how do you expect people who love and worship you, to stand for anything like that. And the bear stuff, and the clanking of chains! . . . [98]

Confident of other outlets for his material, Ed displayed indifference about the Munsey rejection, commenting on July 28, 1917, ". . . sorry you couldn't see the Bridge story because I think it belonged in All-Story; but otherwise it cuts no figure as I sold it immediately." The purchaser, Ray Long of *Blue Book,* paid $600,

Cover of Tarzan and the Jewels of Opar, *1919; J. Allen St. John, illustrator.*

With naked hands
he faced the
maddened Tantor

Illustration of Korak, the son of Tarzan, and Tantor, the elephant, 1918; J. Allen St. John, illustrator.

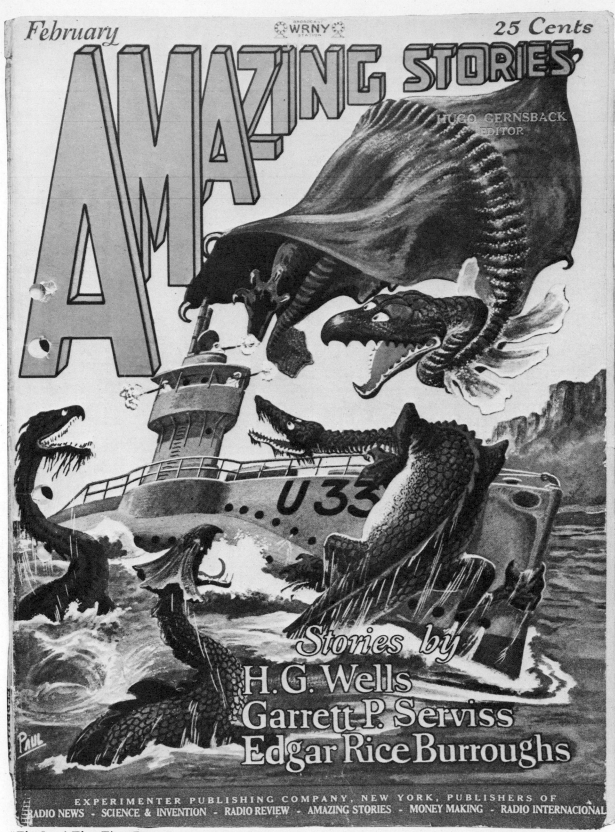

"The Land That Time Forgot" cover of Amazing Stories, *February 1927; Frank R. Paul, illustrator.*

and upon its publication in the March 1918 issue, the story was retitled "The Oakdale Affair."

In two other novelettes of the 1917 period, "The Lost U-Boat" and "Cor-Sva-Jo," Burroughs returns once more to a familiar theme — the discovery of a primitive world teeming with prehistoric monsters and peopled with a hierarchy of strange races. However, he made it plain from the start that he was planning a trilogy. On October 15 he wrote to Long, "Saturday I brought down the first of the three novelettes — The Lost U-Boat; but missed you by a few minutes. Laid the manuscript on your desk...." The master of "withholding," Burroughs deliberately provided an atmosphere of mystery in the first two works concerning the evolutionary process in Caspak, the interior region of the lost island of Caprona. This mystery was resolved in the third story, "Out of Time's Abyss," completed by midsummer of 1918.[99]

"The Lost U-Boat," re-named "The Land that Time Forgot" by Ray Long, is the first of Ed's fictional works to contain a strong condemnation of the Germans; they are painted as subhumans — men without any redeeming qualities. The adventures of Bowen J. Tyler, Jr., (the name is a Burroughs ancestral one, passed down to George Tyler Burroughs, Ed's father) supposedly described in a manuscript found in a thermos bottle floating near the southern tip of Greenland, are launched with the torpedoing of an American liner by a German U-Boat. The succeeding incidents depict the German brutality.

Burroughs, again exhibiting the influence of World War I propaganda, depicted an American traitor almost as despicable as the Baron. The creation of Benson, a sailor who sabotages the submarine, illustrates the wartime attitude of contempt and distrust toward the IWW's.

In "The Lost U-Boat" Ed departs briefly from the story form to present dated reports from the journal prepared by Bowen Tyler. After the manuscript, placed in a bottle, is found (the discovery is made by Burroughs, who as first-person narrator takes part in some of the action), a rescue mission is planned by a new

character, Tom Billings, the protagonist in "Cor-Sva-Jo," the second of the trilogy. And the last work, "Out of Time's Abyss," concentrates upon the adventures of Bradley, one of the British sailors, in his encounters with the ghastly winged Wieroos, the dominant race of Caspak. Here the mystery of the Caspakian seven-cycle scheme of evolution is finally explained. The trilogy appeared in rapid sequence in the *Blue Books* of August, October and December of 1918, under the titles "The Land That Time Forgot," "The People That Time Forgot" ("Cor-Sva-Jo"), and "Out of Time's Abyss."[100]

"The Little Door," a short story written November 17 to 23, 1917, again developed a theme of hatred and revenge against the Germans. It is Burroughs' most violent and bloodthirsty story of the anti-German type. The victorious Germans, invading a small French village, force their way into a home where the young girl Jeanne and her father live. Innocent and childlike, "her life had been one of kindliness and love," and she had no knowledge of evil. It remained for the Germans to teach her about terror and death. Aurele, the family's tottering old servant, and her father are viciously killed.

A Prussian officer seizes Jeanne and makes clear what she must consent to if she wishes to live. Strangely composed, and now apparently unmoved by the sight of her dead father "lying in a great pool of blood upon the floor," Jeanne urges the officer to send his men away, responds warmly to his kisses, and says, "You know nothing of love, you Germans." She leads him to the "little door" of a small room. Once he is inside, she slips out and slams the door behind him. There she pulls upon a silken cord and then drags down upon a heavy manila rope. ". . . From beyond the door came muffled sounds which sent her shrinking against the wall, her palms tight pressed against her ears; but only for a moment...."

Jeanne uses the same tactics to lure, in succession, a lieutenant and then another German officer through the little door into the chamber of doom. Now the terrible shrieks do not affect her and she does not cover her ears. With her dagger she scratches crosses on the door frame of the small room, one for each German.

From then on she stands at the doorway of her home, smiling invitingly at the German officers who pass by, and luring them inside. The German forces are now retreating and the French soldiers are approaching the village. Jules, the man Jeanne loves, has returned secretly and from the house across the street is watching her actions with "burning eyes." Bitter at what he believes to be her wanton behavior, he enters her home, knife in hand, determined to kill her. He pursues her into the room beyond the little door and there an angry growl brings him to a sudden halt. The mystery of the room from which no German ever emerges is finally solved:

In the dim light of the single gas jet in the chamber Jules saw a huge black-maned lion rise, snarling, from the dead body of a German captain. About the floor were strewn helmets and side arms, torn pieces of blood stained, grey cloth and human bones.

The lion, at first menacing toward Jules, recognizes his voice and yields to the command of "Down, Brutus!" The two lovers lock the beast in the room and go to the window where they witness the victorious entry of the French troops.

On December 15, after "The Little Door" had been rejected by *Collier's*, Ed sought Davis' advice: "I am going to send it to you and ask you to tell me what in hell is wrong with it if you don't want it."[101] Once more Ed commented irritably that he "should like to be able to write a salable short story occasionally," but didn't seem to know how. Davis' answer of the eighteenth pinpointed, as usual, the story's weaknesses: "There is nothing the matter with 'The Little Door,' except that behind it is a tidal-wave of bloodshed, horror, and suggestion. There has been so much written about the terrible Boche and his evil impulses that there is nothing more left to the imagination."

Davis' final bit of advice was significant: "Can the war, Edgar, and believe that I am still your peaceful friend and ally."

Despite this sound analysis, Ed stubbornly persisted in sending "The Little Door" out again, this time to *The People's Home Journal*, where it received a firm rejection.[102] The story was never published.

The war situation also encouraged Ed to express his patriotism in verse. In "Little Ol' Buck Private," which at the start announces, "We're marching on Berlin/ We'll stop around at Potsdam/ And please to let us in," Ed concedes that the officers are doing their share, but asks, ". . . who would win the battles/ if 'tweren't for me and you?" The "little old buck private," whether Smith, Schwartz or Murphy, is the one on whom the country depends. In the poem Ed resorts to stereotyped anti-German statements of the period:

We'll get the Kaiser's nanny,
*   We'll get the Kaiser's goat,*
We'll get the Kaiser's army
*   And his damned U-boat.*

A second poem, written shortly after the war, is titled "For the Victory Loan," and in it Ed develops a patriotic and sentimental appeal for support of this 1919 loan. With the war over, and people tired of sacrificing, the poem stresses the rebellious attitudes of Americans; in this case, Ed was probably depicting a real-life resistance to appeals for money. The miser is first shown with his "glittering hoard" whining, "I can give no more. Four times I've given. . . ." But the dancer, pausing "on the ballroom floor," also refuses, crying, "You here again? . . . Away! and let me enjoy life;/I'm tired of hearing of war and strife." The next two stanzas contain similar responses:

A fat man wheeled in his swivel chair.
*   "Just look," he cried, "at that window there!*
" 'Tis thick with posters and flags galore.
*   "I've got to live — I can loan no more."*

A workman held up a grimy hand.
*   "With this," he said, "have I served my land.*

"Four times I've loaned of my savings, too.
   The war is over and I am through."

But Ed reserves his last, climactic stanza to emphasize why Americans must still be willing to sacrifice:

A mother gazed on a star of gold,
   "I gave my best and I'm growing old;
"But God be praised that I still may give
   "That the Peace he died to win may live!"

In contrast to his patriotic exhortations and violent anti-German propaganda of 1918, Ed, almost as though the end of the war had suddenly dispelled the somber atmosphere, allowed his humorous instincts to be released. At the year's end he contributed a piece of burlesque writing to the Coldwater, Michigan, *Daily Reporter,* whose editor was Emma's sister, Leila Hulbert Westendarp. It was a fictitious foreign correspondent's account of a visit to Paris, where a "Local Mystery" received an explanation. Dated December 30, 1918, the article opens:

I arrived in Paris early yesterday morning and found the city not much changed since my last visit notwithstanding the fact that I am assured by trustworthy informants that France has been at war. With the true news instinct that marks the successful correspondent I immediately set forth to run this rumor to earth and, with the assistance of a scoop shovel, I am now able to present to the readers of The Reporter the startling announcement that France has been at war with Germany for four years.

Ed joked about the difficulty of traveling about Paris; the problem was that "this village has no streets, the place being a mess of avenues, places, boulevards and rues, especially rues." He was on the verge of grasping "the meaning and purpose of a rue" when an incident occurred which plunged him into confusion. While dining at a sidewalk cafe he noticed a dissolute old man causing a scene at a nearby table. An inquiry of a French friend as to who the man was, produced an answer — and a

planned pun. The French woman replied, "Rue A, mong-sewer." ("Roué, monsieur.")

Although our "foreign correspondent" is in Paris and would be expected to discuss events in the French capital, he disconcertingly shifts to a report of the discovery of a huge mastodon's tooth in the river near Coldwater, Michigan, — a discovery blared forth in the Paris newspapers. Burroughs describes the mastodon as "a species of preglacial mouse which lived in trees and fed upon flying fishes. . . ." The creature "had but one tooth, not having room in his mouth for any more, which I think that anyone who has seen this tooth will admit is entirely reasonable." Logical reasoning leads to the belief that when the mastodon ate, "it was necessary to remove the tooth in order to get food into his mouth. . ."

To solve the question as to how the enormous tooth came to be deposited in a river near Coldwater, Michigan, Burroughs explained he had consulted two professors in the Department of Paleontology at the University of Paris. From Professors L'Ostete and Tapebaton he received two differing theories. L'Ostete maintained that "M. giganteus" was perched in a tree when he saw a large flying fish approaching; he removed his tooth and laid it carefully upon a branch, then launched into a ferocious attack upon the fish. In the fierce battle that ensued, M. giganteus was carried some distance away. A terrific hurricane arose, and after he had conquered the fish, eaten it, and returned to his tree, he could not find his tooth; it had fallen into the river.

Professor Tapebaton disagreed heatedly with this theory, insisting that M. giganteus was asleep under a tree and was awakened by "the growling of a winged, saber-tooth blue gill." He attacked the animal "without remembering to remove his tooth and . . . while devouring his kill, he swallowed his tooth and choked to death."

For his closing statement Ed saved the one news item that could be considered an "accomplished fact"; he wrote, "I have it upon reasonably good authority that the war is over."[103]

15
GENTLEMAN FARMER

Ed's return to Oak Park, Illinois, had been caused by patriotic motives and his involvement with the reserve militia, but he had no intention of making his permanent home in the Midwest. On December 4, 1918, he wrote to his Los Angeles physician, Dr. W. H. Kiger, "Mrs. Burroughs and I are both very anxious to get back to California. This climate is simply abominable. We had a more or less rotten Summer and entirely rotten Fall and from where I sit it looks as though it is going to be a rotten Winter...." His main concern, as expressed to Kiger, was the flu situation in Los Angeles; he wanted to know whether it would be safe to come there with the children in January: "I wouldn't want to run into another epidemic ... especially as we would have to go to a hotel and live for a month or so where it would be difficult to keep the children from being exposed...."[1]

On December 11, in a letter to his old friend Howard Platt, who had gotten him the job as railroad policeman in Salt Lake City, Ed re-vealed a plan that appeared incongruous for a successful author: "We expect to go to California about February next and I wish to get a ranch and raise swine...." He noted that he would need alfalfa land, and explained that this surprising ambition "to raise stock and live on a farm" was partially motivated by his affection for his brother Harry; Ed hoped they "might be together some day," but stressed that he had not discussed the matter with Harry and did not intend to until something definite materialized.[2]

A week earlier, to Bob Davis, he had also mentioned his plan to leave for California around the first of the year, and to buy a small ranch where he would raise "purebred Berkshire swine." At the same time he commented with aversion about the prospect of further Tarzan novels:

I feel now that I can never write another Tarzan story and I am not posing when I say that I do

ERB's advertisement to sell his property in Oak Park, Illinois, in preparation for move to California.

not see how the reading public can stand for any more of them if they are as fed up on Tarzan as I am. Of course I suppose that it is much harder work writing these stories than it is reading them since I feel that I have said and re-said a dozen times everything that there is to say about Tarzan — this is why the work is so hard, I suppose.[3]

His attitude, later in the letter, was less adamant: "The chances are that I will not write another Tarzan story until I am convinced that it is absolutely wanted by someone, and I have been away from Tarzan long enough to approach him again with a refreshed mind."[4]

Ed's opinion of Southern California, expressed satirically in his 1914 poem "The Climate and the View," and nothing else, had not changed. In trying to persuade his close friend Bert Weston to join him in California, he wrote, "You will not like it at first. It is the experience of a great many people that they return to California a second and often a third time before they finally decide that they wish to live there permanently."[5] His added remarks about California were far from complimentary:

You will soon be disillusioned as to the "perfection" of California's climate. It can be just as rotten there as anywhere and really during the rainy season it is abominable. . . . it has been over-touted and a man goes there for the first time with the expectation of dropping into the Garden of Eden whereas the fact is that southern California is nothing more than desert land, certain spots in which have been reclaimed. The soil is enough to make a man from the Mississippi Valley laugh himself to death, but on the other hand it has for me the advantage of a longer period of sunshine than this climate and the lure of mountains and ocean.

"I would never go to California to make a fortune," he explained, "although I expect to make money out of hog-raising."[6]

To Colonel Charles S. McEntee, his Uncle Charles, who was staying at the Hotel Alvarado in Los Angeles, Ed sent details of the departure:

We expect to land in Los Angeles Monday, February 3rd, having made reservations on the Santa Fe for January 31st and were figuring on stopping at the Alvarado if we can get accommodations. As I understand that you are there again this year am imposing on your generosity to ask you to speak to the management to see if they can reserve us three adjoining rooms.... P.S. Party will consist of my family and maid — Theresa, whom you may recall. Shall bring chauffeur, too; but thought of getting him a room in a private family.[7]

The permanence of this removal to Los Angeles was without question; included in the traveling assemblage were two canary birds and the Airedale terrier Tarzan, and on January 14, 1919, Ed informed Arch Burdick, his insurance agent, that he was shipping the household furniture and the Packard automobile.[8] In trying to allay the concern of his mother about the separation, Ed wrote, "You must not feel that you are not going to see us again as we have been planning on having you and Mrs. Hulbert out as soon as we are located in California."[9]

Ed's departure required a special farewell ceremony by his numerous friends — all sharing with him a membership in The White Paper Club of Chicago. The club, composed of journalists and authors, and dedicated to promoting "friendly intercourse between those engaged in the transformation of white paper into art in any of its printed forms," had adopted its constitution and by-laws on April 11, 1917, and elected its officers and board of governors at that time. The president was Emerson Hough;

secretary-treasurer, Ray Long; and on the board of governors, in addition to these two, were Frank Reilly, James R. Quirk, and Charles D. Frey.[10]

At the banquet held in Chicago's La Salle Hotel on January 28, 1919, Ed was subjected to the banter and practical jokes that the occasion called for. A brochure, titled "Tarzan's Feast of Departure," with cover illustration by J. Allen St. John, contained "The Blackest Page in White Paper History," presumably from the secretary's minutes, reporting a supposed speech of Ed's:

Mr. Burroughs requested the floor, and, on being recognized, spoke as follows: "Mr. President: It seems to me that our club is of such size that 'treating' is out of the question. I move, therefore, that it be out of order for a member to purchase any drinks other than for his own consumption, except in case of a guest or a guest of the club." The motion was seconded and carried. Mr. Burroughs then concluded, with force and feeling: "Gentlemen, I thank you! Waiter, bring me a stein of beer."

Special program of White Paper Club of Chicago honoring ERB; J. Allen St. John, illustrator.

1922 aerial photo of part of Tarzana Ranch, which Ed purchased from estate of General Harrison Gray Otis; shows main residence, to which Ed added other rooms; ERB's stables, dairy barn, creamery, and chicken coop are visable to left of main house; trees surrounding hill on which house is located were mostly rare species imported by General Otis.

In the same brochure was a "night letter" from William Parsons, devised by someone who knew of the dispute that had raged between Burroughs and Parsons about the royalties from *Tarzan of the Apes,* and the production of *The Romance of Tarzan*: "Delighted to hear you are coming to California. Trust that I may continue to produce your stories in motion pictures. I did so enjoy Tarzan and my young lady friends equally enjoyed the parties I gave out of the profits. Bill Parsons." Burroughs' reply, by direct wire to Hollywood, and also someone's invention, was a blunt "Go to hell."

Newspaper accounts of the farewell banquet noted that about thirty members were present, that Hiram Moe Greene, editor of *Woman's World,* was toastmaster, and that Joseph Bray "voiced the sentiment of appreciation to Mr. Burroughs who responded with a promise 'not to forget any of you'." It was reported that Ed "will shortly leave for California, where he will devote his time to an ostrich farm and writing."

A membership list attached to the brochure and headed, "Society for the Prevention of Waste of White Paper," contained the names of such distinguished authors and editors as Howard Vincent O'Brien, Edwin Balmer, Oliver M. Gale, Randall Parrish, and William McHarg. To pay tribute to Ed, an unidentified author had composed a sonnet; titled "Burroughs," the sonnet eulogized Ed as the man who sings "of Nature's voice" with his "wild words."[11]

Upon arriving in Los Angeles in February 1919, Ed at once began his search for the ranch he so strongly desired. During that period the Burroughs moved from the Alvarado Hotel, renting a furnished home at 1729 North Wilton Avenue in Los Angeles.[12] In the last week of February Ed found what he was seeking, but it was a far cry from the "small ranch" he had mentioned in his letters. On March 1 he purchased the country estate of the late General Harrison Gray Otis, founder and publisher of the *Los Angeles Times* newspaper. The estate, called Mil Flores, was located in the San Fernando Valley in the foothills of the Santa Monica Mountains. Details of the purchase were reported in the *Sunday Times* of March 2, 1919: "The estate, created by Gen. Otis near the close of his life, and occupied by him immediately following his presentation to Los Angeles county for a public museum of his Wilshire boulevard home, the Bivouac, was used by him as a place of residence much of the time in the year prior to his death in 1917. . . . The holding comprises approximately 540 acres lying along the south side of the State highway (Ventura road) and toward the western end of the San Fernando Valley."[13]

Concerning the estate house, the article notes that the hill on which it stands "comprises about fifteen acres and is set out to a great variety of rare shrubbery and plants. The world was combed for the greenery on this knoll, hundreds of the plants coming from Asia and Africa." Ed, at the time of the purchase, had explained his intention to rechristen the estate Tarzana, a name which he planned to adopt also as a trade name for any products that were offered for sale. With the estate Ed acquired a small herd of registered Angora goats, living in the hills and deeper canyons. This herd was a project of General Otis, who had been convinced that much of the foothill land, then standing idle, would afford good range for goats. Ed's plans were to continue raising goats in these upper areas, increasing the size of the herds, while using the lower ground for his Berkshire hogs.

Problems beyond the ordinary arose during the moving from Oak Park to Los Angeles and then to the Tarzana Ranch. On March 21, 1919, Ed commented on "the frightful job of installing our furniture which had been shipped from Oak Park, arriving a few days before I closed the deal for a ranch," and added, "On top of this I have had the responsibilities of a going ranch of 540 acres and 500 head of livestock (mostly the goats) with all the help quarreling and everything going wrong. My secretary only arrived from the East Monday and we are now digging into six weeks accumulation of correspondence."[14] The problems with the help, involving disagreements over salaries and work-

North side of Burroughs home at Tarzana Ranch, about 1921.

ing conditions, became quite serious. A number of employees, including the maid Theresa, left Tarzana and returned to Oak Park; the secretary Grace Onthank and her husband Fred, a member of the Oak Park police department who had left his job to accept a position at Tarzana, both departed in a huff, claiming that Ed had reduced their promised salaries and not paid the agreed-upon moving expenses. They especially resented their treatment by Emma, referring in a letter of January 20, 1920, to "the actions of Mrs. Burroughs which you know was the real reason for us leaving." Noting that the situation Ed had "pictured so wonderful . . . had not materialized in the least," Fred Onthank wrote: "We would not have cared, and could have put up with all these things, if you, and especially *yours* had been congenial and treated us at least like white servants should be

treated and not niggers."[15] At a later period, the hard feelings apparently dissipated, the Onthanks returned to Los Angeles, and were given letters of reference by Burroughs.

In spite of these troubles Ed was beginning to relish the things he valued most and had dreamed of for years — the invigorating outdoor life, the pioneer or western environment, and the sense of ownership as he gazed from the knoll of his home to see the valley, the groves and canyons, and the mountain peaks in the distance. In trying to persuade his friend Bert Weston to bring his family and settle in California, Ed wrote in detail about the ranch activities:

The range into which Tarzana runs is very wild. It stretches south of us to the Pacific. We have already seen coyote and deer on the place and the foreman trapped a bob-cat a few weeks ago. Things come down and carry the kids out of the corrals in broad daylight. Deeper in there are mountain lion. I think Collins and Jeff would like it here. I have bought a couple of .22 cal. rifles for Hulbert and myself beside my .25 Remington and automatics, so we are going to do some hunting. Jack has an air rifle with which he expects to hunt kangaroo-rats and lions and I am going to get them each a pony.

. . . There is plenty of room for a golf course and a mighty sporty one too. Also expect to put in a swimming pool and tennis court.[16]

He described his problems wryly and humorously to Joseph Bray, while making it plain that nothing could lessen his enthusiasm for Tarzana:

My secretary and her husband threw up the sponge and departed hence for Illinois last week. I am now my own secretary, hog expert and goat impresario. Also both my goat herders quit Saturday, a coyote killed a kid yesterday, three other kids died, I fired the ranch cook, it rained all over my freshly mown hay and the starter on the Chandler won't work. Other wise we are having a heluva nice time. (I just glanced out the front window to discover that the pole on the rake has broken and that two men have stopped work to look at it, leaving a team and a tractor idle.) But somehow I can't help liking it — I never loved any place in my life as I do this and if anything happens that I don't make a go of it I believe that it would about break my heart.[17]

It is interesting to note that in 1923 Burroughs read and gave to his eldest son a remarkable book entitled *Mother Nature* by William J. Long. Long expressed views about animals that were some fifty years ahead of the current ecological movements. He stressed love of all wild things which he felt have an inherent right to life and should be protected by man rather than slaughtered for the sport. From that time on, Burroughs would not permit hunters on his ranch. He even became a deputy sheriff so he could more easily enforce his no-hunting rules.

While attempting to establish the Tarzana Ranch on a paying basis, Ed was at the same time arranging with his Oak Park real estate agent for the sale of the two homes and a lot.[18] The ranch problems were far from being solved, and to Douglas Rothacker Ed had commented, ". . . God knows I have had enough trouble since I took it. . . . Everything seems to be conspiring to make it difficult for me. . . ."[19] However, he remained optimistic, especially about the success of his livestock project. This abrupt transformation to a gentleman farmer and pig and goat breeder, even if viewed as a temporary situation, appeared strange indeed; the mind and imagination that had created fantastic worlds in outer space was now involved in petty details of animal breeding:

ERB, Emma, and Hulbert with .22 rifles, 1921.

ERB on patio at Tarzana Ranch, wearing a toupee that he finally threw away, May 31, 1922.

...we now have over 250 kids and have only had four die which I think is a mighty good record ... the goat is a mighty hardy animal. I have seen them born on a cold morning after a rain, on a cold, damp ground and in a few minutes they would be up wagging their tails and trying to nurse. If pigs are anywhere near as hardy as these goats we ought to make a fortune in Berkshires. ... just with the natural increase we could start with one sow and at the end of five years have a million pigs but inasmuch as we are going at it slowly, we intend to start with only five sows and at the end of five years God knows how many we will have.[20]

His practicality did not prevent him from responding to the beauty of the ranch setting: "... as I sit in my office I am looking out across green fields and a tree dotted valley to the moun-

tains ten miles away on the opposite side. The roses are in bloom in a long winding border on either side of my driveway down the hill to the county road, and in my orchard the fruit trees are in full blossom. 250 Angora kids are kicking their heels in the corral up the canyon while their mothers are out on the grassy slopes in the mountains at the farthest end of the ranch. ..."[21]

The first signs of the Tarzana Ranch's potential seemed highly encouraging. To Bray Ed wrote, "We started shearing yesterday noon and the fleece from the first hundred goats now commences to look like real money, the first that I have seen with the exception of 34c which somebody paid for a cash meal at the ranch house. ..."[22] The fertility of the land was already demonstrated: "My beans are up, baby limas; my corn is up, Orange County Prolific; my apricots are heavy on the limbs; my new

ERB and sons with their Shetland ponies "Bud" and "Buster," about 1921.

alfalfa is also up, Hairy Peruvian. I thought some of drilling in safety razors with it. My barley is nearly all out and the binders have started on it. . . ."[23]

The ranch also provided the opportunity for Ed to return to horseback riding — an activity he had loved ever since his school days in Chicago and at Michigan Military Academy. Before departing for California he had hoped to acquire a saddle horse; in August 1918 he had met Harry M. Rubey, the new president of the National Film Corporation, who was passing through Chicago on his way to Camp Johnston in Florida for army service. Rubey offered his horse King to Ed as a present and arrangements were made to ship the animal from Fort Collins, Colorado. Rubey stressed that King "is not what I consider a 'show' horse, but a perfect type of cavalry horse. . . ."[24] Although eager to re-

ceive the animal, Ed was unwilling to expose it to injury or "unnecessary discomfort" and insisted that if it could not be shipped without danger, the whole matter should be dropped. To Rubey he wrote:

. . . I certainly have had my heart set on him ever since you told me about him, as I have never owned a thoroughly broken horse . . . write me everything that will be of interest about him . . . I should also like to know just how I should handle him, especially in regard to the proper way to put him through his various gaits. If we succeed in getting him here, I am going to try to get Jimmy Quirk to run his picture in the Photo-Play magazine with a little story. . . .[25]

Ed's love of horses and enthusiasm for riding had been passed on to his family. On October

309

ERB's series of fish ponds or water gardens; building at top left is chicken house; beyond to right is dairy barn and creamery, where Ed had cream separator and butter churn.

10, 1918, in receiving with delight the news that King had been shipped, he informed Rubey, "I have just bought a polo pony for my children and am looking forward with a great deal of pleasure to being able to ride with them. All three down to five year old Jack have been taking riding lessons and appear to take to horsemanship as a duck takes to water. . . ."

The anticipated joy in owning the saddle horse King was not to be realized; the bad news arrived a week later. King had disappeared, apparently stolen. Rubey later wrote, ". . . we have located him and will try very hard to have him shipped as soon as we can get possession of him. . . ."[26] Possibly because of the confusion of the war period, the horse was never sent to Tarzana.

By the following year riding had become an important part of the family life. The children had their own saddle ponies, and even Emma had taken up the sport. Ed offered his friend Robert Lay details of the activities: "Emma rode yesterday for the first time in the morning and again after supper at night, and did very well indeed. I managed by accident to get just the sort of a horse for her — a well-broken, gentle, easy-gaited mare and yet who has plenty of pep or rather, plenty of willingness to go. Emma's horse and mine would not win any blue ribbons at the New York horse show but they are very much what we want out here."[27]

Ed's happiness with the ranch, and his view that his whole life now seemed under a kind of Tarzan "spell," was expressed in his letter of May 8, 1919, to Bert Weston: ". . . We eat and sleep Tarzan. . . . The dog is named Tarzan, the place is Tarzana. . . ." But an unnamed man, mentioned in the same letter, appeared to have the mystic qualities of a soothsayer who was envisioning the shape of things to come: ". . . a

ERB riding with western, or stock, saddle and bridle with curb and snaffle bit with four reins.

guy bobbed up day before yesterday with the plan of a whole village he wished to plant in my front yard — school, city hall, banks, business houses, motion picture theater — and it was labelled City of Tarzana, which sounds like a steamboat."[28]

In the summer of 1919 Ed acquired a new secretary, John A. Shea, a man on whom Ed would depend and whose advice he would seek. Also in this summer the family group was augmented by the arrival of Ed's nephew, Studley Burroughs. The son of Harry and Ella, Studley, who had exhibited artistic talent from his earliest days, had been working in the field of commercial design and illustration. The visit to Tarzana resulted from tragic circumstances; Mary Becker, his wife of only two years, had died in childbirth on April 22, 1919. On the verge of a breakdown, Studley, leaving his infant daughter in the care of his parents, accepted Ed's invitation to stay temporarily at the Tarzana Ranch. Golfing was his favorite hobby, and at the ranch he aided Ed in laying out a nine-hole golf course; Studley also designed a special golf scorecard.[29] He spent less than a year at Tarzana. In March 1920 he received the news that his daughter Margaret Mary, only a year old, was seriously ill with spinal meningitis. His hasty return to Chicago was too late — the child had died.[30]

Studley, who in later years was to illustrate a number of the Burroughs novels, used his artistic skill to create an unusual ex libris (bookplate), devised especially for Ed's personal books. Designed in the period of 1916-20, the bookplate attracted a great deal of attention from Burroughs readers and collectors. The ex libris, quite large (4 inches high by 2¼ inches wide), was described by Studley Burroughs in a letter to Ed:

The central figure is Tarzan, embraced by one of his apes (Kala perhaps) and upholding the Planet Mars, which can be easily identified by its two moons, the Greater and the Lesser. (Not being a landscape artist I omitted the canals.

They are the only things I think I have omitted.)

The pen crossed with the sword indicate what I believe to be your two chief interests at this date. The laurel wreath, of course, depicts a degree of fame.

In the crest below I have symbolized the four most pronounced epics of your career, starting with your days in the Cavalry, and following, in order, your life in the West, your return to the more civilized East, and lastly, your advent in the world of books, magazines, et al. (If anything of moment occurred before this, it was prior to our acquaintance.)

In the panel behind Tarzan may be found my conception of the characters in some of your other bully-good stories.[31]

Ed, who became a bookplate collector at a future period, was pleased to send copies of his own ex libris to those who had the same hobby. He was careful to interpret his bookplate and to provide details about the four objects contained in the crest: "The shield in the lower left hand corner represents what my nephew conceived to be four important epochs of my life — my interest in military affairs being symbolized by the cavalry boot and spur, the cow's skull representing my experience as a cowboy, the automobile wheel my interest in motoring, and the open volume my love of books."[32]

In the winter of 1918, concerned about the Bolshevik revolution in Russia, Ed considered using a fictional approach to alert the public to the menace of communism. It was his first demonstration of the intense dislike and fear of communism that he would display for many years. On December 4, in an inquiry to the Department of Justice, Ed spoke of "the Bolschevik movement . . . an organized effort to spread these doctrines throughout the world for the disruption of existing forms of government." He maintained that if the Bolsheviks were successful, the result would be an end to "all commercial and social progress" with the world being precipitated into "a period similar to that

EX·LIBRIS

ELGAR·RICE
BURROUGHS

ERB's ex-libris, designed by nephew Studley O. Burroughs, depicting main elements of ERB's interests and life work.

which followed the decadence of Greek and Roman civilization." He then explained the fiction he was planning:

I have in mind a novel of the future showing conditions one or two hundred years from now, presupposing a world-wide adoption of Bolshevikism. It is not my expectation to write anything that will revolutionize public opinion as my stories are primarily for entertainment, but if I could obtain information on the I.W.W. movement here and also Bolchevik literature which would permit me to write more intelligently on the aims and practices of these parties, it might be that my story would be of value in setting people to thinking of the results which must follow the continued dissemination of this type of propaganda.[33]

On December 6 a response came from a Mr. Clabaugh of the Department of Justice: ". . . Personally, I seriously question the advisability of confining an article, or series of articles, to the subject to which you refer, as it may do more harm than good. . . ." but Ed, a day later, irked by the rejection, offered a frosty reply: ". . . I doubt if my fiction would be taken seriously enough to do any harm and the only possible value it could have outside of entertainment might be to suggest a line of thought inimical to anarchistic tendencies."

Obviously, Clabaugh's negative attitude could have no effect in dissuading Ed from his project; his alarm over the events in Russia and the actions of the IWW's at home drove him to the task. In a sense, he felt that he was fulfilling a patriotic duty. The story, written April 30 to May 21, 1919, was titled "Under the Red Flag." Its record was a dismal one: during 1919-20 it received a string of rejections from various magazines including *Cosmopolitan, All-Story, Saturday Evening Post,* and *Red Book.* Differing reasons were given; Editor Harriman of *Red Book* referred to "the difficulty . . . of 'Under the Red Flag' . . . which goes far into the future in defining the reaction at that time from a present condition. Somehow, we feel we are serving the country best by allowing our anti-Bolshevik fiction to be reflective sharply of the present instant."[34] Ray Long, on the other hand, noted that the story sounded "too confoundedly impossible" and added, "It was not because of the writing so much as it was because of the subject. In spite of all we know about what Bolshevism does and has done, it seems incredible that anything of this sort could happen to America. . . . plausibility. . . . That's what it seemed to me to lack."[35]

From Bob Davis came another reason for rejection; he contended that the "chief difficulty with 'Under the Red Flag' was its appalling justification." His opinion was that people would benefit by the story, but that "the Pharasees would raise hell with any magazine that resorted to fiction designed to point out the obvious truths." Stirring up the populace, he explained, wasn't either good ethics or good business for magazines; this was the job of the daily press.[36] None of these reasons proved convincing to Ed. In fact, he believed that the editors were reluctant to reveal the truth and were offering subterfuges instead. It was almost as though there were a tacit conspiracy to prevent the publication of a story that was too controversial, too hot to handle. On September 24, 1919, he commented in exasperation to Joseph Bray, "I managed to get an expression from two well known editors and I find that it was not the fact that they didn't like the story but that they were afraid of the effect it would have on the public mind. Personally I think it is ridiculous to believe that a story showing the unpleasant consequences of Bolshevist rule would do any harm." He added, ". . . I intend to try and find somebody to publish it even if I have to publish it at my own expense, as I am personally sore that none of the magazines would take it for such a silly reason."[37]

The past dealings with William Parsons in the production of *Tarzan of the Apes* and the unauthorized second film *The Romance of Tarzan* had increased the caution and skepticism that Burroughs exhibited in re-sponding to all proposals from producers. Yet, in this early period of the film industry, the producers who contacted him were mainly men operating on a shoestring, whose schemes were always the same: they hoped to acquire a Tarzan story, form a company, and then seek capital. Although aware of this procedure, Ed could do little but resign himself to it.

Beginning in May 1918 and continuing for several years, Ed found himself the middle man in a complicated series of film transactions that for manipulation and connivance made all past motion picture projects seem simple and straightforward. Under a barrage of letters from Pliny P. Craft of Monopol Pictures, New York, who was eager to produce *The Return of Tarzan,* Ed's resistance finally weakened. Nevertheless, he was supercautious in clarifying every detail and requirement. On August 5, 1918, he stressed the existing situation, that two films had been made from *Tarzan of the Apes,* the second one ready for September release. Then he stipulated what the contract must contain: a clause confining production to *The Return of Tarzan* only; a financial arrangement similar to that made with Parsons — $50,000 worth of stock, five percent of the gross receipts and a $5,000 cash advance on royalties; and "some voice in the direction of the production." Other provisions, added on August 11, included a request that Ed be employed as co-director, that a maximum of about thirty percent be paid for distribution, and that if two pictures were to be made from *The Return of Tarzan,* the contract must so state, and "reasonable time limits" must be established for the second picture.

With all this agreed upon, and with his salary as assistant director set at $5,000, Ed signed the contract on September 21. Craft's new company was to be called the Apex Picture Corporation. His attempt to change this to Tarzan Pictures Corporation was firmly rejected by Burroughs who noted, ". . . this name is worth more to me than the picture rights to any of the Tarzan stories."[38]

Seemingly all problems had been anticipated; Ed had taken extreme care to avoid any of the difficulties he had encountered with

Parsons. But trouble began at once. With the showing of *The Romance of Tarzan* in theaters, Craft dispatched a threatening letter to the First National Distributors claiming that this picture infringed upon the rights contained in his contract for *The Return of Tarzan*. Craft's claim was that the movie duplicated scenes found in this book. Parsons, upon notification of the supposed conflict, and apparently frightened, arranged for a payment of $3,000 to Craft. Ed's first awareness of the situation was when Parsons, incredibly, wrote to demand that this money be repaid to him.

With Ed now receiving angry demands and accusations from Craft — ". . . how you became induced to authorize the release of the picture, [*The Romance of Tarzan*] under the circumstances, is more than I can understand," the quarrel became increasingly bitter. Inevitably, the lawyers entered the dispute, Harry G. Kosch of New York representing Craft, and Ed using his old firm of Mayer, Meyer, Austrian & Platt in Chicago. Craft's compromise suggestion, based upon his claim that *The Return of Tarzan*, because of Parson's infringement on the plot, had lost most of its movie value, was that Ed should offer him a contract for the balance of the Tarzan stories.[39] On January 6, 1919, Ed proposed his own compromise which Craft reluctantly accepted. Ed wrote: "If you produce a successful Tarzan picture and otherwise fulfill the terms of our present agreement I agree not to dispose of the picture rights to subsequent Tarzan stories until you have had a reasonable opportunity to accept or reject them."

Concerning *The Beasts of Tarzan*, Craft's opinion was that the story could not be produced as a film, but that some of the incidents might be combined with scenes from *The Return of Tarzan* to make an additional movie. To this Ed did not agree. Surprisingly, however, he was amenable to the plan to discard the title *The Return of Tarzan*, and suggested, Tarzan of the Jungle would make a good title and could be used in connection with a subtitle

stating that it was a picturization of *The Return of Tarzan*.[40]

At an earlier period (September 13, 1918) Elmo Lincoln, who had taken the role of Tarzan in both of the Parsons films, had written to urge Ed to join with him in forming a company to produce the remaining *Tarzan* stories. Ed rejected the proposal. Lincoln later became the subject of a discussion between Craft and Burroughs. On January 25, 1919, Craft wrote, "I have made tentative arrangements with T. Hayes Hunter to direct the first picture. . . . He made the *Border Legion* which he has just released through Goldwyn Pictures Corp. I wish you would see this picture and tell me what you think of Hunter as a director. . . . Also let me know if you think Eugene Strong, who plays the lead in 'The Border Legion' would make a good 'Tarzan.' He is handsome and a real actor, but is he big enough for the part? Will the public expect to see a man as big as Elmo Lincoln? Lincoln is now working in some serial picture at the coast. I don't think he is the right man anyway."

In response, on January 28, Burroughs explained how he envisioned Tarzan as a movie character:

In the matter of a man for Tarzan, it may help you some to know that Elmo Lincoln was . . . far from my conception of the character. . . . Tarzan was not beefy but was light and graceful and well muscled. The people who could see Tarzan of the Apes and the Blacksmith of Louvain as identical characters had just about as much conception of my story and of the character as one might expect after seeing some of the atrocious things they did to the picture and the story.

He presented an image of Tarzan that was clear and definite:

In the first place Tarzan must be young and handsome with an extremely masculine face and manner. Then he must be the epitome of grace. It may be difficult to get such a man but please do not try to get a giant or a man with over-developed muscles. It is true that in the stories I often speak of Tarzan as the "giant Ape-man" but that is because I am rather prone to use superlatives. My conception of him is a man a little over six feet tall and built more like a panther than an elephant. I can give you some facial types that will give you an idea of about what I conceive Tarzan to look like though of course it is impossible to explain an ideal. I should say that his face was more the type of Tom Meighan's or Tom Forman's but not like Wallace Reid. In other words, I conceive him of having a very strong masculine face and far from a pretty one.

Burrough's opinion of Elmo Lincoln was more forcefully stated in a letter of March 27, 1922, to his brother Harry:

. . . I have told producers and directors of Tarzan pictures the very same thing that you mentioned in relation to Elmo Lincoln, in fact I have told Elmo himself upon numerous occasions that he was not my conception of Tarzan. . . .

In the letter Burroughs also commented discouragedly about the way his stories were adapted for the Tarzan movies:

The producers never read the stories, and it is only occasionally, I imagine, that the director reads them. In fact, in the making of Tarzan of the Apes, it was forbidden that anyone connected with it read the story, for fear it might influence their work and make it more difficult for the director. Little wonder then that such asinine methods produce such asinine results. As far as I know, no one connected with the making of a single Tarzan picture has had the remotest conception of either the story or the character, as I conceived it. Whatever beauty there was in the character of Tarzan or in the stories themselves, was not brought out, but the pictures paid well in boxoffice receipts, and really that is all that counts.

He matched his criticism of Elmo Lincoln with an equally disparaging opinion of the actress chosen to play Jane Porter: "Miss

Markey is not the type at all. When the time comes if you have several girls in mind and care to do so, you might send me their pictures from which I could give you an idea of the type that really most nearly represents the character as I see it."[41]

Hoping that the dispute with Craft was now settled, Ed wrote to suggest that the Tarzana Ranch could provide an ideal location for a studio. He referred to a friend, Walter Beckwith, who owned "twenty-three of the finest lions you ever saw in your life"; Beckwith was willing to bring the pride of lions to Tarzana if Ed would furnish the cages. Ed explained, ". . . with very little expense we would have a corner on the most expensive part of wild animal production . . . we would have the best lions in the world and could make more or less of a specialty of wild animal stuff."[42]

Any illusion that Craft's grievances were forgotten or, for that matter, that Burroughs was satisfied with the progress of *The Return of Tarzan,* was abruptly dispelled. Burroughs, upon reading the scenario, complained irritably that it bore little resemblance to his story. As in the past, the reasons scenario writers made these drastic changes and deletions baffled him; this familiar practice, which he viewed as outright mutilation of an author's work, was followed because of purely selfish motives: ". . . the only explanation is that unless they do make changes there would be no reason for their employment at a high salary. . . . they have kidded some of you producers into believing that these changes are necessary. . . ."[43]

Unexpectedly, Craft abandoned all attempts at reconciliation, returned angrily to the supposed infringement of *The Romance of Tarzan,* demanded that Burroughs waive his salary of $5,000 as assistant director, and as further compensation, give him a contract for *The Son of Tarzan.*[44] Burroughs' response to Craft, then in Los Angeles, was curt: ". . . talk with my attorney, Mr. Oscar Lawler, for I have had about all the trouble and annoyance on account of motion picture producing that I care to have."[45]

From June 1919 on, the Burroughs-Craft relationship continued in an unbelievable sequence of bickerings, wild threats by Craft, and lawyers' communications. It was only fitting that in the midst of the confusion, Craft should perform the most astonishing action of all. On September 23 he notified Burroughs that he had assigned *The Return of Tarzan* to Numa Film Corporation, a New York outfit headed by Louis Weiss; the corporation was newly formed for the purpose of producing a *Tarzan* movie.[46] Burroughs' exasperation with Craft was further extended into a lesser area. In a moment of mistaken confidence he had given Craft the die which was used for making The Tribe of Tarzan medals. The indignant Burroughs discovered that Craft was freely distributing the medals to boys, contrary to the tribal rules that these medals must be earned. To Burroughs, the idealistic, high-minded purpose of the organization was important. About the boys, on June 9 he wrote to Craft, "They have to win a membership in the Tribe before they are entitled to a medal, and why I should have been so thoughtless as to let you have the die without explaining this to you, I do not know."[47] The value Burroughs placed upon the Tribe was more than matched by the devotion of its founder, Herman Newman of Staunton, Virginia. Upon returning from the war in France, Newman went to Oak Park to look for Burroughs, and not finding him there, traveled to California to Tarzana Ranch.[48]

The sudden death of William Parsons on September 28, 1919, ended the three-way squabble about the conflict between *The Romance of Tarzan* and the projected *Return of Tarzan*.[49] But this did nothing to change the altercation between Craft and Burroughs. Upon the precondition that he "satisfactorily" complete *The Return of Tarzan*, Craft had been given an option on *The Son of Tarzan* until July 1, 1919. With the failure to fulfill the terms, Ed sold *The Son of Tarzan* to The National Film Corporation. From then on Craft continued his harassing actions, dispatching a series of threats to both Burroughs and National Film, attempting to interfere with movie production, and trying to sell his "rights" to D. W. Griffith in Hollywood; his contact there was Elmo Lincoln.[50] Unsuccessful in this effort, he filed a lawsuit against Burroughs, and soon after publicized his plan to form the Tantor Picture Corporation, with its first production to be a fifteen-episode serial titled *The Adventures of Tarzan*. An announcement read, "The new serial . . . will contain new features of unusual interest, chief among these, the casting of Bull Montana as chief of the ape clan. Production will be on the coast."[51]

Craft's lawsuit prompted Ed to hire New York attorney Benjamin H. Stern (Stern & Rubens), but it shortly became apparent that Craft's daring had no limit. On March 10, 1921, *Wid's Daily,* a New York publication, broadcast a full-page ad announcing, in huge black print, "The Real Tarzan is Coming." The film was listed as "The Adventures of Tarzan," and at the bottom of the page, in equally bold type, appeared the amazing affront: "Tarzan Film Company." Traced to a small office in New York through the efforts of a detective, Craft was evasive, but it became evident that these were his latest harassing tactics; the records revealed that no company of this name had been organized.[52]

The legal preparations by Stern & Rubens for the forthcoming court trial brought further contention to the existing film disputes. On December 29, 1921, Ed reacted with anger and outrage to the bill for $1,000 sent to him by the law firm. He wrote bluntly, "I think you have charged me a great deal too much and I am frank in saying that I cannot afford you. I hope it will develop that a mistake was made in this charge, which seems to me fully four times what it ought to be." In reply, Stern & Rubens insisted their charge was reasonable in view of the fact that Craft was suing for $100,000 and that the defense had involved considerable labor and time.[53] Unmollified, Ed noted, "I am no better off than I would have been had I not retained you"; he at once severed his connection with the firm.[54] Actually, Ed's dissatisfaction with Stern

& Rubens may have developed during a long series of communications with Craft and his attorney. In a letter Stern & Rubens had hinted that Ed might settle for a few hundred dollars in order to save the trouble and expense of a New York trial. Ed had been adamant in stating that he would not pay Craft a cent.[55]

The legal affairs were now transferred to Clarence E. Pitts, with the New York law firm of Clark, Prentice & Roulstone, and through their intercession, Ruben & Stern's fee was settled for $500. From then on matters moved quickly. Notified on January 13, 1923, that the case had been placed on the calendar, and that he should plan to be in New York in February, Ed, on the sixteenth, asked for a postponement until spring: ". . . physician advises against my going before April or May." When his lawyers indicated that a doctor's affidavit would be needed, Ed, anxious to have the case ended, changed his mind, arriving in New York on February 18. The action was decidedly anticlimactic. On February 28 the case was dismissed "on merits." Thus the almost four years of charges, threats, and demands were finally halted.

Other film negotiations, while not as complex, followed a similar pattern of bickerings, extensions of time, production failures, and transferences of contracts. The assignment of The Return of Tarzan to Numa Pictures Corporation, headed by Louis Weiss, with the attorney Harry Kosch as secretary, September 1919, brought no tangible result until the spring of 1920. On April 28 Weiss notified Burroughs that the world rights to the completed film had been sold to Goldwyn Distributing Corporation, with the agreement calling for a $100,000 advance and a percentage basis. Numa Pictures, previously granted the privilege of making a second film from The Return of Tarzan, now began dickering with Burroughs on this one. For the fifteen-episode serial the titles of "Adventures of Tarzan" and "Exploits of Tarzan" were suggested; Burroughs preferred the first title.[56]

The matter of a title for the full-length movie to be distributed by Goldwyn, and assumed to be The Return of Tarzan, became a subject of dispute. On June 15, 1920, Numa Pictures wired, "Exhibitors throughout Country under impression Return of Tarzan is reissue. Upon consultation with Goldwyn executives have found it advisable to change title to Revenge of Tarzan. Wire immediately your approval or whether you have better suggestion." Burrough's refusal was prompt: "Cannot approve change of title Return of Tarzan. If McClurg's estimate ten million (10,000,000) Tarzan book readers correct, it would be poor policy to ignore this advantage and the greater millions of newspapers and magazine Tarzan readers." In response, Numa Pictures stressed that the change was "for financial benefit of all concerned," explained that they wanted to attract both the movie public and the book public, and stated firmly, "Using title Revenge of Tarzan adapted from Edgar Rice Burroughs' famous book Return of Tarzan."[57]

Burroughs, equally adamant, wired back, on June 18, "Regret must insist title Return of Tarzan stand unchanged. My professional and financial interests demand this. Suggest you use title "Return of Tarzan, a New Tarzan Story by Edgar Rice Burroughs, Author of Tarzan of the Apes." In the actions that followed, his objection to the new title was ignored. Although Numa Pictures had earlier taken a full-page ad in The Moving Picture World (December 6, 1919), extolling the new film The Return of Tarzan, a later ad informed the trade that "All posters, mats, cuts and other accessories have been changed to read The Revenge of Tarzan," and on July 20, 1920, the film was released under that title.

The Revenge of Tarzan, directed by Harry Revier, featured Gene Pollar, a brawny, 200-pound New York City fireman as Tarzan, and Karla Schramm as Jane. Other roles from the novel included D'Arnot, Franklin Coates; Clayton, Walter Miller; Paulvitch, Louis Stearns; and Countess de Coude, Estelle Taylor.

ERB and children visiting set of The Son of Tarzan, *1920.*

Burroughs again experienced the discouragement of having the movie bear little resemblance to the story.

In dealings with The National Film Corporation through its president Harry M. Rubey, Ed, on September 6, 1919, had agreed to write the synopsis of a fifteen-episode serial based upon *The Son of Tarzan.* After the customary wrangling during which National Film cancelled its option to purchase four of the Burroughs books and decided to concentrate upon *The Son of Tarzan,* Rubey, on November 14, signed the agreement requiring completion of the film in one year. At the end of the year Rubey formed a financial partnership with distributor David P. Howells. Ed had been paid a total of $20,000, but in the arrangements that followed, the plan to have him write the scenario was apparently dropped. Upon reading the synopses of episodes in progress, Ed, as usual, protested the unwarranted changes and made specific suggestions which, also as usual, received little attention.

A further protest by Ed related to the failure to provide the personal publicity that had been promised. In viewing the "leader" for *The Son of Tarzan,* he was dubious about its publicity value, reminding Rubey, on June 14, 1920, of the paragraph in the contract which stated, ". . . the name 'Edgar Rice Burroughs' to appear as author, in letters as large as the letters of any other printed matter therein, and immediately beneath said name shall cause the words, 'Author of Tarzan of the Apes, A Princess of Mars, etc.' . . . ." A week later, Ed, irritated, wrote again to protest the content and make-up of the two-page ad in *The Moving Picture World* of June 15. He objected both to

Roy Somerville, script writer, and ERB on movie set of The Son of Tarzan, *1920.*

320

the unauthorized statement that world rights to *The Son of Tarzan* were controlled by David P. Howells and also to the fact that, once more, his name was not appearing in print as the agreement stipulated. Howells quickly forwarded an apology and a promise to see that future publicity would provide the proper emphasis to the Burroughs name.

Produced in the west coast studios of National Film, with Revier once more directing, *The Son of Tarzan*, a fifteen-episode serial, was a long time in the making, not completed until January 1921. Publicity releases stressed that the film had been very costly because two sets of players were used, one to appear in a prologue which depicted important past events from Tarzan's life. His romance was portrayed, and the prologue contains a scene in which Tarzan and Jane, in England, are married by a minister. The story then continues with Tarzan's son, Korak, then assuming the main role. His part was taken by Kamuela C. Searle, a Hawaiian actor, and others in the cast included P. Dempsey Tabler, Tarzan; Karla Schramm, Jane; Eugene Burr, Paulvitch; Mae Giraci, Meriem as a girl; Manilla Martin, Meriem as a woman; and Gordon Griffith, who had played the young *Tarzan of the Apes* in the 1918 film, now cast in a brief role as ten-year-old Jack.

During the production of *The Son of Tarzan* the actors faced unusual dangers. Tabler and Burr received broken ribs when a rowboat capsized; Mae Giraci was bruised when attacked by an ape; Roy Somerville, who had adapted the story for the screen, had a narrow escape from death; and with the filming of the serial almost at end, an unfortunate accident led to a tragedy. Kamuela Searle, handled too roughly by the elephant that was carrying him, sustained injuries which resulted in his death.

Ed, who was present often on the set while the movie was in production, found himself included in a special scene. In a letter of August 29, 1921, Enzo Archetti, a fan from New Jersey, commented on seeing Burroughs on a "wild horse," explaining, ". . . before they began

the serial from where it left off the week before, it showed you on a wild, bucking broncho. I think you were 'breaking' it. Am I right?" On September 9 Ed responded:

You are quite wrong in assuming that I have a wild horse. As a matter of fact the director and cameraman played rather a mean trick on me. The Colonel is a very beautiful horse in action, but the cameraman turned the camera so slowly that when the picture is shown on the screen it makes the horse appear to be going up and down very rapidly like a rocking horse or a jumping jack. I tried to insist that they take it out of the picture and they promised to do so but failed to keep their promise. . . .

In the fall of 1920 Ed once more experienced the familiar experiences of working with a film company — this time Numa Pictures. The Weiss brothers, Louis and Adolph, were now in control, with attorney Harry Kosch still retained as treasurer. The maneuvers led to arrangements for Great Western Producing Company, a west coast organization, to produce the next scheduled movie — *The Adventures of Tarzan,* with Elmo Lincoln assigned the major role.[58] Publicity for the film, completed in August 1921, advertised it as "picturized" from the concluding chapters of *The Return of Tarzan.* With Robert F. Hill as director, the cast included Louise Lorraine, only sixteen years old, as Jane; Lillian Worth as Queen La of Opar; and Frank Whitson as the villainous Rokoff.

Probably within the period 1920-22 Burroughs wrote a scenario titled "The Savage Breast"; it remained unsold, but two years later he forwarded it to his former secretary John Shea, then associated with William Sistrom at the Hollywood Studios. Sistrom was looking for inexpensive story material for film purposes. At that time, May 1924, Shea returned "The Savage Breast," and on the eighth Burroughs remarked:

You probably remember when I wrote it, and why, and realize as well as I that it is a hack-

On set of Adventures of Tarzan, *1921; left to right: Emma Burroughs, Frank Merrill (who played the role of Tarzan in two later pictures), Elmo Lincoln (who played Tarzan), ERB, and Louise Lorraine (who played Jane).*

neyed subject and none too well done at that, a fact which I knew Mr. Sistrom would realize as soon as he read it, but it was something that I could sell cheap, and that was what I figured you wanted for these four program pictures. . . .

The scenario "The Savage Breast" has apparently disappeared, and there is no information about its plot or characterization.

In March 1920 Ed's dealings with Curtis Brown Ltd., his British agent, brought a new offer, one to dramatize *Tarzan of the Apes* for stage presentation in England. After correspondence with C. B. Fernald of Curtis Brown's London office, Ed, on May 10, signed a contract with Arthur Gibbons for the production of *Tarzan*. Gibbons and Arthur Carlton were

both involved in the enterprise, with Major Herbert Woodgate assigned the task of adapting the novel for the stage. Ed accepted the contract reluctantly, influenced by Curtis Brown's recommendation, and noted that it was against his "better judgement" since he knew nothing about Gibbons or his plans. He also agreed, with some hesitation, to allow the dramatist to use several incidents from *The Return of Tarzan*. The financial arrangements required a $1,000 payment and royalties of ten percent, but problems at once arose with Gibbons seeking a reduction in royalties in the event the play was presented at the Lyceum in London. This request Ed rejected.

The plans called for *Tarzan of the Apes* to be given a trial run in the provinces before the play was brought to London, and on October 4 it opened for a two-week stay at Brixton. Gibbons had ten weeks' bookings to follow at other suburban theaters. At the Brixton opening, as reported by Curtis Brown, the audience was highly enthusiastic: "The jungle scenes were effective and proved distinctly to the taste of the audience. The parts of Tarzan and Kala were both played extremely well, Kala being particularly good."

In the play, with its prologue and four acts, the background and early events of the novel were developed. Surprisingly, Tarzan, age ten, was played by a young girl — Gwen Evans. Actors took the ape roles, Leon Du Bois playing Kerchak, the bull ape, and Edward Sillward in the part of Kala, the she-ape. They both continued their roles when the prologue ended, and the major section of the play presented Ronald Adair as Tarzan and Ivy Carlton as Jane. Adair appeared to be well-chosen for the difficult enactment of a live "stage" Tarzan.

On December 14 Ed was notified that the tour of *Tarzan of the Apes* in England would end that week, but that one performance of the play had been scheduled for London on Boxing Day, the day following Christmas. However, arrangements for this performance fell through, and *Tarzan* was never staged in London. The limited success of the play did not discourage Gibbons from proposing a contract for the production of *The Son of Tarzan*; the financial terms were the same, and Ed, on February 4, 1921, cabled his agreement.

Meanwhile, confusing on-again, off-again notices concerning *Tarzan of the Apes* were being dispatched. The play continued irregularly until June and was then halted because of the "industrial unrest. . . strikes and restricted transport" which hampered business and theatrical activities in England. Gibbons and Carlton still had plans to produce the play in London in the fall of 1921. At that time *Tarzan* made its debut on the New York stage, opening September 1 at the Broadhurst Theater, forty-fourth street and Broadway in New York. The advertised "Dramatic Version" presented by George Broadhurst was in four acts and ten episodes, with British authors Woodgate and Gibbons listed, and with staging by Mrs. Trim-

ble Bradley. Members of the original British cast included Ronald Adair as Tarzan and Edward Sillward as Kala. Lady Greystoke was played by Alice Mosely, and Ethel Dwyer took the part of Jane. The play became more daring than the British version; Broadhurst had real lions on stage — two of them. Jim, the original Tarzan lion, and Beauty, the lioness, were noted as playing "silent but active parts."

The play, in its New York performance, found the public and critics unenthusiastic; its run was brief. To Bray, on September 20, Ed commented about the telegram he had received from George Broadhurst, which stated "the stage version of Tarzan of the Apes is a complete failure and that they are withdrawing it." Ed wrote:

From the newspaper criticisms which I received today I judge that there was no reflection upon the story and that it will do the books no harm. Most of the critics seem to think that the impossible has been attempted and I rather imagine they are right. However, it has been well received in England although it has never played in the West End of London. Broadhurst tells me that he believes he can send out a condensed version on the vaudeville circuit and personally I think it is better adapted to that than to the drama.

Astonishingly, for an author who had set high standards for a serious film production of *Tarzan*, Ed added, "My idea of a paying proposition for the stage based on Tarzan would be a real, honest-to-God Burlesque."

On October 19, in reporting that *Tarzan* was a failure in New York, the Curtis Brown office sent an evaluation:

From the accounts we have had of the production, it seems that it was an adequate one and the play was well cast, but in spite of that the play only ran a short time and all the returns have been sent to you. I am afraid there is little chance of the play going on the road as George Broadhurst feels that the production has shown it is not likely to appeal to American audiences. . . .

Ed's suggestion and apparent approval of an "honest-to-God Burlesque" was hardly an idea that the British producers would have endorsed. In an amusing 1921 sidelight in England, Gibbons and Carlton brought a court action against Dick Mortimer for his sketch, obviously a burlesque or parody of Tarzan, presented at the Victoria Palace in London. The sketch, titled "Warzan and his Apes," featured a cast of a man with a loin cloth, two actors dressed as apes, a pseudo-lion and a "property" baby. The jungle setting consisted of artificial trees and shrubbery. Certain scenes, copied from Tarzan, were done in "dumb show."

Lawton, the attorney for the defendant Dick Mortimer, maintained that the sketch had first been produced in Paris in 1914 and had been running in various music halls since then. Mortimer, an acrobatic gymnast for twenty years, had played the "Tarzan" role in the original Paris sketch. Unbelievably for a British trial, which is expected to be dignified and sedate, this trial, with Justice Avery presiding, was transformed into a burlesque more hilarious than the *Tarzan* sketch. The jokes of Lawton about Tarzan and apes brought rounds of laughter from the spectators, and Justice Avery appeared to enjoy the comic atmosphere. An example of this type of humor was displayed in the cross-examination of the actor who played the role of the she-ape. When the counsel for the plaintiff asked him if he had read the original story, Lawton interposed, "How could he read the manuscript if he is an ape?"

During discussions of the story, a number of references were made to "niggers," and it was revealed that in certain performances of the music hall sketch the "niggers" had been changed in color from black to red because of rumored dangers of race riots. Justice Avery, who had commented that a burlesque might be helpful to the *Tarzan* drama and might "improve the reputation of the original," finally made a decision, to nobody's surprise, in favor of the defendant with no order as to costs. His ruling was based mainly upon the evidence that the sketch had been playing in music halls for at least six years prior to the stage presentation.

In the same years, from 1919 on, legal problems based upon Ed's relationship with William G. Chapman and his International Press Bureau provided additional complications. Chapman had handled some Burroughs newspaper syndications and had also been involved in the submission of *Tarzan of the Apes* to McClurg for publication. The book had been sold entirely through Ed's efforts and through his dealings with Joseph Bray. However, because Chapman had been consulted, Ed agreed to pay him commissions on the royalties of *Tarzan of the Apes* books sold in the United States. Now, Chapman claimed he was entitled to the newly opened foreign rights; to Bray he had insisted that all rights belonged to him and that all arrangements should be handled through him. On May 12, 1919, Bray commented to Ed about Chapman's limited assistance in the past: "It seems to me that he has done pretty well out of 'Tarzan of the Apes.' He has made considerably over one thousand dollars for bringing the manuscript here one morning which we had already practically expressed our willingness to publish."

Ed, noting that he was already paying commissions to Curtis Brown Ltd. on all foreign sales and to McClurg for British sales, refused to pay a further commission to Chapman. There was confusion as to whether Chapman had actually been promised or given some commissions by McClurg's before December 1920. The quarrel inevitably wound up in the hands of lawyers, with Mayer, Meyer, Austrian & Platt defending Burroughs, and Beach & Beach representing Chapman. During years of claims and counterclaims nothing was resolved. Ed, never one to yield or compromise when a principle was involved, refused to settle for a sum of $1800. The trial was finally set for June 1, 1926, in Chicago. Reluctant to appear, Burroughs wrote gloomily to Carl Meyer, "In the first place, I am an extremely poor witness. My memory is very faulty, and I have been in an extremely nervous condition for so long that I am inclined to be rather excitable, so that I make as much of a botch as a witness as I do a dinner speaker, which I can assure you is some botch."[59]

Resigned to the trial, Ed arrived in Chicago on May 29. He had indicated that he might consider a settlement if Chapman relinquished past and future rights to all *Tarzan* enterprises, including drama, films, and newspapers. This was agreed to, and since some compromise was inevitable, Chapman's claims were satisfied through a moderate payment, with the trial ended in its preliminary stages.

A life crowded with business activities — moving his family to California, running the ranch at Tarzana, raising livestock, negotiating with movie producers, and facing legal entanglements — still could not prevent Burroughs from working on new stories. In May 1918, while still in Oak Park, with the war almost ended, he conceived of a Tarzan story based upon the campaign against the Germans in Africa. The influence of anti-German propaganda upon him was strong; his view of German behavior as subhuman and his belief in the atrocity reports were unchanged. With the story in mind he sought information from Bray about published works describing the war in Africa, and at the same time he made contemptuous reference to the German's colonial record.

On May 29 Bray replied that he could find only one book, *Marching on Tonga,* which he was sending, and noted that official accounts of the British government might be available. Concerning the African hostilities, Bray noted, ". . . it would be rather difficult to make much of the campaign, for the Germans were outnumbered I think in every engagement and I do not know of any dramatic happenings. Should you write such a story it seems to me I would use the war merely as a background, and not make too much of it." Bray revealed his calm objectivity in countering Ed's low opinion of the Germans: "My impression is that, except for that excessive veneration for the Fatherland which seems to obsess most Germans, the German colonies in Africa have a pretty good record. Their neighbors did not like them because a German colony simply means the transporting of a bit of Germany to another land. . . ."

Ed, not at all persuaded, disagreed about the "pretty good record" of the Germans and wrote, with some attempt at humor:

. . . although I know nothing about the Germans in Africa, I have learned enough about the Germans in the last four years to know that there aint no such thing as a good German record. Having reveled in hate for the last four years, I should dislike to give up the pleasure derived therefrom by thinking any good thoughts whatever about Germans. Therefore if I write this story, I shall put the wickedest kind of Germans into it and let Tarzan chew their hearts out.[60]

As future events would demonstrate, Ed made a mistake in not adopting Bray's more moderate attitude toward the Germans.

Influenced by the success of the *Tarzan* short stories he had sold to *Red Book*, and the good prices he had obtained, Ed decided to produce the African war stories in a similar sequence. On October 7, 1918, Ray Long tentatively agreed to a series of twelve Tarzan stories, with payment of $450 each for the first six and $500 each for the rest. The story total was later reduced to ten, and at a conference Long suggested that the war background be eliminated. Ed was reluctant to make the change to ten stories; his goal of about 100,000 words was of course based upon plans for a future novel. Nevertheless, he agreed to the reduction, while refusing to accede to the request for a different setting. On October 18 he wrote to Long, ". . . sending you the first of the Tarzan and the Huns stories." He completed five in 1918, and by January 1919 before leaving for California, had sent six stories to *Red Book* Magazine. These appeared serially in *Red Book* in the issues of March to August 1919. The goal of ten stories was never attained. The seventh story, finished at Tarzana Ranch on September

10, 1919, titled "Tarzan and the Valley of Luna," was rejected by *Red Book* and *Cosmopolitan* and wound up in the pages of *All-Story*, appearing serially in the five weekly issues of March 20 through April 17, 1920. All seven of the stories were combined as the book "Tarzan the Untamed," published by McClurg on April 30, 1920.[61]

In the first story, "An Eye for an Eye," Ed disconcerted his readers by creating the apparent murder of Jane by the sadistic German officer Hauptman Fritz Schneider. The scene at the Greystokes' African estate is one of death and destruction, with burned buildings and slaughtered blacks. Here Tarzan recognizes the body of his beloved Jane with the familiar rings still on her fingers. Ed's plan had actually been to have Jane killed, but protests from Bray and Long, and particularly from his wife Emma, forced him to change his mind. To Bert Weston, on May 10, 1920, he wrote:

. . . I left Jane dead up to the last gasp and then my publisher and the magazine editor rose up on their hind legs and roared. They said the public would not stand for it as I was having Tarzan fall in love with Bertha, so I had to resurrect the dear lady. After seeing Enid Markey take the part of Jane in the first Tarzan picture I was very glad to kill her.

It appeared that Ed followed Bray's suggestion on sparing Jane; Bray had urged, "Have her apparently dead if you want to and let Tarzan think that she is dead; however, bring her back in the last chapter and have Tarzan go home and find her in the old place. . . ."[62] In response to Ed's query about the fate of Jane, Bob Davis wired, "Think Bray right" and then wrote, "I think it a good idea to let Mrs. Tarzan survive"; he joked about Ed's creation of the ape-man: "You unchained this damned monkey in a thoughtless moment and now the organ-grinding-son-of-a-gun climbs in the window and chews the rag on the foot-board. When you die and go to hell a delegation of pithecanthropus erectus will greet you at the gate and pick the cooties from your low receding brow."[63]

In *Tarzan the Untamed*, from the very beginning, Burroughs reveals his detestation of the Germans and their "Kultur" as he describes the "cruel wounds and bruises" upon the bodies of the helpless native porters. After the supposed death of Jane, Tarzan embarks upon a spree of revenge against the Germans; imprisoning a lion in a narrow gulch, he confines a German major in the same spot, where he will be devoured by the starved beast. He also accomplishes the feat of forcing a huge lion into the German trenches, and as the trapped soldiers fight madly to escape, "Numa, a terrific incarnation of ferocity and ravenous hunger," leaps upon them, "rending with talons and fangs." Later, Tarzan kills both the men he blames for his wife's death — Underlieutenant von Goss and Hauptman Schneider. The remainder of the novel then departs from the anti-German revenge theme and presents typical Burroughs devices — encounters with hostile blacks and the discovery of a walled city peopled by maniacs whose main deity is the parrot. A romance develops between British Lieutenant Smith-Oldwick and Bertha Kircher, whom Tarzan is forced to protect, although he believes her to be a German spy.

In "The Black Flyer," published in *Red Book*, August 1919, Ed had contrived a scene in which the savage Usanga is taught to fly an aeroplane by Smith-Oldwick. This scene brought a severely critical letter from First Lieutenant Karl de V. Fastenau, stationed with the Air Forces at Wilbur Wright Depot in Dayton, Ohio. On July 31 Fastenau remarked about the "absolute absurdity of Tarzan's latest 'stunt,' " and wrote:

Let me say that I am myself a pilot with some two years experience so am fairly well qualified to criticize this last story from that viewpoint. How can you attempt to foist upon a reading public such ludicrously absurd "stuff" as, for instance, having an absolutely ignorant savage from an African jungle take off a plane after two days of "instruction" (assuming that such an aborigine were capable of receiving it), flying the plane while a man was swaying back and forth on the end of a rope attached to it, having the girl pilot the machine (again assuming that the feat of changing from the rear seat to the front seat while the poor savage was still flying the machine were at all possible), and then to cap it all to have them make a landing and "as it struck among them and mowed through them, a veritable juggernaut of destruction" still have the machine in perfect condition . . . so that the other two characters could fly off.

Fastenau implored, "For God's sake, man, have a heart. It is all so ridiculous that it is really amusing. . . . Your practical knowledge of airplanes and flying is a little less than nil. Stick to your jungle stuff of which you seem to really know but for 'the love of Mike' if you must spring anything so clearly out of your line go out and get a little rudimentary information on the subject first." Fastenau commented, "You are 'getting by' with quite a lot as it is, don't you think?" He added, "I suppose you really are put to it grinding out a new Tarzan story every month so that you have to fill up with such stuff as that referred to for want of new material." The brief reply of August 9, sent by secretary John Shea, offered thanks to Fastenau and an assurance that Burroughs "always welcomes constructive criticism."

Another of the *Tarzan* short stories, "The Golden Locket," appearing in *Red Book*, May 1919, brought a request from William R. Kane, of *The Editor*, for an account of the genesis and development of the story. Kane, on April 25, explained his need for information that would inspire other writers, and in replying to him, rather than focusing upon "The Golden Locket," Burroughs chose to offer general suggestions about writing. He spoke of two methods he had tried, the first one based upon a "very broad and general plot" around which he extemporized, letting "one situation suggest the next." He stated, "I did not know what my characters were going to do or where the plot was heading in the next paragraph; as I was writing merely to entertain I sought to put action or the suggestion of future action into each paragraph."

The second method, in which he plotted his stories more carefully, involved a chart "covering the principal situation and action in each chapter." However, he found the chart difficult to follow, and his writing "became tedious labor" by comparison with his former method. As a result, he returned to the old plan and used it in most of his stories. Interestingly, Burroughs maintained that this system would not work if the story depended upon an "intricate" plot; he believed that in his writing, the action was of most importance and the plot was "merely . . . a simple clothes-horse upon which to hang the action." A consideration of the intricacies of some of his stories, not necessarily in plot, but especially in the lengthy gallery of characters, the complex details of equipment, and the various customs and backgrounds, indicates that this evaluation of his stories as mere improvised sequences of actions is far too limited. Both plot and content could be intricate — for example, in the Martian works, where on occasion the stories were unified around a central theme, and the fact that Burroughs could produce these complicated plots from a general idea, with very little outlining or planning, is quite remarkable.

For the Kane article, Burroughs' advice to young writers related first to their attitude; they were not to take themselves or their work "seriously." He stressed that each writer had his own method of expressing himself — his style. Here Burroughs revealed his own distrust of style, perhaps because of the criticisms of his works as being superficial or nonliterary and his suspicions that style was associated with lofty literary creations, often written for a select audience:

If you take yourself and your work too seriously you will devote too much effort to mastering a style which you believe will insure your success. Forget style while you are writing. Write in the way that interests you most, tell the stories that you are interested in and if you cannot succeed in this way it is because nature never intended you for a writer.

Illustrations by J. Allen St. John, ERB's favorite illustrator.

Through his own experiences he viewed the best writer as the natural or untrained one. He rejected the concept of writing as a craft that required an apprenticeship period, like any other profession, a period in which the writer would develop through careful study, practice, and analysis of other authors' stories. This, Burroughs, a natural storyteller, had never done. A conflict of goals was also involved; he could conceive only of writing to entertain. The subtler and more refined uses of language — those that he might regard as a kind of stylistic pretense — were of course integral to the story's aims and the demands it made upon the reader. If the challenge were intellectual and the goals included a psychological probing of the characters or a perception of social issues, the language and style of the story were not separable from its content. These goals, often associated with realistic or "literary" stories, were beyond Burroughs' scope.

The years from 1918 on brought various events and interests. During August 1918 Ed assigned an option to Red Book Corporation (Story-Book Press) for the motion picture rights to "The Oakdale Affair," receiving $1,000 in payment. The movie, produced a year later by the World Film Company, was a five-reeler starring Evelyn Greeley. In another area, the popularity of *Tarzan* led to a humorous eulogy of the ape-man in a poem in "The Periscope," a column by Keith Preston:

Heroes of Fiction
How many thousand readers greet
Tarzan, half ape, but incomplete.
And wait, with interest never stale,
For sequels to complete his tail!
If sales a trusty index be,
Of vogue and popularity —
A fact you simply can't escape —
The apex goes to this ex-ape.[64]

In correspondence with Paul R. Reynolds, a New York agent who sought to handle his stories, Ed stressed his opinions about illustrators, writing, "There is one man who has absorbed the spirit of the Tarzan stories and who visualizes the characters and scenes almost precisely as I visualize them when I wrote the stories. I refer to Mr. J. Allen St. John of Chicago. . . ." At the same time he remarked, "I have been very much disappointed with the illustrations in the Red Book series. . . ." The artist, Charles Livingston Bull, had drawn Tarzan with a full beard; Ed spoke of this as "entirely ruining the character. . . ."[65]

On occasion he did not hesitate to express disapproval of some aspects of St. John's work. To Bray, who on August 21, 1919, sent him a postal card proof of *The Warlord of Mars*, Ed commented:

I like everything except the man's face and I suppose if you are going to use this for the jacket of the book it's too late to change it, though I hope not. It is not a fighting face, but more the face of a dreamer. . . . His eyebrows are arched too much for one thing and his mouth is not strong enough, nor am I stuck on the dimple in his chin.

Interesting to note, Burroughs' own knowledge of drawing enabled him to pinpoint the features — the eyebrows, mouth, and chin — that had created the objectionable "dreamer" or nonmasculine effect. He added:

I think I can make these criticisms safely for it is the first adverse criticism I have ever had to make of any of St. John's work which, as you know, has always more than satisfied me. The girl is a pippin, although she has too many clothes on for the part. You will recall that Dejah was naked except for the harness. However, I suppose for the sake of the public morality you had to robe her. . . .

Bray agreed with Ed that the man in the illustration, John Carter, did not look like a fighter; he remarked, "Unfortunately, these artists are about the craziest loons the world contains at present. With a few exceptions they are all interested in making pictures rather than illustrating a story. . . . I have an awful time in impressing upon him (St. John) that the illustration on the paper jacket of a book is an advertisement and not a picture for the walls of an art dealer." In Bray's opinion, Frank Schoonover would have done a better job.[66]

Upon returning with his family to Tarzana, after a motor trip through Yosemite to San Francisco, Ed was disappointed to hear of St. John's refusal to change Carter's face; the picture, Ed believed, might harm the book sales. Nevertheless, St. John continued to be his favorite illustrator. On May 18, 1920, Ed wrote to compliment him on his drawings in the *Tarzan* books: "... If I could do the sort of work you do I would not change a line in any of the drawings. I think your work for Tarzan The Untamed is the finest I have ever seen in any book. Each picture reflects the thought and interest and labor that were expended upon it. ..."

With the completion of two stories in September and October 1919, "Tarzan and the Valley of Luna" and "The Efficiency Expert," Burroughs continued his dealings with Munsey and Bob Davis. On October 14, in sending "Tarzan and the Valley of Luna" to the editor, he inquired about the readers' attitudes toward Indian stories and explained an idea he had in mind: "I believe I could make another character similar to Tarzan using a young Apache warrior. There never was a more warlike people. They fought every human from Kansas to Mexico; they could travel on foot all day with mounted men and be fresh at night; their senses were as acute as those of wild beasts; physically they were perfect and many of them were handsome even by our standards. ..." He eulogized the Apaches, noting that before their wars with the white men, they had committed no atrocities; he considered them to be the "herace of the Western Hemisphere" and thought he should write about them "before their power and glory waned."[67]

In the same period, responding to a letter from *The American Boy*, Ed indicated he would like to write juvenile stories and mentioned his custom of telling bedtime stories to his own children; these he kept humorous, noting, "... it was unwise to send them to bed with their heads full of raging lions and sudden death." He brought up an idea of "writing a series of stories around an Apache Indian boy during a period before the Indian country had had been encroached upon by the whites," and explained, "I think I could make of the boy almost as interesting a character as Tarzan, because I have lived for a while among the Apaches... and found... great abundance of material in their exploits. ..."[68]

"The Efficiency Expert," written between September 22 and October 22, 1919, was a 50,000-word story centered about the adventures of Jimmy Torrance in the business and social world of Chicago. In creating Torrance, Burroughs obviously drew upon his own experiences, the years of erratic business ventures, the shifting occupations, and the periods of poverty and unemployment. Torrance in rapid succession becomes a clerk in a hosiery department, a sparring partner for a well-known fighter, a waiter in a cabaret, a milkwagon driver and finally an "efficiency expert." In the last-named role Torrance, who without any previous experience or training is hired to improve the operations of the International Machine Company, duplicates a period in Burroughs' past when, with a combination of effrontery and desperation, he took the position of "expert accountant" for a Chicago firm.

Torrance's success in "efficiently" straightening out the machine company is, in many respects, a dramatic portrayal of Burroughs' own efficiency in the business world, first in his job as a department head for Sears, Roebuck, and then as an adviser for Shaw's System Bureau — where some dubious "efficiency" was demonstrated. The dependence Torrance places upon the small book "How to Get More out of Your Factory," and his amusing glibness in reciting nonsensical jargon from the book, is Burroughs' way of ridiculing the impractical sales books he had read and the slick salesmanship courses he had written.

The autobiographical elements in "The Efficiency Expert" are also evident in the creation of Torrance as a college graduate with a poor educational record, who had concentrated mainly on football, baseball, and boxing. The ultimatum by the college president that he should either start studying or leave school brings to mind Burroughs' expulsion from Phillips Academy and his later problems at Michigan Military Academy. In "The Efficiency Expert" Burroughs disparages the college diploma as a piece of paper of no practical use, or even as a detriment in the business world. Jimmy Torrance discovers, in the story, "that rather than being an aid to his securing employment, his college education was a drawback, several men telling him bluntly that they had no vacancies for rah-rah boys." This was perhaps a defensive reaction resulting from a sensitivity about his own failure to attend college. He may also be flaunting, with an understandable satisfaction, the remarkable success he had made despite his limited education. In a way he *is* Jimmy Torrance; the father of the fictional Jimmy accepts his immature behavior with a resigned amusement — "Well, son. . . it is what I expected" — while, in a comparable response, Ed's father showed disappointment at his son's actions, but also became resigned, making plain his belief that his son would never amount to anything. In returning to this past situation, Ed, as Jimmy Torrance, is redeeming himself, proving that through simple practicality and other qualities superior to education, he had risen to meet his father's expectations.

Sold to *All-Story* on November 17, 1919, "The Efficiency Expert" appeared as a four-part serial in October 1921.

In April 1919, Ed once more launched plans to form his own company. He mentioned his project at the same time in letters to Joseph Bray, Bob Davis, Eric Schuler of the Authors' League, and Ray Long of *Cosmopolitan*. If a production company were formed, the Tarzana Ranch would provide an ideal location for a studio. To Bray, Ed described the existence of a small canyon that was "almost a natural amphitheater," and spoke of his two-part plan to "make a specialty of wild animal productions" and to "attract writers of repute whose stuff is now unavailable." He referred to his friend Walter Beckwith again and his big lion Jimmy "who pulls some of the most hair-raising stuff you ever saw." The idea was to interest a group of well-known authors in joining the company. "I have been jipped, insulted and robbed by motion picture producers. . . ." Ed wrote to Davis, insisting that authors must band together to get a "square deal."

Schuler, in commenting on the plan to form a company that would preserve authors' rights and the integrity of their works, referred to Rex Beach, the president of The Authors' League, who had achieved some success in the motion picture field. Beach's first advice was not to have an "authors only" company, but to include business and technical experts. Ed had written to an old family friend, Judge Adelor J. Petit, about the project; Petit, in the past, had attempted to interest some of his associates in financing the production of *Tarzan of the Apes*. Reminding Petit of the money-making opportunity he had missed, Ed suggested that the judge find backers for this new venture. However, Petit, recovering from a serious illness, explained that he was unable to offer any active aid to Ed. He took the occasion to resurrect the past, and while remarking about Burroughs' fantastic stories, noted jokingly, ". . . I am very much disappointed to think that you have not written the story we talked about some years ago in which you were to weave some romantic tale in which the old Phoenix Distillery would play a part. I think we decided we would have the hero rescue his sweetheart from the old chimney. . . ."[69]

Ed determinedly pursued his correspondence with various individuals and companies from 1920 to 1924, including contacts with the First National Exhibitors Circuit and the W. W. Hodkinson Corporation. He had abandoned his plan to form a company of authors and sought only to find definite outlets for the distribution of the films based upon his own stories that he hoped to produce. However, because of financial difficulties and other problems the project floundered. More years were to pass before a Burroughs production company finally went into operation.

16
TARZANA—
FAMILY,
BUSINESS,
CREATIVITY

To the busy and happy days at Tarzana Ranch, the invigorating days of outdoor living, came a somber touch. On April 5, 1920, Mary Evaline Burroughs died. She had been staying at Tarzana for a month prior to her death, and for a time had been under the treatment of a Christian Science practitioner. As her condition worsened, Mary Evaline asked that she be examined by Ed's physician, Dr. Egerton Crispin. The doctor found that her heart was badly affected and, in addition, discovered a tumorous growth on her kidney. Her death, at age seventy-nine, came shortly afterward. The Burroughs family had shown a preference for cremation, and this practice was to be followed with Ed's mother. The first plan had been to scatter her ashes, but it was decided to place them in a receptacle at the Los Angeles Crematory.[1]

Other family matters during these years included attempts to sell the old Phoenix Distillery property in Chicago. The search for a buyer was being handled by Adelor Petit, with contacts being maintained by Ed's two brothers, Harry, now employed by the National Life Insurance Company in Chicago, and Coleman, residing nearby in Wilmette, Illinois. On April 17, 1920, as a sale failed to materialize, Ed commented gloomily to Harry, ". . . I don't care very much one way or another as the distillery property has always been a hoodoo. It helped to kill Father and I am inclined to think it also helped to kill Mother. . . ." The sales efforts dragged on until 1923 when, in January, Petit succeed in selling the property for $88,000.

At Tarzana the family life exhibited the typical activities and concerns. Joan and Hulbert for a time attended the only elementary school in the area, located about three and one-half miles from the ranch in Marion, a village named after General Otis's daughter; its name was later changed to Reseda. In this early schooling period Ed also created a classroom at the ranch, using the quarters above the garage;

ERB's mother, Mrs. George Tyler Burroughs, at Tarzana Ranch, about March 15, 1920.

there, for several years, the children were instructed by tutors. Ed coached Jack in various school subjects, with emphasis upon spelling and arithmetic, and as the two worked in the study Ed would interrupt his writing to check his son's answers. For a while Joan and Hulbert were given piano lessons by John Shea, the Burroughs' secretary.

Ed's and Emma's method of raising the children appeared on the surface to be one of over-protection, of reluctance to expose them to the rough-and-tumble of ordinary life. However, Ed and Emma were strongly influenced by a deep fear of serious illness. Ed had lost two infant brothers. He himself had been frail as a child. Emma's only brother, Alvin, Jr., had died of appendicitis in his teens. Their son, Jack, nearly died of diphtheria shortly after coming to Los Angeles in 1919. Thus, rightly or wrongly, Ed's and Emma's concern was fear that in the larger public schools their children

would run a greater risk of exposure to disease. And there were no wonder drugs at that time. Ironically, despite these precautions, both Hulbert and Jack apparently contracted mild cases of polio about 1921, but these were not diagnosed as such until years later.

Joan, age twelve, in August 1920 entered the Ramona Convent in West Alhambra, California, not for reasons of religion but to join a friend who was attending there. At the same time, Hulbert and Jack were enrolled in the Page Military Academy. Before the Christmas holidays Joan was withdrawn from the convent; Ed noted in a letter that, because of her "extreme nervous condition" and "physical frailty," she would not return. Her education was continued at the Hollywood School for Girls; on January 4, 1921, Ed reported to Harry that Joan was delighted with the school and that the atmosphere there was much more pleasant than at the convent.[2]

Ed's first approval of the Academy with its military organization underwent rapid change. Jack, age seven, a sensitive and timid child, was unhappy in the disciplined environment. He was soon removed, and Ed, perplexed as to what procedure to follow, commented:

I suppose we are bringing them up all wrong and that they will go to the damnation bow-wows because we don't beat them with sticks and make them go to the schools where they are unhappy, but I have an idea that if a child doesn't get a great deal of happiness during its childhood it never will get it, and they are certainly entitled to all that Nature allows.[3]

He noted his sons' complaints that the boys at the academy were "a bunch of little roughnecks," placed there because of discipline problems at home. While concerned that his sons might be "effeminate," he was not inclined to believe so, explaining that the boys at the military academy were without adequate supervision and did not know how to play, "their idea of a good time being in running around and pushing each other down and fighting." Hulbert, age eleven, would finish out the year at the academy; Ed described his oldest son as

ERB's two new Packards—a sedan and a sports roadster—and a Hudson roadster, with consecutively numbered license plates; bumper on Packard at left includes chrome-plated semicurved ends that could be moved to grip and lock front wheels.

possessing "a more phlegmatic temperament" which allowed him to adjust to the school circumstances.[4]

Ed and Emma soon recognized the need for alterations and additions to the old Otis residence to suit their life-style. The heating facilities of the house were inadequate for a family of five. Ed contracted for the installation of a central steam heating system which necessitated extensive tunneling beneath the house to bring heat to each room.

The most ambitious project was a building to be constructed about one hundred feet west of the main house. This new addition comprised a three-car garage on the ground level and a second story containing rooms for two servants, a photographic darkroom, a workshop, and a study which later was used as a schoolroom where the children were tutored. Later, Ed used it for his writing.

The lowest level of this three-storied building was a combination ballroom and movie theater with a small balcony at one end that served as a projection booth. This large playroom became the center of much weekend social activity. Because of the prohibitive distance to the nearest motion picture houses in those years, Ed brought the movies to his own little theater. Every Friday evening Burroughs and his Tarzana Ranch theater played friendly host not only to his own family and friends but to neighbors of the area. Burroughs was both host and projectionist, screening the popular comedies and features of the day. He particularly enjoyed Charlie Chaplin, Buster Keaton, and Douglas Fairbanks. Following the production of *The Son of Tarzan* as a serial, he personally edited and cut the 15 episodes to a feature length picture in this ballroom-theater. Jack Burroughs recalls the many lines of string in the tiny projection room on which Ed hung the labeled film clips ready for splicing. (Ironically, it was this very Tarzan film, printed on hazardous nitrate base, that spontaneously ignited 38 years later and nearly destroyed the Burroughs office building.)

In that same year, 1920, Burroughs decided to install a swimming pool adjacent to the house. He designed the pool and personally supervised the construction. Recalls Hulbert Burroughs:

In the early 1920's there were no swimming pool contractors in the Valley. My Dad simply determined what size he wanted and instructed a crew of his ranch employees to start digging. Most of the excavation was done with a team of horses and a Fresno scraper with final digging and shaping a pick and shovel operation. It was before the days of Gunite, so wooden forms were built and the cement poured from a wheelbarrow. No filtering equipment was then available so the plan was to periodically gravity-drain the water, clean the pool, and refill.

The pool was a great success as far as we kids and our friends were concerned. We all learned to swim well and it became the natural focal point for many parties for family and friends. However, compared to modern pools with crystal clear filtered water, ours was a mess. No one today would think of swimming in such murky water. Between drainings, the walls and bottom of the pool became green and slippery with algae. Despite the use of copper sulphate, we could never see the bottom. During the mating season, innumerable toads used the pool as a breeding ground. Frequently, luckless rabbits, gophers, and ground squirrels drowned in the dark waters at night. We all should have contracted horrible diseases, but we managed to survive. My Dad had the ridiculous notion that arising early on a cold winter morning for a dip in the pool would, in some mysterious way, prove beneficial. We would line up at the deep end of the pool, Jack and I shivering and trying to muster the nerve for the ordeal. With the exclamation "He who hesitates is lost!" Ed would plunge in, with Jack and I reluctantly following, flailing over those 50 feet of icy waters for dear life.

By the fall of 1921 all of the children had been withdrawn from school; Jack had temporarily been enrolled in the Hollywood School for Girls. Arrangements were now made to

have them tutored at home. Thus, in handling his own children Ed had shown an indecisiveness and an obvious tendency to overprotect them. His actions, in many respects, were the result of *his* conditioning; certainly, as the youngest of four brothers, raised by a father at times stern and domineering, and on other occasions overindulgent, Ed's problems with his own children were clearly predictable.

For Christmas of 1920 Hulbert and Jack received unusual presents from Harry Rubey of the National Film Corporation. They were each given a lion cub, and Joan was presented with two monkeys, described by Ed in one caustic phrase "as tractable as a pair of rattlesnakes. . . ." About the lions, Ed, on December 27 supplied details to his brother George:

ERB's secretary, John A. Shea.

336

They are not very big lions although each of them is capable of devouring three pounds of raw meat a day and tearing it from the bone in a truly lion-like fashion. The children go in the cage and play with them . . . They were brought up with a little female puppy who lives with them in the cage and they are a never ending source of amusement to the children. The monkeys are vicious things and as far as I can see are utterly useless.

Not exactly pleased at the menagerie set up behind the house, Ed remarked, "The only thing that I can imagine that would have been less acceptable would have been an elephant." Burroughs lost little time in finding a more suitable home for the animals.

After taking his first airplane flight, Ed's unenthusiastic comments about it had caused Emma and the children to change their minds about flying. He described the event as a "great disappointment," noting there was "only a knowledge of the danger incurred without any compensating thrill." His main complaint was that "the speed sensation was about what you derive from riding in an automobile at the rate of ten or twelve miles an hour." Although the speed was seventy miles an hour, the plane seemed to be standing still. Used to the excitement of auto driving, he found the plane ride both dull and disagreeable. He was also pessimistic about the safety factors, quoting statistics to George: "for every engine driver killed, one thousand pilots would be killed."

Enjoying pool are Hulbert on left, Emma under umbrella, ERB, Jack, and David Ohrland, Emma's driver, on right, 1921.

Jack Burroughs in lion's den of short-lived Tarzana zoo, December 1920.

Ed's attitude toward flying would be reversed in later years.

Contacts with old friends remained unbroken; in June 1920, Walt Mason, whose poems Ed had long admired, visited the Tarzana Ranch. In 1920-21 Ed corresponded with General Charles King, then living in Milwaukee, describing the ranch and the surrounding hills abounding with quail, deer, and coyotes. Ed noted the presence of mountain lions and spoke of the family's enjoyment in riding along the "many beautiful trails." A letter to King, of course, evoked the past: ". . . I always associate you in my mind with saddle horses, remembering as I do your horsemanship and your love of horses. Mrs. Burroughs and I each have our saddle horse and the children each a Shetland pony, besides which we have a couple of extra saddle horses, so if you do come out I can assure you of a good mount. . . ." When Ed later received a photo of King on horseback, he wrote, ". . . it is really the way I always think of you. I have been bragging for nearly thirty years now of the fact that I once rode under your instruction. . . ."[5]

Ed's political views during the election year of 1920 were forcefully stated in a letter to Bert Weston. Denying any preference for California Senator Hiram Johnson as a presidential candidate, Ed claimed he knew little about politics, but stressed, ". . . I hope to God I never see another Democratic president." Theodore Roosevelt had always been one of his favorites, and because of this he admitted that he "leaned" toward General Leonard Wood as a Republican candidate: ". . . I think he must have imbibed a great many Rooseveltian ideas and ideals and he looks ugly enough to railroad his views through." He became vituperative in expressing his opinion of Woodrow Wilson: "Of one thing I am positive: Johnson, Wood, Lowden, Pershing, or some congenital idiot from a county poorhouse could be no worse than the ass we have had for the last seven or eight years."[6]

Hard reality was shattering Ed's dream of becoming a gentleman rancher — at a profit. In his diary on January 7, 1921, he noted a re-port made by his secretary: "Shea closed books for 1920. Says loss on ranching $17,000 for last year. . . ." The $1,000 cost for a new henhouse was hard to believe. Ed wrote, "those hens will have to work overtime to pay for it . . . resembles a castle . . . the first building of its kind in the world. Concrete slabs or panels nailed to frame studding . . . a better house than most Hollywood bungalows. . . ." The hog-breeding project had turned into a disaster; on March 27 the *Los Angeles Times* announced an auction at the Tarzana Ranch, with the entire herd of pure-bred Hampshire hogs being closed out. The auction, to be held four days later, would include "the aged sow, Floreine 2nd, the sow that was given championship honors last fall at the Los Angeles Livestock Show. . . ."

The attempts to grow crops were equally unsuccessful. Years later, to his friend Charles K. Miller, who had described him as "author and film playwright," Ed responded in wry humor, "you forgot to mention my particular claim to fame — that of Farmer DeLuxe and World's Champion Potato Grower. About twelve years ago I planted an acre of potatoes and, as none of them has ever come up, I am inclined to think that they were planted upside down and are probably making their way slowly toward the Antipodes. . . ."[7]

One of ERB's Berkshire hogs, champion Marimoor Peer, July 1921, and Peter Putz, ERB's pig foreman.

In 1922 Ed arranged to offer for rent the agricultural and stockraising facilities at the ranch; he was finding it impossible to concentrate upon his writing because of the pressure of numerous duties at Tarzana. To his nephew Studley, on July 26, he wrote gloomily, "Our golf course is only a memory, except for a few tees upon which we sweated so three years ago," and about the ranch, "Still have the hogs. Am trying to sell them. . . . We will have nothing left but the dairy cows and saddle horses and the necessary barns and corrals for them. . . ."

In applying for a loan on August 24, 1922, Ed confessed that he did not expect to meet the payments through any ranch income, but at the same time revealed that his earnings as an author, in 1921, had totaled $98,238.28. He noted that the land around him had been selling for subdivision purposes at more than $1,000 an acre, but stated hopefully that he had no plans to dispose of his property: ". . . I wish to retain it intact for my children." However, within a few months he changed his mind; Burroughs' business instincts would not allow him to accept a losing investment or to overlook any money-making possibility. Although he could not afford to expend the time and energy, he soon became involved in an attempt to sell residential and business lots.

In 1922 he formally subdivided approximately fifty acres of his ranch land extending from Tarzana Drive at the foot of the main ranch house hill north to Ventura Boulevard (El Camino Real), bounded on the east by Avenida Oriente and on the west by Mecca Ave. The City of Los Angeles assigned to the subdivision the official designation of Tract 5475. The land consisted of sixty-three commercial lots on Ventura Blvd. and 139 residential lots, many of which were an acre in size and dividable into smaller one-third acre parcels.

The advertising featured the concept of Tarzana as a milieu for artists and writers; this approach Burroughs believed to be a mistake which hampered the sale of lots for homes. On November 8 he commented to Bert Weston, "We rather overdid the high brow stuff in the first advertising. I did not mean it in the way people seemed to choose to interpret it. I wanted decent people in here, not a bunch of roughnecks, and as for an artistic colony, that was a little advertising come-on bunk that didn't pan out very well, possibly because the majority of people are just about as crazy to live with a bunch of authors and artists as I should be. . . ."

Although he was able to sell a few lots, the project languished until the following year. In the interim he decided to intensify efforts to have the ranch used by motion picture companies for location purposes. The ranch had provided a setting for occasional pictures, one of these being described by Ed to Irene Ettrick, a young fan from London, on January 10, 1922: "My children are having a great deal of excitement now because the Universal people are making a picture of the days of Buffalo Bill in the canyon on the back of the ranch. . . ." However, a year later Ed followed a plan to contact the various studios and to advertise the Tarzana Ranch as an ideal location for film-making. A circular, headed "A New Location," was mailed to the studios in January 1923; it mentioned the "Koonskin Kabin" situated on the ranch, an "artistic log cabin," a permanent set which could be used for dressing rooms or other purposes. Rates were listed at $15.00 per day, $75.00 a week. In a letter to Goldwyn Studios, Ed urged the location manager to use the ranch for scenes in *Ben Hur*.

Ed soon acquired film location rights for 3,000 acres adjoining the Tarzana Ranch and made tentative plans, never realized, to build his own movie sets which would be available for all companies. During 1923 and later, various studios, including Vitagraph and Metro, brought crews and actors to Tarzana; the picturesque setting near the Koonskin Kabin was a favorite spot. Despite these uses, the income derived from movie locations was insufficient to make the ranch a financial success.

Although his income from the sale of stories and book royalties was substantial, his expenses as a gentleman farmer of 540 acres had hurt him. Subdivision costs had been a burden and

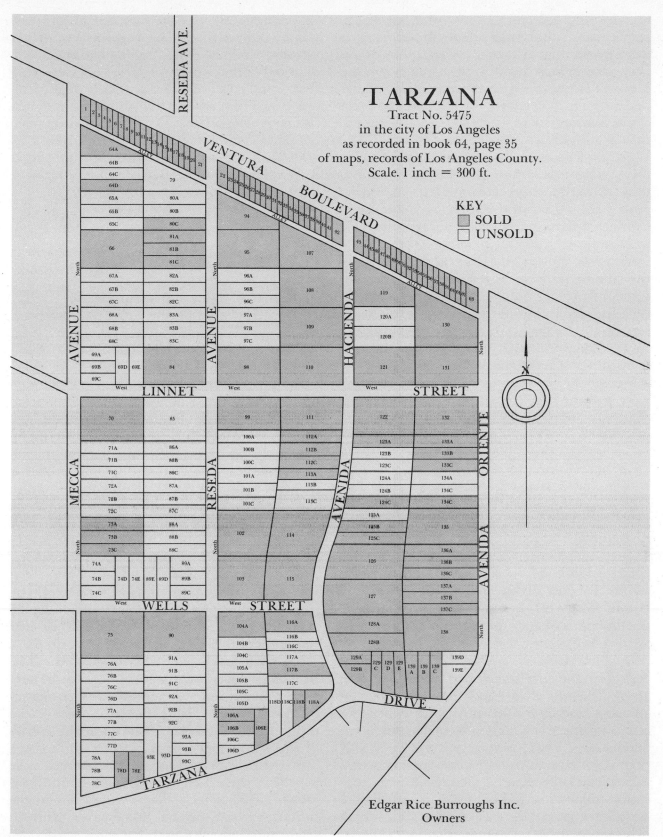

Map of Tarzana.

lot sales disappointing. Property taxes had been on the rise. Additionally, federal income taxes were beginning to take a bigger bite. By his very nature, Burroughs was not a money saver. How could he cut expenses and realize a higher net income? After long consultations with his tax accountants and attorneys, he was advised that he should become a corporation!

In 1922 this was a unique concept. Certainly, so far as is known, no other author at that time had incorporated himself. And so, on March 26, 1923, Edgar Rice Burroughs, Inc., a California corporation, came into being. One week later, in a document dated April 2, 1923, Edgar Rice Burroughs, the author, granted to the new Edgar Rice Burroughs, Inc., all of his rights, title, and interest in his current and future literary rights. In exchange for these assets, he and his family received shares of stock in Edgar Rice Burroughs, Inc., with Ed having controlling interest by virtue of owning one share more than Emma. The three children were given token shares, with their father as trustee. Shortly thereafter Burroughs also granted to the new company the remaining real estate in his Tract 5475 subdivision.

From that time until his death in 1950, Burroughs was a salaried employee of ERB Inc. with all of his literary output becoming the property of the company. Although nothing immediately spectacular resulted from this change, there were decided tax advantages to a corporation as opposed to Burroughs as an individual. The advantages would become apparent in the years to come with the remarkable proliferation of the business into new fields.

With the development of small businesses along Ventura Blvd., and the subdivision of adjacent land by a number of other owners, Ed felt the time was ripe for a further step. On September 7, 1922, in anticipation of his already planned incorporation move and the expected greater sales efforts in lots in Tract 5475, he disclosed to his brother Harry, ". . . I am going to start a town and call it Tarzana. . . ." This unofficial creation and naming of a new town —

the nearest post office was Reseda, California — was announced in the *Los Angeles Examiner* of October 15. The existence of an adjacent subdivision called Runnymede led to some confusion and conflict. The next Burroughs plan was to get official sanction through the establishment of a post office at Tarzana. After making application, on December 12, 1923, he wrote to Representative Walter F. Lineberger in Washington, D.C., to request his assistance:

Tarzana is a name that is associated with this locality and is not only well known locally, but nationally, and even internationally, while Runnymede has absolutely no local significance. . . . Since writing the enclosed, I find that there is a Runnymede postoffice in Kansas, and . . . in New Jersey, while so far as I know there would not be another Tarzana in the world. . . .

The reply of John H. Bartlett, first assistant postmaster general, on April 28, 1924, revealed that unmentioned complications and hidden motives had now emerged. The competition between Burroughs and Melvin S. Daniel, the proprietor of the Runnymede subdivision, who had applied both for the post office and the job of postmaster, was discussed: "The inspector says that within this tract [Runnymede] are 75 very small houses, a small grocery store, three small lunch rooms and a filling station. This section is devoted principally to poultry raising." As limited as Runnymede was, it appeared large in comparison with Tarzana, which was described by Bartlett as "a residential section, consisting of but five homes, including the residence of Edgar Rice Burroughs, who is the promoter of the Tarzana tract."

Bartlett noted that Ed had been frank: "Mr. Burroughs informed the inspector that he concurred on his opinion that there is no necessity for the office and that his chief interest in the proposition, which was advanced by the owners of the Runnymede tract, was to prevent the office being called Runnymede inasmuch as he had been there longer and the community is known as Tarzana." The final recommendation by Bartlett was that no new post office be established; he indicated that both areas, Tarzana and Runnymede, would receive the best service if the mail were handled through a rural route from Van Nuys, a larger adjacent district.

The community itself did not approve the name "Tarzana" until four years later, when on July 20, 1928, at a meeting of the Tarzana Civic League, the resolution was passed; four names had been proposed, and of the 400 members who voted, approximately ninety-five percent preferred "Tarzana." The Civic League next campaigned vigorously for a post office, and on December 11, 1930, Washington sent an official notice of its establishment in Tarzana.

Burroughs' hopes for success in farming had long since dissipated. Soon to become a reality was his planned incorporation and the end of farming. At a well-advertised auction sale on January 15, 1923, most of the livestock and all of the farm tools and equipment were disposed of. Seven saddle mares bred to the famous pedigreed Arabian stallions Letan and Harara were sold, but Ed still retained a number of other horses, including Colonel, his favorite saddle gelding, and Brigadier Rex, a registered saddle stallion. Other livestock at the auction were the dairy cattle and the herd of Berkshire swine, totaling more than one hundred, all registered or subject to registry. Two days later Ed commented to Bert Weston, ". . . it is over and I am through with farming, which is worth the loss, and I believe I could write a book on Gentlemanly Agriculture that would more than compensate me for all that I have dropped in this line of endeavor. . . ."

The Ghostly Script," a work of unusual complexity in which Burroughs devised a bizarre theory and philosophy of the afterlife, was begun on March 16, 1920, discontinued after the completion of five pages that included a foreword and chapter one, and not resumed until ten years later in October 1930. The manuscript at that time reached a total of some thirty-one pages, mainly in rough draft, handwritten form, and it was never finished. Allegorical in its effect, with the events in a supernatural environment clearly applicable to man's

ANNOUNCING THE ESTABLISHMENT OF AN INDEPENDENT
POST OFFICE AT TARZANA, CALIFORNIA, AND OUR
CONSEQUENT CHANGE OF ADDRESS FROM RESEDA, CALIFORNIA
TO
TARZANA, CALIFORNIA

EDGAR RICE BURROUGHS
EDGAR RICE BURROUGHS, INC.

TARZANA RANCH,
TARZANA, CALIFORNIA
DECEMBER 16, 1930

Announcement of Tarzana post office, December 16, 1930.

behavior on earth, the story opens with a foreword again in Burroughs' favorite style, with him as the narrator of happenings communicated to him by another person.[8]

Some eight years after he had started "The Ghostly Script" and allowed it to remain half-forgotten in his files, an inquiry from a fan brought the story theme to life again. On December 27, 1927, Leo Baker of Port George, Nova Scotia, Canada, revealed a vision and perception of a remarkable nature. In an erudite expression of his ideas, he spoke of "the possibility of other forms and modes of life which our limited intelligence would not permit us to appreciate even if they were explained to us," and insisted, "There must be other worlds and other intelligent, living beings. . . ." He confessed having similar thoughts to Burroughs', thoughts "unuttered because of lack of coherent descriptive power. . . ." They had lain "latent" in his brain for years. Then, possibly as "a presumptuous interloper," he offered a tentative suggestion: "Why do you not write a story describing a world within our world. That is to say, suppose there were another world of living beings, inhabiting the same space which we occupy, but on account of being on a different plane, so to speak, not appreciable to us, nor to them. . . ." By way of analogy, Baker noted that before the invention of radio we were not aware of "the countless sounds and noises" that were in the air. Through science we were able to capture and record these. Similarly, could there not be certain elements in "our immediate vicinity" that remain unnoticed because we have not the proper means to detect them?

Highly intrigued, Burroughs, on January 11, 1928, mentioned "the rather remarkable coincidence of your suggestion that I write a story describing a world within our world." He proceeded to explain the theme of "The Ghostly Script," according to the brief section he had written in 1920:

I started a story along similar lines based on a supposed theory of angles rather than planes: If we viewed our surroundings from our own "angle of existence," the aspect of the vibrations which are supposed to constitute both matter and thought were practically identical with those conceived by all the creatures of the world that we know; whereas, should our existence have been cast in another angle, everything would be different, including the flora and fauna and the physical topography of the world.

Thus, Baker's ideas centered about an invisible world existing on a different *plane*, while Burroughs conjured up one based on a newly viewed "*angle* of existence." He wrote to Baker:

The thought underlying the story was that death was merely a change to a new "angle of existence," wherefrom, viewed thus from a different angle, the vibrations that are matter took on an entirely different semblance, so that where before we had seen oceans, we might now see mountains, plains and rivers inhabited by creatures that might be identical with those with which we had hitherto been familiar or might vary diametrically.

Ed confessed that it was a "crazy story," commenting, "There was a reason why I did not finish it, though some day I may do so." Baker, in his letter, urged Ed to read Einstein's "theory of relativity," and noted that "Time, Space, Matter, are all purely relative and are simply artificial factors which we have adopted to suit our orthodox conditions of existence."

With the writing of "Tarzan the Terrible," from August 14 to December 16, 1920, and the customary contacts with the Munsey Company, Burroughs found himself confronted by a changing situation. The story, accepted by Munsey with only a short section completed, was sent to Davis at various times in installments. To Ed's surprise, while the story was still in progress, on December 7 he received a note from Elliot Balestier of *Argosy All-Story* announcing that Davis was no longer with the Munsey Company. He had gone into business for himself, forming the Robert H. Davis Corporation, a New York agency organized to handle the work of a group of well-known authors. By arrangement with Munsey he was assigned all of their syndication dealings and was allowed to represent them in the book and motion picture areas. In responding to Ed's good luck message, Davis wrote, "I thought I had better try my hand uptown among the merchants. I got rather tired of the editorial and reading game. . . ." On January 12, 1921, Ed noted, "You have a lovely letterhead. Every once in a while I used to go into business for myself, the only result, however, being a new letterhead. . . ." He conceded that since Davis's letterhead was more impressive than any he had used, the editor would probably be more successful.

As a sequel to *Tarzan the Untamed*, a novel whose ending revealed that Lady Jane Greystoke, supposedly killed by the Germans, was still alive, *Tarzan the Terrible* continues Tarzan's search for his mate and takes him to one of the strangest of lands, Pal-ul-don, where creatures walk erect like men but have long sinuous tails. A familiar theme, first used in the Martian series, centers about the willingness of intelligent beings to change, and even in a savage world to realize that a life of peace and amity with other beings is preferable to one of constant hatred and warfare. The odd creatures of Pal-ul-don, the pithecanthropi, especially in the clash of black against white, represent simi-

Tarzana Ranch
Van Nuys California
1920   TARZAN THE TERRIBLE   words: 94325
    ~ G.+5 am finished Dec 16 1920 by Edgar Rice Burroughs

pithecanthropus 1, 2, 8, 11
jato - hybrid lion, black and yellow striped, sabre tooth 4
ja - leopard spotted lion - 4
titanic reptiles first mentioned 8, 9
Ta-den - (Tall-tree) white, hairless warrior. Tarzan's first acquaintance-15
Om-at (Long-tail) black, hairy warrior. Tarzan's second acquaintance-15
A-lur (City of Light) Capitol of Pal-ul-don-16   INSERTS
Bu - the moon - 16   A - 7
Waz-don (Black-men)-16.   B - 10
Ho-don (White-men)-16   C - 155
Ko-tan (Mighty-warrior) king of the Ho-don - 16   killed 149
O-lo-a (Like-star-light) Ko-tan's daughter - 16
Dak-at (Fat-tail) chief of a Ho-don village - 17
Ja-don (Lion-man) chief of a Ho-don village and father of Ta-den-17
Bu-lot (Moon-face) a Ho-don, son of Chief Mo-sar(Short-nose)-17
Mo-sar (Short-nose) Chief and pretender to Ho-don throne-17
Es-sat (Rough-skin) chief of Om-at's tribe of Waz-don-18.Killed-33
Pan-at-lee (Soft-tail-doe) Om-at's sweetheart-18
Pastar-ul-ved - Father of Mountains - a peak-19
Jad-ben-Otho- The Great God -19
Jad pele ul Jad-ben-Otho - The valley of the Great God-19
Pal-ul-don (Land-of-man) name of the entire country-20
Kor-ul-ja (Gorge-of-lions) Es-sat's gorge and tribe-22
Kor-ul-lul (Gorge-of-water) Waz-don tribe in next gorge S.E.of Kor-ul-ja-25
Kor-ul-gryf (Gorge-of-triceratops) lair of gryfs-27
Tarzan-jad-guru (Tarzan-the-Terrible)-31
gund bar - chief battle-31
Ab-on - acting gund of Kor-ul-ja during Om-at's absence-35
In-sad) Two Kor-ul-ja warriors who accompanied Om-at,Ta-den & Tarzan in
O-dan) search of Pan-at-lee -.36
An-un (Spear-eye) father of Pan-at-lee -41
Id-an (Silver-spear) One of Pan-at-lee's two brothers-41
In-tan (Dark-warrior) Kor-ul-lul left to guard Tarzan-51. Killed-52.
tor-o-don (beast-like-man) true pithecanthropus, or anthropoid ape of Pal-ul-don.56
  Mention of stranger 22,33,44,60,77,99,116
gryf-27 description-66
dor-son - 87
Dak-lot - one of Ko-tan's palace warriors- 87
Dor-ul-Otho (Son-of-God) -87
Lu-don (Fierce-man) High priest of the temple at A-lur

✓Jar-don (strange-man) stranger - name given Korall by Om-at 119
✓A-ja - lion city - Ja-don's capital - 145
✓Jad-ben-lul (the great water) name of lake at A-lur - 145
✓Tu-lur - (Bright city) Mo-sar's city
✓pal-e-don-so- (place where men eat) - banquet hall - 151
✓au-sat (soft skin) a priest - creature of Lu-don - 154
✓Jad-in-lul - the dark lake
✓Lt. Erich Obergatz - Jane's escort into interior
✓jad-bal-lul - the golden lake - 174
✓Bu-lur - (moon city) city of waz-ho-don (Black-white-men) half breeds
✓iron - 196
✓Waz-ho-don - 189

chapters
I - pg 1
IV - 11
VI - 22
IV - 33
V - 44
VI - 55
VII - 67
VIII - 77
IX - 87
X - 96
XI - 106
XII - 116
XIII - 125
XIV - 135
XV - 146
XVI - 155
XVII - 163
XVIII - 173
XIX - 183
XX - 192
XXI - 202
XXII - 214
XXIII - 223
XXIV - 232
XXV - 241
END - 245

cor
93
152
152
157

Notebook page for "Tarzan the Terrible."

NOTE:

Names of male hairless pithecanthropus (Ho-don) begin with consonant, have even number of syllables and end with consonant.

Female Ho-don — begin with vowel, have odd number os syllables and end with vowel.

Male hairy pithecanthropus (Waz-don) — begin with vowel, have even number of syllables and end with consonant.

Female Waz-don — begin with consonant, have odd number of syllables and end with vowel.

Numerals
1-en
2-enen
3-ad
4-aden
5-adenen
6-adad
7-adaden
8-adenaden
9-adadad
10-on
11-onen
20-ton
30-fur
40-ged
50-het
60-og
70-ed
80-et
90-od
100-san
1000-xot

Application:
sanen-101
sanenen-102
enensan-200
xotsantonen-1121
tonxot-20,000

Back of notebook page for "Tarzan the Terrible," showing Ed's pen and ink sketch of male and female pithecanthropus as he conceived them for mysterious land Pal-ul-don.

lar enmity on earth, and in the story's solution demonstrate that the hostility caused by mere differences in color or appearance and customs, no matter where it occurs, can be eliminated through honest efforts at friendship and understanding. The concept of a primitive religion, one based upon superstition and fear, and one that resorts to human sacrifice, is developed within the same theme of reform or change, and the end of *Tarzan the Terrible* brings the destruction of the priests' power and the promise of a religion of love and humanity.

The oft-repeated Burroughs philosophy of the perfection of nature as demonstrated through her simple creatures, unspoiled by a degenerative civilization, is developed, with some contradictions, in the novel. Tarzan is shown as different from his "fellows of the savage jungle" since he possesses certain "spiritual" characteristics, which, precisely *because* he is a man of civilization, enable him to appreciate the beauties of nature: "The apes cared more for a grubworm in a rotten log than for all the majestic grandeur of the forest giants waving above them. The only beauties Numa acknowledged were those of his own person as he paraded them before the admiring eyes of his mate. . . ."

In his approval of carvings and handicraft of Pal-ul-donian artisans, Tarzan becomes a spokesman for another Burroughs philosophy:

A barbarian himself, the art of barbarians had always appealed to the ape-man to whom they represented a natural expression of man's love of the beautiful to even a greater extent than the studied and artificial efforts of civilization. . . .

And of course one of the greatest qualities of "the simple-minded children of nature" is illustrated in Pan-at-lee's unstinting loyalty: "It has remained for civilization to teach us to weigh the relative rewards of loyalty and its antithesis. The loyalty of the primitive is spontaneous, unreasoning, unselfish. . . ."

In one respect *Tarzan the Terrible* evi-

dences no change — Burroughs' detestation for the Germans remains intense. Erich Obergatz is a "pig-headed Hun," and, as with all Germans, never to be trusted. Obergatz says, "What are promises? They are made to be broken — we taught the world that at Liége and Louvain. . . ." His actions are always villainous, and at the story's end he becomes demented, imagines himself to be a god, and is finally killed by young Jack Clayton.

Tarzan, with his love of nature's beauties, her "picture of peace and harmony and quiet," anticipates modern man's guilt in the pollution of his environment; Tarzan surveys the waters, green landscape and mountains and meditates:

What a paradise! And some day civilized man would come and — spoil it! Ruthless axes would raze that age-old wood; black, sticky smoke would rise from ugly chimneys against that azure sky; grimy little boats with wheels behind or upon either side would churn the mud from the bottom of Jad-in-lul, turning its blue waters to a dirty brown; hideous piers would project into the lake from squalid buildings of corrugated iron. . . .

Burroughs, with this vivid 1920 picture and prophecy of the contamination to come, reveals himself as one who was aware of this serious problem many years before ecology became a national concern. *Tarzan the Terrible,* purchased by Munsey's for $3,000, appeared in *Argosy All-Story Weekly* as a seven-part serial, from February 12 to March 27, 1921.[9]

The writings of 1921 included "Angel's Serenade," a story outline which Burroughs would rework in 1936 and then develop into a 24,000-word story three years later. Its main character, Dick Crode, grows up in the tenement streets of a large city and progresses through early years of petty thievery to become head of a crime syndicate. The title "Angel's Serenade" refers to the song his mother had played on a violin — a song Crode could never forget. Burroughs had originally conceived the story, in outline form, as the basis for a motion picture with the main role assigned to Lon Chaney. On May 15, 1921, he sent two copies of "Angel's Serenade," described as a "rough draft," to Lewis Jacobs of the Century Film Corporation in Hollywood. A month before, Burroughs had contracted with Jacobs for the production of ten stories, five *Tarzan* and five non-*Tarzan*, to be filmed within six years. In offering "Angel's Serenade," Burroughs explained the title:

If you do not happen to recall Angel's Serenade, I may say that it is one of the beautiful old compositions that has survived the ravages of time and the onslaught of many years of popular songs and modern jazz. It was suggested by Mrs. Burroughs, who says that it makes an especially beautiful violin solo.

The story was rejected by Jacobs.[10]

During the year, Burroughs completed a remarkable work, one that for imagination and for complexity of detail and settings exceeded any of his previous writings. In "The Chessmen of Mars," written January 7 to November 12, 1921, he produced an incredible aggregation of characters and creatures and devised Martian customs and practices of unusual ingenuity. His worksheet, one of the most involved he had ever prepared, listed seventy items — people, buildings, rooms, equipment, and geographical references, all briefly identified or explained. Weaving the theme of the game of chess — called *jetan* on Mars — into the story was truly an inspiration. This Barsoomian game is normally played upon a board of a hundred alternate black and orange squares, with the two opponents each allotted twenty pieces in either black or orange. But in "The Chessmen of Mars" the climactic game becomes one of life and death, played on a huge scale. A gigantic jetan board is laid out in the arena at Manator: "Here they play at Jetan with living pieces. They play for great stakes and usually for a woman — some slave of exceptional beauty. ". . . When a warrior is moved to a square occupied by an opposing piece, the two battle to the death for possession of the square. . . ." Each player is dressed according to the piece he represents.

The idea developed undoubtedly from Burroughs' knowledge of chess and his turning to the game for an occasional diversion. During this period his opponent at times had been his secretary, John Shea. In the prelude to "The Chessmen of Mars," with John Carter once more returning to earth, Burroughs, as his nephew, opens with a reference to the game he had been playing: "Shea had just beaten me at chess, as usual. . . ." Burroughs had "twitted" Shea about his skill, mentioning a theory that "phenomenal chess players are always found to be from the ranks of children under twelve, adults over seventy-two or the mentally defective. . . ." It appears, however, that Burroughs preferred to assume the role of a regular loser at chess in the story, a role not indicated in real life. A January 3, 1921, entry in his diary, written before he had begun "The Chessmen of Mars," reads: "Played one game of chess with Shea. Won. If scientific theories are correct it is more of an honor to lose at chess than win. I do not recall ever having lost a chess game — though I have played but few times. . . ." He then jokes about the fact that this ability might establish him within the three classes described in the scientific theory. In February 1922 John Shea left Burroughs' employ and was later associated with the Hollywood Studios whose general manager, William Sistrom, in 1924 accepted an offer to manage the proposed Edgar Rice Burroughs Productions, Inc. The enterprise, launched with a goal of producing stories by Burroughs and other authors, was to be financed by George B. Currier in Los Angeles; however, the organizational plans never materialized.

Concerning the game jetan, Burroughs received a letter of August 6, 1922, from Elston B. Sweet, a convict in Leavenworth Prison. Sweet offered information of unusual interest. After reading "The Chessmen of Mars," he and a fellow prisoner had used the details provided in the story to carve a full set of pieces for jetan. Sweet noted, ". . . We have not only played dozens of games between us, but have succeeded

Cover of The Chessmen of Mars, *1922; J. Allen St. John, illustrator.*

in making the game a favorite among several other prisoners." He inquired whether jetan was being manufactured commercially, and if so, hoped that Burroughs would send him a set. According to Sweet, he and his friend had been sentenced to terms of fourteen and ten years; however, in 1924 Sweet's sentence, commuted to six years, expired, and he was released.

On August 16 Burroughs responded to explain that the two prisoners had made the first set of jetan and that no commercial set had been produced.[11] Reader interest in jetan remained high. Burroughs supplied a further summary of the game for publication in the appendix of the novel, and in September 1927 two young fans, Stephen Lavender and John Creighton of Thomaston, Maine, sent Burroughs a photograph of the jetan board and pieces they had made.[12] A chapter is devoted to jetan in the book *Chess Variations* by John Gollon, published in 1968.

Because of his jetan theme, Burroughs in "The Chessmen of Mars," achieves a unity and intensity not attained in other works which at times could become loosely strung sequences of adventures, battles, and escapes. In addition, the Burroughs imagination is startlingly evident with the creation of the rykors, headless bodies that are mounted by the hideous Kaldanes, living heads without bodies who manipulate the brainless flesh. As explained by Ghek, a Kaldane who later assists Tara of Helium, the heroine of the story, the Kaldanes are part of nature's evolutionary purpose, with the brain becoming larger and more powerful. This process would continue: ". . . in the far future our race shall develop into the superthing — just brain. . . . Deaf, dumb and blind it will lie sealed in its buried vault far beneath the surface of Barsoom — just a great, wonderful, beautiful brain with nothing to distract it from eternal thought."

Because of strong friendship ties with Bob Davis, Burroughs felt he should be given an opportunity, in his new agency, to market "The Chessmen of Mars." However, the price stipulated by Burroughs, as quoted by another agency, was a minimum of $7,500. On March 23,

1921, Davis agreed to contact magazine editors and to "talk about a figure around $10,000." The price, even farther beyond the bounds of realism than the story, brought no takers; the year drew to a close with "The Chessmen of Mars" unsold. On December 12, Charles MacLean of *Popular Magazine* rejected the story, commenting ". . . If he [Burroughs] were to try something not quite so extravagant, something like Jules Verne's submarine story, he would break into a new field and one I think, offering a better chance for his genuine literary ability. . . ." Resigned to the inevitable, Ed, as in the past, returned to his only available market and to a far more modest price; on January 4, 1922, Munsey's bought the story for $3,500.[13]

Davis' venture into his own corporation proved to be brief. To Ed, on November 4, 1921, he explained that while his agency had been even more successful financially than he had anticipated, the business world was not to his liking. "I prefer literature to the counting room," he remarked. "I am something of a lemon as a business man." He revealed that he would return to his old position at Munsey's on the first of the year.

The experience with "The Chessmen of Mars" plunged Ed into a state of gloom; the limited market for his type of fantasy stories was painfully evident. His depression drove him, on November 15, in a letter to Davis, to state once more, ". . . As I wrote Joe Bray today, I think I am through writing Martian and Tarzan yarns. . . ."

Burroughs had long since reached a point of weariness with the Tarzan idea and a discouragement over the clamor from editors and readers for new *Tarzan* works. He could anticipate years of unending sequels to *Tarzan*, an apparent life chore to which he must resign himself. A repeated comment had been, "I want to be known as Edgar Rice Burroughs the author, not Edgar Rice Burroughs the author of *Tarzan*." Past periods of rebellion against this enforced single-track creativity had driven him to try other works, a number of these involving

CHAPTER 28

Jetan (Martian Chess)

Those who have all or part of Edgar Rice Burroughs' Martian series should recognize the name of this game. Possibly some who remember *The Chessmen of Mars* even recall some of the rules. However, most readers probably reacted as I did—they dismissed the game as another of Burroughs' strange flights of imagination, unworthy of a true chess player's attention.

When I was gathering information on the various chess games, I happened to think of Jetan, and decided to include it in the book as a novelty. I made a set of pieces and played out a game. I was surprised to find that the game is quite good—very playable and entertaining. I therefore include Jetan not as a mere novelty but as a respectable game.

The game is supposed to represent (according to Burroughs) a battle between the black race of the south and the yellow race of the north. For this reason the Jetan board is supposed to be placed so that the end with the black army is at the south, and the end with the orange army at the north.

The board itself is of ten-by-ten squares, the squares being checkered orange and black. Positions of pieces are given on Chart 32.

Page of explanation of Martian game of Jetan, *invented by ERB for* The Chessmen of Mars, *as printed in book* Chess Variations *by John Gollon, Charles F. Tuttle Co., 1968.*

realistic characters and settings. At previous times and also in 1924 when he attempted to organize his own motion picture company, his hope had been for the production of non-Tarzan stories; included in these were *The Mucker* and a newly completed story, "The Girl from Hollywood," written from November 16, 1921, to January 7, 1922. The story, first titled "The Penningtons," demonstrated Burroughs' perception of a serious contemporary problem — that of drug addiction — and his daring, both in developing the theme and in setting his fiction in Hollywood.

In "The Girl from Hollywood" he did not introduce the drug theme merely as an expected background for the supposedly depraved movie colony the public so often read about in the papers; instead, he made his heroine Shannon Burke, whose professional name was Gaza de Lure, a drug victim snared by a villainous film director fittingly named Wilson Crumb. After being tricked into snuffing "snow," Shannon descends to complete addiction and is forced to become Crumb's mistress and to occupy a Hollywood bungalow where she peddles cocaine, morphine, and heroin. In contrast to the unhealthful atmosphere of Hollywood, a city painted as a glamor capital that lures naive, movie-struck girls to their downfall, Burroughs uses his Tarzana ranch for another setting — the ranch demonstrating the virtues of a simple outdoor life and the invigorating effects of horseback riding. Rancho del Ganado, so-named in the story, is owned by a Virginian, Colonel Custer Pennington, who lives there with his wife, son Custer, Jr., and daughter Eva. With the narrative placed in the prohibition era, Burroughs inserts another complication in his plot, the storing of a large quantity of stolen liquor on an adjoining ranch, and the illegal activities of Guy Evans, a suitor for the hand of Eva, who is involved in the sale of the liquor.

Burroughs clearly indicates his objections to prohibition in describing Evans' attitude: "Like many another, he considered the Volstead Act the work of an organized and meddlesome minority, rather than the real will of the people. There was, in his opinion, no immorality in circumventing the Eighteenth Amendment whenever and wherever possible." However, Burroughs emphasizes his disapproval of any trafficking in *stolen* liquor.

The deplorable influence of drugs in the Hollywood setting is further developed through the addiction and death of Grace Evans, young Custer's fiancée, who has rejected the pleas to remain in the idyllic surroundings of the ranch, and who insists upon seeking an actress's career in Hollywood. She also falls prey to the dissolute Wilson Crumb.

With the inclusion of certain elements — the description of life at Tarzana, the realistic details about the ranch house, and the horseback rides into the hills and canyons — the story does arouse some strong interest. In Eva, the daughter and darling of the Pennington household, whose doting parents indulged her capricious behavior, Burroughs' real-life model was probably his own daughter Joan.[14]

Although accepted by Davis for magazine publication, "The Girl from Hollywood" received an unenthusiastic appraisal from Joseph Bray of McClurg. While approving Burroughs' motives in writing it — "You pay a deserved tribute to the healthy country life as you have lived it . . ." — Bray felt that the story's appearance in book form would be a mistake. On June 23, 1922, he wrote:

. . . you do not have here a story that will interest people to an extent worth mentioning. You bring the movies into your story. You show the harm an unprincipled man can do and there is no reason to suppose you have overdrawn things. People, however, are not much interested in stories of conditions in Hollywood. . . .

Bray commented about the publication of a number of movie stories in the past months, noting that *Merton of the Movies*, by Harry Leon Wilson, although well-written, was selling poorly.

Bray was also critical of the plot complications involving both bootlegging and drugs. His view of prohibition was quite different from Burroughs':

The bootlegging business you bring in just for the sake of plot development is likewise something in which there is not much interest. I do not know what your attitude towards prohibition is; prohibition is here to stay. Any person who looks at results so far with a clear mind can not escape the conclusion that the country has benefitted greatly from the passing of the eighteenth amendment. . . .

He insisted that the drug theme was not convincing; it seemed illogical for a famous, highly paid director like Wilson Crumb to turn to drug peddling as a business enterprise.

Bray's main fear was of the effect the publication of "The Girl from Hollywood" could have on the other Burroughs books: ". . . it will react against the sale of your books in general and future books in particular." He stressed that the readers expected "lively stories of adventure" from the Burroughs pen, and that Ed should not write stories "in which very little happens." Bray added a frank comment:

. . . I think the publication of "The Girl from Hollywood" would do you a great deal of harm, but let me say in this connection if you want to take the chance, we shall not say no to its publication. My advice, however, would be to forget it as a book. . . .

As a McClurg editor, Bray's concern, naturally, was with sales and profits. He spoke of the decline in sales of Burroughs books recently, and noted that *The Mucker*, about which he had always been dubious, was obviously a money-loser.

Burroughs, having formed his own opinion about the story, was not in the least persuaded by Bray. He had been quite sure that the editor would reject the story, but preferred to give him the "first refusal." Burroughs was positive and impatient: ". . . I intend to have it put in book form before Christmas. It will never be timely again." His most compelling reason, his desire to achieve success in nonfantasy works,

was evident: "I wish . . . to ascertain if there is a market for other than highly imaginative stuff from my pen."

Unwilling to let McClurg publish a book in which they had no confidence, Ed turned to Bob Davis. In the dealings that followed, Davis contacted Carl B. Milligan of Service for Authors, a New York agency that had taken over the Davis corporation. Through Milligan, a contract for the publication of "The Girl from Hollywood" was obtained from The Macauley Company early in 1923, and the book appeared on August 10 of that year.

The reviews of the book contained the strongest criticism ever leveled at Burroughs' writings. Much of this resulted from Macauley's unfortunate selection of a book jacket with a lurid illustration of a partially undressed woman. However, Burroughs was also castigated for the subject he had chosen. The *Chicago Daily News*, on September 5, viewed *The Girl from Hollywood* with repugnance, commenting insultingly about the book and its author:

When we find the vice and depravity of Hollywood dressed up to make a novel with no purpose other than to entertain, we get the strange feeling that something ought to be done about it. . . . In this book he (Burroughs) has taken a timely theme and served it up as so much sensational hash. The jacket on the book pictures a woman dropping a robe to expose her naked shoulders as the camera turns, while a man with leering eyes extends fingers to help take off the robe. Within the jacket is the appealing line: "'Women are cheaper in Hollywood than in any town this side of Port Said,' said a motion-picture director not long ago."

The *News* noted that here was a situation for a great writer, such as Zola, who might present a powerful exposé of vice and realistically depict human suffering. Obviously, the review concluded with contempt: the author must be "more than an Edgar Rice Burroughs, writing feebly for a multitude that sees in a nation's shame nothing more than a cheap diversion. The curse of Hollywood is too dangerous to be played with by men of small talents."

To L. S. Furman, Macauley editor, on October 26, 1923, Ed expressed unconcern over the critical reviews, remarking, ". . . as long as they say *something* I am satisfied." However, he bluntly placed the blame with the Macauley Company:

The illustration on the jacket was suggestive, and to me, disagreeable; while the notice printed inside would lead the book buyer to assume that he was to be regaled with a nasty sex story. Those who like that sort of thing must have been disappointed, while those who do not like it would not buy the book.

He explained that his only regret in connection with the reviews, was that "nearly all of the reviewers seem to have the idea that my book was an arraignment of Hollywood's morals, and was intended to portray a generally existing condition there." Stressing that this was *not* his purpose, he insisted that motion picture people were "clean, hard working people" and Hollywood was "a delightful home community." Whatever vice he had described, existed in all walks of society.

"I hoped that the story would deter young people who had never used narcotics from taking the first step," he wrote, "and that it might hold out hope to those who already were addicts." The reviewers who classified the book as mere sensational entertainment were clearly without perception. The contrast between the tawdry and wretched life of the drug victim in Hollywood as posed against the healthy outdoor life on the ranch was forcefully presented. Burroughs commented sadly about this:

. . . The one big thing I tried to get over, and evidently failed, was a plea for simple, natural, wholesome family life, as typified by the Penningtons. Only a few reviewers grasped this, the majority seizing upon every shred or suggestion of smut they could lay hands upon.

Another project on the 1922 writing agenda was a revision of the unsuccessful "Under the Red Flag," an anticommunist story which, through 1919-21, had suffered eleven rejections.

In the original story of a twenty-first-century world under Soviet domination, Burroughs had created characters and events to match the communist setting. Julian 9th, the main character, had been born in the thirty-first Commune of the Chicago Soviet. The top officials, as listed on the Burroughs worksheets, were Lantski Petrov, president of the United States, elected in the year 2016; Otto Bergst, also shown as Comrade General Bergan, the new commander of the Red Guard at Chicago; Hoffmeyer, an agent of the Bolsheviks; Krantz, the Bolshevik coal baron; and Soord, the new tax collector.

Burroughs had become resigned to the fact that his fictional exposure of the evils of communism was unsalable. He was baffled as to the reasons why, but inclined to suspect that powerful and insidious forces were at work to intimidate editors; their unwillingness to publish the story could be viewed as cowardice or even as a lack of patriotism. His businessman's instincts would not allow him to waste the hours of writing, and since some revision was necessary, he merely changed the setting and turned to the safer and more familiar area of science-fiction. The earth's totalitarian conquerors who by the twenty-first century had reduced an advanced civilization to a primitive, agricultural society, were the Kalkars, sadistic invaders and colonizers from the moon. With this revision, "Under the Red Flag" became "The Moon Men," and with the usual planned sequels the story was shifted in order and became the second of a moon trilogy. The first, "The Moon Maid," was written later in 1922, and the third, "The Red Hawk," did not appear until 1925. All three were combined for book publication as *The Moon Maid* by McClurg in 1926.

Once more utilizing a favorite device, the prologue, to bring the main character Julian into contact with an unidentified narrator, Burroughs, in "The Moon Maid," establishes a bleak setting of a 1967 world finally at peace after a half-century of warfare. Julian and the narrator, whose only role is to be the recipient of Julian's extraordinary tale, meet on the trans-

Cover of The Moon Maid, *1926; J. Allen St. John, illustrator.*

oceanic airship *Harding,* en route to Paris. The day is one of unusual importance — Mars Day — with the earth, after attempts that spanned twenty-two years, at last receiving a message from Mars marked Helium, Barsoom. But in one of the most richly imaginative of all his stories, Burroughs projects his events farther into the future, allowing Julian to recount, through a series of reincarnations, the sequence of happenings that would bring a terrible catastrophe to the earth.

In "The Moon Maid," as Julian tells his story, the incredulous listener learns that the man is really Julian 5th, born in the year 2000, and now returned to earth in one of his reincarnations. Julian explains, ". . . I differ only from my fellows in that I can recall the events of many incarnations, while they can recall none of theirs other than a few important episodes of that particular one they are experiencing. . . ."

Julian reveals that after the fifty years of war ended in 1967, the world had been completely disarmed. Other than those weapons retained by the International Peace Fleet, whose duty was to prevent any preparations for war, "there wasn't a firearm in the world. . . . There was not a gas shell nor a radio bomb, nor any engine to discharge or project one; and there wasn't a big gun of any calibre in the world. . . ." Man had apparently eliminated the war threat on earth. But he had naively failed to foresee another danger, "external sources over which he had no control." Because of the scheming of a warped genius, Lieutenant Commander Orthis, whose sabotage of a flight to Mars forced the airship to make an emergency landing on the moon, an unarmed earth was to find itself helpless to resist an invasion that had never been anticipated — from the moon.

Through the science-fiction theme, Burroughs, always a supporter of the military, was expressing his alarm over our weakened armed forces and his objections to the disarmament proposals of the postwar period. His 1918 articles had stressed the need for the maintenance of a strong reserve army. In these writings and in his opinions he had left no doubt that the prime source of apprehension here on earth was the radical movement socialism or communism. The new and frightening government of Russia, the one he referred to as "Bolshevikism," he viewed as a menace to which the world must be alerted; his "Under the Red Flag," the original version of "The Moon Men," had been written for that purpose. However, Burroughs' later imaginary vision of danger and disaster coming from the moon is both startling and provocative — an idea significant in what it could portend for our future. As the result of an actual disarmament which our world might attain by the twenty-first century, could *we* face the appalling possibility of destructive invasion from another planet?

Perhaps the most remarkable aspect of the moon trilogy is displayed in Burroughs' preparation for the writing, notably in his worksheets for "The Moon Maid." His astonishing capacity for detail and for devising names and places for his exotic civilizations is evident in these pages of planning, but beyond the notes and glossary of terms, he has gone to unusual care to compile a lengthy list of all of Julian's reincarnations, with birth and death dates and other information. From Julian 1st, born in 1896 and killed in France on Armistice Day, and Julian 2nd, born in 1917 and killed in battle in Turkey in 1938, Burroughs proceeds far into the future to Julian 20th. Both Julian 3rd and 4th were killed in service as the line progressed into the twenty-first century; Julian 15th, life span 2259-2309, merits the note "Drove Kalkars from Desert 2309," and the list moves successively through the centuries of reincarnation to end with Julian 20th, born in 2409.

Burroughs' worksheets also contained his drawing of a Va-gas, a human quadruped, described as "A Marauder of the Moon" and "A Lunar Savage," and a page with two drawings, one a cross-section of the moon and the other a smaller area marked with geographical places. He notes the crater where Julian 5th entered the interior of the moon and provides locations of the airship, river, woods, and sea. Interestingly, he had fastened a newspaper clipping to

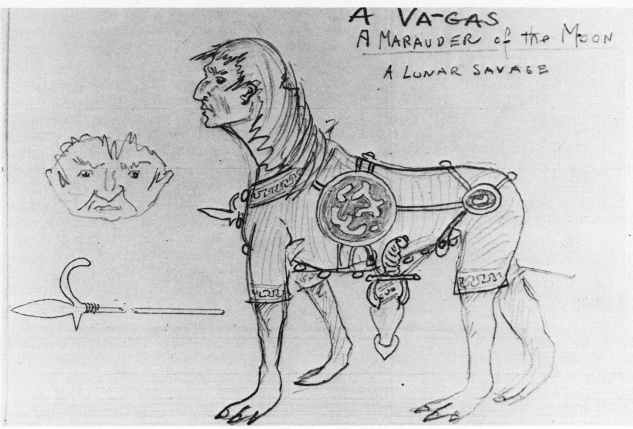

ERB's pencil sketch of a Va-Gas, a lunar savage, for "The Moon Men."

a sheet; its headline read: "Radio Impulses Can Run Plane," and the article reports on the powers of remote radio control and on the instruments displayed at a convention of electrical engineers.[15]

Through his creations in the trilogy, Burroughs expounds other philosophies. In the origin of the Kalkars on the moon, they were first members of a secret society called The Thinkers, "who did more talking than thinking," but who managed to influence the people to rise up and take over the government. The implication of similar dangers from communism is obvious. Burroughs, however, a man of action, is also exhibiting his contempt for the passive intellectuals who merely theorize. As described in "The Moon Maid," The Thinkers "would not work, and the result was that both government and commerce fell into rapid decay." Here Burroughs, in his own way, is jeering at the Communists and especially at the

IWWs of World War I whom he had previously condemned; these radicals were merely idle "thinkers," who wouldn't stoop to hard work and who had impractical and dangerous political solutions for the world's problems.

At the end of "The Moon Maid," with its "frame" structure of a story told to a listener (and narrator), Julian 5th completes his tale and then promises to give an account of the adventures in a later reincarnation — that of Julian 9th. With "The Moon Men," now the second of the trilogy, the conquest of the earth occurs. Julian's bitter enemy, Lieutenant Commander Orthis, who retains his unchanging hatred through a series of reincarnations that match those of Julian, had devoted his twenty-four years on the moon to persuading the Kalkars that an unarmed world was theirs for the taking, and to directing them in the organization of a huge army equipped with new weapons of destruction. In the year 2050, with the aid of an electronic rifle which disintegrated metal through the hurling of radioactive vibrations — "the electrons of the attacked substance increased their own vibratory rate to a point that they became dissipated again into their elemental and invisible state" — Orthis was able to wipe out most of the International Peace Fleet. In the final battle, however, Julian 5th produces his own counterinvention and the two plunge to a flaming death in their airships. "The Moon Men" then tells the tale of Julian 9th, born in 2100 in Chicago, and, in a primitive world surviving on the ruins of the past civilization, governed by the Kalkars with their all-powerful Committee of the Twenty-Four.

Within this setting Burroughs angles unexpectedly for the creation of one of his characters. In "The Ghostly Script" he had exhibited sympathy for the Negroes and had made his main character a Negro sergeant; now he chose to turn to a minority group again and deal sensitively with the Jew, old Moses Samuels, who made a living tanning hides. Moses and Julian, close friends, are united also through their hatred of the Kalkars. All religious worship is forbidden, but the descendants of Protestants, Catholics, and Jews all join to hold services in a concealed church. Strangely, old Moses has saved a tiny image, the figure of a man nailed to a cross, given to one of his ancestors by a Catholic nurse; Julian, presented with the carving by Moses, has no idea what the figure represents, and it remains for the Jew to tell him that the man is the Son of God. The death of Moses is foreshadowed. After terrible torture by the Kalkars, as he lies dying, Julian tries vainly to save him: "Tears came to my eyes in spite of all I could do, for friends are few, and I had loved this old Jew, as we all did who knew him." In the violent revolt that comes at the end of the story, many of the Kalkars are murdered, and Julian notes, "More than once I heard the name of Samuels the Jew. Never was a man more thoroughly avenged than he that day."

Throughout "The Moon Men" the American flag, banned by the Kalkars, but kept hidden and almost worshipped by Julian and his friends, serves as a symbol of their former freedom and as a means of uniting them in readiness for resistance. At the end, Julian 9th kills his reincarnated enemy, now named Or-tis, and is himself killed; but once more, on the completion of his story, he suggests to his narrator that an account of a future life is forthcoming.

The final story of the moon trilogy is set in the year 2430, with Julian 20th leading the struggle against the Kalkars, who have been driven across the continent and are confined in an area adjacent to the sea. The bitter feud between the houses of Julian and Or-tis continues. Titled "The Red Hawk," after Julian, who is the chief of a hundred fierce clans that swear allegiance to his house, the story continues the warfare in a country whose inhabitants have returned to the tribal customs and apparel of the American Indians. Thus oddly, after four hundred years of battles, "the wheel is come full circle," and the United States has reverted to the nomadic civilization of its first Americans. Feathers are worn in the bands that confine their hair, and Red Hawk is so named because he displays the clan sign of his family, a single feather from the redtailed hawk. In various other ways these Americans duplicate Indian customs: they use ocher to paint themselves; their clothing is made of deerskin; they are armed with lances, swords, and bows and arrows; and they take the scalps of their enemies.

For geographical names and places Burroughs on occasion retains those belonging to an ancient America of the twentieth century. With the warfare raging near the Pacific Ocean, there are references to Bear Lake, Cajon Pass, Rustic and Santa Monica canyons, and the capital at Pasadena, near Los Angeles. Corruptions of American names include the tribes of the Kolrados and Utaws, the Nipons as descendants of the Japanese, and the flag handed down through the generations — the Flag of Argon (Argonne).

In contriving an ending for "The Red Hawk" and the trilogy, Burroughs uses a variation of the Romeo and Juliet theme, one of a happy nature. The four-hundred-year feud of the houses of Julian and Or-tis is finally resolved when the two join forces, Americans all, to drive the Kalkars into the sea, and when Julian falls in love with Bethelda, an Or-tis descendant, and takes her for his wife.[16]

Despite his diminished interest in writing further *Tarzan* novels, based both upon his belief that he had exhausted the theme, and his fear that public demand was on the wane, in 1922 he turned again to contrive adventures for the ape-man, this time in the familiar setting of Opar and with the addition of a new African country dominated by gorilla-men. Davis, at *All-Story*, had no doubts about the continuing public fascination with *Tarzan* stories; it was sufficient for him that the new story bore a *Tarzan* title and carried the Burroughs name. His acceptance of "Tarzan and the Golden Lion" was prompt.

On June 14, in thanking Davis for the $4,000 check, Ed commented, "I was not at all sure that you would find the story acceptable, as I was very much disappointed in it myself. . . ." Davis' reply a week later was in his typically bantering tone. He noted that, to him, Ed's confession revealed he was "not entirely without shame." The story, he conceded, was not the best one Ed had written; it had insufficient conflict and consisted mainly of "long treks — going away from here and coming back again." Nevertheless he planned to feature it in the Fortieth Anniversary issue of *Argosy All-Story* with a special four-color cover illustration and the announcement, "Triumphant Return of Tarzan of the Apes."

Earlier that year Ed had signed an agreement with the Munsey Company guaranteeing them the first reading of his entire output of fiction for the two years from May 1, 1922, to April 30, 1924. While he noted that his aim would be to supply them with "one hundred eighty thousand words of Tarzan manuscript," he stressed that this plan was not to be binding. He again disparaged "Tarzan and the Golden Lion" in his letter of June 28 and remarked, "My readers have been too good to me to deserve another 'Tarzan' story as rotten as this last one. . . ."

The novel, written from February 10 to May 31, 1922, served up a familiar fare, but did provide colorful sections in the creation of Jad-bal-ja, the Golden Lion, raised from a cub by Tarzan and trained to attack, retrieve, or kill at his command. Burroughs this time devises an entire group of villains, repeating his past tendency to make his most evil characters foreigners.

In "Tarzan and the Golden Lion" Burroughs again states his philosophy of the decadence of civilization as compared with the simple virtues of nature. The old white man who had been held prisoner by the gorilla-men for many years is advised by Tarzan not to return to civilization, but to stay and help the natives. Should he return, Tarzan says, he will find "deceit, and hypocrisy, and greed, and avarice, and cruelty." For himself, Tarzan explains that he had always been glad to come back to the jungle — "to the noble beasts that are honest in their loves and in their hates — to the freedom and genuineness of nature."[17]

On September 8, 1922, for publication in the special anniversary issue of *Argosy All-Story*, Davis requested a 400-word introduction to "Tarzan and the Golden Lion," in which the Tarzan series and characters would be traced from the first story. The article, as written by Burroughs (1,200 words), contained some interesting data:

Tarzan of the Apes had been rejected by thirteen London publishers before Metheun accepted it. The story (as of 1922) had been translated into Swedish, Norwegian, Danish, Dutch, German, Russian and Arabic, with offers pending for French, Spanish, and Italian translations.

Burroughs also provided some revelations; he was able to clarify the philosophy about Tarzan that he apparently had come to believe:

The life of Tarzan of the Apes is symbolic of the evolution of man and the rise of civilization, during which mankind gained much in its

359

"Tarzan and the Golden Lion" cover of Argosy All-Story Weekly, *December 9, 1922.*

Tarzana's baseball team, about 1922, which ERB helped sponsor; ERB, with white cap, in back row.

never-ending search for luxury; but not without the sacrifice of many desirable characteristics, as well as the greater part of its liberty.

Concerning *Tarzan the Terrible*, written in 1920, he noted:

A year or so before, the late Walter Winans, Esq., of London, commenced sending me clippings relative to purported encounters between white and native hunters, and some huge creature of prehistoric appearance in the swamps of central Africa. Mr. Winans, I believe, was himself convinced of the existence of such a creature. Upon it I constructed the Gryf of Tarzan the Terrible, and wove the story of the Ho-don and the Waz-don and the land of Pal-ul-don....

With "Tarzan and the Golden Lion" Burroughs adopted a new writing practice — the use of the Ediphone. On his worksheet he noted, "Commenced dictating on the Ediphone on page 9 of this mss.," and in connection with "The Moon Maid," a later story, commented that he had used the Ediphone partially and then changed to the typewriter. Finding some difficulty in adjusting to the process of direct dictation, he was inclined to attribute his supposedly inferior writing, during this period, to the new method. To Davis, on September 27, 1922, he confided that he had "discovered the reason" why "Tarzan and the Golden Lion" and "The Moon Maid" were not up to his usual quality: "These two stories I dictated to an

Ediphone. I wanted to give the machine a fair trial, since there is no question but what it would have greatly reduced the actual labor of transferring my thoughts to paper, and it would have relieved me of practically all eye strain, which, with advancing years, I find to be increasing."

He added, "After finishing The Moon Maid, I abandoned the Ediphone and my last story I wrote directly on the typewriter, with the result that I think you will find considerably more action, and at the same time a better knit story." In later years, however, he returned to the use of a dictating machine, the Dictaphone.

The need for a respite from the jungle and fantasy stories prompted him to seek for ideas elsewhere, but in the new writing he resorted to an overused theme — intrigue centering about the monarchy in a miniature kingdom. "Beware," written from August 9 to 31, 1922, features the plotting of revolutionaries to seize power in Assuria. However, Burroughs does devise a new approach, shifting from the Assurian revolution, the death of the king and queen, and the flight of the infant crown prince to a resumption of events twenty-two years later in New York City. In the prologue, where the royal tragedy occurs, the newly born Prince Alexander is saved by Lieutenant Donovan, an officer of the foreign corps. Mrs. Donovan, who herself had given birth to a son two days before, pretends that twins had been born; taking the young prince, she and her husband flee. On board the ocean liner one of the infants dies.

With the passage of twenty-two years, Macklin Donovan, established as a son of the former Assurian officer, becomes the main character. The older Donovan is a police lieutenant, while Macklin, working in the United States Secret Service, is investigating the involvement of wealthy Mason Thorn with a group of Assurians. The interest in Macklin displayed by the snobbish Mrs. Glassock and her daughter Genevieve is motivated by his supposed family prestige and wealth. Macklin is really in love with the exotic Nariva, a mysterious guest.

The story now takes an unexpected direc-

tion. Messages to Macklin, printed notes containing the single word "Beware," emanate from a locked closet. The incidents that follow create an impression of a typical detective story. The mystery involves various secret panels that lead to the adjoining house where the conspirators are operating. At the ending Burroughs prefers to leave the most puzzling question unanswered. Is Macklin Donovan really the Crown Prince Alexander? Only Mrs. Donovan, gravely ill and not expected to live, can supply the answer. But she is in a coma, and whether she ever gains consciousness and makes a statement is not revealed.

In sending the 24,000-word story to Davis, Burroughs suggested that the editor read the prologue last to see what the effect would be. In this case the early events in Assuria would emerge at the end as a type of additional denouement. Davis' evaluation of "Beware," sent on September 12, 1922, was one of blunt disapproval:

. . . I think Beware is the nearest approach to mediocrity that ever came from your pen, and Lord, Edgar, how did you come to fall back among the Russians, the Grand Dukes, Prince Alexander, Crown Princes, then drag them and their descendants along with Saranov down to the present day. That whole bunch smell to high heaven in fiction. . . .

One rejection had never been convincing to Burroughs, and the usual list of submissions followed. Refusals came from *Blue Book* (1922) and *Detective Tales & Weird Tales* (1923). An offer of $230 for the story by *Weird Tales* in 1929 was turned down. Sales efforts continued, and a rejection by *Detective Book* was received in 1938. Finally, in 1939, "Beware" was purchased by Raymond Palmer, editor of *Fantastic Adventures,* for $245. With some of the characters and plot elements changed by Palmer, and the time setting projected to the year 2190, "Beware" was now transformed from a hodge-podge royal intrigue-detective mystery novelette to a science-fiction story and published in the July 1939 issue of the magazine, where it somehow acquired the incongruous title of "The Scientists Revolt."

Miscellaneous writings from the Burroughs pen, both published and unpublished, were produced in the years 1921-25. His article, appearing in *The American News Trade Journal*, April 1921, was a practical one, stressing the required cooperation of the publisher, jobber, retailer, and author in the sale of books and periodicals. But Burroughs first discussed his personal feelings about books: "I like to handle them and to own them. I hate to see them abused. I sometimes fancy that an adult who habitually marks his place in a volume by turning down the corner of a leaf would kick a dog or strike a horse without even provocation of anger." Beyond this emotional attitude toward books, of course, was the "stern necessity" that prompted him to write books, and the dealers to sell them, "the ability . . . to provide for ourselves and our families." He noted that a man does not search for fame; this, perhaps, may come to him later. "It is the box office receipts that really count most while we live." As always, he had a suggestion for increasing book sales. Recognizing the public's interest in the author, Ed proposed that meet-the-author sessions be held each Thursday afternoon at book shops, with selected individuals notified through mailed invitations. In later years he attended many similar sessions at which he autographed copies of his latest book.

Through the years, Burroughs' works had been subjected to severe criticism by those who valued writings of different literary quality. Included in this group were other authors, university professors, and librarians. An article attacking the *Tarzan* stories, published in the March 1922 *Wisconsin Library Bulletin,* had come to Burroughs' attention. The author, Professor Noble, chose to condemn the books, first of all, because of their harmful effects upon children; he also offered scathing comment about certain plot devices, emphasizing their faults and improbabilities. On April 24, in his response to the "rather violent attack" on the *Tarzan* books, Ed presented a logical and convincing argument: The *Tarzan* books were not written for children, though some children were reading them; there was still no evidence that highly imaginative fiction, taken in moderation, was harmful to children. Ed agreed that his works were designed for entertainment, not instruction, adding that the "use of them for this purpose in schools is ridiculous." He had never encouraged this practice. He showed tact in agreeing with Noble that "an exclusive diet of *Tarzan* books would be harmful. . . ."

It is significant to note that in later years after Burroughs' death various schoolteachers were using his books as a means of stimulating an interest in reading. One teacher on a Navajo Indian reservation found the *Tarzan* books to be his best tool for teaching the English language.

In his defense of the imagination Ed displayed a depth of perception: "The power of imagination is all that differentiates the human mind from that of brute creation. Without imagination there is no power to visualize what we have never experienced, and without that power there can be no progress." Although not an educator, he had sound theories on how the child's mind could be developed. Fairy tales, for example, not only stimulate the child's imagination, but "inculcate . . . the first seed of the love of books, and whatever accomplishes this, so long as it carries no harmful teachings, is well worth while." He noted that many adults today derived their first love of literature from reading the *Nick Carter* books. Thus, it was not wise to force children to read books in which they had no interest; they could develop a "subconscious abhorrence" of books. The more intelligent approach was obvious: permit the child to read any story that was not harmful, having confidence that after he had learned to love books, his taste in literature would expand and improve as the years passed. Ed pleaded that children be allowed some voice in choosing what they read — other than those books required in English classes. He remarked, "I have yet to learn of any greater harm resulting from the reading of Tarzan than an injury sustained by an English boy who fell out of a tree while attempting to emulate him."

To Ed's astonishment, from faraway Truro, England, came a statement of support and protest from William G. Hale of the Free Public Library. Indignant over the attack on the *Tarzan* books, Hale, on May 24, addressed a four-page letter to the *Wisconsin Library Bulletin,* offering a point-by-point analysis of Noble's criticisms; Hale sent a copy of the letter to Ed. While thanking him for his advocacy, Ed, on June 20, was doubtful that the *Bulletin* would print the response, and commented, "I understand that American Librarians are laboring under the delusion that their proper duty in life is to safeguard public morals and education rather than to furnish people with reading matter they desire."

Hale, who had been a public librarian for twenty-six years, observed that "the faults found with the Tarzan stories are no worse than the speech with which Kipling endows his animals; they are the legitimate license of the novelist." Hale made specific references to four plot elements derided by Noble: Tarzan's learning to read through a picture book; the unusual strength of a grass rope; Tarzan's manufacture of a knife with the aid of a whetstone; and Tarzan's "nimble and quiet transit" through the trees. All of these, according to Hale, appeared reasonable within the setting, and moreover, they did not exceed the bounds of license allowed to a writer of romances.

Again, Hale established comparisons with Kipling, whom he admired greatly, despite his "improbable soldiers" and his jungle animals who talk "sheer fairy-like stuff." But Hale reserved his most telling blow for the end, what he termed "the real rock of offence in the Tarzan books." It was not the faults of the plot or any defects in the English. Hale confessed that in other American books he had squirmed over such rendering of good English words as "catalog," "program," "colum" and "other docktailed words which make one think of a Manx cat." Nor was the objection by Noble based upon the improbabilities in the *Tarzan* stories. Hale, in a brilliant insight, discloses the real cause behind Noble's distaste for Tarzan:

It is the true and close parallel which Mr. Burroughs draws between the ape and the man showing the essential relationship between the two. Such parallelism vexes the egotism which would fain keep man on a separate plane of creation by himself, disowning the crowd of animal forms from which he has sprung, and to which in moments of primal emotional stress he so plainly reverts.

Burroughs' fervent support of Darwin's theories was of course evident to Hale. To Burroughs, Tarzan's development illustrated Darwin's ideas:

The Tarzan stories constitute the epic of the great evolution of man from the ape, a process in which there were no breaks, no supernatural interventions, but just the irrepressible upward surging of the divine thought through its animal stages from ape to man.

The jungle childhood and growth of Tarzan represents a "similar resume of that evolution to the older and longer one which every animal embryo runs through. . . ." Hale summarized, "In the embryo, we get the whole course of evolution; in Tarzan the course of its mental evolution from ape to man."

Hale continued his penetrating analysis with an appeal:

Let us cast aside this ancient cant of man's separateness. We are not separate; we are close kin to all that breathes; a blood brotherhood exists that will not be denied, and that Mr. Burroughs has rightly and legitimately emphasized and made plain in Tarzan. . . .

Undoubtedly, Burroughs, without articulating it, had been aware of his "blood brotherhood" with the animals, as part of the great plan of evolution, and had demonstrated this in his love of animals, his admiration for their simple virtues, and his solicitude for their treatment by man.

In carrying his logic a step farther, Hale noted that this idea of common origin was what made the appeal of the Tarzan books "so strong and universal"; the public showed an "unconscious approval" of the idea. "Tarzan realizes the jungle life of our ancestors of long ago," Hale maintained. "If he is trash, so are we [even including the professor] for we come of the same stock. . . ." Hale referred to one of Burroughs' favorite themes — the decadence of our supposed "civilization" — in mentioning man's "thinking his way up" from the jungle to the city:

"Up," did I say? What about Upton Sinclair's Jungle, *the abysmal depths of our filthy city brothels and "society" scandals, the atrocities of war, the gaols and the asylums? Any of these in Tarzan's jungle?*

In another letter to Ed, also dated May 24, 1922, Hale turned to a different topic, this time a special interest. He had adopted geology as a hobby, had given a series of lectures on the subject, and in the course of these had done much reading and investigation of the supposed "lost" continent of Atlantis. He now urged Ed to use Atlantis as the setting for a sequence of novels, with emphasis upon the lost continent as an entity in the long chain of human evolution. Hale suggested a "plan of order" in which reincarnation of characters might be utilized to "link distant periods of time." The steps would include the following: the "sheer brute man stage" (ape land) evolving in the south polar area; the beginnings of tools and civilization as man moved westward during the Southern Glacial Period; the separation of races to the Pacific continent, to South Africa, and to South America and Atlantis.

Hale stressed his theory that "the geographical rising and sinking of the continents" had a significant effect upon human evolution. In enclosing two small maps for Burroughs, he noted that the "ghost of Atlantis" was evident in the great mass of submerged land. "Any chart shows a surprising lot of reefs and banks in N. Atlantic which the ordinary land atlases ignore,

showing that old Atlantis is not so utterly gone as some might imagine." He added that "the Azores and Canary Islands seem the best existing points to anchor an Atlantis story to. . . ."

Hale also enclosed a descriptive list of books about Atlantis. The nonfiction group of course included the earliest source contained in *Timaeus,* one of Plato's *Dialogs,* and referred to Darwin's *Coral Islands* picturing a "slowly sinking sea bottom" which would provide some foundation for an old continent in the Pacific. He noted, in addition, a number of fictional works about Atlantis, and offered to send all these books to Burroughs.[18]

Hale's enthusiasm was transmitted to Burroughs who, on June 20, appeared strongly inclined to accept the suggestion to write a series about Atlantis, but not until a future period when present work was completed. Burroughs explained his intention to obtain the listed books by asking his London agent, Curtis Brown, to purchase them. On August 29 he sought Davis' opinion on the choice of Atlantis as a story subject. The editor's reply of September 8 was bluntly negative: ". . . if I were you I wouldn't monkey with that submerged continent. It has already been hit so damned hard that nobody cares whether it ever reappears again." Possibly as a result of this, Burroughs abandoned the idea. Concerning Hale's suggestion that reincarnation of characters be used (to develop the evolutionary sequence), Burroughs had already conceived of this idea in "The Moon Men," completed January 1922, but it is possible that in "The Moon Maid," written in July of that year, with the worksheets listing a lengthy series of reincarnations from 1918 to 2409, Burroughs had been stimulated by Hale, with the result being his greater emphasis upon the reincarnations. But curiously, if a comparison is to be made with Darwin's theories, the "evolution" is in reverse; mankind, on earth, *retrogresses* from an advanced, highly civilized form in the Moon trilogy to the primitive, savage level of the American Indian, as the events of the last story, "The Red Hawk," take place. Burroughs' imagination, perhaps subconsciously, found its own method of adapting Darwinism. In other works, notably his first, *A Princess of Mars,* he had pictured this backward journey, this reversal of man's natural evolution, with the planet Mars returning to barbarism, and again one might conjecture that Darwin's theories provided the inspiration.

Ed's conviction that evolution was a scientific verity, a law beyond dispute, influenced him in 1925 to issue a statement to the press at the time of the Scopes Trial at Dayton, Tennessee. Written for the International Press Bureau and Universal Service, the article appeared in various papers, including the *New York American* of July 6, where it was headed "Evolution held undeniable. Nature's law, says author." Ed's delivered opinion had a tone of impatience with those who needed to be informed of the obvious:

It really does not make much difference what Mr. Scopes thinks about evolution, or what Mr. Bryan thinks about it. They cannot change it by thinking, or talking, or by doing anything else. It is an immutable law of Nature; and when we say that, it is just the same as saying that it is an immutable law of God — that is, for those who believe in God — for one cannot think of God and Nature as separate and distinct agencies.

He went on to explain, "If we are not religious then we must accept evolution as an obvious fact. If we are religious then we must either accept the theory of evolution or admit that there is a power greater than that of God. . . ." His arguments, in the remainder of the article, were based upon the evidences all around us — "the infant into the adult . . . the seed into the plant, the bud into the flower:" these illustrate that all organisms pass through preliminary stages of development to attain a final form. The "marvelous miracle of evolution" is that everything, the entire universe, follows a natural "unfolding." Concerning the human race, a simple consideration of the succession of the Piltdown man, Neanderthal man, and Cro-Magnon man, in progress up the scale of development, makes it clear "that Nature did not produce the finished product originally, but something that was susceptible of improvement. . . ." Ed did not attempt to deny God's connection with this evolutionary plan; the individual could view it as Nature's law or God's law, but above all, mankind must accept "the proofs that God, or Nature, has left for our enlightenment." On an obvious level, those who cannot understand Darwin's theories should be able to perceive how "the entire evolution of the human race" is reproduced "within the womb of every mother."

In other writing of the period, Ed, for Arbor Day, 1922, prepared a speech for presentation to the Uplifters, a social group to which he belonged. Here again he revealed his early awareness of ecology and expressed his ardent support of conservation. Once more he took care to create a combined tone of religion and pantheism in his speech. God may be considered as "The Great Scientist" who maintains a laboratory where He "tries" new forms. All of these experiments are not successful. Evolution is referred to; God discards many forms, and "the object of His changes lies in the direction of eventual perfection." His master works are the earth with its plant life, mineral kingdom, and the great mountains. But in the animal kingdom "He has not done quite so well, if man is his ultimate conception. In fact, He is doubtless rather disappointed."

As an Arbor Day speech, the main subject then became the tree, "a living, breathing thing which in majesty, dignity, and beauty, transcends all His other works. In the tree God has attained perfection." The Uplifters' task for that day was to plant trees. Ed mentioned the eucalyptus, one of his favorites, and one of the most ancient of trees which probably existed in Eocene times, and from that offered a belief: ". . . trees will still be here after man has gone the way of all the countless forms of animal life that preceded him." To Ed it was a "tremendous" thought which suggested the greatness of Nature and the insignificance of man. After all, the saber-tooth tiger who may have stalked

366

his prey in the Tarzana canyons was gone, "although he took very much better care of himself than we do. . . ." Obviously, man will not "persist through eternity," but the trees will. Ed noted, "I can contemplate with equanimity the thought of a manless world; but a treeless world — never!"

Those individuals who in the 1970s began to display a serious concern about the destruction of the earth's surface should appreciate the remarkable fact that Burroughs, through a unique philosophy that united him in love and respect with all of nature, had preceded them by more than fifty years in this concern. In his loving and understanding and fiercely protective attitude toward animals, trees, and plants, he truly exemplified the religious man who in his highest form is described by Coleridge: "He prayeth best who loveth best/All things both great and small. . . ." Burroughs, who as a writer was given to personifying the animals in his stories, thought of his trees in the same way. Toward the oaks, sycamores, and walnut trees on his ranch he felt not only an "affection," but "an intimate and personal touch which implies, at the least, friendship."

The value he placed upon trees was demonstrated in the unusual nature of his alfalfa fields, dotted with sycamores and walnuts. Here the trees made the harvesting more difficult and expensive and were occupying land that could be used for crops. Ed remarked about the foreman who objected to them and who thought he was a "hopeless idiot" when he (Burroughs) insisted that if driven to a matter of choice, he would do away with the alfalfa rather than the trees. He spoke with regret of the huge old oaks, located on property recently subdivided in the Tarzana area, that were now being cut down. To him this was "an odious crime," and he wondered if a law could be enacted that would place all native trees, even privately owned, under the protection of the state. In later years this became a reality in the neighboring community of Encino. Of all his trees, one that he especially cherished was an enor-

mous walnut in his orchard: ". . . I often ride into its shade on my horse in the summer time and I am sure that twelve or fifteen horsemen could stand beneath its branches without crowding."

To the Uplifters listening to his speech Ed offered to donate Tarzana live oaks for transplanting; *Quercus Tarzania,* he noted, was "some tree." He stressed one final thought: we are planting trees for the benefit of our children and our children's children. And through our examples, they may learn to love and treasure trees and to plant them for succeeding generations.

What Ed had viewed or experienced during motion picture production involving the use of animals became the subject of his first article in this field. Titled "Wild Animals in Pictures," the article was completed on March 23, 1922, at the request of E. E. Graneman of Anchor Films in Los Angeles, and appeared in June of that year in the magazine *Hollywood Screenland.* Ed's emphasis, as might be expected, was upon the humane treatment of these animals. They were trained by "masters who have felt and demonstrated an actual affection for their charges. . . . The 'bad' lion, like the 'bad' horse, is usually the result of brutal and ignorant mishandling by a trainer." Ed mentioned watching such trainers as Walter Beckwith, Charlie Gay, and Joe Turner and being impressed by their intelligent and kindly treatment of their animals.

Although conceding that some of the animal scenes are faked, Ed explained that the really thrilling action is bona fide, and the actors, or even the trainers who double as actors, take suicidal chances. He had especially admired the courage of tiny Louise Lorraine. "I have seen a whole bevy of lionesses pass directly over her half naked body, and a full-grown lion spring upon her and throw her to the ground." He described a scene in which Charley Gay, doubling for an actress, was required to dive off a fifteen-foot cliff into a pool with a lioness in close pursuit. The terrified beast had to be driven to the cliff's edge, and as a result, the trainer and the lioness struck the water together. Ed commented that he would hardly have swapped places with Gay who rose to the surface of the small pool to face an infuriated lioness.

Ed recalled his most dangerous personal experience when, at his request, he was allowed inside the arena to witness a scene involving a "particularly vicious lion." He had presumed that the director and leading actor would accompany him but, to his consternation, found himself alone. The director had handed him a large club and said, "Do not run if he comes for you. Just stand still and use this." His actions make it appear that the whole situation was somebody's idea of a practical joke. Ed described what followed:

While I was reviewing my past life and wishing that I had been a better man, they opened the gate at the end of the runway and loosed the lion upon us. . . . I had always considered him a very beautiful lion, but as I faced him in the arena it occurred to me that he had an extremely low forehead and a bad disposition. He was the incarnation of all the devil-faced man-eaters with which I had filled the pages of the Tarzan books.

Moments later the lion was driven back into his runway, and Ed noted, "it was with a sigh of relief that I laid aside my futile war club and stood in the fresh air of the sunshine beyond the limits of the studio jungle."

In a 1,000-word article written for Thomas Ford, literary editor of the *Los Angeles Times,* and sent to him on December 29, 1922, Ed, after reiterating that fiction should not be read for purposes of instruction or enlightenment, made reference to a number of his favorite authors. First mentioned were Mary Roberts Rienhart and Booth Tarkington, but he reserved his highest praise for Owen Wister's *The Virginian,* which, along with *The Prince and the Pauper* and *Little Lord Fauntleroy,* he admitted having read five or six times. Ed wrote:

I believe The Virginian *to be one of the greatest American novels ever written, and though I have heard that Mr. Wister deplores having written it I venture that a hundred years from now it will constitute his sole link to Fame — and I am sure that* The Virginian *will live a hundred years, if the Bolshevists and the I.W.W. permit civilization to endure that long.*

Ed then launched into an attack on "literary people" — he was quite sensitive to their disparagement of his works — and remarked that he had met a few but had "never stayed awake long enough to get acquainted." About them he commented sarcastically, "Literary people do not write. They read what other people write, discuss it, criticise it, quarrel about it and altogether take it much more seriously than the people who write it." They love to meet their favorite authors, he noted, but "sometimes they are happier when they don't":

If one should meet God and find that He wore a dirty collar, ate with a knife and picked His teeth in public he would feel shocked and disillusioned — would one not? Well, of course you can not expect all authors to be better than God. There are some to be sure; but we are in the minority.

Concerning the practice of collecting, termed "a peculiar form of insanity," he recalled how he had saved stamps, coins, and postmarks in his boyhood, and reported that his two sons were now making a "weird" collection of animal bones. The "true spirit of the collector" is revealed in the acquiring of "useless, valueless, discarded things." The "most hideous form" of collecting, according to Ed, was that of uncut books; no individual who really loves books would have an uncut volume on his shelves.

He reserved his most caustic comment for those "modern writers of so called sex stories"; he was quite willing for their books to remain uncut, and to these he added "the complete works of Charles Dickens, each of which bore me to extinction."

A different type of writing, a loosely compiled account of vacation travels, was one that Ed completed during this period. His ten-page

Camp table of willow and quaking aspen built by ERB at Mono Creek, August 27, 1924.

description of a 1924 fishing excursion, into California's Sierra August 22 to September 1, was headed "Notes on Trip to Mono Creek and Porpoise Lake." With his two sons, Hulbert, age fifteen, and Jack, age eleven, Ed left Los Angeles in his Packard roadster, heading northeast, his destination originally Mammoth Lakes, but changed to Mono Creek, a more remote and less crowded area where fishing would be better. As in the past, the first problem was with the car which failed to start the next morning. The handyman had forgotten to place tools in the car, but Ed, a pioneer in long auto trips under the most difficult and primitive conditions (for example, the 1916 cross-country journey), had through circumstances become a fairly skilled mechanic and troubleshooter. He succeeded in opening the carburetor with a jackknife and can opener, and within an hour the trio was on its way.

The article reported the typical vacation events and minor catastrophes:

Fished up Rock Creek . . . Jack fell in the creek and had to go back to camp and change. . . . Jack was sick all night — up three times. Gave him cascara . . . Sunday August 24 we started for Mono Creek with Earl Proebstel as packer and guide. [All rode horses.] . . . took us 7 1/2 hours to reach Mono Creek . . . pleasant afternoon fishing down stream . . . we passed the time until bedtime telling stories . . . the boys asked for a Timothy Twiggs story and one about Mabel, the sub-deb coyote, taking us all back to the bedtime stories I told for many years . . . Mabel; Timothy Twiggs; Arabella, Sophronia and Grandpa Kazink; Percival and Gwendolyn — night after night. . . .

In a 1974 interview at Tarzana, Hulbert recalled some occurrences of the trip:

One afternoon while resting on the bank of Mono Creek, Dad and my brother Jack were doodling in the sand with sticks. It was on this occasion that Dad devised the curious symbol that became his personal mark. He called it the Doodad. It was later used as the now-familiar colophon on the spines of the books his company started publishing in 1930. He frequently signed personal notes and memos with it.

The trip turned into one of illness and suffering for my father. The altitude of near 10,000 feet was the highest he had ever been for any length of time. Although we did not then understand the reasons, he was probably suffering from oxygen starvation.

Ed's main problem was his inability to sleep and shortness of breath. His complaints were repeated: "Followed another night of torture, during which I occasionally lapsed into a semi-comatose condition. . . . I do not understand . . . in perfect physical condition and so physically tired at the end of the day . . . I could swear that I'd sleep on a pile of cobble stones for twenty-four hours at a stretch. . . ."

Recalls Hulbert: "He did not complain at all, and we did not learn of his suffering until much later. He was so unselfish that he did not want to spoil the trip for Jack and me. It is obvious in retrospect that we should have left immediately for a lower altitude. This may have been an early symptom of the heart trouble that developed in later years."

On August 29 Ed noted their arrival at Porpoise Lake, the elevation of their new camp now being about 10,000 feet, and also listed the fishing tally to date: Hulbert, 43 trout; Jack, 4; Ed, 3. Clearly, as Ed commented, Hulbert was "the only dyed in the wool Isaac Walton in the family." Ed's eagerness to forget that he was forty-nine years old, and his overexertions in keeping up with his boys brought him a bad cold. While fishing he had stripped and entered the icy cold water to rescue a fly that had become entangled in a log. He had been ill for three days, unable to eat, and on August 31, as the return trip began, he had to summon all of his strength to make the journey. Perverse fate

Burroughs family at Tarzana Ranch, about 1921; left to right: Joan

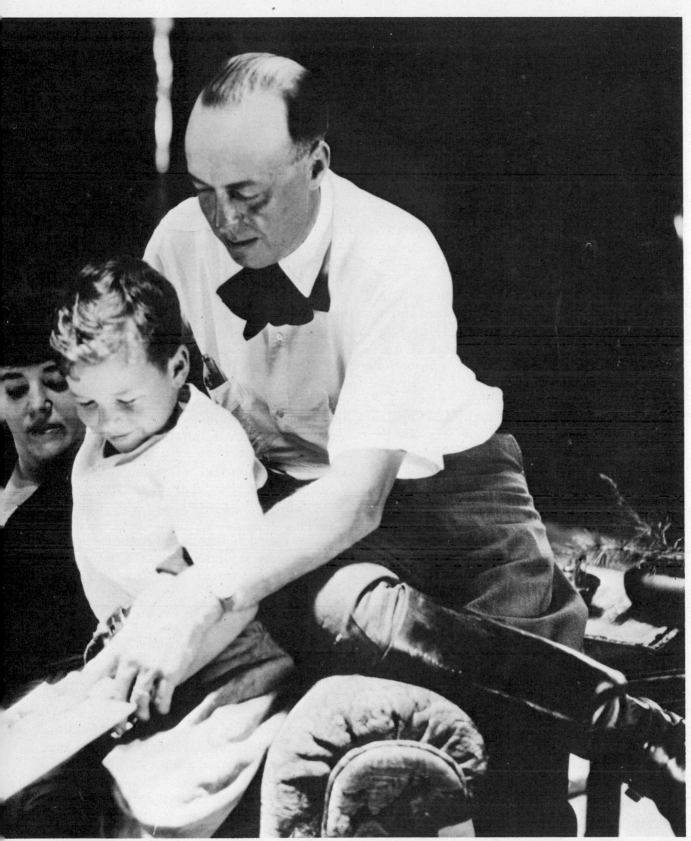

Hulbert, Emma, Jack, and ERB.

made certain that nothing would go easily; a series of car troubles followed. The battery ceased to function and the lights became too dim to view the road. The travelers arrived at Mojave at 2:30 a.m., and near dawn they ran out of gasoline. Luckily, they were on a down grade and coasted to within two miles of Saugus; then they pushed the car the remainder of the way. More pushing followed to make the car start. In his account Ed finally reported reaching home on September 1 — his birthday — and wrote, ". . . I think that in the course of three or four months, if I eat enough and sleep enough, I will approximate normalcy again."

The love of horses and horseback riding, developed from his early years in Idaho and at the military academy, still remained with him. The winding paths, hills, and canyons of Tarzana Ranch provided a unique opportunity for indulgence of this riding hobby. Ed's interest both in the saddle horse and the show horse led to his contributing an article to the *Los Angeles Times* of January 1, 1925, titled "The Saddle Horse in Southern California." Among the group of photos accompanying the article was one of Burroughs mounted upon Brigadier Rex. The article stressed the advantages possessed by the California rider, the rich beauty of nature all about him, the interesting contacts with deer or coyotes or even mountain lions, and the vast area available to the rider. But it also emphasized the healthful aspects of riding, quoting from a statement by Dr. A. J. Ochsner of Chicago who observed that no other form of exercise "so fully affects every nerve and every organ of the human body" as horseback riding does. "Nothing will bring out a healthy glow more quickly or enjoyably. . . . Nothing will more promptly put one's organs of digestion and those of elimination into the way of performing their physiologic work properly. . . ."

After discussing the expansion of horseback riding in Southern California and the growth of private and commercial stables, Ed proudly noted that interest in the horse show was now high and that this sport, especially because of the mild all-year-round climate of Los Angeles, promised to increase rapidly. He then listed prominent residents of the Los Angeles area and the five-gaited, prizewinning horses that they owned.

An unusual form of writing for ERB, a compilation of terms, is titled "Glossary of Hoodlum Language." Although undated, this five-page glossary features many expressions of the prohibition and bootlegging era; the inclusion of these indicates that the glossary was probably written in the mid-twenties. Burroughs' alphabetical list, incomplete, terminates at the "H's." Such expressions as "alky," "blind pig," "chopper," for machine gun, and "gat" are reminiscent of the prohibition-gangster period, but others in the glossary apply to differing types of disreputable activities and rackets. A number of the terms are still understood and used today: Bar flies, big house, beat the rap, broad, cop a plea, dip, fall guy, framed, grapevine. However, most of the expressions, as with the slang or argot of many periods in the past, have long since vanished from the public vocabulary. Some of these are humorous and ingenious:

Ah-ah: *Self-important, attention demanding, e.g. "Tony's broad is an ah-ah dame."*
Big cough: *Bomb containing a heavy charge of explosive.*
Block and tackle: *Watch and chain.*
Butterfly: *A worthless check.*
Caught with a biscuit: *Caught with incriminating evidence.*
Croaker: *A doctor, either physician or surgeon.*
Dance: *To die by hanging.*
Eerbay: *Beer. (Note: so-called "pig Latin" or English words turned around is commonly used among hoodlums when they want to talk in code.)*

In compiling the "Glossary of Hoodlum Language," Burroughs' intention must have been a practical one, to use the expressions in a story he was contemplating or in a series of future stories. He had done some research into the jargon or slang of the criminal classes and lowest elements of society in the past to create

ERB in coaster made by Hulbert, 1919.

vocabularies for characters in "The Girl from Farris's" (1913-14) and "The Mucker" sequence (1913-16).

Always one to speak out bluntly and forcefully in protest against injustice, Ed, in the article "The Absurd Quarantine," attacked the stringent and unreasonable quarantine regulations imposed upon stock raisers and dairy owners. During the period, evidently about 1920 (reference made to the nation's income from farm products in 1919 would appear to establish this date), Southern California was in the throes of a serious epidemic of hoof-and-mouth disease. Apparently, the authorities, in a near-panic, were adopting drastic measures to prevent the spread of the disease. Although the evidence indicated that humans could not contract it, the officials had posted armed guards at various ranches and farms to prevent individ-uals from coming in contact with supposedly diseased animals.

The question, undetermined, was how did the disease spread? Concerning the measures being used, Ed was bitterly accusative: ". . . while they experiment, California is being ruined. . . . There never has been so widespread and strict a quarantine anywhere for anything, and yet the disease hops here and there at will. Do they know the carriers? I doubt it. Cats, dogs, birds are being destroyed ruthlessly. The destruction of bird life alone might so easily upset nature's balance as to cause material losses to the farmer and fruit raiser."

Ed had noted the huge swarms of bees migrating over the fields of the Adohr Dairy, adjacent to his Tarzana Ranch. Since these bees alight on alfalfa blossoms and the cattle are pastured in the alfalfa, could the bees be the

Emma Burroughs, about 1922.

carriers, he wondered. He referred to the "absurd quarantine" that was presently spraying the inside of city dwellers' cars to prevent the spread of the disease. Would it not be more logical, he demanded, to assume that insects, especially the flies, might be the guilty carriers?

To Ed, the severe measures were being enforced to protect the assets of a comparative few — those who owned $12,000 pedigreed bulls. But what aroused his strongest indignation was the statement from the quarantine board that "whoever opposed the quarantine methods . . . was in the same category as the man who, in 1917, opposed the war." An individual who protested was classed as a traitor.

Ed pointed out that rabies had been on the increase in the Los Angeles area for the past five years; this involved the safety of the entire community, and yet no regulations had been passed. To him, the reasons for this indifference were evident. Money and wealthy owners were not involved, as in the hoof-and-mouth situation. Nobody cares, Ed maintained, "if your baby or mine is bitten by a mad dog."

He closed with an angry and defiant charge, "The quarantine as now administered is unfair, unjust, un-American, unconstitutional and absurd — but mostly absurd. If this be treason, make the most of it."

During the period of 1920-25, Burroughs turned occasionally to verse, usually light or humorous, but at times sentimental. Two poems written on December 29, 1920, titled "Sweetheart Eternal" and "Sweet Rose in God's Garden Above," are love poems of a conventional nature.

I loved you when the stars were young
And when the world was new
And every song, as yet unsung,
Welled in my heart for you.

I loved your arms, your soft, brown arms
With copper bracelets bound.
The leopard skin half hid your charms —
The depths that love would sound.

The allusions to "brown arms," "copper bracelets," and "leopard skin," and to "jungle eyes" in a later stanza, indicate that Burroughs may have intended to insert the poem in one of his stories.

"Sweet Rose in God's Garden Above" is a tragic poem, its theme based upon the death of a woman, either real or imaginary:

I dwell on the crest of a mountain
Where the winds volley up from the sea
And clouds sweeping down from the heavens
Leave no one but God there and me.

In February and June 1923, Ed wrote two narrative poems with Western settings. The first, "The Passing o' my Pal, Bill," by Texas Pete (an actual character encountered by Ed in Idaho), was later inserted in "The Bandit of Hell's Bend," written March 30 to May 24, 1923. As recounted by Texas Pete, the poem re-creates a shoot-out between Bill and another cowboy hired by the sheepmen to "git" him. Pete accompanies his friend to a bar where Bill's opponent, a "raw-boned guy," is waiting — but with a girl. The poem develops an unexpected situation:

An' the raw-boned guy wheels and the girl
*   there she squeals:*
"O, fer gawds sake don't shoot, Bill, it's dad!"

Fer the thing she had saw was Bill reach fer the
*   draw*
When the guy she called dad drawed on Bill.

At his sister's cry, Bill freezes, unable to draw, but "thet damn raw-boned guy with the ornery eye" shoots Bill "dead in the door." Texas Pete narrates the end of the tragedy:

But I'm here to opine with this bazoo o' mine
Thet he wont shoot no hombres no more.

Jest a moment, an' where they'd been five o' us
*   there,*
We hed suddenly dwindled to three —
The bar-keep, he was one — the darned son-of-
*   a-gun —*
An' the others, a orphan an' me.

Ed, who through the years had found invitations to join clubs irresistible, on various occasions had composed light verse for club functions. From his earliest period in California he had belonged to the Los Angeles Athletic Club and had later become involved in an authors' group, The Writers. In 1925 he was quite active in the Breakfast Club, and, as its most creative member, was expected to contribute poetry on demand. This varied from two poems written on August 21 to eulogize Thomas E. Campbell, ex-governor of Arizona, who was being granted honorary membership in the club, to a series of verses or lyrics designed to be sung to the melody of Upidee at a Breakfast Club function, "the passing of the oil can," in tribute to the attending oil company officials. Working on the Advisory Committee with Maurice DeMond, Ed contributed a number of lyrics for group singing.

Two other poems, possibly intended for Breakfast Club affairs, were "Hollywood" and "I'm the Guy That Sowed the Sage Brush in the Hills of Hollywood," subtitled "I Knew Him When"; these were written in October and November 1925. In "Hollywood" Ed writes of the famous heroes and great nations of the past that have long since vanished — Agamemnon, the daring Genoese, Babylon, proud Rome — and comments about Hollywood:

Thy standards flaunt the breeze today
As nations flock to homage pay
To thee, the darling of a world;
Our Hollywood!

In the second poem, humorous raillery directed at various acquaintances, Ed remarks, "I could have bought an acre right at Hollywood and Vine/If I had had ten dollars back in eighteen fifty nine" and evokes other memories of the past while noting the changes that had occurred.

Ed's other light verse included "The Wampas," written for the Western Associated Motion Picture Advertisers group attending a Breakfast Club meeting on November 20, 1925. In a satirical view of the film industry, during the same year, Ed composed a poem (untitled) describing a scene in heaven with St. Peter. A "spook," evidently a Hollywood producer or promoter, approaches St. Peter with a plan to expand and glamorize heaven with "pageants and prologs" and "The Great Ten Billion Theater," with films being shown for ten dollars a seat. But upon investigation, the producer loses all enthusiasm for the project:

There are plenty of authors in heaven
And orchestra leaders as well;
But people who act,
Directors — in fact
All the rest of the talent's in Hell."

By 1926 the overburdening pressure of business enterprises and writing projects forced Ed to relinquish his Breakfast Club activities. To DeMond, in referring to these responsibilities plus the problems of two lawsuits, Ed, on April 23, explained that he had no time to write the song requested, and in fact no time to do anything beyond his own business "for at least a year or two."[19]

Poems of a differing type, undated but probably written in the same period, were one in the prosy rhyming style of Walt Mason, whose verses in the Chicago newspapers Ed had long admired. The poem referred jokingly to glamorous movie stars of the times, including Gloria Swanson and Bebe Daniels:

'Twould joy me more than you can guess
to purchase socks for Gloria S., or
lingerie for Bebe D. In fact my sweet
*   philanthropy*
suggests I purchase all their clothes from hats
*   to hose —*
especially hose. But several things discourage
*   me*
and one of these is Mrs. B.

In 1925 Burroughs conceived of a project that would enable him to utilize his motion picture relationships. To Earle Martin of the Newspaper Enterprise Association of Cleveland, on December 17, he wrote, "I have in mind the preparation of a column or half column of studio gossip over my signature, to be furnished weekly, fortnightly or monthly. . . ." He explained that as a member of the board of directors of the Writers Club of Hollywood he heard much "inside studio gossip," noting that most of the board members were employed in the movie field. He stressed that he had "entree" to the studios and was personally acquainted with many directors, producers, and actors.

Ed's idea was to merely conduct a friendly and gossipy column, not to adopt the role of a critic or a reviewer. The column would not be used to provide publicity for individuals; he would prefer to confine himself "principally to the most prominent and widely known members of the profession." The expected question arose: would the "returns" be sufficient to warrant the amount of time he would devote to this column, including the hours he would have to spend at the principal studios? There is no record of a response from Martin; evidently Ed received no encouragement and the column idea was abandoned.

Probably no other author could match the stream of letters that Burroughs received throughout the years from readers and friends. But the constancy and loyalty of these individuals can be attributed to the care Burroughs exhibited in answering all their letters. He sincerely felt that if his loyal fans thought well enough of him and his stories to take their time to write to him, the least he could do was to show his respect and gratitude by replying. Very few of the queries, criticisms, or notes of praise remained unanswered; as though driven by some determination or feeling of pride, he responded to letters of every variety, at first writing personally and later dictating his replies. Among his most tenacious correspondents were three who began in the early 1920s and were still going strong (aided by Burroughs' persistence) from twelve to twenty-five years later. One, in the United States, was Charles K. Miller, a friend of the family and an owner of a clipping bureau in Chicago, while the other two were Burroughs readers abroad, both in England. Through dozens of letters the bond of friendship between Burroughs and Irene

Ettrick and Frank Shonfeld became unbreakable, and yet, most remarkably, he never met either of them.

Miller, from about 1922 on, began reporting various comments in the press and magazines about the Burroughs books and enclosing articles or reviews and items of literary interest. On January 3, 1923, in thanking Miller for clippings, Ed wrote, "I think you must be willfully blind to see only the kindly references to my work. . . . A recent one from my clipping bureau speaks of 'that awful trash, the Tarzan stories . . .' but I manage to bear up and get three meals a day — and pay for them. I hope my critics can do as well." In the passing years other letters from Ed to Miller had typical remarks:

May 17, 1927: "It always flatters my vanity when I hear of an intellectual who admits to liking Tarzan."

June 6, 1929: "Naturally, I am not particularly enthusiastic about book clubs inasmuch as they do not distribute or recommend my books."

August 16: "Inasmuch as no one would ever recommend my books, the book clubs are not particularly harmful to me. . . .

April 29, 1932: "What success I have had is still as much of a mystery to me as it must be to many others."

April 13, 1934: (upon receipt of a clipping) "I noticed also that my name was coupled with those of Twain and Kipling. But did you notice that Tarzan of the Apes and the Bible are on the same list? We are certainly traveling in fast company. . . ."

Irene Ettrick, who at the time of her first correspondence with Ed was about twelve years old — the same age as Joan Burroughs — was the daughter of the Reverend Maughan Ettrick, Rector at Little Ilford at Essex, England. On November 9, 1920, she wrote to acknowledge the books Ed had sent her; in replying, Ed noted

Irene Ettrick of England, who as a child started writing to ERB; their correspondence continued for years.

his hope to come to England some day. For Christmas 1923 Irene's present to the Burroughs family was some English candy, and to her, on January 17, Ed explained that relatives on his mother's side had come from Staffordshire.

In 1924 Ed regretted that he must disappoint her and confessed that he had traveled very little: "I should be able to tell you that I had walked all over Africa, Asia, Europe, and the North Pole, but as a matter of fact I have never been off my own continent. . . ." Irene's communications with Ed had stirred her own literary ambitions, and in May 1925 she sent him a copy of her story "The Deferred Hope" for his comments. As a rule Ed had refused to evaluate stories that writers wished to forward to him, but in this case he read her story and observed, "You have a sense of dramatic values and narrative form which study and experience will unquestionably perfect. . . ."

Irene had suffered some illness, and on February 18, 1926, Ed wrote, expressing his sympathy and answering her questions about hunting: "I cannot derive any pleasure from the taking of a wild animal's life. I would rather shoot a man than a deer, and I used to spend a great deal of time during the deer season riding over my property to protect the deer from a lot of counter jumpers who would just as soon shoot a doe as a buck." In this letter he also noted with a feeling of surprise that Irene would soon be eighteen: "I always think of you as a very little girl, as you were when you first started to write to me." Irene, in May 1926, reported that she was trying to sell some of her stories, without success, and Ed, on the twentieth, suggested that she turn to American magazines and urged a submission to Bob Davis, the Munsey Editor. In December 1927 Ed was pleased to hear that Irene had become a "motion picture actress"; he hoped to have an opportunity to see her one day in a British film.

The correspondence with Irene was maintained regularly throughout the 1930s. On December 20, 1937, Ed acknowledged her Christmas card and wrote, "I wonder if you have a recent snapshot which you will send me?

I have pictures of you since you were a very little girl, and I should very much like to have a later one. . . . I look for you in every English picture we see, but so far I have not been able to recognize you. . . ." In May 1938 Irene told of the death of her father, the Reverend Maughan Ettrick, and on the sixteenth Ed sent a letter of condolence. In December of that year, a card from Irene revealed that she then lived in Brighton, Sussex, England.

Frank Shonfeld, whose first correspondence with Burroughs was probably in 1923, lived in Croydon, England; his father and his grandfather, in accordance with British tradition, had followed the family trade of a tailor, and Frank, at a later period, also had his own tailor shop in Croydon. A dedicated reader of the Burroughs stories, Frank, in his letters, often asked questions about the writings or made comments and criticisms. He had literary aspirations and in 1925 sent a manuscript, without a previous inquiry, to Burroughs who tactfully explained his policy to avoid reading others' creations and returned the manuscript unread. Shonfeld, experimenting with songwriting, in 1926 forwarded a copy of his "Columbine Song" to Ed who replied, "I have absolutely no sense of music whatsoever," and refused to offer any criticism of the song.

Shonfeld undoubtedly took the honors as Ed's most continuous correspondent. In 1937, then a sergeant in the 4th Battery, Queen's Royal Regiment, he was still fascinated by the Tarzan books, and revealed, on March 15, that his tailor shop and house in Croydon were about to be demolished, because of "Town Planning," and that he was now planning to find a new occupation. In 1941, Shonfeld, still in the British army, wrote a lengthy letter describing his attitude about the crisis in England and the war. Deeply impressed by Shonfeld's exemplification of the loyalty and patriotism of the simple English soldier, Ed sent his letter to *Life* on August 1, urging that it be printed; however, the magazine found the letter unacceptable for publication.

AUCTION SALE!

Monday, Jan. 15, 1923, 9:30 A. M.

TARZANA RANCH

Ventura Boulevard at Reseda Avenue

Farm Tools　　　　*Implements*　　　　*Work Horses*
Saddle Horses　　　*Dairy Stock*　　　　　　　*Swine*

TOOLS AND IMPLEMENTS

The principal items offered below are practically new, many of them having been used but a single season. The Case separator, for instance, is a notably good buy, as is, also, the grain drill, the John Deere mower, the side delivery rake, the manure spreader and a number of other implements that are practically as good as new.

Catalog
No.

No.	Description
1	2 small galvanized iron drinking fountains.
1A	1 large galvanized iron drinking fountain.
1B	2 galvanized iron hog troughs, 10 ft. x 13 in. wide x 6 in. deep.
1C	6 hog troughs 2 ft. long, galvanized iron.
1D	1 galvanized iron tank, 2000 gal. capacity.
1E	1 galvanized iron tank, 1000 gal. capacity.
1F	1 galvanized iron tank, 7000 gal. capacity.
2	About 750 feet surface irrigation pipe, 8 1-2 inch.
3	One 1-horse walking cultivator.
4	One 1-horse plow.
5	One 2-gang 14 in. bottoms John Deere moldboard riding plow.
6	One 2-gang John Deere disc riding plow.
7	One 2-gang Emerson disc riding plow.
8	One 3-gang 12 in. bottoms Oliver moldboard riding plow.
9	One 3-section smoothing harrow.
10	One 2-section smoothing harrow.
11	One 4-section spring tooth harrow.
12	One 1-horse garden cultivator.
13	One P & O riding cultivator.
14	One Killifer chisel cultivator.
15	One clod smasher, roller type.
16	One P & O tractor disc with trailer.
17	One 4-horse Fresno scraper.
18	One Thomas hay loader .
19	One Thomas side delivery hay rake.
21	One John Deere mower.
22	One Weber wagon with hay rack.
23	One Sandusky 10-20 Tractor.
24	1 Case 20x28 thresher.
25	One 6 in. 4-ply transmission belt 200 ft. in length.
26	One Ohio No. 9 feed cutter.
27	One Wilson feed grinder.
28	One lister.
29	One P & O No. 140 2-row corn planter.
30	One Van Brunt grain drill.
31	1 John Deere self binder.
32	1 John Deere manure spreader.
33	1 steam cooker.
34	1 small cyclone weed cutter.
35	1 bean cutter.
36	1 pair light wagon shafts.
37	1 H A M M Company feed cutter and blower.
38	1 Fairbanks-Morse 15 H. P. Type "Z" Engine.
39	1 belt, 6 in., 4 ply, 50 ft. in length.

9:30 A. M.　　　　　MONDAY　　　　　January 15, 1923

17
PROBLEMS AT HOME AND ABROAD

The lifelong dream of owning land, a wide expanse of land in its natural and unspoiled state, land without the clutter of people, buildings, and paved roads, had been realized, and yet in a brief period of four years was being relinquished. Raised in the crowded environment of the big city, Ed's first experience with the open spaces and the free, outdoor life had been in Idaho as a young cowpuncher. The experience was a revelation to him. But to the urge for a return to this outdoor life was added a further drive — that of owning something. His background made this understandable. He had grown up in a rented home and had lived, after marriage, in a succession of apartments. In rebellion against the crowded quarters of Chicago he had moved to the quiet suburb of Oak Park, and there, to satisfy his craving for ownership, had purchased a home. The suburban life was a compromise, still not the realization of his suppressed dream. The opportunity had come finally — Tarzana Ranch with its hills and canyons, with all the room for a man to stretch and roam. But what had gone wrong with the dream?

The answer lies in the Burroughs personality. He had originally intended to keep the 550 acres intact, to save them for his children. The key may be revealed in his comment to Bert Weston: "They were subdividing all around me. . . ." Burroughs was never a man to stand by and watch others reap the profits. With the rise in land values and the influx of real-estate agents and homeowners, the money-making fever, always with him, became dominant, overpowering his desire for calm withdrawal and seclusion in the broad, open expanse of Tarzana Ranch. True, he had lost money in his venture as a gentleman farmer and had complained that the taxes and expenses of running the ranch were too high. But his financial situation, at this time, was hardly critical. Payments on the ranch mortgage were of course still due, but the phenomenal sales of his books continued and his income from writing was high. For the years 1919-20 almost two million copies of his books were sold in the United States, while in England his royalties approximated two-thirds of the American receipts for the same years. *Tarzan of the Apes,* although seven years old, had sold 55,000 copies in the last half of 1920. His total income for 1921, including $20,000 paid by Numa Pictures Corporation in advance for movie rights, was close to $100,000. Additional royalties were being received from foreign sales of books translated into Norwegian, Swedish, Danish, Dutch, Russian, German, and Arabic.[1]

Achieving little success in his efforts to sell residential lots, Burroughs, in 1923, decided to assign the entire project to a land developer. As usual, he had too many irons in the fire, and the departure of his secretary John A. Shea, who accepted a position with William Sistrom at the Hollywood Studios — Sistrom was to be the general manager of the Burroughs Production Company which never got beyond the tentative stage — increased his responsibilities. Shea was replaced by G. L. Young. In the fall of 1923 H. B. Currier, a local agent, took over the subdividing of Tarzana. The advertised opening of sales to the general public was announced in the papers as of September 27, with a "great jungle barbecue" to be served by Tarzan himself — Elmo Lincoln — and with Louise Lorraine to be present to sign autographs. Concerning the Ford that was raffled off, Burroughs noted acidly, "The guy who won the Ford didn't buy a lot."[2] A photo, supposedly of Elmo, supplied by the subdivider and printed in a newspaper, was actually someone else; Elmo, irked, refused to appear, and there were threats of a lawsuit.

In 1924 Ed continued to divide his energies in miscellaneous money-making enterprises. The Tarzana Ranch with its picturesque Koonskin Kabin was occasionally being rented to film companies for production, especially of Westerns. That year the ranch was utilized by Phil Goldstone Studios for *The Bar "F" Mystery*

and *Bred in the Bone,* both starring William Fairbanks; by The Vitagraph Company for *The Pioneer* and *Terrible Terry,* starring William Duncan; and by Triograph Productions for *The Squatters,* featuring Bill Patton. No possible source of revenue could be overlooked. That same year the Golden Gate Oil Company was granted a permit to drill for oil. July 23 to 24 the company reported reaching a depth of about 1,300 feet and predicted they would soon find oil. Traces of oil were detected, but never anything in sufficient quantity, and by the fall of 1926 the company abandoned its lease and sold its equipment at auction.[3]

The financial problems were not the only ones encountered during this Tarzana Ranch period. A disturbing family situation, already too apparent, was aggravated by the intensive social life at the ranch. With Tarzana being a unique San Fernando Valley meeting place, the Burroughs family became social leaders in this somewhat isolated area; weekends at the ranch were regularly open house, the guests often including members of the film colony. At these parties the liquor, despite the prohibition law, flowed freely, and food was plentiful. This situation, while exasperating, was not as serious as the problem that centered about Emma. For some years she had found it difficult to limit her dependence upon liquor, and a steady round of parties provided a temptation that was irresistible.

Ed's concern over her increased drinking brought matters to a climax. At this time, in anger and disgust, he proceeded to pour the gallons of liquor into the swimming pool and to announce that the unrestricted open houses at the Tarzana Ranch were finished. The only visitors were a small number of personal friends. The changed situation, now that the free refreshments were discontinued, caused Ed to comment bitterly that it did not take long to find out who his real friends were. Emma, however, could not control her drinking, and in the future this habit would produce a crisis in their relationship.

Early in 1924, Ed committed himself to the most ambitious of his business projects, the sale of 120 acres of the Tarzana Ranch, including the large house and other buildings, for a country club. To his brother Harry, on January 18, he confided the details:

It is to be called El Caballero Country Club, and the aim of the promoters is to make it the finest and most exclusive country club on the Pacific coast. There will be two golf courses and a polo field. Our residence will be used as the nucleus of a larger club house. . . .

He explained that the club promoters were also purchasing one hundred acres from the adjacent Woodrough property on the west, and at the end, commented, "We do not feel so badly about giving up the place . . . since we will have the use of it, without any of the responsibility, and really can enjoy it just as much, if not more than before." Ed informed his brother George, now living in Burley, Idaho, that if the sale were completed, the family would have to leave Tarzana by June 1. He offered a practical reason for the move: "It was necessary, however, that we live in town, as the children are all attending school there, and it is much too far to drive twice a day."

Ed provided a vivid account of the changes taking place in the Tarzana area:

Formerly we were way out in the country, while now everything is rapidly moving in our direction. . . . With the exception of one or two tracts, everything between us and Los Angeles has been subdivided. . . . It is nothing unusual for lots to jump in two or three resales from six thousand and eight thousand to fifteen and twenty thousand dollars. A lot that I purchased six weeks ago for $16,800 I was offered $22,500 for, while the only other similar lot on the street, which lot is a little larger than mine, is being held for $30,000. . . .

"With all these improvements and changes," Ed wrote, "five hundred and fifty acres would have been a very expensive luxury. . . ."[4]

Throughout 1924 and into 1925 Ed maintained activities at a furious pace. The business side of his dual nature now became uppermost, although he did take time to write his longest novel, *Marcia of the Doorstep,* between April 12 and October 13, 1924. As a natural organizer, one who loved to take charge of things and one who was flattered by requests to do so, he found supervisory positions irresistible. To Weston he explained that the office of managing director of El Caballero Country Club had been "wished" on him and that he was obliged to take over the downtown office and handle the membership drive, the building plans, and the club program. He wrote, "I am at the office from about nine to five thirty every day, not even going out for lunch, and when I reach home I am a total loss, being probably the world's tiredest business man."[5]

The assumption of all these responsibilities, with the enforced sacrifice of creativity — he told Harry "I am giving up my writing and practically everything else to put this club across" — resulted, as in the past, from Ed's excessive pride in his business and managerial ability. He could not overcome the tendency, stemming from his years of experience in business and the success of his shrewd bargaining practices with editors, to view himself as The Efficiency Expert. Another factor, strangely enough, was his need for recognition, a need not fully satisfied by his writing achievements. The business judgments and decisions, often hasty and emotional, could be plain miscalculations, as Ed was beginning to understand. Apparently, his vaunted business acumen applied only to his dealings with editors; the future would demonstrate even more clearly that in his financial schemes his lack of success would be paradoxical to his success in the marketing of stories and books. One other point must be emphasized: a harried man is not an efficient man. Ed's habit of undertaking too much, of working desperately under too many pressures, was self-defeating.

To account for his motives in organizing the El Caballero Country Club, one must remember that *his* land was involved, and that he was anxious to devise some scheme for making a profit from the land, after previous projects had failed. The governors and members of the advisory board of the country club, a distinguished group of civic leaders, included bankers, real estate developers, business owners and an attorney.[6] Yet, from the start, the enterprise showed no sign of fulfilling Ed's glowing hopes. A publicized clubhouse opening in July 1924 brought insufficient response; later, the clubhouse was closed, and affairs remained in a state of uncertainty. One problem may have been the membership restrictions. While the club brochure denied any intent toward a "false idea of exclusiveness," yet care was to be taken to find members with "congeniality and harmony of tastes." In order to pay for the land — a total of 236 acres had been acquired, 116 of these purchased from R. L. Woodrough whose property adjoined Burroughs' — membership certificates were to be sold. Life membership cost a minimum of $2,500, and regular members were to pay from $600 to $1,250. To avoid overcrowding, membership was limited to 750; it was by invitation only, and all applications were passed upon by a secret committee before submission to the board of governors. The club's major attractions, obviously to Ed's taste, were to be found in its planned eighteen-hole golf course and polo field; naturally, the emphasis was upon "equestrian features" for those who loved horseback riding.

Ed welcomed the New Year, 1925, on the El Caballero golf links. *The St. Louis Globe Democrat* reported:

Edgar Rice Burroughs, novelist, won the first 1925 golf tournament played in the United States. He defeated L. W. Craig of Los Angeles, 2 up, at 2 o'clock New Year's morning over the El Caballero Country Club's eighteen hole obstacle course. The course was electrically lighted. Playing started New Year's Eve at eight o'clock and reached the finals just after midnight.

That the new year brought no improvement in the financial situation was evident in a letter to Frank Burroughs of January 22, 1925; Ed spoke of "trying to work out the salvation of the Country Club which purchased some of Tarzana. . . ." The duties he had now undertaken appeared beyond the energies of any one man:

I spend practically all of every day in a downtown office. I am also trying to gather up the loose ends of a real estate subdivision which was left in bad shape by an agent and from which I have, up to now, realized little or nothing. In addition there is the regular routine work of my profession . . . on top of it all I had wished on me the chairmanship of the Publicity Committee of the Association which put on the Animal Horse Show here. . . .

In an attempt to rescue the foundering El Caballero, Ed mortgaged his Tarzana property to the extent of $200,000. His attorneys, Lawler & Degnan, on March 4, 1925, noted that the mortgage had been arranged "in order that the bonds secured thereby may be sold for the benefit of the Club. . . . The transaction, therefore, is practically a loan by you to the Club of the proceeds of the bond issue. . . ."

A month later Ed provided a description of his activities to Harry: ". . . plans for a new home in Beverly Hills . . . put unsold lots on the market myself . . . concluding a $200,000 bond issue by Edgar Rice Burroughs, Inc. . . . completed laying eleven miles of pipe in the golf course in El Caballero . . . reopened the clubhouse the first of April . . . feeling that I have too much time on my hands I have recently taken an option on 120 acres close to the heart of town and I am arranging to promote a public golf course . . . between times I am trying to exercise five saddle horses, keep up my reading,

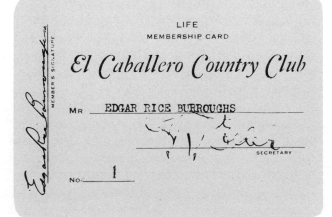

ERB's life membership card in El Caballero Country Club.

and work for the interest of the saddle horse and bridle trail promotion here. . . ."[7]

In the midst of all this Ed had been bombarded by Davis and Bray for a sequel to *The Moon Men* and another *Tarzan* and Mars story. Overwork, as in the past, often brought him to the edge of illness or physical collapse. He had ignored Dr. Crispin's advice, months earlier, to drop everything and go away for a long rest. About this behavior he commented jokingly to Harry, "Being naturally a lazy man, there is only one explanation for my behavior — that I am what the English probably call a bit balmy."

The added project, a public golf course, launched despite the unsolved problems of the El Caballero Club, was called the Rolling Hills Golf Club. Its planned site, a 120-acre tract on El Sereno Avenue, was five miles east of the Los Angeles downtown area and distant from Tarzana.

The Rolling Hills brochure deplored the existence of the private clubs designed for the "Wealthy Few," where memberships could run as high as $2500 (an obvious barb at El Caballero). It stated, ". . . not one man in three hundred can afford to pay such prices for his golf . . . but there are thousands of ardent golfers who can and will be glad to pay from one dollar to three dollars for a game of golf on a first class course which is not overcrowded."

In the promotion of the club, Ed, weighted down with duties, had turned once more to John A. Shea, who resumed his position with Burroughs in the fall of 1924 and was then made vice-president of El Caballero Country Club. Shea was given a dual position as secretary of the Rolling Hills Golf Club, was one of the original subscribers and a stockholder, and handled much of the club business from an office in the Commercial Exchange Building in Los Angeles. Other officers of the club, in addition to Burroughs as its president, were William Sistrom, vice-president, and William P. Bell, the architect who had designed El Caballero Country Club, also vice-president.

The Rolling Hills enterprise, reminiscent of several of Ed's first impractical ventures as an entrepreneur, staggered through a period of public indifference until it was finally abandoned. On April 5, 1926, Ed explained to a friend, "The property is to be opened as El Serrano Country Club as I learned from an article in one of the daily papers recently. I have nothing to do with it."

When their luxurious Tarzana home was adopted as a clubhouse for the El Caballero enterprise, the Burroughs family, in June 1924, moved into town, renting a home at 544 South Gramercy Place, Los Angeles. For transience the Burroughs record would be hard to match; two years earlier Ed had remarked to Harry, "If you keep on moving you will soon equal Emma's record and mine of 22 moves in 21 years. . . ." The future would continue the successive changes to homes or apartments. The financial situation involving the El Caballero Club had been steadily deteriorating. By the fall of 1925 Ed had severed all official connections with the club. Various legal maneuvers followed. The golf course, however, was opened for play in 1926. Hailed as one of the finest courses in the West, it was host to the 1927 Los Angeles Open Golf Tournament, won by Bobby Cruickshank.

The family was now living at 674 South New Hampshire in Los Angeles, but Ed decided to move back to Tarzana where he built a seven-room cottage on a level section in his Tarzana tract at 5046 Mecca Avenue. This was occupied in the fall of 1926, and in wry comment about the change from a "mansion on the hilltop," Ed observed, "The place is so small that we have to go outdoors to turn around, and if we have more than two guests for dinner the table has to be extended out in the living room. . . ."[8] The situation in which a famous author, whose income exceeded that of most other writers in the country, should have arrived at this unhappy state through his own business blunders is surprising but not unheard of; Mark Twain's financial failures are also noteworthy. In a sense Ed had duplicated impulsive actions of his earlier years, and this tendency to devise unsound money-making schemes would lead to further problems.

Golf course at Tarzana; photo by Donald Biddle Keyes.

With the El Caballero Country Club bogged down in a financial morass, a number of years passed in legal battles. In 1929 Ed started foreclosure proceedings. The original $250,000 bond issue was secured by a mortgage on the club property and on 315 acres of adjoining land that Ed owned. In the 1930 settlement Ed received approximately thirty acres, with the club allowed to retain ninety-six acres as a golf course. Ed's property contained the clubhouse, garages, stables, and other buildings. The ninety-six acres ceded to the club constituted a loss of some $50,000. Ed had received most of the land back, including the large home on the hill, his ownings now totaling 345 acres, but his debts were heavy. To Harry, on May 21, 1930, he noted gloomily, ". . . my expense will be not under twenty thousand dollars a year . . . also, I lost some twenty-two thousand dollars last year in mistaken investments, which I made in a hectic effort to get some quick money to save the ranch." On November 17, in writing to Weston, he spoke of expenses of twenty-five thousand dollars to rehabilitate the property, and added, "I think I shall start in unloading, even if I have to take considerably less for the property than I know it to be worth. . . ."

The reference to losses in "mistaken investments" reveals that Ed's penchant for business gambles continued to lead him into trouble. In the summer of 1929 he became involved with two related enterprises, jointly promoted by three men (Heffron-McCray-St. John). One was a plan for a Los Angeles Metropolitan Airport to be constructed in the San Fernando Valley; the other was a plan for the manufacture of an airplane engine by a company to be called Apache Motors. Convinced of the tremendous future of aviation, Ed purchased 1,000 shares of the airport stock at ten dollars a share, plus additional stock in Apache Motors, and persuaded his friend Bert Weston to make the same investment.

The publicity released by the Metropolitan Development Syndicate heralded the certain expansion of the San Fernando Valley, where Tarzana was situated, but here Ed needed no persuasion. On July 3, 1929, he noted that their statements were "conservative," that he had observed the growth of the valley in the past ten years, and that Metropolitan represented one of the safest investments he had ever encountered. Actually, Ed had sold himself; it would almost appear that he was promoting the venture:

. . . What appeals to all of us to a greater or lesser extent is the speculative value of securities . . . doubt if even a wild flight of imagination today would make it possible to visualize the development of the next two or three years . . . impossible to prophecy what heights this stock may soar in view of the increasing air-mindedness of the entire nation. . . .

His most glowing predictions were about the future of the valley. He stressed the airport as a vital requirement for the valley:

Without aviation, there seems little to expect other than a community of small farms, which at best are far from profitable and in this instance almost foredoomed to failure because of the high cost of land and water. With the coming of the Metropolitan Airport, the valley is being rapidly transformed into an industrial aviation center. . . .

He predicted a development not to be attained in his own time: ". . . the center of population of the city will be on this side of the Santa Monica Mountains, and it will no longer be a question as to how far the valley is from Seventh and Broadway, but how far Seventh and Broadway is from the valley. . . ." The prophecy was to be fully realized within the decade after Burroughs' death.

In the first stages of the venture, as always, the reports were optimistic. To Weston, Ed repeated forecasts that the stock would rise to forty dollars a share and that the company was "going to make a lot of money for you." Within a few months his comments became cautious. On October 7, 1929, with the early signs of the stock market crash, Ed wrote to Weston, "The Metropolitan Airport stock went on the market just about the time that the big slump occurred." However, he felt that the good publicity given the airport project would drive the stock upward. Apache Motors had scheduled a Department of Commerce test of the airplane engine, and Ed believed that with the department's approval of the engine, there would be "sufficient orders to make the stock extremely attractive. . . ."

To the Westons, now on a vacation in Cuba, Ed boasted of the rapid growth of the southern California area, adding his opinion, on January 21, 1930, that Margaret Weston had been wise in buying two lots at Miramar. But with the country in the throes of the Great Depression, hopes for the success of the airport venture were vanishing. Concerning Apache Motors, on May 16 the worst possible news was received. From Washington came the report that the 200 H.P. Apache engine had failed the test, disqualifying itself because of supercharger trouble. Production of engines now came to a halt, and affairs of the Metropolitan Airport were tangled in financial confusion. ". . . I feel like hell about the airport and engine company investments, which you certainly would not have made had I not brought them to your attention," Ed wrote in gloom and guilt to Weston.

Because of the deficit, the stockholders had already been required to pay an assessment. Ed opposed later attempts to impose another levy; he offered more apologies to Weston for having involved him in the project, and remarked, ". . . I still think that we would have made some money had the Wall Street slump not taken place." The Metropolitan Airport, Ltd., close to collapse, staggered along into 1931. When efforts to sell shares of capital stock to meet an assessment resulted in no bidders, the only remaining course, as explained in a notice of June 4, was "to liquidate the corporation as quickly as possible and with the least possible expense." Nevertheless, it was not until March 3, 1932, that Burroughs made the final payment on his indebtedness to the corporation.

The world-wide demand for Burroughs' books had resulted in heavy sales of these in foreign translations. To the multitudes of those clamoring for *Tarzan* stories were added, of all people, the Russians. Six of the Tarzan novels — pirated, since the Soviets viewed capitalist copyright agreements with indifference — had been printed in sixty-cent paperbacks. The reading situation in Russia led to a despairing report in a Moscow journal of April 1924:

We are being defeated on the literary front. We publish books and pamphlets about Marxism and our great revolution. We encourage young authors to interpret its spirit and inspire the masses. We even issue cheap editions of the Russian classics. But the public reads — what? — "Tarzan."

Although the total printing was 250,000, the supply was insufficient. A Russian publisher commented, "We could easily sell a million. They read it in offices, read it in street cars, read it in trains, read it in factories. Go to the villages and you find the educated young soldier reading 'Tarzan' to a circle of peasants with mouths agape."

While noting that Burroughs was the Russian favorite, the Moscow newspaper also admitted that a stream of other American and British writers followed him in popularity — O. Henry, H. G. Wells, Jack London, Conan Doyle, and Upton Sinclair. The newspaper was blunt in explaining why no Russian authors were on the list: ". . . old Russian literature is out of date, and the new dry, dull, or too subtle for mass comprehension." Walter Duranty, *The New York Times* Moscow correspondent, had a different and insulting interpretation of the Soviet reading habits: ". . . the newly emancipated Russian nation represents the average cultural level of the American schoolboy between 11 and 16."[9]

A perceptive analysis of the reasons for the Tarzan fascination was given by Axionov, president of the Russian poets' "Soviet," a writer described as "the most sophisticated Russian littérateur." He referred to "the love of fairy tales instinctive in primitive peoples in general and Russians in particular":

Our revolution killed the fairies, just as education killed them in Western countries. But if you dress up Jack the Giant Killer in a sufficiently modern guise to give him at least a semblance of probability, the masses will love him as did their fathers and grandfathers. And to the fact that Tarzan takes his readers away from strenuous, complicated modern life can be attributed the secret of his success.

Axionov then drifted into some ideological ambiguity: "In my opinion this alone proves the necessity for some dictatorship over the proletariat. On the other hand it appears that 'Tarzan' is also extremely popular in America — but comparisons are odious." It should be emphasized that Axionov's point about the importance of the imagination and the delight the average individual displayed in fairy tales and other fantasy creations that transported the reader far from the routine of everyday life, is exactly the point stressed by Burroughs in defending his writings against attacks by American literary experts.

On May 8, 1924, in thanking *Time* editor Henry R. Luce for sending him the magazine's article about Russian reactions, Ed revealed his amusement over the "primitive" Soviet readers, and wrote, "The British are notoriously the worst offenders, even in view of the fact that

Assortment of foreign language editions of ERB's books.

they have been strenuously warned against me by their reviewers (one of whom recently described me as a man with the mind of a child of six). . . ." To Bob Davis, who sent him the *New York Times* report, Ed remarked, "It is evident that Tarzan is overthrowing the Soviet government. I knew when I first wrote the story that it was inspired, but for what purpose it remained for Mr. Duranty to discover."

Concerning the unobtainable Russian royalties, these alone, according to estimates, could have made Burroughs wealthy. Other royalties, however, were pouring in; after the first Tarzan story had been circulated for only six months in Germany in 1924, Burroughs had received the largest royalty check ever paid to a foreign author for a similar period. On June 6,

1925, *The Outlook* of London stated that "contracts have been made for 'Tarzan of the Apes' in no fewer than seventeen languages, including Arabic and Urdu." But Burroughs' own list, sent to Edwin C. King of FBO Studios in Hollywood on December 13, 1926, contains a more accurate count. His books, in translations, were being distributed in at least twenty-one foreign countries: Arab nations, England, British Colonies, Czechoslovakia, Denmark, Norway, Holland, Finland, France, Germany, Hungary, Iceland, Italy, Poland, Roumania, Russia (also published for Russian-speaking people in Belgium), Spain, Sweden, Urdu, Canada. The number of Arab nations reading *Tarzan* was impossible to determine; the British Colonies included South Africa, Australia, and others. Ed supplied a list of all the publishers in these foreign countries.[10]

In the same letter Ed attempted to estimate his total foreign royalties, but conceded that he could not obtain accurate figures. However, based upon incomplete statements, he indicated that sales of his books in the United States and in Great Britain, Sweden, Germany, Hungary, Denmark, Norway, plus the Tauchnitz Continental English Editions, were approximately six million copies.

An inquiry from Florence, Italy, concerning the distribution of *Tarzan of the Apes,* came from the bearer of a famous musical name — Enrico Caruso, Jr. On March 3, 1925, Ed responded:

. . . I am inclined to think that my foreign agents, Messrs. Curtis Brown, Ltd. of London have made arrangements for the Italian book rights. . . . I hope you will be able to see them, or at least communicate with them, however, as I believe that a name so illustrious as yours would add greatly to the selling value of my stories in Italy.

The anti-German sentiments in America and England, aggravated by the distortions of wartime propaganda, were still strong. During the latter part of 1922 Ed had learned of the boycotting of Baron Tauchnitz and his English language paperbacks by outstanding authors. Worried, Ed on January 3, 1923, wrote to Davis, noting that he had just learned of the boycott and that he and Joseph Hergesheimer were "leaders of the opposition," since they had permitted Tauchnitz to publish their works.

Davis, in his reply of the tenth, explained that many American writers during the war "began to boycott the old boy because he was down." Davis defended the baron: ". . . Tauchnitz was about the first foreigner who took American copyrights and paid for something he could have had for nothing. He has done a great deal for literature and for book-making generally. . . ." In advising Ed to continue with Tauchnitz, Davis remarked, "England kicked up a helluva stink and spread a lot of unnecessary odor without reason. . . ." A week later Ed

replied, "My mind is relieved. I thought possibly I had unwittingly become a traitor to my country."

This decision about the German publisher Tauchnitz became a minor matter, but Ed's problems with Germany, based upon his own prejudices, were only beginning. Two years earlier, in correspondence with Enid Watson of the Curtis Brown foreign department, he had revealed the intensity of his anti-German feelings and his indifference to German opinion. The letter of August 23, 1921, to Burroughs quoted a request from Dr. Curt Otto of the Tauchnitz Library:

I regret to find that Tarzan the Terrible *is written in a strongly anti-German tendency, and we shall therefore be glad if you will consent to our issuing* Jungle Tales of Tarzan *instead of it. . . . we should like to publish the third book by Mr. Burroughs as soon as possible. . . .*

On September 9 Ed gave permission for Tauchnitz to issue *Jungle Tales of Tarzan,* unaware, in his statement, that he was predicting the crisis to come: "I presume for the reasons they do not care for Tarzan the Terrible they will not want Tarzan the Untamed." His further remark was tinged with arrogance and contempt: "If they knew half what I thought of the Germans, they would not want any of my books."

The spread of *Tarzan* translations throughout the world, resulting from the remarkably persistent efforts of Enid Watson of the Curtis Brown Agency, continued. On January 23, 1923, Ed wrote to express his appreciation: "You will soon have all the foreign languages exhausted and then what will you do, unless you turn your attention to Mars. . . ." He noted that Mars should provide an unlimited field, since the written languages of all the races were different. About the foreign rights, he was unhappy that the publishers would not guarantee royalties "after they had made their profits," but expressed the hope that Ingolfur Jonsson might get rich on the Icelandic rights.

In March, Enid Watson reported the sale of

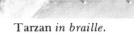

Tarzan *in braille.*

Tarzan of the Apes to *Le Petit Parisien,* a French newspaper, and in July she wrote triumphantly, "After negotiations lasting over several years I have at last found a publisher for *Tarzan* in Germany." She stressed the difficult conditions facing German publishers and felt she should be congratulated for having signed an agreement with Dieck & Company that provided an advance of fifteen British pounds for each book, on a royalty of ten percent. This was the first contact with the Charles Dieck firm. In praise, Ed commented jokingly, "You certainly are blanketing the world with good literature. . . . am particularly interested in the Hottentot rights. . . ."

On September 12, 1923, in response to a request from the Curtis Brown office, Ed granted permission to the National Library for the Blind to braille *A Princess of Mars* and *The Gods of Mars,* with the stipulation that these works could not be sold for profit. Ed wrote, "Some time ago they brailled "Tarzan of the Apes" if I am not mistaken in the title, and I am wondering if they have brailled any other of the Tarzan books." Noting he knew nothing about the process, he wondered if he might ask for a brailled page of one of his books, "merely as a curiosity."

Throughout most of 1924 the German sales increased; on August 1, Charles Dieck wrote from Stuttgart, ". . . we are now at the issue of the third volume. Over 40,000 copies of Tarzan are now on advance orders. . . ." Ed, on September 2, answered to thank Dieck and suggest that the Martian series be considered. An experienced and imaginative publisher, Dieck devised various schemes to promote the sales of *Tarzan*. In a letter of October 10, he informed Burroughs of plans and occurrences in Germany:

. . . towards the end of this month the fourth Tarzan volume, that is "Tarzan's Son," will make its appearance. . . . Of late some writers and publishers are getting jealous of our successful handling of the Tarzan books . . . nearly daily appear criticisms and discussions about the value of Tarzan books. . . . Beginning 1925 we thought to start with "Jungle Tales of Tarzan" and "Tarzan and the Jewels of Opar", shortly followed by "Tarzan and the Golden Lion" and "Tarzan and the Ant Men."

He supplied newsy items: ". . . in Germany two Tarzan parodies have come out; namely 'Tarzan has dreamt' and the 'Tarzaniade'. Both volumes are the products of jealousy, and we are informing the public that these books are erratic and without leaning towards natural conditions or surroundings, but that the original Tarzan books are of good moral standard, as even severe critics could not deny. . . . We came into possession of a very good gorilla death mask and had many copies made in plaster paris, with bronze covering, with which we are supplying the book stores. . . ."

No German protests had as yet been registered about the anti-German themes emphasized in several of Burroughs' earlier stories. These were especially severe in *The Land That Time Forgot*, with references to the "Kaiser-breed" and the depiction of von Schoenvorts, the U-boat commander, as a man without scruples or conscience, and of course in *Tarzan the Untamed*, where a German major is fed to a lion and later an enraged lion is prodded into the trenches to attack the "Huns." However, by the summer of 1924, with the German market expanding, Ed was already exhibiting apprehension over some of the scenes and characterizations he had contrived. On August 8 he wrote Enid Watson:

I wish again to call your attention to the necessity for changes in the text of some of my stories for the German market. The Land That Time

Forgot, for instance, is a story which I believe will be a big seller there. . . . as it was written during the height of hostilities it contains rather bitter diatribe aimed at Germans individually and collectively. As I do not write propaganda, and the sole aim of my work is to entertain, I believe it will be perfectly proper to fit the text to the public we wish to sell to.

"How would it be to make the Germans Austrians," he inquired, "or will these volumes circulate also in Austria; and in any event tone down some of the language I have used?"

In Burroughs' type of fiction a villain was a necessity; the various twists of the plot could not have been devised without one. His standard procedure was to create one, usually of foreign extraction, like the Russians Rokoff and Paulvitch or the Belgian Werper. But at an early period, with the increase of foreign editions of *Tarzan*, Burroughs himself had sensed the general problem that could arise. On January 11, 1921, to Enid Watson he had noted:

In writing my Tarzan and Martian stories I always endeavored to avoid giving offense to any considerable proportion of my readers and therefore many of my villains were selected from the nations least likely to read my books. They were Russian, Swedish and Belgian, not because I harbor any particular dislike of these people but merely because few of my readers would be from these countries.

He observed that now, however, with the many translations, conditions were different. In a joking tone he pointed out that he would not "enjoy" an adventure story "in which the principal characters were all Russians and the dyed-in-the-wool villains American," and then stated the procedure he would prefer: ". . . so far as I am concerned there would be no objection to changing the nationality of the villains, or leaving them without nationality." These comments, four years before the German controversy exploded, in which Burroughs actually authorized the translators to change his villains, demonstrate that the villains were simply creatures of his plot; in general, no prejudice or animosity was involved.

With his war-time German characters, and in at least one other case, Burroughs deviated from his nonpersonal attitude. Here, his contention that he wrote only to entertain was not supportable. Himself an easy victim of war propaganda, he had been led by his prejudices into writing the "bitter diatribe" he mentioned. He had written propaganda, as he had also done, with a different goal, in "Under the Red Flag," published in 1919, with its violent attack on Bolshevism. Davis and other editors, in rejecting this work, had made exactly the point Ed had previously stressed and then violated — fiction was not a proper vehicle for propaganda.

As yet, Burroughs was not concerned with the moral question or the injustice of these indictments of the Germans; his only worry was that German sales might be affected. He was even willing to change his villains into Austrians. Under these circumstances he would have been condemning the Austrians collectively. Granted he needed his villain, but there was a great difference between portraying an individual sadist or murderer and in damning a whole race. This Burroughs would perceive at a later period.

Early in 1925, through the publication of Stefan Sorel's *Tarzan the German-Devourer* (*Tarzan der Deutschenfresser,* Carl Stephenson, Berlin), the German public became aware of the content of *Tarzan the Untamed.* Sorel, in his reading of the English edition — the book had not been published in German — had discovered the scene in which Major Schneider is fed to the lion, and other savage scenes involving the deaths of German officers or "Huns." These actions of Tarzan were in retribution for the supposed murder of Jane. Of course Sorel's exposure of the book and its violent scenes aroused indignation and anger among Germans who had been helpless to refute the wartime reports, obviously Allied propaganda, of their "atrocities," and who had not only lost the war but had been forced to accept the blame for starting it.

On January 30 Dieck wrote in agitation, "Somebody has unearthed the fact . . . that you produced 'Tarzan the Untamed' during the war and that in it the Germans are cruelly drawn. Undoubtedly he has kept silent about it, since it is treated in a volume long suppressed. . . ." Dieck made several suggestions, among them that Burroughs, in his next *Tarzan* story, "might let the Germans come into their right also?" He added, "We want no praise but we would like justice." Dieck also urged that Burroughs write an article "which might breathe of friendliness for the Germans." He promised to "hurl this article" at the press so as to quiet the critics. For incidental information he noted the translation of *A Princess of Mars,* with a frontispiece by Professor Hohlwein, and the plan to release the book about March 15. He mentioned also the scheduled publication of a special volume, *Wild Animals on the Film,* "drawn up by a manager of animal films."

The rising German furor found Ed in the midst of corrections on *The Land That Time Forgot,* soon to be published in England by Methuen & Company. On February 12, 1925, he noted receipt of the first proofs and explained to Curtis Brown that he would have to make changes in the book because of the anti-German sections. While waiting for the second proofs, on February 21 he wrote to Enid Watson, "If they are greatly delayed I wish you would take the matter up with Methuen and see that all inflammatory references to the Germans are sufficiently modified so that they will not necessarily offend. . . ." He referred to the "considerable importance" of his German royalties and the deep resentment against him in Germany because of *Tarzan the Untamed.*

In defense of the *Tarzan* publications, a German officer, Vice-Admiral Daehnhardt, had issued a statement which Dieck planned to use as a preface for one of the books. The *Tarzan* stories were described as "non-political" and Daehnhardt stressed the economic gain to the Germans of the Dieck editions: "Right here in Stuttgart there is the least inducement to turn against it, for a year and a day whole rows of Stuttgart publishers and bookhandlers, Swabian paper mills, etc. have turned running machinery and service to the Tarzan edition. Already the export dealers have protected Stuttgart workers from becoming breadless. . . ."[11]

On February 9, as Dieck realized the situation was becoming extremely serious, he dispatched a cable to Burroughs, "German Tarzan editions now much attacked by our press. Give us quickly good notices that your book 'Tarzan the Untamed' is born during war-bitterness and most of all that you are fond of German people, otherwise your German business will diminish." Burroughs at once wired back "Suggestion dislike Germans ridiculous. Am writing." In his reply to Dieck he explained that during the war he had submitted to much banter from Mrs. Burroughs because for many preceding years the Kaiser had been one of his most admired heroes. Ed wrote, ". . . even as late as the time I wrote The War Lord of Mars, the influence of my admiration for the German Emperor had a great deal to do with the stimulation of my imagination in the conception of that story. The war shattered a great many things, however, from thrones to ideals."[12] He then enclosed a four-page letter addressed, "To My German Readers." In it he recalled the bitterness that had existed between the North and the South during the American Civil War and how, in the passing years, this antagonism had gradually vanished. He predicted that the animosities created by World War I would also be dissipated in the natural friendship of the "two great republics of Germany and America."

Ed did not offer excuses for the anti-German sections in his two novels. "They reflect truly what I thought and felt at the time that I wrote them," he stated, "and because this is a fact I cannot apologize for an honest conviction however mistaken it may have been." He observed, quite logically, that the types of individuals he vilified "were the types that the German people themselves have inveighed most bitterly against . . . the cruel, ruthless, arrogant Ger-

man officer." Ed noted that he had used Russian villains in two of his stories, believing that they would never be translated into Russian. But now that they were, he nevertheless had received no complaints from his Russian readers. Ed stressed, ". . . I have no hesitancy in offending those whom I consider a menace to society regardless of their nationality or of their purchasing power," and added that he would "as bitterly assail" the misconduct of Americans as he would the undesirable or evil actions of Germans, French, or English. In evidence he referred to The Girl From Farris's and The Girl From Hollywood, "in which Americans and American customs are attacked." Burroughs insisted firmly and defiantly:

. . . if I should never sell another book in Germany I should still be as bitterly antagonistic toward Hauptman Fritz Schneider, as all my German friends in this country are and as the vast majority of the German people in Germany are and, I hope, always will be.

Burroughs maintained that of most importance was the pleasure that thousands of Germans derived from his books; this could not be "lessened" because an American writer attacked a "conscienceless militarism that is to be found among certain classes in every great power in the world." In answer to those who accepted Tarzan the Untamed as evidence of his dislike of all Germans, Ed pointed out that he had a German brother-in-law, a native of Hamburg, whose two daughters had recently been guests at the Burroughs' home in Los Angeles, and that in America, among the great many people of German origin, he had made numerous friends. None of these had been offended by his statements in Tarzan the Untamed.

"I hope to visit Germany next year," Ed wrote, "and I have no doubts whatsoever as to the kindliness and cordiality of my reception, which would not be the case if I believed that Hauptman Fritz Schneider was typical of even a negligible minority of the German people."

This explanation and plea by Burroughs had little effect upon the German press which in the spring and summer of 1925 printed a series of violent denunciations of him and his *Tarzan* stories. From such newspapers as the *Berliner Tageblatt, Frankfurter Zeitung, Prager Presse,* the *Berlin Lokal Anzeiger,* and others came these bitter attacks, many of them appealing to the Germans' nationalistic pride. Although Burroughs was being denounced as an individual writer, to the German mind he was representative of all the foreign powers that had defeated and humiliated the German nation:

We have learned much out of the war and who were our former foreign friends. We were not prepared, however, to learn to like the silly admiration for their outlandish literary compositions and which are of so inferior worth and such a lash in our face. It is not otherwise possible that a greater calumny of the German reading public (or insult to the German reading public) could be written than the Tarzan Romance and which is itself such a miserable "Schmierwerk" (botch job)....

In mentioning Burroughs' "noble and holy hate against the Germans and Germany," the article reveals the deep resentment of a defeated country against the victor: "The writing of this calumniator and liar traduces a German Vice Admiral in the innocent minds of our German youth, rather than literary counsel. When will we reach the limit of cringing and fawning upon all of this outlandish volatile foreign domination."

Other attacks were more personal. Concerning the Lion Numa who had devoured the German Major, one newspaper commented, "You will not like Tarzan's action, dear German reader, but you will understand it if Tarzan tells you that this monster of a German Major had murdered and burned the noble wife of Tarzan, the noble monkey-man." The reference is to *Tarzan the Untamed* as the "seventh Tarzan book," containing "deeds accomplished by the dear Tarzan against the overfed German beasts." Six *Tarzan* novels had been published in Germany, and Sorel's book had led the German press to believe that *Tarzan the Untamed* was the seventh in sequence, written in 1925,

rather than 1918. Thus, it was the "same Burroughs who had fattened himself with the proceeds of the German translations" who "six years after the war . . . has written one of the most evil works of wartime literature to insult Germany." The article mentions Burroughs' letter to the German readers and his insistence that he does not dislike the Germans; this is viewed derisively as entirely unbelievable. ". . . Mr. Burroughs really does not have any national sympathies or antipathies. . . ." He is only interested in attracting as many readers as possible and concerned about "hurting his pocketbook." The Germans are given concluding instructions:

Is it after what we have said still necessary, German reader, to tell you that you should hastily throw your Tarzan books into the garbage can and faithfully promise to never touch a Tarzan book again? [Immediately after the publication of Sorel, Tarzan disappeared from the German book stores.]

A book review of Stefan Sorel's *Tarzan the German-Devourer,* (Berlin *Lokal Anzeiger*) comments that the great masses of readers who "became victims" of the *Tarzan* reading fever exhibited poor taste and judgment. This "romantic journey" which increased "with as much rapidity as the prolificacy of rabbits" represents "the greatest piece of stupidity ever thrown on the book market." The author of this "colportage series," referred to as "Mr. Rice Burroughs," is one of the "basest German-devourers existing in the Anglo-Saxon countries."

A lengthy article by Felix Salten, the popular author of *Bambi* and other children's stories, offered a contemptuous estimate of Burroughs' writing ability. In "Tarzan Reflections," appearing in the *Neue Freie Presse,* Vienna, May 3, 1925, Salten, who had started a *Tarzan* book because a friend had referred to Burroughs as "a second Kipling," remarked after reading only a few pages "that the writer . . . lacked practically all the qualities of an author." Burroughs' "cold-blooded, well-calculated complications" could arouse a reader's curiosity, but if one compared his writing, for example, to Conan Doyle's in *Sherlock Holmes,* one could easily detect Doyle's superiority. His books also are "well calculated," but they reveal "a spark of imagination" and "a great many admirable qualities"; none of these are present in the *Tarzan* stories.

Salten's phrases are picturesque: the German people had been seized by a "Tarzan Epidemic"; the books "had been like a literary grippe." They had appeared in different forms, had spared almost no one, but like the grippe, they were "in the process of dying out." The Germans were recovering from "this Tarzan-fever" and they will now be "immune against the infection."[13]

To Charles Dieck, Burroughs now expressed his intention of creating "one of the typical Germans that we all respect here" in his next *Tarzan* story. He promised fervently, "I shall eschew politics forever hereafter." It was plain that the world-wide circulation of his writings made necessary the avoidance of any political viewpoints.

From Enid Watson, on March 25, had come a letter which cast an entirely new light on the virulent German press campaign against the *Tarzan* books. For some time there had been a suspicion that the attacks on Burroughs were not merely motivated by his anti-German sentiments. Miss Watson's view of the situation followed upon an extremely pessimistic statement by Theodor J. Ritter, the Curtis Brown representative in Hamburg, who reported that sale of the *Tarzan* series had come "almost to a complete standstill." Ritter commented, "The bookshops are boycotting the books and the name of Tarzan begins to stink in Germany." He repeated the newspapers' ominous predictions that Tarzan's name would be "obnoxious forever" to the German readers. Miss Watson, however, believed that Ritter's statement was highly exaggerated and overlooked one important factor. The German hostility was not based purely upon Burroughs' supposed "calumny"

or his insults to the intense nationalistic pride. Another more obvious reason could be detected. Miss Watson wrote:

. . . my personal opinion is that this is based not so much on the anti-German attitude as expressed in 'Tarzan the Untamed' but on the jealousy evinced by a certain section of the German press (and not a very important section) at the success of a foreign book in their own country.

Charles Dieck, whose initiative and enterprise had led to the sales of a half-million Tarzan novels, had earlier noted "some writers and publishers are getting jealous of our successful handling of the Tarzan books, and trying through the Press to work against us." The furious newspaper campaign against Tarzan, seemingly organized, with its appeal to German nationalism, was deceptive. The postwar grievances were being deliberately stirred up as a pretext for destroying the sales market for Tarzan books. Of course the press had succeeded. The German people, emotionally susceptible because of the war, had turned much of their anger and hatred against Tarzan and Burroughs.

Ed had begun to suspect that the German campaign was a subterfuge, and Enid Watson's opinion confirmed his. On April 11, 1925, he wrote her to insist that he could not "assume a spineless attitude and retract and apologize ad nauseum." He repeated her view even more forcibly: ". . . the attitude of the German press has nothing whatsoever to do with patriotism or injured German sensibilities but is quite evidently prompted by jealousy of German publishers who did not have the business foresight and sense of values possessed by Mr. Dieck." Feeling he had made a "fair and reasonable" effort at conciliation, Ed lost patience. To Enid Watson he remarked angrily that if the Germans were anything like the Americans, they would have more respect for him if he were to tell those in the press who doubted his explanation, "that they might go to — ." He added, "I was going to say hell, but inasmuch as I am writing to a lady, of course I cannot use that word."

That *Tarzan the Untamed* would never appear in a German translation was obvious; but, as Enid Watson pointed out, its sale in other languages would be difficult to stop. Ed's most pressing worry was about *The Land That Time Forgot,* scheduled for British publication by Methuen. On April 26 he explained his apprehension to Charles K. Miller, noting that the story was written immediately after the sinking of the Lusitania. If the Germans ever read the book, he commented wryly, "I am afraid my life will not be safe should I ever visit Germany."

Inquiries to Dieck about the situation brought a long letter of April 16 describing not only the intense antagonism toward *Tarzan,* but also the effects of the war and Allied propaganda upon the Germans.[14] Dieck's financial position daily grew more serious: ". . . Tarzan has disappeared from the German book market . . . books are being returned to us . . . those who have not returned them do not pay and threaten to send them back. . . ." He explained that plans to publish *Tarzan and the Jewels of Opar* and *A Princess of Mars* had to be abandoned: ". . . we had to withdraw these books, which caused us further great losses. . . ." Dieck offered what was to him the only possible solution: ". . . If you are still anxious to sell your books in Germany, you will have to take some energetic steps, and will have to withdraw the seventh edition also in English speaking countries."

Ed's deepest regret now was about the harm that had been done to Dieck. On May 18, in a general statement addressed to the German press, Ed presented a defense both of his novel and of Dieck's role as publisher; he again stressed that *Tarzan the Untamed* was written "during the heat of an extremely bitter war" and not six years later as Sorel had maintained. He added:

. . . I am sorry, too, that this matter should have brought financial loss to Mr. Dieck . . . who took the stories in good faith without any knowledge whatsoever of Tarzan the Untamed. . . . but perhaps his very success has been his undoing, in the jealousy that it has aroused.

"If I have been stupid in not realizing the harm that Tarzan the Untamed might do," he stated, "I have at least tried to remedy the wrong by instructing my publishers and agents to withdraw this book from circulation as rapidly as possible throughout the world and never to offer it again. . . ." He noted that since his stories were published in twenty countries, his losses would be far greater than any income he could ever derive from German sales. Ed closed, "I know that the German press wants to be fair. I do not ask them to be fair to me but I sincerely hope that they will be fair to Mr. Dieck, a fellow German."

On the same date, in enclosing a copy of this letter to Enid Watson, Ed gave instructions to remove both *Tarzan the Untamed* and *The Land That Time Forgot* from the market in all countries, "insofar as it is possible." If she thought these stories could be rewritten without giving "unnecessary offense," he was willing to do so, after which they might be placed on sale once more. To Eric Schuler, secretary of The Authors' League of America, he sent copies of the German newspaper clippings and of other correspondence relating to the controversy. About this material he noted, "I should like to have it on file with the League in the event that it should be needed in the defense of other American writers from attack on my account."

During August 1925 Ed continued to make inquiries about the German situation, both of Dieck and of Enid Watson. Dieck had succeeded in placing favorable reviews of *Tarzan* books in the newspapers, but these had no effect in reviving the sales. On September 8 Dieck sent a detailed account of events; concerning the royalties for the first half of the year, a matter mentioned by Ed, Dieck replied that these were out of the question. He had suffered heavy losses — "the battle alone has cost me between thirty and forty thousand marks" — and the damage to the firm's reputation was serious.

The German disaster had at least produced one positive result. From here on Ed would display extreme caution in his judgment of all foreigners, both personally and in his fiction. To H. C. Paxton, editor of *The Country*

Gentleman, in discussing new works, Ed, on October 28, remarked that he would like to write a story of the Southwest some day with a Mexican as a hero. His statement indicated a new awareness:

Among the many things we have done to arouse the hostility and antagonism of Mexicans has been our treatment of them in our fiction, where they are nearly always portrayed as heartless scoundrels. I believe that a policy of consideration and fairness toward our sister republic in our literature would do much to lessen this hostility. . . .

However, his social concern was weakened by an added reference to business opportunities: the antagonism "makes it difficult for Americans to transact business profitably in Mexico, where, politicians to the contrary notwithstanding, we are most cordially hated."

On November 6, with German conditions unchanged, Ed depressedly had a suggestion to make to Enid Watson. Having received an opinion that it was he and not Tarzan whom the Germans disliked, he proposed, ". . . we might publish my books in Germany without my name, using instead a German name. . . ." This view of the German hatred as directed toward him was inaccurate, as Dieck, on November 28, pointed out in a letter to Theodor Ritter. Dieck reported that while he faced a "somewhat thankless task" in promoting the *Tarzan* books, still there were signs that some of the bookstores were again making sales. He commented, "Gradually the conviction is penetrating that the whole Tarzan campaign is on a materialistic footing, and has little to do with Idealism." Dieck explained the German enmity; they hated Tarzan, not Burroughs. "The Schoolmasters and their coterie . . . consider him as offal; . . . the National circles have hatred of Tarzan implanted in them because it has brought about attacks on Germany. Concerning the person of Mr. Burroughs they think nothing." Dieck stressed that it was *Tarzan the Untamed* that they wished to "expel from German earth," and added, "in this they are partly right."

Ed was now convinced that the popularity of Tarzan would gradually return to Germany. He expressed the belief to Enid Watson, on January 13, 1926, that once the antagonism had dissipated, the sales of the books would be as heavy as before; the press campaign could have the opposite effect from what was intended, with the publicity arousing the public's interest in reading the *Tarzan* stories. Ed continued, in future years, to reiterate his distrust and rejection of all wartime propaganda. In 1927 he recalled the anti-German reports of World War I and remarked, "I realize that much of this was exaggerated and I know that it does not do any of us any good to foster enmity and hatred. . . ."[15] A request for a statement about propaganda from Henry Goddard Leach of *The Forum,* in 1929, brought a very vehement response from Ed:

Wartime propaganda, including as it did vicious and inexcusable falsehoods sponsored by our Government, has effectively immunized me against all forms of propaganda with the result that in matters concerning which I have no personal knowledge, I believe only that which I wish to believe or that which is commended to my judgement through ordinary processes of reasoning. . . .[16]

To his brother-in-law William Westendarp, on February 28, 1933, Ed made specific references to his past mistakes: "I always regretted the anti-German tone that I permitted to enter two of my stories following the sinking of the Lusitania. I think we must have all been a little stupider than usual during the war, for how any intelligent person could have believed the propaganda stories that we swallowed hook, line and sinker is beyond me." He added, "In some of my later books I tried to atone as best I might by depicting German characters in pleasant and sympathetic roles."

Any hope possessed by Burroughs that certain segments of the German press might modify their vindictive and revengeful attitude toward him and the Tarzan books was quickly dispelled. In 1926, obviously in a further attempt to keep public enmity alive, the press launched an attack directed personally at Burroughs. On April 8, noting that "the campaign against Tarzan has again been revived," Dieck forwarded a copy of an article of April sixth from *Der Mittag*, a Dusseldorf newspaper, headed "The Author of the Sensational Novels "Tarzan" Is a Plagiarist!" According to the article, the original accusation came from the "well-known Russian author" W. Strujski, a Paris reporter for the *Sewodnja* of Riga. The supposed author of a novel that contained the identical Tarzan theme was a French writer, a "Parisian-Bohemian" named Robida, who lived in the Montmartre section some twenty-three years earlier. Robida, a frequenter of bars, would read his works to those present, in exchange for free drinks of absinthe. The article reported, "About fifteen years ago Robida succeeded in finding a publisher who agreed to publish his fantastical novel "The Adventures of Captain Saturnin Fernandoule." A summary of the plot followed:

The French Captain Fernandoule is making a trip to India accompanied by his wife and child. On the coast of Asia the ship was wrecked. The Captain and his family were saved and landed upon an uninhabited island. In fighting wild gorillas, mother and father are killed, and only the child remains alive. Little Saturnin is found by a female gorilla and taken care of. After a good many years a French man-of-war touches the island and the French marines find this half-man, half-ape, take him to the man-of-war and they take him to Paris.

In the *Der Mittag* account, Robida's novel is highly praised. He has described "how in the soul of this creature the battle between beast and human started." Robida's development of this battle is a "psychological masterpiece and the principal attraction of this book." However, Robida wrote in an early period, when a novel of this type could not be appreciated. He died, and both he and his work were forgotten. Ten years later, the article stated, "the reading public had changed its tastes which were more

of a nervous, sharp and nonsensical taste." Burroughs' plagiarism is then described:

Evidently he was well acquainted with the forgotten novel of Robida. He changed in his books the names, the time, added a few more chapters, cut out a few things, and copied almost verbally the already mentioned battle of the soul of man and beast, and thus created of the unknown French novel by Robida, the famous book Tarzan, *for which he collected the nice little sum of six million golden francs.*[17]

The article had referred sneeringly to the "smart English author, Edgard Burroughs," and later to "Mr. Englishman." To Dieck, on April 24, Ed confessed that he "scarcely knew how to reply to such a silly charge" coming from someone who did not even know his nationality or how to spell his name. He was willing enough to concede that such a story might have been written fifteen years ago or fifteen hundred years ago: ". . . there is nothing new in the idea nor have I claimed there was anything new in it. It has been used repeatedly from the time of Romulus and Remus and probably long before." Ed had never seen Robida's novel or had any knowledge of it, but he emphasized that since he read no French, the book could not under any circumstances be a source of information for him. Ed offered a pungent remark: "The lion has fleas but he keeps on going about his business as a successful lion. I have Strujski, Der Mittag, and other minor irritants but I expect to keep on going about my business of being a successful author."[18]

Dieck, in response, noted that the Strujski article had been copied from its original French source by several German newspapers. His letter was encouraging, and to demonstrate that there was still some "affection" for Tarzan in Germany, two "well trained" monkeys were being exhibited under the names Tarzan I and Tarzan II. Dieck had also granted permission to the popular Bush Circus to present a Tarzan pantomime in the shows at Hamburg and Breslau.

Finding it necessary now to obtain further information about Robida and his supposed novel, Ed, on May 20, wrote to his Paris publisher, Artheme Fayard & Cie, enclosing a copy of the *Der Mittag* article (French translation by E. Muller, Burroughs' secretary). Fayard's reply of June 18 contained a surprising statement:

. . . as you request we have made the necessary investigation.

We find, however, that Robida never wrote The Adventures of Captain Saturnin Fernandoule. *We do not even know of any book, by Robida or any other author in which there exists a plot similar to the one you have constructed for Tarzan.*

On July 8 Ed triumphantly forwarded the Fayard letter to Dieck to be used to discredit the plagiarism charges, and at the same time sent an article reporting the controversy to Henry Gallup Paine, Editor of *The Bulletin* of The Authors' League. Titled "An Adventure in Plagiarism," the article quoted the *Der Mittag* statement verbatim and the response of Fayard. Interestingly, Ed, in referring to the numerous queries he had received as to the source of *Tarzan,* revealed that he had thought at last he was "on the right trail" when he wrote to Fayard. Perhaps, unknown to him, there was a work with the *Tarzan* theme. The Fayard reply led to the conclusion that the entire matter, including even *The Adventures of Captain Saturnin Fernandoule,* a "novel" nobody could produce, was a fabrication. In his article Ed emphasized that in addition to searching for measures to punish plagiarists, The Authors' League should find means "for protecting ourselves against those who can now with impunity bring wholly groundless charges of plagiarism against us."

The period 1923-26 became an experimental one, with Burroughs venturing beyond the customary *Tarzan* and Mars stories to utilize new themes and settings. The innovations consisted of his first Western novel; his longest romance, totaling 125,000 words; the Indian story he had contemplated for a long time, centered about the Apaches and their struggles against the white men; and a *Tarzan* juvenile. The period also included two continuing *Tarzan* and Mars adventure stories.

The writing of the Western novel, not at all a project that Burroughs initiated, came through a suggestion from a most unusual source — Sir Algernon Methuen, owner of the British publishing company. In October 1922, after Sir Algernon's suggestion had been forwarded by Curtis Brown, Ed responded, "I have never written a wild west story, although I think I could do it. . . ." He of course had his experiences in Idaho and Arizona to draw upon. The phrase "wild west," as used by Sir Algernon, gave Ed the impression that "the English readers would want the motion picture type of cowboy, which exists only in the pictures." A proposal of this kind from a member of the British nobility was highly flattering to Ed. Still, he exhibited caution, asking, "Has Sir Algernon any special offer to make me on the British book rights on such a story, which might have little or no value here, since the readers on this side seem to prefer my highly imaginative stuff?"

Replying on November 17, 1922, Sir Algernon, even wilier than Burroughs, was careful to make no commitment. He agreed that Ed had the ability to write a good "wild west" story, but added, ". . . if such a book would have little or no value in the States I fear that its success here would not be likely to give Mr. Burroughs sufficient remuneration." He emphasized that the decision lay with Ed.

As in the past, Ed turned to Bob Davis for advice; the editor gave strong encouragement: "You seem to be pretty well equipped to handle rough men, wild animals, and coarse country. I would print a western story from you in a minute. Let 'er go." While Davis' urging may have spurred Ed into the project, it appeared evident that Sir Algernon's request was irresistible. Ed knew that from a sales standpoint the book would be a dubious investment — he had already made that plain. On March 31, in notifying Curtis Brown that he had started "the Wild West story for Sir Algernon Methuen," Ed explained, ". . . I am writing this story with little likelihood of its being very enthusiastically received by my American publishers. . . ." He also felt that "for English consumption" the "rather prosaic life of a cowpuncher will have to be speeded up a bit. . . ."

With the completion of the 81,000-word story on May 24, Ed sent some brief information to Curtis Brown: the story was titled "The Bandit of Hell's Bend"; although not mentioned in the manuscript, the time was about 1885; it contained many of the characters Ed had known in Idaho and when he was in the 7th Cavalry in Arizona; he was sure the story contained "many inaccuracies"; he had tried to use the colloquialisms and slang of the people he had actually known — a hodge-podge group from all parts of the United States; the story was decidedly not a historical novel; he had given it the love interest and happy ending Sir Algernon desired.

To Davis he noted that two other titles had occurred to him — "The Black Coyote" and "Diana of the Bar Y." He also referred to two points he should have researched more thoroughly: as a territory, did Arizona have a sheriff or a U.S. Marshal? And did Apaches circle their enemies on horseback, as the plains Indians did?[19] A unique aspect of the story was the inclusion of original poetry, constructed in ballad form. About these poems Ed commented, "It was easier to compose them than hunt up others and then get permission from the copyright owners to use them."[20]

The plot of "The Bandit of Hell's Bend" involves the competition of two men for the love of Diana Henders, daughter of wealthy ranch and mine owner Elias Henders, who early in the story is killed by the Apaches. At the ranch in Arizona, named the Bar-Y after the old ranch founded by Yale graduates George and Harry Burroughs in Idaho, the hero "Bull," whose last name is never revealed, loses his foreman's job and suffers various misfortunes, all through the connivance of Hal Colby, the devious villain. The story derives its title from the mystery surrounding an actual bandit, "The Black Coyote,"

an outlaw who specializes in stage holdups; his face is covered with a black handkerchief, and because "Bull" also possesses one, many of the townspeople are convinced that he is the bandit. Other complications are introduced with the arrival at the ranch of Jefferson Wainwright, Senior, and Junior, an attorney named Corson, and the sensuous Lillian Manill, all sophisticated big city people who eventually join forces to attempt to swindle Diana out of her ranch and gold mine.

A number of characters who are assigned roles in "The Bandit of Hell's Bend" are freely drawn versions of individuals mentioned in Ed's *Autobiography*. "Gum" Smith, originally "Gum" Brown, is depicted in slapstick fashion and provides comic relief as the cowardly sheriff and saloonkeeper whose favorite order, "Ah depatizes yo'-all" is greeted with derision by the cowboys. Texas Pete, sympathetically described in Ed's *Autobiography*, becomes the balladeer of the novel, singing the "song" lyrics Ed had devised; Pete, as a protector of Diana Henders, emerges as a hero second only to "Bull." In the description of Pete, "a thing of beauty and a joy forever," gaudily equipped with silver-inlaid Mexican spurs that dragged the ground when he walked, spurs that had dumbbells attached to their hubs and "tinkled merrily a gay accompaniment to his boyish heart," Ed was possibly re-creating himself as the greenest of cowhands on his first visit to the Idaho ranch.

In this 1923 novel the Mexicans are referred to as "greasers" and Gregario, an outlaw companion of "The Black Coyote," is called a "dirty greaser." But before the story's end Gregario reforms, helps to trap the villain, and is characterized as "whiter'n some white men." The Apaches appear only in the briefest of scenes, merely skirmishes with the cowboys.

Davis, who had eagerly reminded Ed about "the cowboy story," saying, ". . . that's mine as soon as it is finished," upon receipt of "The Bandit of Hell's Bend," was severely critical. On June 14 he sent three pages of comments and suggestions for revision. He wrote, "You sure have written a conventional Western story here, and drawn little upon your imaginative powers. I can't understand how a bean as active as yours could refrain from butting in and slamming a few novelties into the good old powder-burned frontier." He listed the weaknesses and errors: the dialogue was up-to-date, not typical of the period. Ed had even mentioned a checkbook and the cowboys being paid by check. There was reference to a "black" bandanna, which Davis explained as an impossibility, a bandanna having figures and being either red or yellow. Concerning the sexy scene where Colby clasps half-clad Lillian Manill in his embrace and "beats it for the bedroom," Davis viewed this with a censor's eye: "Shame on you, Edgar. You've got to stop this. You've got to stop it short outside."

The significant weakness in some of Burroughs' writing was as apparent in "The Bandit of Hell's Bend" as it had been in other hasty attempts at realism. He had inserted a few true-life details of setting or character from his background to give some strength to the story. But this superficial approach could hardly provide realism to the characters and their actions, especially within the framework of a trite plot. He had missed an opportunity to recreate the turbulent, colorful Arizona of the 1880s and to depict the exciting cowboy and ranch life of the period. Perhaps the Burroughs goal of making the story as wild and woolly as possible for a British audience may have contributed to this failure. Curiously, although the novel was tailored-to-order for Sir Algernon, it appeared first in print in *Argosy All-Story* in 1924, then in book form for McClurg, June 4, 1925, and finally in the British Methuen edition, January 28, 1926.

In August 1922 Burroughs contemplated turning his writing talents in a different direction. His proposal, sent to Curtis Brown, his British agents, was that he should undertake a series of articles about one of the most picturesque men of the period, a soldier-of-fortune named General Lee Christmas. The astonishing career of General Christmas, his exploits and precarious adventures in Central America, had created public interest and admiration. A locomotive engineer from Louisiana, Christmas, when twenty-eight years old, had fallen asleep at the throttle and crashed his train. His employment opportunities now dim, Christmas left the States, worked for a while on the Mexican railroads and then moved to Honduras. In describing him as "The Last Great Soldier of Fortune," Samuel Crowther in *The Romance and Rise of the American Tropics* provides details of his life and adventures:

There [in Honduras] he and his engine were captured by the revolutionists and he was ordered to run the train for them. He did more than that. He fitted up a flat car as a mobile fort and captured all the engines on the line! That made him a general — one does not much bother about the intermediate ranks in these armies. Also he became superintendent of the road. He organized what he called his machine gun regiment — which was a machine gun and Guy Maloney, a friend of his from the New Orleans police.

But Christmas' wild exploits were just beginning. As a fighting filibusterer he took part in battles in four Central American countries, traveling back and forth between Honduras, Salvador, Guatemala, and Nicaragua. He became bodyguard and chief of staff to a half-dozen presidents. Christmas was wounded many times and reported killed so often that the newspapers, finally skeptical, reserved a special headline for him — Lee Christmas Killed Again! In 1907 he aided President Bonilla of Honduras in a war against Nicaragua. Honduras was defeated, and once more the familiar report appeared — Christmas was dead, so stated the Encyclopaedia Britannica, eleventh edition. The indestructible general was alive and well in Salvador in 1908, and without any scruples proceeded to head an invasion of Honduras. His hectic career of war, forays, and revolutions did not hamper his personal life; he still found time to acquire four wives. His end was not violent. Lee Christmas demonstrated the accuracy of the saying "Generals die

402

in bed." His death was caused by malaria.

Burroughs' admiration for the dashing general was so strong that he offered to go to Guatemala to interview him. On August 31, 1922, he explained to Curtis Brown, ". . . I had planned to write my articles with a view of putting them into book form after they had appeared in a magazine." He noted that the material could be considered as separate articles or as chapters of "a life story." His interest in Lee Christmas was understandable; beginning with John Carter of Mars, Burroughs' favorite heroes were adventurers, men who performed reckless acts without any fear of death. Through these soldiers-of-fortune he had lived vicariously and now the daring general appeared like a storybook warrior fresh out of the pages of a Burroughs novel. Christmas was fulfilling all the heroic actions that Burroughs had dreamed about but never performed; the exploits of Christmas, a real-life adventurer, could provide a vicarious thrill far more exciting than the deeds of imaginary characters.

Unhappily, Ed's proposal to write the series of articles was hedged about with conditions; he had insisted that he must receive a definite commitment from some suitable magazine to accept the articles. On August 25, Lida McCord of the Curtis Brown Agency replied, "We have interested the Saturday Evening Post in your work but they are not willing to make any definite promise until the manuscript is completed." Ed, not inclined to gamble with any of his valuable time, began to cool toward the project and the journey to Guatemala. He was blunt: "I doubt if I would care to undertake the trip without some more definite assurance that I can dispose of the magazine rights, and also, I shall want to know the rate that I would be paid. . . ." A further letter from Curtis Brown on September 21 explained that none of the editors they had contacted would promise to accept the articles sight unseen.

On September 29, 1922, Ed made it plain that he was abandoning the project: ". . . it commences to look as though I might not be able to do anything in this matter for the present, at least, as I understand that Gen. Christ-

mas is expecting to come to the states, in which event it would probably be advisable to wait until I could talk the matter over with him personally." There is no record of any meeting with General Christmas or of any future plan to write the series of articles about this famous soldier-of-fortune.

Once again, with Davis' encouragement, Ed began considering various ideas for a new *Tarzan* story. From Davis in February 1923 came a suggestion: why not place Tarzan among Lilliputians or some type of tiny people? Ed was intrigued by the idea; upon returning from a trip with Emma — in driving they had encountered 24 below zero weather in Wyoming during which he slept in his overcoat and "nearly froze to death," he turned to his own imagination for an original approach to the story. On March 3 he wrote to Davis, "I am thinking of the new Tarzan story and have obtained a copy of Sir John Lubbock's work on ants." But soon afterward he became dubious about the "little men" theme, believing that while the idea might be workable for a chapter or short story, he could not "carry them through a full length novel with Tarzan." He was prepared to adopt an alternative idea: ". . . I had thought of taking Tarzan into Abyssinia where there is a real Emperor surrounded by real warriors, with a system of religious rites already well established. I should like to have your ideas on the subject, and in the meantime, I shall have to read up considerably on Abyssinia. . . ."[21]

Davis found the little men idea highly stimulating. He thought Ed was visualizing the men as "too small," like diminutive pygmies, and commented, "I think if they were two feet high they would be more negotiable." He could picture "the towering Tarzan defending these miniature men against the beasts of the jungle and the discordant elements." The little men would have "their government, their wars, their intrigues, their treasures and their cities." Naturally, the jungle animals would remain in their normal sizes. Davis could envision "a certain intimate understanding between the kings of the little peoples and the giant Tarzan." However, he was willing to settle for Tarzan in Abyssinia and the mysterious religious rites, but urged Ed not to "clutter Tarzan up with a retinue of black people."[22]

Two weeks later Ed confessed to Davis that after scanning various books on Abyssinia, his interest had waned. He thought he might return to the pygmies after all. Davis, approving, offered his ideas. "Turn the women into archers because of their accuracy and indifference to pain. . . ." The pygmies could, as a defense, have a "manufactured odor which they have discovered and perfected." He went on jokingly: "The odor need not be disagreeable as, for example, the kind you emit. I suppose editors smell just like that to authors. . . ." Davis had other practical suggestions.[23]

Ed displayed a more serious reaction to his writing, one that had depressed him before. His feeling was that Tarzan had "shot his wad"; possibly he and everybody else was tired of the subject. Later he complained that the Tarzan story was hard work and wrote, "I think this will be the last. They are not worth the effort I have to put on them now." In the time required for one Tarzan story, he could write three others. "Instead of enjoying my work," he noted, "I am coming pretty near to loathing it. . . . If I had not promised you this one I would chuck it right where it is."[24]

Davis was both distressed and alarmed, demanding, "If you loathe the Tarzan stuff . . . why do you go on with it?" He was concerned about Ed doing a weak job that would not be fair to either of them. However, in response came a more reassuring statement. Certainly the writing was difficult, especially "after having said all there is to say about Tarzan seven or eight times." But Ed had no intention of handing Davis a lemon. Actually, he had found a new angle and was now "having some fun" out of the story.[25] Ed varied the discussions over stories to make an important announcement; to Davis on May 25, 1923, he wrote, ". . . you are

doing business with a soulless corporation." The amazing tripersonality, farmer-businessman-writer was now converted to Edgar Rice Burroughs, Inc.

On November 23 Ed sent the 86,000-word story to Davis, explaining, "I was going to include an appendix and glossary, but thought better of it." He was worried that Davis might object to Tarzan being reduced to the size of the Ant Men, and wrote, "I found it impossible to have him play around with them while his stature remained normal." Davis telegraphed on December 3 to accept the story, but stated, "Esteban Miranda seems totally unnecessary from every point of view. I request his absolute elimination from this story." Davis' reasoning was that with the removal of Miranda, Tarzan's whole adventure would involve the "little people" — a better arrangement.

The editor's request brought a summary rejection from an exhausted Burroughs. Adamant about *any* revisions, he fired back, "Think Miranda Okay. If insist change buy manuscript as is and make change there. I put in five months on story and though I would do almost anything for you I would not work on it again if I never sold it or another. . . ."[26]

The complexity of "Tarzan and the Ant Men" makes it plain that Burroughs' complaint about the "hard work" was, if anything, a mild understatement. The complicated details of the Minunians' customs and social structure required the most intense planning; only a writer with Burroughs' predilection, almost an obsession, for such detail could have created a story of this type. To devise and keep track of the Minunians' names, in itself, was no mean feat. Ed's evident determination to create the longest possible names for the tiniest people, an idea perhaps arising from Swift's concoctions in *Gulliver's Travels* — Brobdingnag, Glubbdubdrib, and Luggnaggian — led him into the amusing realm of names with as many as nineteen letters. The list of "unpronounceables" included King Adendrohahkis, his son Komodoflorensal, the Veltopismakusians, King Elkomoelhago, and the Trohanadalmakusians. On his worksheets Ed had even meticulously placed accents over certain letters in the names, a procedure that was evidently too much for the printer, who chose to ignore them.

The four-page worksheets for "Tarzan and the Ant Men," complete with glossary, chapter headings, word counts, maps, measurements, and dimensions for a pigmy civilization, and drawings of Minunian hieroglyphics provide an astonishing example of Burroughs' capacity for inventive detail. Ed's drawings include a cross section of one of the gigantic dome-houses, constructed in antlike fashion by the Minunians, and Adendrohahkis' Palace, the largest building, is noted as "220 feet in diameter; 110 feet high; 36 stories. Capable of housing 80,000 people. Scale 1/8 inch equals 4 feet."[27]

Although indebted to Davis for the germ of an idea about Tarzan among the pygmies, Burroughs, once he had turned his imaginary powers loose, devised his own combination of plot, subplots and a host of characters, in all a remarkable demonstration of his ingenuity. In the five months of intense work he had transformed the basic suggestion into a complicated story of races, both giant and diminutive, that in its structure far exceeded any previous development of bizarre civilizations with their customs, equipment, and habitations. In the story Tarzan's adventures are launched through a new and foolhardy action. Under his son Korak's instruction he has been learning to pilot a plane, and despite his son's protests insists upon taking off in a solo flight. Beyond the Great Thorn Forest the plane crashes and here the unconscious Tarzan is carried away by a huge Alalus woman, a creature of a primitive race in which the females, massive and heavily muscled, are dominant over the timid males. The young males, between the ages of fifteen and seventeen, after being liberated and chased into the forest, were later hunted and captured by the females for mating purposes. This "unnatural reversal of sex dominance" is changed through Tarzan's efforts, his rescue of an Alalus lad, and his demonstration to the boy of how the brutal females can be defeated. With instruc-

tion in the use of the bow and arrow the Alalus males are able to overcome the mighty muscles and clubs of the women; thus, they assume their role of the dominant male.

From the Alalus, who occupy only a short section of the story, Tarzan moves to his main encounter with the Minunians, tiny creatures who in battle are mounted upon the miniature Royal Antelope. Davis had insisted that the "pygmies" should not be too small — they might then "have the quality of banshees and leprechauns, the habits of gnomes, and the characteristics of fairies." As a compromise, Ed made the Minunians eighteen inches in height. The antelope stood "fifteen inches at the withers." He was also careful to create them as "real pygmies," not the familiar black tribe, but a "lost white race" referred to in myth and legend.

Early in the story Ed makes clear his plan to compare the habits and activities of these little people to those of the ants. This intention had been indicated in his ant research. The movements of the tiny warriors and workers toward the openings of their domelike structures, carry "to the mind of the ape-man a suggestion of ants laboring about their hills." In addition to devoting detail to the complex social organization of the Minunians, and to including the unusual function of the slaves — their adoption as creatures for intermarriage so as to "infuse new blood" into the physically degenerating Minunians — Ed takes obvious delight, as in the past, in describing the superb military maneuvers of these tiny warriors in their combat against their enemies, the Veltopismakusians.

Ed's indignation against the war propaganda that had deceived him and led to his depiction of the Germans as subhuman, impelled him to insert a comment about the noble motives that drove the Minunians out to battle: "No chicanery of politics here, no thinly veiled ambition of some potential tyrant . . . none of these, but patriotism of purest strain energized by the powerful urge of self-preservation. . . ." He then spoke bitterly of "captains of the outer world who send unwilling men to battle for they know not what, deceived by lying propaganda, enraged by false tales of the barbarity of the foe, whose anger has been aroused against them by similar means." This pointed attack upon the "lying propaganda" and "false tales" reveals that by the fall of 1923, more than a year before the German resentment reached its climax, Burroughs was painfully aware of his prejudiced writing.

In "Tarzan and the Ant Men" unique elements of the plot include the reduction of Tarzan to the stature of a Minunian, a feat accomplished by the "wizard" Zoanthrohago; fortunately, the change is not permanent, and despite his miniature size, Tarzan conveniently retains his former strength. The ants themselves had in the past constituted a serious danger to the Minunians. At the lowest strata of the domes, where the dead had been left, the ants had at first been the scavengers; they soon began to attack the living and great battles followed in which the ants were victorious until the Minunians destroyed their nests and their queens.

On December 7 Davis notified Ed that in compliance with his instructions he had "eliminated entirely from this manuscript the person of Esteban Miranda to the extent of eleven thousand words." Miranda was the Spanish villain who had impersonated the ape-man in the previous novel, *Tarzan and the Golden Lion.* Davis maintained that this deletion improved the story "from every conceivable angle." He disapproved of Ed's ending which finds the imposter Miranda claiming to be Lord Greystoke. This obviously indicated that Ed was "setting the stage for a sequel." Davis requested a three-hundred word ending, "bringing Tarzan back to his family in a normal way," and added, "In my humble opinion the Ant People are big enough for another socking good story. Let Miranda remain among the dead."[28]

Ed responded with some mild annoyance about the revision which was costing him five hundred dollars. His failure to even mention a new ending brought a further demand from Davis who spoke coaxingly of the wonderful cover he was preparing for the "Ant People," one that looked like "a segment from 'Gulliver's Travels.' " As usual, Davis' tone was joking and he threatened, "Give me the end of this story or I'll write it myself. The best way to do an author a lot of damage is to finish a story for him."[29] Ed maintained the same humorous attitude, reminding him of the earlier telegram which had stated that "if you did not like my story you knew what you could do." Ed wrote, "If you want me to write the new ending badly enough to pay me for it say so. If not, turn the job over to the office boy. It won't make any difference, for when the story appears in book form it will read as per my original version, than which there can be nothing better!"[30]

In the five-month period from November 1923 to April of the following year, Burroughs, immersed in business activities, the El Caballero Country Club, and the sale of Tarzana lots, could devote little effort to writing. Continuous agreements with McClurg had produced a steady flow of books: *At the Earth's Core* (1922); *The Chessmen of Mars* (1922); *Tarzan and the Golden Lion* (1923); *Pellucidar* (1923). For the latest publication Bray returned to an old Burroughs story "The Land That Time Forgot"; it would appear on June 14, 1924.

Burroughs' two-year contract with Munsey expired in April 1924, and the customary negotiations began. The rate had been five cents a word; Burroughs noted frankly that he could see no advantage to a contract unless Davis either agreed to take all of his work at that price or to raise the rate on the stories that were accepted. An unwritten "gentleman's agreement" was finally arrived at. For a rate of six cents a word, Davis was granted first refusal on all the stories. Concerning those that did not appear to be the type Munsey would want, Ed planned to submit only sections in progress, believing that in the event of rejection, he might not finish the story. However, he proceeded to ignore this plan at once, launching into one of his most untypical stories, and finishing it on October 13. "Marcia of the Doorstep," estimated at some 125,000 words, was the longest work he had ever written.

Cover of Tarzan and the Ant Men, *1924; J. Allen St. John, illustrator.*

Cover of Tarzan and the Golden Lion, *1923; J. Allen St. John, illustrator.*

Cover of Pellucidar, 1923; J. Allen St. John, illustrator.

In his creation of this long novel, Ed was again symbolizing his protest or rebellion against the repetitive sequence of *Tarzan* and other fantasy works that he was forced to write. Although he must have been aware of the extreme difficulty he would face in marketing the novel, he was still driven to complete it. This impulsive action was contrary to the cold-blooded, dollars-and-cents attitude that had long since dictated his writing procedures. But in this case the frustration and the psychological need to be recognized as something more than "Burroughs, the author of Tarzan," were too powerful to suppress. Along with this, despite his often-repeated statements about writing only to entertain, went a hidden dream of creating something that would have a touch of the literary quality, a piece of writing, highly realistic, that might confound the critics who rated him merely as an author of superficial escapism and cause them to view him with a new respect.

The writing of "Marcia of the Doorstep" became a secretive process. In contrast to his usual method of mentioning a contemplated work, sounding out Davis or Bray about it and then discussing its progress, Ed gave no indication at all that the novel was underway. From this, the alternate assumptions could be that he was sensitive about revealing this shift to a new and impractical type of writing, one that broke sharply from his established patterns, or that he desired to keep the work secret, hoping to produce as a complete surprise a novel of unusual strength and appeal. To further insure secrecy, hiding the project even from his secretaries, he wrote the entire 125,000-word novel in longhand on lined legal-size notebook paper. At a later date he commented disparagingly about "Marcia of the Doorstep," explaining that he had written it at a time when his mind "was occupied with other things," financial and business entanglements, and that the "rottenness" of the story was "more or less" a reflection of his "mental attitude" during the period.[31] There may have been some truth in this expla-

nation, but one must deduce that any author who devotes more than five months to a lengthy work is surely motivated by something beyond mechanical persistence — a sustained interest in the story, its characters, and its development.

In the romantic plot of "Marcia of the Doorstep" Burroughs devised involved relationships in a city-life setting and added some background references to the stage and motion picture field. At the same time, he could not resist bringing in one of his much-used shipwrecks with the inevitable mutineers and a landing on a deserted island. Burroughs' past preoccupation with the evils of socialism, Bolshevism, and his contempt for the IWWs is again evident in his occasional lapses into propaganda attacks against "agitators" and their ilk. But most significantly, in the creation of the loathsome villain Max Heimer, the basest caricature of a Jew, Burroughs reveals his susceptibility to the racial prejudice of the times and the stereotype that resulted.

The fortunes of Marcia, an infant left on the doorstep of the Sacketts and raised by them, are the main concern of the story. The story, in its 1906 opening, describes how John Hancock Chase, Jr., the son of a United States senator, is being blackmailed by Max Heimer who has convinced him that on a certain night, after the supposed consumption of too much liquor, he (Chase) had sexual relations with a disreputable woman, Mame Myerz, resulting in the birth of an illegitimate child. Chase, a married man, is unable to pay any more money and is finally driven to suicide.

The reader, of course, is given the impression, after this scene, that the infant is Marcia, who grows up in the home presided over by Marcus Aurelius Sackett, a familiar type of old-fashioned Shakespearean actor. Other members of the household include his wife Clara and an actress, Della Maxwell. Marcus, completely impractical, is childlike in his handling of money and naive in his estimates of human nature. Because of his irregular income, the family lives on the edge of poverty, but despite this,

Tarzana Ranch
Reseda Calif

Copyright
Edgar Rice Burroughs Inc
1924

MARCIA OF THE DOORSTEP
by Edgar Rice Burroughs
Commenced: April 12 1924
Finished: Oct 13 1924
12:34 P.M.

Chapters: 40
Pages: 294
Words: 125,000

Started writing at 8091 Sunset April 30.   Shed T 5-7-24
Started writing at 544 S. Gramercy Pl about June 20 1924

	CHAPTERS		
	The Way Out	I	1
	The Sacketts	II	5
12	Sixteen Years	III	16
30	The Senator	IV	24
42	Mame Myers	V	37
53	Financed	VI	44
63	A Red Letter Day	VII	50
79	An anonymous manuscript	VIII	61
	Della's Letter	IX	70
109	An Invitation	X	77
121	A Little Love	XI	85
133	Good bye!	XII	95
151	Patsy is Bored	XIII	103
162	Jack Chase	XIV	109
173	Gathering Clouds	XV	115
183	Patsy Maneuvers	XVI	121
195	The Squall	XVII	128
207	Helpless	XVIII	134
218	The Derelict	XIX	139
235	Mother Wrecke	XX	149
246	The Stowaway	XXI	156
258	The Last Drop	XXII	162
271	The Eighth Day	XXIII	169
289	Old Friends	XXIV	179
299	Sorenson Comes	XXV	185
311	Cumcrow	XXVI	191
321	LOST	XXVII	198
336	Adrift in Need	XXVIII	206
348	Smoke	XXIX	213
361	A Telegram	XXX	221
370	Off in the Night	XXXI	226
385	The Break Out	XXXII	246
396	Andromeda	XXXIII	243
404	Marcia Sands	XXXIV	249
414	A Frivolous Scar	XXXV	257
429	"Will you be my wife"	XXXVI	265
458	A Confession	XXXVII	270
464	Love's Tragedy	XXXVIII	274
456	The Gorgate Hotel	XXXIX	281
467	The Silver Lining	XL	288

1   John Hancock Chase Jr
1   Max Heimer
1   Louis Kossit - attorney
2   Mame Myers - the woman
3   Billy   Jim   Roger - the three friends of that July night
3   Julia: Mrs John Hancock Chase Jr.
5   John Hancock Chase III
5   Monroe Adams Madison - Chase Butler
5   Marcus Aurelius Sackett
5   Mr Ed Frawley the stage-director
6   Abraham Zinker - owner of the Stock Company
9   Clara Sackett
14   Richard Steele
14   Mollie Steele
15   Marcia Aurelia Sackett - April 10 1906.
15   Della Maxwell
22   Haffington Stock Players
25   183 W. ___th st
25   Orca Steele
29   Senator John Hancock Chase
31   Homer Ashton
42   Judge Isaac Berlowser, Chase's attorney
51   Bloom - a theatrical agent
51   Signor Moussini - vocal teacher
52   Patsy Kellar - (Marcia's friend) Ruth's sister
72   Ruth Ashton - Homer's wife
78   Banks van Spiddle
94   Krause (name mentioned by Heimer)
85   The Marcus Aurelius Sackett Company   Ship's Company
94   Sacketts Com: Boston, Phila, Balto, Wash, Cinn, Ind, St Louis, K.C.
              Denver, SL City, San F, LB, Chgo, N.Y.
16   Edward - the Ashton chauffeur - 129
96   Mr Whitcomb - Dick's boss 140
98   The Lady X - Ashton's yacht   143
98   Tillie an Ashton maid   148
101 Blake, the Ashton butler (Blake) 148
     Mr & Mrs Blair Sacker (guests aquatic) 155
     Captain Dever of the Lady X   210
     Wise a sailor; Trouble makers 212, 213

x Ashton owner
x Sackett
x van Spiddle
x Chase
x Mrs Ashton and Tillie her maid
x Patsy
xx Miss Sacker
x marcia
x Dever Capt
x Jones mate
x Sorenson Engineer
x Wise - sailor
x Slavin
x Hayson sec
x Bledgo
x Olson
x Deeks cre
x Pilkins cre
x Cumcrow
x Schanasky
x Victor Cook

Total 32

Marcus will never consider entering a field that he abhors — the motion pictures. The years have passed; Marcia is now sixteen and Marcus is once more unemployed; but when, in order to pay for her singing lessons, she volunteers to seek work in the movies, Marcus forbids it.

Heimer, appearing at the Sackett home on a legal matter involving Marcus' current play, discovers that Marcia is a "doorstep" baby, perceives the connection with the man he had blackmailed years before, and sees his new opportunity — to go to old Senator Chase and extort money from him. Chase, believing that Marcia is his granddaughter, establishes a trust fund for the girl, with the proviso that the two must never meet, and provides $20,000 for the Sacketts as compensation for raising Marcia. The cunning Heimer manages to swindle Marcus out of most of this money. As treasurer of a Shakespearean touring company, Heimer convinces Marcus that the tour is a financial failure, although it is actually successful, and, as a result, Marcus, believing he has foolishly wasted all of his money, attempts suicide. He is saved by his wife Clara.

Marcia had always assumed she would marry her childhood sweetheart, Dick Steele, but finds herself involved with two men who fall in love with her. Through wealthy acquaintances, the Ashtons, she meets Banks van Spiddle and later accepts an invitation to join these people on a yacht cruise in the Pacific. At Honolulu, where he is stationed, Lieutenant John Hancock Chase, III, the grandson of the old senator, becomes a member of the party. Marcia and Jack Chase fall in love, and here Burroughs creates a situation which raises the problem of incest, since, presumably, unknown to either one, they are really brother and sister.

Judge Isaac Berlanger, a trusted friend of the Chase family, had foreseen the danger of a shipboard romance and obtained the permission of the senator to reveal the relationship. Berlanger cables, but it is too late; the shipwreck has occurred and the ship is abandoned. Marcia and Jack are in a lifeboat with crew members who include a number of dangerous mutineers. Jack courageously keeps these men under control, and after the lifeboat has been adrift for some time the passengers land on a deserted island.

These adventures alternate with an account of the Sackett's troubles at home. Financial problems have driven Marcus to accepting handouts from Heimer. In the meantime, no word is received of the shipwreck survivors. Marcia and Jack eventually are rescued from the island, but upon her return she finds the cable revealing their relationship. Distraught, she leaves without explaining matters to Jack and launches a successful career in the movies as Marian Sands. Fortunately, a letter from Della Maxwell, written on her deathbed, discloses that Marcia is really *her* daughter.

At the end Heimer receives his punishment and is required to make restitution for the money he has stolen from Marcus. Marcia's happy union with Jack is somewhat marred by the tragic death of Dick Steele, who is killed in an airplane crash.

As in other works of the period, "Marcia of the Doorstep" reveals Burroughs' political and social conditioning and his acceptance of the prejudices of the day. There is a repetition of his views in three familiar areas. Radicals and communists are derided. When Dick Steele refers to the "burden" workers are carrying because of "parasites" like the playboy van Spiddle, Della remarks, "Getting to be a regular little Bolshevik, eh?" She points out that van Spiddle's spending creates work for others, and scoffs at the concept of financial equality — a world of this type "would be about as dull and impossible as the orthodox Christian conception of Heaven."

Ashton, in commenting upon the angry complaints of certain crew members, notes that "they've been innoculated with IWW virus" and speaks with scorn of their labor leaders who "live off the fat of the land" and "do it without labor at the expense of the damn fools upon whose ignorance and credulity they play. . . ."

Burroughs demonstrates some prudish morality in Jack Chase's disapproval of women who usurp "the prerogative vulgarities and vices of men," these being smoking, drinking, and swearing. Chase remarks to Patsy that "We all approve of it . . . for the other fellow's women." Yet, "Marcia of the Doorstep" contains an odd, sexually-tinged scene of a type never used by Burroughs. Marcus first hooks his wife's garters and then is summoned by Marcia to come to her room and pull down her brassiere "so it won't show." The un-Burroughesque nature of the brief scene makes it seem that he was doing this in an attempt to emulate the newer style of frank realism in literary stories. He may have hoped that it would make the story more salable, but the scene appears inappropriate and awkward.

In the lifeboat episode the horrifying prospect of cannibalism appears; Burroughs had last resorted to this in *The Return of Tarzan* where a party including Jane and Clayton, adrift in a lifeboat, take part in a gruesome "Lottery of Death." In "Marcia of the Doorstep" Pilkins, one of the sailors, discusses the past of Bledgo, the most dangerous of the mutineers, who had been shipwrecked before; rescued after being adrift for three weeks, Bledgo looked "as fat and chipper as he is today, but they say the boat smelt awful." The bestial, half-crazed Bledgo now runs amuck, attempts to kill one of the men and bites a piece out of his shoulder.

Aware of the excessive length of "Marcia of the Doorstep," Burroughs went through the manuscript making numerous deletions. Long passages, many of them redundant, and even whole pages are scratched out in pencil. A middle section and the long closing scene are reduced through the use of insert pages. On October 30, 1924, in rejecting the story, Davis commented that it would make a first-class book and then added his criticisms:

. . . there is so much diversity, so many characters and scenes, so many threads, the coming together of which is so far apart, that it would be fatal to publish it in a monthly magazine in *serial form. No reader could remember the complications in this novel for a period of five, six or possibly seven months; the time required in view of its length to complete it in serial segments.*

Later submissions produced no results. To Horace Liveright (Boni & Liveright) on June 3, 1925, in sending the manuscript Ed noted he had made "some slight changes" and added dolefully, "I am afraid you will not like the story." Liveright's rejection — "It is not our sort of book. . . ." — confirmed Ed's fears. He was frank in his reply that "people much more experienced than I have told me I had no business trying to write anything other than highly imaginative fiction" and also admitted that he had not sent the story to Bray at McClurg because he *knew* the editor would not like it. Other rejections came from *Redbook,* the *Saturday Evening Post,* and *Love Story Magazine.* Clearly, "Marcia of the Doorstep" was not fated to appear in print.

With the purchase by Davis for $2,150 of "The Moon Men," a revision of the unsalable "Under the Red Flag," came some bantering remarks about Ed's obvious plan for a sequel, made evident in the concluding page of the story. On October 20, 1924, Davis wrote, "The Jews may be 'God's Chosen People,' but you are His chosen author. You could take any one of the psalms, make it 100,000 words in length, and then leave a string dragging for a second verse." About the sequel, its theme being a "feudal state" existing in California of the future, Davis was encouraging, but suggested that Ed use actual locations of the contemporary "Golden West" in developing this story of a region lapsing into decadence. Ed adopted this idea, and on May 14, 1925, sent "The Red Hawk" to the editor.

The summer brought a return to Mars, with the sixth of the series in progress. The story, at first titled "A Weird Adventure on Mars," was finished on November 16. With the invention of a new hero, Ulysses Paxton, an infantry captain in the United States Army, Burroughs makes him the second earthman to be trans-

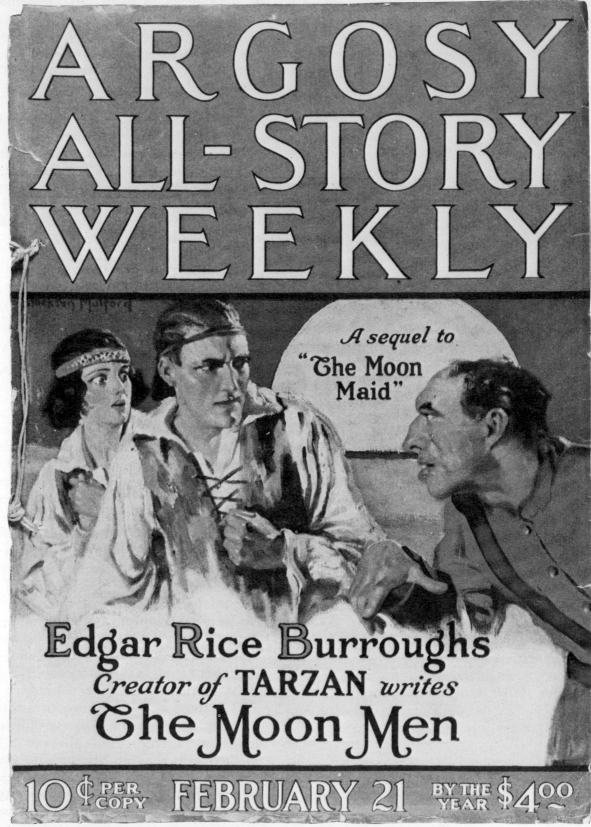

"*The Moon Men*" cover of Argosy All-Story Weekly, *February 21, 1925.*

ported to Mars. From Paxton, as the story opens, comes a letter describing his serious injuries in battle, and how, as he lay on the verge of death, he followed the example of his idol, John Carter, stretched out his arms imploringly toward Mars, and then found himself drawn "through the trackless wastes of interplanetary space."

Paxton at once becomes an associate of the brilliant surgeon Ras Thavas of Barsoom. A very old man, Thavas, in his "House of the Dead," stores the bodies of young men and women, preserving both the living and the dead for use in transplants. The living include the beautiful Valla Dia, purchased as a slave and kept in a state of suspended animation for ten years, at which time her youthful body is exchanged for that of the aged Xaxa the Jeddara (Queen) of Phundahl. In the operation, witnessed by Paxton, the surgeon Thavas demonstrates an astonishing skill: ". . . at the end of four hours he had transferred the brain of each woman to the brain pan of the other, deftly connected the severed nerves and ganglia, replaced the skulls and scalps and bound both heads securely with his peculiar adhesive tape, which was not only antiseptic and healing but anaesthetic, locally, as well." The blood of Valla, reheated, and with a chemical solution added, is then exchanged for the blood of the older woman Xaxa, who is now the possessor of youth and beauty. Thavas, devoid of all sentiment, performs with the detached and objective attitude of the scientist.

Because he believed that the Earthman Paxton, a stranger on Mars, could be trusted, Thavas had chosen him as his assistant. The aged scientist, above all, needed someone who could learn his surgical techniques, and when the necessity arose, exchange his worn-out body for that of a younger man. Paxton, now thoroughly skilled, agrees to perform the operation, but imposes a condition. He had fallen in love with the exquisite Valla Dia at sight and is determined that her body shall be returned to her. Thavas, having no choice, promises to make the transference if Xaxa is brought to his laboratory. The remainder of the story develops from this incredible task Paxton has set for himself. He must journey to the distant Phundahl, somehow kidnap the most powerful woman in the kingdom, Xaxa, and carry her back to the laboratory where the surgery can take place.

In this 1925 story, Burroughs' plot, which may have appeared bizarre, contained the substance of "things to come" in modern transplants. The storage of bodies and vital organs is a present-day medical practice. A description of the transplants could well apply to standard procedures of today or the next decade:

I removed the kidneys from a rich old man, replacing them with healthy ones from a young subject. The following day I gave a stunted child new thyroid glands. A week later I transferred two hearts and then, at last, came the great day for me — unassisted, with Ras Thavas standing silently beside me, I took the brain of an old man and transplanted it within the cranium of a youth.

A further projection of the future is evident in a device called the "equilibrimotor," designed for individual flying. It is described as a "broad belt" which is filled with a Barsoomian ray of propulsion that, by exerting a counterforce against the pull of gravity, helps to maintain a person's equilibrium. The remainder of the apparatus consists of a small radium motor and a sturdy, light wing that can be manipulated with hand levers.

As in *The Gods of Mars,* Burroughs cannot resist ridiculing a blind, superstitious belief in religion. The people of Phundahl worshipped the god Tur, and at the temple followed a ritual which they never presumed to question. Before various idols they might lie prone or bump their heads on the floor, or, on occasion, crawl madly in a circle. In all cases money was dropped in a receptacle.

Burroughs presents a significant aspect of his philosophy in the scene that follows. Paxton, upon hearing the worshippers recite "Tur is Tur, Tur is Tur" before two different idols, remarks that in both cases the sounds are identical. Dar Tarus corrects him, insisting that at first they said, "Tur is Tur," while at the second idol they reversed it. Dar Tarus asks, "Do you not see? They turned it right around backwards, which makes a very great difference." Paxton could not detect the "difference," and because of this, was again accused of a lack of faith.

Of course Burroughs' invention of the word "Tur" for the Phundahlian God is deliberate. The worshippers are really saying, "Rut is Rut." In this scene Burroughs is commenting upon the follies of all blind religious custom, whether on earth or on Mars. But in addition, he is emphasizing a danger. Through years of ritualistic behavior and unquestioning conformity, one may lose the power of seeing things rationally. Paxton, a stranger, not confined in the Phundahlians' particular rut, could apply simple reasoning. About religion as mere jargon chanted automatically, Burroughs is saying that whether one mumbles it backward or forward, it remains meaningless.

With the completion of "A Weird Adventure on Mars," Ed's procedure, as usual, was to submit the manuscript to Munsey. In August 1925 Bob Davis had departed for six months of vacation and travel; his visit to Los Angeles, where he noted his intention to see a "million relatives," included a stopover with the Burroughs family. Replacing Davis was Matthew White, Jr., and his reaction to the Martian manuscript was both unexpected and disturbing to Ed. On November 27, in rejecting the story, White noted, ". . . the present vein you are writing in does not suit the *Argosy* as did your Tarzan stories. We do not find them tense enough in action, rapid enough in action, gripping enough in situations." White indicated that if the choice were his, he would not have accepted "The Red Hawk." Icily formal, in contrast to Davis' bantering remarks, White closed with a statement about writing something "strictly in line with the kind of story the *Argosy* requires. . . ."

Irked and bewildered, Ed put the story aside, uncertain whether to submit it elsewhere. On March 10, 1926, he expressed his feelings to Joseph Bray, explaining that he was a "little sore" about the rejection, "possibly more by the tone of the man's letter . . . than anything else." Because of the extended relationship with Munsey, Ed felt he was entitled to better treatment. He could not restrain his anger: "Therefore, they can go to hell as far as I am concerned until they ask me for another story." He added, "I know it was not Bob's fault, but after all it is the Frank A. Munsey Company that I am dealing with and the letter I received from them was official."

In April, Davis, who had been traveling around the world, returned to his desk; Frank A. Munsey had died. To Ed, Davis remarked that one of the happiest experiences of his trip was "meeting the Burroughs family at their own table." He also advised that two of his books were being published that year, one titled *Over My Left Shoulder*, containing an editor's reminiscences about events and personalities, and the other, *Ruby Robert, Alias Bob Fitzsimmons*, an account based upon Davis' personal association with the prizefighter. In 1897, on assignment from C. M. Palmer, business manager of the *New York Journal*, and with specific instructions from William Randolph Hearst, Davis set out to contact Fitzsimmons before his scheduled fight with Corbett. Hearst, whose plan was to sign Fitzsimmons to an agreement for thirty days prior to the fight and twenty-four hours after, explained the conditions to Davis: "We are paying Fitzsimmons for his silence. He cannot speak to anyone, write to anyone, pose for photographs, or carry on any intercourse whatsoever except through you or in your presence. . . ." For this agreement Fitzsimmons was offered ten thousand dollars, half upon signing and the remainder following the fight. Martin Julian, the fighter's manager, after some persuasion signed the agreement, and Davis at once joined the training group, accompanying them to Carson City, Nevada. He described himself humorously as Fitzsimmons' private secretary. In his book, besides reporting the fight, in which Corbett was knocked out, Davis added colorful anecdotes about Fitzsimmons.[32]

Concerning "A Weird Adventure on Mars," Ed, on April 20, notified Davis that the story had been "packed away" in the vault "with an accompaniment of a few briny tears." Despite his joking, it was evident that he was losing patience with the Munsey Company. He had hoped they would sign an agreement to take his entire output; their refusal to do this and their rejections of "Marcia of the Doorstep" and his latest Mars story put a severe strain upon the relationship. Street & Smith had also returned "Marcia of the Doorstep," and when editor Charles Agnew MacLean, in September 1926, wrote to request Burroughs' submissions for *Popular Magazine*, Ed in annoyance reminded him of this recent rejection. The material MacLean sought was painfully obvious to Ed. MacLean spoke of "a wild hope" that Ed might be interested in doing another *Tarzan* story. Ed forwarded "A Weird Adventure on Mars" to him, and the ensuing correspondence, a contest of price proposals and counterproposals for a *Tarzan* story, lasted for two years and achieved a new record for futility.

On October 30 MacLean had returned the Mars story, commenting that the theme was "too bizarre and shocking." He followed oddly with an admission that it was "extremely easy to read" and confessed, ". . . I kept reading it long after I knew that it would not be advisable for us to publish it." As negotiations continued, Ed determined that if MacLean wanted only a *Tarzan* story, he must pay high for it, and quoted a price of ten cents a word. With the contest moving into 1927, Ed became more irritable: "We seem to be working at cross-purposes. You want to buy a Tarzan story and I want to sell a Martian story. I think you are very foolish not to buy it. . . ." On March 2 MacLean explained that he could not accept the "rather repellent features" of this particular Martian story.[33] During the course of this bickering, Ed had submitted the story to the *Elks Maga-*

zine, where it was rejected. The title change to "Vad Varo of Barsoom" could not make the story more palatable.[34]

The Burroughs response to MacLean's use of "repellent" offered logic and example that were grimly humorous. A story far more repellent, *The Chessmen of Mars*, had been successful in both magazine and book form. In mentioning the kaldanes who were all brain, and "bred" human bodies to carry them about, Ed noted they also devoured these bodies. "They were utterly horrid. There was also another race of delightful people who stuffed their dead and posed them on balconies outside their homes as well as in the corridors of their palaces." The transplanting of brains from one head to another, as described in "Vad Varo of Barsoom," in Ed's opinion was hardly as "gruesome" as the breeding and eating of human bodies. Ed submitted a gambling proposition to MacLean: if the new Mars story did not increase *Popular Magazine's* circulation, the editor would not have to pay anything for it. Despite this free-trial concession, MacLean could not be persuaded to accept the story.[35]

On April 19, 1927, replying to a query by Hugo Gernsback, editor of *Amazing Stories*, about available material, Burroughs offered "Vad Varo of Barsoom" for $1,250. To the struggling Experimenter Publishing Company this was a stiff price. Gernsback, noting that "at the present stage of *Amazing Stories*' development, we would not be justified in paying the amount you ask, ..." made a counterproposal. "Vad Varo of Barsoom" would be published in a yearbook of best stories, issued by *Amazing Stories* in July, and selling for fifty cents, double the price of the magazine. If this were satisfactory, Gernsback would pay the amount demanded. Burroughs quickly agreed, but in the months that followed, a delay in payment brought some heated correspondence.[36] The selection of a title for the story became an immediate problem. On May 9 Gernsback wired for permission to rename it "Xaxa of Mars," stating, "The long name will

417

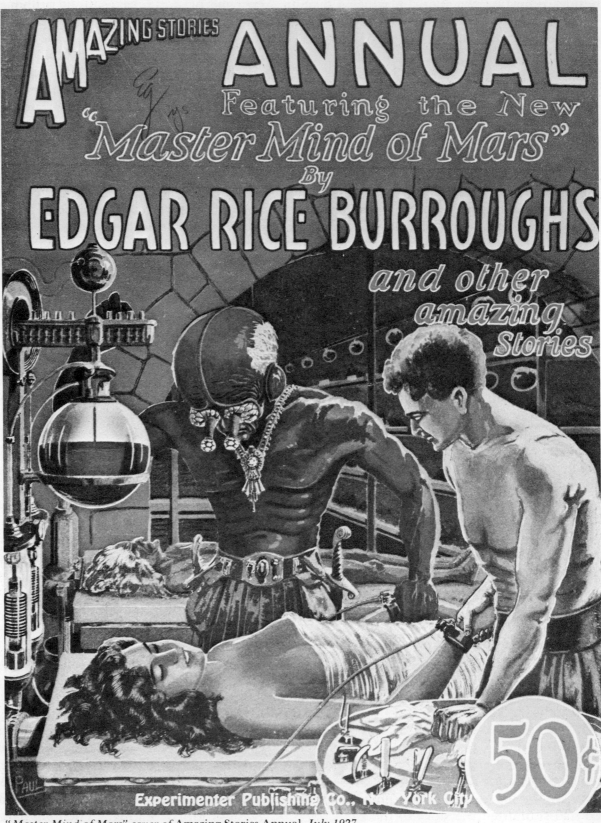

"Master Mind of Mars" cover of Amazing Stories Annual, *July 1927.*

interfere with sale. . . . Word Mars should be in title in our opinion." Burroughs granted Gernsback a free hand, but when the annual appeared, the story assumed a new and final title — "The Master Mind of Mars."

While the MacLean dealings remained at an impasse, Ed, from summer 1926-27, completed and sold two *Tarzan* stories elsewhere. These were "The Tarzan Twins," a juvenile, and "Tarzan, Lord of the Jungle." Through his hesitation MacLean had lost his chance to acquire the latter story, but on October 17 the editor quoted the remarkable rate of ten cents a word for a *Tarzan* story, the highest price he had "ever paid anyone," and stipulated that it must be "really good." That nothing but a Tarzan story would interest him was made evident by his rejection on December 20 of the second of Burroughs' ventures into Indian-white-man conflict, "Apache Devil."

It was not until June 1928 that Ed finished the story, "Tarzan and the Lost Tribe," and sent it to *Popular Magazine.* Based upon the past difficulties, the reaction might have been anticipated. MacLean, seriously ill, was not scheduled to return to work for several months, but the magazine editors, highly disappointed, rejected the story, commenting, ". . . it is not a real Tarzan story, which we had hoped to get from you, and for which our offer was made." Ed had conceived a story of a lost Roman civilization, later to be retitled "Tarzan and the Lost Empire." The editors complained that "almost none of the action takes place in the jungle. . . ." They conceded that the story was "quite fascinating indeed," but claimed, "the balance of appeal is on the side of readers who are interested in archaeology and history (imaginative)."[37] Ed's disgust with the entire matter, the culmination of two years of correspondence, was indicated in his "No Ans." scrawled across the top of the editors' letter.

The cross-exchanges with various editors had often involved wrangling over prices or revisions and had at times produced impatience or exasperation on Burroughs' part; however, this correspondence could produce an un-matched brand of sarcasm and humor, as evidenced by letters between newspaper editors and Burroughs. In December 1926 the *Kansas City Star* rejected "The Mad King" for serialization and added a comment that it was a motion picture scenario. Burroughs, on the seventeenth, wrote to Louis Mecker, serial editor, to express surprise at the statement and to point out that "The Mad King" was a novel, had appeared as a serial in a magazine and had been published by McClurg. He remarked "The motion picture rights to this story have not been sold, nor was it written for motion picture purposes. In fact, none of my stories have been written for the screen, nor am I sufficiently conversant with motion picture production to write a scenario. I am sorry that you were misinformed. . . ."

Mecker, in his answer of the twenty-second, noted the assurance that "The Mad King" *was* a novel and agreed that other newspapers had purchased it with this belief: "All of this only goes to show how preconceived ideas may affect one's convictions. I examined 'The Mad King' myself and came to the conclusion that it was a motion picture scenario, although, like you, I have no technical knowledge of the construction of these scenarios."

Continuing, Mecker turned to Shakespeare for an example:

When Hamlet and Polonius stood gazing at the sky, it was Polonius's opinion that a certain cloud form resembled a whale (if I remember correctly), but Hamlet remarked "Methinks it is a camel," Polonius at once conceded, " 'Tis backed like a camel." You and the Boston Post and the New York World all feel that "The Mad King" is a novel. And sure enough, now that you suggest it, methinks 'tis backed like a novel, but for the rest of it me still thinks 'tis very like a motion picture scenario.

Burroughs, hardly to be outdone in this type of sarcasm, and never one to concede the last word to anybody, proceeded on the twenty-eighth to demolish Mecker: "Many thanks for your delightful letter of December 22nd. The

Cover of Tarzan, Lord of the Jungle, *1928; J. Allen St. John, illustrator.*

Kansas City Star is to be congratulated on having discovered Shakespeare, and I am encouraged to believe that three hundred years hence it will discover the Burroughs classics and commence to increase its circulation accordingly."

An exchange of a lighter nature, involving the *Daily World* of Tulsa, Oklahoma, was initiated on November 18, 1927, when Burroughs inquired why the newspaper had never used his stories serially; he wondered if there were any "condition" that he could correct. From A. X. Hallinan, Sunday editor, came a terse response scrawled on Burroughs' letter: "Not enough sex appeal!"

In the summer of 1926 Burroughs finally began to write a story based upon an idea that had appealed to him seven years earlier. The procedure of making mental notes about story material, filing them away in a corner of his mind, and then reviving the idea at the appropriate time, had been adopted by him on various occasions in the past. An inquiry to *The American Boy* in September 1919 about the market for a story featuring an Apache Indian boy had been followed by a request to the Chicago Field Museum for information about Apache life. In October of that year he expressed his admiration of the Apaches to Davis, referred to "the atrocities committed on them by whites," and sought approval of his idea to create a young Apache warrior "similar to Tarzan." He could turn the Apache into a "regular Tarzan," he explained, through the use of a plot involving a kidnapped white child raised by the Indians.

On October 8, 1925, Burroughs contacted H. C. Paxton, editor of *The Country Gentleman*, and commented about "tying up" his next Western story with the Geronimo campaign. He also spoke of the crossing of the Mormons from Illinois to Utah as another idea. Later he complained about the difficulty of finding information about Geronimo. His hopes for years had been to be accepted by a prestige market of this type, and he made it plain he was writing the story to specifically meet the requirements of the Curtis publication. On June 8, 1926, he was careful to explain a new direction in his story idea: "I find records of innumerable instances in which white children were captured by Apaches and reared by them as members of their own tribes, and in this fact I saw the possibility of a romantic character that might be likened to an Apache Tarzan." Ed noted that with this theme the story "would be written from the viewpoint of the Apache." The plot would center about a white boy who "would be unaware that he was not an Indian"; Ed referred to a true-life situation concerning a white girl abducted by the Indians who afterward married a chief, and who, many years later, upon being captured by the white men, so resembled the other Indian squaws that it was difficult to identify her as a white woman. Ed stressed that he would not start the story until this approach was approved by Paxton, and until the rate of payment was established.

In correspondence with Ed, Paxton, speaking for "The Oldest Agricultural Journal in the World," had indicated that his magazine was not interested in the standard Burroughs fare of *Tarzan* or other-planet works. It was only Ed's shift to the Western, "The Bandit of Hell's Bend," that changed Paxton's attitude. Now, in approving the Apache plot, Paxton and editor Loring A. Schuler commented that there was "abundant foundation for a Tarzan of the Apaches kind of book," but cautioned Ed to limit the flights of his imagination — he would have "to hold far closer to the probabilities" than he had in *Tarzan*. The price was generous, "not less than $5,000 — more if the quality of the tale warranted a better price."[38]

An immediate obstacle to an agreement arose before the story was begun. The Curtis policy required that all rights be sold and that second serial publication in newspapers not be permitted. Book, dramatic, and motion picture rights would be reassigned to the author after the story appeared in the magazine. Ed had stubbornly adhered to his practice of selling only the first serial rights ever since he had unknowingly lost the rights to several of his earliest works. But he was so anxious to break into a media of this type whose reputation was above the *Argosy-All Story,* that he abandoned the rule he had maintained since 1912 and agreed to Paxton's conditions.[39]

In noting the "paucity of authentic information relative to Apaches," especially their "pre-reservation life," Ed claimed he had bought every book on the subject, and after reading and rereading ten volumes had found so many contradictions that he was compelled "to take considerable license" in his writing. He stressed that he was not utilizing his personal knowledge of the Apaches to any great extent, because his experiences had given him "an extremely biased and one-sided impression:" "I knew them then from the soldier's and white man's point of view and even in that day they were still hated and hunted like coyotes or mountain lion, our Apache scouts never travelling across country alone without being in actual danger of being fired upon by the first cowboy or prospector who saw them, and everyone that I talked with being absolutely convinced that there was no good in them."[40]

The precautions Ed had taken to work closely with Paxton and accede to his wishes did not bring the desired result. On December 3, 1926, in a letter distinguished by its vagueness, Paxton and Schuler rejected "The War Chief of the Apaches," describing it as "not quite the serial we should offer our readers." Other phrases were equally meaningless. Without question the story would have "a distinct appeal for many readers"; the choice of a serial "is a matter that calls for prayerful thought." Baffled, Ed sought specific reasons, speculating in confusion about the possible weaknesses in the story. He wondered if his detailed account of the Apache Shoz-Dijiji, in his early years, had been the cause: ". . . I was anxious, probably over-anxious, to develop the reader's understanding of the training and environment of Apaches from childhood to the end that some of their cruel and inhuman practices might not make them wholly abhorrent in his eyes."[41]

He wanted to know if the story was "too horrible" or if the white characters were "too crude," confessing that he thought this might be the problem, and "as a sop," of which he was really ashamed, had arranged for the girl, Wichita Billings, to be taken into the home of an army officer to make her "a little more presentable in the eyes of polite society." He explained he had known many whites of this type years before in Arizona, Idaho, and Utah, and found these pioneers of the '70s and '80s to be "almost universally ignorant, illiterate, uncouth, and unclean," although they often possessed "sterling characteristics" that more than balanced their defects. He added, "Knowing them as I did, I could not honestly place a sweet, marcelled, grammatical heroine in this environment and claim that she was part of it."[42]

On December 28 Paxton explained the reasons for the rejection. Surprisingly, they had little relationship to those Ed had conjectured. Paxton conceded that the white man's dealings with the Indians became "one of the most shameful chapters in American history." But in his opinion the average American still did not understand this and clung to the old view of the redskin as "a savage and heartless marauder." Paxton's remaining comments provided a depressing revelation as to the type of material *The Country Gentleman* fed to its readers. He noted that "Pocahonatas and, to a lesser degree, Squanto are romantic figures; Cooper won sympathy for his redskin characters; but the average reader has no such feeling towards any of the Plains Indians. . . ." Thus, Paxton insisted, a serial written from the Indian's side would have only a limited appeal. Yet, Ed had explained his intention to write the story from the Apache's viewpoint, and Paxton had not objected at that time.

Paxton's main objection, however, was still to come. While admitting that Ed's story could have "geniune literary and historic value," he finally let the cat out of the bag, ". . . the most effective use of savage peoples in fiction is where the red or brown or black man is shown as the staunchly loyal follower of the white leader, and where there is the opportunity for the striking contrast between characters of different races." Plainly, *The Country Gentlemen* wanted nothing to do with realism; the reference to Cooper's sentimental romances about the noble savage made that clear; the desired Indian was a well-tamed, well-behaved "white" Indian. And equally clear was the fact that the magazine would not print a story containing the truth (which Paxton had already conceded) that the Apache was a victim of white aggression, cruelty, and greed.

In his many hours of research, and in the great care he had taken to develop an authentic Apache background, which of course, when combined with Shoz-Dijiji's own viewpoint was bound to create a sympathetic picture of the Apaches, Ed, for Paxton's purposes, had wasted his time. He might just as well have devised a flimsy, trite romance about the Indians, with no concern for realism or for an actual depiction of their customs and habits.

It is true that to a certain extent Ed was writing as a reformer; his indignation about the white man's behavior is forcefully presented. "The War Chief of the Apaches" contains numerous examples of antiwhite propaganda and typical Burroughs comments about the destructive effects of our supposed "civilization":

...fewer men died at the hands of the six tribes of the Apaches than fell in a single day of many an offensive movement during a recent war between cultured nations.

Had he (Shoz-Dijiji) had the cultural advantages of the gorgeous generals of civilization he might have found the means to unloose a poison gas that would have destroyed half the population of Sonora.

Certainly, this condemnation of the white man, and Ed's attempt to interpret the Apache's bloodthirsty deeds as a justifiable retaliation for worse acts committed by the whites, would hardly be viewed by Paxton as acceptable material for his readers.

"The War Chief of the Apaches" is especially remarkable for its details of tribal customs, of religious rites, and of Indian costumes and equipment. All of these become the background to the raising of the white infant, Andy MacDuff, whose father, a Scotch pioneer, and mother, the granddaughter of a Cherokee Indian, had been murdered by the Apaches. The infant, renamed Shoz-Dijiji, grows to manhood unaware of his white blood, and lives under the protection of such great Apache chiefs as Cochise and Geronimo. Burroughs' determination to develop the Apache life faithfully and accurately caused him to copy the most reliable versions of Indian terms he could find. These, undoubtedly formidable for the reader, included such terms as *pindah-lickoyee,* white-eyes; *izze-kloth,* sacred medicine cord; *chidin-bi-kungua,* house of spirits (heaven); and *hodden-tin,* a sacred powder. The story is also complicated by the use of such Apache tribal names as the *Be-don-ko-he,* the *Cho-ko-ken,* the *Chi-hen-ne,* and the *Chi-e-a-hen,* and by a large number of individual names and special words: the hero, *Shoz-Dijiji,* (meaning "black bear"); *Go-yat-thlay,* the Indian name for Geronimo; *Nakay-do-klunni,* the medicine man; *Ish-kay-nay,* the Indian girl; *tzi-daltai,* an amulet; *es-a-da-ded,* a primitive drum. In his adoption of these numerous Indian words and a great many others, taken from supposedly authentic sources, Burroughs has far exceeded the number of words he invented for his Mars and *Tarzan* languages.

Burroughs' understanding of the type of story he did not want, one repeating the cliché of the romanticized and tamed "noble savage," and his extreme care in developing a realistic picture of Apache life, make "The War Chief of the Apaches" an outstanding novel. Unfortunately, in the later sections as he departs from realism and contrives incidents to round out his plot, the story is not as strong. The introduction of a white heroine, Wichita Billings, with whom Shoz-Dijiji falls in love; the convenient death of his Indian sweetheart; the inconsistency Shoz-Dijiji displays in his bloodthirsty mission of revenge against the whites, while at the same time killing members of his own tribe in order to rescue Wichita and her friends; and the unfinished ending with the sequel to

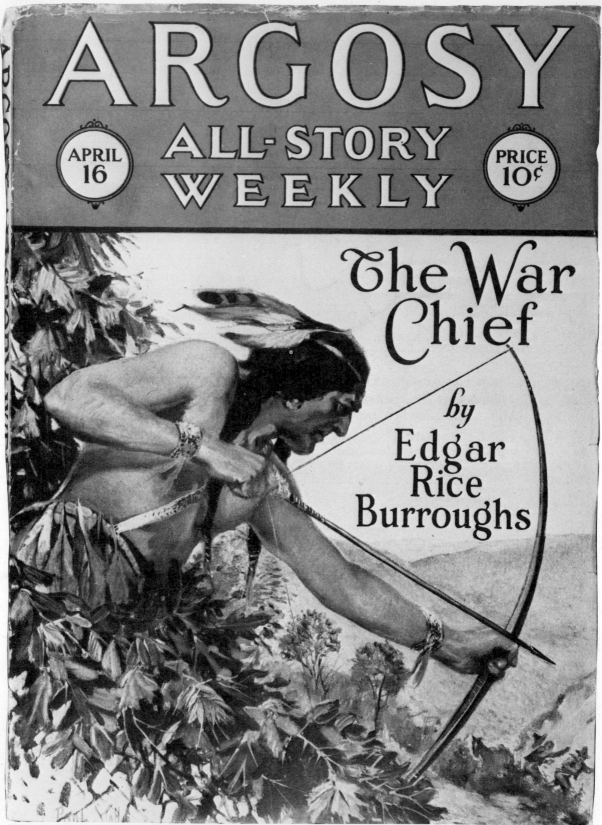

ARGOSY

ALL-STORY WEEKLY

APRIL 16

PRICE 10¢

The War Chief

by Edgar Rice Burroughs

"The War Chief" cover of Argosy All-Story Weekly, *April 16, 1927.*

come—all of these contribute to weakening the powerful effect achieved in the first half of the novel.

Its title shortened to "The War Chief," the novel appeared in *Argosy-All Story* in 1927 and was published by McClurg in the same year. For the book Burroughs compiled a brief glossary. His main research sources, noted on his worksheet, consisted of ten books.[43] In his use of one of the sources, *Trailing Geronimo,* Burroughs corresponded with the author, Anton Mazzanovich, and sent him a copy of *The War Chief.* On November 7, 1927, Ed explained that he had not received *Trailing Geronimo* until *The War Chief* was almost completed, and remarked, ". . . as soon as I did get it I took advantage of the historical information and the local color which it contained." Ed spoke of his days with the Seventh Cavalry at Fort Grant, the Apache scouts he had known there, and the futile efforts of the troops to capture the Apache Kid. He was frank in admitting that the publications about Apache life was often contradictory, and that an informed reader might readily dispute certain points presented in *The War Chief.*

A year later, after he had completed the sequel, *Apache Devil,* Ed somewhat apologetically commented to Mazzonovich, "As a writer . . . you will appreciate the fact that the hero must have redeeming qualities in order to win the sympathy of the reader, and so you can forgive the improbable character as long as I did not make him a full blood Apache, which would have made him impossible."[44]

Hugh Thomason, a former Michigan Military Academy schoolmate, wrote to thank Ed for the copy of *The War Chief.* Explaining that he had known Geronimo well, Thomason described him as "a devil incarnate," and recalled, "One day he sharpened a little pine stick; opened up a small vein in his forearm, and printed his name on his photograph for me."[45] Thomason, himself an author, sent Ed a magazine with one of his stories, published under the pen name "Jack MacLeod." In his reply Ed

listed all his sources and also referred to a book, *Lives of Famous Indian Chiefs,* by Norman B. Wood which stated that Geronimo had blue eyes.[46]

Once *The War Chief* had been completed, the customary dealings with the Munsey Company and McClurg began. Matthew White, the new *Argosy All-Story* editor, had suggested a shortened title, and Ed, on January 11, 1927, noted that the single word "Apache" might create an impression of a Parisian Apache. Ed confessed he was "not keen" about the titles "The Big Chief" or "A Good Indian." On May 23, with only the first novel finished, Ed revealed that his plans included a series of three. He wrote jokingly, "Shoz-Dijiji will not marry the white girl until the third story of the series. I have found that it pays to prolong the agony." He also explained this to Bray: "In the third and concluding volume of the series he [Shoz-Dijiji] will be a cowpuncher or ranch foreman and everything will end happily by his getting the girl. New and original stuff! "[47] After *Apache Devil* had been written, Ed, his plans apparently changed, made no attempt to produce a third story.

While praising *The War Chief,* Bray commented "there is a little too much history in it." He thought the opening was too slow and appeared dubious about the "unpleasant" incidents, such as the scalping of the three prospectors which "creates in one a feeling of disgust." He conceded, however, that the current trend was toward realism and that the War Chief would have committed these bloodthirsty acts. With both White and Bray, Ed became severe about errors or changes in the proofs. Because of the intensive research he had devoted to his Indian stories, he was especially determined that the original manuscript should be followed.

On July 1, 1927, in returning the manuscript and galley proofs of *The War Chief* to Bray, he expressed a blunt disapproval of unauthorized changes in the story. His hesitancies of the early writing period were largely overcome. Having attained success through his own imagination and driving effort, he now could afford to be independent, to be stern with his editors. His letter to Bray, frosty and firm, was a series of instructions that he expected the editor to follow:

The manuscript should be read carefully for grammatical errors, many of which your readers missed.

They should not attempt to alter my copy or change my style. I spent half a day putting back into the galley proof that which had been deleted from the manuscript.

I write into my stories the things that I wish there. If they happen to offend the sensibilities of a proofreader or an editor, I am sorry. but no one has the right to do more than suggest changes — not make them.

In noting that many changes had been made in his books in the past, he accepted the blame, conceding that he had been "too busy or too lazy" to check the proofs carefully. He intended to do so in the future. Concerning items removed from *The War Chief* and then returned by him, he admitted there was one that might bring up a question, a paragraph ending, "Holy Mary sat on the sidelines and rooted for the Mexicans." Ed assumed that the editor had considered this sacrilegious. "It is, however, neither sacrilegious nor disrespectful," he commented. "It is only familiar."

He had often spoken of his deficiency in grammar, and it seemed to him in the matter of corrections, *this* was the proper and necessary province of the editors, but one that they usually overlooked. "I am both faulty and careless in my English and I am very anxious to have my mistakes corrected. . . . but I most emphatically object to having my stuff cut to pieces and whole paragraphs deleted without being consulted in the matter." Interestingly, he expounded his philosophy about the Indians: he had taken great care to treat the Indians fairly in the story, to tell the truth and yet try to win the reader's sympathy. In doing this, he explained, he was compelled to make comparisons between the Indians and the "civilized" whites, these often proving unfavorable to the white man. Above all, he hoped the reader would understand about the Indians, "that everything connected with their life and activity on the war trail was in the nature of religious rites, which puts a very different aspect upon their characters than if it were assumed that they were merely black hearted murderers." He noted that these paragraphs, supporting the Indians' side, were the ones largely deleted. About the glossary of Apache words that he enclosed, he spoke of the various sources from which they had been drawn; none of these could be considered authoritative. ". . . I think there is no authority on the Apache language."[48]

Ed's struggle with McClurg to maintain the realistic aspects of *The War Chief* were far from over. Upon viewing the sample jacket of the forthcoming book, he irately wired his disappointment to Bray. On July 5, 1927, he wrote in disgust:

The figure of the Indian is not of an Apache, it does not look like an Indian and is homely as Hell. I did not mind so much when I saw it on the magazine cover, but I was nearly sick when I saw that you had adopted it for the book, as I was sure St. John would do something really worth while for it.

There is nothing of the atmosphere or coloring of Arizona in the foliage or background; in fact, the whole thing is atrocious and if the picture can kill sales, I am confident that this one will.[49]

Bray's contention that Ed was expecting "an Adonis" on the cover brought an angry reply. Ed referred to his many months of research and to the one hundred dollars he had spent for books. He described the jacket in strong terms: its effect would be to put the story "in the yellow covered, dime novel category at the first glance. It is cheap and tawdry and untrue." Those who see it will feel "that the text is as worthless and as full of errors as the jacket." He was insultingly frank: "You do not have to tell me why this jacket was selected. It was solely because it was bought cheap from Munsey and a couple of hundred dollars saved. If I wrote my stories for you in that spirit, you would not buy them."[50] He admitted that the decision lay with McClurg — he had no voice in the matter. *The War Chief,* published on September 15, 1927, contained the objectionable jacket.

That month an old friend, General Charles King, wrote to praise the book, and in his letter of October 4 Ed noted, "I endeavored to write the story from the viewpoint of an Apache; in fact, as though I were an Apache, and without permitting racial prejudices to influence me." This same attempt to present an objective appraisal of the Apaches was illustrated also in correspondence with John W. LaRue, Literary Editor of *The Cincinnati Enquirer.* After thanking LaRue for a "very kind review" of *The War Chief,* Ed brought up a question suggested by this review: "Are Indians really as dirty as we are accustomed to think them?"

Ed, on September 29, offered a detailed defense of the Indians:

Unquestionably some tribes are less fastidious than others and it is true that they have not the facilities for cleanliness that modern engineering and plumbing have given us, but my experience has been that, with equal facilities, the Indian is as cleanly as the white man.

To support his views, he returned to incidents of the past, recalling the period when he owned a stationery store in Pocatello, Idaho; the store was located inside an Indian reservation. "... many Indians came into my place and, of course, I came in contact with them to some extent. If these people had been infested with vermin, it seems to me I should have acquired a few myself, but I never did." He also remembered how in New Mexico he had purchased a blanket "off the back of a buck," and although he wore it for a week without having it cleaned, he found no evidence of vermin.

His most interesting recollection was about the Apache scouts who accompanied the troops of the Seventh Cavalry in Arizona. Ed insisted they were much cleaner than the soldiers; he spoke of the "considerable time and labor" they would spend in constructing one of their primitive Turkish baths. They prepared a circular excavation and lined it with boulders, upon which they built a fire.

When the boulders became superheated, the embers were removed and a light wickiup constructed around the pit. They then went in with pails of water which they threw on the stones. After this steam bath they took a plunge in the river.

Concerning the ordinary enlisted man of that period, Ed recalled that a soldier in the field for as long as two months might not take a bath at all: "... from personal experience of the pioneer stock that won the West from the Indians, I think I may state, without fear of refutation, that they were about the dirtiest people in the world." Aware of the accusation that the older Indian women were quite fat, Ed responded, "pound for pound, they have not, I think you will admit, much avoirdupois advantage over the fat dowagers hiding behind their diamonds at the opening of a grand opera season."

The last of the 1926 stories, "The Tarzan Twins," Burroughs' first juvenile, was begun on November 16 but not finished until January 15, 1927. A request for a book designed for boys eight to twelve had come from Dr. J. C. Flowers of the Gerlach-Barklow Company, a firm that had acquired the P. F. Volland Company. On receiving Flowers' inquiry, Ed revealed that he had been planning to come to Chicago and would discuss the matter there. The two men met on June 7, 1926, but in the months that followed, Ed was reluctant to commit himself, mainly because of his health (he had been recovering from the flu), and also because of his strenuous writing schedule. In letters to Theodore R. Gerlach, the Volland president, Ed made clear his interest in writing a juvenile, which, he noted, "would be in the nature of an an experiment...", and surprisingly, after saying he could not guarantee completion by March 1927, indicated he might deliver it by the first of the year.[51]

On November 23 Ed submitted an outline of "The Tarzan Twins" to Gerlach and explained that he was writing the story for children about fourteen years old and that he did not intend to change either his style or his subject matter. "I am simply omitting the love interest and using two boys about fourteen years of age as the principal characters," he wrote. "Otherwise, it will be very much like my Tarzan stories." With the story half finished, a suggestion came from Gerlach's office: could one of the twins be a girl? This idea, Ed replied, had occurred to him but he had abandoned it for several reasons. During the Twins' adventures in the jungle, they revert to primitive living and are "practically stripped of clothing." Illustrations of the boys in their scanty, savage costumes would appeal to the young readers, but, obviously, a juvenile book could not feature drawings of a half-clothed girl. Ed also believed that a girl would slow down the action.

Gerlach's displeasure upon hearing that the "Twins" would actually be cousins, brought a reassurance from Ed: this relationship would not detract in any way from the story. Ed then revealed an inspiration that was hardly unexpected. He would devise a sequel with a girl in it, if Gerlach desired one.[52] After the completion of the 21,000-word "Tarzan Twins" and the receipt of a $500 advance royalty, problems at once arose. Volland, in February 1927, complained that the story was too short and requested that from three to seven thousand words be added. Ed replied irritably, stating that an addition of this length would require as much work as he had devoted to the entire story. Experience had also taught him that changes often weakened the original work.[53]

More important reasons for lengthening "The Tarzan Twins" soon emerged. Both Flowers and Margherita Osborne, the editor, agreed that the characters of the two boys had not been adequately developed, and that contrary to the usual Burroughs stories, "The Tarzan Twins" contained little of the vital, colorful African background. Miss Osborne suggested, ". . . you could show some of the wonder and beauty of the native tribes, as well as their outlandishness. . . ." Flowers wanted "the development of manhood in which physical and mental courage were combined." Unfortunately, since the Volland staff had accurately pinpointed the weakness of the story, Ed brusquely rejected the suggestions, making it plain that the payment was the main factor: "I contracted to write a story of a given length for a stated royalty which starts at 5c a copy and increases to 7½c a copy, dependent upon sales. . . . If I had been told that a longer manuscript was desired, the royalties that I should have asked would have been greater. . . ." It would have been far easier, he stressed, to revise the story at the time he was writing it, than to attempt the changes now.[54]

Undoubtedly overawed by Ed's curt rejection, his positive attitude and the prestige of the Burroughs name, Flowers acceded, apologizing for the requested changes. He wrote, ". . . your opinion in this matter should be better than ours. . . . I do not want to take the position of being an able critic in any sense. . . an author like yourself, who has had long years of experience, should be in a much better position to judge. . . ." He agreed to publish the story in its original form.

Volland's unenthusiastic view of "The Tarzan Twins" was duplicated by *Youth's Companion* early in 1927, with a prompt rejection. In proceeding with plans for publication, Volland chose Douglas Grant as illustrator; he prepared the full pages by painting them first in oil on canvas. On August 8 Ed forwarded the dedication for the book: "To Joan, Hulbert and Jack, who were brought up on Tarzan stories, this volume is affectionately dedicated by their father." A month later Ed expressed his approval of Grant's illustrations, and on October 10, *The Tarzan Twins* was published. The book at once won an award from the American Society of Graphic Arts as an example of fine bookmaking, but Ed, while noting his pleasure over this recognition, commented irritably about a different matter: "*The Tarzan Twins* is too fine a piece of bookmaking to be marred by errors which might easily have been obviated by another careful proof reading."[55]

The early sales of the book were encouragingly high; on February 29, 1928, Margherita Osborne, the editor, reported that in the preceding four months 6,715 copies had been sold and that the total would have been greater if *The Tarzan Twins* had been issued with a jacket rather than a box. The dealers claimed that the boxed books were necessarily placed on counters with the juveniles for younger children. By the fall it became evident that the sales were poor; the change from a box to an attractive jacket brought little improvement.

Ed had his own theories as to the failure. These, for the first time, included an admission of the weaknesses in his writing: he believed that he had "unconsciously" been guilty of "writing down" for the juvenile market. He was convinced that children of about fifteen years preferred adult literature. He offered a list of other causes:

. . . the cover illustration was a handicap. . . it showed the boys so very small in comparison to Tarzan, suggesting that it was a book about very young children. . . Another handicap may have been the title, which I believe now should have been "Tarzan and the Twins". . . .[56]

At the same time he attempted a comparison between his book and the children's stories written by Kipling:

I recall the effect of Kipling's "Just So" stories. I do not know that they flopped, although they did as far as I was concerned, notwithstanding the fact that I was an ardent Kipling admirer, and in view of my own experience and what I have learned from it, I think that Kipling made the mistake of writing down to a juvenile audience.

To Volland on April 1, 1929, he mentioned the "unquestioned flop" of *The Tarzan Twins,* and suggested the measures that might be taken to rescue the book. These included enlarging the size of the volume to remove it from the juvenile class and giving it a new jacket with the Twins made larger alongside of Tarzan. ". . . Everything about the character of Tarzan should carry the suggestion of the grim and mysterious dangers of the jungle; neither he nor the boys should be shown smiling." These measures were not carried out, and in the passing years the sales of *The Tarzan Twins* practically vanished. On July 20, 1932, Francis H. Evans, Volland vice-president, noted that the accrued sales since 1927 had totaled only $449, not even equalling the $500 advance Ed had received.

The Tarzan Twins features the escapades of the fourteen-year-old boys Dick and Doc, really cousins, who look alike and are distantly related to Lord Greystoke. The boys, one British and one American, while attending school in England are invited to spend two months on Tarzan's African estate. In the adventures that follow they leave the train to investigate the jungle, become lost, and are captured by cannibals. They make friends of two native prisoners, Bulala, a Negro, and Ukundo, a pygmy. Doc's skill in sleight-of-hand impresses the cannibals and causes them to believe he has magical powers; as a result, the boys' lives are spared. With Ukundo's aid they escape and are later rescued in the jungle by Tarzan and his group of Waziri.

The flimsy story is almost plotless, and as Volland correctly maintained, Burroughs, possibly in his effort to "write down," omitted all of his customary rich detail of the jungle and the animals. Burroughs had commented that boys of about fifteen were reading his adult novels, and he must have been aware that the jungle setting and the personified animals, such as Numa and Tantor, were providing part of the fascination. Yet he devoted no space to this. An even more serious shortcoming occurs because of the light, joking tone of the story. This is produced mainly through the dialogue of Dick and Doc which remains bantering even as they encounter fearful dangers. Because of this, the "perils" create neither interest nor excitement for the reader. *The Tarzan Twins* fails to develop the tension and conflict vital to an adventure story.

18
SOCIAL COMMENTATOR, COLUMNIST

Family responsibilities, mainly the problems encountered in raising three children and planning their education, occupied much of Ed's time. But in these years, as Hulbert, Jack, and Joan moved toward adulthood, Ed was still applying his energies to a multitude of affairs in business, the Tarzana Ranch, and writing. After the large home "on The Hill" had been turned over to El Caballero Country Club, the Burroughs family, from the summer of 1924, lived in Los Angeles. In 1925-26 Ed rented two offices, first at the Commercial Exchange Building in downtown Los Angeles and then at the Hohm Building at Sixth and Western.

Longing to return to Tarzana with its seclusion and outdoor environment, Ed, in 1926, made plans for the construction of a small, low-priced home to be located below the country club. Amusingly, his four-page detailed list — "Rough General Specifications for Inexpensive Home to be Built at Tarzana" — contained a

page of instructions written in Burroughs' familiar blunt and impatient manner. The secretary, William Waterhouse, was told exactly what to do:

The first thing to ascertain is how much we can borrow to build on the lot without any cash payment.

If this house can be built by ERB Inc., start it immediately; and please don't argue.

I want the cheapest thing that can be built that won't fall down under ten years. By that time, I shall doubtless have fallen down. . . .

Streit & Co would be, I am sure, too high priced.

And don't make any remarks about the appearance of the . . . damned thing.

It may be necessary to cut away that part of the large walnut tree which leans at a considerable angle toward the east. If so, save the wood for me.

In his list Burroughs provided details for the

Emma at service porch entrance to home ERB built at 5046 Mecca Avenue, Tarzana; stables at right rear, July 1926.

construction of every part of the house, including installation of screens, an aerial, gas wall heaters, electric switches, an incinerator, a cesspool, venetian blinds, locks, and even bathroom towel racks, and toothbrush holder.

On July 12, 1926, the family moved to the new Tarzana home, its address 5245 (later changed to 5046) North Mecca Avenue on Lot 76 of his tract 5475. In the passing months Ed regretted the economy state of mind that had caused him to build a small home. To his brother Harry, in 1929, he mentioned the "cramped quarters" and wrote, "I made up my mind that life was too short to go on living under the conditions we have put up with for the past three years." He was starting immediately to build additional bedrooms and an extra bath.[1]

During the same period he had moved his office to 5255 (later changed to 5135) Avenida Oriente in Tarzana, but early in 1927 he decided to undertake another building project, this time a combination of three offices and a store. His plans, as indicated to architect Richard M. Bates of Los Angeles, were to utilize the largest office for his study, an adjoining one for a secretary, and one to be rented out to a physician.[2] The project, as visualized by Burroughs, included erecting the store at the front of the lot on Ventura Boulevard, while the offices, set back fifty or sixty feet, would form an ell and allow for an open area with shrubbery or trees. This is the form of the present offices in Tarzana. Burroughs required a Spanish style building with the cost limited to $6,000.[3] His meticulous care in recording dates

Yard and fish ponds at Mecca Avenue house; original Tarzana Ranch home at extreme upper right, September 1927.

and details is revealed in his moving-day note: "Commenced moving from 5255 Avenida Oriente to 18354 Ventura Blvd on Thursday July 14, 1927 — New Office occupied 7/15/27."

Conceived as "an aid to the development of Tarzana," the *Tarzana Bulletin,* issue number one, appeared in August 1927; the editor, Ralph Rothmund, was Burroughs' new secretary. The first issue contained advertisements concerning two Burroughs properties, one seeking a renter for his new store and the other offering a home site in Beverly Hills for sale.[4] The second issue, September 1927, featured a unique article. Titled "Who Cares?" it signalled Ed's return to his old nom de plume —

Normal Bean. Most of the article is devoted to an angry attack upon hunters, the first reference being to those in the state of Utah who have been invited to "slaughter the game" by David H. Madsen, the Fish and Game Commissioner.

The article, in which Normal Bean adopts a chatty style to comment about various items in the news, contains a section about "sportsmen"; Ed describes their actions with sarcasm and disgust:

It is the open season for doves and the early morning landscape is dotted with heroic sportsmen *stalking these fierce denizens of the stubble fields. Compared with English* sportsmen *they are pikers who bring the blush of shame to every right-minded, red-blooded American of the he-man, wide open spaces, for while the*

433

American is trudging around in the dust all morning bagging a dozen handfuls of blood-soaked, bedraggled feathers, the toff with the monocle, up from London for the Scottish grouse season, reclines at ease in a comfortable shelter while beaters herd the birds along until they can be flushed to fly directly above his gun. Some forty years ago John Augustus de Grey, seventh Baron Walsingham, at the age of 78, made a record which, thank God, still stands unbroken: 1070 birds killed in one day with one gun! Had I chanced to be born with the name de Grey I should petition the Legislature to relieve me of the odium.

Burroughs concludes his article by shifting to a lighter topic: "The Los Angeles Times recently ran a front page story of what Lita Grey Chaplin is going to buy in New York. *Who Cares?*"

The two-column *Tarzana Bulletin* (Sep-tember 1927) offers other brief articles on varied subjects. Burroughs' vigorous and some-times explosive style is evident in a number of these, and one must suspect that he wrote most of the Bulletin. The few paragraphs written about wildlife and snakes are obviously from his pen; he again excoriates those who dare to kill animals. His concern now is with protect-ing the wildlife in Tarzana, the deer, quail, doves, roadrunners, and rabbits. "This life is a distinct asset to the value of your property in Tarzana. . . . Help protect it. The pleasure of destroying it (if there can be any pleasure in destroying a beautiful and harmless creature) is ephemeral at best and if it is destroyed it can never be replaced. . . ." He speaks of protecting the wildlife so that "our children" may enjoy it long after we are gone and explains that animals quickly "sense" protection and come to these safe areas to breed. ". . . they become less shy and may be seen and enjoyed by all those who

Front view of office building ERB built for his corporation headquarters in 1927; his ashes are buried at base of tree.

have progressed beyond the stage of the Piltdown man." As in the past, Burroughs spares no insults in his references to these destroyers of wildlife; he views them as some type of low-browed throwbacks to a prehistoric cave age and relishes calling them "Piltdowners." The thought of them turns him violent:

If we are going to rid Tarzana of any wild life let us start in on the Piltdowners. The writer of this has been shagging them off of Tarzana for many years. This morning he ran six off. There should be an open season for Piltdowners extended from January 1 to December 31.

He also pleads for the protection of snakes, "among the most useful creatures that we have," since they destroy certain harmful animals. "Anyone who kills a bull snake, a gopher snake or a king snake should be brained — if he has any brains." Burroughs notes, "Even the much maligned rattler is not such a bad fellow. . . ," but concedes that his poison fangs "put him beyond the pale of protection."[5]

In November 1930 with the return of the spacious Tarzana home to Burroughs — it had been adapted as a clubhouse by El Caballero Country Club — he at first contemplated rehabilitating the home, but finding the repairs too costly, considered building a new one. This plan was also discarded, and in August 1932 he purchased a home in Malibu at 90 Malibu La Costa Beach. There, with an addition completed, he noted, "We are far more comfortable than we were before. . . ." In 1933 he was elected mayor of Malibu Beach. Despite a presumably idyllic location near the ocean, he was not especially fond of his beach home. Several years later, circumstances would lead to its being sold.

The difficulties encountered by Ed's two sons, Hulbert and Jack, in their early schooling, remained unchanged. Despite Jack's unhappy experience at his first military school, Ed, in 1923, enrolled both boys at the Urban Military Academy in Los Angeles. For a while they appeared to be making progress. In a letter of approval Ed noted that his sons were "very much delighted" with the school; his only complaint was about the failure to include French in Hulbert's program. At the time the boys had been entered, Ed had requested the instruction in French, but to his disappointment, he discovered that Hulbert was studying Latin. The overemphasis upon Latin and Greek during Ed's school years had prejudiced him against these subjects. In the fall of 1924 both boys returned to the public schools, with Hulbert attending Los Angeles High School and Jack at John Burroughs Junior High. Embarrassed by this coincidence of the school's name being the same as his, Ed's youngest son avoided enrolling as "John" and listed himself under the informal "Jack."

The boys failed to improve sufficiently in their studies, and in 1926 they entered the Los Angeles Coaching School. The school featured small classes and instruction in fundamentals. Both boys did better in this environment, and Ed was pleased with the results. During this period Jack achieved an early success in creative writing. Undoubtedly influenced by his father's stories, he composed fantastic science-fiction serials, devising plots about monsters coming out of the ocean or about a collision between planets. He provided his own illustrations for these stories. His interest in drawing had been noticeable several years before, when he began copying or tracing the colorful illustrations made by J. Allen St. John. Friday was the storytelling day at the school, and the other students waited eagerly to hear each installment of Jack's serial. Jack was emulating his father's device of the to-be-continued cliff-hanger ending. At this time Jack was also writing poetry and receiving assistance from his father in developing the meter.[6]

Although the boys had improved, Ed was still dissatisfied with his sons' progress. The chief problem was a lack of continuity in schooling due to frequent changes in residences and a consequent change of schools.

Ed's belief that military schools could provide the type of discipline and orderly study that his son Hulbert needed, led him, on April 1, 1927, to send an application to the New Mexico Military Institute. Hulbert was then attending the Los Angeles Coaching School, where he was taking the high school course. In a response a month later, the institute noted that Hulbert was not prepared for entrance to their junior college and suggested that he enroll in their high school. This idea at first seemed acceptable to Ed; he explained that his son had been "handicapped by improper instruction at some of the private schools he has attended, and by changing schools too often."[7] Ironically, the confusion in Hulbert's education, caused partly by Ed's own indecisiveness, continued. By June 8 Ed had changed his mind — the New Mexico Military Institute enrollment was abandoned; now Hulbert would finish his high school work at the coaching school. Assuming that this goal would be accomplished, Ed, on January 17, 1928, sent an inquiry to Yale University concerning his son's possible entrance in the fall. Soon afterward the blow fell. Hulbert's high school work was below par; he was not ready for Yale.

The boys had enrolled at the Los Angeles Coaching School when the family was living at the New Hampshire Street address in Los Angeles. Although they moved back to Tarzana in July 1926, the boys continued at the coaching school in the fall. They had made good progress and Ed did not wish to make another change in schools. However, the daily forty-mile round trip drive to Los Angeles and back was impractical, even though the boys enjoyed driving the Ford Model T touring car. Therefore, in the fall of 1928 Hulbert enrolled as a senior at Van Nuys High School, with Jack following the next year.

Ed's belief in the benefits of an army career led to the next step in the educational process. On April 15, 1929, he wrote to Congressman W. E. Evans in Washington, D. C.: "My two sons would like to take the competitive examination for appointment to West Point. . . ." Nothing came of this plan, and the fall of 1929 found Hulbert attending Pomona College in Claremont, California, while Jack continued his

studies at Van Nuys High School and joined his brother at Pomona a year later.

Unlike Jack, who displayed a fascination with art at an early age, Hulbert, despite some ability in English and creative writing, could find no major goal. In a letter of October 13, 1930, to his nephew Studley, Ed commented about Hulbert's interest in paleontology, but conceded that his son had "no idea what he wants to do after he gets out of college." Ed noted the possibility of Hulbert becoming an archaelogist, while Jack appeared headed for a career in art. "They may never make any money out of either profession," Ed wrote, "but if they enjoy it they will be much happier than they would in business, which to my mind is the most disillusioning and disappointing form of human endeavor."

After graduation from Pomona College, Hulbert, in August 1933, attended the University of New Mexico summer school of archaeology at Jemez Springs. For a while it appeared that his career might lie in this field. However, his indecision and his father's gloomy attitude about it were revealed in Ed's letter of November 6 to Weston:

Hulbert is home fussing around with photography, which this week, he thinks, will be his life's work. I certainly feel sorry for him because he doesn't know what he wants to do, though he feels that he ought to be doing something. I am encouraging him to take up seriously still and motion picture photography, as this will work in well with archaeology in which he is interested. . . .

A position with his father, in which Hulbert managed the radio branch of Edgar Rice Burroughs, Inc., lasted for a brief period in 1934, and following this he turned again to photography and for a time was successful in selling articles and photos to *Desert Magazine* and various other publications.

As a result of their father's interest in autos and his regular acquisition of new ones, the two boys had learned to drive at early ages. A typical scene, remembered by both, is of Hulbert and Jack bouncing along in a Model-T

Ford, en route to either the Coaching School or Van Nuys High School, with Jack, a poetry lover, reciting verses of "Horatius at the Bridge."

At the high school Jack became the most paradoxical of sports editors — one who did not like sports. He dreaded writing up the football or basketball games and usually turned in his assignments at the last possible moment. Hulbert also did some sports writing.

During this period the boys acquired a most glamorous friend, an attractive girl they had observed waiting for the school bus each morning as they drove by. Rochelle Hudson, a movie starlet at thirteen, lived near Ventura Boulevard in the San Fernando Valley at the time and attended Van Nuys Junior High School. In recollection of her meeting with the two handsome boys and her acceptance of a ride to school in their car, she jokingly referred to herself as "a pickup." She became a good friend of the Burroughs family, visited often at Tarzana, and took vacation trips with them. Her unusual situation, a movie star at so early an age and yet a student at a public junior high school, led to problems and unhappiness: the other girls reacted with jealousy or resentment, viewed her as some kind of oddity, and snubbed or ostracized her. The class voted not to let her graduate with them, and she received her diploma without attending the ceremony. Jack Burroughs, at sixteen, drove Rochelle and her mother on a trip to Oklahoma City. In remarking about Rochelle's acting ability, Jack noted, "As we approached Oklahoma City, her southern accent got more and more distinct."

In his four years at Pomona College Jack's achievement was high; he was graduated in 1934 magna cum laude with distinction in art and with acceptance in Phi Beta Kappa. His graduate project, a miniature of a saber-toothed tiger, considered an outstanding piece of work, was placed on exhibition at the Los Angeles Art Museum.[8]

On the subject of college educations in general, Ed had expressed doubts. Years earlier he had noted he was not "awfully hectic" about his children attending college. In his view the purpose of college was to provide an opportunity for the individual to specialize, to work toward a profession. He rejected the concept of the college as a center for general education or for the gaining of prestige.

The performance of his sons had convinced him that too much emphasis was being placed upon examinations. About the two boys he noted, "They work hard at their studies, which we often discuss, and I find that they seem to have an intelligent grasp of the various subjects and I am often surprised at their knowledge, but in examinations they do not ordinarily make good showings. The conditions surrounding an examination, and especially the time limit imposed, seem to constitute a mental hazard that they have difficulty in overcoming."[9] He observed that some people were "slow thinkers," as he was, but that success in life was not attained through "snap judgements."

His sons' enrollment at college had made Ed aware of his own limitations and revived his sensitivity about the value of his writing. To Jack, before his departure for Pomona College, Ed confided his fears. At school Jack would meet literary people who would deride the Burroughs stories. Ed urged his son not to take these criticisms seriously and repeated statements he often made: he had no pretensions about being a skilled or profound writer; his sole purpose was to create entertainment for the reader.

From the 1920s into the '30s both Ed and Emma had various illnesses, some requiring hospitalization or surgery. In August 1923 Emma had an appendectomy, and a year later a series of gallbladder attacks led to surgery on November 24, 1925. Emma later suffered from arthritis. The anxieties resulting from his business entanglements brought Ed close to collapse in 1924. On December 16, his doctor, Egerton Crispin, sent a request to the federal court that Ed be excused from jury duty, explaining that he been under treatment "for pain in his heart following a severe strain of overexertion last summer, and many anxieties

Emma, ERB, Jack, Hulbert, and Joan in Mariposa Grove of Big Trees, California, August 30, 1919.

since." The request was granted. Ed's most serious illness, however, began in March 1930 with intense abdominal pains; after he suffered through a number of months with recurring pain and weakness, the condition was diagnosed as a bladder obstruction. In November Dr. Elmer Belt prescribed surgery. The unexpected complications which appeared later were described by Ed, on February 3, 1931, in a letter to his brother Harry:

. . . Since before Thanksgiving I have made four trips to the hospital, had two minor operations, five doctors and nine nurses — pardon me, six doctors since I just took on an osteopath last week. I still have one of the nine nurses as a hangover, though she hasn't much to do now except to play three handed bridge with Emma

and me. . . . I lay in bed so long that I couldn't walk, and for weeks I could get no relief from pain or rest without taking dope, though I am long past that now, thank the Lord. . . .[10]

The Burroughs' penchant for auto and camping trips, usually hectic events, continued through the 1920s. In August 1925 the family vacation was spent driving to and from the Grand Canyon, a distance of 1,400 miles. They encountered the familiar hazards and heavy rainstorms, and wound up stalled in a muddy ditch. In pushing the car back onto the road, Ed and Hulbert, both clad in their "ice cream" white Palm Beach suits had one of their customary misfortunes. Ed wrote, ". . . his (Hulbert's) feet suddenly slipped from under him and, hitting mine, knocked me flat so that we both sprawled in the red, sticky clay, adding greatly to the gaiety of nations."[11]

In September 1929 the auto-camping trip was to the Ensenada area in Lower California and included only Ed and the two boys. The setting may have been new but the typical mishaps were bound to occur. He and the boys had spent an entire day swimming and beachcombing in the nude on the uninhabited beach, and Ed failed to wear a hat to protect his bald head. On returning, Ed reported suffering from the "grandest case" of sunburn he had acquired in "something like forty years" and added that he was "swelled up like a poison pup." A trip the following September up the Redwood Highway to Grant's pass in Oregon was made in two "Aerocars." Their appearance, he remarked to Bert Weston, "will give you a great laugh when you see them. . . .":

They are trailers that hook on behind a car with a special hitch. The big one, which is called a Pullman and is twenty feet long, was hauled by my old 1921 Packard Roadster. This car contains two lower berths, two upper berths, long divan, lavatory, toilet, refrigerator, clothes press and various drawers and compartments for clothing or what have you. The other trailer, which we used as a commissary car, was hauled by a Ford Pick-up car that I bought for the purpose. It was our dining room and kitchen. We took the cook and his wife, who slept in the commissary car.[12]

The education of Joan Burroughs followed a different direction from that of her brothers; the emphasis from her early years had been upon a preparation for a career in the theater. Her sequence of training for the stage included the Cumnock School of Expression, in 1923, and the Marta Oatman School of the Theatre, 1924-26, both in Los Angeles. Joan played the lead in "Enter Madame," her graduating play at the Oatman School. Because of her voice studies under Yeatman Griffith and her training in dance, Ed commented, ". . . if Joan is fitted for success in any sort of stage work it is along the musical comedy line."[13] On December 13, 1926, in a letter to Louis B. Mayer, with whom he confessed only a "slight acquaintance," Ed requested that she be given a tryout for the part of Kathie in "Old Heidelberg."

Joan's professional stage career was launched with a stock company at the Weber Little Theatre in Ogden, Utah, where, on February 20, 1927, the play "The Whole Town's Talking" opened. Ed and Emma's concern

A Burroughs camp on bluffs above ocean south of Rosarito Beach in Baja California, Mexico, September 3, 1929.

Joan Burroughs as "Kathie" in drama school play The Student Prince, *May 12, 1926.*

over their nineteen-year-old daughter's being far away from home and in the fast and possibly dissolute company of actors caused them to take all sorts of precautions. Emma accompanied her, and Ed hastened to contact M. J. C. Lynch, owner of the New Healy Hotel where Joan was staying, to urge him to keep a special eye on her.

To be present at Joan's opening night, Ed traveled via airplane from Los Angeles, a six-hour flight; he informed a reporter from the *Ogden Standard-Examiner* that he had taken the plane because it was "safer than the Pullman during the present storm."

A week later it became evident that because of internal conflicts and financial problems in the stock company, Joan would not remain with it. Ed even considered driving to Ogden to bring her back, but finally settled for the Union Pacific. Again, his concern drove him to write to the hotel owner, requesting that he reserve a compartment for her on the train. After her return home, in the fall of 1927, she continued her career with the Menard Players at the Glen-

dale Playhouse, performing in both ingenue and lead parts. She demonstrated a newly independent attitude by taking her own apartment in Glendale and coming home only for brief visits. To Bert Weston, on January 17, 1928, Ed expressed doubt that she would stay with the company, "as she is getting nothing from it except experience and a rather small salary." Her involvement with a different company, a month later, was also unhappy, and in commenting humorously about her refusal to return to the Glendale company and replace another girl, Ed wrote, ". . . in the meantime we are trying to wriggle along without her forty dollars a week. . . ."[14]

In the summer of 1926, the chance meeting between Joan and James H. Pierce, a former All-America football player from the University of Indiana, led to a romance that would culminate in marriage two years later. Pierce, who had been a blind date for Joan at an El Caballero Country Club swimming party, at once aroused Burroughs' interest as a prospective Tarzan. Then coaching at Glendale High School on the outskirts of Los Angeles, Pierce was planning to study for a career in law and had little interest in motion pictures. But Burroughs, upon viewing the six-feet four-inch, 190-pound Pierce, was convinced that he had found his ideal Tarzan. Burroughs had never been enthusiastic about Elmo Lincoln in the Tarzan role and was undoubtedly recalling Lincoln when he commented, "Tarzan was not muscled like a strong man or a blacksmith, but rather for speed, agility and endurance."[15] Burroughs envisioned Tarzan as possessing the physique of a Greek God — he must not have bulging or knotted muscles, and his great strength must be combined with speed and agility. Pierce, well-proportioned and graceful, fitted this concept of Tarzan.

Burroughs, using all his persuasive powers, arranged for Pierce to make a screen test at the Film Booking Offices in Los Angeles, FBO — later RKO — Studios. In a letter of July 8, 1926, to Frank Ormston of FBO, Ed noted he was following up on a telephone agreement to send Pierce. A week later Edwin C. King, vice-president of FBO, wrote, "We were interested in seeing Mr. James Pierce whom you sent as a suggestion for Tarzan and the Golden Lion. Mr. Pierce certainly has a marvelous physique and a great face. We made a test, which, as yet, I have not had an opportunity to see. . . ." Burroughs' strong interest in Pierce was evidenced by his statement to Ormston on July 24 that "he comes nearer approaching my visualization of Tarzan of the Apes than any man I have ever seen. If he can only act, I believe that he is a distinct find. . . ."

Pierce won the role, and production got under way in the fall of 1926; the film would be the first full-length *Tarzan* feature and the last of the *Tarzan* silent movies.

The history of the transformation of *Tarzan and the Golden Lion* from a novel to a film includes attempts by two producers, as early as 1923, to acquire rights to the story. W. S. Campbell had approached Burroughs in that year, and in January 1924 submitted a synopsis for the novel. Unable to obtain financing, he dropped the matter, but returned a year later, stating that finances were available. Burroughs sent him a contract with a five-day option, requiring a $10,000 bonus payment. Campbell mentioned that FBO was to act as distributor of the film and negotiations collapsed. In January 1927, after FBO had completed *Tarzan and the Golden Lion*, Campbell filed a lawsuit against the corporation.

During the same period George Merrick of Reputable Pictures Corporation, New York, conceived a novel idea: he would produce a motion picture to be titled "The Daughter of Tarzan." It was to be based upon a "new and original theme," to be supplied by either Burroughs or Merrick. On December 28, 1923, he explained his proposal; if Burroughs created the theme, Merrick would require a synopsis "from which to prepare the continuity for the picture," but, on the other hand, Merrick was willing to write the synopsis and the main idea of the story and to start work immediately. Other clauses guaranteed that "The Daughter of Tarzan"

would be credited as an original script by Burroughs, that he was to receive a $5,000 advance, and that the production cost was not to exceed $75,000, with Burroughs' share set at ten percent of the net profits.

Surprisingly, Burroughs agreed to a unique situation, one that he had not considered in all of his years of writing. On January 5, 1924, he wrote to Merrick, "In the matter of the story, I have suggested that we collaborate as doubtless you have already formulated some plot that will work out well in pictures." In a scrawled footnote he added, "What animals are you planning on using? Can formulate plot better with this information." The "Daughter of Tarzan" idea led nowhere, but in March 1924 Merrick indicated a new interest — he inquired about the rights to *Tarzan and the Golden Lion*. Wearily Burroughs explained that while in "The Daughter of Tarzan" he had agreed to accepting an advance, because it was not to be wholly his story and would require only limited time on his part, in the case of *The Golden Lion* he was insisting upon a $10,000 bonus. This signalled the end to Merrick's proposals.[16]

The arrangements made for the actual production of *Tarzan and the Golden Lion* involved complicated dealings with two related corporations, with R-C Pictures producing the film from the Hollywood office and FBO handling the distribution in New York. The contract was signed by Joseph Schnitzer, FBO vice president, on February 15, 1926, and shortly afterward Ed received his bonus of $10,000. The most distinguished officer of the Film Booking Offices was Joseph P. Kennedy, whose sons would later achieve fame. The announcements of the film release read, "Joseph P. Kennedy Presents Edgar Rice Burroughs' Colossal Jungle Story. . . ." Ed at once contacted his friend Charlie Gay, the founder of Gay's Lion Farm at El Monte, advising him to get in touch with Schnitzer. Ed, who had met Gay when he was handling the lions in an earlier Tarzan movie, was impressed by Gay's kindness in dealing with animals.

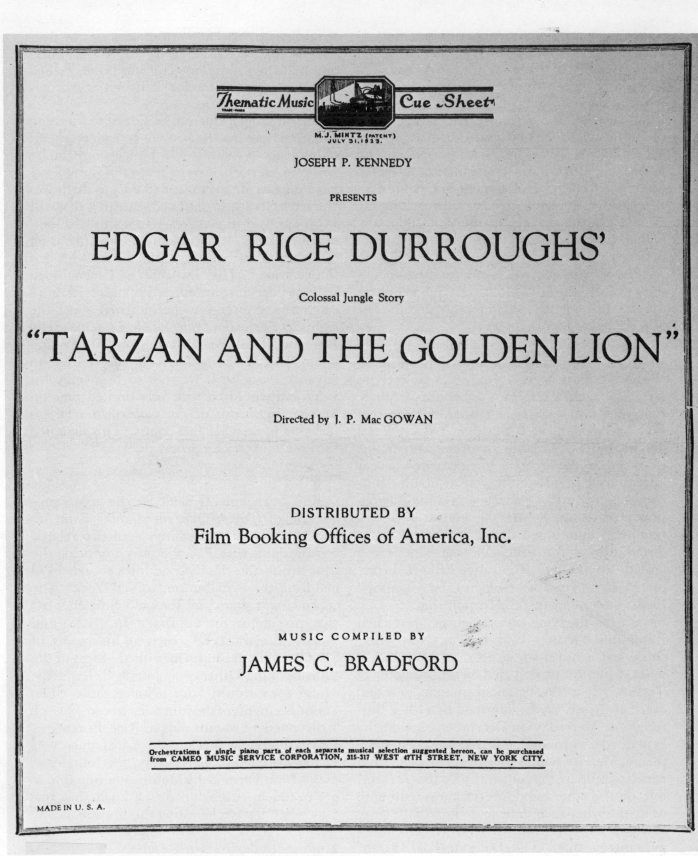

Thematic music cue sheet for FBO film Tarzan and the Golden Lion, *1927.*

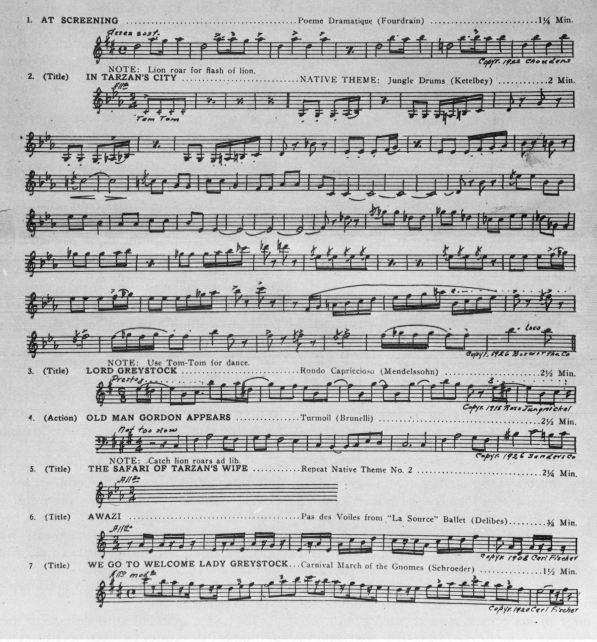

Thematic music cue sheet for FBO film Tarzan and the Golden Lion, *1927.*

In a letter to Charles K. Miller, Ed described the situation at the Lion Farm:

. . . he has about seventy African lions including many young lions and cubs. . . . In the day time his lions are confined in open air arenas, some of which are of considerable size, and he goes into these arenas only with a twig eighteen or twenty inches long and possibly no larger around than a lead pencil. There were a dozen young lions four or five years old in one of the pens and he herded them back and forth with this switch just as one would drive a flock of sheep. While they obeyed him, they seemed to have no fear of him and would come and rub against his legs like big pussy cats. One of his old lions he straddled and rode around the arena. . . .

Ed also wrote to the FBO Studios concerning his friend Louis F. Gottschalk, a former director of the Metropolitan Opera of New York, urging that he be considered when a composer was chosen. Gottschalk had created the scores for a number of successful pictures. However, the music in the completed film was "compiled" by James C. Bradford and consisted mainly of brief excerpts from various published compositions.

Upon returning from a trip to New York where he visited the Film Booking Offices, Ed, in June 1926, was perturbed to read reports that William Wing had been retained to write the scenario for *Tarzan and the Golden Lion*. Past relationships with Wing had been unpleasant, and Ed had even engaged an attorney to collect money owed him by Wing. Ed's letter of the twenty-second, sent to Schnitzer, was one of blunt protest:

. . . the success of this picture means a great deal to me — even more than it does to F.B.O., and I feel that a Wing scenario could add very little to the chances of a successful picture. I know Mr. Wing personally and like him, but I feel that his experience and his work in the past give no indication of any fitness for the proper handling of a scenario for a high grade production, as most of his recent work, I understand, has been along serial lines. If he wrote the scenario

of "Tarzan of the Apes," as stated in the article I read, this fact alone would indicate his unfitness for writing Tarzan scenarios.

The response from Edwin King at the Hollywood studios noted that Wing had been doing considerable work for various producers and that Percy Heath, the FBO script editor, found the first contact with Wing "extremely satisfactory." King, however, was conciliatory and promised to submit the first script to Ed.[17] A week later Ed forwarded twenty original drawings by J. Allen St. John, on loan, to King's office in an effort to help the studio realistically visualize Tarzan and his jungle environment.

During production Ed was present on the set and appeared highly enthusiastic about the film, but after the preview, in February 1927, his doubts began to accumulate. To Schnitzer he conceded that having seen the film several times he "had gone rather cold on it" and was not a good judge, but he had some improvements to suggest, among these "the elimination of practically all of the final fight scene between Pierce and the temple guards." This, he thought, dragged terribly. Ed believed that the picture would be a money-maker and added somewhat unhappily that he wished he knew enough about film techniques — he would like to have directed a *Tarzan* movie.[18]

His objections were to no avail; *Tarzan and the Golden Lion* was produced from William Wing's scenario. The cast included Dorothy Dunbar as Jane, Edna Murphy as Flora Hawks, and Fred Peters as Esteban Miranda. J. P. McGowan directed the film, which, to a reasonable degree, followed the plot of the novel. A man whose later movie roles would mark him as a unique character made his first appearance in this picture: Boris Karloff played a small part as a Waziri chief. Karloff, on May 24, 1927, wrote to thank Ed for sending him a copy of the autographed motion picture edition of the novel.

Ed had responded with delight to the suggestion by Alexander Grosset, of Grosset & Dun-

On set during filming of Tarzan and the Golden Lion, *December 1926; left to right: ERB, Joan Burroughs, J. P. McGowan (director), and Jim Pierce (Tarzan).*

lap, reprint book publishers, that a special motion picture edition be issued. On January 3, 1927, upon receiving the proposal, he wrote to Schnitzer of the R-C Pictures Corporation, ". . . I am anxious to leave no stone unturned to make this edition a success. . . ." He urged Schnitzer to forward a complete set of stills to the publishing firm as soon as possible. However, an inspiration had come to Ed, one that he explained eagerly in the same letter: "In a short time, I am going to ask a favor of you and Mr. Kennedy. I have asked Grosset & Dunlap to prepare twenty-five autographed copies of the picture edition for me, and at their suggestion we are going to have the pages bearing the autographs signed before the books are bound. . . ." The books were to be mailed out to obtain the autographs of Kennedy and Schnitzer, and those of Edwin King, McGowan, and the principal members of the cast; to these were to be added the autographs of both Grosset and Dunlap. "When they are all obtained and the books bound," Ed noted, "I will send a copy to each of those who have been kind enough to autograph them for me." He apologized for the trouble, but remarked, "I believe that the possession of a copy of the book in after years will make the effort worth while." Certainly, the prediction would be borne out. Copies of this autographed edition in existence today are of considerable value. Several copies are in the Burroughs collection. On May 11, 1927, came a letter of acknowledgment from R-C Pictures Corporation for the copies Ed had sent to Kennedy and Derr.

The optimism about the film was brief, and by the summer of 1927 Burroughs exhibited both annoyance and suspicion concerning the incomplete financial reports. He could get no information about the actual returns from each city, and the evidence he could gather convinced him that the film was doing poorly. To Schnitzer he stated, "... I am not surprised. There are reasons for this which you not being on the ground at the time of its production cannot know, but which were very apparent to those of us who were."[19] On August 18 Schnitzer informed Ed that his earnings were only $4,755 as against the $10,000 he had been advanced. The world-wide contracts on the movie, according to Schnitzer, totaled $198,000.

This financial statement appeared incredible to Ed, and he replied with a series of accusations: there was "something wrong" about the returns on the film; FBO was obviously not charging the rentals that it should. Since the movie was being widely distributed, Ed reasoned that the small returns were caused by "block" booking, a method unfair to an author who was receiving royalties. "You will pardon me if I am candid," he wrote, "but I am really very much disappointed in this entire transaction and especially so as I had expected that FBO would take no unfair advantage of me.... Even a poor Tarzan picture should book between three and four hundred thousand dollars at proper rental valuations."[20]

Earlier in 1927 Ed had already concluded that the movie was a poor one. On March 30 he sought his brother Harry's opinion of Pierce's acting and added, "... don't be afraid of hurting my feelings about the picture, which I think is rotten...." To others he made various disparaging comments: the picture was spoiled by poor direction and unnecessary changes; it was far below what it might have been; it could have been a really great wild animal film. At a later period he again spoke of Pierce as the "best" Tarzan, but noted that "poor direction and rather stupid cutting" had seriously weakened his role — "he did not have much of a chance in this picture."[21]

In his recollections of the filming of *Tarzan and the Golden Lion*, Jim Pierce, who performed all of his own stunts, described the various experiences he had had, some amusing and some ticklish or dangerous. His first morning on location he began to run barefoot through the brush — and discovered how painful it was. Pierce said jokingly that the yelp of pain he emitted may have been the origin of the Tarzan yell. At the next filming he wore flesh-colored tennis shoes. Another feat involved crossing a canyon on a rope covered with moss to simulate a moss rope. Pierce naively insisted he could do it and started off, hand over hand, with the yawning canyon a hundred feet below him. He soon discovered he could not maintain a grip on the slippery moss. Luckily, he changed his mind in time to return. The director solved the problem by having baggage hooks attached to his arms, after which Pierce easily crossed the canyon.

In 1934 Burroughs collected information about seven *Tarzans* in writing an article that appeared in the May issue of *Screen Play* and Pierce recalled for Burroughs the day when he

Page from special photoplay edition of Tarzan and the Golden Lion, *Grosset & Dunlap publishers; signatures are of principals involved in film made from novel.*

Jim Pierce as Tarzan in film Tarzan and the Golden Lion, *1926.*

Joan Burroughs and Jim Pierce on set during filming of Tarzan and the Golden Lion, *December 1926.*

unwisely challenged Numa the lion. Pierce, who had been instructed by Charlie Gay, the trainer, never to show fear or attempt to move if anything excited the lions, was taking part in a scene on the veranda of his jungle home. It had been a day of hard work, especially for the lion, who was tired and hungry and not inclined to cooperate any more. The action required Pierce to point into the jungle and command Numa to go in that direction. The trainer, of course, would direct the movements of the lion. Each time the scene began, Numa refused to leave; instead, he turned around and headed for his cage, located behind Pierce. Gay, afraid that the lion might go on a rampage, wanted to stop for the day, but McGowan, the director, angrily insisted upon another take. Pierce noted that all he wanted to do was to get the scene over with as quickly as possible.

On each occasion when Numa had turned toward his cage, Pierce had stepped aside. But after a dozen times Pierce became impatient. He described what followed:

Instead of stepping aside. . . I stood my ground, for some unconscious reason, in front of the door. As the lion came closer to me I saw he was going to go between my legs so I jammed my knees together and he smacked me head on, backed up a few steps and looked at me, mouth open and growling. Of course I had made a foolish, very foolish mistake. The trainer yelled at the lion and rushed madly into the scene cracking his whip and poking at him with his fork, telling me to stand still, for "God's sake stand still."

With his whip and two-pronged fork Gay succeeded in drawing the lion's attention away from Pierce who then moved slowly away until he was outside the wired-in set. He was naturally reluctant to return the next day for more takes, but rest and food had restored the lion's cooperative attitude and the scene was quickly completed.[22]

Pierce recalled that a typical day's work, difficult and dangerous, might require his keeping a few yards ahead of the lion. The blood of chickens was used to set Numa off on the trail,

supposedly in pursuit of Pierce who was to run through the "jungle," scrambling wildly through the brush and leaping over rocks and logs.

The romance between Pierce and Joan Burroughs that had begun in 1926 led to their engagement on July 2, 1928. Pierce recalled humorously how he had been impressed by Joan's driving about in a twin-six Packard and had viewed with disbelief her unusual activity on one occasion. Joan had stocked the car with peaches from the Burroughses' orchards, parked it along Ventura Boulevard in Tarzana, and then attempted to sell the peaches. She made no sales, however; the prospective customers, gaping at the girl who sat in an expensive-looking yellow Packard, could hardly believe that she needed to sell any peaches.[23]

Joan's and Pierce's wedding took place on August 8, 1928, (Pierce's birthday) at the Burroughs' Mecca Avenue home. It was an outdoor affair with a floral altar; the setting, Ed noted with his customary humor, was "between the chicken yard and the corral." At the time, Pierce was employed as a coach at the University of Arizona. On December 24, 1929, with the birth of Joanne Burroughs Pierce at Hollywood Hospital, Ed became a grandfather. Four years later, on August 13, 1934, a grandson, Michael, was born.

The limited employment opportunities in the movie field forced Pierce to seek other types of work. Burroughs provided assistance and financial support. On October 13, 1930, in a letter to nephew Studley, Ed remarked about a new business venture:

. . . Jim has gone into business with an old friend, who has developed a new chicken feed, made from dehydrated oranges, the principal trouble with which is that nobody will buy it, otherwise it ought to be a good business, as the vitamins the oranges contain seem to encourage the chickens to grow husky and propagate their kind with greater frequency and rapidity. . . .

Ed's generous contribution, to the extent of $10,000, was sent to Thomas P. Scully, the founder of California Vitamine Company, on

September 11; a loan, the money was secured by two thousand shares of stock in the company. One stipulation was that James Pierce would be employed at a salary of two hundred dollars a month. The enterprise, as with others Burroughs had undertaken for members of the family, was ill-fated. On February 13, 1932, the company went into bankruptcy.

A major event of the period was Jack's marriage to Jane Ralston on December 12, 1936. Both twenty-three, they had attended Pomona College together and Jane had graduated that year.

The period also brought sadness, first with the death of Frank Coleman Burroughs, Ed's brother, on March 18, 1930. Coleman, 48, had been in the real estate business in Wilmette, Illinois.

Ed had maintained an irregular contact with his brother Harry who, from 1923 on, had been employed by insurance companies in Chicago. One of Ed's repressed hopes was to have Harry and his wife Ella living close by in California. In 1927 Ed tried to arrange a position for Harry as West Coast representative for the Rothacker Industrial Film Corporation, but the plan did not materialize. He had often urged Harry to try writing in his spare time, believing that his brother's colorful experiences in Idaho could provide a rich source of material. On December 18, 1929, Ed wrote:

You are the one who should have been the writer, not I. You have every qualification, nearly all of which I lack, but for God's sake do not try to write fiction, unless it comes to you very easily. There is today a better market for nonfiction than there ever has been in the history of writing.

Ed suggested that Harry begin by describing informally his early days on the Bar-Y cattle ranch: "Put plenty of Sam Land and Mac Harberson in it, of cattle thieves and reminiscences of old timers, a description of Blanco and all of the interesting characters you knew in Idaho. Get Lew in (Lew Sweetser) with his get-rich-quick schemes. . . . Do not forget Emma the cow, nor the red Irish setter you nearly killed with a neck yoke. . . ."

The letter demonstrated Ed's ability to recall these incidents and the picturesque characters of the period. In urging Harry to recreate these exciting years of the past, Ed was undoubtedly aware of his own failures. He had tried, but somehow had never been able to make this rich Idaho background come alive in his own stories.

The second tragedy of the thirties came with the death of Ella Oldham Burroughs, Harry's wife, who was killed in an automobile accident on March 30, 1933, near Ann Arbor, Michigan. They had shared a strong affection, and some years later Harry became involved in unusual psychic experiments as he sought to contact his wife. From his old friend Lew Sweetser, then living in Hollywood, whose wife had died in 1936, Harry heard reports of written messages from the spirit world. Harry placed little credence in the claims that Sweetser's wife had communicated with her husband; in an account published in the *Yale Class Record, 1939 Supplement*, he noted, ". . . I had for years been convinced that there could be no conscious existence after death." He explained what followed:

However, I asked if he would introduce me to the automatic writer through whom he had obtained these messages. He did so and the results of my first interview with her were truly amazing and revolutionary. My long held belief that "death was the end" was destined to be rudely shattered, when I actually received messages from my wife. . . . About Feb. 15, 1937, I received the first of these messages and have had numerous others since then, each tending to confirm my belief in their genuineness. Gone is my conviction that "death ends all." The motive for the deceit on the part of the automatic writer is discounted by the fact that she persistently refused to accept any remuneration for her services.

Ed had also exchanged letters with his

brother George, whose hardware business in Burley, Idaho, was not doing well; toward George, Ed displayed the same willingness to help and a desire to have his brother move to California. He had been writing to friends to seek a business opportunity for George, and on February 6, 1929, commented encouragingly to his brother about the prospect of starting anew. Concerning George's remark about his advanced age — he was sixty-two — Ed stressed his belief that "a man should be about coming into his prime, mentally, at the time that most people think they are through. . . ." Ed insisted that George could develop a successful business under new conditions much more rapidly than he could have done thirty years earlier. "I know that I am a better man both mentally and physically than I have ever been in the past," Ed wrote, "and when we grow older we have the further advantage of being able to find contentment with much less than is necessary to youth. . . ."

The passage of the eighteenth amendment in 1920 and the establishment of prohibition produced an unalterable opposition from Burroughs. He was one who, after a hard day's writing, found relaxation in a late afternoon drink or an evening cocktail with company. He objected on principle to any restraint of this type on the part of the government. On April 15, 1925, in explaining his attitude about the mayoralty election in Los Angeles, he noted his most important reason for being opposed to Judge Bledsoe, one of the candidates: ". . . he is exceedingly intolerant in the matter of the enforcement of the Volstead Act, which I think is doing more harm and resulting in more crime and causing more disrespect for all law than the saloons did at their worst." Ed added frankly about the Volstead Act, ". . . I am opposed to any spirit of intolerance against those who evade it."

Ed commented jokingly about the drinking situation in his own family, noting that he and Hulbert were extreme opposites: "He is absolutely rabid on the subject of drink. Volstead never had a more enthusiastic supporter. It makes a good combination, for Hulbert can do

the temperance act and I can do the drinking for the family."[24]

In several of his novels Ed had stressed the evils of liquor, especially when the hero had taken to drink and gone steadily downhill. The attitude of Charles B. Smith of the *New York Evening World* concerning *The Bandit of Hell's Bend,* which Ed had submitted for serialization, exhibited reluctance to accept the novel because of an antidrinking section. On March 4, 1927, in expressing puzzlement about the newspaper's views on prohibition, Ed wrote, ". . . I cannot see that *The Bandit of Hell's Bend* contained very much propaganda either for or against, although, as I recall it, the hero got in trouble when he drank, and won the girl when he climbed on the water wagon again, which seems to point an excellent moral, but possibly The World is for booze under all circumstances and objected to my taking a rap at it." He ended snappishly, "I think you ought to use *The Mad King.*"

On May 16, 1927, Ed became a sustaining member of The Association Against the Prohibition Amendment, Inc., Washington, D.C. The membership card announced the goals as "Against Bigotry, Fanaticism, Paternalism, Rule by the Minority, and The Volstead Act," and "For Personal Liberty, States' Rights, and Preservation from Mutilation of the Constitution of the United States." Two years later, in a letter to Eric Schuler, executive secretary of the association, who had formerly been the secretary of the Author's League, Ed offered a firm statement of his convictions: "I am just one of the many who believe that any tendency on the part of the Government to interfere in the purely personal conduct of the life of an individual citizen is more dangerous than the evil it is intended to eradicate." As a strong advocate of temperance, Ed pointed out that in this area, and in its goal of prohibition, the Eighteenth Amendment had failed; ". . . because it deprives us of relatively harmless alcoholic beverages, it is making temperance much less possible."[25]

Ed's attitude toward his own drinking varied

through the years, depending upon his state of health and his reaction to a period of temporary overindulgence. An entry of June 12, 1930, in his diary refers to attending the wedding of Marguerite Corwin, the daughter of an old friend: "It was a lovely party. I had a *drink with* the minister. The 18th Amendment is wonderful. . . ." Yet, a September 10 entry revealed a changed attitude: "Alcohol Quit about *this date. . . .*"

He had preserved copies of what appeared to be his favorite verse about drinking:

If on my theme I rightly think,
There are five reasons why men drink;
Good wine; a friend; because I'm dry;
Or lest I should be by and by;
Or — any other reason why.
(*Modified from Henry Aldrich, 1647-1710*)

While Burroughs had always shown a kindness and concern toward all animals, his special love, dating back to his earliest days, had been for horses. His and the family's delight had been in horseback riding; therefore it was undoubtedly with some sadness when in the summer of 1925 he placed all but a few of his horses at auction. The sale, according to a brochure of announcement, resulted from Burroughs' stated plan to convert his stable from saddle horses to polo ponies. This, however, never occurred, nor was it actually his real intention. The real reason was economy — to reduce the number of horses to five, one for each member of the family. The most famous horse on the list for sale was the pedigreed Brigadier Rex, a five-gaited saddle stallion.

After the public auction, held on August 7 at The Breakfast Club polo field, a news story was headlined "Tarzan Horse Is Bought by Mexican Government." The report was that General Hamas Carrillo of the Mexican Army, then in the United States to purchase breeding stock to replenish the saddle horses of his country, had shipped some twelve hundred mares and a number of stallions to Mexico City. But the stallion for which he had paid the highest price, $1,000, was Brigadier Rex. The six-year-old Rex would be set at liberty on the open range where he would become "a veritable king of wild horses."

Those disposed of in the auction included Tarzette, a pedigreed filly, other mares and fillies, Clydes and Percherons, and saddle ponies, a total of sixteen horses that brought $3,915.

Burroughs' popularity as a creator of stories containing colorful animal characters, and his well-known interest in animals, led to unusual requests from newspaper editors. In January 1929, a campaign was launched to acquire an elephant for the Brooklyn zoo, and A. J. Spiro, city editor of the *New York Evening Journal*, wired to ask Burroughs for a supporting article. Ed, in his prompt reply, dispatched the article which opened, "A zoo without an elephant? It can't be done, anymore than you can have a circus without an elephant. It just wouldn't be a circus. Ask any man who was ever a boy." Ed spoke of "the dignity, poise and patience" of elephants which "arouse in many of us a desire to possess similar characteristics"; this would be especially true of children who always want to emulate what they admire. The greatest benefit, however, that children can receive from visiting a "well-stocked" zoo, lies in the power of wild animals to stimulate "that highest faculty of the mind without which there could be no progress, no culture, no civilization." Ed was of course referring to the imagination: "Show me a man who can stand before a cage of lions or tigers, who can watch an elephant, an ape or an armadillo without at least a stirring of the imaginative faculty and I will show you a man with the intellectual attainments of a sheep." Ed reiterated that the Brooklyn Zoo should have an elephant and closed humorously, ". . . while I am just out of elephants and so am unable to donate one, I can still do something to help you get an elephant and I'll furnish its name. If anyone wants to start a guessing contest he will discover that about half the boys and girls in Brooklyn know the name I would donate." The name, obviously, was Tantor.

On February 27, 1932, Ed received a telegram from the city editor of the *Washington*

Star; this time the concern was about NQXGI, a six-year-old gorilla, critically ill of pneumonia in the Washington Zoo. The editor noted that a half-dozen child specialists and veterinarians were attending NQXGI and explained:

NQXGI has been the special pet of all children of Washington who have visited the zoo since he was sent there at the age of two by the famous Chrysler expedition. Since the children have followed the adventures of Tarzan with the great apes through your strip in the Star, we thought perhaps you might send NQXGI a cheering message via The Star....

Ed responded the same day, addressing his telegram to NQXGI:

Have just heard of your illness and hasten to express my sympathy and sincere wishes for your early recovery. You must take care of yourself on the children's account. They would be heartbroken if anything happened to you. If your large corps of physicians feels that a change of climate would be beneficial, I shall be glad to have you visit me on my ranch at Tarzana. We have a lot of banana trees, but we have no bananas today. However, I can promise you warm, sunny days and all the sunkist oranges you can eat, and if you like to ride horseback I will place a good horse at your disposal. Tarzan of the Apes and Bolgani, the gorilla, join me in wishing you an early recovery.

Some years earlier Burroughs had been contacted on an unusual matter, not related to animals. The newspapers of October 26 to 27, 1926, contained such headlines as "Mars Message Waited," with the information, reported from London on the twenty-sixth, that "Thousands of British radio enthusiasts will listen in tomorrow night for possible messages from Mars, which will be in a more favorable position for radio reception than it has been for 100 years." In the period from October 27 to November 4, Mars would be 42,000,000 miles away from the earth. Two years before, when Mars was last near the earth, radio listeners in the United States claimed that strange, unidentified signals were being received, and, because of this,

the wireless league of Great Britain asked its members to stand by for possible messages from the red planet.

Excitement over the event led the British newspapers to devote much space to opinions by various scientists concerning what might be revealed when the earth and Mars came close together. In response to a request from *The London Daily Express,* Burroughs sent a brief statement:

Winds, snows and marshes that astronomers have discovered on Mars indicate an atmosphere. Vast reclamation projects following the lines of interminable aqueducts presuppose rational inhabitants highly developed in engineering and agriculture, naturally suggesting other culture.

Enormous waste spaces, combined with our knowledge of human nature postulate nomadic, warlike and predatory border tribes.

A constant battle for survival has rendered the Martian merciless almost to cruelty. Ages of military service against the apaches of the desert have made him loyal, just, fearless, and self-reliant.

Physically I visualize the Martian of the dominant race as a distinctly human type with strong features, intelligent expression, large chest and slightly less pronounced muscular development than ours owing to the rarer air which he breathes and to less gravity.

In December 1926 Burroughs received notice of the formation of another fan club for young people. Its founder, fifteen-year-old Isaac Boorstyn of Atlanta, Georgia, had adopted the name Edgar Rice Burroughs Club. Replying to Boorstyn that he felt highly honored, Ed also commented approvingly about the inclusion of girls in the club. He promised to send Boorstyn copies of *The Eternal Lover* and *The Moon Maid.* On the twenty-first Boorstyn wrote to express his excitement over hearing from Burroughs:

If a cartoonist had been present when I received your letter he would have sketched the scene and titled it "The Thrill That Comes Once in a Lifetime." I wanted to pinch myself and see if it was real but I controlled myself. . . . Mr. Burroughs I believe you are not aware of the fact that we feel a great love for you. It is the same with boys all through the country. That is why we organized the club.[26]

Several weeks later a request came from The Edgar Rice Burroughs Club for information and photos. Ed sent a picture of himself mounted on Brigadier Rex; it had been taken two years before by a *Los Angeles Times* photographer. In his letter of January 18, 1927, Ed explained that Rex had been sold to the Mexican government: "I hated to part with him . . . but as I ride a great deal in company with Mrs. Burroughs, our daughter and our two sons, I found it undesirable to ride a stallion."

The letter contained much of Ed's philosophy about animals and his desire to protect them: "The coyotes come down every night close to the house, and on many mornings during the summer I could shoot them from my bedroom window, but I would much rather see them than kill them." He described the situation at Tarzana where the wild life had been protected for many years:

. . . hundreds of quail live the year round on the property and are quite tame. We have counted as many as forty on our lawn just before sundown feeding with cotton-tail rabbits and occasionally a jack-rabbit. By putting in lily ponds on my property, I have been able to attract a great deal of beautiful bird life. The birds seem to quickly learn that they will not be molested.

His most perceptive statement, like a confession, revealed the understanding that comes to many individuals only through maturity: "When I was a boy and young man, I wanted to kill things as I think most boys and young men do, but as we grow older we take more pleasure in life than death."

On January 19 Ed wrote to Boorstyn concerning a boy named Jackie Strong who had been lost for three days in the Mount Hood, Oregon, area: "Jackie had read Tarzan of the Apes and the knowledge of what Tarzan had accomplished by himself in the jungle gave him courage. He didn't cry, but built a wall of sticks and lined it with squaw grass to keep out the animals." Ed suggested that Boorstyn write to Jackie in Gresham, Oregon, and offer him an honorary membership in the Burroughs Club.

At the same time Ed forwarded the club information to Theodore Gerlach of the P. F. Volland Company, publishers of *The Tarzan Twins,* urging him to contact Boorstyn. Cooperation between the company and the Burroughs Club could "greatly stimulate" the sale of *The Tarzan Twins,* Ed believed. Concerning a nationwide fan club, Ed, at a later date, proposed to Gerlach that the club be called The Tribe of Tarzan, a name devised by Herman Newman in 1916, when the organization was founded in Staunton, Virginia.[27]

An item in the *Los Angeles Times* recalled the past to Ed, reminding him of his days at Michigan Military Academy and the commandant he had deeply admired. On October 23, 1928, Ed sent congratulations to General Charles King on the occasion of his eighty-fourth birthday. To King, also an author of army adventure tales, Ed wrote, "How well I recall those novels of yours and how I used to devour them. . . ." In February of the following year, after receiving a letter from King, Ed reminisced over "an extremely harrowing incident" in his "checkered career." He had before him the 1892 telegram sent by King to George Tyler Burroughs, with its announcement that Ed had "deserted."

Burroughs' often-stated fears about weaknesses in his writing, his defects in English and grammar, continued to plague him. Several times in the past he had considered paying individuals, either teachers or writers, to correct his work. On one occasion he had sought the advice of Donald Kennicott, *Red Book* editor, after being contacted by a young man who wished to edit his stories. Ed was convinced that his English was "often faulty," but worried that alterations by an outsider might change his "style" — give it "too great refinement."[28] Kennicott, opposed to any corrections of the stories, noted that beyond the minor changes normally made by editors, no writer should have his works "monkeyed with by a third hand"; he agreed that there was a danger of "interfering with spontaneity." Ed was encouraged but still felt that because the reviewers criticized his "rotten English," he should improve; his concern was over the "hundreds of thousands of children of impressionable ages" who were reading his stories.[29] He also asked author Henry Kitchell Webster to recommend a man to correct his manuscripts. Ed confessed, "I venture to say that I do not know a single rule for the writing of correct English," and again voiced his worries about the children who read his books.[30]

The years brought no change in Ed's insecurity. On December 10, 1924, he wrote to Principal Charles Barclay Moore of Franklin High School in Los Angeles: "I have been looking for an authority in English who could give me some assistance in the matter of one of my manuscripts, which would require the reading of what amounts to practically a full length novel and making certain notations there. . . ." The "full-length novel" referred to may have been *Marcia of the Doorstep,* completed in October 1924, and fated to suffer a long string of rejections. Because of this, Burroughs may have sought assistance; the manuscript shows evidence of numerous revisions. To Moore's query about the type of aid he wanted, Ed replied, ". . . checking up in matters of correct usage, the recasting of sentences for force and clearness, as well as plain, everyday primary school grammar in which I am afraid, I am lamentably weak. . . ."[31] There is no record of whether Moore supplied an individual to correct the manuscript.

On August 28, 1927, Jennie Case, an English teacher in Charleston, Illinois, wrote to Burroughs to tell of her enjoyment in reading his novels: "Nothing in literature appeals to me more strongly than an affinity between man and the beasts. . . ." Miss Case, noting that her "special craft was in English," went on to state, "I am no genius — just an old pedagogue with my ear and my eye trained for every blunder in language. I do not read to criticize — but it's just second nature." After mentioning the Burroughs stories' "freedom from English error," she proceeded to qualify: "I wish they might be entirely free." She was presently reading *Tarzan and the Golden Lion* and admitted unhappily that she wished she might have read it "before it was a book — and made it English-perfect."

Miss Case listed errors on six pages, some involving the use of "who" and "whom" and others dealing with simple grammatical slips. In his response of September 12, Ed expressed appreciation, indicating he felt highly complimented that so few errors were found in his works by an "authority" such as Miss Case. He spoke of having studied English grammar for only one month in his life, referring to his experience at West Point: ". . . I tutored for a month, failing miserably after I reached the Point."

Ed once more conceded that he could not remember rules: "I presume I have studied the rules governing the use of who and whom and shall and will hundreds of times since I started writing, but invariably I forget." His one mistake in the use of "don't" for "doesn't," detected by Miss Case, he confessed to be "gross carelessness and the persistence of a bad habit." He hoped that Miss Case would read his new novel, "Tarzan, Lord of the Jungle," soon to start in *Blue Book,* and added unabashedly, ". . . it may cause you to tear your hair, as a considerable portion of the book requires the use of archaic forms, which greatly taxed my ingenuity and would have been, in some instances, quite beyond me had I not had recourse to the Bible, though not for inspiration."

In 1931, with Burroughs now planning to publish his own books, he again sought someone to prepare them for the printer by eliminating errors. He addressed queries to Ralph Trueblood of the *Los Angeles Times* and to Principal J. P. Inglis of Van Nuys High School. Trueblood suggested Mrs. Ruth Burke Stephens, but because of a difference in the payment rates, Ed decided to use the services of Adele Bischoff, a teacher recommended by Principal Inglis. Ed had explained that the work would include at least two novels a year and told Inglis, "I find that it takes me between eight and twelve hours to correct the galley proofs of novels of this length (about eighty thousand words).... I am particularly anxious to find someone who would undertake the work in a confidential nature; show the manuscripts to no one and talk about them to no one...."[32]

The manuscript referred to, Miss Bischoff's first task, was probably *Tarzan the Invincible*, scheduled to be the first book published by Edgar Rice Burroughs, Inc. Ed was pleased with Miss Bischoff's work, complimented her on the "painstaking and intelligent editing," and on July 28, 1931, sent her "The Dancing Girl of the Leper King" for correction. Following this, in September and October, Ed forwarded to her three installments of "Tarzan and the Leopard Men."[33]

Concerning the general criticisms of the Burroughs novels, the disparaging comments by literary columnists and librarians, Ed had long since learned to accept these with a degree of resignation, although not without sensitivity and resentment. His earliest contact with a private library, however, led to an approval and acceptance of his works. With the establishment of the O. Henry Memorial Library in Asheville, North Carolina, in 1925, Ed was requested by Bob Davis to send copies of all of his books. Hesitant, Ed, on March 11, remarked that the library probably wanted only one title from each author, and added, "... I might make myself ridiculous by sending them more...." Insistent, Davis wrote, "I'd hate to see a feeble one-volume contribution from Tarzan's backer, trainer and breeder...." The following month the Asheville Chamber of Commerce thanked Ed for the "entire set" of his books that was to be placed in the Library of American Fiction, dedicated to the memory of O. Henry.

An experience three years later revealed Ed's annoyance with the literary critics. On January 12, 1928, he sought information from Bray about a list of the ten most popular authors of fiction in America, which had appeared in the *Publishers' Weekly*. To Ed's consternation, his name was not included; he noted, based upon Grosset & Dunlap's reports, that his sales were among the three highest in the country, totaling, according to Bray, about seven million copies in the United States and Great Britain. "It is not a matter of injured pride or anything of the sort," Ed wrote, "but one that is at present really important publicity for me...."

On the seventeenth Bray replied, "For some reason every writer about books seems to consider your name taboo. The modern school would visit upon you all the tortures of the Inquisition were it in their power to do so." Ed's answer displayed sarcasm and anger:

I, too, have noticed how my name is always ignored by literary writers, librarians and other members of the intelligensia.... I wonder why they dislike me so much. Is it because I have no personal friends among literary people and because of that am not discussed by them, or if I am not in a friendly way?

I have met a few literary lights. Most of them are egotistical asses or wise cracking smart alecks. I have never seen one literary celebrity that I should care to go on a hunting trip with or in whose company I would wish to be for more than five consecutive minutes, but of course I have not met them all.[34]

Ed's agitation over librarians' attitudes was sharpened by the receipt of a letter from a fan who said that the Burroughs books were to be removed from the shelves of the Syracuse, New York, public library. Recalling the German furor about *Tarzan the Untamed*, he speculated, "... if we were to investigate this and similar other cases we might find that some member of the board, or even the librarian himself, is of German descent. I can think of no other reason why people might be prejudiced against my stories to such an extent that they would wish to bar them from any public library."[35]

Bray sent an inquiry at once to the library, and in the correspondence that followed, Ralph

M. Paine, the librarian, explained that twenty-one Burroughs books were on file, and stressed that no ban upon these books was being contemplated. In fact, he noted, the problem was "to keep them from being stolen from the shelves." He wrote, "I'll bet that Mr. Burroughs would regard this as a compliment. If a boy finds . . . a book which so fascinates him that he is perfectly willing to commit a misdemeanor in order to make that book his own, we can't deny that the author has done something." Paine joked, "We might put Burroughs and Zane Grey and a few others in a locked case and let no one take them out except by special arrangement with the probation officer. . . ."[36]

The banning of his books from the Los Angeles Public Library had long been a source of irritation to Burroughs. On July 29, 1929, upon receipt of a request from Mrs. A. E. Nicely of the Tarzana branch for a set of books, he replied that since the main library had barred his works, he could not grant a request from one of its branches. His response attained a new level of ironic rebuff:

I also feel that books that the Los Angeles Public Library believe might contaminate the morals or literary tastes of their readers should not be tolerated in Tarzana, and when we consider the fact that some hundred million readers all over the world have already been contaminated, we should exert every effort to keep Los Angeles the one bright spot in the literary firmament.

The Burroughs name and works received a special vindication three years later in a way that must have gladdened Ed's heart. The letter from J. C. Powell, Librarian Emeritus of University of California at Berkeley, referred to the collection of writings by *Californian Authors,* a group not accessible to the general public, but intended for the use "of *only* some historian of California literature 100 or 500, or 1,000 years hence." Powell, while noting that extra copies of the novels are purchased for current use, wrote, "We take great pleasure in welcoming you into the circle of authors of the Golden State, and henceforth will consider your future productions as properly belonging in this most carefully preserved collection."[37] Powell requested a copy of *Jungle Girl,* "enriched on the fly leaf" with Burroughs' autograph, for the unique collection. In sending it, on July 26, 1932, Ed expressed his pleasure, stating, "The Jungle Girl and I are naturally appreciative of our election to the Hall of Fame."

Although he rarely indulged in personal criticism of another author, in reply to his friend Charles K. Miller who had sent him clippings about the iconoclastic statements of Sinclair Lewis, Burroughs, on May 17, 1926, was severely condemnatory of Lewis:

I think Lewis is a damn fool, as is any other writer who goes out of his way to offend a considerable proportion of our reading public. He had no more right to stand up in a pulpit before a lot of church people and defy God to strike him dead than I would have to come into your home as a guest and insult some member of your family, which is an utterly impossible and unthinkable thing for a gentleman to do.

Ed emphasized that he held the "same general ideas on religious matters" that Lewis did and had adhered to these for many years, but commented, "I cannot see what good it would do me or anyone else to use my personal opinions as a basis for offending people, simply because I have been successful in selling many books." Ed advocated humorously that the Author's League should appoint a nurse to accompany each successful writer; the nurse would be armed with a large bludgeon, and every time the author opened his mouth, before he could utter a sound, she would hit him on the head.

As the discussion of Lewis continued, Ed conceded that "To be a very great writer may necessitate also being a very great boor." This may occur, he pointed out, because writers are often very much alone; they do not acquire "the veneer of polish" which comes through social interaction. He suggested that authors should cultivate a few friends and "keep their mouths shut." In letters of March and September 1927,

Ed offered further opinions about Sinclair Lewis. His philosophy, as explained to Miller, was that most fiction writers were not equipped to assume the roles of teachers and leaders of thought; they were usually "not too well informed or too intelligent." He reiterated his familiar belief: "The day is long since passed when it is either necessary or desirable to seek for facts or instruction in fiction. It should serve but one purpose, and that is to entertain."

With the 1927 publication of Lewis' *Elmer Gantry,* Ed noted the reports of $150,000 payment in royalties and compared the novel disparagingly to Charles Lindbergh's book:

... "We" should net Lindbergh a million or one hundred and fifty million if the relative importance of the two books governs their sale which, unfortunately, will not be the case. "We" is a tremendously inspiring work that should be read by every man, woman and child in the United States.

It is indicative of Ed's character and values that he would rate highly the work of a man of action, such as Lindbergh, one who was an achiever and a heroic figure (like General Lee Christmas and, in fiction, similar to John Carter), not just a deviser of plots and dialogue.

For a two-week period in 1928, Burroughs, on temporary assignment as a newspaper columnist covering one of Los Angeles' most sensational trials, bombarded the public with a series of explosive statements and accusations. Certainty that the trial of William Edward Hickman, charged with the kidnap-murder of little Marian Parker and the dismemberment of her body, would arouse nationwide interest led the *Los Angeles Examiner* to hire Burroughs to attend the sessions and write a syndicated column giving his personal reactions. The column, appearing January 26 to February 10, presented Burroughs in his most irascible and opinionated mood.

Controversial areas he selected for particular vituperation included the question of Hickman's insanity and the alienists who proposed this theory, the court procedures and the laws, the trial atmosphere, and the heredity and the breeding of criminals.

Burroughs ridiculed the assertions of defense attorney Walsh and the psychiatrists that Hickman was insane. On January 26, at the trial opening, Burroughs wrote:

... Hickman is not normal. But abnormality does not by any means imply insanity. Hickman is a moral imbecile and moral imbecility is not insanity. The moral imbecile is as well able to differentiate between right and wrong as is any normal man — the difference between the two lies in the fact that the moral imbecile does not care what the results may be to others so long as he may gratify his abnormal egotism or his perverted inclinations.

Ed found the alienists' theories incredible and hilarious; on February 1 he noted, "The idea, as it appeared to me, is to prove that Hickman is not guilty of kidnaping and murder because his mother thought she heard strange noises about the house at night." Hallucinations of this type lead to a diagnosis of insanity. Ed jeered at the entire idea: "When I was a young man I thought, upon a certain occasion, I could thrash a policeman. It was a hallucination. Once I had an hallucination that I could write a play. With these facts well established and a matter of record I may now start upon a career of murder." He comically spoke of "the lives of constant danger that all of us married men lead," and inquired, ". . . how many of us are there who do not sleep nightly in the same room with one who hears things about the house after dark? That is, I mean, of course, if we are sleeping where we should."

He thought the funniest bit of information was furnished by Hickman's high school chum; Ed proceeded to offer his own psychological interpretation of this disclosure about Hickman: "He was a boy orator. That was the first downward step, after that came forgery, robbery, kidnapping, murder. I have known all along that something like this was going to happen if some steps were not taken to stem the tide of boy oratory." He quoted supposed statistics from a newspaper that "the 1928 crop of boy orators will mount to the appalling total of 2,000,000"; the perils of a public confronted by this flood of potentially dangerous orators were beyond the imagination.

Continuing his jibes at the alienists, Ed, on January 27, remarked, "As a criminal physiognomist, I shall have to admit being a total flop. I cannot look at the outside of a man's head and say that he is a murderer, yet, after watching Hickman all day I will venture the assertion that if he is crazy, I am Professor Einstein." He humorously exaggerated the alienists' contradictions of each others' theories and their interpretations of incidents from Hickman's past. Ed conceded that the alienists were sincere, and as a result, could only conclude that what he might otherwise describe as "idiocy or knavery" was due to the fact that "psychiatry is as far from being an exact science as is alchemy or astrology and, as such, it has no place in jurisprudence. . . ." He added, ". . . I believe that it can only tend to befuddle the minds of the jury and becloud the real issue."

While inclined to believe that "whatever insanity" existing in Hickman may have come from his mother's side, Ed maintained that the responsibility for "this monster" rested upon the father: "There are lots worse things in the world than dementia praecox. Moral imbecility is worse, and the father who will not admit the obligations of fatherhood and make sacrifices to the end that his boys and girls be better human beings than he, is a moral imbecile."

Ed's observation of the legal maneuvers of the defense and the tactics of the alienists aroused both his impatience and exasperation. "We are the victims of court procedures and of laws that are wrong," he insisted, "and they should be righted by those to whom we look, usually in vain, for such relief." In his impatience Ed resorted to the obvious comments, often made by laymen, who overlook the constitutional rights of the defendant and the necessity to *prove* his guilt in a court of law.

Ed's opinion, stated at the trial opening, was that the procedures might well be abolished; he spoke of "the ponderous machinery of the law . . . the tremendous economic waste . . . represented by the hundreds employed . . . in this hearing who might be profitably employed elsewhere . . . I am moved to wonder if, after all, it is not we who are crazy, and if Hickman and his kind may not be in some respects the only sane people." His point, a typical one, was that the public *knew* Hickman had committed the crime; why waste time and money in an "unnecessary court procedure?"

At times Ed depicted the trial in a farcical light. He referred to Judge Trabucco as "our new guest conductor," and suggested that a master of ceremonies was needed to introduce the celebrities in the courtroom. Concerning the citizens who were unhappy because they could not "crash the gate," he was sorry to disillusion them: "It is a bum show. The lead is a ham and the comedians are a flop. The heavy is all right. He goes around shouting: 'No talking in this courtroom,' and wakes us up every time we lapse into beatific unconsciousness of expert testimony." He believed the alienists provided most of the entertainment, but there were too many of them "in the cast."

From the start Ed emphasized his belief that heredity determined criminal tendencies. His important point was that the hanging of Hickman would be a protective measure for the safety of future generations: ". . . moral imbeciles breed moral imbeciles, criminals breed criminals, murderers breed murderers just as truly as St. Bernards breed St. Bernards and thoroughbreds breed thoroughbreds." He then demanded a general application for his startling theory: ". . . we should not stop with Hickman; in fact, we need not wait to begin with him. The city has plenty of moral imbeciles that we might well dispense with." In his column of January 28 he termed Hickman an "instinctive criminal" and prescribed what must be done about "this new and terrible species of beast":

Destruction and sterilization are our only defense and we should invoke them while we are yet numerically in the ascendancy — if we are. . . . And so I should wish to see Hickman destroyed — not through hate, not through malice, but, with all pity, in the interest of posterity.

On February 10, in the final column of the Hickman trial Ed insisted that "our battle must go on" and we must "discourage the uncaught Hickmans from plying their chosen profession and destroy those whom we do catch." He could not refrain from a last gibe at the alienists: "I am out of a job now; but I am thinking of applying for the position of publicist with the American Society of Psychiatrists."

Ed's dogmatic assertions brought annoyed responses from various readers, one man demanding, "Why don't the reporters *wait* until the trial is over before they bleat as does Burroughs and Adele Rogers St. Johns?" A severely critical comment came from Arthur C. Hannie, University of Illinois psychologist, concerning Ed's reference to Hickman as "a dangerous moral imbecile":

From the standpoint of anyone who is at all familiar with normal and abnormal psychiatry, a statement such as: "For moral imbeciles breed moral imbeciles, criminals breed criminals. . . ." is preposterous. Your wild imaginings as displayed in your works of fiction have no place in a case dealing with stern actualities.

The psychologist turned insulting: "We are sorry to inform you that your deductions concerning human 'imbecility' show just that in your own personal case." He provided scientific data: "It has been proven that a person of morbific mind can marry and beget offspring of high 'moral' integrity. Remember that Jonathan Edwards' grandmother was driven out of the community for gross immorality. This is merely one case out of many that we might quote. Being 'un homme dans l'oeil publique' you should, as a matter of duty, correct this error."

A reader, on February 1, 1928, irate over the Hickman column, took the occasion to make disparaging remarks about Burroughs:

. . . I have read several of your books and if your imagination at times does not border on a stage of insanity, I'm loco myself. I do not sympathize with Hickman but I think that everyone should have a fair and just trial at least, and your attempt at condemning a plea of insanity looks to me like my mother often said — "the kettle calling the pot black." Question: How could any human commit such a crime as Hickman did and still be sane?

Possibly as a further exposition of ideas he had previously expressed concerning the improvement of the race and of government, Ed composed a six-page article (actual date unknown) titled "I See a New Race." The article is visionary and offers a description of an idealistic civilization of the future, stressing a new approach to government and an acceptance of eugenics. The opening pictures a Utopia already achieved:

Only the hills are the same. Everything else is changed. Even the people are different; they are more beautiful, and they are happy. The change did not come in a day. It took a long time, as man's life is measured, and yet only a moment in the span of mankind's life on earth. And it was all very simple.

Adopting a flashback, Ed tells of the deplorable conditions before man began the rehabilitation process. Man, obviously, had not been improving as the centuries passed. Many people even concluded that the masses were "less intelligent than the Cro-Magnon race of paleolithic times," and, even worse, "as the stupid multiplied without restriction, the whole world was constantly growing stupider." A baffling paradox was presented in the brilliant successes of science as against the failure of our governments and economic systems. The reason for this, according to Ed, was that science utilized the best intellects, "leaving government and economics in the hands of pre-Cro-Magnons. . . ." In his severe criticism of our government, he noted that more care was taken in the selection of mail carriers and policemen than in our choice of law makers; the civil servants were required to take examinations to prove their ability, while no standards of competence were established for politicians. Concerning the Congress, state assemblies, and local councils, he observed, ". . . it was chance only that injected even a modicum of intelligence into these august bodies."

With corruption, crime, and poverty rampant throughout the nation, the movement for reform began in a small city; there, a group of dedicated men, aided by scientists, devised a series of intelligence tests for candidates. Although the tests were voluntary, the voters' attitudes indicated that only those politicians who took the tests would receive votes. The results of the tests were published in newspapers before the election, and "those who stood highest received the greatest number of votes." The idea spread gradually to state and then national elections, and in the passing years the entire country came under "the rule of intelligence." The change to follow, involving the masses, was inevitable; it was archaic that age alone should determine a citizen's qualification to vote. Will one who is stupid at twenty be intelligent at twenty-one? "As a matter of fact," Ed responded, "he will probably still be stupid at eighty."

Consequently, intelligence tests were required of all voters. In the earliest period, Ed explained, because of the danger of "disenfranchising practically the entire electorate," the intelligence tests were made extremely simple.

In his program for the improvement of the race, Ed turned next to a procedure he had supported in the past — eugenics. He described the result of a national adoption of this process:

The sterilization of criminals, defectives and incompetents together with wide dissemination of birth control information and public instruction in eugenics resulted in a rapid rise in the standard of national intelligence after two generations.

Prizes were no longer awarded the parents of the largest families — the prizes, in economic and political success, went to the families that produced the most intelligent children. Stupidity became unfashionable.

With the change, an individual's position was determined by his IQ, and the most intelligent were awarded the highest posts in the governing of the country. All positions were based upon IQ with lesser jobs assigned in order on a descending scale.

The same procedure was adopted for private business, but with some unexpected reasoning, Burroughs proposed differing standards for the creative fields: "Literature, art, music, agriculture offer openings for those not sufficiently intelligent to direct the destinies of nation, state, or city. Here adaptability, talent, and personal preference more often determine the calling that the individual adopts; for, with the exception of agriculture, high intelligence in these vocations is not necessary to the public welfare."

Burroughs' next step for the regeneration of the country concerned the problems of crime and welfare that in the twentieth century had reached emergency levels. The solution was the most startling he had offered: laws and legal procedure were the root causes; therefore, "Laws, law courts, and lawyers were accordingly abolished." A person who exhibited an "antisocial nature" or committed crimes was considered "merely as a problem in eugenics." Punishment was not the objective: "No citizen is ever punished by the state under the enlightened procedure of these times; he is either sterilized or destroyed for the welfare of posterity."

The final step in the Burroughs formula related to the new attitude toward religion. As the national intelligence improved, "the people laid aside the arbitrary dogmas of a dozen different religions and clove to the one religion that we all know today — the religion of service to the race." This endorsement of humanism came because all individuals recognized that the goal of God was "the welfare of mankind. . . . he who works to the same end as God works in the noblest field of religious endeavor."

The result of these idealistic goals in the world of the future ushered in "an age of youth." In the twentieth century the world had been ruled by old men, although everybody understood that "man's powers of fresh thinking and constructive action" start to decline in the middle years. Ed noted that "the thirty-fifth year often marked the beginning of the shrinking of the brain." Burroughs closed, "I see a New Race" with a glowing description of the ideal society that had been established:

Today young men rule, using freely the experience and culture of the older men who act in an advisory capacity — a practical application of the Elder Statesmen idea of another day. And so the life of the nation is the life of youth, filled with gaiety and action and happiness and hope — hope for an even better race, for perfection is a goal that we shall never reach.

Only the hills are the same.

Burroughs' acceptance of eugenics, especially for the elimination of the unfit, involved him in a strange correspondence later in 1928. On October 8, William R. Thurston, the author and publisher of *The Great Secret* and *Thurston's Philosophy of Marriage,* sent these books to Ed with a request that he read them to determine whether they contained "a truthful presentation of the subject" and would merit a "wide distribution." Thurston also noted that upon receiving Ed's comments, he would forward George Bernard Shaw's three-page letter with an evaluation of the same books.

In his philosophy Thurston was concerned with curbing "excessive sexual intercourse," both in and out of marriage. His theories, somewhat duplicating those of Malthus, fixed the blame for all of the world's problems on the surplus population which inevitably led to poverty, unemployment, and wars. This surplus, of course, was the result of uncontrolled "sexual excesses." Ed endorsed Thurston's books enthusiastically. He approved of the wide dissemination of the philosophy, but was pessimistic about any influence the books might have. A small percentage of those who read the volumes might be enlightened; "the great bulk of humanity will go on as they have gone on in the past." In this letter of October 25 Ed resorted to the same language that he had used in the Hickman columns:

The result will be, as it always has been, that an inestimable fraction of the world's population will be fit to survive, and, on the other hand, hordes of the unfit, ruled by ignorance and passion, stand ready upon the slightest provocation to engulf and destroy the minority. It is not a pleasant outlook, but it seems to me to be inevitable just so long as we permit mental, moral and physical defectives to live and propagate.

Thurston's philosophy had so deeply impressed him, he observed, that he was asking his children to read both books.

The correspondence continued with Thurston forwarding Shaw's analysis of the books and his own response to the famous author. In his original letter to Shaw, at the time he sent the two volumes, Thurston had referred to the statement by Shaw to the effect that "no man dare tell the truth about marriage while his wife lives." Convinced of the accuracy of this statement, Thurston had undertaken the task of "reporting and distributing the facts" about marriage. He informed Shaw that the reactions to his books had been divided; individuals who disapproved referred to Thurston as "either a mid-Victorian type of idiot, or a mattoid suffering from repressions, engaged in writing merely as a form of sublimation." Thurston was now placing the future of the books in Shaw's hands: if Shaw thought they had merit, they would be widely distributed; if not, they would be suppressed.

Shaw, in his usual brilliant exposition, approved the circulation of the books, but disputed much of Thurston's philosophy as illogical and inconsistent. The opening paragraph displays Shaw's inimitable style:

Your main point, which is, as I would put it, that the real housing problem before the world is how to provide for everybody *over the age of six a separate bedroom with a bolt on the inside, and thereby change marriage from "the most licentious of human institutions" (as I have called it) to a reasonable and wholesome relation, is so enormously important that your book cannot possibly have too wide a circulation to please me, in spite of certain other points in it, which are, in my opinion, either violently overstated or positively wrong.*

He made plain his support of socialism, and listed the points with which he disagreed. He denied that "the poverty of the world, and the slums of the larger cities are . . . due to excessive sexual intercourse, resulting from the present marriage laws." Shaw quoted Henry George's theory that "progress and poverty" resulted from "the institution of private property in land." He also rejected Thurston's contention that sexual intercourse for pleasure alone is harmful to the individual and to the race.

Thurston's main argument had been that the marriage bed artificially stimulates intercourse, and this Shaw accepted as "a sound case." But he criticized Thurston for overlooking Nature's margin for "abuse and waste":

When you consider the fabulous quantity of ova and spermatozoa that Nature provides to do the work of a half a dozen you cannot reasonably contend that her factor of safety in sexual vigour does not allow of intercourse for pleasure alone, even if you deny the mysterious recreative effect which many people find in it, or ignore the distress and obsession they experience when deprived of it.

Shaw maintained that Thurston's theory "would limit everyone's sexual experience to half a dozen acts in a lifetime," and added, "To call that natural is to fly in the face of providence; most people would tell you that nothing more miserably unnatural could be conceived." After rejecting a number of the points made

by Thurston, Shaw returned to the harmful effects of the double bed:

You will be quite in order in showing that the marriage bed forces intelligent people to resort to contraceptives, and that their use certainly reduces intercourse to mere reciprocal masturbation and is probably subtly mischievous. Also, that a pregnant woman ought not to be tempted, and would probably not desire intercourse (as she certainly often does at present) if she were left to herself. . . .

In closing, Shaw wrote,

I have no time to go more fully into the matter; and as my criticism has necessarily occupied much more space than my approval I had better repeat what I began by saying, — that any book which will call attention to this aspect of the housing problem will do a great public service.

Thurston dispatched a frank reply to Shaw's letter. Denying that marriage without sexual intercourse for pleasure only would result in an unhappy existence, Thurston revealed he had "personally discovered that the result is exactly the reverse." He stated, "I am told by the neighbors, with obvious sincerity, that my wife and child are two of the happiest persons in our seaside colony, , , ," He disclosed his startling plan:

It is possible that the experiment of a healthy married couple, under forty years of age, living amiably together without sexual intercourse for pleasure, and without resorting to unnatural sex practices, has been made before, but so far as we know, no record of the result has ever been made public. What we purpose to do is to make the experiment and to leave a public record of the result. . . .

Thurston, with Shaw's permission, proposed that their correspondence should be part of this public record. He revealed that the two books had been translated into "all the vernaculars of India," that the same Indian publisher was printing a new edition in English for distribution in India, and that this edition would have an introduction by Mahatma Gandhi.[38]

Price 25 Cents
Thirty Cents in Canada

JANUARY 1930

THE

BLUE BOOK

MAGAZINE
(ILLUSTRATED)

$500.00 IN CASH PRIZES
FOR REAL EXPERIENCES

DRAGOONS
OF THE AIR
BY NORMAN HALL

TARZAN
AT THE EARTH'S CORE
BY EDGAR RICE BURROUGHS

Also BERTRAM ATKEY
CLARENCE HERBERT NEW
WARREN H MILLER
RAYMOND SPEARS

19
DIVERSE
WRITINGS

The period from mid-1927 to the end of 1929 found Burroughs at a high level of productivity. Beginning with "Tarzan, Lord of the Jungle," he progressed through eight fictional works of remarkable variety. These included three *Tarzans,* one signalling Tarzan's entrance to the inner world at the earth's core; four different sequels, including an Apache novel, a juvenile, and Mars and Pellucidar novels; and a new adventure story with a Cambodian setting.

While Burroughs, in "Tarzan, Lord of the Jungle," repeated his favorite theme of a lost civilization, he provided some unusual aspects to his plot and setting. Deep in the African jungle lie two medieval cities — Nimmr and the City of the Sepulcher. These had been founded by knights from the court of Richard I who in the twelfth century had led an expedition to reconquer Jerusalem from the Saracens. Commanded by Bohun and Gobred, two companies of knight crusaders were shipwrecked on the African shore, but continued their search

for Jerusalem, discovering a hidden valley which Bohun insisted was The Valley of the Holy Sepulcher. Thus, Bohun maintained that the search was ended; Gobred, however, denied this, and the two leaders then proceeded to block each other off, Gobred's followers building a city and a castle to prevent the other from returning to England, and Bohun's forces doing the same to stop the opposing company from moving on in a quest for the True Sepulcher.

For seven and a half centuries the descendents of Gobred and Bohun had remained in their medieval cities in Africa. They are convinced now that any hope of either liberating the Holy Land or returning to England is futile, especially since they have persuaded themselves that a vast army of Saracens occupies the area surrounding their fortified cities. From this background Burroughs creates a type of King Arthur's Court society, complete with armored knights, jousts, and tournaments, and with the inhabitants using the archaic speech of old England. The main character is not Tarzan, but James Hunter Blake, a young American on a photographing and hunting expedition, who gets lost and eventually winds up in the medieval city of Nimmr, where he falls in love with the Princess Guinalda. The plot is complicated by the irrational behavior of Wilbur Stimbol, a wealthy New York stockbroker, and by the villainous actions of a band of Arabs.

"Tarzan, Lord of the Jungle" at times achieves the burlesque tone of Twain's *A Connecticut Yankee in King Arthur's Court*, with Jim Blake introducing modern expressions or colloquialisms that baffle the knights of Nimmr. Blake becomes Sir James when, to humor his hosts, he reveals that his father was a thirty-second degree Mason and a Knight Templar. Concerning the city of New York, unknown to the knights, Blake impresses them by stating that it is sometimes referred to as "New Jerusalem." He explains that in his country those who are not magnanimous to their fallen foes "get the raspberry": ". . . the raspberry is about the only form of punishment that the Knights of the Squared Circle, or the Knights of the Diamond can understand." Sir Dempsey is an outstanding Knight of the Squared Circle, and, to his hosts' astonishment, Blake confesses, "We're all knights these days"; he lists the Knights Templar, Knights of Pythias, Knights of Columbus, and Knights of Labor.

Burroughs' comment to Miss Case that he "had recourse to the Bible" for help in the "archaic forms" was true. His worksheet contains conjugations of "thee," "thou," and "ye" and examples noted as from page 868 of the Bible: "As for me, O Father, I call upon Thee for a witness. That Thou bring them to confusion, etc. . . . Go your way, ye children. I brought you up with gladness." He also lists the conjugation of "wot" with its various (and amusing) verb forms:

I wot; Thou wost, or wot(t)est; He wot or wot(t)eth; We wot; You wost; They witen, or wite.

"Tarzan, Lord of the Jungle," submitted simultaneously in July 1927 to *Liberty, Col-liers, Youth's Companion, Redbook* and *The Elk's Magazine,* was rejected by all; on August 11 it was accepted by Donald Kennicott, *Blue Book* editor, for $5,000, appearing as a six-part serial, December 1927-May 1928.[1]

"Apache Devil," a sequel to "The War Chief," continues the adventures of Shoz-Dijiji as he joins his adoptive father, Geronimo, in the incessant struggle against the white men. Shoz-Dijiji is still unable to subdue his hopeless love for Wichita Billings, who also loves him but cannot summon the courage to overcome the racial barrier — the fear and prejudice of the times. While the romantic interest centers about these two, the real significance of the novel lies in its depiction of Geronimo's desperate plight, the pathos of the small, pitiable band of Apaches who are hunted like animals by both Americans and Mexicans. During one period the band had been reduced to eleven men and women, the only free Apaches still offering resistance.

Burroughs is blunt in his indictment of the white man and in his defense of the Indians. Drawing from authentic sources, he describes the situation in July 1886 when Geronimo had fled to Mexico with "some twenty-five fighting men, a few women and a couple of boys," with the American troops still doggedly on the band's trail:

Outside of their weapons and the clothing that they wore they possessed a few hundred pounds of dried meat and nineteen ponies — the sole physical resources at their command to wage a campaign against a great nation that already had expended a million dollars during the preceding fourteen months in futile efforts to subjugate them, and had enlisted as allies the armed forces of another civilized power.

At the story's end Geronimo tells Shoz-Dijiji of his white blood, and how, after the death of his parents, he had been taken to be raised by the Indians. Burroughs, nevertheless, does not use this to make Shoz-Dijiji more acceptable to Wichita; wisely he shows her rising above racial prejudice and willing to marry the man she believed to be an Indian.

Again, in an effort to reach one of the higher-paying markets, Burroughs, through November and December 1927, submitted "Apache Devil" to *Collier's, Liberty, Popular,* and *Blue Book.* After rejections by these magazines, the novel was sold to *Argosy All-Story* in January 1928 for $4,400.[2]

Despite early indications that his first juvenile, *The Tarzan Twins,* would encounter some sales difficulties, Burroughs could not resist writing the sequel he had planned. Once projected, a sequel became "unfinished business" which could not be left dangling. The brief 22,878-word story, completed on February 20, 1928, was titled "Jad-Bal-Ja and the Tarzan Twins," and it carried Dick and Doc into further adventures, this time involving a group of the crooked bestial men from the golden city of Opar.

While "Jad-Bal-Ja and the Tarzan Twins" generates more excitement and tension than its predecessor, the story still suffers from sketchy writing and from a lack of the rich jungle and animal background so vital to all of the Tarzan works. Submissions of the story to *Youth's Companion* in February 1928, to *American Boy* and *Everybody's Magazine* in 1929, and to *Astounding Stories* in 1930 brought rejections. "Jad-Bal-Ja and the Tarzan Twins," not published in magazine form, appeared on March 9, 1936, as a Whitman "Big Big Book," designed for children.[3] The story was retitled *Tarzan and the Tarzan Twins with Jad-Bal-Ja, the Golden Lion.* The two Tarzan Twins stories were combined in 1963 as a hardcover book by Canaveral Press titled *Tarzan and the Tarzan Twins.*

Ed's dubious view of the value of the Latin courses he was forced to take in his school years had been often expressed. Yet, in establishing a theme for his next Tarzan novel, he revealed the lasting influence of these early Latin and Roman history studies. Time modifies attitudes by giving new perspectives, and Ed's enthusiasm about the Romans and his interest in doing research on a subject which in the past had bored or irritated him was demonstrated in a work of unusual power and ingenuity, "Tarzan and The Lost Empire." The plot is centered about a favorite Burroughs device, the anachronism, in this case involving the existence of two Roman cities (or kingdoms) in the heart of Africa. The cities are actually a continuation of the Roman Empire, with Castrum Mare governed by Validus Augustus, emperor of the East, and Castra Sanguinarius under the rule of Sublatus Imperator, emperor of the West. The founding of the Empire in Africa occurred when, in about 98 A.D., Sanguinarius led a force of Roman soldiers up the Nilus in search of a new country where he might escape the punishment of the Emperor Nerva. At that time Sanguinarius captured a caravan from India and Cathay containing slaves and people of various races, including blacks and those of other skin colors. A combination of these races through the centuries resulted in an empire composed of white Romans who ruled over a motley variety of subjects.

In his complicated plot Burroughs creates a young archaeologist, Erich, the son of Carl von Harben, as the modern man who wanders into the ancient city of Castrum Mare, while Tarzan, in search of Erich, becomes a captive of the Romans in Castra Sanguinarius. Although the two cities are hostile toward each other, the actions of the story are not concerned with war, but rather with the dangers faced by the two men. For Tarzan, Burroughs devises the most spectacular scenes, those in the arena of the Colosseum, when in the games before the bloodthirsty crowd, Tarzan is pitted against men, a lion, and finally six apes, who recognize him and refuse to fight him. At the climax Tarzan and his allies are rescued by a horde of black warriors led by his valiant Waziri. But the real hero of the novel, surprisingly, is the little monkey Nkima who is given an importance he had never before been granted.

"Tarzan and the Lost Empire," with its incidents arranged alternately in the two kingdoms, does produce some confusion and leads

Cover of Tarzan and the Tarzan Twins with Jad-Bal-Ja the Golden Lion, *sequel to only other book designed by ERB specifically for children; it sold for twenty-nine cents, but today is a collector's item.*

to difficulties and an anticlimactic effect in providing a double resolution. In the rejection by *Popular Magazine*, the editors commented:

We found your two cities confusing in their similarity and wondered why they had not been combined into one and placed in opposition to a city controlled by native warriors at the jungle's edge. Then Tarzan could have appeared in his natural surroundings. As it is, the real Tarzan fans who read and like him for the jungle and wild animal, as well as human, interest, would justly resent this.[4]

The suggestion has some merit, but its adoption might have weakened the novel's greatest appeal — its colorful and detailed Roman settings and events. Burroughs' skill in joining syllables to devise original words and names was especially challenged by the need for Latin forms. Such lengthy names as Dion Splendidus, Septimus Favonius, and Maximus Praeclarus were the result. Jack Burroughs, in discussing his father's habit of sounding the words before choosing them, recalls his amusement over the funniest invention — Fulvus Fupus.[5]

The Pellucidar theme had lain dormant for fourteen years after the second story had been written in 1914-15. But because of numerous requests by his readers, Ed, in July 1928, devised an ambitious plan for a Pellucidar revival. He was envisioning a sequence of two stories, one based upon a surprising decision to remove Tarzan from his African environment. To Balmer on July 9, he announced:

It is now my intention to write a sequel to Pellucidar in which I shall pave the way for Tarzan's entrance into the inner world in the next Tarzan story, so that in a way my next two stories will be rather closely interwoven and the Tarzan story will, in effect, be a sequel to the other.

A further reason for this decision was the difficulty in finding new adventures for Tarzan "in the worn out jungles of Africa"; Ed noted, ". . . in the inner world I can introduce him to virgin jungles, peopled by prehistoric creatures worthy of his prowess."

A remark made by a bookstore employee aroused the Burroughs sales instinct and provided additional motivation for his changing Tarzan's milieu. The woman had offered an opinion that "any book with an airplane on the jacket would sell above anything else." Ed explained what followed:

I was casting about for some plan whereby I might connect Tarzan up with airplanes when the thought occurred to me that I could easily work out a scheme for sending him into the polar regions in a dirigible and thus into the northern polar opening into the inner world, thereby getting an airship on the jacket of the book, and in view of the interest concerning the flights of the Norge and Italia in the polar regions I believe that a dirigible would prove as good a lure as an airplane.

In November 1928 Ed completed the 77,000 word "Tanar of Pellucidar," centered about further conflicts and hazards in the inner world. The story is supposedly transmitted on a mysterious radio wave to Jason Gridley in Tarzana. From Abner Perry at "the bowels of the earth" comes an account opening with the departure of David Innes and two companions on a mission to rescue Tanar. The story then becomes a potpourri of strange races and grotesque monsters as a setting for Tanar, who has been captured by the Korsars, the bushy-whiskered buccaneers of Pellucidar.

Tanar's succession of battles and escapes does not establish adequate material for a unified story, and consequently, the novel appears episodic and plotless. There is little original content, but Burroughs does create some unusual races and civilizations.

Other Burroughs innovations include two races with opposite philosophies of life. The inhabitants of Amiocap — the word is actually Pacoima, a San Fernando Valley area, spelled backward — are a people whose existence is based upon love; they do not hesitate to "declare themselves publicly in matters pertaining to their hearts or their passions." The candor of the love-oriented Amiocapians and their happy lives caused Burroughs to compare them to the emotionally-suppressed people of our earth and imply that our attitudes and customs were responsible for "the unnumbered millions of unhappy human beings who are warped or twisted mentally, morally or physically." In contrast to the Amiocapians, the people of the village of Garb base their existence upon hate, not necessarily of strangers, but of themselves. The typical domestic life of these cave dwellers, developed with some humor, consists mainly of shrieking quarrels, curses, brawls, and blows. Burroughs was perhaps parodying the worst aspects of married life on earth. The names devised — Garb (an abbreviation of garbage), Dhung, Scurv, and Sloo — are indicative of the disgusting nature of these creatures.[6]

Ed had been experimenting with "simultaneous" submissions, and on November 24 sent "Tanar of Pellucidar" to *Blue Book* and *Argosy All-Story*. A. H. Bittner, who had replaced White as the Munsey editor, wired an offer of $6,000 on condition that *Argosy* be granted the sequel at the same price; this, Ed rejected. The story was sold to *Blue Book* for $7,500. On December 7 Bittner wrote unhappily, "We dislike very much to see you drifting away from Argosy, but it seems almost impossible to overcome the handicap of our long distance correspondence. . . . Do you, by any chance, contemplate a visit to New York in the next few months?"

In his reply a week later Ed maintained that he had not "drifted" away from *Argosy* of his own volition; he recalled, ". . . Mr. White was not particularly enthusiastic over the brand of deathless literature which I turn out, and when a Martian story was turned down, that was the last straw, as I have always felt that I had no other market for my Martian stories than Argosy All-Story since all five of them had been originally published in your magazines." He doubted that he could visit Bittner in New York, noting that he conducted all of his business matters through correspondence.[7]

Ed, possibly with a touch of nostalgia, must have realized that the old days, the days of close, warm relationships with magazine editors like Thomas Metcalf and Bob Davis, were gone forever. Bittner, as a good will gesture, on June 2, 1928, announced that Munsey was relinquishing the second serial rights to four of the Burroughs stories and was transferring these to Ed "with our compliments." Grateful, Ed spoke of the tone of Bittner's letter which was "reminiscent of the very cordial relations which existed between Bob Davis and myself for many years." He praised the editor's generosity, noting that this action would permit him to realize the long-held hope of controlling all the unsold rights to his stories.[8]

Concerning the two editors whose guidance and influence had been vital, Ed, some years later (1939), commented about both in a letter to a fan. About Metcalf, who had launched him on his career, he wrote, "I have not heard anything from or about him for more than twenty years. He never replied to my last letter to him after he left Munsey." He added, "I never met Frank A. Munsey; but I heard such things about him while he was alive that I never cared to meet him. It was really Bob Davis for whom I wrote in those days. . . ."[9]

After Davis' abrupt and unexplained departure from the Munsey Company in 1926 — he had left once before to go into business for himself and then returned — Ed had lost contact with him. However, during a visit to New York in May 1929 Ed reported meeting him: "He had gone bugs on portraiture, having photographed several hundred celebrities. He was to have an exhibit in New York in June or July, but I have not heard whether he did so or not."[10]

The sequel to "Tanar," at first titled "Tarzan and Pellucidar," was completed early in 1929, and the motive used for launching a series of further adventures was hardly original — another rescue mission, this time to save David Innes, first Emperor of Pellucidar, "languishing in a dark dungeon in the land of the Korsars." Tarzan is persuaded by Jason Gridley to join the expedition; convinced that a polar opening to the inner world does exist, Gridley constructs a huge zeppelin to make the journey, find the opening, and enter the land of Pellucidar. The finished dirigible was named the 0-220, taken from Burroughs' telephone number. The "O" was for Owensmouth, a community in the west end of San Fernando Valley now called Canoga Park.

The perils of Pellucidar, caused by hostile races and swarms of prehistoric monsters exceeding any devised in previous Burroughs novels, are faced separately by Tarzan and Jason Gridley. Among the creatures invented for the story are the Horibs or snake-men, possessors of the three-toed feet and five-toed hands of reptiles, bodies covered with scales and soft, white bellies. Gridley encounters many of the dangers in the company of Jana, the Red Flower of Zoram, with whom he falls in love.

In one unusual aspect, the novel contains an explanation of Tarzan's religious beliefs:

The Lord of the Jungle subscribed to no creed. Tarzan of the Apes was not a church man; yet like the majority of those who have always lived close to nature he was, in a sense, intently religious. His intimate knowledge of the stupendous forces of nature, of her wonders and her miracles had impressed him with the fact that their ultimate origin lay far beyond the conception of the finite mind of man, and thus incalculably remote from the farthest bounds of science. When he thought of God he liked to think of Him primitively, as a personal God. And while he realized that he knew nothing of such matters, he liked to believe that after death he would live again.

Burroughs here is apparently attempting to create a primitive religious philosophy for Tarzan that would parallel the simple beliefs of the natives who shared his jungle environment. As the man who has achieved a oneness with nature, who has become part of nature's great unity, Tarzan must share the faith of her creatures — a faith tinged with awe and wonderment.

In December 1928, while "Tarzan and Pellucidar" was in progress, Ed, at the request of

Edwin Balmer, *Blue Book* editor, forwarded a map of Pellucidar showing the regions described in the previous three inner world novels. Several months later Ed wrote to indicate that with "Tarzan and Pellucidar" he would send some "very crude drawings" that might help the illustrator. He noted, "I often make these, as well as maps, to assist me in carrying the same visualization of unusual animals or characters, as well as locations. . . ." About "Tarzan and Pellucidar" Ed conceded, "It is a bum title."

Because of the introduction of a new device in "Tarzan and Pellucidar," the dirigible, Ed necessarily turned to research. From *The Rigid Airship* by E. H. Lewitt (London, Pittman & Sons, 1925), he compiled five typed sheets of data. In these "Notes on Airships for Tarzan and Pellucidar" he merely listed bits of information that appeared important. After the definitions of the three classes of dirigible balloons, "non-rigids, semi-rigids and rigids," the following items are typical:

The hull, as a whole, forms a skeleton tube, rounded at the nose and tapered at the tail. . . .

A corridor, triangular in form, passes the whole length of the ship at the base. . . .

Propelling power of an airship consists of several gas engines situated in small cars suspended from the hull by wires. . . .

Gold-beater skins are about nine inches square, and are obtained from the entrails of the cow, each animal yielding one skin. A single gasbag of a modern airship would require about 50,000 of these skins. . . .

These notes, filled with dimensions, figures, and lists of parts and equipment, with explanations that at times are a paragraph in length, demonstrate Burroughs' insistence upon some scientific accuracy, and, of course, his familiar obsessive concern with detail.

The account in the February 1929 *Authors' League Bulletin* of the high prices being paid for stories proved disturbing to Ed. On March 15, as he sent "Tarzan and Pellucidar" to Balmer, he remarked, ". . . the price for this story should be somewhere in the neighborhood of sixty thousand dollars. However, it is only eight thousand dollars." Balmer's acceptance telegram attained a new level of adulation: "Heaven never endowed any other with imagination equal to yours, and I read through from start to finish under your sway." On April 18 Ed again complained about the prices he was being paid, this time because of a further article in *The Bulletin:* "When I read that an author got a dollar a word for a serial, and another one two dollars and fifty cents a word, mine almost went out of business. Compared with these plutocrats, I am only a Chinese laundryman. . . ."

"Tarzan and Pellucidar," retitled "Tarzan at the Earth's Core," appeared as a seven-part serial in *Blue Book,* September 1929 to March 1930. The device of having Von Horst, mate of the O-220, vanish somewhere in the wilds of Pellucidar was an obvious indication that a further sequel with a third search for a missing man would be a Burroughs' project of the future.[11]

With a respite of only a few weeks, Ed turned to the writing of another story in the Mars series. Because *Argosy All-Story* had published five previous ones, he felt the series should continue in the Munsey magazine. His irritation over the changes in *Argosy's* attitude after Davis had departed was somewhat tempered by the new, conciliatory approaches made by A. H. Bittner who appeared eager to purchase almost *any* Burroughs story. With Bittner's encouragement, Ed set to work rapidly, and on May 10, 1929, completed "A Fighting Man of Mars." The story, involving a new protagonist, Hadron of Hastor, underwent a complicated transmission, reaching the earth as a result of Jason Gridley's code signals from Tarzana. A response came from Ulysses Paxton, the hero of *The Master Mind of Mars,* an infantry captain who at his dying moment on earth had been transported to the red planet; Paxton, in turn, provided the lengthy tale of the exploits of Tan Hadron and his encounters with bizarre races on Mars.

The abduction of the lovely but supercilious Sanoma Tora, with whom Hadron is infatuated,

is accomplished by occupants of a mysterious airship mounting a gun of astonishing power, one that disintegrates all the metal parts of a plane that attempts to intercept it. As Hadron embarks upon his long search for Sanoma, the emphasis of the story, similar to that of *The Master Mind of Mars,* is upon "science" — science-of-the-future inventions in which Burroughs displays his greatest imagination and ingenuity. The aged scientist Phor Tak, vindictive and paranoid, is the inventor, and his creations are designed only for revenge and destruction:

A rifle projecting disintegrating rays
A blue insulating paint that protects ships and weapons from the rays
A miniature torpedo that, in turn, is attracted by the blue insulating paint, and follows ships and destroys them
A compound which, when painted or spread on objects, renders them invisible

Adapting Phor Tak's inventions, Hadron constructs his own airship, coats it with the insulating paint and then applies the compound of invisibility; the only part of the plane that can be seen is "the tiny eye of the periscope."

In the hands of the half-mad Phor Tak, these devices constitute an appalling menace to Mars and especially to the government of Helium. Hadron's main goal now is to thwart the plans of Phor Tak to conquer the planet and become ruler of all Mars. At the end, when victory is won by Hadron, he destroys Phor Tak's deadly weapons, doing so "to save a world."

Burroughs, in "A Fighting Man of Mars," refers briefly to a game called *yano*; he describes the activities of the warriors in Tjanath, a Martian kingdom: ". . . two were playing at jetan, while others were rolling tiny numbered spheres at a group of numbered holes — a fascinating game of chance, called yano, which is, I presume, almost as old as Barsoomian civilization." (Jetan, a game played with living pieces on a chess-board arena, was invented for *The Chessmen of Mars.*) There is no further mention of yano, nor are any details or rules of the game presented. However, on his work-sheets for "A Fighting Man of Mars," Burroughs made a drawing of an "Ancient Yano mixing jug found near Manator," and beneath it offered some description of the game. A small diagram of a yano court is shown; the seven holes are drawn, with the distance from the players' line marked as "15 Sofads." Burroughs follows with a hand-printed explanation that is partly illegible:

Each player has a numbered sphere. For each play they are mixed and redistributed. The players roll in the order of the numbers on their spheres. If a player's sphere rolls into his own hole he collects 5 from each of the players. If he gets it into "0" he collects 10 from each player. If he misses he places 1 on "0" to be taken by the next player to get "0."

A detailed explanation of the game is contained in Burroughs' notebook. The same yano mixing jug is shown, and the distance to the players' line marked as "15 Sofads." Burroughs points are as follows:

The regulation Yano court is laid out with seven holes, six in a line parallel with Players' Line, the seventh (Zero Hole) 1 ft. in rear of the center of the space between Holes 3 & 4.

A line passing through the centers of Holes 1 to 6 is 15 ft. from Players' Line.

Diameter of holes is 2"; distance between edges of holes is 2".

Yano is played with six balls, numbered from one to six; the balls used in a game must all be of the same diameter and weight; diameter of Yano balls varies from 1 1/4" to 1 1/2".

Six players or less may play.

The balls are placed in a jug and shaken; one ball is then rolled out to each player, whose turn to play is determined by the number of his ball, the lowest number playing first.

Standing behind the Players' Line the players, in their turn, roll or toss the balls toward the holes. . . .

If a player sinks his ball in the correspondingly numbered hole he collects 5 counters from each of the other players; if he sinks it in Zero Hole he collects 10 counters from each of the other players; if he sinks it in any other hole he pays 5 counters to the player holding the ball bearing the number of that hole. (If no player holds this number the counters are placed in the Zero Hole and are claimed by the next player who rolls his ball into the Zero Hole.) If a player misses entirely he places 1 counter in Zero Hole.

All counters in Zero Hole at end of game go to player who has lost the greatest number of counters. A game ends when each player has had five chances. The balls are mixed and redistributed after each play. There can be a greater number of holes and a correspondingly greater number of players, but there must be an even number of holes in the first line and the Zero Hole must always be directly behind the exact center of the line of holes.

The court should be level, with a hard, smooth surface. The Players' Line may be marked with a cord, tightly stretched and pegged down at each end. On Mars it is usually a leather belt from the harness of a warrior.

Burroughs added, "On Earth Yano may be played with golf balls and putters," and he ended the explanation humorously, "I have spoken!"

On May 13, 1929, Ed informed Bittner that "A Fighting Man of Mars" was about to be mailed and that the price was ten cents a word. To his astonishment, on June 8, Bittner sent a rejection with this explanation: "Were this one of the Tarzan stories I should have no difficulty in meeting your rate, but for one of these Mars tales, which we feel appeals to a much smaller audience than your better known work, I am afraid we cannot shoot quite so high." Ed angrily replied that the reason given for the rejection was "both surprising and inconsistent" when compared to Bittner's previous statements. Ed then quoted excerpts from three of Bittner's letters, all of which indicated an eagerness to obtain a Martian story and a belief that a price could be worked out. Ed's old doubts and distrust of Munsey were now reconfirmed.[12] To Balmer at *Blue Book,* he wrote in disgust, "As I told you when in Chicago, I had a hunch that Argosy would not pay the price for the Martian story and I was right." He forwarded the 83,000-word story to Balmer, listing the rate again as ten cents a word. Balmer, also lukewarm about the story, revealed his doubt that it would have sufficient appeal for the readers, but after some consideration, agreed to purchase it for the high price of $8,000. His reluctance was undoubtedly overcome by Ed's comment, hardly subtle, that he could not limit himself to Tarzan stories, and that the editors who wished to buy his material must realize this; the implication helped persuade the Tarzan-hungry Balmer that in this case a diplomatic purchase was advisable.[13]

In an April 1929 correspondence the two men exchanged ideas on the subject of realism. Balmer stated that ". . . there is no actual realism. Every writer, only in varying degrees, constructs his own world, and he attracts people in proportion as they care to live in the world he creates." This version of "reality" Balmer defined as "relative unrealities" and noted that fiction's greatest feat, "the creative fancy of heaven," is "utter unreality" and yet of great significance to mankind. Ed's interpretation was based upon the conflict between his "two minds":

. . . one mind . . . functions in a most logical and reasonable manner according to the accepted standards of logic and reason . . . another mind . . . seems to reason in an equally logical and reasonable manner. This mind insists that all my wildest flights of imagination shall appear consistent, probable and realistic, whereas they do not appear so at all to my other mind. . . .

In business matters, Ed explained, he often, with unfortunate results, accepted the advice of his "second" mind — advice which was contrary to the sounder reasoning of his first mind. Each mind had its own concept of realism, but what the first mind viewed as realism was "entirely lacking in romance and interest" to both

minds. In his conclusion he agreed with Balmer: "Realism is purely relative."

When "A Fighting Man of Mars" had been barely launched, Ed, projecting ahead as usual, was casting about for a theme for his next work. On March 28, 1929, he wrote to Balmer, ". . . I have in mind an imaginative, pseudoscientific conception of the physical geography of Venus and the members of its interesting dominant race in which I could give my imagination full play. Perhaps it would be better to write such a story before giving them another Tarzan. . . ." Balmer's response of April 6 was enthusiastic: "The idea of Venus seems splendid to me in the way you will handle it. . . ." An unexpected circumstance, however, led Burroughs to hesitate about the plan to write a Venus story at that time. On November 5 he commented succinctly to Balmer: "I see where one of McClurg's authors beat us to it in the story of Venus." He added, "However I am a little leery of these Martian type stories. They have always done well in magazines and books, but magazine editors are leery of them for some reason. I think I shall not write any more." (The "McClurg author" referred to may have been Otis Adelbert Kline, whose story *The Planet of Peril,* set on Venus, appeared serially in *Argosy All-Story,* starting June 20, 1929.)[14]

Temporarily discarding the Venus idea, Ed, in the same letter, revealed he was working on a Cambodian jungle story, and explained, "Robert J. Casey's 'Four Faces of Siva' is responsible for it." He listed the content of the latest creation: "It is of Kmer ruins, tigers, wild elephants, another ancient civilization, with a little brown princess and a young American."

From Casey's book Ed obtained some brief information about Cambodia's ancient history and customs, sufficient to provide background for the tale he concocted. Completed at year's end, December 30, 1929, "The Dancing Girl of the Leper King" established a mystic atmosphere for the adventures of Gordon King, a young American doctor, in the jungles of Cambodia. King finds his imagination gripped by his guide's account of the ghosts of his ancestors, the Khmers, who once dwelt in great cities:

Within the dark shadows of the jungle the ruins of their cities still stand, and down the dark aisles of the forest pass the ancient kings and warriors and little sad-faced queens on ghostly elephants. . . .

They, and millions of the ghostly dead, pass forever down the corridors of the jungle. ". . . No man may look upon the ghosts of the dead Khmers and live," the guide says.

King, lost in the jungle, has visions and what he believes to be a hallucination; he watches the passing of a caravan of brown men "with cuirasses of burnished brass," and then, in a "gorgeous howdah" upon the back of an elephant he sees the "sad-faced girl." The caravan vanishes "down the aisles of the jungle in spectral silence." King is convinced that the scene is a product of his delirium, but in the adventures that follow, King finds his queen and becomes a prisoner in the ancient city of Lodidhapura, ruled by the cruel Leper King, Lodivarman. Once more Burroughs creates two warring kingdoms; Beng Kher is King of Pnom Dhek, and it is his daughter, Fou-tan, who has also been captured by the Leper King and forced to become his dancing girl.

The story consists of battles with men and tigers and of rescues and escapes. Amusingly, the fearful Leper King turns out to be a benign villain. Throughout the story he is shown subsisting solely upon mushrooms, and at the denouement, the American, through his medical knowledge, determines that the king is not a leper. He is merely suffering from an aggravated form of dermatitis caused by food poisoning from his diet of mushrooms. After this diagnosis and the elimination of all mushrooms, the sores vanish, Lodivarman recovers, and his entire nature changes. The king had contracted the supposed leprosy one hour after a woman in a crowd had covered his face and mouth with kisses.

On November 27, 1929, with the completion of sixty-eight pages of the story, it was sub-mitted to *Blue Book* for approval. About that time the magazine had been acquired by the McCall Company; Balmer was then made Editor of *Red Book*, and Donald Kennicott took charge of *Blue Book*. Faced by some uncertainty in the purchase of "The Dancing Girl of the Leper King," Burroughs, in January 1930, sent it to *Liberty* and *Elks Magazine*, where it was rejected. Later in the month Kennicott bought the story for $7,000, and with its appearance in *Blue Book* as a five-part serial, May to September 1931, it was retitled "The Land of Hidden Men." Kennicott's main objection was to the word "leper," which he believed would repel readers, but Ed, irked, protested the title change, made without consulting him; he thought there was more appeal in the original title and did not support the editor's distaste for "leper." He wrote:

I recall that Joe Bray prophesied that the word "apes" in the title Tarzan of the Apes would be so repulsive to women that none of them would read the story, while results have demonstrated that there was no justification for his fears.[15]

With the publication by Edgar Rice Burroughs, Inc., in 1932, the book was given a new title — *Jungle Girl*.[16]

In the period of the late 1920's Burroughs received perhaps his greatest satisfaction when, thirteen years after the original appearance in *Argosy*, McClurg published *The Outlaw of Torn* on February 19, 1927. To the literary editor of the *Sacramento Bee*, on March 15, Ed recalled that this story drove him to the hardest "labor" he had ever done. He also noted that Bray never cared for the story, but described him as "one of the princes of the publishing world," and added, "I dedicated this one to him, as you will note from the flyleaf, to make him like it." A few months before publication Bray had been made president of A. C. McClurg & Company. Ed's faith in *The Outlaw of Torn* appeared justified with the report, on March 28, that the 5,000 copy first edition of the book had been sold out — a gratifying record for so short a period. For the window display of *The Outlaw of Torn* for Brentano's Book Store in Chicago, Ed sent a photo of himself at the Tarzana Ranch with the yearling filly named Dejah Thoris. Concerning the novel, he wrote to Maurice Simons at McClurg, "I think it is the best thing I ever wrote, with the possible exception of *Tarzan of the Apes*, and next to it, I believe will rank *The War Chief of the Apaches*."[17]

Since 1917 McClurg had followed a policy of publishing at least two Burroughs books a year; those of the midtwenties were *The Land That Time Forgot, Tarzan and the Ant Men,* 1924; *The Cave Girl, The Bandit of Hell's Bend, The Eternal Lover,* 1925; *The Moon Maid, The Mad King,* 1926; *The Outlaw of Torn, The War Chief,* 1927; *The Master Mind of Mars, Tarzan, Lord of the Jungle,* 1928. By arrangement with McClurg, beginning in 1915, popular reprints of the Burroughs books were published by A. L. Burt Company and Grosset & Dunlap. On September 12, 1927, George Sparks of McClurg presented an astonishing sales total for the United States and Great Britain: "The exact figures to date. . . including *The War Chief*. . . six million, three hundred and fifty-five thousand copies."

Ed's attempt to persuade McClurg to publish one of his older stories, "The Oakdale Affair," which had been made into a film, met with rejection; on July 21, 1927, Bray noted, "There is not enough of The Oakdale Affair to make a book. . . ." A week later Ed requested the return of the story and commented, "The picture will not be anything more than a program picture, I imagine. . . ." The film was retitled *The Warning.*

In his dealings with Methuen & Company, the publishers for Great Britain, Ed, as early as 1921, had disagreed with their procedures. At that time, with the publication of *The Mucker* scheduled, Curtis Brown, Ed's British agent, informed him that the story title would have to be changed, since the word *mucker* had no meaning for an English reader. A minor controversy developed over Methuen's preferred title, *A Man without a Soul.* This duplicated the title of a 1913 Burroughs story. "Is there no word current in Great Britain that answers the purpose of 'mucker'?" Ed inquired. He mentioned several possibilities, including "Billy Bryne, Rowdy" and "The Rough-Neck," and also suggested "hooligan," but admitted that in the United States this term might be associated with Opper's cartoon "Happy Hooligan." Despite his strenuous objections, Methuen, in what they believed to be a compromise, decided to issue two volumes, the first to be called *The Mucker,* the second, *A Man without a Soul.*

Disagreements of a more serious nature followed. In the summer of 1925, disappointed over the British sales and royalties, Ed wished to sever his connection with Methuen, but was persuaded by Curtis Brown to maintain the same arrangements. The indecision continued through 1926, with Ed, on May 20, writing, ". . . please do not place any more of my books with Methuen & Company until further notice. I am keenly disappointed in the returns I am getting and very much dissatisfied with the royalty reports. . . ." He was also annoyed because of the Methuen practice of remaindering large numbers of his books, but again yielded, accepting Curtis Brown's opinion that Methuen could "do better than anyone else."

The next controversy erupted over Methuen's deletions in and alterations of Burroughs' novels. On July 5, 1927, Ed cautioned Curtis Brown about *The War Chief,* referring to the deletions made by *Argosy,* and urged that Methuen use the full text soon to appear in the McClurg publication. About the matter of deletions, he wrote:

. . . I believe I have discovered a possible reason for the diminution of my sales in England. It has never been my custom to read the English editions, but recently my younger son read Methuen's edition of Tarzan and the Ant Men *and called my attention to the fact that it had been very much altered, one principal character being taken out entirely, which necessitated rewriting the entire story.*

"I strenuously object to this procedure," Ed insisted. "It is a liberty that should not be taken with my work. . . ." He stressed that his stories in their original form had been successful in other countries, and instructed Brown to allow no changes in his manuscripts except for corrections of obvious errors.

By 1928 Burroughs was openly expressing his distrust of Methuen & Company. On March 13, after informing Bray that Gernsbach, the German publisher, wanted to publish the novels in small ten-cent paperbacks similar to those issued by Haldeman-Julius — a request which was firmly rejected — Ed proceeded to ask a "confidential" question concerning "the business integrity of Methuen and Company, at least since the death of Sir Arthur." Ed wrote, "They clamor for my books and the reports show sales of practically nothing but remainders. I am quite certain that I am being systematically gipped." A week later Bray replied, "All I can say is that the Company is high class in every respect, and they rank very high in the estimation not only of English publishers, but of American publishers also. . . ." Ed had also commented to George Sparks at McClurg about a supposed "block book sales system" that Methuen was using: ". . . they stimulate the sales of other books on their list by throwing in a quantity of mine at remainder prices." To Pollinger at Curtis Brown he announced, "I shall never be satisfied with Methuen's royalty statements until I have seen a disinterested audit of their books."[18] It should be borne in mind that on past occasions Burroughs had voiced suspicions about the honesty of various firms, had been convinced that film companies were cheating him, and had even requested an audit of the McClurg Company's books. There was no evidence of dishonest dealings by Methuen.

Ed conceded that his stories had "flopped" in England but appeared baffled as to the reasons why. The change to a new publisher, Cassell & Company, brought no improvement, and in April 1929 Cassell returned three of his books, noting their belief that *Tarzan* was "played out" and indicating their unwillingness to accept any more of the Burroughs stories. That month Ed signed an agreement with George Newnes, Ltd., for publication of sixpence editions with British rights. But in January 1930 Curtis Brown wrote to advise that five British publishers had declined to handle Burroughs' writings.

Ed's meticulousness in keeping detailed records of his stories was evidenced in the entries on his worksheets of the numbers of cylinders used for dictation. "Tarzan and Pellucidar," for example, had the entry, "Cyls: 90," while "A Fighting Man of Mars" listed "Cyls: 88-⅔." In his diary Burroughs also

ERB dictating into ediphone, March 1937.

477

noted the cylinders used; typical entries for 1930 were brief: "May 24 Dictated 5 cyl. today — something over 4000 words"; "May 28 2 cyl. today"; "June 3: 1 cyl. today"; "June 9: 5 cyl. today and finished story — *Tarzan and the Man Things.*" Through the years Burroughs used both the Dictaphone and Ediphone; the wax cylinders, after being shaved, were ready for further use. Answering an old friend, O. C. Dentzer, on February 27, 1922, Ed had mentioned purchasing the Ediphone outfit which, at that time, he was not using, but which he planned to use in the future. In later years he responded to an inquiry from the Thomas A. Edison Company as to the advantages of their machine. He noted that in the past twenty-four years he had used *all* methods for producing stories: "I have written longhand and had my work copied by a typist; I have typed my manuscripts personally; I have dictated them to a secretary; and I have used the Ediphone." In all methods, he stressed it was necessary to check the manuscript carefully after it was typed; errors were always present, but he had found that fewer corrections were needed when a manuscript was transcribed from a voice recording. He listed other advantages of the Ediphone: "Voice writing makes fewer demands upon the energy. . . it eliminates the eyestrain. . . the greatest advantage lies in the speed. . . I can easily double my output. . . I can choose my own time for dictating without encroaching on the time of another. . . ." He added amusingly, "I can work Saturday afternoons, Sundays or nights, dictating to a machine. . . that is not resentful of broken engagements and overtime and not planning on what it is going to wear Saturday night." Also, he could have the Ediphone at his bedside "to record those fleeting inspirations that would otherwise be lost forever. . . ." He closed with the most obvious advantage, the economy effected by the use of the Ediphone: "I have been using the same machine for some twelve or fifteen years. . . it has paid for itself several times over. . . ."[19]

A most important event of the period came with the employment of a new secretary.

ERB, right, and Cyril Ralph Rothmund, his secretary and manager

478

William Waterhouse had worked for Edgar Rice Burroughs, Inc., since November 1926, but in June 1927 Cyril Ralph Rothmund assumed the position. In answering an ad for a secretary, Rothmund believed the organization was the Burroughs Adding Machine Company. In the coming years Ed's dependence upon Rothmund in business matters and in family affairs would steadily increase.

One of the strangest of the Burroughs works, an unfinished and untitled manuscript marked "commenced April 6, 1927," opens with three pages in story form and then shifts to a play in complete dialogue with stage directions. That it was intended as a play is evidenced by Burroughs' own drawing of a stage set, a living room with locations of furniture, doors, and stairs indicated. Curiously, a printed box on the page containing this drawing appears to state the theme of the play: "Youth has a right to question the moral mandates of its parents when by their panderings to the follies of the age, weak parents lay themselves open to question." Beneath the drawing Burroughs listed the titles he was considering: "Mary Who?"; "Why Razz the Kids?"; "Holy Bonds of Wedlock." Perhaps the play was designed for his daughter Joan who, at the time, was involved in amateur theatrics.

For no reason related to the action of the play, Burroughs gave most of his characters Spanish surnames. In the twenty-nine-page play Burroughs seems to be striving for a sophisticated atmosphere, an attempt to portray a dissolute society. The social-climbing Mrs. Trepador and her wealthy friends Pansy and Birdie are shown as heavy drinkers and women of loose morals, in contrast to the high-principled Professor and his foster-daughter Mary.

For his plot Burroughs resorts to old devices. Mrs. Trepador's six-month marriage to the wealthy John Dayton had culminated with his death, and she soon wedded a stodgy university professor. Dayton, at the request of a friend, had agreed to rear Mary Quien, a foundling.

Mrs. Trepador views the girl with contempt and tells her that she is illegitimate and "tainted." John Dayton, Jr., a son of Dayton by a previous marriage, returns after a four-year absence to discover that he loves Mary and he announces his intention to marry her; to the socially-aspiring Mrs. Trepador this is unthinkable. In the ensuing furious quarrel that ends the manuscript, Mary decides to leave the Trepador home and John threatens to follow her.

In the shallow contrast of the goody-goody Mary versus the dissipations of Mrs. Trepador and her fast prohibition-era set, and the preaching and moralistic tone of sections of the dialogue, the play emerges as trite and unrealistic.

A second play, definitely written to aid daughter Joan's theatrical career, was completed in the same year. Ed's note of October 19, 1927, to Joan contains an apology for the rough draft of "You Lucky Girl!": "This is the first copy of the original longhand ms. It has not been corrected or revised and is rather rough. Please explain this to Mr. Gould when you hand it to him." Described as "A Love Story in Three Acts," "You Lucky Girl!" reveals Burroughs in a surprising role; he had never hesitated to enter controversial areas, but here he becomes an iconoclast in attacking the cherished marriage concept of woman's subservience to her husband. He ridicules the familiar woman-belongs-in-the-home belief, the contention that child-bearing is her main purpose in life, and the idea that she must accept her life as a mere extension of her husband's. The defense of woman's individuality, similar in certain respects to that adopted by Ibsen in *A Doll's House*, is developed by Burroughs through the conflicts faced by two girls, Anne Mason and Corrie West, who must choose between marriage and a career. In both cases the men involved, Tracy Lord, a movie exhibitor engaged to Anne, and Phil Mattis, the crude villain of the play, a wealthy banker's son whom Corrie plans to marry, are firmly opposed to their future wives becoming actresses.

With the two girls forced to make choices, Burroughs establishes an interesting situation. Anne, already in the theatrical field, unexpectedly capitulates to Tracy, gives up her career and accepts a restricted marriage. Three years later we see her resigned, unhappy, and still dreaming of the stage. Corrie, who had never contemplated becoming an actress, abruptly accepts the offer of producer Barton (partially because of a need to pay for her mother's medical treatments), discards Pettis and his male chauvinism, and leaves Millidge to embark upon a successful career.

Mason and his son Bill attain their life's ambition of owning a Gormley and Packard car agency, but their business is coveted by Pettis who has a villainously underhanded scheme to force the Masons to surrender the agency to him. Further story complications center about Bill, in a martyr's role, accepting the guilt for a robbery actually committed by Frank West, Corrie's brother.

At the story's end Corrie reappears as the celebrated actress Cora Carson to disclose the truth about her brother's act and thus to save the Masons. She and Bill reveal their long-hidden love for each other. Burroughs, in a true triumph for woman's freedom — he might well be considered as an exponent of the current women's liberation movement — has Tracy now confess he was wrong in blocking Anne's career. Anne plans to return to the stage, taking the lead in a Millidge stock company play sponsored by Barton. With both Corrie and Anne combining marriages and careers, a situation unopposed by their complacent husbands, Burroughs unmistakably takes his stand against an old-fashioned, kitchen-domestic, cradle-rocking role for the married woman. In one section of "You Lucky Girl!" he even ventures a step farther, stressing his previously stated views on uncontrolled births. A lengthy speech contains an attack on woman as a mere breeding machine and emphasizes the concern of modern science about the dangers of over-population. Ed offers brief alternate endings for the play, the first one being a love scene between Corrie and

Bill, and the second, a scene in which Anne and Corrie point joyfully at each other and proclaim in unison, "You lucky girl!"

As in the past, Ed did not limit his writing to the area of fiction; from 1926 to 1930 he produced a variety of articles. A brief one of unusual interest, written at the request of F. Romer, president of the Samson Service, Washington, D.C., was about the Colt revolver; the article (about 325 words, no title available), completed February 27, 1926, was scheduled for publication in a small booklet. Ed's opening paragraph is intriguing:

Have you a little Colt in your home? I have three — a Government Model 45 automatic that I packed for years on Tarzana Ranch and with which I missed every coyote in the Santa Monica mountains at least once until finally The Colonel became so peeved that he bucked me off on top of a mountain and left me to walk home — and another, old and rusty six-gun, that Bull might have toted in The Bandit of Hell's Bend. It bears the serial number 70495. Once, being broke and jobless, I annexed a temporary job as railway policeman in Salt Lake City. It was then that 70495 assisted me materially in running boes off the U.P. passenger trains.

Colt number three, Ed's "especial pride," had an eight-inch long barrel and measured fourteen inches from heel to muzzle. It was last loaded by his father over sixty years ago when, as a cavalry officer, he carried it during the Civil War. It had remained loaded — "its funny little percussion caps protruding from the six powder chambers of its cylinder await the sleeping hammer that will fall no more." Ed then revealed that beside the three Colts he owned, his sixteen-year old son Hulbert also owned one. Glancing up at a book shelf, he discovered Colt number five, a pearl-handled revolver with a steer's head carved on one side of the grip; he remembered purchasing it from a cowpuncher "who was broke." He imagined that if he looked around he would find others.

The number of Colts first mentioned had somehow increased, and the article closed with an amusing variation of the opening: "Have you a little Colt in your home? We have five."

Man's need for relaxation and play was the theme of an article written by Burroughs for the *Edgewater Breeze*, a publication of the Edgewater Club in Santa Monica, California. The article of September 25, 1926, headed "Clubs Like the Edgewater a Force for Good in the Community," noted that Americans are living under an intense "nerve pressure," and in their efforts to achieve success they have strained their nervous and physical "power plants"; without some sort of safety valve this "structure of success" could blow up like "an overtaxed boiler." Americans were first learning how to play, Ed remarked, and in his comment about "some of us older generation" who are in danger of never learning and who "forever feel guilty" if they take their noses from the grindstones for just a few hours, he was deploring his own compulsive drive for money and success. As a member of the Edgewater Club, he expressed gratitude for the relaxation he found there (resulting in "increased efficiency"!) and recalled that twenty years ago his family doctor advised patients to "get good and drunk at least once a year if that was the only means they could discover of jolting themselves out of their usual ruts of existence." He did not expect people to agree with this "radical prescription"; the main goal was to find happiness and "sunshine" in life, and some individuals could do so "on the sand and in the surf," while others found theirs in the nightlife at the club.

In response to a request from Louise Sillcox, secretary of The Authors' League, Ed, on May 17, 1927, forwarded an article for the League's *Bulletin*. Titled "The Illustrator and the Author," the article contains a long section of praise for J. Allen St. John's work. Ed is careful to explain that St. John possessed opportunities not as a rule available to other illustrators; he had access to the published magazine stories, could study them and then prepare the illustrations for the books. Usually, the illustrator's only source was the unpublished manuscript which he might retain for a limited period.

Ed observed that his stories were "particularly well adapted to illustration." In this case he was referring to the timelessness of his costumes — certainly the harnesses or clothing of Martians or of Tarzan and the natives would be as acceptable many years in the future as they were when originally created. Thus, they would never become old-fashioned. He believed that younger readers were strongly influenced by illustrations and that those typically found in old books, showing wearing apparel of a former generation, might lessen a child's interest in reading the book.

He recalled the illustrations he had not approved, referring especially to the occasion when Tarzan was drawn with "whiskers," and also to the unrealistic magazine picture of an Apache. One of his complaints related to the practice of "editorial chapter titlers" who, in devising titles, either anticipated the climax or took "all the kick out of the chapters by telling the whole story in the titles." Ed accepted the opinions of the publishers who advised him that illustrations throughout the text did not improve the sales value of a book, but that "a striking jacket illustration" would boost the sales. "For this reason, presumably," he noted, "my books are now illustrated with a single frontispiece, the cover illustration being a reproduction of this in colors." "The Illustrator and the Author" appeared in the *Bulletin* of October 1927.

A request from Walter G. Williamson, Editor of *The Daily Maroon* of the University of Chicago, for an article explaining the origin of the Tarzan idea, brought a response from Burroughs on March 30, 1927. In the brief article Ed noted that throughout history there had always been stories of "human babes reared by beasts" and that these tales had appealed very strongly to his imagination: "I liked to speculate as to the relative values of heredity, en-

vironment and training in the mental, moral, and physical development of such a child, and so in Tarzan I was playing with this idea."

He recalled that several years earlier he had interviewed a young man who claimed he was raised by a band of apes on the coast of Africa. Through this unusual story Dan, the Monkey Man, achieved much notoriety, but commenting frankly, Burroughs believed that Dan's life among the apes was purely fictional and "the result of a misspent youth among the Tarzan books." Ed doubted that any child, without adult protection, could survive in the type of African environment that was described in the Tarzan stories: ". . . if he did, he would develop into a cunning, cowardly beast, as he would have to spend most of his waking hours fleeing for his life. He would be underdeveloped from lack of proper and sufficient nourishment, from exposure to the inclemencies of the weather, and from lack of sufficient restful sleep." Thus, Ed admitted, while he liked to think of Tarzan as a real character, he should be realistically viewed as "an interesting experiment in the mental laboratory which we call imagination." The article appeared in *The Daily Maroon* of May 31, 1927.

The temptation to record details of a summer vacation trip was, as in the past, too strong to resist, and in 1927 Ed expended some 6,000 words to describe the family's travels to Zion and Bryce canyons and the north rim of the Grand Canyon. In commemoration of the 1916 cross-country trip, he chose to title the article "The Eleven Year Itch," recalling, in the opening paragraph, the "itch" that had driven the family to embark on the hectic expedition eleven years before and noting that this form of "mental tetter" had erupted again.

While Ed was given to a humorous reporting of these auto vacation tours and to exaggerating the difficulties that were encountered, still this one far exceeded the others in its steady succession of minor disasters. That all of these mishaps could be compressed into a week's vacation trip appeared incredible. In the familiar transport, two cars and the inevitable trailer, the family departed on August 28, Emma and Ed occupying the six-year-old Packard Roadster, and Joan, Hulbert, and Jack in the Buick roadster. Ensconced in the rumble seat, Jack was in charge of thirteen gallons of water and most of the food. For his son, Ed noted, "the trip was one long orgy of eating and drinking. What he couldn't eat or drink he spilled down his front."

The Packard, besides towing the trailer, was assigned a load appalling to contemplate: "It carried two spare tires on a rear deck, and the well inside the tires was filled with tools, pots, pans. . . . The large luggage compartment. . . was filled with canned goods, an ice chest and about a million other things; on the trunk rack was a trunk in which we carried slickers, rubbers, boots, wash basins, rough clothing, and eggs. . .; the trailer and load weighed 1,202 pounds; Emma and I weighed something and the roadster itself weighs over 5,000 pounds." As they lurched across the Mojave Desert after leaving Baker, it was easy to understand why the steep two-thousand-foot ascent should be a staggering feat for the Packard.

Plagued by bad roads and a never-ending sequence of misfortunes that included flat tires, battery failures, and a leaking radiator, the vacationers also managed to get mired twice in thick mud, and on the return trip, the Packard, surrendering against impossible odds, had to be towed by the Buick all the way in from San Bernardino. The seven-day tour ended at Tarzana on September 4, and Ed noted that they had "slept out" in four states, California, Arizona, Utah, and Nevada; he and Emma had lost seven pounds each. His fifty-second birthday (September 1) was spent in Arizona, and he recalled two previous birthdays in the same state: "My 21st I was somewhere around Fort Grant chasing the Apache Kid with the 'B' Troop of the 7th Cavalry, and I was in Phoenix on my 50th, returning home with the family from the South Rim of the Grand Canyon."

Two letters of March 1929 from Sergeant Cyrus C. Johnson of the Los Angeles Police Department expressed concern over newspaper criticisms of the police and contained a request that Ed contribute an article for the department's bulletin. As a staunch supporter of the police, Ed was aware of "the adverse propaganda that is being circulated" and also of certain newspaper attacks on Chief of Police James E. Davis. Upon receiving a further request from L. D. McGahan, editor of *The Police Reporter,* Ed wrote the article and, in sending it, stipulated that an editorial note must be printed beneath the title:

The following article by one of the highest paid magazine writers in the world is a voluntary contribution to The Police Reporter, prompted solely by the author's sense of civic duty.[20]

In "The Citizen and the Police," appearing in *The Police Reporter,* May 1929, Ed stressed, first of all, that a police department reflects the community: "If it is negligent of its duty, it is because we are negligent of ours. If it is rotten, it is because we are rotten. . . ." Obviously, the police force was not rotten; it was "the victim of rotten and vicious propaganda." Ed observed that he understood the "source and purpose of this propaganda"; its ends were not altruistic but rather "ruthlessly selfish and political." He referred to "the present insidious campaign of calumny directed against the police."

Naturally, he made no claims that the department was "composed of perfect men." He was aware of stories contained in newspapers or broadcast over radio about police negligence and corruption, and he was certain that these concerned only a small fraction of the entire personnel. Much of the remainder of the article was devoted to a defense of Chief Davis, a policeman of twenty years and a "crack shot," acknowledged to be one of the best in the United States. Ed, who still retained an interest in guns and shooting, joined Sergeant Johnson in revolver practice.

Later in the year a request came from Chief Davis for another article, a brief one to be written in rebuttal of a further critical statement. Davis enclosed some statistics for use in the article, but on October 24 Ed noted that "while statistics are what the public needs, it is hard to get them to read"; for this reason, he explained, he had decided to inject a few points into the "easily readable" article he was sending, and in its composition to adopt "a vein of far greater levity than the importance of the subject warrants." Titled "A Scrambled Parable," the article opened in olden times:

Several thousand years ago two nations were at war. The army of one of these nations, led by an experienced and energetic general, was winning signal victories in the field.

To the king came a fool, a traitor, and an enemy spy. On the way to the palace they made a great noise to attract the attention of the citizens and when the king received them in audience they demanded that he recall the general and chop off his head.

The king had all three boiled in oil.

Turning to the present, Ed commented that "many of us regret the passing of the good old days," and pointed out, "We always have fools, traitors and enemy spies, but we do not always have victorious generals or wise kings and less often are they contemporaneous." He developed his analogy by referring to the police chief of Los Angeles who was waging a successful war against criminals. He also referred to the statistics, "open to the investigation of any citizen, whether fool, traitor or spy," compiled by the police department and an insurance company, that demonstrated the decrease in major crimes during Davis' three years as chief. The results achieved by Davis and the esteem in which he was held were sufficient reasons why "we cannot ask the king to recall him and chop off his head."

What we can do, Ed emphasized, is to get together and insist "that the affairs of the Police Department be taken out of the hands of the fool, the traitor and the spy forever, and by that I mean taken out of politics. . . ." He closed with an emotional statement of the procedures he would adopt:

"If I were king" I should abolish the Police Commission and place the affairs of the Department absolutely in the hands of the chief; I

should pay the chief fifty thousand dollars a year and consider that a good chief was cheap at the price; I should appoint him for life and behead him only in the event that he lost too many battles, or resigned; I should muzzle the fool, for he is far more dangerous than the traitor or the spy.

Presumably, Ed's intemperate attitude, his resorting to name-calling, and his assumption that the individuals with opposing views were either fools, traitors, or spies made "A Scrambled Parable" unsuitable for publication. The parable form and the rather strained analogy centered about the king and the "chopping off" of heads did not appear appropriate for the staid *Police Reporter*. On October 28 Ed wrote to Davis to express his indignation over the charges against the Chief printed in that morning's *Los Angeles Times* and to again offer his unwavering support.

After the family trip in September 1929 from Tarzana north to Grant's Pass, Oregon, and back, Ed, delighted over the convenience of the two Aerocoaches he had purchased, wrote a brief article of appreciation. He described the Pullman Aerocoach with its "sleeping accommodations for two life-size adults in lower berths; for two thin people in upper berths; and for one sawed-off, thin person on a transverse divan, forward." The Pullman, complete with refrigerator, lavatory and kitchen stove, was towed behind the "old family dobbin" — the Packard Twin-Six Roadster Ed had been driving for ten years.

In closing his testimonial, Ed wrote, ". . . we had had the comforts of home, combined with the pleasures of camping; we had avoided the annoyances of hotel life and crowds of people. And it had all been made possible by the aerocoaches." The article appeared in *Caravan Club*, an Aerocoach publication, in 1931. Another Burroughs article of the 1929-31 period, titled "My Diversions," is a rambling account in which Ed describes both his activities and philosophies. He explained that horseback riding had been his "principal diversion" all of his life, but he would not term it a "hobby"; he believed he had no hobby in the accepted sense, because his interests were too widespread. However, viewing the matter from a different angle, and based upon a physician's definition that a man's hobby "is the thing he thinks about most," Ed turned surprisingly frank: ". . . then I presume that my hobby is one that is common to most men, for I think most about making money. . . ." His desire for money, he stressed, was not related to possession or power and not even principally to buying things for his family, friends, or "the less fortunate." His most important purpose in acquiring money was actually part of his dream: ". . . it will permit me to carry out a cherished ambition, which is to own a vast tract of land somewhere — land on which there are hills and streams and trees and rolling meadows. . . ." Above all, he sought privacy.

. . . I shall be able to afford to build an unclimbable fence ten feet high. . . . I would have no telephone and no radio. I should like to have a single gate leading into my grounds and this gate would be fastened with a padlock which could not be picked or broken; and I should have a sign on the gate that would doubtless be both rude and profane, but it would inform the world that I was minding my own business and suggest that it do the same.

This yearning for withdrawal or isolation by Burroughs must be viewed dubiously as stemming from his particular mood at the time. His social activities in the past, his numerous club memberships, and his eagerness to be chairman of various committees all indicate that he was not a man with severely introverted tendencies. Burroughs periodically reached states of disgust or extreme dissatisfaction with people and the world, but probing deeper one might suspect that the root causes were feelings of personal rejection (as an author), a belief that individuals often attempted to take advantage of him or exploit him, and a general sense of inadequacy.

The yearning for a Thoreauvian seclusion was only a facade. One who feels he had been hurt by the world may seek to withdraw from it. But in Burroughs' case this withdrawal could only be temporary. The misanthrope, sour and pessimistic, may seek retreat or live as a recluse. Burroughs, however, faced life with a general optimism.

"My Diversions" also describes his emphasis upon physical fitness; he still followed the "seventeen setting-up exercises" of the regular army, doing them and others every morning. The riding and walking in the hills provided further exercise and allowed him "to enjoy one of the most interesting chapters in Nature's book of life." He seldom was able to see the creatures that abounded in the upper pasture, but he knew they were there — "the tiny kangaroo mouse, the great pack rat, the little red fox . . . Mabel the coyote, the wild cat, the deer and the lion. . . ." On many afternoons he would drive his truck — the old Packard Twin-Six towing car with a converted body — up into the hills, skirting the El Caballero golf course as he did so. His pungent remarks about golf indicated that he had lost much of his earlier admiration of the game. He viewed it with exasperation:

Physically, golf is a pleasant diversion for me, but mentally it is hell, and from what I glean from my conversations with golfers I think it is equally as bad for most of them. Imagine a pastime that utterly ruins a man's entire holiday if he chances to hook or slice his first drive. Imagine the pleasure of a pastime that impels people to throw the implements of their diversion as far as they are physically able to, or to break them across their knees, or leap up and down upon them while they foam at the mouth and tear at their hair.

He pointed out that the simple operation of loading flagstones in his truck provided him with as much exercise as golf — minus all the frustration.

Some bitterness toward people entered his writing as he spoke of sitting close to the road runner "in silent communion" and

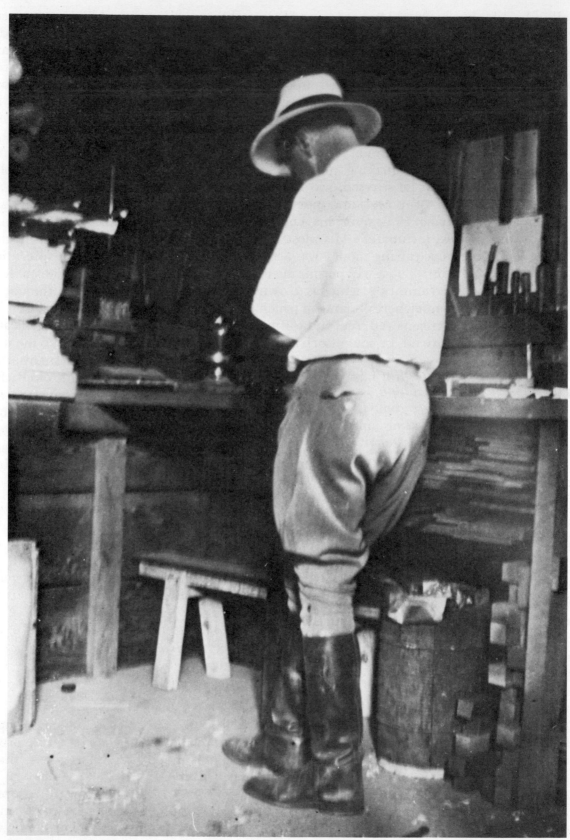

ERB in his workshop at 5046 Mecca Avenue, Tarzana, about 1928; ERB enjoyed working with wood.

noted, ". . . he is a very fine gentleman. . . he is much better company than the majority of the so-called human race. . . ." The English reviewer's comment that author Burroughs had the mind of a child of six Ed now accepted with pride; his mind was interested in simple things, "from which. . . we derive the truest happiness." He spoke finally of his indoor diversions, cards, and most important, books, and explained, "I get all the fiction that a man requires by writing it; therefore, I read none. . . ." His real hobbies and diversions, he added sentimentally, he had scarcely mentioned, but they were evident — his children, Joan, Hulbert, and Jack.

The five-page "My Diversions" has not been discovered in print, although it was written at the request of Max Elser of Metropolitan Books, the company then publishing Burroughs' novels. In sending the article to Elser on October 24, 1929, Ed expressed distaste for "this sort of stuff" which he felt was "painfully egotistical." Yet before signing an agreement with Metropolitan, he had complained that he was not being given enough personal publicity as the author of *Tarzan* and other works. Elser, determined to remedy this deficiency, was publicizing Burroughs through a variety of materials and photos. As his letter to Elser continues, Ed, quite inconsistently, emphasizes his disgust with articles of the type of "My Diversions":

It is natural for us to think that every one is interested in the things in which we are interested, but my mature judgement convinces me that such is not the fact. I do not believe that any one gives a whoop in hell what I do and I am quite positive that if any of these horrible things that I have written should appear in print, I shall have to buy a carload of Murads.

He concluded by remarking that a group of his newest photos "would go well with this inane diversion story."

The script for a slapstick melodrama, written by Ed for a home movie, is headed, "Tarzana Pictures Presents *Them Thar Papers* a superthriller of the wide open spaces outdoors with the doors open." The fact that the cast, in addition to Ed, Emma, and their two sons, lists Miss Joan Burroughs, Mr. James Pierce, and Miss Florence Gilbert, Joan's friend, indicates that the script dates about 1927-28. Tarzana provides a Western ranch setting, and the opening scene, "A quiet Sunday morning," shows the Rexall Kid, played by James Pierce, reclining in a hammock, with Our Nell (Joan Burroughs) chewing tobacco as she approaches. Ed, as "Paw Paresia," enters, shouting angrily "Whar in hell be them thar papers?" Later, after some action that includes wild shooting by Nell, Itchy Ike, the "Villian" (Hulbert Burroughs), arrives at the ranch. He crawls toward the Kid and Nell and hides behind the hammock, where he hears that "Paw will look with favor" upon anybody who gets the papers; Itchy Ike concocts a scheme to acquire these papers and thus win the girl.

When Ike, impatient, kidnaps Nell, Paw summons Gum Jones, the sheriff of Jack Knife County (Jack Burroughs). He hurries toward the ranch, bringing the "bloodhounds" (played by the dog Tarzan, son of Scallywag). The sheriff is accompanied by his daughter Little Hula, whose main occupation throughout the play is "vamping." Little Hula (Florence Gilbert) first vamps the Kid. "When he does not fall for her she tries to vamp Paw. Maw gives her a twelve pound look and she vamps the bloodhounds." Later, she vamps Itchy Ike, and when he is hanged, even attempts to vamp the corpse.

The search for the mysterious papers turns out to be a comedy of errors, with the wrong ones, cigarette papers and fly paper, being delivered to Paw. At the end of the drama the Kid triumphantly produces what Paw has been looking for — the Sunday papers. Giving the Kid and Nell his paternal blessing, Paw cries, "Take her, my boy, and God help you!"

"Them Thar Papers," written as a burlesque of the typical silent film of the period, has the standard camera instructions, including various "close-ups," "long shots," and comical titles to indicate the dialogue.

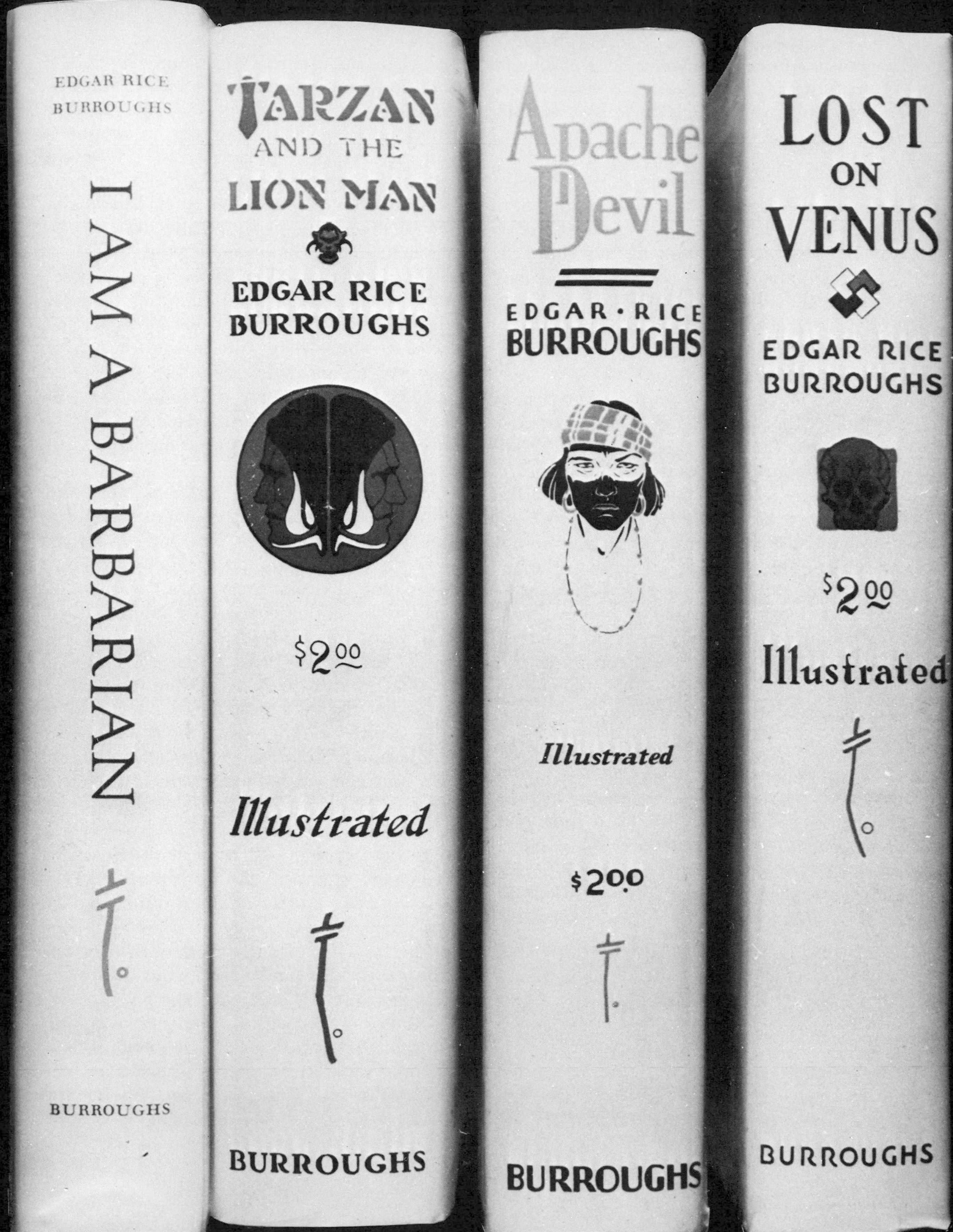

EDGAR RICE
BURROUGHS

I AM A BARBARIAN

BURROUGHS

TARZAN
AND THE
LION MAN

EDGAR RICE
BURROUGHS

$2.00

Illustrated

BURROUGHS

Apache
Devil

EDGAR · RICE
BURROUGHS

Illustrated

$2.00

BURROUGHS

LOST
ON
VENUS

EDGAR RICE
BURROUGHS

$2.00

Illustrated

BURROUGHS

20 MINOR AND MAJOR MONEY-MAKERS

Throughout the years the main sources of income from Tarzan had been the books, magazine stories, and movies, with a secondary money-making enterprise, the newspaper serials, still continuing. Added to this was a Tarzan sideline — various products featuring the famous ape-man name. While many manufacturers and distributors paid the Burroughs Corporation for the privilege, others merely appropriated the name without permission or payment. These even included individuals who assumed the name Tarzan for professional or publicity purposes. Because this unauthorized use of the name was too widespread to restrain or, for that matter, to detect, Burroughs, especially in the early years, came to accept the practice with resignation.

As early as 1921, replying to an inquiry from his brother Harry, he wrote:

No, the Tarzanette lady pays me no royalties. Anyone who seems so inclined merely swipes the name. There was a Tarzan in vaudeville here last year; there is a Tarzan wine manufactured in South America, and a Tarzan Film Company doing business in New York City. I suppose some one will soon invent a Tarzan diaper for boy babies. . . .

Apparently the first permission for the sale of Tarzan merchandise was granted to Davis & Voetsch, a New York toy manufacturer, in 1922; the company devised Tarzan monkeys. On September 27, upon receiving samples, Ed expressed his approval, noting that the entire family liked the toys, and above all "the large ape with the flexible fingers," but he doubted that it could be made at a popular price. Sales for the year totaled only $6,000; the Burroughs royalty was a mere $120.

On one occasion in 1925 Ed was happy to note the unauthorized use of the name Tarzan. To Charles Miller who had sent him clippings about the winning of the American Pacing Derby by a horse called Tarzan Grattan, Ed remarked, "This recalls to me a prophecy which I made to Thomas Metcalf, formerly the editor of All-Story Weekly, some twelve or thirteen years ago, in which I prophesied that some day a race horse would be named Tarzan. . . ."[1] In 1926, upon receiving a sheet of watermarked Tarzan bond paper from Harry, Ed sought the name of the company, informing his brother that while the product had not been authorized, he was "delighted" at its manufacture. To the company he wrote, "I forgive you for using Tarzan without my permission, and it may interest you to know that I am using Tarzan Bond for the manuscript of my latest novel. . . ."[2]

Similarly, Ed had been pleased to approve the request of actor Ken Maynard to name his horse Tarzan, and, in referring to various adoptions of the name, was inclined to view the practice with a tolerant humor:

There was a cafe in Berlin named Tarzan, and some German confectioner sold a Tarzan brand of chocolates. There is a freak down at one of the beach amusement parks called the original Tarzan. Someone registered a dog by the name of Tarzan in the American Kennel Club Stud Book and I just had a hell of a time registering my son's Old English Sheepdog under the same name, but finally got it through. . . .

He added, "These things do not harm me at all, but are helpful in spreading a mild and pleasant publicity. . . ."[3]

A Tarzan reference in the 1931 autobiography of the Prince of Wales was called to Ed's attention by his daughter Joan, about which Ed remarked, ". . . in the wildest flights of my imagination I never expected that the Crown Prince of England would name one of his horses after my meal ticket."[4] Two years later, after Stephen Slesinger, Inc., of New York had been licensed to handle all Tarzan merchandise rights, a problem arose because of Metro-Goldwyn-Mayer's transactions with various manufacturers to produce Tarzan items. A Burroughs note cautioned the film company about infringement and advised that in the use of Tarzan merchandise to promote the movies, the firm must obtain consent from Slesinger.[5]

SHEETA
the Leopard, hereditary enemy
of the Great Apes

NKIMA
the Little Monkey which often accompanies
Tarzan on his adventures

NUMA
the Lion, Tarzan's most
majestic adversary

TANTOR
the Elephant, Tarzan's Great Friend

Caricatures of various animal characters appearing in Tarzan books; John Coleman Burroughs, illustrator.

Sound truck equipped to advertise Tarzan Ice Cream Cups produced by Lily Tulip Cup Company, sponsoring ice cream company in Yonkers, New York, using Tarzan radio show.

An article by Slesinger, published in *The Boys' Outfitter,* June 1934, and titled "Tarzan Enters the Boys' Department," described the tremendous Tarzan popularity which, if utilized, could contribute to improved sales in department stores or clothing stores. Slesinger noted that over thirty-four million copies of the Tarzan books had been sold, and that the Tarzan strips, launched in 1929, were now appearing in 253 newspapers. In using the article as publicity for his licensing enterprise, Slesinger mentioned various Tarzan products: "Tarzan Bread for Energy and Strength," being distributed in two hundred cities; the Lily-Tulip Tarzan ice-cream cup; and Tarzan boys' belts.

By 1939, with the licensing of Parker Brothers for the manufacture of various types of indoor Tarzan games, the number of companies totaled twenty-six, with such items as Tarzan candy, masks and costumes, jungle maps, bathing suits, jungle helmets, yoyos, and archery sets. In correspondence with MGM, Burroughs urged that the company coordinate its publicity on the latest Tarzan film, about to be released, with the distribution of the new Parker Brothers games. Ed also suggested that the likenesses of Johnny Weissmuller and Maureen O'Sullivan be placed upon the Tarzan and Jane plaques soon to be issued.

Other unauthorized adoptions of the name

Tarzan came to Ed's attention. On May 15, 1939, he sent a warning letter to the wrestler who had assumed the name, and in the same year he became concerned about the publicity being given to a Wyoming murderer called "Tarzan." To MGM, Ed complained that this type of publicity gave young people the impression that Tarzan was a gangster. Because this could have a detrimental effect, he volunteered to join with MGM in any action they might pursue.

Most of the money-making ideas had sprung from the Burroughs imagination, but for a new project in the exploitation of Tarzan Ed was indebted to Joe H. Neebe, associated with the Campbell-Ewald Advertising Company in Detroit. Neebe, who also knew Ed's brother Harry, visited Tarzana in June 1927 and at that time revealed an inspiration that had struck him — why not try to create and sell Tarzan cartoon strips?

In August the two men agreed on a financial arrangement which provided for a fifty-fifty split of all newspaper payments, and a month later Neebe's plan to form Famous Books and Plays, Inc., to handle the strips was accepted by Ed, who was to serve on the advisory board. Sample Tarzan strips devised by Neebe brought enthusiastic approval and also a surprising suggestion; Ed spoke of "another angle" which could be profitable — "that is the burlesquing of the same subject that you treat more or less seriously." He could see no reason why the two strips "should not run on different pages of the same paper," with one evoking interest in the other. "I don't know about other authors," he wrote on October 20, "but I would be glad to authorize the burlesquing of Tarzan on the same basis as the more serious treatment of the subject...."

At the same time Neebe disclosed his intention to offer the *Tarzan of the Apes* strips to the Hearst newspapers first, at a rate of $1.50 per day per 10,000 readers. However, the two men were already envisioning another outlet: the Tarzan strips might be highly successful in book form. Since conflicts with the McClurg and Grosset & Dunlap contracts might result, permission had to be obtained from these firms. Obviously, the original book titles could not be used; on November 7 Ed suggested that the cartoon books merely be given numbers, with the first to be called *Tarzan Book No. 1,* from the novel *Tarzan of the Apes,* and others to be titled consecutively.

To aid Neebe in his plan to submit the completed strips to King Features, a Hearst-owned organization, Ed agreed to adapt a letter of endorsement which Neebe composed. In it Ed expressed his delight at seeing the drawings of Tarzan and then wrote:

I confess that I had some doubts as to the ability of anyone to successfully interpret "Tarzan of the Apes" in 300 pictures, and 15,000 words, but I must say that you have made a most successful abridgment of that 150,000 word novel.[6]

Neebe, in his request letter, recalled the evening he had spent at Tarzana in June 1927 "when Tarzan was born as a strip!"

The prospect of the strips appearing nationwide in all the Hearst newspapers placed Neebe in a temporary world of illusion. He dreamed of a huge yearly income, estimating on December 8 that the gross sales could bring a return of $187,200, with the Burroughs' share at $93,600. Ed, who noted the statement, had been too often disappointed in the past years to allow himself any unrestrained dreams; he replied jokingly, "I decided not to do any figuring as I have a weak heart, for with some twenty-eight titles in book form, I can see where we would soon make Mr. Ford take a back seat in the financial world."[7]

The Hearst *Examiner's* assignment of Burroughs to write a column in January 1928 on the Hickman trial had led him to an encouraging hope — they might wish to purchase the Tarzan strips and run them at the same time to achieve maximum publicity. Meanwhile, Neebe had submitted a sixty-four-page portfolio to King Features, its contents producing an excited reaction from the general manager. But the final word still had to come from Hearst —

© 1928 by Famous Books & Plays, Inc. All rights reserved.

| young Lord Greystoke and de of three months sailed over on their way to Africa. l been commissioned to in- te alleged atrocities on black s in a British West Coast n colony. Lord Greystoke nade the investigation, in fact er reached his destination. | Arrived at Freetown, they chartered the Fuwalda, which was to bear them to their final destination. And here, Lord and Lady Greystoke mysteriously vanished forever from the eyes and from the knowledge of man. Two months later, six British war vessels were scouring the South Atlantic for trace of them. | Beyond sight of land, the Fuwalda's captain, with a terrific blow, felled an old sailor who had accidentally tripped him. The swarthy bully's brutality caused big Black Michael to crush the captain to his knees. This was mutiny. The enraged captain suddenly whipped a re-volver from his pocket and fired. | Lord Greystoke struck down the cap-tain's arm, saving Black Michael's life and thus forged the first link of what was destined to form a chain of amazing circumstances ending in a life *for one then unborn* such as has probably never been paralleled in the history of man. | With suspicion of organized mutiny confirmed, they hurried to their quarters. Even their beds had been torn to pieces. A thorough search revealed the fact that only Lord Greystoke's revolvers and ammu-nition were gone. An undefinable something presaged bloody disaster! |

Presenting

TARZAN OF THE APES

by EDGAR RICE BURROUGHS

The Greatest Daily Feature Strip
Ever Offered Newspapers

Syndicated by

FAMOUS BOOKS AND PLAYS, Inc.

First daily newspaper strip of Tarzan of the Apes *when introduced in 1929; feature has been in continuous publication for forty-six years; Tarzan color Sunday page, started in 1931, is also still in publication.*

and it was negative. Because of his affiliation with MGM, he was adamant that a feature should not be accepted for syndication unless the motion picture rights were available to the film company.

On September 22, 1928, Neebe explained gloomily that he had spent more than $2,100 of his own money on the proposition and was with-out funds; he had decided to turn the strips over to an established syndicate: ". . . we have an opportunity to make what I consider a very ex-cellent tie-up with the Metropolitan Syndicate of New York City. . . ." With Maximilian Elser, Jr., as general manager and Earl J. Hadley as associate, the Metropolitan Newspaper Service

had become highly profitable, its best money-maker being the Ella Cinders comic strip. On September 27, Burroughs authorized an agree-ment that would include ten Tarzan novels, and soon after, upon receiving the proofs from Elser, Ed commented that he was "more than pleased" with the work of artist Harold Foster. The first six strips had already been published in the *London Tid-Bits.* Ed at once reminded Neebe of the six Martian stories which could be adapted as cartoon strips.

With January 7, 1929, set as the American release day, the financial prospects appeared excellent. On that date thirteen American newspapers began publishing the Tarzan strip;

493

the Canadian outlets were the *Toronto Star* and *Halifax Chronicle*. But on the twenty-eighth, Neebe, in reporting to stockholders of Famous Books and Plays, Inc., — the firm could pay no dividends — admitted that the strip had not fulfilled the original hopes. It had started slowly and, he believed, it would build gradually into a "big money feature."

Impressed by the seemingly efficient and aggressive activities of the Metropolitan Service, Ed had proposed that the company now take over the newspaper serialization of his stories. While conceding that he had neglected this area for "the past several years," he was frank in stating his dissatisfaction with the Bell Syndicate which had been handling the serials. Responding to Elser's request, Ed sent him a list of more than one hundred newspapers that had purchased stories in the past.[8]

By the spring of 1929 the Tarzan strips were still producing limited returns; Neebe, disappointed, sought a larger commission for Metropolitan, but Ed's response was a firm rejection. Efforts to find a publisher for a strip book were also unsuccessful. Reluctantly, Ed agreed to delay the further syndication of the stories until the performance of the strips could be evaluated. Some encouraging news, however, was soon received. Grosset & Dunlap had decided to publish the Tarzan strips in book form. In August 1929 *The Illustrated Tarzan Book No. 1* appeared, and Ed noted that Foster's work was "splendid" but that he was "not so keen" about the drawings of the "other artist," whose figures were "all wooden, even when supposed to be in action."

In the passing months, through the concentrated efforts of Elser and the Metropolitan Service, the income from the Tarzan strips increased steadily. The main problem, as far as Ed was concerned, lay in the selection of an artist with adequate ability and imagination. In his view, J. Allen St. John towered above the others in the field, but he conceded that Harold Foster had done excellent work on *Tarzan of the Apes*. As the succession of novels continued

to be transformed into strips, Ed did not hesitate to offer blunt comments about the various artists' drawings. For the adaptation of *The Return of Tarzan*, Metropolitan, unable to obtain Foster for the newspaper strips, chose Rex Maxon. In evaluating the cartoons, Ed included the criticisms of his sixteen-year old son Jack. A close student of Tarzan and artistically inclined himself, Jack was disappointed in the drawings, and both he and his father felt that Maxon "could put more character into Tarzan's face. . . ."[9]

Although he had occasionally noted that Maxon's drawings were improving, Ed generally disapproved of the strips. To Elser on January 29, 1930, he wrote, ". . . I have never been wildly enthusiastic about Maxon's work. To me the strips have no character whatsoever and are being carried solely on the strength of the story, which should not be wholly true." He enclosed a lengthy criticism of Maxon and his work prepared by a close friend, a "highly successful commercial artist," who observed that Maxon was "an extremely slow worker" and used poor technique for his figures. In 1931, however, the advent of the latest innovation, the Tarzan Sunday color pages, brought praise from Ed and the remark to George Carlin of the United Feature Syndicate that the work was "very much better." A letter of thanks came from Maxon, and Burroughs, with appreciation, responded, "I didn't know that anyone ever gave a damn what an author thought about anything." Displaying a sympathetic attitude, he was diplomatic in noting the problem Maxon faced in creating daily strips that would "suit" everyone, adding that in the color pages he had "entered more than ever into the spirit of the story."[10]

That summer Neebe reported plans to change the artists who were preparing the strips and mentioned that United Features had contacted Paul Berdanier. Dismayed, Burroughs wrote, ". . . we cannot say very much for him. In fact, we consider him to be worse than Mr. Maxon. Why not get Foster to do the strips? We believe you will admit that the best art work on the strips to date was that done by

Cover of The Illustrated Tarzan Book No. 1 Picturized from the Novel Tarzan of the Apes by Edgar Rice Burroughs, *hardcover book published by Grosset and Dunlap in 1929; contains Hal Foster* Tarzan *daily newspaper strips.*

Foster. . . ."[11] A few weeks later, upon being notified that Foster had agreed to draw the color pages, Burroughs replied that he was "highly elated." Maxon continued to create the daily strips and Ed maintained his unchanging criticisms: ". . . Maxon's work is slipping a little again. What do you think?" In urging that St. John be hired for the strips, Ed remarked ". . . I may be hypercritical as to Maxon's work. . . I felt that if you have the same opinion. . . that I have, my criticisms might fortify any intentions that you may have been harboring to make a change. . . ."[12] He believed that "with a little care and research" Maxon could correct some of his faults; the main weakness was found in his animals: ". . . His antelopes . . . are not as graceful and beautiful as they should be. . . ." Ed suggested that Maxon should obtain pictures of all the animals and study these carefully.

On various occasions Burroughs had voiced his objections, at times in annoyance, to the beliefs of certain critics and reviewers, as well as a segment of the public, that the Tarzan stories were designed for children. Certainly thousands of children read his books, but he wrote them for adults, and the great popularity of the books was caused by their appeal to adults. He was especially sensitive and resentful about assumptions, evident in the critics' statements, that he was a children's writer; these were the same critics, of course, who excluded him from their approved "literary" coteries, and by lowering him to the child's level, they were further disparaging his writing ability. But there was an additional reason for his rejection of the "juvenile" label: if accepted by the public, the editors, and movie producers, it could lead to the destruction of the Tarzan market.

Burroughs had the same attitude toward the Tarzan newspaper strips. On April 17, 1931, in a letter to George Carlin of United Features, he cautioned about the use of children in the Sunday color page and commented, ". . . the only Tarzan story that I ever wrote which is a flop is a juvenile called The Tarzan Twins, written around two boys. My readers, adults as well as children, simply did not seem to want this type of story." He closed with advice: ". . . when we are through with these children in their youth I believe it would be wise to confine ourselves to adults in the future as principal characters." Carlin's response that the Sunday color page was quite different from the daily strip and that the "major focus" of its appeal "lies in the audience of quite small children" caused Ed to express his concern. He was worried about the effect the "juvenile" element in the color pages might have on his book sales. He wrote, "I am constantly endeavoring to impress on the public that the stories are primarily . . . for adults. . . ."

The emphasis upon children in the Sunday page, the featuring of the "Bob and Mary characters," was the subject of a conference held between Rothmund and Carlin in New York. But this meeting and Burroughs' objections had little result, and on June 29, 1931, Rothmund echoed the alarm of the Burroughs organization, mentioning the "considerable adverse comment on the child aspect of the color page," and writing:

It is entirely too juvenile, not at all like anything Mr. Burroughs has ever connected Tarzan with and there is a strong possibility that it will in time relegate Tarzan exclusively to the juvenile class — something that we have been endeavoring and shall direct our future efforts to overcome.

Noting the absence of children in the daily strips, Rothmund observed that the popularity of these remained high and urged that the Sunday page either eliminate the children or age them "another ten years." He attacked "this strictly childish atmosphere" and stated, ". . . it is hurting the entire Tarzan property and may result in its ultimate ruination." On July 7 Carlin agreed to be guided by Burroughs' wishes and wrote, "We will . . . bring to an end the sequences regarding Bob and Mary. Thereafter, we will try to make Tarzan a more adult product." The change could not be made suddenly, but Carlin remarked, "we ought to be able to get the children home to their daddy within the next three or four color pages."

For a number of years Burroughs had been dissatisfied with the royalties paid to him by McClurg; he felt that some change in publishers was necessary, yet he could not drive himself to a final breakup. By the spring of 1929, however, in Ed's mind matters had reached a climax. At various periods he had noted the reports of the large incomes earned by other authors. The disclosure that they were being paid far more than he brought him to a state of impatience and frustration. The author with whom he often made comparisons, especially in his letters to Bray and Davis, was Zane Grey. Ed surveyed with envy the accounts of Grey's phenomenal success and his tremendous income. On April 1, 1929, Ed addressed to Bray a "personal" letter "from one friend to another"; the subject was his royalties:

I understand from Mr. Grossett that I am one of the three best copyright sellers. The last royalty statement shows about two hundred and fifty thousand copies for half a year and yet my income is measly compared with that of many other writers, though I doubt if there are many whose books sell as well as mine. What is wrong?

The obvious inference was that other writers were being paid larger royalties than he. Ed wrote, "Zane Grey, the only writer who probably tops my sales, owns yachts and beautiful summer homes. He cruises all over the world, while I sit here with my nose to the grindstone." Burroughs had chosen to ignore his financial entanglements, his losses in the El Caballero Country Club and other unwise investments, and his "land-poor" situation.

He informed Bray frankly that only their friendship had prevented him from leaving McClurg several years earlier. He believed he should have published his own books; in that way he would have received all of the royalties, instead of splitting fifty-fifty. "I think it was damn poor business that I did not do it," Ed stated, and later in the letter added, ". . . I am not very much of a business man. . . ." He

closed defiantly, "I am getting sick of worrying over finances and I have determined to increase my income in every possible legitimate way."

On April 2 Ed dictated an angry memorandum that seemed both a reminder to prod himself toward new goals and an ultimatum to the world at large. He announced his intention to publish his own books, with Grosset & Dunlap handling the reprints, unless McClurg agreed to a new arrangement with the following provisions:

An increased royalty on first editions.
75% of McClurg's royalty on popular copyright.
All book rights in future works to be returned to him after ten years.
All book rights up to 1924 to revert to him in 1934, and those book rights subsequent to 1924 to revert to him ten years after the date of publication.

Bray, in his response of April 9, maintained that Ed's complaints about his sales and royalties were not justified. All reprint sales, including those of Zane Grey and Harold Bell Wright, had fallen off sharply. Furthermore, the sales of Zane Grey's original editions had decreased in about the same proportion as those of Burroughs. In a long discussion of Zane Grey's success, Bray noted the most important reasons: Grey "contrives to keep his name before the public through his serials"; he has a constant succession of new movies and is associated with one of the best film concerns, Favorite Players. "The last time I saw him, which was several years ago," Bray wrote, "he said he cleaned up annually over a quarter of a million dollars."

Burroughs' main problem, Bray insisted, was his failure to have sufficient stories produced as films. "There isn't a writer of prominence today who doesn't get, I would say, practically all of his stuff used in the movie world. . . . What's the trouble anyway?"

Bray, who explained that he could not afford a California trip, that he was heavily in debt, but that he would not know what to do with a big income if he had it, made an acute observation: he had succeeded in putting McClurg on its feet through economy; he watched expenses "like a hawk." He asked, "Are you doing the same thing? It's all the difference between happiness and worry." He was obviously aware of Burroughs' extravagances.[13]

As the debate continued, Ed admitted his concern about the limited movie production, remarking, "I cannot alter the fact that producers are not interested." The reasons were beyond him, since all of his films had been money-makers. He wrote:

It may be purely a matter of my personality. Some of these people know me and it is very possible that they do not like me. I have been a little bit high-handed with them because I consider most of them ignoramuses and crooks. With one exception, they have practically all gipped me or tried to gip me, and I have many thousands of royalties outstanding that I cannot collect.[14]

Ed made a wry confession: "You were also right about my expenses. They are altogether too high, but nothing short of an act of God can reduce them."

After serving notice that McClurg should make no plans to publish another book until new arrangements were made, Ed emphasized that the best way to increase his sales would be to give him more personal publicity. He recalled that several years before he had suggested that his name appear at the top of every other page in his books. He wanted new photos of himself on each jacket and more newspaper publicity. Bray was willing to cooperate in providing more publicity and even made some concessions on reprint royalties, granting Burroughs seventy-five percent on sales above 50,000, but in the matter of "retroactive" payments — a larger royalty to apply on both new titles and on the sale of old titles from the time the agreement went into effect — he sent a firm refusal.[15] On May 7, 1929, Bray made it plain that Ed's demands were impossible:

What you are asking . . . is that we surrender to you a big proportion of the rights we enjoy in your books under contract with you. Do you think there is any concern in the whole wide world that would do this? I don't. . . . I am sorry, but the old contracts, which at the time they were made were satisfactory to both of us, cannot be altered in accordance with your wishes. . . .

With matters at a stalemate, on May 18 Bray sent an inquiry — would McClurg publish a new Tarzan book or not? Ed decided that a personal conference was necessary and hastened to Chicago; at the same time he set a date for a meeting with Elser in New York. The failure of the Chicago conference was inevitable. Bray could not make any further concessions and Ed would not yield. The end of the McClurg reign as the Burroughs publisher — initiated in 1914 with *Tarzan of the Apes* — was made evident by Ed's succinct entry on a McClurg letter: "Got both Mss. when in Chgo." The stories repossessed were "Apache Devil" and "Tarzan and the Lost Empire."

Upon the elimination of McClurg, Burroughs' plans to publish his own books were temporarily thrust aside, and at the May 28 meeting with Elser, Metropolitan Service became the new publisher. In June a contract was signed and "Tarzan and the Lost Empire," was forwarded to Elser. The popular copyrights (reprints) would be retained by Grosset & Dunlap.

The period of contention with McClurg that culminated in the breakup was matched by a similar period in connection with the Burroughs foreign rights. His unhappiness over his British sales had been steadily growing, and while he had lost faith in Methuen and other publishers, he was also inclined to blame his agent, Curtis Brown. On April 1, 1930, without any forewarning, he sent a curt letter to them: "Please do not place any more of my foreign language rights, as we are making other arrangements for the handling of these. We will also take care of future Tauchnitz titles." Ob-

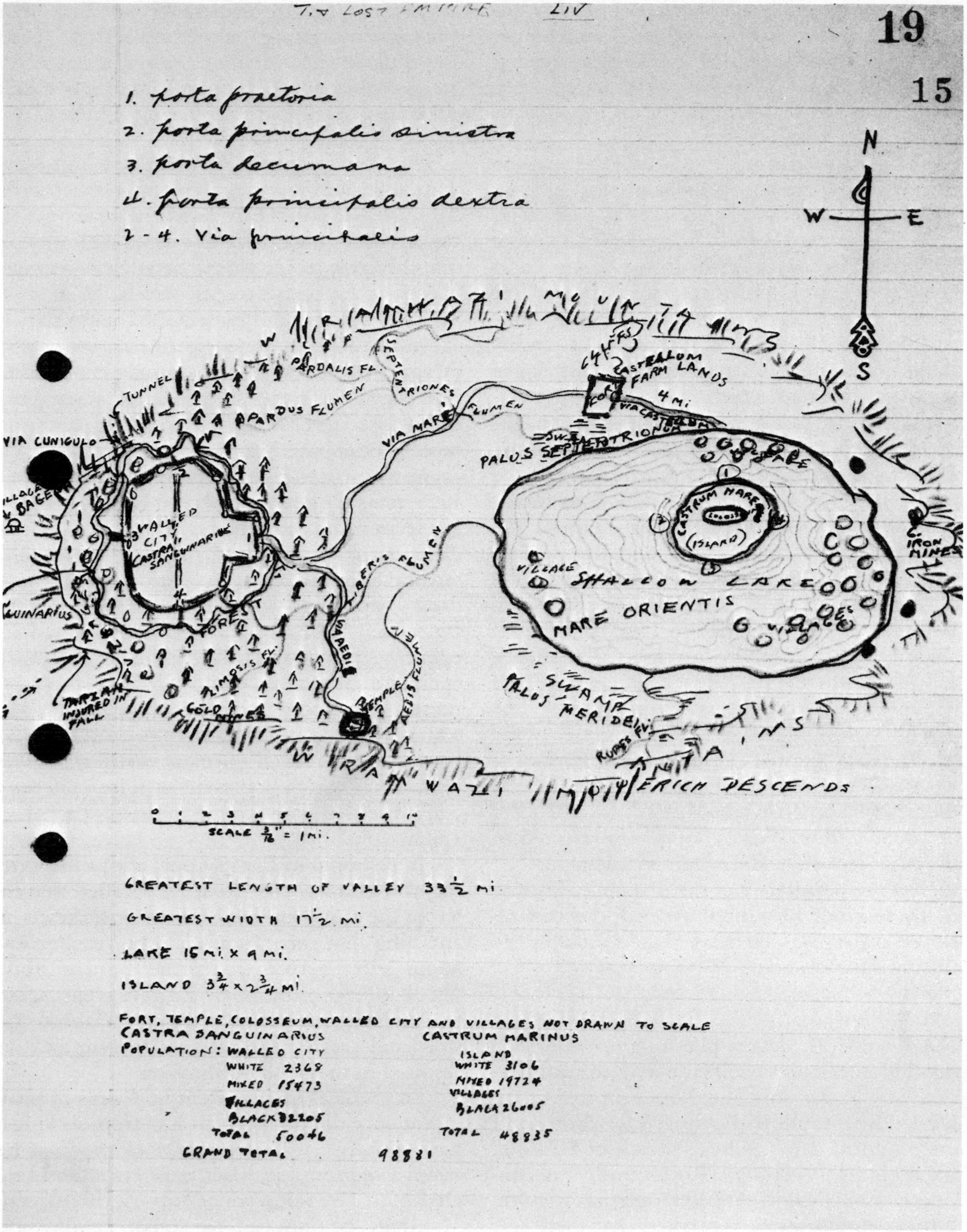

19
15
1. porta praetoria
2. porta principalis sinistra
3. porta decumana
4. porta principalis dextra
2 - 4. Via principalis
N
W
E
S
TUNNEL
VIA CUNICULO
PARDALIS FL.
PARDUS FLUMEN
SEPTENTRIONES
VIA MARE
FLUMEN
FARM LANDS
4 mi.
PALUS SEPTENTRIONALIS
WALLED CITY
CASTRA SANGUINARIUS
CASTRUM MARE
(ISLAND)
VILLAGE
SHALLOW LAKE
MARE ORIENTIS
VILLAGES
IRON MINES
FOREST
TIBERIS FLUMEN
GOLD MINES
TARZAN INJURED IN FALL
TEMPLE
SWAMP
PALUS MERIDE
WAZIRI MOUNTAINS
ERICH DESCENDS
SCALE 3/16" = 1 mi.
GREATEST LENGTH OF VALLEY 33 1/2 mi.
GREATEST WIDTH 17 1/2 mi.
LAKE 15 mi. x 9 mi.
ISLAND 3 3/4 x 2 3/4 mi.
FORT, TEMPLE, COLOSSEUM, WALLED CITY AND VILLAGES NOT DRAWN TO SCALE
CASTRA SANGUINARIUS
POPULATION: WALLED CITY
WHITE 2368
MIXED 15473
VILLAGES
BLACK 32205
TOTAL 50046
CASTRUM MARINUS
ISLAND
WHITE 3106
MIXED 19724
VILLAGES
BLACK 26005
TOTAL 48835
GRAND TOTAL 98881

ERB's map for Tarzan and the Lost Empire.

viously stunned, Jean Watson, whom Ed had praised highly in the past, wrote, "Surely some explanation is due to us of this sudden decision which you have taken? It is not usual for a step of this kind to be taken by an author without giving an agent an explanation. . . ."[16]

The Burroughs reply of May 5 was brusque and coldly formal. Although sales had increased in the United States, they had fallen off greatly in foreign countries, the letter noted; it appeared hardly worthwhile for an agent to occupy any time with these small sales. The foreign rights were "almost worthless" now, and therefore "there was nothing to be jeopardized" by a decision to have the Burroughs organization handle them.

With the publication of new Burroughs novels in the hands of Elser and Metropolitan, Ed, on June 8, 1929, contacted Bray about the possibility of repurchasing all of his book rights. He mentioned his hope of issuing *Tarzan of the Apes* in a gift edition with colored illustrations, in time for the Christmas trade. Replying, Bray informed him that 375,000 copies of the popular reprints had been sold in 1928, and that as far as he could estimate, the rights were valued at "somewhere in the neighborhood of $190,000." Through his launching of the Tarzan strips, Ed had increased the value of the books. Bray quoted the opinion of Grosset & Dunlap that the publicity given the novels by the newspaper strips would result in "plus sales of a half million extra." Bray also referred to the experience of a Metropolitan salesman: ". . . such is the popularity of the Tarzan strips that in three cities he visited recently he had received orders . . . for more than a thousand of the new Tarzan book."[17]

Meanwhile, Elser, planning to release a flood of publicity to coincide with the publication of "Tarzan and the Lost Empire," bombarded Burroughs with requests for photos and biographical data. A brief sketch of Ed's life, assembled by secretary Rothmund, was considered insufficient. At Elser's urging for more, Ed was embarrassed, remarked that there was

"absolutely nothing interesting to record," sent some "uninteresting" details and added: "I am one of those unfortunate people who has never had an adventure. If I go to a fire it is either out before I arrive or proves to have been a false alarm."[18] Concerning the plan to put his picture on the book jacket, Ed protested, and asked that more publicity be given to the Burroughs family. Elser noted Ed's dislike of formal poses, but wrote, ". . . we just can't agree with you . . . that the book jacket should carry a photograph of Jack or anybody except yourself."[19]

Elser's demands for detailed information drove Ed to hastily dictating the *Autobiography* of some 20,000 words, opening with a brief reference to his father's army career, tracing the early days in Chicago, and ending with his success established in 1913. The *Autobiography* was sent to Elser from July to September 1929 in installments; on September 20, with the last section, Ed commented in disgust, ". . . this damn thing bores me to extinction. How could anyone have endured fifty-four such dull and dreary years and still remain sane, I cannot conceive." He had considered the dictated account "merely as an outline for fuller and more complete treatment later," if this were warranted, but upon reading the *Autobiography* was convinced that further effort upon it would be wasted. "With this present installment," he remarked, "which brings me well into the time when I settled down to the business of writing, I shall quit."

In response to Elser's query about the writing of *Tarzan of the Apes*, Ed recalled that he wrote the story "on backs of old letterheads or anything that came handy." The recollection about letterheads is inaccurate; he was thinking of *A Princess of Mars*. Ed gave credit again to the *New York World* which serialized the story and created the nationwide interest that resulted in the book publication.

Ed's typical involvement in dozens of projects at once did not prevent him from seeking a new activity. In a repetition of the past he wired a request that Elser must have found incredible. The telegram of July 17, 1929, read, "I might be induced to accept commission correspondent Russo-Chinese scrap. How about it?" Elser replied, "We have no facilities for handling Russo Chinese war correspondent nor do we know of any New York news organization which not already covered by previous arrangements for far eastern News." On July 18 Ed confessed that he was "rather relieved" when he received Elser's telegram; "It would be wonderful publicity and might tend to increase the value of my book rights as well as my syndicate rights, but the idea of leaving Tarzana left me cold."

Because "Tarzan and the Lost Empire" would be the first Metropolitan book, Ed took extreme care with the proofs sent to him by Elser. He had never objected to corrections of faulty English, but he would not permit other types of changes or deletions. In his list of comments he stressed that he preferred the natural word to the euphemisms chosen by the editor:

Page 145: Changing "murderers and thieves" to "felons" does not suit me. I prefer "murderers and thieves." These words, like "corpse" instead of "body," have more power. They are stronger words and they make a deeper impression.

Page 164: I try to use as little profanity in my stories as possible, but I do not believe that the use of the word "God" as an exclamation on this page is profane, and certainly none of my characters, if they are supposed to be heroic, would ever say, "Heavens!" or "Sugar!" or "Oh Fudge!" Such changes take the guts out of dialogue.[20]

With Ed receiving the number one copy of *Tarzan and the Lost Empire* on September 9, the novel was officially released about a week later, distribution to be handled by the American News Company. Other Metropolitan matters included the "stretching out" of the Tarzan strips, which Ed had approved, believing that they might end too soon, but on October 4, the complaint from the *Toronto Star* that the series was beginning to "thin out" and that they wanted to see advance proofs before accepting the strips caused him to reverse his attitude. At the same time, discouraging reports about

Grosset & Dunlap's Tarzan strip book revealed the sales to be quite low.

Ed sought Elser's advice on what appeared to be an excellent business opportunity. He had been urged to invest in the Los Angeles Monkey Farm, and his knowledge of the success achieved by Gay's Lion Farm made him believe that a second project might be profitable. Elser, opposed to the idea, noted from the literature that the stockholders lacked confidence in the project. He doubted that the connection would benefit Burroughs and thought it extremely inadvisable for the author of *Tarzan* to "bring his following down to earth." He wrote, ". . . Tarzan's background being the great jungles, and his friends the apes who roam through the great jungles, would not the reader illusion be spoiled by the perspective of many readers being focused down to a commercial monkey farm?"[21] Ed agreed at once with Elser's reasoning.

Once more The Tribes of Tarzan, organized originally by Herman Newman, came to Burroughs' attention. A letter from W. L. Foster of the *Pittsburgh Press,* received by Elser, reported that several Tribes of Tarzan were being formed in the Pittsburgh area for boys from ten to eighteen years of age, with the plan to base these Tribes on the principles of Tarzan as presented in the newspaper strip. Foster noted that the Tribes had been instigated by Herman Newman, "who holds copyright on the fraternal workings and general details of the tribe by special permission of Edgar Rice Burroughs." Elser, on October 19, 1929, inquired whether Newman actually held these rights, and on the twenty-eighth Ed replied that he had never authorized Newman or anyone else to take out a copyright on the Tribes.

From Foster, in charge of circulation promotion, came a letter on December 11 with information about the new organization plans, now that Newman had "dropped completely out of the picture." The original formation of large, unwieldy Tribes was abandoned, as was the ritual, and in the new plan the basic group consisted of only eight boys, to be called a "Dotema," with from three to six of these groups to form a "Soceum." These names and those of the officers were adopted from organizations among the Hopi Indian boys; Foster, who disclosed that the son of the chief of chiefs of the Hopi Indians was in Pittsburgh to assist *The Press,* stated that the city's grand Tribe of Tarzan contained about 1,000 boys who had been given the oath. Approving, Ed at once sent various suggestions, the first being that the whole organization be known as the International Tribe of Tarzan, with branches first established in Canada and England. A further idea revolved about the use of an "African totem" for the name of each Tribe, this being an animal or object. Thus there would be a Numa (lion) Tribe, a Tantor (elephant) Tribe, or even a Waziri Tribe. Ed's final suggestion was that President Herbert Hoover be asked to accept the position of honorary president of the International Tribe of Tarzan.[22]

With 1929 almost at end, Burroughs forwarded an unusual request to Elser. Noting that the new Webster's International Dictionary did not include his name in the biographical section, and that *Tarzan* was not listed among the words, Ed asked Elser to contact the publisher. "It is a rather difficult and delicate matter for me to take up," he remarked. Elser, on December 24, promised to send a request to both Webster's and Funk and Wagnall's Dictionaries, and in the revised editions author Burroughs and Tarzan were listed.

The second book scheduled for publication by Metropolitan was "Tanar of Pellucidar," and upon receiving Berdanier's rough sketch for the cover, Ed, as usual, had criticisms to offer. He had not been pleased with Berdanier in the past and made no bones about it now: "Tanar is too effeminate, and in this rough sketch looks like a sap. He is holding the bow in an effeminate manner. His legs are a woman's legs. He should be grasping the bow or spear in a firm masculine grasp." Ed followed with other instructions: "Make Stellara's garb as scant as

possible and do not fashion it like a skirt or bodice. It was only a bit of skin and should not make her look like a ballet dancer, but should permit all of the contours of her body to be suggested. . . ." He conceded that he liked the mastodon, which "forms a striking background for the figures."[23]

On February 12, 1930, with the receipt of the proofs and frontispiece of "Tanar of Pellucidar," Ed was even more forceful in his criticisms: "It seems quite obvious that Mr. Berdanier did not use models. The lower legs and especially the left foot of Tanar are almost deformities. . . . If, however, the price has anything to do with the quality of this work, I suggest that in the future it would be better to pay more for one good illustration to be used on the jacket than to have two inferior illustrations." He reminded Elser again that J. Allen St. John should have been hired. In his stories Ed created his characters in vivid detail so that the readers could visualize them. He therefore felt that a perceptive artist would study the text carefully before preparing the sketches. This was the procedure which St. John followed.

The writers of various articles about Burroughs had been amused to note that the author of *Tarzan* had never been to Africa. Indeed, he had never been abroad and displayed no interest in travel of this type. His farthest journey had been to Cuba, while en route to New York through the Panama Canal. When he did conceive of overseas travel in March 1930, it was typical that it came as a brainstorm — a trip to be undertaken mainly for publicity purposes. To Elser he spoke of "business harassments" which had affected his health; he reported, "I blew up in the doctor's office and nearly passed out. . . ." Another doctor advised him to take a long trip, but this, Ed insisted, he could not afford. He then gave details of the plan that occurred to him:

Linking itself very nicely with the idea of a long sea voyage is the fact that I am starting a new Tarzan story, which necessitates knowing something about Eritria and French Somali Land, concerning neither of which have I been able to find any books or anything in the Encyclopedia Britannica which gives me the information that I desire.

He added, "It, therefore, occurs to me that if I take a trip I might as well go to Eritria and French Somali Land, but that is going to cost something, here is where you come in."

To pay the expenses he proposed to write a "book-length travel story" which Metropolitan would publish and then syndicate; this project would also increase his prestige as an author. The book would be written in a style similar to his *Autobiography,* and would develop the idea "that having discovered Africa some twenty years ago," it might be a good plan for him "to go over and look at it." He asked Elser to advise whether the whole plan was impractical; his own skepticism was evident: "I can just as well take a sea voyage to Catalina Island with probably as good results." Elser was not encouraging and urged him to delay any decision. On the twenty-fifth Ed wrote, "There is no hurry about the African trip. The chances are I will never get much further than the idea, as I seem to be permanently tied down by business matters. . . ."

Several months later the inspiration for a new Tarzan enterprise, one that was truly feasible, came to him. On May 1, 1930, he remarked to Elser, "I have evolved a wild and possibly ludicrous plan of publicity for *Tarzan and the Lost Empire* or any other book you might suggest. . . ." He mentioned the strong interest of the radio public in continued stories, such as Amos and Andy, and then wrote, ". . . there might be possibilities in the reading of one of my books by myself over the radio for fifteen minutes nightly in conjunction with some program having a national hook-up."

The originator of the Tarzan strip idea, Joe Neebe, had severed his connections with the Campbell-Ewald Company, taken charge of another advertising agency branch and dropped that, and then progressed to selling radio programs for Sound Studios Company at their Detroit office. Apparently, he, Elser, and Burroughs were seized by the radio inspiration at about the same time. Upon hearing from Neebe, Ed expressed surprise at the "radio hunch" that had come to all three "simultaneously." Elser's response told of making inquiries in the radio field for several months; he planned to discuss the matter of a Burroughs program with Monte Bourjaily, general manager of a new consolidation — Metropolitan and United Feature Syndicate had just combined. On May 12 Elser made a proposal: he would handle the radio arrangements and grant Burroughs sixty percent of the proceeds. Elser was uncertain about whether Neebe should be compensated, but on this matter Ed was firm. The agreement with Neebe included only the strips; the radio rights were "separate and distinct." Ed would not sign a five-year contract but was willing to try the programs on Elser's terms, using one Burroughs book. Ed confessed that he would prefer not to broadcast personally; although his voice carried clearly, he had exhibited "extreme nervousness" in past broadcasts. He felt, however, that he would overcome this with the use of "familiar copy" and if he were not required to speak extemporaneously.[24]

The hope that some profitable arrangement might be made for a *Tarzan of the Apes* radio program gradually diminished. Elser's 1930 promises to "put Edgar Rice Burroughs over on the radio" had not materialized, and in March 1931, in response to a query about radio rights from Neebe, then with the World Broadcasting System, Ed noted that he had heard nothing on the subject for some time. Actually, a number of proposals to broadcast Tarzan stories had been received, but Ed, judging by past experiences with film producers and other entrepreneurs, had become cautious. He believed the new field of radio could provide great money-making opportunities and he was determined to find a reliable and imaginative organization to handle the marketing of *Tarzan.* Above all, Ed was waiting for presentation ideas that would do justice to the ape-man, and at the end of 1931 he found what he wanted. To Frederick C. Dahlquist, president of the American Radio Syndicate, who had submitted ma-

Jim Pierce and Joan Burroughs Pierce, Tarzan and Jane in highly successful Tarzan *radio show.*

terial, Ed wrote, ". . . we have never had presented to us a plan of presentation which met with our approval until you became interested and developed your ideas. . . ."[25]

In 1932 the radio feature, consisting of transcriptions prepared for a fifteen-minute, six-day-a-week broadcast, was placed on the market. *Tarzan of the Apes* was dramatized using a new technique, a combination of dialogue and narration with elaborate sound effects. The Burroughs family was especially elated because the leading roles were assigned to daughter Joan and her husband James Pierce. Joan made her first appearance as Jane Clayton in the third episode, while Jim, cast as Tarzan, did not appear until much later. His earlier adventures were described by a narrator, since Tarzan, in the book, had not as yet learned to speak English during this period.

To his niece Mrs. Carleton (Evelyn) McKenzie, on February 29, Ed described the sound effects created in the first two episodes: "They

have injected all of the jungle noises, including the roaring of Numa, the lion, the screaming of Sheeta, the panther, the cries of the bull apes, the laughing of the hyenas, the rustling of the leaves, the screams and shots — you can almost hear the blood gushing out of jugulars." Even more than with the proofs of his stories, Ed maintained a close scrutiny over the radio scripts that were submitted to him; his letters to Dahlquist during June 1932 had specific criticisms and requests for changes. Episodes three and four, as with the previous ones, showed an "evident haste and carelessness of preparation," especially in the numerous errors in grammar: "I am sure Mr. Doyle knows better than to use laying for lying and present and past tenses in the same sentence." Ed was pained by Doyle's misconception of the character of Tarzan: "Tarzan must never show fear or terror. He is not supposed to know what fear means."

He was firmly disapproving of the Tarzan "laugh" prescribed in the script, the laugh, in his opinion, being neither necessary nor wise. He wrote, "He never laughed and seldom smiled during his association with the beasts. It is very possible that he might laugh later on when in the society of men, but even then I think it better to keep him always in character, which as I explained . . . should be more or less grim and terrible in a quiet, dignified way." Ed further stressed that "little or no comedy" should be written for the Tarzan episodes, but indicated that he had no objection to comedy "as long as Tarzan had no part in it." He offered limited praise; he could find no fault with "the dramatic presentation of the episodes."[26]

With Burroughs' approval of the radio programs, a three-year contract was signed, granting Dahlquist the Tarzan radio rights and an option for renewal. This agreement, in turn, brought a three-year contract for Joan and Jim guaranteeing their employment for the entire series. As with past projects, however, Ed could not be satisfied with allowing someone else to reap the lion's share of the profits; he was already planning to transfer control of the programs to his own corporation. Ed explained matters to Neebe, whose request for radio rights had been turned down. Dahlquist was required to sell the feature within a certain time; if he failed to do so, the contract was void, and Ed then intended to market the programs himself. He commented, "During the past six months I have learned enough about radio and the demand for Tarzan to know that it is not necessary for me to pay a middleman. This I have already explained to Mr. Dahlquist."[27]

From its inception the sale of the Tarzan radio-transcription series appeared a certainty. Various exploitation gimmicks and give-away items were devised to stimulate the sponsors' interest. Ed arranged for the manufacture of small clay figures of the characters and animals in the Tarzan stories, these to be distributed by the sponsors. Through the efforts of Neebe, now vice-president and general manager of Essex Broadcasters in Detroit, the Foulds Milling Company had purchased the program for five-day-a-week broadcast on Station WKOK. Foulds was reported to have taken an option on all territory east of California and to be sponsoring "the highest priced dramatic broadcast ever put on the air. . . ."[28] The eagerness of large companies to buy the Tarzan series was illustrated in the estimate sent by Ed to his brother Harry; the cost of these programs to sponsors was "simply staggering" and according to the producers could approximate $800,000 a year for forty stations.

Dahlquist was devising every means of publicity to sell the program on the West Coast. To have the records available for sponsor auditions, he offered leading advertising agencies the first six episodes plus the special theme record at a total cost of $17.50. In August 1932 exclusive broadcasting rights in the Tarzan series were purchased by the Signal Oil Company with plans for five-day airings on KPO in San Francisco and KPX in Los Angeles. With the jig-saw puzzle craze sweeping the country, Signal created its own Tarzan Jig-Saw Puzzle Contest, and all materials were distributed at the Signal gas stations.

The soaring Tarzan popularity brought a

Gale Gordon and Joan Pierce in Tarzan radio show.

letter to Burroughs from a British reader; the story it contained was so amusing that secretary Rothmund, on December 31, 1932, could not refrain from "passing it on" to H. E. Ransford of the Signal Oil Company:

A teacher asked a little boy to explain the word 'Tarzan'. The boy said: "It is the name of a flag." "How do you make that out?" asked the teacher indulgently. "Why," said the boy, "the flag of America — Tarzan Stripes."

On September 10 the radio premier on record was presented at the Fox Pantages Theater in Hollywood, where the audience heard the first episode of *Tarzan of the Apes*. Burroughs, daughter Joan, and Jim Pierce made brief speeches. The release date for nationwide radio stations was the twelfth, and a month later, with the program and the puzzle contest a huge success, Signal began the organization of a Tarzan Club, complete with membership card, club button, and a chance to win prizes.

Volume 1. No. 3   PUBLISHED BY THE SIGNAL OIL & GAS CO. IN THE INTEREST OF ITS DEALERS   September, 1932

TARZAN PROGRAM OFF TO FLYING START

WORLD PREMIERE INTRODUCES RADIO TARZAN TO THOUSANDS

Saturday, September 10th, the first Radio Premiere on record presented to radio fans all over the State the first episode in the thrilling adventures of "Tarzan of the Apes," sponsored by the Signal Oil and Gas Company.

Critics and thousands of motorists who jammed the World Premiere Radio Show at Fox Pantages Theatre in Hollywood proclaimed it the most fascinating and colorful radio program they had ever heard.

Among those who participated in the stage show were Jim Pierce, all-American football player and well-known actor, who takes the part of Tarzan in Signal's sensational radio serial; Miss Joan Burroughs, talented actress and daughter of Edgar Rice Burroughs; Mr. Burroughs himself, internationally known author of all "Tarzan" stories, together with the entire Tarzan radio cast, including Lord and Lady Graystoke, Captain Tracy, Cecil Clayton, Yont, Professor Porter, Philander, James

Time Down South"; Cliff Arquette, in his characterization, "Aunt Hat"; Mary Rossetti, versatile singer, and the KNX Rangers appeared in the stage show.

Eddie Lambert, star comedian and producer of the "Nine o'Clock Revue," acted as Master of Ceremonies for the show while Freeman Lang, inimitable Master of Ceremonies at so many Hollywood Premieres, presided over the "mike" to introduce the screen stars as well as the leading lights of radio land.

Included among the guests of the Company were several hundred Signal dealers and their families, Company employees and their families, and representatives from other oil companies, the California Oil and Gas Association and representatives from all the press.

Thousands of radio fans who were unable to attend in person enjoyed the premiere through the courtesy of KNX, who broadcast the entire three

Jim Pierce as Tarzan, Joan Burroughs, daughter of Edgar Rice Burroughs, feminine lead, and Mary, mammoth Chimpanzee from California Zoological Gardens, taking possession of Signal truck in absence of driver.

JIG-SAW PUZZLE CONTEST TO START TUESDAY, SEPT. 20

Signal's Tarzan Jig-Saw Puzzle. The first week's puzzle section.

"Signal Dealer News," a Signal publication to dealers, telling of Tarzan show; Jim and Joan Pierce appear in photo.

By December 1933 the club had grown to 125,000 members. The success of the Signal's Tarzan Club in California brought the realization to Burroughs that some type of national club was needed — above all, one directed by his own corporation. This awareness caused him, on February 1, 1933, to inform Dahlquist of the plans to form an "organization. . . to be known as the Tarzan Clans of America." The letter gave detailed plans:

To this end we are publishing an official guide book which contains, in addition to instructions for forming a Tarzan clan, election of officers

and conduct of meetings, rules for organizing clan and interclan field meets, rules for playing numerous Tarzan games, clan rituals, clan songs, directions for making Tarzan spears, shields, bows and arrows, etc.

If an official guide did appear at that time, its publication cannot be confirmed; the thirty-two page booklet "Tarzan Clans of America" was copyrighted six years later, in 1939. The letter also reported plans to design a Tarzan medal, "emblematic of the locket which Tarzan is supposed always to wear," and explained, "These will be serially numbered so that they may be used as identification tags, thus serving a practicable purpose. . . ."

It was inevitable that Ed's association with Dahlquist should become a repetition of past dealings with other marketing groups. Whether the project was book publishing, syndicating of stories or cartoons in newspapers, motion pictures, or radio programs, the necessity would arise for Burroughs to take over these activities himself. His actions in doing so were based only partly upon a desire for more money or a fear that he was being cheated in the matter of royalties. A stronger motive was his impatience and exasperation with the middlemen on whom he was forced to depend. Almost always he encountered bungling and inefficiency, false, inflated claims and promises, and in the cases of assigned writers or artists, mediocre, unimaginative work. In the operation of new projects the pattern was familiar: an unqualified enthusiasm by Burroughs, a gradual weakening and hesitancy, impatience and growing criticisms, blunt disapproval or even angry charges, final disillusionment — and then the dismissal of the particular agent and the transfer of the project to Burroughs' control. A further motive, possibly a compulsion, was his need to be in charge of things, to demonstrate his ability to organize and to produce better results.

The transition from enthusiasm to rejection followed its expected course in the radio programs, and by the fall of 1933 it was nearing its final stages. On October 26 Ed informed Dahlquist:

As you know, I have never been satisfied with the adaptation of the Tarzan stories for the radio program, and of late they seem to be getting worse. I understand that they are so bad that they have to be practically re-written by members of the cast and the director before they can be recorded.

He wondered if he might take over the adapting with episode 248 and warned that unless the program was improved, "the interest . . . which is already lapsing, will die out completely."

Dahlquist's response was one of surprise and indignation. He noted that Burroughs' com-

plaint was the only one he had ever received, enclosed letters of praise from the largest radio stations, and insisted that Ed's information about rewritten scripts was inaccurate; in the past twenty-five episodes there had been only four words changed and three lines deleted.[29] Ed, obviously biding his time, remarked that any further discussion would be fruitless. He had already contacted Neebe, explaining that the contract with American Radio Features expired in March 1934 and that plans were being considered to take over the programs. He wondered whether Neebe would be willing to handle the selling end.

At the Burroughs offices in Tarzana during the past several years, more and more responsibility and decision-making had been delegated to Ralph Rothmund, Ed's secretary. Now, in the production of the new Tarzan radio serials, he and Hulbert were to assume "the brunt of the campaign." A different approach to the programs involved the preparation of individual thirteen-week serials. Intensive writing and recording followed, and on May 5 Rothmund notified Neebe that a full story in thirty-nine episodes had been completed and purchased by a sponsor and would soon be released. Interestingly, Neebe forwarded a report from the Gem Clay Forming Company about the animal and character statuettes, which said that H. J. Heinz Company had used 43,000; Toddy, Inc., 93,000; and the Foulds Milling Company, almost 300,000.

In July 1934 Hulbert traveled to the eastern cities to make contacts with radio stations and advertising agencies, but in the fall, with the new title of vice-president and authority over the radio branch of the corporation, ERB again sought Neebe's help. In refusing to accept a sales territory, Neebe wrote, "I have returned to my old love the Campbell-Ewald Company with which I was associated at the time I gave birth to the Tarzan strip idea while dining with you at Tarzana."[30]

Ed's preference for the art work of J. Allen St. John, and his efforts in the past to persuade

Bourjaily to replace Maxon with St. John, had brought no results. On December 15, 1931, St. John had revealed his eagerness to get the assignment on the newspaper strips as well as that of illustrator of any books published by the Burroughs Corporation. Ed continued to hope for a St. John collaboration, and in 1933 his ambition to see the Mars stories appear in strips drove him to launch new correspondence. In the fall, St. John prepared samples of a Martian strip for submission to the Hearst newspapers' King Features Syndicate. About these Ed commented, "They have all the St. John art and action." He approved of them highly but thought that John Carter's face should be more ruggedly masculine and more like a fighting man. The St. John work was examined by Hearst himself; his attitude toward running a Martian strip was negative. Informed of the rejection, Ed, on January 10, 1934, noted there was a question of how this new strip might have affected the Tarzan cartoons and wrote, "I am satisfied to let the matter rest and not permit the syndication of this strip at present." Over a period of years other syndicates were approached about the Martian strips, but little interest was displayed. Finally, in December 1941, United Feature Syndicate inaugurated "John Carter of Mars" as a Sunday feature illustrated by ERB's son, John Coleman Burroughs. Unfortunately, the wartime paper shortage forced its demise in the spring of 1943.

The agreement with Elser's Metropolitan Books, Inc., had led first to the publication of *Tarzan and the Lost Empire* (September 1929). Others in order were *Tanar of Pellucidar* (May 1930), *Tarzan at the Earth's Core* (November 1930), and *A Fighting Man of Mars* (May 1931). Despite the friendly, cordial dealings and Burroughs' praise of the Metropolitan sales methods, it was evident that a rift was developing. Elser could hardly fail to be aware of Ed's yearning to publish his own books, while Ed, on the other hand, had known for some time that Elser was dissatisfied with the royalty arrangement. In December 1930 Elser proposed a renewal of the book contract with some changes, and after consideration, Burroughs revealed he was undecided; he pointed out that for more than a year Elser had emphasized his inability to "make money out of the present arrangement" and added, "yet . . . we do not want to relinquish a greater proportion of the popular copyright royalty than we are now giving you." In this letter of February 5, 1931, Burroughs revealed that he had been approached by "one of the oldest and most successful publishing houses in the country" with a tempting proposition. He was strongly inclined to leave Metropolitan and accept this new offer.

To Elser on the twenty-third Ed announced his decision: ". . . we have decided to take over the publication of the Burroughs books ourselves — at least, we will experiment with one book." His comment that Elser had done remarkably well "in view of the nationwide economic depression" brings a realization that Burroughs' action was a daring one (or even a reckless one); this period of the Great Depression was not an auspicious time for the launching of a publishing enterprise. On March 4 Elser made a last attempt to obtain a contract for the next four books, with a sliding royalty of ten to twenty percent and a seventy-five percent royalty on reprints, but this offer was rejected. Ed wrote:

We should like to try our hand at publishing a couple of books. Perhaps at the end of a year we shall be wiser and sadder, but I know of no other way in which we can get the bug out of our system than to give the idea a trial.[31]

The first story scheduled for publication, newly written, was "Tarzan, Guard of the Jungle," then being serialized in *Blue Book,* October 1930 to April 1931. The working title had been "Tarzan and the Man Things," but with its appearance on November 20, 1931, under the Burroughs imprint, it was finally titled *Tarzan The Invincible.* The printing and binding was done by Kingsport Press in Kingsport, Tennessee. This company printed all of the Burroughs books for seventeen years through 1948.

The exploitation of Tarzan through the motion picture medium had in the past provided Burroughs with his unhappiest experiences. His encounters with unreliable producers, many of them conniving and deceitful, had left him with an embittered attitude toward the entire film field. Following his disappointment with *Tarzan and the Golden Lion* he was indifferent to the production of another Tarzan movie, but an agreement he had signed six years earlier would be revived, and as a result, he would have no choice but to accede to the plans for a Tarzan film. In a complicated agreement signed with the Stern brothers and Louis Jacobs in 1922, Ed had sold the motion picture rights to two stories, *Jungle Tales of Tarzan* and *Tarzan and the Jewels of Opar*. A series of bonuses was involved in a required package deal covering both Tarzan and non-Tarzan stories. In 1929 Ed recalled that they paid $20,000 for rights to the two stories, but upon checking his records confirmed that the Stern brothers and Jacobs had paid $20,000 each, for a total of $40,000. At the time, Julius Stern was vice-president and general manager of the Universal Film Manufacturing Company, and now, with Universal Pictures having acquired the rights to *Jungle Tales of Tarzan*, the company planned to produce a serial.

Unfortunately, Burroughs had sold the two stories outright in 1922 and therefore would receive no royalties. His attempts to extract some money from Universal resulted only in their granting him $1,000 for one-time newspaper syndication rights. Opposed to the making of a serial, Ed, at a conference with Carl Laemmle on March 15, 1929, urged the production of a full-length feature, claiming it would have greater box-office appeal, but his objection to a serial was based upon a more important reason — a serial was really equivalent to two features, and Universal would thus be getting two for the price of one.

Ed's preference for a feature was ignored, and he found himself powerless also in the matter of another decision — the choice of a title. Universal was changing *Jungle Tales* to "Tarzan the Mighty"; protests by Ed brought only a weak concession from Robert Welch, the gen-

eral manager. The film opening would read "Tarzan the Mighty, adapted from the famous novel Jungle Tales of Tarzan by Edgar Rice Burroughs." After a fade-out the camera would focus on the book and a hand would be shown turning to the title page. Disgruntled, Ed noted his "impulse was to charge them for the use of the title 'Tarzan the Mighty.' "

Some of the rushes were shown at the Universal lot on June 14, 1928, where Ed met Frank Merrill, chosen for the Tarzan role, and Natalie Kingston, the feminine lead who was playing Mary Trevor rather than Jane Porter. Ed conceded that Merrill might make a good Tarzan, but the scenes he viewed left him in a state of dismay. He commented in a memorandum:

. . . there was only one character that appears in the original work, namely Tarzan, and no suggestion of any episode or action taken from the book.

They have incorporated many characters, including a Lord Greystoke, some pirates, sailors and castaway girl and her little brother, none of which appears in the original work.

They have incorporated a love interest between Tarzan and the girl (Natalie Kingston), which does not exist in the book.

Ed was convinced that this romance would prove harmful to his book sales, noting he had "studiously avoided" the creation of any love interest other than the one between Tarzan and Jane; in addition, they had been married in *The Return of Tarzan*, Jane was still living, and it was hardly appropriate or decent for Tarzan to be involved with another woman. The character of Tarzan, developed through many stories, was Ed's "greatest asset," but he despaired of finding a way to safeguard his interests. Past experiences had made him fearful of long and expensive litigation.

The March 1929 conference between Burroughs and Laemmle exhibited a scarcely repressed impatience and hostility on both sides and a series of threats and counterthreats. *Tarzan the Mighty* was now completed and Universal, already aware that the serial would be a money-maker, was eager for a second Tarzan film. They had no intention, however, of paying Burroughs a large sum of money or granting him any royalties. Laemmle at once stated that the firm could purchase the rights to *The Lad and the Lion* from the Weiss brothers, advertise it as written by the author of Tarzan, and thus assure its success. In fact, as a not-very-veiled threat, Laemmle mentioned he could remake *The Adventures of Tarzan*, but upon being reminded he would have to pay a royalty of five percent to Burroughs, he discarded the idea. Ed's offer to sell Universal an original Tarzan serial for $15,000 with certain restrictions, or to sell rights in *Tarzan, Lord of the Jungle* for $25,000 produced no interest whatsoever. Laemmle had maintained he could purchase the rights to *Tarzan and the Jewels of Opar* from the Stern brothers for $10,000. The conference ended with Burroughs being granted nothing. Universal discovered that the contracts with the Sterns on *Opar* and on *Jungle Tales* were identical, acquired *Opar* from the Sterns, and soon afterward began production on a second serial.

The film, given the illogical and even nonsensical title of "Tarzan the Tiger," was released in a sequence of episodes from October 1929 to February 1930. Frank Merrill again played Tarzan, Natalie Kingston this time taking the role of Jane, and Lillian Worth cast as Queen La of Opar. It was the first Tarzan film to use sound effects, these being of a very limited nature, but one unusual "sound" was originated by Merrill — the blood-chilling yell of Tarzan. Since this second serial was based upon the story he had sold years before, Ed, realizing he was helpless, made little attempt to influence the production of the movie. Efforts to obtain an extra payment for the sound rights were unsuccessful; lawyers on both sides were baffled as to the value of these new rights, whether they had any separate value or whether they were included in the purchase of the story. Thus, the production of the two films *Tarzan the Mighty* and *Tarzan the Tiger* was simply the latest of a series of unhappy experiences that

Ed had almost come to expect in his movie dealings; in a certain respect — his complete lack of authority — the frustration had been even worse than the film disputes of the past. Disgusted, Ed never bothered to attend performances of either of the serials.

Once again a complex agreement granting two individuals the right to produce a Tarzan film led Burroughs into trouble. On January 14, 1929, he signed a contract with G. Walter Shumway and Jack C. Nelson authorizing them to make a serial or feature to be titled "Tarzan the Fearless." The stipulations were that James Pierce, Burroughs' son-in-law, was to star as Tarzan, that the film must be made within seven years, and that before production could begin, a $10,000 payment would be required. Ed was repeating past mistakes with a contract of this type and length. Pierce, despite Ed's warning that he not obligate himself, also signed a contract with the two men.

Shumway and Nelson were unable to obtain funds, and a year passed without any filming efforts, but in 1930 familiar manipulations began with Chadwick Productions of Hollywood acquiring distribution rights to "Tarzan the Fearless" from Nelson and another associate. Unmindful of all the obstacles that had arisen, Burroughs signed a contract with Metro-Goldwyn-Mayer for a Tarzan film, the requirements being that for one year after April 15, 1931, no additional Tarzan picture could be made. As part of the contract, MGM agreed to engage Burroughs as a consultant and pay him $1,000 a week for five weeks, beginning on September 23.

As expected, a dispute soon developed over the original Shumway-Nelson rights; with Ed determined that only MGM would be allowed to make a film, Shumway and attorney Lew Goldstone appeared unannounced at the Tarzana home. Burroughs, who had taken to typing memos (in self-protection) that listed actions and statements of anybody associated with the movie field, described the strange happenings in his memo of October 10, 1931:

I went to the door, and when I saw Shumway I told him that I knew what he had come here

to talk about and that I would not talk to him about the matter. He said they had the money and were all ready to go. I remarked that it was a nice day. Goldstone said that he had come here to tender me $10,000.00. I told him that he would have to talk to Felix [Ed's lawyer]. He said he could not tender the money to Felix. He repeated "I have come here to tender the money. I do tender the money." I said, "I have nothing to say." He did not show me any money nor any check. Mrs. Burroughs and Mr. Corwin were present and heard the entire conversation. . . .

The controversy over the Tarzan film rights remained in dispute while MGM continued with the production of their movie, titled *Tarzan, the Ape-Man*. In reviewing the script to make certain that it did not duplicate the plot elements of his novels, Ed, on November 28, 1931, commented to Bernard Hyman, MGM producer, about obvious similarities: ". . . this story is evidently a new version of Tarzan of the Apes, the motion picture right to which I sold to William Parsons in 1916." Ed then listed the points of resemblance, which may be summarized as follows:

Archimedes Porter (original), American scientist, father of Jane Porter becomes James Porter, African trader, also father of Jane Porter.

In both stories Tarzan sees his first white people and white woman in the persons of the Porter party. Tarzan's inability to understand or speak English, part of the plot of Tarzan of the Apes *only, is also part of the new script.*

Tarzan (original) shows grief over the killing of the she-ape Kala and this is similar to the killing of a she-ape in the new script.

Ed concluded by observing that he could find no similarities between the MGM script and his other Tarzan stories.

Ed viewed these as minor resemblances, as revealed in a later reply to his brother Harry, who, after seeing *Tarzan, the Ape Man*, had wanted to know "why the name was changed." Ed wrote, "It was not. This is supposed to be an entirely different story from Tarzan of the Apes. . . . Also, for this reason, they changed Jane's name to Parker. Really, if you compare the two stories you will find there is little similarity in plot."[32]

Now excited over the money-making possibilities of Tarzan in film form, MGM summoned Burroughs to the studios for a conference with Sam Marx and Irving Thalberg. Because of his previous unpleasant experiences with film producers, Burroughs sent his trusted secretary Ralph Rothmund to negotiate with MGM. The proposal was to make a series of Tarzan movies; Thalberg spoke of a picture a year for three years, with payment beginning at $35,000 and rising to $45,000. Rothmund, with Burroughs' approval, rejected this as being insufficient. While Thalberg seemed willing to increase the amounts, he stressed that the entire transaction hinged upon clearing up the legal tangle over the Tarzan rights. Negotiations must now be conducted with a new individual who had acquired the old Shumway-Nelson contract, Sol Lesser, who in future years would establish a very important relationship with Burroughs. Lesser and his associates finally adopted a conciliatory attitude, agreeing to allow MGM to produce the film, and on March 26, 1932, Burroughs signed a contract with the Lesser group authorizing them to make a picture after the MGM one was out of the way. The situation was now clear for MGM's *Tarzan, the Ape-Man* to be released.

Ed had been delighted by the choice of W. S. Van Dyke to direct the film, and following the preview in February 1932 Ed sent him a congratulatory letter. He expressed appreciation for the "splendid job":

This is a real Tarzan picture. It breathes the grim mystery of the jungle; the endless, relentless strife for survival; the virility, the cruelty, and the grandeur of Nature in the raw.

Tarzan, the Ape Man marked the first appearances of Johnny Weissmuller and Maureen O'Sullivan, and in the letter Ed described Weismuller as a "great" Tarzan with "youth, a marvelous physique, and a magnetic personality." About the "perfect" Maureen O'Sullivan he remarked, "I am afraid that I shall never be satisfied with any other heroine for my future pictures. . . ." He continued with his paean of praise:

. . . Mr. Hamilton and Mr. Smith have added a lustre of superb character delineation to the production that has helped to make it the greatest Tarzan picture of them all. . . . Again let me thank you for the ability, the genius, and the hard work you have put into Tarzan, the Ape Man; *and permit me to express the hope that you may direct my latest Tarzan novel,* Tarzan the Invincible, *when it is filmed.*[33]

On May 31 Ed wrote to Hyman at MGM about the "splendid results" and to report that he had found no adverse criticisms of the film — "even the English reviewers, who ordinarily seem to be suffering from acute indigestion, are praising it highly." He suggested that Tarzan movies be released as seasonal events, each spring, so that people would look forward to the occasion, much as they did to the circus, "to which the Tarzan picture is analogous." He was disappointed to learn, however, that Van Dyke would not direct the next film.

To Bert Weston at the same time, concerning the family's enthusiasm about Maureen O'Sullivan, Ed spoke of her adding "quite a bit to the picture" and pointed out she was far more attractive off the screen than on, "which is unusual for motion picture actresses." Something new, a departure from Burroughs' own practice, was introduced in *Tarzan, the Ape Man.* Ed wrote, "Their pronunciation of Tarzan (Tar-ZAN) was their own. I don't give a damn what they call him as long as their checks come regularly." This unauthorized change — Ed had explained on various occasions that "Tarzan" was accented on the first syllable — may have come about because the stressing of the "zan," with the voice rising in pitch, creates a more mellifluous effect. The accent on "Tar"

produces a harsh sound. The change in pronunciation by some people is the result of the instinctive selection of euphony over cacophony. The Tar-ZAN in the movie evidently caused the Burroughs Corporation to change its official position. On September 30, 1933, in a response to a fan, secretary Rothmund wrote, "The name *Tarzan* is pronounced with the accent on the last syllable — TarZAN."

Tarzan, the Ape Man, adapted to the screen by writers Cyril Hume and Ivor Novello, was based upon incidents that were newly created to avoid any duplication of the familiar Tarzan plot. The last names, as indicated, were also changed. James Parker (C. Aubrey Smith), an African trader, and his youthful partner Harry Holt (Neil Hamilton) embark on an ivory hunting expedition, carrying out their plans to discover the rumored elephant burial ground. The party of course includes Parker's daughter Jane (Maureen O'Sullivan) and in the subsequent adventures Tarzan (Johnny Weissmuller) is involved. Others in the cast are Mrs. Cutten (Doris Lloyd), Beamish (Forrester Harvey), Riano (Ivory Williams), and the chimpanzee Cheetah. The newspaper reviews praised the film highly; it was described as "more exciting than Trader Horn," the picture previously directed by W. S. Van Dyke, "an uncommonly good adventure story" and "a masterpiece of entertainment from all angles."

The Tarzan fever that had gripped the public was demonstrated in the record-breaking attendance throughout the country. To Bert Weston, on May 9, 1932, Ed mentioned the eager crowds in Los Angeles: "The rush was so great Saturday and Sunday that they advertised in this morning's paper that they are forced to put on seven shows a day, starting at about nine in the morning." That night, he noted, he would join Van Dyke and Maureen O'Sullivan in a personal appearance on stage.

The year 1933 found Sol Lesser and his Principal Pictures Corporation competing furiously with MGM in the production of Tarzan films, Lesser's to be a serial, and MGM's, a

Maureen O'Sullivan, MGM's Jane in one of first of its Tarzan *films, in dress made of* Tarzan *Sunday Newspaper pages.*

feature. A controversy had already risen because of the Ken Maynard picture *Come on Tarzan* produced by MGM. In answering Lesser's objection, Burroughs emphasized that Maynard had permission only to call his horse Tarzan, but not to use the name for a movie. When the script of "Tarzan the Fearless" was forwarded by Lesser on January 10, Ed's main concern was to check it for any possible infringement on the Tarzan novels. He approved the script with minor exceptions: Tarzan's popularity was not based upon "sex adventures" and therefore the "sex suggestiveness" in certain scenes should be "toned down"; the Waziri were loyal, intelligent allies of Tarzan and the name should not be used for a cannibal tribe; the chimp "Balu" should be called "Galu."

The stipulation in the contract for *Tarzan the Fearless* that Jim Pierce must be assigned the title role led to a dispute that exhibited comic overtones. Although in May 1933 Lesser gave Pierce a screen test — later viewed by Burroughs — the producer believed that to cast Pierce as Tarzan would be a mistake. Pierce, out of condition, was physically unable to undertake the role. Lesser offered his own version of the sequence of events: the original contract of January 1929 had been given to Pierce as a present after his marriage to Joan Burroughs (July 1928). Efforts by Lesser to obtain Burroughs' help in persuading Pierce to relinquish his right to the Tarzan role brought no result. Adamant, Burroughs insisted that the producer negotiate with Pierce. In their conversations Lesser reminded Burroughs of his son-in-law's excess weight; he maintained that Pierce could not climb a tree and added, "Jane would have to help him up the tree." Lesser followed with a threat that he would play Tarzan as a "sissy" and let Jane be the "strong one." In an interview he stressed that he was seriously prepared to do this, producing Tarzan as a burlesque unless Pierce yielded. Burroughs was unresponsive to Lesser's continuous pleas; to his attorney Max Felix, when a settlement was finally reached, Ed explained the situation (June 8, 1933) and enclosed a copy of the final agreement:

During the last few months Lesser told me frequently that he would like to be relieved of the obligation to use Pierce. On each occasion I told him that I would insist that he use Pierce. More recently he had some tests made of Pierce and asked me to view them. When I looked at these tests he again reiterated his request and attempted to convince me that it would be advisable that Pierce not be used. I again told him that I would not consent.... Lesser did not indicate that he had in mind using Buster Crabbe....

Lesser, at this time, had no success with Pierce, who had enrolled at the Hollywood Athletic Club and was working out frantically in the gym. However, Lesser's persistence, and the fact that Pierce himself may have realized that he could not get into condition, led to the settlement. On May 17 Lesser and his associates Mike Rosenberg and Ben Zeidman outlined the terms of the compromise; they conceded that the original contract (March 26, 1932) had assigned the role of Tarzan to Pierce, but explained, "... we have concluded that a different type to portray said role is desirable." They noted that Pierce was engaged in radio broadcasting at present and would be actively involved in this field for some time. The suggestion, as stated in the agreement, was that Pierce remain "unavailable" and "refuse" to accept the part; on these conditions he was offered $5,000. Lesser stressed that if Pierce were to play the role, his remuneration would be $500 a week for not more than four weeks, and, as a result, he would be losing a substantial sum. Pierce accordingly signed the agreement which confirmed that he would not be available for the role of Tarzan and would "refuse to portray said role."

Buster Crabbe, a 1932 Olympic swimming champion, was now assigned the lead, with Jacqueline Wells cast as Mary Brooks instead of Jane Porter to preclude any possibility of a conflict with previous Tarzan movies and novels. For the musical background and the theme song, later titled "The Call of Tarzan," Ed urged the employment of his friend Louis Gottschalk; Lesser promised an audition, but Gottschalk was not engaged.

Tarzan the Fearless, directed by Robert Hill and released in August 1933, was an odd combination of a full-length feature, running more than an hour, plus eight two-reel episodes that were designed to follow in sequence. The feature was deliberately created with an unresolved ending, since the effect sought by Lesser was of the to-be-continued serial. In many theaters only the feature was shown, and the resulting impression of an incomplete story led to unfavorable comment by the reviewers. The cast, in addition to Crabbe and Wells, included Dr. Brooks (Evalyn Warren), Bob Hall (Edward Woods), Jeff (Philo McCollough), Nick (Matthew Betz), Abdul (Frank Lackteen), and for the villainous high priest, a man who would have numerous film roles in the future — Mischa Auer.

Lesser's *Tarzan the Fearless* was almost completed at the time MGM began work on their film, the chosen title, *Tarzan and His Mate.* In August 1933 Ed was an interested spectator at the studio and reported that "the underwater shot of Weismuller fighting the croc" was going to be "very thrilling." He noted, however, that another underwater shot "may get by the censors and may not"; he wrote, "It shows Jacqueline McKim, doubling for Maureen O'Sullivan, and Johnnie Weissmuller swimming nude under water. It is a very beautiful and artistic shot. The motion of the water partially veils the figures. Their movements under water are naturally slow and extremely graceful. I saw nothing objectionable in it. . . ."[34] On the sixteenth he informed Hulbert that MGM planned to spend a great deal of money on the production: "I am fearful that they are going to spend too much. They are very anxious to make it outshine Lesser's picture to such a degree that there will be no comparison. . . ." In March 1934, with *Tarzan and His Mate* almost ready for release, Ed estimated

the cost of the film at a million and a quarter dollars. MGM publicity in 1937 listed three Tarzan pictures — *Tarzan the Ape Man, Tarzan and His Mate,* and *Tarzan Escapes* — as costing about $900,000 each and grossing $2,000,000 each.

One of the most famous scenes, filmed at "Lot No. 2" at the MGM studio in an area ringed by a heavy corral, was of Weissmuller riding the rhinoceros "Mary." The MGM publicity noted that "despite the statement in encyclopedias that these animals are untamable," Mary was tamed and trained to riding by George Emerson, the studio animal trainer. Mary, who had cost $10,000, was later sold to Ringling Brothers Circus.

In *Tarzan and His Mate* unusual changes occurred after long sections were filmed; Rod La Rocque, partner of Neil Hamilton (playing Harry Holt), was replaced by Paul Cavanagh, and midway in the picture Jack Conway took over the direction from Cedric Gibbons. Others in the cast were Beamish (Forrester Harvey), Saidi (Nathan Curry), and Vanness (Desmond Roberts).

Shortly after the release of *Tarzan the Fearless,* Sol Lesser, on a European trip to promote the picture, made a dismaying discovery. The old 1921 silent film *The Son of Tarzan,* produced by David Howells for National Film Corporation, was being offered for screening all over Europe by Imperial Pictures of New York. The advent of sound and the tremendous possibilities it created for new approaches to the jungle epics had led Imperial to partially transform *The Son of Tarzan* into a sound picture. Dialogue had been dubbed in and music and various sounds had been synchronized. Lesser's hasty wire to Burroughs urged him to take steps to suppress this film which was affecting the prices on *Tarzan the Fearless.* Burroughs cabled Jack Barnstyn, the Lesser representative in Paris, authorizing him to "prevent the showing of this picture"; no firm had been issued a license to distribute the picture, and in the original contract with Howells, only the silent rights were granted.

An old film acquaintance, Elmo Lincoln,

who had contacted Burroughs at various times, wrote to him in 1929 seeking information about the contract with National Film Corporation for the original *Tarzan of the Apes*. Lincoln's last Tarzan role had been in the 1921 *Adventures of Tarzan* and he now hoped to acquire the rights to the first film and reissue it with added sound effects. In his reply of June 6 Burroughs indicated he had no objection to the plan and granted permission to Lincoln to bill the movie as "The Original Tarzan of the Apes," provided royalties and charges for full sound effects were paid. Since Lincoln's early successes, his film fortunes had steadily deteriorated; producers could find no parts for him in the new talking pictures. His projects and his desperate efforts to find some type of employment in the movie industry all led to failure. His dream of reissuing *Tarzan of the Apes* could not be realized, and two years later, on April 30, 1931, as Lincoln continued to inquire, Burroughs wrote, ". . . it will be impossible for anyone to gain control of all of these rights and without all of them I consider the balance to be practically worthless. . . ."

Lincoln's opinion of the MGM *Tarzan the Ape Man* was bitterly critical. On June 5, 1932, he commented to Ed, ". . . the house seemed to think it was a comedy. Why do they portray Tarzan without any dignity? . . . with the right treatment and portrayal, Tarzan could be a romantic, thrilling character, and still have the sympathy of his audiences. . . . I don't like to see him treated as a clown. I still think Weissmuller is a good swimmer." At a meeting with Lincoln, Ed had told of his plans to launch a radio series; Lincoln, in his letter, hopefully suggested that he be cast as Tarzan, but this role was already reserved for son-in-law Jim Pierce. Ed, however, had always exhibited kindness and sympathy for Elmo Lincoln and was sincerely anxious to help him. On June 7 he noted that he had called a "friend" at MGM and urged him to find some opening for Lincoln. Stressing his experience in the filming of Tarzan pictures, Lincoln suggested he could assist MGM with "the adaptation, planning of jungle sets, with animal shots and with the study of Tarzan as a character . . ." He wrote:

. . . I don't believe I ever told you that I gave Hill most of the story and directed much of the adventures that we made for Weiss Bros. My experience in working lions alone would be worth while, as well as the other animals we used. You, like most every one else, think of me only as an actor, but I was always more interested in story construction and the directing of stories than in the acting end of it. . . .[35]

Ed enclosed the letter in a note to M. E. Greenwood at MGM, but the film company appeared uninterested in employing Lincoln. In another 1932 communication Lincoln sought permission to create a vaudeville act that would be centered about the cabin scene in *Tarzan of the Apes,* with the lion crawling through the window after Jane. The request was granted on condition that the name *Tarzan* not be used.[36] Lincoln, who had obtained a film negative of his original *Tarzan,* attempted in vain to have MGM view this; his further efforts to find work in the movies led him to ask for the "return" of the dialogue rights to *Tarzan of the Apes,* claiming that the rights had been promised to him by Burroughs. Explaining that the contract with MGM made this impossible, Ed sent a firm refusal.[37]

The following year brought new arrangements by the Burroughs Corporation in the area of Tarzan cartoon books. Stephen Slesinger, Inc., a New York firm that had been granted certain merchandising rights in a contract of January 1933, had, without authorization, given permission to the Whitman Publishing Company to issue a *Tarzan of the Apes* cartoon book. On December 27, 1933, in a letter to S. E. Lowe, Burroughs noted that Slesinger had acted illegally and was not empowered to sell any publication rights. An exception was a Tarzan coloring book, issued by Saalfield Publishing Company. Negotiations with Whitman soon led to an agreement allowing the publication of Johnnie Weismuller and Buster Crabbe cartoon books, and in 1934 the firm issued a number of ten cent books. The plan had been to begin with *The Tarzan Twins* in a format similar to Orphan Annie and Mickey Mouse with a picture on the right hand page and the words printed on the left. Burroughs approved this and accepted a $1,000 advance royalty; the book, however, did not appear until the summer of 1934 and was preceded by the publication in February of a *Tarzan the Fearless* Big Little Book, based upon the movie, and by *Tarzan and His Mate,* another film cartoon book that appeared soon afterward.

Dealings with Whitman continued, and in 1935 a controversy arose over the publication of a 144-page book merely titled "Tarzan" and issued for the Lily Tulip Cup Corporation. Again, Whitman had obtained permission from Stephen Slesinger, and an argument raged as Burroughs claimed that the contract with Slesinger did not grant him any rights of this type, while Whitman insisted that the authority had been given for the publication of premium and advertising materials. Burroughs had also angrily demanded information about another unauthorized Whitman book, issued for the Mason-Warner Company. Since these cartoon books were already published and distributed, there was nothing that could be done to suppress them. Following this rather shaky start, relations with Whitman improved and continued successfully for more than thirty-five years.

On November 13, 1936, Ed wrote to E. H. Wadewitz of Whitman Publishing Company to inquire whether the firm might be interested in manufacturing a game he had invented. He offered details:

It will consist of a playing field printed on some material such as oilcloth or maybe billiard cloth, and five dice and a dice cup. all of which could be contained in a cardboard cylinder. The six faces of the dice are six different colors, one of which would be white, and no two dice in the set are colored identically.

He enclosed two pages of separate diagrams, the first of a playing "field" composed of a circle twenty-five inches in diameter and marked off into sections like spokes of a wheel. Apparently, when the dice were tossed, they fell into these sections which indicated rewards or penalties. Poker terms were used — "Four of a Kind, Take All"; "Full House, Take 25"; "Two pair, Lose Dice"; "One Pair, Pay 10 and Lose Dice." The playing circle was divided into eleven of these marked sections and had a small circular "pool" in the center. Ed's second diagram was of the set of five dice numbered from one to six and with the colors of the six sides shown as red, blue, yellow, green, orange, and white.

Whitman, in its reply of November 21, stated that the firm would not be interested in manufacturing the unnamed game. They believed that the costs would be too high and also noted that the dice would be a problem; they had no idea how these could be produced, and explained that only the standard wooden dice, used in low-priced games, were available to them. They suggested that Ed contact Parker Brothers, but there is no record of Ed's pursuing the matter any further.

In his criticisms of the Tarzan cartoon strips, and in the numerous comments he had made about the illustrations for his magazine stories and novels, Ed had established himself as a difficult man to please. His high standards and his insistence upon realistic, vibrant drawings, especially where Tarzan and the jungle animals were concerned, resulted partly from his own interest in art, his adeptness at cartooning, and his artist's eye or perception. In 1929 he corresponded with his nephew Studley Burroughs, a commercial artist, to seek his opinion about the newspaper strips. His letter of December 4 to his nephew consisted mainly of complaints about the newspaper artist's drawings and expressed the belief that he was "getting the lion's share of the profits and not doing very good work for what he gets." Ed wrote, ". . . if I were an artist I could make one of these sketches in about fifteen minutes and then have more action in them than Maxon has. What do you think?"

When Studley replied with some detailed criticisms of the strips, Ed was so impressed with these that he forwarded them to the Metropolitan Syndicate as an aid to the improvement of the current cartoons. Aware that Burroughs was about to turn publisher, Studley, on February 19, 1931, offered to illustrate the books. To Studley, Ed held up J. Allen St. John's work as a model for all artists, commenting about the vitality in his figures. The effect Ed valued above all was of action — a powerful, surging action that seemed to emanate from St. John's drawings of Tarzan or the beasts of the jungle. The figures of other artists Ed had often disparaged as being too static.

In the same month Ed wrote to St. John, asking him to quote prices for jacket and frontispiece illustrations, but his quotations were considered too high for a beginning publisher. Ed had chosen to enter the field at the worst possible time, with the country in the grip of the Great Depression, and his financial worries were plainly evident. For Studley he listed prices of $150 for a book jacket, front only, no lettering; $175 for a wrap-around jacket, no lettering; and $75 for a frontispiece. Studley, eager to accommodate his uncle, agreed. Curiously, Ed, who was able at last to obtain the services of the man he had long admired and had eulogized for years as the best of illustrators, placed economy first and chose the inexperienced Studley.

At the time the art work for the first Burroughs publication was assigned to Studley — the novel had so far been titled "Tarzan and the Man Things" and "Tarzan, Guard of the Jungle" — Ed was somewhat apprehensive of the difficulties that might arise. The trauma experienced by Studley in the death of his wife and then of his infant daughter in 1919-20 had left him in a shattered emotional state from which he had never fully recovered. A second marriage, leading to the birth of two daughters, June and Beverly, had produced further personal problems which Studley appeared unable to solve. Added to this were his struggles to achieve a permanent success as a commercial artist. To aid his nephew financially, Ed, in

1930, had given Studley several advances on illustrations to be done in the future. Studley's emotional instability had caused him to seek support through an overdependence upon alcohol. As a result of all of these problems, the possibility of Studley doing creative work on the tight schedule that Ed demanded was, from the start, unlikely.

Studley's early sketches for the first book, finally titled *Tarzan the Invincible,* received Burroughs' approval. In his letter of May 1, 1931, Ed noted the importance of the little monkey Nkima and suggested that his nephew visit the Chicago zoo to acquire a realistic idea of the appearance of an African monkey. Ed, conceding he knew little about monkeys, admitted that he visualized Nkima "as something like the diminutive monk that accompanies the organ grinders." He was anxious to have Studley "determine definitely" what Nkima should look like and explained that "he should really be a pathetic little monkey." About the sketches Ed observed that they seemed to be finished drawings, and he wrote, "I hope you don't spoil them in doing them over again." This statement, indicative of Ed's attitude, could be viewed as a portent of trouble to come. In letters to Studley and other illustrators he dictated his requirements to a most meticulous degree, exhibiting in his tone a positiveness about what he wanted and the high standards that must be met; these explicit and detailed "suggestions" could hardly fail to be disconcerting and frightening to the artists. Studley, already worried and insecure, found himself receiving these precise, lengthy outlines and explanations detailing the action, the costume, and the weapons of the character chosen by Burroughs for illustration, plus requests for additional research to attain authenticity. Practically nothing was left to the artist's initiative or originality.

Ed had cautioned Studley that the illustrations must be finished before August 1, but with the deadline past and no material received, Ed sent an appeal to brother Harry in Chicago. The report was that Studley had taken an assignment for General Motors and could find no time to complete the work. On August 10 Studley was instructed to send the incomplete drawings immediately — only two, jacket and frontispiece, were available. Ed's plans were to have these finished by a Los Angeles artist. The drawings finally arrived, and there were hints that Studley had faced some type of a crisis; Ed had noted, "Glad to know you are out of the woods. . . . try to forget it." Studley was urged to start to work on the next book, *Jungle Girl.* Ed tried to limit his requirements, did not insist that the jacket illustrate any particular story incident, and promised "plenty of latitude." He wanted a book cover that was startling, and explained, "It can be bizarre, it can be anything that will not offend public decency, just so it attracts attention, short of being ridiculous."[38]

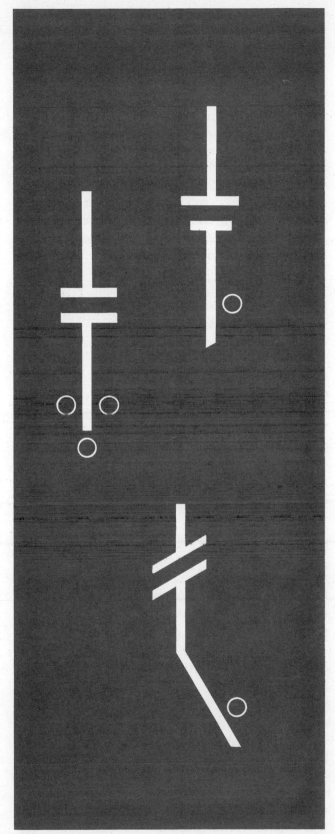

ERB's "Doodad" in three variations.

To provide a little imaginative or original touch to the books he was now publishing, Burroughs decided to use as a logo a design he had devised several years earlier on a 1924 vacation trip to the High Sierra. While Hulbert was fishing in the river, Ed and Jack, sitting on the bank, had taken sticks and were drawing what they called "doodads" in the mud. After remarking to Jack that he wished he might have some trademark for his books, Ed then outlined a figure in the mud (see illustration, upper right).

Before his entrance into the publishing field, Ed and his sons used a similar symbol as a sign or signature for messages. There is some evidence that Ed started this in the horseback riding days at Tarzana; with the "doodad" each member of the family could indicate which direction he had ridden so that the others could then follow. The location of the small circle established the individual's identity; a circle on the lower right side was Ed's signature, on the left was Jack's, and below, Hulbert's (see illustration, middle right; the lower, longer vertical line resembles a spear, and in 1934 diary entries Ed, in some instances, has drawn this spear with the end going through the circle.)

Ed's plan to use the figure as a trademark (or colophon) was not realized in his first privately published book, *Tarzan the Invincible* (November 20, 1931), but with the publication of *Jungle Girl* (April 15, 1932) the symbol appeared on the spine of the dust jacket; it was apparently drawn by nephew Studley Burroughs, then the illustrator. The shape of this little figure had undergone some change (see illustration, lower right, page 519).

Ed made several references to the symbol (by various names) in his instructions to Studley and later to St. John. In one of the earliest of these references, he seemed to delight in the curiosity the figure might arouse; his letter to Studley of March 9, 1932, concerning the illustrations for *Tarzan Triumphant*, contains the word "mysterious":

. . . on the backbone, Tarzan Triumphant, *Edgar Rice Burroughs (in 3 lines), a full length sketch of Tarzan, the word Illustrated, underneath which the price $2.00, the mysterious Burroughs trademark, and at the bottom the name Burroughs.*

On May 26, in forwarding an outline with requirements for the illustrations in *Apache Devil*, Ed reminded Studley, "Backbone same as usual, not forgetting the funny little doodad. . . ." To St. John, beginning in January 1933, he offered similar reminders about the trademark:

I should like to have the general idea carried out as shown on the backbone of the two jackets I am sending you, including the little doo-dad underneath the price. [*January 14,* Tarzan and the City of Gold] *. . . please do not forget to use my little hieroglyph as shown on the backbone of the jackets we sent you. (February 3).*
. . . If there is room for the doodad between the title and the author's name, or directly underneath author's name, it may be put in at very much reduced scale. [*March 7, 1935,* Tarzan and the Leopard Man.]

In the succeeding years the logo appeared regularly on the books published by Edgar Rice Burroughs, Inc., and on the Grosset & Dunlap reprints. Jack Burroughs also adopted it as a personal symbol on his paintings. The logo was usually reproduced on the dust jacket, but in *Tarzan the Magnificent* (1939) and a group of later novels it was printed on both the jacket and the spine of the book.

With the completion of the drawings for "Jungle Girl," Burroughs found himself in financial trouble and facing further problems with Studley. Ed, who had sent several advances to his nephew, explained to Harry, on February 29, 1932, that in the present situation he would have to limit his cash outlay. But of more concern was the fact that Studley's plans for future illustrations appeared uncertain. The question was, did Studley "care to go ahead?" Ed was forced to write to Harry because he could obtain no information from his nephew. In February and March 1932 Ed notified Studley of the next story to be illustrated — "Tarzan Triumphant" — and made it plain that he would again dictate the requirements. Despite his diplomatic praise of his nephew's work, it was evident that "Jungle Girl" had proved disappointing to him. He asked that Studley "use a little different type of feminine pulchritude from that of 'Jungle Girl,'" and wrote, "I should like to have a little more character in the face and less doll-like beauty. . . ." He also had new ideas about Tarzan, whose garment should be changed from a leopard skin to "simple loin cloth or G-string," and added, "The less Tarzan has on the more he will be in character."

Feeling now that Studley needed firm guidance — the "latitude" previously granted not having brought a satisfactory result — Ed sent his most detailed instructions for the jacket, lettering, and four illustrations for "Tarzan Triumphant." The extent of these can be realized through the requirements for "Illustration #1," contained in the letter of March 9:

Lion rearing and burying teeth in face of askari — three-quarter view from rear of lion; beyond lion and victim, the Gunner is seen coming from tent with sub-machine gun in hands. Caption: *A scream of terror burst from the lips of the doomed man.* Note: *If you think better to* omit the Gunner as detracting attention from the principal figures, do so. However, if you show the Gunner, please show him as a black haired young man weighing about 180 pounds. He should be good looking in a sinister way. Remember that he is a tough egg and a killer; yet a character with human appeal that I have tried to make likable throughout the story. As this scene is transpiring at night, he need not wear a hat, but he should have on a short-sleeved shirt, open at the throat, hiking breeches and field boots. This will help to differentiate him from Smith, who wears shorts. The question of the costume for the askari is one rather difficult to handle. These askaris, being the armed guards of the safaris, are often pictured in military uniform. That I do not wish in this instance. I think that you can obtain the desired result by showing this Negro in a cotton shirt falling almost to the knees and with two bandoleers of cartridges passing over his shoulders and crossing at his breast, or . . . with merely a bandoleer of cartridges around his waist.

Instructions for other illustrations were similarly weighted with precise requirements.[39]

Beyond these exacting demands, Studley encountered new problems in the matter of payment; as the depression worsened and the book sales slumped, he received no money from Burroughs for the work he had completed, Burroughs having previously made advance payments. In addition, he was asked to lower his prices for the next scheduled novel, *Tarzan Triumphant*. Burroughs wrote, "When I was in New York . . . Grosset & Dunlap . . . mentioned that we could have very good art work done in New York for $90 the jacket painting . . . This is more in line with what we could afford to pay . . . should like to have your views on this. . . ." At the same time Burroughs contacted St. John, referring to the quotations the artist had offered a year earlier and asking if these could be "reduced considerably." A letter was also sent to illustrator Harold Foster. To St. John, Ed had noted the contingency: "in the event the artist who is doing the work at present will not be able to continue . . ."; he was

obviously doubtful of Studley's interest in preparing further illustrations or of his completing the work on time.

Both St. John and Studley offered reduced prices, and on March 16, 1932, Ed accepted his nephew's bid of $325 for the illustrations for *Tarzan Triumphant*. St. John's price had been somewhat lower, but, to Studley, Ed explained his choice: "Not being much of a business man, and blood being thicker than water. . . ." His decision to continue with Studley was an unwise one that would produce greater difficulties in the future. In the spring of 1932 Studley sent sketches that Ed approved; these revealed careful development of Ed's detailed instructions. On April 5 Ed inquired, "Did you object to my telling you exactly what I wanted? I understand that some artists do. . . ." Although he was pleased with his nephew's work at that stage,

Cover of Tarzan Triumphant, *1932; Studley O. Burroughs, illustrator.*

521

upon receipt of the finished jacket of *Tarzan Triumphant* he voiced his disappointment about "the physique of the model," writing, "He is too prissy and has a belly on him almost as large as mine. . . . let these heroic characters of mine cave in a little below the ribs rather than stick out. *Tarzan Triumphant* looks as though he might be several months along toward an increase in his family. . . ."[40]

To his own exacting standards Ed soon added the suggestions he received from the Kingsport Press, printers of the Burroughs' books, and Grosset and Dunlap. Through their influences Ed had changed his view of the book jacket; the first requirement was that the jacket must have a strong public appeal. In instructing Studley, Ed now became critical of St. John:

If you have any of my former books I wish you would note the almost total loss of outstanding sales value in St. John's jackets. As works of art they seem to me about all that could be desired, but as outstanding, compelling attention attracters they are not so hot. With all the thousands of books on display in a book shop we must bend every effort to have our covers not only artistic but at the same time demanding the attention of the passerby with a loud shriek.[41]

Ed explained he had been surprised to learn that "in about nine cases out of ten it is the jacket that sells the book. . . ."

For the next scheduled novel, *Apache Devil*, Ed again sent precise instructions to Studley. The assignment called for a jacket and frontispiece, same drawing, plus four other illustrations. Details of costume and action left little to Studley's imagination: ". . . a colorful Navajo blanket folded lengthways . . . no bit in pony's mouth . . . no feathers nor war bonnet on rider. . . ." On July 1 Ed noted he was "pleased with the suggested jacket illustrations" and then followed with three pages listing the corrections or changes; he forwarded a copy of *Trailing Geronimo* to Studley, urging him to study the photographs of Apaches, and stating that the war moccasins must be redone, the stock of the

rifle was out of proportion, and, above all, the ponies and horses were all wrong:

. . . *Go down to the stockyards and look at a horse, or better still, swallow pride and ethics and consult some of Frederick Remington's work. It is no reflection upon your artistic ability that your horses do not suit me. There are very few men who can draw a horse in action. Over thirty years ago it was generally believed that Remington carried a kodak; and I am inclined to think that he did, as otherwise it would be practically impossible to portray horses correctly in action from visual observation alone.*

The Apache Devil's horse was supposed to be a pinto, and Ed devoted an entire paragraph to describing how a pinto should be drawn. In re-examining Studley's sketches he noted, ". . . I am inclined to think that one of your horse troubles is that you do not have the nose tapered enough. It is too wide and flat — like a cow's." He followed with a lengthy paragraph, taken from Lummis' *The Land of Poco Tiempo,* giving details of the shape of an Apache war moccasin. About Shoz-Dijiji, the Apache Devil himself, Ed had already stressed that he should be drawn "without an ounce of superfluous fat."

During the summer of 1932 the dealings with Studley had been slowly reaching a crisis. Emotionally unstable, in periods of stress Studley turned to drinking, and as a result he failed to complete the assignments on time. The delay in receiving the illustrations for *Apache Devil* now forced Ed to an action he had so far avoided — he must contact another artist and have him in readiness. On September 17 he inquired of St. John, "We are wondering if your quotation of March 3rd . . . still holds good. We are seriously considering making a change. . . ." On the thirtieth, in a blunt letter to Studley, he laid down the conditions for an assignment on the next book and insisted that he must have an immediate reply. ". . . these transactions must be on a purely business basis," he wrote. "If your work is not satisfactory, I must employ another artist regardless of our relationship." He was offering Studley one more chance:

I was not particularly pleased with the work in Tarzan Triumphant, *and your inability to get work out on time as promised is a very serious handicap to us and I had planned on going back to St. John on the next book. But I like the photostats of* Apache Devil *so well that I should like to have you do the next book for us because you are always very gracious and willing to make the illustrations that I want in the way that I want them. . . .*

Ed's further comment, ". . . I doubt that St. John would brook what he might consider interference with his creative ability," indicated his awareness of the fact that only with his nephew did he have to follow his tactics of dictating the content and style of every illustration. It should be remembered that ERB and St. John worked so well together that he did not have to give St. John such detailed instructions.

Concerning the new novel, *Tarzan and the City of Gold,* Ed emphasized he would allow no deviation from the strict conditions he was imposing. If Studley accepted the work, it must be at the Burroughs offices by January 1, 1933; ". . . If it is not, the order is cancelled and you will receive no pay for whatever you have done up to that time." Studley's preliminary sketches did arrive in November — they were returned with the usual demands for alterations — and a $100 advance that Studley had requested. Meanwhile, on the fourteenth Ed received a letter from his brother Harry revealing that Studley, unemployed, was facing financial difficulties. Ed replied, "I cannot understand what you say about Studley's not having anything to do when we had such a heck of a time getting him to do our work promptly. I heard indirectly that he was drinking again and that was the only reason to which I attribute his very evident neglect of the work he was doing for us. . . ."

With 1932 at an end and no sign of the completed illustrations from Studley, Ed turned the assignment over to St. John. The work did arrive, too late, some weeks later. On January 31, 1933, Ed sent his final comments to Studley about the entire situation: although he had not cared "particularly" for various illustrations he had used them; however, the drawings for *Tarzan and the City of Gold* had not only arrived well past the deadline, but had proved to be disappointing. Ed ventured the hope that he might be able to use some of his nephew's drawings if they did not conflict with those being prepared by St. John, but this seemed unlikely. He credited Studley's account with the full amount charged for the work, while at the same time refusing a request for an immediate payment. In March, St. John sent his completed work, which was enthusiastically received. Ed wrote, "I am delighted with the Tarzan cover and illustrations. . . . I am sure that my readers are going to be glad to see you back again."

Thus, Studley's employment by Burroughs came to an end; his illustrations were contained in four novels, *Tarzan the Invincible, Jungle Girl, Tarzan Triumphant,* and *Apache Devil* (1931-33).

Burroughs' worry and annoyance over the procrastination displayed by Studley in his assignments contrasted with the light and indulgent attitude he adopted toward a scholastic problem encountered by Jack at Pomona College. On October 27, 1933, William E. Nicholl, the dean, forwarded a report of unsatisfactory work by Jack in Mathematics B9a. Jack's grade was "F," but under "Remarks" Nicholl noted, "Case is probably not serious. This work is individual work; he can and doubtless will make it all up." Across the failure notice, Ed wrote some original verse — and undoubtedly sent the sheet to Jack. The humorous poem read:

A young man with a Dante-esque pate
Decided that he'd go Phi Bete;
So he played 'long the path
'Til he'd flunked out in Math
And his papa cried, "Oh, aint that great!"

The years 1930-33 found Burroughs at one of his highest levels of creative output.

Among the completed works were five Tarzan novels. In 1931 alone he finished two Tarzans, started another, wrote a police-crime story and a Venus sequel. In the period of March 18 to June 9, 1930, the novel tentatively titled *Tarzan and the Man Things* was written, its theme being one of political intrigue centered about the actions of Burroughs' favorite villains — the communists. The Russian, Peter Zveri, in order to realize his plan for seizing control of Africa, has assembled a group of communists from various countries. These include comrade Zora Drinov, who later becomes nonpolitically romantic; the Indian, Raghunath Jafar; the Mexican, Miguel Romero; the American, Wayne Colt; and the Filipino, Antonio Mori. Joined with them are Arabs under Sheykh Abu Batn and a large number of African blacks. The scheme, as part of an international plot to weaken the capitalist countries through a series of wars and revolutions, is to maneuver Italy into a war with France. At the moment that a supposed French plot to invade Italian Somaliland is revealed to the Fascist government by communist agents in Rome, Comrade Zveri's forces, disguised as French soldiers, would cross the border into the Italian colony. With the other capitalist powers distracted by problems at home, the communists would then succeed in establishing a group of autonomous soviet states throughout Africa.

Since a large amount of money is needed to finance the operations, Zveri plans to loot the treasure vaults of Opar. Informed by little Nkima, the monkey, of the presence of a group of armed men, Tarzan spies upon them, follows them to Opar, and works to frustrate their schemes. As the story progresses, the presumed theme of a world-wide soviet conspiracy is abruptly abandoned; Burroughs, in his contempt for the communists, refuses to allow them to be sincere even in their Marxist goals. Zveri, the dedicated communist leader, emerges as an egomaniac, a man possessed by a desire to become Peter I, Emperor of Africa, and motivated, oddly enough, by uncontrollable capitalistic urges to corner a huge pile of money. To Zora, whom he plans to make his Empress, he

cries, "Yes, I am crazy for power, for riches, and for you." Later, when Zveri suggests that he might make Mori, the Filipino communist, into a grand duke, and Mori, astonished, remarks that the grand dukes were "wicked men who ground down the working classes," Zveri replies, "To be a Grand Duke who grinds down the rich and takes money from them might not be so bad. . . . Grand Dukes are very rich and powerful. . . ."

In *Tarzan and the Man Things* a romance develops between Comrade Zora and the American "communist" Wayne Colt, and Burroughs, as usual, reserves certain revelations about the two until the end. To complete the novel, Ed required some prodding from Donald Kennicott of *Blue Book*; the publication, owned by McCall's since 1929, had been purchasing a series of Burroughs novels and paying record prices. On May 20, 1930, Ed, aware of his promise to Kennicott, wrote, "The Tarzan story is not coming along very well; in fact it is not coming at all. I have had a great many other things upon my mind and, in addition, have felt none too well for several months. . . ." On the thirty-first he noted that Kennicott's letter had "awakened" him to the necessity of "getting busy"; he now felt certain the manuscript would soon be finished. It was forwarded to Kennicott in two sections, 135 pages on June 11 and the remainder on the twentieth. The story, for which *Blue Book* paid $8,000, was retitled "Tarzan, Guard of the Jungle," and appeared in the magazine as a seven-part serial, from October 1930 to April 1931. In scheduling the novel as the first to be published by Edgar Rice Burroughs, Inc., Ed planned to use his original title, but changing his mind, on June 26 announced a new title to Elser — *Tarzan the Invincible*. The book made its appearance on November 20, 1931, with cover and frontispiece illustrations by nephew Studley.[42]

The certainty that his non-Tarzan stories would be difficult to market could not prevent Ed from turning on occasion to differing themes. To Kennicott, who had left no doubt that he wanted only Tarzan stories for *Blue Book*, Ed wrote on June 26, 1930, about his work on a Western. He was writing it "in an entirely different vein" from anything he had done before: "I am in the fourth chapter and so far only one person has been killed. I am trying to make it more ladylike in the hopes of getting it into some... publication like *Red Book*. The chances are that I shall not be able to sell it at all." The 60,000-word Western, written June 14 to July 12, was titled "That Damned Dude"; its plot, fairly routine, centers about the stratagem devised by Buck Mason, the Deputy Sheriff of Comanche County, New Mexico, who is falsely accused of the murder of Ole Gunderstrom. Mason vanishes from the area and is thought to have fled to evade arrest, but actually he is seeking the real murderers; in this task he becomes "Bruce Marvel" and turns up at the TF Dude Ranch, owned by Cory Blaine. In playing the role of Marvel, Buck wears outfits that are incongruous for the western range; his English riding boots and breeches and white polo shirt provoke derision and contempt in the other guests at the dude ranch, while his assumed ignorance about horses and riding and his "sissy" attitude make him appear as a pitiable tenderfoot and earn him the appellation of "that damned dude."[43]

For "That Damned Dude" Burroughs pursued lengthy and determined marketing efforts which for years resulted only in failure. When a submission to *Collier's* on July 18, 1930, brought a rejection, Ed returned to an old standby, Munsey's *Argosy*. But there was little enthusiasm for what A. H. Bittner, the editor, described as "a good, usable regulation western story." On September 9 Bittner noted that *Argosy*, which accepted few westerns, wanted them to be "unusual and outstanding." His final point was painfully familiar: "Our readers expect the Tarzan type of story from you and it certainly would disappoint a great many of them to hand them a western story under your name."

A year later, at Rothmund's initiative, an inquiry was dispatched to Don Moore, the new managing editor of *Argosy*, concerning "That Damned Dude"; Rothmund referred to Burroughs' past popularity in the magazine and wrote, "... I am sure that your readers would appreciate to have him back again...."[44] Moore, delighted at the prospect of a Burroughs reappearance in *Argosy*, announced that the magazine could use "a large quantity" of his stories, both *Tarzan* and interplanetary, but that a Western would be acceptable only if it could follow one of his popular fantastic novels.[45] In the negotiations that followed, Moore mentioned the discouraging failure of the Tarzan stories to bolster *Blue Book's* circulation — it had reached a low point of 118,000, about half of its past record — but added that he was willing to gamble "heavily" and would pay ten cents a word for a new Tarzan novel. Burroughs at once replied with a three-story package offer: Tarzan and Venus stories, plus "That Damned Dude," the price to be 7½ cents a word. Moore, who had previously indicated he "might" consider paying three to six cents a word for "That Damned Dude," at once rejected the blanket price scheme. At the end of 1931 and the first part of 1932 *Argosy* purchased the two fantastic stories it had desired, "The Pirates of Venus" and "Tarzan and the City of Gold." But Moore carefully avoided all reference to "That Damned Dude." On January 5, 1932, Burroughs brought up the story again, mentioned the special non-Tarzan rate of 7½ cents he had granted and insisted that Moore, because of past concessions made to him, should be willing to purchase the story at that rate. Moore's steadfast refusal brought an annoyed letter: the definite understanding had been that of the three stories to be published by *Argosy*, one would be "That Damned Dude." The price was lowered to six cents a word, and when Moore still remained adamant, Burroughs, on February 8, via Rothmund, offered an astonishing proposal: Considering that the Western was not "outstanding," any plan to publish it under Burroughs' name would not be desirable; it would only "reflect" upon him. Therefore, in adopting a suggestion that Moore had advanced earlier, the story could be published under a pseudonym. Burroughs wrote,

"This is the only way that I would want it published now. . . ." He asked that Moore re-read "That Damned Dude" with the idea of "using a fictitious author's name," and again reduced the price to a flat figure of $2,500.

Moore now seemed hesitant and on February 23 Burroughs dispatched the manuscript to him, noted he would be "eagerly looking" for the $2,500 check, and advised that since the story was to appear under a pseudonym, it should be copyrighted by the Munsey Company and then transferred to the Burroughs Corporation. On March 10 all of the two years' incredibly persistent efforts to sell the story came to nothing. Moore firmly stated his "final judgement," insisting, "the story is not for us under any name or at any price. It is much too conventional and leisurely. . . ." The Burroughs office replied weakly, "We appreciate your frank opinion of this story, as a result of which we have put an N.G. tag on it. . . ."[46]

But the marathon marketing saga of "That Damned Dude" was not finished yet. Four years passed, and in the summer of 1936, with *Argosy* now headed by a new editor, Jack Byrne, the story was again submitted. On August 8, 1936, in rejecting it, Byrne conceded that the story was "entertaining" but that he now had on hand a year's supply of long Westerns. Earlier that year Burroughs had received a letter from Leo Margulies, editorial director of Standard Magazines, who nostalgically recalled the past:

I started off as office assistant to the one and only Bob Davis in 1920 in the Robert H. Davis Corporation, and we handled some of your stuff. In particular I remember Bob Davis giving me one of your Martian stories to take home to read. Eventually it sold to good old All Story, *a grand magazine then. The years roll by. And here I am the editorial director of fourteen pulp magazines. . . . I know it is almost an impertinence to ask whether you have anything on hand. . . . Our rates are nothing to brag about, but maybe, who knows, you may have a yarn that everybody else is afraid to publish. . . .*[47]

Burroughs' response brought a quotation from Margulies of a maximum two-cents-a-word rate. On April 17 the novel "Back to the Stone Age" was forwarded to Margulies with an accompanying hint that *more* than the maximum rate would be required. After some hesitation — the story was overlong and had no central plot — Margulies offered $1,000. This was rejected by Burroughs, and in the continuing saga of "That Damned Dude" a passage of three more years was required before Burroughs suddenly recalled his previous correspondence with Margulies and thought of his unsold Western. The old Standard Magazines had by then become Popular Library and Margulies now had some thirty magazines on his list. On August 23, 1939, "That Damned Dude" was sent to Margulies and his offer of $500 was promptly accepted by Burroughs. Margulies had noted that "with some editorial changes" the story could be made "to conform to our policy." On October 12 he revealed publishing plans for the March 1940 issue of *Thrilling Adventures*; "That Damned Dude," a three-part serial, would be retitled "The Terrible Tenderfoot." Its sale and appearance in print culminated more than nine years of sales attempts and demonstrated that in the matter of unsold properties Burroughs had a memory exceeding that of his elephant Tantor. In 1941 "That Damned Dude," transformed to "The Terrible Tenderfoot" by Margulies, became *The Deputy Sheriff of Commanche County* when it was published in book form by Edgar Rice Burroughs, Inc.

In the original 1931 agreement signed with Don Moore, *Argosy* editor, Burroughs was allowed only one other market — *Blue Book* — for the sale of Tarzan and other fantastic stories for a year's period. Some months before the Munsey agreement Ed had written *Tarzan and the Raiders* (February 27 to May 20, 1931). On his card index he noted, "Ralph (Rothmund) took ms. to NY to submit to *Cosmopolitan* and *Colliers*, or to *Blue Book*. . . ." As in the past, Ed's hopes of breaking into the top slick magazine field did not materialize. The story wound up with Kennicott at *Blue Book*, who on June 13, wrote, ". . . depression has hit hard. . . willing to accept $7,000. . .?" He also commented, "most readers will share my disappointment that our beloved Tarzan himself and his wild-animal comrades appear so little. . . halfway through. . . found that Tarzan appears on only one-fifth of the pages. In the last half of the story he's a bit more prominent. . . ." Concerning the title, Kennicott inquired, "How does 'Tarzan Triumphant' strike you. . .?" Ed rejected the offered price, demanding $1,000 more, and on June 19 Kennicott wired, "Confess unconquerable taste for Tarzan stop Eight thousand it is." Under the title of "The Triumph of Tarzan" the novel ran as a six-part serial in *Blue Book*, October 1931 to March 1932. For the book, published by Burroughs on September 1, 1932, the title became *Tarzan Triumphant*.

The novel demonstrates some plot ingenuity with certain bizarre events launched through the use of an imaginative prologue describing one Augustus the Ephesian, for whose background Burroughs journeys 1800 years into the past.

Tarzan Triumphant contains a Russian communist villain, this time Leon Stabutch who, in an unusual scene, is shown taking direct orders from Stalin for the assassination of Tarzan. Stalin insists that Peter Zveri must be avenged; Zveri's communist plot was thwarted in *Tarzan the Invincible*. Other characters pair off into romantic situations, with Danny "Gunner" Patrick, a Chicago gangster, falling in love with the golden-haired Jezebel, and Lafayette Smith, a geology professor, becoming enamored of Lady Barbara Collis. Tarzan is involved in his usual series of mishaps, escapes, and hairbreadth rescues of the others.

The Burroughs organization had plans to publish two books a year, and because of this ambitious schedule the selection of sales representatives to handle the various territories became extremely important. Burroughs had

seldom approved of any of the companies or syndicates with which he had dealt in the past, but in 1932 he began an association with Michael S. Mill that lasted for many years. Mill, hired as a publishers representative for the metropolitan area of New York, the New England states, New Jersey, Philadelphia, Baltimore, and Washington, D.C., was guaranteed a twelve and one-half percent commission; the first books to be promoted were *Jungle Girl* and *Tarzan the Invincible*. While all orders for books were transmitted to the Burroughs offices in Tarzana, the shipping was arranged through warehouses of the printer, the Kingsport Press in Tennessee and New York City. Distribution rights were assigned to the American News Company and Baker & Taylor, both of whom were granted special discount rates. At a later date, because of problems with the Kingsport Press in handling the New York area, shipping and billing for this territory were transferred to the American Booksellers Association.

The correspondence between Mill and Ralph Rothmund, almost voluminous, produced an amusing exchange as a result of a phrase used in *Tarzan Triumphant*. Mill, adopting the attitude of a censor, objected to the content of a sentence on page 307 of the novel: "I shall never cook for any white bitch." On November 18, 1932, Rothmund responded, "I called this to Mr. Burroughs' attention, and his reaction to it was that the words 'white bitch' are properly used. They were meant for a 'white dog.' Bitch is a perfectly good word in good standing, and is listed in Webster's International Dictionary. Bitch means dog, and it is proper to use it in that sense." Burroughs, as on other occasions, opposed efforts to substitute prissy or genteel words for the blunt, natural ones he had chosen.

In his earlier years Burroughs had sought to vary the steady and exhausting diet of long novels by writing a number of shorter works. His hopes of attaining even a limited success through sales of some of these stories had not been realized. Nevertheless, in 1931 he wrote a 6,500-word crime story, completed in only two days, June 12 and 13, titled "Calling All Cars." For his setting, as the story opened, he turned to the San Fernando Valley adjacent to Los Angeles and described the unplanned and unblending hodgepodge of architecture adopted for the Valley homes:

The explosion of hot air, which was the latest Los Angeles realty boom, covered the floor of a valley with bungalows, duplexes, Italian villas, and mortgages; it drove them up winding canyons and over summits and spewed them out across other valleys; it scattered residences up the sides of the Santa Monica Mountains, leaving many perched precariously, and isolated, upon hilltops. The architecture was varied — often beautiful, occasionally weird, sometimes awful — but the mortgages were all alike.[48]

In "Calling All Cars," a crime story with a light touch, Burroughs offers a style that is smoother and more sophisticated than in any of his previous works. The problem, however, lies in plot defects.

The story suffered the fate of other Burroughs short stories. A first submission to the *Saturday Evening Post* brought a rejection, and in the fall of 1931 the story found a similarly negative reception at *Cosmopolitan* and *Liberty*. Burroughs' fondest hope had been, for years, to place stories in these high-paying prestige markets. His secretary, Ralph Rothmund, especially bombarded *Liberty* with a succession of stories. On November 14, 1931, D. E. Wheeler, a *Liberty* editor, in his rejection of "Calling All Cars," made it plain that he perceived the plot weaknesses: "To us, it is a mistake to build up such a dramatic situation and then have it come out a hoax." *Colliers*, another magazine that had received several Burroughs manuscripts, also rejected the story, and in 1932 it was returned by H. N. Swanson, Editor of *College Humor*. "Calling All Cars" never achieved publication.

Continuing his steady writing pace, Burroughs next produced *Tarzan and the Leopard Men*, completing the 80,000 word novel in a two-month period — July 9 to September 25, 1931. The Leopard Men, a secret order of natives who gathered under their chief Gato Mgungu to perform "abhorrent rites," donned leopard-skin hoods and wore steel claws as they prowled the jungle in search of human victims. The blacks they killed were mutilated, parts of the corpses being cut away to be used in their cannibalistic orgies. In providing for Tarzan's role, Burroughs selected an over-used device, the familiar loss of identity after an injury. Tarzan, struck by a heavy tree limb, suffers amnesia, is named Muzimo — the protecting spirit of a departed ancestor — by a native who has become his friend, and comes to call himself by that name. Throughout most of the novel Muzimo, who pits himself against the bloodthirsty Leopard Men, is involved in hand-to-hand combat or the rescuing of his friends. Burroughs creates two white men, Old-Timer and The Kid, whose real names are not disclosed until the end. The feminine half of a romantic situation is a white girl who accepts the native name of Kali Bwana; she is searching for her brother, and in a not-very-surprising discovery he turns out to be The Kid. With the brother and sister Jerry and Jessie Jerome reunited, the story ends as the Old-Timer, not really very old, and Jessie plight their love.

Still pursuing the elusive prestige markets, Burroughs in 1931 sent *Tarzan and the Leopard Men* to *Collier's* and *Cosmopolitan*. With their rejections he turned to *Blue Book*, but in the 1932 correspondence that followed, Kennicott bemoaned the effects of the depression on magazine sales and offered only $5,000 for the story. Some weeks of dickering ensued, and in April of that year Burroughs finally accepted a compromise price of $6,000.[49]

An idea for fantastic adventures on a new planet, discarded by Burroughs in 1929 because of a story published by another author, was revived two years later. Despite Otis Adelbert Kline's use of a Venus setting, Burroughs, in 1931, adopted the cloud-covered planet as a background for a novel containing some unusual types of pseudo-scientific devices and stressing a theme of social or class conflict. The

Tarzan for President

A CITIZEN who had grown desperate with the multiplicity of schemes to end the depression, and who was well wearied with political pettifoggery and propaganda, recently wrote a letter to a New York newspaper. The desperate citizen had a brilliant and simple suggestion which the newspapers liked well enough to pass on to its readers.

"Let us," said the writer in effect, "elect Tarzan to the Presidency. He at least went places and did things."

Unfortunately we cannot, In this difficult world, have many of the things we want. We cannot, for example, have Tarzan for President. We can, however, have him for a job that is individually more important to us: we can have him for a friend in need, and for a needed refuge and solace from humdrum things, we can go on safari with him in his own primitive and refreshing world.

Next month this champion adventurer in all the realm of fiction comes back to you in a new novel—"Tarzan and the Leopard Men." With him comes his familiar spirit the little monkey Nkima riding through utmost peril on his shoulder; with him too come Numa the lion and Sabor the lioness and all the rest of that goodly jungle company we have known and loved so well. With him also come many new and interesting people, friends and enemies alike. You may count upon renewing a true and tried fiction delight when you turn to the next issue of the Blue Book Magazine.

TARZAN will have good company: an absorbing mystery novelette by Henry C. Rowland entitled "Murder on the Eastern Shore," as well as many specially attractive stories by such writers as Clarence Herbert New, Warren H. Miller, Henry La Cossitt, Arthur K. Akers, Edgar Jepson and the like.

—*The Editor.*

"Tarzan for President," article published in Blue Book Magazine, *July 1932, as buildup for appearance of ERB's new Tarzan novel, "Tarzan and the Leopard Men," in August issue.*

most important of the Burroughs inventions, an everyman's fountain-of-youth dream, was the "serum of longevity," perfected on Venus a thousand years before the arrival of the protagonist, Carson Napier. "It is injected every two years and not only provides immunity from all diseases but insures the complete restoration of all wasted tissue."

Other devices include a deadly R-ray handgun and a cannon that discharges an even more destructive T-ray, capable of disintegrating any object it strikes. For the propulsion of the Thoran navy, Burroughs created his own atomic energy:

... the very useful element 93 (vik-ro) is here again employed upon a substance called lor, which contains a considerable proportion of the element yor-san (105). The action of vik-ro upon yor-san results in absolute annihilation of the lor, releasing all its energy.

It was noted that the "annihilation" of a ton of coal liberates eighteen thousand million times as much energy as combustion would. Because of this Venusian discovery, "Fuel for the life of the ship could be carried in a pint jar." The Venusians also possess navigational instruments that utilize radioactivity drawn from the nuclei of certain elements, the gamma ray being the most important of these. The ray, which upon encountering an obstruction records the "retardation" that follows, is used to determine distances and ocean depths for the Amtorian navies.

In the novel *Pirates of Venus*, written October 2 to November 6, 1931, Carson Napier, who was raised in India by the mystic Chand Kabi, has acquired a telepathic ability which enables him to converse with people at a distance or to project mental images through space. For the proper contact an individual with "psychological harmony" was needed, and Burroughs proved to have this quality. Napier, a young man, gives details of a life of varied activities: he has returned to America, has been graduated from Claremont College in California, has become an airplane stunt man in the movies, and after acquiring a fortune has

developed an interest in rocket cars culminating in the construction of a gigantic rocket on Guadalupe Island. His original hope had been to journey to Venus, but because of scientific reports that this planet has extremes of temperature too hazardous for man and, above all, that Venus is apparently without oxygen, he has decided to travel to Mars. He then reveals his purpose for the "psychological" link with Burroughs: once upon Mars, with little chance of returning, he must establish telepathic communication with someone on earth.

These plans for space travel are explained to Burroughs and his secretary Ralph Rothmund by Napier at the offices in Tarzana, and with arrangements now made for Ed to be the "medium" through whom all future adventures will be transmitted, Napier embarks upon his one-man rocket trip. Ironically, because of a failure to provide for the gravitational pull of the moon, the rocket veers off course, and some weeks later Napier finds himself hurtling toward Venus — the planet he had first rejected as his goal. In parachuting downward through the clouds, he discovers that the scientists were wrong; Venus does possess sufficient oxygen to support life.

The first Venusians encountered by Napier surprisingly resemble normal earth beings. He learns that Venus, called Amtor, is divided into three main areas, and these, as drawn in concentric circles on a map of the planet, consist of Trabol, a temperate zone region, Strabol, a tropical country near the equator, and Karbol, a frigid region surrounding one of the poles. Napier also finds that he is on a large island, the country of Vepaja, where the inhabitants have built their homes far above the ground in huge trees. To establish passage and communication, they have connected the trees with wide causeways. The reasons for these strange dwellings are explained to Napier. Centuries earlier Vepaja was a great prosperous country extending from Strabol to Karbol. Unfortunately, a group of malcontents composed of the lazy and incompetent and the criminal classes, under the leadership of a man named Thor, began a propaganda campaign to create discord and dissension. The secret order known as Thorists preached a gospel of class hatred called Thorism. Their subversive efforts led to a bloody revolution and the overthrow of the Vepajan government. A small number of people, including members of the cultured class, escaped with their leader or "jong" to this uninhabited island where, for their own safety, they constructed the tree cities.

Burroughs' hatred of communism and his contempt and mistrust of labor leaders (or "agitators") caused him to create a revolution without any socialistic or reform motives, one led by Thor, a laborer and actual criminal, who gained a large following from the "ignorant masses"; large numbers of people were thus easily duped. Here Burroughs reaffirms his belief that the average man, the citizen in a democracy, is often incapable of making intelligent choices or decisions.

Curiously, the revolution occurred in a Vepaja that was "prosperous and happy." The many people who followed the false leaders did so because of only one motive — they disliked the upper class. And even more curiously, these individuals, drawn from the three other classes, were weak and naive enough to be influenced by malcontents described as "envious of those who had won to positions which they were not mentally equipped to attain." This is a sad reflection upon the intelligence of a cross-section of the citizens; they were not only simple-minded and gullible (having no motive other than jealousy for revolting), but they were willing to join with others who were also stupid and to accept orders from a mere laborer.

In creating the society of Vepajans who had withdrawn to their island, Burroughs devised his own solution to the class conflict. "We have learned our lesson," Danus says, "that a people divided amongst themselves cannot be happy. Where there are even slight class distinctions there are envy and jealousy." The answer is plain: the people must be socially equalized, adjusted to a homogeneous mass. Danus explains, ". . . We are all of the same class. We

have no servants; whatever there is to do we do better than servants ever did it. . . ."

The Vepajans' use of "the serum of longevity" produced another problem which led to a solution Burroughs had proposed in the past. "As none grew old and none died," the Vepajans were confronted by an overpopulation danger. Burroughs' answer was of course mandatory birth control, with children allowed in quotas of sufficient number to balance the only deaths that occurred, those caused by war or violence.

The *Pirates of Venus*, taking its title from a brief sequence in which Napier, aided by mutineers, seizes a Thoran ship and then turns to piracy against other vessels of the communist nation of Thora, becomes a typical romance with Napier falling in love with Duare, the inaccessible daughter of the jong. In the unresolved ending, as Duare is carried to safety by a birdman and Napier is captured, Burroughs' plan for a Venus series is evident.

Possibly because of his creation of a new planetary setting, his first space adventure away from Mars (except for *The Moon Maid* trilogy), Burroughs prepared a detailed map of Venus. Besides three main areas, the circular map contains a number of islands, their names entered in English and in the Amtorian alphabet. Also one of Ed's inventions, the alphabet corresponds to our twenty-six letters, and on his worksheet, with its glossary of characters, objects, and places, he meticulously translated by hand the long list of items into the Amtorian letters.

The 60,000-word *Pirates of Venus*, part of a prearranged triple sale to Don Moore, *Argosy* editor — a kind of written-to-order agreement with a *Tarzan* story to follow — brought an approving statement from Moore who felt that the Venus setting could launch "a very successful series." However, on November 24, 1931, Moore suggested the addition of two incidents which he believed would improve the first two magazine installments. Surprisingly, Burroughs, who as a rule was unwilling to accept editors' ideas for revision, agreed to make the changes.[50] Moore had already stressed his plan to celebrate the Burroughs return to *Argosy* with a Tarzan story first; *Pirates of Venus* was

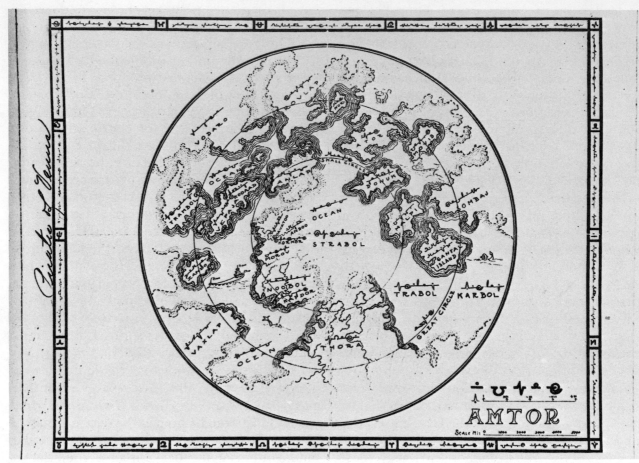

Ed's map of Amtor in The Pirates of Venus; *around periphery of map are words in Venusian language invented by ERB.*

held until *Tarzan and the City of Gold*, already begun, had been published; the Venus serial ran from September 17 to October 22, 1932, in *Argosy*.

Responding to Moore's query, Burroughs sent a brief outline of the latest Tarzan story, noting its Abyssinian setting; the City of Gold where lions were bred for racing, hunting, and war; and the expected white queen, this time half mad, who falls in love with Tarzan. At the climactic grand hunt, as Tarzan runs the gauntlet with Belthar, a huge lion, in pursuit, Jad-Bal-Ja, who has tracked his master over hundreds of miles, arrives at the last moment to save him.[51]

Tarzan and the City of Gold, written November 21, 1931, to January 7, 1932, was forwarded to Moore in two sections. Upon sending the first half, Burroughs explained his intention to use the title for the forthcoming book. The title was especially appropriate because of the plan to write a companion story and call it *Tarzan and the City of Ivory*.[52] Burroughs' often-revealed disgust about mankind appears, as in the past, through Tarzan's reflections. In *The City of Gold* Tarzan believes contentment to be the highest goal and "health and culture the principal avenues along which man may approach this goal." Man, however, can only be viewed with contempt because he is "wanting in either one essential or the other, when not wanting in both." Despite man's "vaunted mentality," his vices place him upon "a lower spiritual scale than the beasts, while barring him eternally from the goal of contentment." In a later dialogue,

Venusian alphabet created by ERB for his Venus novels.

when Gemnon remarks that beasts are "different," Tarzan responds, "Yes; they have left all the petty meannesses to man." The comparison is aptly made:

"We are what we are born," rejoined Gemnon; "some are beasts, some are men, and some are men who behave like beasts."

"But none, thank God, are beasts that behave like men," retorted Tarzan, smiling.

A most unusual scene, a type not previously used by Burroughs, is one of flashback with Tarzan, a prisoner in a dungeon of the City of Gold, releasing his memories which "roved the jungle and the veldt and lived again the freedom and the experiences of the past." Tarzan travels back to his childhood with Kala, the she-ape who had suckled him; recalls the later tragedy of her death; and remembers the animosity

he and old Tublat, his foster-father, had displayed toward each other.[53]

In *Pirate Blood,* an unusually brief 34,000-word novelette written February 22 to May 5, 1932, Burroughs creates a determining theme based upon his own belief in the influence of heredity upon human beings. The introduction, presenting deceptively casual dialogue, provides clues to the story's direction. Three characters, John Lafitte, Frank Adams, and Daisy Jukes discuss heredity and eugenics. Lafitte's achievement, both in his college studies and on the Glenora football team, could never approach that of the brilliant Adams who became student body president and captain of the debating team. Significantly, Lafitte, who did poorly in his chosen field of law, excelled in boxing, rifle shooting, and military science. Adams' ancestors included lawyers, diplomats,

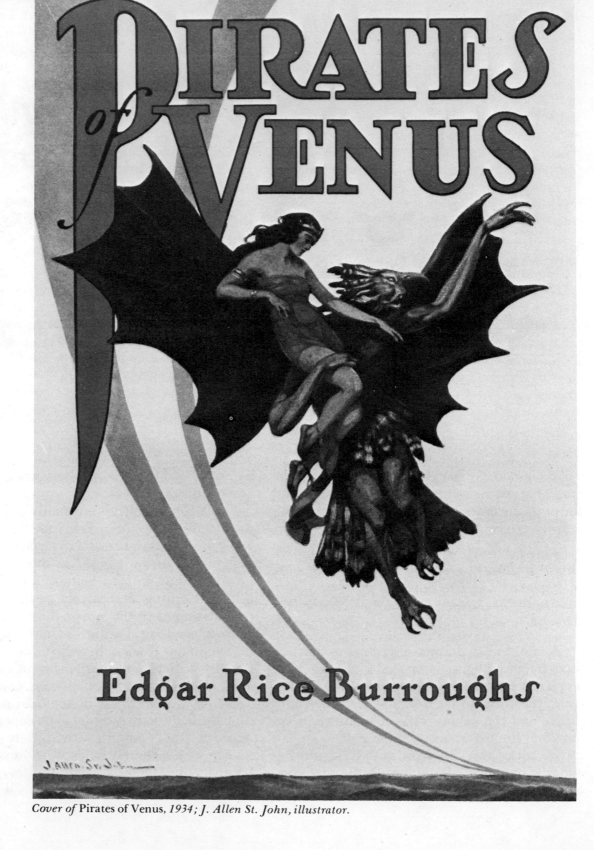

Cover of Pirates of Venus, *1934; J. Allen St. John, illustrator.*

and two United States presidents, while Lafitte's only forebear of record was the pirate Jean Lafitte. Daisy reveals her knowledge and fear of her ancestry — her descent from the disreputable Jukeses.

It is evident that Lafitte and Adams believe in inherited characteristics. They both speak sadly of Daisy who has the blood line of old Max Jukes which has produced paupers, prostitutes, and criminals for two hundred years. The passing years bring no success to John; he fails the bar examination, and becomes a policeman. Meanwhile the Jukeses and Adamses become wealthy when oil is discovered on their properties. The final blow to John comes when Daisy, the girl he has always loved, discloses her plan to marry Frank Adams.

Burroughs next proceeds to the action of the story, centered about the protagonist, John Lafitte. Burroughs does try to indicate some skepticism about heredity in his reference to the effects of environment and training upon the long line of admirals descending from Commodore Perry. Lafitte, pursuing Bill Perry, a cashier who has absconded with the bank funds, finds himself in the balloon in which Perry is making a getaway. The balloon drifts far across the Pacific, Perry suddenly turns mad and leaps out, and John, now the sole passenger, parachutes to an island where a notorious pirate, The Vulture, is located. There Lafitte feels a bond drawing him toward The Vulture. Neither loyalty nor affection is involved. It is simply a matter that blood will tell — the piratical instincts of old Jean Lafitte have seized control of him.

John falls in love with La Diablesa, The Vulture's mistress; takes part callously in the capture of vessels and the slaughter of the people aboard; and later joins The Portuguese, a rival of The Vulture. Daisy reappears as the Queen of Diamonds, a prostitute from the brothels of Singapore. The blood of old Max Jukes had brought her to this sorry state, she explains bitterly, while revealing she had never married Adams, and had always loved John. She notes that the "curse of blood" had made him a pirate and destroyed her and she cries, "I

wonder if we can ever escape our putrid blood streams...." Then she commits suicide. At the story's end, after The Vulture and The Portuguese are killed, John Lafitte and La Diablesa become a respectable married couple.

The strength of *Pirate Blood,* its development of a unifying theme not as a rule displayed by the Burroughs novels, was not sufficient to make it palatable to the magazine editors. Neither a fantasy nor a realistic tale, it was too atypical of the Burroughs style. On May 20, 1932, a lengthy letter sent to four top publications — *American, Colliers, Cosmopolitan,* and *Liberty* — contained a sales pitch that preceded the offering of *Pirate Blood.* Noting that the editors had come to consider Burroughs' stories as designed principally for juvenile reading, the letter stressed that this was contrary to the facts. Much of the fan mail came from adults — doctors, lawyers, bankers, and other professional people. Assuming that the editors had not clearly understood this, the letter went on to refer to the newly written *Pirate Blood:* ". . . before submitting . . . should like to have you advise us whether you would care to consider. . . ." No encouragement was received from the magazines. The story was nevertheless forwarded to *Liberty, Colliers,* and *Cosmopolitan* in June 1932, where it brought quick rejections. On April 28, 1938, *Pirate Blood* was returned by *Argosy,* and a year later, by Leo Margulies of *Popular Library.*[54]

In the 1931 agreement Burroughs and *Argosy* were obligated to the extent of three stories. With the completion of *Tarzan and the City of Gold* and *The Pirates of Venus,* all that remained was the prearranged Venus sequel. Don Moore, *Argosy* editor, was blunt in stating the type of story he wanted and expressed disappointment about the second installment of *The Pirates of Venus;* it did not contain sufficient action and excitement. His concept of a successful story was one "crowded" with incidents, plot, and "especially invention." Urging Burroughs on, he wrote, "The more fantastic creatures and imaginative scenes of action that he can pack into this sequel, the greater momentum the series will have. . . ."[55] Moore had hoped to receive one-half of the sequel, *Lost on Venus,* by October 1932, but Burroughs instead sent the full work on November 18. It was greeted with delight by Moore who remarked that it was "at least twice as good as The Pirates of Venus." He confessed in this letter of the twenty-eighth that he had felt ". . . *The Pirates* . . . was generally rather slow. . . ." Nevertheless, he suggested a number of changes in this sequel, some centered about "The House of Seven Doors," and one plot change which, without question, produced a better device than Burroughs' original one. Without argument Burroughs agreed to these and on December 6 sent revisions on a number of insert pages.[56]

Moore's importuning for "Action . . . Action . . ." undoubtedly influenced Burroughs in his writing of *Lost on Venus,* for the completed work became a sequence of violent encounters, battles, shootings, and hairbreadth escapes, with Napier facing hostile Venusians, weird creatures, and monsters in every possible shape. Without a stronger unifying theme, the story develops as a series of exciting adventures. But Burroughs, as always, manages to contrive some strikingly original characters and situations. Most interesting are the living dead, those whom the warped Skor has "resurrected from the grave." Synthetic life has been "instilled" into them, and in their dead minds are only the thoughts that "Skor transmits to them by some occult, telepathic means." These variants of the zombie (or possibly precursors) have no blood in their veins. They talk, appear to reason, and at times take independent action, even when Skor is not controlling them; he has implanted a "system of conduct and ethics" into their dead brains. Amusingly, Skor explains that certain specimens of his living dead appear very dull, "because they were dull people in life."

In a number of encounters Napier realizes, to his consternation, that one cannot "kill" the dead. When he views these men as they float helplessly upon their backs in the river, he believes they will drown, until the girl reminds him that the dead cannot drown. When Napier

later shoots an arrow through one of them, the creature only laughs. An incongruous situation is created when Mal Un, one of the walking corpses, is caught in the city of Havatoo. His sentence is decapitation and cremation, which produces "a mirthless laugh. . . from the dead mouth of Mal Un." Napier is chilled by the thought of a dead man laughing because he is sentenced to death.

From the familiar battles with monsters and primitive creatures Burroughs turns abruptly to an advanced civilization on Venus. The modern city of Havatoo, with auto freeways and elevated walks for pedestrians, has automated vehicles energized through power transmitted on three frequencies from a central station; in this way traffic regulates itself. For the citizens of Havatoo, who exhibit "extraordinary perfection of form and feature," Burroughs has again resorted to his theories of eugenics. The Havatooans display the results of generations of scientific breeding. They had been "misruled" by politicians, and half the population had lived in poverty and vice and had "bred like flies." A great "jong" (emperor) who came to the throne took over dictatorial powers and rejuvenated the nation:

. . . he wiped out the politicians . . . he appointed the greatest minds of Havatoo — physicists, biologists, chemists, and psychologists. . . . He encouraged the raising of children by people whom these scientists passed as fit to raise children. He saw to it that the physically, morally, or mentally defective were rendered incapable of bringing their like into the world; and no defective infant was allowed to live.

The jong, before his death, devised a new government without laws and without a king. A quintumvirate, called Sanjong, is now in charge; it consists of a biologist, a psychologist, a chemist, a physicist, and a soldier. Since the inhabitants of Havatoo have been "bred" into a race of people "who know the difference between right and wrong," no rules of behavior are required and the Sanjong's function is merely to guide. With man-made laws eliminated, only natural laws are in existence and these are understood by all the citizens. When on rare occasions an individual acts harmfully or against the natural law — and here Burroughs restresses his belief in the inheritance of defective or evil characteristics — he does so because the undesirable genes "have not all been eradicated from the germ cells. . . ." The person is then tried by a court which is not hampered by "technicalities nor precedent. . . ." Burroughs' numerous, frustrating experiences with lawsuits, especially involving film producers, and his impatience with legal maneuvers and entanglements, are made evident in this reference to the Havatoo court procedure. All facts are considered, but the heredity of the defendant is of extreme significance; verdicts of the Havatoo court — unlike the interminable court processes on earth — are "final and without appeal."

Perhaps Burroughs' equally frustrating experiences with the hired help both at the Tarzana Ranch and at his office in the earlier days, a problem many Americans have shared, led to his next social invention in Havatoo. Supposedly, class barriers did not exist; in the military the officers and soldiers mingled freely, and as regards the menial jobs of ordinary life, a man who may be a street sweeper suffers no social exclusion. He is judged only on how he performs his duties, his civic morality, and his culture. Furthermore, Napier is informed that "necessary and useful work is never distasteful to the man best fitted to do it." But with this explanation the Havatooans begin to display inconsistency. The five upper classes live in a strange segregation, all the physicists housed in one section of the city, the chemists in another, and the other intellectuals grouped in another. The purpose here is to have them associate with one another and to "mate with their own kind." Thus the laws of heredity are applied; each class, whether physicists, psychologists, or another, is constantly improved because of this selective breeding. The warriors or soldiers are also privileged to join these segregated classes. The large mass of the "common" people

live in the Yorgan district. For this society without social distinctions Burroughs has apparently created a ghetto. While the distasteful jobs, such as street cleaning, are performed with the aid of machines, still these tasks are relegated to the yorgan class, with each one taking his turn as his contribution to the public welfare. The highly intelligent people of the upper classes naturally prefer creative work. Somehow these Venusians seem little different from the class-conscious earthlings.

The yorgans, who evidently are condemned to the real segregation in Havatoo, are also excluded in the choice of rulers or "guides." Concerning the quintumvirate, Burroughs notes, "There is a tendency to breed Sanjongs among five of the six classes into which the people of Havatoo are naturally divided." It is true that all classes are encouraged to mingle and to intermarry; Herlak explains that "the high moral and mental standards of the people" are maintained in this way and that otherwise the yorgan class would deteriorate badly while the other classes would "diverge" greatly from one another, emerging with no common basis for understanding.

Deeply impressed by the perfection of this society, Napier compares the Havatooans with citizens of his own planet: ". . . I thought of the mess that Earth-men have made of government and civilization by neglecting to apply to the human race the simple rules which they observe to improve the breeds of dogs and cows and swine." Napier's earth-created defects almost result in his elimination; because of his "inherited repressions, complexes, and fears" and the fact that his germ cells are "replete" with "vicious genes," he is considered a menace to the future generations on Venus. The scientifically-obsessed Havatooans are barely persuaded to allow him to live.

Perhaps in an ironic comment on human nature in all societies, or with a realization that these cold-blooded, super-logical Venusians need an emotional outlet, Burroughs contrives (as entertainment) a bloody spectacle in the arena. Before an enormous crowd two factions of warriors, equipped with swords and shields, engage in a "game" in which many are wounded and killed. This irrational behavior can only be viewed with incredulity. Napier, appalled, remarks, ". . . the whole thing seemed so out of harmony . . . here was the highest type of culture and civilization that man might imagine suddenly reverting to barbarism. It was inexplicable." Stunned by the "savage enjoyment" of the spectators, Napier seeks an explanation from Ero Shan whose response is based upon a familiar philosophy about war: "We have few wars. . . . For ages war was man's natural state. It gave expression to the spirit of adventure which is part of his inheritance . . . man must have some outlet for this age-old urge. . . ." Ero Shan insists that if the citizens are denied both war and dangerous games, they will turn to crime or quarrels with each other. Without this necessary release for violence and aggression, "man would stagnate, he would die of ennui."[57]

The plot of *Tarzan and the Lion Man,* a novel that opens and closes in Hollywood, is concerned with the filming of a Tarzan movie in the jungles of Africa where the crew and cast encounter many dangers and misfortunes. For the final chapter, a tongue-in-cheek, highly amusing account of Tarzan's actual experiences in movieland, Burroughs may have been indebted to Ernest V. Heyn, editor of *Modern Screen.* On August 31, 1932, some five months before Burroughs began his *Lion Man* novel, Heyn wrote to request a story "on some aspect of Hollywood or motion pictures." Suggesting the title "If Tarzan Came to Hollywood," Heyn outlined his idea:

. . . if your famous character were to be set in the midst of the sometimes glamorous, sometimes barbarous life of the film capital, his reactions would be of extreme interest to the motion picture fan because, to some extent, his would be the same reactions as those of the fan. . . . you would be able . . . to give some very interesting sidelights on motion picture personalities, their places of meeting, dining and playing. When

you picture the reactions of a primitive man in Hollywood, you would be able to view that village from a fresh viewpoint and could make it additionally interesting by treating this imaginary trip around the town in semi-fictional form.

Heyn noted that his limited budget permitted him to offer only three hundred dollars for the article, but pointed out that *Modern Screen's* recent contributors included such distinguished personages as Booth Tarkington, Mrs. Franklin D. Roosevelt, and Vicki Baum.

Further correspondence followed, but no article was forthcoming, and on October 17 Rothmund replied to explain that Burroughs was "very busy" and to add, ". . . he has many story ideas of his own, so that if he writes anything that is suitable to Modern Screen, the manuscript will be sent to you." Burroughs, as always, had "his own ideas"; a suggestion by another person, when accepted, was usually altered or transformed, and it emerged imaginatively improved. Heyn's title, "If Tarzan Came to Hollywood," provided the inspiration for an ending to *Tarzan and the Lion Man,* but Burroughs, instead of describing the reactions of the primitive ape-man to the sophisticated film capital, chose to treat the matter satirically and create a scene in which Tarzan, unidentified and known only as John Clayton, winds up in a Tarzan movie — assigned only to a bit part.

In *Tarzan and the Lion Man,* written February 9 to May 30, 1933, the film company project to produce a movie deep in the heart of Africa causes the expected complications. With the main characters, Stanley Obroski, a world champion marathon runner, chosen to play Tarzan, and the spoiled, vain Naomi Madison selected for the feminine lead, the company, conducting "the strangest safari Africa has ever seen," attempts to force its masses of equipment through the tangled jungle and encounters natural disaster and death from the poisoned arrows of the Bansutos. The plot is launched with excellent possibilities, but soon adopts trite situations for its development, turning again to the exchange of identities, this time with Tarzan pleased and amused at the chance to impersonate Obroski.

Burroughs' intention to allow no story to be complete without its weird, anachronistic race leads him to devise creatures so bizarre and outré as to strain the tolerance of even the most flexible science-fantasy readers. In this case the creatures are gorillas who talk English, occupy a medieval city, and are called by such sixteenth-century British names as Wolsey, Cranmer, Buckingham, and King Henry the Eighth.

The real power in this strange city is wielded by the man who calls himself "God." Very old, he was originally a white man, but he now reveals certain gorilla characteristics — patches of black skin and hair, heavy fangs, and hands with long, curved claws. The man explains how the gorilla society came into existence (Burroughs once more resorts to a breeding device), telling of his early days in England, his fascination with the theories of Lamarck and Darwin, and his encounter in Austria with a priest named Mendel. They exchanged ideas, and God conceded that Mendel had given him some help but insisted, "Doubtless he got more from me." In 1857, with the mystery of heredity "practically" solved, God had published a monograph outlining his discoveries, centered mainly about the functions of the body cells and germ cells. He had learned that the genes, the carriers of heredity, "never die": indestructible, they are "the basis of all life on earth, the promise of immortality throughout all eternity." His experiments with genes led him to an astonishing action:

In 1858 I managed, through bribery, to gain access to a number of tombs in Westminister Abbey; and from the corpses of former kings and queens of England and many a noble lord and lady I extracted the deathless genes.

Later, facing blackmail by a man who knew about these "extractions," and embittered by the contempt of other scientists and the "persecution" of the government, he grew to hate all men. Fleeing England, he came to Africa and transferred his experiments to the gorillas.

Anesthetizing them, he removed the germ cells and substituted the human cells he had brought from England. No change in the gorillas was observed until a number of generations had passed; then he detected signs of greater intelligence. Other indications of the gorillas' evolution upward were soon noted (an opportunity too good for Burroughs to miss) as "they quarreled more, were more avaricious, more vindictive." Quite obviously, they were entering the realm of humanity. God now trained the young to speak English; sent them out to instruct the others; provided the gorillas with a background in agriculture, architecture, and construction; and directed them in the building of a large city named London upon a river that he naturally called the Thames.

In describing the evolution of his gorilla subjects, God comments angrily about their ingratitude: "I gave them laws, I became their god, I gave them a royal family and a nobility. They owe everything to me, and now some of them want to turn upon me and destroy me. . . ." The gorillas have become "very human"; they are "ambitious, treacherous, cruel — they are almost men." God explains his transition from a handsome Englishman to a grotesque half-man, half-gorilla. He had discovered a method of perpetuating his youth. This involved the segregation and transference of body cells from one individual to another. Unfortunately, he had been forced to use the cells of young gorillas; and as these multiplied within him, he began to acquire the gorilla characteristics. At this stage of his story, told to Tarzan and Rhonda Terry the actress, both of whom are his prisoners, God reveals his dreadful plans. With their body cells he can reverse the process and again become a normal human. In disclosing this, God, obviously mad, tells of his intention to absorb their body cells quickly by eating them.

With Tarzan and the movie company returning to Hollywood, Burroughs, in the last chapter, cannot resist the opportunity to ridicule the blundering ineptness of film producers. Tarzan, incognito as John Clayton, and a possible candidate for the lead in a Tarzan film, is sent to Prominent Pictures for an interview. There, Ben Goldeen, the production manager, surveys him critically and snaps, "Not the type. Not the type at all." Instead, Cyril Wayne, a famous adagio dancer, is signed for the role; Tarzan accepts a minor part as a white hunter. At the filming the scene is to depict Wayne, the heroic ape-man, with the aid of a double, rescuing the panic-stricken white hunter from a charging lion. As the scene develops, the supposedly tame lion goes wild and menaces Wayne. The white hunter (Tarzan) then springs to the rescue, leaping upon the lion's back and killing the animal. The angered, indignant Goldeen cries, "My God! You've killed our best lion. He was worth ten thousand dollars if he was worth a cent. You're fired!"

The marketing of *Tarzan and the Lion Man* created a new, unexpected relationship between Burroughs and Michael Mill. A letter of March 17, 1933, contained a query about the submission of future stories to "leading hardcover magazines." Would Mill be interested in trying to sell these stories to such publications as *Collier's* and *Cosmopolitan*? Sales to the low-paying pulp magazines, usually easy to make, were not included. To Mill's offer that he would peddle the manuscripts' first magazine rights for fifteen-percent commission, Burroughs agreed and in June forwarded *Tarzan and the Lion Man.* In effect, he had made Mill his literary agent — this despite his oft-repeated, adamant statements that he would not allow agents to handle his material.

Following a *Collier's* rejection of the *Lion Man,* Mill contacted *Liberty* and in August advised Burroughs that the magazine seemed interested in the story and wanted "our lowest figure." On the eighth, Burroughs wired, "Have never sold magazine with Liberty's circulation and have nothing to go by. Believe twenty-five thousand reasonable figure. . . ." Of course the price was too high, and the story was rejected at once. Editor Fulton Oursler noted that a Tarzan serial was too much of a speculation, since *Liberty* could run only one serial at a time. Aware of some uncertainty, Mill offered a price compromise, but no decision was reached. Shortly afterward, *Tarzan and the Lion Man,* submitted by Mill, was returned from *Cosmopolitan.*

Earlier, queries had come from Moore, the *Argosy* editor, who was eager to purchase another Tarzan novelette. On February 21, 1933, Moore was notified that a new Tarzan work had been launched but that it was not "Tarzan and the City of Ivory." Moore had hoped for a continuing agreement to supply stories to his magazine, but Rothmund emphasized that *Argosy's* insistence upon limiting the novels to 65,000 words posed a problem. This was not a satisfactory length for book publication; in fact, Burroughs was accustomed to writing novels of 75,000 to 80,000 words. Moore insisted he had "assumed" that Argosy would receive a number of Burroughs stories.

It all leaves me with a grave doubt as to how far I can depend on our understandings in the future; and of course I cannot afford to build up any series or arouse expectations in our readers of future stories which they will never get. . . .

He further remarked, "It would be a better policy for us . . . to wean our readers away from Mr. Burroughs. . . ."[58] In response, Burroughs reminded Moore that the 1931 agreement had simply called for the delivery of three stories, and that this requirement had been met.[59] Impressed by Mill's determined sales efforts, Burroughs still hoped that one of the high-paying magazines might purchase the story; however, in September 1933 rejections were sent by *Saturday Evening Post* and *American.*

The following month, *Liberty,* in a surprising reversal, revived its desire for a *Tarzan* serial and began negotiations once more. Now fearful of losing his first sale to a prestige magazine, Burroughs, in what might be described as a capitulation rather than a compromise, dropped the price to $10,000, and the sale was made. Mill's commission was $1,500. *Tarzan and the Lion Man* ran as a nine-part serial, November 11, 1933, to January 6, 1934. The appearance in *Liberty* was Burroughs' greatest success, financially and in the matter of prestige. The British magazine *Tid-Bits* also purchased the story for two hundred pounds.[60]

In one respect *Liberty's* publication of the serial proved to be a severe disappointment to Burroughs. He complained to Mill about the "complete absence of advance exploitation"; the magazine had printed only a small box announcement in the preceding issue. Ed commented irately that he had agreed to the low price because Oursler had mentioned plans for "extensive promotion work" that would cost several thousand dollars. Ed viewed this as a promise which had not been kept, but Mill responded that *Liberty's* "promotional work" amounted to "approximately what Mr. Oursler outlined to us over the phone. . . ."

The book publication of *Tarzan and the Lion Man* September 1, 1934, brought some diverse opinions from Mill and Burroughs. In creating the jacket, St. John was influenced by comments from the Burroughs offices that too much "sameness" in style was leading to monotony. Accordingly, he devised an entirely different jacket; the details were sent to Mill: ". . . a double-headed design in three colors — red, black, and gold, the lettering being in gold. The flaps and jacket back will be printed in blue. . . [I] really think we will have a very attractive and dignified looking book."

Mill, upon reading the blurb on the jacket flap, could hardly believe the sentence he had discovered: ". . . we are going to tell you that Mr. Burroughs believes this to be the poorest Tarzan novel he has ever written. . . ." Mill could not perceive how a derogatory statement of this type would aid the sale of the book. On February 11, 1935, he offered his philosophy to Burroughs:

. . . in my humble opinion, it is not the type of blurb that should go on the front flap of a jacket. . . . good bookmaking calls for a front flap which contains a description, not in superlatives, but merely facts and what the story consists of. This, after all, is what the reading public is interested in. . . . This is clever advertising writing, but again . . . while this type of blurb would appeal to some people, many of the readers would not "get" the cleverness but remember only that Mr. Burroughs did not think it so good, even though Liberty *purchased it as a serial. . . .*

Disagreeing, Burroughs answered on the sixteenth:

You would be surprised to note the comment it aroused among book reviewers. Practically everyone without exception mentioned it, and it apparently aroused their curiosity for they took to the book with avidity and then mentioned that it was one of the best Tarzan yarns yet written. . . .

A comment by an author, prominently displayed on a book jacket, disparaging his own work, was certainly something new. As a gimmick with shock-effect, however, it may have realized its goal of stimulating interest.

On the twenty-fifth Mill noted that his only concern was about the jacket's effect upon "the average layman," adding, "I am more interested in this than I am in the effect that it has on the literary critics, ninety percent of whom take a keen delight in trying to bring out their own brightness and belittle the other fellow's. . . ." In further letters he stressed his belief that Burroughs' concept of the new type of jacket was faulty; above all, an action jacket was needed, an all-around one that carried the picture from the front flap clear around to the back flap.

Mill's next sales attempts were unsuccessful; the manuscript of "Swords of Mars," delivered to *Liberty*, brought a brief evaluation from Gordon Fulcher: "Liberty has a very warm regard for Mr. Burroughs but in his present Martian flight it was felt he shot beyond our limited firmament. . . ." Mill reported their opinion that the story was "too fantastic" for them, and his efforts to sell it to *Cosmopolitan*, *American*, and *Pictorial Review* also led to failure.

Mill resumed his critical role later when "Swords of Mars" appeared in book form. On August 29, 1936, he wrote:

. . . We had a number of criticisms regarding the jacket on Swords of Mars and Tarzan's Quest because we have a semi-naked woman thereon. This criticism came particularly from buyers in juvenile departments; and while the sale in these departments is not so great, I would suggest that on future jackets we try to avoid this. . . .

His objection received short shrift from Rothmund:

Neither Mr. Burroughs nor I can see any objection to what some book buyers have termed a "semi-naked" woman on our recent jackets. The girl in each instance is sufficiently clothed. To put more clothes on her to satisfy the sensitive feelings of a few would utterly ruin the illustration for the majority.

It was Burroughs' writing pattern, now almost ingrained, that drove him again to leave Tarzan and resume the Mars series. "Swords of Mars" was written November 6 to December 15, 1933; its plot involved the perils faced by John Carter in his efforts to break the power of the assassins and their terroristic guild. The first of the Burroughs inventions for the novel is a plane equipped with a mechanical mind (or brain) that responds to thought waves. These "waves" or directions may be transmitted from a distance by an individual who is outside of the plane, and the plane will then operate automatically, proceeding to the specified destination or performing any required maneuver.

The evil inventor, Fal Sivas, explains its function to John Carter, who, needless to say, learns to control the plane and later appropriates it, after his wife, Dejah Thoris, has been kidnapped. A new element enters the story with Sivas' plans to journey to Thuria, one of Mars' moons, where there are "mountains of gold and platinum and vast plains carpeted with precious stones." John Carter's further adventures occur when in search of his wife he lands on Thuria and there encounters the hideous cat-men, creatures with one large eye and two mouths, who actually purr, meow, and leap about gracefully like cats. The Invisible Foes are Carter's most dangerous adversaries; through their hypnotic powers they have willed themselves to be invisible to others. The task of Carter, in which he succeeds, is to focus the power of his will so as to break through the mental barrier surrounding him.

Mill's persistent but fruitless efforts to sell "Swords of Mars" to a top magazine continued for six months; on June 20, 1934, he returned the story to Burroughs. The only markets available now were the pulp magazines. On July 18, implying that he had just completed the story, Burroughs informed Don Moore at *Argosy*, "We will have ready within the next few days for submission to magazines a new Edgar Rice Burroughs manuscript, *Swords of Mars. . . .*" The reply came from the new editor, Frederick Clayton, who found the seven and one-half cent per word rate impossibly high and also noted that even though Tarzan outdrew John Carter in magazine circulation, *Argosy* could not afford the Tarzan rates either. Clayton emphasized that Burroughs' insistence upon coupling the two types of stories, and his demanding that editors must purchase the Mars series in order to acquire a Tarzan novel, forced him to reject all of the works.[61]

Negotiations with *Blue Book,* conducted at the same time, led to a sale. On August 16 Kennicott wired, ". . . so anxious to have Mr. Burroughs back in the book we are going to rob the till and make it Fifty-Five Hundred." A proposal that Kennicott avail himself of the list of 1,500 fans on file at the Burroughs offices was accepted. In September 1934 a form letter announcing the scheduled appearance of "Swords of Mars" in the November *Blue Book* was circularized; composed by Kennicott, the letter stated: "The courtesy of our mutual friend and author, Edgar Rice Burroughs, has made it possible for me, as Editor of Blue Book Magazine, to send this letter to you, as a special admirer of Mr. Burroughs' imaginative talent." "Swords of Mars" ran as a six-part series, November 1934 to April 1935.[62]

At the Tarzana offices expanding activities and the increasing complexity of business dealings led to the delegating of more responsibility to secretary Rothmund. But by 1933 these duties had grown too heavy for Rothmund alone, and on August 13 of that year a new assistant, Mildred Bernard Jensen, was hired. The presence of these two signaled the end of the old Burroughs tendency to use temporary help and brought in many years of permanence and reliability.

During this same period Burroughs experimented with a new type of fictional writing. "Murder, A Collection of Short Murder Mystery Puzzles" features Inspector Muldoon, master detective and mathematical genius who displayed evidence of his remarkable talent at an early age: "At nine, he could mentally multiply numbers of six or seven digits, or extract square or cube root, almost instantaneously."

Muldoon's crime-solving technique was based "on his ability to carry a complicated array of figures in his mind and to correlate them instantly and accurately. . . ." Seven of the mystery puzzles form a collection which includes a table of contents and an introduction by Burroughs, but two additional ones, "The Red Necktie" and "The Dupuyster Case," were preserved separately. The puzzles, varying in length from three to twelve pages, all pose "whodunit" questions at the end; the collection of seven contains an appendix which supplies the solutions to the murders. Presumably, Burroughs' plan for publication was to present the puzzle as a challenge to the reader, and then to furnish the solution in the next magazine issue.

The puzzles involve brief scenes in which all the murder suspects are gathered in one place, and Muldoon's only function is to cross-

C. R. Rothmund dictating to Mildred Bernard Jensen who worked as stenographer and secretary for ERB for many years, March 1937; Mrs. Jensen transcribed many of ERB's stories from the wax cylinders of his ediphone and dictaphone.

examine them until he discovers the guilty party. There is no action, and the murderer is revealed through the minor clues found in the individuals' replies. Burroughs did not intend these puzzles to be stories in any sense, but, even so, his concept of a puzzle without characterization, plot, or suspense, and with the solutions based upon trivial points, could not be successful. Among the suspects conveniently grouped together and waiting to be questioned, Muldoon always finds at least one person who knows the murderer and refuses to name him, but who is willing to play games with the detective and offer the answer as a kind of riddle.[63]

Four of the nine murder mystery puzzles were published in *Script,* a Beverly Hills magazine owned, published, and edited by Rob Wagner, a good friend of ERB. "Who Murdered Mr. Thomas?," "The Red Necktie," and "The Terrace Drive Murder" appeared in 1932, and "The Lightship Murder" in 1935. Writing dates are not specifically established except for clues contained in some of the puzzles. "The Dupuyster Case" refers to "the evening of September 17, 1932," and "The Gang Murder" mentions "the Year of our Lord 1940." In another source, a diary entry under 1935, Burroughs notes, "Nov. 5 Stayed home all day & wrote 'Murder at Midnight' — a mystery puzzle...."[64]

For *Script,* Burroughs also contributed several articles, one of these resulting from a correspondence with Homer Croy, who was temporarily editing the magazine while Wagner was on vacation. Burroughs, in a bantering exchange, had mentioned his acquaintance with the lovely movie star Thelma Todd. On June 29, 1932, he sent a brief article to Croy and noted the enclosed "photographic proof" that he was "not kidding." The "proof" was a photo of Thelma Todd and Burroughs; he wrote on an attached slip, "Thelma Todd being looked after by Ed Burroughs while Rob Wagner is fishing for tall blondes at Tahoe." The 400-word article, titled "The Birth of Tarzan, by his poppa" was supposed to contain the familiar information Ed had supplied to numerous magazines, but instead he jokingly made

Thelma Todd the main topic. In the article he creates the impression that he is trying to write about Tarzan but is unable to keep from thinking about more exciting subjects.

... he (Homer) shares the popular conception that I can't write about anything but Tarzan. ... I am an authority on she-pulchritude. The older we get, the more we get that way ... and even now, young as I am, I don't care what color they are so long as they're blond.

Oh, yes, I almost forgot Homer. It was twenty year, come Michaelmas, that Tarzan first broke into print. We were living in Chicago then, and I had just taken up golf. And speaking of golf reminds me of the hit Thelma made a week ago Sunday when she came out to Tarzana Golf Course to present the trophies to the winners in her tournament (adv.). Every one fell in love with her.

He later apologizes, "I trust that I have not bored you with these intimate details concerning the birth of Tarzan, but when I get to writing about him I just don't know when to stop." Ed recalls the accusations by English reviewers that he had stolen the idea from Kipling. "The truth is that we both stole an identical idea from the same source, a source that antedates the founding of Rome; but being a less conscience-less plagiarist than Rudyard, I substituted a she-ape for the she-wolf." He soon turns again to write ecstatically about Thelma, and closes the article humorously,

If there is anything further that I can tell your readers about Tarzan, Homer, please don't hesitate to call on me, for there is no one I more enjoy writing about than Th — Tarzan.

Script for July 9, 1932, featured one of Burroughs' most unusual articles, a wildly imaginative autobiography filled with hilarious incidents that never happened. Headed "Edgar Rice Burroughs Tells All," the article opens, "I was born in Peking at the time that my father was military advisor to the Empress of China, and lived there, in the Forbidden City, until I was ten years old." (See pages 786–7.)

On January 26, 1934, in response to Wagner's request, Burroughs wrote a brief article to celebrate *Script's* fifth birthday. In the letter Ed commented, "I am not so hot on birthday articles. As a matter of fact, I have been growing to loathe birthdays more and more during the last twenty years." The article, titled "Symbol of a New Day" in its February 17 publication, contained reminiscences about the past and the steady succession of inventions that had changed society. Ed recalled when telephones were not a necessity and when gas was the sole source of illumination for the cities. He remembered, "When I was no longer a boy, the majority of business letters were written in longhand and copies were made in an iron letterpress with a steering wheel on top." With some exaggeration, after noting he had witnessed the birth of such things as the automobile, aeroplane and radio, he insisted that the success of *Script* was more significant than any of these.

Not so many years ago Script would have been banned as sacrilegious and obscene. That it is not banned today suggests that we are becoming more honest, less hypocritical, that bigotry is giving way to a fair open-mindedness....

Script's tenth anniversary brought another contribution from Burroughs, this time a 500-word story with a humorous ending. Written January 14, 1939, the story, in a deliberately exaggerated Burroughs jungle-Tarzan style, describes the strange actions of Um-gah, the king ape who for no apparent reason goes suddenly berserk, screaming, roaring, and killing members of his own tribe. From nearby, Tarzan rushes to the scene, battles Um-gah, hurls him to the ground, and forces him to surrender. The reason for Um-gah's abrupt violence is revealed at the story's end:

"Ula bango gin mula mule?" demanded Tarzan, or *"What the hell's eating you, you big bum?" "Can you blame me?" pleaded Um-gah. "Some so-and-so swiped my anniversary number of* Script."

As with many of his other stories, Ed also included observations about mankind. In the quiet of the jungle (before Um-gah's strange actions) Usha the Wind whispers through the trees and sets them to "gossiping — breathing softly the peace and the beauty of Nature primeval undefiled by man, the Devil's *coup de maitre.*" Ed's typed suggestion to Wagner, "... you can title this," resulted in the story being called "Even Apes Fight for It."

Burroughs of course wrote other articles in the 1930-33 period; the best-known of these, containing a restatement of his philosophy about writing, was a *Writer's Digest* assignment. Titled "Entertainment is Fiction's Purpose," the article was forwarded to Aron Mathieu, the magazine's business manager, on April 21, 1930. Burroughs noted he was filling the request and explained that because the article was in danger of being overlong, he did not "go very fully" into all of his methods. From a modest opening assertion — "... I do not possess... a conscious knowledge of the technique of story writing" — he continued. "The best that I can do, therefore, is to discuss frankly my own methods, which will be utterly valueless to professional writers and of doubtful value to anyone else."

His first emphasis is not upon writing approaches, but rather upon physical and mental fitness; "the retention of a youthful and elastic mind," a requisite for the writer of "highly imaginative fiction," may be achieved by keeping the body in good condition and the mind "responsive to a diversity of simple stimuli." He had avoided any "single" hobby, believing that it might exert too narrowing an influence upon a fiction writer who, above all, must develop an interest in many things. He offered, as an example, the stamp collector who may devote too much time and thought to a hobby that could provide no actual knowledge for the writing of stories.

Ed's advice about reading evidently stemmed from his own practices; the analysis of stories by other writers, a procedure adopted by many authors as a means of self-improvement, he found purposeless. "The fiction writer should read almost anything other than fiction," he insisted. For entertainment he should rather seek variety, as many activities as possible. Amusingly, he used the phrase invented by his two sons — "monkey-minded." The fiction writer should "caper erratically through the forest of human knowledge, swinging from tree to tree, tasting the fruits of many." Burroughs' personal library with its astonishing diversity demonstrated his omnivorous reading habits, his "monkey-mindedness."

Familiar assertions appear in the article: the writer should not take himself or his work too seriously; fiction, except for its entertainment value, is "an absolute unessential." The most dogmatic of his statements followed: "I would not look to any fiction writer, living or dead, for guidance upon any subject, and therefore, if he does not entertain, he is a total loss."

In his cynicism about humanity and even the contempt with which he sometimes viewed the masses, he evaluated the reader frankly: ". . . you may rest assured that he does not wish to be instructed. He does not wish to have to think, and as fully ninety percent of the people in the world are not equipped with anything wherewith to think intelligently, the fiction writer who wishes to be a success should leave teaching to qualified teachers. . . ." Some of Burroughs' bitterness over his exclusion from the select circle of literary writers is evident in these statements. Though he closes by advocating "a high plane of business integrity and professional ethics," he still feels prejudice against "literary" works; a writer is expected to maintain these high standards, he insists, "without any vain and silly illusions" that fiction has any purpose other than entertainment.[65]

In 1930 Burroughs devised an unusual piece of writing, unrelated to anything he had previously done. His diary for May 11 contains the entry, "Originated '83' (or 'Tarzana')"; this referred to Tarzana Bridge, a card game he then proceeded to describe in detail. His ten-page manuscript, "Tarzana Bridge," has various sections: an introduction, list of terms, explanation of twenty rules, remarks on bidding, remarks on play, and two pages offering a brief history of the origin of cards. That he hoped to have these instructions for a new bridge game published, or the game itself issued in some form, is indicated by his 1930 copyright and the marking, "First Edition." The first name considered for the game, "83," is based upon rule thirteen, "Value of Cards in Accounting," which lists ten, jack, queen, king, and ace of the suit bid as worth ten points each, the cards numbered nine to two as worth one point each, and a companion queen worth twenty-five points: the total number of points is eighty-three. Under certain rules a winning player could collect eighty-three points from each of the others.

Tarzana Bridge, Ed explains in his introduction, was designed to take the place of Auction or Contract bridge, especially when from five to seven players are involved. The fundamentals are easily learned, even by an individual who has no previous knowledge of bridge; the new game arouses a stronger interest because of the importance it places upon skill rather than chance. Ed remarked, "Perhaps its greatest appeal lies in its elimination of partnership play, the cause of much needless anger, recrimination, domestic infelicity, and general unhappiness."

In the section titled "A Matter of History," Ed adopts a humorous tone to summarize the origin of cardplaying. Noting that this origin was "lost in antiquity through either the carelessness or modesty of the inventor," he observes, "Being neither careless nor modest, I purpose to record here the date, occasion and intimate details of the invention of Tarzana Bridge. . . ." The belief that cards had existed in India from time immemorial, he comments, is not unreasonable "when one considers the countless generations of Indian concubines who must have required some form of amusement while sitting around waiting for their numbers to be called." Concerning all those who claimed to have invented cards, "the conscientious historian may only remark: 'Who cares and what of it?' "

After some brief references to the game of whist, a forerunner of bridge, Ed trumpeted the arrival of "that historic date, Sunday, May 11,

1930," and wrote "I had lumbago. The last time I had lumbago I wrote a play — which I still own. This time I invented, evolved, created, composed (or whatever it is you do to a card game) Tarzana Bridge." For the benefit of historians, he wishes to record that the first game was played at Tarzana on May 13 — "and, perhaps, the last."

Upon sending Tarzana Bridge to Max Elser of Metropolitan Books, then publishing the Burroughs novels, Ed offered a plan to use the game in a publicity campaign. On May 20 he suggested that a small edition be printed and distributed to the newspapers carrying the Tarzan strips. The type of book he had in mind, he informed Elser, would resemble the one titled *The Heart of Bridge,* by Staples. He evaluated the section on card history jokingly:

(It) was written to permit the book to bulk a little bit larger than it otherwise would have. It is unnecessary as text and does not have to be read, and I thought of inserting a note to this effect, as, for example: "The following does not have to be read. It was inserted only to make the book larger."

Following some correspondence in June with Elser about some revisions in the game, all reference to Tarzana Bridge disappears, and there is no record of the game being printed in the newspapers.

At the request of *Writer's Digest* Ed once more contributed an article, this time titled "Literary Rights." The 2,000-word article, sent to the *Digest* on December 29, 1931, explained Burroughs' progress from an early ignorance about an author's rights to a later knowledge gained through painful experience. He had been aware of the importance of book rights and had retained these, but had not known about second serial rights for magazines. As a general protection for the writer, Ed emphasized the necessity of having all stories copyrighted in the author's name or having the magazine copyright legally reassigned to the author.

A writer should also try to anticipate the future and the new opportunities that could arise. Ed noted that the idea of dramatic rights in *Tarzan of the Apes* had not occurred to him when the novel was written; yet the value of these became evident later when the play was performed in England. Thus, an author must protect these potential values. He wrote, "Equally remote were the possibilities of profiting from foreign and translation rights. A kindly providence who looks after infants, inebriates, and young authors, or the fact that nobody thought they were worth anything, preserved my foreign and translation rights to me. Afterward, my foreign royalties were, at one time, greater than my United States royalties." In this 1931 period he had already taken steps to protect his television rights: a special clause had been inserted in one of his film contracts. He had an accurate vision of the future: "... long before my copyrights expire television rights will be worth a fortune...."

He turned whimsical in his predictions:

Perhaps in my radio contract I shall insist upon the reservation to me of the interplanetary rights. Why not? Radio rights and sound and dialog rights would have seemed as preposterous twenty years ago; and with my intimate knowledge of conditions on Mars and Venus, I, of all men, should anticipate the value of broadcasting Tarzan to the eager multitudes that swarm our sister planets.

Reserved for a last discussion was an important proposal — the literary rights should revert to the author. Real estate and other possessions are leased by the owners for definite periods, and this same practice should be followed with literary properties; no publisher should obtain rights extending for decades into the future. Ed was of course recalling his struggles to reacquire the rights to his early novels, and he was especially concerned about the increased value of a work, a value which could produce no financial return for the author unless he had some control over his own property. In the article, titled "Protecting the Author's Rights" when it appeared in the 1932 *Writer's Yearbook,* Ed suggested that radio contracts be limited to three years and film contracts to not more than ten years. About the stealing of literary rights he remarked, "I have had rights purloined in Italy, Russia and India, and, of course, New York; but naturally a man cannot be expected to watch all the thieves on this planet when so much of his time is spent on Mars and Venus."

A 1930 interview broadcast on radio station KTM has proved to be an interesting source of Burroughs information and opinions. Orme's query about the development of a successful writer brought a categorical reply: "... there is something inherent in the successful writer that cannot be acquired by people who do not naturally possess it. It cannot be taught." His scorn for critics is revealed in his next statement; the fact that individuals cannot be trained to write is demonstrated by those highly educated individuals who fail as authors and often become critics or reviewers. Humorously, he offers his philosophy about humans: "... the majority of people, having nothing with which to think, are merely entertained, while most of the others are too intelligent to look to fiction for anything more than simple relaxation." It should be noted that he was not at all reticent, even on a radio broadcast, to insult the masses. His contempt for fiction writers who dare to be "authoritative" is also repeated. These individuals are not qualified to educate people; "... a great many of them," he remarked, "are not so well balanced, mentally, as to inspire me with any great amount of confidence." He based this conclusion on what the press revealed about those writers who rose to "heights of asininity" in their attempts to gain publicity.

Questions by Orme produced further strong opinions: "I see no pleasure or sportsmanship in shooting dove or quail; the man who shoots one of the beautiful deer that are yearly growing scarcer in our hills, and can boast about it, should have both his heart and his head examined — there is something wrong with them." About Prohibition, to which he had been adamantly opposed, he now displayed some uncertainty. "In the Literary Digest poll I voted for repeal, but possibly modification would be better. The fear that I entertain in relation to modification, however, is that it might result in another form of prohibition."

One of the most fascinating of the Burroughs articles, "The Tarzan Theme," printed in *Writer's Digest,* June 1932, achieves an intellectual and imaginative level not attained in his others. He discusses the first Tarzan story, offers his views on heredity and environment, and presents his familiar attack on "civilized" man who exhibits the terrible vices and defects that are alien to the animals. A most convincing reason for Tarzan's appeal to the public is "the constant urge to escape ... not alone the narrow confines of city streets for the freedom of the wilderness, but the restrictions of man-made laws, and the inhibitions that society has placed upon us." Naturally, we seek to emulate the people we admire; "... we would each like to be Tarzan," Ed writes. "At least I would; I admit it." This yearning, which in the past caused people to dream of being like Theodore Roosevelt or Jack Dempsey, also is associated with heroic fictional characters who become "flesh and blood" to us. Thus, these characters, such as d'Artagnan, and of course Tarzan, have elevating and inspiring influences upon people.

A brief article titled "What is Good Fiction?" was written by Burroughs as copy for the inside back flap of the jacket for *Jungle Girl,* published in April 1932. Here he lashed out scathingly at the writers he most detested, those who tried to "pose as prophets or leaders or teachers." His attack is more violent than the preceding ones:

Men who defy God from a public pulpit, men who punch one another's nose at social gatherings, men who seek fame by defaming their own countries and consorting with their countries' enemies, "fresh guys," "smart alecks," "village cut-ups," are not the types of men to whom I would look for leadership or enlightenment, however much I might enjoy their fiction.

He continues in the same vein: "Nearly every novel that has helped to mold public opinion has been rank propaganda and, like all propaganda, extravagant and inaccurate and, consequently, harmful. Each represents the personal opinions of a single individual, and the personal opinions of very few individuals are worth much more than your own. . . ." He next states that there *are* authoritative books, written by men thoroughly versed in their subjects, and these works should be consulted. This type of man, who has an important message and knows his subject, does not lessen the value of this message by writing it in a fictional form.

On occasion when Ed took a bypath into humor, he was not above poking fun at his "meal-ticket" — Tarzan in his natural jungle environment. Written on March 3, 1933, "Tarzan and Jane, a Jungleogue" was a 5,000-word play that featured characters from the original *Tarzan of the Apes*. Those present included Professor Archimedes Porter, Samuel Philander, William Clayton, Esmeralda, and two familiar animals, Numa the lion and Terkoz the bull ape. The plot, humorously embellished, is a sequence from the novel, with Jane, her father and the others, after being put ashore by the mutineers of the *Arrow,* finding Tarzan's cabin with his warning note. In the play, presumably designed for amateur production, Ed has suggested props and sets and inserted stage directions. Among these he mentions a runway or chute for the lion and piles of rotting logs and boulders for jungle realism. Movements of the characters are prescribed: "Tarzan listens off R. Crosses and enters L. Enters lion chute L." and similar instructions.

Another of the many vacation trips, this time to California's Death Valley, is humorously reported in a nine-page article titled, "The Death Valley Expedition of the Intrepid Thirty-Threers." With the opening "The spirit of the Forty-Niners lives again!" Burroughs sets the amusing theme in which he contrasts the obstacles and dangers faced by the original gold rush pioneers with the "sufferings" of the intrepid Burroughses. "To reduce the possibility of greatly increasing the number of bleached bones which already clog the trails into the valley," he writes, "we limited the personnel of the expedition to four." A description of the four explorers follows:

Pomona College loans us two able scientists, Hulbert Burroughs and John Coleman Burroughs, both experts in comparative anatomy. The former was the leader of the expedition, having been unanimously chosen for this position by himself. The latter was the official photographer. The services of Emma Hulbert Burroughs were finally obtained after a vast outlay in hats, shoes, sportswear, and a complete pharmacy; and she was signed up as expert radio operator. The fourth member of the expedition, Old Burroughs, went along for the ride. He was the life of the party.

The expedition "assembled" five miles east of Point Dume, "a smuggler's rendezvous known locally as Malibu La Costa Beach." Ed is referring to the family home at Malibu. The "goggle-eyed natives" who witnessed the departure included Joan, Florence Dearholt, Mrs. Alvin Hulbert, and Jessie Hulbert. The family trips were always by automobile, and on this occasion they drove in a Lincoln Twelve Sedan, which, Ed noted, was especially equipped to visit the two fashionable department stores, Robinson's and Bullock's Wilshire, and thus was "ideal for a trip to Death Valley."

Departing on the morning of April 3, 1933, the adventurers "limped" into "the tiny desert outpost of Barstow" that afternoon and then pushed on: "Into the valley of death rode the Burroughses." Their agonies were vividly pictured in Ed's words: "We were stranded in this arid waste without iced water and only a few cookies." Soon Furnace Creek Inn came in view. "Would the desert tribe give us shelter?" Their primitive accommodations consisted of large, luxurious rooms and the use of the pool. On April 6, in their exploration of Death Valley, they arrived at Dante's View, an elevation of 6,000 feet. Earlier, Hulbert and Jack, who

ERB, Emma, and Hulbert in Death Valley at lowest point of North America, April 1933.

were eager to collect salt crystals, could not find any and finally settled for two bottles of salt water.

They faced new challenges on the return journey. "At 7 a.m. April 7, 1933, we set out in search of the Pacific Ocean." The appalling difficulties that awaited them were compared to those encountered by the explorers William Manly and John Rogers who struggled for two weeks "to cross burning waterless deserts and formidable mountain ranges to reach Los Angeles." The Burroughs family covered the distance to Malibu in nine hours and twenty-five minutes. At the close of the account of these "intrepid thirty-threers" Burroughs noted, "If we accomplished nothing else, we have at least proved the value of a college education and brought two bottles of salt water to the Pacific Ocean."

Much of Burroughs' poetry in the past had been light verse, satirical or joking, of the type composed for the Los Angeles Breakfast Club, or the kind, many years before, that he had contributed to the *Chicago Tribune* columns.

However, in late 1929 or the first weeks of 1930 he began writing a long poem that was far different from his early creations. Titled "Genghis Khan," the narrative poem with its Mongol-Asiatic setting describes the birth and rearing of Timujin, destined to be "the future Ruler of All Men." The poem, incomplete, is composed in heavy, formal language and arranged in a series of fourteen-line stanzas. Timujin's story, recounted in twenty stanzas, begins with Houlan, his mother, who upon her wedding ride with her groom had been captured by the fierce Yesukai, Khan of Yakka, carried away to become his mate. From this union came Timujin, and the rigorous Mongol life served its purpose — hardening him and inuring him to suffering and danger. He was "born to the iron of Gobi's savage womb," and the same savagery governed his childhood:

So early weaned from woman's milk to mare's,
And thrust by elders from the warming fire
To fight the cur pack which, with bristling
*   hairs,*
Dispute with him the food they all require

Growing up, he tends the horse herds, and the many hardships he endures prepare him for his destiny:

The attributes that are to make him known
In glory fear nor hate may ever dim —
The Scourge of God, who mastered every
*   throne;*
The Perfect Warrior he, whose god was gore;
Who slew a brother in the days before
His beard; who was to slay his millions more.

With the story of Timujin's struggles unfinished, Burroughs, on January 24, 1930, sent the poem to W. F. Bigelow, editor of *Good Housekeeping;* the accompanying note read, "Will you kindly read the enclosed beginning of an epic of Genghis Khan and advise me if you might be able to consider it for publication, upon its completion, possibly in serial form?" The letter was signed with a pseudonym: Edar Burr c/o C. R. Rothmund, Box 625, Reseda, California. "Genghis Khan" was returned, and on the rejection card Secretary Rothmund made an amusing notation: "RR/The cat came back B/" The poem was also rejected by *The Forum*. After the rejections Burroughs filed the poem away, and Genghis Khan's further adventures were never described.

Typical light verses of a later period include "Dear Old Eight-Two-Three," written while Burroughs was convalescing at the Good Samaritan Hospital in Los Angeles. Dated December 3, 1935, the poem humorously tells of his confinement in Room 823 and of the routine to which he must submit:

Miss Collins comes at seven,
And Fansie comes at three,
The night nurse at eleven
To dear old eight-two-three.

They rub me and they scrub me;
They change my silly shirt;
They jab me with their needles
To ease my every hurt.

In the poem's five quatrains Burroughs also describes himself gazing wistfully out the windows where the mountains are "smiling and beckoning" to him.

An unusual request from W. B. Halley, Jr., of *The Courier-Journal* and *The Louisville Times* motivated Burroughs to write a "political speech" for Tarzan. On October 22, 1935, Halley explained plans for an election:

. . . the candidates will be the characters of the comic pages of these two papers. They will all compete for the office of Oompah which is defined in Nebster's Fictionary as "A big noise, hence, a ruler, male or female, of comic characters."

Naturally, Tarzan would be a candidate, and Halley noted that Maxon had already sent several posters for use in the campaign. Halley suggested "some speeches for Tarzan who is planning to announce on a Nude Deal Platform."

Willing to aid in this promotional gimmick for the cartoon strips, Burroughs composed a 600-word campaign speech, but chose to have it delivered by little Nkima, the monkey, rather than Tarzan. Nkima, representing his beloved ape-man, was of course in favor of a Nude Deal or any similar type of "unclothed" platform. In his speech he bragged that "ouah party's candidate for Oompah" is a man "who can run on any platform, barefooted." He spoke humorously of the planks of this platform:

If our candidate is elected we promise to make the tailors walk the first plank, the haberdashers the second plank, the shoemakers the third plank. Then there is a plank on which to exhibit bigger and better fig leaves, and we are going to remove the tariff on fig leaves, G strings and loin cloths.

Nkima continued, "if our party triumphs at the coming election, we promise you that there will be a nude eel in every frying-pan."

Ed could not resist some political barbs. Under the Nude Deal, according to Nkima, more Democrats would be put on the dole — "if they are not all on now" — and all those who are discontented should rest assured that "Tarzan is for the Reds." Nkima explained, "Wholeheartedly and unashamedly, he is for the Reds — the Rhode Island Reds, fried, with mashed potatoes and gravy, Southern style." In closing, Nkima expressed certainty that Tarzan would be the next Oompah. Sound effects had been inserted in the speech, and these, in the last lines, described the feverish reactions: "Prolonged, prolonged cheering, followed by riot squad with tear-gas bombs, and Waziri warriors with white plumes." Despite Nkima's unquestionably inspired speech, Tarzan failed to win the election; Dick Tracy was chosen "Oompah of the Comics." The large advertisement with Maxon's illustration, appearing in the two newspapers on November 5, was headed "Down with Lion Politicians!" In urging the support of Tarzan, it claimed that he was the only one "who has had first-hand experience in dealing with Ethiopian situations," and denied the rumor that "Mr. Tarzan's candidacy is being opposed by the Animal Rescue League."

21
PERSONAL CRISIS AND ADJUSTMENT

The man who created the heroic exploits of John Carter and Tarzan embarked upon a daring exploit of his own in 1934. The setting was neither a distant planet nor the familiar terra firma, but the skies over the earth. Ed's diary for January 5, 1934, had the entry, "First flying lesson today about noon. Jim Granger, Instructor, Clover Field." On the student pilot's permit, issued December 29, 1933, Ed's age was shown as fifty-eight, his weight 189, and his height sixty-nine and one-half inches. In order to keep his lessons secret and prevent Emma from worrying, he assumed the pseudonym of "Smith."

For his first flight, in a Kinner Security low-wing monoplane, the altitude was 4,000 feet, the air bumpy and the student "scared stiff." He reported, "Granger said I surprised him. Evidently I did fairly well. Think I'm going to like it. I flew the ship after he took off and got altitude. At the end of the lesson I throttled down and made a 90 degree turn down toward

field until close; then Granger took controls and landed. No safety belt or chute today. Like stepping into an auto and driving off."

His diary contained a series of entries continuing through February 12 to record his flying progress. On the second lesson Granger commented that Ed worked too hard; "I was tense and nervous," Ed wrote. "Got very tired. I don't seem to acquire much confidence, but then I have flown only one hour. . . ." He noted he had met a Mrs. Gillespie on the field and had asked her if she flew — and then discovered she was Ruth Elder, the aviatrix. Other entries, almost daily, were soon encouraging:

I like gliding best, as the noise of the motor and blast of the prop annoy me . . . am still very tense and can't make my feet behave. Too much imagination has its drawbacks. When flying I envy the cow. . . .

Legs behaved until the last few minutes. I like these lessons and am losing my nervous-

ERB standing by tail of his airplane bearing his colophon on rudder, 1934.

ness.... I am making landings in about half the time of the average pupil ... my nervousness is about gone now....

He had met a Mrs. Clark and watched Jim Granger take her up for instruction. He commented, "She must be as old as I, yet she flies; so why not I?" He had a discouraging day: "Forgot to put down my goggles again. This is the third time.... I think I'll never learn to fly. I take off fairly well now, but that is comparatively simple. It is the landing that gets me — and that damned right rudder." On January 20 he reported that his "pet secret" was out; Emma learned he was flying, possibly getting the information from a manicurist in Burbank. "Exit Mr. Smith," Ed wrote.

Emma and Hulbert became spectators for his tenth lesson — after they had dared to fly with Granger and Mrs. Clark in a Stinson plane. "Emma said she was not afraid. It was her first flight." Confident in his skill now, Ed ordered a Security Airster plane, noted it would be ready in a week and granted an interview to a *Los Angeles Times* reporter and cameraman who came to the airfield. The plane arrived on February 10 and on the twelfth Ed made the climactic entry in his diary: "Soloed perfect. Got my wings. Great thrill." Ed's earlier successes had immediately inspired Hulbert to start flying lessons, Jack was eager to begin, and on March 10 Emma took her first lesson.

To celebrate these stirring events, father and son Hulbert, following his first solo flight, sponsored a Solo Dinner, "tendered to the staff and pupils of The Pacific School of Aviation," and held at the Hollywood Athletic Club on February 15. Special aviation dishes were devised for the menu:

Aquaplane cocktail, Happy Landing Dressing
Soup de Empennage de Boeuf
Fuselage de Bossy, Broiled, Maitre D'Hotel
New Peas en Tailspin
Potatoes au Ground Loop
Clover Field Salad
Parfait de Solo

The day after the Solo Dinner twenty-five-year-old Hulbert was involved in a different type of aviation affair, one that was a near-catastrophe. Flying the brand new Security Airster, named the Doodad after Ed's trademark, Hulbert attempted a landing at Clover Field in Santa Monica, lost control of the plane, struck the tenth-hole flag on the adjacent golf course, and then crashed to the ground. Luckily, he suffered only minor injuries. Ed described the incident in his diary: "... Started a ground loop after landing; tried to take ship up but hit trees on golf course and crashed. ... not badly hurt. Suffering from shock. Ship pretty badly wrecked. Both wings gone, front of fuse cage damaged, engine mount twisted, prop broken, tailskid a wreck. Do not know yet extent of damage to engine, if any."

In letters to his brothers Harry and George, Ed explained that as his son landed, a gust of wind lifted the plane by one wheel. He made the mistake of trying to take off again, and instead of cutting his motor, opened it wide. The plane rose some fifteen feet and then crashed into the golf course. Ed commented wryly about the new plane, "I had the pleasure of flying it for five minutes." It now gave the appearance of something "run through a meat grinder," but as long as Hulbert's injuries were not serious, "none of us gave a damn about the ship." Undeterred by the accident, Hulbert resumed flying two days later.

Not sufficiently experienced for long-distance flights, Ed, on March 26, refused an invitation to fly to Coronado for a visit with Bert Weston, but on April 5, three months after he had begun his lessons, he remarked in his diary, "... I am very well satisfied with my progress. I doubted then and for some time thereafter that I could ever fly without nervousness. Under ordinary flying conditions I am no more nervous than in an automobile, and in some respects I am more at ease. I have no more fear. It has done a great deal for me in restoring much of the self-confidence that I felt in youth." That day he piloted his son-in-law, Jim Pierce, to Tarzana.

To Homer Croy at *Script Magazine* Ed mentioned his plan for a transcontinental trip, admitting, however, that while on a flight to Pomona College to visit his son he had become lost, circled over El Monte until he was almost out of gas, and then returned home. On October 3, 1934, the flying instructor, Jim Granger, for whom the Burroughs family had developed a deep admiration, was killed in a plane crash. For the front of Ed's Pilot Log Book, Granger had written a laudatory inscription: "Your natural ability to grasp the ideas of this writer, your patience and kind appreciation of his efforts made the work of teaching you to fly a genuine pleasure for your, 'Instructor'."

During the period from summer 1933 to spring 1934, because of a situation that had grown intolerable, Burroughs, in his personal life, was nearing a crisis. The early days when he and Emma had shared the hardships, facing poverty and adversity together, had united them in love and understanding. But the sharing of affluence and success had brought insoluble problems. The image presented to the world by Ed and Emma in their marriage, one of a stable, unchanged relationship, had for some time been nothing more than a pretence. The strained home life, hidden from outsiders, and even from Ed's brothers, was of course no secret to Joan, Hulbert, and Jack.

The main problem, a continuous source of unhappiness, was Emma's drinking. Her increasing dependence upon liquor had driven her more deeply into alcoholism. They had diverged greatly, Ed's interests expanding, his tastes changing, while Emma's remained the same. It was not only that he had retained a youthful outlook, but actually that the emphasis in his life was upon youth; this was evident, first of all, in his determination to stay young through sports — horseback riding, golf, and later, tennis. His possession of a youthful spirit — granting that this stemmed from his need to prove his masculinity — was demonstrated in his learning to fly at the age of fifty-eight. His physical vigor was certainly atypical for a man of that age, and in his associations he made it plain that he preferred the company of younger people.

In her early years Emma's charm and vivacity made her heaviness of minor importance, but naturally, as she grew older, this tendency toward overweight lessened her physical attractiveness. The old days of sharing, of closeness, when Ed depended upon her, consulted her about his writings, brought his triumphs and failures home to her, were gone. It was a familiar story: she was not *needed* by her husband — at least in the way she had been needed in the past. About her drinking and its effect upon Ed, Jack Burroughs explained, "My father was sensitive and idealistic about women. He wanted them to be like his heroines, fine and virtuous. The idea of his wife as a victim of alcohol was difficult for him to accept. His generation thought that drinking by women was immoral."[1]

Though the rift had existed for a long period, and despite the quarrels and recriminations, and the fact that he had left home several times, Ed was unable to make a decision. Undoubtedly his concern about his children, how they might be affected, and how they would react to a separation made him hesitant. To drive matters to a crisis and force a decision, a new factor was needed. It developed through an association that began in 1927. At that time Ed had his first dealings with Ashton Dearholt, a cousin of Waterson Rothacker, a film producer and friend of the Burroughs family. On February 14, 1927, Ed noted a visit from Dearholt, who had come to discuss a proposal he had offered to Pathe; this was to produce five pictures from Burroughs' novels with Jack Holt in the leading roles. The novels were *The Outlaw of Torn, The Mad King, The Mucker, The Bandit of Hell's Bend,* and *H.R.H. the Rider.* Dubious, Ed explained he would prefer to use Jim Pierce, and since Dearholt indicated that Pathe would pay only $10,000 each for the film rights, any further discussion was a waste of time.[2] Dearholt's wife, Florence, had accompanied her husband to the Burroughs home, and on March 11 Ed sent a set of photos taken during their visit.

The relationships with Ashton and Florence (Gilbert) Dearholt continued. Seeking a movie career for her daughter, Mrs. Gilbert brought Florence and brother Eddie from Chicago to Los Angeles in 1918. At the age of fourteen, Florence, who looked eighteen, was offered film roles at the Fox Studios. For many years she played leads in the Van Bibber stories of Richard Harding Davis and worked in comedy parts also at the Christy Studios. She had played a more serious role in *The Johnstown Flood* for Fox Studios. However, after her marriage to Dearholt she gave up her career, devoting herself to the raising of her children, Caryl Lee and Lee.

Florence's association with the Burroughs family came mainly through her friendship with Joan; the two spent much time together. In that period, while Florence knew Hulbert, Jack, Emma, and her sister Jessie, who was visiting at the Tarzana home, she had little acquaintance with Burroughs himself. Ed Gilbert, Florence's young brother, an avid reader and collector of Burroughs' books, formed a friendship with Jack and joined him on vacation trips.

In business matters, Burroughs soon began to value Ashton's ability and his connections in the movie field. On September 4, 1929, Ed forwarded to him a film idea or outline, unidentified, commenting, "I think the enclosed would make a bully comedy for some chap like Wally Reid, if there is anyone who has taken his place, but, of course, as far as the story is concerned, it is absolutely out of my line. I would not know how to handle it any more than I would know how to write a treatise on the Einstein theory. Why don't you do it yourself?"

The Dearholts and Burroughses met at various social functions and exchanged visits throughout 1930. On August 17 Ed noted in his diary, "Ashton Dearholt out with his new land yacht. . . ." The "land yacht," a mobile home which Ashton himself had constructed, provided a way of life for the Dearholts for almost a year; they wrote to Ed as they traveled to San Diego, Yuma, and Palm Springs. In response, Ed remarked, "I often think of you all and have wondered when you will tire of gypsy-

Florence Dearholt and her two children, Caryl Lee and Lee Ashton, about 1933.

ing. I like a little of it, but I am afraid that it would pall on me after awhile, but then, of course, you are not a hundred years old." The following May, Ashton notified Ed that the vagabond days were over; he and Florence were taking an apartment in West Hollywood.

Dearholt's newest business venture, in September 1932, was *The Standard,* a Hollywood film publication issued by Standard Casting Directory. The magazine, in existence for eleven years, and tottering financially, furnished information and publicity for those in the film or entertainment industry. Dearholt urged Burroughs to send news items for the Hollywood Bulletin "which reaches hot spots in the picture business. . . ." In suggesting that Joan and Jim purchase space in the publication, Dearholt wrote, ". . . the *Standard* will cover every radio station, sponsor's office, as well as advertising agencies." Stressing this latest emphasis upon radio programs, Dearholt informed Burroughs, ". . . the Feb.-March issue can carry Tarzan's messages to the hottest spots in radio."[3]

In the summer of 1933 Dearholt announced

Ashton Dearholt and Florence Gilbert Dearholt on outing with ERB prior to divorces, about 1933-34.

that he had taken over the bankrupt *Standard*, had "a chattel mortgage on everything of value," and planned to make the magazine a profitable enterprise. His letter of July 24 to Burroughs revealed he was seeking a partner: "When you are squared around would like to have a talk regarding 'Hully'.... I need a young man with 'Hully's' education—possible ability—willing to work — who can make new contacts with artists, directors and writers financing his activities — receiving his compensation by an interest in business and percent of net earnings...." He disclosed another requirement: "An investment of about $2,000 is needed...." Apparently neither Ed nor Hully (Hulbert) was interested in the proposition. Dearholt, abandoning *The Standard*, took employment with RKO Studios, and in September 1933 embarked on a three-month assignment in Guatemala to reorganize RKO's floundering film company there.

Still in turmoil over his personal problems, Burroughs, in the summer of 1933, made plans to take a vacation alone; ostensibly this vacation was to serve as his retreat from the tensions of business, provide him a chance to meditate over his writing, and allow him to recuperate from a total exhaustion. The desire to be alone was actually motivated by his need to reflect clearly about his marriage and somehow force himself to a decision. Past vacations had always been taken with Emma or the children. The destination was Springerville in the White Mountains of Arizona, and to Hulbert he explained that this was to be his "thinking" trip. On July 9, before starting, he noted in a letter to Jack that he had purchased a quarter interest in a gold mine in Cochise County, Arizona, and hoped to inspect the mine during his travels. Transportation called for a veritable caravan: Hulbert's trailer loaded with mess equipment was to be hitched to Ed's luxurious Cord automobile.

After a July 13 departure Ed soon found that the combination of the excessive weight and long steep grades was too much for the Cord; his only choice was to detach the trailer and leave it for a return pickup. Once at his vacation site, his loneliness and his longing for his children became quickly apparent; he was not used to being separated from them. A habitual letter-writer, he was driven by this loneliness to an even greater-than-normal rate of correspondence. Long letters to Hulbert and Jack, signed affectionately "O.B.," described his activities. For several years he had been using these initials in letters to his children; following a minor quarrel with a man in Tarzana, the man had referred to him in exasperation as "Old Burroughs," and Ed, delighted over the epithet, adopted it for his own.

To Jack, on the eighteenth, he described his stay with the Steinbergs at their ranch lodge on the Little Colorado River, located eleven miles from Springerville, saying he had been accepted as a member of the family: "We all wash in the same tin basin, use the same home-made shower, and the same two holer — though not all at the same time." The days passed with much outdoor activity, crawling into caverns to search for Indian relics, riding horses on the steep mountainsides, and climbing about rocky

ERB and his front-wheel drive Cord automobile, 1934.

cliffs. In August on the tenth and fourteenth Ed wrote to brother Harry and Bert Weston, noting he had been away for three weeks "taking a rest." The "thinking" retreat undoubtedly refreshed and invigorated him, but upon his return the family situation remained unchanged, and it was clear that he could not, as yet, take any serious action.

From Dearholt came a query: would Burroughs consider sponsoring an expedition to make motion pictures, if this could be done without infringing upon his MGM contract? Ashton explained that RKO wanted to use the Burroughs name. Intrigued, Ed decided to explore the legal angles. Ashton was in Guatemala, and his wife, Florence, and Joan were vacationing in Palm Springs. In November 1933 Florence sought Ed's help in arranging passage to Guatemala for herself, the two children, Lee and Caryl, and a maid.

Early in 1934 events combined to finally drive Burroughs to the long-delayed decision.

The entries in his diary record not only his actions, but give more than a hint about things to come:

February 19: Left home at dinner time.

February 20: Came to live at The Garden of Allah, Villa 23.

February 22: . . . Went to Palm Springs with Florence.

The separation from Emma had come. That an interest in another woman had been steadily developing — an interest Ed may not have wished to admit to himself — became evident in the light of future happenings. In fact, for a long time he had firmly repressed the affection he felt for Florence. He had watched her at a distance, and, as revealed to her later, could recall how she looked when she walked down the lawn and on other occasions. He claimed to have fallen in love with her at first sight, years before she hardly knew he existed.[4] These feelings undoubtedly spurred him toward an action he was reluctant to take. The separation was reported by Hulbert to brother Jack, then at Pomona College:

However hard it is to tell you I think it best that you know before you come home. Mamma and Papa have separated. I have seen for years, as I suppose you have to, that they have been far from happy together. What they propose doing I cannot say, but Mama will probably stay here. Naturally, things are quite confused but I think eventually they will both be happier apart than they were together the past year or so.[5]

Urging his father to return home, Jack offered reasons why there should be a reconciliation; on the twenty-eighth Ed discussed the problem in a lengthy letter to his youngest son: "Innumerable times in the past I have weighed all the arguments you have set forth in your splendid letter, but against them rise the countless hours of hideous suffering I have endured for thirty years." Ed's surprising reference to thirty years of suffering, even if an exaggeration, creates a picture of a marriage in which husband and wife were bound together by vows and circumstances for many years, rather than by a mutual love and respect. Naturally, we are being presented with a one-sided version of the marriage. In continuing the letter, Ed releases deep emotions: "There have been many happy moments, but always in the background was the specter of fear of what I knew would inevitably come the next day or the next. I dreaded always to come home; or if I were home, I dreaded the coming of your mother. Perhaps I have been overly sensitive, but I am as I am."

I never wished to make your mother unhappy; I do not now. Yet I cannot forget that she knew how horribly unhappy she was making me. If she had loved me as much as you say, she could not have done it. She would never have treated a dog as unkindly as that. Love makes many sacrifices; and it dies hard, but it can be killed.

With the "comparatively few years left," he emphasized that he intended to live his own life in his own way. He believed that in the same way, Emma would be happier leading her own life, doing "the things she wants to do without fear of criticism," and added, "Were we to live together again this thing would always stand between us, and all the family relations would be as strained as they were last Sunday." Here, of course, are further references to Emma's drinking habit. Ed noted the possibility that he and his wife "might live together again. . . . Perhaps after a while neither one of us will wish to; perhaps we may discover it will work out after all. But we should have time."

He believed that Emma's action in leaving the house and going to a hotel was "a frank declaration of her preference," an indication of "at least a subconscious desire to end a relationship that has been . . . extremely strained for years." Ed stated his desires firmly; concerning visits, he wanted no set day or time for coming; he wanted "no more obligatory ruts"; he would not return at this time — to do so "would put the seal of perpetuity" on his "unhappiness." In order that Emma might keep occupied, he urged that she take up flying — "I have done nothing in years that gave me so much to think about pleasurably. . . ." Or she might drive back to Coldwater, Michigan, to visit her mother. He confessed that "some heroics have crept into this letter" and apologized to Jack: "I did not mean them to, for after all this is 1934, and sentiment is passe — if that is how it's spelled."[6]

The efforts by the Burroughs children to persuade their father to try a reconciliation proved unsuccessful; he insisted that Emma must arrange for a divorce. However, Hulbert and Jack continued their attempts to bring their parents together again. Through Murray Hulbert, Emma's cousin and a New York attorney, a Los Angeles lawyer, Michael Shannon, was contacted. His belief that everything might be "cleared up with clever handling" proved encouraging to son Hulbert who, in a letter of March 21 to his brother, remarked, "Papa is magnifying the troubles too much. . . ." The plan suggested by Hulbert was to prevent any precipitate action and to consult with the family physician, Dr. Charles E. Phillips; the purpose, in Hulbert's words, was to find "the subtlest way to deceive father."

Ed's health problems at this time — he was suffering from a bladder condition which had not responded well to treatment — led both Dr. Phillips and Hulbert to conjecture that this sickness might be "the basic cause of his mental warping, if such it can be called." Unduly frightened by this illness, possibly because the specialist had over-stressed its seriousness, Ed had refused to travel anyplace where a doctor might not be available. Phillips believed that a long vacation trip might change Ed's entire outlook, and he suggested a journey to Central America or a joint motion picture expedition to the South Seas with writer Norman Foster, husband of Claudette Colbert. Hulbert wrote, "The big problem is to stave off the divorce idea and to cleverly and diplomatically implant the trip idea." Hulbert also hoped to persuade Ed's attorney, Max Felix, to discourage divorce proceedings in the hope of an "eventual reconciliation." Yet Hulbert, frankly pessimistic about the result, felt that his father would return only because of his longings to be with his children: "I cannot see how Papa and Mamma can ever really be contented together."

During this period Ed spent much time with the Dearholts. Entries in his diary reveal a situation now involving four people:

March 2: Had dinner with Florence & Ashton

March 7: The Dearholts and Miss Holt are coming to dinner.

March 8: Drove to Gay's Lion Farm. . . . Florence, Ashton and Ula Holt went with me.

March 9: Went to Florence's party in the evening.

This soon-to-be-explained puzzling foursome consisted of Ed paired off with Florence Dearholt and her unconcerned husband Ashton paired off with Ula Holt, an actress who would later play a role in a Tarzan movie. On March

29 came an announcement of a divorce decree granted to the Dearholts.

All hope of reconciliation between Ed and Emma now ended. She, Hulbert, and Jack stayed in the Malibu home, and Ed leased a house at 2029 Pinehurst Road in Los Angeles. He and Florence were together as often as possible, and her name was prominent in his diary:

April 4: Dinner at Florence's. Show at Ritz. . . .

April 8: Up at 6:30 a.m. Got Florence at 7, and brought her down to breakfast. Took her to Speyers at 8 . . . telegram from Florence at 10 p.m. from Sacramento.

April 13: Wired Florence at Gold Beach.

April 14: Ula Holt and Ashton came to dinner.

April 17: Moved today from Garden of Allah to 2029 Pinehurst Road.

April 19: Telegram today. Florence will be home Sunday and take dinner with me.

April 22: Florence came home. We dined at the Vendome.

By the end of the month the two were calling, writing, or meeting almost every day.

In the midst of this personal dilemma, with his marriage of more than thirty years being shattered, Ed was also confronted by pressures to make important business decisions. The continuing anxiety over too many projects that in the past had brought him close to collapse was now aggravated by the family situation, and these combined problems turned him into a harried, disturbed man. This was hardly a period for him to consider a new business venture. Nevertheless, matters were brewing, and the first step came in the spring of 1934 when Dearholt headed a company called Romance Productions, Inc., located at the Mack Sennett Studios in Hollywood. Associated with him were George W. Stout and Ben S. Cohen, and the avowed purpose of the company appeared to be nothing more than to produce a Tarzan serial. Their proposal brought a quick rejection; the letter of May 4 stressed that because of the warm friendship between Dearholt and Burroughs, a special consideration had been given to the proposal. Nevertheless, the policy was to refuse permission for *any* serials and to concentrate upon film features. Yet about a week later the Burroughs office made a complete reversal, agreeing to sell to Romance Productions the talking motion picture rights to an original Burroughs story and allowing a serial of "not more than twelve episodes totaling twenty-five reels." Ed was careful to preserve all other rights, including television. The required payment was $20,000.

More manipulations were in order. With MGM failing to exercise its option for further Tarzan films, Dearholt gleefully and abruptly launched a new project. Romance Pictures was abandoned and on July 31 he wrote to Ed, "In order to produce the highest type of motion picture chapter play featuring the same Tarzan principals and covering their experiences in various foreign countries, I would suggest the formation of a new corporation to be called Tarzan Productions, Inc." The corporation, under a continuing license from Burroughs, would purchase one story a year at a cost of $40,000. Dearholt presumably was well aware of Ed's long-suppressed ambition to found his own film company. In fact, as amply demonstrated in the past dissatisfaction that Ed had expressed with his publishers, syndicates, editors, illustrators, and agents, and his compulsion to control all of these outlets or functions, there was an inevitability about his entrance into movie production.

Plans to form the new corporation were soon underway. Even before the contracts were drawn up an office was established at 8476 Sunset Boulevard in Hollywood with Dearholt in charge. The contract, listing George W. Stout, Lee Ashton Dearholt, and Ben S. Cohen as "Promoters" and Burroughs as "Owner," reported the formation of Burroughs-Tarzan Enterprises ". . . to produce, distribute and/or exhibit talking motion pictures based on the stories and characters written and created by Burroughs." Sixty percent of the stock was to be divided equally among the three promoters, with Ed being granted the remaining forty percent. On September 12 the agreement was sent to Attorney Max Felix and on the twenty-fourth the California incorporation was completed.[7] On the company letterhead, some months later, Stout was listed as president; Cohen, vice-president; Dearholt, vice-president in charge of production; and Nat G. Rothstein, director of advertising and exploitation.

Ed made it plain that he was delegating all responsibility to these men. In August 1934, replying to a request for employment in the planned movie, he noted that this matter would be handled by Dearholt: "I am not interfering in any way with the work that can be done so much more ably by experienced motion picture men. . . ." With the launching of a campaign to find a new actor for the Tarzan role, numerous applications poured into the Tarzana office; all of these were referred to Dearholt. Also in August, before the film contract had been signed, the newspapers were reporting the plans for an expedition to Guatemala. On the sixteenth Louella Parsons' column told of the search by "Tarzan's papa" for an "unknown" to take the lead in future "jungle operas":

Burroughs tried to borrow both Weismuller and Crabbe and when that wasn't possible he sent his partner, Nat Rothstein, out on a countrywide tour of colleges to locate a new Tarzan. . . . his first picture with his own hand-picked Tarzan will be "Tarzan in Guatemala". . . .

Ed confirmed this tentative movie title in responding to an inquiry from the Grace Steamship Company: "Yes, we are going to make 'Tarzan in Guatemala' and actually in Guatemala in order to get authentic backgrounds." He indicated that the company would travel by the Grace Line.[8]

The quest for a new Tarzan culminated in October 1934 with the selection of Herman Brix, a former University of Washington football and track star and an American Olympic athlete. On the twenty-fourth Dearholt informed Burroughs, "Herman Brix has outclassed every other applicant, in our opinion. . . .

Burroughs-Tarzan Enterprises offices, Sunset Boulevard, Hollywood, 1935; ERB is standing directly beneath the name Burroughs *that appears in the sign on the building.*

He has stage presence, considerable picture experience, and is an individual who can be handled. Subject to your approval, we are now ready to sign him on five year, optional contract, starting at $75 for first twenty weeks, and $100 second twenty weeks, and so on." Dearholt also noted tentative arrangements to employ the chimpanzee "Jiggs" at a cost of $2,000 for the movie. This would also include roles for Jiggs' owners, Mr. and Mrs. Gentry, with the woman scheduled to play the part of Queen Maya in the Lost City. Burroughs at once approved all of these selections.

Seeking publicity angles, Dearholt urged Ed to consider writing a novel titled *Tarzan in Guatemala* which could be illustrated by still pictures from the movie and then published at the time of the film release in September 1935.[9]

Unreceptive, Ed reminded Dearholt that the plans called for a low-priced Whitman publication of *Tarzan in Guatemala*; this would be better for tie-ins than a two-dollar novel. For the exploitation of the picture Ed suggested a Tarzan Clan campaign with copies of the Official Guide to be distributed at the theaters. Ed mentioned the fact that Signal Oil had enrolled 125,000 members in their coast Tarzan Clans. He added, "I have now entirely run out of ideas. In fact I have not had a new one for so long that I suspect someone has been practicing birth control on my idea procreator."[10]

In November 1934 Dearholt was still having casting problems and reported "trying to close with a Miss Dale Walsh, who promises to be everything we need for the ingenue." Miss Walsh later won the role of Alice Martling, daughter of an archaeologist who comes to the Guatemalan jungle in search of the Green Goddess, a priceless Mayan relic. For the juvenile role Dearholt noted the signing of twenty-two-year-old Harry Ernest, then playing the boy bugler in the Ronald Colman picture, *Clive of India*. The ambitious Dearholt disclosed his choice of the first non-Tarzan novel to be adapted for a film; he informed Ed, "Now outlining 'Mad King' so writers can start treatment."[11] Responding, Ed was doubtful:

Are you all quite sure that The Mad King *is the best selection for the first non-Tarzan? I think this would bear a little investigating. . . . I am best known for highly imaginative fiction. Would a Prisoner of Zenda picture by me have much pulling power? There is nothing very new or original about it. I like the story. I think it would make a good picture. I just raise this other question so that we may all consider every angle of the question.*[12]

With the expedition scheduled to sail for Guatemala at the end of November, Dearholt and Stout were feverishly involved in their most serious problem — the arrangements for financing the enterprise. Dearholt's previous assurance to Burroughs that Pathe would provide the finances now proved to be only wishful thinking. Frantic negotiations with the bank led to the only acceptable agreement: Burroughs would receive his promised $20,000 advance, but for the needed $50,000 loan the rights to *Tarzan in Guatemala* must be assigned to the bank as collateral. In the event that the loan was not paid and the bank assumed ownership of Burroughs' story, he was guaranteed the right to repurchase it from them for the original $50,000.[13]

The first animal scenes, shot at the Selig Zoo in Los Angeles before the expedition departed, were enthusiastically reported by Dearholt: ". . . wild, confusing, but productive — saw rushes last night and lion fight had old-fashioned guts. Tarzan looks fine and uses his head. 'Jiggs' definitely holds one's interest."

Preparations for the voyage included the fingerprinting of Jiggs, the chimpanzee, who would take the role of Nkima.

Soon after the departure of the expedition with twenty-eight actors and a menagerie of trained wild animals, the film title *Tarzan in Guatemala* was discarded; on December 11, 1934, *Variety* noted that the company's first production would be called "Tarzan and the Green Goddess." But the title uncertainty continued, with Burroughs-Tarzan Enterprises unable to make a final decision. In a lengthy analysis of four possible titles, BTE was highly critical of "The New Adventures of Tarzan." It was too similar to the title of a previous picture. . . they might release their silent version simultaneously with the release of our picture. . . the title in no sense differentiates this Tarzan picture from all other Tarzan pictures, since every exhibitor knows that Tarzan pictures are adventure pictures. . . ." The greatest objection, however, was the effect this title might have upon future films — they could not all be called "Adventures of Tarzan." With this type of reasoning, the best title became apparent: "Tarzan's 1935 Adventures." This would establish the film as the very latest and newest, and since BTE planned to produce a Tarzan movie yearly, the only change necessary was in each succeeding date. Tarzan films would thus become annual institutions like the *Ziegfeld Follies*. After all this agonized quibbling and petty analysis, BTE proceeded at once to ignore its own logical conclusions; by the summer of 1935 the title somehow became *The New Adventures of Tarzan*.

The Dearholt expedition, aboard the liner *Seattle*, encountered incredible difficulties beginning with the landing on the Guatemalan coast in December 1934 in the midst of a storm. San José had no harbor, and the passengers and freight had to be lowered into boats with a crane. This unloading, done three miles from shore in a rolling sea, included a four-ton sound truck. The first location at Chichicastenango, on a plateau 8,000 feet above sea level, required an eighteen-hour trip to cover only one hun-

ERB in 1934.

ERB reading in his den at Malibu; at his feet is Tarzan, his son Jack's Old English sheepdog, 1934.

ERB and granddaughter Joanne Pierce, 1934.

ERB developing a hearty laugh, March 26, 1937.

ERB playing bottle pool at Malibu home, 1934.

dred miles. The sound truck first had to be towed and pushed up the steep grade and then, in the descent, plunged downward at high speed and at times out of control. At 2 a.m., with the expedition still high in the mountains, a violent tropical storm began and in the deluge that followed, all of the electrical equipment stopped functioning. The last twelve miles were driven in the dark. The company used three locations, the Mayan ruins at Tikal, old Spanish capital of Antigua, and Guatemala City, called the "little Paris" of Central America.

The New Adventures of Tarzan, adapted by Charles F. Royal and Edwin H. Blum, with screen play by Royal, was directed by Edward Kull and W. F. McGaugh. In addition to Herman Brix as Tarzan, the cast consisted of Ula Vale (Ula Holt); Major Martling (Frank Baker); Alice Martling (Dale Walsh); Gordon Hamilton (Harry Ernest); Raglan (Don Costello); George (Lewis Sargent); Bouchart (Merrill McCormick); and Nkima, played by Jiggs. The part of Raglan was played by Ashton Dearholt when actor Don Costello became too ill to continue. Designed as a serial in twelve episodes, the film opens with Tarzan in the African jungle, where he saves the life of a demented Frenchman who then informs him that D'Arnot, Tarzan's close friend, is lost in the wilds of Guatemala. En route to Guatemala by ship, Tarzan meets a group headed by Major Martling, an archaeologist who hopes to find the valuable Mayan relic, the Green Goddess. Included in the group are Alice, Martling's daughter, Ula Vale, a woman of mystery, and Raglan, a villainous explorer.

The movie contained familiar plot elements of the Burroughs novels. There is a hidden lost city and a Queen Maya (shades of La of Opar) who, with dagger poised to sacrifice Tarzan on the altar, naturally falls in love with him and spares his life. However, the film introduces a subplot with incidents not typical of the Tarzan stories. Smuggling of firearms and ammunition is involved, and the secret service is on the trail of the guilty parties and a ship carrying a contraband cargo. A clever secret service agent, unidentified, but mysteriously referred to as Operator No. 17, is revealed in Episode Twelve to be Ula Vale.

The rushes sent by Dearholt from Guatemala received an enthusiastic approval from Burroughs, who, on January 7, 1935, wrote, "You have some wonderful shots, and with the sets, crowds and backgrounds it looks like a million dollar picture. It would certainly have cost MGM that much if they had made it on their lot. . . ." He suggested some improvements; Dale Walsh's voice was "too sharp and babyish," and Brix appeared too self-conscious, was taking the part too seriously, and needed to relax. Overly optimistic, Burroughs spoke hopefully of accumulating a working surplus out of the first profits and being able to finance future pictures without seeking loans. But two months later, when the uncut film arrived, the dreams of "a million dollar picture" were rudely shattered. In a memorandum of March 5, he appraised the film candidly:

. . . what we have to work with consists of the story and the Guatemalan background. MGM, with little or no story, made two successful pictures because of the tremendous amount of action injected. We must face the fact that we have little or no action in our picture; and what impressed me last night was the fact that we had sacrificed both the story and the scenic shots in an effort to achieve action that either was not there or not worth while, and what action there is is not particularly thrilling.

The picture should be recut with many of the picturesque background shots retained and with some of the sequences shortened. "In other words," Ed admitted sadly, "we should try to build up a picture with what we have." Although he was familiar with the story, he noted he could not "vizualize" certain scenes because of "missing progressions." His only enthusiasm was for the chimpanzee Jiggs, whose actions "were far more interesting than a great deal of the stuff we had in." He referred to

Jiggs' smearing of the cold cream over his face and head and his finding of Ula and leading her toward the temple. Ed conceded his mistake in suggesting that an educational sequence should be deleted; a "cow sequence" instead should have been removed. It had "absolutely no bearing upon the picture" and would produce nothing but ridicule from the audience.

The enthusiasm over the rushes had been so strong that neither Ed nor the others could possess any doubts that the complete movie would be a success. But BTE now had to accept a distressing fact — *The New Adventures of Tarzan* had serious defects. The hectic and expensive Guatemalan expedition had not been justified. Ed commented, "As the picture now stands, there is not a great deal to show that it might not have been made in Hollywood. . . ." Disturbed over a "very noticeable weakness," noticed too late, Ed wrote, "Tarzan is unquestionably a subordinate character," and further explained Tarzan's minor role: ". . . the big climax at the end of the picture features the comedian. He is the real hero and the rescuer of the party. I should have caught this in the script months ago, but it did not strike me forcibly until I saw it on the screen last night."

Throughout the years Burroughs' evaluations of most of the Tarzan films had been severely critical. Irked over the failure of the producers and writers to adhere to the original plots and characterizations, he had reacted varyingly from pained resignation to bitterness, contempt, or sheer disgust. In his attitude toward the filmmakers, whom he often regarded as a group of bunglers, he exhibited a positiveness, a certainty that if given the chance, he could produce a film far superior to the others.

The Guatemalan film venture, however, revealed his limitations and lack of experience in this specialized area. On numerous past occasions he had observed or conceded that writing scenarios and making films required skills and perception that were beyond him. The novelist's creations were not effective through simple transference to the screen; they needed someone with dramatic understanding and vision who knew how to select,

reshape, and transform the original ideas, how to adapt them for a visual medium. Burroughs' rueful confession of his inability to detect the glaring weaknesses in *The New Adventures of Tarzan* during the production illustrates another point. The special difficulties of appraising a film while it is in the making, with the producer closely involved, working on separate sequences, are quite evident. This is far different from the opportunity granted an outsider, such as Burroughs who in the past had viewed the completed pictures, analyzed them as a whole, and discovered the obvious failures.

Although Ed and Emma were separated, the situation remained confused, with no divorce proceedings initiated; she had refused to accede to his request that she arrange for the divorce. Meanwhile, he continued to spend his time with Florence and her relatives and friends. His involvement in a steady round of social affairs and his nervous state and subsequent illness are revealed on his 1934 diary pages:

May 18: Taken sick. Vomited twice on way home. Went to bed. Florence came and insisted upon calling doctor. Doctor Chase came — just a little stomach upset. . . .

May 23: Took Paul Speyers to Breakfast Club.

May 24: Took Ashton & Ula to dinner at Levy's. Dropped in to see Florence.

His acquaintance with Florence's family, the Gilberts, is indicated in a later entry:

July 16: To May & John's for bridge with Florence. . . Mrs. Gilbert, Eddie & Claire came. Brought Florence home and let her read Hulbert's letter. At 3 a.m. I phoned Hulbert in Chicago to take the first plane home.

July 17: 3 hrs. sleep last night. . . .

Ed's main concern was about the attitudes of his two sons; he had not seen them since leaving home, but he was aware of their dismay and their inclination to blame him. He could not rest until the old closeness was restored:

July 18: Hulbert arrived this morning. He and Jack came home with me and we discussed matters. They now understand and are reconciled. . . .

July 24: . . . Dinner at home with Florence, Hulbert and Jack. . . .

With this problem settled, Ed, Florence and her children, and Mrs. Gilbert left for a vacation trip to Big Basin at Santa Cruz. He was careful to note the decorum of the arrangements:

July 29: Arrived at Inn in time for luncheon. Mrs. Gilbert, Florence & the children have connecting cabins #43 & 44. I have #39 on another street.

The later activities included a drive to San Francisco with Florence, bicycle riding for two, and a stopover at Yosemite. Upon returning home the whirl of social affairs was feverish: luncheon at the Ambassador with Florence and Esther Speyer, an evening at the fights, a drive to Santa Barbara and to Agua Caliente, and even visits with Ashton. With the expiration of his lease on the home at Pinehurst Road, Ed, on October 20, moved temporarily into the Dearholt apartment in West Hollywood. His months of romancing with Florence brought him to the next, obvious step. On October 21 he noted, "Left for Las Vegas, Nev. . . ." The reasons were unmistakable, but Ed was avoiding publicity. The story in the *Los Angeles Times* of October 28 was vague; headed in a tongue-in-cheek fashion, "Tarzan Author Studies Nevada," the story read: "Edgar Rice Burroughs, writer, has taken up temporary residence here. Although most temporary residents of Las Vegas are here to get quick divorces, Burroughs said he came here to get atmosphere for a story." But Walter Winchell, in his column of the twelfth, stated matters in his familiar, blunt style: "A man named Edgar Rice Burroughs is at the Apache Hotel. . . for the usual reason — after 34 years of marriage.

ERB, Florence, and her two children, about 1935-36.

His next bride will be Florence Dearholt of Queens Road, Hollywood. Please check if he is the Tarzan author. . . ."

The monotony of waiting in Las Vegas was alleviated by playing tennis, doing a little writing and "watching gambling" at one of the clubs. Ed had noted he was "terribly lonely" but phone calls between him and Florence helped, and soon she began to make regular trips to Las Vegas. Ed also returned for brief visits to Los Angeles. On November 11, when Florence and he decided to drive back to Las Vegas together, Ashton obligingly volunteered to take care of the children. Emma, still stunned and incredulous about the happenings, had moved with her two sons to 10452 Bellagio Road in Bel-Air. She was in communication with Ralph Rothmund, the Burroughs secretary, who spoke of "too long a story to tell." She still hoped that Ed would return to her, and on November 21, in a letter to Jack, mentioned, "something to bring Ed to his senses before too late." Later, it appeared she was going to contest the divorce, and Ed's diary entry of November 27 reported: "Bad news from Ralph. No help from one who brought this hell on me and is evidently bent on ruining me. . . ."

On December 4 Ed's six-week residency was ended, and with Emma deciding not to offer any objections, the suit was filed the next day and a quickie divorce granted on the sixth. In testimony given behind closed doors, according to the newspapers, Ed accused his wife of "extreme cruelty." Emma's attorney, in explaining the plans not to file a countersuit, accepted Ed's belief "that incompatibility of temperament precludes the continuance of a happy and satisfactory marriage relationship." A property agreement had already been reached, with Emma receiving a generous settlement.

In writing to his brother George, Ed stressed that continuing "incidents" lasting for many years — "during which I twice previously left home" — had led to the separation. Florence's relationship had naturally brought accusations against her; but Ed insisted that she had nothing at all to do with it:

At the time Emma and I finally separated, Mrs. Dearholt had no reason to believe that she would be separated from her husband or that he would give her any grounds for divorce. It was a mere coincidence that their separation and divorce followed so soon after my separation. Mrs. Dearholt and her husband have been two of my best friends for years and it was natural that we should be thrown together when I was alone. He and I are still the best of friends. . . .[14]

Ed deplored the fact that he had not heard from Harry for a year and commented, "He was very fond of Emma and probably, like all of my other friends, he has heard only one side of the story, which is all anyone will ever hear as far as I am concerned."

The collapse of Florence's marriage, as she recalled, came abruptly as a result of Dearholt's consuming interest in the actress Ula Holt, cast in the role of the mystery woman in *The New Adventures of Tarzan*. Florence, stunned, reacted with shock and disbelief when Ashton brought Ula back with him from Guatemala and indicated his desire to have her stay in his home. After the separation, Florence and Ed, both in deep distress — sufferers in common — were drawn to each other. "We were two lost souls that got together," Florence said.[15] Ed's misery and guilt were so strong that [he told her] he was "ready to shoot himself." More than once in the passing weeks he credited her with saving his life. His sharpest anguish was about Hulbert who now, because of the separation, was left with the burden of the problems at home. The most difficult situation, of course, centered about Emma and the despair which drove her to increased dependence upon alcohol. Florence recalled the "terrible obligation" Ed felt toward his oldest son. "He wept over Hulbert," she said. Ed's unhappiness was so great that she suggested he might wish to return to Emma. His response again was that he would "shoot himself" before going back to face the same insoluble problem.

Having finally reached a decision, the two made plans for a new life together. Ed was staying temporarily in a house at 7933 Hillside Avenue in Hollywood. They selected an engagement ring, and at a special Christmas breakfast held at the Gilbert home announced their engagement. With the arrival of the new year, 1935, Florence and Ed began house-hunting; the one they chose, then occupied by Maurice Chevalier, was in Beverly Hills at 806 North Rodeo Drive. The publicity for the marriage was unavoidable. His diary noted the events:

March 31: Drove over to 5th Ave. and saw Frank McNamee (the attorney). Everything set for Thursday.

April 1: Two Times men out on front porch for several hours with a camera.

April 4: Florence & I flew to Las Vegas on Western Air Express. . . Frank McNamee met us. We went directly to the court house and were married at 10:20 by Judge Wm. Orr. Mrs. Keller and Frank were witnesses.... Flew back to L.A....

Another diary entry of February 20 had noted Florence's thirtieth birthday; thus, Ed, who had turned fifty-nine on September 1, 1934, was marrying a woman about half his age.

The next day the newlyweds boarded the *S.S. Lurline* for a honeymoon in Honolulu. On the ship, where they dined at the captain's table, they were joined by Jeanette McDonald and her mother, and upon arriving at Honolulu on April 11, they received a special greeting from Florence's friend, Janet Gaynor, who sent leis out to them before the ship docked. Later activities included a first swimming lesson for Florence, Ed's first surfboarding experience, and a visit with Janet Gaynor at her cottage. On May 11 they boarded the *Lurline* again, this time for the voyage home, and returned to Los Angeles on the sixteenth.

The fact that in the passing weeks they spent an afternoon with Dearholt, Florence's ex-husband, who was working at the zoo with the Tarzan company, was not considered at all unusual. In July 1935 Ashton and Ula Holt were married. The men remained business associates and close friends, and the newlywed couples were together on various occasions — at their homes, at social affairs, or on the tennis courts. Toward Ashton, who was always welcome to visit his two children, Caryl Lee and Lee, Ed never displayed any jealousy. In November Ed entered the hospital for surgery, the problem being a recurrence of the old bladder trouble that had plagued him in the past. A long period of convalescence followed. At the Good Samaritan Hospital, Ed, probably sensitive over the nature of his illness and anxious to avoid publicity, was entered as "John B. Downs"; the statement of charges was made out to "Mr. J. B. Downs alias E. Rice Burroughs, 6442 Lexington." Florence, under severe strain from worrying and waiting at the hospital, was close to a nervous collapse. In this situation Ed turned to the man he most trusted under the circumstances — Ashton

Dearholt — and called him to pick up Florence and take her home.[16]

Fascinated by the desert atmosphere, the sun and the unlimited tennis opportunities, Ed and Florence decided to stay in Palm Springs, and in October 1935 they rented a home on Arenas Road, for eight months only, from Harold Hicks, a Realtor., The weeks that followed were filled with social activities, but the tennis courts became the center of attraction. Ed's diary reported the events and new acquaintances:

Oct. 16: Met Charles Farrell and Ralph Bellamy in Harold Hicks' office and joined the Racquet Club.

Oct. 17: Tennis at Racquet Club at 9 with Harold Hicks and John Lamb. Rode bicycles in afternoon....

Oct. 20: To Racquet Club in afternoon. Florence played doubles with Mrs. Paul Lucas against Mrs. Ralph Bellamy and Mrs. Charlie Farrell (Virginia Vallee).

Ralph Bellamy and Charles Farrell, famous as screen and stage actors, were also business partners in the development of the Palm Springs Racquet Club, which at first consisted merely of a group of tennis courts. Bellamy recalled with amusement that when he and Farrell sent out a list of invitations to join the club, with the fees established as fifty dollars for a single membership, and seventy-five dollars for a family, plus nine dollars dues yearly, only a few individuals responded. They proceeded to raise the charges every two months, and when these reached $650, they had a long waiting list. The club became a paying proposition later, with Farrell selling it and then taking it back several times. Bellamy, however, as the club expanded to include a restaurant, with a large staff and an orchestra, found the responsibilities too time-consuming; he severed his association with the Racquet Club.[17]

Florence and Ed returned to Los Angeles from Palm Springs in May 1936. In the temporary choices of living quarters, Ed gave the impression of being determined to maintain the typical moving pattern that had marked his past. A brief stay at 2315 North Vermont Avenue was followed by six months' residence at the Hearst-owned Chateau Elysee at 5930 Franklin Avenue, and then, in June 1937, a change to the Sunset Plaza apartments in Hollywood. This transience in the couple's residences would continue in the years ahead.

Ed's feelings toward Florence were sentimentally expressed in a unique form in the writing and publication of *Swords of Mars* in 1936. He devised the first word in the prologue and in each of the twenty-four chapters that follow so that the first letters in these words form an acrostic. Printed to stand out in a heavy bold type, these first letters, beginning with a T in the prologue, compose an affectionate message: "To Florence with all My Love Ed."[18]

The Tarzan sequels were of course inevitable, and the latest, number nineteen, at first titled "Tarzan and Jane," was written May 13, 1934 to January 19, 1935. It parallels the loosely plotted pattern of the previous stories, this time concentrating upon the hazards that confront Jane and a group of acquaintances after their airplane crashes in the jungle. Jane, merely a passenger on the private plane of her wealthy friend Kitty, seeks to return to the Greystoke African estate. Kitty's goal is to find a witch doctor who according to rumor possesses a formula "for renewing youth and inducing longevity." Others in the party are Prince Alexis Sborov, who has married Kitty solely for her money — he naturally becomes Burroughs' indispensible foreign villain; Tibbs, an English butler who cannot be ruffled; Brown, an American pilot; and Annette, the French maid.

Tarzan's adventures are of the usual type, consisting of encounters with hostile natives, but a new element has been added with the creation of the Kavuru, white savages who possess a strange hypnotic power. They lure their victims, young girls between fourteen and twenty, with a weird call, place them under a spell, and then reserve them for a horrible fate. To brew an elixir of life, they use "the pollen of certain plants, the roots of others, the spinal fluid of leopards, and, principally, the glands and blood of women — young women." Kavandavanda, the high priest of the Kavuru, blond and extremely handsome, is also half mad. Because of the elixir, the secret of deathless youth he had discovered, he is immortal. As he reveals to Jane, his captive, he has lost track of his age — he may be a thousand years old.

Tarzan and his friend Brown, in their attempts to rescue Jane, fortunately discover another airplane whose pilots have been killed by the natives. To reach the Kavuru temple, located in a deep canyon inaccessible by land, they fly over the area and then parachute to earth. At the end, with Kavandavanda dead and Jane saved, the surviving members of the party — Brown, Annette, and Tibbs — accompany the Greystokes to their estate, carrying a box of pellets that can provide eternal youth. They decide to divide them into five equal parts, but Jane's question leads to a change: " 'Aren't you forgetting Nkima?' asked Jane, smiling. 'That's right,' said Brown. 'We'll make it six parts. He's sure a lot more use in the world than most people.' "

Rejected by *Liberty* and *Collier's*, "Tarzan and Jane" was sent to Frederick Clayton, *Argosy* editor, in the hope that the magazine would pay the $5,000 it had originally offered for a new Tarzan work. On April 29, 1935, Clayton returned the story, complained that it was too "stereotyped," and commented: ". . . the contrasting 'high society' life seemed out of place. In fact the technique of alternating chapters of this side of the plot and then of the jungle elements strikes us as being outmoded. . . ."

With no remaining markets, the story was forwarded to Kennicott at *Blue Book*; he approved it except for the device of sacrificing young girls to produce an elixir of youth, stating that it was "a bit morbid and sensational" and better designed for the movies. He also proposed to change the title. On the twenty-seventh Burroughs accepted the offer of $3,000,

BLUE BOOK

Magazine   October   15 cents

A *new* **TARZAN** *novel*

Edgar Rice Burroughs, H. Bedford-Jones,
William Makin, Robert Mill, William Chester.

"Tarzan and the Immortal Men" cover of Blue Book, *October 1935.*

and with the publication in *Blue Book*, October 1935 to March 1936, the new title became "Tarzan and the Immortal Men."[19]

In the editing of the manuscript, a new practice was initiated. The separation between Ed and Emma created a need to provide her with financial support, and from a business and tax standpoint, this could be best accomplished by assigning Emma the task of copyreading the stories and listing her as an employee of the corporation. A note of February 7, 1935, addressed to Emma at her Bel-Air home (10452 Bellagio Road), referred to "Tarzan and Jane" being forwarded for "corrections and notations."[20] However, the "employment" of Emma, under the circumstances, could produce few if any positive results. On August 28, 1935, Rothmund wrote to complain:

It has been a long time since we have noticed any corrections or comments made by you in connection with the various scripts we send you, and so we are anxious to know whether or not you read these scripts as carefully as they should be read. On several occasions after the scripts have been returned by you, we discovered typographical and grammatical errors. . . .

Rothmund noted the considerable time devoted to the "transmission" of these scripts and the expense of postage. Emma, in her disturbed condition, suffering from the shock of the separation, was in no state to perform an assignment of this nature. A statement of January 11, 1936, to the accountant revealed that Emma received a salary of $21,600 for the previous year.

With the book publication date set for September 1, 1936, the title for the latest novel — last called "Tarzan and the Immortal Men" — remained uncertain. In correspondence with St. John, the illustrator, Rothmund cautioned him to await further instructions before doing any lettering.[21] Burroughs, away from the office for two months, visited St. John in Chicago in July and spoke of the book scheduled for the following spring. But a sudden change of plans brought a deep disappointment to St. John: the Burroughs organization would have a new illustrator — young John Coleman Burroughs. Throughout the years Ed had lauded St. John's work and offered it as a model for all illustrators to follow. However, the time had arrived to draw upon Jack's artistic skill. On September 28 Ed wrote to St. John:

. . . it has always been the ambition of my son, Jack, and myself that one day he would illustrate one of my books. He is doing very excellent work, and I am having him illustrate the Spring book for us. However, he stands in the same position that any artist must; and if the work is not satisfactory, I shall have to have it done elsewhere. . . .

Jack commented at the time that he was well aware he had not yet attained the ability of a St. John, but was deeply grateful to his father for the unprecedented opportunity afforded him. He was a dedicated man and worked hard to justify his father's faith in him. He matured rapidly as an artist, and the illustrations he did for ERB's 1948 Martian novel, *Llana of Gathol*, were superb. He illustrated a total of 13 Burroughs books.

St. John's final book jacket and illustrations appeared in the fall of 1936 with *Tarzan's Quest*, the title at last chosen; the suggestion for the title came from Mildred Bernard, the Burroughs secretary.[22] With *The Oakdale Affair and The Rider*, a combination of two 1918 magazine stories, Jack produced the first in a long series of illustrations for his father's novels. The book, published on February 15, 1937, was viewed dubiously by Michael Mill, the Burroughs sales representative, who commented, ". . . I am having a terrific struggle with the *Oakdale Affair*. I have received quite a lot of adverse criticism on account of the 'two novels in one' idea. The trade say that two novels in one are not successful because there is no way to classify them. . . ."[23] Later, Burroughs offered gloomy agreement: ". . . I note that the total sale was nothing to brag about. . . . I take it that buyers are not sold on two short novels in one book."[24]

The fifth of the Pellucidar series, titled

ERB and son John standing by John's painting of dust jacket for ERB's book containing two stories, October 23, 1936; the book, The Oakdale Affair/The Rider, *was published by Edgar Rice Burroughs, Inc., February 15, 1937.*

Back to the Stone Age, written January 26 to September 11, 1935, recounts the adventures of Lieutenant von Horst who had been left behind when the dirigible 0-220 departed from the inner world. The novel is a series of battles with savages and monsters, including the Trodon, a gigantic winged marsupial that deposits its captives in its pouch, then proceeds to paralyze them by injecting a poison with its needle-sharp tongue. Von Horst, one of the victims, is taken to a cavern where a horrible death awaits him. Helpless to move, he is in the nesting place of the young Trodons, and as they emerge from their enormous eggs, he realizes that he and the other victims are to serve as food for these hideous creatures. Von Horst's escape and his subsequent perils in this primitive world include his daring action in saving Old White, a mammoth, by removing thorns from the animal's feet; Old White then becomes his friend and protector. Because of his love for the barbarian slave girl La-ja, von Horst refuses to return to the earth's surface with rescuer David Innes, deciding, instead, to remain with La-ja and become chief of the Lo-har cave dwellers.[25]

Back to the Stone Age displays little of the accustomed Burroughs inventiveness. Assembled over a long period — eight months is indeed a long time for a novel of this type — the story may owe its faulty development to the turmoil of Ed's personal life in these months, his guilt and mental conflict after the divorce, and the pressures and changes that accompanied his remarriage.

Following a rejection by *Liberty*, the novel was sent to *Blue Book* and *Argosy*. On January 24, 1936, Kennicott, apologizing for holding *Back to the Stone Age*, wrote to Rothmund, ". . . I have known and loved his work for so many years, that it is very difficult for me to let go of a story of his. . . ." *Blue Book* was facing financial problems; Kennicott hoped that some "change of conditions" might permit him to purchase the story. He noted, however, that it did not "rank with Mr. Burroughs' best":

It starts in the middle of things, with no attempt to explain Pellucidar or his characters' presence there, or to win sympathy for his hero. Indeed, the last Pellucidar story we printed, had Tarzan as the leading figure, and as far as material which came to us is concerned, Mr. Burroughs never bothered to get Tarzan out again. . . ."

From *Argosy*, where the circulation had fallen severely, Frederick Clayton explained that the top price for any serial would be $2,500. It was soon clear that he was not impressed by *Back to the Stone Age*, and Burroughs, worried, offered to write a prologue for the story.[26] Clayton was undecided, and after a month's wait, he returned the manuscript on March 16. Available markets were now exhausted and the sales chances appeared dim. However, in June 1936, Jack Bryne, replacing Clayton as the *Argosy* editor, offered to accept the novel on certain conditions: ". . . the story needs rather extensive editorial revision to put it in shape for us. We can, by reference to the other Pellucidarian stories we have published, work out a prologue that will be a good introduction to the story." Concerned about the political situation abroad, Bryne indicated that because of anti-German sentiment he would discard the name "von Horst" and change the nationality of the hero. Because of these complications, *Argosy* would pay only $1,500 for *Back to the Stone Age*.

In this period of uncertainty the manuscript had been forwarded to Leo Margulies at Popular Library.[27] On June 11 Margulies wrote to offer a proposal: ". . . it has been a tough story to decide on. Frankly, . . . this isn't the best story Mr. Burroughs ever wrote. However, it is a good yarn and certainly worth publishing." Margulies noted that *Back to the Stone Age*, much too long (80,000 words), could not be used in *Thrilling Wonder*, but might be adapted for *Thrilling Adventures*: "Its biggest fault is its lack of one good central plot. As a matter of fact it hasn't got a plot." This would be a serious disadvantage if the story were to be run as a long novel, but Margulies' plan was to divide it into a series of short novelettes. Obviously, revisions would be needed. Margulies concluded, ". . . we would be quite happy to undertake this job if we could get the story at our price. I can offer you one thousand dollars. . . ."

With *Argosy's* higher offer already received, Margulies' proposal was rejected.[28] Burroughs, agreeing to sell the story to *Argosy*, offered no apparent objection to the indicated revisions. On June 23, however, an explanation of von Horst's German background was sent by Rothmund:

. . . Mr. Burroughs mentioned that he laid the foundation early in the story that von Horst's father was an English Special Agent in Germany, that he took the name von Horst and brought his son up under that name. His son knew his father and mother were English; and as he was going to work into the same special agency himself, he kept the name believing that there would be no question raised in the minds of the Germans as to his nationality. It may be that you will want to bring this out in your build-up for the story.

Since a great many readers had requested a von Horst-Pellucidar sequel, Rothmund felt that these details, if included in the changes, would improve *Back to the Stone Age* and provide the necessary transition for the readers. The novel was published as a six-part serial in *Argosy*, January 9 to February 13, 1937, under the title

"Seven Worlds to Conquer" cover of Argosy Weekly, *January 9, 1937; book title:* Back to the Stone Age, *1937.*

of "Seven Worlds to Conquer," but with the book publication on September 15 of that year, the original title was resumed.

To match the determination, or plain stubbornness, demonstrated in the efforts to sell a manuscript retitled "The Brass Heart" would be an arduous undertaking. In 1930 Burroughs had written a western, "That Damned Dude," which at the time had proven unsalable. Five years later, when a series of submissions was launched, the story was given the puzzling, unrelated title of "The Brass Heart." Rothmund, evidently at Burroughs' instructions, listed the author under the nom de plume of John Mann. The return address used was also Rothmund's, 20441 Arminta Street in Canoga Park. On certain occasions when Burroughs resorted to pen names, he was trying to determine whether the editors might accept a story by an unknown writer on its own merits; he suspected that the name Burroughs on a story could bring automatic rejections, without a careful reading, because the editors assumed the work was a typical fantasy, not a type they wanted, or because they feared the price would be quite high. It is significant, therefore, that the pen name was attached to a story of lesser quality, one for which a lower price would be accepted; one might also reason that Burroughs preferred to have a mediocre work appear under a nom de plume.

Using a form letter, with a dotted line prepared for the insertion of the editor's name, Rothmund, beginning on August 17, 1935, submitted "The Brass Heart" to nine publications, and in November to fifteen others. Outright rejections were received from all. Sales efforts were not successful until 1939 when "That Damn Dude" was purchased for *Thrilling Adventures* and appeared the following year as a three-part serial, retitled "The Terrible Tenderfoot."

Burroughs' lack of resistance to the drastic changes made in his stories by the *Argosy* editors was of course surprising; in the earlier years he had been adamant in his refusal to allow any unauthorized revisions. But new factors and a changing situation were now involved. The novels, even the Tarzan ones, were more difficult to market. The prestige magazines, with the exception of *Liberty*, had never valued the Burroughs works, and the pulp magazines, with circulation declining, were extremely selective in their purchases and limited in their budgets. There never had been a variety of markets for fantasy works. As demonstrated with *Back to the Stone Age*, the Burroughs office was simply forced to compromise in order to make a sale. However, there were other causes for the new situation. One was overproduction — Burroughs was writing and distributing too many works. The book publication schedule of two or more a year had glutted the market. On January 28, 1937, Mill noted discouragedly, ". . . in practically every instance a buyer will say, 'Oh, another Edgar Rice Burroughs book. We can't sell that. We haven't been able to do anything with his last two books. . . .'" In several instances Burroughs stubbornly ignored the opinions of editors and chose mediocre works for publication; examples were *Back to the Stone Age* and later *The Lad and the Lion*. Naturally, the resulting sales were poor.

The extent of the revisions by Jack Byrne, *Argosy* editor, and the plaintive but helpless attitude that Burroughs displayed may be noted in the correspondence. On November 16, 1936, Ed wrote, "I thought *Back to the Stone Age* was a pretty hot title, but if you like *Seven Worlds to Conquer*, hop to it." He then commented about the changes in *Tarzan the Magnificent* (retitled in *Argosy*, September 19 to October 3, 1936):

After reading the first installment of Tarzan and the Magic Men in Argosy, I find that you like change, so inasmuch as you are going to change the story you might as well change the title too, but please have a heart and tell your re-write man not to change my style entirely. In twenty years I have never permitted one of my characters to "husk" and I doubt if I ever used "aye" except in the dialogue of a sailor.[29]

Some months later, on January 27, 1937, Ed had some biting comments to make about the newly published "Seven Worlds to Conquer." He recalled his previous protests about changes and then remarked:

In glancing over the first installment of Seven Worlds to Conquer, *I sensed that it has been largely rewritten. Perhaps the stories are improved, but they are not in my style, which evidently some people have been foolish enough to like.*

He followed by quoting from a letter he had received from an *Argosy* reader:

That last Tarzan novel surprised me. No, not its shortness, but its difference in style of writing; somehow I felt that its philosophies were not exactly reminiscent of Mr. Burroughs' writing style. Could this novel have been written by Mr. Burroughs' elder son? Cheer up, however — it was quite an enjoyable tale.

Ed added in wry amusement, "You see, there is at least one deluded individual who likes my stories the way I write them."

The next in the Tarzan series, written by Ed at the home he and Florence had rented in Palm Springs, was evidently completed in March 1936. The writing dates are not indicated on his worksheet, but on April 1, he sent the story, titled *Tarzan the Magnificent,* to Fulton Oursler at *Liberty.* Ed remarked about the shortness of the story (42,000 words) and, oddly, apologized for the earlier work, *Tarzan and the Lion Man,* that had previously appeared in *Liberty*: "... it was not until I received comments from readers and the reviews of *Tarzan and the Lion Man* that I realized it was not up to the previous standard that I had established for Tarzan...." In his opinion *Tarzan the Magnificent* was "a much better story." Oursler, however, did not share this view and promptly rejected the work.

The action of *Tarzan the Magnificent* is launched as Tarzan discovers a twenty-year-old message, an appeal for help from Lord Mountford, whose disappearance with his wife

had remained an unsolved mystery. His note reveals their capture by the wild women of Kaji, the birth of their daughter a year later, and the death of his wife, killed by the Kaji. These wild women, who possess "strange, occult powers," desire only white men whom they lure to their plateau. The Kaji also own an enormous diamond weighing six thousand carats. Soon after finding the message Tarzan encounters Stanley Wood, an American writer, who had organized an expedition to search for the missing couple and had met the dying Mountford and heard him speak incoherently of a white girl. Helpless to resist a magnetic power stronger than their own wills, Wood and his party had been drawn to the plateau of the Kaji and there made prisoners. The mysterious power, wielded by the witch doctor Mafka, actually emanates from the enormous diamond Gonfal. Wood had met the Queen of the Kaji, Gonfola, a creature of "radical contradictions" who at one moment was "all womanly compassion and sweetness" and the next, a veritable she-devil. They fell in love, and Gonfola helped him escape, but now he intended to return for her and to rescue the others in his party, Van Eyk, Troll, and Spike.

Following the *Liberty* rejection, *Tarzan the Magnificent* was sent to Kennicott at *Blue Book.* On May 29, 1936, in returning the story, he noted it was not "up to the quality that we had learned to expect" and added, "I miss Tarzan's pleasant friendships and adventures among the animals, and find the long range hypnotism of this strange native tribe not wholly successful, as a motif." With further persuasion by Rothmund, Kennicott moved from a $500 to a $750 offer and on June 12 wired, "Element of miscegenation puts Tarzan at discount for us...." Kennicott was obviously fearful of the reader reactions to the black and white breeding. However, he again referred dubiously to the "absentee hypnotism." His offer was at once rejected as too low.

A more acceptable price of $1,500, still a compromise because of the story's shortness, was finally received from Jack Byrne of *Argosy.* The agreement that he would be allowed "certain minor revisions" resulted, as previously explained, in changes far in excess of "minor."[30] Eager to aid in publicizing the new Tarzan story, the Burroughs office informed Byrne of the list of two thousand fan names maintained at Tarzana, a list that was circularized at least twice a year when the novels were published. The suggestion was that Byrne send copy about the forthcoming serial, to be retitled "Tarzan and the Magic Men," and that this copy would be mimeographed and distributed on the Burroughs letterhead to the fans. Byrne agreed, and the one-page publicity, composed in the first person and signed by Ed, announced the story's appearance in *Argosy* of September 19 and spoke of Tarzan's return to the magazine in which he had started: ". . . I give [*Argosy*] so much credit for making Tarzan one of the most sensational characters in fiction." On his own part, Byrne devised various circulars with clever cartoons. Headed and signed by *The Red Star News Company* of New York, these circulars were distributed to all the magazine dealers.

In a period of only three days, March 22 to 25, 1936, Ed completed a 5,000-word story titled "Elmer." Establishing Pat Morgan, an inventor and former war pilot, as the narrator of a sequence of bizarre events, the story opens with reference to a vanished athlete and movie star, Jim Stone. Morgan describes his invention of a revolutionary airplane engine and a new type of concentrated fuel; his attempts, without success, to sell these to the United States Government; and his decision to accept an offer from the Russians and fly his plane to Moscow. He is accompanied by Dr. Marvin Stade whose experiments with animals, freezing them and thawing them out, had brought objections from the SPCA and the Department of Health; angered, Stade has arranged to conduct his experiments in Russia.

En route, the plane, its engine failing, is forced to land in a desolate area of Siberia. There, after a torrential rain has washed away the face of a cliff, the pair make a startling discovery: embedded in a solid block of ice is a prehistoric man, a cave-dweller of the stone age. Caught in a blizzard, the man, numb with cold, had fallen asleep and had been covered by the great glacier that swept over the area. Now, after 50,000 years, Jimber-Jaw — so-named because of his resemblance to a Yellowstone Park grizzly — comes to life, his revival achieved through a transfusion and injections of adrenalin, pituitary fluid, and sex hormones from sheep, administered by Dr. Stade. In his delirium he mutters the one word, *Lilami,* and as he convalesces and learns to speak English, he reveals that Lilami is the woman he loves and the one he somehow intends to find.

Their plane now repaired, Morgan and Dr. Stade return to the United States with Jimber-Jaw, who is given the name of Jim Stone and soon becomes an unbeatable wrestler and boxer. Later he is signed to a film contract. Something in the appearance of Lorna Downs, a movie star, convinces him that she is his lost Lilami. A frivolous, superficial type, Lorna, seeking fun, accepts his attentions for a while, but when he discovers her being kissed by another man, he reverts to his cave-era tactics, turning violent. Lorna, in a rage, calls him a "big boob" and a "tank-town Romeo" and tells him the affair is over. Jim had already become aware of the low morals of the Hollywood set. To Morgan he remarked about the women, "They are without shame. They go almost naked before men. In my country their men would drag them home by the hair and beat them." He observed that the men and women were alike; they both smoked, drank, swore, and gambled. The women, out all night, could not be fit "to look after the caves and children next day." He insisted, "They are only good for one thing, otherwise they might as well be men. . . . In my country such women are killed. No one would want children from them."

After his rejection by Lorna, Jim disappears, and some weeks later his body is found—in the frozen-meat room of a cold storage warehouse. Morgan reported, "He was resting on his side, face against his arm, and I've never seen a man, alive or dead, more peaceful. The note pinned to his coat, addressed to Morgan, read, 'I go to find the real Lilami. And don't thaw me out again.'"

"Elmer" was returned by *Collier's* on April 6, and it was not until the fall of 1936 that an editor displayed interest in the story. Sent to Jack Byrne of *Argosy* on October 30, "Elmer" brought an offer of only $250, a price that Burroughs was forced to accept.[31] The name "Elmer" came from a human skull given to skull collectors Hulbert and John Burroughs by Ed's physician, Dr. Elmer Belt. The name was chosen in his honor. In the original manuscript, Jimber-Jaw, the cave man, had been called Elmer Stone in his wrestling and movie careers, the name "Stone" being an indication of Ed's humor, presumably based upon the Stone Age. The original contains no Dr. Stade; instead, the scientist is named Dr. Wilson Lord. On February 17, 1937, notified of Byrne's intention to change the story title to "The Resurrection of Jimber-Jaw," Ed wrote, " 'Elmer' may not have been so hot, but I think that 'Jimber Jaw 'is a hell of a name." The story appeared in *Argosy* on the twentieth, and on March 5 Byrne replied:

So "Jimber Jaw" is a hell of a name? Well, maybe it is—but it certainly fitted the cover of that recent issue much better than "Elmer" would have done. I don't want to outrage your sensibilities, but doggone it, we've got to sell magazines. . . .

"The Resurrection of Jimber-Jaw," not published in book form until many years later,[32] exhibited ingenuity in its frozen-man idea and Jim's reactions to modern society. The theme, of course, represented Burroughs' familiar condemnation of the fast movie crowd.

Because of the briefness of "Tarzan and the Magic Men," Burroughs quickly completed a sequel, "Tarzan and the Elephant Men," December 1, 1936, to March 8, 1937, and forwarded it to *Argosy*.[33] The first part centers about the actions of the villainous white hunters Spike and Troll who soon capture Gonfala. The story returns to previous settings at Cathne, the City of Gold, and Athne, the City of Ivory, with Tarzan again made prisoner and forced into the arena, The Field of Lions, where he saves the life of the tyrant King Alextar of Cathne who is attacked by an enraged lion. Other adventures follow at Athne, with all the characters, including Stanley Wood and Gonfala, facing dangers.

On March 29 Byrne expressed his disappointment with "Tarzan and the Elephant Men" and, in this and a later letter, offered Burroughs some perceptive advice about writing. His indictment of the story was severe: ". . . too many characters, with too many objectives . . . the whole situation is be-clouded throughout and the suspense so diffuse that it does not catch hold . . . escapes are haphazardly achieved . . . the one you have used for the climax is the old Daniel-in-the-lion's-den that appeared in your last Argosy story." The mistake, Byrne felt, resulted from this attempt to combine too many themes:

I don't think, for instance, that you were particularly interested in the Stanley Wood-Gonfala business; you must have revived it in a weary moment. Then, when you bring in all the business of the City of Gold which appeared such a long time ago you added an additional burden from which the story never recovered. I read the tale carefully twice over, and I'm still a bit bewildered as to what actually occurred. None of the minor characters created the least spark of interest in me and I thought that Tarzan went through his paces with a complete lack of verve. . . .

Byrne then shifted to some blunt analysis of the faulty direction Burroughs was taking in his Tarzan tales: ". . . you are making a mistake in your latter day tendency to make Tarzan into a deus ex machina who blunders into minor situations that concern rather uninteresting characters and proceeds to solve these difficulties after passing through a certain amount of danger to himself. Tarzan needs to have some really personal interest to motivate him, I believe. I'd like to see you give him a definite shot of re-invigoration along these lines, at least."

Byrne, unquestionably correct, here demonstrated a remarkable insight into the causes of the deterioration of the later Tarzan stories. The reader wanted a Tarzan with a compelling motive for his actions, even if this motive were only a need for money, as in the early journeys to Opar. But unfortunately, all of these goals, including the trite, repetitious searches for a missing Jane, had been badly overused.

In reply, on April 5, Ed conceded discouragedly, "I think the trouble is that I am rather fed up on the type of stories I have been writing for over a quarter of a century. I have said everything that I can think of saying about Tarzan, and said it over and over again." But he could not refrain from returning to a past argument —that a great many editors had been mistaken in their refusal to accept *Tarzan of the Apes* for book publication. On April 8, Byrne further summarized the weaknesses of "Tarzan and the Elephant Men," attributing its failure to Burroughs' "lack of interest. . . in this particular situation." He remarked that the story had no theme and explained, as most significant, "Tarzan is a lesser figure here because you have given him a background of people of no importance; his achievements are minimized in our minds because he has nothing fine or real to fight for." Speculating in another direction, Byrne suggested that Ed's writing philosophy needed some reexamination:

I wonder if I am reading between the lines correctly, and diagnosing the difficulty as a need for plot stimulation. Haven't you been playing the lone wolf too long, and failing to throw your plot ideas against the sounding boards of other minds so that the ghost of them can come back to you enlarged a hundredfold?

The criticism, quite bold, as Byrne admitted, considering Burroughs' great success, was certainly an important element in the diagnosis of Ed's writing problems. Byrne had actually hit the nail on the head. Writing as a "lone wolf," neither communicating nor sharing ideas with other authors, ignoring trends and changing tastes, and above all, choosing not to read modern fiction, Burroughs, through this complete isolation, had become stagnant. He had also led a sedate life for many years, a life without adventures or unusual experiences needed as a background for writing. As a result, his stories lacked originality and inspiration.

Ed, on April 12, expressed appreciation of Byrne's "diagnosis of the illness that seems to have afflicted 'Tarzan and the Elephant Men.'" Byrne had also stated frankly his belief that the story could be sold to an editor who was concerned more with the publicity value of the Burroughs name than with the quality of the writing. He warned against letting "the exigencies of a present situation" dictate a course which would weaken the future reputation of the Tarzan works, but Ed, in his marketing, as always, had more than one iron in the fire and had earlier informed Kennicott of the story in progress. Although "Tarzan and the Elephant Men" was a sequel to "The Magic Men," which had appeared in *Argosy,* Kennicott was willing to purchase it for *Blue Book.* After some dickering — the maximum offer was $1,500 provided the story could be run as a serial and not complete in one issue, as Ed desired — an agreement was reached. "Tarzan and the Elephant Men" was serialized in *Blue Book,* November 1937 to January 1938; a year later the 41,000 word story, too brief for a book, became the last half of *Tarzan the Magnificent,* published September 25, 1939.

Carson of Venus, the third in the Venus series, is a lengthy novel which recounts the perils Carson and his sweetheart Duare encounter in their uncertain quest for the island of Vepaja. The story opens with a minor digression, seemingly unrelated to the major plot, with Carson meeting the Samary, a tribe of cave-dwellers ruled by brawny warrior women. This idea of reversed roles, with the dominant Amazon terrorizing and beating the timid, submissive males, had been previously used by Burroughs. When Carson and Duare arrived at Sanara, the capital of the empire of Korva, the main theme emerges; in this case, for a long section of the novel, Ed contrives and effectively develops a unified theme, something he had failed to do in many of his preceding novels. A totalitarian group, described as "a strange cult," led by the sadistic Mephis — the name, as noted by Ed, was derived from "mephitis, an offensive smell" — had seized almost all of Korva and imprisoned the true ruler. These Zanis, blind obedient followers of Mephis, obviously symbolized the Nazis whose ruthless control of Germany was evident at the time (1937). Mephis represented Hitler, and Burroughs' satire of the mechanical "Heil Hitler" is indicated in the counsel given to Carson:

". . . it is obligatory upon all loyal citizens to preface every greeting and introduction with the words Maltu Mephis. Please, never omit them. Never criticize the government or any official or any member of the Zani Party. Never fail to salute and cry Maltu Mephis whenever you see and hear others doing it. . . ."

The resemblance to the Nazis, exhibited in the shouts of "Maltu Mephis" and in the "incessant chanting" of these words by the crowds that gathered to greet their "beloved" dictator, was also displayed in the character of the Zani Guard, duplicates of the storm troopers. Most of these were described as "surly boors—an aggregation of ignorant thugs, bums and gangsters." Burroughs shows an awareness of the psychological reasons behind their prejudices: "They resented the fact that we were cultured; and the very fact that we were cultured seemed to feed their suspicions of us; and because they felt their inferiority, they hated us, too."

Nazi-like regulations are further revealed in the performance of the one play shown at the one hundred theaters in Amlot, the capital of Korva, at the same time. The play, the life of dictator Mephis, consists of 101 episodes, each a night's performance, and all citizens are required to attend the theater at least once every ten days. In another area, the "schooling" of young boys, similar to the Hitler Youth, was purely military drill.

A Burroughs work rarely failed to produce some innovations, and in *Carson of Venus* the Amlot theaters were of a most unusual nature. The audiences, seated with their backs to the stage, observed the action as it was reflected in a huge mirror placed on the back wall:

[This action] by a system of very ingenious lighting stands out brilliantly. By manipulation of the lights the scenes may be blacked out completely to denote a lapse of time or permit a change of scenery. Of course the reflections of the actors are not life size, and therefore the result gives an illusion of unreality reminiscent of puppet shows or the old days of silent pictures.

This odd method of watching a play had originated in the past when the acting profession was in disrepute; to be seen on the stage was considered a disgrace, and accordingly, this system was devised so that nobody could stare directly at the performers.

Burroughs may also have invented airplane bombing raids. Both Carson and Duare, whom he teaches to pilot a plane, fly over the Zanis and drop the deadly R-ray and T-ray bombs. The love shared by Carson and Duare appears hopeless because of the law of Vepaja that forbids any man to even speak of love to the virgin daughter of the emperor. The penalty for both is death, and at the end, with Duare sentenced to die, she and Carson fly to the kingdom of Korva.

Carson of Venus, written July 24 to August 19, 1937, was sent to the four prestige magazines—*Liberty, Saturday Evening Post, Collier's* and *Ladies' Home Journal*—and rejected by all. Ed then began negotiations with *Blue Book* and *Argosy*. In September Kennicott's offer of $2,000 for the serial rights was rejected; the concern of all magazine editors was in the drawing power of the story, and on the twenty-seventh, Kennicott commented that Ed's last work "didn't give the newsstand sales any special kick." Ed responded, "Maybe if I were paid more for magazine rights I would write better stories. There is a thought. . . ."[34] *Argosy* now remained the only market, and Jack Byrne's bid of $3,000 was accepted. *Carson of Venus* appeared as a six-part serial, January 8 to February 12, 1938; book publication came on February 15, 1939.

"Carson of Venus" cover of Argosy Weekly, *January 8, 1938.*

Now the publisher of his own works, Burroughs could not resist the temptation to revive old stories and prepare them for book form. Turning to *The Lad and the Lion*, written in 1914, sold to William Selig for a film, and published in *All-Story* as a three-part serial from June 30 to July 14, 1917, Ed set to work to expand the original 40,000-word novelette. In the period of August 20 to 31, 1937, he added 21,000 words, and in September offered the work to *Argosy* and *Blue Book*. To Byrne he mentioned the story's new title — "Men and Beasts" — and explained that it "incorporated" the novelette *The Lad and the Lion*, but insisted, "It is practically an entirely different story."[35] On the twenty-second he informed Kennicott of the revision to a full-length novel and added details about the new manuscript, "Men and Beasts":

While it incorporates the novelette, "The Lad and the Lion," it nevertheless, in its present form, is so different as to make it hardly recognizable; and as a new generation of readers has developed since 1914, it is as good as a new story. We feel it is only ethical to tell you this, although we are certain it will react unfavorably in your decision....

Both magazines were unreceptive to the novel, Kennicott noting first of all that *Blue Book* could not accede to the request to publish the work before the scheduled appearance of the book on February 15, 1938, and stressing that despite the revision, the story would be a reprint: "... some readers have long memories, and are sure to call an editor if they think he is trying to slip old stuff over on them...."[36] In rejecting "Men and Beasts," Chandler Whipple, the new *Argosy* editor (Jack Byrne was now managing editor of all the Munsey titles), offered similar reasons.[37]

With the book publication in 1938, the original title, *The Lad and the Lion*, was resumed. The addition of some 20,000 words did not strengthen the novel; that certain elements of the early Tarzan books were being repeated was obvious. On occasions when Michael, the lad, is seeking his mate or when he has killed his foe, in imitation of Tarzan's savage cry of the bull ape, he roars like a lion. The story's peculiar structure is somewhat confusing, with alternate sections describing Michael's adventures and then shifting to events at the royal court thousands of miles away. The two plots appear indirectly related, and no unified effect is achieved.

In "Tarzan and the Forbidden City," a 67,000-word novel completed in little more than a month, October 10 to November 18, 1937, Burroughs assembled unoriginal plot devices developing from a search for the missing young Brian Gregory that leads to the city of Ashair with its "Father of Diamonds." Once again Tarzan, with no personal goal, embarks upon a rescue mission, in this case assisting Gregory's attractive sister Helen and their father. Complications are introduced by the villains, naturally foreigners, the Eurasians Atan Thome and Lal Taask; associated with them at first is the woman Magra, who abruptly shifts from her evil role to come to the aid of the Gregorys. Familiar elements include Tarzan's startling resemblance to another man, Brian Gregory, and the incidents that follow: the two-cities-at-war situation, Tarzan's inevitable assignment to the arena, and the inescapable altar scene with the priest ready to plunge the knife into the helpless victim. Perhaps the most amazing incident occurs when Tarzan, facing an attack by two lions, seizes one animal from behind, swings it over his head, and hurls it at the other charging lion.

Ed does apply his imagination to devise the interesting underwater scenes. The Ashairians, in their valley of Tuen-Baka, had invented a diving helmet, and this later led to the building of their temple beneath the waters of a lake. A great geyser of air was discovered shooting up from a hole in the lake's bottom, and, as a result, a plan was adopted to construct the temple around the air geyser:

The most difficult part of the work was the capping of the air geyser, but this was finally ac-

complished; then the building of the temple commenced. It took a thousand years and cost twice that many lives. When it was completed and tightly sealed, it was, of course, entirely filled with water; but when the valve that had been installed in the geyser cap was opened, the water was forced out of the temple through a one-way valve. Today, the geyser furnishes pure air for the temple and actuates the doors of the air chambers.

A group of priests, called ptomes, wear underwater suits and are equipped with tridents, used normally for fishing. In the action that follows, Tarzan, also wearing a watersuit and carrying a trident, battles the ptomes at the bottom of the lake. In a duel with a ptome, Tarzan feels "like one in a bad dream, who makes strenuous efforts but accomplishes little or nothing."

On November 18, 1937, without attempting his policy of seeking the highest bidder, Burroughs mailed "Tarzan and the Forbidden City" to Chandler Whipple, *Argosy* editor. Conceding that the novel had much exciting material, Whipple noted that the most interesting sections were the later ones dealing with Tarzan's adventures in Tuen-Baka:

We feel, in fact, that the latter chapters contain material unusual enough to warrant a further build-up at the expense of a certain amount of boiling-down of the first one hundred pages. If it is satisfactory to you that we attempt these changes, we shall be able to offer you three thousand dollars.[38]

Burroughs made no protest about the planned revisions, accepting the price indicated. Upon its publication in *Argosy* as a six-part serial, March 19 to April 23, 1938, the novel somehow acquired the baffling title of "The Red Star of Tarzan." No reference to a "red star" appears in the work, and a conjecture that Munsey's dealings with The Red Star News Company, a New York magazine distributor, may have produced this incongruous title, seems too remote for serious consideration. The defects of "Tarzan and the Forbidden City" in its original form were further compounded by Whipple's drastic patchwork revision. How much of the novel's disjointed structure — its effect of bits-and-pieces and broken sections jumbled together — existed in Burroughs' manuscript, and how much resulted from the rewriting in the *Argosy* offices, is impossible to determine. Knowledgeable Burroughs students have long had doubts that ERB wrote this story. The drastic revisions by Whipple may be the explanation. The book was published in 1938 under its original title and included illustrations by John Coleman Burroughs, the first he had created for a Tarzan novel.[39]

" 'Two Gun' Doak Flies South," an adventure novelette with comic overtones, was the kind of story that Burroughs enjoyed creating as a change of pace from the customary fantasies. Written between December 1, 1937, and January 31, 1938, with a pen name of John Tyler McCulloch apparently used for some submissions, the 29,000-word story provides an opportunity for Ed's own style of satire and biting humor. Stock characters, created for the purpose of ridicule, include Mrs. J. Witherington Snite, a huge, domineering woman referred to as "the lady hippopotamus," whose millionaire husband owns a chain of restaurants. Among others in the cast are Wilbur Klump, the Candy King, a "real sugar daddy," and his wife Gladys, twenty years younger, who obviously married him for his money. An "intellectual appearing young man" is revealed as the snobbish and pretentious E. Allan Smith, a *New York Times* book reviewer.

These and other colorful characters, joined by young Jerry Hudson, the hero, and Larry Maxton, the heroine, are all passengers on a TWA flight bound for New York, but fated never to reach there. In the action Ed anticipates a familiar modern crisis, the skyjacking of the airplane, this being accomplished by a gangster named "Trigger" Schultz. The background of Jerry and Larry, who are accidently together on the plane, began with their fathers Jeremiah Hudson and Larry Hill Maxton, oil and mining tycoons and close friends, who many years earlier had made an unusual agreement. This occurred after Maxton, who had always wanted a son, found himself with a daughter; even though he named the girl after himself, this could not compensate for his disappointment.

Hudson, trying to console him, suggested that it might be a blessing in disguise, as his son could marry Maxton's daughter, thereby giving each of them a son and a daughter; so they shook hands on it and entered into a gentlemen's agreement. . . .

The two young people, now grown up (they had not seen each other for fifteen years), are notified of the marriage plans. They at once reject the idea, but Larry is persuaded to travel to California to meet Jerry. Some hectic events follow. Larry's plane is late, and when Jerry, imbibing too many drinks while waiting, fails to be there, she arranges to take another plane back to New York. Pursued by the police because of his erratic driving, Jerry winds up as a stowaway on the same plane and assumes the alias of "Joe Doak." Unaware of the old family ties, the two become newly acquainted as Joe and Larry. Because of his escape from the police, Jerry is believed to be a criminal; taken with the idea, he accepts the sobriquet of "Two Gun Doak."

With the stage set for the skyjacking by "Trigger" Schultz, the action then proceeds with an enforced landing at the gangster headquarters in Mexico, where, under the leadership of The Big Shot, Tony Turino, the gangsters and their "molls" are staying. The illegal activities conducted from the Mexican location include bootlegging, dope-running, and the smuggling of Chinese into the United States.

The plane passengers face an uncertain fate. Jerry, accepted by the gangsters as one of their ilk, is allowed to pilot another plane back to the States to collect supplies and ransom money, and during his absence the Mexican soldiers arrive to rescue the passengers. Jerry is still presumed to be a gangster, and the Mexicans are waiting to seize him, but upon his return he is warned in time by Larry, and the two escape in the plane. Ironically, each still unaware of the other's true identity and the family associa-

tion, they are in love and planning to marry, just as their fathers had intended.

In his characterization of the married couples and of the gangsters and their women, Burroughs created and exaggerated a situation which had been a familiar source of humor in many stories and cartoons. The spectacle of the dominant, overbearing wife and the intimidated or henpecked husband is one that readers have encountered often. It is illustrated in the J. Witherington Snites and even more so in the relationship of the Klumps. When Wilbur sings with the group in his off-key voice, his wife Gladys tells him to "shut up" and he subsides.

ERB's gangster characters reveal themselves as coarse and crude and become obvious stereotypes of the period. But in their associations with their "molls" they exhibit a surprising submission and inferiority.

Ed could not resist the opportunity to lash out again at overly refined literary writers. E. Allan Smith, when reminded that this experience with the gangsters should provide him with material for writing, views the whole matter with disdain, doubting that he could "utilize anything like this. . . . 'The importance of fine writing is more or less of a fetish with me. I deplore the modern tendency toward slovenliness of style, vulgarity of situations, and the general luridity of conception — if you get what I mean.' " Smith, it is noted, fails to mention that all of the magazine editors have rejected his stories, and that even those "lurid" ones, submitted to the pulps, have been returned.

In his sales efforts for " 'Two Gun' Doak Flies South" Ed followed customary procedures, sending the story first to *Liberty*. The note of rejection read, "It has some amusing moments, but, as a whole, it's a pretty inexpert job. . . ."[40] On February 25, 1938, the story was returned by *Cosmopolitan* and two years later, in June 1940, by *Blue Book*. Marketing attempts ended. Never published, the story later was retitled "Mr. Doak Flies South." The Burroughs files contain a version with the original "Two Gun" title, headed "outline of a story"; this eighty-four page manuscript is written in play form with characters' names followed by dialogue. Some plan may have been considered to submit this adaptation for radio broadcast or for a film scenario.

One of Burroughs' most remarkable works, deserving of such superlatives as a dazzling feat of the imagination or a tour de force in the field of science fiction, was "Synthetic Men of Mars," completed in late July of 1938 or the first days of August. Burroughs had not hurried this 70,000-word novel, begun on March 2, and in it, as though newly inspired, he crowded all of the accumulated detail of Mars — the rich scenery, the barbaric atmosphere, the weapons and equipment — and against this background devised a plot of spectacular originality, woven about the bizarre laboratory creations of the master scientist of Mars, Ras Thavas.

On August 4 the story was sent to Jack Byrne at *Argosy,* but in the same month it was also submitted to *Liberty* where its rejection was inevitable; "Synthetic Men of Mars" was simply too wildly imaginative for the staid, general readers of this slick magazine. Bryne reacted to this amazing novel with admiration bordering on awe: ". . . the most interesting and imaginative story you have done in the past five years," he commented on the sixteenth. He added:

I make this statement even though the chances are heavy against its publication in Argosy. *It's not that I wouldn't be delighted to have it, but rather that I am unable to make you a satisfactory offer for it. . . . My absolute maximum for serials is $200 per installment ($1,200) in this case. . . .*

Byrne wrote, "I would count it as an amazing stroke of luck, of course, to get such a story as 'The Synthetic Men' at this price. . . ."

Before this offer could be considered, Ed and Florence had scheduled their vacation, and on August 19 the two departed on the *Lurline* for a stay in Honolulu. Unable to contact Burroughs, Rothmund forwarded the novel to *Blue Book,* on September 15, where Kennicott noted with regret the "heavy inventory" which precluded any chance of their accepting another serial.[41] On September 29, in a sudden decision, Ed and Florence boarded *The Empress of Japan* at Honolulu, embarking for a visit to Vancouver; from there they later drove down the coast, arriving home at Tarzana October 11.

Rothmund had remarked to Byrne that the offer for "Synthetic Men of Mars" was "so low" that he could not assume the responsibility for accepting it.[42] Shortly after Burroughs' return he approved the sale to *Argosy,* and "Synthetic Men of Mars" appeared as a six-part serial, January 7 to February 11, 1939.

In the novel the serious injuries suffered by Dejah Thoris following an airplane collision lead to John Carter's involvement in the events that develop, but the main character and narrator is Vor Daj whose tale of the search for Ras Thavas, the brilliant surgeon, who must "mend" Dejah Thoris, is transmitted over the Gridley Wave to the radio at Tarzana. En route to the friendly city of Duhor, Carter and Vor Daj, because of a faulty automatic compass, find themselves approaching hostile Phundahl, and the sight of huge flying malagors, giant birds, each with a mounted warrior, is a sign of impending danger. Forced to land, Carter and Vor Daj refuse to surrender and are attacked by five grotesque "horrific creatures":

They seemed the faulty efforts of a poor draftsman, come to life — animated caricatures of man. There was no symmetry or design about them. The left arm of one was scarce a foot long, while his right arm was so long that the hand dragged along the ground as he walked. Four-fifths of the face of one was above his eyes, while another had an equal proportion below the eyes. Eyes, noses, and mouths were usually misplaced; and were either too large or too small to harmonize with contiguous features. . . .

In the ensuing battle Carter and Vor Daj make a startling discovery; the creatures are impervious to pain or shock, cannot be killed, and even when they are run through with a sword, or when an arm is severed, they continue to fight. Decapitation may render some of them hors de combat, but in the fight the headless body still ran about "cutting and slashing" aimlessly, while the head "lay gibbering and grimacing in the dust." Captured, Carter and Vor Daj soon learn the complete story. The hormads are the creation of Ras Thavas who had founded the city of Morbus in the Great Toonolian Marshes. Here in his laboratory Thavas had perfected the secret of producing human beings from human tissue. The hormads resulted from these experiments.

Events, however, had taken an unexpected and terrifying turn. Although most of the hormads were mere unintelligent robots, a few who had developed normal brains banded together to seize control of Morbus. Ras Thavas was now a prisoner in his own city. The hormad leaders had conceived a plan to conquer the world through the production of an army of millions of their creatures. Food was no problem; they were fed with an animal tissue that grew with great rapidity in another culture. The details about the hormad production reveal the seriousness of the situation:

There are several million hormads on the island. . . . It is estimated that the island can accommodate a hundred million of them; and Ras Thavas claims that he can march them into battle at the rate of two million a year, lose every one of them, and still have his original strength undepleted by as much as a single man. . . .

Those hormads, "grossly malformed" and "utterly useless," were "sliced into hundreds of thousands of tiny pieces" and dumped back into the culture vats. "They grow with such unbelievable rapidity that within nine days each has developed into a full-sized hormad. . . ."

For the plan to conquer the world, Ras Thavas has apparently solved the problem of transporting an enormous hormad army. Through experiments with malagor tissue and a special culture, he can produce enough of these gigantic birds to carry the hormads into battle.

In the creation of the hormad theme and the fascinating details that accompany it, Burroughs certainly was inspired. Once he had launched the idea, his imagination knew no bounds. The ruling hormads of Morbus, seven "jeds," aware of Ras Thavas' great surgical skill, have forced him to transfer their brains into the skulls of seven handsome officers; thus, instead of being deformed like the other hormads, they have the appearance of normal men. In transferring the brain of Tor-dur-bar, a hormad, to the powerful body of Gantun Gur, an assassin, the standard technique is followed: the blood is drained from both bodies and replaced by a colorless liquid preservative. After the scalps are removed, Ras Thavas saws through the skull of each "with a tiny circular saw attached to the end of a flexible, revolving shaft." At the end of the four-hour operation, with the brain transplanted, the severed nerves and ganglia are connected; the skull and scalp are restored and bound with an adhesive material which is both antiseptic and anaesthetic; then from Gur's veins the liquid is withdrawn, and the reheated blood, plus a chemical, is returned. Tor-dur-bar's brain, now released from its repulsive body, occupies the body of Gantun Gur.

A startling and original twist to the plot, one that dominates the future action, is now devised: Vor Daj, believing that Janai, the woman he loves, is being held by the Council of Seven Jeds, and aware that only a hormad may be chosen as a guard for one of the Jeds, persuades Ras Thavas to transfer his brain to the body of Tor-dur-bar. As a result of the operation, Daj now has a great torso poised on short legs, a right arm reaching below his knees, and a left arm slightly below his waist line. His face is grotesque:

My right eye was way up on my forehead, just below the hairline, and was twice as large as my left eye which was about half an inch in front of my left ear. My mouth started at the bottom of my chin and ran upward at an angle of about 45 degrees to a point slightly below my huge right eye. My nose was scarcely more than a bud and occupied the place that my little left eye should have had. One ear was close set and tiny, the other a pendulous mass that hung almost to my shoulder. . . .

Burroughs has still one more astonishing development in the plot. The churning culture in Thavas' vats of life has become uncontrollable. The mass of living tissue, multiplying at a fearful rate, fills the room, bursts through the windows, and billows out into the courtyard. Vor Daj's first concern is that the tissue may engulf and destroy his body, stored on a slab in some secret chamber. Not only is the entire island of Morbus now facing destruction by this enveloping mass, but, as Thavas explains ruefully, ". . .it might cover the entire surface of Barsoom, smothering all other forms of life." Only fire can check the expanding tissue.

The suspense and excitement of "Synthetic Men of Mars" is somewhat marred by Burroughs' insertion, late in the novel, of scenes involving the ludicrous kingdom of Goolie, whose inhabitants oddly combine human characteristics with kangeroolike qualities; they have long, powerful tails and are given to making prodigious leaps. The women, being marsupials, lay eggs and carry them in a pouch on their abdomen, where the young are later hatched. The male Goolians are shown comically as cowards and braggarts, described by Vor Daj as "the most useless race of people I have ever encountered, expending all their energies in boasting and little or none in accomplishment." About the Goolians Burroughs commented, "There are lots of people in the world like the Goolians, but some of them are never found out."

The late 1930s also brought several articles from Burroughs' pen, the most unusual being "Man-Eaters," not to be confused with the 1915 story "The Man-Eater" or "Ben, King of Beasts," published as a six-part serial in *The New York Evening World*. In the opening section of the 3,000-word article about lions, Ed recalled his own experiences as he viewed the filming of several Tarzan movies. But in emphasizing that lions were "unpredictable" in their reactions to humans and could exhibit behavior varying from excess timidity to daring and ferocity, Burroughs turned mainly to examples contained in printed sources. Details of the courage of lions

and of the instances when they had become man-eaters are drawn from *The Book of the Lion* by Sir Alfred E. Pease, *The Man-Eaters of Tsavo* by Lieutenant-Colonel J. H. Patterson, and *Is Nature Cruel?* by J. Crowther Hirst. Hirst quotes statements by a number of men who had been mauled by lions and includes an account by the missionary David Livingstone. Burroughs had used several of these references in his earlier article "The Tarzan Theme" published in 1932.

In recounting his experiences on movie sets, Burroughs told of the danger he and his daughter Joan, then a small child, had faced when a lion became panic-stricken: "A great deal of trouble was experienced in getting the lion to approach the camera at the right angle. Half a dozen men were chasing him around with whips, firing blank cartridges at him, whooping and yelling. It would have been quite enough to have wrecked the equanimity of a stone Buddha. It wrecked the lion's. . . ."

Dashing toward the camera, past it, and *beneath* the leg of the cameraman, the lion leaped the protective fence and ran toward Ed and daughter Joan. Previously cautioned to stand still if this type of emergency arose, Ed pushed his daughter behind him. "I stood very still. By comparison, a tombstone would have been dancing a merry saraband." Fortunately, the animal was too frightened and nervous to attack anybody.

On location at the MGM studios Ed watched a cameraman trying to film a lioness charging directly into the camera. A large wooden box, supposedly lion-proof, had been built with a hole in front; through this hole the camera shot was to be made. The cameraman and his assistant presumably were safe inside the box. The performance demanded of the lioness appeared incredible:

The plan was to start her with a rush from the opposite end of the arena, have her run for her cage, to reach which she would have to leap to the top of the camera box. The resultant shot would have shown a head-on charge of a lioness, with the beast rising in air to seize its prey at the

Cover of Synthetic Men of Mars, *1940; John Coleman Burroughs, illustrator.*

end of the charge. Marvellous! That is if the lioness had understood what was expected of her, but she didn't. . . .

The terrified animal approached the camera box, saw the hole, and scrambled inside to hide. They later discovered the cameraman in one corner of the box with the camera on top of him and the lioness in the other corner. The assistant had wriggled out of the hole at the same time that the lioness came in. But no one was hurt; again, the lion had demonstrated its unpredictability.

At the old Selig Zoo in Los Angeles the filming of a lion sequence led to a tragedy: "The lion was supposed to leap from a platform onto a man dressed in some kind of skins. I do not know why a dummy was not used. It seemed impossible to get the lion to leap from the high platform; so a device was rigged up wherewith a current of electricity could be shot through the lion. . . . It was a splendid idea, and it worked to perfection. The lion leaped onto the man and killed him."

The section of the article devoted to lions as man-eaters offers details of the beasts entering tents to grasp their victims and even an instance of a lion opening the door of a railroad car, seizing a man, and hurtling with a great crash through a window, carrying the man along. Burroughs closes the article with a humorous defense of man-eaters, observing that because of their large bodies and enormous vitality they required great quantities of food; they were not endowed with "alimentary processes fitting them to assimilate broccoli, artichokes, avocados, or spaghetti," and so they were forced to eat meat. The killing of humans for meat may appear ruthless, Burroughs conceded, but he had some joking comments to make about this:

. . . you must remember that lions have no packers to do their killing for them. Doubtless our methods seem ruthless to pigs, cows, chickens, and sheep. However, I am going right ahead eating prime beef; and I accord to the man-eaters their inalienable right to go on eating us, provided they can catch us.

"Man-Eaters," completed on March 18, 1937, as noted in Ed's diary, was submitted to various top publications in April and May, including *This Week* and the Chicago Tribune New York News Syndicate, and in June to *Liberty*. The article was rejected by all of these, but was finally purchased by the *Los Angeles Times* and appeared in the *Sunday Magazine* of August 22, 1937.

Another 1937 article, first titled "The Author-Publisher," was Burroughs' response to persistent requests from Editor Mathieu of the *Writer's Digest*. Unable to generate any enthusiasm about the chore or to find a subject that could prove stimulating, Ed rambled uncertainly in the opening section; he gave the impression of a man in a complaining or dissatisfied mood:

This bird, Mathieu, has been after me for an article since the late Pleistocene; and he is as pertinacious as a New Jersey mosquito. He has finally drawn blood. What else he has got remains to be seen, but I am afraid not much. My profession does not seem so thrilling as it did eighty or ninety years ago. It is even difficult for me to recreate that moment of cosmic import when I first saw a story of mine in print, the moment that, for me, put the "s" in cosmic.

Noting that he had left a blank space at the top of the page for a title, he added, "it corresponds perfectly with a similar area in my mind where a title should be." He confessed he did not know what to write about. ". . . I shall start off on the subject of book publishing, and if that can't be padded into an article I'll wander into some other field of interest to writers — possibly food."

Once he had turned to publishing and its problems, he began a discussion of costs, refuting a statement in a *Los Angeles Times'* column that an author could produce his own book for five hundred dollars. The preliminary costs, comprising the various plates and dies and the payment to the illustrator for the jacket painting and other drawings, totaled more than $1,000, and the costs of printing and binding were still to come. In reference to sales and the supposedly "eager" public awaiting the book, he stressed that the individual readers were not the ones on whom a publisher had to concentrate: "You have to sell a few thousand keen, hard-boiled buyers for retail stores who already have some forty thousand books on their shelves that they can't sell."

The most interesting section of the article concerned the illustrations in the current book *The Oakdale Affair and The Rider,* done by Jack Burroughs. Ed explained that the assignment had been "very tough," requiring that Jack portray both novels in a small area of the front cover. Ed described Jack's conscientious attention to detail and his determination to closely relate his drawings to the text:

An instance of the former is the hangman's knot in the frontispiece for The Oakdale Affair. That bothered him for days until he recalled that when he was a child I had tied one for him among other knots that I had learned during my cow-punching days; so, if it is wrong, the fault is mine; for he brought a piece of rope to my office, and I tied one for him.

Ed recalled an "amusing contretemps." After Jack had completed a painting of a particular scene in the book, the discovery was made that the two characters, as indicated in the text, were supposed to be wearing gypsy costumes. Rather than having the illustration done over, Ed changed the text, eliminating the gypsy clothes.

At the end of the article Ed offered a frank admission: he had been too "greedy" for higher royalties in the past and this had resulted in "killing" the large sales of his two-dollar editions. As a book publisher, he now realized that the margin of profit was small, and he felt guilty about not allowing a fair profit for his previous publisher who, because of this, had lost interest in exploiting the original editions. He confessed sadly that if he had understood at the time and had made the necessary compromise in royalties, he would not have turned to the publishing of his own books.

Something unique for Burroughs, a political speech, was his contribution to the campaign

ERB at work in Tarzana office, March 26, 1937.

for the reelection of Mayor Frank L. Shaw of Los Angeles; the speech was delivered over radio station KFI on April 30, 1937. In supporting Shaw, Burroughs emphasized that he did not know the mayor and in fact had never seen him. He based his defense of Shaw on the record, turning specifically to the topics of employment, bonded indebtedness, taxes, crime, gambling, and the police force. A list of Shaw's achievements followed. The mayor had created employment for a large number of people; he had kept the city's bonded indebtedness down — 94 American cities had a higher per capita debt than Los Angeles; of 45 large cities, Los Angeles had the lowest tax rate for municipal government. Shaw inherited a serious crime situation and directed measures against it; perhaps the gauging of his success could be done best by noting the number of arrests: about two thousand more arrests were made, during Shaw's administration, for gambling, lottery, and prostitution than had been made in the previous administration.

On the problem of gambling, Burroughs insisted that efforts to blame Shaw were illogical; the people themselves had legalized betting at the race tracks and thus had given a great impetus to gambling in other forms. Yet, gambling was still of negligible importance in the city. Burroughs' greatest enthusiasm was for Los Angeles' "splendid police department." In his eulogy of the police he shifted to his pet anathema — communism — to warn of impending danger "through the activity of those subversive forces that have bored their way into our labor unions, our schools, and even our hospitals."

Certain that Shaw would be reelected, Ed nevertheless noted humorously that his support might prove a great handicap. "I voted for Teddy the time he lost, I voted for Hughes, I voted for Landon; the last horse I bet on threw his jockey and ran around the track in the wrong direction." To remind the citizen of how important one vote could be, Ed described his only experience as a candidate, recalling the year 1904 in Parma, Idaho, when he ran for the board of selectmen of the village. He cam-

paigned by asking voters to save him from the embarrassment of receiving only one vote. The election was a "landslide" for Ed, 49 to 48 — the "one" vote had done it.

The Burroughs persistence in remarketing old manuscripts was again demonstrated in 1937 with efforts to stimulate interest in his unfinished *Autobiography*. On March 20 he sent a form letter to various magazines, including *Harper's* and *Liberty*, offering to sell first rights to the manuscript; pictures of Burroughs "at various states in his life" could be published with the *Autobiography*. Apparently, the editors were uninterested.

In a radio interview of January 23, 1938, on KFWB in Hollywood, Ed responded to familiar questions and produced some fresh reactions: He had planned to write only two Tarzan novels originally. In the first two he had said "all there was to say about Tarzan." Bob Davis, the Munsey editor, believing the Tarzan theme was exhausted, offered the idea of a new character, the son of Tarzan. Not keen on the idea, Ed, to please Davis, wrote "The Son of Tarzan" and was convinced that with this novel the series was definitely finished. "But it wasn't," Ed said, "and now I find Tarzan's son more or less of an embarrassment to both Tarzan and Jane, as well as myself."

During the interview some statistics emerged: Tarzan strips were being printed in about 300 newspapers; Tarzan appeared in book, magazine, or strip form in some thirty-five foreign countries and had been translated into about fifty-eight languages or dialects. From the interviewer (Carver) came an unexpected question: "Tell me, Mr. Burroughs. As man to man, now, remember: Does Mrs. Burroughs — well — does she call you 'Tarzan'?" Ed's reply was indignant:

No, she does not. You know, there is a class of people who call men 'brother' and women clerks in stores who call their customers 'dearie', and I would class any one in this category who called me 'Tarzan'.

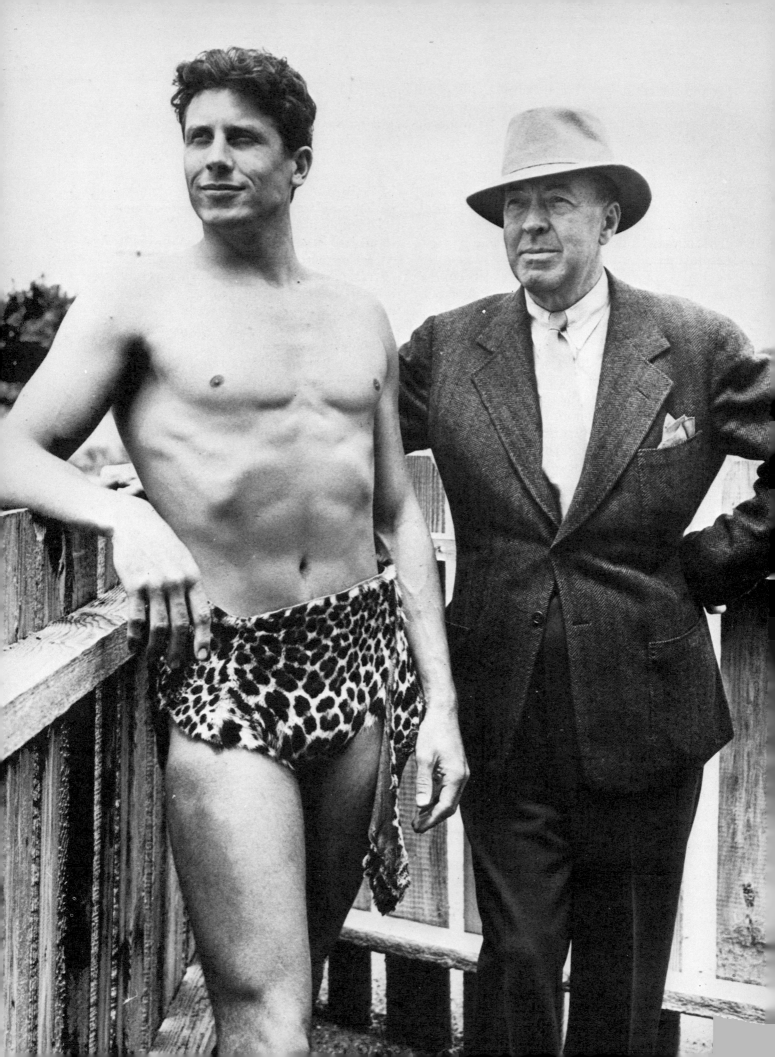

22 BURROUGHS-TARZAN FILMS

With the formation in 1934 of Burroughs-Tarzan Enterprises for film production, the business activities were divided, the book and magazine transactions being directed separately by Edgar Rice Burroughs, Inc. By late 1935 the film company, headed by the trio of Dearholt-Stout-Cohen, was called Burroughs-Tarzan Pictures (BTP), and the stationery listed the location at 8476 Sunset Boulevard in Hollywood. A new representative, Jesse Goldburg, reported to be "the most dynamic to date," was engaged in January 1936 to handle exploitation and publicity.

The main film property was *The New Adventures of Tarzan*, but the corporation's goal was to produce a number of non-Tarzan movies. Ashton Dearholt, as in the past, had a variety of projects in mind and his letters to Burroughs were filled with glowing predictions. BTP's grandiose plans, with their setting of a shoestring budget, appeared as incongruous and fantastic as the best of Burroughs' stories.

Vague film schemes, involving works viewed as good possibilities, could not lead to any serious production efforts. Ashton, in his letter of January 4, 1936, noted, "Contracts are ready to be signed on 'Dark River' and 'Typee'...." He referred to "experiments" on "Monk film" and a month later remarked, "Still monkeying on the Monk." This was probably a movie titled "Three Wise Monks," never completed. In January he also predicted that shooting on "The Drag-Net" could start in two weeks, and apparently this film, featuring Rod La Roque, was finished on February 20. A play by Willard Mack, "The Drag-Net," was acquired through a six-feature deal with William Selig. Ashton also spoke of preparing an airplane picture and a Coast-Guard special, this with the "full cooperation of the government."

The airplane story with a World War I background was titled *The White Glove*, and on March 19 Ed exhibited a dubious attitude about the script:

Thinking about The White Glove. Some of the scenes between Maddox and the German ace, and Maddox and Armstrong seem a little too melodramatic. Perhaps I am wrong; but please read them over with this thought in mind. I think we should always be careful to avoid laughs in the wrong places. You know I have had over twenty years experience in trying to keep people from laughing at comedy, and perhaps this has resulted in a complex. Ridicule will kill anything.

In May 1936 preliminary shooting on *The Phantom of Santa Fe*, done at the Tarzana Ranch, was completed, but Ashton's problems with this movie and one titled *Tundra* were just beginning. To seek outlets for the films, Ed was dispatched to Chicago and New York in the summer of 1936. In Chicago he stayed with his old friend Fred Mandel, Jr., well-to-do department store owner. Ben Cohen, also in New York to contact distributors, complained about the quality of the work on *The Phantom*: "... I received... the worst print of the Phantom which has been made to date, it being the lab's first print. The color and sound were poor and, in addition, it contained a very bad scratch throughout most of the two reels."[1] Concerning *The Phantom*, a type of "Mark of Zorro" film in color, Ashton noted on July 21 that the quality was "greatly improved" and that the movie would be shown at the California Theater within three weeks. He was now pessimistic about its future: "It should make money but at its cost, and knowing its history, producers of *Lonesome Pine* will never be made jealous."

To Burroughs, Ashton admitted that the reactions in New York to *The Phantom* had been "consistently bad," and in the passing weeks the situation, if it were possible, even worsened. "Phantom kickbacks have caused many of our boosters to lose confidence," Ashton wrote. "It is apparent that we must re-record the first reel and replace those first reels now in fifteen exchanges. This is the only way to protect our investment." An additional $5,000 loan would be needed. The first reel of *The Phantom* was run at the Egyptian Theater on August 2; Ashton remarked that the color "was beautiful enough, but sound and synchronization were pitiful."[2] Eight hours of hard work would be required to correct this condition.

Tundra, a story of survival in Alaska, was highlighted with a colorful display of wild animals, but the difficulties were similar to those of *The Phantom*, the most insoluble problem being finances. Ashton wrote of "pounding Tundra night and day to a finish." He had added several hundred feet of "marvelous Alaskan stock stuff" to the film and complained that "every hour we are held up on Tundra is hurting, for it's a hot weather picture."[3] The money problems were so acute that no salaries had been paid for three weeks and BTP had reached a point where the numerous debtors could not be stalled further. On August 3, with *Tundra* near completion, Dearholt wrote in gloom and desperation to Burroughs:

Not meeting obligations will soon destroy every inch of ground that we have gained in our entire period of struggle. Success is still a money problem, one of about fifty thousand dollars is my guess. Such an amount would quiet creditors, also give "Tundra" and "Phantom" a chance to bring in necessary earnings, getting "Three Wise Monks" recorded, reviving credit enough to get "White Glove" completed and "Murder at the Carnival" ready for continuity. ...

The letter made it obvious that BTP had reached the end of its rope; "It's a mighty black picture," Ashton confessed: "... all our noses are flat into a wall of disheartening facts." The needed $50,000 "might as well be fifty million for we have exhausted every possible chance to borrow and used what security we have until it screams for help."

As endorser of notes and guarantor of loans, Ed was now in an unhappy position. He stood to lose $7,000 in notes and might be forced to assume responsibility for a $60,000 bank loan.

A debt of $27,500 to Phil Goldstone, if not paid through the receipts from *Tundra*, could result in his seizing *The New Adventures of Tarzan*, the property of Burroughs. This would be a serious loss. Without question, Burroughs' ventures in movie production and his association with Dearholt could be termed financial disasters. Neither of the two had sufficient experience in the film field to understand its pitfalls or to realize that even with the largest companies, film-making was the most erratic of gambles. The close friendship between him and Dearholt had undoubtedly influenced Ed in his decisions. He had overvalued Dearholt's ability and, as in the past, had acted impulsively in launching a new enterprise. Of course he had been driven by his ambition to control his own films. This would be the end of another of Burroughs' dreams.

Following the release of *Tundra*, an educational film, in August 1936, it became evident that here, at least, was a BTP production that deserved a measure of success. The magazine reviews expressed strong approval, the *Hollywood Reporter* noting that this was an animal picture "unlike anything ever filmed before," and praising it with such terms as "first-run calibre," "stirring, suspenseful," "great emotional wallop." The *Reporter* commented, "Filmed in the wild country of Alaska, it is one animal picture that is believable and not obviously faked."[4]

Tundra, with scenes actually shot during the six-month location in Alaska, was plotted around a flying doctor who was on his way to an isolated plague-ridden settlement when his plane crashed. He then started a 400-mile trek across the arctic snow, marshes, and glaciers. With him were two bear cubs, and the mother bear following in pursuit. Much of the photography featured wildlife, with views of animal warfare and shots of wolves, musk-oxen, caribou, and others. The role of the doctor was played by Del Cambre; the story and direction were by Norman Dawn and the screenplay by Charles F. Royal and Norton S. Parker. The New York *Motion Picture Herald* of August 29 described *Tundra* as "educational entertainment which rates well above the classification of a travelogue," referred to the film's "pictorial and dramatic values," and summarized it as "extraordinary entertainment for any bill."

The *Herald*, in a photo captioned "On to Malaysia," showed Burroughs, as board chairman of BTP, signing an agreement to be cosponsor of a movie titled *Asia Roars*.[5] This was probably BTP's last project. William J. Richard, the other sponsor, was president of the California Zoological Society which planned a seven-month expedition to the Malay Peninsula, with departure set for February 1937. Clyde E. Elliot, director-producer, planned to broadcast a series of short-wave programs from the jungles as part of the publicity; Jesse Goldburg was supervising the production.

Throughout the late thirties Burroughs and Rothmund conducted a persistent campaign to persuade the motion picture companies to consider various stories as film vehicles. The submissions were numerous and some interest was at times exhibited, but none of the stories was accepted. The 1937 list included "Seven Worlds to Conquer"; "Elmer"; "Back to the Stone Age"; "The Oakdale Affair"; and "The Rider." In 1939 a stream of story synopses, many only one page long, was dispatched to Columbia and Twentieth Century-Fox; a number of these had been submitted years earlier. Those most determinedly marketed were *Jungle Girl*, *Outlaw of Torn*, *The Mucker*, *Apache Devil*, and *The War Chief*. All of the stories were judged unsuitable for film production.

Burroughs had also arranged for his movie submissions to be handled by the William Morris Agency in Beverly Hills. In July 1939 "Mr. Doak Flies South" and "Angel's Serenade," sent there to James Geller, brought rejections from the film companies, and Burroughs revived a story he had written in 1915:

This morning one of my sons called me up to remind me of a story I wrote twenty-four years ago when the World War was young. He

Advertisement for film Tarzan and the Green Goddess, *released in 1938 by Burroughs-Tarzan Enterprises; film was reedited from* The New Adventures of Tarzan, *a film produced in 1935.*

thought it was very timely now that another world war is brewing. . . . By changing a couple of dates, the story might have been written today. I am enclosing a very brief outline of it. . . .[6]

The story, "Beyond Thirty," is projected to the year 2150 when after The Great War much of civilization has been destroyed and the American continents, by an edict, are separated permanently from Europe and Asia.

In returning "Beyond Thirty" Geller described it as "a bit too strong for Hollywood," and claimed that the cost would be prohibitive.[7] A request from Sam Marx of Columbia Pictures for synopses of sixteen stories led Burroughs to rewrite the synopsis of "Beyond Thirty," give it the title of "It Might Happen Here," and forward it to Marx. Burroughs felt that only he could do these synopses, and he wrote all sixteen one-pagers himself.[8] All of them were returned.

The collapse of Burroughs-Tarzan Pictures was inevitable. Sometime in 1937 the corporation went out of business, but BTE continued to function. From the serial *The New Adventures of Tarzan* a feature film was cut and assembled and additional material added; the completed work was called *Tarzan and the Green Goddess.* An agreement with Jesse

600

Goldburg established him as special representative for the sale and exploitation of this motion picture.[9] BTE, however, was in serious financial trouble; its debts were unpaid and heavy judgments were lodged against it. In this crisis, Jesse Goldburg through his vigorous worldwide distribution of the BTE Tarzan properties came to Burroughs' rescue. Goldburg, who had been accorded a fifty percent commission, produced enough return on the films to pay off the large Citizens Bank note which Ed had endorsed.[10]

Tarzan and the Green Goddess demonstrated its audience appeal in England, as indicated in a review of the *Daily Express*, December 22, 1937, which noted that the film did "better business. . . than any film has the right to do in the week before Christmas." The writer explained that the Tarzan movie had drawn people out of their homes and away from the popular Gracie Fields radio broadcast. On July 26, 1938, Goldburg, responding to a claim for money due on *Phantom of Santa Fe* and *Tundra*, emphasized that these were the properties of BTP, now defunct, but that Burroughs-Tarzan Enterprises was still very much alive and distributing *Tarzan and the Green Goddess*. A year later, a query from the tax office brought a reply revealing that BTE was finally out of business: "No money is received by Burroughs-Tarzan Enterprises, Inc. and as the corporation is no longer actively engaged in business, and has no office nor employees, accounts for the fact that no books are kept. . . ."[11] By tacit agreement, Goldburg, who had formed his own organization, United Screen Associates, was granted sole rights to the two Tarzan movies, *The New Adventures of Tarzan* and *Tarzan and the Green Goddess,* on the same fifty percent basis. The appreciation for Goldburg's success in liquidating the bank loan was so great that Burroughs and Rothmund indicated their willingness to have Goldburg retain "all the surplus income."[12]

Because of his contacts at the movie studios, Goldburg acted as Burroughs' agent in submitting an unusual synopsis in 1938. Completed on December 19, this one-page synopsis titled "Heil Hitler!" offered a "Suggestion for a story of what a humanitarian Hitler might accomplish for Germany and the World." Burroughs devised a plot involving one of the "doubles" that Hitler supposedly utilized to impersonate him at various affairs:

One of these doubles bears such a startling resemblance to Hitler that their intimates cannot tell them apart.

Fifteen army officers conspire to assassinate Hitler. To hide their crime, they take the perfect double into their confidence. The assassination takes place at Hitler's country estate. The body is disposed of, and the perfect double assumes the role of Hitler.

His masters are the fifteen officers, who prove to be as ruthless as Hitler. Only they know that he is not Hitler. He purges them, so that he may continue as Fuhrer. He inaugurates reforms. He commences to ameliorate the condition of the Jews. Goebbels and other Jew baiters combine to discredit him. He purges them.

Master of Germany, he removes all bans against Jews; restores free speech and free press; restores Austria to her former position as an independent state; returns the Sudeten to Czechoslovakia; enters into a pact with France and Great Britain that insures the peace of Europe and the World.

On January 9, 1939, in returning the brief synopsis "Heil Hitler!," Goldburg wrote, "The story editors of Fox, Warner Bros. and Paramount agree that your story would be dangerous at this time. . . ." If Burroughs recalled the earlier rejection of an antitotalitarian story, "Under the Red Flag," and he probably did, he may have viewed this disapproval of "Heil Hitler!" as a second example of editorial cowardice. In 1919 he had felt certain that the editors were being intimidated by radical forces in this country, and, in filing away "Under the Red Flag," he had noted on the manuscript, "Preserve this original of Under the Red Flag which was rejected by editors for fear of the Bolshevistic agencies in the U.S."

Following Burroughs' dismal experiences in the production of two Tarzan films, MGM resumed the Weissmuller-O'Sullivan series it had launched in 1932 with *Tarzan the Ape-Man*. After *Tarzan and His Mate* (1934), and a hiatus of two years, MGM's series continued with *Tarzan Escapes* (1936); *Tarzan Finds a Son* (1939); *Tarzan's Secret Treasure* (1941); and *Tarzan's New York Adventure* (1942). In 1937 Sol Lesser turned to the making of Tarzan movies, hiring Olympic decathlon champion Glenn Morris to take the lead and Eleanor Holm, formerly on the Olympic swimming team, to play the role of Tarzan's sweetheart. Lesser would dominate the Tarzan screen field from 1943 on with a long series of films, and the association between Lesser and Burroughs would become one of trust and respect. The friendship that developed between Ed and the Lesser family was a close one, on a first-name basis, with Sol, his wife Faye, and his son Bud.

For its 1939 movie, first titled *Tarzan in Exile*, MGM, through writer Cyril Hume, initiated a daring plot. Tarzan and Jane (Weissmuller and O'Sullivan) discover a young boy whose parents have died in a plane crash. They raise the boy, played by five-year-old Johnny Sheffield, and, as the plot develops, their temporary son is revealed to be the heir to a fortune; at the story's end he returns to civilization. But producer Sam Zimbalist, using Hume's screenplay, called for Jane to die from a spear wound. Protests from hosts of fans and from Burroughs caused MGM to change the script, and when the movie, finally called *Tarzan Finds a Son,* was released, the ending showed Jane recovering.

On August 22, 1939, Ed received an interesting letter from Harry Monty who had done all the doubling and stunt work for Tarzan's young "son" in the film. Monty offered details:

I am 32 years old, 53 inches tall, weigh 89 pounds and am known professionally as the Midget Strong Man with the most Muscular Perfect Physique of any small person in the World. I have worked many years on the stage doing strong acts, muscular posing, feats of strength, aerial work, and am an all around gymnast. . . .

He had not read any of the Tarzan books, but had heard a great deal about Burroughs and wanted to meet him. Ed urged Monty to stop in at Tarzana.

Although Zimbalist's plan to eliminate Jane had aroused Ed's ire, he later expressed his approval of *Tarzan Finds a Son*, commenting on August 29 to the producer, ". . . I am only sorry that you are not going to do them all. Whoever makes the next one has certainly got a mark to shoot at. . . ."

Burroughs, the creator of an unending list of projects, produced his latest inspiration at the end of 1936. He conceived of a "live talent program" for radio and on December 19 wrote to F.H. Winter at the Radio Recorders, Inc., to explain the idea and seek assistance. The setting for the program would be the editorial office of *The Tarzana Tribune* with Burroughs himself playing the role of a columnist. Others in the cast of four characters would include a small-town editor-publisher, a dumb stenographer, and an office boy. Ed noted that the editor should be a "querulous, fault-finding, sarcastic man who does nice things surreptitiously and doesn't want anyone to know about them." The stenographer should be "a good-looking blonde with one of those foolish voices that seem always to get a laugh." Ed hoped that Winter would help him in finding this cast. On the twenty-first Ed wrote to the J. Walter Thompson Agency to explain the same program. In taking the part of the columnist, under his own name, Ed planned radio scenes in which he would discuss his daily column with the editor who would give caustic comments about it. Sections of the column, written in a light tone and containing remarks about the news, quips, and gags, would be read aloud on the air. The human interest would center about the problems and family troubles of the stenographer and office boy.

Ed could further envision a "publicity tie-

Theatre lobby card for MGM film Tarzan Finds a Son, *1939.*

in" and "merchandising hookup" through actually publishing the *Tarzana Tribune* in a magazine format. Advertising by the sponsor and other firms would be carried, and the *Tribune* would be sold on subscription. Ed had chosen the title "I See by the Papers" for his radio program.

The demonstration records, made on January 4, 1937, presented the office boy, played by Harry Gibson, and Mabel, the stenographer, played by Mrs. Gibson. A week later, when the recording was submitted to the J. Walter Thompson Agency, Ed entered a wry note in his diary: "Listened to records of 'I See by the Papers.' Awful!" The result was a distinct absence of interest by the agencies or sponsors, and

on February 2, seeking another outlet, Ed wrote to George Carlin at the United Feature Syndicate to inquire about the possibility of running "I See by the Papers" as a regular newspaper column. Carlin, explaining that the market was "over-columned" and that United Feature was handling eleven of them by such authors as Eleanor Roosevelt, Westbrook Pegler, Heywood Broun, and others, insisted that Ed's creation could not be accepted for syndication.[13]

With his usual tenacity Ed refused to abandon his plan for a radio program, and in 1939 he concocted another one, this time a one-character show in which he would comment about news events and broadcast responses, jokes, and verses from listeners. To Paul

Rickenbacher at the Thompson Agency he described the program as patterned after Bert Leston Taylor's column in the *Chicago Tribune*. He recalled how thrilled he had been when he "made the Line."[14] For the proposed fifteen-minute, once-a-week broadcast, Ed invented the title "Quiet, Please!" and prepared sample pages containing his humorous and at times opinionated remarks. The emphasis was upon quiet — Ed vehemently expressed his objections to noise. He evidently planned to open each program with a quotation about noise and the need for quiet, and three of his sample programs were headed with a famous line from Schopenhauer: "A man's ability to endure noise is in inverse ratio to his intelligence."

The other quotations came from varied sources, including the Bible:

And that ye study to be quiet. . . .
                    (1 Thessalonians iv. 11)

[Following this Ed remarked] *"I commend this Biblical admonition to saxaphone players and the leather lunged, flannel mouthed guy who always sits directly behind one of my ears at the football games, wrestling matches, and fights.*

All's quiet on the Western Front.

Be plain in dress and sober in your diet. In short, my dearie, kiss me and be quiet.
        (Lady Mary Wortley Montagu 1690-1762)

And join with thee, calm, peace and quiet.
                        (John Milton)

But whoso harkeneth unto me shall dwell safely, and shall be quiet. . . .
                        (Proverbs 1:33)

The best doctors in the world are Dr. Diet, Dr. Quiet, and Dr. Merryman.
                        (Jonathan Swift)

In the sample columns, all headed with quotations emphasizing quiet or decrying noise, Ed inserted his own pungent complaints about the situation:

I think I shall organize The Society for the Elimination of Unnecessary Noise and Noise Mak-

Front cover of brochure used by Edgar Rice Burroughs, Inc., for promoting new radio program.

ers. Any volunteers? We might start in by liquidating the noise makers. I like that word in its Stalinesque connotation, as much as I dislike admitting that I like anything born of Communism.

Radio is a source of much useless, and senseless noise. . . . the ideal solution would be to adopt a Constitutional Amendment banning all loud speakers and making it mandatory upon radio listeners to go back to the old earphones.

Every Columnist should have a Cause, I am told. I have one. I have espoused the cause of Quiet.

All those wishing to join the Society for the Elimination of Unnecessary Noise and Noise Makers may send their applications, together with their nominations for candidates for liquidation, to me at Tarzana, California. The Society is offering a tickless watch as a prize to anyone who will invent a noiseless motor to go with the invisible airplane which has just been invented.

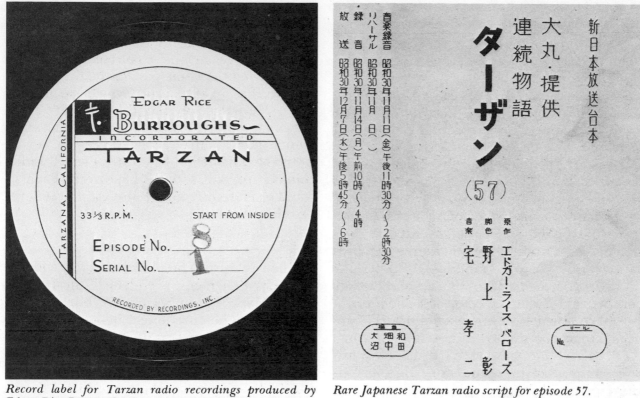

新日本放送台本

大丸・提供
連続物語
ターザン
(57)

原作　エドガー・ライス・バローズ
脚色　野上孝二
音楽　宅　彰

編曲　大畑和田
　　　沼中田

リール No.

音楽録音　昭和30年11月11日（金）午後11時30分～2時30分
リハーサル　昭和30年11月　日（　）
録音　昭和30年11月14日（月）午前10時～4時
放送　昭和30年12月7日（水）午後5時45分～6時

Record label for Tarzan radio recordings produced by Edgar Rice Burroughs, Inc.

Rare Japanese Tarzan radio script for episode 57.

In studios of Radio Recordings, Inc., Hollywood, during recording of a Tarzan episode, March 31, 1937; left to right: Jack Brundage, Chang Winters, and Hulbert Burroughs.

The saddest sound that ere did cut
The silence and disturb:
The traffic copper's "putt-putt-putt"
That pulls you to the curb.

In the area of politics Ed saved his choicest barbs for his pet abominations, Franklin and Eleanor Roosevelt, Hitler and the Nazis, and, of course, the communists. One of his columns contained the joke about the psychiatrist who died and sought entrance into heaven. St. Peter welcomed him, saying, "You're just the man we're looking for. We've a very bad case here. God has been running around for the last three days saying that he's Franklin D. Roosevelt." Ed's abhorrence for Harry Bridges and Frances Perkins, the secretary of labor, was evidenced in several comments: "I understand that they are trying to recall the Governor of California. Well, what if they do?—Harry Bridges will still be economic dictator of the State. He's Ma Perkins fair-haired protege, you know."

Gloomily predicting that Roosevelt would be elected for a third term, Ed described the weaknesses of the other candidates. A man must look like a president. Dewey did not, and he suffered the handicap of a moustache, a facial appendage which had been brought into disrepute by Hitler and Stalin. Taft did not look like a president, and unfortunately, people still recalled that his father, "while a very swell fellow, was not much of a President." Ed's only praise was for Hoover: "The cards were certainly stacked against him during his administration. He got the worst breaks of any president. He is a highly intelligent, conservative man, the type we need to drive the bats out of the Capitol dome. . . ."

Jokingly, in his columns Ed announced his own candidacy for president. His give-away platform contained inducements that far exceeded those offered by the other candidates: "Fifty dollars a week for everyone eligible to vote; thirty dollars every Thursday for those who vote twice; a fried chicken in every dinner pail; a car in every garage; a garage for every car; no taxes; no budget. . . ."

While noting with regret the death of Douglas Fairbanks, Ed delved into the past to provide some surprising information, not previously disclosed by anyone: "Fairbanks came very near playing the name part in the first Tarzan picture, Tarzan of the Apes, which was made in 1918. He wished to play the part; but 'Billy' Parsons, stupidly, wouldn't pay the price Fairbanks asked. What a box office Tarzan he would have made!" The "Quiet, Please!" radio-column program, as with "I See by the Papers," could produce no sponsor interest; it was never broadcast.[15]

The late thirties produced a correspondence with Cyril Clemens, president of the International Mark Twain Society, Webster Groves, Missouri. The first letters between Clemens and Burroughs, written in 1933, led to Ed's acceptance of an honorary membership in the Society; on June 28, 1933, he wrote, "From boyhood I have been an admirer of Mark Twain, his works being among the first that I recall having read as a child. . . ." On August 8, upon acknowledging the certificate of membership, Ed forwarded a copy of *Apache Devil* for the Society library. When the correspondence resumed in 1937, Clemens notified Ed of his unanimous election to the society's fiction committee. In this letter of July 14, Clemens noted that Hugh Walpole was chairman of the committee. Clemens, who was writing a biography of G.K. Chesterton, inquired, "Do you recall the first time you met him either in the flesh or through his books? He held your work in high esteem." Clemens also quoted the passage from Kipling's *Something of Myself* that praised Burroughs and the Tarzan idea.[16] Enclosing a list of three books he had written, Clemens offered to send them to Ed; the books were *Mark Twain's Religion, An Evening with A. E. Housman,* and *A Visit to George Santayana.*

On the twenty-first, appreciative of his election to the fiction committee, Ed added the information that he had not met Chesterton, could not recall the first time he had read his works, but greatly admired him. He requested a copy of *Mark Twain's Religion* and on August 3, upon receipt of the book, expressed his gratitude, noting especially Clemens' inscription on the title page. The correspondence between the two men again resumed in later years; in response to a request from Clemens, Ed, on January 31, 1940, agreed to participate in a memorial to Zane Grey, whose works "will live forever as authentic records of days that are fast disappearing." Concerning another author, Booth Tarkington, Ed remarked to Clemens that while he had never met Tarkington, he admired his works and viewed him as "our greatest novelist."[17] In 1948 Clemens notified Burroughs that because of his "outstanding contribution to American literature," he had been unanimously elected a *Knight of Mark Twain*.[18]

Once more, this time in 1939, Burroughs renewed his support of an organization for the youth; in his revival of the Tarzan Clans of America he made no secret of the fact that publicity and promotion were his main goals. A five-page informational statement, issued for distribution, stressed the business and sales benefits to be derived from the nationwide Clans. Burroughs referred first to Signal Oil's earlier promotion of The Tribes of Tarzan, noting the financial success of this project: "With 125,000 young people plugging for the sale of Signal commodities their gasoline gallonage alone increased over 300%." The popularity of the novels, films, and newspaper strips that kept the names of Tarzan and Burroughs "constantly before the public" should be exploited in every possible area: the 190 newspapers should "make use of their local Tarzan Clans by means of contests" thus increasing the demand for their comic sections; Principal Productions (Sol Lesser) which used the Signal Oil Tarzan Tribes to promote *Tarzan the Fearless* should "enthusiastically endorse" the Clans, as would Twentieth-Century Fox; book publishers, including Grossett & Dunlap and Whitman, would of course take part in the Clan publicity; for radio sponsors the Tarzan Clan idea was "an absolute natural in the exploitation of

many commodities"; the Clans "might enroll 2,000,000 young people who would be enthusiastic 'pluggers' for the sponsor's merchandise."

Later, it was Burroughs' plan to publish the *Tarzan Magazine*, containing fiction and articles for young people; it would be sold on newsstands and "its advertising space should prove valuable to publisher, sponsor and motion picture producer alike." The first publication, however, was a 1939 printing of the *Official Guide of The Tarzan Clans of America,* a thirty-two-page booklet containing the rules; various items relating to the Clans, including poem-songs; and at the end, an English, Ape-English dictionary. Curiously, instead of the expected drawing of Tarzan, the cover displayed a native chief, his savagery stressed with dangling earrings and a feather in his hair; one upraised arm flourished a spear while the other held a shield. The cover design had been adapted by Jack Burroughs from a St. John illustration in *The Beasts of Tarzan.*

In sending the proof of the *Official Guide* to MGM on May 10, 1939, Burroughs noted the printed reference to appointments of a chief of chiefs, a chief of subchiefs, a chief medicine man, and a chief high priest. The plan was to make Johnny Weissmuller the chief of chiefs, and permission for this was sought from MGM. Ed observed, ". . . it might be good publicity for Johnny and for the picture [*Tarzan Finds a Son*]". . . He added, ". . . it might not be a bad idea to appoint Maureen O'Sullivan chief high priestess." The *Guide*, Ed explained, would have a "very limited first printing" and only one advertisement in a magazine; from this minimum effort Ed would determine its success. If MGM had plans to use the booklet extensively, the first printing would be increased.

MGM promptly sent permission for Johnny Weissmuller to be titled chief of chiefs, and, for Ed's approval, returned an article publicizing Weissmuller and the film *Tarzan Finds a Son*.[19] The article, bearing the Burroughs name, was apparently composed jointly by Ed and MGM. In it, while conceding that an author is "the worst critic of a motion picture," Ed reported his attending the preview of *Tarzan Finds a*

Assortment of foreign language newspapers publishing Tarzan strips or Sunday pages.

Son. He liked the picture "tremendously" and once more mentioned Tarzan's special appeal—"the body perfect, the body potent and masterful." Lasting from early childhood is our admiration for Jack the Giant Killer and for David in his defeat of Goliath. "All women like their mates to be drawn from the Tarzan mould in some form." We indulge in hero worship of champion athletes, and on the screen Weissmuller is "what we all hope to be and Maureen O'Sullivan is the women of the audience themselves."

Hopes that MGM would embark on an extensive campaign to publicize the Clans and the *Official Guide* were not realized. On June 12 MGM requested merely sixty copies of the booklet, promising to distribute these to the theater managers who in turn would forward them to the newspapers. Burroughs himself had launched the promotion of the Clans when, on May 24, using the list of young people who had previously corresponded with him, he mailed a circular describing the new Clans. A membership application was enclosed, and those who joined were offered a remarkable bargain: one dollar would pay for a membership card, an *Official Guide,* a Burroughs novel, the initiation fee, and the yearly dues. The two-dollar novel and the other items were actually worth $3.35.

By the fall of 1939 the Tarzan Clans circular was headed with "Johnny Weissmuller, Chief of Chiefs" at the top left and "C.R. Rothmund, Chief Scribe" at the right; it also bore Burroughs' personal signature as the Founder.[20] A variant form merely provided for a signature by the chief scribe. On June 26, in response to a query from Dewey Bloom of Toronto, Canada, Burroughs noted that although the Clans had been created primarily for American youth, he would welcome a Canadian branch, offering them the same one-dollar membership combination.

The *Official Guide,* its contents being the work of Burroughs, demonstrated both his imagination and his aptitude for organization. Following a precise table of contents, the booklet provides specific instructions for the formation of clans, the duties of officers, the procedures at meetings, the initiation ritual for new members, the Tarzan Pledge, the Tarzan Clan Grip, and the method of rating the members. The emphasis was upon ethics, behavior, and physical fitness. The Tarzan Pledge required members to be helpful, obedient to their parents and others, loyal, courteous, trustworthy, and even cheerful; the youth were asked, as a safety precaution, to be careful; to maintain clean speech, clean sport, and clean habits; and above all to uphold the laws of the United States and "never be a traitor to it by word or act."

The *Guide* contained a detailed section of sports and games, including "Tarzan in the Tree," and instructions for clan and interclan field meets. The song-poems, or lyrics, evidently composed by Burroughs, were titled "Tribal Hunting Song," "The Song of Manu the Monkey," "The Song of Numa the Lion," and "The Song of Usha the Wind." It would appear that the songs were chants, with no specific melodies intended. A description of the Clan Dance was presented, and from a practical standpoint, details were given on making a spear, a shield, and a tom-tom. The final four pages of the *Guide* featured the Dictionary of the Ape Language, totaling some 500 words.

Other 1939 items include a proposal from Charles F. Lorenzen of Oak Park, Illinois, that an Edgar Rice Burroughs Museum be established in this small town, a suburb of Chicago, where Ed had lived and written various novels. Lorenzen, in his letter of March 24, told how he and William Gardner, an old friend of the Burroughs family, had conceived the idea of purchasing the home and turning it into a "museum, shrine or memorial...." Mistakenly, Lorenzen believed that Ed had written the "first Tarzan stories" there. On the twenty-seventh Ed replied to thank Lorenzen but to stress that this honor was not deserved. He noted the faulty premise and explained that *Tarzan of the Apes* was written in Chicago; however, nine stories, either wholly or in part, were created at the Augusta Street address, where Ed lived from May 1914 to August 1916, and of these stories, four were Tarzans. In noting that he later

moved to two other Oak Park addresses, Ed added that in Oak Park he had written wholly, or in part, a total of twelve stories.

Lorenzen, not deterred from his project, believed that the creation of a number of Tarzan stories in Oak Park justified the founding of a museum there. He foresaw no difficulty in purchasing the Augusta Street home, but emphasized that either an endowment or trust fund would be required to maintain the museum. To contact and coordinate various civic groups, some money would be needed for expenses; in his letter of March 31 he suggested that Burroughs might be willing to "temporarily support" this promotional activity by contributing $500. Burroughs, in reply, reiterated his previous objection: since the first Tarzan stories were not written in Oak Park, there was no reason to establish the museum.[21] This statement caused Lorenzen to abandon the project.

To Burroughs, the passing years had brought the inevitable succession of deaths of friends and relatives. On March 17, 1933, death came to General Charles King, the commandant of Michigan Military Academy whom Ed had so deeply admired. A few years later, on January 31, 1937, Ed received a letter from King's son Rufus, a retired U.S. Navy commander. In it he mentioned: "While going through the personal effects of my dear old Dad, in straightening out his estate, I came upon several books you had sent him and the photos of your daughter and son among his cherished possessions...." King, now employed by the Metropolitan Life Insurance Company, had moved to San Diego and was eager to visit Burroughs at Tarzana. From his father, King had inherited a love for horses, and upon noting that the photos displayed Ed's son and daughter "on those beautiful horses," he wanted to see the animals.

The letter from King's son stirred old memories for Ed; sentimentally, he wrote of his hero worship for the general: "I used to try to emulate him. In the riding ring I rode my fool head off and nearly killed myself a couple of times in my anxiety to live up to what he expected of me as a horseman. . . ."[22] About the horses, Ed explained sadly, "Tarzana Ranch is no more — subdivided and sold; and my horses are gone, as I do not ride any more. I have taken up tennis instead, giving up something I could do reasonably well for something I cannot do at all."[23]

The death of Joseph E. Bray, former president and chairman of the board of A. C. McClurg & Company, on December 28, 1939, also revived recollections of the past and especially of the year 1914, when, after numerous rejections, *Tarzan of the Apes* was accepted for publication. Bray had been described as the "discoverer" of Burroughs and had received credit for being the first editor to show an awareness of Tarzan's unique appeal. Yet he had at first rejected the story in 1912 with a vague excuse about its "availability," and the correspondence that occurred two years later leads to the conclusion that Herbert A. Gould, a McClurg employee and friend of the Burroughs family, deserves the major credit for the publication of *Tarzan*. In reply to a query from Ed about the reputation of another company, Gould, on March 3, 1914, suggested that *Tarzan of the Apes* be resubmitted to McClurg. Ed accordingly decided to try again.

On January 19, 1933, Gould, then seventy, sent his recollections to Burroughs; Gould wanted corroboration, and in detailing the events, noted, "I feel so certain about this version, that I have made a wager with myself, that your remembrance will coincide with mine." Upon receipt of Ed's query, Gould reported contacting McClurg's publishing department: "I talked the matter over with them and they consented to publish it (i.e., Tarzan), if I could get the manuscript." In his letter of the twenty-fourth Ed confirmed the information supplied by Gould. Bray had first advised that Tarzan, while successful in magazine form, was "wholly unfitted" for a book. Ed recalled the opinion he had sought later from Gould and what had followed:

. . . doubtless on the strength of your having

taken the matter up again with Joe (Bray), I received a letter from him to the effect that they had so many calls from their retailers for Tarzan of the Apes . . . that they were willing to publish it.

In the same letter Ed attributed Tarzan's initial success to the wide newspaper syndication of the story; he credited *The New York Evening World,* first paper to print *Tarzan,* for this "start." He might have also given credit to editor Albert Payson Terhune, but before this, and above all, to Thomas Metcalf, *All-Story* editor, for the original acceptance of *Tarzan of the Apes* in 1912.

Another death, that of an old childhood friend, Robert D. Lay, was acknowledged by Ed in a telegram of January 2, 1940, in which he spoke of being "terribly shocked." Lay had been Ed's classmate at Michigan Military Academy. But the death of Harry Burroughs, Ed's brother, on January 21, 1940, while not unexpected, inspired a profound sadness and reminder of the vanished years. To Bert Weston, with whom he had maintained his most lasting friendship, Ed wrote, "That leaves only George and me of our generation."[24] Harry had stayed with his brother George in Fontana, California, for a while; in November 1939 Ed had visited Harry who was in a Chicago hospital for a cataract operation. Ed described his brother's lengthy illness:

Harry had been hospitalized for eight months with sclerosis of the spine. As he was practically blind, almost entirely helpless, and his case hopeless, we all felt that his death was a release from an intolerable condition which he must have hated, though he never once complained. He was one of the finest men I ever knew. . . .[25]

Harry died at the home of his daughter Evelyn (Mrs. Carlton McKenzie) in Quincy, Michigan.

A year later Edna, George's wife, who in August had been committed to a mental institution, died in October 1941. Some months earlier, with his wife's death certain, George invited his old friend Lew Sweetser to share the Fontana home.[26]

23
WAR CORRESPONDENT

Active and happy in the years following their marriage in 1935, Ed and Florence encountered only one disturbing factor. This was the complete rejection of Florence by Joan, whose sympathies and concern remained with her mother, Emma. In the future, Joan, who had been Florence's close friend, would never speak to her again. Jack, on the other hand, neutral in the controversy, regularly visited the newly married couple. And Ed, who had always liked and understood children, developed a pleasant relationship with Lee, who was six years old at the time of the marriage, and Caryl Lee, who was about four. The attachment between Caryl and Ed — she soon accepted him as the father she strongly needed — became very close; she called him "Ebby," a pet name she invented in her childhood.[1]

Because of her new father's movie associations, Caryl had an early acquaintance with celebrities. At the Sunset Plaza apartment Ralph Bellamy became a "kind of stepfather"

to her, and there at the pool both she and her brother Lee were taught to swim by a distinguished expert — Johnnie Weissmuller. The affection shared by Ed and Caryl was illustrated in another way; as though he were seeking to recreate the early years with his own children, Ed told her the same to-be-continued stories he had recounted to Joan, Hulbert, and Jack. Grandpa Kazink reappeared, this old man who could pull anything he wanted out of his flowing beard, and soared about in his Model-T flying machine. Both Caryl and Lee listened in fascination to Ed's serial, the story that was often left dangling with its cliff-hanger ending.

For Caryl, as he had done for his own children and for his niece Evelyn, Ed devised a combination of poetry and original illustrations, in this case using an ordinary hard-cover notebook. On the first page is an ex libris, a drawing of three palm trees bending toward the water, and beneath this bookplate is marked

613

"Li'l B Her Book." The pages follow with these entries: "Copyright in Benbow June 16, 1937. Finished?" and "This is an edition of one copy of which this is No. 1." Below them Ed has drawn a large version of his own logo and has placed "Big B Printing Company" at the bottom of the page.

A contents page lists only "The Ballad of the B's," page seven, and "It's Ants," page fifty. A separate title page has in bold print "The Ballad of the B's." The "B" of course stands for the Burroughs family, and this reference and Ed's pet name for Caryl — "Li'l B" — demonstrate his affection for her and his willingness to accept her as a "Burroughs." The poem, "The Ballad of the B's," and the accompanying illustrations, done colorfully in water colors of orange, red, brown, green, and yellow, are on pages eight to fifteen. The ballad evidently narrates the happenings on an Arizona auto trip:

> Like cast iron pot
> The sun was hot
>   Twixt Needles and Berdu
> And you were off
> That day at Goff
>   And off at Needles too
>
> And we were two
> And one was you
> And Flagstaff far away
>   And that was when
>   That it was then
> A hairpin saved the day
>
> The wind she blew near Kingman town
> She nearly blew the damn trees down
>   Where we were camped that night
> And tortured souls came out of holes
> And shrieked around the bending boles
>   And laughed as we took flight
>
> We stalled and stopped upon a grade.
> While strong men fainted in the shade
>   You pooshed and grunted in the heat,
> And fought for every inch you made.
> There were no strong men there nor shade,
>   But I sat in the driver's seat.
>   (For the last time.)

Ed's drawings include one of a small girl lying prostrate in the heat, while an iron pot in the sky above her sends down torrid rays. Another drawing shows the roadster, a trailer attached, struggling up a steep grade, and a girl, presumably Caryl, pushing behind. The caption beneath this watercolor drawing reads, "You pooshed."

The pages in the notebook are blank until pages fifty and fifty-one where Ed has created a poem titled "It's Ants" and a drawing that follows. The poem deplores the restlessness which drives people to leave one spot and travel to another:

> I wonder what is wrong with us
> And why the dither and the fuss
>   That we should travel anywhere
>   To get from here to go to there,
> Nor give a continental damn
> Just so we can be on the lam.
>   Cuelebra Cut! Kailua hut!
>   We liked Havana also, but
> We didn't find sands point so bad,
> Nor all the planters punch we had
>   With Mr. X and his Miss Z
>   Beside an azure tropic sea;
> And I will bet that some pretext
> Will take us on to Shanghai next.
>   It seems there's something in our pants.
>   My diagnosis is: It's Ants.

Toward the end of the book Ed drew a second, small-sized logo and entered a final note: "Florence bought this June 9, 1937."

Another poem, which Ed scrawled on a small slip of paper and gave to Caryl, repeats several phrases found in "The Ballad of the B's," but proceeds from there to joke about liquor and create a mock-horror effect with resemblances to Poe:

> The night was gone
> Then came the dawn
>   Naked and stark forsooth
> Like cast iron pot
> The rim was hot
>   And there was no vermouth.
> Oh, hideous gods

With swollen pods
  In thee there is no truth
  But list to the shriek
  Of the cursed weak
   Oh god, there's no vermouth
In the fetid swamp
We wriggle & romp
  And snakes crawl from our eyes
We hate the earth
That gave us birth
Apparently, part of the poem is missing.

The odd, macabre atmosphere of the poem serves as a reminder that during this period Ed was still suffering from the fearful nightmares that had occurred at various times throughout the years. The noises and frightened cries he emitted during these nightmares were so startling and disturbing that Florence found it difficult to sleep in the same room with him.

While Ed did not attain the closeness with Lee that he had with Caryl, there was nevertheless a friendly father-son relationship, with trips to ball games and to boy scout affairs. At school the problems Lee encountered with his studies must have reminded Ed of his difficulties in the early years. And the remedy was the same one that Ed's father had applied — the firm atmosphere of a military school. In fall 1937 Lee was enrolled at Hollywood Military Academy in Brentwood, but his reaction to the strict regulations was decidedly unfavorable and he was soon removed.

Following Florence's major surgery in June 1939 and the recuperative period, the family moved to the luxurious Beverly Hills home formerly occupied by attorney Jerry Giesler. At 716 North Rexford Drive, where the family moved on August 31, the rental was $300 a month. Ed's diary of the next day, September 1, noted, "My birthday [He was sixty-four].... The World War II broke today."

In this period Ed's most serious health problem became evident. The cause, a familiar one, the attempt of an older man to keep up with a young wife, was exhibited in his unwillingness to limit his activities and to avoid overexertion.

A diary entry of May 18, 1937, illustrated this lack of moderation: "We took the children boating . . . I rowed for about two hours. 2 sets of tennis after lunch. Nearly dead. Old angina pains after I got to my room. They come and go. Some day I'll go with them. . . ." The angina attacks recurred; in November 1939 he reported, "Have had several slight heart attacks today."

At the same time the problem of finances returned to plague him. Accustomed to spending freely, he had often incurred heavy expenses; but now he was required to maintain two establishments, the second being Emma's home in Bel-Air. Before his marriage to Florence, he had frankly laid down conditions. She recalled, "It was clear that we would have nothing. Emma came first — I understood this."[2] She remembered also how he would display anger when he found her tidying up; he objected to his wife doing this type of work. "We pay people to do that," he said. Florence thought it was natural for a woman to perform these household chores.

Some eight months after he had leased the home in Beverly Hills, Ed came to an abrupt

ERB playing tennis, March 27, 1937.

decision. His expenses made the present situation intolerable, and because of the European war he had lost a significant part of his income. He would move to Hawaii where he could practice economy, especially in his social obligations, and where living would be generally cheaper. On April 18, 1940, Florence and the children sailed on the *S.S. Matsonia* — her Packard sedan was also aboard the ship — and on the twenty-fourth, after renting the Beverly Hills home, Ed embarked on the *S.S. Monterey*.

In a letter to his brother George, Ed gave more explicit details about the sudden change: "I reached the end of my rope, financially, on the mainland; and had to do something about it quick; so I rented our house at a good profit and came here, where it is costing me about one third as much to live."[3] With Europe at war, he explained, thousands of dollars owed him in foreign rights were now tied up overseas; it was doubtful that he would ever receive this money. He had also been informed that his income from France and England for the Tarzan films would be suspended for the duration, as well as the payments from all foreign countries on books, magazines, and cartoon strips.

The plan to limit social activities in Hawaii became impossible at once. To George, Ed remarked, "I intended to crawl into a hole and pull the hole in after me when I got here, but that was easier thought than done. We have many friends here; and Tarzan is very popular on the Islands, with the result that they won't let us alone."[4] The letter contained his assessment of Oahu which he described as "an immense fortress," with every point "heavily fortified," and added, "Our navy is great, but our army is pitifully undermanned and underequipped."

Ed, always prolific in his correspondence, launched a steady stream of letters soon after his arrival at Honolulu. Most of these were to relatives and old friends, including Bert Weston and Virginia and Charles Farrell. The postmark was "Lanikai, Oahu," and Ed revealed that he had taken a house on Kailua Bay, "smack on the ocean." To Bert he disclosed the rental, $125 a month, and claimed that he must now live on a "paltry $250." His office was located in a small room in the garage. Concerning the beach house, evidently a ramshackle affair, Ed noted Florence's discouragement, "She will not admit that it is a house."[5] A diary entry of June 25 contained an economy note: "I washed my car — first time in over 20 years. . . ." At this time Ed sent an odd communication, a chain letter, to Weston, with instructions to mail it to "nine other victims." The letter, originally dated 1930, had evidently been circulated in the past. It appeared that each individual was asked to enclose a dollar in the letters he mailed; perhaps the money-making aspects of the scheme appealed to Ed. In his letter of September 12 to Weston, he wrote, "Forgive the chain letter. It is the first time I ever did anything like that, but the doggone thing was so worded that I couldn't turn it down. My dollars have not started rolling in yet. If I get one, I'll break even."

Above the long list of names was an admonition: "This is that part of the chain of which you are a link. Your nine letters should go out within nine days, or may God have mercy on your soul." The names were arranged in two parallel columns, the first individuals being the senders, and opposite them, the receivers of the letter. Many famous names were included:

Senator Heflin	to	Bernard Shaw
Bernard Shaw	to	Arthur Train
Arthur Train	to	C. G. Dawes
C. G. Dawes	to	Henry Ford
Henry Ford	to	Col. Lindberg

Others among the forty names were Dorothy Dix, Artistide Briand, Ramsey McDonald, and John Barrymore. Ed was shown last on the senders list, with H. T. Weston as his receiver.

The beach house produced a new problem: the area was infested with scorpions, centipedes, and rodents. The diary reported happenings during a July 4 fireworks celebration on the beach: "Florence stung on heel by centipede. Called Betty Mitchell and was told to apply an epsom salt compress. After killing the first centipede for Florence, she found another in her bathroom. This made the fourth we have killed here. Something tells me we shall move." Florence, understandably on edge, had been appalled by another regular occurrence: the rats, slithering across the roof of the dilapidated house, would peer down through the cracks.

None of these disturbing factors could stop Ed's writing schedule. On May 4 to 5 he noted his work on the outline of a Venus story, on July 16 he wrote ten pages of a "Mr. Dinwiddie" story, and on the twenty-fourth he started a new Martian novel. But any longer stay in the beach house was impossible, and on August 28 the family moved to 2623 Halelena in Honolulu, with Ed, a week later, taking an office at 1298 Kapiolani Boulevard. There he turned determinedly to writing. His diary reported the completion of two works, one of 20,000 words, on September 6, featuring John Carter, and the other, on the fifteenth, with David Innes as the hero. With the arrival of his dictaphone outfit on September 26, the feverish writing pace even intensified and on the thirtieth he noted, "Mrs. Jane Morse started typing for me."

Ed and Florence had renewed old friendships soon after arriving at Hawaii. Among the first were Rochelle Hudson and her husband, Hal Thompson; Rochelle revealed her interest in playing the lead in *Jungle Girl*, the Burroughs novel that had been sold to Republic in April. When the film appeared, however, in 1941, as a fifteen-part serial, Frances Gifford took the lead role. The movie bore little resemblance to the book. Thompson, who, with his wife Rochelle, saw Burroughs "every day or evening for several months," recalled the discovery that Ed had known his late father in the Spanish-American War. During the long conversations Ed used the word "scientifiction" to categorize his writings, a term he claimed to have coined.[6]

The most surprising occurrence on Hawaii was the chance meeting of Ed and Bob Davis, former Munsey editor, who, from 1914 on, had purchased many Burroughs stories. Davis, retired for some time, was staying at Kailua Beach, and he proceeded at once to query Ed about the past, with a view to using the answers for a "short and simple biography." Written with a humorous touch, the biography appeared in Davis' *New York Sun* column, July 20, 1940, and reported at the opening how Davis "found the great simianologist and author of 'Tarzan' strolling through his Hawaiian jungle at Lanikai." In the article, an informal exchange of questions and answers, Ed discussed the origin of *Tarzan*, noted that a British reviewer had described Burroughs as having the mind of a child of six, gave details of his writing methods, and joked about his penchant for taking chances: ". . . at 56 I took up flyin'; at 59, tennis; at 61, skiing. . . ."

The impending 1940 presidential election became a main topic in Ed's letters to George and to Bert Weston. Ed had often expressed his dislike and distrust of Roosevelt and his detestation of liberalism, particularly as displayed by Eleanor Roosevelt. He felt tremendously enthusiastic about Wendell Willkie whose nomination "offered the first ray of hope" he had seen for eight years: "I had about given up all hope of the Republican party developing anything resembling real Presidential timber. . . . Willkie symbolizes everything that has made America a great country — youth, strength, intelligence, business acumen. . . . I hope he doesn't disappoint us as FDR has."[7] Ed succumbed to his emotions in making a prediction: "I feel that he will be elected — especially if FDR runs for a third term. There must be millions of conservative people who are congenitally opposed to any third term for a President."[8] After the election, in response to Weston, who had also predicted a victory for Willkie, Ed wrote sourly, "This is the people's country; if the people wish Mr. Roosevelt as President who am I to oppose their will?"[9]

With the American apprehension over Japan especially strong in the Islands, and the war danger increasing, Ed revealed some of his fears in a letter to Irene Ettrick, a London fan with whom he had corresponded for many years: 'If the Islands get statehood, as they are trying to, I have prophesied that in ten years they will have a Japanese Governor and there will be Japanese senators and representatives in Washington. They are very strong politically . . . and they cling to their language, religion and customs. . . ."[10] He made plain that he had no faith in the Japanese loyalty: "I imagine that every Japanese here has relatives in Japan, and I am sure that their hearts are there." He noted that a Japanese ship loaded fifty tons of "comfort bags" for the soldiers in Japan. Despite the noncommittal statements of the army and navy officers he had met, Ed was inclined to believe that war was near: ". . . the consensus of opinion among civilians . . . [is that] we shall be at war with Japan within a matter of weeks, perhaps days."[11]

Although Ed maintained his daily writing schedule, the evening social affairs were, if anything, more numerous than on the mainland. Among the large group of friends were two from the movie field — actor John Halliday and actress Janet Gaynor. Card-playing had always been a strong Burroughs interest, and here the emphasis was upon bridge. Florence recalled Ed's fascination with the game: "He lived for bridge in the Islands. At evening affairs it was usually drinks and then 'Let's get to bridge'. His horror was conversation; he couldn't stand to just sit and talk. . . ."[12]

With his second marriage Ed adopted a new attitude toward his writing. The old days when Emma and the children read and commented on his stories were gone; now he did not discuss his writing at all with Florence. His days at the office, from nine to four, were like a routine job, kept separate from his home life. Florence perceived that he was never elated over his work: "When people referred to him as an author, he would always downgrade himself." His strong feelings of inferiority were evident to her. This at times led to jealousy and bitterness. She remembered an incident when she mistakenly tried to joke with him about Ernest Hemingway. They were dining at a restaurant in Hawaii when Hemingway and Martha Gellhorn walked in. Adopting an awestruck attitude, Florence pretended to swoon. Ed, furious, announced he was going over to get an introduction for her. "Obviously, you need to meet this man," he said. Although he did not talk to Hemingway, he never forgot the incident and would frequently say, "Maybe you and Ernest Hemingway should get together on some island sometime." Florence naturally was unaware of Ed's deep resentment toward "literary" writers and his anger at the critics who had excluded him from literary circles and disparaged his writing.

The attraction she had found in Ed at the start was not because of his fame; through her work in the movies she had known many celebrities. What appealed to her was his "wonderful sense of humor." He had changed her life. Dearholt, her first husband, had treated her as a little girl or child, had been too demanding. With Ed the days were all fun and good times. She also approved the special type of "Burroughs" humor — "show yourself in a derogatory manner, deflate yourself."

The marriage seemed to work well in California, but in Hawaii the early signs of trouble were apparent. The "economy" life, Florence noted, "wore on him." Her diagnosis was that he found the limitations "difficult." However, the problems, obviously, were more complex than this. Florence, with deep feelings of guilt, blamed herself for not understanding, for not having better psychological perception. Her protected background and lack of exposure to complex human problems, and, of course, her age, did not prepare her for this intense situation. Ed, disturbed by the separation from his children, and still not able to overcome the trauma of his divorce from Emma, might plunge himself into a life of fun and games, but he could not bury his inner agonies.

Ed called Florence "Mamma," and she especially remembered his repeated exhortation: "Come on, Mamma, have another drink. Let's have fun." At the time of their marriage, sensitive to the difference in age as far as the

618

public attitude might be, she deliberately dressed in an older fashion. Photos of the period show her in dresses soberly and conservatively styled. Ed soon began to pass responsibilities on to her; he seemed like a child and she the serious, older one. His constant plea was for fun — more fun. In their relationship, however, she became aware of some of his phobias. He had developed a "horror" of notoriety — perhaps because of the publicity produced by the divorce and remarriage. In addition, after reading a newspaper account of a kidnapping for ransom, he became acutely nervous that he might be the target of such a criminal attempt.

The tension between Florence and Ed was soon apparent to any observing outsider. Rochelle Hudson, in the hours she spent with the two, was convinced that the marriage "wouldn't work out," and would "just run its course." She had noticed that Florence was "sharp and impatient" with him, and that he in turn would "dawdle deliberately" or do other things to irritate her.[13] Hal Thompson recalled his appraisal at the time: "Florence and ERB seemed so ill-mated that it was obvious that the marriage wouldn't last."[14]

The increasing tension brought a new problem — that of Ed's excessive drinking. He had been a social drinker and one who stayed away from liquor during his writing hours; in the past he had always been "bright as a dollar" and ready for work the next morning. The first change came when he began to drink heavily in the evenings: "Any visitor was an excuse for drinking."[15] As the situation worsened, he kept a case of liquor under his bed at all times. Continuous scenes and quarrels erupted between him and Florence. She could not perceive the causes for his drinking. "I wasn't smart enough to know, not experienced enough," she confessed. "My great regret is that I didn't have brains enough to know what was behind it."[16]

Ed had always been a man of repressed emotions, hardly one who would reveal his inner thoughts to anybody, even his children. Certainly, with his attitude toward psychia-trists, he would be the last person in the world to seek psychological help. His life from the early years had been one of discipline and self-control — the qualities that represented masculinity. An emotional release, a pouring out of his buried feelings was contrary to this male stoicism and thus unthinkable.

Their home and social life changed. Florence remembered, "Because of his drinking, he could no longer manage himself at the table. The children began to irritate him. For the first time in our marriage age began to enter into it." The evening affairs, the guests being mainly army and navy acquaintances, became nerve-racking to her, and Ed "acted up." She had never cared for drinking, and now with Ed drunk almost every night, she was forced to do all the driving. She dreaded driving his huge Pierce Arrow convertible over the mountain roads in the dark.

The crisis, certain to arrive, came because of Ed's curt and impatient attitude toward Lee. Although Ed had never punished Lee physically, Florence recalled that on this occasion the child was quite afraid of him. After the quarrel that followed, she felt that a separation was unavoidable: "I told him I was going to leave and never return," she said. The end of the marriage was recorded in Ed's diary on March 14, 1941: "Florence & the children sailed on the Lurline at noon. . . ." To Weston, on the twentieth, Ed told of meeting Prince Ilaki Ibn Ali Hassan, a professional wrestler and long-standing Burroughs fan. Ed had corresponded with the prince for some time, and now, because the letters were "very amusing," he was forwarding them to Weston. Hassan (whose real name was Agis I. Mihalikas), Ed noted, was a successful pulp writer and had become a "prince" because his father owned 3000 goats in Arabia. In the letter Ed informed Weston of Florence's departure, but concealed the truth: "It is so difficult to get reservations and the possibility of war with Japan so definite that we thought it best to get them off while we could. I shall finish up my business here and follow in about a month. . . ."

The shock of the separation was profound.

At the Niumalu Hotel, where Florence and Ed had moved in December 1940, Ed would reveal his tormented feelings only in his diary: "March 27: Had a very bad night last night from worry about Florence and finances. Early this morning when I awoke I thought I had had a slight stroke in my sleep. (I think of the cutest things) My arm still feels funny — the left one — sort of numb. . . ." His life became one of complete withdrawal: "April 8: Mabel White asked me to dinner for tonight but I regretted. Bill Mitchell called up and asked me over for the weekend. I declined. I have no wish to go anywhere or see anyone. To bed 7:30."

He adhered to a routine of a movie every day and going to bed early every night, with all invitations declined. On the twelfth he wrote, "I just realized that I go for days without speaking except to say 'morning' a few times and to order my meals. . . . To my surprise, I do not mind being a sort of recluse." On May 3 he noted his weight at 189; he had lost eleven pounds in a month. He decided to swear off drinking: "I am selling the few bottles (of Scotch) I have left to the Harmons." In refusing an invitation to a cocktail party, he commented, "I don't drink, I don't like to talk, and I don't like to listen to other people talk. . . ."

He was confronted by another health problem. On June 2 he wrote, "Had a bad night last night and am scared; my old trouble seems to be returning. . . ." The "trouble," involving the bladder, caused urinary difficulties; he had previously undergone surgery for this condition. After a consultation with Dr. Paul Withington, Ed received treatment from a urologist, Dr. R. O. Brown. In a report of July 2 to Rothmund, Withington explained that with the aid of sulfathiozal Ed improved rapidly and insisted upon leaving the hospital, against the doctor's advice. A recurrence of the same illness forced his return to the hospital in July and in August, 1941.

His diary recorded "something amusing": "I haven't had a drink with alcohol in it for 2 mos. and have seldom felt better. Withington told me to start drinking again! . . . So I had 2 big highballs before dinner. . . ." He also aban-doned his life as a recluse, went out to play bridge, had another highball, and stayed up until 10:50. The aftermath was unpleasant: "Lay awake nearly all last night and am back on the waterwagon, Dr. or no Dr. I know when I feel well and I feel like hell this morning."

The advice to resume drinking led to an even worse reaction later. When he faced the prospect of returning to the hospital, Ed imbibed liquor with a vengeance: ". . . I drank five highballs and went to see ball game. . . . When I came home I drank 3 more highballs. I'm either going to kill or cure myself." After his first discharge from the hospital, he was under the care of his friends Wayne and Mary Pflueger.

On July 23, while he was struggling to recuperate, the *Star Bulletin* called to disclose some bad news: Florence had filed suit for divorce, charging him with mental cruelty. Ed had no intention of returning to the mainland, and he delegated the legal matters to Rothmund and Attorney Max Felix. In the passing weeks, with Ed's long illness causing concern at home, Hulbert decided to join his father, arriving on September 7. Soon afterward the illness flared up again, and Ed was in the hospital for brief periods in September and October.

In explaining the separation to his brother George, Ed noted that Florence and he had a premarital understanding that either party could "call it off" at any time without objections from the other, and the two would remain friends. "I only hope that she contemplates remarriage," he wrote. The divorce suit now prevented his return home: "This demand of Florence's lawyer for $1,000 a month for her and a fee of $5,000 for himself may make me stay put indefinitely, as he cannot get service on me as long as I remain out of California."[17] His finances were so bad, he insisted, that he had been forced to remain in Hawaii because he could not pay for his transportation home; he had borrowed the money for the fares of Florence and her children.

From Hal Thompson, who with his wife

Rochelle Hudson had left the Islands in June 1940, came an inquiring letter; Thompson, now living in the San Fernando Valley, had presumed that Ed was back in California. On August 14, Ed responded, "Since you left I have been in the hospital three times, had my car telescoped by a five ton truck with ten tons of crushed rock on it, and quit drinking (three times). Don't some people have all the fun. . . ." To Rochelle, who later wrote, Ed explained that he was sitting in his parked car, about to start it, when the truck smashed into the rear of the car, propelling it ahead into a Packard. Fortunately, nobody was injured. Appreciating her concern, Ed spoke of his fondness for her, writing, "You are still, and always will be to me, the sweet little high school girl that Hulbert and Jack were also so very fond of. . . ."[18]

Earlier, probably because of his health problems and the occurrence of several heart attacks, Ed wrote an unusual letter to Rothmund. Dated April 19, 1941, the letter, a mixture of the sentimental and coldly practical, first expressed appreciation for Ralph's friendship and spoke of "what a pleasure it has been to work with you all these years." Ed added, "I often wonder how in Hell you have put up with me." He then gave instructions to be followed after his death:

My personal desire is that there shall be no funeral and no services. . . .

I do insist, though, on cremation and that my ashes be not retained. I think it is possible to carry cremation to a point where no ashes remain. If this is true, that is what I wish; but if there be any residue, I suggest that it be buried under one of the live oak trees in the back pasture; the children will know the one. . . .

If my mother's ashes have not been previously disposed of, it might be a good idea to inter them with mine. . . . If arrangements cannot be made to bury my ashes in the back pasture, bury them under the big black walnut tree on my pet lot.

At the bottom of the letter was a brief note, dated four years later:

9 May 1945: Bury them beside my Mother's under the tree in the office yard.

What I wrote in the first person above more than four years ago about my appreciation of your enduring friendship not only holds today, but could be greatly amplified. Outside of my children, you are unquestionably the best friend that I have.

On August 12 Ed sent a request to his children, urging them to elect Ralph Rothmund president of Edgar Rice Burroughs, Inc., "and, if the means are available, pay him a salary commensurate with his worth." He had first considered leaving some stock in the corporation to Ralph, he explained, but had decided the stock should remain in family control. In lieu of this, he suggested that Ralph receive salary increases and bonuses each year, and in the event of his death, that provision be made for his wife.

On May 2, 1941, while still living his life of a "recluse," Ed dispatched an acrimonious letter to the *Honolulu Star-Bulletin*. The subject was the Hawaii Legislature, and in denouncing it he reached new heights of derision, contempt, and vituperation. The insulting tone was evident in the first lines:

To a man up a tree, where I shall probably have to take refuge after writing this, it would appear that the childish antics of the Territorial Legislature, fortunately adjourned, constitute a very strong argument against conferring Statehood upon Hawaii; for it has conclusively proved that the Territory is not prepared for even partial self-government.

After stating that this indictment could be applied to all of the state legislatures, he repeated an accusation he had previously made—Americans use an "utterly ridiculous system" to select "the giant intellects who spend our money and make the laws for us."

. . . in nearly every large city of these United States of America a noble and ambitious citizen wishing to become a street cleaner must pass an

examination and, among other things, must be able to read and write; but not so with those whom we elect to make our laws, spend our money and guide our destinies.

Noting that the Constitution does not require that even the President should be able to read and write, he commented that we could elect to our highest office "a congenital idiot who could neither read nor write and spend all his time unravelling his socks." Then he really leveled his choicest insults at the Hawaiian lawmakers. Of course, he explained, he was being absurd about the Presidential election danger. But concerning the territorial and state legislators, he had this to say: "Perhaps we would all be better off if they confined their activities to unravelling their socks; but, unfortunately for us, they are not all congenital idiots: there are many borderline cases who have studied oratory in high school."

He emphasized that his criticism was not mere "captiousness," but was really a diagnosis of "what is wrong with democracy." He believed America might be destroyed by "a political ineptitude such as wrecked France... or almost wrecked Great Britain." His solution, offered in previous articles, was based upon a test for prospective lawmakers:

... before any person, otherwise qualified, may become a candidate for any elective or appointive office, he shall pass a comprehensive intelligence test to determine not what he knows about Greek literature, or the name of the seventh President of the United States, or who said, "You may fire when you are ready, Gridley," but to prove just how much native intelligence he has — the kind of horse-sense intelligence that Will Rogers had.

He had no faith in the present intelligence tests that determined one's IQ. "Many ten year old children pass them with flying colors, but I don't wish any ten year old children to make laws for me." He saved some jeering comments for the last:

I believe that if our bulbous-domed psychologists went into a huddle they could evolve such a test as would at least keep a majority of the nit-wits out of public office.

If this fails, we can put the street cleaners in our legislatures. At least, we know that they can read and write.

With the printing of the letter on May 5, 1941, in the Star-Bulletin, the editor added a note inviting Burroughs to outline the type of intelligence test he would advocate for legislators. In his reply Ed conceded that a solution to the problem of "what the hell is the matter with democracy" would depend upon minds "far better equipped" than his:

Unfortunately for democracy, I am only a member of that extremely low form of animal life, slightly above the amoeba — a fiction writer; but there are an infinite number of colossal encephala in these United States which could produce an intelligence test that would be an intelligence test and not merely a test of acquired knowledge.

Nevertheless, he offered a plan: An examining board, to be selected, would consist of psychologists, logicians, engineers, lawyers, and representatives from other professions who deal with "practical problems."

I would shoo all fiction writers and school teachers as far away from such a board as possible, as such people are usually impractical; and I would make it a capital crime for a politician to come within 75 mm. range of the board.[19]

The results of the tests would be published in the newspapers prior to election day. Ed finally commented, "... then, if the people wish to elect nit-wits, as they very possibly would, they would get just the kind of legislation they deserved."

In his diary, on May 17, he noted with satisfaction that according to his friends, the Pfluegers, the article was viewed favorably in the governor's office. To his brother George he reported that "considerable comment," mostly approving, had resulted from the publication. He had one further evaluation of the lawmakers: "This legislature is something that only Gilbert & Sullivan could have conceived. They are far more proficient with the hula and the ukelele than they are with legislating."[20]

As 1941 drew to a close, Burroughs' personal problems and, in fact, all civilian affairs became of minor concern. The fateful month of December brought the Japanese attack on Pearl Harbor and the United States' entrance into the war. Always the writer, Burroughs could not be expected to overlook the opportunity to give his own account of the momentous Sunday, the seventh. Curiously, almost as though fate owed him something, as though fate were making amends for what it had deprived him of, it had now arranged for him to be in the right spot at the right time. His complaint, often restated, was that nothing had ever happened to him; he had found no adven-

tures, and what was worse — to use his own comparison — he was the pursuer of fire engines who always managed to arrive after the fire was put out. Now, at age sixty-six, Burroughs was granted one last chance — he had finally arrived at the "fire," this time a real conflagration, while it was burning.

In his article, "Came the War," he first described how Hulbert had come to Hawaii "to enjoy the peace and quiet of The Paradise of the Pacific." Hulbert had also come to care for Ed when he was ill. At 7:55 Sunday morning, December 7, they heard distant sounds of firing, but believed these to result from practice exercises listed in the newspapers. They proceeded with their customary activity, paddle tennis, playing on the hotel court which provided a clear view of the coast from Diamond Head to beyond Pearl Harbor and Barbers Point.

From the court they noticed the bomb bursts over Pearl Harbor and Hickam Field, and saw the "dense, black smoke" billowing up. They thought this was a practice smoke screen, and when anti-aircraft shells exploded in the sky and the ships at sea began firing, they were "thrilled by the realistic maneuvers the navy was staging." A man hurried over to tell them that the Japanese were attacking. But they didn't believe him; they thought it was "just another rumor." However, when a bomb fell near a supply ship standing off-shore near the hotel, Ed and Hulbert were startled into belief. The radio announcement followed: "Then we commenced to appreciate the gravity of the situation. It was about this time that Hulbert and I lost interest in tennis."

Ed observed the antiaircraft shells bursting over the area. "Many of our civilian casualties were caused by our own fire," he wrote. "But of course that could not be helped. I saw remains of an automobile that had been struck by an antiaircraft shell almost in the heart of downtown Honolulu and completely destroyed."

Following a radio call for all able-bodied men to report for duty, Ed, Hulbert, and a friend, Anton Rost, joined Patrol 2, Company A, 1st Battalion, stationed on the wharf at the

ERB greeting Hulbert aboard S.S. Mariposa, Honolulu, September 7, 1941.

623

ERB, at right, watching Pearl Harbor and Hickam Field, Sunday morning, December 7, 1941.

warehouse of Honolulu Tuna Packers Ltd. The three men were assigned to sentry duty from 10 p.m. until 2 a.m. Ed's desire for action had been quickly realized; it was Sunday evening, the seventh, with the Japanese attack still fresh, and he and Hulbert were already part of the war effort. In writing, he chose, as usual, to look on the lighter side. For months, since the separation from Florence, he had been going to bed around seven o'clock, "sleeping a paltry ten or eleven hours and waking up tired." Now he must carry a heavy Springfield rifle and do sentry duty until the early hours of the morning. He jokingly decided he should have "reenlisted in the cavalry" and chosen a war "that was carried on only during Chris-

tian hours." Indicative of the general confusion was the issuing of dark blue arm bands to the civilian sentries; these were "totally invisible after dark" and obviously had been "well thought out by master minds."

Later, Ed and Hulbert were detailed to guard twenty-two enemy aliens confined in a wire enclosure on the wharf. Ed's attitude was revealed in his comment that these men were supposed to be "dangerous saboteurs and fifth columnists"; he obviously did not believe these accusations. After midnight, already exhausted, Ed was assigned as one of the guards to march forty Japanese — "enemy aliens" — to the Immigration Station, a long distance away. He described his physical condition: ". . . both

624

my collar bones had caved in beneath the weight of my Springfield, and my feet had practically ceased to exist as such, being merely two pains." Luckily, he was able to return to Kewalo Basin on a truck.

The general nervousness and overtaxed imagination of the civilian guards led to spasmodic firing at no particular targets. Ed observed a machine-gun detachment on the roof of Felix's Cafe on Fisherman's Wharf "blasting away" toward Pearl Harbor, ten miles distant. Concerning the same gunners, who fired at the rocks above the water's surface in the lagoon in the belief that the rocks were boats, Ed, amused, offered another reason for this action: ". . . it is fun firing a machine gun!"

Relieved of duty at about two a.m., Ed and Hulbert attempted to sleep on the cement floor of the tuna company warehouse. "The air was filled with the aroma of departed tuna, cigarette smoke, sweat of various ethnological groups, and a part of the 27th Infantry that had been on duty for several weeks without benefit of baths." The next morning, when an alarm was sounded, and many people crouched behind sandbags with their guns pointing, Ed noted he was an exception, refusing to lie down even when Hulbert tugged at him. He wrote, "I was not animated by any excess of courage, but by a definite conviction that if I once got down, I should never be able to get up again."

Toward the end of his 2,800-word article "Came the War," Ed remarked, "About eight o'clock, having gotten the war off to a good start, we went home." He was touched by Hulbert's pleasure — that father and son had done sentry duty together. In the summons to the defense of his country, Burroughs, at sixty-six, indifferent to the dangers of further heart attacks, was concerned only with his military obligations. On December 23, in a letter to his sister Joan, Hulbert spoke of his pride in his father:

He is way past the age for any such active duty, but he didn't hesitate a minute. He seemed thrilled and anxious to do what he could. I think he has always regretted that he missed out during the Spanish-American War the time he wanted to join Teddy Roosevelt's Rough Riders, and then again during the last war. And so he was much pleased that he was finally able to carry a gun for his country in this present war.

Hulbert added, "It seemed strange that after all these years he and I would be walking the same sentry beat on this small island far out in the Pacific."

Hulbert, after his arrival at Hawaii, had maintained a steady correspondence with Rothmund, sending long reports about his father's condition. Before the Pearl Harbor attack, Hulbert had noted Ed's steady improvement: "I think I've talked him out of his habit of drinking more than was good for him. He has not had anything now for about three weeks and he is a hundred percent better already. . . ."[21] Ed found himself in the annoying position of having to wait for his monthly check until "both wives" were paid. Hulbert wrote, "The other day he said he only had thirteen dollars left in the bank."[22] In October 1941, and earlier, Hulbert referred to the divorce suit as the main obstacle to his father's return home: ". . . once the FGB matter is straightened out. . . he'll be quite happy." After Pearl Harbor, Hulbert, worried, wanted his father to leave Hawaii and urged Rothmund to persuade Ed to do so. Planning to enlist, Hulbert was reluctant to enter the armed forces until his father had left. But Ed now refused to return. "His feeling. . . is that he is doing some good here, whereas in LA he could do none," Hulbert explained. Since Florence was displaying a conciliatory attitude in the divorce matter — "no attachments will be forthcoming" — this barrier to Ed's return did not exist anymore.[23]

Eager to make some contribution to the war effort, Ed soon was offered the ideal opportunity. Summoned to General Headquarters by Lieutenant Colonel Kendall Fielder, whom he had previously met at cocktail parties, Ed was asked to write a daily column for distribution to the local newspapers and press services as a civilian morale booster. The assignment was a happy one, a request for a Burroughs specialty; no other writer could equal his skill and celerity in producing a series of this type. He demonstrated his speed at once:

December 12: Came back to office & wrote article (6 copies) which I took back in afternoon for approval. It was broadcast over KSU and KGMB this evening.

His decision to comment on the lighter side of the war was evident in the title of the column, "Laugh It Off"; it first appeared in the *Honolulu Advertiser* on December 13, and on that day, after bringing column number two to Colonel Fielder's office, Ed noted in his diary, "I am now a War Correspondent with a green arm brassard and a red C and an official identification card. Am *I* getting up in the world!" For several issues the column was published in both the *Advertiser* and the *Star-Bulletin*, but Ed soon arranged for the latter paper to have exclusive rights to the column.[24]

While adopting a light tone in the "Laugh It Off" columns, joking and reporting funny incidents, Ed also inserted serious comments and war pep talks. In the first issue he noted that there was no sabotage, merely silly, unfounded rumors; on the fifteenth he included praise of the Red Cross girls and even more strongly of the Filipinos who, for twenty straight hours, without rest, had been digging trenches at Kewalo Basin. On the twenty-fourth he cited the loyalty of four Japanese house servants who informed their employer of their intentions to work without pay for the duration. Later, when they were given their salary, they insisted upon returning it.

In following his main goal of cheering people up, Ed included many humorous stories. Among these was a report of the owner of three dogs who feared that fifth columnists had poisoned the water; he sampled the water first before allowing the dogs to drink. As one of the blackout problems, there was the incident of the three-year-old who cried out from the bathroom in the dark, "Mommy, I can't find my way home!"

The "Laugh It Off" columns appeared uninterrupted until January 28, 1942, when they were discontinued. Ed, restless, was seeking a more active war role. He may have been stimulated by Hulbert's enlistment, on January 18, as a photographer in the Army Air Corps. A few weeks later, after drilling and taking part in gas mask practice with the Businessmen's Military Training Corps, a civilian organization, Ed was introduced to Colonel Bourland, and asked to be public relations officer for the Corps.

In a publicity article, "The BMTC," Ed described the functions of the corps, then consisting of a regiment of four battalions:

The training of the regiment is pointed toward two principal objectives, which are always kept in mind: Fifth Column activities and invasion. Its very presence on the Island will be a deterrent to the former. Its other regular and little less important work lies in co-operation with the police and, in event of air-raids, the air-raid wardens. . . .

The members, whose average age was forty-two, in civilian life were mainly executives or professional men. Sixty-four percent had previous military training, "ranging all the way from ROTC to West Point," and twenty-five percent had served in armies of various countries.

Ed, who on February 22 had noted he was a corporal in the BMTC, two days later revealed that Colonel Bourland had promoted him to second lieutenant. It was quickly evident that Ed would not be happy, especially in the military, until he received a position of authority. On March 2 he wrote, "I have been assigned to drill all regimental rookies — at my own request. . . ." At the first session he was disgusted at the small turnout: "Only 14 there, owing to usual civilian non-efficiency. . . ." He drilled them for an hour. His new job brought special privileges: ". . . got permit to carry .45 Colt and travel anywhere on the Island at any time, day or night."

On Hawaii, both when Florence was present and after her departure, Ed, except for his period as a "recluse," led a social life far busier

ERB, third from left, interviewing officers involved with BMTC; left to right: Colonel Frank Steer, Lieutenant Colonel Goldsmith, ERB, Colonel Earl Bourland, Colonel Craig, and Brigadier General Tom Green.

and more varied than any he had followed on the mainland. Because of the island's position as a military outpost, it thronged with both army and navy personnel, and among these were a number of officers who became Ed's friends. One of the first he had met, soon after he had moved to the Niumalu Hotel, was Brigadier General Thomas H. Green, then executive assistant to the commanding general. Green actually occupied a post under martial law equivalent to that of governor of Hawaii. The Niumalu Hotel consisted of an informal arrangement of thirty cottages clustered around a central dining room placed among palm trees; this stimulated a friendly mingling among the guests.

In his association with the BMTC and his activities as a columnist, Ed visited General Green regularly at his office and accompanied him on inspections. At times, late at night, when Green had finished his duties, Ed came to see him and offer suggestions. Concerning the BMTC, Green recalled that most of the members were older men, and because many of these had "protruding" stomachs, the BMTC was nicknamed Opus Guard, *opus* being the plural for Hawaiian *opu*, "stomach" or "belly." After leaving Hawaii in 1943, Green kept in touch with Burroughs.[25]

Both Green and two of Ed's civilian friends, Sterling and Floye Adams, as residents of the Niumalu Hotel, remembered especially Burroughs' nightmares and how they disturbed and frightened the nearby guests. Green recalls being told by Ed that these nightmares supplied material for stories, a point that is still in dispute. This was supported by Sterling Adams, head of the FBI in Honolulu:

Those who resided close to Ed's shack recall numerous occasions when Ed would have wild nightmares and emit sounds not unlike his "Tarzan of the Apes." Afterwards, Ed would tell us that he actually dreamed up some of the characters and plots for his stories and would arise in the night and jot down notes while the thoughts were fresh in his mind. We always wondered if he was being factual. However, he was writing about one novel each year at the time and, having read one of his works of that period which he autographed, I can believe that the characters were born out of one of his nightmares.[26]

In an amusing contest involving coded messages, Burroughs pitted his ingenuity against that of the army, his friendly opponents being General Green and Colonel C. A. Powell of the Signal Corps. Burroughs launched the battle in September 1942 in response to a challenge sent by Green: the Signal Corps boasted it would need only fifteen minutes to decipher any message Ed could create. Naturally, there was a wager, two drinks, to be furnished by the loser. Ed was eager to win *any* contest, and his old research habits took over. In his diary on the fourteenth he wrote, "Tried to get books on Cryptology, but found Military Intelligence had withdrawn them all for the duration." He forwarded his "Undecipherable Cipher" to Powell, who unexpectedly sent one devised by the Signal Corps. On October 3, in a letter headed, "Subject: Two drinks," Ed conceded he was completely baffled by the coded message, but still artfully dodged the payment of the bet:

Before I pay 'em, I want to know if that thing you sent me is a bona fide message in cipher, or just a hoax.

The message in the Burroughs Undecipherable Cipher, which I handed General Green, and which you so far have been unable to decipher, is no hoax. Regardless of collusion and a barefaced attempt to confuse the issue, the General still owes me a drink. So far, he has put off paying it until I had gone on the wagon, and there was no more hard likker in town.

To Green, who was stationed at Iolani Palace in Honolulu, Ed, on the twelfth, noted that the Signal Corps had failed to decipher his message in the fifteen minutes they predicted: "... no proof of this has been forthcoming during the three weeks they have had it. ..." Nevertheless, Ed reported, he had "improved and streamlined" his system:

I am enclosing another message, with which you are at liberty to irk them. If they can't do any better with this than they have with the other, perhaps I have something the Army might use to advantage. It is unfortunate that there is such a shortage of hard likker, as otherwise you and I might drink off the Signal Corps for some time.

The "message" naturally was composed in Burroughs' favorite form — light verse:

The Signal Corps has little flags
Sometimes it wigs again it wags
I do not doubt that if they heed 'em
The Signal Corps can really read 'em
But what its cryptographers sigh for
Is the key to Burroughs famous cipher

On the sixteenth Powell replied, still with no indication that he had solved Burroughs' code, to explain that the Signal Corps message was no hoax: "We were merely trying to level the wager to more even terms, as we did not believe it fair for us to do all of the work. It is very easy to make a code, but not so easy to decipher with the small text on hand." Powell added that he was asking Ed to "break" his code "at the same time we slave over the so-called Burroughs Undecipherable Cipher." Since the Signal Corps code had been constructed to resemble Burroughs', Powell insisted it should be easy to solve.

While there is no record of whether the corps ever decoded Ed's message, on the twenty-first, in a letter to Colonel Powell, Ed surrendered:

. . . Having already given the best years of my life trying to decipher that. . . thing you sent me, I suggest that you drop in about 5 p.m. some evening soon and collect two drinks while I still have two drinks — which won't be long. Bring Green with you. He knows the way. I'd like to have you stay for dinner too.[27]

Again at the Niumalu Hotel, Ed formed a close friendship with another officer, Brigadier General Kendall J. Fielder, chief of military intelligence under General Short; Ed had originally contacted him in seeking a correspondent's identification card. Fielder, affectionately referred to as "Wooch" by his friends, had acquired this peculiar nickname while on the football team at Georgia Tech. It resulted from a newspaper error in a headline which was supposed to read, "Watch Fielder," but instead came out, "Wooch Fielder."[28] Fielder described the activities at the Niumalu Hotel:

. . . the residents. . . each night about eight would assemble in one of the cottages for a game of whiskey poker. When I could sneak off from my office at Fort Shafter I would join them. Ed loved these games with a passion. . . . he was the boss of the play and ruler on all technicalities.[29]

Because of the blackout and the curfew requirements, everyone but officials was to remain indoors, and card games, parties, and drinking became favorite pastimes. The liquor was rationed, but Fielder was able to bring unallotted bottles from the officer's club for the "whiskey" poker games. In noting that the group was "not a bunch of drunks" and that he had never seen them "get out of hand," Fielder commented, "Ed probably loved a drink as much as anyone and could hold quite a bit, but he rarely showed it much."[30]

In the summer of 1942 a friendship developed between Ed and Phil Bird, a lieutenant in the 64th antiaircraft brigade. On September 3, Bird wrote to express his appreciation for the courtesies Ed had shown him and the members of the brigade:

First, you honor us by speaking before our Intelligence School; then you send me a first edition, autographed copy of one of the best damn books I've read in a long time. . . . Not content with the above-mentioned, I have merely to mention the fact that I am having a three-day pass, and lo and behold there is a house with all the trimmin's — not to mention a guest card at the best club on that side of the island. . . .

Ed and Phil Bird began to see each other frequently; on one occasion, as he accompanied Bird to the Naval Air Base at Kaneohe, Ed was allowed to fire one round from a three-inch anti-aircraft gun. Later, the two men visited the 369th Negro Brigade, commanded by Colonel Hooper. To reciprocate, Ed, in preparing a radio script designed for a BMTC recruiting broadcast on KGU, wrote in a part for Bird. The program, on September 30, 1942, included Helen Hess, Gene Woodruff, Colonel Bourland, Lieutenant Bird, Sergeant Trinidad, and Burroughs.

Ed continued to channel his energies in two directions, on the drill field and tennis courts. That he had conquered his illnesses, at least temporarily, was demonstrated in his return to vigorous tennis playing, almost every day. But dissension had arisen over the BMTC program, with Ed angry about the treatment of this civilian group by the regular army. On March 18 he sent a protesting letter to Colonel Bourland, listing his complaints and at the same time resigning his position. Bourland at once rejected the resignation. Evidently, disparaging comments had been made about the BMTC's war role, for on March 21, Ed's diary reported, "At dinner Capt. May came to explain his remarks about me & B.M.T.C. I told him he was a louse. He is." The army's attitude toward the BMTC was a condescending tolerance or even a complete unawareness of its existence. Bird, in recalling how he met Burroughs, noted that the BMTC had come to the battery area and been refused entrance; upon calling his commanding officer to complain about the BMTC, Bird was informed that Ed was in charge. Irked, Bird went to Ed's office to discuss the matter. There, Bird's anger soon dissipated. They became friends and Bird remembers that Ed put his arms around him. But Bird still banned the BMTC from his battery area.[31] Acceding to Bourland's request, Ed remained with the BMTC.

Other matters requiring his attention included the property settlement with Florence, "received, signed and mailed" on March 23, and a new CBS program for the mainland to be beamed weekly on KGMB; Ed agreed to write the scripts and on April 1 completed the initial one. Hulbert, promoted to corporal several weeks before, was a photographer with the 7th Air Force at Hickam Field. Unhappy over his son's lowly rank, Ed, on March 25, wrote for the second time to General Henry H. Arnold in Washington; he urged the "reinstatement" of his son's ROTC commission that had been twice recommended, but never granted. He explained, "I am writing you without his knowledge or that of his commanding officer, whom I do not know. Under present conditions, it is necessary to send an officer with him on all his assignments. Rather a waste of man power...." On June 12 Hulbert received his commission as 2nd Lieutenant, but his father still outranked him. Ed's promotion to major in the BMTC had been granted earlier, on April 14.

Never one to be hesitant about expressing his opinions, especially on military matters, Ed, on March 9, addressed a letter to Senator Hiram Johnson; in it, he emphasized that as a legal resident of California he was writing Johnson about the peril facing the state as a result of the weak defenses at Hawaii. Because of the Australian "feint" by the Japanese, the Islands had been left "practically undefended." He noted that this was not the opinion of a civilian but of the experienced officers with whom he

was in contact. "I am informed that the island of Maui is defended by a single battalion; the Big Island, Hawaii, by a single regiment! It is these and the other outlying islands that the Japanese would first invade...." Few other civilians or officers would have presumed to dictate war policy, yet Ed laid down the precise requirements for the defense of the Islands:

...All the bombers and protecting fighter planes that can be accomodated on our present flying fields.... And in addition to these we need adequate reserves of both.... Our land forces here should be brought to full wartime strength and reinforced by several full divisions. We need much more mobile artillery than we have, and we need a great many more medium tanks....

It did not appear incongruous to Ed that a civilian, unacquainted with the complex global war problems faced by a nation that was forced, while unprepared, into a huge European-Pacific conflict, should dare to offer a complete Hawaiian defense plan to those whose knowledge of the situation far exceeded his.

In addition, he voiced his concern about the "enemy alien" groups on the Islands; these totaled 159,000, he claimed, and he pointed out that in two of the regiments, twenty-five percent of the enlisted men were of Japanese extraction. These, and all of the Japanese officers "should be evacuated to the Mainland." His susceptibility to the blind panic and prejudice of the period was revealed in his statements:

There may be many loyal citizens among them, but their staunchest supporters cannot tell which are loyal and which are not. They are in our armed forces, they are in our homes, they are employed within military and naval reservations. They are a Damoclean sword hanging constantly above our heads.

In closing, he expressed his conviction "that something must be done, and done immediately, if these islands are not to fall to the enemy...."

Varied news had been received from home. A telegram of April 28 from Rothmund must have evoked disturbing memories: Ashton Dearholt had died the day before. Rothmund also noted that the property settlement between Ed and Florence had been signed, and later the *Honolulu Advertiser* reported the granting of the divorce from Florence on May 4: "The young Mrs. Burroughs told the court that the sixty-eight-year-old author told her he considered their marriage a mistake." Happier news came with an announcement of the birth of a son to Jack and Jane on June 22, 1942. The choice of a name led again to Ed's favorite— John—the second in the Burroughs family.

Ed's dogged determination was illustrated in his tour of inspection with Major Frank Steere, Hawaiian Provost Marshall. On April 30, after driving into the hills, the two men walked through hazardous terrain to inspect gun emplacements, fox holes, and observation posts. Ed wished to survey the land in preparation for his planned BMTC exercises. He wrote in his diary, ". . . an interesting hike for a guy in his 67th year. I fell down three times and fell hard. I grabbed cacti for support and am still an animated pin cushion." But the 67-year-old "guy" was not the only one having trouble: "Steere fell twice and nearly fell a third time—into a four-feet deep machine gun nest. . . ."

Although Ed, through his military activities, had acquired many friends among the officers, during his sojourn on Hawaii, he had also formed numerous civilian friendships. Among these were the Pfluegers, Wayne and Mary; "Duke" and Lyda Willey; and Bill and Betty Mitchell. These and others had been deeply concerned about him during his illness. His friends at the Niumalu Hotel included Sterling and Floye Adams. Sterling, an FBI agent at the time, knew Ed well and corresponded with him for a number of years. He recalled the opportunity Ed had missed when Fred Biven, the manager of the Niumalu Hotel, tried to sell the property:

They were anxious to dispose of the hotel and spacious grounds for any reasonable fee— Biven once mentioned $250,000 as an accept- *able figure. A group of Ed's friends, all in moderate income brackets, sought to prevail on Ed to put up the money so that we might purchase this prize property. Ed, partly serious and partly in jest, stated he could ill afford such a venture with all the alimony payments he was making. This property now housing the Hilton Hawaiian Village complex is presently worth millions.*[32]

In listing others who had known Ed—Sue Brown and Henry Mahn, who were later married; Jack and Eleanor Jenkins, Peg Martin, Doctor Carden and his wife Midge—Sterling Adams recalled the poem Ed had written about the Niumalu group, titled "Heil Freddie:"

Grande Hotel de Niumalu-
On-the-Sewer beside the sea,
Where the idle wealthy wallow
In barbaric luxury.

The poem then goes on to list twenty-five first names of the hotel guests, and explains that the guests stayed because the hotel was so cheap.

Ed's impatience with the limited participation of the BMTC members had been steadily growing. In his intense patriotism he demanded an individual's complete dedication to the service of his country. His attitude is revealed in an article titled "Oahu: Singapore or Wake?" printed in the *Honolulu Advertiser*, May 19, 1942. Here, after noting the succession of Allied defeats and disasters, and praising the efforts of the armed forces, he assailed the civilian apathy: ". . . We're sitting on our fat tails and letting 'George do it.' . . . Right up to the present moment we have been licked. . . . We are still being licked. . . ." He berated the civilians: "This is an all-out war. Can't we ever get that through our thick heads? It was an all-out war for the boys who died here December 7. It was an all-out war for the boys who starved and died on Bataan and Corregidor. . . ."

"How much of your time are you giving without remuneration?" he inquired. "That is the measure of your patriotism, your loyalty, and your intelligence." He then turned to a blunt attack on the BMTC, explaining that because he was proud of the organization, he could not be accused of unfairness or prejudice; he commented upon the amount of time spent by BMTC members:

The most conscientious of them give an average of about twelve and a half percent. That is a long way from 100 percent, all-out effort. . . . There is a too large minority which gives little or no time. Having received their pistols and passes, they absent themselves from drills. They are the slackers. BMTC wishes to replace these with 100 percenters.

Oahu, he insisted, faced a serious danger, not only of being raided, but of an attempted invasion. Because of this, the BMTC should give at least eighteen hours weekly to training. In conclusion, he noted that Oahu's "place in history lies in our hands"; he asked, "Shall we go down in history as another Singapore or another Wake?"

The departure of Hulbert on September 7 for Air Force bases in the South Pacific as a documentary and combat photographer may have been one factor that drove Ed to a final decision about the BMTC. He was envious, wanted to be where the real war was occurring; the civilian Corps had become too much like playing at war. General Fielder commented, "As long as there was a job to be done, Ed was right in there, for he was a doer." But with the American forces now on the offensive, there was little danger of another Japanese raid. Fielder had recalled that Ed overtrained the BMTC members with too many long hikes and drills and too much emphasis upon rigorous calisthenics. Ed, as always, was a hard taskmaster. Fielder believed the group was "kept going too long and got to the point where some of the leaders were there for personal aggrandisement." By September 1942 it became evident that the BMTC had little function as a defense unit.[33]

Ed's desire for an active role in the war zone led him to a new goal; he sought now to be a war correspondent for the United Press. Meanwhile, the BMTC situation continued like a comedy of errors, with Ed resigning again (in a huff) on September 10. Colonel Bourland acted as conciliator and Ed accepted a new position as liaison officer. He was merely marking time, however, waiting impatiently for his correspondent's credentials to be issued. Help came from Frank Tremaine, head of the United Press in Hawaii, but Ed had also written to his old friend, George Carlin, of the United Feature Syndicate. On October 23, with the approval still not received, Ed wrote in his diary, "Am now all ready to go—almost. I know that, at my age, it is probably a fool thing to do. My decision, then, is not based on faulty judgement. I want the experience. If I don't come back, I am at least definitely expendable. So it won't make any difference. . . ." He also reported Hulbert's return from the Solomons where on Guadalcanal he had been under "every known brand of fire—ack-ack, Zeros, bombing, land artillery, and naval guns."

On November 2 Ed sent a thank-you letter to Carlin: the United Press credentials had arrived. Carlin responded, "Your example in always seeking fresh adventure at an age when most of your contemporaries are content to give up and just stay waiting is an inspiration to me and gives me a goal at which to aim." Quoting Ed's fervent statement—"I hope to God I can make good"—Carlin expressed his admiration for the humility with which Ed was tackling the assignment.[34] At a meeting with Tremaine, Hulbert, and others the discussion centered about where Ed should go. The consensus was that he should travel to New Caledonia first and then work back to the New Hebrides and Fiji Islands; they agreed he should write feature articles unless unusual spot news occurred.

Now an accredited war correspondent at the age of sixty-seven, Burroughs waited for his army approval and assignment to a plane. On November 6 he noted the start of his autograph album which he planned to carry with him. On the thirtieth, at the suggestion of Frank Tremaine, he completed an article reporting on a year of martial law in the Islands. Important announcements came through on December 4: Hulbert received a promotion to 1st Lieutenant, and Ed was informed that he would depart the next morning. To signal the start of his new duties, he initiated the first in a series of war diaries; this one, dated December 4, 1942, to January 19, 1943, would record happenings in New Caledonia and Australia. An entry of December 5 told of the plane trip and landing:

. . . . a G87 transport plane similar to B-24. . . eleven passengers—nine Lts., a civilian and I. . . passed autograph book around and then had to do a lot of autographing myself. . . ate four sandwiches. . . played bridge. . . landed at Canton Island. . . went right to Mess Hall and ate a big dinner. . . 28 miles around the island—one tree. No women. . . drinking from 4 to 9 p.m. Only 4 drinks per man. . . .

From Canton Island Burroughs was flown to New Caledonia, and at the capital city, Noumea, was astonished to discover an old friend. The naval lieutenant who sat down next to him at the officers' mess stared with disbelief, and so did Burroughs. Hal Thompson, Rochelle Hudson's husband, cried, ". . . what are you doing here?" Thompson, recalling the meeting and the fact that they did not immediately recognize each other, had some interesting memories:

ERB had aged considerably in the little over two years since we'd seen one another, and I had been badly wounded in the meantime. . . . I do recall an amusing incident: ERB was wearing a knapsack slung over one shoulder, and he said it contained all his valuables, and never left his side. He showed me the contents: five bottles of Scotch packed in a bed of socks and shorts. . . .[35]

Burroughs' continuing travels brought him to Sydney, Australia, on December 24, 1942, where he spent only a brief period, returning to New Caledonia on January 10, 1943. He had hoped to be flown back to Hawaii, but on January 30 was notified that he would return directly to Pearl Harbor on the destroyer *USS Shaw*. On the thirty-first, after boarding the ship, he discovered somewhat apprehensively that the *Shaw* had previously been stranded on a reef and badly damaged: "Temporary repairs had been made, but her keel was badly wrinkled, some of her plates were sprung, and she had holes in her bottom that had been patched up with concrete. And she had but one screw. The Shaw was practically a wreck. . . ." The captain's assessment was hardly reassuring; he told Ed that if the ship were to drop depth charges, fire the guns, or run into a bad storm, she might very well sink. "Some of the crew never laced their shoes during the whole cruise," Ed wrote, "except when we were in port. This and the fact that many of them wore black sox so as not to attract sharks, added zest to the voyage. . . ."[36]

In the long return trip the *Shaw* docked at Suva, in the Fiji Islands, then journeyed to Tutuila in the American Samoas, where Ed visited the town of Pago Pago and noted, ". . . I saw the Sadie Thompson hotel. Through the windows, I saw Sadie's room—or what might have been."[37] On February 28, aboard the *Shaw*, Ed wrote, "Jack's birthday — 30 years old. On Joan's birthday I was in Noumea. On Hulbert's, in Honolulu. I should like to be in Chungking on my next one."[38] The *Shaw* arrived at Pearl Harbor on March 2, and later, as expected, Ed completed a detailed account of the entire trip, requiring sixty pages to tell the whole story. Titled "The Diary of a Confused Old Man, or Buck Burroughs Rides Again," the account was begun in April 1943 and not finished until June 8. The ending summary revealed that army chaos had made Burroughs a noncorresponding war correspondent:

I had been gone three months, had a wonderful time, and written twenty-five stories, practically none of which have ever reached United Press. They have so notified Frank Tremaine, UP Bureau Chief in Honolulu. We think they may be mouldering in the War Department in Washington, where Colonel Stead asked me if he might send them direct.

Burroughs' treatment by the navy—they refused to recognize his army credentials or to accredit him as a navy correspondent — led him

ERB enjoys interviewing members of 112th U.S. Cavalry on Colonial Highway, New Caledonia, 1942.

to compose a second letter to Senator Hiram Johnson. For an undetermined reason, Burroughs decided not to mail the letter, but it is valuable for its explanation of his attitude and motives. Feeling ignored, rebuffed and insulted, he opened his attack on the navy by demanding that it be thoroughly investigated by Congress. In this letter of April 4, he insisted that the navy, through its actions, had aroused general antagonism. The situation was caused by the "autocratic attitude of high ranking naval officers."

He continued in withering terms to assail the navy's "fostering" of "egomania." Naval officers assumed they were endowed with greater intelligence than army officers and that "all civilians, are, by comparison, morons." He also scored the navy for its reluctance to make changes, for clinging to "the fetish of tradition."

After experiencing the blind, dictatorial policies of the navy in the Pacific Area, Ed returned with a deep resentment. He described instances of the navy's contemptuous treatment of correspondents, who were prohibited from traveling by air; because of this, Burroughs waited from October 21 to December 5 for transportation back to Hawaii. He noted the suppression of one of his dispatches because he did not have naval credentials, and reported, for the same reason, his exclusion from the Pearl Harbor Naval Base:

I called attention to the fact that Pearl Harbor is overrun by Orientals and that it was unwarranted to discriminate against a white American citizen in favor of people of alien blood and ancestry. Of course, I got nowhere.

Amusingly, a source of Ed's antagonism toward the Navy was its "unbelievably selfish attitude in the matter of liquor distribution." He complained bitterly that although the naval officers received a weekly allowance of three to four bottles of whiskey, the army and the civilians had been allotted none. He wrote indignantly, ". . . now the navy has made it an offense punishable by court martial for a navy officer to buy whiskey for an army or civilian friend." Most distressing was a report about 40,000 cases

of scotch and bourbon purchased on the mainland for the use of the army and civilians in Hawaii — these cases appeared destined to remain tantalizingly distant, since the navy refused to transport them.

Ed finally offered his solution to the problem: he advocated the elimination of the navy as a separate branch; there should be only the United States Armed Force with identical uniforms and ranks, and a secretary of the armed force would replace the secretaries of war and navy. In closing he wrote, "The foregoing might suggest that I hate the navy. I do not. . . . But there is something wrong with the navy as a whole; and because this is America, I have the right to say so to the end that whatever is wrong be discovered and corrected."

In one of his United Press stories, sent from the South Pacific and published in the newspapers, Burroughs voiced his objection to the policy of free mail for servicemen. His contention was that mail from home, an item of first importance to the soldiers, was being delayed because of the thousands of sacks of unnecessary letters that had to be delivered; he insisted that the free mail was an "ill-advised measure" that encouraged the sending of many unimportant letters. To his attack on the free mail service he added a critical view of the soldiers' spending habits: "The men have plenty of money. They can afford to pay full postage. . . . I have seen them shooting craps. Outside of a national bank, I have seldom seen more money. . . I have seen them paying five dollars for a 50-cent grass skirt. . . . on another island the men were paying one and two dollars a bottle for beer and twenty-five to thirty dollars a bottle for whiskey. . . I'm sure none of them would object to paying postage on letters home. Money means practically nothing to these boys."

In stressing that his only purpose was to halt the unnecessary mail so that a lot of "poor kids" could "hear from mom, or pop, or honey," he stated his objection to "well-meaning people who have banded themselves together to write to men they don't know, who don't give two whoops about receiving letters from them. All that these misguided souls do is clog the postal service. . . ."

His aggressive and controversial opinions did not go unnoticed. On March 17, 1943, three soldiers stationed overseas, after reading the article, used strong language to display their disgust with him:

. . . In the first place you should be ashamed to say such things about fellows who are overseas. I wouldn't even show my face in public after such a thing as you say.

When do you see the armed forces gambling in front of a bank, or paying such a high price for a drink? Haven't you any mercy for a friend or son or some relative that is in the service? . . . We have to pay insurance, laundry, taxes, and some allotments. So what do we have left to spend? Just enough to buy cigarettes, stationery, and go to a movie.

They closed explosively: "We just hope to see you some day, so we may give you our piece of our mind. You low down skunk, good for nothing." The letter was signed Pfc. Wm. F. Hovan, Pfc. Dallas Hebert, and Pfc. Edward F. Kelley.

On April 1 Burroughs sent his reply to the "Commanding Officer, Co. A, Replacement Bn.," enclosing the soldiers' letter and commenting:

You will note. . . that they hope to see me some day, that they may tell me some more of what they think of me.

This is an excellent idea, and I should be delighted if you would arrange a meeting at your convenience and theirs. It would be only fair to them and to me.

I am interested, because I hate to think that a single soldier should continue to doubt my friendship and interest in the enlisted personnel of our armed forces.

The months he had spent in the hazardous South Pacific area whetted Ed's appetite for adventure and excitement. His hope that he would soon receive permission from the army to return to the war zone was not realized and he waited in Honolulu, bored and restless. A year passed without any word, and he followed his normal activities of writing stories, corresponding with friends and relatives, and attending social functions. His interest in the military brought him new acquaintances among the top-echelon officers. The arrival of 1944 established a record for him — he had written no fiction since March 1943.

On February 16, 1944, he noted that his autograph books were a main source of interest; he was now using his fourth book and had recently "added Admiral Halsey and Harold Stassen" to his list of "victims," having spent an afternoon with them. He wrote, "I now have 572 autographs, and have met an average of thirty people a month whose names appear in my diary but not in my autograph book. . . ."[39]

Although he wrote no stories, he continued to produce articles on various aspects of the war, presenting his typically controversial views. The problem involving the large number of Japanese in the Hawaiian Islands had been a subject of heated discussion ever since Pearl Harbor. Burroughs had listened to many opinions and had sought to appraise the situation. In 1942-43 he was easily influenced by the irrational and prejudiced opinions of the period and, as a result, jumped to hasty conclusions. In an article titled "What Are We Going to Do about It?" probably written early in 1943, he was positive in asserting that the two sides of the controversy represented mere expediency versus true patriotism:

. . . what to do about the 159,000 people of Japanese descent now living in the Hawaiian Islands. . . . Non-Japanese residents are divided. On one side are those whose judgement appears totally eclipsed by dividends or politics. They are the wishful thinkers who shrink from losing the workers from the fields or the voters from the polls. On the other hand are the majority of the kamaainas, malahinis, and army and navy officers who shrink from losing the Islands. . . .

The statement, often heard, that newcomers, such as he, were offering uninformed opinions, brought a barbed retort: "some people do not require a lifetime to arrive at intelligent judgements." On the other hand, there was a day when people spent their entire lifetime on this planet and still thought the world flat." He made no bones about his doubts of the Japanese, "159,000 potential Fifth Columnists, 57,000 of whom are males of fighting age." Those dependent upon Japanese votes were the only ones who believed "that any considerable part of the Nisei would be wholly loyal to the United States in the event that Japan should attempt an invasion of the Islands." There is no question but that he was influenced by his associations with the military.

This defense of the Nisei was "so much optimistic propaganda" emanating from the Islands and Washington; those most responsible were the "powerful moneyed interests" in Hawaii who were largely dependent upon Japanese labor. Another factor was the great percentage of Nisei voters, and concerning the Islands' delegate to Washington, Sam King, Ed commented that the man's pro-Nisei attitude had resulted in his being called "Sampan" King. He quoted the view of a friend who had been educating young Japanese-Americans for many years and who, because he had "treated them as equals," had acquired their trust and confidence. He sought their opinions about Nisei loyalty:

They told him that 80% of the Nisei hoped that Japan would win. They said that they were like football fans standing on the side lines rooting for their team... under American domination they could never hope to hold other than minor positions in the business world, in addition to which they were socially ostracized. They believed that if Japan takes the Islands all that would be changed. As they put it, they would then be "top men."

Thus, Ed could predict the actions of the Nisei if the Japanese launched an invasion. Most of the Nisei had ROTC training, and at the Japanese language schools they attended, "it is doubtful that loyalty to America was any part of the curriculum." The Nisei were also abject followers of the doctrines of Shinto, described by Professor Sakamaki of the University of Hawaii as a "fake religion" which was really a "Japanese nationalist and propaganda cult," designed "to assist in Japanese military and economic domination."

The combination of Shinto philosophy and the natural resentment of the Nisei at the "social ostracism" would of course turn them against the United States. Ed insisted that not eighty percent, but one hundred percent of them, were "rooting for Japan." He referred to the title of his article in offering a solution:

But what is to be done about it? Many army and navy officers and responsible civilians believe that the entire 159,000 should be evacuated to the Mainland and American volunteers brought here to replace those evacuees essential to the carrying on of all vital economics of the Islands.

It would be a tremendous undertaking, but the Islands are worth the effort....

This solution, hastily and emotionally derived, was also supported by his contention that the recruiting of the Territorial Guard and BMTC had only one purpose — not to fight "in Australia or Iraq," but "right here on the Island of Oahu." His assumption was that these units would be engaged in a desperate battle against the Fifth Columnist Nisei in the not-too-distant future.

By the fall of 1943 he had begun to examine the problem more rationally. He now regretted his earlier comments, and his intention was to write another article analyzing the situation and proposing a solution. He prepared carefully, discussing the matter with civic leaders. In a November 3, 1943, memo he commented:

"Nisei Problem. Interviewed Edward W. Carden, President, Bank of Hawaii. He believes that the ideal solution of the Jap problem would be total liquidation of the race—world wide. A practical solution would be the voluntary

transfer of several thousand Nisei yearly to the Mainland, preferably the middle west. . . . He thought that intermarriage might eventually solve the problem, and called attention to the fact that many white soldiers were marrying Japanese girls. . . ."

A memo of November 19 reported an "hour's talk" with Cyril Damon on the Japanese question: "It is economically and physically impossible to deport all Japanese. . . . just a spark might be required to set off one of the worst race riots here that the US has ever known." If a Japanese were to spit on an American soldier, particularly one returning from the war front who might be "mentally irresponsible," this could lead to a riot. Damon spoke of the American attitude: ". . . our innate sense of superiority and our unconscious display of this feeling antagonizes all Orientals."

To George Waterhouse of the Bishop National Bank of Hawaii, Ed, on November 3, agreed that the first goal was *winning the war*. But he rejected the idea that post-war planning should be laid aside. That he had devised a tentative solution to the Nisei problem was evident in his reference to one that would not "engender bitterness and hard feeling" and might even be welcomed by many young Japanese-Americans. He was frank in revealing his uncertainty about whether this solution would work.

A first draft of his article, completed in December, was passed by army and navy censors, but Ed also desired the support of the Honolulu Chamber of Commerce. His description of the article to Frank Midkiff brought a dubious response; even a "tacit approval" appeared impossible without knowing the entire content of the article. But to Midkiff, on December 20, Ed admitted he had been mistaken: "At first this (solution) was difficult because of the bitterness of my feelings toward all things Japanese, but my research and investigation materially altered my attitude. . . ."

The 1,500-word article, titled "Our Japanese Problem," appeared in the magazine *Hawaii* on June 30, 1944. The change in Ed's attitude was demonstrated in his first reference to the 285,000 Japanese living both on the mainland and in Hawaii. "The question is, do these people present a really serious problem, or only an imaginary one?" Gone was the dogmatic tone and the crying of alarm about the Japanese menace. He proceeded at once to a humble confession:

My approach to the problem was colored by bitter prejudice. I believed that every person of Japanese ancestry should be deported, and not without reason. As long ago as 1935, on the occasion of my first visit to the Islands, the Japanese problem was one of the chief topics of conversation among whites of long residence here. They entertained two fears. One was political domination of the Islands by the Japanese. The other was that the Japanese would rise in a body and massacre the whites in the event of war with Japan.

Following this explanation of the sources of his prejudice, he made a complete refutation of his earlier opinions:

Yet weeks devoted to research and to discussion of the subject with the very few civic leaders who would discuss it at all have aroused in my mind a question as to the existence of a real postwar Japanese problem in Hawaii.

He then produced factual support: Despite the war, the Island Japanese *did not* "rise and massacre the whites"; the fear of domination by the Japanese because of their supposed high birth rate was dissipated by statistics indicating that this rate was declining; the impudence of a few young Japanese was of no importance; "The vast majority of the older Japanese, citizens and aliens alike, are cooperative and courteous — as they have always been."

He cited statistics on convictions for the various crimes; among the seven principal nationalities, including whites, in the Islands, the Chinese had the best record for fewest crimes of murder and manslaughter and the Japanese were second. In connection with all other crimes, the Japanese were revealed as the most law-abiding of the racial groups.

Ed commented on the claims of "resistance to assimilation": ". . . I assume [this] refers to social intercourse and inter-marriage. That cannot be justly charged against them without first proving that they have resisted assimilation more than we have, which is rather doubtful." He also scoffed at their "potentiality for harm"; they comprised only .002 percent of the United States' population. "If you lived in a community of five hundred people, one of whom was a Japanese, who might or might not be a loyal citizen, would you live in very great fear of him?"

As far as the Islands were concerned, with large numbers of Japanese employed as craftsmen, domestic workers, farmers, fishermen, proprietors of stores, auto mechanics, and plantation workers, "it would be economic suicide to deport all these people." He now revealed a state of uncertainty:

My research knocked my preconceived theories into a cocked hat. I approached the subject in the honest conviction that all Japanese should be deported after the war. I thought we were faced with a very serious situation. Now, I don't know. When one comes to analyze it, it doesn't appear very serious.

From an analysis of the issues he proceeded to divulge his solution, its basis to be found in the "many highly educated, brilliant and presumably loyal American citizens of Japanese descent — economists, scientists, doctors, lawyers, engineers." A number of these, he presumed, "would volunteer to go to Japan to install a system of government along democratic American lines, under the guidance of a United Nations commission, that would make Japan a decent neighbor in the community of nations." Under his plan others might later migrate "to the homeland of their forefathers in the knowledge that they could still enjoy the way of life to which they had been accustomed in America." These would consist of merchants, artisans, teachers and missionaries.

The solution, he maintained, was "definitely realistic," would benefit the United States, and might even be to the advantage of the Japanese-Americans. He urged that we not judge our Japanese citizens by those "Japs" we were fighting. *Ours* have been altered physically through "a couple of generations of American living," and are larger and better looking than those prisoners he saw in the South Pacific area. He believed that the Japanese-Americans were also "spiritually different." Those who volunteered to migrate to Japan would benefit in one important way: they would "escape from that discrimination with which all racial minorities in all countries have to contend, for they would constitute the ruling class of the country, backed, if necessary, by the armed forces of the United Nations."

Burroughs also expressed his admiration for the thousands of Japanese who were in Italy, "fighting and dying at the side of other Americans," and insisted that he could not "conceive of repaying them by disenfranchisement and deportation." His solution, to persuade the Japanese, both citizens and aliens, to return to their "homeland" was based on the assumption that the United States was not their country. He wanted them to enjoy the American way of life, to which they had grown accustomed, but in another country.

Here again, Burroughs was venturing into complex areas, often where sociological or psychological understanding was needed, to express his opinions. He had repeatedly described the views of mere fiction writers as valueless and had derided them for daring to intrude into the practical world and offer opinions on national events or politics — yet he chose to ignore his own advice.

In March 1944 the long waiting period came to an end. Through the efforts of a new friend, Brigadier General Truman H. Landon, commanding general of the 7th Bomber Command, Air Force, Ed once more journeyed to the war front. Leaving Honolulu on the twentieth, he flew to Tarawa in the Gilbert Islands, proceeding from there, a week later, to Eniwetok in the Marshalls, where he visited six atolls and many islands. He was an ob-

ERB interviewing Brigadier General Truman H. Landon, commander of 7th Air Force Bombers, Gilbert Islands.

server on two daylight missions, watched through a camera well as the 500-pound bombs dropped on Japanese installations, and shared the hardships of life in the field. To his friends Oscar Oldknow and Donald Jackson he sent details of his activities:

Had a swell time. . . . Lost six or seven pounds, got sunburned, rode in amphibious jeeps, picket boats, and a rubber raft. Got marooned twice in amphibious jeeps while attempting water jumps between islands — once for two hours, again for three. . . . The only thing about the trip I didn't like was doing my own laundry work. . . . God never intended me to be a laundress. . . .[40]

One of his greatest pleasures was in discovering his son Hulbert, now a captain, on Kwajalein Island. It was their first time together in a war zone.

Ed and General Landon worked together on the back-breaking job of digging an air raid shelter. About the general, Ed reported, "He stands in line with his mess kit at chow with everyone else, taking his turn." Expressing his

admiration for Landon, a "West Pointer with 6,000 hours flying time," Ed claimed, "He can fly any plane made, is also a bombardier and navigator."[41]

Ed found most amusing the occasions when he posed for photos with his arms around young "Micronesian belles" clad only in grass skirts. ". . . a young ATC pilot would yell at the jeep driver every time he saw a native woman without her shirt on; then we would all jump out and be photographed."[42]

After a stay on Kwajalein Island Ed's assignment was finished, and from Tarawa he returned on a hospital plane carrying wounded soldiers, arriving in Honolulu on April 24, 1944. He had flown 7,000 miles on the trip. He had continued his special war diaries filled with details of happenings in the war zones: *Diary #2* was dated January 19 to March 19, 1943; *Diary #3*, March 20 to April 5, 1943; and at a later period, *Diary #4*, Tarawa-Kwajalein, March 10, 1944, to February 1, 1945.

Ed resumed his civilian life and made plans for new stories. Items of interest included a note from George Carlin of United Feature Syndicate suggesting a future novel in which Tarzan would be pitted against the Japanese. Ed was not very receptive to the idea: ". . . it is something to think over, but for my own part I didn't like very much his previous experience in fighting the Germans in North Africa. . ."[43] However, by June 10 he had started writing such a story and on September 11, 1944, had completed *Tarzan and the Foreign Legion.* As a correspondent he was still receiving no cooperation from the navy; in a note to General Green he remarked, "Guess I have been on my last assignment. The navy (Admiral Nimitz in person) ordered me back from the Marshalls the last time I was out. . . ."[44]

The contrasting events of life, both happy and sad, were soon to be demonstrated in the inevitable birth-death cycle. On June 2, 1944, another son, Danton, was born to Jane and Jack Burroughs. On the eighth, Ed's brother George died at Fontana, California. George's retirement there had been part of his dream to live in his later years on a ranch and raise

ERB and Hulbert examining windmill washing machine an ingenious GI invented to take advantage of Pacific winds.

oranges and chickens. In a touching coincidence, Lew Sweetser, who had been George's closest friend for many years in Idaho, died the next day. The two men, inseparable in life, were also inseparable in death — their plans to be cremated together were carried out.

A ceremony which Ed found thrilling was reported by him in a long letter prepared in quadruplicate and sent to Carlin, Weston, Oldknow, and Jack Burroughs. It was a special assembly and review, in July 1944, in honor of a visit to Honolulu by President Roosevelt and General MacArthur.

Some weeks later Ed turned again to the controversial Japanese problem, this time spurred by the actions of the Nevada representatives at the American Legion convention in Chicago. A statement in the *Honolulu Advertiser*, written by Jazz Belknap, was severely critical of the resolution introduced by Nevada at the convention; Nevada demanded that the Legion support national legislation to deport all alien Japanese at the close of the war. Ed had lost some of his previous uncertainty and was now ready to take an aggressive, forceful stand. In his article, printed in *Hawaii*, September 1944, he voiced his approval of Belknap's criticisms: "... (he) and I see eye to eye in this matter, and we both see red that any American should suggest that the parents of men who volunteered to fight in our armed forces should be deported. ..." He spoke of the

War on Venus	22,044	
The Living Dead	20,030	
The Fire Goddess	20,280	
Captured on Venus	23,600	
	85,954	
Escape on Mars	21,415	
Black Pirates of Barsoom	19,880	
John Carter & the Pits of Horz	20,000	
	147,249	
Tiger Girl	20,801	
Men of the Bronze Age	20,738	
Hodon and O-aa	20,727	
	209,515	
Beyond the Farthest Star	21,574	
	231,089	
Invisible men of Mars (Nov 24th)	21,489	
	252,578	*545,356*
Tarzan and the Castaways	37,209	289,787
	XXXXXX	
Tangor Returns (Dec 21 1940)	20,695	20,695
	XXXXX	310,482
Misogynists Preferred (Jan 8 1941)	4,000	4,000
	XXXXX	314,482
Wizard of Venus (Oct 1941)	19,836	
I am a Barbarian (Sep 1941)	65,000	
Skeleton Men of Jupiter (Nov 1941)	22,000	
More Fun! More People Killed! (Mar 1943)	20,727	
Uncle Bill (May 1944)	1,787	
Tarzan and "The Foreign Legion" (Sep 1944)	80,000	209,350
	XXXXXX	523,832
Savage Pellucidar (87-4) Oct 1944		20,000
		543,832

ERB's tabulation of stories he wrote in Honolulu during four-year period.

Japanese-Americans he had recently met and "how very fine and American" he found them. His article (titled "What Price Tolerance?") ended with a demand for national legislation that would award automatic citizenship "to the alien parents of any man who served honorably in the armed forces. . . provided they qualify in other respects."

At the Bel-Air, California, home the problems relating to Emma Burroughs had grown steadily worse. The shock of the separation and divorce had plunged her into periods of heavy drinking. As her health deteriorated, she required treatment by doctors both at home and in various institutions. Emma's inability to handle her financial affairs and her tendency to spend money foolishly led to a strict supervision by her son Jack and Rothmund. The family, having heard that Christian Science could aid in the cure of alcoholism, tried to interest Emma in the faith, but without success.

On November 5, 1944, Emma died unexpectedly of a stroke. Understanding the misery and suffering she had endured as a victim of alcoholism, Ed viewed her death as an escape from an agonized life. To Weston and Ted Landon he noted, "It was a relief, as her condition was hopeless. . . ." He was granted a forty-five-day travel order by the army and Hulbert received a thirty-day leave; on November 17 they boarded the same plane for a return to the States. It was the first Christmas in eleven years that Ed had spent with his children and grandchildren. Also at the family gathering were grandchildren James Michael Pierce and Joanne Pierce and two grandsons (Jane's and Jack's) that Ed was seeing for the first time. The home stay, however, produced a compli-

ERB working on story at Honolulu office, November 21, 1941; in this office ERB wrote most of the stories he sent to his secretary-manager Ralph Rothmund, Tarzana, for retyping and submission to magazine editors.

cation he had hardly expected. At the end of December he underwent surgery for a hernia, and a month of convalescence followed.

While in California Ed visited with Florence and Caryl Lee. Florence had remarried; her husband, Dr. Alfred Chase, was a physician who had treated both Ed and her. In recalling the meeting with Ed — they had lunch at Perino's — Florence remembered that he looked robust and handsome in his uniform and that he greeted her with a "big bear-hug." They met only once, and she never saw him again. Ed returned to Hawaii on February 3, 1945, with Hulbert arriving there ten days later.

Soon after Florence and the children had left Hawaii and returned to the mainland, Ed began writing letters to Caryl Lee, for whom he had developed a deep affection. That he wanted very much for her to retain his name

was evident from the start of the correspondence when he addressed her as "Miss Caryl Lee Burroughs." In October 1942, after Florence had married Dr. Chase, Ed inquired, "Are you going to change your name again, or keep mine? I should like very much to have you keep it, if you care to." A month later, after receiving a letter from her, he noted, "I see that you have changed your name. Nevertheless, you will always be Caryl Lee Burroughs to me." At that time, Caryl, about ten years old, had probably been instructed to use the name of "Chase."

Ed's eagerness to have Caryl use his name was evident even two years later when, on January 15, 1944, he wrote, "You seem to have a bad time trying to remember to sign your letters to me, Caryl Lee *Burroughs*. You don't have to use my name if you don't want to. You said that you did. My feelings won't be hurt

Thanksgiving photo of entire family at Joan's home in Sherman Oaks, 1945; front row, left to right: Hulbert Burroughs, John Ralston Burroughs, and James Michael Pierce; second row, left to right: Joan Burroughs Pierce, Jane Ralston Burroughs (John C. Burrough's wife), Jane's son Danton, ERB, and ERB's granddaughter, Joanne Pierce; back row, left to right: John Coleman Burroughs, Marion T. Burroughs (Hulbert's wife), and James H. Pierce.

either way. Just keep on loving me, as I do you." The following month he chided her, "I am glad that you want to keep my name, but I think you should learn how to spell it. It is *not* Bourroughs. You should know that."

The correspondence, maintained throughout the years that Ed spent in Hawaii, included his letters to Caryl when he traveled, as a correspondent, to the war zones. His persistence in writing to her — most of the effort was on his part — revealed an anxiety or even a fear that they might lose touch with each other. He often sent her presents:

Did you get the grass skirt. . .? Am sending you this enclosed check for your birthday. . . a few little things by parcel post. . . souvenirs of my trip South. . . the pikake necklace is made of shells gathered and strung by ex-cannibals of the Fiji island of Vita Levu, where I acquired it. . . there is also a so-called Australian "black opal" that I picked up in Sydney. . . . The little sea horse was made by natives of Vita Levu from the shell of a tortoise. . . enclosed is a little Christmas remembrance. . . .

On August 4, 1943, Caryl revealed that she was attending the private Marlborough School for Girls. In his response Ed's main concern was that she might become too "snobbish." He cautioned, "Don't let it change you any. There are lots of fine girls whose parents cannot afford to send them to private schools. Because you will be going to one, don't let it give you the idea that you are better than they. : . ."[45]

At school, Caryl persisted in listing her last name as "Burroughs," contrary to the wishes of her mother. The strong attachment between Caryl and Ed, her tendency to view him as her only father, created conflict at home. In recalling her adoption by Dr. Chase, who had the kindest of intentions toward her, Caryl noted the bitter contest that ensued: "I didn't want him to adopt me. . . said something like hell, no, in court. . . I was supposed to have some choice, but actually had none. . . got adopted anyhow."[46] The rebellion that characterized her actions caused her to have little motivation for any schooling. Her brother Lee was also an indifferent achiever at school. At this time Caryl developed an interest in horses; her fascination with horses and dogs would strongly influence her future life. She remembered how, in her defiance of her mother and adopted father, she refused to stay home but would spend her days at the horse barns in Burbank. Amusingly, she also described, as part of her rebellion against her luxurious home, the hobby she deliberately chose, collecting skulls.

Burroughs, following his return to Honolulu, resumed writing his "Laugh It Off" column. His 1945 diary noted on the twelfth the report of President Roosevelt's death and on May 8 the announcement of V-E day. The columns in the magazine *Hawaii* contained the typical chatty comments about war, politics, and other matters. Surprisingly, in a "Laugh it Off" column, written on April 14 (*Hawaii*, May 1945), Ed included strong praise for a Democrat, President Truman:

Since he was nominated for the vice presidency it has become the fashion to belittle him. He takes office with two strikes on him.

I was studying a newspaper portrait of him yesterday. His is a strong, intelligent, pleasant face. It is the face of a man one might intuitively like and trust. All my life I have been a Republican, but I cut that portrait out of the Advertiser and pinned it on my wall, something I have never done with the portrait of any other president.

Ed's admiration for Truman, the blunt-speaking, rugged individualist, was easy to understand; this type of independence and even the tendency to be "cantankerous" was something Ed respected.

In the same issue Ed referred to his "consistent" disappointment in the *Encyclopaedia Britannica* because of the information it omitted. In his past research on Indians he had been unable to find a reference to the Yaquis of Mexico. He also recalled his interest in writing a biography of the famous soldier of fortune,

General Christmas, and his perusal of the *Britannica* account about the general — an account which reported Christmas' death, when he was very much alive. Ed wrote, "The latest edition ignores the general completely. The compilers evidently felt that a man who wasn't dead when they said he was did not deserve immortalization."

Ed also responded angrily to an accusation made by George Seldes, editor of *In Fact*, "An Antidote for Falsehood in the Daily Press." The April 2 issue of the publication, in an article headed "Writer Aids Nazis," referred to a "Laugh it Off" column in the *Honolulu Advertiser*; Seldes wrote that Burroughs, "creator of Tarzan, as imbecile a piece of fiction as ever appealed to morons, not only attacks our ally Russia, but suggests that as soon as America is through with the Japanese it would be a good thing to fight Russia." Seldes commented,

Technically this is not treason. The U.S. Govt. in its pamphlet "Divide and Conquer" exposes all those engaged in attacking one of our allies — Britain, China, Russia — as aiding the enemy. Mr. Burroughs was investigated by certain of his colleagues who have aided the OWI.

Ed caustically evaluated Seldes as a journalist who was "right on his toes every minute." The article being criticized by Seldes had appeared in the *Advertiser* on October 21, 1942; "Mr. Seldes, always on the ball, discovered it about two years and six months later." Ed continued, "But either Mr. Seldes never saw the article or he is afflicted with ideological astigmatism, for I did not suggest that it would be a good thing to fight Russia at any time. That statement is an unequivocal lie. As a matter of fact, I said many nice things about Russia." Seldes' statement, Ed insisted, was libelous, but a law suit was not being contemplated for at least one good reason: ". . . I should have to go to New York, the whole proceedings would cost a great deal of money, and about all I could hope to get out of it would be an apology and several soiled collars." He added that it was "rather stupid" of Seldes "to

imply that Tarzan readers are morons." This was an insult to millions of Americans, "many in the armed forces, who have loved Tarzan books."

In a letter to Rothmund about the same matter Ed noted that the accusation of "attacking one of our allies" might better apply to Russia. He referred to his original article, "Whatsoever a Man Soweth," which opened, "Russia reproaches us. She reproaches us for the paucity of aid we have given her." The remainder of the article assailed Russia for her subversive attempts in this country. The American people have chosen their own form of government: "They do not wish Communism, and they demand that in the future Russia leave them alone." This insistence that Russia stop her propaganda efforts in the United States led Ed to hint at the possibility of a future war:

Before one plane or one bullet was sent to the aid of Russia, we should have demanded this assurance from the Russian government. If such assurance was not demanded and received, then some day we shall have to fight to win it. That would be tragic; for we like the Russian people, and we do not want to fight them.

Seldes' accusation seemed to be based on this statement and had some substance behind it.

The discussion of Seldes and Russia contained in the letter to Rothmund, April 24, 1945, was concluded with a comment to the Burroughs stenographer at Tarzana, Mildred Bernard. Some three years earlier the FBI at Honolulu had come to see Ed. He had noted the visit in his diary: "It was about *Mildred* who had been reported as saying the President ought to be shot. After talking with me, they said they would drop the matter." Referring to Seldes' charge, Ed added, "I, too, have been investigated and by my 'colleagues'!"

His "Laugh it Off" columns for May and June 1945, in *Hawaii*, included another vigorous attack on the "Japanese Exclusion League" and even a semihumorous plan for postwar Germany. On April 15, 1945, under the heading "What to Do With Germany," he noted that every "knucklehead" had a plan, so he would not hesitate to offer his. He disapproved Morganthau's suggestion as being too "sadistic" and argued that the Burroughs scheme was "far more subtle": "I would make Germany a Jewish republic. . . . Under this plan Jews who thought they were getting the worst of it could move to Germany. . . ." He pointed out, however, that not all Jews would move, because "all Jews are not fond of Jews." He based this opinion on a statement by a Jewish friend, made in the late '30s; the man, when asked to subscribe to a fund to get the Jews out of Germany, declared, ". . . he would subscribe twice as much. . . just to keep the Jews in Germany, . . . three times as much to send American Jews to Germany, and. . . double that if they would send his relatives to Germany."

Ed conceded there was "danger" even in his plan: "The Jews are a clever race. That is one reason why they are disliked by less clever people. They would build up a rich and powerful nation that would need 'living room.' Then up pops a modern Joshua, and — bingo!" His view was that all races would follow the same pattern of discrimination once they became dominant, and he cited the situation in Liberia, with the Negroes' mistreatment of the "indigenous tribes," as an example of this. The only solution was for someone to "pop up with a plan to change human nature."

Ed's three-month's visit to California had created in his personal life a situation with all the elements of a new romance. His seriousness about this attachment worried Jack, who on April 9, 1945, sent a lengthy letter to Hulbert; it contained information and a plan of action:

Off the record — There are reasons which make me believe O.B. is contemplating another marriage. The object of his present affliction is, I think, the person whom he met on his recent visit here and with whom he managed to spend no little time. I can see nothing but trouble and unhappiness here again for him if he follows through with this idea, which I'm
sure is in his mind. Now, for the first time in years, he is free of worry — financial or otherwise.

Jack, commenting on his father's improved condition, praised Hulbert and Rothmund for "all this good work," which he feared might be "destroyed": ". . . if he marries this person, there is little likelihood that he could stand another marriage like his last."

Jack's proposal, in part, was that his father be "sidetracked temporarily from his almost fanatic desire" to return to California, where presumably he might decide to get married. "The longer we can stall him," Jack wrote, "the more certain he will be to cool off in regard to this. . . woman over here." Hulbert, in his reply of the seventeenth, registered incredulity: "If what you say is true, I give up!" During the visit at home with his father he had noticed "that the old biological urge had been stimulated in O.B.," but he had not viewed the involvement as a serious one:

From my conversations with OB over here I felt certain that he was through with marriage forever. He said he was interested only in what he called "innocent flirtations," but certainly not marriage. You have not given me enough information as to why you think he is contemplating another fiasco for me to discuss this thing intelligently.

Hulbert rejected any scheme that would resort to subterfuge; he insisted, "I prefer to ask OB outright what his intentions are. And if they confirm what you say, I shall speak quite frankly and to the point."

Some weeks later it became evident that Jack's fears were well founded: Ed was considering another marriage. A letter from him to his children, asking for the return of certain shares of stock in the corporation so that he could retain control "purely for sentimental reasons," was interpreted quite differently by Hulbert. He commented to Rothmund, "I did . . . wonder why he had suggested this, knowing as he did that certainly none of his offspring would ever use our shares to the detriment of the business. A recent letter from Jack suggests the grave possibility that he may be contemplating another marriage. . . . Conversations with him here on the subject — in an objective vein — indicate that he is not opposed to another marriage and that it is his own damned business. . . ." Hulbert believed that his father's effort to regain the stock was motivated by a concern that his children, through combined action, might move to drastically reduce his income so that a marriage would be impossible.[47]

The attempts by his children to convince him that his marriage plans were irrational, especially with the woman he had in mind, aroused Ed's ire. In a letter of angry protest, forwarded in triplicate, he wrote, "I have never sought to interfere in your private lives or dictate whom you might or might not have as friends. But I have a well grounded conviction that one or more of you have not accorded me a like courtesy. And I deeply resent it." He went on even more bluntly, "Until a competent court has judged me a mental incompetent I shall continue to choose my own friends and live my own life. I grant you the same right."[48] He reminded them of their mistakes — "None of you is in a position to throw stones" — while admitting, "I have done many fool things and shall probably continue to do so. . . ." But he would not tolerate any "invasion" of his "personal rights."

Any serious thoughts of marriage were apparently dissipated as the passing days brought an unanticipated privilege. In the midst of his boredom — he complained that life was "pretty much in a rut" — the navy displayed a change of attitude. Unaccountably, he was accepted as a correspondent for the navy, and on May 25, 1945, embarked from Pearl Harbor on the *U.S.S. Cahaba*, a fleet oiler commanded by Captain Burnbaum. He described activities aboard the ship and the procedures in fueling destroyers, cruisers, carriers, and battleships, his dispatches for the United Press appearing in various newspapers.

On the two-month cruise the *Cahaba* stopped at the Ulithi Atoll in the Caroline Islands, where Ed went ashore and was shot at by a sniper. From a navy gig he watched a kamikaze flier dive directly into a nearby ship. In returning by air, his pilot for the first part of the trip, to Guam, was Lieutenant Tyrone Power. In all, Ed flew 5,000 miles, covered 11,000 miles on the cruise, and arrived at Honolulu on July 15. The articles reporting his experiences were printed in the *Advertiser* in July and August.

Soon after his return he faced a health problem; his diary noted the symptom of trouble in the future: "July 23 Angina Pectoris, or whatever it is, hurts like hell today. . . ." On August 10 came the important announcement, relayed by Hulbert from Hickam Field: the war was over. The official date in Hawaii was the fourteenth, and at the Niumalu a lively celebration began. With Ed were the Willeys, Hulbert, and his fiancée Marion Thrasher. The revelers later adjourned to the home of Louise Rogers, an island realtor. Ed wrote, "Feel fine this morning. We had another celebration at Willeys."

Ed also had an unexpected experience with the police. As he started to back his car into a stall in a parking lot, the place was snatched from under his nose by another motorist. Angered, Ed called the man a name and in other strong language ordered him to get out. His diary entry of the seventeenth reported the consequences:

About 10:30 two policemen came in a police car and arrested me. They took me to the police station. Phil [Bird] & Lt. Middleton followed in Phil's car. I was booked and posted $25.00 bail.

Inclined to view the whole affair as a joke, he added, "We had a good time, and it was like old home week." However, in court the next day his attitude was quite different. He pleaded not guilty to the charges the man had preferred against him, and the trial was set for the twenty-second. "It was very humiliating," Ed wrote. At the scheduled trial Ed was advised by the prosecuting attorney and bailiff to "walk out"

ERB interviewing Japanese captive, Mayor Meyasato Sieii of Zamama Shima, Kerama Retto; left to right: Mayor Sieii; interpreter, Private Shigemii Yamashita of Honolulu; Colonel Roamer W. Argo; Captain F. A. Rhoads, USN; and ERB.

and forfeit his bail, since a group of reporters was waiting and adverse publicity would undoubtedly result. Ed took this advice and the matter was dropped.

In the meantime Hulbert had received orders to return to the mainland and in a radiogram to ERB announced his discharge as a major in the air force. The action that followed was not unexpected. Marion arranged to return home at once to marry Hulbert. Ed, in turn, began his own packing, but his angina attacks now were more severe. On September 13 he noted, "Took a codeine tablet and a sleeping pill. . . . I am having these attacks too frequently and wish I were home." A few days later, after treatment by Dr. Carden, he was ordered to bed, and a nurse, Miss Wilson, took charge of him. The seriousness of his condition was evidenced in his confinement to bed for

more than a month. Toward the end of October he was sufficiently recovered to make final preparations for his departure. On the twenty-eighth he shared farewells with a host of friends, boarded a plane, and landed the next day at Hamilton Field, where he was greeted by Jack and Lieutenant Middleton.

The return to a civilian life in a postwar world was revealed in his diary entry of November 4:

House-hunting. Finally found something that will do nicely until I can build. The prices are outrageous — $15,000 for a 2-bedroom house on ½ acre. Later: Got it for $14,000. Hully bought a house.

At the year's end, on December 26, Ed moved into his new home at 5465 Zelzah Avenue, Encino.

THE INVISIBLE WHEEL OF DEATH by Don Wilcox

See BACK COVER

AMAZING

STORIES

JANUARY 20c

JOHN CARTER
AND THE
GIANT OF MARS
by EDGAR RICE
BURROUGHS

HAMILTON ★ CABOT ★ O'BRIEN ★ HARRIS

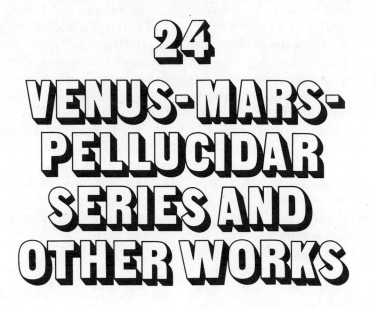

24
VENUS-MARS-PELLUCIDAR SERIES AND OTHER WORKS

In the fall of 1938 Burroughs had resumed his inner-world series, this time in the 60,000-word novel *Land of Terror*, whose main character, David Innes, appears to wander aimlessly about this prehistoric land. The plotless story, mainly a succession of perils, produces the usual bizarre races. The warrior women of primitive Oog — as in the past, Burroughs enjoys his slapstick scenes about huge hairy women who dominate their effeminate men — are given such names as Rhump and Fooge. Innes also encounters the mad Jukans; the man-eating giants of Azar; and in the way of monsters, gigantic ants with bodies six feet long. Captured by one of the creatures, he is dragged down into a chamber beneath a huge anthill, where, in the nick of time, he is rescued by a colossal ant bear, as large as an elephant; inserting its powerful tongue into the subterranean chamber, the antbear licks up the enormous insects. Adventures with the black Ruvans and their erratic floating islands com-plete David Innes' wanderings.

Completed on April 17, 1939, *Land of Terror* received its most accurate evaluation from A. Worthington Post, *Argosy* editor who succeeded Chandler Whipple. The story was not sent to Post until September 29, and in rejecting it Post wrote:

. . . I think you will agree that the development is distinctly haphazard, consisting as it does of little more than a series of escapes, captures and rescues. Too, the lack of a constant menace and of sustained suspense; the fact that David has almost no definite objective at the outset, and that later his whole aim is simply to get out of the trouble he has gotten so aimlessly into; the abrupt appearance and disappearance of various more or less principal characters — all these only to help to increase the disjointed effect of the narrative.[1]

Post also noted the novel's lack of originality: "Smaller touches and scenes are almost duplicates of similar situations from earlier Burroughs yarns published in Argosy. The ending left a great many loose threads and seemed inconclusive...."[2] A rejection also came from *Blue Book,* with Kennicott writing, "... war fiction will supply enough of the terror element ... non-war material should afford the reader some sweetness and light and variety...."[3]

Burroughs was surprisingly candid in his agreement with Post: "I think you are entirely right. I had exactly the same feeling while I was writing the story, but for some reason I didn't seem to be able to do anything about it."[4] However, he at once diagnosed the cause of his problem, not only with *Land of Terror,* but with other mediocre works of this type. "Perhaps the trouble is that it is one of a series which should have been concluded with the last story instead of trying to carry on without any logical reason." Burroughs, in these later years, was writing without inspiration, doggedly grinding out stories for whatever market he could find.

Because of limited outlets and recent rejections he had lost much of his earlier confidence. He made an offer to Post that years before would have been inconceivable: "If you think some one on your staff could whip it into shape, I will be glad to consider a plan to that end...."[5] On October 19 Post replied that while he would like to revise the manuscript, under his present staff conditions he could not undertake the task.

Meanwhile, Burroughs had forwarded *Land of Terror* to Leo Margulies at Popular Library. On November 24 Margulies returned the story, noting it was unsuited for *Thrilling Wonder Stories.* His criticism resembled Post's: "... a continuity element is lacking. There's really no plot... the entire thing being developed by a series of incidents and adventures. Result — the suspense needed to generate interest in a serial is lacking." Margulies also observed that the "scientific highlights" of Pellucidar were only fleetingly touched. He believed that the last seventy-six pages were "fairly appealing,"

and these might be revised into a twenty-thousand word novel. If the story was not sold elsewhere, he would consider it again: "I'll buy the chunk I like...."

Rejections by Editor Raymond Palmer of Ziff-Davis Publications, January 2, 1940, and *West Magazine,* January 23, completed the unsuccessful record of *Land of Terror*; although it never appeared in a magazine, on May 1, 1944, it was published as a book by Edgar Rice Burroughs, Inc.

While *Land of Terror* was still in progress, Ed devised another project and proceeded to sound out both Kennicott at *Blue Book* and Byrne at Munsey's to obtain their reactions. He spoke of writing four fifteen-to-twenty-thousand-word Tarzan stories in 1939:

I have in mind combining the Northwest Mounted Police and super-sleuth ideas, and making Tarzan something of a jungle Sherlock Holmes. In each story he would solve a mystery, such as the murder of a Colonial official; or a search for a royal big-game hunter, who has become lost; or a diamond shipment that has been stolen; or perhaps the apprehension of a white-slaver who had stolen a girl, and the rescue of the girl.[6]

He felt that Tarzan's "superman characteristics" and his facility in uncovering clues — turning Tarzan into a detective — might provide a fresh twist to the old plots.

The contemplated new role of Tarzan as a jungle detective, proposed so enthusiastically by Burroughs, was viewed by the two editors with the mildest of interest. Aware that a high price would be demanded, they were also painfully aware of low magazine sales and strained finances. Kennicott, on the sixth, observed that Tarzan's popularity in the strips and movies had produced an adverse effect upon the magazine stories; in the newer media Tarzan was fresh and appealing, while in magazines the novelty had "worn off." He admitted that Ed's idea might improve reader interest, but emphasized that *Blue Book*'s top price was $500

652

"in these degenerate days." From Munsey, where matters were chaotic, came an offer of two cents a word.

Nevertheless, Ed launched his project, described as the "New Tarzan Series." He quickly wrote the 16,000-word "Murder in the Jungle," January 10 to 18, 1939, and followed with "Tarzan and the Champion," July 17 to mid-August, 1939. Abandoning his plan to produce four stories, he finished the series at Honolulu with the 37,000-word "Tarzan and the Castaways," November 26 to December 13, 1940. Apparently, with this last novel he also turned away from his concept of an under-20,000-word series.

"Murder in the Jungle" did feature Tarzan acting as a detective. The story centers about his evaluation of various clues, first when an Italian aviator is found dead in his plane and the wound in his throat indicates that the bullet came from above, or, as Tarzan concludes, from another plane. One of Tarzan's assets as a sleuth is his sense of smell, and when the wind carries the strange odor of gasoline to him, he discovers a second wrecked plane, but in this case the pilot had bailed out.

Toward the end of the story Tarzan sniffs the breeze to detect the odor of a dead man, which is coming from a camp, and with the discovery of the body of Lieutenant Cecil Giles-Burton, the murdered British pilot, he proceeds to interpret the clues that lead to the killer. The detective story, with its requirement for an original plot, subtle devices, and a surprising dénouement was not Burroughs' forte. His problem was compounded by the fact that the jungle offered too limited a setting for a murder mystery, and Tarzan, because of his typical, restricted associations, had little opportunity to do any real detecting.

In marketing "Murder in the Jungle" Ed's first submissions, as in the past, were to the high-paying magazines, *Liberty*, *Collier's*, and the *Saturday Evening Post*. The successive rejections came in February and June, 1939. When Munsey also returned the manuscript in August, the only remaining outlet was Margulies' Popular Library. After holding the

story for several months, Margulies, on October 25, gave an evaluation and a conditional acceptance. He had hoped that the first Tarzan story to appear in *Thrilling Adventures* would be "full of Tarzan." Instead, as his letter revealed, in Ed's original manuscript Tarzan entered the story late and was referred to as "The Stranger," apparently a misdirected attempt to make a "mystery" out of the easily identifiable Tarzan. Noting the story was unacceptable "in its present shape," Margulies wrote:

... I took the liberty of turning it over to one of our editors for a revision job. It was revised according to what we think a Tarzan story — and this particular story — should be like. ... Naturally, I cannot take the liberty of using our version unless it receives your okay. ... most of the changes have been made in rearranging the story, and making Tarzan a much stronger and more prominent character. ...

Margulies also "rearranged" the title to "Tarzan and the Jungle Murders."

Ed promptly accepted the Margulies version, except for some corrections of errors in the names of animals.[7] The payment of $300 was only two cents a word. The story appeared in *Thrilling Adventures* in June 1940.

In the second of the series, "Tarzan and the Champion," the main character, One-Punch Mullargan, heavyweight champion of the world, chooses to take his vacation in Africa and hunt big game. Mullargan, "a notoriously dirty fighter," is an ignorant, stereotyped New York pug who communicates in broken English or "Brooklynese." He carries his indifference to sportsmanship to the jungle where his idea of hunting is to pursue zebras and elephants in an automobile and blast them with a machine gun. Naturally he runs afoul of Tarzan; in the fight that ensues, the world champion finds he is no match for the ape-man.

Later, when the two men have been captured by the Babango cannibals, Tarzan is outraged by Mullargan's statement about the suffering, wounded beasts: ". . . they're only animals. We're human bein's." In answer, Tarzan presents Burroughs' familiar philosophy:

"*. . . You are worse than the Babangos. You had no reason for hunting the zebra and the elephant. You could not possibly have eaten all that you killed. The Babangos kill only for food, and they kill only as much as they can eat. They are better people than you, who will find pleasure in killing.*"

At the story's end, when Joey Marks, Mullargan's manager, offers Tarzan "one hundred G's" to return to New York and become a prizefighter, Tarzan merely stalks away.

With the writing of this story Burroughs quite evidently discarded his plan to create his jungle-sleuth series; in the brief, 10,000-word story there is no murder and Tarzan does no detecting. The unsuccessful "Jungle Murders" had taught Burroughs that the task was impossible. After the expected rejections from *Liberty, Collier's*, and the *Saturday Evening Post*, "Tarzan and the Champion" traveled to editor Post at Munsey's where it received a criticism that had been offered before. The early tales centered always around Tarzan: "He was menaced, he got in danger, and while he frequently rescued others, his own perils were always the chief attraction. . . ."[8] Post complained that Tarzan now was being "kept off the stage a good deal of the time," and when he did appear, he was like a miraculous deity who saved others without very much effort; as a result, suspense was lacking. Tarzan had become an "avenging angel," and this "superheroic" role weakened the interest in him as a person.[9]

Some dickering followed at *Blue Book,* the final market. Kennicott, referring to the "scant 100,000 circulation," noted he could not compete with the "slicks." His top offer of $250 was accepted by Rothmund on November 16, 1939, and the story appeared in *Blue Book* in April 1940.

The last of the series, "Tarzan and the Castaways," included a lengthy assortment of characters, and the action, first aboard a ship for almost half the story, is followed by a setting on a South Pacific island where Burroughs utilizes a favorite device — an anachronistic return to a lost civilization. A group of Mayans migrated from Yucatan in 1452 and transferred their ancient society to the island of Uxmal where they built the familiar walled city, called Chichen Itza.

The unusual opening of the novelette, in Mombasa, finds Tarzan in a desperate situation; an injury, causing a brain lesion, has left him speechless. He has been captured by Arabs, placed in a cage, and delivered to the German Fritz Krause aboard the tramp steamer *Saigon.* Krause, a dealer in wild animals, has a varied cargo for transport to New York, including elephants, orangutans, tigers, and others. He plans to exhibit Tarzan in the United States as a wild man.

All of the standard Burroughs plot elements are crowded into the story. A mutiny, with the second mate Schmidt taking over the ship, is soon followed by piracy, with the seizure of an English yacht. Schmidt has a mania for putting everything behind bars, and the British passengers are assigned to cages adjacent to Tarzan. Abruptly recovering his health and his speech, Tarzan escapes from the cage and, with the aid of first mate De Groote and others, recaptures the ship.

The sequence brings Burroughs' next device — the storm and shipwreck and the landing on the island of Uxmal. Encounters with the primitive Mayans ensue, which include the familiar high-priest-altar-beautiful-girl-sacrifice scene with Tarzan coming to the rescue. Before the story ends the entire foreign assemblage of villains is eliminated in a wild gun battle.

The Burroughs concern for animals is demonstrated in Tarzan's actions when the *Saigon* is wrecked on the reefs of the island. Once all the people are safe ashore, Tarzan sets about freeing the animals. To Colonel Leigh's protest about the "dangerous beasts of prey," Tarzan replies, "Their lives are as important to them as ours are to us, and I'm not going to leave them here to die of starvation."

In the 1940 "Tarzan and the Castaways," with Germany and England at war, Burroughs again lapses into his characterization of Germans as a subhuman species. The story, forwarded to Rothmund from Hawaii, was submitted by him to Munsey.[10] An approval finally came on February 26, 1941, with Post offering only $450 for the novelette, and commenting, "If this seems a rather startling figure to offer for a Burroughs story, it is because we feel that a great deal of work would have to be done on the manuscript here in the office, and while there are features in the story that attract us, there are also a great many which will make it a thorny manuscript to edit. . . ." Burroughs accepted the price, and the story, retitled "The Quest of Tarzan," appeared as a three-part serial in *Argosy*, August 23 to September 6, 1941.

Burroughs' persistence, his practice of resurrecting and revising old, unsuccessful stories, exceeded all of his past efforts when, in 1939, he turned to a third version of "Angel's Serenade." The story, launched with a mere outline in 1921, was revised on May 19, 1936, and then expanded to 24,000 words in 1939. The sentimental account of Dick Crode's early life, showing the misery of mother and child in a squalid tenement neighborhood, continues with his inevitable drift into petty thievery and traces the steps in his rise, as a criminal "mastermind," to become head of The Syndicate. The opening scene of "Angel's Serenade" finds Dick, a small boy, and his mother June facing starvation and turning to music for a brief escape from their troubles. Dick dances while his mother plays the violin and later, at bedtime, asks her to play his favorite lullaby, "Angel's Serenade," a song that would haunt him throughout the years.[11]

At the story's end, Dick, determined that nobody else should have Betty, the daughter of his mother unknown to him and her second husband, is at the Tavish home, unseen, with gun raised and about to shoot her, when June in the sitting room begins to play the violin;

the song, of course, is "Angel's Serenade." Shocked, Dick has a vision of his mother playing as he, a child, sat at her feet. He realizes that June is his mother and turns away, a broken man. The solution he chooses is death — by his own hand.

For "Angel's Serenade" Burroughs devised an unusual structure. The sections are divided according to years and months. After the opening, headed 1914, part two follows in 1916, part three in 1919, and part four in 1939. This last section was written by Burroughs in his final revision-addition, April 25 to June 13, is the longest, occupying most of the manuscript, pages twenty-six to seventy-nine. While the theme of the song "Angel's Serenade" provides a unity to the story — something often lacking in his fantasy works — and while the plot is carefully and logically developed, the overly sentimental tone and the unrealistic characters — like individuals drawn from a melodrama — overpower the good qualities of the story. "Angel's Serenade" never appeared in print; records indicate a rejection from *Liberty* on July 7, 1939. A year later, on May 6, the story was sent to Michael Mill, publisher's representative, who had been promoting the sales of Burroughs' books to the dealers. Mill stated frankly that he could see no market for a work of this type.

Once more resuming the jungle setting, Burroughs wrote "Tarzan and the Madman," January 16 to March 22, 1940, producing a loose collection of incidents and devices that were too stale for further repetition. Again, there was a Tarzan impersonator, a temporary "madman" named Rand, who loses his memory and identity after a plane accident and assumes he is Tarzan. There is the familiar lost and decadent civilization, the founder, on this occasion, being Cristoforo da Gama, a brother of the famous Portuguese explorer. Christoforo and a group of his musketeers, pursued by a horde of Moslems, had found sanctuary in an African valley, where they built a castle and established a kingdom named Alentejo, after a province in Portugal. Hundreds of years later, the kingdom, with its "chocolate-colored" descendants — resulting from the intermarriage of Portuguese and native — still survived and was ruled by another monarch who called himself Christoforo da Gama.

Tarzan continues his latter-day role as an off-stage rescuer, and other characters include Sandra Pickerall, an English girl, who naturally is made a goddess in the savage kingdom; and a customary high priest, Ruiz, who indulges in human sacrifice; a communist named Minsky who spouts nonsensical anti-capitalist jargon; and an Englishman, Francis Bolton Chilton. Indispensable to all Tarzan novels is the conflict between opposing kingdoms or races, and in this case Alentejo is constantly at war with the black descendants of the original Moslems; named the Gallos, these Negroes are ruled by a sultan.

An unusual circumstance relating to "Tarzan and the Madman" concerns the existence of a Burroughs Dictaphone wax cylinder, the only remaining one, saved by son Jack for possible historic significance. On the cylinder, rerecorded by RCA, Ed's voice can be heard dictating a brief section of the novel, about 1,500 words. At the start, after announcing "Cylinder Sixteen," apparently his standard procedure, he proceeded to dictate at a fairly fast rate. Although he was improvising the story, he had sources, brief notes or references, prepared in advance. In his notebook, for example, the story appears in a condensed form of about fifty handwritten pages. This served to fix the structure and characters in Burroughs' mind. The notes were intended mainly as reminders, especially to provide the continuity, to make certain he was following the incidents he had already planned. Evidently, in most of his dictation, he had the story elements well arranged in his mind and he could dictate or improvise for long periods without glancing at any notes. On occasion he glanced down at the papers on his desk, which might be mere glossaries of characters and their roles.[12]

"Tarzan and the Madman," covering fifty source pages in Ed's notebook, seemed to be a rough draft longer than he usually prepared.

The first three pages are identical with the printed version, indicating that he wanted a carefully polished opening and chose to write it out exactly rather than improvise it. The notebook reveals that from a summary of one or two sentences he might improvise a long section as he dictated. For example, in the notebook Burroughs wrote, "Next morning Gantry, Crump and Minsky discuss the voice in the night. Gantry is afraid. He decides to turn back." From this short statement Burroughs created and dictated more than a page, some 350 words, mainly dialogue between the men.

Burroughs' confidence in Mill, who had really become his agent, was again demonstrated when, on March 28, the manuscript was forwarded to him. Mill submitted it to six of the top magazines, but it was returned by all. Later, when the Burroughs office sent it to Munsey, editor Post, on November 26, 1940, analyzed the obvious defects: "Tarzan doesn't seem to be Tarzan anymore. The present manuscript seems almost completely to lack the motivation and excitement of the earlier Tarzan pieces. Its plot, though it does contain large helpings of action, is pretty repetitious with its constant capture, escape, re-capture pattern." A more serious fault, according to Post, was Tarzan's limited role; "under fifty percent of the wordage" centered about his actions. He became a "safety net" in the rescue of others, his own problems or perils being of little significance. Other rejections came from *Blue Book* and Ziff-Davis in 1940 and from Standard Magazines and Street & Smith in 1941. Never appearing in a magazine, it was finally published as a hardcover book by Canaveral Press in 1964.

One of Burroughs' most exhilarating tales, a type of situation comedy, is "The Strange Adventure of Mr. Dinwiddie," in which a Walter-Mitty-like character, a nonentity, the most insignificant of men in real life, has his one moment of glory — because of a mistaken identity. In creating the character of Abner Dinwiddie, Burroughs exhibits an awareness of environmental influences. As a boy working in his father's grocery story, Abner was denied all the normal experiences: "His only social contacts had been kitchen-door and over-the-counter; and being naturally shy, he had not profited by these. Other boys went swimming and fishing; they played baseball and football; but not Dinwiddie." He found his escape from the dull world of commerce (as Burroughs did) in his imagination:

All day Abner Dinwiddie was a cringing, apologetic slave to the penurious, grubby little man who had fathered him, and the small town patrons of his grimy grocery store; but at night, after he had taken off his thick lensed spectacles and gone to bed, Abner Dinwiddie came into his own. Then he became a dashing Hussar or a magnificent Mountie rescuing beauteous damsels from black hearted villains.

When his father died, he modernized the store, expanded his operations, became prosperous, and married Sarah, the thirty-five-year-old spinster.

Sarah dominated Abner to such a degree that he lived in fear of her. "He was so afraid of her," Burroughs wrote, "that she probably died a virgin, while Mr. Dinwiddie was rescuing beauteous damsels underneath the same counterpane." After twenty years of marriage, Sarah died and Abner, a Shriner, attended conventions at which he indulged in his one hobby — collecting menus. These he kept in a brief case which he carried on all his travels. For the next Shriner convention, set in Honolulu, he booked passage on the *Lusonia*, as did a certain Admiral Arnold Dinwoodie, who then cancelled his voyage at the last moment. Abner, assumed to be an admiral by the ship's personnel, found himself saluted by officers and invited to share the captain's table. And the beautiful Sonia Doughlev contrives to make his acquaintance, displaying an unusual interest in him. She becomes the girl who had occupied his dreams. Later, Sonia's romantic advances are revealed as a cover-up for her nefarious activities; she bursts into Abner's room in her negligee and her screams summon

a supposed "husband." Abner is terrorized into handing over his briefcase, presumably filled with specifications about the Navy's new bomb sight. The chagrin of the two spies when they discover the collection of menus can well be imagined. A Honolulu paper reports the "very clever work of Mr Abner Dinwiddie of Utropolis, Kansas," in helping to capture three international spies.

"The Strange Adventure of Mr. Dinwiddie" set a record for a Burroughs story. The 5,700-word manuscript was completed in a one-day span — July 16 to 17, 1940. It was marketed under a new nom de plume, that of John Tyler McCulloch, a combination of Ed's favorite first name with two family names that could be traced back several generations, and the mailing address became Ralph Rothmund's — 20441 Arminta Street, Canoga Park, California. However, the story encountered a long string of rejections and was never published.

While Ed was following his usual intensive writing schedule, his corporation continued its own unvarying project, the publication of spring and fall books. The two 1940 novels, published February 15 and September 15, were *Synthetic Men of Mars* and *The Deputy Sheriff of Comanche Country*, with illustrations by John Coleman Burroughs. The latter book, published when Ed was in Hawaii, carried a dedication to Mary Lucas Pflueger, a close friend in Honolulu. With the war erupting in 1941, and the resulting paper shortage, no Burroughs books appeared until 1944 when *The Land of Terror* was published on April 15.

Although Ed had achieved little success in his planned series of *Tarzan* novelettes, this new concept appealed to him, and in 1940 he undertook a strenuous writing feat, nothing less than a goal of four-story sequences for each of his fantasy worlds — Venus, Mars, and Pellucidar. That these writing projects may have been conceived by Rothmund is indicated in a letter of July 6, 1940, to editor Palmer at Ziff-Davis Publishing Company. Rothmund had acknowledged receipt of payment — $400 —

for "John Carter and the Giant of Mars." In his letter to the editor he spoke of a plan he was submitting to Burroughs; he stipulated that he would only do so if Palmer offered a preacceptance for the stories. Rothmund described his plan:

To have Mr. Burroughs write three 20,000-word novelettes, each a complete story in itself; and later when we plan to issue the stories in book form, we would have Mr. Burroughs write a chapter to connect the first two novelettes and another chapter to connect the second and third novelettes, which would give us approximately 65,000 to 70,000 words for book publication. These additional chapters, of course, would not be submitted to you, as they would be written primarily for book publication.

He then explained that these novelettes were to feature John Carter of Mars, Carson Napier of Venus, and David Innes of Pellucidar. Burroughs, in his New Tarzan Series launched and

John Coleman Burroughs, October 1962.

then abandoned a year earlier, had planned a similar four-story sequence featuring the ape-man.

Once Palmer had agreed to the proposal, Burroughs set to work on the Venus series. He chose, however, to alter Rothmund's plan, eliminating the chapters that were to be written later as connectives and establishing his goal as four 20,000-word novelettes. Burroughs' remarkable writing discipline and the flexibility of his imagination were illustrated in his shifts between the three fantasy worlds, leaving one series incomplete while turning to another or working on two series at the same time. After finishing "Captured on Venus," the first of the Napier series (May 4 to July 20, 1940), Ed wrote the "Frozen Men of Mars," the first of the John Carter series, July 24 to September 6, and then shifted to the first of the Innes series, "Hodon and O-AA," later titled "The Return to Pellucidar," September 7 to 15. Overlapping stories included "The Living Dead" (Venus), October 15 to 22, "Savage Pellucidar," October 2 to 26, and "Men of the Bronze Age" (Pellucidar), October 6 to 13. But in this period, the amazing creative feat also included the beginnings of other stories from differing series: "Escape on Mars," October 24 to 30, and "Beyond the Farthest Star," October 24 to November 5, a new setting on the planet Poloda.

The novelettes of the Carson of Venus series, titled "Captured on Venus," "The Fire Goddess," "The Living Dead," and "War on Venus," were designed for magazine installments, each with an ending effect, while at the same time maintaining the continuity needed for the future novel. In their wanderings, Carson and his sweetheart Duare, traveling by plane, are involved in perilous situations that are created by his blundering, impulsive actions. The novel follows the Burroughs pattern: dangers encountered with bizarre races, battles with either Carson and Duare captured or separated, the escape of one or both, and then new perils with other semihumans. For the four novelettes Burroughs first devises the

Myposans, creatures with fish characteristics, gills and webbed feet, protruding lips and "pop" eyes, who walk, talk, and wear heavy beards. Carson and Duare become slaves of these fish people; at the auction because he is a troublemaker, Carson is sold for a mere $5.90. Certain "weird looking fishes," detected swimming in a pool, are revealed to be Myposan "children," brought into the world by the females. After developing hands and feet, they slough their tails, become amphibians, crawl on land, and acquire heads and faces. Finally, as Myposans, they walk erect, but still have gills instead of lungs. At the end of the first story Carson rescues Duare from the depths of a pool, where Tyros, the Myposan tyrant, has dragged her.

In the second episode, with Duare left temporarily with the Timals, a group of friendly aborigines, Carson, once more imprudent, watches a battle between the ships of Myposa and Japal and allows his plane to drop too low; the plane's propeller is damaged by a catapulted rock, and after landing, Carson and his friends Kandar and Doran are imprisoned in Japal. Later, they lead Japal warriors in a battle against strange invaders, the Brokols, who are of a "sickly greenish hue," completely hairless, and even more repulsive because of "a little knob of flesh" on top of their bald heads. At the city of Brokol, Carson views orchards of small trees and discovers "diminutive Brokols dangling in the air by stems attached to the tops of their heads." This of course explains the odd "knobs" that remain on all of the Brokols. However, most unusual is Carson's meeting with Loto-El-Ho-Ganja, a name translated as "The Fire Goddess," who puzzlingly appears as a normal earth woman, without any of the hideous features of the Brokols. Loto, struggling to recall strangely suppressed memories, speaks the words "United States" and "New York" and then cries the name "Betty" many times. Finally, in excitement, she calls, "Now I have it! Brooklyn!" Loto mysteriously disappears from Brokol, and Burroughs inserts an editor's note in the story to report what is called a "remarkable coin-cidence." An odd news item had appeared in a Brooklyn newspaper: "The body of Betty Callwell, who disappeared twenty-five years ago, was found in the alley back of her former home here early this morning. The preservation of the body was remarkable, as Miss Callwell must have been dead for twenty-five years. . . ." Betty had experienced some unexplained transmigration (in the flesh) to Venus, presumably after her death; her body now had returned to Earth. She had been reincarnated as Loto, the Fire Goddess, in a second life that had lasted twenty-five years.

For the third novelette about Venus, Burroughs, repeating his airplane-failure device, has Carson and Duare land in another city where they are greeted by happy, laughing people. The warm hospitality of Voo-ad is a welcome change, in contrast to the antagonism and violence that the two had met at other cities, but they soon discover they have been tricked by this mask of friendliness. Drugged and paralyzed through food eaten at a banquet, Carson and Duare are carried to an enormous domed building; there a horrible fate is planned for them. On platforms are specimens of beasts and reptiles, supported by props or scaffolding, and on the wall hundreds of paralyzed human beings are suspended "in ingeniously devised slings which distributed their weight equally to all parts of their bodies.

The Vooyorgans, though not weird, non-human creatures, do, however, exhibit their strangeness through a "well-defined reddish line," resembling a birthmark that runs down the exact center of the face and body. Later, when one of them begins to shiver, reels drunkenly, and falls to the floor, the function of the red line is revealed. Screaming and groaning, the creature starts to divide, splitting apart along the reddish line: "With a last, violent convulsion, the two halves rolled apart. There was no blood. Each half was protected by a thin, palpitating membrane, through which the internal organs were clearly observable. . . . That both were still alive was evident, as I saw their limbs move." Through the use of an antidote Carson and Duare overcome their paralysis and, before escaping, restore the other human specimens to their former selves. These were all warriors and were "Hell-bent on revenge" against the deceitful Vooyorgans. As Carson and Duare soar away in their plane they see the red flames of destruction rising in the sky.

In the final novelette Carson, Duare, and Ero Shan view, from the airplane, what appears to be a battle fleet on land and, in dropping lower, are amazed to see units resembling dreadnoughts, some being seven or eight hundred feet in length and others being smaller and comparable to cruisers and destroyers. Once more the "jinx" is with them: their plane is damaged, they land, and they are taken captive. Carson, held by the Falsans aboard their huge flagship, discovers that a battle is about to start with the Pangans; although all of the units are on land, the maneuvers are similar to those used by fleets at sea. Called *lantars,* the ships are equipped with t-ray and r-ray guns and with shell-hurling guns, which in the case of the dreadnoughts might send shells weighing a thousand pounds to a distance of fifteen miles. Tiny wheeled torpedos, self-propelling, effective only at a close range, are used to damage the heavy caterpillar belts on which the lantars run. To Carson, the most exciting vehicles were the small scout ships, whose main function was to destroy enemy torpedoes and launch their own.

Apparently content with this creation of the land-battle fleets of the Falsans and Pangans, Burroughs, in this last section on Venus, did not extend his imagination to produce any bizarre races other than the Cloud People, hairless, with skins the color of corpses, who in a brief appearance prove to be friendly. At the end of the novelette Carson and Duare are safe and ready for further adventures. Since by pre-agreement Raymond Palmer of Ziff-Davis was to receive the Venus and other novelettes, the marketing problem was simplified. In the order of acceptance, the stories brought the following amounts: "Captured on Venus," $472; "The Fire Goddess," $405.60; "The Living Dead," $400.60; and "War on Venus," $440.88. Appearing in *Fantastic Adventures* of March, July,

and November 1941 and March 1942, the stories, except for the first, carried the original titles; "Captured on Venus" was renamed "Slaves of the Fish Men."[13]

A controversial story, one that stirred Burroughs fans to much critical comment, was titled "John Carter and the Giant of Mars." Not part of a series, the 20,000-word novelette was sent to Ziff-Davis on June 29, 1940, and was published in *Amazing Stories,* January 1941. The letter to Palmer spoke of "the new Edgar Rice Burroughs . . . John Carter romance," but the fans, to whom every Burroughs sentence broadcasts his inimitable style, were convinced that he had not written the story. On November 27, 1940, Rothmund prepared a memo for Burroughs, then in Hawaii, and mailed it to him. About the story (the January issue was on the stands on November 10) Rothmund wrote, "Criticisms have been coming in, one at a time for the past week or more, and today two more were received." These, similar to the others, were quoted. The first, from Frank J. Brueckel of Milwaukee, posed a question about the authenticity of both "The Giant of Mars" and *Tarzan and the Jungle Murders.* Brueckel remarked, "Somehow I managed to get Tarzan & the Jungle Murders read, but with Giant of Mars I've got to stop a couple of times on each page and go for a walk around the block. . . ." He later added a firm opinion: ". . . well, as I said before, you didn't write it, so that explains everything."

A letter from Lorin Nunnely of Fayetteville, Arkansas, displayed a dubious attitude: ". . . if you will pardon my frankness, it did not have the usual tang of Burroughs style." Rothmund's closing statement in the memo also strongly implied that the story was *not* by Burroughs: "The above two, as did the others, sensed the fact that you did not write The Giant of Mars. Apparently, you put a little too much 'English' on your words for anyone else to duplicate. I simply give you the above as an interesting sidelight."

In later years the continuing speculations of the fans produced an answer from Hulbert Burroughs, indicating that this story had origi-

"Slaves of the Fishmen" cover of Fantastic Adventures, 1941.   "Goddess of Fire" cover of Fantastic Adventures, 1941.

"The Living Dead" cover of Fantastic Adventures, 1941.   "War on Venus" cover of Fantastic Adventures, 1942.

These four magazine stories were combined in the hard-cover book Escape on Venus, 1946.

nated in a collaboration between Ed and his younger son Jack; the work involved was a book for Whitman Publishing Company:

This story appeared under the title, John Carter of Mars, in Whitman's Better Little Book No. 1402. Whitman had a very set formula for this — exactly 15,000 words — with text so arranged that the drawings on the opposite page depicted what was being told in the text. My Dad was never happy to write to such a strict formula. Apparently, therefore, he worked with my brother on it. John also did all the illustrations for the book.[14]

Hulbert then explained that when *Amazing Stories* requested a Martian work, Ed and his son Jack added a new ending of some 6,000 words to the story. If the two collaborated, as Hulbert suggested, this would have to have been done by correspondence — creating a number of difficulties. No record of this appears in Ed's letters from Honolulu or in Jack's well-preserved letters to his father.

In its wildly conceived plot, "John Carter and the Giant of Mars" breaks the bounds of any fantasy Burroughs ever devised. Pew Mogel, a synthetic man created by his master, Ras Thavas, has escaped from Morbus with other synthetic men, all of them traveling on the backs of the huge malagors, the birds of transport. Having learned all of Ras Thavas' secrets, Mogel has transferred the brains of red men, exiled criminals, into the powerful bodies of white apes. He has also constructed the giant Joog, 130 feet tall, "modeled from the organs, tissues and bones of ten thousand red men and white apes." Joog, whose veins contain a serum that makes all tissues self-repairing, is "practically indestructible. No bullet or cannon shot made can stop him!" With the giant and his army of white apes, Mogel now plans to conquer all of Barsoom. The apes, equipped with rifles, cannon and atom-guns, form an invincible air armada as they ride the winged malagors. They dive in "true blitz-krieg fashion" to blast the warriors on the ground.

From an armored howdah atop the giant's head, Pew Mogel, through short wave, dictates the actions of Joog who exceeds King Kong's wildest feats, wielding an enormous tree trunk to smash the planes of Helium. But the most bizarre concoction of all is John Carter's scheme to destroy the swarms of ape-mounted malagors. Using two thousand parachutes, Carter arranges for the planes to drop Martian rats through the skies; when the rats, hereditary enemies of birds, appear above the malagors, these flying creatures scatter in panic, fleeing the battlefield.

The incredible sequence of actions, like a Burroughs plot gone berserk, may convince the reader that Ed did not write the *Giant of Mars*. But the style offers a more definite evidence: the constant short, awkward sentences create a monotonous effect; there is little attempt at paragraph unity; and typical Burroughs elements, description, background details, and philosophical comments, are lacking. The story is thin and flimsy, a bare skeleton. Whether "John Carter and the Giant of Mars" was written in its entirety by Jack Burroughs, or created by an unknown editor at Whitman Publishers with a section later added by Jack, is difficult to ascertain; certainly, the short, staccato sentences, suitable for a cartoon-book style, indicate that much of the story was designed for this purpose. The faithful Burroughs devotees, who never forget any detail of the master's writing, base their rejection of the story on its reference to a three-legged Martian rat, a glaring error, since Burroughs, in *The Chessmen of Mars*, describes *ulsio*, the rat, as "many-legged".

With the completion of his novelette series centered in Venus, Ed's next locale was Mars. His contemplated title for the future book was "The Frozen Men of Mars," and the first story, written July 24 to September 6, 1940, was called "John Carter in the Pits of Horz." Rothmund, in sending it to Ziff-Davis on September 20, noted that Burroughs was "not very keen" about the title and had offered two other suggestions, "Llana of Gathol" and "The Horror Pits of Horz"; he was willing, however, to accept any better title that Palmer might devise. The remaining stories of the series were "The Black Pirates of Barsoom," September 27 to October 2; "Escape on Mars," October 24 to 30; and "Invisible Men of Mars," November 18 to 22. Why Burroughs felt compelled to adopt this furious writing pace of four to six days for each 20,000-word novelette is simply explained — Burroughs needed the money.

With the creation of a foreword in the first story, Ed displayed careful writing; his practice had usually been to polish the forewords or openings of his novels, and in this case, after describing the restful atmosphere of Lanikai on the Island of Oahu, he muses about old Hawaii and its kings and chiefs. He then imagines that he sees the great conqueror, Kamehameha, come striding toward him. Moments later he discovers that a strangely garbed warrior *has* appeared, but he is not Kamehameha; John Carter, his kinsman, has returned and is eager to tell the story of the beauteous Llana of Gathol.

The Burroughs inventions in this four-part Mars series include, first of all, the "dead" city of Horz where the last survivors of a previous race, the Orovars, had taken refuge from the attacks of the green men. Now the Oravors kept their existence secret and killed any stranger who might see them and betray their presence to their enemies. Imprisoned in the Pits of Horz, John Carter and his friend Pan Dan Chee find that the remnants of an ancient civilization, men and women who had lived more than a hundred thousand years before, had been maintained in suspended animation by the hypnotic powers of a mad creature who rules these underground pits. When Carter kills the madman, the spell is broken and the men and women arise from the chests where they had been confined. They had been a maritime people, but now, completely bewildered, they learn that during the countless ages of their imprisonment the five great seas of Mars had dried up.

In "The Black Pirates of Barsoom," the second of the series, John Carter once more encounters the First Born of Barsoom, black men, the oldest race on the planet who trace their lineage to the Tree of Life. Captured and taken to the city of Kamtol, Carter is subjected to an "examination" by a strange machine and later learns that his individual "nerve index . . . unlike that of any other creature in the world" has been recorded. A master machine, controlled by the dictator Doxus, generates short wave vibrations that can be "keyed" exactly to an individual's nerve index; once this is done, the person has a severe paralytic stroke and dies almost instantly. The nerve index of every adult in the Valley of the First Born has been recorded. By these means Doxus reigns supreme, the entire population at his mercy. Doxus, the only man whose index has not been recorded, and his assistant Myrlo are the only ones who know the location of the master machine and how to operate it. John Carter's goal, of course, is its destruction.

Escape on Mars" continues the perils of Carter and Llana, with Burroughs returning to a previous device, the equilibrimotor, a type of "life belt" used for individual flying; it is filled with a Barsoomian propulsion ray and has a radium motor. Burroughs also returns to one of his most terrifying creatures, the huge, white-furred, six-limbed "apt" whose enormous eyes, designed for the animal's cave habitat, each contain several thousand ocelli. A new product of the Burroughs imagination, centered in the domed city of Pankor in the Arctic, involves the "frozen in" warriors. Out in the bitter cold Carter sees what appear to be thousands of frozen corpses, hanging heads down, like the carcasses of animals in butcher shops: "Each corpse was encased in ice, a transparent shroud through which their dead eyes stared pleadingly, reproachfully, accusingly, horribly. Some faces wore frozen grins, mocking Fate with bared teeth."

At first shuddering at the thought that the corpses were to be used for food, Carter watches as they are revived through heat, massaging, and hypodermic injections. These warriors, the accumulation of a hundred years, captured, frozen and retained in cold-storage, constitute

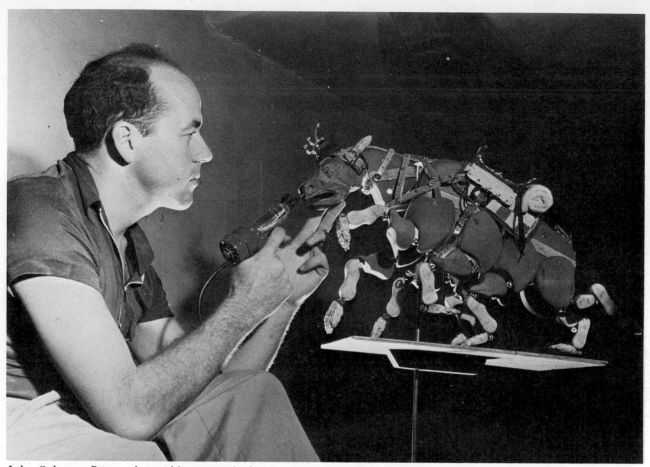

John Coleman Burroughs working on articulated model of Martian thoat, *September 1941; he created this model to assist him in doing the illustrations for his father's book about Mars.*

an army of more than a million men — an army designed to aid Hin Abtol in his scheme to conquer all of Mars.

For the final episode Burroughs creates a race with most unusual powers, the inhabitants of Invak, a city in The Forest of Lost Men, who have learned the secret of invisibility. Within the city, itself concealed beneath a vine-covered roof, the Invaks become visible as they walk through specially lighted corridors, but once they appear in the open, they vanish from sight. A humorous note is added as Kandus further explains the situation: "Unfortunately, there is a hitch," he said. "We can see you, but we can't see each other any more than you can see us." This accounted for the grumbling and cursing Carter had heard in the forest — the warriors were running into each other.

Through the girl Rojas, who falls in love

with him, Carter obtains the invisibility spheres for himself and Llana. To achieve this, he does something that no Burroughs hero has ever done — falsely encourages the love of a woman whom he really does not care for. This is a startling violation of Burroughs' code for his supermen, especially since Carter is a married man with his love pledged to the incomparable Dejah Thoris. Naturally, as the effect of the spheres wears off, both Carter and Llana reappear in the solid flesh.

In publishing the novelettes in *Amazing Stories*, Palmer changed two of the titles; the sequence is the following: "The City of Mummies," March 1941; "Black Pirates of Barsoom," June 1941; "Yellow Men of Mars," August 1941; "Invisible Men of Mars," October 1941. The novel, combining all four novelettes, was published as a book and issued on March 26,

"The City of Mummies" cover of Amazing Stories, 1941.

"Black Pirates of Barsoom" cover of Amazing Stories, 1941.

1948. It was titled *Llana of Gathol* and dedicated to Ed's wartime friend at Honolulu, John Phillip Bird.[15] *Llana of Gathol* was the final book illustrated by John Coleman Burroughs. Some say the illustrations compare favorably with the best of St. John's.

The next four-story sequence, taking place in the inner world of Pellucidar, consisted of "Hodon and O-aa," written September 7 to 15, 1940; "Men of the Bronze Age," October 6 to 13; "Tiger Girl," November 6 to 10; and "Savage Pellucidar," not completed until four years later, October 2 to 26, 1944. The typical adventures, loosely devised, involve David Innes, the Emperor of Pellucidar and his sweetheart Dian, but these are alternated with conflicts and perils faced by Hodon, The Fleet One, and the girl O-aa, with whom he falls in love.

The character of Abner Perry as an eccentric, inept, but lovable old inventor is established in previous Pellucidar works; however, on this occasion, he outdoes himself in committing inexcusable blunders. After building and inflating a huge balloon, he forgets to fasten the mooring rope properly. The balloon, with Dian aboard for a supposed trial ascension, soars away. Naturally, he had forgotten to attach a ripcord, so that Dian could not release the gas and make a gradual landing. Another humorous character is Ah-gilak, a wizened old man from Cape Cod who, following a shipwreck, has drifted into Pellucidar through the North Polar Opening.

Burroughs had devoted some thought to the development of Ah-gilak as a picturesque old scoundrel. Concerning the shipwreck of the

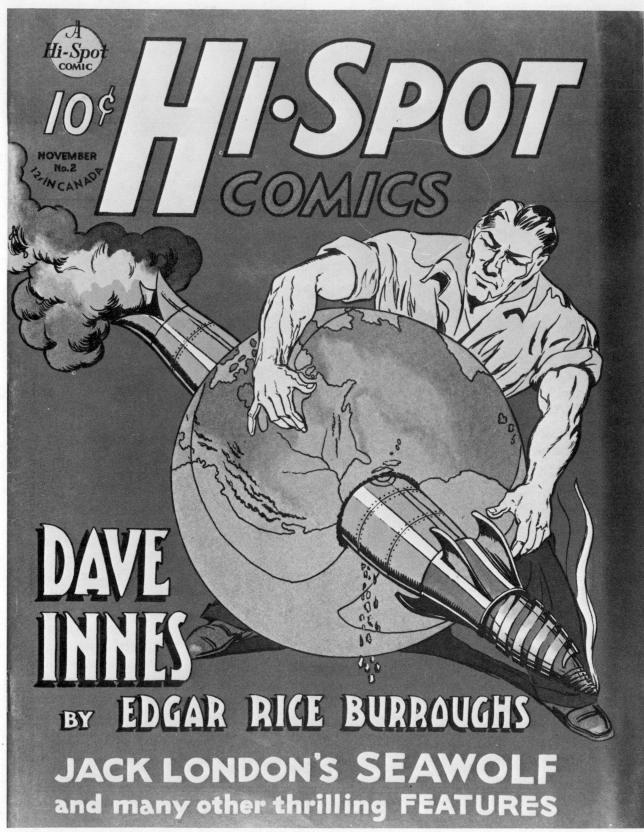

Cover of Hi Spot Comics, 1940, featuring a Burroughs Pellucidar story; John Coleman Burroughs, illustrator.

First page of "Dave Innes of Pellucidar."

Cover of Llana of Gathol, *1948; John Coleman Burroughs, illustrator.*

Dolly Dorcas in the Arctic in 1845, Ah-gilak, now 153 years old, persisted in giving lip-smacking accounts of the gruesome events that ensued. He spoke complacently of his cannibalism to O-aa and Hodon:

"Do you eat human flesh?" demanded Hodon.

"Well, you see I sort o' acquired a taste for it after the Dolly Dorcas was wrecked. Ole Bill was a mite tough an' rank, but there was a Swede I et who was just about the nicest eatin' you ever see. Yes, I eat what the Lord furnishes. I reckon I'm goin' to enjoy both of you."

The old man expressed a hope that he would be able to avoid eating them, since he enjoyed their company. When O-aa reminds him of this, he responds, "Yes, I'm sort o' torn between two loves, as the feller said: I loves to eat an' I loves to talk." Later, when Ah-gilak and the others are trapped in a cave without food, he speaks again of cannibalism, insisting he will be "the last man" because he is "too dod-burned old and tough to eat." Waiting outside are the sabertooth men, black savages equipped with long tails and tusks "that curve down from the upper jaw to below the chin." Ah-gilak complains of the selfishness displayed by David, Hodon, and O-aa: "If we don't eat each other, the sabertooths are goin' to eat us; an' I'd think you'd rather be eaten by a friend than by one of them critters."[16]

In the second novelette, "Men of the Bronze Age," Burroughs inserts one of his familiar caustic comments about civilized man as he refers to the "propaganda of terror" to which the primitive natives of Lolo-lolo submitted:

Remember, they were just simple people of the Bronze Age. They had not yet reached that stage of civilization where they might send children on holy crusades to die by thousands; they were not far enough advanced to torture unbelievers with rack and red hot irons, or burn heretics at the stake; so they believed this folderol that more civilized people would have spurned with laughter while killing all Jews.

Bringing the Pellucidar series to an end, the novelettes appeared in *Amazing Stories,* the first, retitled "The Return to Pellucidar," in February 1942, the next two in March and April, and the final one, posthumously, twenty-one years later, in November 1963.[17]

Apparently feeling too confined in the worlds of Mars, Venus and Pellucidar, Burroughs envisioned an entire new solar system as a setting for an adventurer from the earth. With his novelette "Beyond the Farthest Star" almost finished — it was again designed to launch a three- or four-part series — he became aware of a number of astronomical problems and sought the advice of an expert. On November 1, 1940, he began a correspondence with Professor J. S. Donaghho, also living in Honolulu, obtaining his name from a friend, Dr. Livesay. Ed wrote, "The problem is in relation to one of those very profound classics which I have been inflicting on a very tolerant world for a quarter of a century," and explained the nature of his enclosed pencil sketch: ". . . a diagram of an imaginary solar system consisting of a small sun and eleven equally spaced planets. An atmosphere belt rotates about the sun at the same speed as the planets."

To Donaghho he posed four questions concerning the orbits of the planets, their visibility at night and day, the type of ocean tides that might be produced on a certain planet, and the particular visibility to other planets of a "sphere" about eight thousand miles in diameter. On the first point, noting Burroughs' interest in planets that would describe a circle rather than an ellipse in their orbits, Donaghho replied:

Any planet could revolve around the sun in a circle, if it had a certain velocity, of a value depending upon the combined mass of the sun and the planet. As a result, the required velocity for two planets of different mass would not be the same, so your planets must all have exactly the same mass, or they will not remain equally spaced.[18]

Burroughs' second question involved a supposed Planet P: to its inhabitants, what other planets would be visible at night and day? Donaghho concluded that if an observer stayed up all night, and if the weather was clear, he would have a chance to see all of the planets in one night. Daytime visibility was quite uncertain; possibly only two, or at the most, four of the planets might be seen then. The third question, about the tides, was the most important one to Burroughs who commented, "What I wished to determine was whether the tides would be so terrific as to preclude all forms of ocean navigation." Donaghho's response was disconcerting:

The tidal efficiency of the sun varies inversely as the cube of the distance. So, at a distance of 1,000,000 miles, its efficiency would be about 800,000 times as great as the distance of the earth. So the tides would not only preclude all forms of ocean navigation, but would, in all likelihood, sweep daily over the whole of the continents, thus precluding all forms of life!

As to the visibility of a sphere 8,000 miles in diameter, Donaghho explained, "Such a sphere . . . would not be visible at all if cloudless. If filled with clouds, it would be visible, but to what distance would be very difficult to determine." The professor then dealt a shattering blow to Ed's vital invention for his planetary system. Ed had conjured up an atmospheric belt, doughnut-shaped, that would serve all eleven planets. Donaghho viewed this as a scientific impossibility:

Now, I hope that your atmospheric belt is not an essential part of the plan, as I must assure you that it would not "stay put". If the planets did not have as much atmosphere as they could hold (a fairly definite amount), each one would draw in from the surrounding belt enough to fill out its quota, and the rest would be diffused in all directions. . . .

Ed reacted with dismay to this information, but also faced his contretemps with some amusement: "The total loss of the atmosphere band desolated me, especially inasmuch as I had already used it in the first installment of the story. In the next installment, I shall alibi myself out of it with as much ease as was displayed by the daring young man on the flying trapeze."[19] The "first installment," the 21,000-word "Beyond the Farthest Star," was written October 24 to November 5, 1940. The correspondence between the two men, who were never to meet, appeared completed until Ed, reexamining Donaghho's most recent letter, became aware of a possible misunderstanding. On November 18, referring to the professor's opinion on the tides, Ed wrote, ". . . I cannot tell whether you based your deductions on the assumption that my imaginary sun was of the same size as our own sun, or not. It is supposed to be very much smaller, just large enough to give forth enough heat to maintain a rather springlike temperature on the planets, which are one million miles distant."

Ed had truly uncovered a differing interpretation, for Donaghho at once answered to explain his natural assumption — that the sun of the planetary system and the planets themselves were of the same mass as our sun and earth; Donaghho now offered a new theory: "If the mean density of your sun were the same as that of our sun, and its diameter about 20% greater than that of the earth, on a planet whose mass was the same as our earth, and at a distance of one million miles, it would raise tides about the same as ours." He also estimated that the tidal effects of the planets upon each other might "slightly reduce" the effect of the sun. "As a result, to produce tides equal to ours, the diameter of your sun might have to be some 25% greater than that of the earth."[20] Expressing his pleasure in replying to Ed's questions, Donaghho remarked, "This has been fun!"

In the final letter of the correspondence, on November 23 Ed wrote, "You have proven yourself a real benefactor to the human race of Poloda (Planet P) by lowering the tides so as to permit ocean navigation." However, the atmospheric problem had not been solved, and Ed commented jokingly, ". . . there are two schools of thought on Poloda: One adheres to the Donaghhoan theory, while the other, hopefully anticipating inter-planetary navigation, clings stubbornly to the Burroughsian theory." Concerning the fun Donaghho had found in the queries, Ed stated, "I find fun in the imaginings which prompt them; and I can appreciate, in a small way, the swell time God had in creating the Universe."

For "Beyond the Farthest Star" Ed composed a brief foreword, and in it he repeated a device he had used in his "Ghostly Script": invisible hands, presumably from a spirit that was transcending the barrier of death, depress the typewriter keys with a "bewildering rapidity" and an amazing story appears on the blank paper. The protagonist, a pilot shot down behind the German lines in 1939, chooses to remain unidentified. He knew he was dead — a machine-gun bullet had penetrated his heart — yet he found himself naked amid strange surroundings, discovering soon that through transmigration or metempsychosis he had journeyed to the planet of Poloda, 450,000 light-years from the earth. On the continent of Unis, in the city of Orvis, he is first assigned to the home of Harkas Yen, a psychiatrist, who gives him the name of Tangor, and there he makes friends of Harkas' son and daughter, Don and Yamoda.

Tangor, bewildered by the strange movements of buildings that plunged downward like elevators, hears the sounds of guns and detonation of bombs and becomes aware that a war is being waged. In explaining, Harkas mentions a "happier world," many years before, when men lived and worked on the surface of the planet. "But within ten years after the Kapars launched their campaign to conquer and rule the world, every city in Unis and every city in Kapar and many cities on others of the five continents were reduced to rubble. It was then that we started building these underground cities that can be raised or lowered by the power we derive from Omos [The Sun of Poloda]."

The war between the Kapars, who have subjugated almost every nation on Poloda, and the Unisans continues with unabated fury. Harkas describes the situation:

What they have done to us, we have done to them; but they are much worse off than we.

Their people live in underground warrens protected by steel and concrete; they subsist upon the foods raised by subjugated people who are no better than slaves, and work no better for hated masters; or they eat synthetic foods, as they wear synthetic clothing. . . .

The Unisans' periodic offers of an honorable peace were rejected by the Kapars whose goal was nothing less than the "total destruction" of Unis.

Tangor, who seeks to join the Unisan air forces, is informed by Harkas that he will probably be accepted. Because of casualties which appear incredible, there is a constant demand for flyers. Harkas notes average losses of 100,000 men a month. Appalled, Tangor inquires why the nation has not been exterminated. "There are six million adult women in Unis and something like ten million babies are born every year," Harkas says. "Probably a little better than half of these are boys. At least five million of them grow to maturity, for we are a very healthy race. So, you see, we can afford to lose a million men a year." When Tangor, still shocked, comments about what effect this must have on the mothers, Harkas replies stoically, "It is war; and war is our way of life."

The attitude of the mothers is illustrated by Harkas Yen's wife; in describing her, Tangor paints a horrifying picture:

She is a sad-faced woman of about sixty, who was married at seventeen and has twenty children, six girls and fourteen boys. Thirteen of the boys have been killed in the war. Most of the older women of Unis, and the older men, too, have sad faces; but they never complain nor do they ever weep. Harkas Yen's wife told me that their tears were exhausted two generations ago.

Through ideas advanced in numerous articles and stories Ed had left no doubt about the type of political and legal systems he approved. The contempt he displayed for politicians was matched by the disgust he felt for lawyers and the legal processes, and beyond this he exhibited a profound distrust for the masses, the electorate, who to him seemed incompetent to choose their own representatives. In the creation of Unis he naturally seized the chance to invent an ideal government. Unis is ruled by the Janhai, a commission of seven men who are elected to serve until they are seventy years old; then they may be reelected. Only if a vacancy exists may elections be held. The Janhai has extraordinary powers, appointing all judges as well as governors of states; the local officials are all appointees, the governors selecting the mayors who in turn choose the remaining officeholders. Ed noted, "There are no ward-heelers in Unis."

The seven members of the Janhai head the regular departments, such as war, state or commerce, and they elect one of their group to serve as Eljanhai, or high commissioner, for a period of six years. Thus, he really becomes the ruler of Unis, with far more power than a president. This is especially true since there is no Congress. As a requirement for office-seekers, Ed adopts one of his favorite devices — the intelligence test. The Janhai and all appointees on all levels "must submit to a very thorough intelligence test, which determines the candidate's native intelligence as well as his fund of acquired knowledge; and more weight is given the former than the latter."

Ed's impatience with lawyers and the courts led him to contrive the type of legal procedure he approved. The first case reported, involving a murder, brings a request from the defendant to be tried by a judge. Approvingly, Harkas Yen remarks, "He is either innocent, or the killing was justifiable. When they are guilty, they usually ask for a jury trial." Here Ed reveals his distrust of juries and his doubt that they can weigh the evidence impartially.

The defendant is described as a man who "in a fit of passion . . . had killed another who had broken up his home." The verdict pronounced by the judge and the elapsed time were amazing: "In fifteen minutes he was tried and acquitted."

The Unisans, forced to direct all production into the war effort and the building of cities, have long since abandoned clothing styles; the standard garment is made of indestructible plastic, and no person may possess more than three of these. The suppression of frivolity has also led to limitations on pleasure and recreation. Harkas Yen claims that in the past, the unrestricted pursuit of pleasure weakened the Unisans and other nations and contributed to the Kapars' victories. In Unis, however, culture is preserved. "We would not permit art, music, and literature to die," says Yen.

Burroughs' superpatriotism and his contempt for those opposed to the growing power of the military and the obvious war pressures — this was late 1940 and the conflict raged in Europe — was again made evident in a dialogue with Harkas Don. Tangor remarks, "In my country we have what are known as pacifists, and they have a song which is called, 'I didn't raise my boy to be a soldier.'" Don's reply indicates that this craven attitude would be rejected scornfully even by the women: "If our women had a song, it would be, 'I didn't raise my son to be a slacker.'"

In preparation for this series with its new planetary setting Ed devised more than eight pages of glossary, statistics, alphabet, and maps. The system of eleven planets, each 7,000 miles in diameter, that were in orbit around Omos, the sun, received the Unisan name of Canapa. Ed referred to this system as Globular Cluster N.G.C. 7006, 220,000 light years from the earth, and noted that the name had been derived from a book by Sir James Jeans, the distinguished British astronomer. His statistics about time on Poloda include the following: The recorded history antedates the year *1* by 5,000 years, but before this consists largely of legend; there are 300 days to the year, 30 days to the month, and 10 days to a week. He invented the Unisan numerals and an alphabet of 25 vowels and double consonants.[21]

The Burroughs map of Canapa shows the perfect circular orbit of the eleven planets that are only one million miles from their sun, Omos. The planets are Poloda, Antos, Rovos,

Vanada, Sanada, Uvala, Zandar, Wunos, Banos, Yonda, and Tonos. With the creation of this extensive system Burroughs revealed his future writing hopes — in eleven worlds he had unlimited settings for all the bizarre civilizations he cared to invent. Three other maps were of Unis and the eastern and western hemispheres of Poloda, the remaining four continents, all with syllable endings like Un*is*, being named Epris, Heris, Karis, and Auris.

These pages of details and statistics provided some realistic substance to the Unisan civilization in "Beyond the Farthest Star," but actually, other than short sections of reference or explanation, the material does not receive sufficient emphasis to make the Unisans or other races in any way unique. In the Mars stories, notably *A Princess of Mars* and *The Gods of Mars,* the Burroughs details about the green and red men, the incubators, the atmospheric plant, and the equipment provide fascination and color. Burroughs had long since run out of these ideas. The style of "Beyond the Farthest Star" was mere thin, brief reporting of events, language used casually and without excitement. Even the social and legal systems were developed sketchily. Perhaps this was a result of the hasty writing; the novelette was completed in twelve days while Burroughs, at the same time, had spent six days in finishing the 21,000-word "Escape on Mars."

The incidents of "Beyond the Farthest Star" involve Tangor's role as a pilot of a pursuit plane for the Unisan air force, and much of the story consists of battles with the fleets of Kapar planes. With the story offering only the barest hint of a romance between Tangor and the girl Balzo Maro, it sets some sort of record for Burroughs, who in his other works has always managed to introduce romantic elements in the early chapters.

The second of the projected series, "Tangor Returns," was a novelette of 20,695 words written in only five days — December 17 to 21, 1940. In it Burroughs provides more exciting adventures for Tangor, who, with the conniv-ance of the Unisan Commissioner of War, becomes a double agent, accepting the scheme of the traitress Morgra Sagra to flee to Kapara; there, presumably, the pair will hand over vital military secrets to the enemy. Tangor's real mission, however, is to steal the drawings of the Kapars' most valuable device — a power amplifier that will allow them to fly great distances from Poloda. The Eljanhai, Unis' ruler, in explaining why the amplifier is so important, reveals plans for "an amazing and stupendous project." Tired of the perpetual war, Unis intends to send an expedition to one of the closest planets, either Tonos or Antos, and if a suitable environment is discovered there, Unis hopes to transport all of its people to the new planet. The Unisans' staggering plan, "a heroic migration unparalleled in history," was a Burroughs theme for the future, an idea held in abeyance.

In creating Kapara, where Tangor arrives with the treacherous Morga Sagra, Burroughs has incorporated the worst elements of two dictatorships, those of Stalin and Hitler. The secret police, headed by Gurrul, "the most feared man in all Kapara," represent the Soviet OGPU (MVD) or Himmler's Gestapo, while the dictator, Pom Da, who had ruled for ten years and is described as "a cruel and cunning monster who had ordered many of his best friends and closest relatives destroyed," is a counterpart of Stalin. A fourteen-year old boy, Horthal Gyl, the son of Horthal Wend, the inventor of the desired power amplifier, becomes a type of fanatical Hitler youth, a boy who has been indoctrinated to reject his parents' love as "maudlin sentimentality . . . not for Kapar men," and who wishes to be admired only because he is "hard." Dedicating himself, body and soul, to the state, he spies upon his father and without qualms turns him in to the secret police for execution.

Again, in this second novelette of the series, the romantic aspects are ignored. Tangor, having escaped from Kapara with the secret amplifier, is prepared to undertake a most hazardous mission; to test the amplifier, he will fly to the planet Tonos, 570,000 miles from Poloda. At the story's end, as he prepares to depart, a sentimental farewell scene between Tangor and Yamoda, Harkas' daughter, gives promise of a future romance. They kiss for the first time, and Yamoda, who had previously been a kind of "beloved sister," now somehow seems "different." This is only a brief indication of awakening love, however. Burroughs concludes the story and the series — the contemplated third or possibly fourth novelettes were never written — with an editor's note: "I wonder if Tangor ever reached that little planet winging its way around a strange sun, 450,000 light years away. I wonder if I shall ever know."

In marketing "Beyond the Farthest Star," the first of the two novelettes, Burroughs at once ran into difficulties. A first submission to Ray Palmer at Ziff-Davis brought a rejection, and with the return of the story from Munsey, on January 10, 1941, editor Post included a discerning evaluation:

It seems to be merely a long travelogue about a fictitious and not extremely interesting planet. I think you will agree with me that about eighty percent of the story is description and that there is little plot or suspense and only spurts of action.

In February came rejections from *Liberty* and from Standard Magazines where Margulies also offered pertinent criticism:

The story's initial premise is too far-fetched for our science fans. . . . How the story came to be written, why the hero fails to die, how he is suddenly whisked away to a world light-years away, and how the hero can suddenly speak the alien language — all these elements, unexplained in the story, make it far from convincing. The hero's adventures on the alien world are rather ordinary.[22]

Conceding that the action was "fairly good," Margulies maintained, however, that "the bulk of the hero's experiences are not imaginative enough for a pseudo-science novel." He concluded, "The far-fetched foundation of the story, plus the mundane quality of the hero's exploits, remove it from within our scope. . . ."[23] On September 3 "Beyond the Farthest Star" was

purchased by *Blue Book* for $400 — Kennicott agreed that the story had "the element of novelty" — and it was published in the issue of January 1942. "Tangor Returns," the second novelette, apparently was not submitted to magazines; its appearance in print, posthumous, would be some twenty-four years after it was written.[24]

One of Burroughs' occasional excursions into humor and satire, "Misogynists Preferred," produces the inevitable consequences, aided by fate and natural instincts, that result when men who abhor women and women who detest men try to escape each other. The 3,300-word story, written in only three days, January 5 to 8, 1941, is launched when John Alexander, wealthy, eccentric, and a misogynist, inserts an ad in the newspaper: "*Wanted:* Men without family ties to join scientific expedition to be gone for two years; need some with scientific and some with seafaring experience; must be in excellent physical condition; misogynists preferred. . . ."

Alexander is described as a man "who likes to dig for things," but also a man to whom all women were anathema; he had made one fortune, lost it, and then made another. In between, his wife "had stuck nobly by him until he lost his money and then run out on him. Every time he thought of her, he could feel his blood pressure rise." Responding to Alexander's ad and joining him on the expedition are two unemployed actors and an ex-sailor, all of them with deep grievances against women. James, Alexander's Negro servant, is scheduled to accompany the group. The five men board the yacht *Henry VIII* and after an uneventful cruise arrive at their destination — an uninhabited Pacific isle. The carefree misogynists are now at "an Eveless Garden of Eden . . . a place of peace, sans gabble, lipstick, red toenails, permanents, and perfume at forty dollars a drop."

Meanwhile, Minerva Johnson, a wealthy man-hater, has proposed a plan to three attractive girls who share her antipathy toward the male sex. They would all like to "get away some place where there wouldn't be a single one of the odious creatures." Minerva's Negro maid, Hibiscus Washington, would join them.

The story takes its expected, coincidental turn. The *Naiad,* damaged in a storm, becomes a helpless derelict and drifts toward the island home of the misogynists. Later, a hurricane wrecks both of the yachts; the women are forced to come ashore and the men cannot escape from the island. Burroughs writes, "Let us, with charity, draw an impenetrable veil across the ensuing eighteen months during which five misogynists and five man haters were compelled to live together on a lonely volcanic isle."

An excerpt from the log of the *SS Westwind,* whose captain detected smoke arising from the island of Nui Papaya and sent a boat to investigate, presents the denouement. The people on the island wanted stores and provisions, but declined an offer to be evacuated. Some not-very-surprising statistics follow: "There were fifteen people on the island: five men, five women, and five babies, one of them black."

Burroughs' characters in "Misogynists Preferred" were given to quoting poetic lines that disparaged either men or women. In the Epilogue, the final line of the story, man has the last word: "Woman's at best a contradiction still."

While "Misogynists Preferred" provided some entertaining moments, the story was not sufficiently original to find a market. Its submission, under the pen name of John Tyler McCulloch, brought rejections, in February 1941, from *Esquire, New Yorker, Romantic Story,* and Hillman Periodicals. The story was never published.

Resuming the Venus series, again with a plan for three or four novelettes, Ed began "The Wizard of Venus" on January 23, 1941, but did not finish the story until October 7 of that year; during this period he interrupted his work on this manuscript to devote six months to the completion of the 65,000-word "I Am a Barbarian."

The Arthurian legend with the magician Merlin, who through his spells could transform his enemies into animals, such as pigs, provided Burroughs with the germ of an idea for his "Wizard of Venus." Carson Napier and his friend Ero Shan, once more fated to encounter accidental perils in an anotar (airplane), make a forced landing near a structure which resembles a medieval castle. They are viewed with fear and hostility by the people who live adjacent to the castle. Napier and Ero Shan are suspected of being wizards and of being in league with Morgas, a magician, who supposedly has turned individuals into zalders, a type of herded animal usually raised for food.

The Lord of the castle, Tovar, informs the two men that his lovely daughter Vanaja has been turned into a zaldar by Morgas, the evil Wizard. To prove it, he even shows them a small zaldar, resembling a pig, and insists that this animal is Vanaja. The astonished Napier views Tovar and his wife Noola with suspicion, believing it best to humor individuals "who are the victims of mental disorders." However, matters become quite serious when their weapons and plane are seized and they have no choice but to proceed to the castle where Morgas, the Wizard of Venus, lives.

Summoning up the occult powers he had acquired through the teachings of Chand Kabi, the East Indian mystic who had tutored him in the early years, Napier uses these to combat Morgas. The girl Vanaja, as Napier suspected, has not been transformed into a zaldar, but is a captive in Morgas' castle. Through his power to project images of himself, Napier deceives Morgas into a wild chase after phantoms; finally, Napier wills a herd of zaldars to appear, in Morgas' vision, as ferocious lions. The Wizard, seeking escape, leaps to his death from the summit of the castle.

A first rejection came from Munsey where Post, on November 3, 1941, described the story as lacking suspense and "short on both menace and action." Post remarked, "Once Carson's occult agility has been established his heroic deeds seem singularly unexciting." On the twenty-fourth the novelette was returned by Ziff-Davis, and a year later, in October 1942,

"The Wizard of Venus" received its final rejection from *Blue Book*.[25]

Burroughs' fascination with Roman history had led him, in *Tarzan and the Lost Empire*, written in 1928, to devise the strangest of anachronisms — a Roman civilization, its ancient customs unchanged, existing in the heart of Africa. This interest was revived in 1941, but Burroughs, instead of a fantasy work, chose to create a pseudohistorical novel about the Roman emperors. The main character, son of a chief of the Britons made captive by the Romans, becomes the personal slave and companion to a four-year-old boy whom he calls "Little Boots." Only ten himself, Britannicus soon realizes that he is serving the grandnephew of the emperor, one who bore a name that would be indelibly recorded on the pages of history — *Caligula*.[26]

The early chapters of "I Am a Barbarian" arouse strong interest and give promise of a fascinating novel, but far too much space is then devoted to the childhood periods of both Caligula and Britannicus and to the portrayal of the decadence of the Caesars and the depravity and sadism of the half-mad Caligula.

The last section of the novel depicts Caligula's "diabolic cruelties" rising to a horrifying climax. "None was immune except the army, which he greatly feared. He sought to destroy the entire Senate piecemeal. . . ." Britannicus was forced to witness many of the executions, but he then becomes involved in the slaying of the tyrant.

At the story's end Britannicus knows that he must flee from Rome to escape the retribution that will come. The closing lines merely state, "What followed the assassination of Caius Caesar Caligula in the twenty-ninth year of his life and the fourth of his reign, you may read in your history books — probably greatly garbled, as is all history." The indefinite ending, with Britannicus' actions uncertain, indicates that Burroughs probably was retaining an option for a sequel. His fascination with the bloodthirsty Caesars might have motivated him to use their

later reigns as a setting for another novel, with Britannicus still the main character.[27]

While "I Am a Barbarian" was still in progress, Burroughs began writing the most unusual work of his entire career. The humorous stories he had created in the past, including those intended for children, demonstrated that his imagination could soar just as widely and wildly in the invention of comic situations and characters as it could in the fantasy world. But in "Uncle Miner and Other Relatives" Ed wrote a series of portraits about a family whose antics left no doubt that they were completely mad. Without question, Peavy Peaberry, the narrator of the crazy events, and his father, grandparents, and relatives were insane — at times hilariously so.[28]

One can only speculate about Burroughs' motivation in writing a work of this type. He started "Uncle Miner and Other Relatives" probably in July 1941, shortly after he had been discharged from the hospital. The past months had been severely traumatic for him; in March Florence had left him, sailing from Honolulu to the mainland. The end of the marriage left him in deep depression, and to make matters worse, his mental turmoil was soon accompanied by physical problems — some slight heart attacks and then the return of his old trouble, a bladder infection. Between June 5 and July 8 he spent two periods in the hospital, where surgery was performed. In the preface to "Uncle Miner and Other Relatives," titled "An Appreciation," he described his hospital experience:

This tender and appealing autobiographical sketch was written by a noted savant immediately after his discharge from the Queen's Hospital in Honolulu, where for three weeks he was shot full of various derivatives of the poppy flower by hypodermic and orally, was given a general anesthetic that burned his lips, the inside of his mouth, his throat, and his lungs, was operated on by a surgeon named Brown, and was filled so full of sulfathiazole by a doctor named Withington that it ran out of his ears.

I AM A
BARBARIAN

BY EDGAR RICE BURROUGHS

Cover of I am a Barbarian, *1967; Jeff Jones, illustrator.*

It is doubtless that to these various contributing factors we owe this touchingly sentimental contribution to American belle lettres.

Oddly, he signed this preface "Joe Louis."

Burroughs had periodically attempted to vary his subject matter and style, hoping to escape the confines of the jungle and the fantasy worlds to which the editors and the public had relegated him. His efforts in realistic writing had not been successful, and all that remained was satire and humor; it was these that he chose to experiment with, stretching and exaggerating them into madness — humor gone berserk. The behavior of Peavy and the other Peaberrys reminds one of the old-time slapstick comedies where the most outrageous violence can be committed without being taken seriously. Although "Uncle Miner and Other Relatives" had an ingenious variety of characters and situations, it could not inspire any interest in the editors. It remained unpublished, with the records showing only one rejection, from the *New Yorker,* on August 28, 1941.

With "The Skeleton Men of Jupiter," written October 25 to November 20, 1941, Burroughs once more indicated plans for a series of three or four novelettes. On this occasion he returned to John Carter of Mars, who at the outset is kidnapped by "things" that were not men, human skeletons whose "black eye sockets looked out from grinning skulls." The strange aircraft on which Carter is placed soars away from Mars at an "appalling speed," traveling 14,000 miles in little more than a minute. He soon discovers the destination — Sasoom, the Martian name for the planet Jupiter, 342 million miles distant. Carter records the appearance of the skeleton men:

Parchmentlike skin was stretched tightly over the bony structure of the skull.... What I had thought were hollow eye sockets were deep set brown eyes showing no whites.... The nose was but a gaping hole in the center of the face ... so tightly was this skin drawn over their torsos that every rib and every vertebra stood out in plain and disgusting relief. When they stood directly in front of a bright light, I could see their internal organs.

U Dan, a Martian aboard the aircraft, apologizes to Carter and explains the reasons for the kidnapping. It appears that Vaja, the girl U Dan loves, has been captured by the villainous Multis Par and taken to Jupiter. On this distant planet the skeleton men, the Morgers, are planning to conquer all of Barsoom. To save the life of Vaja, U Dan has been forced to follow Multis Par's instructions; the Morgors need information about the war techniques of Helium and the man to supply this is John Carter. U Dan, without choice, has arranged for the kidnapping of Carter who in turn will also have no choice but to cooperate, for Dejah Thoris is soon to be seized by the Morgors and carried to Jupiter.

When Carter scoffs at the ability of the Morgors to defeat Helium, U Dan tells him of the invisible airships: "Perhaps two million of them will invade Helium and overrun her two principal cities before a single inhabitant is aware that a single enemy threatens their security. . . ." U Dan then explains how the Morgors make their ships invisible through the use of "magnetic sand composed of prismatic crystals":

. . . they magnetize the hull; and then from countless tiny apertures in the hull, they coat the whole exterior of the ship with these prismatic crystals. They simply spray them out, and they settle in a cloud upon the hull, causing light rays to bend around the ship. The instant that the hull is demagnetized, these tiny particles, light as air, fall or are blown off; and instantly the ship is visible again.

On Jupiter, events proceed rapidly. In an escape attempt Dejah Thoris, Vaja, U Dan, and other prisoners get away, but Carter is recaptured. Later, he too escapes and makes his way to the friendly country of Zanar, where, at the end of the story, Dejah awaits him.

The submission of "The Skeleton Men of Jupiter" to *Blue Book* on January 19, 1942, brought a rejection from Kennicott, who returned "I Am a Barbarian" at the same time. Referring to the war then raging, the editor commented, "I feel that there is so much real horror in the world, that our readers would rebel at the fictional horror which characterizes both these stories. . . ."[29] Some months later the novelette was accepted by Palmer at Ziff-Davis, the payment being $400; "The Skeleton Men of Jupiter" appeared in *Amazing Stories,* February 1943.[30]

Burroughs had begun a new Carson of Venus story on December 2, 1941, but the bombing of Pearl Harbor five days later, and the United States' entry into the war, caused him to abandon fiction writing for two years. The Venus story, with an opening of a little more than two pages completed, describes Carson and Ero Shan, in their anotar, flying "into the unknown," their destination the city of Sanara, where Carson has left his beloved Duare. The brief section is mainly expository, referring to their adventures with the "mad Wizard of Venus," his death and the dissolving of his "malign hypnotic powers," with the final freeing of all his subjects.

The two men pass over the vast, uncharted regions of Venus. Among the series of adventures and mishaps, there is a hint of danger in the sight of "Gargantuan beasts." The story breaks off with the men excitedly discovering a ship moving on an unknown ocean beneath them: ". . . the first work of man that we had seen since taking off from Gavo."

In this same brink-of-Pearl-Harbor period, Burroughs wrote an odd article, a hybrid piece that was a combination of fiction and prediction. His positive, superpatriotic opinions, aided by his unrestrained imagination, led him to compose "Fall of a Democracy," a 2,400-word article that prognosticated a bleak future world under totalitarian control. The situation appeared almost as a preliminary to the kind of world he had created in *Beyond Thirty.*[31]

He summarized a succession of disasters. Among these were: Hitler and Stalin formed a military alliance to crush England; the defeat of Russia was attributed to the perfidious British; the combined Axis armies forced Turkey, Vichy France, and Spain to declare war on Great Britain; in North Africa, the British forces were destroyed; America was terrified; the Isolationists were victorious in the November elections; neutrality measures were enacted; the British fleet attacked and crushed the American Atlantic fleet; the Japanese entered the war, seizing China, Hong Kong, Singapore, the Dutch East Indies, and the Philippines; Russia occupied Alaska; South and Central American governments seized Mexico; states west of the Mississippi seceded from the Union; hostile armies approached Australia, Canada, and Hawaii, and America's end was made inevitable.

Completed in October 1941, "Fall of a Democracy" was rejected on the twenty-second by *Liberty* and on November 13 by *Collier's.* A submission to George Carlin at United Feature Syndicate brought a note and refusal addressed to Rothmund. Burroughs sought publication by United Press. Carlin, on December 18, wrote, "Mr. Burroughs' *Fall of a Democracy* arrived here right on top of the news of Pearl Harbor. The news, of course, killed all possibility of using the article, but, in the light of events, the article had plenty of thrills of its own especially in the third from the last sentence, 'From the West Japan had crept closer.' " Carlin explained that even under normal circumstances the United Press could not purchase material of this type; there was simply too much demand for coverage of day-by-day events, and articles with a fictional basis properly belonged in magazines.

The Pearl Harbor attack, as Carlin indicated, made the article valueless. But this was a charitable comment about "Fall of a Democracy"; Burroughs, who in numerous past instances had assumed the role of political seer, was driven by his prejudices to compose this article with its series of predictions.

After a two-year war hiatus, Burroughs, aboard the destroyer USS Shaw en route to Honolulu, conceived an idea for a comic detective story; started on February 24, 1943, "More Fun! More People Killed!" was finished ashore on March 30. Any doubt that this is the wildest of parodies on the "whodunit" can be immediately dispelled by a consideration of its list of fifteen characters. Fourteen of these die in the course of the story. One of them is murdered by two mad competitors-in-crime, Bill Loveridge and Shandy Mason; they in turn eliminate each other. Sister Jennie has been poisoned by a certain Miss Sploor prior to the beginning of the narrative. Tessie Sploor, her violent homicidal tendencies displayed in the past, is "a demure little spinster of 68" who has killed her father and mother with an ax.[32]

In 1944 Burroughs devised realistic background elements for a horror story. In "Uncle Bill," a brief 1,787-word narrative written in only two days, May 19 to 20, Ed chose a "Young Woman named Mary" to summarize the one event in Aunt Phoebe's life.[33]

After returning from the Tarawa-Kwajalein mission in 1944, Ed, at the suggestion of George Carlin, conceived an idea for a *Tarzan* novel with a new setting. With the Netherlands East Indies now invaded and conquered by the Japanese, a fresh and exciting background awaited Tarzan, one with peril unlimited and, above all, with a dense jungle that matched his African habitat. This was the Island of Sumatra, and in using it for his novel "Tarzan and 'The Foreign Legion,'" Ed did some research. His foreword to the novel offered a statement of indebtedness: "My knowledge of Sumatra at the time I chose it as the scene of a Tarzan story was pathetically inadequate; and as there was not a book on Sumatra in the Honolulu Public Library, nor in any of the book stores, it bade fair to remain inadequate." He acknowledged information given him by various Netherlands government officials of India, Honolulu, and New York, and expressed gratitude to his "good friend" Captain John Philip Bird, who arranged a first meeting with the Netherlanders.

His worksheets, in addition to the customary glossary of characters, included two pages of details headed "Notes For Tarzan Sumatra Story." These listed geographical features, dimensions, and population ratios of the different races, and, as might be expected, devoted much space to the large variety of animals. For the animals that were vital to any Tarzan tale, the tiger and elephant, Ed prepared special notes. The Siamang gibbons had evidently aroused his interest for he wrote, "largest of the gibbons, great gymnasts, can make a terrific sound. Pouch in throat swells up like toy balloon, giving call a booming quality that makes it carry long distances in jungle." The Sumatran forest was described: "Enormous straight trunked trees, ensnared by giant creepers, vines, and huge air plants made a thick canopy overhead." He also noted certain savage natives — the Kubus; the Battas, who were cannibals; and the Orang-lu and Orang-lubu.

The 80,000-word "Tarzan and the 'Foreign Legion,'" completed on September 11, reports, at the opening, the efforts of Hendrik van der Mer to evade the Japanese; he is accompanied by his wife Elsje, daughter Corrie, and two faithful Chinese servants. Van der Mer's wife dies of fever, and he and a servant are callously bayoneted to death by the Japanese, but Corrie and Sing Tai escape temporarily. Tarzan first appears as Colonel John Clayton, an observer on the Liberator plane *Lovely Lady,* which is flying over Sumatra. The plane is shot down and Tarzan parachutes into the jungle, joined by Joe Bubonovitch, Tony Rosetti, and Jerry Lucas. Later, when the group is augmented by some loyal Dutchmen, it is called the "Foreign Legion," for its membership includes a Russian, an Italian, an Englishman, a Eurasian, and an American, Jerry, who is part Indian. The emphasis in the novel upon Oklahoma and Jerry as an Oklahoman is a tribute to Burroughs' friend Phil Bird, a native of the state. As in past stories, Tarzan becomes a rescuer, the godlike figure who descends at the crucial moment. The love affairs occur between Jerry and Corrie and between Rosetti and the lovely Eurasian, Sarina.

In "Tarzan and 'The Foreign Legion'" Burroughs does not produce an individual villain, as in his previous stories, but instead presents all of the Japanese as villains of the most despicable sort. Here he has forgotten a lesson of the past and the vow he made after his unfortunate indictment of the Germans. In this respect Burroughs revealed himself to be just as susceptible to World War II propaganda as he was to the propaganda of the first war. But with the Japanese he goes to even greater lengths, exhibiting them both as callous, sadistic monsters and as comical and ludicrous cowards.

The Japanese "sub-men" display confidence only when the odds are in their favor; against the superb fighting of Tarzan or the Legion they flee in confusion or, when the situation is desperate, blow themselves up with hand grenades. Burroughs' emphasis upon hatred of the Japanese, although this is disapproved by some of the Legion, makes hatred appear to be an inspired feeling. Tarzan's natural instincts place him above hatred — the emotion had come only once in his life, when Kala, the she-ape, was murdered by Kulonga; yet Corrie, the Dutch girl, says she wants to hate the Japanese: "I often reproach myself because I think I am not hating bitterly enough." Jerry cannot share her feelings, and later she tells him that hate will make her "a better woman": "I do not mean petty hatreds. I mean a just hate — a grand hate that exalts . . . a common, holy hatred for a common enemy."

In a brief section of "Tarzan and 'The Foreign Legion'" Burroughs provides an explanation for something that had long provoked comments and questions from *Tarzan* readers. This was the matter of the ape-man's unchanging youth. Tarzan reveals his belief in certain powers possessed by witch doctors and then recalls how, many years before, he had saved the life of a young black man; identifying himself as a witch doctor, the man persuaded Tarzan to agree to his "treatment": "It required a full month of concocting vile brews, observing solemn rituals, and the transfusion of a couple of quarts of the witch doctor's blood into my veins." Dr. Reyd, who has listened to this account, guesses Tarzan to be in his twenties. Burroughs, cagily avoiding any mention of an exact age — how could the jungle superman retain his glamor if his age placed him in the senior citizen bracket? — makes Tarzan's answer evasive: "That which I have told you occurred many years ago."

Tarzan also recalls another experience involving the achievement of perpetual youth. Certain "white fanatics" in Africa, described by Burroughs in his novel *Tarzan's Quest*, followed a practice of kidnapping young girls, killing them, and using their glands to prepare a compound. Tarzan reported that at the time, in rescuing some of the girls, he had obtained a supply of this compound. "Those who have taken it," he said, "including a little monkey, have shown no signs of aging since."

"Tarzan and 'The Foreign Legion'" develops into a series of adventures, without any unifying theme other than a common hatred of the Japanese and the Legion's eventual goal to travel to the sea and escape to Australia. At the story's end, with the group afloat on a prau, they are shelled by a Japanese ship and hurled into the water; a British submarine appears suddenly to save them.

Rejected by *Blue Book,* on November 28, 1944, and by Popular Publications, new owners of Munsey's *Argosy,* a year later, "Tarzan and 'The Foreign Legion'" never appeared in a magazine. Dedicated to Ed's friend Brigadier General Truman H. Landon, it was published by Edgar Rice Burroughs, Inc., August 22, 1947. In the book Ed pokes fun at another wartime friend, Colonel Kendall J. Fielder, picturing him dressed up as a "witch doctor."

Among the miscellaneous pieces written by Burroughs in the early 1940s is "An Autobiographical Sketch," assembled to fill a request of Raymond Palmer, Ziff-Davis Editor. The 750-word article was printed in *Amazing Stories,* June 1941, the same issue that contained Ed's "Black Pirates of Barsoom." Although the tone is humorous, the information about Ed's early years is accurate. The reference to his first ancestor, however, must be taken with a grain of salt; this ancestor, Coel Codeveg, a third-century King of the Britons, came to light in the genealogical investigations done by a researcher

Cover of Tarzan and "The Foreign Legion," *1947; John Coleman Burroughs, illustrator.*

for Burroughs. He mentioned the distinguished Codeveg with amusement, remarking, "as soon as you start writing your autobiography, you start bragging," and then he added, "You don't say a word about Stephen Burroughs who was such a notorious forger and jailbreaker in early New England days that a book was written about him. I probably inherited my bent for writing from him."

Ed carried his autobiography through his school days, his cowpunching period in Idaho, and his stint with the 7th U.S. Cavalry. He continued with a list of his varied occupations. In mentioning the thirty years he had devoted to "writing deathless classics," he noted that he had not "learned one single rule for writing fiction," but presumed that since his stories entertained and relaxed him, they would do the same for many other people.

Found in the Burroughs file of the 1940s is a Tarzan parody that Ed wrote, titled "Tarzan's Good Deed Today." It is a play and a satire for young people and appears as though Ed were having a good time with members of his own Tarzan clan. At the end of the play, Ed gives bizarre instructions on how to make costumes for Tarzan, the natives, and other characters.[34]

A one-page article, written by Burroughs in 1942 for a series titled "Famous Living Americans and Their Homes," was viewed with disapproval by the French-Stamats Company, publishers of *Perfect Home* magazine. Burroughs, hardly stimulated by the chore, sent the article from Honolulu to Rothmund on February 21 and advised, "If you don't like it, can it. . . ." His attitude was revealed in the comment that this was "a hell of a subject to a guy who ain't got no home to enthuse about." The French-Stamats Company, rejecting the article, noted its failure to do Burroughs justice: "His writings are customarily so vivid and moving and individual."

Ed's statements in the brief article were somewhat ambiguous. After recalling that his father had never owned a home, living always in a rented house, Ed, remembering his earlier years, explained that a need for a pride in ownership and a sense of permanency had motivated him to purchase homes later, two in Illinois and two in California. "But I have never lived long enough in one place to acquire a solid sense of permanency," he said. "And home and security seem almost synonomous, for home is sanctuary." Following his insistence that his homes were "real homes in every respect other than permanency," he concluded by stating, "And so, to me, home is where the children are and love and companionship and dogs and security and horses and ownership and white rats and books and permanence."

Burroughs also tried his hand again at writing verse. Two serious poems, one written when the war was raging in Europe and the other after the United States' entry into the war, are titled "Skunk in Defeat" and "A War-Job Striker to a Soldier."[35] In another poem, of a lighter nature, "Mud in your Ai, or May 1940," he makes an amusing attack on the supposedly idyllic Hawaiian setting. The poem was sent to Hulbert on the twenty-fourth; it contained some footnotes defining Hawaiian words — *mauka,* meaning inland, toward the mountains; *makai,* toward the sea; and *buffo,* "a repulsive toad that swarms over our yard nights."

On the beach at Lanikai, lovely, lovely Lanikai,
Where the mud comes down from mauka, from
  mauka to makai;
Where the piebald fishes ply through the mud
  at Lanikai;
There's where I love to be beside the yellow sea
With my water-wings and slicker, and
  umbrella over me.
Where the liquid sunshine tumbles and the
  thunder rumbles, rumbles
And a cloud-burst is a sun-shower on the beach
  at Lanikai.
I love the buffo buffo and the rain upon
  my roof, oh!
And the mildew and the rust and the typhoon's
  throaty gust
And the roaches, and the ants that have crawled
  into my pants.
I love it! oh, I love it! I cannot tell a lie,
From Kalama and Kailua all the way to
  Lanikai.

25
LAST
YEARS
WITH THE
FAMILY

For Burroughs, now at his home in Encino, life assumed a sedate pace, his interests and activities revolving about his family. The excitement of the war period and the arduous months as a correspondent were behind him and he was happy to relax in the peace and quiet of southern California. The author whose characters faced constant peril and performed heroic feats on distant planets had avoided travel and adventure for most of his adult life, except for his brief automobile vacation trips. He had finally embarked, however, upon his most daring personal exploit, as a war correspondent, at age sixty-seven, when his youthful vigor and endurance were gone.

This overexertion, which he later regretted, had caused his severe attacks of angina pectoris. To Captain Burnbaum of the fleet oiler *USS Cahaba,* Ed mentioned his first heart attack on the ship and the second one that had seized him in Honolulu. "I guess I ran up and down too many ship's ladders for an old man," he wrote.[1]

On Hawaii and during his missions as a correspondent he acquired a host of friends, and at home he devoted much of his time to answering the stream of letters. His remarks to Donald Jackson, who became a congressman, and Phil Bird, both now civilians, were typically humorous: "Oh, how are the mighty fallen! All you snooty majors have been cut down to size. You were very pretty in your uniforms. I hope your wives still admire you in your natty civies. . . ."[2] He also had heard of the seismic wave that swept ashore in Honolulu, caused much damage in the harbor area, and forced his friends to flee from the Niumalu Hotel. Ed noted, "Evidently, I got out of the Niumalu just in time."[3]

He maintained a regular correspondence with Honolulu friends Duke Willey and Louise Rogers. Ed's fondness for liquor — Dr. Carden's medical report, following the angina attacks, stated, "Whiskey has been allowed thruout for its vaso-dilator effects" — led him to gloat over the abundance of liquor in California

Family gathering at ERB's Encino home; left to right: ERB, Mike Pierce, Joan Pierce, Marion Burroughs, Jack Burroughs and wife, Jane, October 1946.

in contrast to the shortage still existing in Hawaii. To Louise Rogers he wrote, "Not bragging, but just to make you envious: I now have cases of rum, gin, sherry, cognac, sauterne, bourbon, scotch, some Cointreau, creme de menthe, benedictine; and the other day I got a case of Ballentine's; but I had to buy two cases of sherry and a case of rum to get it."[4]

The wartime paper shortage, still severe, was posing publication problems. Ed joked about his paper-saving device:

You will note that I write on both sides of the paper while you waste an entire 8 1/2 × 11 sheet. It hurts me when I ponder the fact that we have orders for thousands of the famous Burroughs books that we can't fill because some

people take two sheets where one would do. We have an order in for 100,000 books, which is a piddling order; but we can't hope to get them before 1947 — if ever.[5]

Still weak from his overexertions in the Pacific, Ed spent much of his time resting. To Bert Weston he explained, "My life, if you are interested, consists in sitting. I tried to do something more strenuous the other day and had another heart attack; so I have taken up sitting again."[6] The sitting, during many evenings, was enlivened by family gatherings with Hulbert showing old movies and Laurel and Hardy comedies. Ed's diary entries included a note on September 1, 1946, his seventy-first birthday: "The children gave me a party at

"Happy Birthday, dear antique . . . September 1, 1946" (ERB's caption; he was 71); front, left to right: Joan Pierce, ERB, and Mike Pierce; back, left to right: Joanne Pierce, Jane Ralston Burroughs, Jack Burroughs, and Marion T. Burroughs.

Joan's and presents. It was a wonderful birthday." On the twenty-fifth he reported viewing a film supplied by Sol Lesser — *Tarzan & the Leopard Woman.* And on October 13, continuing a past practice, he entered a reminder: "Father was born 113 years ago. . . ." A comment of the twentieth told of a visit by four fans, "A Mr. Evans and his daughter, Mr. Ackerman, and 'Tigrina', a pretty blonde." (See page 802.) On November 20 Ed disclosed that Michael Mills had come to discuss the "reprinting of 27 Burroughs books to be priced at $1 or $1.25."

In his Hawaiian correspondence Ed acknowledged with sadness the receipt of the death notice of Dr. John Carden: "He had the same thing that he treated me for — angina

pectoris. He is another one of several of my physicians whom I have outlived."[7] He sent a sympathy letter to Mrs. Carden.

Ed maintained his relationships, both social and business, with Sol Lesser, his wife Faye, and their son Bud. In resuming the production of *Tarzan* films, after MGM had issued three of them from 1939-42, Lesser, for RKO, completed *Tarzan Triumphs* (1943), *Tarzan's Desert Mystery* (1943), *Tarzan and the Amazons* (1945), and *Tarzan and the Leopard Woman* (1946). The part of Tarzan was played by Weissmuller, who had been transferred from MGM, but the female roles were assigned to various actresses, including Francis Gifford, Nancy Kelly, and Brenda Joyce. Because of his popularity, Johnny Sheffield, the boy, Tarzan's adopted son, would appear in eight successive films, three earlier ones for MGM, and the remainder, the last being *Tarzan and the Huntress* (1947), for Lesser-RKO, with Weissmuller and Brenda Joyce still playing the leads.

Rothmund, concerned about British criticisms of the *Tarzan* movies that showed "distinct signs of weariness" and were "beginning to wear very thin," voiced the same objection to Lesser that Ed had previously made. The spectacle of a happy or joking Tarzan brought dismayed protests, with Rothmund writing:

I did not like "Tarzan and the Amazons." . . . You had Tarzan laughing continually. He never laughs; he only smiles, and this very rarely. He talked too much and too fluently for Tarzan, and on one or two occasions you had him telling funny stories. Brenda Joyce, as Jane, was terrible. She was dressed as if to go to a Hollywood night spot. She even had a permanent wave and other similar modern-day, feminine attractions. She giggled too much. . . .[8]

Rothmund added, ". . . it is a mistake to deviate too far from the standard Tarzan tradition, and I think the opinion of the British editorial writer . . . is correct when he says that the Tarzan fantasy is beginning to wear very thin."[9] Following the preview of a Tarzan film produced by Sol Lesser and his son Bud, a movie critic referred to the film as "the evil of two Lessers."

Lesser promised to advise the writer of the next Tarzan picture of these "constructive" criticisms, but noted that "the challenge for new and adventurous things for Tarzan to do is a wearisome task."[10] The film *Tarzan and the Amazons*, he explained, was exhibiting great box office appeal both here and abroad: "When I was in London they showed me evidences that the picture would gross in excess of $620,000, and here in the domestic market we are showing an increase of about 10%."[11]

Burroughs' general feeling of fatigue and the recurrence of angina pains prevented him from resuming a regular writing schedule. His health was poor. Associated with his heart trouble was arteriosclerosis, and what was diag-

ERB chatting with Sol Lesser and screen writer Richard Siodmak, Palm Springs, California, about 1947.

nosed as Parkinson's disease. He was overweight and in his seventy-first year. All of these problems sapped his strength to the point where he lacked energy to do very much. Despite all of this, an attempt at a story, the first since his return to the mainland, was noted in his diary on May 2, 1946: "Started 'Xonthron'. . . ." No further mention is made of this mysterious work. However, on September 7 he launched a new Tarzan novel, untitled.[12] Burroughs completed about 15,000 words (83 pages) before abandoning the project.

The correspondence with Caryl Lee, Florence's daughter, had continued while Ed was at Honolulu, and following his return they exchanged letters again. Caryl's main interest was still in horses, and when, in August 1946, she asked Ed to buy one for her, he responded, "I have been out of touch with the horse market for so many years that I wouldn't know where to look for a good one. And you probably won't find a good one that is cheap."[13] But the strong affection he felt for her was evident in his next questions: "Why have you never called me on the phone? I have asked you to several times. There must be some reason. Wish I might see you again. . . ."[14] Later, Caryl revealed, "I don't want to call because Mom always listens in on my telephone conversations. . . ."[15]

Caryl, whose desire for a horse could not be suppressed, commented hopefully that "somebody" might be "real generous on Christmas" and if the present were to be a horse, she would not be inclined to argue. On October 16, in response to her request that he drive over to pick her up, Ed explained, ". . . my condition has been such recently that I go nowhere." He urged her to visit him or telephone him. Caryl's never-ceasing suggestions about the horse caused Ed, on November 11, to write that he was sorry to refuse her: ". . . if your parents wanted you to have one they would buy it for you and pay the stable charges. They are as able to do so as am I." He noted he was feeling better and promised to see her soon. Addressing him as Dear "Ebby," the name she had always used, Caryl, on December 4, wrote, "Well last Friday I was fifteen. Everybody thinks I'm older but I'm not." Ed remarked, "And I haven't seen you since you were thirteen," and added, "I hope you get your horse before you throw a fit."[16] Concerning the birthday "remembrance" he sent, Caryl reported putting it in her savings account "to buy a horse which I will probably never get."[17]

It was not until January 1947 that Ed felt well enough to make the trip. In his diary, on the tenth, he noted:

Drove in to Marlborough School and picked up Caryl Lee. . . . She had a friend with her whom I had to drive home. . . . Then I got lost and drove halfway through Santa Monica — Stupid! Took Caryl Lee home for lunch, and then to King Midas Ranch to look at Palominos. . . . It was a hard drive for me. . . .

The strong attachment between the two continued, with Caryl's affection for Ed becoming even stronger as she grew older. Her visits were regularly recorded in his diary:

June 1, 1948: Caryl Lee came out to the office to see me. Florence brought her.
June 8: Caryl Lee and a friend : . . came out. They stayed for some time. . . .
July 15: Caryl Lee dropped in to see me at the office. . . .
October 17: Caryl Lee came to see me. . . .

Ed's fondness for her was demonstrated in the care he took to save all of the Valentine and "I Love You" cards that she sent him. On January 4, 1949, he wrote to thank her for remembering him at Christmas, and a month later, in a note to a Honolulu friend, he remarked, "Caryl Lee drops in to see me occasionally. She is quite a young lady and very pretty and very sweet. . . ."[18] Caryl's love for animals decided her future career; she became an animal trainer, working especially with dogs, and was employed at the movie studios.[19]

Since 1934 Edgar Rice Burroughs, Inc., and the Whitman Publishing Company had been joining forces to issue the Big Little Books,

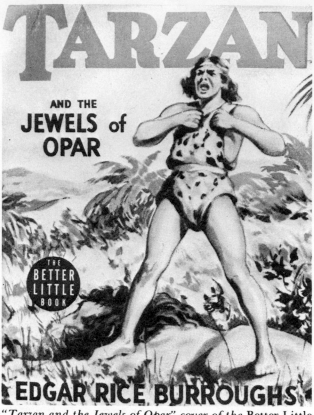

"Tarzan and the Jewels of Opar" cover of the Better Little Book, *Whitman Publishing Company, 1940.*

Better Little Books, and Tarzan and Mars stories. The story lines used in these varied children's books were not all Ed's creation; however, in a number of these the continuity and the illustrations were the work of Jack Burroughs. While the emphasis was upon the adventures of Tarzan, Mars, Venus, and the Inner World also provided settings for the stories. Some were published in comic magazines, such as *Crackajack Funnies,* by United Feature Syndicate, and in the comic pages. Typical Whitman Better Little Books of the 1940s were *John Carter of Mars; Tarzan the Untamed; Tarzan the Terrible; Tarzan and the Golden Lion; Tarzan and the Ant Men; Tarzan, Lord of the Jungle; Tarzan and the Lost Empire;* and *Tarzan in the Land of the Giant Apes.*

The correspondence between Lloyd Smith of the Western Printing and Lithographing Company, of which Whitman was a subsidiary, contained references to the "Tarzan one-shots"; three of these were scheduled, with Eleanor Packer doing the editing. In a letter of May 7, 1946, Rothmund wrote:

We were successful in securing a writer for her by the name of Rob Thompson, who has written our Tarzan phonograph album scripts which we have produced for Decca Records, as well as several of our Tarzan radio serials. He knows Tarzan, is not occupied with anything else at the present, and so can swing right into the job.

Two Tarzan "one-shots" appeared in 1947, *Tarzan and the Devil Ogre* and *Tarzan and the Fires of Tohr,* both taken from the Tarzan newspaper strips. Letters between Smith and Rothmund discussed the possibility of a twenty-five-cent pocketbook to be titled, "My Life with Tarzan," by Edgar Rice Burroughs. On June 22, 1947, Rothmund indicated uncertainty about the book:

I have had another talk with Mr. Burroughs on this, and it is felt that this is something that had better wait until some later date. I might add that the idea is one that we have mulled over in our minds for a number of years, and we have always felt, as we still do, that it should wait.

In August 1949 *The Cave Girl* was published by Dell as a paperback.

A lengthy relationship with writer Rob Thompson had begun in the early 1930s when he undertook to write the script for the radio serials. After this assignment was ended, Thompson did no work for Burroughs for a number of years. By 1947 complaints were being received from newspapers that the Tarzan comic strips had lost their popularity. Pessimistic comments came from various areas of the country:

. . . the belief prevailed here that Tarzan had — for the present generation, at least — outlived its usefulness and its popular appeal . . . in the last poll Tarzan ranked fourteenth among all our Sunday "comics".

We've had an idea for some time that Tarzan has spent itself. By this I do not mean that the comic is necessarily not as good as it used to

Board of Directors of Edgar Rice Burroughs, Inc., February 15, 1947; left to right: John Coleman Burroughs, C. R. Rothmund, ERB, Joan B. Pierce, and Hulbert Burroughs.

be, but that it has lost its appeal, possibly through age. . . .

. . . it was rated by the previous managing editor at the bottom of the list of what we were using. . . .

. . . declining interest in your feature . . . Tarzan was replaced by Lil Abner. . . .

An all-time low for subscribers to the daily Tarzan strips was reached that year, the total falling to eighty. On June 30 Rothmund wrote, "There have been as many cancellations in the first six months of this year as there were in the entire year of 1946. This shows an increase in cancellations of the Daily of exactly 100% from last year." Burroughs, alarmed, had been studying the Tarzan strips and had sent a note of disapproval to Laurence Rutman at the United Feature Syndicate. Concerning the week's strip that he had examined, Burroughs remarked, ". . . instead of being titled Tarzan, it should have been called Big Louie. It is not a

Tarzan strip. Practically no animals and no jungle. . . . I feel that this work casts such a reflection upon my name and my character that it may work a great deal of harm to both my books and my pictures."[20] He conceded he was "partially to blame" for not having noticed this before, and confessed that he had not read the scripts "for years." As an example of Tarzan's appeal in his "natural setting," Ed referred to Dell's fifty-two-page all-Tarzan magazine, just issued, which sold its 450,000 copies in less than a week.

As always, the remedy in a failing venture was to apply the "new broom" procedure. Ed wrote, "I think that we should have new writers and new artists, and that we should return Tarzan to the jungle where he belongs."[21] Figures quoted on the Tarzan strip income showed that before the 1947 decline had set in, the totals had risen from $3,344.99 in 1929 to $19,681.03 in

Cover of Tarzan of the Apes, *no. 5, Harold Foster's* Tarzan *daily newspaper strip, Dell Publishing Company.*

1946. It was at this time that Ed mentioned Rob Thompson, "a man whom we like," as the one to take over the continuity of the strips. Rex Maxon, now being paid $45 for writing the daily strip continuity — he had started in 1943 but had previously done art work and continuity on Tarzan — was to be dropped from the series. Burne Hogarth, receiving $50 a week for the Sunday page, would assume the daily strip art work beginning on September 1.

With Burroughs and Rothmund undertaking a close supervision of the strips, Thompson's writing chore became a difficult one. In fact, the correspondence, with United Feature included, turned into a series of complaints, requests for changes, placing of blame — Hogarth was the target for some of this — and pleas by Thompson for more money. The letters of 1947-48 to Thompson revealed that Ed was outlining or dictating the story contents and issuing a steady stream of criticism; the tactics

were reminiscent of Ed's association with his nephew Studley. Thompson exhibited remarkable patience in facing disapproval and continuous demands for improvement. Burne Hogarth, after thanking Burroughs for his letter welcoming the artist's "reappearance on Tarzan," stated, "Believe me, Tarzan is almost a part of me," but added, "I should like to reiterate my desire to use my own judgement wherever possible in order to make the picture material more clear to the reader."[22]

In May 1949 it became evident that United Feature, represented by Laurence Rutman, general manager, was dissatisfied with the continuity on the strips. Phoning from New York, Rutman contended that the story was "lousy" and that a new writer was needed. The writing was described as "too slow moving," the stories as "very much the same," and the names as "very difficult, confusing and unpronounceable."[23] Thompson, on May 12, responded with a lengthy defense of his work and a frank statement that he did not want "to lose the job of writing the Tarzan strips." He even expressed willingness to "take on a collaborator, a professional action-adventure writer," if Burroughs would agree. Thompson continued with his assignment for another year, and it was not until May 12, 1950, that Rothmund, yielding to demands from United Feature, notified Thompson of intentions to hire a new writer. "We have always deferred to the judgement of the Syndicate in matters relating to comic features," Rothmund wrote. The plan now was for Hogarth to assume both the writing and illustration of the daily and Sunday Tarzan features.[24]

Adapting himself now to a quiet, uneventful life, Ed found little inclination or energy for writing. In 1946 an old story, retitled "Night of Terror," was launched on a series of submissions; it was the unchanged version of "More Fun! More People Killed," written in 1943.[25]

Following a first rejection from the *Saturday Evening Post* on December 26, 1946, "Night of Terror" was returned by *Collier's* on February

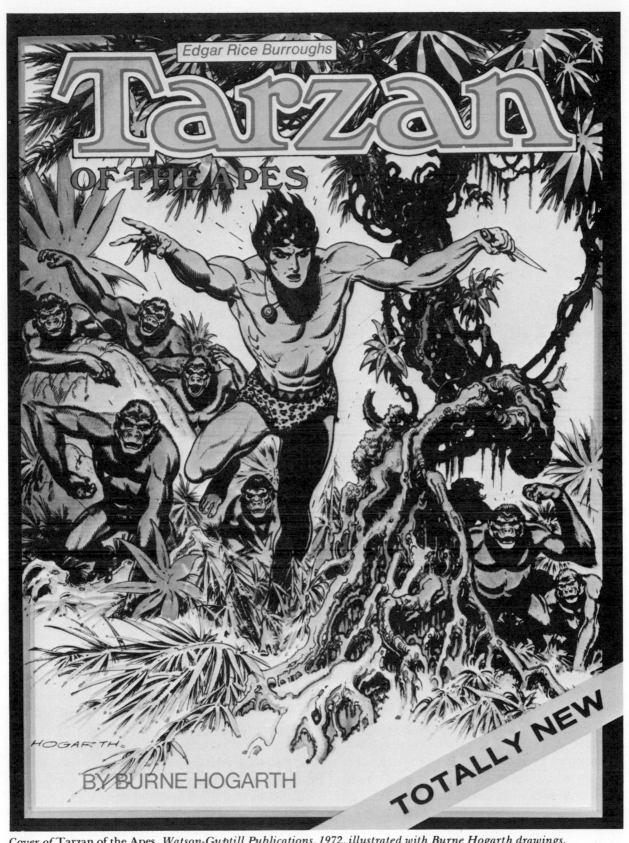

Cover of Tarzan of the Apes, *Watson-Guptill Publications, 1972, illustrated with Burne Hogarth drawings.*

28, 1947, by *Cosmopolitan* on March 28, 1947, and by *Ellery Queen's Mystery Magazine* on January 12, 1950. The story was never published.

Social and business matters occupied Ed's time during 1947. To replace his old wartime Buick, brought back from Honolulu, he purchased a new convertible Roadmaster coupe. At an office meeting he was advised that the government would demand of the corporation a $25,000 excess profits tax for both 1943 and 1944. On July 3 he entered a statement in his diary: "My RCA television set was installed this afternoon. I watched an LA-Hollywood baseball game at Wrigley Field — the first television picture I had ever seen. . . ." From then on it was television almost every evening, with Ed watching boxing, wrestling, and baseball. On September 1 he noted his seventy-second birthday and the customary family gathering to celebrate it.

Ed turned briefly to writing in October, but the nature of the work was puzzling. On the nineteenth he wrote in his diary, "Worked at office on Tarzan Sunday, finishing a 6 weeks story in one week — about 14 hours work." The last Tarzan novel, begun in 1946, had never been finished, and there is no other record of a Tarzan work. The entire day, on December 10, was devoted to correcting the *Llana of Gathol* page proofs; the book, a combination of four Mars novelettes, was published by Burroughs on March 26, 1948.

Ed's correspondence remained as extensive as ever. A note from Brigadier General Truman Landon, now at the War College in Washington, thanked Ed for the copy of *Tarzan and the 'Foreign Legion,'* the inscription, and the book's dedication, to Landon. In acknowledging the honor, Landon praised the "high degree of technical ability" Ed had acquired during the Pacific War and his demonstration of this ability in the novel. The plane that carried Colonel John Clayton (Tarzan) and others of the combat crew was a B-24 Liberator, similar to the ones Ed had flown with Landon. However, two minor criticisms of details in the novel were offered by Landon: "I've never been able to

fly a B-24 at 20,000 feet, loaded, on three engines; we never found it necessary to fill in Signal Corps photographers as members of combat crews since we had good ones of our own."[26] Ed accepted Landon's comments gratefully, and concerning the general's dubious view of the novel's title, remarked, "Three of us jammed our brains for months trying to find a better title, but were unable to improve on the one we chose. . . ."[27]

An invitation from Sol Lesser to be his guest at Palm Springs brought a comical response from Ed, who chose to emphasize the drinking hazards (since December 1946 he had been on the water wagon): "It would be nice to come down there and get cockeyed with you; but some time ago I stopped drinking entirely, and my recollection of Palm Springs leaves me the impression that there could be absolutely nothing for a non-drinker to do down there. I might come down and have a nitro with you. . . ."[28]

Ed might have established some kind of a record for continuous correspondence throughout the years, both with his readers and friends. A British fan, Frank Shonfeld of Croydon, England, who had begun writing to him in the 1920s, continued for the rest of Burroughs' life. On February 14, 1947, replying to Shonfeld's complaint about a futile search for a Burroughs book, Ed admitted, "I am rather glad that you are unable to get The Mad King. I am not very proud of that story. . . ." From his friend Bert Weston, who had remained in touch with him for more than thirty-five years, came a note telling of what a "great day" March 28 had been — the day Weston had visited Ed in Encino. In his letter of May 6 Weston noted that Ed appeared "much the same"; the years had not changed him, and Weston remarked in awe, ". . . after all the . . . things you have gone through during the war . . . you are the damndest man I have ever known also the most colorful and most lovable. . . . When I saw you 3/28/47 I wanted to pound on your back, hug you and perhaps hold your hand. . . ."

A letter to Burroughs from Germany revealed that the widow of Charles Dieck, who

Last meeting of ERB and longtime friend Bert Weston and wife Margaret, April 1947.

had published Tarzan books there, faced a desperate financial situation. Ed sent the letter to his niece, Marjorie Wesrendarp, so that her husband could translate it. Mrs. Dieck, in her appeal, spelled her name differently, and Ed checked with friends in the military in Germany to confirm her identity. To Marjorie, on June 12, he wrote, ". . . I shall send her something, for my relations with Mr. Dieck were very pleasant, and he made me a great deal of money."

A review in the *Los Angeles Examiner* of the film *Tarzan and the Huntress* contained a paragraph which Ed perused with astonishment:

Tarzan, impersonated by Johnny Weismuller, who has played the character 11 times, once *again moves back to his original setting, the jungle, where the late Edgar Rice Burroughs first imagined him.*

Concerning the term "late," Ed, on April 26, 1947, sent an inquiry to the paper and sought further information: "I have been an Edgar Rice Burroughs fan for many years, and I am grieved to learn of his death. Will you kindly advise when, where, and under what circumstances it occurred." After signing the letter, Ed dispatched a copy to Sol Lesser.

The year 1948 found Ed's health once more shaky. On February 12 he contracted "Virus X" and was given penicillin and sulfa "without results except for an allergic rash." On the fourteenth he noted, "I got worse and quit the medicine. Took Bourbon instead." He had actually started the year with a resumption of drinking; to a Honolulu friend he remarked, "You know we angina pectorials have to keep our arteries dilated. And you know how I hate the stuff. . . ."[29] Following his switch to bourbon, his temperature became normal and he began to get well. Later in the year, his most serious health problem returned; on October 1 he wrote, "Angina pains all afternoon. Took nitro-glycerine but the pain didn't stop entirely until I started on bourbon. . . ." The drinking continued: "November 17 — Had a bad night . . . drank bourbon highballs until 11 p.m. . . . December 1 — Lousy night and I feel like hell. I drank two cups of strong coffee and lay awake practically all night. I guess I'll have to go back to Bourbon — I did."

The year also brought a car accident in which, luckily, nobody was injured. Burroughs was apparently careless in entering the traffic on busy Ventura Boulevard from the driveway of his office; the *Los Angeles Times* of April 9, 1948, reported with regret the unhappy fate of three "new" sedans in the collisions that ensued:

A similarly new sedan of the same make . . . was unable to stop in time . . . [This] car struck the rear of a third new sedan of the same make . . [the] car then collided with Burroughs' rendering all three neither shiny nor new.

The accident was clearly ERB's fault. His once keen eyesight had been failing him. His narrowed peripheral vision and lack of good depth perception caused him to misjudge the distance and speed of the other vehicles. As a result of this accident and a realization of the hazards of driving at his age (72), his long love affair with the automobile came to an end. From the secondhand Velie of 1913 to the Buick Roadmaster of 1948 had been an eventful thirty-five years.

1948 was the presidential election year, and Burroughs, as in the past, gave his fervent support to the Republican Party. His detestation of the Democrats, the New Deal, and liberalism, still unchanged, was demonstrated in his daily routine: each afternoon he would leave the office in time to be home for the radio broadcast of one of his idols — Fulton Lewis. The first trust he had placed in Truman — Ed had pinned his photo to the wall of the cottage in Honolulu and commented that Truman had an "honest face" — quickly changed to disapproval and disgust. The election, during which he and the family, with the exception of Joan and Jim, voted for Dewey, was of course a terrible disappointment. Ed noted the results succinctly in his diary:

November 2: Voted this A.M. — Straight Republican ticket.

November 3: Truman elected.

Following the disastrous results, when daughter Joan came to Ed's home crying in jubilation, "We won! We won!," Ed, usually self-controlled in matters involving his family, exploded in anger.[30]

As 1949 opened, Ed's health began a steady deterioration. To nephew Studley and his friends he confided that he had avoided a physical checkup for nearly three years: ". . . I don't expect to have another one until I get a pain that I can't explain or that frightens me. I am afraid to put myself in the clutches of doctors. . . ."[31] A query about his health from "Prince" Mike Browning, a wrestler whose real name was Agis I. Mihalakis, caused Ed to respond, "Really, the only thing wrong with me is antiquity." Concerning wrestling on television, he observed, ". . . the more I see of it, the more I think it stinks. . . . But then, if 10,400 morons are entertained by the silly antics that one sees in the wrestling ring today, far be it from me to complain. . . ."[32]

A new and even more discouraging physical symptom now appeared. On March 14, 1949, following a thorough examination, Ed received a diagnosis from Dr. Buell H. Sprague:

The electrocardiograms showed evidence of heart damage, which is the result of the attacks that you described. However, we believe that your principal difficulty is due to a condition

Auto wreck of 1948 on Ventura Boulevard; ERB's car is on left in front of a corner of his office.

ERB's last California automobile operator's license.

called Parkinson's syndrome, or paralysis agitans. The weakness, muscle spasticity and the type of gait that you have are typical of it. Tremor or shaking of the arms and hands is usually more evident than it is in your case, which makes your case a little more difficult to recognize.

Sprague advised that no cure existed for this condition, but suggested the use of a drug called Benedryl to alleviate the symptoms. Ironically, Jack Burroughs contracted the same disease approximately twelve years after his father's death.

Ed's deep despondence at this complication was indicated in his reply to Weston, who had

697

Illustration of ERB and some of his literary characters; Al Williamson and Reed Crandall, illustrators.

698

also complained of old-age symptoms, but had noted a little improvement: ". . . if you are recovering from old age, more power to you! I am not. I have paralysis agitans, and am pretty nearly through getting around at all. I have a folding wheelchair that isn't any good unless somebody pushes me around."[33] He added, "I am too low even to dictate a letter, Bert; so I'll say goodbye." To his niece Marjorie he wrote, "I've got some doggoned form of paralysis that has more or less crippled my hind legs and apparently my brain also, as I haven't enough energy or ambition even to dictate a long letter. . . ."[34] The plans he had formed to build a new, larger home in Tarzana he now abandoned. Life, almost totally static, was reduced to sitting or lying, reading, watching television, and chatting with his family.

With Ed, at the year's end, being in precarious health, he was not informed of a tragic circumstance — the unexpected death of his nephew Studley. A diagnosis, possibly faulty, had brought Studley to the hospital for surgery. Following the operation for a hiatus hernia, Studley, age 57, died suddenly of an embolism on December 23, 1949.[35]

That month, following a serious heart attack, Ed was placed in an oxygen tent, but, with his old determination still intact, he refused to yield to discouragement or abandon hope. By January 1950 he improved sufficiently to be removed from the oxygen tent and even to write to a friend and apologize for the brief period of despair: "I am sorry if I gave you an idea I was unhappy in my last letter. With three wonderful children and five wonderful grandchildren, my life is certainly not dull. . . . they tell me I am getting on fine."[36] A note from Weston, vacationing at Coronado, brought a reply from Rothmund, who on March 2 reported talking to Ed: ". . . [he] especially enjoyed seeing the excellent snapshot . . . he . . . told me to mention that he is 'hopping in and out of oxygen tents.' "

On Sunday, March 19, 1950, Ed finished his breakfast and sat in bed, reading the comic pages. He was alone, and death came to him suddenly and quietly. The discovery was made by his housekeeper who, by prearrangement, notified his family and his physician, Dr. Herman Seal. Ed's desire for cremation had been expressed often in the past and in 1945 he left instructions that his ashes should be buried beside his mother's; he wrote, ". . . bury them under the big black walnut tree on my pet lot." The cremation took place at the Chapel of the Pines in Los Angeles, and on March 27, his son Jack Burroughs removed the ashes. According to Ed's wishes, they were buried beneath the tree that shaded the offices in Tarzana.

So in this final action Ed's life continued. He was now part of the nature he had worshipped and sought to protect — the nature whose creatures he had always viewed as superior to man. Shortly before the end he had said, "If there is a hereafter, I want to travel through space to visit the other planets."

Ed was seventy-four when he died — five months short of his seventy-fifth birthday. Life's road had been a long one. He traveled from a Chicago childhood to frustrating schooldays, to danger and adventure in Arizona and Idaho, to the tedium of business offices, and to the strange, wild creation of fantastic characters and events on paper. His greatest journey, forever to be appreciated by his host of readers, began in his imagination. It took him to the jungles of Africa and allowed him to soar through space and arrive, unconcerned with all boundaries and limitations, at his own teeming worlds. At first *his* worlds, they quickly became the pleasure and dream worlds of others — the eternal legacy of Edgar Rice Burroughs.

# NOTES

Chapter 1: The Creative Decision

1. ERB's *Autobiography* (unpublished ms.), p. 46.

2. "How I Became an Author," written by ERB for the Fine Arts Supplement of the *Chicago Examiner*, April 4, 1918.

3. From a biographical sketch of ERB, requested by William G. Chapman, who was handling ERB's newspaper syndications. On April 10, 1914, Chapman wrote:

Please detach yourself from your personality and write about a half a column sketch of Edgar Rice Burroughs. The American Press Association wants this for announcement purposes. Cast your modesty to the winds and write the sort of sketch that I might write if I had the same knowledge of you that you possess of yourself. No one will know you wrote it, in fact it will be attributed to me....

On April 13, ERB responded, "I don't believe that I can write that Edgar Rice Burroughs stuff for you; but there is a fellow who knows me who will tackle it, though what the devil of interest he can find to say I don't know. . . ." The "fellow" who wrote the biography remains unidentified, although the homey and adulating tone of the biography creates a possibility that Ed's close friend, Herbert (Bert) T. Weston, may have written it. There is no record of it having appeared in print in 1914, although Chapman had replied to say, ". . . The article will do you some good as it will be given a tremendous circulation. . . ." A lengthened version of the sketch, with five paragraphs added at the end to bring ERB's achievements up to date, was published in the *Book News Monthly* of August 1918 and titled "The Creator of Tarzan."

4. "How I Became an Author," *Chicago Examiner*.

Chapter 2: Childhood and a First Adventure

1. From a humorous autobiography written at the request of R. A. Palmer, editor, *Amazing Stories*. It appeared in the issue of June 1941 with ERB's "Black Pirates of Barsoom."

2. This was the first in a series of eleven steps in "My Wonderful Military Career," compiled and illustrated by ERB in 1897. (See section on his experiences with the U.S. Seventh Cavalry.)

In his *Autobiography* Ed jokingly refers to William Carpenter "Billy" Camp, his Brown School playmate, as "a nationally known marital expert, having married, among others, the actress Alita Proctor Otis and Mrs. Thorne of Montgomery, Ward & Co." He also recalls Bev Waters who "makes nearly all the steel lockers in the world and is another one of the lousy rich." ERB had referred to the Brown School as having a "roster that sounded like Who's Who"; Lillian Russell had also attended there.

ERB wrote twice to the Brown School on the occasion of its Diamond Jubilee in 1932. His letter, dated July 12, 1932, was to Principal William J. Page: "One of my brothers recently sent me newspaper clippings relative to Brown School's Diamond Jubilee which I found tremendously interesting, recalling as they did the days that I had spent at Brown School."

After mentioning that his wife Emma had been graduated from the school, Ed recalled, "Three of her older sisters and three of my older brothers also attended the school at various times." Ed pointed out that no mention was made of Florenz Ziegfield, also a former pupil. "One of the memories of the school that most deeply impressed itself," he wrote, "is of 'Daddy' Wood and his disciplinary methods. As I recall the band of youthful highbinders he had to deal with, I sympathize with him now, but at the time I did not. . . ."

To the editor of the school newspaper, *The Brown Spot*, Ed wrote on December 16, 1932: "The Brown Spot came to me today as a very pleasant surprise and a reminder of a dim and distant past when I was a pupil at Brown."

Ed commented about the neighborhood and noted, "Our three children were also born on Park Avenue, near Robey. . . ."

3. The businesslike tendency of the family and, of course, George Burroughs' pride are illustrated in his notation beneath Ed's letter to his father: "Recd at 'Riggs House' Washington, D.C. Feby 19th 1882 G.T.B."

4. In a taped account, George Burroughs, III, recalls this reason why both brothers entered Yale at the same time. Marie Burroughs, also taped, reveals that Harry, anxious to put childhood things behind him, sold his stamp collection for about $500. This is an indication of how prosperous the family was at the time.

5. The poems are in the Burroughs manuscript collection at Tarzana, California.

Once there was a man who thought himself quite grand
There was a dagger in his belt and pistol in each hand
But when he saw a poor blind mole
He climbed far up a very tall pole
But before he reached half way to the top
One of his pistols he had to drop.
But at the bottom it hit the pole
And going off shot dead the mole.
Then this grand man came sliding down.
And carried the mole in to the town
And told the people (the wicked knave)
That he was good, and strong, and brave
He told them too he killed the mole,
But never mentioned climbing the pole.

At the bottom of the page beneath the poem Ed illustrates the remainder of the incident. The buildings of the town are outlined in a skillful perspective to provide a background for the cowboy who now stands, mustaches pointed, with a gun dangling from his right hand. His left hand, held out, also clutches a gun, and extending from it is a stick — on which the dead mole is draped. A careful observer, Ed missed no details. In both drawings of the man, the dagger is shown at his waist, and his blouse, pants, and long heavy boots are clearly sketched.

Ed addressed another letter to "My Highly Educated Brothers" and drew comical cartoons representing George and Harry, one on each side of the page. They are shown with top hats, canes, and formal coats. One has an enormous handlebar mustache while the other wears both mustache and beard. Ed has printed in large letters "89 S.S.S.!" the S's stand for "Senior." His original poem then follows:

In eight teen hundred and eighty nine
For my brothers to be seniors it will be time
And then you bet their hats will shine,
In eight teen hundred and eighty nine.
From September eighty seven to September eighty eight,
Will be the first and last of their Junior date.

On the other side of the page he offers a poem titled "Chicago":

The snow is falling thick and fast
In Chicago
And I hope every gust will be the last
In Chicago
And it falls on every side walk
In Chicago
And the lazy folks talk
In Chicago
How tired they will get
Before it will melt,
In Chicago.

Poems which may not have been contained in letters to his brothers include one about a certain Mr. Roach who "will be the next mayor of Chicago." Ed ends by stating, "And when Roach has the key/No more red flags will you see." He goes on to write "Dear Reader if you want to be killed just turn over and read what is on the back of this paper." He has composed a poem titled "Horses and Dogs":

Horses are large
And horses are small
Some horses kick
But hurrah for them all.

Dogs are good,
And dogs are bad.
Dogs are solom,
And dogs are sad,
Some dogs snarl,
And some dogs bite,
Some dogs are playfull
And their all right.

Joyce Burroughs, the daughter of George Burroughs, III, was fascinated by her famous relative and in 1942, at the age of thirteen, wrote a brief biography of ERB, possibly as a school project. In it she mentions his letter-writing to his brothers at Yale and his illustrations: "On one letter he illustrated a boy sitting on a telephone pole out of the reach of angry hands and it was labeled: 'Me, when you find out I wrecked your sailboat.'"

6. Reported in Joyce Burroughs' biography. Her account appears to be confirmed by the same information on a tape by George Burroughs, III.

7. At that time, by the fall of 1888, George and Harry had moved into the new Chi Phi Fraternity House, just completed. An article in the Sunday *Register* describes it as one of the finest fraternity houses in Yale; it was situated on York Street near Elm. The Chi Phi Fraternity itself was claimed to be the oldest in the country, founded in 1824 at Princeton. "Those who are fortunate to occupy the new house," the article stated, "are George T. Burroughs, Jr., Harry S Burroughs. . . ."

The house was of brick, three stories high. In the elegantly furnished parlors were "velvet moquet" carpets, and the walls were covered with the new cartridge paper of a fashionable tint, matching the carpets. The house was heated by steam, and hot and cold water was furnished to every room. A system of "lighting gas by electricity" was used, and all the rooms had "electrical call bells." The luxury in which the two boys lived is

again an illustration of Major Burroughs' ample income at the time.

On June 27, 1888, George wrote to his mother; the letter was headed Chi Phi Fraternity, Omicron Chapter, New Haven, and was about plans for coming home, evidently for the summer. These plans were being changed; he wrote, "Sweetser is going home today & Rice will probably not go through Chicago until after we get to Beaver Lake. . . ." In a P.S. he writes, "Yale yesterday won the deciding game in the base-ball series & consequently again holds the championship."

8. Letter from Ed to Joseph Emerson Haven, American Consulate, Florence, Italy, April 20, 1931. Haven, who had lived on the west side of Chicago, had written ERB on March 31. ERB responded ". . . the district you mention was in the stamping grounds of my childhood."

9. Reported in an unidentified clipping contained in the old Hulbert album.

10. Ibid., in another clipping.

11. Stated in "When 'Tarzan' Went to Harvard," written at the request of Elsie Schobinger, whose father was the principal and Ed's professor at the school. At the time the article appeared in the *Harvard Review*, Anniversary Issue, 1865-1940, the school was located at 4731 Ellis Avenue in Chicago.

12. Letter to Elsie Schobinger, August 3, 1939.

13. "When 'Tarzan' Went to Harvard," *Harvard Review*, Anniversary Issue, 1940.

14. In his *Autobiography*, in speaking of the emphasis upon Latin and Greek in the schools, Ed wrote about Harvard, ". . . Professor Schobinger was putting into practice the brilliant idea of teaching boys Greek and Latin Grammar before they learned English, which is one of the reasons why I know nothing about either Latin, Greek or English."

He referred to this practice in other schools he had attended as a joking explanation of his defects in writing and grammar. In "When 'Tarzan' Went to Harvard" he adds, "then I went to Andover and studied Greek and Latin all over again; so, having never studied English, I conceived the brilliant idea of taking up writing as my profession." He often repeated this jibe at himself.

15. Quoted from "How I Wrote the Tarzan Books," ERB's account, date unknown. On the subject of "epidemics" he wrote in his *Autobiography*, "Unquestionably my destiny is closely interwoven with pestilences, which may or may not account for my having become a writer."

16. In a flurry of letters dated September 3, 7 (two letters), and 15, the conscientious Schobinger sent George Burroughs a certificate of moral character for Ed, a list of his grades, and letters of explanation and apology. George Burroughs had written to him on September 6 to ask for Ed's grades, since the first letter did not contain them. On September 7 Schobinger wrote, "I wrote one before and sent it by mail to your address on Washington Boulevard. It was dated Sept 3d; but as Edgar had only told me of his wanting a certificate of moral character I had put in nothing about his standing. As you mention this specially, however, I have supplemented the new certificate by the averages drawn from our books, and shown as the cards we sent you weekly."

The entire matter offers an illustration of George Burroughs' close supervision of his son, and of his thorough attention to the smallest details.

17. Edgar Rice Burroughs' *Autobiography*, unpublished, is a fifty-page manuscript, unpaged. Extracts and passages from it, some sent out by the Burroughs office, have appeared in a number of publications. A first reference to ERB's intention to write his autobiography was made in a letter of August 24, 1925, to his friend W. H. Gardner: ". . . So many people are writing about their own lives now that I am afraid the public is going to tire of autobiographies. I think that work is one for extreme

old age when we are through with active work, so in a few years I shall probably start my autobiography...."

With the syndication of the Tarzan cartoon strips by The Metropolitan Newspaper Service headed by Maximilian Elser, Jr., there was evidently a demand for the autobiography. Elser requested it some time in 1929, as indicated by ERB's direct comment to Elser in the *Autobiography*, page 17:

This, my dear Elser, hurts me more than it does you. Of all the punk jobs that anyone ever wished on me, this attempt to write the outline of my life that you have asked for is unquestionably the comic worst. It is deadly, due unquestionably to the fact that nothing interesting ever happened to me in my life. I never went to a fire but that it was out before I arrived. None of my adventures ever happened. They should have because I went places and did things that invited disaster; yet the results were always blah....

The *Autobiography*, completed toward the end of 1929, was referred to by ERB in a letter to his brother George, December 9, 1929:

That autobiography was a nightmare for me. The publishers asked for it and kept after me until I wrote something. Then I decided to write it as fully as I could and in detail. At that I never finished it. though I had about twenty thousand words when I gave up the ghost. This they condensed to what is appearing in the newspapers....

In a letter to brother Harry, Ed, on December 18, 1929, explains:

The autobiography, as published, was very much abridged. In some twenty thousand words, which took me only a little way into my literary career, I carefully narrated everything that I could recall that my publishers might have some leeway in the matter of selection of the material they wished....

I got a grin out of your references to originating appropriate replies to remarks and questions relative to the autobiography. I have a hell of a time, being neither witty nor quick at repartee. I have to content myself with merely looking foolish, which I can do quite naturally.

The *Autobiography* extends only to the year 1913 and actually offers little detail about the first important sales of stories, merely referring to them. Its most valuable sections are about the early years at Michigan Military Academy and the experiences with the Seventh Cavalry and those in Idaho. Of special appeal is ERB's humorous and self-deprecating style.

In later years a number of attempts were made to sell the *Autobiography*. On March 20, 1937, identical letters were mailed to *Liberty* magazine and to *Harper's*, stating: "Would you be interested in purchasing the First American and Canadian magazine rights in Edgar Rice Burroughs' autobiography, in connection with which we could possibly submit pictures of Mr. Burroughs at various states in his life?" Both magazines turned down the offer. As late as 1963 copies of the *Autobiography* and "Memoirs of a War Bride" were sent to *American Heritage Magazine*.

18. In the humorous article appearing in *Amazing Stories*, June 1941, ERB explains his greenness during those early Idaho days:

Somewhere along the line I went to Idaho and punched cows. I greatly enjoyed that experience, as there were no bathtubs in Idaho at that time. I recall having gone as long as three weeks when on a round-up without taking off more than my boots and Stetson. I wore Mexican spurs inlaid with silver: they had enormous rowels and were equipped with dumb bells. When I walked across a floor, the rowels dragged behind me and the dumb bells clattered: you could have heard me coming for a city block. Boy! was I proud!

Since Ed went to Idaho in 1891, and again to the Mule Shoe Ranch some time after his discharge from the army in 1897, possibly for the spring roundup of 1899, some of these recollec-

tions may apply to this later period.

19. The horse may have been the "locally notorious man killer, Black Pacer," mentioned in "The Creator of Tarzan," *Book News Monthly*, August 1918.

20. ERB was always concerned about any mistreatment of animals and was opposed to indiscriminate killing by hunters. He loved dogs but had evidenced a dislike for cats.

21. From a five-page autobiography written for Conroy Gillespie of the *Spokesman-Review*, Spokane, Washington, May 17, 1935. ERB apologized for the article, referring to it as a "very rough outline," and on page five at the end wrote in his P.S., "This is terrible, but if you can make anything of it, more power to you."

The account opens with a statement that ERB as a boy had ridden for "Sweetzer Brothers & Pierce" of Cassia County, Idaho. Lew Sweetser (spelled with an *s*, not a *z*) appears to be the only one otherwise mentioned as being part of the firm of Burroughs & Sweetser.

22. Ibid.

23. Ibid.

24. ERB's *Autobiography*.

25. Ibid.

26. *Spokesman-Review*, May 17, 1935.

27. Ibid.

28. Ibid.

29. Ibid.

30. Ibid.

31. ERB's *Autobiography*.

32. In his *Autobiography* ERB writes, "From murderers, horse thieves and badmen I was transported to Phillips Academy, Andover, Mass. I presume there must have been another epidemic somewhere."

Chapter 3: Schooling, Rebellion, Discipline

1. Taken from the Phillips Academy catalogue of June 1892 which added a further warning statement, "The school is not a suitable one for boys who are idle, wayward or averse to study, or for such as require the supervision of a teacher and the routine of a schoolroom to enforce industry and fidelity."

The academy in 1969 attained its 191st year. In a decision made in the late fifties, the school adopted a policy of admitting the best 250 candidates each year "regardless of their ability to pay tuition." In 1965 the "Schoolboys Abroad" program was established; one hundred eleventh-graders are sent abroad each year to study in Rennes, France, or Barcelona, Spain, "under the joint sponsorship of Andover, Exeter, and St. Paul's."

2. Information obtained through correspondence with Charles W. Smith, alumni secretary of Phillips Academy, and with the special assistance of Mrs. Waters Kellogg, associate archivist.

Frank Coleman Burroughs, born in 1872 and closest in age to ERB, may have gone to a private school in Chicago before enrolling at Phillips Academy. A brochure saved in Ed's school papers advertises a preparatory school at 43 South Sheldon St., Chicago, September 20, 1884, with John M. Bell B.A. as master. The courses of study for junior, middle, and senior years are based upon subject matter, with fees of $100, $150, and $200. Since Ed would have been only nine years old at the time, it's doubtful that he attended this school.

3. Phillips Academy catalog, 1969.

4. Ibid.

5. Ibid. Charles Smith's letter of December 19, 1968, states that "School opened September 11 in 1891 and broke for recess on December 11, reconvened on January 15, 1892, until March 22...."

6. Ed's older brothers George and Harry had studied at Sheffield Scientific School of Yale University, but they had not attended Phillips; only brother Frank had attended, as indicated, from 1890 to 1892.

7. "A Horrible Example of The Man Who Could Not Say No" was written by ERB for the *Sesqui-Centennial Record* at the request of A. Porter Thompson who, on November 27, 1927, asked for a story "on any subject," adding, "it need not be more than three pages." In a little over two pages ERB recalled his days at Phillips, treating the whole subject of his brief, undistinguished scholastic record humorously. Thompson had hoped for something about Tarzan. Since the deadline was April 1928, ERB's article, presumably, was written between December 1927 and April.

The *Record*, a large paperback of 96 pages, commemorates the 150-year period from 1778 to 1928. ERB's article (he is listed as Edgar Rice Burroughs '94) is rather brief, beginning on page 13 and continuing on page 68. A cartoon drawn at the top of the article shows a table labelled The Morrill House Eating Club. Figures are drawn at the table and ERB is the second one from the left. Ten boys are shown; the cartoon is arranged as follows: Andy Gilmour; Edgar Rice Burroughs, '94; "Gus" Thompson, '92; S. C. Conde, '95; Frank Burroughs, '93; May Morrill (in background); Wirt Thompson, '94; Mancel Clark, '94; B. F. Rice, '93; "Art" Foote, '92.

The contributors to the *Record* include Ring Lardner; Walter Pritchard Eaton; Commander Richard E. Byrd; Archibald B. Roosevelt, '13 (President Roosevelt came to Andover for his son's graduation in 1913, according to a photo notation); Senator Hiram Bingham '94; Samuel Merwin; William Beebe; Louis Untermeyer (a poem); Sir Wilfred Grenfell; and William Lyon Phelps. These are not all alumni; some had been lecturers at the school and others had sons or relatives there.

The *Record* contained congratulatory letters and telegrams from prominent persons: William Howard Taft — two of his sons had attended Phillips; Oliver Wendell Holmes, Justice of the Supreme Court and son of Oliver Wendell Holmes, Andover 1825; Henry L. Stimson, 1883; and Herbert Hoover. Telegrams were sent by Charles A. Lindbergh and Dwight W. Morrow.

8. ERB's *Autobiography*.

9. Excerpt from *The Phillipian*, the school paper, September 16, 1891, as supplied in correspondence with Charles W. Smith and Mrs. Waters Kellogg, December 19, 1968.

10. Ibid.

11. In his article for the *Sesqui-Centennial Record* ERB wrote, "Beside me are copies of the Philo. Mirror for the Fall Term of '91 and for the Winter Term of '92. I have not opened these for lo, these many years. Perhaps it would have been just as well if I had never opened them. They contain poems and numerous illustrations of my composition, the less said concerning which the better, except that they point the horrible example of the man who could not say no."

The reference to "poems and numerous illustrations of my composition," if interpreted correctly, indicates that ERB had more than one poem in these issues. However, according to Mrs. Kellogg, only one poem could be assumed to be his. She writes, "There were only two poems, besides the first prize poem, in the Winter issue. I am assuming that the 'Possum et Coona' one, of which I have made a photocopy is by Burroughs, as the other one was about Latin Commons which would not have any connection with him."

The total cuts by ERB in the *Mirror* of Fall 1891 are as follows: (1) Table of Contents illustrations; (2) "Out of Sight," p. 46; (3) "A Pony is a Nice Thing to Have," p. 62; (4) "Head Reducer," p. 66; (5) "Ye Long Haired," cut heading the football poem, p. 67; (6) Horses and chariot with football players; (7) Girl waving farewell, p. 74; (8) Individuals and street scenes, p. 84; (9) Football player, p. 96; (10) "Street Teams," p. 101;

(11) "P.A. Police Force," p. 111; (12) "Prospective," couple holding hands while picture is being taken, p. 113.

The cut "Out of Sight" presents a back view of three men, one gazing off into the distance as a ruse to draw the attention of the other two away from the bottle he has concealed behind his back. The "Street Teams" shows two players striking each other. Ed, to complete his rowdy conception of how football is played informally off the gridiron, added an imaginary "Morton Street Team" lineup. The "P.A. Police Force" is a cut of five students, drawn from a back view, who are carrying police clubs and a banner reading, "Keep back of the second line."

The *Mirror* of Fall 1891 contains (Ed's copy) the well-known *ex libris* Edgar Rice Burroughs, the bookplate of Tarzan, and a special background created by Studley Burroughs. Ed is listed as a member of the Tennis Association, p. 80.

12. Ed's name is spelled incorrectly in *The Phillipian*, but in an unidentified clipping reporting the same election, the name has been corrected.

13. "A Horrible Example, or The Man Who Could Not Say No." *Sesqui-Centennial Record*, Phillips Academy.

14. ERB's scrapbook of his school days has a number of clippings revealing his possible social activities. An invitation reads, "Mr. E. Burroughs invited to Friday evening dancing class, Nov. 6, 1891 at 7:30, 164 Warren Ave., every second Friday under direction of Mr. and Mrs. Horace W. Beek."

Whether Ed was able to return to Chicago from Phillips to attend any of these is not known. A Concert Hall Program, pasted into the book, is a "plugger" for Gaffney's Concert Hall at 99 West Madison Street, Chicago. Entrance is free. The program, commencing August 16 (no year) lists a "very funny Burlesque" entitled "The Piano Player's Mistake," a performer of "contortions and dislocations," and among other acts, a Miss May Clifford, "The Hebrew nightingale." Friday night was amateur night. The fact that Ed had gone to the trouble to paste these into his scrapbook would indicate that he had attended some of these performances.

An amusing clipping headed "Eye Flirtations" reveals the romantic interests or fads of this period: "Winking right eye" means "I love you," while "Winking left eye" means "I hate you." The list includes interpretations of "drooping eyelids" and "placing right forefinger to right eye." There are also "hand flirtations."

15. Ed's interest in sports and betting is disclosed also in a pink card pasted into his scrapbook: "I Warren Wright do bet E. R. Burroughs that John L. Sullivan will knock James J. Corbett out in the 25th round or before — Bet Theatre Ticket for the Grey Mare before Sunday. (sgnd) W Wright."

In the fight which went 21 rounds on September 7, 1892, at New Orleans, Corbett knocked out Sullivan and Ed won the bet. Beneath the card containing the bet, the ticket stubs for "The Grey Mare," September 10, are pasted.

16. In the *Sesqui-Centennial Record* ERB again produced his familiar joking reference to the emphasis upon Latin in his school curriculum:

. . . In the matter of writing books I was as ill prepared as I had been to play a guitar in the Mandolin Club. In early youth, before I had studied English grammar, I was taken out of public school and placed in a private school, the head master of which believed in the active application of the theory of evolution, so he started at the bottom, with Greek and Latin leading up to English and I left his school before I had progressed as far as English, and left without knowing much about Greek or Latin, either. I attended other private schools and had tutors before I came to Andover, but they all ignored English grammar. When I came to Andover it was presumed that I had already studied English grammar, so they started me in on the Greek and Latin again.

So, in casting about for my life's work and being unable to say no, I chose that particular line of endeavor for which I was signally ill equipped....

17. According to Charles W. Smith, alumni secretary, there was no mention of the reason for ERB's dismissal in the minutes of the faculty meetings of 1891-92. He commented, "It may have been a private matter between Dr. Bancroft and Mr. Burroughs."

Ed was later notified of the proposed formation of an alumni association in Chicago. A notice dated January 16, 1892, mentioned that an association existed in New York and that "Phillips men now residing in Chicago want such an association." The reference was to a plan "whereby old Phillipians visiting Chicago in 1893 may be able to meet classmates and Friends residing there." This was obviously in connection with the World's Fair in Chicago. An announcement of a meeting on January 25, 1892, at the University Club Rooms, 116 Dearborn St., included signatures of George F. Root, 1835; Leslie Lewis, 1862; and Victor Lawson, 1871.

18. In his *Autobiography* ERB states, ".... He (my father) had received me with open arms and with no reproaches when I was fired from Andover...."

19. Autobiographical article for R. A. Palmer, editor, *Amazing Stories*, June 1941.

20. In a letter to Frank S. Hough, M.D., The Sibley Hospital, Sibley, Iowa, April 27, 1934, ERB wrote, "... As I recall it, I entered Michigan Military Academy in 1891." It was actually 1892. The letter continues:

Colonel Rodgers [sic] was then head of the institution and remained so until several years after I left.

Adelbert Cronkhite was commandant when I entered the academy. He was followed by General Charles King, the writer, and we afterward had Major General Frederick S. Strong.

When I was assistant commandant, Captain Fred A. Smith of the Twelfth Infantry was commandant. Professor Butts was headmaster during my term at Orchard Lake.

In his *Autobiography* ERB states that "During my plebe year an army officer by the name of Adelbert Cronkhite was Commandant for a part of the time." No dates are established, and ERB first describes events in connection with King before mentioning Cronkhite. According to his letter above, this description of events would be in reverse chronological order as though King had been the first commandant.

21. ERB's humorous comment, often repeated, about not having studied English grammar because the emphasis was always upon Latin or Greek, may be somewhat exaggerated. As a junior middler, he was required, according to the catalog of 1892, to take two hours weekly of English composition, and in successive terms the catalog listed studies in punctuation and declamation. It is true, however, that Latin and Greek occupied a total of ten hours weekly.

The catalog reveals, in a list of enrollments by states, that most of the students came from Michigan and Illinois — forty-four each out of a total of 155. The military routine was typical: Reveille, first call, 6:05 a.m.; Second call, 6:15 a.m.; Evening call to quarters, 7:00; and Reading and Letter Writing, 7:00 to 7:30. A further reminder was Study, 7:30 to 9:00. Tattoo was at 9:00 and Taps at 10:00.

Under the heading of Financial is the statement that "the charge for instruction, room, board, washing, mending underclothes, fuel lights, use of arms and equipments is $450 per annum." An additional charge for "Horsemanship" (optional) is $40 per term or half-year. Uniforms, to be furnished by parents, together with certain incidental expenses, add an estimated $150 to the regular charges. In an amusing cautionary note, evidently based upon experience, parents are urged not to give their children too much spending money.

The Michigan Military Academy calendar of 1892-93, listed

in the catalog and elsewhere, has some slight variations in dates:

Catalog		
Sept. 14	Sept. 13	First term begins.
November	November	Thanksgiving Recess of one day.
Dec. 17	Dec. 22	Holiday Recess begins Fri. night.
Jan. 2	Jan. 8	Holiday Recess ends at Tattoo.
Jan. 29	Jan. 28	First Term ends.
Jan. 30	Jan. 29	Second Term begins.
June 14	June 13	Second Term ends.

An Easter vacation, although not on the calendar, was granted.

Members of the three companies whom ERB mentions, or with whom he had contact in later life, include the following: Company A, W. W. Waterman, 1st Lieut.; Company B, F. L. Buel, Corp.; Company C, C. C. Matteson, 1st Sgt., W. C. Risser, Corp.; Company D, L. B. Slosson, Corp. In the Register of Cadets, ERB is listed as "Sc." and "Chicago." Friends from Chicago included Charles Stafford Dickerson, Charles Cramer Matteson, and Willis Clark Risser. Other friends include David Linley Auld, Atchison, Kan., and Leonard Joseph Ullman, Cleveland, Ohio.

22. Bob Lay, Ed's roommate at MMA, took part with Ed in the riding exhibitions at the Detroit Riding Club, and both Lay and Weston also joined Ed on the MMA football team. The lifelong friendship resulted in regular visiting and correspondence, especially with Bert Weston, who wrote numerous letters and received many from ERB. Robert D. Lay was later president of the National Life Insurance Company in Chicago.

23. The reason for the extended vacation is not known. Ed may have been ill. But it appears unusual for a parent to ask for an extension so soon after his son has enrolled at a new school. Later, in King's letter of April 18, 1892, after Ed had gotten into trouble, King made a caustic remark about Ed's returning from his vacation "a week or more behind." George's indulgence toward his son again seems evident.

24. Quotations from ERB's *Autobiography*.

25. Ibid.

26. ERB's scrapbook contains a news item about the wedding, headed, "Nuptials of Miss Ella Frances Oldham and Henry Studley Burroughs." The marriage took place in the Burroughs home on Washington Blvd., the ceremony being performed by the Reverend Dr. Thomas.

Ella's background was described: she was a southern girl, and her father, who had fought in the Confederate Army, had died a number of years earlier. Her future was determined by a chance stopover in Chicago to change trains. She was met at the depot by Mary Evaline Burroughs who promptly took her home. Ella's plans to go to a drama school in New York were forgotten and she lived with the Burroughs family until her marriage. The two oldest brothers, George and Harry, both fell in love with her, but she chose Harry.

The newspaper reported that their permanent residence would be in Yale, Idaho, "where the groom has extensive interests in a cattle ranch."

Information about Ella obtained from Katherine Burroughs Konkle (Frank's daughter), reveals that Ella had been orphaned when quite young; her father had been a Mississippi riverboat captain.

27. Ed's liking for fun and pranks was shown in the membership certificate in the "Amalgamated Association of Liars," saved in his scrapbook. Dated February 14, 1893, it states that "This certifies that Ed R. Burroughs has been elected a member of the above society, having passed a very successful examination." It is signed M. R. S. Levy, president.

In the book following the certificate Ed saved a collection of newspaper clippings containing tall tales of the familiar exaggerated type. One is headed "The Tale of an Arizona Liar," while another, from the *Tombstone Epitaph*, describes Arizona's petrified forests, saying that animals who venture into it are turned to stone. Frogs and snakes become petrified when they wander into the springs, and the writer even goes so far as to tell of the cattleman who stood in a certain spring while bathing, then became conscious of peculiar sensations; after a few weeks his feet became petrified and he couldn't walk.

28. ERB's *Autobiography*.

29. Hugh Thomason became a good friend of Ed's and remained in touch with him for many years. Thomason turned to writing and in 1929 sent ERB a copy of a story published in a magazine. He used the pen name of "Jack McLeod." (See Thomason in later accounts.) His name is listed in ERB's memo book with Troop E, 6th Cavalry, Ft. Myer, Va.

30. Event 6, Competition Drill in U.S. Cavalry Tactics (Class 4), according to the program. Nine competed.

31. The first prize was a Siren Whistle Cane, contributed by Roehm & Son, the program states. Ed had marked his program "2nd prize" and "Horse received red ribbon."

32. Quoted from "How to Become a Great Writer," by Alva Johnston, *Saturday Evening Post*, July 29, 1939. ERB was quite thrilled about the biography, praising it highly, and even leaping to its defense when it was criticized. On September 5, 1939, ERB wrote to *Variety* magazine:

In your issue of August 23 there appeared an article captioned "Footnote on Burroughs" which questions the accuracy of Alva Johnston's Saturday Evening Post story on me. I leap to the defense of Mr. Johnston; and, at the same time, question the accuracy of your informant.

Mr. Johnston interviewed me for hours at a time over a period of several days, and I do not recall that he took many notes. It is not strange, therefore, that there are minor inaccuracies, minor exaggerations, and minor under-statements in his article, which, when the manuscript was submitted to me, I did not consider of sufficient importance to correct.

To his brother George, on July 31, 1939, ERB praised the biography, referring to it as "the finest publicity that I have ever received." When submitted to him before printing, he wrote to Wesley Stout of the *Post*, on June 21, 1939, to speak approvingly of the article, saying, "I feel that it is quite correct." He also wrote to Johnston on July 27 to thank him "for the excellent article" and then sent a telegram (June 16, 1939) to Stout which read, "I knew Johnston would turn in a good article. He is a swell person. . . ."

33. From "Tarzan and His Empire," a projected article for the *Post* written by Green Peyton. This article was rejected by ERB. Comments about it are that it was "rather weakly done, and has a great many errors in it, as well as omissions of items that would make it much more interesting, and inclusion of others that detract from rather than add to its interest."

ERB made notations on the typed copy in connection with statements that he disapproved or felt were inaccurate. Peyton's comment that "Burroughs had been a failure at every enterprise he touched" was marked "This is not true." ERB showed annoyance over this statement on other occasions, but never succeeded in squelching it. ERB's stint in the cavalry was listed as "three months"; he changed it to a year. (It was actually about ten months.) The item about his being an accountant for "a patent medicine company" was changed to "construction company." There were other corrections. However, in the uncorrected portion, assumed to be accurate, Peyton writes well and produces bits of information that do not appear in Johnston's article.

In regard to the "electrical carriage," it appears that ERB was not the only member of the family to drive it on the World's Fair grounds. In a letter of April 12, 1969, Katherine Burroughs Konkle reported that ". . . Mother and Dad (Frank Burroughs) who were then engaged to be married drove a battery-driven 'horseless carriage' around the fair grounds at Grandfather's request."

34. Lineup pasted into ERB's scrapbook.

35. *The Adjutant* 7 (November 1865):2.

36. In the fall of 1895 Ed, now graduated, returned to MMA as an instructor.

37. ERB's *Autobiography*.

38. Ibid. Ed phrases it, "The fact that two of my older brothers were graduates of Yale kept me from accepting, with the result that I never went to college."

39. Ed's collection of school papers includes three books which he evidently used for drawing practice. These paperbacks are by a German, Wilhelm Hermes, and published in London, 1862. They contain outline drawings of all types of animals, done with lines and shadings. When or where these were used is not known.

40. *The Adjutant* was published monthly, subscription for the school year being $1.50. The issue of December 1895, vol. 7, no. 3, as well as the June 1895 issue, contains a special first page with actual signatures of all the editors reproduced in print. Ed's signature is first, and his friend Herbert Weston's is also included.

41. ERB's *Autobiography*.

42. *The Urbanite* publication of Urban Military Academy in Los Angeles 1(April 4, 1924):10. Ed's article, written at the request of the editors, was titled "Out of Time's Abyss." He had evidently contributed this recollection of the "duel" to the Academy publication because his sons Hulbert and John were attending there.

43. Ibid.

44. Ibid.

45. Ibid. Here, Ed recalls, "Springfield rifles at twenty paces"; in his *Autobiography* he mentions "fifty paces."

46. Ibid.

47. Ibid.

48. Ibid.

49. Ibid.

50. ERB's *Autobiography*. Here, Ed wrote, "One of the headlines reads, 'Duel with carbines at ten rods'."

51. Ibid. Ed also saved newspaper clippings with accounts of the duel; these were dated December 14 and 15, 1893.

52. Ibid. Here Ed also mentioned a previous excursion to Detroit when the corps was taken there to see DeWolff Hopper in a current play. "I shall never forget the thrill that I experienced when he ran my name into some of his lines," Ed wrote. "Between acts he recited 'Casey at the Bat' for us. If a vote had been taken when we left the theater that night it would have unanimously proclaimed DeWolff Hopper the greatest actor that the stage had ever produced."

53. Ibid.

54. In his *Autobiography* ERB adds, "Thus was Edwin Booth's reputation as the greatest American tragedian permitted to remain unquestioned." Ed preserved the telegram in his scrapbook. Address to his father at 646 Washington Boulevard, Chicago, its date is undecipherable, but appears to be March 22, 18--[?].

55. Ed Rohrbaugh, ERB's close friend, was with him on the football team, playing left guard. His name is included in ERB's small memo book on a page of names and addresses. Rohrbaugh is listed at Seligman, Arizona, and at 432 E. Monroe St., Phoenix, Arizona. They evidently kept in touch after ERB left Michigan Military Academy.

56. His estimate of Commandant Strong and Colonel Rogers undoubtedly contained some emotional bias. The colonel was

pleased to supply a reference for him at a later time.

57. In Ed's scrapbook are pasted torn parts of another letter from his father, date undetermined, which refers to "troubles with your teachers . . . very humiliating to me . . . reduced in ranks. . . ." The topic may be Ed's repeated problems at MMA and his reduction to "Cadet Private Co. A."

The scrapbook contains several telegrams from George Burroughs to his son, dates illegible but in January of the 1890s. One reads "Wire immediately if matters are satisfactorily adjusted or not. Father" A second reads, "Telegram recd come home at once we'll plan later. Father."

58. A souvenir program of the Detroit Horse Show, April 25 to 27, 1895, shows Cadet Captain E. R. Burroughs at the top of the list of those taking part in these later exhibitions, events no. 1, 4, and 6. Herbert Weston was cadet lieutenant, and Hugh Thomason was still the drillmaster.

59. The notification lays down specific conditions: "Should you be found deficient in studies at the semi-annual or annual examination, or should your conduct reports be unfavorable you will be discharged from the military service. . . ." The signature appears to be Geo. D. Ruggles, adjutant general, for the secretary of war.

60. A clipping in ERB's scrapbook, date unknown. One of the headlines reads, "Belief That One or Both Will Pass."

61. In his *Autobiography* Ed explained, "I had a revolver, but I had thoughtfully left it under the seat of my buggy."

62. At this point in his *Autobiography*, Ed, disgusted with his attempt to write the story of his life, breaks into the narrative with a statement to Max Elser. (See Notes, Chapter 2: Childhood and a First Adventure, n. 17.)

63. In reference to these midnight marches, ERB, in his *Autobiography*, writes, "Most of this happened while Captain Fred A. Smith of the regular army, who was then commandant, was ill and I was acting Commandant." Smith had been in the 12th Infantry.

Chapter 4: The Seventh Cavalry and Beyond

1. The letter is written on the letterhead of the American Battery Company office, 25 South Canal Street, Chicago. Officers are listed as Jonathan Abel, president; Geo. T Burroughs, vice-president; B.W. Kendall, secretary; Wilson Ames, treasurer. The factory is listed as being at Oregon, Illinois.

2. As revealed later in Ed's discharge, the army in error entered his age as twenty-one and eight-twelfths at the time of enlistment. He was twenty and eight-twelfths years of age.

3. The memo book, a type of small pocket-sized book given free as an advertisement by the Edward Ely Company, tailors at 163 Wabash Avenue in Chicago, contains varied entries and addresses of friends. The cover reads, "This belongs to Burroughs of 'B' Troop 7th U.S. Cav. Ft. Grant, Arizona." The earliest entry appears to be Sunday, December 27, 1895, when he lists his weight, dressed, as 175¼ pounds. He keeps a record of his weight as it rises to 177 pounds in April 1897 and drops to 159 pounds in July 1897.

The book contains birthdays of his parents and relatives. His friend Bert Weston's birthday is noted as April 15, 1876, and Weston's address is 11 Grove St., New Haven, Connecticut. Ed. H. Rohrbaugh is listed, and Frank C. Burroughs' address is shown as c/o Millan-Osborn Spice Company, Denver.

Notations of engagements include reference to "dinner at home" and the fact that "Weston arrives." "Wed. 1st" at Hulberts is noted. Jessie and Emma Hulbert both are entered with their address at 194 Park Avenue, and Ed has also listed a Miss Elsie Bell and Helen R. Coffin. Other entries include Ed's carbine number and his bicycle number with a cyclometer notation following.

4. This recollection is also in a letter to Hugh Thomason of November 20, 1929, in response to Thomason's letter, and the same reference to Ed's riding is contained in his *Autobiography*. In the letter Ed writes, "We may not have been long on scholarship but we sure could ride, back there in the days of the old cavalry squad." (He is speaking of the days at MMA.) To Thomason concerning his experience at Ft. Grant, Ed wrote, "Fortunately, I had been very careful not to mention that I could ride, which was much better than having bragged about it. . . ."

5. About the watch Ed notes in his *Autobiography*, "[It is] the same watch that I pawned the night that the plebes all ran away from Orchard Lake to escape hazing, and being a saving soul, I still have it, as I still have the penholder that I had when I was in school at Orchard Lake and with which, incidentally, I wrote my first story, 'A Princess of Mars,' and also many other stories, including 'Tarzan of the Apes.'

6. In his scrapbook Ed saved several post exchange chits. One, marked "No. 1 Fort Grant, A.T. July 7th 1896," reads, "On next Pay Day I promise to pay the officer in charge of the Post Exchange Two Dollars. Value received." It is signed by E. R. Burroughs and witnessed by O. M. Leach, first sergeant, Troop B, 7th Cavalry. The holiday dinners were paid for by profits from the men's canteen (Post Exchange).

Information contained in *Old Forts of the Far West* by Herbert M. Hart, Bonanza Books, New York, 1965 reveals the following about Fort Grant: Old Camp Grant had existed before about 1873 in a very crude and unhealthful site. This was abandoned and a better site chosen at the foot of Mount Graham. However, even here the conditions were bad. Buildings of timber or of adobe could not keep out the rain and were in constant need of repair. Some enlisted men lived in tents. A "Lake Constance" was constructed under orders from Brevet General Anson Mills, 1888 commander. There had been a shortage of water, and Mills, at a cost of $16,000, installed a water and sewage system and built the cement-lined lake in the middle of the parade ground (the lake was named after his daughter).

Nevertheless, the Camp Grant post was severely criticized in 1890 in a secretary of war report: "The quarters for the enlisted men at this station are of inferior construction, contracted and uncomfortable. The stables for the cavalry are in bad condition, needing much repair for the proper protection and comfort of the animals occupying them." The fort had three troops of cavalry and two companies of infantry; these totaled twenty-three officers and 240 enlisted men. There was a reservation of 42,341 acres. Fort Grant soldiers were involved in the 1880 period Apache War, with many patrols being sent out. The soldiers joined General Crook's campaign into Mexico.

The New Camp Grant site is presently occupied by the Arizona State Industrial School.

7. Ed responded to a letter received from Colonel Laurence C. Brown, Ninth Coast Artillery District, Presidio of San Francisco, January 15, 1930, forwarded by *Red Book* magazine. On January 29 Ed wrote and recalled Brown as being one of the enlisted men at Fort Grant when he was there and congratulated Brown upon having achieved his goal of a commission: "I still have a bunch of cancelled canteen checks that recalls the wild debauchery of 'The May Have Seen Better Days Club.' As I recall it if we got one square meal and a bottle of red wine a month we were going some."

Ed answered a letter from W. L. Burroughs of Charlotte, N.C. (no relative) who had inquired about the old Fort Grant days. Ed's letter of March 26, 1936, refers to the "The May Have Seen Better Days Club."

8. A large assortment of sketches and drawings or watercolorings are still preserved. Ed, with his eye for the picturesque, also

drew the Indians, and commented about the appearance of the Apache women in his *Autobiography*: "We saw little or nothing of their women, though several that I did see among the younger ones were really beautiful. Their figures and carriages were magnificent and the utter contempt in which they held the white soldier was illuminating, to say the least."

9. Other drawings or sketches by ERB include such subjects as a cavalry instructor, first sergeant Troop F 6th Cavalry, Pease's horse, Walters' horse, and varied cowboys and horses.

10. Whether the "mistake" referred to was Ed's inconsiderate and abrupt departure from the academy at a time when Rogers was depending upon him, or whether the reference is to a quarrel or one of Ed's previous escapades, is difficult to tell.

11. The existence of "two very fine openings in Commercial lines" is doubtful. Ed seemed to have no prospects of employment, and this appears as an obvious attempt to present a case for discharge. (The later reference to Ed's mother being in "poor health" may also be a similar device.)

12. A letter to ERB from W. L. Burroughs, Charlotte, North Carolina, in March 1936, mentions a different reason for Ed's discharge:

This morning an old army sergeant whom I soldiered with back in the nineties dropped in my office and our conversation started at Fort Sheridan III when the 7th U.S. Cavalry and the 15th U.W. Infantry left that post for Arizona and New Mexico. He asked me if I remembered Edgar Burroughs of Troop "B" 7th Cavalry, said he was discharged during the summer of 1896 at Fort Grant Arizona account of a "Tobacco heart"....will be delighted to know for certain that we soldiered with so distinguished a person back in the nineties.

In Ed's response of March 26, 1936, he said, "...seldom have been in touch with any of the men I soldiered with since I left Fort Grant...."

13. Under his military record there are a number of comments by S. R. H. Tompkins, first lieutenant, 7th Cavalry, commanding Company "B":

Recommendations: A very intelligent soldier
Marksmanship: 3rd class
Physical Condition when Discharged: Good
Battles, Engagements, Affairs or Skirmishes: None
Remarks: Service honest and faithful

14. This recollection was reported in the *Albuquerque Journal* of December 3, 1939, at a time when ERB was in Albuquerque and there met Hugh Herbert, "the creator of 'woo-woo'" for the first time. Herbert was a fellow passenger on the train and Ed asked to be introduced to him (they had never met although both lived in Los Angeles). Ed recalled coming through Albuquerque in 1896 "in charge of a train of cattle."

15. A bicycle license dated August 5, 1897, was issued to ERB in Chicago. The bicycle is described as a Reliance brand with a "Diamond" frame. Ed's address is shown as 646 Washington Street.

16. His scrapbook contains a student's ticket issued by the Art Institute of Chicago to Edgar R. Burroughs, stating "Good only until July 1, 1898," and signed by N. H. Carpenter, secretary.

In a letter addressed to his niece, Marjorie Westendarp, in care of Harry Burroughs (Marjorie, an art student, was being given some financial help by Ed), ERB inquires about the Art Institute. His letter, dated October 22, 1921, asks:

The next time you write us will you please tell me where the classes are held. I have not yet been able to get it through my head as to whether the school is conducted by the Art Institute or in the Fine Arts Building. The classes I attended were in the old Art Institute Building which I think was on Michigan and Van Buren, or Harrison; and then later I entered a class in the new Art Institute although I only went for a few lessons....

17. Stated by Marie Burroughs, Studley Burroughs' widow, in a taped interview. She recalled that when Ed was put in a life class he stayed there only one day. "He wanted only to draw horses," she said, "and they wouldn't let him."

18. The report of the application to Theodore Roosevelt is mentioned in the biography of ERB by Alva Johnston, *Saturday Evening Post*, July 29, 1939. It has been repeated in numerous articles. ERB valued Johnston's biography, considering it one of the best, and made no attempt to contradict the Roosevelt story. Johnston's biography also reports that ERB received a commission in the Nicaraguan army which he couldn't take because "his family interfered." There is no documentary evidence of this.

Green Peyton's biography of ERB, written for the *Post* and then rejected by ERB, contains a statement about Ed not being able to get to the Rough Riders in time (presumably from Idaho) and about his refusing to join a group of volunteers going to the Philippines from Idaho. ERB, in his corrections of this article, did not delete this.

19. The information contained in the "Local Brevities" was contributed by Dale R. Broadhurst, a Burroughs fan, who traced these items in the files of the *Pocatello Journal*. His original report to Hulbert Burroughs was dated September 13, 1964.

20. The "Local Brevities" also contains the following item dated July 20, 1898:

Lewis Swester [sic] is in town today on his way to Omaha with 14 car loads of cattle which Swester, Burroughs and Sparks loaded at American Falls yesterday. Mr. Swester says that the cattle are in fine condition this year and that prices are keeping up in good shape.

21. The "Local Brevities," as compiled by Dale R. Broadhurst, include numerous other publicity items about the store:

You can rent a camera by the day or week at E. R. Burroughs'. (August 10, 1898)
E. R. Burroughs, the stationer, spent a couple of days in Salt Lake on business this week. (August 27, 1898)
They are Dead Right! Junius Brutus 10c Havanna cigars, Burroughs sells them. (August 27, 1898)

Many of these were repeated; the last one, according to Broadhurst, was dated October 22, 1898.

22. Quoted from a letter to Herbert Hungerford, editor, *The American News Trade Journal*, February 12, 1921. This recollection was published in the *Trade Journal* of April, 1921, within a long article which offered suggestions to the bookdealers.

23. Kipling's poem and the parody, fastened together in ERB's scrapbook, were evidently printed in the same newspaper, probably the *Pocatello Tribune*, at the same time, to enable the reader to make comparisons. The complete poems follow:

THE BLACK MAN'S BURDEN

[A Parody]

(The following clever lines, in imitation of a recent very celebrated poem, are the composition of one of the well-known young men of Pocatello. — Ed.)

Take up the white man's burden,
* The yoke ye sought to spurn;*
And spurn your father's customs;
* Your fathers' temples burn.*
O learn to love and honor
* The white God's favored sons.*
Forget the white-haired fathers
* Fast lashed to mouths of guns.*

Take up the white man's burden,
* Your own was not enough;*

He'll burden you with taxes;
  But though the road be rough,
"To him who waits," remember,
  "All things in time shall come;"
The white man's culture brings you
  The white man's God, and rum.

Take up the white man's burden;
  'Tis called "protectorate,"
And lift your voice in thanks to
  The God ye well might hate.
Forget your exiled brothers;
  Forget your boundless lands;
In acres that they gave for
  The blood upon their hands.

Take up the white man's burden;
  Poor simple folk and free;
Abandon nature's freedom,
  Embrace his "Liberty;"
The goddess of the white man
  Who makes you free in name;
But in her heart your color
  Will brand you "slave" the same.

Take up the white man's burden,
  And learn by what you've lost
That white men called as counsel
  Means black man pays the cost.
Your right to fertile acres
  Their priests will teach you well
Have gained your fathers only
  A desert claim in hell.

Take up the white man's burden;
  Take it because you must;
Burden of making money;
  Burden of greed and lust;
Burden of points strategic,
  Burden of harbors deep,
Burden of greatest burdens;
  Burden, these burdens to keep.

Take up the white man's burden;
  His papers take, and read:
'Tis all for your salvation;
  The white man knows not greed.
For you he's spending millions —
  To him, more than his God —
To make you learned, and happy,
  Enlightened, cultured, broad.

Take up the white man's burden
  While he makes laws for you,
That show your fathers taught you
  The things you should not do.
Cast off your foolish feathers,
  Your necklace, beads, and paint;
Buy raiment for your mother,
  Lest fairer sisters faint.

Take up the white man's burden;
  Go learn to wear his clothes;
You may look like the devil;
  But nobody cares who knows.
Peruse a work of Darwin —
  Thank gods that you're alive —
And learn the reason clearly:—
  The fittest alone survive.

                    Edgar Rice Burroughs

THE WHITE MAN'S BURDEN
by Rudyard Kipling

Take up the White Man's burden —
  Send forth the best ye breed —

Go bind your sons to exile
  To serve your captives' need;
To wait in heavy harness,
  On fluttered folk and wild —
Your new-caught, sullen peoples,
  Half-devil and half-child

Take up the White Man's burden —
  In patience to abide,
To veil the threat of terror
  And check the show of pride;
By open speech and simple,
  An hundred times made plain,
To seek another's profit,
  And work another's gain.

Take up the White Man's burden —
  The savage wars of peace —
Fill full the mouth of Famine
  And bid the sickness cease;
And when your goal is nearest
  The end for others sought,
Watch Sloth and heathen Folly
  Bring all your hope to nought.

Take up the White Man's burden —
  No tawdry rule of kings,
But toil of serf and sweeper —
  The tale of common things.
The ports ye shall not enter,
  The roads ye shall not tread,
Go make them with your living,
  And mark them with your dead.

Take up the White Man's burden —
  And reap his old reward:
The blame of those ye better,
  The hate of those ye guard —
The cry of hosts ye humour
  (Ah, slowly!) toward the light: —
"Why brought ye us from bondage,
  Our loved Egyptian night?"

Take up the White Man's burden —
  Ye dare not stoop to less —
Nor call too loud on Freedom
  To cloak your weariness;
By all ye cry or whisper,
  By all ye leave or do,
The silent, sullen peoples
  Shall weigh your Gods and you.

Take up the White Man's burden —
  Have done with childish days —
The lightly proffered laurel,
  The easy, ungrudged praise.
Comes now, to search your manhood
  Through all the thankless years,
Cold, edged with dear-bought wisdom,
  The judgment of your peers!

24. Autobiography.

25. Quoted from ERB's letter of February 18, 1929. The information concerning the quarrel in the saloon and the blow from a policeman's billy club was given by Jack Burroughs, ERB's youngest son, in an interview of January 11, 1970. Jack had been told the details of the strange incident of the keys and recalled these details throughout the years. He also remembered being told that as a boy of twelve, ERB had fallen while riding his bike and had hit his head on the pavement. ERB had then driven home in a daze, not remembering how he got there. He had a scar on his head as a result of the accident.

26. Letter of February 18, 1929.

27. Ibid.

28. In his letter to Colonel Laurence C. Brown, Ninth Coast Artillery District, Presidio of San Francisco, on January 29, 1930, Ed refers to his attempts to get a commission and remarks, "My own failure to obtain a commission either during the Spanish-American War or the World War was a keen disappointment to me, but I have been long since resigned to my fate and am probably very much better off as it is, for I doubt if I was temperamentally fitted for that profession."

29. From the projected biographical article by Green Peyton, intended for the *Saturday Evening Post*, but not approved by ERB.

Chapter 5: Marriage, Wanderings, and Reality

1. Ed's scrapbook displays cards that show he was a member of the prestigious Ashland Club in Chicago in 1899 and 1900.

2. Brief biography of ERB requested by William G. Chapman, an agent. ERB, on April 13, 1914, had protested that he couldn't write it, but had a friend who would "tackle it." Chapman replied, "...you're too modest. However, your friend doubtless will have more to say than you anticipate. Have him get busy, please, *instanter*, as time presses. The article will do you some good as it will be given a tremendous circulation."

Why the biography, requested in 1914, should turn up in *The Book News Monthly*, August 1918, under the title "The Creator of Tarzan" and without any author's name has not been explained (the "friend" remained unidentified). Chapman was later at odds with ERB over commissions, and a lawsuit followed.

3. In ERB's letter of December 9, 1922, to his friend Charles K. Miller, he refers to Emma's musical training: "...Mrs. Burroughs studied with Madam Duff at the same time that she was training Mary Garden and Fanchon Thompson and had a wonderful future, which was wrecked by matrimony...."

Joan Burroughs Pierce, in a letter of April 4, 1969, states, "Emma Burroughs' only schooling was at Brown. Her voice studies were extensive and continued until her brother Alvin's death when all schooling abruptly ended for all the girls, as far as I know." His death was caused by appendicitis.

4. Emma Theresa (Mrs. Alvin) Hulbert on February 22, 1928, responded to ERB, making it plain she was answering *his* request for genealogical information about the Hulbert line. She explained she was born on one side of the river in Rochester, New York, and Alvin on the other. She wrote, "Dr. Henry Webster Jones was the attendant (physician). His Grandfather was the Great Noah Webster of Dictionary fame. He was not the attendant at Allie's (Alvin Jr.) birth, as the Grandfather's Funeral was at that time. I remember he said, having another physician might bring a change in the sex. So Allie came...."

The genealogical chart, handprinted, covered two pages and was headed, "From the Drake Family England to America 1360-1895 by Louis Slaughter Drake Privately printed (Mssrs. David Clapp & Son. Boston 1896, 291 Congress St Boston)." Thus the interest that ERB showed in genealogy in his printing of his mother's memoirs in 1914 continued in 1928.

5. In March 1928, possibly for genealogical data, Emma Theresa Hulbert requested a copy of her daughter's birth certificate from the Department of Health in Chicago. The certificate, issued on March 6, 1928, the usual copy of the original, lists Emma Theresa's age as "24 at last birthday." Since the certificate was first issued at daughter Emma's birth on January 1, 1876, this would make her mother's birth date approximately 1852. However, the genealogical chart shows her born on July 24, 1850, and Joan Burroughs Pierce, in her letter of April 4, 1969, lists Emma Theresa's birth date as 1850.

6. Written by ERB to his nephew Studley Oldham Burroughs, March 22, 1946. In connection with this, ERB stressed his philosophy of "You lead your life, and I'll lead mine...."

7. The invitation, printed in flowing script, reads, "Mr. & Mrs. Alvin Hulbert announce the marriage of their daughter Emma to Edgar Rice Burroughs, Wednesday, January thirty-first, nineteen hundred. Chicago."

A year earlier, on March 5, 1899, Emma had been one of the witnesses at the marriage of her sister Jessie (Jessica Drake) Hulbert to Charles Warren Nichols in Milwaukee, Wisconsin. The marriage of Jessie ended in divorce on January 11, 1904. The decree of divorce, in the Circuit Court of Cook County, lists Nichols as guilty of "extreme and repeated cruelty"; Jessie was granted the right to resume her maiden name.

8. A letter of October 18, 1902, addressed to Ed at 35 South Robey Street in Chicago, is from the New York Life Insurance Co., Chicago, office of F. A. Jackson, cashier. A check for $10.15 is enclosed as the "net amount of the loan" due Ed on his policy. He had borrowed $52, but after deduction of the premium and interest, his balance was only $10.15. It would appear that he borrowed to pay his premium.

9. A photo in Emma's old album is marked "Ed after typhoid 1902." An additional reference to Ed's illness is contained in a letter from his friend Bert Weston, who on March 16, 1912, speaks of a note from Emma and writes, "That was nice of Emma. It is the first time we have heard from her since you nearly died with the Thypoid phever."

10. Much of the information about the houseboat and the mining operations was contained in the notes of Grace Moss Burroughs, supplied by Katheryn Burroughs Konkle, her daughter. Other information came from Marie Burroughs. A photo of the men's smaller houseboat reports that it needed more caulking. Another photo of the large houseboat in the old Burroughs family album is marked Idaho 1898.

11. Letter of April 12, 1969, from Katheryn Burroughs Konkle. She recalls the special election booth and equipment set up on the banks of the Snake River for the Sweetser Burroughs Mining Company in November 1900. William McKinley and Teddy Roosevelt were running against Bryan and Stevenson. The Burroughs family's Republican sympathies were evident, but their main interest was in Roosevelt and they later turned from the party to support him in 1912. A charter membership certificate for the Progressive Party, issued to ERB in 1912 as a receipt for a one-dollar contribution, displays pictures of Roosevelt and his running mate, Hiram W. Johnson.

An indication of the exhausting and dangerous tasks the brothers faced in their gold dredging in Idaho is contained in Coleman's letter of December 1, 1899, to Grace Moss, soon to be his wife. Written on the stationery of the Sweetser-Burroughs Mining Company, Minidoka, Idaho, it describes a typical emergency. He and Harry Burroughs had gone up the river with a tug to bring back a load of coal. They loaded the barge and prepared to return:

As the wind had been blowing pretty hard all morning we were somewhat afraid to start back especially as the barge was very heavily loaded... the wind seemed to be dieing out so we made up our minds to start back as there was still plenty of work to do before everything would be ready for the house warming.... In some way two of the three rudders on the tug had become disconnected from the main rudder and when I tried to head the boat down river it would not mind the helm at all and we drifted into the trough of the waves broadside.

As the wind began to blow a "regular gale" both the tug and the coal barge were deluged with waves more than six inches high above the sides of the boats. Both Harry and Coleman had to stand in water up to their knees in the barge and bail with buckets, while Walter Sparks stood in the flooded barge trying to keep its nose headed toward the shore. "As the water was about 13 feet deep at that particular place," Coleman wrote, "we were all enjoying some pretty serious thoughts at that time." After several hours of desperate work in the cold water, the men were at last able to make the boats fast. They then built a fire to dry their clothes. Coleman wrote:

. . . I took off my trousers, shoes and sox and built a tripod in front of the fire with long willows and hung my wet duds up to dry, shortly after the boys decided to follow suit. I never saw anything that looked as funny as we did sitting there on that pile of drift wood, half dressed (or less) with that tripod hung full of waving trousers, sox and shoes, and first a cloud of sand blowing over us, then one of ashes from the fire and last but not least a snow storm.

They couldn't finish that day, and the next day had more trouble with the rudders and had to drift ashore and work in the cold water to fix them before they finally returned.

Coleman's letter to his fiancee was addressed "My Precious Little Girl," and he told of his lonesomeness. Of the other women aboard the houseboat, his favorite was Nell (Ella), Harry's wife. Coleman wrote to Grace, "I really think that if I could always have you and Mother and Nell I would never care to see any other woman in the world." He soon returned to Chicago for his marriage to Grace on January 24, 1900.

12. Information contained in a long typewritten letter dated at top, June 6, 1900, Minidoka, Idaho (but not completed on that date), and sent by Coleman to ERB, reveals that the situation on the houseboat, especially among the three wives (Edna, George's wife; Ella, Harry's wife; and Grace, Coleman's wife), was one of constant friction. The letter was a series of complaints about the behavior of Edna, who supposedly refused to help in the household duties. A remark was made also that Edna, before marriage to George, "did not care whether she got George or Lew (Sweetser)." Upon returning from her wedding trip on February 5, 1900, Edna again, according to Coleman, neglected her share of the work. There was trouble also with Freda, wife of Walter Sparks, who at one time left the houseboat abruptly and didn't return until a month later. In a situation where four couples (or more), plus two children, were crowded into close quarters, squabbles of this sort appeared inevitable.

The resentments became so bitter that George suggested the three brothers should separate when the chance arose. Coleman remarked about George that "all George cared for any of us was simply for what he could get out of us and now that the time had come when we are of no further use to him he is going to cut loose from us." Coleman cautioned Ed to "be very careful of this letter and *do not lose it* as its content reflect somewhat on our family credit, but *do not* destroy it as I may want the folks to see it." At the bottom he wrote, "Just finished this today June 17th."

13. Ella's stress upon her family line and the ancestry traced back to George Washington had caused both family competition and amusement. (See Appendix 2, pp. 780–86.) The date of the family booklet, evidently before 1900, establishes that Ella's interest in her ancestry had existed far earlier than had been supposed. Evelyn (Marie) McKenzie, Ella's daughter, in a letter of May 1, 1970, recalls that her mother had once again probed into her genealogy when she applied for membership in the DAR, about 1920. This was the chapter in Coldwater, Michigan; Leila Hulbert Westendarp, very active in the DAR, had persuaded Ella to complete her records and join.

In the family booklet ERB uses the term "bull" to indicate an error by him. He writes, "this is a bull on Uncle Ed," or, "two bulls on Uncle Ed." This apparently means he made an error in a cartoon or in lettering and presumably tore out the page, leaving only the reference to the "bull." He also drew small figures of bulls to explain his mistake.

The family booklet contains a variety of cartoons and poems by Ed. One, according to Evelyn McKenzie, was written before she was born:

And if it is a Girl, sir
I'll dress her up in blue
And send her out to Saltonstall,
To coach the freshman crew.

This and other references to Yale are of course because George and Harry attended Yale and were oarsmen on the crew.

14. Another poem and series of cartoons concerning the Idaho days tell the story of Waupi, a small town where all the miners and cowboys went for a good time:

Mamma's Lullaby.
Bye Baby, bye, bye;
Papa's gone to Waupi
He'll get a skate
And come home late;
Mamma'll meet him at the gate;
To run a flat-iron at his pate;
Bye Baby, bye, bye.

To "get a skate" means to be liquored up.

A cartoon showing Grandfather (Major George Burroughs, Sr.) on a bicycle refers to the occasion when he did purchase a bicycle with resulting humorous comment by the family. Ed's poem is beneath his cartoon:

Words fail us at a sight like this;
No verses come to save
When we behold Grandfather
Scorching down the pave.

In a poem and cartoon dated September 12, 1895, Ed jokes about Grandfather's change in attitude toward boats. Presumably in this Idaho period Major George had remarked "in accents soft and tender" that he would like to sail in the *Defender*. "What a change ten years has wrought," Ed noted, mentioning that years before, Grandpa had been so fearful while in a boat, that George had to row "with one oar on the shore."

15. Evelyn McKenzie expresses the belief that the "Snake River Cottontail Tales" were written for both Studley, her brother, and her and that they were given to her when her family lived on the houseboat. Ed's fondness for wordplays and puns is illustrated in another of his poems in which a pinto Cayuse is talking to Mrs. Bunnie. The cayuse asks for money, claiming he hasn't tasted food for several days. He brags about his past as a horse who has bucked many riders and "given them all the shakes." Mrs. Bunnie replies:

Good morning Pinto Cayuse, you who used to pass right by us,
Your appetite's improving of your ways.
If you starve a little longer your manners may grow stronger.
Since you're such a wondrous bucker
Why don't you Buckwheat cakes?

16. Evelyn McKenzie recalls that as a child she had used the tiny measurements of gills, drops, and pinches to prepare the foods; the recipes had turned out successfully. Ed drew full-page cartoons to accompany each recipe. Those recipes for nut candy, molasses candy, and others list such measurements as a gill of sugar, one-fourth gill of water, a gill of molasses, a pinch of chopped nuts, etc.

17. The promissory notes were a sequence marked "60 days after date I promise to pay to the order of F. Coleman Burroughs fifty and no/100 Dollars ($50.00) with interest at the rate of 6% . . . per annum from date, for value received." They were numbered one through six, and the days arranged in a progression thirty days apart, e.g. "90 days after date. . . 120 days after date. . . ," etc. The phrase "for value received" may have indicated a cash loan, an actual purchase of the railroad tickets,

or a combination of both. Another possibility is that Coleman may have paid some of Ed's debts or even paid for the household furnishings that were carried along. Ed never paid the debt, and in 1908 his father revealed that he had retained the notes for a long period and had paid them off without telling Ed about it.

18. The newspaper story, saved in Ed's scrapbook, is unidentified. It describes the mining operations:

Those somewhat familiar with their operations say they ship large quantities of gold, some of it being sent to the Boise assay office, while part is sent elsewhere.

The plant consists of a sand pump and burlap machines set upon a flatboat. The sand and gravel are pumped up from the bottom of the stream and run over the burlaps. The dredge works against the bank so that some of the material comes from the bottom of the river and some from the bank.

There is an immense amount of placer land in that vicinity and success in working it will lead to the inauguration of extensive operations there. The American Falls camp is only some 2 miles further up the river and it seems that that is one of the best sections of the entire Snake river valley for placer mining operations, though the country along the stream from one side of the state to the other is all rich.

That George held a position of esteem in the state of Idaho is evidenced by his appointment by Governor Steunenberg, in a letter of February 10, 1900, to represent the state at the International Mining Congress at Milwaukee, Wisconsin, on June 19, 1900.

The existence of another dredging company is revealed in the finding of letterheads reading, "Please ship to Yale Dredging Co. Minidoka, Idaho, the following items by. . . ." Possibly at an earlier period only George and Harry (and Lew Sweetser?) were involved in the Yale Dredging Company, again named after their alma mater or their cattle ranch at Yale, Idaho. The backs of this stationery were used by Ed to write his fairy tale, "Minidoka 937th Earl. . . ."

19. Recalled by Marie Burroughs, Studley Burroughs' widow, in a taped interview, January 3, 1968, at Tarzana, California.

20. In a letter to a fan, Albert Burch of Medford, Oregon, on August 12, 1939, Ed offered this information and added, "I worked on the Stanley Creek and Oregon Dredges."

Various snapshots in the old Burroughs family album show Ed and Emma during the Idaho period en route to the Stanley Basin or leaving it. One marked "en route to the Stanley Basin on the U.P. 1903" shows ERB, wearing a bowler hat, with Rajah, their dog. There is one of Rajah and Emma in the station yard at Omaha in 1903 and one of ERB and Rajah from the U.P. Baggage Car in May 1903. A man named Meecham, evidently a friend and a driver of a freight wagon in Idaho, is shown with the Burroughs family in a number of pictures:

Going into Stanley Basin from Mackay, Idaho, 1903 (Emma in front seat of stage)

Meecham and ERB, Idaho, July, 1903

Emma & Meecham en route from Stanley Basin, Idaho, July, 1903

Coming out of Stanley Basin, July, 1903

Meecham and ERB at a ghost city in Idaho, 1903 ("Meecham drove us out of Stanley Basin")

ERB, Rajah, and Meecham on road from Stanley Basin, 1903

ERB, Emma, and Rajah at Nampa, Idaho, July, 1903

21. This anecdote is recounted by George Burroughs, III, in a tape recorded on December 22, 1968. The story was used by his daughter Joyce Burroughs Goetz in a biography of ERB written when she was thirteen.

22. The brief biography, published in the Press Club's *The Scoop* for November 7, 1914, was released on the occasion of

admitting new members to the Press Club. ERB was one of these and his photo is at the top of the page. Writing from Oak Park, Illinois, Ed refers to Lederer's hopes of "making a cartoonist of me" and adds, " 'a damn poor one', I think you said over the phone the other day. The Lord has doubtless entered a merit mark to your credit that you didn't." ERB's certificate of life membership in the Press Club was dated February 18, 1915.

23. Ed writes:

Many erstwhiles since a portion of Idaho was ruled over by an extremely illnatured and wicked Brady called Pzvrtjhk. The Prime Minister and a few of the Brady's favorite nobles who still had heads for everyday wear called him Smith for short. The common herd were wont to address him as "O Sire", or "O Brady". All the civilized world was divided into kingdoms ruled over, in North America, by other Bradys, or Haras, or Malleys, or Conners, but it was many erstwhiles later that the title King became popular. Even to this day you will see some of the descendants of these ancient monarchs bearing the noble titles of their forefathers and hods.

In continuing, Ed explains that "this story deals only with the Bradydom of Smith and the Connerdom of Bil which lay directly south of Basalt the land of Brady Pzvrtjhk." Once the highly imaginative tale is launched, Ed soon maneuvers it into all sorts of wild twists and inserts a variety of fantastic devices. "In that age," he writes, "all things were measured by hops and the standard hop was that hop which the Brady's Own Royal Engineer General could take at 4 o'clock in the morning of the fourth day after donning his Shoes of Office." To use any other standard except the "Cooney Hop" for measuring anything was a capital offense.

Our hero, The Earl of One Mile, a nobleman of Connerdom, is in command of a crack regiment — Conners' Own Royal Light Cow Guards. "In those days cows were swifter than horses and the horse-boys of the plains rounded up the vast herds of range horses on their vicious little horse-cows."

The youthful Earl, only eighteen, is ordered out with his regiment to take part in the battle against the Basaltines. The order reads, "proceed to the front with all possible dispatch and annihilate somebody."

In developing the story, Ed uses all the familiar elements of the fairy tale: magic and magical spells, a beautiful damsel to be rescued, and terrifying monsters to be destroyed. The Earl of Minidoka is given the power to speak to the animals and to understand them. He is warned of impending dangers by the Little Horned Toad and also by a repellent creature called a "Hoo-body" who appears suddenly before him on the ceiling:

He had heard all his life about the Hoobodies, but he had never seen one before. Hoobodies are not pretty and they can walk just as well on the ceiling as they can on the floor. That is because they have hollow feet like flies. Hoobodies have ingrowing faces and green hair; it is really only grass. When a Hoobody gets bald he ploughs up the top of his head, plants some more hair and goes out and gets rained on. Hoobodies live to be very old and unless they get notification from Box B they stand still and do nothing. Some times they stand in one spot under a sage brush for a thousand years at a time till the dust covers them all up but their hair.

Ed has the Hoobody and other creatures talk in rhyme. For instance, after being accused by the Earl of "talking ragtime," the Hoobody replies:

You may say what you think, yea or nay.
You may not even think what you say,
 Or fib yourself blue, green, and pink.
You may dress up your thoughts in varieties of clothes;
It dont cut any ice, for the Hoobody knows;
 The Hoobody knows what you think.

The Earl is informed that his initiation the next day into

the Knights of the Spring of Fire includes a requirement that he go out to battle the Hookie-Dookie, "a fierce Paleozoic monster who holds the keys to the Spring of Fire." At the cave of the monster he is joined by a young knight wearing a coyote's head mask. The knight volunteers to help him, and as they enter the flames and fumes of the cave, the knight removes the mask and turns out to be the beautiful Princess Bodine, previously rescued by the Earl. The Earl is aware of the Hookie-Dookie's two vulnerable places:

A Hookie-Dookie is full of hot air instead of blood and if you puncture the end of his red nose he will collapse like a balloon and that is the end of him but if you cut off the rattle on the end of his tail it will take him thirteen seconds to die and in that time he can have one wish and he is pretty sure to wish something unpleasant for the one who kills him.

In the wild fight that follows, the Hookie-Dookie is pinned down with a half-nelson, after which Bodine produces a key-hole saw, sits upon the monster's tail, and cuts off his rattle. Unfortunately, in his last breath he makes his wish and changes poor Bodine into a coyote. The Earl acquires certain powers of the Spring of Fire, but now faces the heroic task of finding and destroying a new monster, the Rhinogazarium, who in his dying moments would remove the spell from the lovely Bodine.

The Earl again summons the Hoobody who explains to him that the Rinogazarium is really the handsome young Rhi, changed to a monster by his jealous brother Ab. However, upon turning into a monster, Rhi had immediately "dispatched" his brother and thus assumed "The Power of Ab," which gave the holder the ability to change at will the species of any animal. It was this power that the Earl of Minidoka must seek.

Arriving at the "Edge of the World" where the monster lived in the Castle in the Air, the Earl signaled a challenge by using his "pocket projector for wireless telegraphy." The Rhinogazerium came out at once:

Bellowing and tearing out huge hunks of space with his massive horned snout he lumbered down the ether path bordered with wild atmosphere kicking up great clouds of ozone and weather. When within about three hops of Minidoka and earth he ground his feet into the Climate and came to a sudden stop.

The Earl knew that in order to overcome the monster he must get him down to Earth "before the Sun bobbed down behind the world," while the Rhinogazerium, too foxy to be trapped, intended to stall around until dark, for only then could he exercise his Power of Ab. His plan was to turn Minidoka into a "toothsome shote and assimilate him." Since the two were at a distance, the only possible battle was one of words. The Earl threatened, cajoled, and pleaded without success, and the day passed with the pair arguing and calling each other names. With the night approaching, the Earl cunningly proposed a tug-of-war and managed to hurl his lariat so that it tightened about the monster's enormous, protruding eye. Snared, and in terrible pain, the Rhinogazerium had to surrender his Power of Ab to Minidoka, who immediately used it to change Bodine back to a beautiful princess. He also restored the monster to his original form — the handsome young Prince Rhi.

Up to this point in the story Ed had merely allowed his imagination and sense of humor to run wild, but in the section that follows he makes a surprising change which appears like a sudden inspiration. He had been having fun with the popular fairy tale devices, but now he turned to satire and to a subject that had always aroused his deepest feelings: man's treatment of the animals. The incidents he creates are not only fantastic and amusing; they expose man for what he has done and indict him for his cruelty and indifference to the sufferings of animals.

Bodine, Rhi, and the Earl journey to the land of Nevaeh (heaven) down a yawning abyss into the center of the earth.

Here is the place where all good animals — and bad people — go when they die. The keeper of the door of Nevaeh, "an old white elephant with a great long white beard," is named Tnias Retep (St. Peter spelled backward). After ushering them in, he assigns a little monkey to be their guide. He is Anthropop, very old, and the Father of Monkeys. He leads them up a wide street "paved with old horse shoes, blinders, chains, iron bars, and everything else that animals don't like.

Here in animal heaven the roles are reversed, the animals are dominant, and man faces retribution and must experience the agonies he has inflicted on his helpless creatures:

They had not gone far before they met a heavily loaded wagon stuck in a bog of Lepages Glue and clay. A big fat horse sat on the box with a great heavy whip and he belabored a thin, rawboned, knee-sprung, underfed man, who, panting and lugging, tried to pull the enormous load out of the hole.

Man's brutality is vividly painted:

Finally the horse fell in the street one day from exhaustion and the big brute man got down from his seat and kicked him in the belly and stamped his heel into his face. The poor horse never got up again, fortunately for him, so we gathered him here to his fathers.

Later, when the man dies and tries to "break into Heaven," he is barred by St. Peter. His punishment, laboring to pull the heavy load out of the mire, has lasted for a thousand years. He receives the same treatment he gave the horse:

Presently the horse will get down and put a nose bag on him with a quarter of a spoonful of mouldy oats in it. At three o'clock every afternoon the man falls down from exhaustion and the horse gets off the box and kicks him in the belly for half an hour.

On the sidewalks are throngs of animals shopping and promenading. "Many of them had naughty little boys on chains. Puppies and kittens ran along pulling the little boys' ears and biting their legs. It was lots of fun for the puppies and kittens, but then the naughty little boys had their fun on Earth."

The Earl, Bodine, and Rhi are conducted to the theater where they see a stage melodrama in which the villain is a Numidian lion. Later, grand opera is presented with the roles performed by "a band of cats who were laboring under the impression that they could sing." Several musical lines are quoted:

Was it a Boot Jack Tabbie
Or only a bottle of cream?
Back! Back! My onliest Tommy
For things are not what they seem.

In a plainly derisive view of grand opera, Ed remarks, "This is only a few inches of it, the original is seven miles long." Evidently disgusted with the caterwauling, Anthropop ordered the bulldog stage manager "to ring off the cat show and put on something less classical."

Here Ed inserts "a simple evening lullaby" titled "What are the Wild Waves Saying?" This lengthy poem in its style and in the coining of nonsense words demonstrates the influences of the British writers Lewis Carroll and Edward Lear. Ed uses Lear's method of combining syllables taken from normal words to create new humorous ones:

"The Sea Cow... guppled in her spacious maw...."
"She fraggled out his squirmy hair...."
"This sploshy man, so gue and pink...."

Other coined words and expressions include "the ghersters," "flabble tail," "hingling skulls," "surled," "hearsesome," "googers."

At the zoo, where Anthropop next leads Minidoka, Bodine, and Rhi, they are shown the lagoon where again the roles are reversed, this time between fish and humans. In the lagoon men and boys are disporting themselves while winged fish with halos sit on marble copings and angle for "the tender little boys, baiting their hooks with chocolate creams and plain tastes of honey":

...one little boy was hooked through the cheek and drawn ashore wriggling and squirming. The fish tore the hook from his cheek and throwing him into a bag full of other little boys rebaited his hook and went to fish again.

The "fisheries exhibit" continues at the great Central Lagoon where Jonah is required to swallow the whale every afternoon at three o'clock. In an obvious gibe at the accuracy of the biblical tale, Anthropop reports a conversation with the repentant Jonah:

He told me in confidence the other afternoon that if he could live his life over on Earth he'd try and be more truthful in the future and even if temptation should assail him and get the better of him he'd confine his imagination to French sardines.

Ed shows no limit to his imagination in devising punishments "to fit the crime" for humans who had mistreated animals. In another building men, women, and boys are caged and guarded by an African lion who strikes some of the men across the nose with the butt of his whip. The highlight of the day's entertainment for the spectators comes when one of the men is forced to open his mouth and the lion places his head inside.

The women also have punishment waiting for them: "...down one great avenue fled the shades of a thousand thousand thousand women pursued by the beasts and birds whose furs and feathers had bedecked the women on Earth."

Their visit to Nevaeh completed, the trio is returned by magic to their camp where Minidoka continues his adventures, this time receiving a golden box and key from the Little Horned Toad; in a moment of peril all he need do is open the box, but he loses the key and is captured by enemy forces. He still retains the Power of Ab, however, and is being watched over by the Hoobodies who arrive in a swarm to rescue him. Returning to his camp, he finds that his trusted companion Rhi is attempting to woo Bodine who repulses him with the indignation of a heroine in a melodrama. Minidoka and Rhi now engage in a duel which goes on for fourteen days until the Earl, aided by an eclipse of the sun, conquers his opponent and changes him into a green-eyed monster called Jealousy, turning him loose "to prey upon people with guilty consciences."

Minidoka has also changed thousands of enemy troops into cockroaches, and now, since they are becoming a nuisance, Bodine implores him to transform them into "something soft and brown and nice that couldn't possibly frighten your Bodie." On a sudden inspiration he agrees to make them animals with long ears and white tails "so that one can always tell which way they are going." Ed comments as an aside, "Now you know how Idaho came to be infested with cotton tails and Jack rabbits."

At this point, disgusted with a land overrun with Jack rabbits and "dead croton bugs" (cockroaches), the Earl decides to change part of it:

...he turned loose the Spring of Fire and covered the whole Bradydom three hundred feet deep with melted rock and glass. If you should ever happen to be on the old Oregon trail where it crosses the modern Raft River at the old Bowers Ranch near Yale in Cassia County you will see where Minidoka checked the flow of lava at the boundary of his Connerdom. The bluffs are not three hundred feet high now of course; time has crumbled them away, but the old ford is still used and when you cross Raft River you ride right up on top of lava beds which bury millions of dead croton bugs and jack rabbits.

Concerning Ed's use of the names *Brady* and *Conner* in his fairy tale, one can speculate as to whether they referred to actual persons whom he knew in the Minidoka area or elsewhere. His poking fun at the Irish may have been a type of private joke that related to individuals who were closely associated with him.

There appears to be no other reason why he should choose such names as Cooney, Brady, and Conner.

Ed's facility in concocting names that were unusually rhythmic, colorful, or comical, which was strikingly evident in his later works, both the Tarzan and other worlds series, is noticeable at this early period. He liked to experiment with odd syllables and combine them to produce strange words that sounded realistic in the bizarre settings he created. He had a keen ear for original phonetic combinations.

The complete poem, as contained on pages 63–65 of "Minidoka 937th Earl...," follows:

WHAT ARE THE WILD WAVES SAYING? AN EVENING LULLABY FOR THE CHILDREN

The sad sea waves rolled in upon
The Oyster's feather bed.
"We'd like to can the mush faced man
"Who's asking what we said.
"We yearn to serve him in a jug
"Or frizzled on a red hot mug,
"Or fried in grease instead.
"He is too soft for any good
"Excepting, as a breakfast food,
"The Sea Cow may be fed."

2

The Sea Cow oped her lanthern jaw
And guppled in her spacious maw
The man, without ado.
She fraggled out his squirming hair
And gapped his teeth beside her there.
She left his bones all raw and bare,
But, O, it made her blue.
It made her blue to glean and think,
This sploshy man, so gue and pink,
Was of the Corbi's crew.

3

The Corbi, that ill fated craft,
By noxious, noisome breezes waft,
As loaded down with dead and daft
She cruises round for blood.
Her master sabers all who come
Except the lordly Borogum,
Who dines and wines on mud.
The ghersters lark aboard this bark,
With hingling skulls and eyeballs stark,
The Slaves of Great God Crud.

4

The Knockers god, and those who wail
His flaming eye and flabble tail
Pursue them round the world.
He shageth him of syphon head
Puts hunch backed bugs upon his bed,
As wailing wails he fills with dread
The hushful one and surled.
With sink-hole eye he passes by
And in his wake they writhe and die,
All withered, choked, and curled.

5

And so the lordly Borogum
With Crud and hearsesome ghersters come
All down the center aisle,
And pick their bones as white as stone
Till every snarling skull, with moans,
And ghastly groans, each sin atones.

Then all shoot craps awhile,
Until a merry little crap
Gets sore at being that, mayhap,
And googers with a smile.

Buried also in the ruins of the ancient capital of the Bradydom of Pzvrtijhk is the golden palace, and Ed remarks "they are digging in Snake River today for the fine pieces that were filed off when it was built and dumped into the river to be got rid of."

This reference to digging for gold in the Snake River could date the fairy tale within the 1903-04 period when ERB was in Idaho and involved in his brothers' gold mining enterprises. The title "Minidoka" and the use of letterheads from the Yale Dredging Company further reinforce the choice of this period. However, Ed may have saved the old letterheads and written the story later in Chicago.

24. An old family photo album has a picture of Gladys Sammons, Buster, the dog, Emma and Rajah, marked Parma 1904. Gladys, presumably, was the wife of R. K. Sammons, the clerk of the village. Other photos of the period show Ed and Emma's home at Parma, a small wooden frame house, 1903-04. ERB appears in another photo with a horse named Joseph, Parma 1904. One photo is marked "Residence, Parma about April 1904." Two snapshots of ERB show him sitting at a typewriter, evidently in his Parma home, one marked "Parma, Idaho, 1903," and the other "Parma about February 1904."

25. This explanation of the failure is offered by George Burroughs, III, on a tape recorded December 22, 1968.

26. This account is contained on a tape made by Marie Burroughs during an interview at Tarzana, January 3, 1968.

27. Photos and cards show two addresses in Salt Lake City — 111 North First West and 111 North Fifth West Street. Whether this is an error, or whether Ed and Emma changed their address (or whether the street numbers were changed) is difficult to ascertain. Photos show the living room of their home at 111 North Fifth West Street "about July 1904," in two cases. Another photo of the home at 111 North First West has a note about existing there from April to October 1904. There is a card addressed to Emma at 111 North Fifth West, dated July 25, 1904, from Margaret Weston.

28. Mentioned in a long biography assembled from clippings by Leon Tebbetts and printed in the *Sunday Telegram*, Portland, Maine, in late 1933, possibly September or October.

29. In a brief article written at the request of F. Romer, President of the Samson Service, Washington, D.C., March 2, 1926, ERB states:

I am glad to send you a few words on the Colt because I have always owned one and have always liked them..." He reports that he now has three — "*one, an old rusty six-gun bears the serial number 70495*" — and adds, "*Once, being broke and jobless, I annexed a temporary job as railway policeman in Salt Lake City. It was then that 70495 assisted me materially in running boes off the U.P. passenger trains.*"

30. ERB's *Autobiography*

31. Ibid.

32. Ibid.

33. Ed's care in saving the letterhead of the American Genealogical Society might indicate that he was at one time associated with this business as well as with the firm of Moss & Burroughs; the fact that they both occupied the same office provides some support for this theory. However, since his name does not appear on the Genealogical Society's letterhead, one could assume that Moss & Burroughs and the Society merely shared space in the office. Earl C. Moss was a brother of Grace Stuart Moss, Coleman Burroughs' wife. Thus it was not surprising that he and Ed should go into business together. But the activities of the two forwarding agents, or what items they handled, cannot be determined.

The Woman's Temple, where the office was located, was erected by The Woman's Temperance Building Association, organized by Mrs. Matilda B. Carse in 1892 as a memorial to Frances B. Willard, the founder of The Woman's Christian Temperance Union. Situated at 120 South La Salle Street, it was razed in 1926.

Attention was first focused upon these letterheads because Ed had used them in writing certain stories. An analysis of the evidence drawn from them, plus whatever information we have about Ed's writings, offers solutions to the perplexing problem of time — both as to when Ed was involved in these enterprises and as to when he wrote his first story. (Previously, it was noted that the fairy tale "Minidoka" was written on the backs of old stationery.)

An examination of these facts leads to two possibilities: upon leaving Chicago in May 1903, he carried the American Genealogical Society letterheads with him to Idaho, using them to write "Minidoka" there; or, upon returning from Idaho in the fall of 1904, he brought the stationery of the Yale Dredging Company and his Pocatello photo bills and proceeded to write "Minidoka" some time afterward. In this case he also used old letterheads of the Genealogical Society which presumably were available to him in Chicago.

However, evidence of a more specific nature may be used to establish the time of his first story. On the back of a Genealogical Society letterhead, page six of "Minidoka," is a stamped date — February 24, 1904. Further significant data is contained in the fairy tale. At the end Ed writes, "They are digging in Snake River today...." This indicates that "Minidoka" was written (at least partly) during Ed's Idaho period, when the gold dredge was in operation, but more likely it represents literary license. Another time reference should be observed: in a margin of "Minidoka" (page 62) Ed has noted, "lapse of about a year." This, and the other evidence, leads to the conclusion that "Minidoka" was completed within the years 1903-05.

The stamped date of 1904 on the letterhead of course supplies proof that the American Genealogical Society was in existence prior to this time, since Ed must have carried these letterheads with him from Chicago. And finally, one might conclude that Moss & Burroughs, located at the same office, was in business during the same period, prior to the 1903-04 stay in Idaho.

If this reasoning is accepted, the next use of these letterheads, about seven years later, raises a question to which the answer is somewhat surprising. In writing "Under the Moons of Mars," Ed used the backs of stationery from both the American Genealogical Society and the firm of Moss & Burroughs. A yellow envelope with a return address reading American Genealogical Society, 1102 Woman's Temple, has also been preserved; the envelope contains a pen point, and on the front of the envelope is a brief notation: "This pen started the 1st 120 pages of MSS Under the Moons of Mars, my first story ERB." That "Under the Moons of Mars" was written in 1911 has been definitely established.

34. Autobiographical article, *Los Angeles Times*, November 3, 1929. King, a colonel at the time he became commandant at Michigan Military Academy, was given publicity in an article in a Pontiac newspaper of March 18, 1892. The headline reads, "Col. King is Coming. The Author of 'A War Time Wooing' will become commandant of the Michigan Military Academy, at Orchard Lake, Next Week."

Information about his background was offered in the article:

His time, of late years, has been given to literary work, largely." His father was General Rufus King, "under whom the now famous soldier and author entered the army as a drummer boy and saw considerable service in the war as a mere boy...went to

West Point — graduated as officer — in Indian country — was one of the best Indian fighters — and was wounded, near death, in battle — he was retired as Captain in the regular army — "A part of his time while in active official duty was spent as instructor in West Point Academy." Colonel King assisted in preparing Upton's Tactics; in fact, the manuscript of the book was in his handwriting. He is regarded by regular military men as the best posted man in military tactics in the country, in all lines — cavalry, infantry, artillery, and signal service. After leaving the army he held the position of military instructor and professor of military engineering in the University of Wisconsin.

In recent years he has made his home in Milwaukee and has been active in state military service in Wisconsin, acting as inspector general of state troops. . . ."

Col. King is the intimate friend of Col. Rogers of the military school, and is well known there as a visitor. His position will be not merely instructor in military tactics, but that of commandant. The reports of army officers sent to visit and inspect the Michigan Military Academy show it to be second only to West Point in point of thorough military training. Col. King's services will make the institution second . . . in the world.

35. King's novels of the West were quite popular in the period from the 1880s to the turn of the century. *The Colonel's Daughter*, published in 1883, is described as one of his best. A reviewer in the *Readers' Digest of Books*, Macmillan Company, New York, 1929, comments that "The author disclaims all charms of rhetoric and literary finish in the conversation of his characters. They 'talk like soldiers' in a brief plain speech. For that reason, perhaps, they are natural and human. The author has depicted army life in the West with the sure touch of one who knows whereof he writes. 'The Colonel's Daughter' is preeminently a soldier's story, admirably fitted in style and character to its subject-matter."

36. The family album has a photo of Arch O. Burdick and Emma at 88 Park Avenue in 1901, and another of Burdick, Ed, and Rajah at 88 Park Avenue in 1902. ERB wrote to Burdick, his insurance agent, from Los Angeles on January 14, 1919, to report his new address.

37. All these addresses are obtained from the backs of photos or from cards sent through the mail; these are in the album whose first page is inscribed, "Emma Hulbert Burroughs 194 Park Avenue Chicago from 1904 to 1907." A photo from the album showing Emma, Fly (the dog), and Rajah at 194 Park Avenue "about 1902" has a notation, "now #2005."

38. In a letter to Bunn from Blanchard the strict time schedule for the shipping of merchandise, after receiving the customer's order, is emphasized. It is noted that Mr. Burroughs will have to watch carefully as "Mr. Doering has set a nine hour schedule for handling correspondence, in which schedule the Stenographic Department is allowed four hours. Nine hours from the time a piece of mail is stamped into a merchandise department, it must be finally disposed of by that merchandise department. . . . Mr. Doering seems to be very insistent that this schedule be maintained."

39. ERB commented in the same letter, "I think Mr. Doering is the only member of the organization with whom I have kept up my acquaintance. Even then he was the really big man of the merchandising organization and that was a great many years ago."

On March 18, 1922, Doering wrote from River Forest, Illinois to tell how much he enjoyed reading *The Mucker*. (ERB may have sent him a copy.) Doering remarks about the "really charming character in our friend 'Bridge,'" indicating that 'Bridge' may have represented a real-life person they both had known.

Doering offers a humorous criticism about the fact that in *The Mucker*, Maw, the old farmer woman, hides her bank notes in the family bible, saying, "you know perfectly well that she would be more apt to have a *Sears, Roebuck* catalog on the little marble top table and hide them in that. Oh! the opportunity that you missed — I mean that *we* missed!"

ERB responded on March 23, 1922:

In all humility I acknowledge the justice of your criticism and accept the merited rebuke. That I should have been guilty of such a glaring error covers me with mortification, for lives there an enlightened man who does not know that the Sears, Roebuck catalog has supplanted the family bible from pole to pole. Please forgive me.

On November 20, 1925, in response to an inquiry from Fred M. Schukraft of Oak Park, Illinois, Ed spoke of the homes he had occupied in Oak Park, saying, ". . . just before we came West we lived in the old Doering house on North Oak Park Avenue, near Ontario, I think. . . ." In a letter to Charles Lorenzen, Oak Park, March 27, 1939, ERB states, ". . . rented the home at 325 No. Oak Park Ave. where I resided from April 30, 1918, to January 31, 1919, at which time I moved to California. . . ." This establishes the location of the Doering house and makes it clear that ERB only rented it.

40. Ed's screed, though in rhyme, as was the original to which he was replying, was a prose form. The full screed follows:

'Twas all very well for the ninety and nine, while they roamed this mundane sphere, but it wasn't so funny bye and bye, when they reached those golden gates on high, and St. Peter remarked that oysters and pie weren't served in Heaven with beer. "Come higher," he cried, "you intelligent ghost, with elegant coat and vest, why those certainly must be Seroco pants, (as one could tell by a passing glance;) I know your appearance will surely entrance the legion of the blest. The balance of you may go to a place where fires are furnished free, and burn the wads you ached to blow, when you were in the world below, because you hadn't the brains to know Sears-Roebuck quali-tee." Then up spake one of the ninety and nine: "O! look at this stove pipe hat, you surely can tell that it's certainly swell, and would look much better in Heaven than — well — the place where sulphur and brimstone smell — St. Peter, you must see that!" But St. Peter frowned, as he looked all around, and he shouted, "You idiot, hark! that hat was first bought from roebuck sears, by the merchant who started the gibes and jeers, but he added the price of twenty-two beers; before you bought it, you easy mark!

The word "before" in the last line was scratched out and the word "then" written below in ink to replace it. No other corrections are shown, and thus the reference in the letter to "taking a few liberties" cannot be clarified.

41. The speculations are centered about the incidents in *Tarzan of the Apes*, beginning with the raising of the baby Tarzan by Kala, the she-ape. The fingerprints of the baby, accidently recorded at the age of six months in the diary of his father, Lord Greystoke, are then discovered and compared to those of the grown Tarzan. The famous telegram from D'Arnot, "Finger prints prove you Greystoke. Congratulations," provides a climax to the novel and establishes Tarzan's identity.

From this evidence comes a rather startling theory that the idea for the famous *Tarzan of the Apes* was already germinating in Burroughs' mind as early as 1907 and that he was seeking fingerprint information to support his imaginative plot. His inquiry for a book on child care in 1907 may be interpreted not as a mere desire to prepare for the arrival of his first child, but rather as research for his projected novel. He felt he had to know something about raising children, since he was planning the story of the infant Tarzan and would have to provide realistic details of his "care and feeding," even by a she-ape! While the theory is ingenious, the circumstances of 1907 do not appear to support it. At this time the writing of stories seemingly had not even occurred to Ed; nothing in the records indicates any writing plans as early as 1907. He turned to writing, in desperation, four years later.

42. Ed sets this humorous tone at once in the opening:

Babies born in captivity sometimes live to a great age. This is not true, however, unless certain precautions are taken to receive them properly when they arrive. If a baby is expected in cold weather the house should be slightly heated. Authorities differ on the exact temperature to be maintained in the stork reception room. Some say 190 degrees while others adhere tenaciously to the 212 degree theory. Experience has taught the author that the two hundred twelvers are in the majority. If the stork is to visit a frame house on a cold night, and all ordinary means for attaining the requisite heat fail, the house should be set on fire. This plan is efficacious in several directions. It not only produces a gentle heat, but also makes it unnecessary to provide artificial light should the baby arrive after dark. . . .

The total destruction of the house would make no difference, the article continues, since "papa" would not have enough money to keep the house after paying for the baby.

Various suggestions follow for the care of the baby. A light diet is recommended: "If buckwheat cakes are to be eaten, under no circumstances should maple syrup be allowed with them. The restriction is necessary on account of the frequent adulteration of genuine maple syrup. However, were strictly pure maple syrup obtainable it would be no more injurious to a young baby than buckwheat cakes." Mainly for reasons of economy, the infant should not be given intoxicating liquors. Since a baby drinks every two hours, and the price of a drink is fifteen cents, the cost in a year could be staggering.

Nurses require careful supervision: "Most nurses will drug the baby when they wish to quiet it and stick pins in it when mamma is trying to." The nurse may also, in a spirit of humor, leave the baby lying on a chair where visitors could sit on it; this should be avoided since a visitor might be frightened or offended.

The doctor, who is quite unimportant, should be selected for his appearance, the Van Dyke, biblical type being preferred so that the infant can play with the beard. The family is urged not to scrutinize the doctor's prescriptions too closely, or else he may be embarrassed: "Some doctors can read their own writing, but these are usually novices and cannot be trusted. The more experienced a doctor the poorer his chirography. When they reach the top of their profession they are unable to write at all. This has undoubtedly saved many lives."

The first advice given to the mother is that all dinner and theater engagements should be cancelled for several days after the baby arrives. This is only in order to watch the nurse. The mother should choose talkative old ladies for companions; they are given to recalling sudden deaths: "most old ladies have lost children in infancy who had all the symptoms of yours." One should be kind to these old ladies and encourage them to "dilate" on this subject.

Concerning the baby's name, Burroughs noted the difficulty of choosing one that would satisfy everybody. One plan was to number the babies consecutively and permit them to select their own names later:

This idea was highly elaborated by a systematizer for a large corporation. He arranged to number his children in series. The first series running from 1 to 25; the second series to be similarly numbered but prefixed by the first letter of the alphabet, and so on. This system allowed of more than a sufficient range of names for ordinary families. The inventor, in order to prove its merits, was forced to give up his position and move to Utah.

Chapter 6: Frantic Years and a Taste of Success

1. Alva Johnston, "How to Become a Great Writer," *Saturday Evening Post*, July 29, 1939.

Attempts to obtain specific information about ERB's numerous business projects in Chicago have not produced anything definite. Miss Margaret Scriven, librarian of The Chicago Historical Society, has supplied whatever information was available in the Chicago city and business directories of the period. Concerning Dentzer, ERB's partner, the city directories from 1900-1908 do not list this company. No listing was found of the E.S. Winslow Company, for whom ERB had worked.

The mystery of the Moss & Burroughs enterprise of "Forwarding Agents" remains unsolved. According to Miss Scriven, there is no listing of the firm. From her data, the following items of some importance were obtained: Earl C. Moss was first listed in the directory in 1890 with home address only; 1895, as a mech. engr.; 1897-1903 as a mech. engr.; 1904-05 as a salesman; 1906-09, as an engr.; 1911-13, as a cons. engr., one address shown as 135 Adams. (These listings are from the city directories and the telephone directories.)

Listings in the city and telephone directories contain the following information about ERB: he was first listed in 1894, with home address only; 1897, as a cashier, 42 W. Quincy; 1899-1903, as a treasurer, Am. Battery Co.; 1905-09 as a mgr., 138 Jackson Blvd.; 1910-11, at Stace, Burroughs, & Co., 309 Michigan Ave., Edward Stace, pres., Edgar Burroughs, Sec., mfgs. agents 309 Michigan; 1912, as Burroughs, dept. mgr. 16th floor, 5 N. Wabash; 1913, as Burroughs, with a home address only in city directory but Stace, Burroughs & Co. appearing in telephone directory; 1914-16, with only Stace, Burroughs & Co. listed in the telephone directory and no personal listing for ERB.

There is no listing in any of the directories for The American Genealogical Society.

2. Alva Johnston, "How to Become a Great Writer."

3. The clipping, headed "This is My Birthday," may be from the *Chicago Tribune*. Others whose birthday fell on this day were James A. Rose, Secretary of State of Illinois, and Victor Elting of Winnetka, a well-known attorney at the time.

4. ERB's *Autobiography*. There he wrote, "It was while I was with Stace that our second child was born — Hulbert — so I had another reason for wanting to get rich quick."

There is no explanation of why, in the case of daughter Joan and son Hulbert, the family tradition of giving middle names was not followed. When the second son was born, he received the name of John Coleman Burroughs.

5. Alva Johnston, "How to Become a Great Writer." In a letter of April 25, 1946, to a Mr. Waddell who had inquired about Mr. Paullson who had presumably worked for Dr. Stace, ERB answered, ". . . a great many years ago, I was employed by Dr. Stace as Office Manager where Mr. Paullson was also an employee. That was nearly forty years ago; and I have known nothing concerning The Physicians' Cooperative Association or Mr. Paullson since that time. . . ."

6. ERB's *Autobiography*.

7. Ibid.

8. The money owed to the John M. Smythe Company may have been some type of installment payment, possibly for furniture, and the reference to "girl" may mean a cleaning girl in the home, perhaps to help Emma at the time Hulbert was born.

9. On the envelope for the Christmas cards was a printed return address: "Offices: Suite 550, 309-11 Michigan Avenue, Chicago." The nature of this business has not been ascertained.

An old letterhead, on the back of which ERB had typed a

three-stanza "Joan's Pick-Me-Up-Song," contains the heading at the top left:

BURROUGHS
Bookkeeper
Office Manager
Credit Man
Correspondent
Advertising Manager
Confidential Man
Purchasing Agent
Sales Manager

The address shown is 82 Sherman Street, Chicago. This business is also unidentified.

A Christmas card with one of ERB's own cartoons, showing Santa Claus clinging to a tree while below him an enraged reindeer is snorting and butting the tree, has the following typed statement: "Uncertainty as to the movements of a certain stock has decided Santa Claus to remain where he is for an indefinite period. We are therefore sending you only our best wishes for A Merry Christmas and A Happy New Year." The card has no date.

10. ERB's *Autobiography*.

11. Ibid.

12. A business card, still preserved, shows the New York Office at 44-60 E. 23rd St., and the London office at 34 Norfolk St., Strand, London.

13. Alva Johnston, "How to Become a Great Writer."

14. ERB's *Autobiography*.

15. Ibid. In a letter to Thomas Metcalf, Munsey editor, ERB on May 30, 1912, explained that he got around to the Champlain Yardley office (a stationery company owned by his brother Frank) about two or three times a week. He may have been working there part time while also holding a job at Shaw's *System* or may have merely used the facilities of his brother's company for his story writing.

16. Alva Johnston, "How to Become a Great Writer."

17. Ibid.

18. Emma and Ed may have stayed with her folks for a period after their marriage in 1900; it is possible that he wrote "The Violet Veil" then.

Chapter 7: The Outlaw of Torn

1. Ed's awareness of the value of money and his emphasis upon meeting his obligations were illustrated in his letter of September 28, 1911 to Metcalf, written from 222 W. Kinzie St. in Chicago. Ed was concerned after his stenographer returned from mailing the revised "Martian Princess" story to Metcalf, to discover that the postal clerk had mistakenly charged only 12 cents postage, whereas it should have been 56 cents. He believed that the same error had been made by the clerk when the original ms. was mailed to Metcalf, and now wanted to pay Metcalf if the postage due had been collected from him. Metcalf replied on Oct. 6 to state that he didn't understand about the postage and that he believed Ed didn't owe him any money.

2. Ed's suggestion for an ending, on August 26, 1911, was vague and unconvincing, and Metcalf countered with an idea of his own. It stimulated Ed to think of a far better one. Ed's statement to Metcalf about writing an ending "along lines of your own suggestion" is more diplomatic than accurate. The ending was original, and he did not accept Metcalf's suggestion that Dejah Thoris die at the final moments.

Ed did follow Metcalf's orders in shortening the first chapters and felt it necessary to write the entire story in the first person.

3. In this letter of November 6, 1911, in which Ed accepted the offer of $400 for the story, he gave references and also explained he was secretary and advertising manager of the Champlain-

Yardley Company and that they would guarantee the originality of anything he submitted to Metcalf.

4. Also in the November 6 letter Ed inquired as to when the first installment of "Under the Moons of Mars" would appear. Metcalf, on November 20, replied that it would be published in the February *All-Story*. When it appeared, it was serialized in six parts, running through July of 1911.

Ed had written to his close friend Herbert (Bert) T. Weston about the publication of the story. A long letter from Weston, dated December 26, 1911, discusses the story and other matters. Margaret, Weston's wife, and her children, had been scheduled to stop off in Chicago (en route from New York to Beatrice, Nebraska), to visit ERB, but her son's illness prevented it.

Weston refers to Ed's "nom-do-plumb" of Normal Bean and writes, "This being an agricultural, and not a literary community, I fear that I am going to have some difficulty in getting hold of the issues of that same publication for some months back. However, I am after it, and have hopes... I am simply crazy to read that Moon story." Weston went into a lengthy eulogy on ERB and about Ed's "charm," speaking of it as a salable product. About ERB, Weston wrote in his homey language, "Margaret and I have many times said that anybody with the least descernment [sic] would be simply tickled to death to get hold of any part of ERB that they could (not physically me boy) and if people only knew about him they would pay mighty well for whatever smaller parts he might conclude to market." Weston thought "that Normal Bean" was the funniest thing he had ever heard.

5. Ed may have taken Metcalf's letter to the library with him, for at the bottom of the letter he had noted the books and their call numbers — *Forest Lovers* by Hewlett, *Ivanhoe* by Scott, and *Men of Iron* by Pyle.

6. On November 20, Ed, in his answer admitted, "I am a bum waiter," and went on to complain about the "Outlaw of Torn," "The pitiful part of it all is that I am too dense to see what is wrong, or how to remedy it — I certainly tried. I think my mistake lay in attempting to patch it up. I should have forgotten everything except the plot, and then rewritten it from the beginning. . . . I really wish though that I knew just how and where it is weak."

He was experiencing the anguish familiar to all writers who face the task of making revisions based upon an editor's vague explanation. On December 12, 1912, he wrote a long letter again extolling the virtues of "The Outlaw of Torn":

As to the Outlaw of Torn. I wish you knew how very much I am hoping for a favorable decision. There are several reasons. Not the least is my firm conviction that the plot alone will make the story a success. I am largely influenced in this belief by your own belief in the value of the plot, and you certainly know what is good and what is not.

Ed proceeded to offer other reasons why the story should be accepted, including even an assertion that once its success was established, he would write "several other good tales of the same period." He pointed out that in spite of all the praise he had received from Metcalf and the readers of *All-Story*, he had given no indication of "an enlarged ego" — he still saw his work with all its crudities exactly as he saw it before anybody approved it. He stressed that it is not the style or "the handling" that counts — it's the story itself, as with the Tarzan story: "It was an accident that I happened to get the story into my head, but the fact remains that the 'story' is interesting regardless of its dress. The *story* was what 'got' the readers — the story of the Outlaw of Torn will get them, for it *is* an interesting story."

Not inclined to let go, Ed wrote, "Every story you print must be more or less of a gamble. You took a big chance on Under the Moons of Mars. As a matter of fact would you be taking as great a chance today on The Outlaw of Torn? . . . why not give The Outlaw of Torn the benefit of the doubt?"

All of Ed's persuasive eloquence had no effect upon Metcalf who on Dec. 18 answered, "I have come to my decision in regard to "The Outlaw of Torn" and it is with regret that I have to say I do not like it. I am sure that no one in the world except yourself is as sorry for the attitude that I have to assume."

7. The three manuscripts are still preserved in the Burroughs files. From the 215 pages, all handwritten, of the original manuscript, the one marked "original typed mss." was reduced to nine chapters and 114 pages. The third expanded version had the first eleven pages handwritten; then a mixture of writing and typing followed.

The expanded work, completed February 2, 1912, underwent further revisions and deletions before the later publication. A long descriptive section, obviously inserted by Ed for medieval atmosphere, lasted for about two pages and described the furnishings of the armory in detail and also the suits of armor hanging on wooden pegs. In one section Ed writes:

At each side of the room was a great fireplace above which were reproduced in colors the king's arms and his motto:

"Ke ne dune ke ne tine ne foret ke desire.
"Qui non dat quod habet non accipit ille quod opta."

The lengthy descriptive section precedes the first reference to Sir Jules de Vac, in charge of the armory.

8. The "dead king's bones," described in the original longhand and typed versions as being buried in "Westminster," were given a new location in the expanded form of February 1912. Here "Westminster" is lined out and "the Cathedral of Worcester" is substituted.

9. Ed's annoyed statement in his letter of February 2 to the effect that he wouldn't use the name *Normal Bean* anymore, came at the time when this revised manuscript was completed. He probably changed the "Normal Bean" listed in the box. His last use of "Normal Bean" in story correspondence may have been in the letter of November 29, 1911.

10. This opening first appears in *New-Story Magazine* of January 1914, running serially through May 1914 (five issues). ERB's copy is labeled "6415 Augusta Street, Oak Park, Ill." The magazine version appears to be somewhat longer than the form that was finally published by McClurg in 1927.

11. Whether Ed ever received any additional money at the rate of two cents a word is doubtful. He wrote Sessions on August 6, 1914, to inquire about the reader response and mentioned the matter in a postscript. On November 21 he wrote again, reminding Sessions that he had overlooked the postscript. In a letter of October 5, 1915, Ed stated that he had received only $500 for *The Outlaw of Torn*.

Chapter 8: Tarzan of the Apes

1. Letter of March 6, 1912, to Metcalf from 2008 Park Avenue.

2. On April 5, 1938, ERB prepared a one-page cast of characters from *Tarzan of the Apes* and also listed important information:

"Tarzan" coined about Dec 19, 1911 on page 71 of ms. Greystoke was originally Bloomstoke.
Tiger first mentioned on pg. 50; changed to lioness in book after magazine publication.
Foreword written after 95 pages of ms. had been written, probably on Dec 22, 1911.

3. Ed's inquiries in 1907 about books on fingerprinting and on the care of infants have led to speculations that he may have been creating his Tarzan plot at that time.

4. From August 14, 1911, when he sent his first story to Metcalf, through the end of November 1911, he used the address of the Champlin-Yardly Company, 222 West Kinzie St., Chicago. (Letters of November 6 and November 17 were initialed ERB/H

at the bottom, indicating that a company secretary had done the typing.) Afterward, he preferred to use his home address, except that on March 6, 1912, he asked Metcalf to return the manuscript of *The Outlaw of Torn* to the company office. In 1912 Metcalf, on occasion, wrote to him at the Kinzie St. address, and Ed, on May 30, 1912, requested that the editor use his home address at 2008 Park Avenue.

5. ERB's *Autobiography*.

6. Ibid.

7. The Munsey files contain a card notation that a check for $700 was mailed to ERB on June 26, 1912. Ed's private card index of sales also shows the $700.

8. In this letter of June 26, 1912, Metcalf requests with some annoyance that Ed never again use "such appallingly thin paper," since by the time he read it and the clerical department handled it, "the manuscript looked like a very much disheveled cabbage." He also suggested that Ed never write with single spacing. On June 28 Ed responded, "You need not have cautioned me against thin paper. I have cussed it all the way back to the Wisconsin paper mill that made it. I finally had the girls single space because the thought of doubling the number of those infernal sheets appalled me. I shall stick to 8½ × 11 16# double spaced hereafter."

Ed's pen name was not misspelled in the advance publicity in *All-Story* of January 1912 on the Table of Contents page which reads, "In February will appear the first installment of *Normal Bean's Under the Moons of Mars* a surprisingly vivid interplanetary romance...."

9. Letter to Rose Martino, Waterbury, Conn., February 21, 1925.

10. Letter to Arthur Rhenisch, Oak Park, Illinois, December 2, 1918. Rhenisch had sent ERB an original story synopsis on "The Freeing of Opar."

11. "Edgar Rice Burroughs, Inc.," article in *Writer's Digest*, August 1949.

12. Interview on Radio Station KTM, Los Angeles, 1931.

13. "Edgar Rice Burroughs, Inc.," *Writer's Digest*, August 1949.

14. Oliver Poole, "Romance Isn't Dead," *Writers' Markets & Methods*, March 1938. (Contains an interview with ERB.)

15. Letter of August 12, 1939, to Donald Herne, Kansas City, Kansas.

16. Letter of February 13, 1931, to *The Bristol Times*, Bristol, England.

17. ERB's letter of March 31, 1937, to Altrocchi. Ed had read books on mythology when he was a child.

18. Altrocchi's letter of April 2, 1937.

19. ERB's letter of April 5, 1937.

20. Altrocchi's letter of October 9, 1937.

21. ERB's letter of October 11, 1937.

22. ERB's letter of June 15, 1939.

23. Altrocchi's letter of June 19, 1939.

24. ERB's letter of June 21, 1939.

25. Altrocchi's completed work, a collection of essays published by Harvard University Press in 1944, was titled *Sleuthing in the Stacks*. The individual essay relating to the Tarzan theme, "The Ancestors of Tarzan," is one of a group of seven discussing the authors and their works or themes.

26. ERB's letter to *The Bristol Times*, February 13, 1931.

27. Titled *Something of Myself* and added "For My Friends Known and Unknown," Doubleday Doran & Company, 1937. The Index lists "Tarzan of the Apes," p. 235, but there is no listing of Burroughs. The reference to *Tarzan* is in Chapter 8, "Working-Tools," the last chapter.

28. ERB's letter of February 13, 1931, to *The Bristol Times*.

29. Contained in information supplied by ERB for Hardware Mutual Casualty Company's house organ, "Contact," October 3, 1935.

30. ERB's letter of March 30, 1927, to Walter Williamson, managing editor of the *Daily Maroon*, University of Chicago.

31. "The Creator of Tarzan," *Book News Monthly*, August 1918.

32. Ibid.

33. "Romance Isn't Dead," *Writers' Markets & Methods*, March 1938.

34. Green Peyton, unpublished article of October or November 1938, intended for *The Saturday Evening Post*.

35. "The Tarzan Theme," *Writer's Digest*, June 1932.

36. Ibid. A quote of Livingston's *Missionary Travels and Research* as quoted in *Mother Nature* by William J. Long.

37. William J. Long, *Mother Nature*.

38. "The Tarzan Theme", *Writer's Digest*, June 1932.

39. ERB's letter of March 30, 1927, to the *Daily Maroon*.

40. Ibid.

41. Interview (Nickerson), Radio Station KGMB, September 3, 1940.

42. "Table-Talk," June 1913. The letter came from Boston, Massachusetts, and was signed *The Author of "The Dominant Chord."*

43. "Table-Talk," June 1913, signed H.J.B., Capetown, South Africa. Under the same date a letter from San Francisco from M.A.D. commented, "G.T.M. of Massachusetts says there are no tigers in Africa. He speaks true, but there is the cheeta, very similar to the tiger, and as mighty, if not braver than the tiger."

44. Complaints about the ending of "Under the Moons of Mars" and of "Tarzan of the Apes" appeared in a number of issues:

What we want is more stories like "Tarzan of the Apes." We want the sequel to it. The story is a bean, but, oh my, the ending is absolutely punk. (C.T.B. Winston-Salem, N.C., March 1913)

First "Under the Moons of Mars" kept us looking for more. Then "Tarzan of the Apes" made us call for more, not "The Gods of Mars" — Well I am so provoked that I will have to wait until he feels inclined to give us the rest. Oh, I am too angry to write any more. Please shake him good at your first opportunity. (Mrs. T. B. F. Anderson, So. Carolina, July 1913)

... I shall never again, if I know it, read a novel written by the above author. Mr. Burroughs must possess a peculiar sense of humor or a very much perverted idea of what constitutes properly the ending of a story. ... With Mr. Burroughs ingenuity and resources there can be no excuse for such work, and if the author sees fit to continue his custom of disappointing his readers at the end of each story, he will eventually find himself very much in disfavor among the readers of the splendid All-Story Magazine. Human nature, Mr. Editor, is very much alike. ... (J.A.D. Cleveland, Ohio, July 1913)

... when the end of a story would make a lady swear, that's some provoking.

Mr. Bean must have grown tired or had a grouch, hence the ending of the Ape-man. The author floats along upon a sea of ideas, when "all at once" the think feast is over — and end — that's all. ... (Mrs. A.C.P.F. January 1913)

Let him marry the girl he loves. I know an author like Mr. Bean can arrange it to the satisfaction of all the characters of the story, and by so doing can square himself with the readers of your magazine, and also furnish another corking good story. But don't make it a serial. (W.C.C. Boston, Mass., March 1913)

... never saw anything in print that could get on the same block with it up to the last page — but gee! — the finish is rotten.

Yours for a better finish. (F.G.R. Spokane, Wash., January 1913)

Can't you persuade Mr. B. to write a sequel to this story, wherein T. will be treated as his character deserves?

It don't make much difference what becomes of Clayton. Miss Porter can simply break the engagement, or, for all I care, Mr. B. can kill Clayton in a train-wreck. ... (J.O.B. Detroit, Mich., December 1912)

A letter dated September 14, 1912, forwarded to Ed from the Munsey Company, was from the soldiers of the Tenth Infantry, U.S. Army, Las Cascadas, Panama.

Your October number of "All-Story" is fine — let me send you the voice of hundreds of soldiers here, for "Norman Bean" or in his correct name "Edgar Rice Burroughs" and his great story of "Tarzan of the Apes;" everybodys talking about it — and every one thinks it's great; some say that "Bean" should write another about "Tarzan" because he lost the girl — while others wonder if he can get used to living in civilization. What about it Mr. Editor?

Yours for the other Story

Ed's response, dated November 13, 1912, was printed in *The Pioneer*, published weekly at Camp E. S. Otis in the Canal Zone (issue of November 24). Ed referred to the letter forwarded to him:

Although I have not attempted to reply to any letters unless they were addressed to me personally I should be very glad indeed if you should be able to locate the man who wrote that letter and tell him how much I appreciate it — more than any of the letters that have come to the Editor and to me from all over the world.

And the reason I appreciate it so much is that I soldiered myself — "B" Troop 7th Cavalry, Fort Grant, Arizona — and know what a God-send an interesting story is after the day's work is done, and a fellow gets to longing for the lights along Broadway or Clark Street, or the sight of some nice girl back in Oshkosh or Benton Harbor.

If you find him, give him my best regards, and tell him that I am working on a sequel now, — he asked about that in his letter.

Ed's printed letter in *The Pioneer* was headed with an explanatory statement: "The following letter was received by the sergeant major this week and is published in the hope that it will meet the eye of the writer of the letter mentioned by Mr. Burroughs."

45. See Chapter 1: The Creative Decision, concerning the ending ERB first devised for "Under the Moons of Mars," Metcalf's suggestion, and ERB's final choice of a more original, unfinished ending.

46. ERB's letter of March 6, 1912, to Metcalf.

47. Metcalf's letter of September 18, 1912.

48. Ibid.

49. ERB's letter of September 20, 1912, to Metcalf.

50. Metcalf's letter of October 11, 1912. He outlined a plot for the Tarzan "sequel" which included Tarzan trying to live, unsuccessfully, in some "effete metropolis, like London, Paris or New York," and later introduced a young woman who had also been marooned in the wilderness and had grown up to be a savage.

51. ERB's letter of September 20, 1912, to Metcalf.

52. Ibid.

53. Letter of November 19, 1912, initialed F.D.

54. Reilly & Britton had acknowledged receipt of "Tarzan of the Apes" on November 4, 1912. ERB later noted at the bottom of the letter, "Called on Mr. Reilly Jan. 15, 1913, and left letters of comment" (letters of praise from readers). He next noted, "March 4, 1913 — By phone Mr. Reilly explained that the syn-

dication of Tarzan of the Apes by the N.Y. World had killed it for their purposes."

In a form letter dated November 6, 1912, Dodd, Mead and Company, Fourth Avenue and 30th Street, New York, acknowledged receipt of a "manuscript," undoubtedly "Tarzan of the Apes." The company name was signed and initialed "M." On December 18, 1912, another form letter was sent to ERB, rejecting the manuscript without offering any specific reasons. Phrases used were "we are unable to make you a proposal for its publication" and "for our purposes it proves to be unavailable." The letter is merely signed "Dodd Mead Co."

55. There is no record of a response from General King.

Chapter 9: The Prolific Period

1. ERB's worksheet for "A Princess of Mars" contains a note that the sequel was started on July 14, 1912.

2. See pages 708-9, note 23, for what has been identified as ERB's parody of Kipling's poem "The White Man's Burden."

3. In the same letter of October 9, 1912, he thanked Metcalf for a clipping from the *New York World*, commenting jokingly, "We're getting famous. The pinnacle however remains to be attained in the naming of a race horse after Tarzan." Ed added, "I was talking with a commission man here last night whom you would never imagine read damphool stories, but he had recently finished Under the Moons of Mars and was very keen for the sequel." Metcalf, in his letter of October 11, remarked, "... the time will come when let alone naming racehorses 'Tarzan', the word 'Tarzan' will become a generic term for anything that is a huge success."

4. Letter of October 30, 1912. Ed was paid $750 for all serial rights to "The Gods of Mars." By his calculations, at one cent a word, he should have received at least $860. Metcalf promised to pay an additional $100 later.

5. ERB's worksheet for "The Gods of Mars" contains a glossary of the new terms and names and a Table of Time (Martian) with complex calculations. He concocted Martian units of time such as the tal, xat, zode for seconds, minutes, and hours, with the padan being one Martian day. Ten teeans make one ord — a year. The figures are irregular and do not parallel the earth units of time, e.g. one xat equals 2 minutes, 57.3 seconds, while a zode equals 2 hours, 27 minutes, 42 seconds. His glossary first lists Old Ben or Uncle Ben, "the writer's body servant [colored]," who is mentioned once in the foreword.

6. On November 18, 1912, "The Avenger" was mailed to Courtland H. Young, 124 East 25th Street, New York. Young has not been identified and there is no record of a reply. The rejection by The Associated Sunday Magazines was signed merely "The Editors." The letterhead describes the magazine as "Issued every week cooperatively and simultaneously as a part of the Sunday Editions of 12 newspapers." Included were the *Chicago Record-Herald*, the *New York Tribune*, the *Boston Post*, the *Washington Star*, and the *Baltimore Sun*.

7. The writing time is noted on the original manuscript: "Started October 3 at 2008 Park Avenue finished October 5 10:50 P.M."

8. "The Fool's Mother" contains a real-life reference to another character, Texas Pete, whom Ed had known in his Idaho days. Pete is mentioned in Ed's *Autobiography*. (See Chapter 2: Childhood and a First Adventure.) He later appears in ERB's Western novels, "The Bandit of Hell's Bend" along with "Gum Smith;" Smith is portrayed as a cowardly sheriff and cunning villain. The book contains original verse by ERB, the words for Texas Pete's sentimental song. In "The Fool's Mother" Penwell remarks to the Kid, "You all remind me of Texas Pete. He sure could kill the booze too."

Ed was still trying to sell "For the Fool's Mother" years

later. A letter of July 26, 1919, to M. B. Gates, editor of *The People's Home Journal*, New York, mentions enclosing the story and another one, "The Little Door." In this letter ERB writes, "I have an idea that I am not a short story writer but I also have a desire to become one in order to fill in between the longer stories, which are rather tiresome writing...."

9. ERB used both the British word *grey* and the American word *gray*.

10. There appear to be no reasons for ERB's choice of a French setting for his story other than the original interest in French characters that he had shown in "Tarzan of the Apes" with his introduction of the French cruiser and Lieutenants D'Arnot and Charpentier. ERB's foreign language background had been in Latin and Greek, which he acquired in his school studies. In "The Outlaw of Torn" ERB had created the French fencing master Sir Jules de Vac and had made him the most evil of villains. ERB's use of French words in both "The Outlaw of Torn" and "The Return of Tarzan," other than the names of his French characters and the Paris street, the "Rue Maule," was limited to the phrase "Mon Dieu."

The reasons Tarzan should have learned French first, with D'Arnot as his tutor in "Tarzan of the Apes," have been unexplained. In the story D'Arnot first teaches him such words as *homme*, *singe*, and *arbre*, while Tarzan quickly learns to say "Mais oui."

ERB's device in "Tarzan of the Apes" of having Lord Greystoke's diary written in French — he never explained why an English lord should prefer to write in French — was presumably used to prevent Tarzan from reading the tragic account of his parents' death and possibly guessing his parentage early in the book, and of course to allow a Frenchman, D'Arnot, to read the diary and make the discovery at the end of the book, together with the all-important fingerprints. Tarzan, who had learned to read English and had read other books that were preserved in the cabin, found the French diary a mystery. ERB comments in the novel:

Poor little ape-man! Had he but known it that tiny, baffling mystery held between its sealed covers the key to his origin; the answer to the strange riddle of his strange life.

The puzzle as to why ERB should have resorted to the complicated roundabout device of the French diary and the French language brings up the question as to which came first into his mind — the diary, which then made the Frenchman D'Arnot necessary to the plot, or D'Arnot himself, who then may have given ERB the idea of creating the incident of the diary in order to let D'Arnot play an important role.

ERB's choice of a Frenchman and the Paris setting may also be attributed to the French interest in criminal detection, begun with Bertillion, and their use of fingerprints for this purpose. In 1912 the French Police placed more emphasis upon fingerprints and scientific criminal detection methods than the American police did.

11. Metcalf's letter of November 9, 1912. He commented that he liked the beginning of ERB's outline "down to the point where Tarzan takes passage for the Congo," but after that, objected to the mutiny. He wrote, "You see the way you have done here, you first have the ship wreck and the mutiny, in which Tarzan and Miss Strong are concerned and then a little later you have practically the same sort of a stunt with Jane and Clayton."

12. Ibid.

13. Letter of November 25, 1912. Metcalf sent ERB another batch of "Tarzan" letters from readers.

14. Ed commented, in this letter of December 5, that he had removed the first shipwreck and the mutiny and had discovered "a really logical way to push Tarzan overboard." He presented the plot details about Rokoff basically as they occurred in the

manuscript. He wrote, "Then I may change my plan of putting Tarzan into the Foreign Legion, and instead intrust him with a secret mission for the Minister of War...."

He spoke of his plan to have Tarzan travel to a "great walled city" in the interior of Africa, remarking that "it will also give Tarzan the much needed opportunity of accumulating a fortune without working for it." Ed explained, with a humorous note, "He (Tarzan) will have adventures with this strange race, learn something of their history (which I can assure you will add vastly to the sum total of the world's knowledge)...."

15. This would later become "A Man Without a Soul," completed on May 10, 1913, and in later book form titled "The Monster Men." On his worksheet ERB referred to it as "Number Thirteen," based upon the main character who was the result of laboratory experiment number thirteen. He also titled it "Number Thirteen" in his letter of May 20 to Metcalf, at the time he mailed the manuscript.

16. Letter of December 10, 1912.

17. Letter of December 20, 1912.

18. ERB's worksheet, containing a list of characters not used in "Tarzan of the Apes," also includes Algerian towns and hotels with the page numbers. There is also a list of chapter headings and a relief map of a section of Eastern Algeria, drawn by ERB. The completion date is shown as January 8, 1913, 9 p.m., with the estimated words as 98,640.

19. ERB's letter of January 9, 1913, in which he advises that he has mailed "The Ape-Man," shows careful insertions in ink, done obviously to correct his grammar or to correct typing errors. A comma, an apostrophe, and a question mark are added in ink. ERB was to remain sensitive about his "pretty rotten" English in later years.

20. In his letter of January 15, Ed seemed reassured by Metcalf's reply, promising to get a copy of Sherman Adam Hill's rhetoric "tomorrow."

21. ERB wanted to know whether to sell the book rights for cash or for a royalty. Reilly & Britton had posed this question. Ed inquired of Metcalf:

What would be a reasonable cash price?
What would be a reasonable royalty?
What points, if any, should an author guard against in entering into a contract?

Ed expressed a fear that because he was a new author, he might be offered a "bottom figure," and wrote, "...I should like to feel sure of my ground if I thought it wise to suggest other terms than those offered by them."

22. Letter of January 20, 1913.

23. In this letter of January 24 he also inquired about the additional $100 Metcalf had promised him for "The Gods of Mars." It is not clear whether Metcalf sent it or not.

24. This was in a letter dated February 7, 1920, and in a reply to a "fan" who signed himself "Subnormal Bean" and turned out to be Ed's brother Harry. Ed opened by stating, "I beg to acknowledge receipt of your blurb of February 1st and to assure you that I always appreciate constructive criticism from my readers — both of them." Harry's letter is not in existence and the "Dr. Abbot" whose theory was presumably quoted in some newspaper or publication, has not been identified.

25. Ed had followed the suggestions contained in Metcalf's letter of November 25, 1912, about having Tarzan return to the civilized world of men and then renounce it. He had also used Metcalf's suggestion of having Tarzan "running the natives" and becoming "the ruler of the native village." Tarzan became "King of the Waziri." Concerning his leadership of the natives, Metcalf had written, "Perhaps you could have that first and then have him go from the blacks to the animals and so on down the line, until he is reclaimed from his downfall by the

reappearance of the heroine." When, on December 5, Ed had detailed his plot and included the section of the fabulous gold city of Opar, Metcalf, on December 10, had replied, "I think you have just the right idea for a sequel now and I am sure it will be a corker."

26. While Metcalf approved the Opar section, he of course had no idea that it would be so brief and occur so late in the story. He may have also felt that the finding of the gold ingots was an obviously contrived device to make Tarzan a wealthy man.

27. Letter of February 26, 1913.

28. In this letter of March 1 Ed had commented, "It is only natural that I should wish to sell my stuff where I can get the most for it, and that I should wish to enlarge my market, and that I should try to dodge rewriting stories that I believe to be as good as I can write."

He reminded Metcalf of the months "wasted in trying to fix up The Outlaw of Torn," adding, "... you will see why I hated to think of repeating the thing with The Ape-Man."

29. Letter of January 27, 1913.

30. Letter of January 30, 1913.

31. Letter of February 22, 1913.

32. Letter of March 10, 1913. Ed stated, "Yours of the 7th is more than fair — in fact I think you have always been fair to me. I have not meant to imply anything to the contrary." He explained that now there were other demands for his work, mentioning Street & Smith and referring indirectly to the *American Magazine*, and went on to say that if he accepted Metcalf's proposition he would have no chance to enlarge his market. He might lose the syndicate rights and the chance for book publication. He wrote, "I learned this latter fact when the publisher who has been considering Tarzan of the Apes for several months phoned me last week after he returned from New York that he had discovered that Tarzan had been running in The World and that that killed it for his purposes."

33. Letter of March 17, 1913.

34. Letter of September 6, 1913.

35. The Munsey Company had sold second serial rights for "Tarzan of the Apes" to the following papers or organizations: *New York Evening World; Philadelphia Inquirer; Pittsburgh Press;* Scripps-McRae League, Cleveland; Scripps California Papers, *Los Angeles Record* and *Sacramento Star;* American Press Association, New York City; and *Memphis* (Tennessee) *Press.*

36. Terhune addressed Ed in care of System, Chicago, indicating that he may have obtained the company name from Metcalf or the Munsey Company and also that Ed was probably still working for Shaw's business publication.

37. On the matter of serial rights, ERB had run into some annoying problems with the Munsey Company who on occasion were ambiguous (either intentionally or unintentionally) about what rights they were entitled to. Ed had begun to adopt an attitude of caution in his dealings with Metcalf and an attitude of carefulness in having a clear statement of what he was selling. In his letters of March 22, 1913, to Metcalf he mentions sending the manuscript of "The Cave Girl," and after stressing that the check endorsement should cover only first serial rights, he adds, "If it is within the range of your system I should be glad to have the rubber stamp omitted and be permitted to sign a receipt."

The rubber stamp on the back of the check evidently made it appear that all rights were being surrendered.

38. In his letter of March 17 ERB had inquired about the possibility of obtaining the Chicago newspaper serial rights to "Tarzan of the Apes." On March 20 Metcalf explained that Munsey was apparently dickering for the Chicago newspaper rights, adding, "I rather doubt whether the concern would be

willing to let the rights revert to you, and another thing, you very likely imagine that we get a great deal more money for these second serial rights than we do. I don't mean to say that we practically give them away and then sob ourselves to sleep every night, but in each individual case our remuneration is not so great, although taken as a whole we may not come off so badly."

On March 22 Ed responded, "About Tarzan newspaper rights. I don't want them if you are negotiating for their sale here. . . ." Later, on June 1, he wrote to Metcalf in the matter of syndication to inquire about Ralph Danenhower who wished to handle the newspaper serialization of Ed's stories. Danenhower had been head of Munsey's syndicate department. On June 5 Metcalf replied with an enthusiastic endorsement of Danenhower. However, ERB never used Danenhower's services.

39. Letter of May 4, 1913.

40. Letter of May 12, 1913.

41. ERB received the check on February 14, 1913, and the story was published as "At the Earth's Core" in *All-Story* of April 4 to 25, 1914. *All-Story* had been changed to a weekly, selling for ten cents. In his workbook Ed had prepared three sheets for "At the Earth's Core," the first a glossary of characters and locations, the second a typed list of categories — characters, animals, tribes, and geographical places with the chapters and page numbers where they are first mentioned, and the third, dated January 14, 1913, containing data about the Inner World.

On the sheet Ed had listed what seemed to be alternate titles for the story. He typed the words "interior," "buried," "abysmal," "subterranean," "entombed," "intombed," and "sepulchral" (i.e. "Interior World," "Buried World," etc. were the possibilities). The dimensions of the "Inner World" were shown — area, diameter, circumference, etc. as compared to the earth. The measurements of "The Inner World" were smaller than the earth, and the land and water areas were reversed. "The Inner World" contained ¾ land or 124,110,000 sq. mi., and ¼ water, or 41,370,000 sq. mi. Ed showed the earth as 53,000,000 sq. mi. of land and 144,000,000 sq. mi. of water.

On the same sheet the speed of the prospector was listed as follows: 611 feet per minute; seven miles per hour; 167 miles per day; 500 miles in three days. There is also a table of "Order of Stratification" showing the various epochs and periods. Ed had noted, "Igneous, or iruptive rocks running through all." A handwritten note states, "The Mahars are Rhamphorynchi, a genus of pterosaurs."

In addition to the initial payment of $420, Ed received another $320 for an addition written October 13 to 24, 1913, containing sixteen thousand words.

42. Letter of February 22, 1913.

43. Ed sent "The Cave Girl" to Terhune on July 21, 1913, remarking, "I know you will pardon my delay...I have been working on another story or two, and when I get interested I am likely to neglect other things. . . ." Terhune's reply was dated July 24.

"The Cave Girl" appeared in *All-Story* as a three-part serial; the cover illustration was by Clinton Pettee in the first issue. It ran from July through September 1913.

44. From a taped recording of Mrs. Carlton D. McKenzie, Harry Burroughs' daughter, made in Charlotte, North Carolina, by Hulbert Burroughs, July 12 to 13, 1969.

45. Letter of May 19, 1913. In requesting information from Terhune about what to charge other newspapers, Ed wrote, "I do not know how to figure it, and in fairness to you I do not wish to let others have it for less money than you are paying. Of course if I could charge them more — and get away with it — that would be better still, but I do not want to ask more than the story would really be worth to them."

Ed's main concern, as in the past, was the date of payment.

In the letter of May 19 to Terhune he had been worried about the late release of serial rights by Street and Smith to "The Return of Tarzan." The November issue of the magazine came out on October 5 and yet they had indicated that the rights would not be released until November 15. Ed wrote, "I hope this change in their plans will not interfere with the sending of the check."

46. In this letter of May 26 ERB had asked if Danenhower was "all right." There is no record of Terhune's reply.

47. Letter of April 9, 1913.

48. In this letter of May 24, 1913, ERB computed the number of words for "Number Thirteen" ("A Man without a Soul") as 58,254.

49. Sent to Metcalf on March 22, 1913.

50. Letter of February 22, 1913.

51. In a postscript of his letter of March 1, 1913, to Metcalf — this was the long letter in which ERB responded bluntly to the editor's angry accusations over the sale of "The Return of Tarzan" to Street and Smith — ERB added:

Say, I just happened to think that the best proof of my friendship is the fool letter I wrote for you the other day. I am not humorously inclined — Mr. Clemons [sic] niche in the hall of fame is secure in so far as I am concerned — so when you asked me to write a witty letter it was only my self-sacrificing loyalty that kept me from telling you to go to the devil. I hope it was what you wanted — and that it was well balanced.

The letter, as published in *All-Story* "Table-Talk" of May 1913, follows:

It has been with feelings of considerable amusement that I have read your various references to me and other writers in your highly interesting "Table-Talks."

I am constrained to believe, however, that a continuation of this policy cannot fail to produce in the minds of magazine readers an entirely erroneous impression, since the natural inference is that writers associate, on terms of equality, with editors.

Pray do not assume from this that I consider myself at all superior — though I do feel that there are certain ethical properties which should, outwardly, be rigidly observed by professional men in so far as their clientele is concerned.

As a matter of fact I am really quite democratic — I would even go to lunch with a publisher, under certain, more or less obvious conditions.

I am quite sorry not to have been able to see you the last time you called — I trust that my secretary made my apologies in perfectly good form.

By the bye, before closing I feel that I must speak of a very delicate matter. It is, in fact, no less than that my man complains that you sometimes keep him waiting as long as ten minutes when he delivers a manuscript to you before you make out the check.

I do not wish to appear harsh, but I must insist that this must not occur again — James's time is very valuable.

As my car has just been announced, I shall have to close, but it is with every assurance of my continued favor that I subscribe myself, sir,
Very respectfully your obedient and humble servant,
Edgar Rice Burroughs

The only change from the wording of ERB's original letter was in the word *car* in the next to the last paragraph. Ed had written, "As my bus has just been announced...".

In the same May 1913 "Table-Talk" a letter was included from writer Jack Brant who told how he got his ideas for stories while he was duck hunting; he explained that after nine hours of "work" waiting for the ducks he usually returned home with "half a dozen mallards and an idea."

52. Letter of June 14, 1913, to A. L. Sessions.

53. The publication of an article on Newell Convers Wyeth together with a portfolio of his works, in *American Heritage*, October 1965, was instrumental in bringing the matter of the *New Story* Tarzan illustration to the attention of Hulbert Burroughs, Edgar Rice Burroughs' son. The article made reference to Wyeth's "early Tarzan" and included a small cut of the cover design. Interest in the works of Wyeth had been stimulated as a result of the exhibition of approximately 125 of his paintings, on display at the William Penn Memorial Museum in Harrisburg, Pennsylvania, from October 13 through November 28, 1965.

With the aid of Reverend Henry Hardy Heins, an enthusiastic Burroughs fan and compiler of *A Golden Anniversary Bibliography of Edgar Rice Burroughs*, the Wyeth illustration was located. The original of the cover design for the August 1913 issue of *New Story*, the one containing the third installment of "The Return of Tarzan," was found at the Graham Gallery in New York. The history of its travels was fascinating. Conde Nast Publications of New York had merged with the firm of Street & Smith and included in the properties acquired was a large collection of original cover paintings. A number of these were placed with the Graham Gallery, and of course the *American Heritage* article revealed the existence of the Wyeth illustration. Wyeth had done two other cover designs for Burroughs' stories — one in the June 1913 first installment issue of "The Return of Tarzan" and another for *New Story* of January 1914 with ERB's "Outlaw of Torn." The Graham Gallery, however, did not have these and had no knowledge of their location. (Letter of November 2, 1965, to Reverend Henry Hardy Heins)

A letter from Paul H. Bonner, Jr., of Conde Nast Publications, dated February 18, 1966, disclosed that his firm had no further information. He stated, "As to any other Tarzan paintings, I'm afraid there weren't any.... the rest (outside of those placed with the Graham Gallery) were given to Street & Smith employees. I saw them all, though, and there were no other Burroughs illustrations as far as I could tell."

Negotiations for the purchase of the August 1913 illustration of N. C. Wyeth were initiated by Hulbert Burroughs on November 3, 1965, in a letter to James Graham of the Graham Gallery. He explained, "We have in our collection something over 150 originals of illustrations done for the Edgar Rice Burroughs novels, which we hope eventually to make a part of a proposed Edgar Rice Burroughs Memorial Library or Museum, in Tarzana, California." He then inquired if the painting were for sale, and if so, what the price would be. Hein's correspondence with the Graham Gallery had already established the price — $1,500.

On November 5, in a telephone conversation with Graham and in a confirming letter, Hulbert Burroughs arranged for the purchase of the painting.

Later, in a letter of January 5, 1966, Paul H. Bonner of Conde Nast Publications, sent a signed statement guaranteeing the reproduction rights of the Wyeth painting to the Burroughs organization and stipulating that these reproduction rights would not be granted to anyone else, with the exception that Conde Nast retained the right "to reproduce the painting in its own publications if it so wishes."

N. C. Wyeth did no further illustrations for Burroughs novels, other than the three done for *New Story*, but the August 1913 illustration of Tarzan was used in the dust jacket of *The Return of Tarzan* when the book was published by McClurg in 1915.

Thus N. C. Wyeth's original oil painting, titled "Man in Jungle with Bow and Arrow," which ERB might have purchased for $100 in 1913, was finally acquired by members of his family in 1965 for the price of $1,500.

54. Metcalf had been away on his vacation, and on September 2, 1913, wrote to explain why he had not read Ed's stories "The Avenger" and "For the Fool's Mother." These had been acknowledged on August 18 by M. Herald, Metcalf's secretary. Metcalf wrote, "... I am sorry to have been so slow, but of course you understand. I wonder if you would mind explaining the matter to your sister-in-law, whose stories I shall read as soon as I may."

Ella's early interest in writing poetry had been illustrated in her poem dedicated to Major George Burroughs and his wife Mary Evaline, printed in the *Memoirs of a War Bride*. The poem of fourteen lines, all rhyming couplets, was dated November 23, 1914. In later years four of Ella's poems were published in a volume titled *Illinois Poets*, an anthology of writings by sixty-four poets, Henry Harrison, publisher, New York, 1935. The poems are titled "Wing-time, Ring-time," "Inca Love Song," "Midsummer," and "The Song." Ella wrote conventional poetry, using rhyme and meter.

55. At the meeting with Metcalf ERB mentioned his two short stories, "The Avenger" and "For the Fool's Mother," and Metcalf agreed to read them. On August 16 ERB wrote to tell the editor the stories were being forwarded, and commented, "The Avenger is the gruesome one. For the Fool's Mother I intended as the first of a series of complete stories with The Prospector as the hero...." Metcalf returned these, remarking in his letter of September 10, 1913, "I guessed 'The Avenger'. It seemed to me it was straining a point anyway. I was not entirely convinced by 'For the Fool's Mother.' "

During the New York visit Ed also saw A. L. Sessions, editor of *New Story*. The most important topic of their discussion was "The Outlaw of Torn," but Ed mentioned the new Tarzan story he was planning. "The Beasts of Tarzan," and indicated that he wanted $3,000 for it. Sessions, eager to get the story, appeared willing to pay the price. Ed also left a copy of "Tarzan of the Apes" with Sessions who had promised to submit it to Appleton and Company. Whether he did so is not known.

56. Letter of December 5, 1912.

57. In "Number Thirteen" ("A Man Without a Soul") Ed was experimenting with new settings, as he had done in "The Return of Tarzan" with his use of Eastern Algeria. The action in "Number Thirteen" takes place in one of the islands of the Pamarung group, described on Ed's worksheet as "off the coast of Borneo at the mouth of the Koti River about 4 degrees S Lat 117 degrees 30' E Long." The list of characters on the worksheet is brief, but there is a separate sheet titled "Words in Number Thirteen" which calculates the words carefully by pages and lines (e.g. "words per line 11.35," "words per page 336"), evidently based upon the original manuscript. On a third sheet ERB has drawn a small map of "The Island" with the scale and directions indicated. Differing word counts are given on the worksheet and card index: 58,254 and 59,150. Ed received $1,165 for the story.

58. ERB's worksheet lists the dates as "Commenced June 7, 1913, Completed July 8, 1913."

59. Metcalf's letter of July 19, 1913, and Ed's response of July 21.

60. Letter of August 1, 1913.

61. Letter of August 5, 1913.

62. McWeeny's letter, dated July 18, 1913.

63. One of Ed's original inventions is the Mahar "band"; since the large reptiles cannot hear, the "band" presents a program of "music without sound":

Their technic consisted in waving their tails and moving their heads in a regular succession of measured movements resulting in a cadence which evidently pleased the eye of the Mahar as the cadence of our own instrumental music pleases our ears. Sometimes the band took measured steps in unison to one side or the other, or backward and again forward — it all seemed very silly and meaningless to me, but at the end of the first piece the Mahars upon the rocks showed the first indications of enthusiasm that I had seen displayed by the dominant race of Pellucidar. They beat their great wings up and down, and smote their rocky perches with their mighty tails until the ground shook. Then the band started another piece, and all was again as silent as the grave.

"That was one great beauty about Mahar music," David Innes commented in the story, ". . . if you didn't happen to like a piece that was being played all you had to do was shut your eyes."

A remarkable scene captures the full horror of the religious rites of the Mahars held in a "mighty temple of hewn rock" whose lower floor was "an enormous tank of clear water." Here the Mahars swim about while slaves, both men and women, are clustered on small islands of granite. The ceremony begins when the queen slides off her large rock and swims toward one of the islands:

Raising her hideous head from the water she fixed her great, round eyes upon the slaves. They were fat and sleek, for they had been brought from a distant Mahar city where human beings are kept in droves, and bred and fattened, as we breed and fatten beef cattle.

The queen begins to exert her hypnotic powers, fixing her gaze upon a plump young maiden. "Her victim tried to turn away, hiding her face in her hands and kneeling behind a woman; but the reptile, with unblinking eyes, stared on with such fixity that I could have sworn her vision penetrated the woman, and the girl's arms to reach at last the very center of her brain."

As the queen continued to stare, her head moved to and fro, summoning the girl toward her:

To the water's edge she came, nor did she even pause, but stepped into the shallows beside the little island. On she moved toward the Mahar, who now slowly retreated as though leading her victim on. The water rose to the girl's knees, and still she advanced, chained by that clammy eye. Now the water was at her waist; now her armpits. Her fellows upon the island looked on in horror, helpless to avert her doom in which they saw a forecast of their own.

The Mahar sank now till only the long upper bill and eyes were exposed above the surface of the water, and the girl had advanced until the end of that repulsive beak was but an inch or two from her face, her horror-filled eyes riveted upon those of the reptile.

The two vanished beneath the water, but soon the reptile queen emerged, backing toward the surface and drawing the maiden with her. Although the girl had been under water long enough "to have drowned her thrice over," there was no sign "other than her dripping hair and glistening body, that she had been submerged at all." David Innes described how "again and again the queen led the girl into the depths and out again, until the uncanny weirdness of the thing got on my nerves so that I could have leaped into the tank to the child's rescue had I not taken a firm hold of myself."

The ceremony finally reaches its awful climax:

Once they were below much longer than usual, and when they came to the surface I was horrified to see that one of the girl's arms was gone — gnawed completely off at the shoulder — but the poor thing gave no indication of realizing pain, only the horror in her set eyes seemed intensified.

The next time they appeared the other arm was gone, and then the breasts, and then a part of the face — it was awful. The poor creatures on the islands awaiting their fate tried to cover their eyes with their hands to hide the fearful sight, but now I saw that they too were under the hypnotic spell of the reptiles, so that they could only crouch in terror with their eyes fixed upon the terrible thing that was transpiring before them.

With the queen's ceremony completed, the other Mahars entered the tank and began "upon a larger scale, a repetition of the uncanny performance through which the queen had led her victim."

While "The Inner World" is a fascinating example of Ed's inventiveness, the story itself drifts into a series of incidents that appear unplanned or hastily improvised. Careful, logical development and explanation are missing, and the unfortunate result is that the work does not give a unified impression. The scientific background and atmosphere which Ed created in the *Mars* stories as part of a compact, organized civilization are also missing here. The "Inner World's" hodge-podge of weird races and customs lacks this organization; consequently, it does not achieve any convincing realism. The most important reasons for the failure in realism are the tone and style of the work: Ed chooses to adopt a casual or even jesting tone and a style of writing that permits intruding and irrelevant comments by the main character. All of this weakens the suspense and feeling of impending danger that are so vital to a story of this type. (This effect was powerfully created by Ed in the Mars series.)

In addition, the main character, David Innes, is without color, and although he achieves heroic actions, he is not created with the individualism and superheroism of John Carter. His love affair with "Dian the Beautiful" is only sketchily developed — she is not present during long sections of the story. Certainly, in the narration she does not resemble the "incomparable" Dejah Thoris, and the love between Dian and David Innes, instead of being "deathless," appears trivial.

Interestingly, Ed manages to slip into the story some references to the schools he had attended, although he devises incidents that did not actually occur. David Innes, facing death, is reflecting:

I recalled numerous acts of my past life which I should have been glad to have had a few more years to live down. There was the affair in the Latin Commons at Andover when Calhoun and I had put gunpowder in the stove — and nearly killed one of the masters.

In a later section, when Innes' life depends upon the accuracy in which he hurls a large stone at a hyaendon, a ferocious wolf-dog, he recalls his past again:

At Andover, and later at Yale, I had pitched on winning ball teams. My speed and control must both have been above the ordinary, for I made such a record during my senior year at college that overtures were made to me in behalf of one of the great major-league teams; but in the tightest pinch that ever had confronted me in the past I had never been in such need for control as now.

The familiar comparison and its accompanying philosophy that Ed had stressed in the *Tarzan* stories — the hypocrisy and insincerity of civilized man as opposed to the basic honesty of nature's simple creatures — are once more developed in "The Inner World." Concerning Dian, who fought to survive in a savage world, Innes notes that she was without culture or refinement as we know it, but she was "good, and brave, and noble and virtuous. And she was all these things in spite of the fact that their observance entailed suffering and danger and possible death."

A less inspiring example of modern woman's behavior is offered:

I couldn't help but compare Dian's action with that of a splendid young woman I had known in New York — I mean splendid look at and to talk to. She had been head over heels in love with a chum of mine — a clean manly chap — but she had married a broken-down, disreputable old debauchee because he was a count in some dinky little European principality that was not even accorded a distinctive color by Rand McNally.

Innes' trip back to the surface in the iron mole that bored its way "up through the crust of the earth from the inner world of Pellucidar," and his determination to return to that world in a quest for his beloved Dian, set the stage for a planned sequel. (His bringing with him of a Mahar, "a rhamphorhynchus of the Middle Olitic," recalls a similar incident in A. Conan Doyle's *The Lost World*, when a pterodactyl was brought back by Professor Challenger as proof of the fantastic journey he had made. Ed, as previously noted, had recalled reading a "part" of *The Lost World*; it was published in 1912, a year before "The Inner World" was written.) Casual and undeveloped references to mysterious places in "The Inner World," including "The Darel Az," "The Land of Awful Shadow," and "The Dead World," a procedure Ed followed in "A Princess of Mars," offer a hint that these places might be woven into a future story.

"The Cave Girl," Ed's story of "a young man from Bosting," was a shorter work in which he again, without compunction, returned to the "castaway" theme he had over-used in "The Return of Tarzan." Waldo Emerson Smith-Jones, "an animated encyclopedia" with a weak body, pipestem arms, and skinny legs is washed overboard from a steamer's deck and hurled upon the shore of a remote island. Here in Waldo's association with the beautiful little savage, Nadara, Ed proceeds to develop a plot with a clever reversal: Waldo, a poor specimen of manhood with a hacking cough, faces a necessity to measure up to the faith and admiration (unwarranted) of his cave girl. Undertaking a rigid back-to-nature training program, he develops a physique of heroic proportions and with it acquires an incredible courage and daring.

The popularity of the Tarzan theme — the emphasis upon the "natural" man — appears to have influenced Ed to use a variation of it in "The Cave Girl." Certainly Terhune's request for stories "with the scene laid in the jungle," and Ed's awareness that readers and editors both were clamoring for more of the theme of nature's simple perfection versus the decadence of civilization, were the important factors that drove him to this repetition.

64. The sequel, naturally titled "The Cave Man," was not written until the summer of 1914; in the A. C. McClurg & Co. book, published in 1925, the two were combined under the title of "The Cave Girl."

65. "Number Thirteen," titled "A Man without a Soul," was published in *All-Story*, November 1913.

In a long letter to "Table-Talk," printed January 1914, a reader, "H.B.H.," after commenting that the story was great, wrote:

But for the love of Mike — what has come over our friend Mr. Burroughs? For once he has really put a very agreeable ending to a story of his. Honestly, for a while I was almost afraid to start this particular story, fearing I would have to throw the book down in disgust on account of having such entertaining stories as he writes spoiled by the tantalizing endings he has almost invariably "tacked on."

H.B.H. went on to say that Burroughs had demonstrated that "he does not have to spar for an ending, but is really capable of writing stories that have the real twang and logical ending with 'everybody living happily ever after'...."

66. ERB had informed Metcalf on June 1 that the sequel to "The Gods of Mars" was "progressing nicely." On June 5 the editor cautioned, "This time I think you had better wind it up, don't you? You might as well leave them very happily married. Of course, if anyone wants more of it later on, we can carry on a sequel in which we have the son as the hero." ERB's story with its first Martian happy ending has been considered the third in a completed trilogy.

ERB's card index shows that on July 19, 1913, he received $1,141 in payment for the first serial rights from the Munsey Company. "The Warlord of Mars" ran in *All-Story* issues from December 1913, with cover design, through March 1914.

67. Before he had made any contact with Sessions, ERB, on December 24, 1912, had sent "The Outlaw of Torn" to Street & Smith. It had been rejected, possibly by another editor, since Sessions could not recall having read it. In his *Autobiography* ERB wrote, "It...was rejected three times by Street & Smith and rejected by several other magazines...."

68. Sessions' letter was dated February 28, 1913, and on March 28 the editor wrote, "...we are unable to make use of your story 'The Outlaw of Torn' in the New Story Magazine...."

69. See Chapter 7: The Outlaw of Torn.

70. Letter of August 15, 1913.

71. In this letter Ed also stressed that he intended to produce a story of the highest possible quality, writing:

Whether you make a contract with me or not I am going to try to make this as nearly as good as Tarzan of the Apes and The Return of Tarzan as a sequel can be with the hope of improving on both stories if it's in me. I realize that the Tarzan stuff is what put me on the map, and that if I fall down on the next Tarzan story it would have been better for me never to have written it at all.

Chapter 10: A California Sojourn

1. ERB's *Autobiography*.

2. Letter of September 10, 1913, addressed to ERB in care of Gen. Del. San Diego. Metcalf inquired about the additions to " 'The Inner World,' the elaboration to the center part of 'The Inner World,' " that Ed had promised to write.

3. Letter of September 23, 1913, from San Diego.

4. Ibid. Ed asked Metcalf to send galley proofs of "The Man Without a Soul" to Terhune at the *Evening World*. He also inquired about making arrangements to get a "stated number" of galley proofs for his stories when they were printed, about twenty-five copies each, and wanted to know the price. Ed had promised to finish his present story as soon as he got settled and to send "the balance of The Inner World."

5. Chapman's letter of September 22, 1913, was addressed to ERB at the new San Diego address in response to ERB's letter of September 17. Ed enclosed a copy of a letter from Williams of the Pittsburgh Press concerning "The Cave Girl."

6. Letter of December 1, 1913, containing the same inquiries about "The Cave Girl" and "The Return of Tarzan." In ERB's letter of October 3, he had advised Chapman that he could release "The Cave Girl" on October 15. Ed stated, "I must admit that I am not exactly crazy about the idea of assuming half the expense of putting the story in type if Mr. Sessions fails to make good his promise to me." He noted that there had been a number of unsolicited requests for the story and he could have sold to these people directly and simply sent them copies of the magazine, thus not having to pay forty percent to Chapman. He expressed his opinion that Chapman should bear the expense, writing, "If this additional business amounts to anything at all, shouldn't it be ample to cover the expense of the sales campaign?"

7. The fifty copies cost $33, which Chapman agreed to pay. The American Press Association would not pay more than $200 for the ready-print and plate rights, Chapman explained; he had quoted Scripps-McRae $250 but didn't expect to get more than $150. "Unfortunately there is only one New York Evening World; I wish there were more papers with the same spirit," he wrote.

8. Letter of October 2, 1913.

9. Letter of October 10, 1913. "Pretty fine cover design on the November number, and the line drawing for the caption is a pippin," Ed commented. He promised to start on an addition to

"The Inner World" at once.

10. Ibid.

11. The map of Barsoom, marked " #XVI," is drawn on two separate pages and saved in ERB's workbook. He had noted "Always give Lat first."

12. The glossary had twenty-three proper names and twenty-eight common names.

13. Letter of September 23, 1913, from Coronado.

14. Letter of October 24, 1913. ERB instructed, "As to the mss: If you will draw your blue pencil through the top line ('made it possible etc.') on page 50 of the original mss you will find that the additional matter slips in between pages 49 and 50 without further change." ERB's addition to the center part of "The Inner World," according to his workbook, was written October 13 to 24, 1913; it consisted of 16,170 words and payment was $320. No maps were attached to "The Inner World" in the workbook, but two maps were attached to "Pellucidar" later in the workbook.

15. Ibid.

16. Ibid. ERB's workbook shows "The Mucker" as being written from August 16 to October 9, 1913 — a total of 68,392 words.

17. Ibid.

18. Ibid.

19. Letter of October 23, 1913.

20. Ibid.

21. Ibid. Metcalf also commented, "Half way through your story you work very hard to make perfectly clear the 'Mucker's' character and psychology. You do this almost to the point of tautology. When it comes to a time when the 'Mucker's' character must undergo considerable change you ignore any particular subleties and jump from one high spot to another, and so to me at least, though possibly not to the average reader, the effect is not particularly convincing."

22. Letter of October 29, 1913.

23. Sessions' letter of December 8 reads, " 'The Mucker', regret also that the story is not, in our opinion, quite what we want as a serial...." The "also" refers to Sessions' previous rejection of "The Outlaw of Torn."

24. Noted in ERB's card index as rewritten December 18 to 21.

25. Letter of January 13, 1914.

26. Ibid. Ed wrote, "I was greatly surprised by the announcement in yours of the 7th that The All-Story is to become a weekly. There have been so many requests in Table Talk for a change to the fortnightly basis that that would not have surprised me much.... I have often wondered that anyone could have the patience to complete a serial with installments a month apart — I know that I never have." He now "viewed with horror" Metcalf's "Herculean Labors" and remarked, "The idea of having to read four times as much bunk as you then had to is positively staggering...."

27. ERB's card index shows "The Mad King of Lutha," estimated at 40,000 words, written from October 26 to November 24, 1913; the payment of $880 was received on December 8. "Nu of the Neocene" was written from November 27 to December 17; the payment of $600 was received on January 13, 1914. The latter story appeared first in All-Story on March 7, 1914, with the cover design. "The Mad King" appeared on March 21, 1914, also with the cover design.

28. In chapter six of "The Mad King" Ed, through Barney's dialogue, makes reference to "Burket's coal-yard on Ella Street, back in dear old Beatrice...." Ed may have devised "Ella" from Ella Oldham Burroughs' name, but "Beatrice" refers to Beatrice, Nebraska, home of Ed's old friend Bert Weston.

29. Letter of December 2, 1913.

30. Letter of December 8. Ed commented, "After what you say about the readers tiring of the Martian stories I am a little leery of attempting another. Guess I had better wait a while — what would be your advice in the matter?"

31. Ibid.

32. Letter of January 12, 1914.

33. Letter of January 13.

34. Ibid.

35. Ibid.

36. Letter of January 12.

37. Ibid.

38. Letter of January 19.

39. Ibid.

40. Ibid.

41. Ibid.

42. Letter of January 29, 1914. Metcalf wrote, "... there is always the Munsey Magazine to consider and you may rest assured that anything you send us will be considered with that magazine in view first of all. In case of any acceptance by them, the amount will be considerably higher than I can ever pay in The All-Story."

43. Letter of February 3, 1914. Metcalf, on January 29, had stated, "I don't remember anything about your third Tarzan story. It seems to me that it ought to come to me, though I don't know what arrangement you have made with the other people. It is hard work, as you state, to carry on this sort of argument by letters. It is too bad I can't see you and talk to you personally."

44. Letter of February 3, 1914.

45. As listed in ERB's card index, where an additional $135 is also shown, received on July 9, 1914, for changes.

46. "The Eternal Lover" also signals the first appearance of the infant Jack, named after ERB's youngest son John (Jack) Coleman Burroughs. In the story he is of course the son of Tarzan and Jane and in his later jungle episodes is renamed Korak by Akut, his ape companion.

After publication in *All-Story*, March 7, 1914, "The Eternal Lover" drew varied reader comments:

... I have always wondered whether before writing such stories as "The Warlord of Mars" and "The Eternal Lover" he (ERB) goes on a spree, or whether he injects enough cocaine to make himself believe he is living in the prehistoric ages. How a man in his right senses can write such stories is beyond me.

... The ending is not satisfactory to me, and probably not to others of your readers who take an interest in human life and its progress.... It is unthinkable that any educated woman could sink into barbarity, or that such a one as Nu could exist among the savage tribes of Africa.

I'd like you to get in behind Edgar Rice Burroughs to finish "The Eternal Lover," published in March 7 issue. It ended entirely too abruptly; liked the characters and story, and would like to know what became of Nu the son of Nu and Victoria Custer. And which way did Barney Custer go — east or west?

... "The Eternal Lover." I'm inclined to believe that you would not have accepted that story from a new contributor.

I am afraid that Mr. Burroughs exhausted his imagination on that class of story after writing "Tarzan" — that story was a masterpiece.

47. Ed, in his letter of January 13, 1914, thanks Metcalf for the check. Metcalf's letter was dated the seventh.

48. Letter of January 13. On January 12 Metcalf had written to apologize for having lost track of Ed's characters: "I have, of course, by this time discovered my egregious mistake in regard to

the characters Barney Custer and the others...."

49. Ibid.

50. Letter of February 10, 1914. In California Ed sent his manuscript by Wells Fargo, whereas in Chicago he used the Adams Express.

51. Letter of August 21, 1913.

52. Ibid.

53. Ibid. Ed wrote to Sessions, "If you change your mind and decide to order this story in advance you can figure on having enough instalments to go ahead with by the last of January." Evidently at the time Ed saw Sessions in New York the editor had promised to submit "Tarzan of the Apes" to a book publisher. Ed now inquired, "Did you do anything about submitting Tarzan of the Apes to Appleton & Company? I left a copy with you the afternoon I left New York — you were out at the time." There is no record of the manuscript being sent to Appleton or of any response from the company.

54. Letter of February 16, 1914.

55. Ibid.

56. Ed's worksheet "#XIII" notes that "Beasts of Tarzan" was begun on January 7, 1914, and finished February 9, 1914. At the top of the sheet words are estimated at 56,760, about two and one-half cents a word, making $1419. But Ed marks "Recd $2,500.00." As with other worksheets, Ed noted that he was listing new names and places not in other Tarzan stories. At the bottom of the sheet he had written, "Suggestions for titles: Bwana Tarzan. Bwana Tarzan & his People. The Apes of Tarzan." At the top he had entered the latitude and longitude of Jungle Island as nine degrees, forty-five minutes South; eleven degrees, ten minutes east.

According to his card index, 13,500 words were added to "The Beasts of Tarzan" for the book.

The story appeared in *All-Story Cavalier Weekly* as a five-part serial, May 16 to June 13, 1914.

57. Letter of March 3, 1914. Ed thanked him for the "Mucker" check, saying "I think your suggestions improved the story immensely."

58. Ibid.

59. Letter of March 5, 1914, indicating that the manuscript was mailed the day before.

60. Letter of March 20, 1914. Metcalf had sent him a letter about the cover designs. Ed also inquired, "Am I to understand from yours of the 13th that 60,000 words stories will be acceptable from me? I have been keeping them down lately because I thought you preferred the shorter ones...."

61. Ibid.

62. Ibid.

63. Letter of March 5.

64. "The Girl from Harris's" was begun in Chicago on July 14, 1913. Ed's worksheet lists this data:

Stopped August 13 1913 67 pgs written
Resumed March 6 1914 (San Diego)
Finished March 19 1914 (11:45 AM) San Diego
13 chapters 136 pages 44,880 words

The story was published as a four-part serial in *All-Story Weekly*, September 23 to October 14, 1916, with the title changed to "The Girl from Farris's." Ed's card index shows the payment to be $1,087 as of April 6, 1914. On July 10, 1914, Ed referred to the story as "Farris" and began alterations and revisions.

65. Letter of March 7, 1914. Ed wrote, about "The Eternal Lover," "Who painted the cover? It's as pretty a picture as I've seen in a long time. Looks something like Wyeth's work, but I don't see his name. If you think of it tell your Art Editor to thank the artist for me — even if it isn't any of my business."

66. Letter of March 13, 1914. Concerning "The Cave Girl" Ed wrote:

I wish that I had finished up The Cave Girl at one sitting, as it seems to me, without giving the matter much thought, that it is going to be dinged difficult to write a sequel to that story. In fact I never had any intention of doing so, as I thought the ending logical and satisfying. Then there is going to be some mighty tactful handling required to get Nadara past Mrs. Grundy with even a shred of reputation left to her....

67. Letter of March 24, 1914.

68. Ibid.

69. Letter of February 25, 1914. Metcalf had responded, "I cannot imagine where the other copy of "The Beasts of Tarzan" can have gone because it did not come here...."

70. Letter of March 3, 1914.

71. Letter of May 2, 1914.

72. Ibid.

73. Letter of April 6, 1914.

74. Ibid.

75. Ibid.

76. Ibid.

77. Letter of May 22, 1914.

78. Ibid. ERB added:

That, of course, would mean nothing to them; but I am loathe to stultify myself by submitting further mss to them under the circumstances. I am writing you, dear Metcalf, as I would talk if I could see you, because I believe in your friendship and loyalty to me, and because, if there is a way out of the difficulty I know that you will be ready to help me to it.

79. Letter number two, May 22, 1914, to Metcalf. ERB also wrote, "A. C. McClurg & Company are to publish Tarzan of the Apes in book form on June 17th." Emma received her first edition of the book on June 7, as an advance copy. Ed also asked Metcalf if he would arrange to have the book mentioned in "Heart to Heart Talks" in *All-Story*.

80. Letter of June 10, 1914.

81. Letter of June 23.

82. Letter of March 4, 1914.

83. Ibid.

84. The one-cent a word rate quoted in Ed's telegram would have actually totaled $250 for the 25,000 word "Eternal Lover." He asked $300 in his letter of March 13 and finally settled for Terhune's terms — $200, getting less than one cent a word.

85. Letter of March 20. Terhune also further informed Ed: "By the way, I gave Stern & Co., (playbrokers and moving picture managers) your address today; and advised them to try at once to secure from you the dramatic rights on Tarzan."

86. Another town mentioned, Goliath, is purely fictional. In the story Secor leaves Ketchum and takes "the first train south for Shoshone and Goliath." At the Palace Lunch Room there, he meets June Lathrop, working as a waitress. Goliath is described as "a thriving town of three or four thousand inhabitants."

87. It has not been determined whether Ed did actual research in the vernacular of the Chicago streets for "The Girl from Harris's" and "The Mucker." Based upon his past practices and research habits, it would appear likely. His "Glossary of Hoodlum Language," containing terms of the prohibition era, was probably compiled in the 1920s.

88. Ed's letters of April 6 and 7, 1914, contain complaints about underpayment. In the first letter, after reporting, "We got back Tuesday," he notes that he found a check for $670 for "The Lad and the Lion" and added:

Someone has blundered. It should have been about a thousand dollars, more or less. All my records are in transit now, but I recall that I figured on this amount in case you took the story. Either the words were erroneously estimated or the wrong rate applied. I am returning the receipt unsigned, so that one for the correct amount may be sent me with the check for the balance.

Since Ed's card index shows a payment of $940 for "The Lad and the Lion," Metcalf apparently sent a check for the balance. The story, on his worksheet, is listed as 40,000 words, and writing dates are February 12 to March 4, 1914. A hand-drawn, one-line map shows the Caravan Trail, with the French Camp, canyon, and mountains marked. The tents of Ali-Es-Hadji are also marked, and at the farthest point south is entered the "Gorge." (An attached page lists later additions to "The Lad and the Lion," written for the book and marked "Commenced August 20 1937 Finished August 31 1937." It lists 21,000 words.)

The story appeared in three parts in the *All-Story Weeklys* of June 30, July 7, July 14, 1917, after being held three years to coincide with the release of the Selig movie.

In the letter of April 7 Ed discusses the word count and payment for "The Girl from Farris's." He notes that he had forgotten to enclose the receipt for "The Lad and the Lion" for the correction he had demanded "yesterday," and writes:

With it is another — that of The Girl from Harris's. Smatter? Have you changed my rate, or employed a new card estimator? I have been figuring an average of 330 words per page for a long time and it has always hit quite close to your mark until these last two stories. Of course all my notes and data are some where on the Santa Fe, and I cannot give exact figures, but as I recall it The Girl From Harris's ran 58,000 words. This 330 word average took into account white space at start and finish of chapters, and was the result of the careful counting of many pages from several stories. My marginal stops are set precisely alike for all mss, so there can be very little variation. How about it?

He sought Metcalf's opinion of "The Girl from Harris's":

Would you mind handing me a word of comment on The Girl From Harris's? I ask it because the story is so very different from anything else I have written, and I was so positive that you would not care for it that I should like to know what there was about it that did *appeal to you, as, since you have accepted it, I have come to think that it may be a better story than I thought it.*

Whether Metcalf sent any comment on the story is not known.

89. Ed's action is described by David Eisenberg in John I. Tucker, "Tarzan was Born in Chicago," *Chicago History*, Spring 1970.

90. In his letter of March 2 Ed also wrote to Kidd, "If the time seems ripe now I would have no objection to taking the matter up with you. I am sure that the story would have a reasonably good sale, for it has had considerable advertising in both the All-Story magazine in which it has been mentioned several times in almost every issue for the past year and a half; also in The New Story magazine."

91. Letter of March 3, 1914. Ed wrote,

I realize that I am asking a great deal of you to answer such questions as these, but it means quite a lot to me to know, and you may depend upon it that I will not abuse your confidence.

While I can get an R. G. Dun report on them it wouldn't cover the particulars that are of greatest moment to me — the intangible moral assets that a man knows safeguard him when he deals with a house like McClurg.

The original rejection of "Tarzan of the Apes" had come from Joseph E. Bray, a man with whom Ed had had no contact. About him Ed wrote, "I wish Mr. Bray (?) had liked the yarn a bit better. I think he was half minded to take it at that — he wrote me a very complimentary letter when he rejected it. By the way, just what is his name? His initials are J.E.B."

92. Gould's reference to "last fall" is not clear; "Tarzan of the Apes" had been originally rejected by McClurg on October 31,

1912. Whether Ed had sent it again later and received a second rejection is not known.

Gould identified Bray, stating that he has had "a great deal of experience in buying, selling and publishing of books...." Concerning the firm of Stewart & Kidd, Gould added, "Please understand that this is not said with an idea of underestimating their desire and good intentions, but the question of capital enters largely into transactions of this nature. What I am telling you is done for old time's sake, and between us only." In his letter of April 7, 1914, to Metcalf, Ed had stated, "I had been thinking of putting out Tarzan myself, but all of a sudden up pop three publishers who wish to consider it — so I am waiting while they consider. When they have each turned it down I may take a whirl at it myself." While not identified, the three publishers were probably Stewart & Kidd, McClurg, and Bobbs-Merrill Company. The latter rejected the story on November 19, 1912, but there is evidence that the firm was reconsidering. Ed refers to a letter from Chapman dated April 15, 1914, concerning Bobbs-Merrill. Ed had also written to Chapman on March 3, 1914, about the firm of Stewart & Kidd. Chapman discussed the firm but then suggested that Ed contact Paul R. Reynolds, a literary agent, presumably to find a publisher for "Tarzan of the Apes."

A series of seven letters between ERB and Chapman are discussed in Ed's letter to Bray on February 5, 1925, at the time of a lawsuit by Chapman. Ed had sent the copies of these letters to Bray. Among them was Ed's letter of January 15, 1914, asking Chapman about the advisability of Ed's publishing "Tarzan" on his own account. On January 21 Chapman replied to discourage the idea, urging Ed to wait until a publisher made an offer.

93. Letter of April 24, 1914, from Terhune. The exact date of Ed's war-correspondent request is not known.

94. The agreement included a ten-percent royalty for the first five thousand; twelve and one-half percent for the second five thousand; and fifteen percent for the third five thousand and over. There was a royalty advance of $250. Chapman received a ten-percent commission.

95. In this letter of May 2, 1914, Ed wrote, "I have been trying to persuade the Evening World to send me copies containing press notices relative to Tarzan or myself, against the time I should find a publisher. Now, I have found one — McClurg & Company. They are going to get the first Tarzan story out this summer, and I need all the dope I can get for them...."

96. The sales are as follows:

Collected in summer of 1913 in Chicago

"Return of Tarzan"	$1,000
Evening World	300
"The Inner World"	420
"The Cave Girl"	600
"Number Thirteen"	1,165
"The Warlord of Mars"	1,141
	$4,626

Collected in California

"The Mad King"	$1,000
"Nu of the Neocene"	600
"The Mucker"	1,450
"The Beasts of Tarzan"	2,500
Chapman syndication	150
Addition to "Inner World"	320
	$6,020

Chapter 11: The Writer at Home

1. Ed had claimed this when advertising the home for sale later. He listed the cost as $8,500 and described the home as on a lot forty-five feet by one hundred and thirty-six feet, with two baths,

three toilets, a sleeping porch, and "a fine garage with running hot and cold water, drain and hot-water connection with the house."

Ed had previously lived in Oak Park from April 11, 1910, to April 1911 at 821 South Scoville Avenue.

2. John (Jack) Coleman Burroughs, interview of January 11, 1970.

3. Biography requested by William Chapman on April 13, 1914, and published in the *Book News Monthly*, August 1918.

4. Recollections of Jack and Hulbert Burroughs.

5. Ed's loose-leaf workbook contains a sheet for every story written (with the exception of "The Outlaw of Torn"); these sheets are chronological and contain pertinent data. A number of them include hand-drawn maps or diagrams. This record does not include his detailed card index which also lists royalties.

6. From information furnished by Mrs. Carlton D. McKenzie (Evelyn Burroughs).

7. By Alva Johnston, "How to Become a Great Writer," *Saturday Evening Post*, July 29, 1939.

8. Recollections of Jack and Hulbert Burroughs.

9. Ibid.

10. Name inserted in proof of *Writer's Digest* biography, August 1949, and also recalled by Hulbert and Jack Burroughs.

11. Recounted by Joan Burroughs Pierce. At the Tarzana Ranch, the outdoor environment may have led to this interest in coyotes.

12. *Writer's Digest*, August 1949.

13. Ed had never liked cats and according to his sons had even fired out the window of his Oak Park home at a cat, evidently missing it.

14. Information obtained from Hulbert and Jack Burroughs. Joan learned to play the piano and Hulbert took singing lessons. Concerning the nightmares, Jack Burroughs, in later years, had the same type quite regularly. He claimed that they stopped after his second marriage.

Alva Johnston, in his *Saturday Evening Post* biography of July 29, 1939, developed the idea of Ed's daydreams as sources for his writings, especially in reference to his early start:

He was too poverty-stricken to pay for any of the tired business-man's relaxations, but he hit upon a free method of making himself feel better. When he went to bed he would lie awake, telling himself stories. His dislike of civilization caused him frequently to pick localities in distant parts of the solar system. Every night he had his one crowded hour of glorious life. Creating noble characters and diabolical monsters, he made them fight in cockpits in the center of the earth or in distant astronomical regions. The duller the day at the office the weirder his nightly adventures. His waking nightmares became long-drawn-out action serials.

15. Interview with Hulbert and Jack Burroughs. In the outline for his *Autobiography*, following his statement of his first sale, Ed wrote one word — *neuritis*.

16. In this letter, obtained from Herbert Weston, Jr., Ed also wrote, "Anyhow, it costs one and one half bucks per bottle and is absolutely guaranteed to be harmless.

"Dr. Earle pooh-poohs the idea that it helped me and so do I; however it was a remarkable coincidence that immediately after commencing to take it the pain left me for the first time in years and I have been steadily improving since. To show what a narrow minded chump a man can be, I quit taking it because they doubled the price. . . ."

Writing from his Oak Park office at 1020 North Boulevard, Ed explains that as soon as the war is over he intends to leave Oak Park with its cold weather and return to Los Angeles.

17. Ibid.

18. Letter of April 30, 1919, to Father Dom Cyprian, Order of St. Benedicts, Waukegan, Illinois, who had commented on the correct uses of the words "novitiate" and "novice," causing Ed to refer to the dictionary in this response to indicate that the two words were about the same. Cyprian also referred to an article in the *Chicago Tribune*, evidently containing an implication that Ed must be using drugs or alcohol to do his type of writing. Ed replied:

I did not see the Tribune article you mention, but I am so often jokingly accused of seeking inspiration through alcohol or drugs that I sometimes think there must be those who seriously suspect me of one or the other. I have had my share of the former; but except on a single occasion when a surgeon gave me morphine to allay pain following an operation I have never had any of the latter — and it did nothing for me that time. . . . At the time I wrote my first stories — A Princess of Mars and Tarzan of the Apes — I had been high and dry on the water wagon for five years. Now I like my beer and for that reason am sorry to see July 1st coming. . . .

19. Letter of November 8, 1922, to Harry Burroughs. There also had been a report that on his second trip to California in 1916, when a dentist pulled certain teeth, the neuritis had cleared up. The outline for his *Autobiography* reports. "In '16 I drive to California for my health." Perhaps this was a reference to the neuritis.

20. Letter of May 17, 1945, Honolulu, to Studley Burroughs. Ed said that strangely the bursitis which he had in 1942 left him during one of his army flights to New Caledonia.

21. In the Yale University Fiftieth Year Supplement, Harry had written, "Operated placer gold dredges successfully on Snake River, Idaho, and later, disastrously in Stanley Basin, North Central Idaho, at the foot of the eternally snowcapped "Saw Tooth" range — the Alps of America, with glaciers and terminal moraines that would have delighted the heart of Professor Verrill."

22. Information obtained from George T. Burroughs, III, and from Yale records.

23. In a letter dated September 30, 1969, Harry's daughter Evelyn McKenzie, the incident is explained:

Dad wanted to drive the rig to the Snake River the next day to wind up some final matters. He was wearing dark glasses constantly on the doctor's orders — and he seemed to be safe. But it snowed during the night. The sky was cloudy and Dad started back. About half way home the sun came out brightly on the snow and he suddenly realized that he had left his dark glasses in the office at the River. He went on with the bright reflection from the snow hitting him — by the time he reached home the damage was done. . . .

She noted that his wife Ella had to lead him around and feed him. His eyes were covered with medicated cotton pads and then bandaged heavily, with a folded silk scarf placed over the bandage. Yet the pain was intense. A lighted lamp carried through the hall, even with heavy portieres covering the doorway, would cause sharp pain. The doctors feared brain damage. They conjectured that Harry's violent weeping spells may have had a healing effect and may have saved his reason.

24. In Idaho Harry traveled to and from Parma and Boise, where Dr. Buffem had his offices. Ed and Emma lived near his brother in Parma at the time. Dr. Buffem believed in the old-fashioned practice of bleeding patients. He drew blood from Harry and kept weakening him. Finally, Harry was taken to the best eye specialist in Chicago, a doctor who was credited with saving his sight. However, he would always be sensitive to light. Dr. Buffem, when Evelyn was eight, took out her adenoids.

25. During his long period of illness, Harry received financial help from his father, Major George.

26. According to Evelyn McKenzie, the family moved to an apartment in the South Side district of Woodlawn and later to Hyde Park. Evelyn and Studley attended Lewis Institute (Evelyn for two years) before going to Hyde Park High School.

27. Letter of May 21, 1969.

28. Letter of January 8, 1970. Frank and Grace Stuart Moss had three children: Grace Stuart, born October 6, 1904, in Chicago; Marjorie, born August 15, 1908, in Chicago (she died in infancy on June 21, 1909); and Katheryn, born September 4, 1909, in Chicago (Mrs. Alexander Konkle).

29. Ibid. Mrs. Konkle, in her reminiscences, recalls that while her father, Frank, was in the stationery business, presumably the Champlin-Yardley Company, he had offered Ed scratch paper and a corner of his office. "It seems that Ed had read some yarn just released, and throwing it down in disgust said, "If I couldn't write better than that, I'd go — (do something or other)" — to which he was challenged, "Why don't you?" Ed accepted the challenge and the offer of paper and desk space, and not too many moons later he was launched on his writing career.

30. Information from Biographical Record, Class of 1889, Yale University. Sweetser had been born in San Francisco, had attended Urban School there, and had spent a year at the University of California before completing his education at Yale. His family had settled in California in 1850, and his grandfather, Joseph B. Sweetser, raised one of the first big apple orchards with 95,000 fruit-bearing trees. He married Clara Hawkins, known as "Aunt Clare" to the family, on February 15, 1902, in Salt Lake City.

31. Ibid. Sweetser, a man of wit and droll humor, describes his career in the Yale Graduate Record. Concerning the Sweetser-Burroughs ranch and other activities, he wrote, "We found our mechanical education of vast assistance in the cattle business. Pretty soon, George built a gold-saving dredge on Snake River, which we continued in operation for many years, with some degree of success; in fact, we operated two, the second one somewhat of a frost. . . ."

About his withdrawal from the race for governor of Idaho, he wrote, "Some say my nomination and election were conceded." Information furnished by George Burroughs, III, indicates that Sweetser had a brilliant career facing him and would have probably been governor, but at a convention was taken aside by Senator Borah who told him that he'd have to give up his ambitions because of his wife Clara's alcoholism.

For the Yale Record Sweetser wrote, "About 1892 or 1893, with the assistance of Senator Fred Dubois, also a Yale man, the Burroughses and I effected the establishment of a postoffice at our ranch, which was named Yale. This postoffice still persists, although we have disposed of the property."

Sweetser maintained that you could include the phrase "went broke" after every one of his business enterprises. These were numerous and of an astonishing variety, scattered all over the country.

32. In H.E.K.'s column, "In the Wake of the News," Ed was jokingly referred to as Dr. Normal Bean. The reference to him as Normal Bean, the "rising young novelist," also in this column, made it plain that his nom de plume had been penetrated.

33. Date unknown. The topic of the world's series might have been the contest between the Chicago Cubs and Philadelphia in 1910. The Cubs played in other world's series between 1906 and 1908.

34. Marked October 13, year unknown. This announcement was headed "Our Staff Begins to Swarm." "In the Wake of the News" appeared on the Tribune's sports page. A short poem in the column by I.J.G. refers to "Staff" world's series members and includes these lines:

And Doctor Bean and Sambo Brown
For wit and brains deserve a crown;

35. The poem, printed in "The Wake," is undated.

36. Date unknown, but the reference to Oak Park indicates that this was in the second Oak Park period, beginning on May 11, 1914, although there is a possibility of the early period, 1909 to 1910.

37. The poem was printed on February 3, 1914. Ed, after his yearning appeal for "A Line-O'-Type or Two," and one he evidently missed in California, was offered reassurance, presumably, in Taylor's title — "Nay, It Hath Not Gone." Beneath his original poem, following an asterisk, Ed had typed "Help!"

The second San Diego poem, again humorously critical of Southern California, was printed in "A Line-O'-Type Or Two" on March 30, 1914, and titled "The Climate and the View":

When one first comes to southern Cal
And gloms the cloudless blue,
   One swallows nearly everything
   While listening to the natives sing
The Climate and the View.

And when one's robbed and bilked and bled
And flimflammed through and through,
   The native tries to ease the pain
   By bleating loudly and amain
Of Climate and the View.

The lean and hungry realty man
Adheres to one like glue,
   He has not eaten for a year,
   Yet still one hears him bravely cheer
The Climate and the View.

And when one comes to leave for home,
And bids the south adieu,
   One must admit, would one be fair,
   That Sunny Southern Cal is there
With Climate and with View.*

Normal Bean

*And nothing else.

38. These two poems, printed in "A Line-O'-Type Or Two," are without any author's name and are titled "Musca Domestica" and "The Martyrs." The first one, composed of four eight-line stanzas and a final rhyming couplet, presents a vivid picture of the disgusting fly:

Baby bye, here's a fly.
We will watch him, you and I;
Lest he fall in Baby's mouth,
Bringing germs from north and south.

The fly's filthy habits are described: "I believe with six such legs/ You or I could walk on eggs;/ But he'd rather crawl on meat/ With his microbe-laden feet." At the end of the poem the fly is about to be swatted. "Musca Domestica" is marked beneath its title "Republished by request" and asterisked "Of the International Anti-Fly Association."

"The Martyrs," printed October 23, 1909, is a humorous poem criticizing the C. B. and Q. Railroad. Those who wait "in the shed of the C.B. and Q." are the real martyrs:

Its menagerie air is the natural lair
   Of the germs of pneumonia and grip,
Of pellagra, bronchitis, and ev'ry old 'itis,
   Of peevishness, pimples, and pip.
They swarm on the people who come to this place.
   Which smells like a gym or a zoo —
The martyrs who wait for the ump-umpty-eight
   In the shed of the C., B and Q.

Whether this poem, consisting of three eight-line stanzas, and the "Musca Domestica" were written by Ed is not known; they may have been the work of B.L.T. The tone and language are typical of Ed's verse. The fact that they were saved in his scrapbook may or may not be of significance.

Other poems saved in his scrapbook, also from "The Line" but undated, are titled "The Clark Street Cable," described as the ballad of "the guy with the fishy eye" whose work is "to watch the beautiful botch/ That's known as the Clark Street rope"; a poem titled "Decorative Therapeutics" that tells of the effects of environment upon health — the importance of choosing furniture and bric-a-brac properly; and a short poem titled "Be Careful How You Say It," concerning the pronunciation of "volplane."

The poem "Hooks for Men!" by Normal Bean was printed, but column and date are unknown. It consists of five four-line stanzas and describes how both he and the dog have been dispossessed, with the two babies, "two tiny towheads" taking over all the belongings and closets. Of course he admits that he doesn't mind this "servitude."

A poem titled "A Warning and a Plea to Beachey," dated November 20, 1913, was written by Ed at Coronado. A typed copy is saved in his scrapbook; it is not known whether the poem was printed. Ed has noted on one side: "Written after watching Lincoln Beachey practicing for several days before he looped the first loop looped in an aeroplane." Hulbert Burroughs has recalled the incident in a note to Stanley Vinson, September 20, 1965, explaining that in this California period, although he was only four years old, he could remember having seen "the earlier flier Lincoln Beachey make what we called then a loop-the-loop...."

Ed's poem protests about the fact that he can't write and that he finds himself standing at the back window all day, "boob-like," watching Beachey circle over the house:

My labors for my daily bread
Have lately gone to pot.
 My children clamor to be fed;
But I can hear them not.

. . . .

 Half bathed, the baby squawks amain,
Exposed the while to croup,
 While friend wife hugs the window pane
To glom the loop-the-loop.

 My spacing bar and key board beck;
My pants are out behind;
 My editors weep on my neck;
But I am deaf and blind.

At the end Ed implores Beachey to "go otherwhere" and says, "Or, Beachey, list! On bended knee/ A supplicating goop/ Beats his bald pate and begs of thee;/ For Pete's sake loop-the-loop,/ And then beat it.

A poem addressed to B.L.T., dated June 11, 1914, a typed carbon, humorously develops the idea that to make "The Line," one has to write poetry, not prose: "Though worlds may pause in cosmic flight/ To hear what I would say/ You let them keep on pausing as/ You turn my prose away"; In closing Ed writes, "So I am now constrained to think/ The prose stuff that I wrote/ Was sadly utilized by you/ As brain food for the goat." The poem is signed Normal Bean; Ed's protest indicated that he had been sending prose to "The Wake," but no copies of this have been found.

A lengthy poem of eleven four-line stanzas, in typed form, signed Normal Bean, again offers a defense of sports; its setting is in heaven with St. Peter confronting a would-be entrant. St. Peter asks the "old party with saucy side-whiskers" what he has done to deserve a place in heaven. The old man replies:

 I have ruined a hundred good fight games
Besides closing a race track or two,
 And forced the unwilling ten thousands
To do as I liked them to do.

 And whenever I've seen a new pastime

That I thought wouldn't interest me
 I've hollered and shouted and bellered
'Til I've frightened the same up a tree.

St. Peter rejects the old man's application for entrance, commenting sarcastically:

 You have overlooked tennis and bowling;
Likewise, checkers and golf and croquette,
 And also some wicked old ladies
Who sit and drink tea and crochet.

 And I'm sure there are several millions
Whose pleasures in life you've not crabbed;
 And there's oodles of cush in reforming
That an A.I. reformer'd have grabbed.

 I'm afraid you can't play in the finals;
You've foozled too dinged much by far,
 And I'm sure they don't want you in hades
So you'd better go sit on a star.

 For putting the kibosh on pleasure
Because it's not pleasure to you
 Doesn't give you the high-sign to heaven,
Or an oar on the heavenly crew.

Ed here reveals not only his partiality for sports but his distaste for narrow-minded reformers. It is not known whether the poem was printed.

A four-line poem, evidently used to autograph a book presented to Bert Leston Taylor — in this case probably a copy of the first edition of *Tarzan of the Apes* — was preserved in Ed's scrapbook:

You may not read it, B.L.T. —
This book what I have wrote —
But if you throw it on the floor
I hope it gets your goat.

The verse is signed with Ed's nom de plume; with the receipt of the book, Taylor obviously knew that Burroughs was Normal Bean.

Other verses designed for book autographs, saved by Ed, are ones to Bert Weston and his family and to the Chicago Press Club. The verse to the Westons reads:

I'm trying to think of something bright
Upon this fly leaf to indite
 To make The Weston Tribe conceive me
 To be some witty gink, believe me!
But now, at last, I must, forsooth,
Reveal to Bert and Mag the truth.
 And why, indeed, should I delay it?
 With naught to say, I haste to say it.

To the Press Club, in presenting a book, probably *Tarzan of the Apes*, Ed wrote as an autograph:

Wend, magnum opus. to the Press Club shelves,
Rewarding who for greater knowledge delves.
Upon they way — a gift to them from me,
Since Led'rer says they will not pay for thee.

Lederer had remarked that he once wanted to make a cartoonist of Ed. Lederer, evidently an official, is referred to in *The Scoop* of November 7, 1914, when Ed was admitted as a new member.

A brief printed reference to Normal Bean, probably in "A Line-O'-Type Or Two," is in Ed's scrapbook: "Speaking of Normal Bean, the rising young novelist, this line occurs in the cast of 'the Girl at the Gate': 'Normal Beane, a down and outer.' Fred Donaghey claims that William Gaston's contract, signed last May, calls on him 'to play the part of Normal Beane in a new and brilliant musical comedy, etc.' Which sounds plausible enough — all but the n. and b." The date is unknown. Ed's poetry scrapbook contains miscellaneous poems by other writers, including a 1914 poem by Rudyard Kipling, clipped from a newspaper, titled "For All We Have and Are," that exhorts the readers to support the war against Germany and states, "The Hun is at the gate." Kipling pictures the law of the sword as "knitting mankind." He refers to nations that go "To meet and break and bind/ A crazed and driven foe." Other poems are by Ed's friend, Walt Mason, a poet that he highly admired and by Elmer Allen Bess.

39. Dated September 20, 1927. Foster & McDonnell, at 728-734 West Sixty-Fifth Street in Chicago, published the *Southern Economist* and operated radiophone WBCN. In speaking of Ed, Dougherty said, "I have often thought of him when occasion would permit me to read one of the Tarzan stories, and have hoped that I might congratulate him on the success he has had. You may be assured that I will review this latest story of his as though it were an 'order from the boss' and will forward same to you after finishing my reading." Dougherty added that he felt as though he were entitled to an autographed copy of Ed's next book "for services rendered in the past, for I was conscientious in my endeavors and placed his efforts before B.L.T. whether he made The Line or not."

40. Letter dated October 1, 1927. Ed offered Dougherty an autographed copy of a book, saying, "If you do not care to wait until next Spring, select one from the enclosed list and I will be glad to forward it to you....." On October 22, 1927, Dougherty addressed Ed at 306 Hohm Building, Sixth & Western Avenue in Los Angeles, and explained that he would prefer to have Ed choose a book for him. He also inquired about Ed's brother Harry. On October 29 Ed replied to say he was sending an autographed copy of *Thuvia, Maid of Mars*, since this was the next one of the Martian series that Dougherty had not read. He informed Dougherty that Harry was with the National Casualty Company at 1607 Howard Street in Chicago.

41. Ed's worksheet shows that he began "Thuvia, Maid of Mars" on April 16, 1914, at 1006 South Michigan Avenue in Chicago, the office of the Physicians Co-Operative Association, run by his former partner, Dr. Stace. Ed was evidently using the office for his writing. His brother Harry had been office manager for the association. On May 22, 1914, after the shift at Munsey's, Ed had written to Metcalf, "I started a Carthoris story some time ago but have stopped writing it awaiting a reply to my inquiry relative to its length...." In the changeover Ed's letters had not been answered.

42. Letter dated June 15, 1914.

43. Ibid.

44. Ibid.

45. Letter of June 19, 1914. Ed wrote that he expected to reach New York Tuesday, the twenty-third, via Twentieth Century.

46. Letter of June 16, 1914. Ed added, "This, with what I previously sent you, makes an additional 5400 words."

Ed's dealings with the Munsey Company in the final revisions of "The Mucker," and in the absence of Davis, led to a comedy of confusion. On September 9, 1914, H. C. Durant wrote to state, "We have struck a little snag in the editing of your story, 'Mucker Harding.'" Durant then quoted a paragraph from the story referring to two characters named Divine and Clinker and mentioning a "scheme" involving Simms. Durant wrote, "The above is the first allusion to 'Divine and Clinker.' There is absolutely nothing to tell the reader what the scheme is or how and when these two characters came into the story."

On September 18 Ed replied:

Mr. Metcalf wanted The Mucker shortened, and in doing this I must have cut out a few essentials. I think the best way to get around this is to resubmit the deleted portions that you may select what you desire.

The page numbering is horribly mixed but you should have little difficulty in fitting in the new stuff with the instructions that accompany it.

I notice that you refer to the story as "Mucker Harding." If you have changed the name of the story, should it not be Mucker Bryne? Harding is the girl's name.

On September 24, associate editor A. R. Ingalls responded to explain that they had taken Ed's deletions and had inserted "a few paragraphs here and there" that cleared up the story. Parts of Ed's plot, Ingalls noted, were being changed. Ingalls stated that the story title was not being changed — that an error had been made. He listed other revisions and remarked that Theriere's conversation had been made "a little more Frenchy."

47. Letter of June 20, 1914, in which Ed noted that the manuscript had 45,210 words.

48. Letter of June 12, 1914.

49. Letter of July 13, 1914.

50. In this letter of July 21, 1914, Ed had written "Commencing page 103 you will find new matter and again on Page 135-a." The original manuscript, still in the Burroughs' files, shows 135-a to be a half page, and on it Ed reveals that Ogden Secor was really a foster son. Beginning with the title page, the H's in Harris have been lined out with F's inserted above in pencil. In the manuscript Ed missed some of these changes. No explanation has as yet been found for the change in this name.

On July 10 Ed had referred to the revision of "The Girl from Harris's" as "the sort of job I hate." He added, "What little extra coin it brings doesn't begin to cover the labor involved. Don't you think that it would be nice next year to raise the rate for alterations? Sort of time-and-a-half for over time, as it were...."

51. "The Girl from Farris's," House of Greystoke: Kansas City, Missouri, 1965, p. 68.

52. Ed's comments to Davis on the flyleaf are not known.

53. Ed thanked him in a letter of July 10, 1914, saying, "Many thanks for the list of 'het up' Tarzan fans. McClurg is going to circularize them....," Bray's letter to Ed was dated May 21, 1914, and two days later Ed responded, "I have written All-Story as you suggest, but as they don't seem inclined to be very friendly of late I doubt if they will honor my request...." This was during the shifts at Munsey's and the dispute over serial rights to "The Beasts of Tarzan."

54. The magazine, dated August 8, 1914, was sent to Ed on August 5 by J. F. Rose, Davis' secretary. The letter is on page 170.

55. Letter of June 24, 1914, which Davis printed verbatim in *All-Story-Cavalier*, "Heart to Heart Talks," August 8, 1914. The heading read, "Tarzan Burroughs Outlines His Plans For The Future." Ed's letter included an unexplained postscript, possibly written to stimulate reader interest:

P.S. — Just in receipt of a letter from London. If my informant is correct a terrible tragedy has occurred in the life of my old friend* Tarzan; but I cannot bring myself to repeat the rumor until I have further evidence, when I shall hasten to give you all the facts.

*and meal ticket (in letter but not printed)

56. Ed's last letter from him had been on May 8, 1914. Ed had written to him on May 22 on story matters, but a later response came from Davis.

57. In this letter of July 8, 1914, Ed wrote that he had just returned from "a ten days tour in Michigan" to find Metcalf's letter of June 28 waiting for him. He had undoubtedly spent some days at the Hulbert farm in Coldwater where he had vacationed in the past. Ed also wrote, "In any event, please let me hear from you occasionally, and do not forget me just because you are no longer condemned to read my stuff...." Ed listed his Oak Park phone number.

58. Letter of September 19, 1914.

59. Ibid. Ed also mentioned Chapman's plan to start a newspaper campaign on the Tarzan series, adding that he hoped for the cooperation of Tillotson of the Munsey syndication department. Tillotson had refused to furnish a list of the papers that had purchased "Tarzan of the Apes."

60. Ibid.

61. Ibid. Mrs. George T. Burroughs was listed at 2525 Eastwood Avenue, Chicago.

62. Letter of September 21, 1914.

63. Ibid.

64. Ibid.

65. Ibid.

66. Letter of September 23, 1914.

67. Ibid.

68. Ibid. Ed wrote, "Am starting on the sequel to The Mad King with considerable relief as I am getting damned sick of the forests primeval. I want to make this a bully story, if it's in me."

69. Letter of September 30, 1914.

70. Ibid. Ed noted, "Shall do as you request about submitting an official word count with future mss."

71. Letter of November 1, 1914. A word count was enclosed. Ed explained, "The total lines are the result of actual count — the words are estimated from an actual count of every tenth page."

72. Ibid.

73. Letter of November 11, 1914.

74. Ibid.

75. Ibid.

76. Ibid.

77. Ibid.

78. Ibid. Davis, always diplomatic, wrote, "If anything in this letter seems to be peevish, it is not meant to be so. It is just a little man-talk from one to another."

79. Letter of November 14, 1914. Ed reported that he had read Oppenheim's story, "The Curious Quest of Mr. Ernest Bliss," in the *All-Story Cavalier* and thought it was "bully."

80. Letter of November 16, 1914.

81. Ibid.

82. This took place in an exchange of telegrams, November 16, 1914.

83. Since the article "What is the Matter with The United States Army?" is undated and presumably unpublished, these statistics help establish the date of writing as about September 1914. Official army statistics reveal that in 1914 the army's strength totaled close to 98,000 men, with 5,000 officers and 93,000 enlisted men. In the several years preceding 1914 the total approximated 85,000. Thus Ed's reference to "85,000 recruits" appears to place this article in the 1914 period. This is also supported by Chapman's letter of September 25, 1914, mentioning the "Army MS." received. Ed's reference to the "Krupp guns" may have related to those manufactured for the German Army in the plant under Frau Berta Krupp in 1914 or earlier. These large bore guns were publicized as "Berthas" or "Big Berthas."

84. Ed had launched his article by posing a question that he believed should precede the one contained in his title. He demanded, "What is the United States Army for?", and replied, "To quell internal disorders and to repel invasion, of course. How simple! Yet how often is the regular army called upon to do either, and when it is, what proportion of its insignificant force ever is employed?" He then returned to his own experiences: "And in the mean time what is it doing? I cannot say accurately what it is doing today, but when I was in the 7th Cavalry that part of the United States Army that was in my immediate vicinity was largely engaged in building boulevards in Arizona!"

He defined his "new purpose" for the army: ".... It is to make the standing army of the United States a great military school. A school from which thousands of young men will graduate yearly into peaceful vocations yet with the knowledge and training that will fit them when necessity confronts us to step into the firing line fit and ready."

He indulged in a number of angry comments about laboring and ditch digging: "Ditch digging is as bad for the officers as it is for the men. It keeps the officers in idleness when they should be actively engaged in the instruction of their troops." He was obviously recalling his commanding officer at Fort Grant in referring to the "four years of ditch digging, or police duty, or whatever you wish to call the day laborers' work that many commands are compelled to perform at the caprice of some commanding officer who is too fat, or too lazy, to get out and direct practice maneuvers."

In his three-year plan, Ed obviously favored the recruit's service of the last two years in the National Guard. He spoke of "the relative result upon a young man of four years in the regular army as compared to one year":

At the end of four years the discharged soldier who does not reenlist starts in civil life under a terrible handicap. Four of the best years of his life have been devoted to a profession that is without remuneration outside the army — unless he chooses to become a professional ditch digger — and he finds himself too far behind men of his own age to hope to keep pace with them in pursuits commercial.

He stressed that both the recruit and the army would be better off if the young man spent one year in service and then (supposedly in part time) trained with the National Guard for two years, while at the same time turning to some "productive trade or profession." Ed admitted that the cost would be an obstacle and that the army "has hard enough work now to get even the miserable little appropriations that are doled out to it." He claimed that under his plan the army might be made even smaller than it was and still have a more effective fighting force, or a better solution might be to ask the various states to share in the expense.

85. Bunker's letter to McClurg was dated August 19, 1914.

86. ERB's fondness for Macauley's "Horatius" was passed on to his youngest son Jack who in January 1970 was still able to recite long passages from the poem by memory. Jack maintained that his father's style of writing had been strongly influenced by the Latin studies of his early school years and by the works of Macauley.

87. The dates of the four completed stories were as follows: "Thuvia, Maid of Mars," April 16 to June 20, 1914; "The Cave Man," July 23 to August 17, 1914; "Sweetheart Primeval," August 21 to September 14, 1914; " 'Barney' Custer of Beatrice," September 26 to November 1, 1914.

88. Data on "Thuvia, Maid of Mars," taken from Ed's worksheet and card index, is as follows: manuscript of 153 pages, 45,210 words; check for $1,150 received from Munsey's on June 27, 1914; appeared in All-Story Weekly April 8, 15, 22, 1916. Surprisingly, the story was held almost two years by Munsey before printing. The worksheet contains a lengthy list of characters with the page numbers on which they appear. On the sheet Ed has marked "correcting Tarzan" and bracketed dates from April 23 to May 1. Evidently he was correcting the proofs of "Tarzan of the Apes" for McClurg. The book was published on June 17, 1914. Thus, the actual time Ed had devoted to the writing of "Thuvia...." should be shortened by seven days.

89. Data on "The Cave Man," a sequel to "The Cave Girl," is as follows: manuscript of 125 pages, 41,270 words; check for $975 received from Munsey's on September 4, 1914; appeared in

All-Story Cavalier March 31, April 7, 14, 21, 1917. Ed's card index shows that the *Tacoma News-Tribune* paid $40 for the story on December 21, 1918.

90. "The Eternal Lover" was originally titled "Nu of the Neocene." In a later paperback publication the full title for original and sequel became *The Eternal Savage* (Ace Books Inc. 1963).

91. Nu, paddling in a boat, is confronted by a "monstrous shape"; the animal attacking him has a "huge reptilian head," and later "a mighty tail" rises out of the water. Another reference is to the "hideous flying reptiles" of the Mysterious Country. However, none of these monsters receive prehistoric names; these were evidently deleted.

Ed creates the strange "hairy, tree-people":

They differed from the greater ape-folk in that they went always upon two legs when on the ground, and when they were killed and cut up for food they yielded one less rib than their apeish prototype.

92. Ed's worksheet lists "Sweetheart Primeval" with 50,000 words and 142 pages of manuscript. A notation of "From October 26, 1913" could indicate that a section of the story may have been done earlier. The index shows that on October 2, 1914, Munsey paid $1,075 for the story; it was noted that this was for 43,000 words "a/c deletion." The story appeared in *All-Story Cavalier* January 23 to 30 and February 6 and 13, 1915.

In his workbook, for "Sweetheart Primeval," Ed had three sheets: the first, a usual one, listing characters, dates, and so on; the second, a hand-drawn map of the area; and the third, a typed word count of ten percent of the pages, used to establish an average of 11.9 words per line multiplied by 3,795 lines actual measurement, making a word total of 45,160 words. This was the method that Ed had described as inaccurate. His goal was 50,000 words; he had planned to make it but, due to faulty counting, had fallen short.

93. Bert Weston, in a letter of December 26, 1911, to Ed, makes it plain that bridge playing, in which he has a moderate interest, is a very important activity in Beatrice. He writes, ". . . I had to go to a very stuffy bridge party, at which were all the 'best' of Beatrice, mostly older than I though not better. These best ones take bridge, like everything else, seriously." Bert, who had told his brother Ralph about Ed's writing under the name of Normal Bean, was playing bridge with "the Lady Auction Champ of North 7th Street." His brother, in passing, asked if he had heard from "Normal" lately. Bert, losing track of the game, "asked the L-A-C what trump was, and a little later many were whispering together and looking my way."

94. On his worksheet Ed had estimated 50,000 words, 160 pages for "'Barney' Custer of Beatrice," but a word count on a second page listed total lines as 4,751, average words per line as 11.15, total words as 52,974, and price as $1,324.35.

His card index notes that the story was returned by Davis on November 13 for changes and that these were made. An advance check for $500 was received on November 16 and the balance of $825 on November 27. The story appeared in *All-Story Weekly* August 7, 14, 21, 1915.

Ed has listed Margaret and Bert Weston in his cast of characters on his worksheet.

95. In preparing worksheets for "Pellucidar," the sequel to "At the Earth's Core," Ed went into his most extensive detail, requiring seven pages for his glossary of characters, word count sheet, detailed action-by-action outline of two typed pages, list of additions to the original, and two maps. On the glossary page he has drawn a large picture of Gr-gr-gr, the chief of the brute-men (almost six inches high). The word count sheet shows 5,166 lines, 60,919 total words, and $1,522.98 price. The card index lists a check for $1,522 received on January 22, 1915. "Pellucidar" appeared in *All-Story Cavalier* May 1, 8, 15, 22, 29, 1915.

The list of character additions notes that the land surface of Pellucidar is 124,110,000 square miles. The outline of "Pellucidar" is dated November 18, 1914, evidently prepared five days before Ed started to write the story. It is headed, "To have 60,000 words, 168 pages, 18 chaps." For the first time Ed lists a detailed plan for his story; he describes events step-by-step in a series of phrases and sentences. For example, the outline opens:

I was about to go lion hunting when I recd the following letter. Letter from reader of At the Earth's Core. He stumbled on cairn and telegraph wires. Heard click of inst.

Ed continues in this style, in some cases scratching lines he has typed; these deletions indicate minor changes in the plot.

The two maps of Pellucidar may have duplicated some of the drawings Ed sent to John S. Phillips, editor of the *American Magazine*, on January 23, 1913, when he submitted a section of "The Inner World." (See Chapter 9: The Prolific Period.) The first map, not as detailed as the second, has an "x" next to the Inland Sea to indicate the "Point at which prospector emerged at end of 1st trip." A tunnel beneath the mountains is also marked. A dotted line shows the cruise of the Sari. Other locations are noted: "Where I found Perry;" Phutra; Mountains of the Clouds; Great Ocean, Amoz, and Anoroc.

The second map of Pellucidar shows Korsar Az and Amicap at the extreme northwest. Beneath this, to the west, are Mahar City, the Lidi Plains, and the Land of the Awful Shadow. In the book, as the enemy Hoojans advance, Innes remarks that Perry has dubbed them "Hoosiers" and has even gone so far as "to christen this island where Hooja held sway Indiana; it is so marked now upon our maps." Ed's map does show the small island marked "Indiana." Sojar Az, the great sea, is shown in the southwest, and toward the east, the Unfriendly Islands. The Lural Az, another sea, appears on the far east.

96. The 1914 stories are "The Beasts of Tarzan," 56,760 words; "The Lad and the Lion," 40,000 words; "The Girl From Farris's," 44,880 words; "Thuvia, Maid of Mars," 45,210 words; "The Cave Man," 41,270 words; "Sweetheart Primeval," 43,000 words; "Barney Custer of Beatrice," 52,974 words; and "Pellucidar," 60,919 words. "The Girl From Farris's" was half-completed in 1913 (67 pages). With the addition of 5,400 words on "The Mucker," the total for 1914 is 390,413 words. The amount of money received for the eight stories, not counting syndications, plus $135 for "The Mucker," totaled $10,709. "The Mucker," in its original form, had been completed in 1913, resubmitted to *All-Story* on February 8, 1914, and on February 26 Ed received a check for $1,450. The check for "Nu of the Neocene," in amount of $600, was also received in 1914, on January 13.

Chapter 12: Film Frustration

1. Dated March 23, 1914, from 102 W. 38th St., New York, it was sent to the San Diego address and then forwarded to Chicago.

2. April 6, 1914. The fact that Ed's interest in motion picture writing had been aroused at an earlier date is indicated in his letter of July 21, 1913, to Metcalf: "Can you direct me to someone from whom I can get a copy of a moving picture play so that I can see the proper form in which these should be presented. I should also be very grateful to you if you would suggest someone to whom I might submit a play of this kind. . . ."

There is no record of Metcalf's reply or of any play written or submitted by ERB at this time.

3. Letter of June 30, 1914. On July 15, Mrs. Wilkening wrote to thank Ed for a page from *McCall's Monthly* containing remarks about *Tarzan of the Apes*.

4. Letter of August 27, 1914. Concerning the gap in correspondence — her last letter had been July 15 — Ed said he had begun to fear that Mrs. Wilkening was ill. On August 29 she asked for three additional copies of *Tarzan* and acknowledged these on

September 2. On September 10 Ed sent a followup: "... let me know how you are progressing...."

5. Letter of November 11, 1914.

6. Ibid. About the placing of his name at the beginning of each reel, Ed commented, "I do not know how the producers look upon this; but, realizing the value of legitimate publicity, I am very strong for it...."

7. Letter of November 12, 1914.

8. Letter of November 16, 1914.

9. To his letter of November 28 to Mrs. Wilkening, Ed had added a pencil notation on his copy: "Mrs. Wilkening was in Chgo Dec 2 or 3 when I consented to show 'Tarzan of the Apes' to Selig — also 'The Lad & the Lion' — see correspondence with Selig Polyscope Co."

10. In the same letter Ed explained that Selig could keep the copy of *Tarzan* but that the manuscript of "The Lad and the Lion" was his only copy and he wanted it back.

11. Letter of December 3, 1914.

12. Ed offered to contact Sacher, whose New York address was 116 Nassau Street.

13. Letter of January 16, 1915, to Mrs. Wilkening in New York. In her telegram of the same day, inquiring about the price he desired for "The Lad and the Lion," she had stated, "Cannot advise you as I have not read the story." Ed's telegram of January 16 read, "Do not know. See letter Monday."

14. Letter of January 16, 1915.

15. On January 18 Mrs. Wilkening responded, "Mr. Selig is coming to see me... I am very glad to hear that you like him and I am not surprised, as he is one of the finest men I have ever met...."

16. Mrs. Wilkening received her commission in a letter of February 5, and, in acknowledging on the eighth, said she expected to see Selig in New York, upon his return from Panama, and would take up the matter of *Tarzan* with him.

17. Letter of February 8, 1915. Correspondence between ERB and Schuler of the Author's League of America was launched with a letter of January 7 from Schuler, sent at Mrs. Wilkening's suggestion. Schuler sent a circular about the league and an application blank. Ed noted at the bottom, "Mailed application January 29, 1915." On February 1 Schuler acknowledged it, stated he would place it before the executive committee at its next meeting, and notified Ed he was sending a copy of the Yearbook and the January *Bulletin*.

Distinguished authors on the league council included Samuel Hopkins Adams, Gertrude Atherton, Rex Beach, Gelett Burgess, Hamlin Garland, Ellen Glasgow, Jack London, Ida M. Tarbell, Booth Tarkington, and others. The executive committee consisted of Rex Beach, Gelett Burgess, Ellis Parker Butler, Harvey J. O'Higgins, William H. Osborne, Arthur C. Train, and Louis Joseph Vance. Train was also the general counsel for the league.

18. Letter of February 8, 1915.

19. Ibid.

20. Ibid.

21. The author of "No Business-Man" in the March *Bulletin* used the letter X. It was evidently the policy of the *Bulletin* to assign letters as signatures for received communications.

In his letter of March 9 to Schuler, Ed commented that the *Bulletin* was valuable, "so valuable, in fact, that were it the only work accomplished by the league it would more than compensate any writer his expenditure for yearly dues."

22. The "fourth story" mentioned by Ed was "The Return of Tarzan." This was the story for which the *New York Evening World* paid $300; the *World* is also the newspaper he refers to as maintaining a nationwide syndication service.

23. In the article titled "Syndication," printed in the league's April 1915 *Bulletin*, Ed also stressed his belief that "no book or magazine publisher will permit the question of ownership of the second serial rights to any manuscript to stand in the way of their acquisition of the first serial rights, if they want them. If they don't want the first serial rights, it is certain that the second will prove no inducement." He pointed out that if "an unknown writer of very ordinary fiction" (referring to himself) can make good money on his second serial rights despite competition from publishers' syndicating bureaus and the low prices they accepted, then any writer could receive money for some of the second serial rights now being given away.

24. Letter of May 16, 1915, from Stockbridge, Mass.

25. Letter of May 20, 1915. Ed had a series of suggestions for the hoped-for bureau. "This bureau could issue a weekly or monthly bulletin of offerings, giving a brief synopsis of each manuscript, number of words, rights already disposed of and those for sale. This could then be mailed regularly to the larger newspapers, to The Scripps-McRae League, The American Press Association, The Western Newspaper Union, and similar organizations." A similar bulletin would be distributed to the photoplay producers listing manuscripts suitable for the movies. Ed also saw the necessity for a "series of personal follow-up letters to newspapers specially interested in the work of any particular writer."

Aware of authors' jealousy, he suggested that all work be listed impartially and in alphabetical order. This jealousy, he conceded, could be "the one big stumbling block in the way of a profitable and satisfactory arrangement between writers."

His vision extended farther: "Way in the back of our heads we could harbor the hope that some day the bureau could develop into that ideal (for the writer) organization — an authors' publishing house, by means of which we could not only get our royalties, but also a share of the profits from our books."

Ed noted that as a former department manager for the A. W. Shaw Company, publishers of *System*, The Magazine of Business, he knew there was money in a "sanely conducted magazine and publishing business combined."

26. Ibid. Eaton's reply on May 23 showed a keen disappointment, although he adopted a joking tone:

Alas! You may be Moses, but you still seem to be on the hinter side of the Red Sea! I thought you were going to take all my stories, and make $700 apiece for me out of 'em. Bitter, bitter blow. Seriously, from my abysmal ignorance of the whole subject, I don't see why somebody who has reached my age and magazine standing should never have sold a second serial right, except either from stupidity of his own, or lack of opportunity. I'm guilty of the former, no doubt, but also think there's something in the latter explanation. Therefore, I don't see why, if enough writers of standing should band together, they couldn't, as you suggest, benefit themselves by having a sufficient line of goods to make the newspapers, etc. interested. I, certainly, for one, would be glad to come in with a sufficient number of writers of standing to give the thing a chance, and also to chip in a bit for initial capital. But I'm infernally ignorant of business, particularly such a business, and can offer only vague suggestions. Why don't you formulate a plan in your head, and sketch it in The Bulletin, asking for those interested to write to you? We might get a line on the chances, and, if good, get together at the League of Publishers' convention in the Fall.

Fringstance, I've a series of stories beginning in the June American *which are supposed to be popular. I have retained all 2nd rights, etc. But I've not the faintest idea what to do with 'em. I don't even know who buys such things. It seems rather ridiculous. What do you do in such a case?*

Ed marked Eaton's letter "Ansd 6-2-15," but there is no record of the answer.

27. Letter of February 4, 1915. Rice, at the time he had received the story, on November 27, 1914, had explained that he was having it made into a scenario.

28. Ed's letter of June 8 was in response to Lorimore's of the fifth. The prize contest evidently was in connection with a California "exhibition."

29. Letter of June 8. Schuler responded to Ed with copyright information. He had on April 14 addressed Ed as "Mr. Burrows," but now had his name right. On June 4, 1915, in a long letter, Schuler made it plain that stories could not be copyrighted before publication. An author could copyright his story after publication by mailing two copies of it to the office in Washington with the required fee, but Schuler felt this was unnecessary, since an author's "common law rights effectively protect his property interests in a manuscript before publication." On June 12 Schuler wrote again, worried that he had not made the matter clear. He noted that while manuscripts of stories could not be copyrighted, there were exceptions in lectures and musical and dramatic compositions. Books also could not be copyrighted before publication, Schuler noted, and again stressed that Ed's idea of securing copyright protection was not possible. Schuler added that he was seeking information about Alec Lorimore.

30. Letter of June 30, 1915.

31. Letter of March 16, 1915. Friedman's letter, requesting the price for "all Photoplay rights and Concessions to 'Tarzan of the Apes,'" was typed on the letterhead of "N. Friedman Big Store" of Ottumwa, Iowa.

32. Terhune had inquired about the possibility of obtaining a new, unpublished Tarzan story.

33. Letter of May 12, 1915. Ella's address was listed as 1526 East 65th Place, Chicago.

34. Letter undated. There is no record of whether Ella actually had a movie tryout with Selig.

35. Letter of August 13, 1915.

36. Letter of August 17, 1915.

37. The manuscript of "The Prospector" is marked "completed August 24 to 25, 1915." These dates, if accurate, might indicate that Ed would not have had time to submit this synopsis of "For the Fool's Mother" to Selig with the other listed materials that he had returned on August 27. Thus Selig's reference to a "Western" story as one of the submitted ones might apply to the original "For the Fool's Mother." Earlier, on April 20, 1915, Selig had rejected "The Cave Girl."

38. Letter of August 28, 1915. The comedy synopsis "The Lion Hunter" is undated, but since "His Majesty: The Janitor," dated August 16 to 17, 1915, was sent to Selig first, it could be assumed that "The Lion Hunter" was completed some days later.

39. Letter of September 2, 1915, addressed to Anthony P. Kelly. Ed wrote, "Wanted to have a talk with you about the enclosed scripts and wired you at New York yesterday to know if you would be there Friday, intending to run down and see you. The Western Union reported back that you were in California." Ed referred to his dealings with Selig, noting they were satisfactory, but remarking that "a recent change in organization necessitates my dealing with a stranger instead of with the men I am acquainted with, and under the circumstances I believed this would be a good time to learn whether or not my stuff could be used by the Universal." He explained that he had not been required to write the scenarios and was furnishing only "outlines." He mentioned a plan to "start for Los Angeles some time the latter part of the month" and hoped to meet Kelly personally.

In a letter of September 2, 1915, to Kelly, Ed described the two synopses:

The Mad King *is a synopsis of the story by the same name, and its sequel,* Barney Custer of Beatrice, *which have appeared in magazine form. I imagine that it should make five reels, or more.*

The Lion Hunter *is a wild animal comedy which I wrote with the idea of getting a savage beast into it without making it imperative that the actors appear in the same scenes with the animals during production. I wrote it for a one reel production.*

Ed noted that he expected to start for Los Angeles "some time the latter part of the month" and hoped to meet Kelly there, adding that he planned to discuss the movie possibilities of "The Return of Tarzan" with Kelly.

40. Letter of September 21, 1915. Ed gave Berst his habitual sales talk about his books, magazine stories, and nationwide syndications.

41. Letter of September 23. Berst obviously could not use "The Mad King" in Ed's synopsis form. The synopsis of sixteen pages included "The Mad King," as published in *All-Story Weekly* of March 21, 1914, and the sequel, "Barney Custer of Beatrice," *All-Story weekly,* three parts, beginning August 7, 1915. The synopsis, a paragraph-by-paragraph summary, is divided into Book One and Book Two. There is no attempt to divide it into scenes or to give any camera instructions. It opens with a brief exposition of events that preceded the story:

About twenty-one years before the opening of the story Victoria Rubinroth daughter of the King of Lutha, eloped from her father's court with a young American by the name of Custer, beating her father's cavalry across the northern border by a small margin.

The young couple came at once to America, settling in Beatrice, Neb., where they still reside. A son and daughter were born to them — Barney and Victoria.

There are only occasional lines of dialogue.

42. On October 10, 1915, Ed sent a followup letter to Kelly, writing, "Something over a month ago I sent you two scripts — The Lion Hunter and The Mad King — with a letter explaining why I would appreciate the courtesy of an early decision." Ed noted that he had received a second letter "from the producer (Selig) who made me the original offer for these," explaining that he had been waiting for a response from Kelly. He wanted to know if Kelly intended to make an offer for either of the stories.

43. Letter of March 31, 1915, referring to Romeike's letter of the twenty-sixth. Ed discontinued the service on June 2, 1917, but resumed it at a later period.

44. Letter of May 12, 1915.

45. Letter of November 3, 1915.

46. Letter of November 17, 1915. Meyer, replying to Ed's letter of the eighth, wrote:

...I wish to say that I consider your Tarzan of the Apes a story which will greatly appeal to the German Taste regardless of the nationalities of the novels hero and his friend. The German is broadminded enough to judge a book simply for its merit, he rightly claims, that art in any form, music literature and so far are international. So for instance even at present times Shakespares masterpieces are played at the leading Berlin theatres, and French and Russian dramas are on these repertoires as well. Meyer's opinion of the German objectivity and ability to judge a work "simply for its merit" is interesting in the light of the furor that occurred later in Germany over Burroughs' *Tarzan the Untamed.* Meyer stated that he had done translations from the English since his early youth and had written for "Feutlleton short stories." He offered to send Ed a translation of any chapter from *Tarzan of the Apes* for comparison and criticism. Under his proposal, Ed would receive fifty percent of the profits. The letter was sent from 661 East 29th Street, Paterson, New Jersey.

47. Letter of November 28, 1915.

48. Letter of December 2, 1915. Schuler wrote, "I should not advise in any case the payment of $150.00 for the translation. These matters are usually done the other way around; that is, the translator pays the author a lump sum for the translating rights, or he makes the translating on his own responsibility, and shares the proceeds equally with the author."

49. Ed wrote, "I wish the story was to appear in Munsey." He valued the prestige of *Munsey's Magazine* far above *All-Story*. The "great Kathlyn" referred to is Kathlyn Williams who was rated as the Queen of the Serials before Pearl White became popular.

50. Letter of November 11, 1915.

51. Letter of December 1 to Selig. Ed wrote, "Am sorry that I could not see my way to accepting your Mr. Berst's offer for this scenario. . . ."

52. The seven-page, typed synopsis of "His Majesty, the Janitor" was written August 16 to 17 at 414 Augusta Street, Oak Park. In his writing Ed stressed certain comical actions of the characters which make it appear that he was aware of the importance of these small actions in creating a slapstick effect. For example, Jerry "slaps a piece of sticky fly-paper over the wound on the fat man's head" or, when a woman protests over his behavior, he "picks up garbage can and slams it down over her head, the contents covering her." The complete plot is Chaplinesque in style. For his concept of Jerry the janitor as a character, Ed adopted and exaggerated a prototype — the old-time apartment building janitor who ruled his domain and his tenants with the supreme authority of a king.

Because of the movie form, Ed prepared a cast of characters with descriptions. Jerry is created as a small man with "burnsides or a fringe around under his chin." Returning to his hackneyed plot of the commoner and king who had almost identical appearances, Ed noted that Fromage I, King of Edam, "should be same height as Jerry, but made up as fat man, so that his clothes will hang queerly on Jerry. Face should be made up to resemble Jerry's. Should wear crown and a pair of cavalier boots with large spurs. The balance of his costume might conform (with exaggerations) to medieval styles. Carries scepter."

The feminine lead, hardly a romantic type, is Princess Birdie of Camembert, listed as "an ancient lime," and described as "tall and muscular," with further instructions — "A man should take this part." Remaining characters are the King of Camembert, "A perfect demon of a man," various fierce-looking prime ministers, the apartment house tenants, the king's subjects, "a brigandish looking lot," and a number of minor participants.

The action is launched on a sweltering summer day when Jerry, asleep in the basement, dreams of a cold winter scene, and then half-awake, "builds a roaring fire under the steam-heating boiler." Angry protests come from the tenants. Jerry, who never goes anywhere without his broom, a weapon that he wields with deadly effectiveness, responds violently to the tenants' complaints. He stalks through the apartments, walloping men and women alike with his broom, and stumbling about to sow a path of destruction with broken chinaware, statuary, and furniture. Haughty as only an all-powerful janitor can be, he is completely indifferent to the rights of others: ". . . a man is sleeping on porch. Jerry steps on his face as he passes over him. Man awakes, angry, but when he sees who it is he goes down on his knees with palms together in supplication. . . ."

On his afternoon off, carrying his broom, Jerry visits the amusement park, and there, following another one of his practices, flirts with a nursemaid and kisses her. When she screams, a policeman appears and a chase begins. Jerry finds a large balloon, its basket empty and moored to the ground by a single rope, and to escape the policeman, climbs into the basket and severs the rope. The balloon soars through the sky toward the royal palace of Edam where King Fromage I is shown as a coward who submits to insults and beatings by his ministers, by his subjects, and even by a dancing girl who slaps him in the face and knocks him down when he attempts to kiss her. The palace janitor who comes to clean the throne room is equally contemptuous of the king and sweeps him out the front door with the "other rubbish."

The mob gathered at the palace gates has already forced the king to remove the tariff from mousetraps. Now, complaining that the river which runs through Edam to the sea is carrying all the water out of the country, "they demand that the king have the river run in the opposite direction on Mondays, Wednesdays, and Fridays." The prime minister, by choking the king, gets him to agree to meet the people's deputation. As the king lies sobbing on a couch, Jerry, tumbling out of the balloon, falls through the ceiling of the palace into the throne room. They soon discover their astonishing resemblance. Jerry is happy to change places with Fromage, especially after the king paints an enticing picture of the populace "strewing flowers in his path and going down on their knees before him." Jerry dons the king's clothes and struts about, waiting for the deputation to arrive.

The deputation's behavior is quite unexpected; instead of kneeling, the people shake their fists at Jerry and the leader "grabs him by the throat and pins him in a corner of the room, where he reads the petition relative to the changes in the course of the river."

Jerry is only momentarily taken aback. Dropping his sceptre, he seizes a broom and goes on a rampage, while the deputation, flabbergasted by the incredible change in their cowardly king, scatter in all directions. When the prime minister enters to begin his customary browbeating tactics, Jerry applies the broom to him. Later, riding the minister as a saddle horse, he leaves the palace to charge the mob outside and disperse them with his broom. Jerry is now accepted with awe and respect as the monarch of Edam.

Princess Birdie soon arrives with her father, the fierce and powerful King of Camembert. Arrangements have been made for a marriage ceremony uniting the two kingdoms, and Jerry, who has anticipated a beautiful young maiden, is appalled to discover that the princess is old and ugly. His efforts to force Fromage to resume the throne are unsuccessful, and intimidated by the ferocious King of Camembert, Jerry has no choice but to marry the princess. She is more than a match for him, seizes authority, and beats him up when he rebels.

In desperation, both Jerry and Fromage flee the kingdom. The last scene takes place in the basement of the apartment house: *Jerry is there in the king's clothes, with a Janitor nameplate on the front of his crown. Fromage I stands beside him with Asst Janitor on the front of the silk hat he wears. They have their arms about each other's neck and are smiling happily.*

53. "The Lion Hunter," a five-page synopsis, is undated, although marked "414 Augusta St., Oak Park, Ill." After being rejected several times, it had evidently been sent to William G. Chapman, Ed's syndication agent, for stamped in the left-hand margin is "From W. G. Chapman 118 North La Salle St. Chicago, Ill." Ed uses more script and camera form here, such as camera directions: "Show Algernon dressed as African, big-game hunter, stalking quarry through jungle. Show lion turning and running away. Closeup show horror stricken expression on de Sachet's face."

54. Ed had retained the title "Ben, King of Beasts" for the novelization of this synopsis as he submitted the story to Davis and to Sessions, editor of *New-Story*, in June 1915. It is not until August 1915 that he mentions the new title of "The Man-Eater." The plot is concerned with Ben, a lion who has the memory of an elephant and who never forgets the man who

saved his life. At the same time he is implacable in his pursuit of the villain, Scott Taylor, who has killed his mate. The complications are launched when Virginia Scott, the heroine, faces the necessity of proving the marriage of her father and mother in order to inherit the fortune of her grandfather, Jefferson Scott. Her parents had been married by a missionary in Africa, and the marriage certificate, the important evidence she needs, is still in the archives of the mission. A certain Robert Gordon, however, had been a witness to the marriage, and a letter is mailed to him in New York asking that he forward an affidavit. The letter has been intercepted by Scott Taylor, the only other heir (and the villain), who intends to thwart any effort to confirm the marriage.

Robert Gordon has died, and the letter is received by his son Dick, who is wealthy, idle, and bored. On the spur of the moment he decides to go on a hunting trip to Africa and recover the precious paper for Virginia. He is followed by Scott Taylor and two of his rascally friends; the three are determined to murder Gordon, if necessary, and to obtain the marriage certificate. Virginia, learning of the plan, and anxious to warn Gordon, also departs for Africa.

The scene shifts to a steamer and then to the interior of Africa where Dick Gordon finds the important paper. At this point the real hero, a huge black-maned lion, enters the story. His mate has been killed by Taylor, and the lion, bent upon revenge, is trailing the man by his scent. The animal falls into a native lion pit, is rescued by Gordon, and in turn refuses to harm Gordon when he stumbles and lies helpless on the ground. Arriving in Africa, Virginia is seized by Taylor and his friends and kept prisoner in their tent. The lion, on the trail of Taylor, plunges into the tent, and in the melee that follows, Virginia escapes into the jungle. Taylor has luckily eluded the lion. Virginia and Gordon meet, fall in love, and after other perils, return to civilization. The lion, caught and caged by a trapper, is by coincidence on the same ship, and during the voyage he and Gordon become fast friends. In America the lion is sold to a traveling circus and named Ben, King of Beasts.

Taylor, still in pursuit of the paper, arrives at the Scott family home in Virginia with one of his confederates, enters the house, and when Gordon discovers him, they fight. At the same time, after the circus train is wrecked, Ben escapes and also turns up at the Scott home. Taylor stuns Gordon and seizes the marriage certificate, but Ben, mad for revenge against the man who shot his mate, pursues and kills him.

Gordon, happy to see his old friend again, buys the lion from the circus owner. In the ending, Ed describes a typical romantic Hollywood fade-out:

As they stand on either side of the mighty beast, their fingers locked together in his shaggy mane, the sleepy keepers chance to turn their eyes away. Gordon leans across the lion's shoulders from his side, Virginia from hers, and their lips meet in a long kiss above the savage loyal head of Ben, King of Beasts.

55. Letter of April 23, 1917, from Davis to Selig.

56. Ibid.

57. In this letter of April 23, 1917, Davis wrote, "If you wish to take advantage of this date and get some publicity on the cover of our magazine, it will be necessary for you to send me photos immediately, in order that we may make the plates."

He also noted that he was sending a copy of the letter to Burroughs. The cover of All-Story Weekly, June 30, 1917, has a drawing of the Lad and a lion; apparently no photos were used. The Selig Polyscope Company was at 58 East Washington St., Chicago.

58. Sent by Davis from 8 West 40th Street, New York.

59. Letter of May 17, 1917.

60. Ibid. The matter had been made clear to Mrs. Wilkening also, Ed explained, "through whom the picture rights were sold, that release could be made prior to publication only through

arrangement with you [Davis]." Ed wrote, "I also have copy of a personal letter I wrote Mr. Selig under date of December 3 1914 explaining this phase of the matter, precisely two months to a day before the agreement was dated."

61. The Lad and the Lion" was directed by Al Green. Others in the cast were Colonel Vivier (Cecil Holland); Marie (Gertrude Oakman); Captain Tagst (Frank Clark).

62. Quoted from a printed movie review of May 26, 1917, author and name of publication unknown. A review of the film in The Moving Picture World, June 2, 1917, by James S. McQuade, offers an enthusiastic evaluation of the film:

Director Al Green has succeeded in visualizing Edgar Rice Burroughs' adventure story with fine realism. The story calls for marine views that include shipwreck, fire aboard another vessel at sea, its abandonment by the crew and the escape of the sole survivor and a captive lion from the wreck; an Arab village and the desert surrounding it; wild, picturesque scenes along the shore nearby, and desert brigands dashing across the sands on their Ishmaelite adventures. All these invest the pictured story with an atmosphere that succeeds in carrying the spectator away beyond his or her accustomed ken, forming perfect surroundings for the action of the photoplay.

Vivian Reed is described as "charming in the dress of Nakhla" and bearing the role "with becoming grace and pride." Of Will Machin's role as the Lad, the reviewer appeared impressed by the handling of the lion-man relationship; Machin's actions "will cause many to wonder; for this animal is really a fierce brute that resents intimacy from all but his trainer." The film release was through K-E-S-E, Inc.

63. The synopsis was written August 23 and 24, 1915. The stereotyped characters, the over-sentimentalized story, and the unoriginal plot offer ample reasons for Selig's rejection of either this synopsis or "For the Fool's Mother," from which the synopsis was developed.

64. Frank (Coleman) Burroughs' wife, Grace, and George Burroughs' wife, Edna, had turned to Christian Science. Mrs. Carlton (Evelyn) McKenzie, Harry Burroughs' daughter, commented on the situation in a letter of May 27, 1970:

I can't tell you whether Aunt Edna or Auntie Grace was the first, but they both became interested in what was then a fairly new religion when I was a small girl; and converted their respective husbands to it.
... those four remained interested in Science all their lives (especially the women). They — especially Auntie Grace — tried hard to convert my parents — and grandmother finally became interested after Grandpa's death and when she went to California became a devoted Scientist and died believing it.

"Grandmother" is Mrs. George T. Burroughs, Sr. Her husband died February 15, 1913.

Chapter 13: Auto-gypsying

1. Spears evidently answered questions sent into the column "Hunter-Trader-Trapper" in Camp and Trail. He noted he'd been "over a good part of the eastern states seeking material for stories...." He mentioned routes, free beaches, and camp sites.

2. Assuming that ERB would write on the trip, Spears remarked, "If you have any particular line of stories in view, perhaps I could tell you short cuts to the material...." He explained that he had been "running around for twenty years, at intervals...." He also advised Ed to carry a muzzle for the Airdale pup, "to hang around his neck, if you happen to land in a Rabies quarantine." He urged Ed to "drop in and look over my own accumulation of story plunder."

3. Detroit Journal (Magazine Page), July 22, 1916. The four photos printed for this feature article include one of Burroughs; one of Tarzan, the Airedale pup; one of the traveling outfit

packed on "Calamity Jane" and "Happy Thought," with "Their Tamer, Louis Ziebs"; and one of "the morning after at Camp Despair, near Rolling Plains, Ind."

4. The Sears, Roebuck order, dated May 6, 1916, totaled $47.60 and was marked "Ship cheapest way."

5. Spears' letter of May 29, 1916. His reference to gypsying may have inspired Ed to call his diary of the trip "Auto Gypsying;" however, in a letter of April 19, 1916, to Davis, Ed wrote, "...I want to spend the summer touring in a wild attempt to slough this damned neuritis which has made life one Hell for the past two years. We are planning on starting east in June with two cars, one for the fambly and a light truck for the camp equipment, and leading a regular Gypsy existence for a couple of months or more." Ed noted that he expected to reach New York and visit the Munsey office. On May 8 Ed wrote to Davis, Symmes & Schreiber, New York attorneys, asking George Schreiber for campsites within fifteen or twenty miles of New York City. On the eleventh Schreiber replied to say he could not supply any and suggested the sport's editor of *Outing*. A June first ERB letter to the Department of Agriculture at Albany, New York, concerning rabies quarantines brought a detailed answer on the third from J. G. Wills, chief veterinarian.

6. Letter of May 29, 1916. Spears gave his address as 26 Arthur St., Little Falls, New York.

7. Letter of June 12, 1916. Spears also noted that the roads in Ohio and Indiana were in bad shape because of rains.

8. Portland, Maine, was where Ed's brothers George and Harry had been born. The typed itinerary marked a stopover at Jay Brown's home and also at Raymond Spears' home.

9. George Burroughs had at first agreed to accompany the group, but had changed his mind. About the problems related to putting up the tent, Ed wrote, "I had helped put it up but once before when practicing with George in a neighbor's back yard before George got cold feet at the thought of the hard labor of the trip and resigned his job as my chauffeur." Ed was careful to describe and number all his Kodak pictures, listing the numbers in his diary of the trip.

10. About Michigan, Ed added, "I went to school at Orchard Lake, Michigan, for five years and travelled about the lower peninsula playing football in the Fall and as manager of the baseball team in the Spring, and about the only unpleasant feature of those trips which I can recall is the railroad service...."

11. Camp Branch was evidently named after the Branch family. Julia Hulbert, Emma's sister, had married Roy Branch.

12. Marjorie Westendarp, ERB's niece (the daughter of Leila Hulbert Westendarp), is mentioned in the diary as are Margaret (Peggy) and Judson, the Branch children. Dorothy Westendarp Aitchison, still living in Coldwater, Michigan, is Marjorie's sister.

13. On the twenty-eighth they drove 140 miles to Oak Park. Ed wrote, "It was an awful trip, hot and dusty. Tarzan and I have lame eyes from the wind and dust. He, because he insists on sticking his head out of the car all the time, being fearful that he will miss something, and I, because I have been foolish enough to drive with the wind shield raised, or, rather, lowered."

14. Hulbert's birthday was on August 12.

15. A familiar problem, encountered at Camp Point where the family had to stay at a hotel, was in sneaking Tarzan into the room. "He is the best of hotel dogs," Ed wrote. "Never makes a sound all night...." The man who had towed both cars charged Ed only five dollars. In the diary Ed commented a number of times that surprisingly, people along the routes had been moderate in their charges and had not tried to rob him, as he had feared.

16. On August 16 Ed noted he had met Mr. Hodgston and Mr. Mahon, the latter having purchased Mark Twain's boyhood

home and presented it to the city. Mahon accompanied Ed around town and gave details of Twain's life. Later, Ed took Emma and the children to Mark Twain's home. Kodak photos numbers 28 and 29 in Ed's diary of the camping trip show the family in front of the Twain home.

17. The truck tipped against an abutment of a bridge and it took two hours work with a block and tackle to get it through a hundred yards. It also stalled on numerous occasions. On the matter of never getting an early start Ed explained the seemingly endless packing chores that faced the family each morning, including tying up seven bedrolls, strapping up seven cots, rolling up blankets, carrying out a trunk and eight suitcases, and preparing twelve canvas bags. Then they had to take down the tent and pull up the stakes, drain the kerosene stove and strap it down, and begin to load dozens of miscellaneous items.

18. At Emporia, Kansas, they camped in the yard of the Moons, a Quaker family. The Moons, who came there in 1858, are described by Ed as "not precisely rolling stones," He then tells of his own traveling tendencies and the effect upon his family:

Jack, in his three and a half years, has probably travelled and seen more than old Mr. Moon has since he landed here in 1858; yet the Moons seem happy and contented, though no more so than Jack. Undoubtedly I shall always roll, at least as long as I have the price of rolling, and drag my family with me until they are old enough to anchor for themselves, I often think of a remark Jessie once made to the effect that she "wished Emma and Ed would light." It is now quite hopeless, I fear, as Emma, who was formerly quite a home person, has been inoculated with the mad virus and is becoming somewhat of a roller herself.

Walt Mason's home was at 606 West Twelfth Street. He autographed a copy of his latest book for ERB. Still preserved in Ed's collection and titled *Walt Mason, His Book*, it contains Mason's note to ERB "With Best Wishes" and Ed's note below: "Aug 28 1916 at Walt Mason's home Emporia, Kansas, while enroute to Los Angeles on camping tour." The book, with an introduction by Irvin S. Cobb, was published by Barse & Hopkins, New York. The poems, written in Mason's prose-rhyming form, are numbered from 17 through 189. The dust jacket contains a photo of Mason at the typewriter.

19. Concerning Bryan, it should be recalled that George T. Burroughs, Sr., switched to Bryan from McKinley in 1896, the only time the elder Burroughs had voted Democratic.

20. The bad roads, rain, and breakdowns in Kansas caused Ed to comment, on September 2, "Tomorrow, God willing, we shall be out of Kansas. We entered it August 25th and shall leave it on the tenth day — an awful long time to be in Kansas." He described Kansas as "the most tiresome, prosaic, monotonous, unromantic state in the Union...." He spoke of the one good "crop" Kansas had this year — a crop of "Fords from Oklahoma — the roads are lousy with them." He wrote, "Forders are proud and haughty folk. Almost everyone else is cordial and returns our salutations as we pass... but the Forders, especially the Forders from Oklahoma, stare at us with prideful disdain...."

21. About Joan's illness, Ed wrote, "The little thing lay perfectly still and at one time Emma thought she could detect no pulse." After the doctor had assured them it was not serious, "Emma broke down." Ed noted, "I had done mine in the drug store where I could make a holy show of myself. That night we decided finally to abandon camping out...." On September 8 Hulbert was sick with symptoms that were the same as Joan's, but soon recovered.

22. Ed, described the dangerous driving west of Albuquerque on narrow roads with sharp curves and commented, "Emma is remarkably game. If she feels fear, and I know she must at times, she never shows it until the danger is past; nor does she make driving hideous for me by constant advice and direction,

as I have heard is the habit of many estimable and well-meaning ladies. No man could ask or find a better driving companion than she. In this respect I have always been more than fortunate, as Emma's mother and mine are both game and delightful passengers. Doubtless they resign themselves to their fates when they enter my car. . . ."

23. Ed noted that this day, September 18, had been "a day of disaster." There was rain and a whole series of car troubles, with the group forced to return to the Harvey House at Winslow. On the nineteenth he reported, about the Packard Twin Six, "This is our first tire trouble since leaving Oak Park — almost 3,000 miles of actual mileage. The Twin passed her 13,000 mile mark yesterday."

24. He wrote, "Emma has driven a couple of times for short distances; but she is rather afraid to tackle it on bad roads, for the Twin is heavy and far from an easy car to steer."

25. At San Bernardino Ed went into a bookstore and found the owner, named Le Roy, to be exceptionally courteous and helpful. He took them to a hotel, The Plaza, and they saw him again the next day.

26. In this letter of October 25, Davis advised Ed, "Don't be lured by Walt Mason into writing any great historical novels. You would put a crimp in history from which it would never recover. . . ."

27. Letter of October 30, 1916.

28. Ibid.

29. Letter of December 3, 1916.

30. Sent on June 4, 1918.

31. Letter of June 7, 1918.

32. Ibid. About Ed's criticisms of Kansas, Davis replied, "What would happen if fragments of that diary crept into the Kansas newspapers? Suppose William Allen White and Walt Mason knew what you thought about Kansas and its environs? I guess one of the best sellers we ever had would jump off the earth."

33. Bates had introduced Ed to Lester Poyer who would be returning to Los Angeles. Poyer's father was the Republic representative in Los Angeles.

34. Letter of December 21, 1916. Ed explained that he had been at the exposition at San Diego and added, "Mrs. Burroughs and I recently had the pleasure of helping in the welcoming of young Mr. Poyer at Universal City at the end of his long trip." Poyer evidently drove a Republic truck across the country.

35. A comparison between ERB's original "Auto-Biography" and the printed version reveals that minor corrections and deletions were made, presumably by the Republic Company. First Paragraph: ERB "between the factory and the junk pile" was printed, "between the factory and their ultimate burial ground — the junk pile."

36. "The womb of our mother, The Factory" is ERB's original phrase; when printed, this changed to "from our mutual birth-place — the wonderful Modern Factory."

37. On the camping trip the Burroughs family did hoist a flag at the end of each day. The "Auto-Biography" describes how Joan or Hulbert would get out the phonograph and records and play music. The pieces were "seldom classical" and were named "Are You From Dixie?," "Do What Your Mother Did," "Hello, Hawaii, How Are You?" and others. The truck "tells" how the kerosene stove caught fire and blazed "up to the canvas top." The Boss had to use a pyrene gun to extinguish the fire.

38. The truck's "reference" to the fact that it was "the most popular entry in the Great Motor Truck Show of Los Angeles" indicates that Ed entered it in the show after his arrival.

Ed's copy of "An Auto-Biography" is autographed "Emma H. Burroughs From Husband E. R. Burroughs." The printed copies have a photo of ERB, which he furnished at the company's request. On December 21, to Somerville, he noted that he had asked "Windsatt of Oak Park, Illinois, who made my latest portrait to send you a print." The prints were pasted into the booklets.

39. Previously, on December 14, 1914, Davis had written, "In the January 23rd number I am starting 'Sweetheart Primeval,' with the greatest cover ever wrapped around a magazine. . . ." A copy was sent to ERB by Davis on January 20 who noted, "See the flying peloshi. . . ."

40. Letter of January 25, 1915.

41. Letter of January 28.

42. Ed stipulated that the agreed price was three cents a word and counted the story as 100,000 words.

43. Accepted in telegram of May 26. On June 2 Ed wrote, "You are at liberty to make the changes you mention. On page 227 you might have him fire once, dropping the nearer sentinel, and with a word in the pointed ear of his slim Arab ride the hoofed death down upon the other, trampling him into the dust of the roadway — ah, ha!"

44. Letter of April 29, 1915.

45. On June 28 Ed replied, ". . . Sure! I'm sorry you aint got no sense, and there are four more, you say? It must be the Brazil building you moved into. . . ." He spoke of "praying for the five blooming idiots who do not know a ripping good story when they see it."

46. Sent to Davis on August 26, 1915.

47. Letter of September 7, 1915.

48. "Beyond Thirty" was sent to the *Saturday Evening Post* on August 10, 1915. The rejection from the *American Magazine* came on August 24.

49. Letter of September 29, 1915.

50. Ed made the offer of $500 for "Beyond Thirty" in his letter of October 5. On October 20 he acknowledged Sessions' check for the amount and wrote, "Under separate cover I am sending you by mail mss. of 'Tarzan and the Jewels of Opar,' the Tarzan story of which I wrote you. . . ."

51. On January 13, 1915, Ed answered Terhune to explain that he hadn't any unpublished Tarzan stories; he stressed that the price suggested by Mr. Tennant was far too low, less than one third of what he had been receiving.

52. Ed's letter of March 17 pointed out that he had come down in the past for *The World*; he mentioned selling "The Beasts of Tarzan" for much less than it was worth, "simply because of my friendship for you and The World."

53. Letter of January 12, 1915. Ed wrote, " 'The Cave Girl' I do own. If you think you can do anything with her it might be well to try her on your list, as there seems to be reason back of your argument relative to the newspapers paying for photo-play stories."

54. *The Return of Tarzan* was dedicated to Ed's mother — Mrs. George T. Burroughs, and *The Beasts of Tarzan*, to his daughter Joan. On January 23, 1915, Bray sent ERB three samples of the chapter illustrations, done by St. John, for *The Return of Tarzan*, noting that Ed "ought to be satisfied with his manly proportions."

55. The form letter, as revealed in the one sent to the Western Newspaper Union in Chicago, inquired, "Would you be interested in the first serial rights for plate service of the novelization of a wild animal scenario that I have written for the Selig Polyscope Company?" Ed explained, "The film will be released, I understand, this coming winter. . . ." His card index shows that "The Man-Eater" was rejected by Associated Newspapers and Illustrated Sunday Magazine. In a letter of August 19, 1915, to Selig, Ed wrote, concerning the synopsis, then named "Ben, King of Beasts," "I have called the novelization 'The Man Eater'

since sending you the original mss., but am in hopes that your people have found a better title, or will find one."

56. Terhune paid $350 for "The Man Without a Soul."

57. Ed spoke of his total proceeds on a story, if sold directly to newspapers, as being about $5,000 for the serial rights, adding that if Mr. Smith were even ten percent correct there should be fifty newspapers that would pay $100 for the first serial rights. There is no record of a reply from Terhune.

58. Letter of December 12, 1922, to George F. Haas, Shively, California.

59. Letter of December 14, 1934 from Funk; reply of December 20, from Ed.

60. Letter of August 1, 1940, from Merriam; letter of August 5, 1940, from Rothmund.

61. Letter of August 15, 1940, Lanikai, Oahu, Hawaii.

62. Burroughs' wax cylinder, used for his dictaphone, was discovered and rerecorded by RCA for the Burroughs Corporation. It contains a section of "Tarzan and the Madman" with ERB dictating the story, January 16 to March 22, 1940.

63. Ed noted about "Tarzan and the Jewels of Opar," "I should like to dispose of it in time to meet a few million dollars worth of obligations."

64. Letter of November 26, 1915.

65. Sessions estimated "Tarzan and the Jewels of Opar" at 50,000 words and offered two cents a word. Ed's worksheet lists it as 60,000 words.

66. Letter of November 29, 1915.

67. Ibid.

68. Davis commented about "Tarzan and the Jewels of Opar," "If you do not feel like making a counter-proposition, say so frankly. Do this always with me. You and I know that neither can afford to bump the other. It is your move."

69. Letter of December 7, 1915.

70. On December 1 Ed had written Davis, "As I haven't heard anything in reply to my wire relative to the last Tarzan story I take it that you don't want it...." Davis telegraphed to request Ed to hold the story "until Saturday"; Ed agreed to wait "a few days longer." On the ninth Davis wired an acceptance.

71. Completed December 5, 1915, "H.R.H. the Rider" was sent to Davis on the sixth with Ed totaling it as "a trifle under 40,000 words." His card index showed the story as 38,000 words. On December 31 Davis insisted that the story was not worth more than $800, and under the terms of their agreement asked Ed to say yes or no.

72. Letter of October 25, 1915, from S. L. Goldsmith, 105 Bool Street, Ithaca, N.Y., sent to the Munsey Company; a copy was forwarded to ERB.

73. Letter of November 3, 1915, from Theodore Kelly of 230 Linden Avenue, Ithaca, New York; a copy was forwarded to ERB.

74. "The Son of Tarzan," written January 21 to May 11, 1915, is listed as 100,868 words. The payment was $3,000 and the story ran in six parts in All-Story Weekly, beginning December 4, 1915.

75. "The Man-Eater," written May 13 to June 10, 1915, contained 37,000 words. It was sold directly to The New York Evening World on October 18, 1915, for $350 and appeared in issues of November 15 to 20, 1915, six in all.

76. "Beyond Thirty," written July 8 to August 10, 1915, is estimated at 40,000 words. Ed's card index notes that it was submitted simultaneously to Colliers and the Saturday Evening Post and rejected, then submitted to American, Associated Sunday Magazine, and Munsey and rejected by all. First serial rights were then sold to New Story on October 18, 1915. The story appeared complete in one issue of All-Around Magazine,

formerly New Story, in February 1916.

The story is concerned with the adventures of Commander Jefferson Turck. While on patrol duty in his ancient and ill-equipped Coldwater, Commander Turck encounters a bad storm, sabotage from a jealous officer, and a breakdown of his engines, and cannot prevent the aerosubmarine from entering the forbidden area. Later, Turck and three of his men embark in a small boat on a fishing trip and find themselves abandoned by the Coldwater. They have no recourse except to head for what Turck recalls as the coast of a vaguely-remembered country called England.

The men land at Devon and instead of the great civilization that once existed there, discover nothing except wild vegetation and buried ruins. They run into large numbers of Felis Tigris, the huge fierce tiger of ancient Asia, and on the Isle of Wight encounter primitive men who have never heard of England and inform them that the country is called Grubitten, an obvious corruption of Great Britain. Traveling up the mouth of the Thames toward London, they find no sign of the teeming life and industry of the big city; all is silent, and bands of wild animals, including antelope, lions, and elephants, wander at will. The inhabitants, when discovered, prove to be savage and unfriendly, and Turck is made a captive.

Later, "Beyond Thirty" becomes a series of battles, mainly against lions, and repetitive incidents involving escapes from hostile natives. The usual love interest around a "savage" girl is created. The girl is Victory, titled Queen of "Grabriten" (a second form of the corrupted name of the country).

Some original scenes are introduced, but they receive only superficial development. The former Germany is occupied by the black Abyssinians under Emperor Menelek XIV, who has a standing army of ten million men, and Ed's ironic version of the empire makes the white people slaves, as many as fifteen million of them. In a further adventure Jefferson Turck and Victory meet the yellow men and their ruler, an emperor whose domain includes "all of Asia, and the islands of the Pacific as far east as 175W." Only the briefest of references is made to this empire.

The provocative plot of "Beyond Thirty" deserved a full, imaginative development; it was unfortunate that Ed did not devote the time and thought that might have made it one of his best stories.

77. "Tarzan and the Jewels of Opar," written September 6 to October 19, 1915, totaled 60,000 words and appeared as a five-part serial in All-Story, beginning November 18, 1916.

78. "H.R.H. the Rider," written October 25, 1915 to December 5, 1915, is listed as 38,000 words. The story ran in All-Story Weekly in three parts, December 14 to 28, 1918. Payment was $800. On October 8, 1919, the story was sold to Western Farm Life for $25.

In his workbook Ed drew a map of the kingdoms of Karlova and Margoth, marking the hunting lodge, the bandit's lair, the inn, and the Roman Road, in addition to the cities of Vitza, Demia, Klovia, and Sovgrad.

A reference by Hemmington Main to an actual person in the story is to "Garrigan of the late Chicago Press Club."

79. On December 31, 1915, Davis wrote, "A woman of Mrs. Bass' class and nature would probably know that a Crown Prince even of a small European kingdom, couldn't contract anything but a morganatic marriage with a commoner, even if he wanted to. Also it seems doubtful that in two adjoining kingdoms, the combined area of which is probably less than Cook County, that the faces of the rulers of both would not be familiar."

80. Letter of November 20, 1915.

81. Letter of December 11, 1915. In appealing for all future Tarzan stories, Davis stressed that he was constantly "advertising Tarzan and his whole damned family" and selling a great many

books for Ed. He requested that Ed keep him informed and let him know in advance when an offer came from another magazine.

82. Letter of December 15, 1915.

83. Ibid. Davis had pointed out on December 31 that while there were stories selling for five cents a word that did not "pull" as well as *Tarzan*, still *All-Story* was buying Ed's "entire output," and as a result, he was doing as well as "anybody in the game at the present time."

Chapter 14: Writer-Patriot

1. Letter of December 4, 1916.

2. Letter of December 21. The scripts may have been "The Lion Hunter," "His Majesty, the Janitor," and "The Mad King."

3. Letter of March 7, 1916, from Davis; letter of March 14 from ERB.

4. Letter of March 14. Ed added, "I know where I can hire the practical producing experience which I lack. I also know that I can produce Tarzan with such aid. From present indications there will be no difficulty in raising a couple of hundred thousand beans for production."

On April 5 ERB wrote to Eric Schuler of The Author's League, New York, to explain his plans for a new film company, not only to produce *Tarzan*, but to be "a holding company for the production of both old and new work of well-known writers." He again stressed that it must be a company in which writers could place "implicit confidence." The company must conduct business like reputable publishing houses, "without any juggling of royalties or shrewd business practices."

On April 6 Ed repeated details of this plan to Davis, emphasizing that "the finished film will not cause an author to weep tears of rage and mortification, for he will be one of a committee of three who must pass upon every foot of film before it is accepted." Of course the first work of the company would be the production of Tarzan of the Apes, "probably in about five reels." Ed noted that he would take no royalties on *Tarzan*, but only the same profits on his stock holdings that the others would receive. He explained, "What I propose asking is a piece of the stock and a reasonable salary as president of the company, for I shall practically stop writing and devote my time to the company. The salary I shall ask is less than my writing has brought me for the past two years."

A suggested list of officers and directors for the company, a number of whom had not yet been approached, included the following: Robert D. Lay, vice-president; Watterson Rothacker, vice-president; Ray Long, secretary; David H. Watkins, treasurer. Directors, in addition to the above, were Robert H. Davis, James R. Quirk, Jack London, George Barr McCutcheon, and Rex Beach.

On April 7, to Davis, ERB gave further explanations. Although all the capital, he maintained, could be raised among a few men, he wanted the stock scattered among the others he had listed, to insure that these people, who had influence in literary circles, would help keep the proposition upon a "high level," far above what the "present-day producers" were doing. Ed discussed his ability as an executive, mentioning his experience with Sears, Roebuck Company, where "without friends or influence" he advanced in less than three months from an "extremely minor position to the head of a department of two hundred and fifty people." Ed also offered brief resumes of the qualifications of the men he had chosen for officers. Watterson R. Rothacker, the head of his own film company, was described as the "father of the industrial motion picture business." James R. Quirk was noted as treasurer of *Photoplay Magazine* who, Ed had been told, owned a third of the stock. Watkins was noted as "the man whose enthusiasm has persuaded me to go to

the proposition." Concerning London, McCutcheon, and Beach, Ed explained that these men would be desirable both as stockholders and as writers who would submit original stories. He admitted, "They have not been approached, and may never be."

5. In rejecting the chance to be either a director or a stockholder in the proposed company, Davis explained that once he became interested in anything, "half measures disappear"; he would think only of the company and neglect his job at Munsey's. Also, Munsey's had a wide business with motion picture houses throughout the country, and any connection Davis might have with Ed's company could lead to suspicions that he was biased in that direction.

6. Letter of April 19, 1916, to Davis. Noting that he had been busy moving his office from The Loop back to his home, he added, about his gypsying tour, "I rather expect we will touch N.Y. City, and if you won't be too ashamed I may blow Prince Albert in your face for a few minutes...."

On April 21 he wrote to Hobart Bosworth in Los Angeles to announce that he was abandoning his plan for producing *Tarzan* and would spend the summer touring to regain his health. He apologized to Bosworth, saying that he might accept the offer of a producer and stating, "You were so highly spoken of as a managing director that I was anxious to interest you...."

7. Letter of April 14, 1916. Again, he informed Watkins of his plan to relinquish the idea of forming the company and to devote "...all of the next year to trying to get back my health...." About the rights to *Tarzan*, Ed stressed that there must be a time limit inserted in any contract, and if the picture were not produced within this period, the rights would revert back to Ed. Also, the royalty must be based upon gross rentals.

8. With his letter of June 12, 1916, Ed returned the signed contract to Parsons, noting that he did not want the $50,000 in capital stock until Parsons had raised at least that amount so as to insure production. He noted that the paragraph stipulating that Parsons must turn over to him the "finished film" was ambiguous. All Ed wanted was "reasonable proof" of finished production. He added that all he expected was a "square deal," and wrote, "Any damned contract is at best but an incentive to chicanery and a provocation for litigation." He enclosed letters to men who might be able to find a market for some stock and at Parsons' request sent a couple of photos of himself.

9. Parsons addressed Ed at "Clear Water" Michigan and referred to Kodak prints of the tour that he had received. Henry Carr was president of the Cook County Realty Board. Parsons claimed that at the next stockholder's meeting all those mentioned would be placed in the board of directors and that Richard Strongman of the Woolworth Company would be included.

10. Lay's letter of October 2, 1916, was sent to Ed at the Hollenbeck Hotel in Los Angeles. Lay enclosed Parsons' check of $500 with notice that this extended the time of payment of the required $5,000 to October 6, and with a further $500 on that date, the balance of $4,000 was to be extended to December 1, 1916.

11. On October 3, Lay sent the second Parsons check for $500 and added a personal note: "How is that for a collector. I think you will get the rest by 12/1. Don't think I have anything to do with the company because I haven't and won't. Just acting for you so you can get the money. Such a valuable life should be insured." Lay was secretary of the National Life Insurance Co.

12. Parsons, in this letter of October 5 to Ed at the Hollenbeck Hotel, mentioned his suggestion to Lay that Ed take the presidency and that Parsons become vice-president and general manager.

13. Ed's letter of October 7 was written from 355 South Hoover Street, Los Angeles. Concerning his brother Frank, whose

address was listed as 228 Wood Court, Wilmette, Illinois, Ed explained, "I have not written to him on the subject and do not know that he would care to undertake the work; but I should prefer him to another if he is at liberty."

14. Ed also stated that he liked Los Angeles, but unfortunately "the rainy season set in some two months ahead of time this year." He noted that he and Emma had seen Griffith's *Intolerance* the evening before at Clune's Auditorium, had found it a "magnificent spectacle," but not "as full of thrills and heart throbs as The Birth of a Nation."

15. The first use of the stationery appeared to be in Parsons' letter of July 21, 1916, to Ed. Parsons wrote, "Just got out our stationery and stuff. What do you think of it?" The letterhead contained no list of officers, with only Parsons shown as president and the address at 218 West 42nd St., New York.

16. Letter of October 18. The National Film Corporation stationery now showed executive offices in the Steger Building, Chicago, and New York offices at 1600 Broadway. The stationery still contained the Arting silhouette of Tarzan and the phrase "The Wonder Story of the Age."

17. In this letter of October 18, Parsons mentioned Charles F. Lorenzen of Oak Park, the head of the largest tile manufacturer in the West, as a hoped-for president of the company. The letter, handwritten, indicated clearly Parsons' agitated state of mind.

18. Letter of October 18. On the twenty-third Parsons wrote Ed at the Hoover Street address in Los Angeles explaining that he had previously offered to issue the stock to Ed who didn't want it at that time. Parsons said he would issue it on receipt of instructions and suggested that some of it be issued in Frank Burroughs' name so that he could act for Ed.

19. Letter of October 24.

20. Ibid. Ed enclosed a photo of himself and wrote, "Please be careful how you use it. I don't want it on letter heads or anything of the sort."

21. Lay informed Ed of the resignation in a letter of October 24, and stated that Ed should not accept the presidency. He added, "I do not believe that Mr. Parsons would consider letting anyone but himself control the affairs of the company...."

22. In his letter to Ed, October 28, Parsons enclosed the certificate for 10,000 shares. He explained he was still searching for a president and noted that he had issued $2,500 worth of stock to Robert Lay for services "which he promised to perform." Ed's letter, acknowledging receipt of his stock, was dated November 7.

23. The nature of the operation is not known.

24. Letter of January 9, 1917.

25. Letter of February 21, 1917. The bound volume of fan letters contained those that had been sent to Ed personally and a larger group that had been sent to *All-Story*. Not all of the letters mentioned *Tarzan* specifically.

26. The sample circular letter sent to Ed was dated March 12, 1917, and was addressed to Dr. J. Elizabeth Tompkins, 3213 Groveland Ave., Chicago. She was evidently one of the fans who had written a letter to Ed or to *All-Story*.

27. To Ray Long, in a telegram of March 20, 1917, Ed wrote, "Home April third." The telegram also referred to the series of Tarzan short stories: "Mailing eleven today. Substitute if possible or change ten there. I have no copy here to work from." Long had complained about the ending of story number ten.

In a previous telegram to Parsons, dated November 18, 1916, Ed had mentioned another trip, probably a short one: "All plans made for auto trip about first." Ed was in Los Angeles.

28. On March 4, 1917, W. H. Gardner, in Chicago, wrote to Ed in Los Angeles to describe the home at 700 Linden Ave., Oak Park, that he was offering for sale:

...occupies half a block at the Northeast corner of Augusta St. & Linden Ave, having a frontage of 132 ft. 9 in. on Augusta and 135 ft. on Linden Ave. My original price on this property was $26,000, but in order to be sure of the sale... I have reduced this to $23,000.... The Billiard Room in the basement is of figured Gum and panelled to the height of the doors and has a large boulder fireplace. The entire first floor is trimmed in selected, genuine Mahogany of the very best quality and figure, excepting the kitchen, which is white enamel. The second floor is trimmed in white enamel with genuine Mahogany doors and the third floor is trimmed in white enamel with Birch Mahogany veneered doors. We have four good rooms on the third floor... plumbing is of the best, the glass is plate and the workmanship on the building is as good as can be produced. The construction of the house is double wall, reinforced concrete with slate roof.... would not be necessary for you to wait until April, when, I understand, you expect to be in Oak Park....

29. Both advertisements in *Oak Leaves* carried the miniature engraving of Arting's *Tarzan of the Apes* in the upper left-hand corner. The ad of May 5 was headed, "Do You Invest for Profit or Do You Loan Your Money at 3% So the Other Fellow Makes the Profit?" A description of *Tarzan* as a moneymaker followed, with reference to the *New York Evening World*, the Munsey magazines, and McClurg & Company. Speaking of Tarzan, the ad stated, "He has made his creator independent." Potential investors were urged to take the advice of famous financiers about opportunities in investing. Marshall Field, J. Pierpont Morgan, Andrew Carnegie, and others were quoted in general statements, the theme being the importance of investing in "new things." The Oak Park representative listed was Charles A. Gleason, Fiscal Agent, 254 Clinton Avenue. The ad of May 12 featured *Tarzan* as "The Wonder Story of the Age" and stated that "a small block of the treasury stock of the National Film Corporation of America" was being set aside for distribution in Oak Park, with the price set at $5.00 a share.

Other publicity broadsides put out by Parsons (not ads) included a sheet referring to endorsements of the National Film project by the investment journal *National Banker* and also by the *American Dentist*. The latter periodical, in accepting an ad for the project, stressed belief in the integrity of the company and its officers. Another broadside told the story of *Tarzan* and then quoted comments from various newspapers, including the *Galveston News, Pittsburgh Gazette, San Francisco Argonaut,* and others.

30. Parsons' letters were written from the studio in Los Angeles, Santa Monica Boulevard and Gower Street, and sent to Coldwater, Michigan. He wrote, on August 2, "I have before me your letter of the 28th ult., and will take this occasion to say that I don't like it.... I was in Chicago and you knew it but you could not arrange to see me, and as I was very busy practically day and night, naturally, I did not have the time to see you." On August 3 he wrote, "... I was very much disappointed from the help that we received from you...." He stressed that his only goal was to make a success of the movie, not for Burroughs' sake, but for the sake of the people who had invested their money.

31. The *New York Times*, February 3, 1918, noted that production required eighteen months to complete; 300,000 feet of negative were exposed, and 9,000 feet used at the Broadway Theatre in New York.

32. *The Moving Picture World*, August 11, 1917.

33. Letter of September 25, 1917, to Julian Johnson, in which Ed also wrote, "Parsons has broken off diplomatic relations with me and recalled his minister. He thinks I am a damnfool and I know that he is. I got my $5,000 out of it; but he used my name to sell stock and I want to see that the stockholders get a square deal, — if I can."

34. Letter of September 25 from ERB; letter of October 19, 1917, from Rumsey.

35. Rumsey explained, "... I have never tried to sell any stock, but myself and associates invested extensively in the National Film Corporation with its 'Tarzan of the Apes' and it bore influence throughout the State and others invested." Rumsey added, "I have learned to have a deep regard for you and want to assist you in every way within my power...."

36. A receipt from Watkins stated that he had purchased stock certificate 354 from Burroughs and was aware that ERB had appointed Parsons as his proxy to vote this stock for a period of two years from (about) November 29, 1916. On January 3, 1918, Ed wrote to the collector of internal revenue: "... I accepted $50,000 in capital stock of a producing company for the motion picture rights of one of my stories. I held this stock for about a year, receiving no dividends or other income from it; I then sold it for $5,000 cash, or at a loss of $45,000. Must I include this in any way in my return?" There is no record of a reply.

37. Durling's inquiry is dated September 30; reference is made to a Mr. Cohn who was to be Durling's partner in the company. Ed suggested that the two men get The Authors' League to endorse them. To Edna Schley, Cinema Exchange, Los Angeles, in reply to her letter of October 4, Ed wrote on October 15, "I have had all the dealings I care to have with motion picture producers."

38. Letter of January 22, 1918.

39. About the film, the *New York Times*, January 28, 1918, commented, "The domestic narrative intertwined with the jungle story grows tedious," while the *Chicago Daily News* of May 16, 1918, reported that Elmo Lincoln was miscast in the role of Tarzan, and that Enid Markey "also finds her duties beyond her conception. She is as lost in her part as she is in the forest when rescued." The *Chicago Herald Examiner*, May 19, 1918, described *Tarzan* as a "satisfying novelty," conceded that the producers had achieved a "remarkably atmospheric result," and added that "the jungle scenes are consistently vegetated, wherever they were gleaned from...." The *Examiner* reported that *Tarzan* was being held over for a second week at the Colonial Theatre in Chicago.

40. On May 13, 1918, Ed wrote to Carl Meyer and enclosed a copy of the agreement he had signed with the National Film Corporation. The agreement stated clearly that National could not sell or assign its rights without the consent of "the party of the second part" (Burroughs). They had however sold the distribution rights and according to Ed were receiving fifty percent of the receipts from the distributing company. He contended that his royalties should be figured on the gross receipts. National had also promised to pay his royalty every month, but Ed noted, "they have made no payments whatsoever though it is reasonable to believe that the gross receipts have been in excess of $100,000."

41. On June 2, 1918, Kitty Kelly, in answer to ERB's inquiry, replied that she had read about the new Tarzan film in some press material sent out by Mabel Condon in Los Angeles. Ed followed with a request for information from Condon and then sent Kitty Kelly's letter to attorney Meyer. Still baffled, Ed on June 4, wrote to P. P. Craft of Monopol Pictures, New York, who was interested in producing "The Return of Tarzan." Craft had reported hearing of a second film and on June 5 he sent Ed the article from *Variety* of May 31.

42. Ed's dealings with Levey also involved a claim against William Wing, the *Tarzan* scenario writer, who had evidently borrowed $500 from Ed. Levey had been engaged to collect on the note. Wing and Ed had been quite friendly for a time and had seen each other at the athletic club. Wing was waiting for money owed him by Selig. Impatient, Ed wanted to attach Wing's property (owned by his wife who was seriously ill) and his car. To Levey on April 20, 1918, Ed wrote: "Keep after him. If he can afford to play around the Athletic Club he

should be able to pay his debts." Information about Parsons and the new film had come from Wing.

43. Letter of June 18, 1918, sent to Ed's new office at 1020 North Boulevard in Oak Park. On June 8 Ed had written to Carl Meyer and enclosed P. P. Craft's letter, the *Variety* page, and other clippings Craft had forwarded to him concerning the new film, Ed wanted Parsons enjoined from distributing or exhibiting this film or some type of financial settlement.

Mabel Condon, replying to Ed's inquiry of June 4, wrote on July 11, "... the National Film Corporation is putting into film form the second half of your book 'Tarzan of the Apes.' It is to be a sequel to the first half of the book as issued by them on the screen under your book title 'Tarzan of the Apes.' Thus, this company is producing only material that it purchased from you in your story 'Tarzan of the Apes'."

44. Letter of July 24, 1918.

45. Ibid.

46. Letter of July 30, 1918, to Parsons in Los Angeles. On August 5 Ed wrote to the First National Exhibitors' Circuit in New York to acknowledge the receipt of $2,500 from Parsons in connection with the second film. He gave them permission to use the name "Romance of Tarzan." To Parsons on August 5 he stressed that that second picture must not interfere with his other stories and must be a continuation of "Tarzan of the Apes."

47. Letter of August 7 to Parsons.

48. Ibid. On June 8, 1918, in a letter to P. P. Craft of Monopol Pictures, Ed wrote, "I saw Tarzan of the Apes for the first time last night...."

49. Letter of November 27, 1916.

50. Letter of December 3, 1916. Ed also sought a statement from Davis to be sent to Parsons who had requested "letters from men well known in literary circles expressing their personal opinions of Tarzan as a picture proposition."

51. Letter of December 20. About Davis' reluctance concerning "The Tribe of Tarzan," Ed referred to him as a "pin-head," adding, "Here the First Tribe of Tarzan writes me that about their first official act was to subscribe for the All-Story Weekly and you won't even recognize the poor kids." On December 29 Davis replied that he would run the announcement.

52. Letter of January 19, 1917 to Davis. Ed called Baum "The Wizard of Oz."

53. In a letter of March 19, 1918, Ed wrote to Denison at the *Chicago Herald*, explaining that he had also taken up the matter with McClurg and the company was willing to cooperate, but only a newspaper could "properly handle the plan." The *Herald* replied that though the idea was an excellent one, they were presently "tied up with the Junior Jackie Club."

54. McClurg's *Bulletin* noted that Herman Newman had organized the first tribe sometime in 1916 in Staunton, Virginia, the birthplace of President Wilson. Through Newman's efforts other tribes were formed in many cities. The work of each tribe is kept secret ("I will divulge the secrets of the tribe to no one but my parents"), but all members practiced in running, jumping, wrestling, and treeclimbing. They also sought to "perfect themselves in roping, spearing, and archery in emulation of Tarzan of the Apes, who carried a grass rope with which he lassoed Numa the Lion and Sheeta the Panther." Newman's address was given as 319 Prospect St., Covington, Virginia.

55. McClurg's *Bulletin*, August, September, 1918.

56. Davis' letter of January 20, 1916. He jokingly mentioned Ed's "total lack of reverence," confessed he was "rather interested in the idea," and would be willing "to help Cain out and set him up as... respectable...."

57. Letter of January 24, 1916.

58. Ibid.

59. Ibid. Ed wrote, "I could make the story strongly religious, with a moral and all of that, and still fill it with excitement and action of the primeval jungle sort. If I could do that well enough it might make a story that would go to beat the band, or I could make it slightly satirical. Which would you prefer?" In a later paragraph he commented, "My idea is that the Bible does lots of people a lot of good and that a familiar story of biblical characters might boost the circulation of the bible and All-Story at the same time, not that either of them need it, being neck and neck now at the top."

60. On February 23, 1916, while working on "The Mucker," Ed inquired of Davis, "Hast thought any thoughts concerning Mr. Cain of Nod? I shall be ready to get at him in a month or so...."

61. Letter of December 19, 1916, addressed to Ed at 355 South Hoover Street in Los Angeles, Davis added, "London is too big a man to be left unsung, no matter who plays the accompaniment; and when it comes to pounding a banjo hard, Edward, you are there with both hands. There can be no doubt about the chorus who will join in. Go to it."

62. Letter of January 20, 1916.

63. In this letter of April 10, 1926, to an unnamed London fan, Ed stated he was trying to find out if the poem appeared in any of Knibbs' published works. "Out There Somewhere" is included in a collection of Knibbs' poems, *Songs of the Outlands: Ballads of the Hoboes and Other Verse*, Houghton Mifflin Co., 1914.

64. Ed's worksheet shows that "Out There Somewhere" ("The Return of the Mucker") was begun January 24 and finished March 15, 1916. The writing was done at his office in the First National Bank Building in Chicago. The story ran in *All Story Weekly*, June 17 to July 14, 1916. On March 28, 1916, Davis wrote, "...sending you a check for $1,725.00, topping your word count by four words, bringing the grand total up to sixty-nine thousand. [Ed had listed 68,996.] I like your character Bridge very much. I suppose you planned that son-of-a-gun for the purpose of writing a sequel to 'The Mucker'. You're that artful and heathen Chinee in your tactics that no one can skin you out of a future...."

65. Whether Knibbs visited the Burroughs family in Los Angeles is not known.

66. Again, in answer to Arnold Pratt, a New York fan, Ed on March 14, 1927, noted that Knibbs' poem "Out There Somewhere" made such an impression on him that he "could not refrain from using it in the story." Ed forwarded the letter to Houghton Mifflin Company, the publishers of Knibbs' poems and commented, "...Mr. Pratt candidly admits that the best part of my book was Mr. Knibbs' poem, and also that he liked Knibbs better than either Kipling or Service...." On April 9, 1926, Ed wrote to Houghton Mifflin Company to inquire if the firm had published a book of poems by Knibbs and stated, "I should also like to have Mr. Knibbs' address if you can send it to me. I have been trying to get in touch with him for some time but cannot find his Los Angeles address and have not seen him for a couple of years." In 1933, responding to a request by J. P. Carrington of Pasadena for information to be used on a radio program, ERB recalled that Knibbs' poem had always been one of his favorites.

67. Letter of April 12 from Davis; response of April 19, 1916, from Ed.

68. Letter of December 10, 1929.

69. Ibid.

70. Ibid.

71. Letter of October 28, 1920, to Dom Cyprian, O.S.B., Old Catholic Church, 810 W. Ohio Street, Chicago.

72. Letter of January 11, 1921, to Harry Burroughs in Chicago. Ed added, "It is needless to say that the sun is shining and the cook has not intimated that she is about to leave. Tomorrow things may be different."

73. Letter of October 19, 1938, to F. S. Chase, Waterbury, Connecticut.

74. Letter of October 1, 1929.

75. Letter of May 2, 1927, to *The Forum*, New York. Obviously, the question was a loaded one, with its deliberate references to "forcing" religion into the schools; it appeared worded to create an unfavorable reaction.

76. Ibid. Ed's statement, along with a number of others on both sides of the question, was printed in *The Forum* of July 1927.

77. ERB's religious attitude was explained by his sons Hulbert and Jack in an interview of January 11, 1970. However, Harry's daughter Evelyn (Mrs. Carlton) McKenzie insists that ERB was not an atheist.

78. Ed's notebook outlines the series of "New Stories of Tarzan" (Jungle Tales). The writing dates were as follows: no. 1, March 17 to 21, 1916; no. 2, May 8 to May 25, 1916; no. 3, May 26 to June 1, 1916; no. 4, "Commenced Camp Branch" (Mich.), July 7 to 13, 1916; no. 5, finished October 13, 1916 (no starting date shown), at 355 So. Hoover St., Los Angeles; no. 6, November 1 to 5, 1916 (this and the remaining stories all in Los Angeles); no. 7, December 8 to 11, 1916; no. 8, December 22 to 29, 1916; no. 9, February 7 to 8, 1917; no. 10, February 12 to 28, 1917; no. 11, March 5 to 11, 1917; no. 12, March 14 to 18, 1917. The stories were purchased by Long, *Blue Book* editor, for $350 each. Ed's card index shows the total words for the twelve stories to be 75,025. The stories appeared in *Blue Book*, one a month, from September 1916 to August 1917, inclusive.

In correspondence with Long while the stories were being written, Ed, on February 9, 1917, inquired whether the editor could use any "motion picture fiction," explaining, "I mean fiction written around incidents of the motion picture industry. I ask because I chance to know a fellow here who ought to be able to turn out great stuff in that line. He is Billy Wing, one of the oldest and best scenario writers. Formerly he was a newspaper man and fiction writer...." On February 15 Long noted that number nine was "certainly a peach of a Tarzan story" and replied that he could use motion picture fiction of a humorous nature — nothing serious. On March 20, in a night letter, Long wrote, "Much disappointed in ending of Tarzan number ten. Rest of story is excellent but in all our announcements in advertising we have featured that each story will be complete. Could you send us special delivery new ending making this complete story...." Ed had evidently relapsed into one of his "sequel-type" endings. On the twenty-first he telegraphed Long that he was mailing number eleven and requested that Long "substitute if possible or change ten there" since he had no copy to work with.

79. Letter of November 16, 1916. Long wrote, "This last story was the first one over which I have not been enthusiastic.... We are keeping the story because I realize perfectly that you can't strike twelve on every one of the stories; I am simply figuring that this one brings the average about even, because some of the others certainly have been bell ringers...." In sending the story on November 7, Ed noted, "Mrs. Burroughs likes it better than the last, and I hope you will. Walt Mason sent me a very clever Tarzan pome, entitled That Tarzan Person. You'd orter buy the magazine rights of it. I have written asking permission to use it opposite the title page of Bray's next Tarzan book. If granted it wouldn't interfere, would it?"

80. Letter of November 21, 1916.

81. Letter of February 10, 1917.

82. Letter of January 22, 1917, to Joseph Bray. Concerning the British edition, Ed commented, "If I get 10% it sounds reasonable; but if I only get 1.2% I am not hectic." He stated that if *Tarzan* were published in England, he would like to have the copy checked by an Englishman to "correct any glaring local errors." He wrote, "I think I spoke of a lord as 'Sir John', for which, according to English jurisprudence, I should properly be hanged. Doubtless an Englishman would find other things that would make hanging seem too mild an expiation." On January 26 Bray offered to send advance royalties to aid Ed in his medical bills. Ed's reply of February 10 referred to Jack's sickness and the quarantine. He also authorized Bray to go ahead on the British edition and closed with regards to The White Paper Club.

83. Ed's enrollment in the school was mentioned in a letter of recommendation dated April 2, 1917, written by proprietor Jacob Vogt, 1870 West Washington Street, Los Angeles.

84. Letter of February 10, 1917.

85. Letter of March 9, 1917, from Milwaukee, Wisconsin. On March 19, upon receiving a copy of *The Son of Tarzan* from ERB, King wrote, "Appetite and digestion remain unimpaired, my dear Burroughs, in spite of the three score years and ten and then some, so the Son of Tarzan comes most opportunely. The only thing about it which *I* cannot eagerly swallow is the flattery on the fly leaf. Mrs. King fairly turned it down. And yet I rejoice in believing it an honest expression however undeserved...."

86. Letter of March 19, 1917.

87. Other letters of recommendation included one from Charles King, dated April 21, 1917, referring to Ed's military experience and to his success as a writer; one from Carl Meyer of the law firm of Mayer, Meyer, Austrian & Platt in Chicago; one from Forrest Crissey of "Meadowcroft," Geneva, Kane Company, Illinois; and a brief humorous statement by Emerson Hough, the author, one of doubtful value for Ed's purposes. On March 13, 1917, from Chicago, Hough wrote, "You will make an excellent officer of volunteers. You ride, shoot, and speak the truth. I hope you get a commission."

88. Letter of June 4, 1917.

89. Ibid.

90. "Bridge and the Oskaloosa Kid" was sent to Davis on June 13, 1917. On August 24, Ed wrote to Davis from Coldwater, Michigan, to comment that his vacation was nearly over and he hadn't "written a line" and added, "We go home a week from today." He explained he had requests for another Tarzan serial, but "the trouble is I have to make them so damn long to make a book. I hate myself before I get half through with a hundred thousand word story...."

91. Ed's letter of October 17, 1917, and Jerle Davis' letter of the eighteenth. Davis noted that the Western Newspaper Union's editor-in-chief, Wright A. Patterson, "cronies around a bit with your friend Mr. Chapman."

92. Whether the newspapers printed Ed's three articles is not known. Among other military activities, a card issued to Ed reveals that he was a charter member of the Oak Park Defense League in 1917.

93. The exact dates of some of these articles of the 1917-18 period are not known. "Do Boys Make Good Soldiers," containing a reference to Camp Steever at Lake Geneva, Illinois, where Ed had attended August 12 to 25, 1918, was apparently written after that date. "Patriotism by Proxy" appeared in *Oak Leaves* of May 25, 1918, while the date of "Who's Who in Oak Park," saved on an *Oak Leaves* galley proof, is not known. Concerning "A National Reserve Army Proposed," Ed, on June 18, 1918, wrote to Eric Schuler of The Authors' League, enclosing the article and stating, "I understand that there is some bureau

or association composed of authors that has means of giving wide publicity to patriotic propaganda." He urged that Schuler forward the article to "the proper person." Thus, it is evident that the article was written months before its publication in the *Army and Navy Journal.*

94. In "Patriotism by Proxy" Ed announces a recruiting office at 1020 North Boulevard, Oak Park, where his office was located. He was severely critical of Oak Park's support of the militia and of the community's failure to subscribe money to it.

His attitude toward the Germans was revealed also in a letter to his friend Bert Weston in Beatrice, Nebraska, October 25, 1918, in which Ed wrote, "It looks very much as though the filthy Hun would have to lie down and surrender within the next six months but I think he will only do it after a complete and thorough licking unless a gleam of intelligence manifests itself among the German people to the end that they rise up in their wrath and massacre the entire darned military class...."

95. Concerning one clergyman who had preached against enlistment in the U.S. Army, Ed commented, "The last I heard of him he hadn't subscribed for a liberty bond, and he has a German name that smells to heaven." On the galley proof this last clause was deleted, possibly by ERB himself.

96. Ed gave high praise to the young Captain Babcock at Camp Steever for his ability to enforce discipline "with tact and good judgement" and because of the "vast amount of military information this young man possessed." In referring to the regular army officers who had instructed him in the past — Strong, Cronkhite, Smith, and King — Ed maintained that this "boy of twenty who trained me at Camp Steever was their equal in every way...."

On August 28, 1918, to Bert Weston, Ed mentioned Camp Steever and the training activities: "I put in an interesting and profitable two weeks...." On September 4 he described the camp and its activities to Weston; Ed had returned because he wished "to see the battalion from the outside." He also remarked, "I notice in a new draft law that bald-headed men with three children are to be put into A-1 class so I suppose you and I will soon be in the front line trenches." About Evelyn, Harry's daughter, who had completed a course for "overseas long distance telephone," Ed noted she had become "a fluent French conversationalist."

97. The name of the publication in which "Peace and the Militia" appeared is not known. "Go to Pershing" was written for the Military Training Camps Association of the War Department, Office of Civilian Aide to the Adjutant General.

98. Letter of June 27, 1917. Davis commented, "To me, Bridge, in the sequel to 'The Mucker' was a very splendid character, well worth a great story. In this yarn he doesn't justify his promise. Honestly, do you think that bear could pull the chain stuff on Bridge for one second? You *do* not!"

99. The writing dates on the trilogy are as follows: "The Lost U-Boat" ("The Land that Time Forgot"); September 8 to October 13, 1917; "Cor-Sva-Jo" ("People That Time Forgot"), October 23, 1917 to February 8, 1918; "Out of Time's Abyss," May 23, 1918 to July 16, 1918. *Blue Book Magazine* paid $1,000 for each of the three stories. The long time period on "The People That Time Forgot" may be partially accounted for by *Blue Book's* return of the manuscript for revisions. Word counts were 40,000 on the first two and 36,700 on the last story.

Ed's worksheets on these stories were heavily detailed with lists of characters, names of prehistoric monsters, and descriptions of the various races. As in other stories, a dog was a necessary companion; the airedale, Crown Prince Nobbler — "Nobs" — is the first character listed. On the worksheet of "The People That Time Forgot" Ed has drawn a figure of a Galu woman in order to show the details of the costume. "Out of Time's Abyss" includes notes on the Wieroos, a small drawing of the quarters of the Wieroos, and a full page hand-drawn map of Caspak and the Island of Caprona, prepared on a scale of ten miles to the half-inch. The island's dimensions are 130 miles wide by 180 miles long, with the Great Inland Lake shown as 60 miles wide by 120 miles long. Other features, painstakingly marked, include the site of Tippet's grave; the locations of the Band-lu, Ga-lu, Sto-lu, Ba-lu, Kro-lu, and A-lu; Fort Dinosaur; the Rocky Plateau; the Subterranean Channel; and the Wieroo City of Human Skulls.

Publication dates for the trilogy in *Blue Book* were August, October, and December, 1918.

100. In preparing to write the first story of the trilogy, "The Lost U-Boat," Ed encountered a problem of possible duplication of the plot of a story by another author. On September 11, 1917, he sought the advice of Davis, explaining, "The first of last week Ray Long and I were talking about stories. He had one in mind and I promised to try to put it on paper. I started it and yesterday I bought a copy of the All-Story Weekly and read the announcement of Mr. Stilson's Polaris and the Goddess Glorian. Then I stopped writing and called up Long. He suggested that I write you." Ed then followed with a brief outline of his story and asked Davis if it sufficiently resembled Stilson's to warrant "abandoning the idea." The outline was as follows: "A U-boat is captured by an American. It becomes lost and reaches, by subterranean channels, a warm pocket in the Northern ice pack. Here is discovered the remnants of a pre-Cambrian race of amphibious, reptilian humans. Their bodies are covered with hard scales which resemble armour." Ed stressed that he had never read any of Stilson's stories, and of course could not have read "Polaris" since it hadn't as yet appeared, but he noted, "something in the announcement [is] so suggestive of my idea that I hestitate to go ahead until I have some assurance from you that I can do so safely." On September 13 Davis responded with an outline of Stilson's forthcoming "Polaris." In the story Polaris and his friends are aboard an American gunboat and pick up a man clothed in golden armor. Later the gunboat is destroyed by "a sort of golden U-boat." The U-boat rescues the men and takes them through a subterranean passage to the landlocked island of Adlaz, populated by descendants of the Atlantean colonists. A Goddess Glorian has the secret of immortality.

On September 17 Ed commented to Davis, "I guess I'll have to spin on one wing and flatten out somewhere else...." Whether he planned at that time to abandon the lost U-boat story is not clear. Perhaps, since Stilson's story appeared to be quite different, Ed contented himself with making certain changes in the projected story to make sure that there would be no duplication.

Correspondence relating to the trilogy reveals that Long was more demanding than Davis in the matter of revisions. He requested a new ending for "The Lost U-Boat." On November 2, 1917, Ed sent it and wrote, "... it merely follows page 96. I have left off the original closing paragraph by the narrator, or rather by the finder of the manuscript as I cannot see that it adds anything to the story. If you wish to use it you have it on the original page 97." A request for revisions in "Cor-Sva-Jo" found Ed quite compliant; on February 25, 1918, he wrote, "Just as soon as I get my income tax return off my chest I'll get busy with the changes you suggest for Cor-Sva-Jo. Being much relieved that you liked it at all I haven't a murmur to murm anent your criticisms...." On May 16, 1918, Donald Kennicott, Long's secretary, informed Ed that Long didn't like the title "The Lost U-Boat" and that the magazine would call the story "The Land That Time Forgot." Ed responded that he had no objection.

Again, with "Out of Time's Abyss," Long requested revisions, noting that the story was a "corker," but only for those who had read the other two. The new story needed an introduction, as though it were "the first story in the series instead of the third"; it was also necessary to introduce each character as he appeared. On August 2, 1918, replying to Long's suggestions of July 24, Ed sent the additions. He wrote, "This is my first attempt at dictating copy and the manuscript that I am sending is the first draft just as it came off my stenographer's machine."

101. "The Little Door" was sent to *Collier's* on November 23, 1917, at which time Ed commented, "I have in mind several short stories built entirely around the animal characters used in the Tarzan stories—particularly about Numa the lion. Will you let me know if you would care to see these?"

102. The manuscript was sent to *The People's Home Journal* on July 26, 1919, along with "For the Fool's Mother." In rejecting both on October 15, the editor remarked, "The war interest in 'The Little Door' rather spoils it for us—and the western story has hardly enough plot interest...." Ed had also submitted the 2,800-word "Little Door" to *Short Stories* on June 28, 1919, without success. The story was never published.

103. The article in the *Coldwater Daily Reporter*, listed by ERB as "Paris, December 30 — (By Special Cable)," contains no date of publication. The armistice for World War I was on November 11, 1918, and Ed's report of the war finally being over, plus the additional evidence of an ad on the page of the *Reporter* announcing a meeting of the Southern Michigan National Bank to be held on January 14, 1919, provides evidence that the article was published in January 1919. Coldwater, Michigan, had been a summer vacation spot for the Burroughs family and the Hulbert family for many years. In the notes for his *Autobiography* Ed disclosed that in this period he had bought a country place in Coldwater.

Chapter 15: Gentleman Farmer

1. Dr. Kiger, in his response, explained that the flu quarantine had been lifted in Los Angeles and that the death rate was lower than that of a month earlier; however, quite a few cases of the flu were still being reported. On December 4, 1918, Ed had written to the France Investment Company in Los Angeles about finding a ranch where he could raise hogs. His preference was for a place not over thirty miles from town and one that might be leased with an option to buy later. The company's reply of February 28, 1919, was too late; he had purchased Mil Flores Ranch.

2. To Platt, Ed noted that he would have about twenty thousand dollars in Liberty Bonds and cash available and that he was counting upon an annual income of about twenty-five thousand dollars from his book royalties.

3. Letter of December 4, 1918. Ed spoke of a plan to write a story consisting of three complete novelettes, "the time of which will be in three different periods of the future." He inquired whether he could submit this story to Munsey's and to Ray Long at *Cosmopolitan* at the same time.

4. Ibid. Ed stressed that any plan to write a *Tarzan* story in the future for Munsey's depended upon the offer of a "good price" and added that he "ought to have about $10,000."

5. Letter of December 9, 1918.

6. Ibid. In speaking of the children's education, Ed noted that it might be difficult to send them to school if the family were to live on a ranch about thirty miles from Los Angeles. He added that if Bert would come to the area and buy an adjoining farm, they could "build a little school house and prorate the professor's salary," using the school for the children in both families. An article by Roselle Dean, *The Oak Parker*, January 18, 1919, reported that Burroughs would leave on January 31 for a ranch near Los Angeles and remarked that it was "a far cry from stories to swine." In the same issue there is a story of a farewell party for Joan Burroughs, with the "hosts assisting" listed as Hulbert and Jack Burroughs, and with story-telling contributed by Ella Burroughs. Joan, age eleven, is shown in the photo of a group of children.

7. McEntee, Ed's uncle, had married Caroline Studley, George T. Burroughs' sister who had died December 18, 1915, in

Chicago. On December 20, 1918, Ed wired Sergeant L. Floyd Bruner, stationed at Camp Wadsworth, South Carolina, to inquire whether he wanted his former position as a chauffeur and would be willing to accompany the family to California; if so, Bruner would have to get a furlough and discharge at once. The matter was evidently arranged.

8. Details contained in letter to S. G. Neff, New York, March 21, 1919. To McEntee, on January 23, Ed revealed his worry over Tarzan, his Airdale terrier, and whether the dog would be allowed to stay in the Alvarado Hotel overnight until he could be placed in a dog hospital where he had been treated earlier. He wanted McEntee to get permission from Corwin, the hotel owner.

9. Letter of January 21, 1919, from Ed to his mother who was then staying at Wilmette, Illinois, with Ed's brother Frank. On January 17 Ed had commented in a letter to Bert Weston about the problem of moving to Los Angeles and leaving parents behind: "Every time we go away, and we have gone a great many times, there is always that same suggestion that we shall never see our surviving parents again but we always do." Bert had been concerned about leaving his in-laws, the Collinses, in case he decided to come to California. Ed pointed out that, as an example, Mrs. Hulbert, living in Coldwater, Michigan, only 150 miles away from Chicago, was still isolated and could become ill and die before any members of her family could reach her. Before departing for Los Angeles, Ed placed both of his homes for sale; these, in Oak Park, were at 700 Linden Avenue and 414 Augusta Street. A vacant lot on Ridgeland Avenue north of Augusta was also listed for sale.

10. This information was obtained from a two-page brochure describing the rules and regulations of the White Paper Club.

11. The sonnet to Burroughs opened, "The winds have talked to him confidingly; The trees have whispered to him...." He was pictured as a man in communion with Nature. Later lines read, "Apes cluster round his thoughts; and twitterings / of bug and monkey, in an endless May, / Are mingling with the wild words he sings." In the club program, St. John's cartoon shows a monkey riding on the back of a pig, which appears to be soaring into space. This was an obvious joke on Ed's plans to raise pigs in California. A dedicatory page that follows shows a pig playing a harp with the following poem printed at the top of the page:

The Heavenly Occupation

Departed Souls, so goes the ancient story,
Just Play their Harps, and Sing like Muratore.
Tonight that Sceptic, Science, stands the Test:
It sees our friend Ed Burroughs "Going West"
And prophecies that in Elysian Togs
He will lay down his Lyre, and just raise Hogs!

Jibes at Burroughs with reference to both pigs and apes then have been devised. These include Four Ways to Cook an Author, from "the private recipes of Lordhelpus, captive chief of the Cannibal King of Tarzanta"; a page in miniature from "The Descent of Man," supposedly an "advance proof from a new work by Charles Darwin, Jr.;" and on a later page, the cast of characters for a play titled, "Tarzan, the Monkey Wrench or the Relation of Nothing to Nothing." Beneath, the play is described as "An Idyl of the South Seas." Among the characters listed in this White Paper Club play are Tarzan, Don Kennicott; Old Quittum, Second Mate, Emerson Hough; Assistant Cannibal, Edwin Balmer; John Jones, a visiting Elk, Ray Long; Colonel Shoutum, FROG.S, Watterson Rothacker; GoGo Getum, Colonel's native valet, J. Allen St. John; Lord Godhelpus, a tourist, Joseph E. Bray; Bayrly Thair, an East India merchant, I. K. Friedman. In the play, probably never presented, was listed an entire Tarzan family — brother, cousin, father, uncle, and

grandfather Tarzan, and also Doctor Tarzan, a monkey scientist. "Robinson Caruso" was identified as "Tarzan's father by marriage."

A page of humorous song lyrics to be sung to popular melodies, such as "Tipperary" or "There's a Long, Long Trail," contains references to Tarzan, apes, or pigs. A back page illustration on this White Paper Club program shows a monkey perched upon a stack of books, holding a candle aloft in one hand, and clutching a money bag in the other. The monkey's long tail is wound about a pen thrust into an ink bottle.

A telegram of January 23, 1919, received at the banquet, was from Emerson Hough: "I don't see why any man should want to leave Chicago and move into a mission building with cafeteria attachment in a country where we have to climb a tree for water, dig in the ground for wood, and spell Hickory with a Jay. Still I have always noted primordial tendencies in Edward, and for some reason, don't blame him for wanting to move out closer to the movie studios, so he can exercize his well marked prehensile tendencies...."

12. A letter of April 12, 1919, to Mrs. Z. H. Rubenstein of Los Angeles, notes the enclosure of a check for $200 for rental of the property at 1729 North Wilton Place from April 12 to May 12. This indicates that Ed was still paying rent for the home, evidently by some type of agreement or lease, even though he had moved to Mil Flores. In a letter of March 14, 1919, to Bert Weston, Ed notes that he has been living in a furnished house in Hollywood. He explains that the Mil Flores house contains eighteen rooms and six baths, stands on a hill about half a mile from Ventura Boulevard, and is of Spanish architecture, built around a patio.

13. The *Times* presented photos of the house from various angles. The article notes that "The late owner indulged his love for the rustic and picturesque by building back against the hills in a sheltered hollow a house of logs, which he christened the Koonskin Kabin, and in which he was wont to extend a delightful hospitality to former comrades-in-arms and intimate friends...."

14. Letter to S. G. Neff, New York.

15. Fred Onthank, writing from the Oak Park Police Department, had a series of bitter accusations against Burroughs. He accused ERB of cutting the promised salary for the two from $190 a month to $100 and of reducing "our bungalow to a dirty Mexican eating house...." Mrs. Grace Onthank, in a letter written on May 5, 1919, spoke of her "slipping away" as quietly as possible because of the difficult situation at the ranch. She insisted she had only stayed because of the "future" that had been promised her husband, a future that never materialized. She had put up with "the dirt, filth, and all the inconveniences incident to living in the Koonskin Kabin...."

Ed had referred sarcastically to the "loyalty" of the four employees he had "imported from Illinois," and in a letter of January 8, 1920, to Fred Onthank, had written, "Practically the only thing that you and Mrs. Onthank could have given me to have made you of any value whatsoever here was loyalty. This you absolutely with-held in both word and deed, as I discovered to some extent while you were here and to a much greater extent after you had gone." He claimed that although Onthank was to finance his own trip to Los Angeles, he had advanced the money for it, including freight on the furniture, and that Onthank still owed him $236.30. He remarked that "I hoped that after mature thought you and she would realize that the injury you had done me was one that only a sincere and honorable apology might mitigate...." Onthank angrily rejected any thought of an apology by his wife.

16. Letter of March 14, 1919. ERB urged Bert to consider buying one of the ranch sites on either side of the Tarzana Ranch; he also mentioned plans to visit mutual friends, the Balls, in Hollywood.

17. Letter of April 28, 1919.

18. Letter of April 1, 1919, to Tom Roberts.

19. Letter of March 20, 1919.

20. In this letter of March 28, Ed expressed regret at Bert's statement that he could not come to California. Ed mentioned an adjacent site which was offered for $350 an acre and urged Bert to at least buy it as an investment. He described the success he and Onthank were having in raising the goats.

21. Letter of April 1, 1919, to Earle E. Martin, Scripps-McRae Union, Cleveland.

22. Letter of April 15, 1919.

23. Letter of May 8, 1919, to Weston. Ed wrote, "... I have acquired three dogs in addition to Tarzan. There is Don, a mongrel sheep dog who was on the place and stayed. There is Jack, a full blood sheep dog I bought to make the goats nervous, and Lobo, another sheep dog, that a Spaniard gave me. Lobo I love. Emma says he has soulful eyes. A wag would call him a sad dog. He is six months old and appears to have been born without any friends; but there is something about the little cuss that gets under my skin."

24. Letter of September 21, 1918.

25. Letter of September 24, 1918.

26. Letter of October 29, 1918.

27. Letter of August 12, 1919. Ed referred to the golf course he and Studley had constructed as "the sportiest course in existence." He noted that each of the children had a Shetland pony and that these ponies are "seldom if ever properly broken," and as a result the children, especially Jack, were having trouble handling the animals. Jack's pony did whatever he pleased, and, because of this, Ed reported that "Jack sits in the saddle and screams most of the time, neither enjoying the trip himself to any great extent nor permitting anyone else to."

28. Ed stated that "three motion picture men" had come to the ranch in the past two days to talk about *Tarzan* films.

29. Information taken from taped interview with Marie Burroughs, Studley's third wife, at Tarzana, January 3, 1968. Studley remained in Chicago, doing freelance illustrating.

30. Margaret Mary Burroughs died on March 31, 1920, at the age of one year and twenty-three days. She had been cared for by Harry and Ella while Studley was in Los Angeles. Studley and Mary Becker were married in Chicago on June 5, 1917.

31. The letter is undated. Studley's original design of the bookplate is in the Burroughs office in Tarzana.

32. Letter of March 10, 1931, to Mrs. Cornelia Eames Anthony, West Chicago, Illinois. Other letters in which ERB tried to establish the date when the ex-libris was made were as follows: in 1934, "about 16-17 years ago"; in 1937, "about 22 years ago"; in 1939, "about 25 years ago." The date, thus uncertain, could be between 1915 and 1917.

33. At the close, Ed inquired, "I will greatly appreciate it if you can suggest where and how I may obtain the literature I desire and if you will tell me candidly if you think, outside of its entertainment, a novel of this sort would be helpful."

34. Letter of September 13, 1919. On September 5 Ed had written to Harriman to seek "a candid expression" and asked, "Is it the story itself, or is it the subject with which it deals that made you decide against it?" He noted that he expected to finish a Tarzan novelette "within a day or two."

35. Letter of July 2, 1919, in reply to Ed's letter of June 22.

36. Letter of September 17, 1919.

37. In the letter to Bray he asked if Bray would consider publishing "Under the Red Flag" as a book, "using the fact that it had been rejected by various magazines and quoting what these two editors said without using their names.... In other words, make a propaganda book out of it, and give it a lot of publicity." Obviously, the idea did not appeal to Bray.

38. Letter of October 5, 1918. Ed added, "If I give permission to you to incorporate under the name 'Tarzan Pictures Corporation' and you were to produce other pictures, you would of course feature the name of the corporation which would be only natural so that in a little while the word would be entirely meaningless to the motion picture public as far as my stories were concerned...."

39. Letter of December 20, 1918. On the twenty-first Craft wrote again to report that he had consulted with Charles A. Logue, an outstanding scenario writer, about the conflict between *The Romance of Tarzan* and *The Return of Tarzan*, and Logue had advised the creation of an entirely new scenario containing incidents that had not been used previously.

40. Letter of January 28, 1919, to Craft.

41. Ibid.

42. Letter of April 14, 1919.

43. Ibid.

44. Letter of April 19, 1919. Craft insisted that Parsons paid him $2,000 and gave $300 to Kosch. Since Ed was dissatisfied with the scenario, Craft asked him to advise what scenes should be used and then explained his plans to have T. Hayes Hunter, a writer who had just completed *Desert Gold*, a Zane Grey movie, do a new scenario.

45. Letter of April 21, 1919.

46. Letter of September 23, 1919. Craft noted that he had first thought a serial would be best, but when he arrived in New York he found that too many serials were being produced; as a result, he decided to make a feature film "which could be done quickly." Craft had been in the hospital for some time and had lost the services of Hunter who had signed with Goldwyn.

47. To Craft, then at 330 South Grand Ave., in Los Angeles, Ed stated his intention to handle the Tribe of Tarzan project personally. He asked that Craft return the die to him or tell him how he could obtain it.

48. Letter of March 31, 1919, to Bray.

49. On October 1, 1919, Harry Rubey notified Ed of Parsons' death and reported that the board of directors would remain the same but R. C. Middlewood of Wyoming would join the board and Rubey would become president. A rumor had circulated, unverified, that Parsons had committed suicide.

50. Telegrams of July 28 and 30, 1919; Craft was in Dallas, Texas.

51. *Wid's Daily*, February 10, 1921. The title, *The Adventures of Tarzan*, had been mentioned by Harry Rubey in a letter of September 24, 1919, to Ed. The proposition was that Ed would write a fifteen-episode serial of that name or "a similar name which shall be agreed upon...."

52. Letter to ERB from Stern & Rubens, New York lawyers, April 8, 1921. The firm sent a detective to the office and other people, supposed movie exhibitors, who attempted to book the proposed Tarzan picture. Craft stated that his company was "not yet ready to do business."

53. Letter of January 5, 1922.

54. Letter of January 14, 1922. Ed, stating that he would pay the lawyers, wrote, "I am financially unable to do so at this time, and I regret that you will have to wait until I can pay you."

55. Letters of April 8, 15, 1921.

56. Letter of November 17, 1920, from Kosch of Numa Pictures Corp.

57. Telegram of June 17, 1920.

58. Letter of February 17, 1921, from Louis Weiss of Numa

Pictures. Weiss also wrote, "We have acquired the interests of Messrs. Merrick and Cohen ... excepting their distributive rights... and in the future my brothers and myself will be the sole owners of this Corporation...." Legal matters would still be handled by Kosch.

59. Letter of October 21, 1925.

60. Letter of May 31, 1918. Ed thanked Bray for forwarding "Marching on Tanga." In this letter Ed also inquired about H. G. Wells' "Martian stuff" and when it appeared; he was concerned because a critic had claimed *A Princess of Mars* resembled Wells' novels. Ed stated that he had never read the particular Wells' novel referred to by the critic. On June 1, Bray insisted that Ed's works were not "in any sense borrowed from H. G. Wells' Martian stories."

61. Data on the stories is as follows: no. 1, "An Eye for an Eye," 10,504 words, August 9 to October 17, 1918; no. 2, "When the Lion Fed," 9,067 words, October 18 to 30, 1918; no. 3, "The Golden Locket," 9,323 words, October 31 to November 23, 1918; no. 4, "When Blood Told," 10,362 words, November 27 to December 10, 1918; no. 5, "The Debt," 11,842 words, December 11, 1918 to January 15, 1919; no. 6, "The Black Flier," 11,187 words, January 15 to 24, 1919; no. 7, "Tarzan and the Valley of Luna," 48,506 words, August 7 to September 10, 1919. *Red Book* paid $450 each for the first five and $500 for "The Black Flier;" on November 17, 1919, "Tarzan and the Valley of Luna" was accepted by *All-Story Weekly* for $3,000. It appeared from March 20 to April 17, 1920. ERB's worksheet contains a drawing, presumably of a river, with compass directions inserted.

62. Letter of December 3, 1919.

63. Letter and telegram of December 1, 1919.

64. Sent to Long by ERB on November 1, 1918.

65. Letter to Reynolds of June 9, 1919.

66. Quotes and opinion from Bray's letter of August 27, 1919.

67. Davis offered no encouragement at the time or when ERB mentioned the matter again on December 5, 1919.

68. Letter of September 12, 1919, to Griffith Gordon Ellis, editor. Ed added, "While the price you could pay me is considerably below what I am now getting I believe I would be willing to write stories of about thirty five hundred words for $100.00 apiece.... for the pleasure that I would get out of this work as well as for the possible later book value of such a series...."

On September 17, Ed wrote to the curator of the Field Museum in Chicago: "I am trying to find a work on Apache Indians that will give me the details of their customs and habits of life prior to their considerable contact with our own race...." He inquired about how they obtained their food, the preparations, their dances and the purposes of these, methods of warfare, enemy tribes, and marriage customs.

69. Judge Petit's letter from Chicago, dated May 9, 1919, was in response to Ed's of April 19 and continued the proposed story plot; the heroine had been thrown into the old chimney by the Greek wool-pullers "who refused to release her until I repaired the roof for them. I have had some Wool-pullers as tenants for some time and the battle I have had with them to determine who should repair the roof from time to time."

Other letters concerning the projected film company were as follows: to Bray, April 15, 1919; to Davis, April 18; to Schuler, April 18; to J. D. Williams, First National Exhibitors' Circuit, December 16, 1919, and January 3, 1920; to Ray Long, April 18, 1919.

Chapter 16: Tarzana — Family, Business, Creativity

1. On June 30, 1933, Ed wrote to Harry, "... I have had mother's ashes kept at the Los Angeles Crematory Association pending some decision as to what to do with them. I have in mind burying them on the hill at the ranch for I thought that we were going to live there permanently, but inasmuch as we are not going to live anywhere permanently it seems unwise to make such a disposition of them. Any plan that you have will meet with my approval."

He then revealed plans for his own burial: "If we still have the ranch when I die, I am going to have a hole dug with a post hole auger under an oak tree on the back part of the ranch and my ashes put in loose; that is, not in a container. There are two beautiful oak trees back there where I have spent considerable time, and while I have no sentimental reactions in the matter I thought that that would be an easy way to get rid of me as any, and no bother in the future for anyone, and some part of the ashes would probably go up into the trees...."

On February 12, 1941, Ed wrote to his brother George about Mary Evaline's ashes which had remained at Pierce Brothers Crematorium for the past twenty years. Ed explained he was worried about what would happen to them after he died: "I imagine that I am the only person in the world, with the possible exception of Ralph (Rothmund, his secretary), who knows that they are in existence or where they are; nobody has ever inquired; nobody has even mentioned them...." Writing from Hawaii, Ed again, on March 6, noted to George, "About Mother's ashes: I think the sensible and practical thing to do is have them scattered as, I believe, Father's were. They are not Mother, and after we are gone they will have not even a sentimental value for anyone else."

He again brought up the matter of his own planned cremation: "My ashes are to be scattered after I am gone, and if I die over here some friends of mine have promised to scatter them on Kaneohe Bay where I have been with them many times on their cruiser. It's not for sentimental reasons, but just an easy way to get rid of something absolutely worthless...."

On September 15, 1944, a permit was obtained from the California Bureau of Vital Statistics for the removal of Mary Evaline's ashes; permission was granted to John Coleman Burroughs, ERB's son, to transport the remains to the Evergreen Cemetery in Chicago. However, at the bottom of the form, a handwritten memo dated October 13, 1944, states the following: "Today the cremated remains of Mary Evaline Burroughs were buried at 18354 Ventura Blvd., Tarzana, California, in the ground at the south side of the walnut tree growing in front of the building at that location." It is signed "John Coleman Burroughs, Joan Burroughs Pierce, C. R. Rothmund." Thus Mary Evaline's remains were buried in the front yard of the Burroughs offices in Tarzana. The requirements that the form issued by the California Department of Vital Statistics must be filled in by the person receiving the remains at the destination and that the signed form must be returned to the California Bureau were apparently ignored. Whether the family ever intended to transport the ashes to Evergreen Cemetary in Chicago is not known.

2. In the letter Ed commented about the marked difference in the atmospheres of the convent and Hollywood School. "At the Hollywood School the children run and play and laugh and make all the noise they want while at the Convent they were always tiptoeing around and whispering in low tones, and when I talked in an ordinary tone of voice or laughed while I was there Joan was always fearful that I would be put out. The long, black habits of the Sisters always seemed to me depressing and I do not believe that it is the proper environment for growing children...." He mentioned some of Joan's "famous" friends, including Jim Jeffries' daughter Mary Jane, Francis X. Bushman's daughter, and the Cecil DeMille girls.

3. Letter of January 4, 1921, to Harry.

4. Ibid.

5. Letters of January 8, 1920, and January 4, 1921, to King.

6. Letter of May 10, 1920. Earlier, on October 26, 1918, to Weston, he had commented about Woodrow Wilson, "If you were delighted with Wilson's letter to the Kaiser, what do you think of his appeal to the American people to vote the Democratic ticket? They could stand me up against a stone wall in the morning for what I think about it. . . ."

7. Letter of June 25, 1931.

8. In "The Ghostly Script" Burroughs states his skepticism about the existence of any occult or metaphysical forces until certain experiences with a ouija board bring surprising results: after intense concentration upon the board, he succeeds in making it move without placing his hands on it, and while this is occurring, realizes, through his blurred mind and vision, that he has drifted into a trance. This trance then returns to him later when he is seated at the typewriter, working on a new novel. Upon inserting a fresh sheet of paper, he finds himself floating vaguely, and, helpless to resist, sits with his hands in his lap and watches the keys click away by themselves. His only role is to insert sheets and to start "in blank amaze." When the machine stops, it leaves "in its wake such a story as no human imagination might conceive." Burroughs then presents an account of class divisions in a transitional "world" of the hereafter called Halos. The actual discontinuance for ten years, after chapter one, is made a part of the story; the mysterious communicator suddenly stops his spirit typing and then, years later, as suddenly resumes it.

At the beginning of the narrative we encounter strange words, created to describe the transition from our present state to the state that humans call "death." Burroughs notes that the story contains words "that are to be found in no mortal dictionary, whose definitions I may conjecture, but not know." His language and theme and the atmosphere he achieves are reminiscent of Poe: ". . . know the truth, you who have derided and questioned. There is no death. There is only change. In the vast, illimitable span of forever there can be no future and no past — all is one great eternity of present. . . ."

What are the changes that take place when we fade from this earth? The "fluilations" that are you — your ego or soul — become dissipated, "but you will not be dead — your fluilations will merely have changed to new angles to which the senses of your present, conscious contemporaries fail to react." Man goes through various stages.

With the brief development of a complex philosophy, Burroughs then shifts to the main character of his narrative, a man who had been "dead" about twenty years. For his protagonist he chooses a Negro: "I was a colored man, a sergeant in the United States Infantry and I fell on San Juan Hill with a bullet in my heart. I was forty-seven years old." In telling his story, the black sergeant (unnamed) describes himself awakening to a scene similar to those created by Burroughs in his Martian series. The sergeant appears to be in a prehistoric world, "upon the sward of a mighty forest . . ." with "steaming earth," the trees "strange and hoary giants with boles, and foliage of hues such as no spectrum of your knowledge are separated." He observes in surprise that three great suns are suspended in the heavens, and conjectures that he has been transported to "some far distant solar system." But this is not the case. Since there is not time, space, or matter, one cannot accept a definition of systems or worlds that are separate.

In being "born again" the black man notes that he now would "probably be termed a white man, though here there are no distinctions of color or race. . . ." He explains that merely "differing degrees of radiance" exist and states, "I am of a high degree of radiance though there are others more radiant." As the story develops, Burroughs then introduces one of his favorite schemes — a hierarchy of classes.

The individual's position or classification on one of the levels of the hierarchy is made evident by his "radiance." The Negro, in dictating his story, explains, "Caste lines, then, that are really determined by relative approximation to perfection are objectively apparent in varying degrees of radiance." Details are given of the five degrees of radiance, those with the least, called the Maxteles, being the "dullest": "They are the drudges, the servants of all other castes. They are not hated, they are not abused except by the Psamaftogenes, but theirs is a hopeless existence of drab, unending labor." The Maxteles constitute the majority, "seventy-five percentum of all those who have paused here for the moment in the eternal journey toward perfection. . . ."

Of the Psamaftogenes, next in the scale above the Maxteles, the protagonist comments, "fortunately for us they are much fewer in number . . . , for they are recruited almost exclusively from the criminal class of your existence. . . ." They total fifteen percent of the population. Although they are criminals, few of them have been guilty of taking an individual's life. "But there are other murderers among them — the murderers of youth, and love, and happiness — hypocrites and slanderers and bearers of false witness."

On a plane above the Psamaftogenes are the Xarocens, a group to which the black sergeant belongs; they make up five percent of the inhabitants. Although they were "far from perfect" in their worldly lives, they had striven to improve themselves, and above all had avoided doing any wrong or harm to a fellow man.

As the "managers, the superintendents, the captains, the enforcers of law," the Xarocens are subject to the orders of the Corophines, those with more radiance who are above them, a group who contain only two percent of the population. The Corophines, makers of the laws and developers of the resources of this mystic world, have been rewarded for their attainment of higher virtues in their previous lives. But they, as with the other classes, are not perfect and all are still struggling to overcome "the same desires, emotions and passions" experienced by humans on earth. Although the four classes know where they came from, they do not know why they are suspended in this after-death state or what their next destination will be. Perhaps the Harods, the final two percent of the world called Halos, could provide the answers.

Religious attitudes of those in the afterlife of Halos appear remarkably similar to those expressed by people on earth. Some deny the existence of the supposedly all-powerful Harods, while others "would gladly die in defense of their belief in them."

With the development of the story, the black man returns to the past, his years spent as a slave on a Virginia plantation and his association with his young mistress Priscilla, whom he worshipped. In the Negro's words, Burroughs discloses his support of a misconceived theory about the racial problem:

The great tragedy of our lives was the freedom that the Civil War brought to us — the freedom that we did not then know how to use; that the black man has not yet learned how to use, nor ever will, because it is the freedom of an alien race in a foreign clime.

The African's only freedom might have been found in Africa where he once enjoyed it. . . .

For this problem of the "alien" in white society, Burroughs then offers a surprising solution: "Only extinction through intermarriage with other races in the lands to which he has been carried will get the Negro back his freedom, and then he will no longer be a Negro." That Burroughs' sympathy lies with the black race is evident; his creation of the Negro as the main character in the story demonstrates that. He further reveals his feelings by an indictment of the white plantation family: "They are still of Earth: still the victims of narrow prejudice."

The story shifts to Halos and soon loses the philosophical strength and appeal established at the beginning; as though uncertain of his goal or of how to unify the story, Burroughs proceeds with irrelevant actions before finally abandoning the narrative.

9. For "Tarzan the Terrible," 94,235 words, the worksheets contain a glossary of characters in the Pal-ul-don language with English equivalents — for example *Bu-lot* (Moon-face) and *Es-sat* (Rough-Skin) — and some geographical names also listed in the two languages. A separate page explains that the names of the male hairless pithecanthropus (Ho-don) begin with a consonant, have an even number of syllables, and end with a consonant. Names of female Ho-dons begin with a vowel, have an odd number of syllables, and end with a vowel. Names of the male hairy pithecanthropus (Waz-don) begin with a vowel, have an even number of syllables, and end with a consonant. The names of female Waz-dons begin with a consonant, have an odd number of syllables, and end with a vowel. The page also lists the system for numerals from one to eleven, and then by tens — from twenty to 100 (for example, 1: en, 2: enen, 3: ad, 4: ad-en, 5: adenen; using a method of doubling syllables. 100 is san; 1000 is xot; and the system in numbers above 100 is as follows: 101 is sanen; 102 is sanenen; 200 is enensan; 1121 is xotsantonen; 20,000 is tonxot.

ERB's drawings on these worksheets include upright figures, about five inches high, headed "Pithecanthropus Male and Female Ho-don," shown with clothing and accoutrements. The male is holding a large club and is equipped with a knife in a scabbard. In both cases the long tails are shown. On another page ERB has drawn a large map of Pal-ul-don with compass directions. Quite detailed, the map includes mountains, valleys, cities, and places where important actions occurred. Marked are the Valley of Jad-Ben-Otho, A-Lur, Kor-ul-Gryf, Tarzan's entrance spot and route, the place where Jane landed, the morasses, and many other cities. *Tarzan the Terrible* was published by McClurg on June 20, 1921.

10. To Jacobs, Ed wrote, "If you and Mr. Chaney find the plot satisfactory I should be very glad to go over the outline with Mr. Chaney carefully any time at his convenience. Since writing it many new ideas have suggested themselves to me, as they doubtless will to Mr. Chaney after he reads it over...." On September 9, 1921, to B. H. Stern, Ed explained that Lewis Jacobs had "recently" contracted for ten of his stories.

11. In his letter Sweet also wrote, "Only a soldier of fortune, such as we have been for some years, can really appreciate the true value of your stories, as we dream much, and act at any time there is occasion, or when hazardous Adventure calls. Such a man, I believe, was your 'hero,' John Carter, War Lord of Mars." Sweet added that if he and his friend were released in the future they might be able to make ERB a "paying proposition" for the game of Jetan, "as played on a large scale with wrestlers and boxers as the 'pieces,' instead of the swordsmen who played the game to the death, on bloody Mars." Sweet reminded ERB that if he forwarded a set of Jetan pieces, he should not expect any payment, as they were without funds.

ERB, in his response, wrote, "I think I have a copy of the rules somewhere among my papers, and if I can locate it I will send it to you.... Your idea of playing with boxers and wrestlers is an excellent one. To these might be added fencers...."

12. On September 7, 1927, ERB wrote to Lavender and Creighton, "A great many people have written me telling me that they have played Jetan with home-made pieces, but you are the first to send me a photograph of a Jetan board and the pieces used. Insofar as I know, it is the only photograph of its kind in existence." He expressed the wish that the photo had been larger and more distinct and requested another print to be sent to his publisher. On November 25 the two boys wrote to explain that new pictures of the Jetan set were being sent to ERB. ERB, on December 5, noted that the boys' letter was postmarked

"Andover," and he wondered if they were students at the academy. He mentioned that he had attended there.

13. Davis, in business for himself, had contacted Ray Long at *Cosmopolitan* about "The Chessmen of Mars," but Long was not interested. ERB's detailed worksheet includes a glossary of some seventy-five names and places and reminders of story incidents. The 93,000-word story was printed as a seven-part serial in *Argosy-All Story Weekly*, February 18 to April 1, 1922, and published as a book by McClurg on November 29, 1922.

14. Davis did not approve the title, "The Penningtons," when the story was sent to him. On February 28, 1922, ERB noted that his working title had been "Shannon," which he "really liked." He thought "The Penningtons" had dignity and sounded like a best seller. On March 10 he sent Davis a list of eleven titles, including those that contained the word *snow* for dope, such as "Fetters of Snow," "The Snow Slave," "The Demon of the Snow." Other titles were "Rancho del Ganado," "The Little Black Box," and of course "The Girl from Hollywood," which was finally chosen. Davis' suggestion was "The Needlewoman," which ERB rejected at once.

Purchased by Davis for $3,500, "The Girl from Hollywood" appeared in *Munsey's Magazine* as a six-part serial, from June to November 1922. Joseph Bray, McClurg editor, rejected the story, and it was published as a book by the Macauley Company, August 10, 1923.

15. The newspaper clipping, dated "Chicago, April 22," reported also that "Wireless radio impulses... can drive an automobile around the corners of a distant country road without any hand at the wheel...." These findings were revealed at a convention of the American Institute of Electrical Engineers at the Drake Hotel in Chicago by F. W. Dunmore of the United States Bureau of Standards.

"The Moon Maid," 61,910 words, was written June 7 to July 20, 1922, and accepted by Davis for $3,100. It appeared as a five-part serial in *Argosy-All Story Weekly*, May 5 to June 2, 1923, and was published by McClurg on February 6, 1926. Concerning the Ediphone, a note on ERB's worksheet reads, "Dic to Pg. 80, Typewritten from Chap. VIII."

16. "The Moon Men," originally "Under the Red Flag," 40,618 words, was rewritten starting January 24, 1922, and appeared as a four-part serial in *Argosy-All Story Weekly*, February 21 to March 14, 1925. Juana St. John, the girl whom Julian 9th loves, is of course named after the illustrator J. Allen St. John. Burroughs' love of horses led him to give the stallion Red Lightning an important role. On his worksheet he listed two other titles: "Under No Flag" and "Under The Hawk's Wing." "The Moon Men" was not purchased by Davis until October 20, 1924; it brought $2,150.

"The Red Hawk," the last of the trilogy, written April 20 to May 14, 1925, totaled 38,500 words and was bought in 1925 by Davis for $2,310. It appeared as a three-part serial in *Argosy All-Story Weekly*, September 5 to 19, 1925. The McClurg novel, *The Moon Maid* (1926), contained the complete trilogy.

17. "Tarzan and the Golden Lion," 79,884 words, appeared as a seven-part serial in *Argosy All-Story Weekly*, December 9, 1922 to January 20, 1923. McClurg published the book on March 24, 1923. ERB's worksheet has his small drawing of the Palace of Diamonds with the Tower of the Emperors marked; compass directions are also shown.

18. Other works on Atlantis listed by Hale are *Atlantis, the Antediluvian World*, Ignatius Donnelly, S. Law & Co., London, about 1882; "Atlantis," a lecture by Pierre Termier, Smithsonian Institute Report for 1915; "Story of Atlantis," Scott Elliott, Theosophical Society, London, 1896; *Queen Noo*, by Le Peongeon, and other books by him on the Mayas; *Island Life* by Alfred R. Wallace. Fiction listed included *Lost Continent* by Cutliffe J. Hyne; *Queen of Atlantis*, Pierre Benoit; *Atla, a Story*

of the Lost Island, Mrs. J. Gregory Smith, Ward and Downey, England, 1887; *When the World Shook*, Rider Haggard; *Last Lemurian*, Scott; *Lemuria*, Donnelly.

To stress the "blood brotherhood" of all living creatures, Hale wrote, "... Burroughs has rightly and ultimately emphasized and made plain in Tarzan... that brother-nature that makes us grin when we're pleased, pull back the corners of our mouths when we are 'fierce,' our hands clench when forcibly expressing an argument and our arms or legs make rapid motions of clutching and climbing when drowning, and all the rest of the manifold instincts we show with our brothers of the 'animal creation.'

19. Ed, on October 3, 1925, responded to a letter from William V. Thompson of the Hollywood Athletic Club concerning an application for membership by Maurice DeMond. Thompson's letter made it plain that DeMond was suspected of being a Jew, and, as a result, his application was being held up. In defense of DeMond, whom Ed praised highly, Ed noted that he had been involved with the same problem in sponsoring DeMond for The Writers, another club, "to which he was elected after a most thorough investigation." Ed offered to appear before the board of the Hollywood Athletic Club and furnish information about DeMond and wrote, "To the best of my knowledge he is not a Jew, but an American of French descent and he is an Episcopalian. Whether or not he is a Jew is immaterial to me, but even if he were, the main objection which I understand to be held against Jews in the Hollywood Athletic Club could not apply in his case as his friends, the people he might bring to the club house, are among the nicest people in Los Angeles and at such times as I have been entertained in his home I have never seen a Jew among his guests."

Chapter 17: Problems at Home and Abroad

1. Information obtained from Letter of August 24, 1922, to Edward Caldwell of the California Joint Stock Land Bank, San Francisco, when ERB was applying for a loan. ERB revealed that his first foreign translations had occurred only about two years before and that now there were the seven listed.

2. ERB made this comment to Ralph Rothmund, who became his secretary in 1927 and remained with him and the Burroughs Corporation for many years. Rothmund, in a note to ERB, had referred to the *Reseda News* celebration of its twenty-seventh birthday and reprinting of an item of September 27, 1923, announcing the opening of the Tarzana Tract and the presence of all the celebrities. Rothmund noted, "After 26 years, this is all news to me." Burroughs also wrote on the sheet, "You didn't ask me."

3. On October 7, 1926, to R. L. Woodrough, a Tarzana neighbor, ERB sent notification that the Golden Gate Oil Company had abandoned its Tarzana lease. He wrote, "It may interest you to know that yesterday afternoon the man who is pulling the casing brought me down a bottle of oil that came from between three and four hundred feet. It is quite rich in gasoline." The man, named Haggard, who had worked in many wells in the Valley, said this was the first gas that he had ever seen.

In 1924 ERB evidently owned a lot, number twenty seven, tract 3819, at the southwest corner of West Sixth Street and Muirfield Road. He was offering it for sale for about $25,000, according to notes to brokers dated May 27 and September 15. It was sold in December 1924 to I. Eisner Co., a California Corporation.

On May 21, 1926, ERB wrote to a realtor to offer for sale a lot in Beverly Hills, lot 4, tract 6981, on Ridgedale Drive at the corner of Hanover, for $37,000. He had planned to build a home there, but earlier, on January 9, had notified a realtor that he had given up the idea. He referred to Mrs. Burroughs' health

and the order of her physician to live in the country, and commented, "We are therefore planning on returning to Tarzana Ranch."

4. Letter to George Burroughs, February 19, 1924.

5. Letter to Bert Weston, November 12, 1924.

6. The governors and members of the advisory board of the El Caballero Club included Merritt H. Adamson, owner of Adohr Dairy Farms; Alphonzo E. Bell, developer of Bel-Air Estates; L. W. Craig and W. D. Longyear, both officials of the Security Trust & Savings Bank; G. R. Dexter, an attorney, and various others.

7. Letter of April 3, 1925.

8. Letter to Charles K. Miller, October 27, 1926.

9. *New York Times*, April 16, 1924.

10. The list of his foreign publishers includes, for 1926, Arabic: Sayed Hofez & Abdul, Rahman Ghamrawi, Alexandria, Egypt; England: Methuen & Co., London; British Colonies (including South Africa, Australia, and so on, except Canada): Methuen & Co., Czechoslovakia: L. Sotek, Prague II.; Denmark: Steen Hasselbach, Copenhagen, Denmark; Norway: Steen Hasselbach, Copenhagen, Denmark; Holland: Messrs. Weltman, The Hague, Holland; Finland: Kustannusliike Minerva O-Y, Helsingfors, Finland; France: Artheme Fayard & Co., Paris; Germany: Dieck & Co., Stuttgart, Germany; Hungary: Fovarosi Konyvkiado Reszvenytarsasag, VI, Budapest, Hungary; Iceland: Ingolfur Jonsson, Reykjavik, Iceland; Italy: R. Bemporad & Figlio, Florence, Italy; Poland: Trzaska Evert i Michalski, Warsaw, Poland; Roumania: Alex Filotty, Bucharest, Roumania; Russian: Edition des Nouveautes de la Litterature Etrangere, Esneux, Liege, Belguim. Published for Russian-speaking people in Belgium; Russia: Pirated in Soviet Russia. No records available; Spain: Tarzan Series: Gustavo Gili, Barcelona, Spain, and Martian Series: M. Aguilar, Madrid, Spain; Sweden: Lars Hokerbergs Bokforlag, Stockholm, Sweden; English on Continent: Bernhard Tauchnitz, Leipzig, Germany; Urdu: Mo. Azeez Ahmed, Qamer Munzil, Neotani. Dist. Unao, India; Canada: A. C. McClurg & Co., Chicago, Illinois.

11. Quoted by Dieck in letter of January 30, 1925.

12. Letter of February 9, 1925.

13. Salten also commented with contempt about *Tarzan the Untamed*: "Only the one volume which appeared during the war, the book wherein Tarzan hunts for Germans in Africa and kills every German he can get into his clutches like vermin, this one volume the German public did not see. Why should they? This wonderful work would have only brought about a great loss for the author and his German publisher. And business is business." Salten continued with his criticisms of Burroughs' writing: "... never has an author described the wonderful rich vegetation of the tropics any poorer than did Edgar Rice Burroughs." He had severe comments about ERB's animals: they are "made human" — all the "fine instincts of the animals were unknown or inconceivable to the good Burroughs...." The scenes and actions do not develop from the character of the animal. "These male and female lions, gorillas, leopards and elephants behave like characters in a comedy like 'The Old Mrs. Birch-Pfeiffer.' They 'turn' or become 'converted' whenever the story demands it, with disregard to their natural habits and instincts." Salten was also critical of Tarzan's learning to read and write — "all alone, all by himself."

Salten explained that because Germany was cut off for four long years from the rest of the world "through the blockade of war and for four additional years through the blockade of poverty," this led to a yearning for exotic distances and adventures that contributed to the success of Tarzan "and the utter failure of the German literary taste and judgement." Tarzan could have killed the wicked villain easily "a dozen times," but he does not do it for then the story would end. One actually feels ashamed, Salten wrote, how often and without motive "this villain escapes and how this only happens so that another Tarzan book may be written. The speculation for good business is shown so plainly and shamelessly." Salten accused ERB of stealing his idea from Robinson Crusoe and from Rudyard Kipling. Finally Salten said of the Germans, "It seems strange that a race which has scarcely escaped the horrors of war... could give itself to this thirst for blood as celebrated in the orgies of the Tarzan books."

14. Dieck went into detail about the German character. "The German as a whole is good-natured, too good-natured, which manifests itself frequently in weakness. As a whole he does not hate his enemies. Our soldiers went to war in 1914 with a certain enthusiasm, but without hate towards the enemy, not even towards the French, from whom throughout history we had to endure so much hardship." Dieck maintained, "The well known song of hatred against England was written by a Jewish writer and did not find much appreciation, except in a few papers." Dieck conceded that there were some German officers who were "haughty and unpleasant boys." He also noted that the Germans were very proud of their colonies and the success they had attained, and quite sorry to have lost them. In all armies in the colonies it may happen that an officer becomes a drunkard, but Dieck believed that this happened more often in the French and Belgian armies than in the German.

15. Letter of September 14, 1927, to John H. Bell of Whitman, Massachusetts.

16. Letter of February 15, 1929. ERB also wrote, "...as fountains of truth, newspapers and magazines no longer gush for me. Propaganda's greatest weakness lies in the fact that it is one-sided and self-seeking and in these respects has no relation whatsoever to truth. It will not fool all of the people all of the time."

17. The *Der Mittag* article, to explain why Robida's book had never been popular, noted, "...Robida was born too many years ago and he lived in an age where Foxtrot, shimmy and everything that is exotic was not 'modern,' nor did the people know anything about Jazz orchestras. Literature was simpler, and in this I refer to 'the literature of the streets.' Then came war, revolution, and life changed considerably. Soon afterwards the bookstores started offering in colored bindings the books of *Tarzan*." The article also claimed that almost the entire French press was attacking "the English author" and accusing him of plagiarism, but "Mr. Englishman does not reply to any of these articles. Possibly he considers it wiser to keep quiet."

18. ERB also wrote, "I have made millions of friends all over the world; for over fifty years I have been in a position to wear good clothes and eat three square meals a day, and to maintain my self-respect and the respect of those who know me. I did this before a single copy of my books was sold in Germany and I expect to continue to do so if Germany never buys another Burroughs book." He stressed that his only regret was that Dieck should have suffered a financial loss. He hoped that the withdrawal of *Tarzan the Untamed* all over the world would make clear his regret for having hurt Dieck and the German readers.

19. Letter of May 25, 1923. He wondered if Gum Smith should have been made a U.S. Marshall. Ed reminded Davis that Munsey was now doing business with a corporation, Edgar Rice Burroughs, Inc.

In correcting the galley proofs of *The Bandit of Hell's Bend*, Ed, on April 17, 1925, explained to Bray that in using the original verse he had adopted "quotation marks in accordance with an archaic form, which I learned at school some thirty or forty years ago." Whoever had corrected this copy had "balled it up" still more. Ed noted that he had now corrected it again and put it in exactly the form he wanted; he urged Bray not to change it. He also included, with this letter, about two pages of "Publicity

Notes" for McClurg to use in exploiting the book. These notes gave details about the actual characters used in the book, men who were part of Ed's past. These men were Gum Smith the sheriff, Wildcat Bob, and Bill Gatlin. Ed wrote, "Gum Smith the sheriff, and Wildcat Bob are drawn with more or less fidelity to life, though they are paraded under assumed names. The broncho, Gimlet, who threw Carson is described under his own name. He was at one time one of ERB's string of eight horses."

Bill Gatlin, the stage driver, was endowed with a vivid imagination, as evidenced by the samples of his stories told in *The Bandit of Hell's Bend*. One of his stories was about "the ridin'est woman I ever seen." She was a widow who had lost both legs in some sort of an accident, yet whose chief diversion was riding wild, bucking broncos that no one else could conquer.

Ed devoted much space describing his horse Whiskey Jack and his trials and tribulations with this horse, as recounted also in his *Autobiography*. Ed wrote, "I named him 'Whiskey Jack' much to the disgust of a dignified older brother who rechristened him 'Black Pacer.' I have ridden all my life, ever since I was four years old, and I have ridden a good many horses but I think that in many respects 'Whiskey Jack' was the most wonderful animal I was ever on, although he was not much of a lady's horse."

The Bandit of Hell's Bend, written March 30 to May 24, 1923, was purchased by Munsey for $4,070 and appeared in *Argosy All-Story Weekly* in six installments, September 13 to October 18, 1924. It was published by McClurg on June 4, 1925, and by Methuen on January 28, 1926.

20. Letter of February 11, 1932, to Mary A. Conklin, Coldwater, Michigan. The poems were titled "The Passing 'o My Pal Bill" and "The Bad Hombre." Ed wrote in response to her letter, "I never had the pleasure of meeting your grandfather, but then I was only in Coldwater for short periods during a few summers...."

21. Letter of March 31, 1923.

22. Letter of April 5, 1923.

23. Letter of April 30, 1923. Davis also wrote, "You got off the track by trying to make the people too small. If they are too diminutive, they have the quality of banshees and leprechauns, the habits of gnomes and the characteristics of fairies." He suggested that one branch of the pygmies be albinos and offered a "rather ingenious feminist trick" in the novel by having a group of pygmy Amazons travel under the slogan "Warriors First" in case of battle, turning their attention to the males first instead of the females. He added, "I suppose the golden lion will come into this story. Why not have the golden lion serve as a mount for the brigadier-general of the pigmy army...? The thing that makes the pigmies effective is their numbers. They literally swarm when they start to scrap."

24. Letter of September 24, 1923.

25. Letter of October 10, 1923.

26. Telegram of December 4, 1923.

27. "Tarzan and the Ant-Men" was begun on June 20, 1923, and finished November 22, 1923, with a note on the worksheets, "No work from July 12 to September 3." The words here are listed as 86,800, but Davis' elimination of 11,000 words with the removal of Miranda brought the magazine total down to 75,000 at a payment of $3,750. The larger, original work was used for the book publication by McClurg on September 30, 1924, but the British Methuen editions from 1925 on duplicated the *Argosy All-Story* version, February 2 to March 15, 1924. Ed's drawings, in addition to the ones of the palace, include a small map of the area, the Thorn Forest, Ugogo River, and other places.

28. Davis congratulated Ed on the wild females he had injected into the story. He wrote, "Sometimes I don't think you are aware of how great you are. Your pretense that literature is an

offense and that you loathe writing is an incontrovertible lie." He remarked, "...down deep under my coarse exterior I hold you in reverence."

29. Letter of January 9, 1924. In urging that Ed write the 300-word finish, Davis also asked, "...quit submitting the damned rotten verse written by Baron Ireland." Describing the cover, he said, "One of the diminuendoes looks very much like you. He's got a toothpick in his mitt for a spear, has an impudent, long upper lip and carries more than a trace of murder in his eye; altogether a tough baby."

30. Letter of January 30, 1924.

31. Letter of January 3, 1927, to Joseph Bray.

32. *Bob Davis Recalls: Sixty True Stories of Love and Laughter and Tears*, D. Appleton & Co., New York, 1927, contains lively personal experiences and anecdotes. One of these is an account of a dinner "prepared" by Sam Davis, Bob's brother, and Mark Twain in Virginia City, Nevada. The two men faked the dinner for the two sisters they had invited. The men arranged with a widow to cook the dinner and then brought each course down through the fire escape into the kitchen. Everything went well, with the sisters believing that the men had cooked the dinner, until Sam, carrying the roast duck, slipped and the duck fell on the sheriff below.

33. On March 2, 1927, MacLean commented, "I do think that your strongest hold is on something of the type of Tarzan... that idea being founded more or less on the evolutionary theory, has a sort of reality for people that the stories of other planets do not carry.... When you get right absolutely away from the earth and from reality altogether into the domain of complete fantasy, there is a loss somewhere."

34. "Vad Varo of Barsoom" was sent to the *Elk's Magazine*, John Hilder, managing editor, on November 17, 1926, and rejected December 9, 1926. The title change had confused W. J. Waterhouse, ERB's secretary at the time. He wrote on the rejection slip, "I find no sheet for Vad Varo. Will you give me rest of information." ERB wrote, " 'A Weird Adventure on Mars' XLVIII. Change name to *Vad Varo of Barsoom*."

35. Letter of March 11, 1927, from Ed. He pointed out that Bray had told him that *Tarzan of the Apes* was "too gruesome"; he also quoted six cents a word for the Mars story.

36. Ed had been in correspondence with Gernsback in 1926 concerning the "science-fiction" that Gernsback wanted for his *Amazing Stories* Magazine. On March 30, 1926, Gernsback bought "The Land That Time Forgot," second serial rights, for $100, running it from February to April 1927. After the purchase of "The Master Mind of Mars" on May 2, 1927, ERB waited a month for the payment which did not arrive. Inquiries that followed brought no money but "trade acceptances" from the Experimenter Publishing Company. On July 12 ERB wrote to say he could not accept these in lieu of the check that had been promised. Ed noted that he understood about the slack season but the company should have indicated in advance that it intended to pay with these acceptances which would then bear interest of seven percent. On July 18 Ed wired agreement to take the trade acceptances at seven percent, signed by the president and treasurer, with the interest totaling $1,266.01. The payment must have been made, for on January 17, 1928, when Gernsback inquired about the Burroughs story "Beyond Thirty," ERB quoted a price of $800 for second serial rights. Gernsback, astonished at the price, protested, reminding ERB of the $1,250 he had paid for first rights to "The Master Mind of Mars." ERB explained that "a combination of circumstances" had permitted Gernsback to get this story, and that the opportunity would probably not arise again.

37. The editors further criticized the story: "We found your two cities confusing in their similarity, and wondered why they had not been combined into one and placed in opposition to a city controlled by native warriors at the jungle's edge. Then Tarzan could have appeared in his natural surroundings. As it is, the real Tarzan fans who read and like him for the jungle and wild animal, as well as human, interest, would justly resent all this."

38. Letter of June 16, 1926. Paxton noted that "no criticism of Tarzan of the Apes is intended" and that he had always considered the story as "a first-rate piece of imaginative writing." The first interest in ERB's stories had been indicated by *The Country Gentleman* on September 14, 1925, with reference to the "shift" from his old style of fiction to a Western story, *The Bandit of Hell's Bend*, which the magazine found "highly entertaining." In this inquiry to McClurg, *The Country Gentleman* wished to know if ERB had another book planned.

39. Letter of November 2, 1926.

40. Ibid. Ed stressed that he had "adhered very closely to the facts" and had not given his imagination the free rein he allowed it in his *Tarzan* and Martian stories. His first goal was to be entertaining, as always; the novel was "in no sense an historical novel" because the "chronology" was "more or less mixed." Still, nearly every incident, battle, or raid was taken from a reasonably authentic history of the times. An ethnologist could find the story "replete with glaring errors." This was caused by the unreliable translations of the Apache language into Spanish and then into English, often done by "extremely ignorant and illiterate men." The spellings of names and words vary, never being identical in any two works; much of the information seems to have been compiled from memory, rather than from notes taken at the time. He referred to the Indian Chief Juh, whose name was pronounced "Who" or "Hoo" and spelled as "Whoa" in one work.

41. Letter of December 13, 1926.

42. Ibid.

43. The research sources for *The War Chief*, listed on Ed's worksheets and in a letter of January 20, 1930, to Hugh Thomason, are *The Marvellous Country*, Samuel Woodworth Cozzens (1874); *Thrilling Days in Army Life*, Genl. Geo. A. Forsyth (1900); *The Frontier Trail*, Col. Homer W. Wheeler (1923); *The Land of Poco Tiempo*, Chas. F. Lummis (1913); *Annual Report of the Smithsonian Inst.* (1920); *Annual Report of the Bureau of Ethnology* (1887-8); *Lives of Famous Indian Chiefs*, N. B. Wood (1906); *Trailing Geronimo*, Anton Mazzanovich (1926); *Geronimo's Story of His Life*, S. M. Barrett, ed. (1906); and *Life Among the Apaches*, John C. Cremony (1868).

Ed also listed his "note book" as a source, and gave various page numbers in the notebook.

44. Letter of August 17, 1928.

45. Letter of December 13, 1929. Ed had replied to Thomason on November 20, 1929, to inform him that the only Orchard Lake, Michigan Military Academy friends he still kept in touch with were Woodrough Ball, whose parents were living in Hollywood, and Bert Weston and Robert Lay. He thanked Thomason for his letter and "the pleasant memories it aroused...."

46. Letter of January 20, 1930.

47. Letter of August 6, 1927.

48. Letter of July 1, 1927, to Bray. On July 27, Ed wrote to Bray, "I have not as yet received any assurance from you that The War Chief is going to be published as written. If it is not, I am going to the mat with A. C. McClurg and Company as I certainly would never wish to quarrel with you."

49. In a second letter of July 5, Ed, hoping that McClurg would arrange for a new jacket illustration, urged Bray to get "The Land of Poco Tiempo" by Charles F. Lummis for information and also get "Geronimo's Story of His Life," edited by S. M. Barrett; this would have photographs that would "suggest Apache types." "Trailing Geronimo," by Mazzanovich, he noted, had a reproduction of a photograph of Geronimo and "some reproductions of stills made during the filming of a western

picture and some actual photographs of Apaches taken in the 80's. . . ." Ed added, ". . . before going into battle Apaches strip to G string and war band. Lummis' book is considered an authority and goes into detail in the matter of war paint and ornaments worn in battle or on the war trail."

50. Letter of July 8 from Bray; letter of July 13 from Ed. The dust jacket and title page were the work of Paul Stahr, taken from the cover of *Argosy-All Story Weekly* of April 16, 1927. "The War Chief" ran in the magazine for five issues through May 14.

51. On December 1, 1926, Ed sent copies of the agreement to Gerlach. He granted book rights only to Volland, for United States and Canada. Dr. Joseph C. Flowers was the company treasurer.

52. Letter of December 7, 1926. On December 21 Ed wrote to Gerlach to reassure him that he would not offer "The Tarzan Twins" to any other publisher. Ed commented, ". . . if you cannot make a success of them, no one else could." On January 14, 1927, he informed Gerlach that as the story neared its end, some changes would be necessary. The plot as he outlined it was the same as in the published work.

53. Letter of February 9, 1927.

54. Letter of March 4, 1927. Ed emphasized that through experience he had learned "it is not wise to rewrite" and also, he could only write in his own way; when he attempted to write in accordance with another's suggestions, the work was never satisfactory. All stories by all authors, he noted, could be improved, but this would lead to an endless series of changes. Stories written "freely and spontaneously" are usually better than those containing changes made later. The question about a longer book, brought up by Dr. Flower, received a firm answer: considering the age of the children who would read the book, a shorter one would be better and sell more; it would also lead to a greater demand for a sequel. He suggested larger type and numerous illustrations, claiming these would appeal to children rather than "a formidable array of text."

In the same letter Ed reported to Flowers that Dr. Stace, who was an old associate from the early business years, had called at his office and told his secretary that Mrs. Stace had died on Sunday, February 13. Ed had been out of the city during Stace's visit. References to Stace, who was leaving for Spain, and to another man named Brock, made it clear that Ed and Flowers had known each other for some time before the Volland contacts and that they had mutual friends.

55. Letter of December 28, 1927.

56. Letter of January 26, 1929.

Chapter 18: Social Commentator, Columnist

1. Letter of June 14, 1929.

2. Letter of March 22, 1927, to Bates.

3. Ibid. On June 20, 1927, Burroughs wrote to R. D. Condit of the Navajo Indian Rug Company to urge him to rent the store.

4. The site, at the corner of Ridgedale and Hanover Drives in Beverly Hills, was purchased by Ed to build a home there; he later changed his mind.

5. The *Tarzana Bulletin*, August 1927. Editor Ralph Rothmund reports, under "Building Notes," the construction of the new store and office building at 18352 Ventura Boulevard, the property being substantially the same as the present offices. Reference is made to the "beautiful old walnut tree in the center of the yard" in front of the office and to the Burroughs study which "he recently christened by completing therein his eleventh Tarzan novel."

6. All information obtained from taped interviews with Hulbert, Jack, and Joan Burroughs.

7. Letter of May 19, 1927. In his inquiry of April 1, Ed noted he had heard of the institute through Congressman Rex B. Goodcell, whose son would attend the school. On May 12 a letter from the New Mexico Military Institute informed Ed, "Your son is not prepared for entrance to our Junior College. . . we shall be pleased to have him enter our High School. . . ."

8. Jack had studied painting with Nicolai Fechin, a well-known Russian painter, and had taken a few lessons with W. Elmer Schofield.

9. Letter of November 22, 1929 to Macurda-Drisko Schools (L.A. Coaching School), Los Angeles.

10. The condition, called epididymitis, involved an inflammation related to the testicles. Two operations were performed at the Hollywood Hospital, one in November 1930 and the second in January 1931. Ed's total bill was $2,551.45.

11. Letter to Charles K. Miller, September 3, 1925.

12. Letter of September 13, 1930.

13. Letter to Marta Oatman, January 5, 1926.

14. Letter to Weston, March 19, 1928.

15. Letter of December 14, 1926, to Austin Schreffler, a fan, Manteno, Illinois.

16. Letter of September 15, 1925.

17. Letter of July 12, 1926. King apologized for having missed Joan's performance in "Enter Madame" and remarked that he would be happy to meet her and give her a screen test at F.B.O.

18. Letter of February 7, 1927, to Schnitzer. Ed also wrote, "I always see so many opportunities for improvement that I think no one else could possibly see, but as I have not the necessary technical knowledge, that possibility is definitely out."

19. Letter of July 27, 1927.

20. Letter of September 7, 1927. On September 22 Schnitzer replied to explain that he had made up a list of all the bookings on *Tarzan and The Golden Lion*, including the theaters, towns, and prices, and he was sending this to Ed. He denied that any block booking method was being used; an exhibitor could buy any picture he selected. He also denied Ed's "insinuation" that F.B.O. was "taking unfair advantage" of him. He said he was also disappointed at the volume of business.

21. Letter to Cadet Herbert T. Weston, Jr., April 18, 1929, at Culver Military Academy, Indiana. His father and mother were visiting with Ed at Tarzana at the time. Ed requested that Herbert, Jr., ask the cadets at Culver to write to offer their opinions as to the type of man who would make the best movie Tarzan based upon the Tarzan pictures they had recently seen. Ed noted that he had not seen Frank Merrill in *Tarzan the Mighty*, although he met him on the lot, but that "neither his face nor his conformation seems to me to quite fulfill the requirements of the character as I had visualized it."

22. Information from Pierce's letter of January 8, 1934, to Ed, written from 1710 North Fairfax Ave., Los Angeles, and also from a taped interview with the Pierces on January 19, 1968.

23. Taped interview of January 19, 1968.

24. Letter of January 13, 1926, to Bert Weston.

25. Letter of March 28, 1929, to the association, then in New York. Ed scoffed at the claims of the Republican Party and the Anti-Saloon League that the prosperity was due to prohibition, and added, "Personally, I think we are prosperous in spite of prohibition and both major parties, the selfishness of whose representatives in Congress forced prohibition upon us."

26. In his reply to Boorstyn on December 21, 1926, Ed suggested that the club activities should include hikes and athletic contests; he also suggested that members might try writing a short play based upon a Burroughs book and then present the play. Ed mentioned competition in essays and in the play, with the

prize to be an autographed copy of his book.

27. Letter of September 26, 1927, to Gerlach. He asked Gerlach to help with membership cards and in organizing the club, the goal being to stimulate sales.

28. Letter of March 30, 1921, to Kennicott about the request of Milton Ford Baldwin.

29. Letter of April 8, 1921, from Kennicott; Ed's reply, April 15, 1921.

30. Letter of April 15, 1921, to Webster. Ed added that he would not want to correct his English "at the expense of whatever style I may have or to lose that which you call prose rhythm, which often times may represent as much as an hour's work upon a single sentence before it swings to my satisfaction...."

31. Letter of December 29, 1924.

32. Letter of April 28, 1931 to Inglis.

33. On September 23, 1931, in sending the first three chapters of "Tarzan and the Leopard Men" to Miss Bischoff, Ed wrote, "As to the punctuation, unless Mr. Burroughs' punctuation would be considered incorrect by all good authorities, please do not make any changes in it. If it is merely a matter of personal preference, please give the punctuation in the manuscript the benefit of the doubt. Please correct all colloquialisms in all cases except quotation...." On September 30, four additional chapters of the same novel were sent, and on October 2, 1931, three more followed. Ed at this time stated that his chauffeur would pick up the corrected manuscript and asked that the white girl in the story, "Bwana Kali," be renamed "Kali Bwana."

34. Letter of January 21, 1928.

35. Letter of February 10, 1928.

36. Letters from Paine dated February 27 and March 2, 1928.

37. Letter of July 22, 1932. Powell noted that for more than sixty years the library had been gathering all published writings by Californian Authors, now a "very extensive collection." The works of fiction are "further segregated and kept in a room with two locks and keys."

38. Copies of the Shaw letter (undated) and Thurston's responses were sent to Burroughs on November 1, 1928. On November 8 ERB acknowledged the letters and commented that Thurston's books deserved "wide distribution." Shaw's letter, sent from 4 Whitehall Court, London, referred to the "reckless" statement that "one hundred western soldiers are equivalent in fighting power to ten thousand Chinese." Since Thurston himself admitted that marriage in both China and in the West were the same, Shaw wrote, "... even if your outrageous exaggeration were an exaggeration of the truth, it would prove that some other cause than the marriage institution common to both east and west must be the right explanation." Concerning Thurston's contention that "the law should ordain that the man shall have sexual intercourse with the woman only when and if she desires it," Shaw wrote, "You say that if she has been properly educated she will be qualified to regulate this matter. But suppose she desires it when the man does not desire it! Is not he, 'if properly educated,' also qualified to regulate his part of the matter? Everybody, male or female, would be qualified to regulate everything on earth 'if properly educated.' The retort is obvious: "If ifs and ands were pots and pans there'd be no need for tinkers." Shaw noted that he shared Thurston's "intense dislike of contraceptives" and remarked, "I cling to the hope that when high human cultivation reduces natural human fecundity from its present rabbit-like profusion in the slums, married couples will not have more children than they desire as the result of unstinted natural intercourse. But it is quite useless to denounce contraceptives at present, and quite impossible to convince people that the harm they do — if any — is greater than the harm they prevent. You know how con-

flicting the evidence is, if you can call it evidence when it is mostly merely opinion." In a P.S. Shaw wrote, "Thank you for the books. As you see, I have read them attentively."

Thurston's economic theories were stated in his second letter to Shaw: "The economic superstructure of the world rests on the ability of the individual man to provide the necessities of life, together with a surplus, which surplus may be used for luxuries, or saved, or invested at interest. The greater the vitality of the man or of any group of men, the greater will be the individual and the collective surplus...." Thus, if men drain themselves of their vitality through sexual excesses, "the ability of the masses of men to produce this vital surplus will decrease as their age increases. Also, the gradual over-population, with more people to feed, will increase prices, glut the labor market and reduce wages, and this in turn will further handicap the individual in his efforts to create a surplus." War then often follows, the nation's surplus is then wiped out, and as Thurston stressed, the United States could find itself in China's situation, "where 98% of the population have no surplus and live... in filth and squalor." He then rejected Henry George's theory, supported by Shaw, relative to the private ownership of land, and insisted that sexual excesses were the obvious cause of poverty.

Chapter 19: Diverse Writings

1. "Tarzan, Lord of the Jungle," 70,622 words, was written May 13 to July 22, 1927. Ed's worksheet notes the story was started at his office at 5255 Avenida Oriente and completed at the new office, 18354 Ventura Boulevard, where he moved on July 14. On the sheets he had listed various Arab words: the word of peace — *salaam aleyk*; the answer — *aleykom es-salaam*; *beyt* — abode, tent, house; *byut* — plural, etc. He had made a small circular drawing of the City of the Sepulcher, "The Wood of the Leopards, Nimmr," and marked "The Cross."

2. *The Apache Devil*, 73,333 words, was written August 4 to November 20, 1927. The worksheets note this: "Lost 4 wks. in September vacation, Lost 3 wks. in October illness." Ed was trying his new scheme of simultaneous submissions to a group of magazines. On the sheets he drew a cow with the brand of the Billings Ranch, the Crazy "B." The story appeared in *Argosy-All Story*, May 17 to June 20, 1928.

3. On September 28, 1939, ERB Inc. sent an inquiry to S. E. Lowe of the Whitman Company concerning *Jad-Bal-Ja and the Tarzan Twins*, referring to the book's publication and sale for twenty-five cents. The letter recalled that the books in this series had not sold well and that Whitman "never again published a Tarzan book at 25c." With plans now to publish out-of-print non-Tarzan books at low prices, from fifty cents down to thirty-nine cents, ERB, Inc., wanted to know if this would conflict with the Whitman ten-cent Tarzan books. *Jad-Bal-Ja and the Tarzan Twins*, written January 17 to February 20, 1928, has this worksheet entry: "22 days out." On October 15, 1930, Ed queried Munsey editor Bittner about accepting the story, but on the twenty-seventh Bittner rejected the idea, writing, "In the first place we never publish stories which have already come out in book form, secondly, we are not at all interested in juvenile fiction."

4. Letter of June 14, 1928.

5. "Tarzan and the Lost Empire," written March 29 to May 26, 1928, consisting of 66,402 words, was purchased by *Blue Book* for $5,000 and appeared in the magazine October 1928 to February 1929.

6. *Tanar of Pellucidar*, 77,825 words, was written September 13 to November 21, 1928. The worksheet notes that the story was "Commenced Thurs. Sep. 13, 1928, at 9 Sea View Terrace, Santa Monica, Finished Wed. Nov. 21, 1928, at 18354 Ventura Blvd., Tarzana." The story was published March to August 1929.

7. Letter of December 14, 1928. Earlier, on August 22, Ed had commented, "It would certainly be nice to be back in Argosy, but other magazines will pay so much more for my stuff than the Munsey Company that I have been pushed out into the cold world." On August 27 Bittner replied, "I was not aware that your work had drifted out of Argosy because of the matter of rate — thought that matter was adjusted to your satisfaction. . . . Frankly, what rate does interest you?" On September 10 Ed conceded he was "up in the air" on prices. Noting he had recently been offered "sixty times" what he used to receive, he also referred to a report of somebody's story sold for $75,000. "If you know what my stories are worth to you, let me know."

8. Letter of June 14, 1928. The four stories whose second rights were being returned to Ed by Munsey were "Under the Moons of Mars," "Tarzan of the Apes," "The Gods of Mars," and "At the Earth's Core."

9. Letter of July 31, 1939, to Don McGrew, a fan, San Francisco.

10. Letter of November 29, 1929, to Louis Gottschalk.

11. "Tarzan and Pellucidar" (retitled "Tarzan at the Earth's Core"), 79,446 words, was written December 6, 1928 to February 7, 1929. The worksheet lists "Cyls. 90," a reference to the Ediphone cylinders. A typed note gives the final word count and is signed by Ralph Rothmund. The $8,000, the largest sum Burroughs had received for a story, was paid in two installments, April 2 and 10, 1929.

12. He had seen Bittner in New York on May 29 and Bittner told him that the story was "acceptable."

13. In this letter of July 10, 1929, Ed mentioned the "Martian terms" used in the story; these appeared to be a "drawback" to Balmer, but Ed assured him that the fans found them stimulating. He offered to furnish a glossary, if necessary. He stressed that before Balmer decided against this story, he should also remember "that it is to my interest to find a publisher who will take these stories which I have found by experience sell well in book form. . . ." He also noted that every time he made a "pleasant connection" with an editor, the man gets another job or the magazine gets another editor. He was referring to the change with Balmer now editor of Red Book and Kennicott the new editor of Blue Book.

"A Fighting Man of Mars," 83,633 words, was written February 28 to May 10, 1929, and appeared in Blue Book, April to September 1930. The card index records the $8,000 in two equal payments, September 14 and November 4, 1929, but also lists $400 balance received February 24, 1930. The worksheets list "Cyls. 88-2/3" and contain details of the game of Yano, called "The Game of Spheres and Holes."

14. Sam Moskowitz, an author and Burroughs fan, has described a supposed Burroughs-Kline "feud," developed over the writing of Venus stories by both men. However, the evidence shows that Burroughs conceived the idea of a new Venus series first, as stated in his letter of March 28, 1929, to Balmer, and before Ed could possibly have known Kline was creating a Venus story. Ed never mentioned Kline by name.

15. Letter of March 24, 1931, to Kennicott.

16. "The Land of Hidden Men" (Jungle Girl), 67,443 words, was written October 2 to December 30, 1929. The worksheets lists "Cyls. 74 plus longhand mss," and again there is a special word count by Rothmund.

17. Letter of April 1, 1927.

18. Letter of March 20, 1928.

19. Letter of March 5, 1935.

20. Letter of April 8, 1929.

Chapter 20: Minor and Major Money Makers

1. Letter of July 29, 1925. Miller owned a clipping bureau.

2. Letter of July 19, 1927.

3. Letter of October 19, 1928, to Joe Neebe.

4. Letter of February 21, 1931, to Chas. K. Miller.

5. Letter of August 9, 1933, to Greenwood at MGM.

6. The suggested letter composed by Neebe was contained in his letter of December 21, 1927. He requested that Ed send it on his letterhead and make any changes that he saw fit or that would improve it. On December 28 Ed notified Neebe he was enclosing the requested letter. Neebe had said previously that the completed book would have sixty strips, a ten weeks' run.

7. Letter of December 13, 1927.

8. List attached to letter of December 28, 1928.

9. Letter of June 6, 1929.

10. Letter to Carlin, February 25, 1931; letter from Maxon, March 3, 1931; Ed's response, March 9, 1931.

11. Letter of August 5, 1931.

12. Letters of December 15, 1931, and March 1, 1932, to Bourjaily at United Feature Syndicate.

13. In his letter of April 9, 1929, Bray noted he had published Zane Grey's first book, The Last of the Plainsmen, and that another Grey novel, The Short Stop, was also on the McClurg list. Grey had written this for Bray when Bray was working on Outing Magazine. Bray remarked that Grey had "fooled around during his early connection with the movies with rather disastrous results." He recalled that when he saw Grey several years ago, Grey had claimed his annual income was over a quarter of a million dollars. Bray enclosed a card listing Ed's royalties with McClurg: $15,406 in 1924; $16,730 in 1925; $22,978 in 1926; $21,478 in 1927; $22,478 in 1928.

14. Letter of April 15, 1929.

15. Letter of April 24, 1929.

16. Letter of April 22, 1930.

17. Bray, in this letter of June 29, 1929, commented about the newspaper strips, presently using The Return of Tarzan: "If they use up all the books in this strip business they will hardly be through for five years at least, and then, . . . the Mars series is almost as good." He believed that the strips would be very popular overseas. He enclosed a detailed account of books published and total royalties from May 1924 to May 1929 as supplied by Grosset & Dunlap. On July 5 Ed requested the total popular copyright sales for the past five years, showing the number of copies and the amount of royalties. On Bray's letter Ed marked "Total pop. 14 years, 3,892,607; Av. per year 278,044; @ 5½c per copy $15,292.42; 5 yr. period, $76,462.10."

18. Letter of July 10, 1929.

19. On June 24, 1929, Ed had commented to Elser about a different type of illustration for the inside of the book covers that had presented a "standing repetition of my face." He wanted to have photos and scenes of people related to him. He spoke of a photo of his son Jack "with his bobtail 'Tarzan, Son of Scallywag.'" He believed the photo would attract more attention, especially with a story beneath it, than any photo of himself. He also mentioned a photo of Jack with a coyote he had shot, and other pictures of members of his family and himself on horseback. ". . . nothing, it seems to me, would appeal more to the class of readers whom I interest than the relationship which exists between myself and my children." This might have a beneficial effect upon the relations between other fathers and their children, he noted. On August 2, 1929, Max Elser addressed the "first letter of Metropolitan Books, Inc." to Ed; the lawyers had notified Elser that the name was now approved legally in New York. The name Home Book Club, Inc., evidently the previous organization with whom Ed had signed a contract, had now been changed to Metropolitan Books, Inc.

20. Letter of August 9, 1929, to Elser.

21. Letter of October 23.

22. Letter of December 19, 1929, to Elser.

23. Letter of January 18, 1930, to Elser. About Tanar, Ed had other requests: "He should have a shock of black hair, long but without any suggestion of effeminacy. If permissible, he should wear only a G-string of dark fur, the end hanging down almost to his knees in front...." He also added, "I do not like the saber-toothed tiger at all. It suggests nothing terrible or ferocious, nor is there any action in its pose."

24. Letter of May 17, 1930, to Elser.

25. Letter of January 5, 1932.

26. Letter of June 6, 1932, to Dahlquist. In a letter of June 8, Ed commented to Dahlquist about a radio scene in which Tarzan removed a tick from the mouth of a lioness and noted that he believed it to be preposterous. He had never heard of a tick embedding itself in an animal's mouth; they are usually found on the body. He could not imagine Tarzan clinging to the lioness' back and removing the tick with a hunting knife. He suggested that the writer, Doyle, find another situation. He added a page of comments on episode fifteen: "Do not make any of the animals in the story female unless I have so indicated...Sheeta is supposed to be a consistent and fearless enemy of Tarzan. If you have him run away in terror now, how can you use him later as a menace?" He also commented on episode sixteen: "Too much natural history—sounds stilted.... Try and develop Jane into a decent character. She is too blah in these scripts...."

27. Letter of June 20, 1932.

28. Letter of September 6, 1932, to Mrs. D. W. Jeffries, Chicago.

29. Letter of October 26, 1933.

30. Letter of August 31, 1934.

31. Letter of March 9, 1931.

32. Letter of May 20, 1932.

33. Letter of February 19, 1932.

34. Letter of August 14, 1933, to his son Hulbert.

35. Letter of July 15, 1932, to Burroughs.

36. Letters of September 8 and 15, 1932. Lincoln's act was to be called King of Beasts or King of the Jungle.

37. In December 1932 with Lincoln, then living at 1900 Franklin Street in Hollywood.

38. Letter of October 1, 1931.

39. Other instructions were painfully detailed:

Illustration #2: Tarzan lifting a shifta above his head to hurl him at other shiftas pressing close. Caption: A white giant who fought with his bare hands. Note: The shiftas in this and other illustrations should be costumed after the Abyssinian manner. Also, please see if you can get the Abyssinian saddle and horse trappings more or less correct. If you will refer to the June 1925 issue of National Geographic Magazine you will find all the horse trappings you will need. And by referring to Page 122 of the book Savage Abyssinia *by James E. Baum, you will notice illustrations of shiftas and their costumes.*

40. Letter of August 5, 1932.

41. Letter of May 24, 1932, to Studley, then at 19 Pearson Street, Chicago.

42. The worksheet lists 80,000 words for *Tarzan the Invincible* and under cylinders, "69 plus longhand mss." For the publishing of his books, Burroughs contracted with the Kingsport Press. In his publicity he notes that the book represents "the outcome of what might be called a long-distance publishing venture." Burroughs was at Tarzana, Studley Burroughs in Chicago, the printer, Kingsport Press, in Tennessee, and the advertising agency, Chas. H. Denhard, in New York. The publicity release also reports, "Burroughs has the faculty of suggesting much to the imagination of the adult mind without transgressing the dictates of polite society or arousing the *libido* of the adolescent." This euphemistic language expresses Burroughs' anxiety over any emphasis upon sex in his writings.

43. "That Damned Dude" suffered a series of rejections: August 1930 by *Elks Magazine*; September 1930, by *Liberty*; November 5, 1930, by *Ladies' Home Journal*; November 21, 1930, by Doubleday, Doran; September 20, 1930, by *The Saturday Evening Post*; November 4, 1931, by *Blue Book*; and May 1937, again by Doubleday, Doran.

44. Letter of August 24, 1931.

45. Letter of September 10, 1931.

46. Letter of March 23, 1932.

47. Letter of February 19, 1936.

48. The home of Jephet Seegar, situated on "the steep escarpment of a hilltop and Hollywood," illustrated the incredible effort of the architect to combine as many features of European origin as possible. "Its motif was an ornate Gothic doorway, reminiscent of the entrance to the Cathedral of Amiens...." But the ensemble became an odd potpourri of "Gothic, Spanish, French, Italian and middle Iowan." This home of Jephet Seegar was unusual in another respect, Burroughs noted humorously: "It possessed no mortgage, for where mortgages crossed the path of rich, retired Jephet Seegar, bachelor, they discovered him in the role of mortgagee, never mortgagor." From one of his wrought iron, Italian balconies Jephet had a magnificent view; ahead of him was an area that stretched "from the high, white tower of the city hall down to the blue waters of the Pacific, with the peaceful mysterious hills of Catalina looming just off shore and, sometimes, even far San Clemente in the distance." At night the expanse was "like a splendid glittering rug of a billion gleaming jewels spread in regal magnificence from Hollywood to the Baldwin Hills." Burroughs closed this colorful description by commenting that Jephet "had no need to look so far afield for satisfying beauty when he could appease the artistic cravings of his soul with a Gothic entrance, a chateau tower, or a green tile bathroom with a red plush toilet seat."

As the plot develops, certain actions occurring on the second floor carry a hint of a crime. There are "sounds of voices raised in altercation," "the banging of a door and then ominous silence." The elderly butler, Maddox, locks the door of the room containing Jephet Seegar, mutters, "The old fool. I warned him!" and proceeds downstairs. There his behavior is strange; he spends much time checking all the window catches, as though in fear of burglars; then he sits down to listen to the shortwave police broadcasts on his radio. Maddox had been Seegar's servant and companion for ten years, and his master had treated him generously both in wages and gifts. A stingy man, Maddox saved all his money; he had no faith in banks and hoarded his savings in a secret hiding place. He "lived in a state of constant apprehension" that this hiding place might be discovered by burglars.

With Maddox continuing to listen to police calls on the radio, through his thoughts, new elements, quite puzzling, are introduced. He dreads the next day: "There would be telephone calls and people coming to inquire for Jephet Seegar, and Maddox would have to lie to them. He hated lies." A cleaning woman, recently hired, is scheduled to arrive. By the second day everything will be all right, he believes; but what will he do tomorrow? As Maddox meditates, half-asleep, he hears a car, and from the front window sees it stop in front of the house. A man and woman approach the entrance, but as their flashlight focuses on the front porch, Maddox opens the door and points a revolver at them. Despite their protests, he orders them into the house and ushers them upstairs, locking them in a room. There, from an adjoining room, the pair see a trickle of red coming from beneath the door. The two, who are revealed as young and romantically involved, go out to the balcony to peer at the street below, realizing there is no escape.

Meanwhile, Maddox has called the police, and the wail of the siren signals their approach. The young couple, when found, disclose that they were merely on a treasure hunt organized at a party at a nearby home. The instructions that brought them to the house consisted of a poem, written on a piece of paper:

There is a house upon a hill
Where dwell the landed gentry.
Follow the road at the old blue mill,
And search the Gothic entry.

The couple inform the police of the suspicious red fluid coming from under the door. When the door is opened, Jephet Seegar is discovered lying in what seems to be a pool of blood. Maddox, who has the key to the room, is of course suspect until he explains that Seegar was given to drinking bouts and that in order to sober his master up, he had served him the usual tomato juice and crackers. The police, upon closer examination, realize that Seegar is lying dead drunk in a pool of tomato juice.

At this stage, with apparently no crime committed, and the reader disappointed over a much-ado-over-nothing situation, the story takes an ingenious turn. Seized by a sudden fear, Maddox rushes to the basement, finds that the window has been forced, and at once perceives the appalling truth: his lifetime savings have been stolen from the hiding place beneath a floor board. He stiffens and then slumps in a heap upon the floor. In a clever denouement the real criminals are disclosed: The young girl, most cunningly, had contrived to meet the young man a week earlier and at the party had suggested the treasure hunt and planted the poem of instructions that brought them to the Seegar home. The entire scheme had been a ruse to divert Maddox' attention while the girl's associates, informed of the hiding place by Mrs. Blump, the cleaning woman, had entered the basement to steal the money.

The young man, blissfully unaware that he has been tricked and used by a girl who cares nothing about him, leaves in a rapt state, announcing he will see her the next day. She watches him depart, mutters, "Oh, yeah?" under her breath, and hurries away to join her criminal confederates, two men and a blowsy, middle-aged Mrs. Blump. One of the men pulls the girl onto his lap, kisses her, and tells her that the butler's money totaled $25,000, "thanks to you and Ma Blump," he says. Burroughs reserves an ironic paragraph for the end: "Jephet Seegar slept peacefully in his hillside home in Hollywood; two floors below, the body of Maddox slowly stiffened in the awkward posture of death. In the home of the police commissioner a young man dreamed of a girl, and in the south part of the city the girl finished another highball and went to bed with a dapper youth with sleek hair."

49. *Tarzan and the Leopard Men* appeared in *Blue Book* August 1932 to January 1933 and was published by Burroughs on September 7, 1935. The worksheet contains a note, "Script for M-G-M (6-8-38)," and lists two additional characters added for the script.

50. For the story, "The Pirates of Venus," purchased for $4,500 by Munsey, Moore's suggested changes were described: "On page 30, for instance, would it not greatly improve the story to have Carson Napier attacked, not by Targo, but by some other, new fantastic creature which, perhaps, was fleeing from the Targo just as Napier was. The people from the Tree City could then dash out to the rescue of Napier just as he felt himself hopelessly alone in this new world...."

Moore's second suggestion followed: "...to introduce some action into Napier's long period of getting acquainted with the Tree people and the mysterious girl. Why would it not be logical to have a stray party of Thorians (probably not identified to Napier as yet) make a vain attack on or near the Tree City? This would nicely plant the eventual kidnapping of the Princess,

besides giving one good action scene in the interesting but rather quiet second part."

In his November 30, 1931, letter Ed referred to his previous telegram agreeing to make the changes and to forward these sent in the early part of that week. The changes, enclosed, were in the form of inserts, following Moore's suggestions. A further letter of December 3 to Moore discussed the disagreement over the word count of the "Pirates of Venus." Ed had calculated 60,000 and Moore only 57,500. He explains his method of counting, originally established by Bob Davis; it was really estimating, after counting only fifteen to twenty full lines. Ed insisted that while the actual count was 57,500, "yet the space this story will take in your magazine will be equivalent to sixty thousand words." The book *Pirates of Venus* was published by Burroughs on February 15, 1934.

Ed also offered Moore a choice of titles for the next Tarzan story, listing four suggested titles: "Tarzan and the City of Gold," "Tarzan and the Lion People," "Tarzan the Courageous," and "Tarzan Courageous." On December 15, 1933, to brother Harry, Ed reported that the "Pirates of Venus" was running in *Passing Show*, a London magazine, with the sequel already sold to the same magazine. A publication in Holland had requested it, and the story was wanted for a Turkish translation. "'Tarzan and the Lion Man,'" published in *Liberty*, had been sold to *Tid-Bits* in London.

51. This outline was in Ed's letter of December 15, 1931.

52. Letter of December 22, 1931.

53. The 65,000-word "Tarzan and the City of Gold" was purchased by Munsey for $6,500 and ran in *Argosy* from March 12 to April 16, 1932. On his worksheets Ed has drawn a map showing such features as Onthar, Thenar, the Crater of Molten Lava, the Field of the Lions, Plain of the Elephants, Pass of the Warriors, Cathne, City of Gold, and Athne, City of Ivory. Also marked is the point where Tarzan and Valthor reached the Valley. The book *Tarzan and the City of Gold* was published by Burroughs on September 1, 1933.

54. See letter of September 19, 1939.

55. Letter of September 20, 1932, from Moore.

56. On the twenty-eighth Moore sought more action in the "House of Seven Doors." He suggested that "the hero, fleeing from the snakes, might dash into one corridor, propping the door open with the table; be chased out of it by the tharban, which engages in a desperate and hopeless fight with the snakes as our hero leaps on to the rope." Around page 140 Moore also suggested a plot change: "Just as Carson Napier is about to be sentenced to death, he remarks about his trip from another world coming to a strange conclusion; this remark leads the judges to question him and give him a last-minute reprieve." Ed adopted this idea, rather than the one he had originally used, where the girl learns of the plan to have Napier killed and announces that such a man must not be allowed to die. Here, Moore maintained, the suspense had been killed and the reader was able to forecast everything that would happen. On December 6 Rothmund wrote to indicate that Burroughs had made these changes, and inserts were attached.

57. The 63,000-word "Lost on Venus," written August 6 to November 12, 1932, ran in *Argosy* March 4 to April 15, 1933. It was purchased by Moore for $5,065. The book was published by Burroughs on February 15, 1935.

In his letter of December 20, 1932, Moore noted that his manuscript department counted the story as 67,500 words and that since this exceeded the number usually printed in six installments, he was going to try an experiment and run "Lost on Venus" in seven installments. He stressed that he liked this story better than "The Pirates of Venus" and explained that he was making some minor changes in the editing of the story; he was inserting a "suggestion" two or three times during Carson's travels with Neva that he was longing for Duare and worrying about her welfare. Moore thought this was not brought out quite enough and resulted in a weakening of the Carson-Duare suspense. "As it is, he very ficklely forgets her while sojourning in Utopia with Neva. . . ."

The worksheets, marked "90 Malibu La Costa," the beach home where Burroughs wrote the story, contain a detailed drawing of The City of Havatoo in Noobol, showing the Civic Center and all the adjacent streets or districts where the differing classes lived. The districts are listed as: Civic Center, first circle; Sentar, for biologists, second circle; Ambad, for psychologists, second circle; Korgan for soldier (officer) class, second circle; Katlto for chemists, second circle; Kantun for physicists, second circle; Yorgan for common people, third circle; shops and factories, fourth circle. The various schools, placed on the map by numbers, are listed below the map, e.g., number one, School of biology; number two, School of Psychology, etc. Counting two numbers for preparatory schools, there were seven schools in all.

58. Letter of March 14, 1933. Here Moore also wrote, ". . . it would strike me as a distinct breach of faith to have you sell a Carson Napier or 'Tarzan and the City of Ivory' to another magazine unless we had had the option of purchasing it at the rates agreed upon. Moore conceded that Burroughs' view about the word length needed for books was a valid one; if Argosy were certain of receiving Tarzan and Venus series regularly, Moore would be willing to "stretch serialization over seven installments" to use 75,000 words, which would be a better length for book publication. He would not continue building up a series which might be switched to a competitor at a moment's notice. On March 22, Burroughs replied to stress he had kept his agreement and that it had always been "particularly repugnant" to him to be tied down by contract; one of the greatest advantages "is my independence." He added, "I shall never do it again — with you or anyone else." Tarzan's audience, he pointed out, was not based upon his appearances in Argosy, but rather on the twenty year combination of strips, newspaper serials, books, motion pictures, and radio broadcasts.

59. Letter of March 22, 1933.

60. The worksheets for the 70,000-word "Tarzan and the Lion Man" list other royal and noble gorilla characters that have roles in the novel. These include all six of Henry's wives. Ed has drawn a map again showing the entrance to the valley with its monolithic column and red granite outcropping. The Valley of the Diamonds is shown; the barren cone-shaped hill is marked; and numbers on the map locate the various settings where the action occurred (e.g., number one, Arab camp from which the girls escaped; number two, Rungula's village, etc.). *Tarzan and the Lion Man*, published in book form by Burroughs, appeared on September 1, 1934.

61. Letter of August 6, 1934. Rothmund had typed a note at the top of Clayton's letter; the note was addressed to Burroughs: "I held this Argosy letter pending the outcome of the Blue Book negotiation. Now that Blue Book has purchased the Mars story, it doesn't make any difference to us what Argosy's views as to the Martian stories are, as I see it. As the attached letter does not call for a reply, I believe it wiser to simply file it and leave Argosy in the dark as to the Tarzan mss. What do you think?" Burroughs marked "O.K."

62. The 78,000-word *Sword of Mars* was published in book form by Burroughs on February 15, 1936.

63. In "Who Murdered Mr. Thomas?" a strand of hair taken from the dead man's coat is the main clue, and a guest replies to Muldoon in this riddling fashion:

"It is not fair to assume that it was a strand of the killer's hair. As a matter of fact the killer had the same color hair as one of the guests who was absent from the room at the time of the murder."

"So you know who the killer is?" demanded Muldoon, but the man closed up like a clam and would say no more.

Later, when the butler explains that three people were in the room with Mr. Thomas and then names only one, Muldoon asks, "Was the color of the killer's hair the same as that of either of the two present?" The butler answers, "No; but the other two had the same color hair." Upon receiving this information, Muldoon quickly arrests the murderer, and the puzzle ends with the question, "Whom did Muldoon arrest?" Burroughs produces a solution that is so complicated that the reader emerges more baffled than he was with the puzzle itself: "The killer did not have the same color hair as either of the two men, and as he had the same color as one of the guests who was absent from the room it must have been the same color as Miss Mill's, which was black, as she was the only woman guest absent from the room; therefore the killer had black hair."

Muldoon's vaunted mathematical ability which enables him to solve crimes by "correlating" various figures is demonstrated quite ludicrously in "The Bank Murder." In grilling the suspects about the murder of Morgan, the bank examiner, Muldoon, for no logical reason, ignores the important questions and seeks to know only the ages of the persons involved. King, the teller, "about the coolest proposition" one could find, replies, "If I were four years younger, I'd be one year older than that man there who is twenty years younger and much poorer than the man sitting at the desk and who has the same name as he." This attempt by Burroughs to create clues based upon numbers leads to unreal situations and dialogue that verge on the ridiculous. Further questioning in "The Bank Murder" provokes similarly garbled responses:

"What is your name, doctor?"

"My name is the same as the only man in the room who is exactly fifteen years younger than Thaddeus James and five years older than Ralph James.

[*Dialogue next involves Thaddeus James.*]

"How old are you?" asked Muldoon. "I suppose you are seven years older than some one else who is eight years younger than some other person."

James smiled. "No," he replied; "I am twice as old as the young gentlemen whom King describes as being poorer than I."

"Well, that helps a lot," said Muldoon; "now we are getting some place."

No reply is without numbers: "I have known him for one-third of his life and one quarter of mine; I first met him when Ralph was ten years old." And to provide the final clue (obligingly) that identifies the culprit, Burroughs writes, "The man who killed Mr. Morgan was five years older than I." Muldoon points at the guilty man, unnamed, and the puzzle closes with the question, "At whom did the Inspector point?"

In "The Terrace Drive Murder" and "The Lightship Murder" Muldoon's questions, again designed to produce the instantaneous clues that lead to the solutions, are concerned with both the ages and the relationships of the suspects. Again, one person present knows who the murderer is, refuses to tell, but is quite cooperative in giving hints about the guilty party. "Foley, you're lying to me — you know who committed this crime. Come on — out with it!" Muldoon orders, in "The Terrace Drive Murder." Foley blurts, "Yes, I know, but I'll never tell." Later, when Muldoon in a friendly fashion inquires, "I was just wondering if the murderer were very well acquainted with the deceased," Foley answers, "Yes; at one time they were engaged to be married." The solution, as with the previous puzzles, is of an unbelievable complexity, for example:

Elwood was the deceased's nephew.

Elwood's mother was an only child; therefore Elwood had no uncle nor aunt on that side.

Elwood's father had no brothers; therefore, his mother being an only child, he never had an uncle; therefore, the murdered person, whose nephew he was, must have been his aunt.

Even more so in "The Lightship Murder" the solution hinges upon the relationships of the five MacTeevors who were aboard the lightship on the night of the murder. Admitting she knows who committed the murder, Esther announces, "I won't tell. You couldn't never drag it out of me." She follows this by giving Muldoon the clue he seeks: "It was in the blood — the mother's blood; 'twarn't in my blood nor in the MacTeevor's." Burroughs' one-page solution offers several paragraphs unraveling the relationships (for readers with determination) before presenting the dénouement: "Esther said the murderer had murder in his blood but that there was no such criminal strain in her blood nor in the MacTeevor's; therefore the blood strain must have come from Carrie, and as Andy is the only one with her blood in his veins and as Carrie was in her bunk when the murder was committed, Andy must be the murderer."

"The Dark Lake Murder" presents a different type of clue for the solution; since Mr. Thayer was shot from behind and slightly above, the position of each suspect was important. Mrs. Thayer, the only person standing behind the murdered man, was on the porch, gazing down. Obviously, she alone could have fired the bullet that angled downward. In "The Gang Murder," concerning the question of who "croaked" Louis "Spike" Finie, Kid Meghan "won't peach on a pal" but is quite eager to test Muldoon's reputation; the Kid offers a riddle: "The father of the guy that croaked Spike Finie is Tony's father's son." The brilliant Muldoon at once identifies the culprit.

The last and longest (twelve pages) of the puzzles in the collection, "Murder at Midnight," provides a setting at Palm Springs and a solution again based upon the suspects' ages. Sidley obligingly explains, "The man who killed de Veny was nearer forty than he was thirty-five." The two puzzles not included in the collection, "The Red Necktie" and "The Dupuyster Case," are developed in the same vein with emphasis upon petty clues. A mystery without a murder, "The Red Necktie," centers about the attempt to bribe Judge Racket. An incredible courtroom cross-examination by the prosecuting attorney leads to riddle games involving ages and numbers: "I am five years older than that other defendant over there who is twenty years younger and much poorer than the defendant who has the same name as he. ... If I were five years younger I should be just your age. ... I have known him for one seventh of my life and one sixth of his. ... He is as much younger than you as he is older than the defendant whose name is the same as yours." The Dupuyster Case" is marked in Burroughs' handwriting: "not finished — too long and too complicated." It contains a rather farfetched solution. With Hutton, the butler, and Miller, the valet, the prime suspects, the solution is determined by the fact that Hutton is color blind; the murderer, after killing Dupuyster, had wiped the knife on a blue handkerchief. "Dupuyster had on blue socks and tie and a green handkerchief was in his pocket. Miller, a trained valet, would not have selected a green handkerchief to replace the one on which he had wiped the bloody knife. Hutton, who was color blind, might have. So Muldoon arrested Hutton."

64. The unfinished "Dupuyster Case" contains a short explanation before the story opens: "In most of these mystery puzzles only a single conclusion may be deduced from the clews given. In this one the solution is not a mathematical certainty, as it is based upon circumstantial evidence that points to the guilty party. The question therefore is, which person would a clever criminologist charge with murder?" Page ten outlines the remainder of the story, showing the reasoning that leads to the solution. Two more pages of handwritten notes follow.

65. "Entertainment is Fiction's Purpose" appeared in *Writer's Digest*, June 1930.

Chapter 21: Personal Crisis and Adjustment

1. Interview with Jack Burroughs, January 11, 1970.

2. Letter to Emma, then at Ogden, Utah, with Joan, who was performing in a play.

3. Dearholt's letter to Ed, Joan, and Jim, January 13, 1933.

4. Taped interview with Florence (Tillman), May 21, 1969.

5. Letter of February 21, 1934.

6. In this letter of February 28 to Jack, Ed devoted a page to a discussion of flying: "I hope that you boys won't give up flying if you still wish to fly. Hulbert seems to have lost interest. If he really has, then he should give it up; but if not, I hope he continues, for he is going to make a great pilot; as I think you are too after seeing how well you did Sunday. I had a fine day today. Made all pretty good landings — three at . . . field and one at Clover. It was very windy — a cross wind at Clover. Hully ground looped, and I think that discouraged him. But we all do that, even old aces — I have done it twice. . . ."

7. *Variety* reported on November 27, 1934, that 2,000 shares were issued. Directors in addition to Stout, Dearholt, and Burroughs included H. A. Cummings, A. S. Wright, Alfred L. Armstrong, C. J. Staley, and A. D. De Muth. Presumably, these new men had added capital to the company.

8. Letter of August 27, 1934, to Robert H. Patchen of the Grace Line. Patchen was a friend Burroughs had known in his early years.

9. Letter of October 30, 1934.

10. Letter of November 1, 1934 to Dearholt.

11. Letter of November 13, 1934.

12. Letter of November 15, 1934.

13. Burroughs, playing it safe, on November 13, 1934, had procured a signed agreement from George Stout, assigning all rights to Romance Productions to him, and also assigning rights to Romance's boy scout film serial, "Young Eagles."

14. Letter of December 14, 1934, to George, who was in Burley, Idaho. George, on December 10, wrote to say, "It was with almost incredulity that I learned of the difficulty in your family and that it has led to a divorce from Emma, for I had supposed that your home life was more than usually serene and satisfactory." Evidently, Emma's drinking problem had been a well-kept secret; neither George nor Harry was aware of it.

15. Taped interview with Florence, May 21, 1969.

16. Ibid.

17. Taped interview with Ralph Bellamy, September 4, 1968.

18. Revealed in interviews with Ed Gilbert and Florence, October 9, 1968, and May 21, 1969.

19. "Tarzan and Jane," according to the worksheet, totaled 80,000 words, was started at 2029 Pinehurst Avenue on May 13, 1934, and was completed at Tarzana, January 19, 1935.

20. This was sent by Rothmund, who said that, because of the expense of postage, these could be picked up by Johnson.

21. Letter of March 20, 1936.

22. Taped interview, March 16, 1968.

23. Letter from Mill, January 28, 1937.

24. Letter to Mill, May 21, 1937.

25. An odd, undeveloped section of *Back to the Stone Age* relates to the Gorbuses, a race of albinos encountered by Von Horst (pages 94 to 99, *Ace* paperback) and to the uses by Durg of two English words, *cleaver* and *dagger*. Horst is baffled by this. The primitive tribe had no weapons at all; how could Durg know what a cleaver and a dagger were and above all, where did he learn the English words? Durg and Torp, in their quarreling, reveal themselves as murderers. When Von Horst explains that he comes from another world, Durg says, "I knew it. It must be

that there is another world." He then indicates his belief that once the Gorbuses lived in a happy world, but because of evil actions they were sent away from it to live in their present dreary world. They receive fleeting glimpses of a previous life "out of the dim background of almost forgotten memories." They were different then, Durg says. He then talks of the murders he committed in this previous world or life: "I can see the three that I killed with the cleaver — my father and the two older brothers — I did it that I might get something they had; I do not know what. They stood in my way. I murdered them. Now I am a naked Gorbus feeding on human bodies. Some of us think that thus we are punished." When Horst inquires about "cleavers," Durg explains that he had used a cleaver in his family murders and that he had murdered another man with a dagger. "He had on blue clothes with shiny buttons." Thus we see that in a previous life Durg had killed a policeman. In this peculiar section Burroughs is creating a kind of reincarnation, but one in which murderers go to this special Hell for punishment, becoming Gorbuses. All of them are murderers; Torp had killed seven women in his previous life.

Burroughs then extends the philosophy of "killing" beyond the murder of a person. An old woman had killed the happiness of people, a man and a woman who loved each other very much. She is now punished as a Gorbus. A man killed his wife's love; love is described as "more beautiful than life." Durg says, "I am glad that it was men that I killed and not happiness or love." Horst replies, "Perhaps you are right. There are far too many men in the world but not half enough happiness or love."

26. Letter of February 1, 1936.

27. Sent on April 17, 1936.

28. Letter of June 25, 1936.

29. In the letter of November 14, 1936, Byrne asked Rothmund to rush details of "the means and method by which Von Horst reached Pellucidar" and something about the background of the trip to the inner world. Byrne could not find this information; he explained his plan to write a brief prologue to introduce the new Pellucidar story and also noted he was calling it "Seven Worlds to Conquer." Byrne wrote, " 'Not a bad title,' says he, clapping himself on the shoulder." Burroughs' letter of the same date gave a paragraph of background information about Von Horst.

30. Ed's worksheet for "Tarzan the Magnificent" reveals that he had done research about diamonds. The Gonfal, the great diamond of the Kaji, is noted as 6,000 carats, worth 1,884,000 British pounds, or $9,420,000. An attached sheet lists weights and values of two other diamonds: "Cullinan Diamond: 3025 ¾ carats (1 ¾ lbs) Found 1905. Star of the South: 254½ carats Found 1853. When cut weighed 125 carats. Bought by Gaikwar of Baroda for 80,000 British pounds. Uncut equals 314 Brit. pounds per carat. At this rate the Cullinan would be worth 950,085½ Brit. pounds, or $4,750,427.50." He then followed with weight and value of the Gonfal, based upon the previous figures, and added, "The Great Emerald of the Zuli might have been worth twice this."

31. "Elmer," as noted on the worksheet, was written in Palm Springs and Tarzana. In an exchange of telegrams Ed tried to obtain $500 for the story, but Byrne refused to raise the price. On November 10, 1936, Ed finally agreed to the $250.

32. "The Resurrection of Jimber-Jaw" was published in 1964, Canaveral Press, as one story in *Tales of Three Planets*.

33. "Tarzan and the Elephant Men" was sent to Byrne on March 10, 1937.

34. Letter of October 1, 1937.

35. Letter to Byrne of September 2, 1937.

36. Letter of September 28, 1937.

37. On October 25, 1937, Ed noted that he hadn't expected *Argosy* to take the story "inasmuch as the time was so very short." On January 6, 1938, Byrne wrote to Rothmund to explain that Whipple was the new editor and that Byrne was managing editor "of all our titles since early last fall."

38. Letter of December 9, 1937.

39. On his worksheet, Burroughs notes, "Strip continuity: September 2, 1937, to September 30, 1937."

40. Letter of February 3, 1938, from *Liberty*.

41. Letter of September 29, 1938. The letter also contained the comment that the Mars novel "didn't hit us quite hard enough to overcome this excess of mss. in stock."

42. Letter of August 23, 1938.

Chapter 22: Burroughs-Tarzan Films

1. Letter of July 24, 1936, from Cohen to Dearholt and Stout.

2. Letter from Ashton, August 3, 1936.

3. Letter of July 21, 1936.

4. Review of August 22, 1936.

5. Photo and caption, January 9, 1937.

6. Letter of July 20, 1939.

7. Letter of July 21, 1939.

8. *Beyond Thirty* was sent to Marx on November 10, 1939; other synopses were sent on November 15 and 17.

9. Agreement of May 18, 1937.

10. The Citizens National Bank note was paid off on June 28, 1940. Goldburg's letter of May 27, 1950, refers to getting Mr. Burroughs "off the hook" on his endorsement of the $100,000 note of BTE, which note was secured by the negatives of the BTE pictures...." Goldburg, in a letter of February 19, 1938, to Jimmy Fidler at MGM, spoke of Fidler's project to produce a series of shorts dealing with motion picture celebrities of the past. Goldburg explained that he owned original negatives of eight single reel subjects directed by D. W. Griffith, with such stars as Lillian Gish, Mary Pickford, Jack Pickford, Blanche Sweet, Lionel Barrymore, and Harry Carey; these were produced "over twenty-five years ago." Goldburg wished to sell these.

11. Letter of April 8, 1939.

12. Goldburg's letter of May 27, 1950, from Goldburg to Rothmund. The letter dealt with protests by RKO and Sol Lesser over the exhibition of the old BTE-*Tarzan* films; they claimed that the BTE films "seriously interfered" with the income of their pictures. Goldburg called the claims ridiculous, noting that his films were more than ten years old, "without a box office name," and were exhibited only at rare intervals in neighborhood theaters for short runs. On October 4, 1950, Goldburg wrote again to Rothmund who had threatened legal action. Goldburg, irked, reminded Rothmund of how Burroughs was rescued when Goldburg "was called in to salvage the BTE films and liquidate the loan. In recalling the promises of Burroughs, Goldburg spoke of the corporation's tendency to forget: "That wasn't so in the year *1939* when the pictures were turned over to me after the bank's loan was liquidated. That was the year when Ed Burroughs wrote his acknowledgement of his obligation to me, *seven* years before your agreement with Sol Lesser."

A memo of December 30, 1959, from Mildred Jensen, Burroughs' secretary, to Rothmund, reported that Jesse Goldburg had died in September 1959. She tried to contact him about the film *Tundra*, for submission to Warner Brothers.

13. Two sample programs of "I See by the Papers" were recorded on one disc and Burroughs prepared a script to go with each. The script was preceded by a note to the announcer: "The two sample programs recorded on this disc contain

references to news that was current at the time they were written; when broadcast they will be brought up to date." The scene is set in the offices of the Tarzana Tribune owned by Herman Grooch. Other characters are Mabel, the stenographer, and Jimmy, the office boy. Burroughs himself is a character in the play; he has been employed by Grooch to write the daily column "I See by the Paper." Burroughs reads a letter from a reader who describes the new column as the "worst drivel" and also calls him a "tool of the capitalists." Another letter refers to the Tribune as a "Red sheet... that takes orders direct from Moscow." The remainder of the script involves jokes and comments about news items. The two scripts, about thirteen pages each, adopt a light, disparaging tone about the new column and Burroughs' writing. He does launch a serious attack on the shipping strike and the economic effects caused by it and, of course, attacks Harry Bridges.

To Carlin, on January 20, 1937, this time for a projected newspaper column, Ed sent three pages of sample items for "I See by the Paper." Some of these items were versions of the same ones used in the two recorded programs. Ed's daily "verse gem," his own composition, was about Aimee Semple McPherson and Wally Simpson:

Said Aimee to Wally,
"I'm off you, by golly;
Just believe me, I'm in a rage
Because all the mob'll
Forget my new squabble
Since you pushed me off the front page."

Other items included a "Society for the Prevention of Cellophane." Ed complained about the difficulty of opening cigarette and gum packets. In mentioning the birth and death of Francisco Goya, Ed referred to Goya's war etchings and noted there was no "romance" in war. "If you are thinking of starting a war, go first and look at Goya's etchings."

14. Letter of January 25, 1940.

15. The "Quiet, Please!" sample columns in the Burroughs files total nine separate ones, each consisting of typed sheets of four or five pages.

16. Kipling's reference to *Tarzan* and its author is quoted in Part 3, Chapter 2, p. .

17. Letter of October 29, 1946.

18. Letter of February 6, 1948. On June 21, 1949, in what was probably his last letter to Clemens, Ed wrote, "Naturally I am deeply honored by my nomination to honorary membership in the International Mark Twain Society."

19. Letter from Don McElwaine, publicity department, May 23, 1939.

20. The only remaining copy is dated September 18, 1939.

21. Letter of April 10, 1939.

22. Letter of February 2, 1937.

23. Ibid. Ed also wrote about King, "I was not the only boy at Orchard Lake who worshipped him — we all did. In every way he was our ideal cavalry officer; he was just and fair and a stern disciplinarian. He piled so much punishment on me that if it had not been remitted I'd have been walking it yet, but I knew that I deserved it. It is too bad that there are not more men who understand the psychology of boyhood as he must have."

24. Letter of February 20, 1940.

25. Ibid.

26. In this undated letter to his friend Lew Sweetser, George told of Edna's illness and her inevitable death to come. He explained that Edna's nurse, Mrs. Murray, was a splendid cook and that she insisted Sweetser come at once, since it would be little work to cook for an extra person. George noted to Lew, "Your board and keep would cost you nothing."

Chapter 23: War Correspondent

1. Taped interview with Caryl Lee (Cindy Cullen), November 2, 1968.

2. Taped interview, May 21, 1969.

3. Letter of June 14, 1940.

4. Ibid.

5. Letter to Bert Weston, June 27, 1940.

6. Letter of December 27, 1968, from Hal Thompson, sent from Malaga, Spain.

7. Letter to George Burroughs, July 10, 1940.

8. Ibid.

9. Letter of November 7, 1940.

10. Letter of November 17, 1940.

11. Ibid.

12. Taped interview, May 21, 1969.

13. Taped interview, November 27, 1968.

14. Letter of December 27, 1968.

15. Taped interview with Florence, May 21, 1969.

16. Ibid.

17. Letter of August 10, 1941.

18. Letter of September 3, 1941, to Rochelle Hudson.

19. Letter of May 6, 1941, to the *Star-Bulletin*.

20. Letter of August 10, 1941, to George.

21. Letter of October 20, 1941, to Rothmund.

22. Ibid.

23. Letter of December 24, 1941, from Hulbert to Rothmund.

24. Noted in his diary of December 17, after he had made phone calls to the editors of the publications.

25. Tape-recorded recollections of General Thomas H. Green, retired, now living in Moravia, New York. Green, after leaving Hawaii, became judge advocate general of the war department in Washington, was later promoted to lieutenant general, and in 1969 was a part-time instructor in law at the University of Arizona in Tucson.

26. Letter of February 4, 1969, from Adams who was in Honolulu.

27. The Burroughs Cipher plus unidentified coding charts are preserved in the Burroughs files.

28. Fielder, captain of the Georgia Tech team, was second-string all-American quarterback and twice all-Southern quarterback.

29. Quoted from General Fielder's letter of December 12, 1968, from Honolulu.

30. Ibid.

31. Interview with Bird at Tarzana offices, July 1968.

32. Letter from Adams, February 4, 1969.

33. Letter of December 29, 1968, from Fielder.

34. Letter of November 27, 1942.

35. Letter of December 27, 1968.

36. Details of Ed's entire Pacific assignment from December 4, 1942, to March 2, 1943, are contained in his sixty-page account, completed on June 8, 1943.

37. Ibid.

38. Ibid.

39. Letter of February 16, 1944, to Major H. J. Freeman, who had written Burroughs to explain that he also had an autograph book.

40. Letter of April 26, 1944, to Donald Jackson.

41. Letter of April 2, 1944, to Oscar Oldknow. Landon, also a

Californian, lived with his wife near Bel-Air.

42. Letter of May 3, 1944, to Bert Weston.

43. Letter of May 23, 1944, to Carlin.

44. Letter of July 11, 1944.

45. Letter of August 17, 1943.

46. Taped interview, November 2, 1968.

47. Letter of April 28, 1945, to Rothmund.

48. Letter of July 25, 1945.

Chapter 24: Venus-Mars-Pellucidar Series and Other Works

1. Letter of October 13, 1939.

2. Ibid.

3. Letter of September 21, 1939.

4. Letter of October 17, 1939.

5. Ibid.

6. Letters of January 4, 1939, to Kennicott and Byrne.

7. Letter of October 30, 1939.

8. Letter of November 17, 1939. The story was sent to Post on October 28. Rejections came from the *Saturday Evening Post*, September 6; *Liberty*, September 26; and *Collier's*, October 20.

9. Letter of November 17, 1939.

10. Rothmund noted in his letter of December 27, 1940, that he had just received the manuscript from Hawaii that day.

11. In the course of the story we learn that whatever love had existed between Jake Crode, Dick's father, and his wife June, who had married him against the wishes of her family, had quickly vanished; she feared him because of his drunkenness and brutality. The events that changed Dick's life began when his father, after savagely beating his mother, shot and killed the policeman who tried to arrest him. Later, Jake Crode was hanged. While June, critically injured, remained in the hospital for two months, Dick was placed in a juvenile home. He soon ran away and alone in the city turned to living by his wits. Recovering, June, with the aid of Dr. Benjamin Tavish, who had fallen in love with her, tries unsuccessfully to find her son.

Dick's apprenticeship in crime now commences; at the age of seven he works for Jeb Ward, a Faginlike beggar who fakes blindness. At street corners Ward plays on his harmonica while Dick dances, and afterward the little boy passes the hat among the spectators. Dick's most traumatic experiences with animals are to permanently affect him. Desperately in need of something to love, he acquires a kitten at the juvenile home, only to have it taken away from him. Later, his dog Bum, a mongrel who is his sole friend, is picked up by the dog catchers; Dick, in a frenzy of grief and rage, runs wildly after the wagon for blocks, screaming and hurling things at it. He takes a vow: "Everything I love gets it in the neck. Well, never again — I ain't goin' to love nothin' anymore."

As the ruthless head of the Syndicate, he now adopts the name of Dick Crouque; a man without pity, kindness, or any of the softer emotions, he holds control over his underlings through fear. Crouque's only interest — an obsession — is in music and dancing. But because of his childhood experiences with an alcoholic father, he had never touched liquor and has a deep contempt for those who drink. When, at a party for the Syndicate members, a pretty girl urges him to sip her drink, he stares at the glass, sees the indistinct images of a man, woman, and child, and the upraised hand of the man as he strikes the woman. This scene from the past — his father, Jake Crode, striking his mother — is burned in his memory. He curses and smashes the whiskey glass into the girl's face.

June Crode through the years had lived happily with her husband, Dr. Tavish, and Betty, his daughter by a previous marriage. By coincidence, Crouque, suave, well-dressed, un-
suspected as the Syndicate leader, meets Betty, and despite his vow, falls in love with her. She is impressed, finds him tempting, but really loves Don Vance, an FBI agent who is Crouque's most dangerous adversary. Curiously, when mother and son, June and Dick, meet after a separation of twenty-five years, they have only a troubled sense of familiarity; neither recognizes the other.

12. Some information about Burroughs' writing and dictaphone methods were obtained from Mrs. Mildred (Bernard) Jensen, his secretary.

13. Writing dates of the *Venus* series are as follows: "Captured on Venus," May 4 to July 20, 1940; "The Fire Goddess," September 16 to 24, 1940; "The Living Dead," October 15 to 22, 1940; "War on Venus," November 12 to 16, 1940.

14. Letter of May 6, 1964, from Hulbert Burroughs to Vernell Coriell.

15. The first section of the novel was retitled "The Ancient Dead." The payments were as follows: "John Carter and the Pits of Horz," $400; "The Black Pirates of Barsoom," $397.60; "Escape on Mars," $428.30; "Invisible Men of Mars," $429.78.

16. Reminders about Ah-gilek's New England dialect are noted on Burroughs' work sheet for "Savage Pellucidar." Here Burroughs lists: "Ah-gilak's expletives and colloquialisms: dodburn; tarnation; goldarn; Gad and Gabriel; two shakes of a dead lamb's tail; as the feller said; no more sense than a white pine dog with a poplar tail; didn't know him from Adam's off ox."

17. The novel, never published by Burroughs, appeared also in 1963 in Canaveral Press, hardcover, titled *Savage Pellucidar*. Burroughs had intended the novel to be called *Girl of Pellucidar*. In a note attached to the original manuscript Burroughs left instructions pertaining to a map he had drawn; this was to be used as a frontispiece when the four novelettes were published in book form. Two maps were referred to, both drawn by Burroughs, and he also included a jacket blurb he had written for the contemplated book. He enclosed a dedication page "To my first grandson James Michael Pierce."

18. Letter of November 4, 1940. Donaghho lived at 913 Alewa Drive, Honolulu.

19. Letter of November 7, 1940.

20. Letter of November 20, 1940.

21. The worksheets for "Beyond the Farthest Star," eleven pages in all, contain many details: the Unis population is 130 million, "about sixteen million adult women, bearing ten million children a year, over half of which are boys, of whom some five million grow to maturity." Ed also noted the plane production: "40 plants with ten assembly lines each, each line turning out one plane per hour for a ten hour day during 27 working days per month — 270 planes per month per assembly line; 2,700 per month per plant, 108,000 per month for 40 plants." Ed's reference to the Island of Despair, off the southern tip of Unis, indicates a possible plan to use this for adventures in a future story.

22. Letter of February 24, 1941.

23. Ibid.

24. It was published by Canaveral Press, in 1964, in a Burroughs collection, *Tales of Three Planets*. "Beyond the Farthest Star" is included.

25. *The Wizard of Venus* was not published until 1964, when it was included in *Tales of Three Planets*, Canaveral Press.

26. In the story the child Caligua conceives an instant attachment for Britannicus, wanting his "slave" near him at all times; on the first night, when the two are separated, Caligua's shrieks and screams continue until Britannicus is allowed to sleep near him, on a mattress placed at the foot of his cot. Agrippina, Caligua's mother, who detests Britannicus, has to accede to her son's wishes; on several occasions, after Britannicus has run away to avoid being put to death by Agrippina, he is saved and

restored to his position because of Little Boots' tantrums and demands that he be returned.

One scene has remained forever in Britannicus' memory, that of his father and mother, following in chains behind the chariot of the Emperor Germanicus: "Their chins were up, their bearing that of conquerors rather than the conquered. They looked neither to the right nor to the left. It was as though they walked among human scum that they would not lower themselves to look upon. They did not deign to glance at an emperor of Rome." He watched with tears in his eyes and notes later, "And so they passed on. I never saw them again. . . ." Britannicus' hatred of Rome is born in that moment but grows even more intense when he learns that his parents have been strangled and their bodies hurled into the Tiber: ". . . hatred of Rome and the Caesars surged through me — a great wave of bitterness that has never receded. . . . and alone, I then dedicated my life to one purpose — vengeance: someday I would kill a Caesar."

During the ten years that he and Caligua live in Rome, Britannicus follows the same studies as his master but becomes a far better student. At the library he has access to the works of Cicero, the poet Quintus Horatius Flaccus and the historian Titus Livius. He recalls, "I also read in the Greek, the works of the philosopher Aristotle, the poet Homer. . . the dramas of Aristophanes and Euripedes. . . but that which gave me the greatest pleasure of all was a study of the amazing works of Euclid, the great Greek geometrician."

27. Records show only one submission of the manuscript to Edwin Balmer at *Red Book*, February 2, 1942, by Rothmund. The novel was never sold and was published posthumously by the Burroughs corporation in 1967. A foreword lists works that "were consulted;" there are thirteen of these, used for research, and they include, *History of England*, by Trevelyan; *Caesar's Commentaries; Lives of the Twelve Caesars*, by S. Baring-Gould; and *Women of the Caesars*, by Gugliemo Ferrero.

28. With Peavy Peaberry as narrator, the first two characters, Aunt Ellie, who lives on a chicken ranch near Van Nuys, California, and her husband Uncle Miner, make their appearance. Aunt Ellie, "a little eccentric," flourishes a meat cleaver as she pursues Uncle Miner into town, but this in only a minor homicidal tendency; later she uses the same cleaver to dispose of her friends Birdie and Gwendolyn, the victors in a bridge game. She and Peavy bury the bodies in the backyard. The title of chapter one, "The Summer Resort," soon becomes clear when Peavy decides to visit Uncle Miner who is staying "over at Patton." After arriving at a large building — Peavy knows it is "a very exclusive place" because he has trouble getting in — he finds that Uncle Miner had a pleasant room: ". . . as a protection against burglars, there were iron bars at the window. It seemed to me that that was very thoughtful of the proprietor of the summer resort." Later Peavy makes an astonishing discovery: Uncle Miner is in an insane asylum.

Peavy, a cum laude Harvard graduate (Burroughs seizes the chance to deride college education), recalls his disappointment at not making the football team. In tryouts, at right tackle, he had bitten several of the opposing left tackles; and the coach removed him for taking the game too seriously. The next day Peavy reported for practice with a thirty-eight calibre automatic tucked under his jersey. Since the purpose of the game was "to carry the ball through the opposing team," he planned to do this in the simplest way: he would shoot all of the players that got in his way. He was excused from football practice until further notice. The coach announced, "When I want you, I'll send for you," but Peavy complained that in the four years he spent at Harvard, he was never sent for.

The portraits of Grandma and Grandpa Peaberry provide some detail about Grandpa's inventions. Grandma quits financing them when she finds he has invented a parachute that goes up instead of down. He has also devised a mousetrip that lets the mouse out after it was caught. An invention of this type,

Grandpa claims, "would stimulate the demand for mousetraps as it would insure an unending supply of mice." Grandpa's latest project is a door that cannot be opened. "It is going to effect a great saving in hinges and locks," he says. "Every theater in the United States will install them at all fire exits." Other Grandpa Peaberry inventions include a nonrefillable bottle, which is, in fact, two-in-one, and thus twice as efficient; he has simply melted and fused the necks of two bottles, making them air-tight. Concerning his invention of a glassless window, Grandpa notes, "It will be light and therefore easy to raise and lower. It will be far less expensive than a glazed window, and it will let the mosquitoes in where you can get at them to kill them."

With the depiction of Peavy's father, a painter, Burroughs turns to a subject which had previously been a source for ridicule, modern painting. Father has a high respect for Salvador Dali, mentioning especially the fur-lined bathtub the great artist had built. At a meeting the two men compare their work, and Dali concedes that he has no idea what any of Father's pictures represent. Because of this, Dali is deeply impressed, maintaining that Father has founded a new school of art and is years ahead of his contemporaries. The work of the best artists, according to Dali, is still in its infancy; unfortunately, objects on their canvasses can occasionally be recognized. But in Father's paintings "no one could identify anything but the frames." Dali suggests, "If you could just do away with the frames." Father speaks of Dali's cleverness in throwing his fur-lined bathtub through a show window in New York. Peavy, enthusiastic, agrees that Dali was clever — "Clever as a Peaberry!" For years Father has been cleaning his brushes on a piece of canvas. On a visit to Philadelphia, Father wires a request to have his painting "Catalina on A Clear Day" sent there as a contest entry. Instead, Fulgencia, the Filipino houseboy, who cannot tell one painting from another, ships the piece of canvas used for brush-cleaning; ". . . it created quite a sensation and took the Grand Prize."

Peavy, suddenly enamored of the idea of becoming an inventor, sits down to think and has an inspiration. He will invent the telephone first, follow with the electric light the next day, and after that will invent the milk bottle. With these projects completed, he calls a number of attorneys to inquire about getting patents; they offer no encouragement, but he finally finds a man named Zog who agrees to seek patents for Peavy's inventions. The charge is a thousand dollars, which Peavy pays in four monthly installments. At the end of that time, when Peavy goes to Zog's office, he finds the "attorney" is gone — and so is his furniture. A dark man with a turban sits at a desk gazing into a glass ball. He at once asks for two dollars, which Peavy pays, and then the man demands, "What do you want to know?" Peavy replies, "I want to know where Mr. Zog is." Staring into the glass ball, the seer says, "I see a tall, dark man riding over the desert on a Camel." Peavy comments, "Now, Mr. Zog is a short, red headed man; and people don't ride Camels, they smoke them; so I knew this man was a fraud. So I picked up his glass ball and hit him over the head with it and went home. I have decided not to be an inventor."

Another member of the eccentric Peaberry family, Aunt Minerva, after leasing an apartment for two years, begins playing phonograph records continuously, on full volume, from six in the morning until ten at night. When the landlord comes to protest and demands, "What in hell do you think you're doing?" Aunt Minerva replies, "I'm practicing on my orchestra." The tenants start to move out of the eighteen-apartment building, and in three months Aunt Minerva is the only occupant left. The landlord cannot make the payment on his mortgage and the bank forecloses on the property. However, even the bank is powerless to cope with Aunt Minerva, who still has a year and nine months to go on her lease. She continues "practicing on her orchestra."

Uncle Emerson, described by Grandma Peaberry as "a biological error," engages in a "pretty little romance" in meeting and courting Aunt Lena. At the time of the "romance" he is in the psychopathic ward of Bellevue Hospital in New York, and Aunt Lena is an out-patient. Lena's parents are wealthy, and after they have followed Uncle Emerson's suggestion and have made out wills leaving all their money to Lena, they die mysteriously of "ptomaine poisoning." Lena, nervous about events, prepares a will that leaves the money to her two children. When Emerson begins taking "a deep interest in the children's diet," she adds a clause to her will; it stipulates that in case her children do not survive her, the money will be used to "endow a home for old maids with two or more children." She expresses her implicit trust in Emerson, but admits he is "*so impulsive.*"

Peavy suffers his most frustrating experience in dealing with the draft board and the army. Upon being summoned by the draft board, he at once expounds his plan for "carrying on" the war: "... we should first take Greece, then invade Abyssinia, after which we should conquer England and then encircle Arizona." The Board listens to Peavy's plan, goes "into a huddle," and emerges to announce that he is classified "F4." He is advised to go home and wait for a call from them. Peavy's telegrams to the secretary of war and to President Roosevelt produce no result, so he decides to enlist; however, having an aversion to entering the army as a private, he proceeds to the Western Costume Company and rents a general's uniform. The salesman persuades him not to rent a sword, pistol, and rifle, claiming "it would lower the dignity of a general to carry anything."

At the recruiting office, where all the soldiers salute him, he meets a "very disagreeable-looking man" who is wearing "three bars and a little square" on the sleeve of his shirt. The man wants to know, "Why the scenery?" and Peavy explains, "... private soldiers are always the ones who do all the work and get killed, while a general never does any work and never gets killed. That is why I have decided to enlist as a general." The man at once calls police headquarters and says, "They's a nut here; come an' get him." (Peavy inspects the other people in the room, notes that none of them looks crazy, but feels that "you can't always tell ... just by looking." He wonders who it is.)

He is told to sit down and is assured that a "staff car" will call for him soon. "What war do you want to go to?" the man asks. Peavy reveals that he has "read a great deal about Gettysburg," and understands it is "very scenic." He thinks he will choose *that* war. He is informed that General Grant will be "tickled to death" to have him. When the police car arrives, Peavy is quite disappointed; instead of being taken to the "Gettysburg war," he is carried to the psychopathic ward of the General Hospital. The doctor says, "Why, hello Peavy! You're here again?" Peavy is annoyed by the "stupid" question, since anybody can see he is there. He has met many psychiatrists and is convinced they are all nuts; of course, that is the reason they are kept in insane asylums.

Peavy's cousin Wilfred combines the unusual qualities of a poet and a firebug. In writing poetry, he reverses the normal procedure, starting all his lines with small letters and ending them with capitals. He is also the first to insist that in reading poetry aloud, one should not pronounce the punctuation marks; a line of poetry is ruined when one says, "Comma, or semicolon or comma-dash" at the end.

Cousin Wilfred's prize-winning poem, "erysipelaS" (with his original style of capitals at the end of the lines), is quoted:
the moon is red the moon is red the moon is reD
my soul crawls on its belly my soul crawls on its bellY
the puppy has worms the puppy has worms the puppy has
  wormS
hortense the beautiful hortense the fair is down in the cellar
  shoveling coaL.

Wilfred's pyromania is launched when he first tries to set fire to the Empire State Building. He wastes ten boxes of matches, has no success, and complains to a policeman, "The damn fool who built this building must have used asbestos — it won't burn." Wilfred is put away in a place where he finds plenty of time to write poetry. Later, when he returns, he sets fire to Aunt Ellie's home, Grandpa Peaberry's beard, the Hollywood Hospital, and Peavy's house.

The strain of madness in the Peaberry family is quite clearly demonstrated in the behavior of Cousins Andrew Jackson and Percival. Andrew Jackson is rushed to the hospital after he insists he is a machine gun and swallows a box of .22 longs. While there, he keeps pounding his stomach as hard as he can, determined to make the cartridges go off. When nothing happens, he complains that something seems to have gone wrong with his mechanism. "I think a fifth columnist has been tampering with it," he says. "I think the doctor and a horse-faced nurse are Nazi spies."

Cousin Percival Peaberry's talent as an interior decorator has been evidenced in his early years when he drew pictures on walls and wrote things there. Peavy explains, "... they put him away in a sanitarium because of some illustrated verses with which he decorated the walls of the toilet of a young ladies' seminary. He had dressed up in girl's clothes to get into the seminary." After his release, Percival visits Peavy's home where he embarks at once upon a redecorating project. Looking at the living room, Percival screams, "I can't stand it!" and then tears down all the draperies, moves the furniture, and throws the rugs out the window. In the dining room he demolishes the table with a hammer, describing this process as "distressing"; when things look too nice they must be "distressed." "Everything in a home should look as though it were found in a junk yard," Percival explains. He smashes the mirror with a hammer and then examines it approvingly: "... that is better — now it is an antique."

Peavy, delighted over this "good clean fun," finds a hatchet and joins Percival, and they proceed to "distress" all the remaining furniture. Elated, Peavy says, "I never had any idea that being an interior decorator was so exciting." With nothing left to "distress," Peavy studies Percival and cries, "You look just too awfully new." Percival dives through the window, and Peavy, hatchet in hand, pursues him, calling, "... when I catch you, I am going to distress you." The police intervene, they are both thrown in jail, and later they are brought to Patton. Peavy, conceding he has a "nice room," nevertheless spends his days out in the yard with Napoleon, George Washington, and Jesus Christ. "It makes me feel that I am getting somewhere in the world socially," he confesses.

In the final chapter of "Uncle Miner and Other Relatives," titled "God Help America," Peavy reveals that a place has at last been found for his talents: "I did not work on my autobiography while I was in Patton. I had nothing to work with. There was nothing in my room but padding. I remained at Patton for two years. Then I came to Washington, where I now am. It is worse than Patton.

When I got to Washington, some one told me that we were at war. With Bulgaria, I think. I should be at the front directing things, but the President had other plans for me when he sent for me to come to Washington. He put me to work in OPA.

29. Letter of February 27, 1942.

30. The worksheet for the 22,000-word story lists various details: "Speed of Morgor interplanetary ship: 2,000,000 mi per day; 83,000 mi per hour; 1,383 mi per minute; 23 mi per second. Time of trip between Mars and Jupiter: About 18 earth days."

31. In the article Burroughs states that following the assumed defeat of Russia by the Nazis, the Soviet Government, in a negotiated peace, would cede all of its European territory to Hitler and retreat beyond the Urals. Thus, by 1942, Hitler

768

obtained vast areas of Russia, including her valuable mineral reserves, and was then ready for his next conquests.

America would soon face a crisis, and for this and the desperate events to come, Burroughs blamed the Isolationists and "America Firsters;" he had gone to some pains to produce (and invent) statistics:

In August 1941, more than 58% of the people had been ready to accept armed intervention; more than 76% had been ready to follow President Roosevelt's foreign policy even if it led to war. Following the publication of the Russo-German peace terms, only 24% were still willing to accept armed intervention, and less than 24% were still willing to back Roosevelt's foreign policy to the point of war.

Because of this change in public attitude, the Isolationists succeeded in having a new Neutrality Act passed, banning the shipment of all commodities to Great Britain and her allies.

Burroughs then summarized the disasters that followed. Hitler and Stalin formed a military alliance to crush England; the defeat of Russia was attributed to the perfidious British: "This Jewish-Capitalistic race of warmongers sought only the annihilation of Soviet Russia!" The combined Axis armies then annexed all of the Middle East and forced Turkey, Spain, and Vichy, France, to declare war on Great Britain. In North Africa the British forces were destroyed: "This was in the fall of 1944. America was terrified. Herbert Hoover, Alfred Landon, Burton Wheeler, John L. Lewis, Charles Lindbergh fed this terror. Some of them were sincere, if mistaken, patriots." Astonishingly, Burroughs pro-war attitude drove him to support the detested Roosevelt in his demands for aid to the Allies and to attack prominent Republicans whom he had long admired.

The November elections in America brought great victories for the America First Party; while the Democrats and Republicans together still maintained a majority in both houses, "the President and Vice President... were both rabid Isolationists..." Neutrality measures were at once enacted, with all convoying forbidden and an embargo placed upon the shipment of all arms to the Allies. The President withdrew American troops from Iceland, from Cuba and all of the West Indies islands, and from South and Central America. In the spring of 1945, helpless without American aid, the British Isles were invaded and conquered.

Burroughs next concocted fantastic events. The British fleet, refused permission to enter Canadian waters to refuel for a voyage to Australia, attacked and crushed the American Atlantic Fleet. The Japanese entered the war, seizing China, Hong Kong, Singapore, the Dutch East Indies, and then the undefended Philippines. A Russian ultimatum to the United States demanded the return of Alaska; the President tried to persuade Russia to buy the territory, but the Soviet "saw no reason for paying for something that belonged to her." America, fearful of offering any resistance, stood by while Russia occupied Alaska. The South and Central American governments, after making trade agreements and military pacts with the Nazis, invaded and seized Mexico. The isolationist president ordered the army and navy to withdraw from Hawaii. "It took several months, during which Japan could afford to wait patiently."

Conditions at home now became chaotic. Because of the isolationists, America had been cut off from trade with the rest of the world. Unemployment was high, food shortages occurred in the East, and riots followed. The midwest states were accused of hoarding, and the President threatened to send troops to force them to "disgorge" foodstuffs. Texas offered to help Kansas, Nebraska, and Iowa to repel this "invasion." Burroughs referred to prominent persons, in some cases unidentified, who came to a realization too late:

A man named Landon, disillusioned, bitter, flew from Washington to Kansas to urge resistance. In Palo Alto, California, an old man was awakening from years of lethargy to preach revolution.

Had he awakened too late? In Chicago, another old man, a man who had been a general in the army of the United States, committed suicide in his palatial home in Highland Park. In Washington, a man named Lewis gathered about him the politicians, the fifth columnists, the Communists, the Fascists, the Bundists, and the racketeers, hoping to make himself dictator. A democracy was tottering.

With Texas assuming the leadership, the governors of all the states west of the Mississippi and the top army and navy officers met at Austin and issued a manifesto announcing that these states had seceded from the union. "The new declaration of independence was signed by twenty-two governors, seventeen generals and thirty-one admirals." The new capital of the United States of Western America was established at Denver. The nation now completely disintegrated, with the fifth columnists, Communists, Fascists, and others "who had ruined the country," converging on Washington to take control. The starving people turned violent, breaking into stores, homes, and warehouses to seize food, and then, arming themselves, also marched on Washington.

Meanwhile, the external dangers grew critical. One Japanese fleet had sailed south to invade Australia, while another was enroute to the Hawaiian Islands. Canada, after "conversations" with the Axis Powers, massed troops at the strategic border points, in readiness to pour across. On the south the Axis forces were surging north through Mexico and would soon enter the United States. At the conclusion of "Fall of a Democracy" the final conquest was not described, but America's end was made inevitable:

From Canadian waters on our northwest, the still mighty British fleet gazed southward along the Atlantic coast. An Axis fleet rendezvoused in the Carribbean, looking toward the north. From the far north, the shadow of the Bear That Walks Like a Man fell athwart the Pacific Coast. From the west, Japan had crept closer.

A democracy was falling.

The America Firsters had triumphed!

32. The characters, almost all inmates or guards from two asylums, find shelter in a private home during a storm and their arrival launches a series of murders. On Burroughs' worksheet, where he has listed brief identifications, some typical examples of the murdered guards and inmates can be noted:

Smith — asylum guard & bus driver — killed by Bill, pg. 25. Shadrach Brown — Negro congenital idiot, killed by Shandy, pg. 40.

J. Wentworth Hollinsby — Paranoic with delusions of grandeur — killed by Bill, pg. 43.

Oscar Larsen — He likes to take things apart, but can never get them together again — killed by Shandy, pg. 45.

Kiru Komoto — Japanese homicidal maniac — killed by Bill, pg. 47.

Max Schmaltz — He thinks he is a Gestapo Agent — killed by Bill, pg. 47.

The zany quality of the story is illustrated by an unexpected inclusion of another "character," the thirteenth to be disposed of: "The Author — Killed by Shandy, pg. 62." Two columns at the bottom of the worksheet provide tallies of the murder victims, with Shandy's Score shown as seven, and Bill's, six. The Author (Burroughs) is the last in Shandy's column, but in a later version of the story, "Night of Terror" (1946), she fails to kill him and the contest ends in a tie.

Burroughs took care to draw a floor plan of the house where the murders occur; the X's he inserted to "mark the spot" indicate that six of the bodies were found in the living room, six in the back halls, and one in the trophy room. His 20,000-word story "More Fun! More People Killed!" remained unpublished.

33. In "Uncle Bill," Mary and her brother Bob, their parents dead, had come to live with Aunt Phoebe in 1919. Staying with

her in the "two story and attic clapboard house in the little New England town of Wesford, they became aware of the all-pervading presence of Uncle Bill, who had disappeared many years before. Following Lee's surrender in 1865, Uncle Bill, a captain on General Meade's staff, had obtained a leave of absence and returned home. Aunt Pheobe recalled how, at the end of his leave, she had driven him to the station, and Mary describes her Aunt's unfailing belief that Bill would come back: "That is what kept her young. I don't want your Uncle Bill to come back to an old woman, she used to say. For sixty-eight years a light burned every night and all night in the reception hall. . . so that if Uncle Bill should come back after dark he wouldn't have to grope his way about blindly."

Growing up in these surroundings, with Aunt Phoebe speaking of Bill constantly, Mary and Bob "just took it for granted that he might come home at any minute." But in telling the story, Mary describes the terrible change that had occurred "one day in 1934, ten years ago." With Aunt Phoebe away in Boston on business, Mary and Bob, then fifteen and sixteen, entered the attic, where they had never been before. Curious, Bob untied the rope around a large trunk, forced the lock, and flung the lid back. "In the trunk was the mummified corpse of a man, clad in the Civil War uniform of a captain. There was a round hole in the skull between the eyes — a bullet hole."

Aunt Phoebe, returning at that moment, stood at the foot of the stairs. When she asked in a strange voice, "What did you find?", Bob answered, "Uncle Bill." The next morning Aunt Phoebe was found dead, a half-empty box of sleeping tablets near her bed.

Despite some successful touches of realism, the story becomes merely a horror incident, the ending anticipated as soon as Bob and Mary discuss the attic. The viewpoint adopted by Burroughs, with Mary, the narrator, merely summarizing events, destroys the necessary suspense and of course weakens the characterization. Aunt Phoebe does not receive the individual development needed to explain her actions, and since the relationship between her and Uncle Bill is never established, the reader can conceive of no reason for the murder. Sent to the *Saturday Evening Post* and *Liberty* in August-September 1944, and to *Cosmopolitan* in November, "Uncle Bill" was rejected by all three.

34. With Tarzan in the African jungle are "three big bad apes," Ketchut, Killut, and Eetut, and the enemy turns out to be Buck Gordon, a white hunter. While Tarzan and his ape friends, smelling the white man, set off to find him, Gordon and three natives are stalking Wappi, the antelope. Wappi, personified, remarks, "Some guy with a gun is on my trail. I'll circle around behind him and see what he looks like."

When Gordon complains, "Ef we doan get meat purty soon we-all'll starve to death," the natives insist that they won't they have "smelled the blood of an Englishman" and plan to eat him. Buck hastily reveals he is an American from Chicago, and the dismayed natives announce that "if he's from Chicago, he's too tough to eat." The play develops a theme of animal protection, for when Gordon is about to shoot Wappi, Tarzan yells, bounds in, and kills Gordon. At the end Tarzan says, "Now I'm an Eagle Scout. I've done my good deed today."

"Tarzan's Good Deed Today" appears to be Burroughs' idea of a satire on a play for young people, almost as though he were having fun with members of his own Tarzan Clan. This is especially evident in the outrageous instructions that follow the play: "Tarzan should wear a leopard skin loin cloth. If the mother of any of you or of your friends has a leopard coat, a nice loin cloth can be cut from it. After the play, it can be sewn back in. If the lady has a sense of humor she will think it a great joke. A large, sharp butcher knife from the kitchen can be used as Tarzan's knife." About the apes' costumes, the young people are advised that "lovely large ears can be cut from a pair of your father's shoes or riding boots and fastened on with

adhesive tape." For the natives, who usually wear ornaments, the young peoples' mothers' jewelry should be appropriated: "Diamond bracelets and rings would sparkle beautifully behind the footlights."

The youth were also instructed to improvise makeup for the natives: all the corks in the medicine cabinet should be burned, and the resulting charcoal should be mixed with their mothers' cold cream and then spread on the face and "other exposed parts of the body." Ed suggested, "Any excess charcoal left on the hands may be wiped off on the living room curtains." To contrive horns for the antelope, the young dramatists should break "a couple of legs off a Ming horse." The tail could be made from a piece cut from an old ermine coat, but "if you can't find an old ermine coat in your mother's fur closet," Ed wrote, "or if her friends are too stingy to contribute one, a new ermine coat will do just as well."

35. The first poem, "Skunk in Defeat," composed on January 15, 1941, proceeds without restraint to describe how revolting the Nazis are:

The skunk came out and looked about and waved his gorgeous tail;
The people ran, each ev'ry man; the bravest there did quail.
The skunk would strut and wave his butt; a chesty skunk was he.
He looked around that well known ground to see what he might see;
Then from on high up in the sky there came a horrid stench;
The skunk did quail and lower his tail, and e'en his face did blench
He held his nose with little toes and ran away from there,
For who could hope to fairly cope the stink that filled the air?
He beat it then to hidden den to lay him down and die;
And what, you think, that awful stink? 'Twas a Nazi flying by!

Ed's ardent patriotism and his antiunion sentiments were revealed in the poem "A War-Job Striker To A Soldier." The worker's complaints about the long hours, and how tired he is at night are contrasted ironically with the soldier's fate. The worker grumbles:

I have to pay a lot of silly taxes
So guys like you can fight the bally Axis.
  You, soldier, only have to die.

In the four-stanza poem, the last line sounds a dirgelike refrain, with the soldier's death made inevitable:

I have to work for all the coin I get.
My gas and hootch are rationed, yet
  I do not ever grouse, not I.
If things aren't run exactly as I like,
Believe me, brother, I can always strike.
  You, soldier, only have to die.

Hard as my lot, my friend, I feel, alas, .
That you are just a . . .silly ass
  Who must have let his chance pass by
To get a cushy job with lots of jack
Instead of one from which you won't come back;
  For, soldier, you are going to die.

But if, perchance, you should survive the strife
And come back to your kiddies and your wife,
  I promise you that I will try
To force you in the union that I'll run;
And then your one regret will be, my son,
  That in the fray you did not die.

Chapter 25: Last Years with the Family

1. Letter of November 29, 1945.
2. Letter of December 9, 1945, to Donald Jackson.
3. Letter of April 4, 1946, to Phil Bird.

4. Letter of May 30, 1946.

5. Letter of May 30, 1946, to Louise Rogers.

6. Letter of May 1, 1946.

7. Letter of December 27, 1946, to Louise Rogers.

8. Letter of August 22, 1945, to Lesser.

9. Ibid.

10. Letter of August 27, 1945.

11. Ibid.

12. Ed turned to foreign villains, Igor Gromovitch and Fritz Blomberg, for this story. He repeated his device of introducing Negro characters for comic effect and included two blacks with the names of Woodrow Wilson Jones and Franklin D. Roosevelt Brown.

The story, a patchwork of the many typical incidents and characters, opens with Tarzan, after five years in the R.A.F., returning to his native jungle. He at once assumes his role of protector and rescuer of helpless individuals who cannot cope with the natural jungle hazards or with the nefarious schemes of Gromovitch and Blomberg. Tarzan's wards have a decidedly familiar ring about them. Eugene Hanson, Ph.D., an archaeologist, had been a navigator on a heavy bomber during the war, and in the course of a flight had spotted the ruins of an ancient city. With the war ended, Hanson proposes to investigate these ruins. His daughter Jean, a beautiful blonde, accompanies him, and the two are to meet other members of the scientific expedition in a rendezvous at the ruins. Another character needing Tarzan's protection is Rex Hunt, a young American big game hunter, whose guide, Hi Small, quickly reveals himself as an unscrupulous scoundrel, eager to join the villains in any dishonest venture.

Gromovitch and Blomberg, described on Burroughs' worksheet in the phrases "smaller heavy" and "larger heavy," are as typically and familiarly evil as they can get. They treat their native carriers brutally, lashing and beating them; call blacks "niggers" — Gromovitch's sneering remark, "I ain't afraid of a bunch of niggers," is marked "cut" on the manuscript — and seize the food and ammunition of the Hansons, leaving them to face death in the jungle. The villainy of Gromovitch is apparently compounded by his communist beliefs; he protests about the "damned bourgeois" and "too much fraternization with the bourgeois prisoners," while Blomberg, a fellow traveler, uses the term "comrades."

The two Negroes, whose identifications on the worksheet are "larger black heavy" and "smaller black heavy," have at first joined Gromovitch and Blomberg in their evil plans. Deserters from a U.S. transport, the two black men had jumped ship at Tunis. To avoid possible arrest, they had assumed new names, acquiring the ones they now possessed, by a simple procedure — "rolling de bones." Jones and Brown soon redeem themselves, springing to the defense of Jean when Gromovitch attempts to manhandle her. Jones announces, "Her and me both Americans and nobody ain't goin' to beat her up while Ah'm aroun'." He later says, "We Americans must stick together."

Burroughs duplicates ideas from other works. Future events are predictable; for instance, there is reference to "a golden hoard in the fabulous ruins of Ur." Native cannibals appear in the persons of the Mburis. Jad-bal-ja, the golden lion, makes almost as many rescues as Tarzan. The incidents, completely unplotted, consist of a drab sequence of individuals facing jungle perils or capture by the villains; Tarzan descends from the tree-tops whenever the danger becomes really acute. At the end of the 4400-word story section, Nyama, the native girl who has escaped with Jean, indicates, in her statement, that there is nothing new coming up. She and Jean have been separated: "I have not seen her since, and have no idea where she may be."

13. Letter of August 7, 1946.

14. Ibid.

15. Letter of November 5, 1946.

16. Letter of December 5, 1946.

17. Letter of January 3, 1947.

18. Letter of February 17, 1949.

19. Caryl's first name became "Cindy," and, following her marriage, she used the last name of "Cullen." She was later divorced.

20. Letter of June 16, 1947.

21. Ibid.

22. Letter of September 6, 1947.

23. Rutman's words were quoted in a memo of May 10, 1949, from Rothmund to Burroughs.

24. Thompson was a resident of Van Nuys, California, with his address shown at 6449 Peach Avenue.

25. In the story, after Shandy Mason and Bill Loveridge, seeking refuge in a storm, enter an old house, they are joined by a group of guards and inmates from the insane asylum at Millridge. Because of a fire at the asylum, the inmates were being transported to a new location, but when the bus broke down, they also were brought to the house for shelter. The action that follows is nothing more than one murder after another, until all ten of the guards and inmates are killed. It then becomes apparent that the murderers are Shandy and Bill, themselves escapees from an asylum for the criminally insane, who have actually devised a gruesome contest to see who can kill the most people. At the end, in a strange viewpoint shift, the author Burroughs, as a visitor to the same house, enters the story in a first-person narration scene and escapes being murdered only because Shandy's gun falls on an empty chamber. (In the original "More Fun! More People Killed!" the story's bloody finish shows the author as Shandy's last victim. Mortally wounded by Bill, whom she has killed in a shoot-out, she still manages to murder Burroughs in her dying gasp and emerge the victor in the contest, the score (with both participants counted) being seven to six.

26. Letter of August 4, 1947.

27. Letter of August 7, 1947.

28. Letter of November 14, 1947.

29. Letter of January 5, 1948.

30. Burroughs' political attitudes and actions were recalled by Marion Burroughs, wife of Hulbert, in a taped interview, September 9, 1968.

31. Letter of February 1, 1949.

32. Letter of February 17, 1949.

33. Letter of April 26, 1949.

34. Letter of May 6, 1949.

35. Taped interview with Marie Burroughs, Studley's widow, who noted her belief that the operation had resulted from a faulty diagnosis.

36. Letter of January 10, 1950, to an unidentified friend.

APPENDIXES

1. Major George and Mary Evaline

To those who come after — a long time after — this volume will tend to make George and Mary Burroughs more than merely a rather vague conception of two names. It will bring you in whose veins flows the red blood of the Puritan and the Pioneer, bequeathed to you, uncontaminated, by these two, a livlier [sic] sense of reality of these ancestors of yours. It will depict them as living, breathing people, who lived and loved as you, let us hope, shall live and love, through fifty years of prosperity and adversity; a personification of what might justly be emblazoned upon the arms of the Burroughs — Loyalty and Constancy.

The pride of the Burroughs family in its ancestry and blood inheritance is evident in this second paragraph from a foreword to a small "volume" titled "Memoirs of a War Bride." The foreword, headed "To Posterity," was written by Edgar Rice Burroughs in 1914, the same year he had arranged for the printing of his mother's reminiscences. Mary Evaline, who had dedicated the "Memoirs" to the memory of her husband, who had died only a year before, described her marriage to George Tyler Burroughs and the events that followed when she joined him at the war front (for further information, see Appendix 2: Genealogy, pp. 780–86).

The Burroughs family had long been aware of their descent and, as Edgar Rice Burroughs had expressed it, "the red blood of the Puritan and the Pioneer" that flowed in their veins. His emphasis on what had been "bequeathed" to the family, and especially his use of the word "uncontaminated," implies a disdain for the more "common" blood. The attitude revealed in this stuffy language — the ancestral pride — was not at all unusual for the early 1900s. But time inevitably modifies attitudes, and Edgar Rice Burroughs, changing, and aided by a natural inclination to deflate matters pompous, was able to view the subject of genealogy with amusement.

From the early stress upon ancestry had come an interest in formal genealogy, illustrated by the outline contained in the back of Mary Evaline's "Memoirs" that traced her descent from seventeenth-century England down to nineteenth-century America when the two lines, Zieger and Burroughs, were united in marriage. A chronology of the Burroughs family's descent from the distinguished Rice family of England is also recorded. The ancestral pride was reinforced by an intense patriotism about the military achievements of the men during the Revolutionary War and with the Continental Army in the years that followed. The Coleman branch, on Mary Evaline's side, had been active in the Continental Army and in various Virginia regiments. Ed Burroughs was impressed by the military exploits of his ancestors, and he was proud of his father's record as a major in the Union Army during the Civil War. This military heritage influenced his thinking most of his life. On his own copy of the "Military Record of the Coleman family during the War of the Revolution," dated September 13, 1900, when he was twenty-five, he proclaimed, "This Record Belongs to E. R. Burroughs."

In the 1920s, apparently determined to clarify certain elements of the Burroughs line, Edgar initiated research. This revealed that the Rice branch had its origin in Deacon Edmund Rice, a Pilgrim from Buckinghamshire, England, who settled in Sudbury, Massachusetts, in 1638. Through the marriage of Abner Tyler Burroughs and Mary Rice in 1827, the two families were then joined. The activities of Ella Oldham Burroughs, the wife of Edgar's favorite brother Harry, may have stimulated this new interest in genealogy. For various reasons, including a desire to be accepted for membership in the Daughters of the American Revolution, Ella traced her ancestry and proved she was descended from Colonel John Washington, George Washington's grandfather, through Elizabeth, George's aunt and the colonel's third child.

There are indications that Ella's success created a kind of friendly rivalry between Ed and her in establishing genealogies linked to famous ancestors. Ed's continuing research led to the discovery of three related pedigrees of the Rice family of England. The first was traced back to Coel Codevog, King of the Britons; the second, to William the Conqueror of England; and the third, to the Saxon Prince Egbert and Alfred the Great. With these discoveries Ed began to treat the entire genealogical situation humorously. In fact, the subject of ancestry and pedigrees became a family joke. The competition to determine whether the Oldhams or the Burroughses could trace their lines farther into the distant past brought a letter from brother Harry that boasted of his wife's ancestry traveling back "through a long line of Kings of Denmark to one who flourished in the year 80 B.C." Concerning William the Conqueror's line, from which the Burroughs family was supposedly descended, Harry challenged, ". . . can't you trace William's back to some date prior to 80 B.C. I don't ask much. Nothing unreasonable. Would be contented with 79 B.C."[1]

Edgar's later attitude about his family descent is best illustrated by his letter to David E. Burress of Pendleton, South Carolina:

None of my Burroughs ancestors seemed to have set the world on fire, and I think my father was the only one who ever made a great deal of money.

The only one I have ever been able to brag about was Steven Burroughs, but I am not descended directly from him. He is reputed to have been the greatest forger and jail breaker in the Colonies. He even had a book written about him, which I saw in the Chicago Public Library.[2]

Concerning John Burroughs, "who seemed to have strayed off into Connecticut and died there in 1756," Ed admitted that he could neither read nor write and that he signed his will with an X. John, "a generous soul," Edgar commented, bequeathed to Sarah, his well-beloved wife, "two cows to dispose of as she thinks best." In one of his typical jokes Edgar added, "I may not be descended from John, but I mention him as possible proof of the power of heredity. Many critics say that I can't write either."[3]

Thus, the early seriousness about ancestry and much of the pride of family descent had been dissipated by the casual and democratizing influences of later years.

The marriage between George Tyler Burroughs and Mary Evaline Zieger, originally planned for the autumn of 1861, had been delayed because of the outbreak of the war. With the firing on Fort Sumter in Charleston Harbor and President Lincoln's proclamation calling for 75,000 volunteers, George, then employed by a New York importing firm, had gone to the nearest armory and had enlisted at once. The fact that he had reduced vision in one eye, from which he could see only light and shadow, did not deter his joining the army. The handicap had resulted from an accidental injury when his sister Caroline Studley had thrown an object which had struck him in the eye. Assigned to Company G, 71st New York State Militia, he had taken part in the Battle of Bull Run, and after the disastrous rout of the Union forces, he had returned to his position in New York. There he waited impatiently for a commission that finally arrived, and in December 1861 George was made acting regimental

quartermaster of the New York 43rd Regiment.

In 1863, George, now a captain, was determined to wed Mary Evaline; he obtained a leave to join her in Iowa, and on February 23 their marriage took place in Iowa City. "He arrived on a Wednesday," she wrote in her "Memoirs." "We were married on the following Monday, at 12 o'clock, and after a wedding breakfast left at once for Washington." She joined her husband at the war front and for various periods remained near him or at Washington. On June 22, 1865, George received his discharge from the Union Army with the title of brevet major, and, soon after, he and Mary made their home in Portland, Maine. In the autumn of 1868 they came to Chicago, a city that Mary noted, ". . . was ever afterward our home."

Concerning his father, George Tyler Burroughs, and the city of Chicago, which was to provide the setting for all youthful memories, Edgar wrote:

My father was born in a house in Massachusetts that was built in 1741. His father owned it. My father never owned a house of his own. He lived for forty years in the same rented house in Chicago, although he was a wealthy man and could easily have afforded to own a home.

I was born in that rented house . . .[4]

As though convinced that their roving days were over, George and Mary Burroughs seemed content to allow the big city to swallow them. The house that George rented in 1868 was on Chicago's west side, first numbered 650 Washington Boulevard, later changed to 646. If renting creates an impression of transience, this was certainly disproved in the years that followed. The Burroughs family and Chicago seemed inseparable.

The marriage of George and Mary had a singularly one-sided result: they could produce only boys. Of the total of eight, two were stillborn and two, Arthur McCulloch and Charles Stuart, died in infancy.[5] The remaining four were George Tyler, Jr.; Henry (Harry) Studley; Frank Coleman; and Edgar Rice. In a sad recollection of a lost brother, Edgar wrote, "The earliest event in my life that I can recall clearly is the sudden death of an infant brother in my mother's arms. I do not recall exactly when this occurred, but I think it was in my second or third year. . . ."[6]

The youngest of the four, born in Chicago on September 1, 1875, Ed was called "Eddie" by his brothers and later "Ed," the name he preferred.[7] Two of his brothers were born in Portland, Maine, George Tyler, Jr., the oldest, on August 31, 1866, and Henry Studley on May 23, 1868. Frank Coleman was born in Chicago on May 14, 1872. The selection of the boys' middle names continued a tradition of choosing from British ancestors on both sides of the family. But the exact method used for apportioning the names of Tyler, Coleman, McCulloch, and Studley to the boys is not clear, and no particular reason can be discovered for reserving the celebrated Rice name for Ed.

Before settling down in Chicago, George and Mary had briefly tried their fortunes in Portland, Maine, where George went into business, in 1866, with two partners, John B. Hudson and H. B. Masters. The business cards, indicating that George was head of the company, read:

George T. Burroughs & Co., *Plain and Ornamental Furniture, Feather Beds, Mattresses & c., Lancaster Hall, Portland, Me.*[8]

With his arrival in Chicago two years later, George had sufficient capital to launch a new type of business. A stock company was formed and the Phoenix Distillery went into operation. Shares were divided equally among four men: Jonathan Abel, president; George T. Burroughs, vice-president; Ben W. Kendall, secretary; and Wilson Ames, treasurer. The venture, remarkably successful, established George as a prosperous businessman, and the Burroughs family was welcomed into the activities of the upper class society in Chicago of the 1870s and 1880s.

Abner Tyler Burroughs, George's father, who, since his birth in 1805 had lived at the family home in Warren, Massachusetts, and had occupied himself with farming, in 1868 decided also to locate in Chicago.[9] A man of sixty-three might normally have been considered in his declining years, but Abner proceeded to demonstrate that he possessed the durability and longevity of his ancestors. A newspaper story in April 1896 was headed, "Abner Tyler Burroughs, Oldest Voter in Chicago," and beneath a sketched portrait of Abner, his adamant political opinions were quoted:

The Ninth Precinct of the Twenty-Fourth Ward claims the oldest voter in Chicago in the veteran Republican, A. T. Burroughs, No. 294 East Erie street, who will celebrate his ninety-first birthday on May 26.

"Father" Burroughs turned out to vote yesterday, walking half a block to the polling-place. It was the first time he had been out of doors since the last November election.

As the veteran entered the polling place men removed their hats, expressed gratification at his coming, and gave him cordial greetings.

"I shall be 91 years old next month," said Mr. Burroughs, "and I have never lost but one vote since I became 21. That was at the time of Carter Harrison's last race, when I was sick abed."

Although bent with his years, Mr. Burroughs went about his task with alacrity. Assistance was offered him upon entering the booth, but he said he "could do his own voting, thank you."

"A sermon in patriotism," said a bystander.

Mr. Burroughs came out of the booth so quickly it caused fresh comment.

"Did you have much trouble scratching candidates?" asked an old acquaintance.

"Since there has been a Republican party," Mr. Burroughs replied, "I have never voted any other ticket, and before that party was born, as an old-time Whig, I voted for straight Republican principles."

Mr. Burroughs is a native of Worcester County, Mass. He has dwelt in Chicago twenty odd years. He is now living with his children, Mr. and Mrs. Charles S. McEntee, and it is one of his regrets this son-in-law is a Jeffersonian Democrat, whom two decades of missionary effort have failed to regenerate.[10]

With three generations of the Burroughs family settled in Chicago — grandfather, father, and four sons — the family adapted itself to the big city's climate — its stifling, humid summers and erratic winters which often produced violent storms and blizzards. At these times there might be snow piled three feet high or, when the thermometer fell to ten below, the streets would be surfaced with ice, and the miserable pedestrians would slide and teeter while a raging wind off Lake Michigan hurled blasts at them like explosions.

The Burroughs family, of course, was immersed in Chicago's daily happenings, its ordinary activities, its exciting events and catastrophes. During the terrible days of the eighth through the tenth of October in 1871, when fierce yellow flames lit the sky and huge clouds of black smoke settled over the city, George and Mary and two of the children climbed to the roof of their Washington Boulevard home to watch the fire consuming the city to the east of them.[11] By the time the great Chicago fire ended, about one-third of the city with an estimated 18,000 buildings was destroyed.

George, a vigorous, active man, was not one to limit himself to his responsibilities at the Phoenix Distillery. It was natural for him, part of a family tradition, to become involved in political, civic, and social affairs. Through the 1870s and 1880s he took part in important functions of all types. An invitation of November 8, 1879, impressively worded, requests the presence of Major George T. Burroughs and "Ladies" to "assist in a reception given to General and Mrs. U. S. Grant, by the Society of the Army of the Tennessee, at the Palmer House, Thursday Nov. 13th." The Committee on Reception, a group of officers, was headed by General P. H. Sheridan.[12]

Typical examples of George's political activities include his appointment as United States Supervisor of Registry and Election in 1880 and his selection as a delegate to the Republican Convention in the same year. In 1887 the records show him officiating as vice-president of the citizens' and businessmen's Republican Ratification Meeting of April 2, and in 1888 he attended the Republican National Convention in Chicago.

In these busy and prosperous days George was also the somewhat autocratic ruler of a household that occupied the large three-story brick home on Washington Boulevard. He was well able to indulge his wife and four sons in all the upper-class comforts. There were two maids to attend to the domestic tasks, and the family had the use of a carriage and "pair" with a coachman — "all very beautifully turned out."[13] The home, to George as its patriarchal head, was a place not only for raising four boys, but for keeping the family closely united. It would become a place for reunions. Sons might grow up and leave, but they would gather again in the old home; some of their children would be born there and also return to live there.[14]

Major George left no doubt, of course, as to who would give the orders and make the decisions in the family. But while he was described as "a very strong and dominant figure in the family," it was also recalled that on occasion, if Mary Evaline thought he was going too far, "just a quiet word from her to the effect of 'That's enough, George,'" ended the matter at once.[15] Toward his sons he was strict, prescribing firm standards of discipline, and they, although not without affection for him, responded with respect and even some fear. With the years he mellowed, losing some of his sternness and inflexibility, and his sons, themselves growing up and acquiring more understanding, developed a deeper affection for him.[16]

George, the prototype of the self-made businessman who had achieved success through hard work, determination, and the willingness to take risks, was proud of his success, his place in life, and his ample income. As a prosperous merchant, respected in business and society circles, he wanted his sons to have all the advantages of his position and income. While attending Yale, Harry and George, Jr., were granted an allowance of $150 a month, plus tuition and other expenses. Upon graduation, they would be provided with money for whatever business or career they chose.

The distillery remained a profitable operation for many years. Other Chicago distillers ran into financial difficulties and went bankrupt. A scandal resulted, and prosecutions were launched by the federal government for evasion of the internal revenue laws. Some distillers were fined and imprisoned and their property confiscated. On February 17, 1880, the *Chicago Tribune* reported the aftermath of the government's actions:

The Chicago distillers accused of "irregularities" in their dealings with the United States Government are endeavoring to compromise the claims against them. It is well understood hereabouts that these distillers are insolvent, and most of them have obtained their discharges in bankruptcy from all their indebtedness except to the United States.[17]

The article went on to offer a plea for the distillers and to urge a government compromise so that the companies might accept their losses and resume operations. There appears to be no evidence that the Burroughs distillery was involved in the government prosecutions. But on August 3, 1885, the Burroughs company met a far more serious misfortune. The *Chicago Tribune* headline blared: "The Phoenix Fire a Loss of One Hundred Thousand Dollars with an Insurance of Thirty-five."

The huge fire was described as a disaster:

The fire at the Phoenix Distillery yesterday morning left nothing but the warehouse and the wine-room standing. These structures were saved through the well-directed efforts of the fire department, and thus a very great additional loss to the firm and to the insurance company was averted. The distillery, including the fine machinery and roller mill, was completely destroyed, nothing of the building being left.

It was noted that the firm had recently spent over $25,000 in new improvements and had "made the distillery probably the most complete in the United States." The company was estimated to have made as high as $80,000 a year in profits.

The *Tribune* gave further details:

The cattle sheds were also completely destroyed, and the total loss will not fall far short of $100,000, upon which the insurance is but $35,000. The firm carried $40,000 insurance up to a short time ago, but allowed $5,000 to lapse within a short time, owing to the high rate charged by the companies on the risk.

During an interview George Burroughs was reported as viewing the situation philosophically and even humorously, remarking:

"I am out of the whisky business for the present. The loss is a heavy one, but we can stand it, and we shall go right on and rebuild. We did a very profitable and large business, which, of course, must be somewhat interrupted. If we get out with a loss of from $50,000 to $60,000 I shall feel satisfied. I have been out of town, and only came in yesterday, and I suppose that the show was got up for my benefit. But the exhibition was expensive, to say the least. I don't know the origin of the fire, and I don't think anybody else does. . . ."[18]

Whether the Phoenix Distillery was completely rebuilt is uncertain, but within a few years George turned to a new business, the American Battery Company, manufacturers of storage batteries used principally for train lighting and signaling.[19] But his fortunes were on the decline and his income would never again equal the amount he earned from the distillery.

As a respected former army officer and prominent businessman George became involved in numerous public and civic matters. On July 2, 1881, the country was shocked when President James A. Garfield was shot and critically wounded. He clung to life for two months, dying on September 19, 1881. The assassin, Charles J. Guiteau, was a disappointed officeseeker and a "Stalwart," a supporter of Chester A. Arthur, the vice-president. Guiteau's purpose was to make Arthur the president. During the trial George was summoned to Washington to testify, as an "expert" for the defendant. He appeared at the trial sessions of November 14 and 28.[20]

On May Day, 1886, Chicago, the center of labor agitation, became the focus of nationwide attention. The Knights of Labor, an organization of 700,000 members, had planned May Day demonstrations in all the major cities. In Chicago, May Day was celebrated without any serious disturbance, but a crisis arose when the police killed four people outside the McCormick reaper plant two days later. On the following night, when a protest meeting was held in Haymarket Square, someone hurled a bomb at the police. Seven persons were killed and others were injured. Eight "anarchists" were seized and charged with inciting the crime.

George and Mary Evaline followed the long trial with interest.[21] It extended over sixty-two days, from June 21 to August 20. All of the anarchists were found guilty: four were hanged, one (Louis Lingg) committed suicide, and the remaining three were sentenced to prison for life. The records indicate that George attended sessions of the trial.[22] Later, a special permit card issued by C. R. Watson, Sheriff, read:

Admit
Geo. T. Burroughs
    Anarchists
To Witness Execution at Cook County Jail,
    10 A.M. November 11th, 1887.[23]

In the passing years George continued active both in the American Battery Company and in his civic duties.[24] In a news story of May 17, 1888, George's unusual actions in connection with James M. Johnson, a Negro, are described. Johnson served in the Confederate Army, was discharged because of sickness, and was sent to Richmond to recuperate. There George Burroughs, then a major and quartermaster, took an interest in him and decided to help him. In May 1865 Johnson was brought to the Burroughs home in Warren, Massachusetts, and "was made practically one of the family." He was "given the privilege of education, and his efforts to improve his mind received the most generous and hearty encouragement."[25]

Johnson went to work for Charles McEntee, a brother-in-law of George Burroughs, first in Albany, New York, and then in Chicago, where McEntee founded a chain of shoe stores. The industrious Johnson had been saving his money, and when business turned bad and the stores were being closed down, he stepped in to buy the last two. The news story commented that "both these stores are models in their arrangements and do a large and prosperous business."[26]

The Burroughses' long record of support of the Republican Party, of a fierce, unwavering faith in Republican principles, was abruptly broken in the McKinley-Bryan campaign of 1896. The overriding issue was the maintenance of a gold standard as opposed to the free coinage of silver. McKinley, the Republican "gold" candidate, was bitterly attacked in Bryan's speeches in which the battle lines were clearly drawn between the "struggling masses" and the "idle hoarders of idle capital." Picturing the workers as victims of a destructive gold system, Bryan used his familiar, impassioned oratory to cry out that the laboring man could be saved only through the coinage of silver. His emotional indictment of the Republicans and McKinley, in which he created his "cross of gold" metaphor, aroused a national furor: "You shall not press down upon the brow of labor this crown of thorns, you shall not crucify mankind upon a cross of gold."

Bryan's fervor and his display of support for the workingman, plus the Burroughs family's intense dislike of the Republican boss Mark Hanna, led to their surprising switch to the Democratic Party. The decision was prominently featured in the news:

Wants a Change
George T. Burroughs, Business Man, Tires of Hanna & Co.

Among the many who are flocking to the standard of William Jennings Bryan from the republican party are George T. Burroughs and his son Harry S. Burroughs.

Mr. Burroughs is a distiller who needs no introduction to the business world. He is a representative Chicagoan, who, since he attained his majority, has always voted the republican ticket. Seeing in this campaign the principles of the party of Lincoln sold to Hanna for McKinley votes, he decided to vote with the people. Accordingly on election day he, accompanied by his son, will go to the polls and vote for Bryan and free silver.[27]

With the nineteenth century drawing to a close, George was still involved with the management of the distillery but had concentrated much of his efforts in his American Battery Company. For publicity purposes George arranged a demonstration of his batteries at the World's Columbian Exposition of 1893 in

Chicago. The award presented by the judges referred in glowing terms to George's product as "the only storage battery made in this country deemed worthy of any notice whatever."[28] Although George's business acumen and imagination appeared as strong as ever, the superprosperous days were at an end. A period of financial caution, of adjusting to new realities, loomed ahead.

Notes

1. Quotes from Edgar's letter of February 12, 1921, in which he restates Harry's challenge.

2. Letter of April 25, 1945.

3. Ibid.

4. Mary Evaline's pencil entry at the beginning of her scrapbook reports: "The house on the old family homestead of the Burroughs family was built in 1741. It was the second house built in Warren, Mass. Mr. Danforth Keyes being built a year earlier."

The quoted passage in the text was written by ERB in response to a request of the publishers of *Perfect Home* magazine in 1942, when ERB was in Honolulu. In a letter to his secretary Ralph Rothmund, ERB wrote, "Attached is copy for French Stamats Co's *Perfect Home* magazine. Read it over. If you don't like it, can it; if you do, ask Mildred [Jensen] to make a clean copy and send it in. I might remark, in passing, that that is a hell of a subject to ask a guy who ain't got no home to enthuse about." ERB's father had lived and raised his family in a home rented from W. H. Gardner, a man with whom ERB had dealings later.

In turning the article down, French-Stamats wrote, "Frankly, we don't think this article does Mr. Burroughs justice and we dislike very much to have it represent him. His writings are customarily so vivid and moving and individual. . . ."

5. While there is no printed record of the two stillborn children, Mrs. Carlton (Evelyn) D. McKenzie, Harry Burroughs' daughter, has supplied this information and believes it is accurate.

6. From a letter written to Mrs. Ruth Wood Thompson of New York, on January 31, 1935, who had inquired about early recollections for her booklet "First Memories."

7. A birth certificate, issued by Robert M. Sweitzer, County Clerk of Cook County, Illinois, establishes the birthplace as 650 W. Washington St., in Ward 13, and lists the father's occupation as "distiller" and the attending physician as Dr. E. Dyson. A copy of this certificate, obtained later, was dated December 19, 1927.

8. The business card is preserved in Mary Evaline's scrapbook.

9. Abner Tyler Burroughs' disposal of his farm and all possessions in Warren, Massachusetts, is revealed in a large handbill, saved in Mary Evaline's scrapbook. This "broadside" had been distributed on October 7, 1868, with its announcement in heavy black print that a "Great Auction Sale" would be held on Tuesday, October 20, at "nine o'clock a.m." The handbill offered every conceivable bit of information, first about the farm of A. T. Burroughs:

. . . situated in Warren, Mass., 1-2 miles South-East from the depot. The farm will be sold entire or in lots to suit the purchaser and consists of about 125 acres of Land suitably divided into Mowing, Pasturage, Tillage and Woodland, well watered with a 2½ story dwelling house, barn and other Out-Buildings thereon. . . .

Personal property followed, and included such items as "one fine carriage and saddle horse. One light, shift seat top Carriage. Two light, open buggies. One Milk Wagon. Five light, silver mounted harnesses, two of which are nearly new. One pair heavy ox harnesses. Three Ladies' saddles. Two McClellan Saddles. One English Saddle with bridles & c."

Under "Stock and Farming Tools" were listed "one large yoke of fat oxen, 11 Winter Milk Cows, 1 Ox Sled, Wagon," and various pieces of equipment and machinery. Among them was a "Potatoe Planter which furrows, cuts, drops and covers at the same time." Evidently Abner was through with farming and the farm country, for the handbill also offered "1 large, fine wolf-skin Robe, 2 Buffalo Robes, 1 Fancy lap Blanket, 4 nice Horse Blankets, 1 India Rubber Horse Cover. . . ." Farm produce for auction included "12 bbls. Cider, 50 barrels assorted Winter Apples, 100 bushels of Potatoes" and other items. All the family furniture and belongings were also to be sold. Details of the sale completed the handbill:

Shed No. 14 at the Congregational Church. Sale to commence promptly at 9 o'clock, with furniture and farming tools. All the above can be seen on the premises previous to the day of sale. Terms made known at time and place of sale.

    A. T. Burroughs
    C. S. Hitchcock, Auctioneer
    T. Morey, Printer. West Brookfield, Mass.

10. This story, newspaper unidentified, appeared in April 1896 and was saved in ERB's scrapbook. Abner Tyler Burroughs, born May 26, 1805, died on July 9, 1897.

11. Described in a letter from Mrs. Evelyn McKenzie, dated November 19, 1968.

12. The invitation and banquet ticket are in Mary Evaline's scrapbook.

13. Letter of Mrs. Carlton D. McKenzie, February 20, 1968. In a taped interview of July 12 to 13 at her home in Charlotte, N.C., Mrs. McKenzie gave further information about the two homes of Major George, the first at 646 Washington Blvd., and the second at 1418 Jackson Blvd. She recalls, as does Hulbert Burroughs, that the major always employed Irish girls to work in the house; two sisters were named Katie and Lizzie Sheridan. The major was very considerate toward them and in one case, when an Irish girl married the coachman, George got him a job with the police. The family recalled that the girls always waited on them "hand and foot." The Burroughs family had never employed Negro servants.

Both homes were three-story and Mrs. McKenzie recalls the dining room upstairs, a dumbwaiter, kitchen off the first floor, and a basement. There was an outside long flight of stairs, and underneath were doors going into a vestibule.

14. Ibid. Evelyn (Mrs. McKenzie) and her brother Studley were both born in the Chicago home on Washington Blvd. At a later period of difficulty, when Harry Burroughs was ill, he and his wife Ella, Evelyn, and Studley lived in the Jackson Blvd. home on the third floor for some time, with Major Burroughs helping them.

15. From a letter of George T. Burroughs, III, January 19, 1969. In recalling his visits to the Chicago home, George remembered that the family attended Sunday and holiday dinners at the first home. Major George was in charge and ruled the household firmly; George III said "the Major reminded him of 'Life with Father.'" He took it for granted that he knew best what was to be done. George III recalled that the Major liked steak for breakfast, and as a result they all had to eat steak for breakfast. Evelyn Burroughs describes the Major as a "martinet," but quite devoted to his family. At nine p.m., she recalls, when he went to bed, everybody had to follow suit, and all lights went out. He was very firm about meal times; a Chinese gong, kept in the house, was struck promptly at twelve noon, six p.m., and 7:30 a.m. for breakfast.

Marie Burroughs, in her recollections, referred to Major George as "The Fiery Major" and described him as "very much the patriarch."

16. Letter of George Burroughs, III. Joan, ERB's daughter, characterizes Major George as a "harsh" man, one whom her father respected for his military record, but not a man who shared close feelings with his son Ed, especially in the early years. She believes that the Major was partial to George, Jr., and Harry because Ed had never gone to college and the Major felt he would never be a success.

17. The article is in Mary Evaline's scrapbook. George Burroughs, III, presently living in Oakland, California, has taped responses to questions which indicate that the distilleries suit by the U.S. Government may have been an antimonopoly suit. As he recalls it, the government insisted upon breaking up the combination of small distilleries and forcing them to go back to their original plants. It is not certain whether the Phoenix Distillery was involved in this antimonopoly suit.

18. Both the article and an artist's sketch headed "Ruins of the Phoenix Distillery," from the *Chicago Tribune*, August 5, 1885, are pasted in Mary Evaline's scrapbook.

19. According to Evelyn McKenzie, the Major suffered severe business reverses in connection with the distillery because of dishonest practices by a partner.

The American Battery Company, for which George, Harry, and Ed all worked at various times, evidently manufactured an electric bicycle lamp or a battery for this type of lamp. A cartoon drawn by ERB on a letterhead of the company, dated April 14, 1897, shows a man on a bicycle on which is mounted a lamp and battery. Another man is covering his eyes and saying, "So bright — I am blind," as the bicycle approaches.

As described in The Chicago World's Fair Columbian Exposition, the company also experimented with an electrical auto which was demonstrated on the Fair grounds.

20. Two notes are contained in Mary Evaline's scrapbook. The first is an official form dated October 27, 1881, Criminal Docket No. 14056, stating, "United States vs. Charles J. Guiteau" and "The President of the United States to George T. Burroughs":

You are hereby commanded to appear before the said court on the 14th day of November 1881 to testify for the defendant. R.J. Meigs Clerk. all

This is marked as a "copy" in Burroughs' handwriting. The second is a handwritten pass stating:

Marshall Henry — Please admit bearer, one of our experts —
Geo. Scoville
Washington D.C. Nov. 28th 1881 for admission to Guiteau trial

It is not known what the nature of George Burroughs' testimony for the defendant was or in what area he qualified as an expert. It may have been because of his knowledge of guns.

21. Mary Evaline saved numerous articles about the anarchists in her scrapbook; most of them have artist's photos or sketches of the accused men and of the jurors.

22. A handwritten pass for George Burroughs reads:

Officer in Charge
Judge Gary's Court
Please admit —
George Burroughs to Court Room
Give him as good seat as possible & oblige
Gleason

23. On the back of this special permit card George had listed the men and their sentences:

A. R. Parsons — American
August Spies — German
Geo. Engel — do [ditto]
Adolph Fischer — do
The above were hung
Louis Lingg, German suicide
Sam Fiedler — English

Michael Schwab — Bavarian
committed to imprisonment for life
Oscar W. Neebe German descent-
born in N.Y. 15 years in Penitentiary

24. In an order dated October 5, 1889, signed by C. R. Watson, sheriff, George was notified to appear in the criminal court of Cook County to serve as a Petit Juror.

An unidentified newspaper article, headed "Opposed to Fanaticism," reveals that George was excused from jury duty in this case because of his frank admission that he was prejudiced against all Catholics:

The juror (Burroughs) then threw a bombshell into the defense by saying that he belongs to three military societies, the Masons, and the American League.

Q. Have you any prejudice against those men because they are Irish Catholics? A. Not more than I have against French or German Catholics. I have no prejudice against the individual, but I have against the religion.

Q. Do you consider that a well-founded opinion? A. Yes, sir. I do not believe in fanaticism anywhere.

In answer to the court, the juror said, not withstanding the defendents were Catholics, he would endeavor to give them a fair and impartial trial, and he thought he could do so, but he was not clear about it. He would be more apt to doubt the credulity of a Roman Catholic in behalf of a member of the same religion, as they were clannish. He believed he could give the men a fair and impartial trial, and would endeavor not to let his prejudice affect his judgment, but he could not say whether it would.

The judge agreed that George Burroughs' answer "hardly comes within the statutory requirements," but commented acidly, "... I think the gentlemen have made a mistake in challenging him...."

25. The biography of Johnson includes a photo of the man and offers comments about his appearance: "It might hardly be gathered from the portrait that Mr. Johnson is a colored man, for as features and intelligibility go he shows little trace of that origin."

Considering the prejudice of the times, it is quite remarkable that Burroughs and McEntee gave such generous aid to the man and that they were so willing to accept him as an equal.

26. The two stores in Chicago were originally at 276 West Indiana and 660 West Madison Streets; after they were sold to Johnson, he moved the Madison Street store to 389 Indiana, his residence. It was run by Mrs. Johnson.

27. Clipping in ERB's notebook, newspaper and date unknown.

28. The award of the judges read:

We affirm that the "American" battery has been examined and tested by us, and found worthy of an award for its excellency of design and construction, and for its efficiency and indication of durability.

Wilbur M. Stine   W. Lobach

Under George Burroughs' ownership, the American Battery Company was located at various addresses during the years. In 1894 letterheads show the office at 25 South Canal Street and the factory at Oregon, Ill. At this time the officers were the same ones who had been in charge of the distillery: Jonathan Abel, president; George T. Burroughs, vice-president; B. W. Kendall, secretary; Wilson Ames, treasurer. Other addresses (earlier) include 188 Madison Street, Chicago, with the factory at 353-361 Twentieth Street, and also 42 West Quincy Street. A card at this address read, "Highest Award granted at World's Columbian Exposition, Chicago, 1893." In later years ERB worked for the company as treasurer. A stamped form shown in ERB's small memo book lists George Burroughs as president of the company, but an employee's pass to the Exposition lists him as vice-president.

2. Genealogy

Printed copies of "Memoirs of a War Bride," written by Mary Evaline, the mother of Edgar, George, Henry (Harry), and Frank, were distributed to all the members of the family. The original handwritten manuscript is still preserved at the Burroughs office in Tarzana, California. Dated Chicago, June 23, 1914, the *Memoirs* were first addressed to "My dear son Edgar," but this is scratched out with an insertion beneath of "My dear sons," evidently not in Mary Evaline's handwriting.

That Ed was the prime mover in having his mother write her memoirs and in arranging for the publication is quite clear. However, there is evidence that all the brothers collaborated in preparing the book for the printer and in assembling the genealogical sections. They were also aided by their uncle Charles S. McEntee (married to Caroline Studley, Major George's sister, on December 21, 1865) who submitted corrections on the genealogy. Brother Harry's undated note to Ed reads:

Must hustle to get this in mail box. 1st page enclosed contain all information on Father's side I can dig up as far back as the Family Bible goes. Please note my criticism of the Title Page and if you think it valid call Studley [his son] or Nellie [his wife] up here and OK it as he has it roughed in in pencil only and can easily change it.
How would this sound
> *in this year of our Lord*
> *Nineteen Hundred Fourteen (?)*
Everything else fine.
Foreword is a peach
unanimous sentiment

Studley Oldham Burroughs, who had done the title page of the "Memoirs," and who was born in Chicago on December 26, 1892, was an artist and professional illustrator. His sister Mary Evelyn, later Mrs. Carlton D. McKenzie, was born on March 12, 1895, in Chicago, and still possesses the old family bible referred to, with its list of births, marriages, and deaths in the back.

In sending a scrawled list of all the Rice ancestors, Charles McEntee wrote, "Harry asked me to send you this history of your family on your fathers side. I hope you can make some use of it. We have no records of the Burroughs side of the family."

On January 13, 1915, he wrote to Ed from 85 East Elm Street, Chicago, heading the letter "Dear Nephew" and requesting a copy of the "Memoirs" for "The Loyal Legion Library" in Chicago. He noted that in the book, now printed, he had detected a few errors and would correct these in the copy when he received it, "for should Army of the Potomac Men read it, they would note the errors at once." (The nature of the errors is not known.) He praises Mary Evaline for her accuracy and urges Ed that "whenever you see my friend Mr. Miller at the Club do not fail to make yourself known to him, he is a great admirer of you, and he is well worth cultivating." Charles K. Miller, McEntee's friend, and owner of a clipping service in Chicago, later corresponded regularly with ERB.

While the name of the printer cannot be stated with certainty, since none appears in the book, a letter from The Ralph Fletcher Seymour Company, The Alderbrink Press, Fine Arts Building, Chicago, saved by ERB, offers a possible clue. Dated November 24, presumably 1914, and addressed to Edgar Rice Burroughs, it states:

We have estimated the cost of your books to be about $225.00 for about 50 copies.
We have figured on the best stock and the best binding with about 64 pages of type.

The writer, "M. Hopkins," appeared willing to negotiate if the price was considered too high.

Mary Evaline's "Memoirs" had outlined whatever information the family possessed in 1914, but at the end of 1920 or first part of 1921, further research was initiated. A letter from Joseph Edwin Woods, a genealogical researcher from Barre, Massachusetts, indicated that the earliest individual he could trace in the Burroughs ancestry was one Joshua Barrus who lived in Brookfield, Massachusetts, in 1717. Barrus' only record was his payment of a tax of eighteen shillings and three pence. Woods' compilations revealed that three variations of the name "Burroughs" had first appeared — "Barras," "Burras," and "Burrows."

The most remarkable person to be listed in Woods' chronology of the Burroughs family in America was David Burras of "Winsor," Connecticut, born in 1746 or 1747. In the account of his military activities, interestingly reported by Woods, David's name becomes "Burrows":

The published record of "Soldiers and Sailors of Massachusetts who served in The War of The Revolution" shows: "David Burrows private in Captain Joseph Cutters Company of Volunteers which marched from Western or Oakham to join General Gates in the Northwest Sept. 24, 1777. He served 18 days.

David, who later became a deacon, reached the age of 91 or 92. By the time of his death in 1838 his name appears to have been changed to "Burroughs."

In a letter of March 15, 1922, from Henry C. Burroughs of Aikin, Maryland, details of the Burroughses' British ancestry were offered. Henry, presumably a relative, based part of his information on a pamphlet printed in 1894 by Lewis Ames Burroughs, another in the family line. Henry believed that Jeremiah Burroughs, one of four of that name who emigrated to the Colonies in the seventeenth century, was the original Burroughs ancestor. Jeremiah is mentioned in *Savage's Genealogies* as having reached Scituate, Massachusetts Bay. He is first referred to in 1647 and died in 1660.

The information compiled by both men, Henry C. Burroughs and Joseph Woods, seems reasonably accurate, although it is not extended to the twentieth century. Burroughs' list of births ends in 1755, while Woods' continues on to 1843. The two accounts indicate that the family had settled or lived in various Massachusetts towns, including Brookfield, Enfield, Bridgewater, Warren, and others. It was also clear that John was a favorite male name. In England a John Burroughs, possibly Jeremiah's brother, left Ipswich, county of Suffolk, where he had been born in 1606, and reached Salem, Massachusetts, in 1634. Jeremiah showed his preference for the name by calling his son "John"; and the succeeding generations produced John Burroughs, II, and John Burroughs, III, who was the first to leave the state. He moved to Winsor, Connecticut, in 1718.

ERB's copy of the "Memoirs" has Henry C. Burroughs' letter attached. It contains copies of two wills by John Burroughs, II, and John Ensign Burroughs, III. In the will of John Burroughs, II, two of his cows are left to his wife "to dispose of as she thinks best." John Ensign Burroughs' will is signed only with his "mark"; evidently he was unable to write.

Following a respected British tradition, the Burroughs family adopted ancestral names from both sides as middle names for the male descendents. From Mary Evaline's branch the names McCulloch and Coleman were taken, while the Burroughs line supplied the names Rice, Tyler, and Studley. It was interesting to note that this pride of ancestry was associated only with the lines that could be traced back to England; in the case of Josiah Zieger, Mary Evaline's father, who was of Dutch descent, no attempt has been made to pass the name down to present generations. The Burroughs family today can offer no explanation for the method used to assign the middle names of Tyler, McCulloch, Coleman, Studley, and Rice to the men.

Abner Tyler Burroughs, who introduced the celebrated Rice name into the family when he married Mary Rice in 1827, was responsible for a line, it is claimed, that may be traced all the way back to Deacon Edmund Rice, a Pilgrim from Buckinghamshire, England, who settled in Sudbury, Massachussetts, in 1638. Researchers maintain that the line is noted for a remarkable list of distinguished Americans. Notable among these is Calvin Coolidge, whose ancestor was a John Coolidge, an early settler in Watertown, Massachusetts. His son Jonathan Coolidge married Martha Rice, a granddaughter of the celebrated Deacon Rice. Other famous descendants of the Rices, according to the researchers, are Julia Ward Howe, Harriet Beecher Stowe, Mary Baker Eddy, Samuel F. B. Morse, and Clara Barton.

ERB on January 12, 1921, mentioned receiving a book on the Rices from Charles McEntee, who appears, as previously shown, to have had a strong interest in Rice genealogy. The book, referred to in Woods' letter, was considered very rare. It was titled "A Genealogical History of the Rice Family," by A. M. Ward, 1858. On March 5, 1925, an article in the *Christian Science Monitor* told of the famous descendents of Deacon Edmund Rice, revealed as the result of research by Mrs. Mary Barber Schuneman of East Orange, N.J. She had traced the genealogy of President Coolidge back to the Rice line. The mention of a book by Charles Elmer Rice, *In the Name of Rice*, caused a flurry of interest; he was flooded with letters and demands for the book which was then out of print. He made up a form letter rejecting the requests for his book but offered to send copies of three pedigrees tracing the Rice line back some thirty-five generations. The charge for this was ten dollars.

On May 1, 1925, obviously in response to a request by ERB, he had sent a copy of the book with this autograph: "To my distinguished Kinsman Edgar Rice Burroughs with the profound admiration of Charles Elmer Rice." He also sent the form letter with its request for payment, but wrote at the bottom: "Nothing on the above applies to you — I only send it to show you what I have been obliged to do to keep at bay a mob of women who desire to join the order of the Crown — or be related to Mr. Coolidge." The three pedigrees, compiled by Charles K. Winslow, were sent to ERB by Rice.

A further article on January 15, 1926, in the *Monitor* was headed by an engraving of a pen and ink drawing of the Deacon Rice Homestead in Wayland, Massachusetts, the homestead shown as it was constructed in 1650. The article again discusses the lineage of the Rices, the famous descendents, and details of the Rice Homestead.

The book *By the Name of Rice*, based upon information compiled by Dr. Charles Elmer Rice, president of the Union Theological Seminary of Alliance, Ohio, and a sixth great-grandson of Deacon Rice, provides an amusing addition to the Burroughs family research. Issued in 1911 by the Williams Printing Company, Alliance, Ohio, the book states on its title page "Done briefly by omitting some 15,000 names that can be had upon application to the Author." The book is additionally described as *An Historical Sketch of Deacon Edmund Rice The Pilgrim (1594-1663)*. This exhaustive study by Dr. Rice had by 1885 covered 1,400 families or 7,000 individuals. The book, a paperback, seven and one-half inches high by five and one-fourth inches wide, has ninety-six numbered pages, with two additional pages containing letters from Thomas Hart to his beloved Betsy Rice (Hart), actually 100 pages in all. On the back of the title page is the notation, "Entered according to Act of Congress in the year 1910 by Charles Elmer Rice, in the office of the Librarian of Congress at Washington," and beneath this, "Limited edition, of which this is number 617" (ERB's copy). It bears the signature *Chas. E. Rice.*

In Dr. Rice's three pedigrees of the Rice Family of England, the first is based upon information belonging to a descendant, Lord Dynevor, that establishes a first royal ancestor — Coel Codevog, King of the Britons. The line, followed to its twenty-fifth generation, revealed the existence of a Rice ap-Griffith FitzUryan who married Katherine, daughter of Thomas Howard, Duke of Norfolk. The heir was Griffith ap-Rice, the direct ancestor of the twentieth century Lord Dynevor. The succession then obviously continues through other British Rices to the American Rices.

The second pedigree traced the descent of Thomas Howard, Duke of Norfolk (whose daughter had married Rice ap-Griffith FitzUryan), all the way back to William the Conqueror of England. With the final pedigree, that of the Saxon princes, the line began with Egbert, 802-839, continued through Alfred the Great, and by the twenty-third generation had joined with Thomas Howard, 2nd Duke of Norfolk. In this way Dr. Rice demonstrated that the three distinguished lines had met and had been united through the Rices: the first, descending from the King of the Britons, was connected with the Howards; whose ancestor was William the Conqueror; and the third line of the ancient Saxons also met with the Howards. The blood of all these eventually flowed in the veins of the good Deacon Edmund Rice who traveled overseas to establish his pedigree in Sudbury, Massachusetts.

The pedigrees, *A, B,* and *C,* as supplied by Dr. Rice, are one page each with separate title pages. At the end is a statement of authorities of which there are three: (1) *By the Name of Rice,* (2) *The Peerage of Great Briton and Ireland,* by Sir Bernard Burke, 1914, Lord Dynevor, and (3) *Dictionary of the Landed Gentry of Great Britain and Ireland,* Burke, 1851. This statement bears the signature of *Chas. K. Winslow.* On the title page of pedigree A, Record of the Rice Family of England, is this explanation: "As abstracted from various authentic sources, including an illuminated pedigree of the family of Rice, in the possession of Lord Dynevor, drawn and attested in the year 1600, by Ralph Brooke, York Herald, and continued to the present time by Dr. Charles Elmer Rice."

In his genealogical research Dr. Rice had assembled statistics that gave encouragement to all descendants: the Rices had an astonishing record for longevity. Ages in the eighties were quite common and many of the Rices lived to the late nineties. An example was Ephraim Pratt, born in 1687, who became the husband of Martha Rice. He attained the age of 116 years, five months, twenty-two days, and died in 1804. From this union came four sons who lived to be over ninety years of age and two daughters who were between eighty and ninety years old. Gershom Rice, who died in 1768 at the age of 101 years, had fourteen children, twelve of whom lived to a great age. Their aggregate age was 1,000 years.

The interest in the Rices is heightened by the individualistic style of Dr. Rice in his book. His droll wit and humor, his habit of inserting sprightly anecdotes, jokes, and good-natured observations about people and life make the book delightful. His three-page preface has this opening comment:

"Oh that mine adversary had written a book," quoted the afflicted Job; and let him tackle the Rice family chronology, say I, and Nemesis has him by the scruff. There are too many Rices and few of them are wildly enthusiastic upon the question of their origin....

In speaking of the "apathy" encountered while he was seeking information about the Rice line, he remarked, "At first it seemed a futile and frenetic search, likely to be 'a great cry for little wool,' as the Devil said when he tried to shear the pig." But later he found that these "antipathetic" relatives were only "sporadic cases" and that the majority were quite willing to aid him. "Among the descendents of Deacon Edmund Rice," he wrote, "I have found almost every famous New England name. On page 92 Dr. Rice uses the ironic heading, "Whom the Gods Love, Die Young," and beneath it, "For why should youth and beauty in the grave lie low?" and then proceeds to offer a long list of Rices who lived past 90. In addition to Ephraim Pratt, from 1710 to 1848 approximately 86 Rices lived past 90, and a number of these lived from 96 to 99.

The marriage of Abner Tyler Burroughs to Mary Rice in 1827, presumably at Warren, Massachusetts, brings us to relationships nearer in time, closer to the modern branch of the Burroughs family. The records of the seventeenth and eighteenth centuries show that families on both sides were fairly large, averaging five or more children. (In the case of John Burroughs III, of Windsor, Connecticut, there were eight children — five boys and three girls.) The family of Abner and Mary, typical of their ancestral pattern, consisted of six: Mary Louise, Sarah Ann, George Tyler, Henry Rice, Abner Tyler, and Caroline Studley.

George Tyler Burroughs, Edgar's father, was born on October 13, 1833, at Warren, and little is known of his early years except that he attended an academy at Monson, Massachusetts, conducted by the Reverend Charles Hammond. Its source, an article, undated, pasted in Mary Evaline's scrapbook, tells of the return of Yung Wing to the village of Monson, Massachusetts, to attend the funeral of his old missionary friend, Dr. Samuel R. Brown, "under whose advice and protection Yung Wing himself, with two other Chinamen, named Wong Shing and Wong Fun, left China thirty-three years ago to receive a Christian education in America." They were taken into the Brown home and Reverend Charles Hammond was their teacher at the academy. A handwritten entry at the bottom of the article explains, "I attended the School at Monson, Mass., with the three Chinamen, herein mentioned. G.T.B." The article quotes four lines of a popular hymn written by Mrs. Brown, and next to it George Burroughs inserted the dates "1880 or 1881," presumably the period of publication.

A card preserved in Mary Evaline's scrapbook reveals that in later years George went into business in Columbus City, Iowa, as a merchant, together with N. G. Fitch. He and Mary had possibly met in the city or its vicinity when she was teaching school, or he had gone there to be near her. His marriage to her in 1863 brought a new family line to join the Rices and Burroughses, and for the first time the British blood was diluted with Dutch blood. Mary's mother had in 1835 married Josiah Zieger, a descendant of one of the Dutch settlers of Western Pennsylvania who had emigrated to Indiana after the Civil War.

Mary Evaline could also be proud of a British ancestry, for as shown in her *Memoirs*, her descent could be traced back to John Inskeep of Staffordshire, England. Of his two sons, one became a judge and settled in New Jersey, while the other moved to Virginia. In 1749 a marriage of Sarah Inskeep to John McCulloch introduced a new family name. The line continued with the wedding of Sarah McCulloch, the daughter, to Jacob Coleman, and it was completed when Mary Coleman and Josiah Zieger were married.

Mary Evaline's military record of the Colemans during the American Revolution contains an impressive roster. Jacob Coleman, her great grandfather, served in the seventh and ninth Virginia Regiments from 1779 to the war's end. Others who enlisted were John Coleman, Ensign Second Virginia Regiment, 1779; Richard Coleman, Second and Fifth Virginia Regiments, 1776 to 1780; Samuel Coleman, Eighth Virginia Regiment, 1776 to 1780, when he was killed at Camden; Whitehead Coleman, Second Virginia Regiment, 1776 to 1783; and Wyatt Coleman, Second Virginia Regiment, 1778 to 1792. In addition, on her father's side, Jacob Zieger had served in the First and Second Pennsylvania Battalions from 1775 to 1777, while from the McCulloch branch, Thomas, a lieutenant in the Virginia Riflemen, had died in 1780 of wounds received at King's Mountain. In Mary Evaline's genealogical notes Jacob Coleman is also listed as a first lieutenant in the eighth Virginia Infantry.

John McCulloch Coleman, Mary Evaline's grandfather, had moved from Kentucky, first to Terre Haute and then to Eugene, Indiana, a small town on the Vermillion River. There, Mary recalled information about her birth: "I was born at a point on the Vermillion River between Perrysville and Eugene where a huge boulder on the brink of the river marked a point known as The Indian's Leap. I have forgotten the legend, however." In the 1830s her grandfather moved again, taking his two daughters Eliza and Nancy who later became the wife of Judge Springer, to Iowa City, then the capital of Iowa. Some years later he persuaded Mary's parents to join him in this new country. In her notes Mary mentioned her travels: "My Father and Mother, with their three children, nine, four, and two years of age made the trip in the old style emigrant wagons. . . ." The four-year-old was Mary Evaline herself, called MEB, and on the journey she was stricken with typhoid fever.

The events that were most strongly impressed upon her memory occurred in her fourteenth year. Her grandfather, John McCulloch Coleman, took her to Indiana to spend the winter with her cousins, the Groenendykes. When she returned the following summer, she was sent to join her mother, brother, and sister at the home of her uncle, Judge Springer, in Columbus City, Iowa. The change brought a painful awareness that her father and mother had separated and that the old home was broken up.

In the fall her grandfather placed her in a preparatory school founded by the Methodists — Cornell College — located at Mount Vernon. There she passed two happy years. The studies were designed to prepare her for teaching. "Just before my seventeenth birthday," she wrote, "I opened a private school where I taught for a couple of years, children from six to sixteen. Later I was associated with the principal of public schools of Washington, Iowa. I remained until a short time before my marriage."

During the Civil War, Mary Evaline's life became crowded with excitement and adventure. At her son's request she tried to recreate the experiences from 1861 to the end of the war, recording the events in her neat, flowing handwriting. Her original genealogical notes, in preparation for her "Memoirs" (supplied by Katherine Burroughs Konkle, Frank Coleman's daughter), include a letter written by ERB when he was sending these notes, on April 19, 1920, from the Tarzana Ranch, to his brother Frank at 1204 Forest Avenue in Wilmette, Illinois:

I am enclosing typewritten copy of the genealogical notes Mother was working on. The longer one is a copy of her original pencil manuscript, the other a copy of practically the same thing which she had made in ink with minor changes.

I am sending similar copies to each of the other boys.

The completed "Memoirs of a War Bride" offer

a very sketchy account of the Civil War period which Mary was trying to recall from memory. Her story covers fifty-five pages, and the section that follows is written by her husband. Headed "Personal Anecdotes of the Civil War," and narrated by Major George T. Burroughs, it describes a "Night Ride with Moseby," "A Close Call," and "The Beginning of Sheridan's Ride." The genealogical data follows. At the front of the volume, beneath photos of George and Mary, is a fourteen-line poem constructed in rhyming couplets, written by Ella Oldham Burroughs, Harry's wife, and dated November 23, 1914. In ERB's copy of the book, entries of all the family births, marriages, divorces, and deaths were added on pages at the end, as they occurred.

The "Memoirs" was addressed to her sons in the introduction:

You have asked me to record, as far as my memory will permit, some of the events in which your Father and I, one or both, participated during the Civil War. Most of these (incidents) occurred in the earlier years of the conflict, before our marriage; for, after I went to Washington as his wife, he was careful to run no unnecessary risks, as he had so often done before.

She recounts that at the time of her planned marriage to George Tyler Burroughs in 1861 he had been employed in the woolen department of Bliss, Wheelock and Kelley, a large New York importing house. He had selected their future home, then being built in the suburbs. After Lincoln's election and the Southern secessions came the firing on Fort Sumter in Charleston Harbor. President Lincoln issued a call for 75,000 volunteers, and about this Mary Evaline wrote, "Your Father was on his way to his place of business, when, buying his morning paper, he saw the head-lines announcing the call. He proceeded at once to the nearest armory or place of enlistment, and entered his name on the list."

George then went directly to his firm and informed Mr. Bliss of his actions. As a result, "flattering offers were made if he would re-consider his decision; but finding him determined, his partners complimented him on being the first one of their employees to enlist, and offered him anything in the store which he might need for his outfit."

Sworn in on April 19, he was assigned to Company G, 71st New York State Militia. Upon hearing that the Massachusetts 8th Regiment had been attacked in the streets of Baltimore, the colonel of the 71st chose a route to avoid the city, disembarking at Annapolis and marching to Washington. Disturbances had also occurred in Washington, and the 71st was assigned there to maintain order.

When the 71st marched toward the front, to the area where the Battle of Bull Run was to take place, George was in the hospital at the time. Mary Evaline explained that "... soldiers felt the effect of change of climate, water and foods," the assumption being that George had dysentery. "Invalids were ordered to remain behind," she said. "Eluding nurses and guards by climbing out of a window near his cot, your Father joined his company. He was reprimanded, but allowed to remain."

After the disaster of Bull Run on July 21, the soldiers of the 71st, bewildered and in disorder, managed to reach Washington within the next two days. In the front rank of the battle George felt a bullet pass through his blouse. It struck and killed the man behind him. He prized the bullet-torn blouse as evidence that he had really been under fire, and when he went to sleep, put it carefully away. He awoke to discover that the blouse had been stolen.

The military engagement had been short, and with no further assignment George returned to New York and his position at Bliss, Wheelock and Kelley's. But he exhibited the impatience with inaction and the eagerness to serve his country that had been typical of the Burroughs family in past generations. Mr. Bliss was willing to use his influence with his brother-in-law Colonel Baker to procure a lieutenancy for George in a regiment being formed in Albany. The appointment came through, and in December 1861 George was made acting regimental quartermaster of the New York 43rd regiment.

What followed was a year of "watchful waiting," and during this period George's almost impossible job was to provide food for the men. The food had to be carried over Virginia roads that were "veritable quagmires" in the winter and early spring. George would often remain on horseback for twenty-four hours, sleeping in the saddle. Mary Evaline recalls that George "at times dismounting, would rest against a tree-trunk, with his horse's bridle wrapped around his wrist, and sleep until the grazing animal tightened the bridle enough to waken him."

The front line action that George had hoped for did not come, and deeply discouraged he continued to perform his quartermaster's duties. It was only through the efforts of Colonel Baker's wife (she sang for the governor at a social function and exacted a promise of a favor in return) that George's commission finally came through. On February 19, 1863, he was promoted to captain and placed in charge of the Commissary of Subsistence under Brigadier General Thomas H. McNiel. George, now determined to wed Mary Evaline, obtained a leave to join her in Iowa. Only four days later, on February 23, their marriage took place in Iowa City. "He arrived on a Wednesday," she wrote. "We were married on the following Monday, at 12 o'clock, and after a wedding breakfast, left at once for Washington."

The newlyweds spent one day in Chicago and another at Wheeling, West Virginia, where Mary

Evaline met George's three sisters — Louise, an assistant principal of the Young Ladies' Seminary; Sarah, a teacher of drawing and painting in the same school; and Caroline, who was studying French and music. Because of travel delays, they didn't reach Washington until the day his leave expired. They had to part almost immediately, and Mary was left alone in the capital city.

Her real adventures began in June when George obtained a pass for her to visit the front. She was brought to their temporary home in camp, near Falmout, on the Rappahannock River opposite Fredericksburg. A new one-hundred pound gun called the "Lincoln" was mounted on a bluff overlooking Fredericksburg. Mary and her party rode up a hill to watch the huge cannon in action. Minutes later a shot from the Confederate battery hurtled through the air and landed nearby, plowing up the ground. They were all covered with dirt. Later, upon returning, they found that a shot had also struck close to their tent.

Camp was to be broken, and an order came through for all civilians to leave. Mary Evaline was not one to yield easily. In her "Memoirs" she recalled, "I appealed to General McNiel to let me stay till the army was opposite Washington which we knew would be only a few miles from that city. He argued that I would experience hardships in the tent life of a moving army — but in the end gave a reluctant consent on condition that I should on no account permit the general of the army to see me. Your father knew how to manage that matter, for he kept himself informed of the location of army headquarters."

She accompanied the men, riding on a white pony. When it began to rain, she was persuaded to climb into the army wagon. She found lying in the midst of the tent poles and other equipment very uncomfortable and insisted upon returning to her pony. She rode through the steady rain wearing a poncho, a type of rubber blanket with a hole in the middle for the head.

On a later occasion while standing with a group of officers, she heard a warning cry. The officers closed in around her hurriedly so that she couldn't be seen. She didn't realize until afterward that General Hooker was passing and that she was almost discovered. The general of the Army of the Potomac exchanged salutes with the officers, unaware of her presence.

Upon her return to Washington Mary Evaline met a number of her relatives, including her uncle, Samuel Coleman. She received a letter from George urging her to go to his father's home in Warren, Massachusetts, since Washington might soon be under siege. En route she stopped in New York to meet George's brother, Henry Rice, and then proceeded to Springfield, where, at the Massasoit House she was surprised and alarmed at George's unexpected arrival. He was supporting himself with a crutch and a cane. "While placing his wagon train in a safe position," Mary explained, "he was seriously injured by the repeated kicks of a vicious mule from which he could not escape owing to the narrow pass through which he must make his way to command." Later his leg became swollen and intensely painful.

Reaching Warren on July 1, Mary decided to stay there, and she made no more visits to the army during the remainder of 1863. She did have an opportunity to be at a reception given by the President and his wife. She recalled that she shook hands with Mrs. Lincoln and "touched the hand of the Great Emancipator."

After the fall of the Confederate capital of Richmond, Mary visited the city and went to its "White House," the former residence of Jefferson Davis. The home, a typical Southern mansion, was thronged with people, many of them souvenir-hunters. Reflecting upon her actions, Mary was somewhat ashamed to admit she had followed the examples set by others and had taken a large heavily-fringed "tidy" from a chair. Fearful of discovery, she permitted her escort to slip it under his coat. She described the situation:

This was quickly done; but later we realized that if it was discovered in his possession it would subject him to humiliation and censure if nothing worse for, military guards were all over the house instructing the visitors to remove nothing. How our party of nearly a hundred could bring away vases, statuettes and other small and large articles without detection will always be a mystery to me. The only possible solution lay in the fact that the federal soldiers placed on guard felt as we all did, that in view of all we had suffered from the uprising of the South, we were entitled to anything which the president had left in his sudden flight.

Mary returned to Washington to find a telegram announcing that her mother and sister were seriously ill. On the morning of her arrival at Nevada, Iowa, she heard the horrifying news of the assassination of President Lincoln. With this came good news — her mother and sister had passed the crisis and were recovering. George obtained a leave to join her in Iowa, and on June 22, 1865, after they had traveled once more to Washington, he received his honorable discharge as a brevet major.

The war and all its adventures being at an end, Mary and George went to visit relatives in Warren, and from there journeyed to Portland, Maine, where they remained until the autumn of 1868. Two of their sons, George, Jr., and Henry, were born in Portland. From then on Chicago became the permanent home of the Burroughs family. In addition to George's father, Abner Tyler Burroughs, the family was joined by George's brother Henry Rice, who had previously lived in New York. His home, near the Burroughs family, was at 580 Washington Boulevard. A newspaper notice, date unknown, announces his death on March 18, 1904, at age 67, in Chicago. The Massachusetts and Maine papers are asked to copy. Beneath the notice, in ERB's handwriting, is noted, "My Father's brother."

The Burroughses' family pride and patriotism caused them to keep detailed records of the war service of Major George T. Burroughs, Sr. In the Civil War he had entered service as a private in Company "G" of the 71st Regiment, New York State Militia, enlisting on April 19, 1861. In the advance on Manassas, June 16 to 21, he had seen action at Sudley Springs and at the Battle of Bull Run. He was mustered out at New York City on July 31, 1861, but on December 16 reentered service with a commission as first Lieutenant, 43rd New York Volunteer Infantry, "Albany & Yates Rifles." He was acting regimental quartermaster from December 1861 to September 1862. After various battle campaigns, he was detached from his regiment and assigned to duty as acting commissary of subsistence on the staff of General F. L. Vinton and then with a commission from President Lincoln was made captain and commissary of subsistence on February 19, 1863.

He remained throughout the war and was present in numerous campaigns. After resigning on June 22, 1865, and receiving an honorable discharge, George T. Burroughs was breveted Major U.S. Volunteers on June 24 "For Faithful and Meritorious Services During the War."

After the war he joined various military organizations. In 1867 he was elected an Original Companion of the First Class of the Military Order of the Loyal Legion of the United States, Commandery of the State of Massachusetts, and was one of the thirteen Original Companions of the Illinois Commandery. In Illinois he was also a member of Post No. 5 of the Grand Army of the Republic and a life member of Apollo Commandery No. 1, Knights Templar. He was also a Freemason, joining in Portland, Maine, on April 6, 1867.

3. Edgar Rice Burroughs, Fiction Writer: An Autobiographical Sketch

I am sorry that I have not led a more exciting existence, so that I might offer a more interesting biographical sketch; but I am one of those fellows who has few adventures and always gets to the fire after it is out.

I was born in Peking at the time that my father was military advisor to the Empress of China and lived there, in the Forbidden City, until I was ten years old. An intimate knowledge of the Chinese language acquired during these years has often stood me in good stead since, especially in prosecuting two of my favorite studies, Chinese philosophy and Chinese ceramics.

Shortly after the family returned to the United States I was kidnaped by gypsies and held by them for almost three years. They were not unkind to me, and in many respects the life appealed to me, but eventually I escaped and returned to my parents.

Even today, after the lapse of many years, I distinctly recall the storm-torn night of my escape. Pedro, the king of the gypsies, always kept me in his tent at night where he and his wife could guard me. He was a very light sleeper, which had always presented a most effective obstacle to my eluding the clutches of my captors.

This night the rain and wind and thunder aided me. Waiting until Pedro and his wife were asleep, I started to crawl toward the tent flap. As I passed close beside the king, one of my hands fell upon a hard metal object lying beside him; it was Pedro's dagger. At the same instant Pedro awoke. A vivid lightning flash illuminated the interior of the tent, and I saw Pedro's eyes fixed upon me.

Perhaps fright motivated me, or perhaps it was just anger against my abductors. My fingers closed upon the hilt of his dagger, and in the darkness that followed the lightning I plunged the slim steel blade deep into his heart. He was the first man I had ever killed; he died without a sound.

My parents were rejoiced by my return, as they had long since abandoned all hope of ever seeing me again. For a year we travelled in Europe, where, under a tutor, I pursued my interrupted education to such good effect that I was able to enter Yale upon our return.

While at Yale I won a few athletic honors, annexing both the heavyweight boxing and wrestling championships; and in my senior year I captained the football team and the crew. Graduating summa cum laude, I spent two years at Oxford and then returned to the United States and enlisted in the army for a commission from the ranks.

At the end of two years I received my appointment as a second lieutenant and was attached to the 7th Cavalry. My first active service was with Custer at the battle of the Little Big Horn of which I was the sole survivor.

My escape from death during the massacre was almost miraculous. My horse had been shot from under me, and I was fighting on foot with the remnant of my troop. I can only guess at what actually occurred; but I believe that the bullet that struck me in the head must have passed through the head of a man in front of me and with its force spent merely have stunned me.

I fell with my body between two small bowlders; and later a horse was shot above me, his body falling on top of mine and concealing it from the eyes of the enemy, the two bowlders preventing its weight from crushing me. Gaining consciousness after dark, I crawled from beneath the horse and made my escape.

After wandering for six weeks in an effort to elude the Indians and rejoin my own people, I reached an army post, but when I attempted to rejoin my regiment, I was told that I was dead. Insistence upon my rights resulted in my being arrested for impersonating an officer.

Every member of the court knew me and deeply deplored the action they were compelled to take; but I was officially dead, and army regulations are army regulations. I took the matter to Congress but had no better success there; and finally I was compelled to change my name, adopting that which I now use, and start life all over again.

For several years I fought Apaches in Arizona; but the monotony of it palled upon me, and I was overjoyed when I received a telegram from the late Henry M. Stanley inviting me to join his expedition to Africa in search of Dr. Livingston.

I accepted immediately and also put $500,000 at his disposal, but with the understanding that my name or my connection with the expedition was not to be divulged, as I have always shrunk from publicity.

Shortly after entering Africa I became separated from the relief party and was captured by Tippoo Tib's Arabs. The night that they were going to put me to death I escaped, but a week later I fell into the hands of a tribe of cannibals. My long, golden hair and my flowing mustache and beard of the same hue filled them with such awe that they accorded me the fearful deference that they reserved for their primitive gods and demons.

They offered me no harm but kept me a prisoner among them for three years. They also kept in captivity several large anthropoid apes of a species which I believe is entirely unknown to science. These animals were of huge size and of great intelligence; and during my captivity I learned their language, which was to stand me in such good stead when I decided, many years later, to record some of my experiences in the form of fiction.

I finally escaped from the cannibal village and made my way to the coast, where, penniless and friendless, I shipped before the mast on a windjammer bound for China. Wrecked off the coast of Asia, I eventually made my way overland to Russia, where I enlisted in the imperial cavalry. A year later it happened to be my good fortune to kill an Anarchist as he was attempting the assassination of the Czar; for this service I was made a captain and attached to the imperial bodyguard.

It was while in his majesty's service that I met my wife, a lady-in-waiting to the Czarina; and when, shortly after we were married, my grandfather died

and left me eight million dollars we decided to come to America to live.

With my wife's fortune and mine, it was unnecessary for me to work; but I could not be idle; so I took up writing, more as a pastime than as a vocation.

We lived in Chicago for some years and then came to Southern California, where we have lived for more than thirteen years at that now famous watering place, Tarzana.

We have eleven children, seventeen grandchildren, and three great-grandchildren.

I have tasted fame — it is nothing. I find my greatest happiness in being alone with my violin.

4. List of ERB's Complete Works
Working List of ERB's Works

The information in this list has been taken from information compiled by Hulbert Burroughs and is on file at Edgar Rice Burroughs, Inc., Tarzana, California. Hulbert Burroughs has used as his major source ERB's notebook, and the number preceding each work corresponds to that assigned by ERB. The sequence of numbers does not always coincide with the chronological dates of writing. In such instances it can only be assumed that ERB may have started a story but did not complete it until after he had written something else. For example, the story listed as number 35 ("For the Fool's Mother") was actually written on October 3, 1912, placing it during the period that ERB wrote *The Gods of Mars*; it should logically have been numbered 4 or 5. It is likely ERB laid it aside and forgot it until 1919. A footnote in his notebook on the page devoted to number 91-1 (*The Wizard of Venus*) states: "Between the dates that I started and finished this story, I wrote *I am a Barbarian* (65,000 words) between April 11 and September 27, 1941. I have no record of writing anything during February and March." The first title shown for each story is ERB's working title and may or may not be the final title.

1. "Dejah Thoris, Princess of Mars" (by Normal Bean)
Date written: 1911
Magazine title: "Under the Moons of Mars"
Magazine reprint title: "Carter of the Red Planet"
Magazine published in: *All-Story,* February to July 1912
Book title: *A Princess of Mars*
Date book published: 1917, A. C. McClurg & Co., first edition, hardbound
Book illustrator: Schoonover
2. "The Outlaw of Torn"
Date written: Fall 1911, rewritten 1912
Magazine Title: "The Outlaw of Torn"
Magazine published in: *New Story,* January 1914
Book Title: *The Outlaw of Torn*
Date book published: 1927, A. C. McClurg & Co., first edition, hardbound
3. "Tarzan of the Apes"

Date written: December 1, 1911, to May 14, 1912
Magazine title: "Tarzan of the Apes"
Magazine published in: *All-Story,* October 1912
Book Title: *Tarzan of the Apes*
Date book published: 1914, A. C. McClurg & Co.,
   first edition, hardbound
Book illustrator: Arting

4. "The Gods of Mars"
Date written: Started July 14, 1912
Magazine title: "The Gods of Mars"
Magazine published in: *All-Story,* January to May
   1913
Book title: *The Gods of Mars*
Date book published: 1918, A. C. McClurg & Co.,
   first edition, hardbound
Book illustrator: Schoonover

5. "The Ape-Man"/"Monsieur Tarzan"
Date written: December 1912 to January 1913
Magazine title: "The Return of Tarzan"
Magazine published in: *New Story,* June to November 1913
Book title: *The Return of Tarzan*
Date book published: 1915, A. C. McClurg & Co.,
   first edition, hardbound
Book illustrator: St. John

6. "The Inner World"
Date written: January to February 1913
Magazine title: "At the Earth's Core"
Magazine reprint title: "Lost Inside the Earth"
Magazine published in: *All-Story,* April 4 to April 25,
   1914
Book title: *At the Earth's Core*
Date book published: 1922, A. C. McClurg & Co.,
   first edition, hardbound
Book illustrator: St. John

7. "The Cave Girl"
Date written: February to March 1913
Magazine title: "The Cave Girl"
Magazine published in: *All-Story,* July to September
   1913
Book title: *The Cave Girl*
Date book published: 1925, A. C. McClurg & Co.,
   first edition, hardbound
Book illustrator: St. John

8. "Number Thirteen"
Date written: March 31, 1913, to May 10, 1913
Magazine title: "A Man without a Soul"
Magazine published in: *All-Story,* November 1913
Book title: *The Monster Men*
Date book published: 1929, A. C. McClurg & Co.,
   first edition, hardbound
Book illustrator: St. John

9. "The Prince of Helium"
Date written: June 7, 1913, to July 8, 1913
Magazine title: "The Warlord of Mars"
Magazine published in: *All-Story,* December 1913 to

March 1914
Book title: *The Warlord of Mars*
Date book published: 1919, A. C. McClurg & Co.,
   first edition, hardbound
Book illustrator: St. John

10. "The Mucker"
Date written: August 16, 1913, to October 9, 1913
Magazine title: "The Mucker"
Magazine published in: *All-Story Cavalier,* October
   24 to November, 1914
Book title: *The Mucker* (includes "The Mucker" and
   "Out There Somewhere," story 26)
Date book published: 1921, A. C. McClurg & Co.,
   first edition, hardbound
Book illustrator: St. John

11. "The Mad King of Lutha"
Date written: October 26, 1913, to November 24,
   1913
Magazine title: "The Mad King"
Magazine published in: *All-Story,* March 21, 1914
Book title: *The Mad King*
Date book published: 1926, A. C. McClurg & Co.,
   first edition, hardbound
Book illustrator: St. John

12. "Nu of the Neocene"
Date written: November 27, 1913, to December 17,
   1913
Magazine title: "The Eternal Lover"
Magazine published in: *All-Story,* March 7, 1914
Book title: *The Eternal Lover*
Date book published: 1925, A. C. McClurg & Co.,
   first edition, hardbound
Book illustrator: St. John

13. "The Beasts of Tarzan"
Date written: January 7, 1914, to February 9, 1914
Magazine title: "The Beasts of Tarzan"
Magazine reprint title: "Tarzan Returns"
Magazine published in: *All-Story Cavalier,* May 16 to
   June 13, 1914
Book title: *The Beasts of Tarzan*
Date book published: 1916, A. C. McClurg & Co.,
   first edition, hardbound
Book illustrator: St. John

14. "Men and Beasts"
Date written: February 12, 1914, to March 4, 1914
   (21,000 words added for book: August 20 to
   August 31, 1937)
Magazine title: "The Lad and the Lion"
Magazine published in: *All-Story Cavalier,* June 30
   to July 14, 1917
Book title: *The Lad and the Lion*
Date book published: 1938, Edgar Rice Burroughs,
   Inc., first edition, hardbound
Book illustrator: J. C. Burroughs

15. "The Girl from Harris's"
Date written: July 14, 1913, to March 19, 1914

Magazine title: "The Girl from Farris's"
Magazine published in: *All-Story Cavalier,* September 23 to October 14, 1916
Book title: *The Girl from Farris's*
Date book published: 1965, House of Greystoke
Book illustrator: Frazetta

16. "Carthoris"
Date written: April 16, 1914, to June 20, 1914
Magazine title: "Thuvia, Maid of Mars"
Magazine published in: *All-Story Cavalier,* April 8 to 22, 1916
Book title: *Thuvia, Maid of Mars*
Date book published: 1920, A. C. McClurg & Co., first edition, hardbound
Book illustrator: St. John

17. "The Cave Man"
Date written: July 23, 1914, to August 17, 1914
Magazine title: "The Cave Man"
Magazine published in: *All-Story Cavalier,* March 31 to April 21, 1917
Book title: *The Cave Girl* (includes "The Cave Man" and "The Cave Girl," story 7)
Date book published: 1925, A. C. McClurg & Co., first edition, hardbound
Book illustrator: St. John

18. "Sweetheart Primeval"
Date written: August 21, 1914, to September 14, 1914
Magazine title: "Sweetheart Primeval"
Magazine published in: *All-Story Cavalier,* January 23 to February 13, 1915
Book title: *The Eternal Lover* (includes "Sweetheart Primeval" and "The Eternal Lover," story 12)
Date book published: 1925, A. C. McClurg & Co., first edition, hardbound
Book illustrator: St. John

19. " 'Barney' Custer of Beatrice"
Date written: September 26, 1914, to November 1, 1914
Magazine title: "Barney Custer of Beatrice"
Magazine published in: *All-Story Cavalier,* August 7 to 21, 1915
Book title: *The Mad King* (includes "Barney Custer of Beatrice" and "The Mad King," story 11)
Date book published: 1926, A. C. McClurg & Co., first edition, hardbound
Book illustrator: St. John

20. "Pellucidar"
Date written: November 23, 1914, to January 11, 1915
Magazine title: "Pellucidar"
Magazine published in: *All-Story Cavalier,* May 1 to 29, 1915
Book title: *Pellucidar*
Date book published: 1923, A. C. McClurg & Co., first edition, hardbound

Book illustrator: St. John
21. "The Son of Tarzan"
Date written: January 21, 1915, to May 11, 1915
Magazine title: "The Son of Tarzan"
Magazine published in: *All-Story Cavalier,* December 4 to 25, 1915
Book title: *The Son of Tarzan*
Date book published: 1917, A. C. McClurg & Co., first edition, hardbound
Book illustrator: St. John

22. "Ben, King of Beasts"
Date written: May 13, 1915, to June 10, 1915
Magazine title: "The Man-Eater" (In Evening World Magazine)
Magazine published in: *New York Evening World,* November 1915
Book title: Included in *Beyond Thirty* (number 23) and *The Man-Eater* (number 22)

23. "Beyond Thirty"
Date written: July 8, 1915, to August 10, 1915
Magazine title: "Beyond Thirty"
Magazine published in: *All Around Magazine,* February 1916
Book title: *The Lost Continent;* also included in *Beyond Thirty*
Date book published: 1963 (*The Lost Continent*)
Book illustrator: Frazetta

24. "Tarzan and the Jewels of Opar"
Date written: September 6, 1915, to October 19, 1915
Magazine title: "Tarzan and the Jewels of Opar"
Magazine published in: *All-Story Cavalier,* November 18 to December 16, 1916
Book title: *Tarzan and the Jewels of Opar*
Date book published: 1918, A. C. McClurg & Co., first edition, hardbound
Book illustrator: St. John

25. "H.R.H. the Rider"
Date written: October 25, 1915, to December 5, 1915
Magazine title: "H.R.H. the Rider"
Magazine published in: *All-Story,* December 14 to 28, 1918
Book title: *The Oakdale Affair* and *The Rider* (stories 25 and 28 are combined)
Date book published: 1937, Edgar Rice Burroughs, Inc., first edition, hardbound
Book illustrator: J. C. Burroughs

26. "Out There Somewhere"
Date written: January 24, 1916, to March 15, 1916
Magazine title: "The Return of the Mucker"
Magazine published in: *All-Story Cavalier,* June 17 to July 15, 1916
Book title: part 2 of *The Mucker* (see story 10)
Date book published: 1921, A. C. McClurg & Co., first edition, hardbound
Book illustrator: St. John

27. "The New Tarzan Stories"
Date written: March 17, 1916, to March 18, 1917
Magazine title: "The New Stories of Tarzan"
Magazine published in: *Blue Book,* September 1916 to August 1917
Book title: *Jungle Tales of Tarzan*
Date book published: 1919, A. C. McClurg & Co., first edition, hardbound
Book illustrator: St. John
Stories: "Tarzan's First Love" (written March 17, 1916, to March 21, 1916); "The Capture of Tarzan" (written May 8, 1916, to May 25, 1916); "The Fight for the Balu" (written May 26, 1916, to June 1, 1916); "The God of Tarzan" (written July 7, 1916, to July 13, 1916); "Tarzan and the Black Boy" (written October 13, 1916); "The Witch Doctor Seeks Vengeance" (written November 1, 1916, to November 5, 1916); "The End of Bukawai" (written December 8, 1916, to December 11, 1916); "The Lion" (written December 22, 1916, to December 29, 1916); "The Nightmare" (written February 7, 1917, to February 8, 1917); "The Battle for Teeka" (written February 12, 1917, to February 28, 1917); "A Jungle Joke" (written March 5, 1917, to March 11, 1917); "Tarzan Rescues the Moon" (written March 14, 1917, to March 18, 1917)

28. "Bridge and the Oskaloosa Kid"
Date written: January 10, 1917, to June 12, 1917
Magazine title: "The Oakdale Affair"
Magazine published in: *Blue Book,* March 1918
Book title: *The Oakdale Affair* and *The Rider* (stories 25 and 28 are combined)
Date book published: 1937, Edgar Rice Burroughs, Inc., first edition, hardbound
Book illustrator: J. C. Burroughs

29. "The Lost U-Boat"
Date written: September 8, 1917, to October 13, 1917
Magazine title: "The Land That Time Forgot"
Magazine published in: *Blue Book,* August 1918
Book title: *The Land That Time Forgot* (contains stories 29, 31, and 32)
Date book published: 1924, A. C. McClurg & Co., first edition, hardbound
Book illustrator: St. John

30. "The Little Door"
Date written: November 17, 1917, to November 23, 1917 (2,800 words)
Unpublished

31. "Cor Sva Jo"
Date written: October 13, 1917, to February 8, 1918
Magazine title: "The People That Time Forgot"
Magazine published in: *Blue Book,* October 1918
Book title: Included in *The Land That Time Forgot* (the book contains stories 29, 31, and 32)
Date book published: 1924, A. C. McClurg & Co., first edition, hardbound

Book illustrator: St. John
32. "Out of Time's Abyss"
Date written: May 23, 1918, to July 16, 1918
Magazine title: "Out of Time's Abyss"
Magazine published in: *Blue Book,* December 1918
Book title: included in *The Land That Time Forgot* (the book contains stories 29, 31, and 32)
Date book published: 1924, A. C. McClurg & Co., first edition, hardbound
Book illustrator: St. John

33. "Tarzan and the Huns
Date written: August 9, 1918, to September 10, 1919
Magazine title: "Tarzan the Untamed"
Magazine published in: *Red Book,* March 1919
Book title: *Tarzan the Untamed*
Date book published: 1920, A. C. McClurg & Co., first edition, hardbound
Book illustrator: St. John
Stories: "An Eye for an Eye" (written August 9, 1918, to October 17, 1918, *Red Book,* March 1919); "When the Lion Fed" (written, October 18, 1918, to October 30, 1918, *Red Book,* April 1919); "The Golden Locket" (written October 31, 1918, to November 23, 1918, *Red Book,* May 1919); "When Blood Told" (written November 27, 1918, to December 10, 1918, *Red Book,* June 1919); "The Debt" (written December 11, 1918, to January 15, 1919, *Red Book,* July 1919); "The Black Flyer" (written January 15, 1919, to January 24, 1919, *Red Book,* August 1919); "Tarzan and the Valley of Luna" (written August 7, 1919, to September 10, 1919, *All-Story Weekly,* March 20 to April 17, 1920

34. "Under the Red Flag"
Date written: April 30, 1919, to May 21, 1919; rewritten January 24, 1922
Magazine title: "The Moon Men"
Magazine published in: *All-Story,* February 21 to March 15, 1925
Book title: part 2 of *The Moon Maid* (the book contains stories 34, 42, and 47)
Date book published: 1926, A. C. McClurg & Co., first edition, hardbound
Book illustrator: St. John

35. "For the Fool's Mother"
Date written: October 3, 1912, to October 5, 1912 (although listed as story 35, the date of writing indicates that the story should have been listed either as story 4 or 5)
Unpublished

36. "The Efficiency Expert"
Date written: September 22, 1919, to October 22, 1919
Magazine title: "The Efficiency Expert"
Magazine published in: *All-Story,* October 8 to October 29, 1921

Book title: *The Efficiency Expert*
Date book published: 1966, House of Greystoke
Book illustrator: Morrison and Frazetta

37. "The Ghostly Script"
Date written: Started March 16, 1920
Unpublished

38. "Tarzan the Terrible"
Date written: August 14, 1920, to December 16, 1920
Magazine title: "Tarzan the Terrible"
Magazine published in: *All-Story,* February 12 to March 27, 1921
Book title: *Tarzan the Terrible*
Date book published: 1921, A. C. McClurg & Co., first edition, hardbound
Book illustrator: St. John

39. "The Chess Men of Mars"
Date written: January 7, 1921, to November 12, 1921
Magazine title: "Chessmen of Mars"
Magazine published in: *All-Story,* February 18 to April 2, 1922
Book title: *The Chessmen of Mars*
Date book published: 1922, A. C. McClurg & Co., first edition, hardbound
Book illustrator: St. John

40. "The Penningtons"
Date written: November 16, 1921, to January 7, 1922
Magazine title: "The Girl from Hollywood"
Magazine published in: *Munsey,* June to November 1922
Book title: *The Girl from Hollywood*
Date book published: 1923, The Macaulay Co., first edition, hardbound
Book illustrator: Monahan

41. "Tarzan and the Golden Lion"
Date written: February 10, 1922, to May 31, 1922
Magazine title: "Tarzan and the Golden Lion"
Magazine published in: *All-Story,* December 9, 1922, to January 20, 1923
Book title: *Tarzan and the Golden Lion*
Date book published: 1923, A. C. McClurg & Co., first edition, hardbound
Book illustrator: St. John

42. "The Moon Maid"
Date written: June 22, 1922, to July 20, 1922
Magazine title: "The Moon Maid"
Magazine reprint title: "Conquest of the Moon"
Magazine published in: *All-Story,* May 5 to June 2, 1923
Book title: *The Moon Maid* (also includes *The Moon Men,* story 34, and *The Red Hawk,* story 47)
Date book published: 1926, A. C. McClurg & Co., first edition, hardbound
Book illustrator: St. John

43. "Beware!"
Date written: August 9, 1922, to August 31, 1922

Magazine title: "The Scientists Revolt"
Magazine published in: *Fantastic Adventures,* July 1939

44. "The Bandit of Hell's Bend"
Date written: March 22, 1923, to May 24, 1923
Magazine title: "The Bandit of Hell's Bend"
Magazine published in: *All-Story,* September 13 to October 18, 1924
Book title: *The Bandit of Hell's Bend*
Date book published: 1925, A. C. McClurg & Co., first edition, hardbound
Book illustrator: Modest Stein

45. "Tarzan and the Ant Men"
Date written: June 20, 1923, to November 22, 1923
Magazine title: "Tarzan and the Ant Men"
Magazine published in: *All-Story,* February 2 to March 17, 1924
Book title: *Tarzan and the Ant Men*
Date book published: 1924, A. C. McClurg & Co., first edition, hardbound
Book illustrator: St. John

46. "Marcia of the Doorstep"
Date written: April 12, 1924, to October 13, 1924 (125,000 words)
Unpublished

47. "The Red Hawk"
Date written: April 20, 1925, to May 14, 1925
Magazine title: "The Red Hawk"
Magazine published in: *All-Story,* September 5 to 19, 1925
Book title: part 3 of *The Moon Maid* (the book contains stories 34, 42, and 47)
Date book published: 1926, A. C. McClurg & Co., first edition, hardbound
Book illustrator: St. John

48. (1) "A Weird Adventure on Mars," (2) "Vad Varo of Barsoom"
Date written: June 8, 1925, to November 16, 1925
Magazine title: "The Master Mind of Mars"
Magazine published in: *Amazing Stories,* July 1927
Book title: *The Master Mind of Mars*
Date book published: 1928, A. C. McClurg & Co., first edition, hardbound
Book illustrator: St. John

49. "The War Chief of the Apaches"
Date written: August 19, 1926, to November 12, 1926
Magazine title: "The War Chief"
Magazine published in: *All-Story,* April 16 to May 14, 1927
Book title: *The War Chief*
Date book published: 1927, A. C. McClurg & Co., first edition, hardbound
Book illustrator: Stahr

50. "The Tarzan Twins"
Date written: November 16, 1926, to January 15, 1927

Book title: *The Tarzan Twins*
Date book published: 1927, The P. F. Volland Co., first edition, hardbound
Book illustrator: Grant

51. "Tarzan the Invincible"
Date written: May 13, 1927, to July 22, 1927
Magazine title: "Tarzan, Lord of the Jungle"
Magazine published in: *Blue Book*, December 1927 to May 1928
Book title: *Tarzan, Lord of the Jungle*
Date book published: 1928, A. C. McClurg & Co., first edition, hardbound
Book illustrator: St. John

52. "Apache Devil"
Date written: August 4, 1927, to November 20, 1927
Magazine title: "Apache Devil"
Magazine published in: *All-Story*, May 19 to June 23, 1928
Book title: *Apache Devil*
Date book published: 1933, Edgar Rice Burroughs, Inc., first edition, hardbound
Book illustrator: S. O. Burroughs

53. "Jad-Bal-Ja and the Tarzan Twins"
Date written: January 17, 1928, to February 20, 1928
Book title: *Tarzan and the Tarzan Twins with Jad-Bal-Ja, the Golden Lion* (Sequel to *The Tarzan Twins*, story 50; both stories were published together in the 1963 Canaveral Press edition of *Tarzan and the Tarzan Twins*. See story 99)
Date book published: 1936, Whitman Publishing Co., first edition, hardbound
Book illustrator: Juanita Bennett

54. "Tarzan and the Lost Empire"
Date written: March 29, 1928, to May 26, 1928
Magazine title: "Tarzan and the Lost Empire"
Magazine published in: *Blue Book*, October 1928 to February 1929
Book title: *Tarzan and the Lost Empire*
Date book published: 1929, Metropolitan Books, Inc., first edition, hardbound
Book illustrator: A. W. Sperry

55. "Tanar of Pellucidar"
Date written: September 13, 1928, to November 21, 1928
Magazine title: "Tanar of Pellucidar"
Magazine published in: *Blue Book*, March to August 1929
Book title: *Tanar of Pellucidar*
Date book published: 1930, Metropolitan Books, Inc., first edition, hardbound
Book illustrator: Berdanier

56. "Tarzan and Pellucidar"
Date written: December 6, 1928, to February 7, 1929
Magazine title: "Tarzan at the Earth's Core"
Magazine published in: *Blue Book*, September 1929 to March 1930

Book title: *Tarzan at the Earth's Core*
Date book published: 1930, Metropolitan Books, Inc., first edition, hardbound
Book illustrator: St. John

57. "A Fighting Man of Mars"
Date written: February 28, 1929, to May 10, 1929
Magazine title: "A Fighting Man of Mars"
Magazine published in: *Blue Book*, April to September 1930
Book title: *A Fighting Man of Mars*
Date book published: 1931, Metropolitan Books, Inc., first edition, hardbound
Book illustrator: Hugh Hutton

58. "The Dancing Girl of The Leper King"
Date written: October 2, 1929, to December 30, 1929
Magazine title: "The Land of Hidden Men"
Magazine published in: *Blue Book*, May to September 1931
Book title: *Jungle Girl*
Date book published: 1932, Edgar Rice Burroughs, Inc., first edition, hardbound
Book illustrator: S. O. Burroughs

59. "Tarzan and the Man Things"
Date written: March 18, 1930, to June 9, 1930
Magazine title: "Tarzan, Guard of the Jungle"
Magazine published in: *Blue Book*, October 1930 to April 1931
Book title: *Tarzan the Invincible*
Date book published: 1931, Edgar Rice Burroughs, Inc., first edition, hardbound
Book illustrator: S. O. Burroughs

60. (1) "That Damn Dude," (2) "The Brass Heart," (3) "The Terrible Tenderfoot"
Date written: June 14, 1930, to July 12, 1930
Magazine title: "The Terrible Tenderfoot"
Magazine published in: *Thrilling Adventures*, March to May 1939
Book title: *The Deputy Sheriff of Comanche County*
Date book published: 1940, Edgar Rice Burroughs, Inc., first edition, hardbound
Book illustrator: J. C. Burroughs

61. "Tarzan and the Raiders"
Date written: February 27, 1931, to May 20, 1931
Magazine title: "The Triumph of Tarzan"
Magazine published in: *Blue Book*, October 1931 to March 1932
Book title: *Tarzan Triumphant*
Date book published: 1932, Edgar Rice Burroughs, Inc., first edition, hardbound
Book illustrator: S. O. Burroughs

62. "Calling All Cars"
Date written: June 12, 1931, to June 14, 1931 (6,531 words)
Unpublished (?)

63. "Tarzan and the Leopard Men"
Date written: July 9, 1931, to September 25, 1931
Magazine title: "Tarzan and the Leopard Men"

Magazine published in: *Blue Book,* August 1932 to January 1933
Book title: *Tarzan and the Leopard Men*
Date book published: 1935, Edgar Rice Burroughs, Inc., first edition, hardbound
Book illustrator: St. John
64. "The Pirates of Venus"
Date written: October 2, 1931, to November 6, 1931
Magazine title: "The Pirates of Venus"
Magazine published in: *Argosy,* September 17 to October 22, 1932
Book title: *Pirates of Venus*
Date book published: 1934, Edgar Rice Burroughs, Inc., first edition, hardbound
Book illustrator: St. John
65. "Tarzan and the City of Gold"
Date written: November 21, 1931, to January 7, 1932
Magazine title: "Tarzan and the City of Gold"
Magazine published in: *Argosy,* March 12 to April 16, 1932
Book title: *Tarzan and the City of Gold*
Date book published: 1933, Edgar Rice Burroughs, Inc., first edition, hardbound
Book illustrator: St. John
66. "Pirate Blood" (by John Tyler McCulloch, one of ERB's pen names)
Date written: February 22, 1932, to May 5, 1932
Book title: *Pirate Blood*
Date book published: 1970, Ace Publishing Corp., first edition, soft cover
67. "Lost on Venus"
Date written: August 6, 1932, to November 12, 1932
Magazine title: "Lost on Venus"
Magazine published in: *Argosy,* March 4 to April 18, 1933
Book title: *Lost on Venus*
Date book published: 1935, Edgar Rice Burroughs, Inc., first edition, hardbound
Book illustrator: St. John
68. "Tarzan and the Lion-Man"
Date written: February 9, 1933, to May 30, 1933
Magazine title: "Tarzan and the Lion Man"
Magazine published in: *Liberty,* November 1933 to January 1934
Book title: *Tarzan and the Lion-Man*
Date book published: 1934, Edgar Rice Burroughs, Inc., first edition, hardbound
Book illustrator: St. John
69. "Swords of Mars"
Date written: November 6, 1933, to December 15, 1933
Magazine title: "Swords of Mars"
Magazine published in: *Blue Book,* November 1934 to April 1935
Book title: *Swords of Mars*
Date book published: 1936, Edgar Rice Burroughs, Inc., first edition, hardbound

Book illustrator: St. John
70. (1) "Tarzan and Jane," (2) "Tarzan and the Immortal Men"
Date written: May 13, 1934, to January 19, 1935
Magazine title: "Tarzan and the Immortal Men"
Magazine published in: *Blue Book,* October 1935 to March 1936
Book title: *Tarzan's Quest*
Date book published: 1936, Edgar Rice Burroughs, Inc., first edition, hardbound
Book illustrator: St. John
71. "Back to the Stone Age, A Romance of the Inner World"
Date written: January 26, 1935, to September 11, 1935
Magazine title: "Seven Worlds to Conquer"
Magazine published in: *Argosy,* January 9 to February 13, 1937
Book title: *Back to the Stone Age*
Date book published: 1937, Edgar Rice Burroughs, Inc., first edition, hardbound
Book illustrator: J. C. Burroughs
72. "Tarzan the Magnificent"
Date written: 1935 or 1936
Magazine title: "Tarzan and the Magic Men"
Magazine published in: *Argosy,* September 19 to October 3, 1936
Book title: *Tarzan the Magnificent* (also includes story 74)
Date book published: 1939, Edgar Rice Burroughs, Inc., first edition, hardbound
Book illustrator: J. C. Burroughs
73. "Elmer"
Date written: March 22, 1936, to March 25, 1936
Magazine title: "The Resurrection of Jimber-Jaw"
Magazine published in: *Argosy,* February 20, 1937
Book title: part of *Tales of Three Planets* (book contains stories 88-1, 88-2, and 91-1)
Date book published: 1964, Canaveral Press, Inc., first edition, hardbound
Book illustrator: Roy Krenkel
74. "Tarzan and the Elephant Men"
Date written: December 1, 1936, to March 8, 1937
Magazine title: "Tarzan and the Elephant Men"
Magazine published in: *Blue Book,* November 1937 to January 1938
Book title: *Tarzan the Magnificent* (also contains story 72)
Date book published: 1939, Edgar Rice Burroughs, Inc., first edition, hardbound
Book illustrator: J. C. Burroughs
75. "Carson of Venus"
Date written: July 24, 1937, to August 19, 1937
Magazine title: "Carson of Venus"
Magazine published in: *Argosy,* January 8 to February 12, 1938
Book title: *Carson of Venus*

Date book published: 1939, Edgar Rice Burroughs, Inc., first edition, hardbound
Book illustrator: J. C. Burroughs

76. "Tarzan and the Forbidden City"
Date written: October 10, 1937, to November 18, 1937
Magazine title: "The Red Star of Tarzan"
Magazine published in: *Argosy,* March 19 to April 23, 1938
Book title: *Tarzan and the Forbidden City*
Date book published: 1938, Edgar Rice Burroughs, Inc., first edition, hardbound
Book illustrator: J. C. Burroughs

77. (1) " 'Two Gun' Doak Flies South" (by John Tyler McCulloch) (2) "Mr. Doak Flies South" (by Edgar Rice Burroughs)
Date written: December 1, 1937, to January 31, 1938 (26,700 words), unpublished

78. "Synthetic Men of Mars"
Date written: March 2, 1938 to ?
Magazine title: "The Synthetic Men of Mars"
Magazine published in: *Argosy,* January 7 to February 11, 1939
Book title: *Synthetic Men of Mars*
Date book published: 1940, Edgar Rice Burroughs, Inc., first edition, hardbound
Book illustrator: J. C. Burroughs

79. "Land of Terror"
Date written: October 17, 1938, to April 17, 1939
Book title: *Land of Terror*
Date book published: 1944, Edgar Rice Burroughs, Inc., first edition, hardbound
Book illustrator: J. C. Burroughs

80. (1) "New Tarzan Series, 1939," (2) "Murder in the Jungle"
Date written: January 10, 1939, to January 18, 1939
Magazine title: "Tarzan and the Jungle Murders"
Magazine published in: *Thrilling Adventures,* June 1940
Book title: part of *Tarzan and the Castaways* (book includes stories 80, 82, and 89)
Date book published: 1964, Canaveral Press, Inc., first edition, hardbound
Book illustrator: Frazetta

81. "Angel's Serenade"
Date written: outline written May 13, 1921, and revised May 19, 1936; story written April 25, 1939, to June 12, 1939 (24,000 words)
Unpublished

82. "Tarzan and the Champion"
Date written: July 17, 1939 to ?
Magazine title: "Tarzan and the Champion"
Magazine published in: *Blue Book,* April 1940
Book title: part of *Tarzan and the Castaways* (book contains stories 80, 82, and 89)

Date book published: 1964, Canaveral Press, Inc., first edition, hardbound
Book illustrator: Frazetta

83. "Tarzan and the Madman"
Date written: January 16, 1940, to February 22, 1940
Book title: *Tarzan and the Madman*
Date book published: 1964, Canaveral Press, Inc., first edition, hardbound
Book illustrator: Reed Crandall

84-1. "Captured on Venus"
Date written: May 4, 1940, to July 20, 1940
Magazine title: "Slaves of the Fishmen"
Magazine published in: *Fantastic Adventures,* March 1941
Book title: *Escape on Venus*
Date book published: 1946, Edgar Rice Burroughs, Inc., first edition, hardbound
Book illustrator: J. C. Burroughs

84-2. "The Fire Goddess"
Date written: September 16, 1940, to September 24, 1940
Magazine title: "Goddess of Fire"
Magazine published in: *Fantastic Adventures,* July 1941
Book title: *Escape on Venus*
Date book published: 1946, Edgar Rice Burroughs, Inc., first edition, hardbound
Book illustrator: J. C. Burroughs

84-3. "The Living Dead"
Date written: October 15, 1940, to October 22, 1940
Magazine title: "The Living Dead"
Magazine published in: *Fantastic Adventures,* November 1941
Book title: *Escape on Venus*
Date book published: 1946, Edgar Rice Burroughs, Inc., first edition, hardbound
Book illustrator: J. C. Burroughs

84-4. "War on Venus"
Date written: November 12, 1940, to November 16, 1940
Magazine title: "War on Venus"
Magazine published in: *Fantastic Adventures,* March 1942
Book title: *Escape on Venus*
Date book published: 1946, Edgar Rice Burroughs, Inc., first edition, hardbound
Book illustrator: J. C. Burroughs

85. "The Strange Adventure of Mr. Dinnwiddie"
Date written: July 16 and 17, 1940 (5,700 words)
Unpublished

86-1. (1) "The Frozen Men of Mars," (2) "John Carter and the Pits of Horz"
Date written: July 24, 1940, to September 6, 1940
Magazine title: "The City of Mummies"
Magazine published in: *Amazing Stories,* March 1941

Book title: *Llana of Gathol*
Date book published: 1948, Edgar Rice Burroughs, Inc., first edition, hardbound
Book illustrator: J. C. Burroughs

86-2. "The Black Pirates of Barsoom"
Date written: September 27, 1940, to October 2, 1940
Magazine title: "Black Pirates of Barsoom"
Magazine published in: *Amazing Stories,* June 1941
Book title: *Llana of Gathol*
Date book published: 1948, Edgar Rice Burroughs, Inc., first edition, hardbound
Book illustrator: J. C. Burroughs

86-3. "Escape on Mars"
Date written: October 24, 1940, to October 30, 1940
Magazine title: "Yellow Men of Mars"
Magazine published in: *Amazing Stories,* August 1941
Book title: *Llana of Gathol*
Date book published: 1948, Edgar Rice Burroughs, Inc., first edition, hardbound
Book illustrator: J. C. Burroughs

86-4. "Invisible Men of Mars"
Date written: November 18, 1940, to November 22, 1940
Magazine title: "Invisible Men of Mars"
Magazine published in: *Amazing Stories,* October 1941
Book title: *Llana of Gathol* (after completing story 86-4, ERB changed the title for eventual book from "Frozen Men of Mars" to "Swordsman of Mars"; however, it finally became *Llana of Gathol*)
Date book published: 1948, Edgar Rice Burroughs, Inc., first edition, hardbound
Book illustrator: J. C. Burroughs

87-1. "Hodon and O-aa"
Date written: September 7, 1940, to September 15, 1940
Magazine title: "The Return to Pellucidar"
Magazine published in: *Amazing Stories,* February 1942
Book title: *Savage Pellucidar* (the book was scheduled for publication by Canaveral Press in November 1963; ERB's tentative title for stories comprising 87 in book form was "Girl of Pellucidar")
Date book published: 1963, Canaveral Press, Inc., first edition, hardbound
Book illustrator: St. John

87-2. "Men of the Bronze Age"
Date written: October 6, 1940, to October 13, 1940
Magazine title: "Men of the Bronze Age"
Magazine published in: *Amazing Stories,* March 1942
Book title: *Savage Pellucidar*
Date book published: 1963, Canaveral Presss, Inc., first edition, hardbound
Book illustrator: St. John

87-3. "Tiger Girl"
Date written: November 6, 1940, to November 10, 1940
Magazine title: "Tiger Girl"
Magazine published in: *Amazing Stories,* April 1942
Book title: *Savage Pellucidar*
Date book published: 1963, Canaveral Press, Inc., first edition, hardbound
Book illustrator: St. John

87-4. "Savage Pellucidar"
Date written: October 2, 1944, to October 26, 1944
Magazine title: "Savage Pellucidar"
Magazine published in: *Amazing Stories,* November 1963
Book title: *Savage Pellucidar*
Date book published: 1963, Canaveral Press, Inc., first edition, hardbound
Book illustrator: St. John

88-1. "Beyond the Farthest Star"
Date written: October 24, 1940, to November 5, 1940
Magazine title: "Beyond the Farthest Star"
Magazine published in: *Blue Book,* January 1942
Book title: part of *Tales of Three Planets* (book contains stories 73, 88, 91; ERB planned 88 as the first of a series of three or four novelettes to be combined as a book)
Date book published: 1964, Canaveral Press, Inc., first edition, hardbound
Book illustrator: Roy G. Krenkel

88-2. "Tangor Returns"
Date written: December 17, 1940, to December 21, 1940
Book title: part of *Tales of Three Planets* (book contains stories 73, 88, 91)
Date book published: 1964, Canaveral Press, Inc., first edition, hardbound
Book illustrator: Roy G. Krenkel

89. "Tarzan and the Castaways"
Date written: November 26, 1940, to December 13, 1940
Magazine title: "The Quest of Tarzan"
Magazine published in: *Argosy,* August 23 to September 6, 1941
Book title: *Tarzan and the Castaways* (contains stories 80, 82, and 89)
Date book published: 1964, Canaveral Press, Inc., first edition, hardbound
Book illustrator: Frazetta

90. "Misogynists Preferred"
Date written: January 5, 1940, to January 8, 1940 (4,000 words)
Unpublished

91-1. "The Wizard of Venus"
Date written: January 23, 1941, to October 7, 1941
Book title: *Tales of Three Planets* (contains stories 73, 88, and 91; "The Wizard of Venus" and 91-2

were planned as the first of a proposed three or four novelettes in a new Venus series; 91-2 was interrupted five days later after the beginning of the Japanese attack on Pearl Harbor, which ERB witnessed from the waterfront at the Niumalu Hotel in Honolulu)

Date book published: 1964, Canaveral Press, Inc., first edition, hardbound

Book illustrator: Roy G. Krenkel

91-2. "A Venus Story"

Date written: December 2, 1941 (two and one-half pages; unfinished)

Unpublished

92. "I Am a Barbarian"

Date written: April 11, 1941, to September 27, 1941

Book title: *I Am a Barbarian*

Date book published: 1967, Edgar Rice Burroughs, Inc., first edition, hardbound

Book illustrator: Jeff Jones

93. "The Skeleton Men of Jupiter"

Date written: October 25, 1941, to November 20, 1941

Magazine title: "Skeleton Men of Jupiter"

Magazine published in: *Amazing Stories,* February 1943

Book title: *John Carter of Mars* (combined with "John Carter and the Giant of Mars," story 98)

Date book published: 1964, Canaveral Press, Inc., first edition, hardbound

Book illustrator: Reed Crandall

94. (1) "Night of Terror," (2) "More Fun! More People Killed!"

Date written: February 24, 1943, to March 30, 1943 (20,727 words)

Unpublished

95. "Uncle Bill"

Date written: May 19, 1944, to May 20, 1944 (1,787 words)

Unpublished

96. "Tarzan and the 'Foreign Legion'"

Date written: June 10, 1944, to September 11, 1944

Book title: *Tarzan and "The Foreign Legion"*

Date book published: 1947, Edgar Rice Burroughs, Inc., first edition, hardbound

Book illustrator: J. C. Burroughs

*97. "Unnamed Tarzan Novel"

Date: September 7, 1946 (incomplete at time of ERB's death; consists of eighty-three typewritten pages)

Unpublished

**98. "John Carter and the Giant of Mars"

Date written: 1939 or 1940

Magazine title: "John Carter and the Giant of Mars"

Magazine published in: *Amazing Stories,* January 1941

Book title: *John Carter of Mars* (combined with "The Skeleton Men of Jupiter," story 93)

Date book published: 1964, Canaveral Press, Inc., first edition, hardbound

Book illustrator: Reed Crandall

***99. "Tarzan and the Tarzan Twins"

Book title: *Tarzan and the Tarzan Twins* (contains *The Tarzan Twins,* story 50, and its sequel *Tarzan and the Tarzan Twins with Jad-Bal-Ja, the Golden Lion,* story 53)

Date book published: 1963, Canaveral Presss, Inc., first edition, hardbound

*Not listed in ERB's notebook; manuscript was assigned this number by ERB

**Not listed in ERB's notebook

***Not listed in ERB's notebook

Note: Unpublished stories: 30, 35 (?), 37, 46, 62 (?), 77, 81, 85, 90, 91-2, 94, 95, 97. Stories not published in magazines: 50, 53, 66, 79, 83, 88-2, 91-1, 92, 96.

Novels (listed in order of publication)

Tarzan novels

Tarzan of the Apes
The Return of Tarzan
The Beasts of Tarzan
The Son of Tarzan
Tarzan and the Jewels of Opar
Jungle Tales of Tarzan
Tarzan the Untamed
Tarzan the Terrible
Tarzan and the Golden Lion
Tarzan and the Ant Men
The Tarzan Twins
Tarzan, Lord of the Jungle
Tarzan and the Lost Empire
Tarzan at the Earth's Core
Tarzan the Invincible
Tarzan Triumphant
Tarzan and the City of Gold
Tarzan and the Lion Man
Tarzan and the Leopard Men
Tarzan and the Tarzan Twins with Jad-Bal-Ja, the Golden Lion
Tarzan's Quest
Tarzan and the Forbidden City
Tarzan the Magnificent
Tarzan and "The Foreign Legion"
Tarzan and the Tarzan Twins (combines *The Tarzan Twins* and *Tarzan and The Tarzan Twins with Jad-Bal-Ja, the Golden Lion*)
Tarzan and the Madman
Tarzan and the Castaways
Tarzan and the Valley of Gold (Fritz Leiber)

Martian novels

A Princess of Mars

The Gods of Mars
The Warlord of Mars
Thuvia, Maid of Mars
The Chessmen of Mars
The Master Mind of Mars
A Fighting Man of Mars
Swords of Mars
Synthetic Men of Mars
Llana of Gathol
John Carter of Mars

Venus novels

Pirates of Venus
Lost on Venus
Carson of Venus
Escape on Venus
The Wizard of Venus

Inner-world novels

At the Earth's Core
Pellucidar
Tanar of Pellucidar
Tarzan at the Earth's Core
Back to the Stone Age
Land of Terror
Savage Pellucidar

Apache novels

The War Chief
Apache Devil

Miscellaneous novels

The Mucker
The Girl from Hollywood
The Land That Time Forgot
The Cave Girl
The Bandit of Hell's Bend
The Eternal Lover
The Moon Maid
The Mad King
The Outlaw of Torn
The Monster Men
Jungle Girl
The Oakdale Affair and the Rider
The Lad and the Lion
The Deputy Sheriff of Comanche County
Tales of Three Planets
    Beyond the Farthest Star
    Tangor Returns
    The Resurrection of Jimber-Jaw
    The Wizard of Venus
I am a Barbarian
Pirate Blood
The Efficiency Expert
The Girl from Farris's

Miscellaneous Works

1. "A National Reserve Army": written August 31, 1918; 1,000 words; published in *Army-Navy Journal*

2. Article re Scopes trial: 600 words; published by International Press Bureau

3. "Autobiography of Edgar Rice Burroughs" (incomplete): 15,000 words; unpublished

4. "Came the War (WWI)": 2,700 words; unpublished (?)

5. "Diary of an Automobile Camping Trip Undertaken by the Burroughs Family in 1916": unpublished

6. "Edgar Rice Burroughs Tells All" (humorous autobiography): written July 9, 1932; 1,000 words; published in Rob Wagner's *Script*

7. "Fall of a Democracy": 2,100 words; unpublished(?)

8. "His Majesty, The Janitor" (outline): 2,100 words; unpublished

9. "I See a New Race": 1,800 words; unpublished (?)

10. "Late News": published in the *Coldwater Daily Reporter*, Coldwater, Michigan

11. "Laugh It Off!": regular column in the *Honolulu Advertiser* during World War II

12. "Little Lessons for Little Learners — 1. Jonathan's Patience" or "How Fortune Came Through Faith (A Sunday School Story)"

13. "Minidoka 937th Earl of One Mile Series M.": written before 1911; unpublished

14. "Murder, a Collection of Short Murder Mystery Puzzles" (17,400 words): (1) "Murder at Midnight," unpublished; (2) "Bank Murder," unpublished; (3) "The Terrace Drive Murder," *Script Magazine*, 1932; (4) "The Gang Murder," unpublished; (5) "The Lightship Murder," *Script Magazine*, 1935; (6) "The Dark Lake Murder," unpublished; (7) "Who Murdered Mr. Thomas?" *Script Magazine*, 1932; (8) "The Red Necktie" (800 words), *Script Magazine*, 1932; (9) "The Dupuyster Case" (3,000 words), unpublished

15. "Night of Terror": 18,000 words; unpublished

16. "Out of Time's Abyss": article for *The Urbanite*, school paper of Urban Military Academy where Hulbert and John C. Burroughs attended, 1924-1925

17. "Patriotism by Proxy": 1,700 words; article published in *Oak Leaves*, May 25, 1918, Oak Park, Ill.

18. "Peace and the Militia": published in *The Oak Parker*, November 16, 1918, Oak Park, Ill.

19. "Quiet Please!": nine articles for proposed ERB newspaper column that never materialized, 1939

20. "Radio Interview": sponsored by the Texaco Star Theatre (Ken Murray) October 18, 1939

21. "Selling Satisfaction" (an anecdote by Normal Bean): 900 words; unpublished (?)

22. Speech delivered at Flag Day exercises, Oak Park,

Ill., June 14, 1918

23. "The Absurd Quarantine": article probably prepared for a Los Angeles newspaper, regarding hoof and mouth disease epidemic in San Fernando Valley, California, in early 1920s

24. "The Avenger": 3,600 words; unpublished

25. "The Citizen and the Police": 1,500 words; published in the *Police Reporter*, 1929

26. "The Death Valley Expedition of the Intrepid 33ers": written in 1933; 2,700 words; unpublished

27. "The Eleven Year Itch" (humorous): 5,500 words; published in Rob Wagner's *Script*

28. "The Lion Hunter" (comedy outline): written in 1915; 1,500 words; unpublished

29. "The Prospector" (outline): 3,300 words; unpublished

30. "The Zealots": written in 1915; unpublished

31. "Them Thar Papers": script for home movie filmed on Tarzana Ranch, starring family and friends; Tarzana Pictures Presents, about 1933

32. "Uncle Miner and Other Relatives": 22,800 words; unpublished

33. Unfinished play (29 pages)

34. "Wanted — Good Citizens": a call for volunteers — Illinois Reserve Militia, Oak Park, Ill. 1918

35. "What Every Young Couple Should Know": 3,300; unpublished

36. "What Is the Matter with the U.S. Army?": 2,196 words; unpublished (?)

37. "You Lucky Girl!" (3 act play): unpublished

Tarzan Motion Pictures

1. *Tarzan of the Apes,* produced in 1918 by National Film Corporation of America, starring Elmo Lincoln and Enid Markey

2. *Romance of Tarzan,* produced in 1918 by National Film Corporation of America, starring Elmo Lincoln and Enid Markey

3. *The Return of Tarzan,* produced in 1920 by Samuel Goldwyn, starring Gene Polar and Karla Schramm

4. *The Adventures of Tarzan,* produced in 1920 by Weiss Bros., starring Elmo Lincoln and Louise Lorraine

5. *The Son of Tarzan,* produced in 1920 by National Film Corporation of America, starring P. Dempsey Tabler, Kamuela Searles, and Karla Schramm

6. *Tarzan and the Golden Lion,* produced in 1927 by FBO (RKO), starring James H. Pierce, Dorothy Dunbar, and Edna Murphy

7. *Tarzan the Mighty,* produced in 1928 by Universal Pictures Co., Inc., starring Frank Merrill and Natalie Kingston

8. *Tarzan the Tiger,* produced in 1929 by Universal Pictures Co., Inc., starring Frank Merrill and Natalie Kingston

9. *Tarzan the Ape-man,* produced in 1932 by Metro-Goldwyn-Mayer, starring Johnny Weissmuller and Maureen O'Sullivan

10. *Tarzan the Fearless,* produced in 1933 by Serial Prod. Corp. (Principal Productions, Inc.), starring Buster Crabbe and Jacqueline Wells.

11. *Tarzan and his Mate,* produced in 1934 by Metro-Goldwyn-Mayer, starring Johnny Weissmuller and Maureen O'Sullivan

12. *The New Adventures of Tarzan,* produced in 1935 by Burroughs-Tarzan Enterprises, Inc., starring Herman Brix and Ula Holt

13. *Tarzan and the Green Goddess,* produced in 1936 by Burroughs-Tarzan Enterprises, Inc., starring Herman Brix and Ula Holt

14. *Tarzan Escapes,* produced in 1936 by Metro-Goldwyn-Mayer, starring Johnny Weissmuller and Maureen O'Sullivan

15. *Tarzan's Revenge,* produced in 1938 by Principal Productions, Inc., starring Glenn Morris and Eleanor Holm

16. *Tarzan Finds a Son,* produced in 1939 by Metro-Goldwyn-Mayer, starring Johnny Weissmuller and Maureen O'Sullivan

17. *Tarzan's Secret Treasure,* produced in 1941 by Metro-Goldwyn-Mayer, starring Johnny Weissmuller and Maureen O'Sullivan

18. *Tarzan's New York Adventure,* produced in 1942 by Metro-Goldwyn-Mayer, starring Johnny Weissmuller and Maureen O'Sullivan

19. *Tarzan Triumphs,* produced in 1943 by Lesser-RKO, starring Johnny Weissmuller and Nancy Kelly

20. *Tarzan's Desert Mystery,* produced in 1943 by Sol Lesser Productions, Inc.-RKO, starring Johnny Weissmuller and Frances Gifford

21. *Tarzan and the Amazons,* produced in 1944 by Sol Lesser Productions, Inc.-RKO, starring Johnny Weissmuller and Brenda Joyce

22. *Tarzan and the Leopard Woman,* produced in 1946 by Lesser-RKO, starring Johnny Weissmuller, Brenda Joyce, and Acquanetta

23. *Tarzan and the Huntress,* produced in 1947 by Lesser-RKO, starring Johnny Weissmuller, Brenda Joyce, and Patricia Morrison

24. *Tarzan and the Mermaids,* produced in 1948 by Lesser-RKO, starring Johnny Weissmuller, Brenda Joyce, and Linda Christian

25. *Tarzan's Magic Fountain,* produced in 1949 by Lesser-RKO, starring Lex Barker and Brenda Joyce

26. *Tarzan and the Slave Girl,* produced in 1950 by Lesser-RKO, starring Lex Barker and Vanessa Brown

27. *Tarzan's Peril,* produced in 1951 by Lesser-RKO, starring Lex Barker and Virginia Huston

28. *Tarzan's Savage Fury,* produced in 1952 by Lesser-RKO, starring Lex Barker and Dorothy Hart

29. *Tarzan and the She Devil,* produced in 1953 by Lesser-RKO, starring Lex Barker and Joyce McKenzie.

30. *Tarzan's Hidden Jungle,* produced in 1955 by Lesser-RKO, starring Gordon Scott and Vera Miles

31. *Tarzan and the Lost Safari,* produced in 1957 by Lesser/MGM, starring Gordon Scott and Betta St. John

32. *Tarzan's Fight for Life,* produced in 1958 by Lesser/MGM, starring Gordon Scott, Eve Brent, and Rickie Sorensen, first color film

33. *Tarzan the Ape-Man* (remake), produced in 1959 by Metro-Goldwyn-Mayer, starring Dennis Miller and Joanna Barnes

34. *Tarzan's Greatest Adventure,* produced in 1959 by Lesser-Paramount (Banner Productions), starring Gordon Scott, Sara Shane, and Scilla Gabel, made in Africa

35. *Tarzan the Magnificent,* produced in 1960 by Lesser-Paramount (Banner Productions), starring Gordon Scott, Betta St. John, Jock Mahoney, and John Carradine

36. *Tarzan Goes to India,* produced in 1962 by Banner Productions, Inc./MGM, starring Jock Mahoney, fllmed in India

37. *Tarzan's Three Challenges,* produced in 1963 by Banner Productions, Inc./MGM, starring Jock Mahoney, filmed in Thailand

38. *Tarzan and the Valley of Gold,* produced in 1966 by Banner Productions, Inc./MGM, starring Mike Henry

39. *Tarzan and the Great River,* produced in 1967 by Banner Productions, Inc./MGM, starring Mike Henry

40. *Tarzan and the Jungle Boy,* produced in 1968 by Banner Productions, Inc./MGM, starring Mike Henry

5. Reminiscences of Hulbert Burroughs

My father and mother showed great foresight and wisdom in making Tarzana Ranch our home during our formative childhood years. The outdoor life and close proximity to the world of nature greatly influenced me. To a boy of ten, fresh from the suburbs of Chicago, it was an exciting new world to explore.

Not long after we settled in our new home, my father started teaching the entire family to ride horseback. His training at the Michigan Military Academy and at Fort Grant, as well as on the ranch in Idaho, made him well qualified. He bought Shetland ponies for each of us children. All of us were at first frightened of the animals and this new experience; and until we learned to control the animals ourselves, my father frequently rode beside us, leading one or more of the ponies with halter ropes. Some of our early riding experiences were frightening. I recall one occasion when Joan's pony decided to lie down and roll in the dust. Joan, in tears, tumbled off. Jack's pony was prone to bucking unexpectedly. This terrified Jack, who was only about seven at the time. My pony was great until it came time for us to turn back toward the stables. Every experienced rider is familiar with the eagerness of a horse to return to food and water. "Bud" knew he was stronger than I; and once he took the bit in his teeth, he took off at a dead run. I was too inexperienced to control him. All I could do was ride it out and hope I would not be scraped off by the low-hanging branches of an oak or walnut tree. As a result of our experiences with these half-trained little ponies, Dad soon graduated us to full-sized and properly trained horses. He was convinced that most ponies make poor saddle animals because they are too small for a grown man to ride and properly train.

In the approximately ten years we lived on the ranch, Dad was a vigorous man, always engaged in some activity or project. A typical day usually started with a horseback ride at the first light of dawn before breakfast. Dad usually arose at 5 a.m., seldom later than 6. Both of my parents believed in the adage "early to bed and early to rise." Usually the entire family started the day together. We had two basic riding trails. The first person to the stables wrote on the blackboard in the tack room which trail he had taken and what time he had started. With that information, those who followed would be able either to catch up or to intercept him on the return trail.

These early morning rides were always exciting and invigorating. In the early 1920's the Santa Monica Mountains were unspoiled and there was an abundance of animals. On almost every ride we would see coyotes, deer, rabbits, quail, and other birds. On rare occasions we might catch fleeting glimpses of a wary mountain lion or bobcat.

I have strong recollections of my dad during those ranch years. Because horseback riding was a daily occurrence, most of the time he wore riding clothes. English-style breeches and boots, a leather jacket, and felt hat were his customary attire. On the early morning rides he usually packed a Colt .45 automatic pistol, acquired when he was an officer in the Illinois Reserve Militia. One morning this .45 was cause for considerable embarrassment. He was riding alone on his favorite horse, Colonel, following a trail through chaparral along a hogback. In the trail just ahead he spotted a large rattlesnake warming itself in the morning sun. Dad reined Colonel to a stop, unholstered his gun, and took aim at the snake. At that moment Colonel either sensed the snake or was startled by something else. In any event, he suddenly shied to one side. Dad instinctively moved his right hand to join his left on the reins. The quick movement of his gun hand caused him to squeeze the trigger. As the .45 discharged only a few inches from his ears, the horse fell as if pole-axed. Thinking he had shot and killed his horse, Ed rolled clear. Almost immediately the frightened but unhurt Colonel scrambled to his feet and headed for home. As an old cowhand and excavalryman, it was an embarrassed Ed Burroughs who had to walk a couple of miles home.

Although he was thoroughly familiar with the western, or stock, saddle, as well as with the McClellan cavalry saddle, he preferred the flatter English style. It was his opinion that it required more skill and horsemanship to ride the flat saddle than the western rig. Furthermore, it was more comfortable. We all eventually graduated to the English saddle.

Occasionally some visitors to the ranch would be inclined to brag about their riding ability. Dad did not like braggarts, and for them he had a special horse — not really mean or dangerous, but a bit unruly and unpredictable. Riding this animal was usually a chastening experience and served to separate the men from the boys.

Dad was inclined to be grumpy and somewhat disagreeable in the morning before breakfast and not very talkative. We learned to accept this and did our best to avoid irritating him. Usually he spent the mornings at his office, working on his stories. He was well disciplined in his work habits and kept regular writing hours.

I do not recall his exact daily schedule, but I do know that he seemed to be involved in a multitude of activities. Although he had farmhands to do most of the labor on the ranch, he planned and supervised everything that went on. He found time to encourage Jack in his growing interest in clay modeling and drawing. Whenever one of us demonstrated an interest in some particular subject or activity, he immediately gave encouragement by either working with us or obtaining books for us. I still have the bird and animal books he gave me during my young naturalist years. When Joan showed an interest in singing, he arranged voice lessons for her.

Dad's creative urge was not limited solely to his writing. He not only was a good cartoonist, but he enjoyed working with his very capable hands. His workshop was well stocked with tools which he encouraged Jack and me to use. He enjoyed making things of wood — most of which were of an inventive or imaginative nature. We still have an ingenious little automatic pop-up cigarette dispenser he made. He used cigarettes most of his life; yet strangely he never inhaled. For many years he rolled his own,

using the little booklets of cigarette paper and drawstring pouches of Bull Durham tobacco. He took pride in being able to roll a cigarette with one hand. Later he switched to Prince Albert. With the advent of factory-made cigarettes he gave up rolling his own.

Like most successful men, my father was restless and dynamic. His mind was constantly active, and almost by compulsion he had to be involved in something constructive and interesting. He enjoyed stone masonry and was proficient in this skill. On the slope of the hill just below his house he built a series of five cement fish ponds bordered with white flagstone he had excavated from Jackknife Canyon on the ranch. A small waterfall cascaded down his realistically arranged rocks into the highest pool, with the overflow from each pool tumbling over the rocks to the next lower pool. The ponds were planted with water lilies and hyacinth and stocked with an assortment of goldfish.

Most meals were family affairs. My father and mother tried to make these occasions constructive, fun, and interesting. Dad was a prodigious reader and would frequently use the evening mealtime for sharing with us the interesting books he had been reading — usually books on travel and exploration in distant lands. He was very articulate, and his natural storytelling ability enabled him to recount most graphically the exciting episodes of these books. We frequently played word and guessing games at the table. Almost every evening after dinner, Dad spent an hour or more reading. His ability to concentrate was a source of wonder to me. When he was engrossed in a book, we'd almost have to throw something at him to gain his attention. I believe it was this power of total concentration that was the secret of his speed in story-writing.

As children we were engrossed with his stories and delighted in identifying with the characters. He liked to recount Jack's experience with meat. Mom and Dad had difficulty persuading Jack to eat cooked meat. He wanted to eat it raw because that's the way Tarzan ate it! One day he noticed Jack following him across the yard on his hands and knees with his nose to the ground. Dad asked Jack what he was doing. "Following your scent spoor," Jack replied.

With my father as the leader and active participant, we frequently played outdoor games on the lawn after dinner. Employees usually joined us in a softball game which Dad called "One Old Cat." Often Dad would take the whole family for an auto drive on the dirt road up the main canyon because he enjoyed seeing the rabbits and quail in the early evening. Always patriotic, he installed a tall flagpole in the front yard. In the evening the lowering of the flag was a family affair.

Dad had inherited from his father the gene for

pattern baldness and was self-conscious about this. He had started losing his hair while still in his twenties, and by the time we moved to California there were only a few hairs on top of his head. Whenever possible he wore a hat to hide his head. Finally, not long after moving to the ranch, he bought a toupee at a shop called "Zan's" that advertised WIGS-ZAN-HAIR. Hairpieces in those days were not what they are now, and his *looked* like a toupee. On one occasion his friend Bill Kiger, a doctor with a sizeable paunch, started kidding Dad about his toupee. Irritated, Dad retorted, "At least I don't have to wear a corset yet!" He was such an active man and perspired copiously in warm weather, and the toupee became an intolerable nuisance. Finally he had had enough. I can well remember the day he threw it away in disgust: "To hell with the damned thing!" he exclaimed.

This self-consciousness about his baldness was but one manifestation of a deep sensitivity and feeling of inferiority. Another source of embarrassment to him was the unevenness of his front teeth, and he developed a habit of partially covering his mouth with a hand when he laughed. At times he was thought to be unfriendly or at least uncommunicative among strangers. Actually I believe this was but another example of his natural reticence.

Dad was always warm and loving with his children. He gave us a considerable amount of freedom, though he was a very careful and concerned father. Joan recalled that her only memory of his being angry with her was in 1932 when she confessed to having voted for Franklin D. Roosevelt for president.

He told us bedtime stories almost every night when we were children. They were in serial form, to be continued each following night. He always began exactly where he had left off the night before. "Arabella, the Coyote" and "Grandpa Gazink and His Flying Machine" were among our favorites.

He trusted us and granted us much independence to use our judgment. Joan was sixteen when she started going out on dates, and she often commented that Dad never told her to be home at any certain hour or what to do or not to do. He had confidence in our ability to take care of ourselves. He was stubborn when he made up his mind about something. He demanded respect from us and got it. In the matter of religion he said we were free to choose our own church when we became adults. He did not attend church, and neither did we.

After he contracted Parkinson's disease and suffered further heart attacks, he stayed at home most of the time with a housekeeper-nurse. He was lonely and used to call Joan nearly every day at five o'clock to remind her to come over for their private cocktail hour. In his declining years he enjoyed television and particularly liked the wrestling matches. He used to grunt and groan with the wrestlers and insisted that the matches were genuine.

Although for years Dad was roughly handled by many so-called literary critics, many have since come to recognize the literary merit of his stories and the impact he has had. Sam Moscowitz in his *Under the Moons of Mars, A History and Anthology of "The Scientific Romance" in the Munsey Magazines, 1912–1920* (New York: Holt, Rinehart, and Winston, 1970, page ix), makes this comment:

The publication of Under the Moons of Mars *by Edgar Rice Burroughs in The All-story Magazine in 1912 brought onto the magazine scene a writer whose instantaneous and phenomenal popularity shaped the policies of the early pulp magazines, making them the focal center of science fiction and inspiring a school of writers who made the scientific romance he wrote the most accepted form for more than twenty years.*

In August of 1962 the prestigious Oxford University Press of London published a condensed version of this novel in its *Stories Told and Retold* series. Henry Hardy Heins, an ERB authority and compiler of *A Golden Anniversary Bibliography of Edgar Rice Burroughs,* has commented: "We look upon the Oxford *Princess* as an extremely significant milestone in Burroughs publishing history. This was the author's first novel now brought out in its golden anniversary year as a *schoolbook* by the venerable Oxford Press."

I have often thought of the prediction Thomas Newell Metcalf made in his letter of October 11, 1912, written shortly after publication of *Tarzan of the Apes* in the October 1912 issue of *All-Story* Magazine: "We . . . have no doubts that the time will come when let alone naming race-horses 'Tarzan,' the word 'Tarzan' will become a generic term for anything that is a huge success. . . ."

6. "Of Beans and Rice," Forrest J. Ackerman

It may be that I am the only person on Earth who ever had the notion of asking Bela Lugosi to actually sign the name "Count Dracula"; Boris Karloff, in his own hand, to write "Frankenstein"; Fredric March, academy oscar winner, to give me the filmic autographs of "Dr. Jekyll and Mr. Hyde" rather than his own.

And on that long distant day when I saw the literary idol of my youth for the next to last time, in his own cottage in Tarzana, I went with the premeditated intention of asking him to sign one of my rarest possessions, not "Edgar Rice Burroughs," not even "Norman Bean" as it had been erroneously printed on his earliest work, but "Normal Bean" — the play on words as he had intended it.

With me that day, as I recall, on that pilgrimage to pay homage to the Master, was a science fiction fan of the time, a young girl who had adopted the name "Tigrina." When she left, she took with her a copy of *Princino de Marso* with probably the only inscription ERB ever gave in the artificial language of Esperanto: "Tigrina, Vere Via [Truly Yours], Edgaro Rajs Buroz."

And I, well, I had three treasures with me, and as I handed their creator the first — a virtually mint copy of the original magazine publication of *Tarzan of the Apes* — I asked him, "Now, Mr. Burroughs, instead of signing this with your own name, would you put the pen name on it for me that you first intended to use?"

He indicated he would be glad to oblige, but he was carrying on a conversation as he started to write and before he knew it had automatically signed his name in the usual manner.

One down, two to go.

I handed him my second treasure: *Under the Moons of Mars* by Norman Bean, February 1912 issue of the *All-Story*. As deferentially as I could, I pointed out that he had not signed my first magazine "Normal Bean" as I had requested. (Incidentally, at that time it had never entered my "bean" that the significance of *his* Bean was the slang-of-its-day for gourd, noggin, head. I mentally interpreted it as meaning "being," as a human bein'. It was only years later that I was disabused myself of this erroneous notion that I was carrying around in my bean.)

Again Mr. Burroughs' attention was distracted and again he signed his name normally. When I pointed this out, he did, as an afterthought, squeeze in "Alias Normal Bean" after his name and just above the printed title of the magazine.

Two down, one to go.
Ballpoint in hand, Edgar Rice Burroughs wrote:

*To
F.
J.
Bean*

"Oh, no! What have I done?!"

What he had done couldn't be undone. Nor would I have had it any other way, else I never would have had the fun of telling this anecdote to countless ERB fans who've visited me, of relating it at a Dum-dum held during a World Science Fiction Convention, of bringing laughter in my home to the lips of his son Hulbert, of having the privilege of being included in this unique volume.

What had he done? He had given me a new name, to add to Weaver Wright and Spencer Strong and Fisher Trentworth and Fojak and 4sJ and Dr. Acula and a score or more others by which I have been known in this life.

"Never mind," I reassured him instantly. "For you, Mr. Burroughs, I'll change my name!"

So he enclosed the "Bean" in parentheses, added "Ackerman," concluded with "All good wishes," and signed his name one more time "Edgar Rice Burroughs."

And that is the story of how a poor but honest farm boy came to the big city, met a childhood hero and was rechristened F. J. Bean, editor of *Famous Monsters of Filmland;* F. J. Bean, editor of *Perry Rhodan;* F. J. Bean, creator/curator of the Science Fantasy Museum. When your name's on the product, you're mighty picky about whom you choose to honor.

Mr. Bean thanks you, Mr. Rice!

THE AUTHOR

Irwin Porges — author, historian, musician, and world traveler — grew up in Chicago, where Edgar Rice Burroughs spent so many years. Born in 1909 in Maywood, Illinois, Porges saw his first poems and stories in print when he was ten years old. He grew up at a time when boys swung from limbs, lassoed fence posts, and screamed strident calls as they fought imaginary apes and lions in imitation of their hero — Tarzan.

The author became a professional musician after his graduation from Lake View High School in Chicago, served in the Air Force during World War II in Africa and Italy, moved to California after his discharge in 1945, and obtained his degrees at the University of Southern California and the University of California at Los Angeles. He taught English, literature, and creative writing at Valley College in Van Nuys, California, for twenty-three years, meanwhile writing articles, short stories, and books.

At Van Nuys, as in Chicago, Porges was near a Burroughs base of operations, and he sought to penetrate the mystery of Burroughs the man and the writer. Fascinated, Porges became convinced that prior stories about ERB were only exaggerated and contradictory bits and pieces. After one look at the Tarzana, California, warehouse packed with ERB memorabilia, Porges knew that the real Burroughs had not been touched. He then embarked on the project that has resulted in *Edgar Rice Burroughs: The Man Who Created Tarzan*.

The author had two "secret weapons" for writing this colorful and definitive look at ERB. One was his wife, Cele, a gifted researcher, who spent nearly three years culling information from the extensive library at Tarzana. The other was unlimited permission to use this library with the full cooperation of Hulbert and Jack Burroughs, sons of ERB. All these factors, along with Porges' skill in piecing together the massive amount of information and reducing it to usable size, have resulted in this captivating book, the first and only true and definitive account of the life and work of this remarkably successful author.

Porges has published more than fifty articles and stories and has written four other books, including a sociological study, *The Violent Americans,* and a biography, *Edgar Allan Poe, 1809–1849,* now in its second printing.

The Editor

803

INDEX

810

---

*Relationship to
Edgar Rice Burroughs

This book has been set in
Baskerville and has been printed on Crown Book 60#
at Brigham Young University Press, Provo, Utah 84602. It is bound in
Sierra Parima, dark green, spine: Tanaline Ten, black shoe grain. It is stamped
with gold foil. The endsheets are Multicolor Antique, Spring Green,
and the dust jacket is KromeKote Litho C1S 70#.